CONTEMPORARY Management

Eleventh Edition

Gareth R. Jones

Jennifer M. George
Jesse H. Jones Graduate School of Business
Rice University

McGraw
Hill
Education

CONTEMPORARY MANAGEMENT

Published by McGraw-Hill Education, 2 Penn Plaza, New York, NY 10121. Copyright © 2020 by McGraw-Hill Education. All rights reserved. Printed in the United States of America. No part of this publication may be reproduced or distributed in any form or by any means, or stored in a database or retrieval system, without the prior written consent of McGraw-Hill Education, including, but not limited to, in any network or other electronic storage or transmission, or broadcast for distance learning.

Some ancillaries, including electronic and print components, may not be available to customers outside the United States.

This book is printed on acid-free paper.

5 6 7 8 9 BMI 21 20 19

ISBN 978-1-260-56573-7
MHID 1-260-56573-4

Cover Image: ©G.LIUDMILA/Shutterstock

mheducation.com/highered

BRIEF CONTENTS

AUTHORS

Gareth Jones currently offers pro bono advice on solving management problems to nonprofit organizations in Houston, Texas. He received his BA in Economics/Psychology and his PhD in Management from the University of Lancaster, UK. He was formerly Professor of Management in the Graduate School of Business at Texas A&M University and earlier held teaching and research appointments at Michigan State University, the University of Illinois at Urbana-Champaign, and the University of Warwick, UK.

He continues to pursue his research interests in strategic management and organizational theory and his well-known research that applies transaction cost analysis to explain many forms of strategic and organizational behavior. He also studies the complex and changing relationships between competitive advantage and information technology in the 2010s.

He has published many articles in leading journals of the field, and his research has appeared in the *Academy of Management Review,* the *Journal of International Business Studies,* and *Human Relations.* An article about the role of information technology in many aspects of organizational functioning was published in the *Journal of Management.* One of his articles won the *Academy of Management Journal's* Best Paper Award, and he is one of the most cited authors in the *Academy of Management Review.* He is, or has served, on the editorial boards of the *Academy of Management Review,* the *Journal of Management,* and *Management Inquiry.*

Gareth Jones has used his academic knowledge to craft leading textbooks in management and three other major areas in the management discipline: organizational behavior, organizational theory, and strategic management. His books are widely recognized for their innovative, contemporary content and for the clarity with which they communicate complex, real-world issues to students.

Jennifer George is the Mary Gibbs Jones Professor of Management and Professor of Psychology in the Jesse H. Jones Graduate School of Business at Rice University. She received her BA in Psychology/Sociology from Wesleyan University, her MBA in Finance from New York University, and her PhD in Management and Organizational Behavior from New York University. Prior to joining the faculty at Rice University, she was a professor in the Department of Management at Texas A&M University.

Professor George specializes in organizational behavior and is well known for her research on mood and emotion in the workplace, their determinants, and their effects on various individual and group-level work outcomes. She is the author of many articles in leading peer-reviewed journals such as the *Academy of Management Journal,* the *Academy of Management Review,* the *Journal of Applied Psychology, Organizational Behavior and Human Decision Processes, Journal of Personality and Social Psychology, Organization Science,* and *Psychological Bulletin.* One of her papers won the Academy of Management's Organizational Behavior Division Outstanding Competitive Paper Award, and another paper won the *Human Relations* Best Paper Award. She is, or has been, on the editorial review boards of the *Journal of Applied Psychology, Academy of Management Journal, Academy of Management Review, Administrative Science Quarterly, Journal of Management, Organizational Behavior and Human Decision Processes, Organization Science, International Journal of Selection and Assessment,* and *Journal of Managerial Issues;* was a consulting editor for the *Journal of Organizational Behavior;* was a member of the SIOP *Organizational Frontiers Series* editorial board; and was an associate editor of the *Journal of Applied Psychology.* She is a fellow in the Academy of Management, the American Psychological Association, the American Psychological Society, and the Society for Industrial and Organizational Psychology and a member of the Society for Organizational Behavior. She also has coauthored a textbook titled *Understanding and Managing Organizational Behavior.*

PREFACE

Since the tenth edition of *Contemporary Management* was published, our book continues to be a leader in the management market. This tells us that we continue to meet the expectations of our existing users and attract new users to our book. It is clear that most management instructors share with us a concern for the need to continuously introduce new and emerging issues into the text and its examples to ensure that cutting-edge issues and new developments in the field of contemporary management are addressed.

In the new eleventh edition of *Contemporary Management,* we continue with our mission to provide students the most current and up-to-date account of the changes taking place in the world of business management. The fast-changing domestic and global environment continues to pressure organizations and their managers to find new and improved ways to respond to changing events in order to maintain and increase their performance. More than ever, events around the globe, rapid changes in technology, and economic pressures and challenges show how fast the success and even survival of companies can change. For example, the increasing complexity of the exchanges between global companies has profoundly affected the management of both large and small organizations. Today there is increased pressure on managers to find new management practices that can increase their companies' efficiency and effectiveness and ability to survive and prosper in an increasingly competitive global environment.

In revising our book, we continue our focus on making our text relevant and interesting to today's students—something that we know from instructor and student feedback engages them and encourages them to make the effort necessary to assimilate the text material. We continue to mirror the changes taking place in management practices by incorporating recent developments in management theory and research into our text and by providing vivid, current examples of how managers of companies large and small have responded to the changes taking place. Indeed, we have incorporated many new and contemporary examples in the new edition illustrating how founders, managers, and employees in a variety of types of organizations respond to the opportunities and challenges they face. These examples drive home to students how essential it is for them to develop a rich understanding of management theory and research and the ability to apply what they have learned in organizational settings.

The number and complexity of the strategic, organizational, and human resource challenges facing managers and all employees have continued to increase throughout the 2010s. In most companies, managers at all levels are playing catch-up as they work toward meeting these challenges by implementing new and improved management techniques and practices. Today relatively small differences in performance between companies, such as in the speed at which they can bring new products or services to market or in how they motivate their employees to find ways to improve performance or reduce costs, can combine to give one company a significant competitive advantage over another. Managers and companies that use proven management techniques and practices in their decision making and actions increase their effectiveness over time. Companies and managers that are slower to implement new management techniques and practices find themselves at a growing competitive disadvantage that makes it even more difficult to catch up. Thus many industries have widening gaps between weaker competitors and the most successful companies, whose performance reaches new heights because their managers have made better decisions about how to use a company's resources in the most efficient and effective ways. In the rapidly changing and dynamic environment facing organizations today, effective managers recognize the vital role that creativity and innovation play in successfully anticipating and responding to these challenges as well as seizing the potential opportunities that they bring while mitigating the threats.

The issues facing managers continue to intensify as changes in the global environment, such as a tightening of the U.S. labor market and rising wages in China and other countries, impact organizations large and small. Similarly, increasing globalization means managers must respond to major differences in the legal rules and regulations and ethical values and norms that prevail in countries around the globe.

Moreover, the revolution in information technology (IT) continues to transform how managers make decisions across all levels of a company's hierarchy and across all its functions and global divisions. The eleventh edition of our book addresses these ongoing challenges as IT continues to change at breakneck speed, especially in the area of artificial intelligence, blockchain technology, data analytics, and cybersecurity.

Other major challenges we continue to expand on in the new edition include the impact of the steadily increasing diversity of the workforce on companies and how this increasing diversity makes it imperative for managers to understand how and why people differ so they can effectively manage and reap the many benefits of a diverse workforce. Similarly, across all functions and levels, managers and employees must continuously search out ways to "work smarter" and increase performance. Using new IT to improve all aspects of an organization's operations to boost efficiency and customer responsiveness is a vital part of this process. We have significantly revised the eleventh edition of *Contemporary Management* to address these challenges to managers and their organizations.

Major Content Changes

Encouraged by the number of instructors and students who use each new edition of our book, and based on the reactions and suggestions of both users and reviewers, we have revised and updated our book in the following ways. First, just as we have included new research concepts as appropriate, so too have we been careful to eliminate outdated or marginal management concepts. As usual, our goal has been to streamline our presentation and keep the focus on the changes taking place that have the most impact on managers and organizations. In today's world of instant sound bites, videos, text messaging, and tweets, providing the best content is much more important than providing excessive content—especially when some of our students are burdened by time pressures stemming from the need to work long hours at paying jobs and meeting personal commitments and obligations.

Second, we have added new management content and have reinforced its importance by using many small and large company examples that are described in the chapter opening cases titled "A Manager's Challenge"; in the many boxed examples featuring managers and employees in companies both large and small in each chapter; and in the "Case in the News" closing cases.

Chapter 1, for example, contains new and updated material on the way recent changes in IT and the products and services that result from it are affecting competition among companies. The chapter features a new opening feature about Microsoft CEO Satya Nadella and his quest to reboot the tech giant by encouraging staff to adopt a mind-set that is constantly learning and improving, retooling products and services to encourage efficiency and innovation, and placing a high value on diversity in the workplace. New chapter highlights include features about working as a city manager, managing a large emergency room facility, and recovering from a companywide ethical scandal at Wells Fargo. The chapter also contains an updated discussion and examples about managing a diverse workforce, including America's best employers for diversity.

Chapter 2 opens with the story of how Comcast is rethinking the customer experience in an effort to sustain competitive advantage. The chapter continues to cover traditional management theories and how they have been modified to address changing work conditions in the global environment today. In addition, a new discussion focuses on the theory of dynamic capabilities, which encourages managers to use the organization's past experience to shift focus when situations demand a different approach.

Chapter 3 updates material about the manager as a person and the way personal characteristics of managers (and all members of an organization) influence organizational culture and effectiveness. The chapter opens with a new "Manager's Challenge" on Geisha Williams, the CEO of PG&E (one of the country's largest gas and oil utilities) and the first Latina to run a *Fortune* 500 company. There is also new content about personality assessments, including the Myers-Briggs Type Indicator and the DiSC Inventory Profile, as well as chapter features on promoting ethical values in the hotel industry and understanding emotional intelligence in various cultures.

Chapter 4 provides updated material about the unethical and illegal behaviors of managers from various industries. We have updated our coverage of the many issues involved in acting and managing ethically, including an opening story about Tesla and its involvement in building microgrids to help restore power in Puerto Rico after the island suffered devastating damage from recent hurricanes. We also discuss new issues in ethics and provide conceptual tools to help students understand better how to make ethical decisions. We highlight issues related to worker safety, environmental responsibility, and regulations to protect consumer safety. Finally, we have updated coverage of the ethics of nonprofits and their managers as well as added chapter features on Accenture's new chatbot that is helping to guide employee ethical behavior and a global organization that protects home-based apparel workers in foreign countries. The ethical exercise at the end of every chapter continues to be a popular feature of our book.

Chapter 5 focuses on the effective management of the many faces of diversity in organizations for the good of all stakeholders. A new "Manager's Challenge" highlights the strategies Intel uses to effectively manage diversity in the workplace. We have updated chapter content, examples, and statistics for such issues as age, gender, race and ethnicity, disabilities, sexual orientation, and the pay gap between women and men. In addition, we have added a new discussion about implicit bias and how it affects most people's actions and decisions in an unconscious manner. The chapter also provides expanded coverage of the way managers can leverage the increasing diversity of the population and workforce to reap the performance benefits that stem from diversity while ensuring that all employees are treated fairly. Finally, the discussion about sexual harassment has been revised to include recent statistics and information about the #MeToo movement, which impacts women in many different work situations.

Chapter 6 contains an integrated account of forces in both the domestic and global environments. A new

"Manager's Challenge" describes the challenges and opportunities Amazon faced as it tried to expand its e-commerce business to India. The chapter has also been revised and updated to reflect the way increasing global competition and free trade have changed the global value creation process. The chapter uses examples from the fashion industry, electronics industry, and the music-streaming industry to illustrate these issues. In addition, a new section describes the GLOBE project, which extends Hofstede's work on national culture by examining additional dimensions that may impact how business is conducted in a variety of cultures and countries. The chapter also has an updated discussion about the challenges faced by expats in moving abroad, as well as strategies utilized by companies in an effort to become key suppliers to emerging global businesses.

Chapter 7 discusses the vital processes of decision making, learning, and creativity in organizations and their implications for managers and all employees. The chapter opens with a new "Manager's Challenge" on how creativity and the ability to learn helped the management of 23andMe, an online genetic screening service, adapt its business when roadblocks almost derailed the company. We also include a discussion of the position of chief sustainability officer and examine how managers can make decisions to help ensure their actions contribute to sustainability. Also, we continue our discussion of social entrepreneurs who seek creative ways to address social problems to improve well-being by, for example, reducing poverty, increasing literacy, and protecting the natural environment. In addition, we expanded the discussion of strategies for creating and sustaining a learning organization and added features on decision-making strategies at a beauty-products startup and Western Union's successful approach to constant learning throughout the organization.

As in the last edition, **Chapter 8** focuses on corporate-, global-, and business-level strategies, and **Chapter 9** discusses functional strategies for managing value chain activities. These two chapters make clear the links between the different levels of strategy while maintaining a strong focus on managing operations and processes. Chapter 8 continues the discussion of planning and levels of strategy, which focuses on how companies can use vertical integration and related diversification to increase long-term profitability. A new opening story describes the strategies put in place by Marriott International CEO Arne Sorenson and his management team to expand the company's growth over the next few years. The chapter also includes updated examples of business-level strategies that focus on low-cost strategies in a world in which prices continue to be under pressure due to increased global competition. In Chapter 9 we continue to explore how companies can develop new functional-level strategies to improve efficiency, quality, innovation, and responsiveness to customers. We also added a discussion on the importance of value chain analysis for managers within any organization to help increase efficiency, reduce costs, and strengthen collaboration among various functional activities. In addition to coverage of TQM, including the Six Sigma approach, we include a discussion of the importance of customer relationship management (CRM) and the need to attract and retain customers especially during challenging economic times.

Chapters 10 and **11** offer updated coverage of organizational structure and control and discuss how companies have confronted the need to reorganize their hierarchies and ways of doing business as the environment changes and competition increases. In Chapter 10, for example, we discuss how McDonald's CEO Steve Easterbrook made major organizational changes, including a move to the city for the company's corporate headquarters, in an effort to revitalize and re-energize the company's culture and overall business. We also continue to highlight examples that show how companies are designing global organizational structure and culture to improve performance. In **Chapter 11** we continue this theme by looking at how companies are changing their control systems to increase efficiency and quality, for example. More generally, how to use control systems to increase quality is a theme throughout the chapter.

We have updated and expanded our treatment of the many ways in which managers can effectively manage and lead employees in their companies. For example, **Chapter 12** opens with a new "Manager's Challenge" that highlights how Home Depot's strategic focus on hiring and retaining top workers in a tight labor market continues to pay off for the home improvement retail giant. The chapter also discusses best practices to recruit and attract outstanding employees, the importance of training and development, pay differentials, and family-friendly benefit programs. In addition, there is treatment of the use of background checks by employers, the use of forced ranking systems in organizations, and issues concerning excessive CEO pay and pay comparisons between CEOs and average workers, and updated statistics on U.S. union membership. Finally, we added a discussion on the recent trend of companies doing away with annual performance appraisals in an effort to provide real-time feedback and foster ongoing conversations about job performance, expectations, and growth and development. **Chapter 13** continues coverage of prosocially motivated behavior, including examples of people who are motivated to benefit others. It also discusses the many steps managers can take to create a highly motivated workforce and the importance of equity and justice in organizations.

Chapter 14 highlights the critical importance of effective leadership in organizations and factors that contribute to managers being effective leaders, including a discussion of servant leadership. A new "Manager's Challenge" describes the effective leadership demonstrated by the two recent CEOs of the Dana-Farber Cancer Institute. There is also a discussion of how managers with expert power need to recognize that they are not always right. The chapter also addresses how emotional intelligence may help leaders respond appropriately when they realize they have made a mistake, and it gives updated examples of leadership in a variety of organizations. Expanded and updated coverage of the effective management of teams, including virtual teams, is provided in **Chapter 15,** which opens with a new "Manager's Challenge" that highlights how the U.S. Army has set up special teams to expedite innovation and cut through bureaucratic red tape, which historically has been a huge obstacle within military management and operations. The chapter also covers the problems that arise because of a lack of leadership in teams.

Chapter 16 includes coverage of effective communication and how, given the multitude of advances in IT, it is important to create opportunities for face-to-face communication. There is also information on the ethics of monitoring email and Internet use, including statistics on Internet usage both in the United States and in other countries around the world. Finally, there is also a discussion of social networking sites and why some managers attempt to limit employees' access to them during the workday. **Chapter 17** includes an updated discussion of the vital task of effectively managing conflict and politics in organizations and how to negotiate effectively on a global level. There are many new examples of how managers can create a collaborative work context and avoid competition between individuals and groups.

Chapter 18 has been revised and refreshed to discuss recent advances in information technology that continue to change the way we do business and the way we manage people. For example, a new "Manager's Challenge" describes how software that applies artificial intelligence is being used as a management coaching system—ongoing feedback from employees defines areas in which a manager needs to improve his or her leadership. Other recent innovations such as data analytics, blockchain technology, and machine learning are also explored. In addition, cybersecurity and data privacy are highlighted as ongoing issues managers will need to address as technology continues to evolve quickly and impact their roles and responsibilities in any organization.

We feel confident that the major changes we have made to the eleventh edition of *Contemporary Management* reflect the changes occurring in management and the workplace; we also believe they offer an account of management that will stimulate and challenge students to think about their future as they look for opportunities in the world of organizations.

Unique Emphasis on Contemporary, Applied Management

In revising our book, we have kept at the forefront the fact that our users and reviewers are supportive of our attempts to integrate contemporary management theories and issues into the analysis of management and organizations. As in previous editions, our goal has been to distill new and classic theorizing and research into a contemporary framework that is compatible with the traditional focus on management as planning, leading, organizing, and controlling but that transcends this traditional approach.

Users and reviewers report that students appreciate and enjoy our presentation of management—a presentation that makes its relevance obvious even to those who lack exposure to a real-life management context. Students like the book's content and the way we relate management theory to real-life examples to drive home the message that management matters both because it determines how well organizations perform and because managers and organizations affect the lives of people inside and outside the organization, such as employees, customers, and shareholders.

Our contemporary approach has led us to discuss many concepts and issues that are not addressed in other management textbooks, and it is illustrated by the way we organize and discuss these management issues. We have gone to great lengths to bring the manager back into the subject matter of management. That is, we have written our chapters from the perspective of current or future managers to illustrate, in a hands-on way, the problems and opportunities they face and how they can effectively meet them. For example, in Chapter 3 we provide an integrated treatment of personality, attitudes, emotions, and culture; in Chapter 4, a focus on ethics from a student's and a manager's perspective; and in Chapter 5, an in-depth treatment of effectively managing diversity and eradicating sexual harassment. In Chapters 8 and 9, our integrated treatment of strategy highlights the multitude of decisions managers must make as they perform their most important role—increasing organizational efficiency, effectiveness, and performance.

Our applied approach can also be clearly seen in the last three chapters of the book, which cover the topics of promoting effective communication; managing organizational conflict, politics, and negotiation; and using information technology in ways that increase organizational performance. These chapters provide a student-friendly, behavioral approach to understanding the management issues entailed in persuasive communication, negotiation, and implementation of advanced information systems to build competitive advantage.

Flexible Organization

Another factor of interest to instructors is how we have designed the grouping of chapters to allow instructors to teach the chapter material in the order that best suits their needs. For example, the more micro-oriented instructor can follow Chapters 1 through 5 with Chapters 12 through 16 and then use the more macro chapters. The more macro-oriented professor can follow Chapters 1 and 2 with Chapters 6 through 11, jump to 16 through 18, and then use the micro chapters, 3 through 5 and 12 through 15.

Our sequencing of parts and chapters gives instructors considerable freedom to design the course that best suits their needs. Instructors are not tied to the planning, organizing, leading, and controlling framework, even though our presentation remains consistent with this approach.

Connect®

Students—study more efficiently, retain more and achieve better outcomes. Instructors—focus on what you love—teaching.

SUCCESSFUL SEMESTERS INCLUDE CONNECT

FOR INSTRUCTORS

You're in the driver's seat.

Want to build your own course? No problem. Prefer to use our turnkey, prebuilt course? Easy. Want to make changes throughout the semester? Sure. And you'll save time with Connect's auto-grading too.

65%
Less Time Grading

They'll thank you for it.

Adaptive study resources like SmartBook® help your students be better prepared in less time. You can transform your class time from dull definitions to dynamic debates. Hear from your peers about the benefits of Connect at **www.mheducation.com/highered/connect**

Make it simple, make it affordable.

Connect makes it easy with seamless integration using any of the major Learning Management Systems—Blackboard®, Canvas, and D2L, among others—to let you organize your course in one convenient location. Give your students access to digital materials at a discount with our inclusive access program. Ask your McGraw-Hill representative for more information.

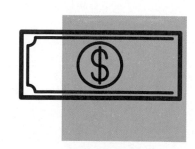

©Hill Street Studios/Tobin Rogers/Blend Images LLC

Solutions for your challenges.

A product isn't a solution. Real solutions are affordable, reliable, and come with training and ongoing support when you need it and how you want it. Our Customer Experience Group can also help you troubleshoot tech problems—although Connect's 99% uptime means you might not need to call them. See for yourself at **status.mheducation.com**

Effective, efficient studying.

Connect helps you be more productive with your study time and get better grades using tools like SmartBook, which highlights key concepts and creates a personalized study plan. Connect sets you up for success, so you walk into class with confidence and walk out with better grades.

©Shutterstock/wavebreakmedia

> **"** I really liked this app—it made it easy to study when you don't have your textbook in front of you. **"**
>
> - Jordan Cunningham, Eastern Washington University

Study anytime, anywhere.

Download the free ReadAnywhere app and access your online eBook when it's convenient, even if you're offline. And since the app automatically syncs with your eBook in Connect, all of your notes are available every time you open it. Find out more at **www.mheducation.com/readanywhere**

No surprises.

The Connect Calendar and Reports tools keep you on track with the work you need to get done and your assignment scores. Life gets busy; Connect tools help you keep learning through it all.

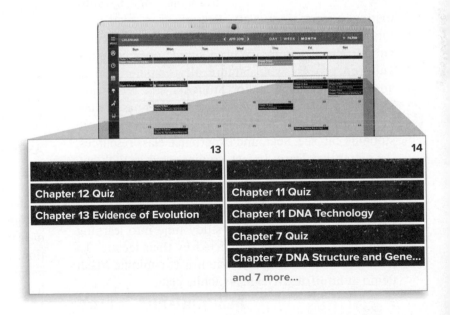

13		14
Chapter 12 Quiz		Chapter 11 Quiz
Chapter 13 Evidence of Evolution		Chapter 11 DNA Technology
		Chapter 7 Quiz
		Chapter 7 DNA Structure and Gene...
		and 7 more...

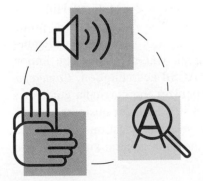

Learning for everyone.

McGraw-Hill works directly with Accessibility Services Departments and faculty to meet the learning needs of all students. Please contact your Accessibility Services office and ask them to email accessibility@mheducation.com, or visit **www.mheducation.com/about/accessibility.html** for more information.

Course Design and Delivery

 **CREATE** Instructors can now tailor their teaching resources to match the way they teach! With McGraw-Hill Create, **www.mcgrawhillcreate.com**, instructors can easily rearrange chapters, combine material from other content sources, and quickly upload and integrate their own content, such as course syllabi or teaching notes. Find the right content in Create by searching through thousands of leading McGraw-Hill textbooks. Arrange the material to fit your teaching style. Order a Create book and receive a complimentary print review copy in three to five business days or a complimentary electronic review copy via email within one hour. Go to **www.mcgrawhillcreate.com** today and register.

 **TEGRITY CAMPUS** Tegrity makes class time available 24/7 by automatically capturing every lecture in a searchable format for students to review when they study and complete assignments. With a simple one-click start-and-stop process, you capture all computer screens and corresponding audio. Students can replay any part of any class with easy-to-use browser-based viewing on a PC or Mac. Educators know that the more students can see, hear, and experience class resources, the better they learn. In fact, studies prove it. With patented Tegrity "search anything" technology, students instantly recall key class moments for replay online or on iPods and mobile devices. Instructors can help turn all their students' study time into learning moments immediately supported by their lecture. To learn more about Tegrity, watch a two-minute Flash demo at **http://tegritycampus.mhhe.com**.

 **BLACKBOARD® PARTNERSHIP** McGraw-Hill Education and Blackboard have teamed up to simplify your life. Now you and your students can access *Connect* and Create right from within your Blackboard course–all with one single sign-on. The grade books are seamless, so when a student completes an integrated *Connect* assignment, the grade for that assignment automatically (and instantly) feeds

your Blackboard grade center. Learn more at www.omorenow.com.

 **MCGRAW-HILL CAMPUS™** McGraw-Hill Campus is a new one-stop teaching and learning experience available to users of any learning management system. This institutional service allows faculty and students to enjoy single sign-on (SSO) access to all McGraw-Hill Higher Education materials, including the award-winning McGraw-Hill *Connect* platform, from directly within the institution's website. With McGraw-Hill Campus, faculty receive instant access to teaching materials (eTextbooks, test banks, PowerPoint slides, animations, learning objectives, etc.), allowing them to browse, search, and use any instructor ancillary content in our vast library at no additional cost to instructor or students. In addition, students enjoy SSO access to a variety of free content (quizzes, flash cards, narrated presentations, etc.) and subscription-based products (e.g., McGraw-Hill *Connect*). With McGraw-Hill Campus enabled, faculty and students will never need to create another account to access McGraw-Hill products and services. Learn more at **www.mhcampus.com**.

ASSURANCE OF LEARNING READY Many educational institutions today focus on the notion of *assurance of learning,* an important element of some accreditation standards. *Contemporary Management* is designed specifically to support instructors' assurance of learning initiatives with a simple yet powerful solution. Each test bank question for *Contemporary Management* maps to a specific chapter learning objective listed in the text.

AACSB TAGGING McGraw-Hill Education is a proud corporate member of AACSB International. Understanding the importance and value of AACSB accreditation, *Contemporary Management* recognizes the curricula guidelines detailed in the AACSB standards for business accreditation by connecting selected questions in the text and the test bank to the eight general knowledge and skill guidelines in the AACSB standards. The statements contained in *Contemporary Management* are provided only as a guide for the users of this product. The AACSB leaves content coverage and assessment within the purview of individual schools, the mission of the school, and the faculty. While the *Contemporary Management* teaching package makes no claim of any specific AACSB qualification or evaluation, we have within *Contemporary Management* labeled selected questions according to the eight general knowledge and skills areas.

MCGRAW-HILL CUSTOMER EXPERIENCE GROUP CONTACT INFORMATION At McGraw-Hill Education, we understand that getting the most from new technology can be challenging. That's why our services don't stop after you purchase our products. You can email our Product Specialists 24 hours a day to get product training online. Or you can search our knowledge bank of Frequently Asked Questions on our support website. For Customer Support, call **800-331-5094** or visit **www.mhhe.com/support**. One of our Technical Support Analysts will be able to assist you in a timely fashion.

ACKNOWLEDGMENTS

Finding a way to integrate and present the rapidly growing literature about contemporary management and make it interesting and meaningful for students is not an easy task. In writing and revising the various drafts of *Contemporary Management,* we have been fortunate to have the assistance of several people who have contributed greatly to the book's final form. First, we are grateful to Michael Ablassmeir, our director, for his ongoing support and commitment to our project and for always finding ways to provide the resources that we needed to continually improve and refine our book. Second, we are grateful to Haley Burmeister, our product developer, for so ably coordinating the book's progress; and to Debbie Clare, our marketing manager, for giving us concise and timely feedback and information from professors and reviewers that have allowed us to shape the book to the needs of its intended market. We also thank Jessica Cuevas for executing an awe-inspiring design; Kathryn Wright for coordinating the production process; and Iliya Atanasov (Rice University) and Marcie Lensges (Xavier University) for their assistance with research. We are also grateful to the many colleagues and reviewers who gave us useful and detailed feedback and perceptive comments and valuable suggestions for improving the manuscript.

Producing any competitive work is a challenge. Producing a truly market-driven textbook requires tremendous effort beyond simply obtaining reviews of a draft manuscript. Our goal was simple with the development of *Contemporary Management:* to be the most customer-driven principles of management text and supplement package ever published! With the goal of exceeding the expectations of both faculty and students, we executed one of the most aggressive product development plans ever undertaken in textbook publishing. Hundreds of faculty have taken part in developmental activities ranging from regional focus groups to manuscript and supplement reviews and surveys. Consequently, we're confident in assuring you and your students, our customers, that every aspect of our text and support package reflects your advice and needs. As you review it, we're confident that your reaction will be, "They listened!"

We extend our special thanks to the faculty who gave us detailed chapter-by-chapter feedback during the development of the eleventh edition:

Amy S. Banta, Ohio University

Charles Buchanan, The Ohio State University

Alex Chen, University of Central Arkansas

C. Brad Cox, Midlands Technical College

Susie S. Cox, University of Arkansas at Little Rock

Justin Gandy, Dallas Baptist University

Shahbaz Gill, University of Illinois–Urbana Champaign

Paul D. Johnson, University of Mississippi

Rusty Juban, Southeastern Louisiana University

Marcie Lensges, Xavier University

John E. Lewis, Midlands Technical College

Renee Nelms King, Eastern Illinois University

Sandy Jeanquart Miles, Murray State University

Ronald Purser, San Francisco State University

Bruce Wayne Richardson, Northeastern State University–Broken Arrow Campus

Steven A. Stewart, Georgia Southern University

W. Alexander Williams Jr., Texas A&M University–Commerce

And our thanks also go to the faculty who contributed greatly to previous editions of *Contemporary Management:*

Jerry Alley, Aspen University

M. Ruhul Amin, Bloomsburg University of Pennsylvania

Lindy Archambeau, University of Florida

Kelly Barbour-Conerty, Parkland College

Gerald Baumgardner, Pennsylvania College of Technology

Charles W. Beem, Bucks County Community College

James D. Bell, Texas State University

Danielle R. Blesi, Hudson Valley Community College

Susan Blumen, Montgomery College Department of Business and Economics

Jennifer P. Bott, Ball State University

Edwin L. Bowman, Principal, Manhattanville College, Purchase, NY

Charley Braun, Marshall University

Reginald Bruce, College of Business, University of Louisville

Murray Brunton, Central Ohio Technical College

Judith G. Bulin, Monroe Community College, Rochester, New York

Barry Bunn, Valencia Community College

Aaron Butler, Warner Pacific College ADP

Gerald Calvasina, Southern Utah University

Bruce H. Charnov, Hofstra University

Alexander Chen, University of Central Arkansas

Jay Christensen-Szalanski, University of Iowa

Jason W. Coleman, Wesley College

Joy Colarusso, Daytona State College

Renee Y. Cooper, Fashion Institute of Technology

Robert Cote, Lindenwood University

C. Brad Cox, Midlands Technical College

Marian Cox Crawford, University of Arkansas–Little Rock

Susie S. Cox, University of Arkansas-Little Rock

Cheryl Cunningham, Embry-Riddle Aeronautical University-Daytona Beach

Teresa A. Daniel, Marshall University

Thomas W. Deckelman, Owens Community College

Richard S. DeFrank, University of Houston

Fred J. Dorn, University of Mississippi

D. Harold Doty, University of Southern Mississippi

Max E. Douglas, Indiana State University

Sandra Edwards, Northeastern State University

Stewart W. Edwards, Northern VA Community College-Annandale

William Eichenauer, Northwest State Community College

Scott Elston, Iowa State University

Richard Estrella, California Polytechnic University

Valerie Evans, Kansas State University

Bagher Fardancsh, Piaget Consulting

Carla C. Flores, Ball State University

Andrea Foster, John Tyler Community College

Dane L. Galden, Columbus State Community College

Jim Glasgow, Instructor, Villanova School of Business

Monica Godsey, University of Nebraska

Selina Griswold, The University of Toledo

Kathy Hastings, Greenville Technical College

Karen H. Hawkins, Miami Dade College

Travis Lee Hayes, Chattanooga State Technical Community College

Samuel Hazen, Tarleton State University

Kim Hester, Arkansas State University

Perry Hidalgo, Gwinnett Technical College

Anne Kelly Hoel, University of Wisconsin-Stout

Robert C. Hoell, Georgia Southern University

Jenni Hunt, Southern Illinois University-Edwardsville

Irene Joanette-Gallio, Western Nevada College

Carol Larson Jones, Cal Poly Pomona, California

Coy A. Jones, The University of Memphis

Gwendolyn Jones, University of Akron

Kathleen Jones, University of North Dakota

Rusty Juban, Southeastern Louisiana University

Jordan J. Kaplan, Long Island University School of Business

Joanne E. Kapp, Siena College

Renee N. King, Eastern Illinois University

Deanna R. Knight, Daytona State College

Mike Knudstrup, Florida Southern College

Susan Kowalewski, D'Youville College

Cynthia J. Lanphear, University of the Ozarks

Jim Long, Southwestern Oklahoma State University

Joyce Lopez, Missouri State University

Margaret Lucero, Texas A&M-Corpus Christi

Nicholas Mathys, DePaul University

Daniel W. McAllister, University of Nevada-Las Vegas

Christy McLendon Corey, University of New Orleans

Chrisann Merriman, University of Mary Hardin-Baylor

Douglas L. Micklich, Illinois State University

Sandra Jeanquart Miles, Murray State University

Carol T. Miller, Community College of Denver

Don C. Mosley Jr., University of South Alabama

Clive Muir, Stetson University

Troy V. Mumford, Colorado State University

Bahaudin G. Mujtaba, Nova Southeastern University

Jane Murtaugh, College of DuPage

Nanci D. Newstrom, Eastern Illinois University

Catherine Nowicki, International Business College

John Overby, The University of Tennessee at Martin

Karen Overton, Houston Community College

Eren Ozgen, Troy University, Dothan Campus

Fernando A. Pargas, James Madison University

Marc Pendel, Miller College of Business, Ball State University

Susan A. Peterson, Scottsdale Community College

Gary Renz, Webster University

L. Jeff Seaton, University of Tennessee-Martin

Gregory J. Schultz, Carroll University

Marc Siegall, California State University-Chico

Randi L. Sims, Nova Southeastern University

Michaeline Skiba, Monmouth University-Leon Hess Business School

Frederick J. Slack, Indiana University of Pennsylvania

M. James Smas, Kent State University

Gerald Smith, University of Northern Iowa

Marjorie Smith, Mountain State University

Susan D. Steiner, The University of Tampa

Warren Stone, University of Arkansas at Little Rock

Cynthia L. Sutton, Metropolitan State College of Denver

Laurie Taylor-Hamm, California State University, Fresno

Sabine Turnley, Kansas State University

Isaiah O. Ugboro, North Carolina A&T State University

Velvet Weems, Landingham, Kent State University

John Weiss, Daytona State College

William K. Wesley, Golden Gate University

Elizabeth Wilson, Georgia Southwestern State University

Jan Zantinga, University of Georgia

Please note that these lists do not include the more than 200 faculty members who reviewed or contributed to earlier editions of the text.

Finally, we are grateful to two incredibly wonderful children, Nicholas and Julia, for being all that they are and for the joy they bring to all who know them.

Gareth R. Jones

Jennifer M. George
Jesse H. Jones Graduate School of Business
Rice University

CONTENTS

Chapter 3
Values, Attitudes, Emotions, and Culture: The Manager as a Person 56

A MANAGER'S CHALLENGE

CEO Illuminates a New Path for PG&E 57

Overview 58

Enduring Characteristics: Personality Traits 58

The Big Five Personality Traits 58 | MANAGER AS A PERSON: Openness to Experience Helps Lee Thrive 61 | Other Personality Traits That Affect Managerial Behavior 62 | Additional Personality Assessments 63

Values, Attitudes, and Moods and Emotions 64

Values: Terminal and Instrumental 64 | ETHICS IN ACTION: Promoting Ethical Values in the Hotel Industry 65 | Attitudes 65 | ETHICS IN ACTION: Subaru Protects Jobs and the Environment 67 | Moods and Emotions 68

Emotional Intelligence 70

MANAGING GLOBALLY: Emotional Intelligence across Borders 70

Organizational Culture 71

Managers and Organizational Culture 72 | The Role of Values and Norms in Organizational Culture 74 | Culture and Managerial Action 77

Summary and Review 79

Management in Action 80 | Building Management Skills 80 | Managing Ethically 80 | Small Group Breakout Exercise 81 | Be the Manager 81 | *Bloomberg Businessweek* CASE IN THE NEWS: The Undergrad Fixing Finance 81

Notes 83

Part Two | The Environment of Management

Chapter 4
Ethics and Social Responsibility 86

A MANAGER'S CHALLENGE

Musk Steers Tesla Ahead While Helping Others 87

Overview 88

The Nature of Ethics 88

Ethical Dilemmas 88 | Ethics and the Law 89 | Changes in Ethics over Time 89

Stakeholders and Ethics 90

Stockholders 91 | Managers 92 | Ethics and Nonprofit Organizations 93 | Employees 94 | Suppliers and Distributors 94 | Customers 94 | Community, Society, and Nation 94 | MANAGEMENT INSIGHT: Keeping Things Clean and Green 95 | Rules for Ethical Decision Making 97 | Why Should Managers Behave Ethically? 99

Ethics and Social Responsibility 101

Societal Ethics 102 | ETHICS IN ACTION: Sourcing Diamonds Responsibly 102 | Occupational Ethics 103 | Individual Ethics 103 | Organizational Ethics 104 | ETHICS IN ACTION: Chatbot Provides Ethical Guidance 106

Approaches to Social Responsibility 107

Four Different Approaches 108 | MANAGING GLOBALLY: Protecting Home-Based Workers 109 | Why Be Socially Responsible? 110 | The Role of Organizational Culture 110

Summary and Review 111

Management in Action 112 | Building Management Skills 112 | Managing Ethically 112 | Small Group Breakout Exercise 113 | Be the Manager 113 | *Bloomberg Businessweek* CASE IN THE NEWS: The Greening of Throwaway Stuff 113

Notes 115

Chapter 5
Managing Diverse Employees in a Multicultural Environment 118

A MANAGER'S CHALLENGE

Inclusion for Women Engineers at Intel 119

Overview 120

The Increasing Diversity of the Workforce and the Environment 120

Age 121 | Gender 122 | Race and Ethnicity 123 | MANAGING GLOBALLY: SodaStream's Oasis of Diversity 124 | Religion 124 |

Chapter 6
Managing in the Global
Environment 152

A MANAGER'S CHALLENGE

Amazon Primed for Success in India 153

Part Three | Decision Making, Planning, and Strategy

Chapter 7
Decision Making,
Learning, Creativity, and
Entrepreneurship 180

A MANAGER'S CHALLENGE

Creativity and Ability to Learn Keep 23andMe
Strong 181

Chapter 8
The Manager as a Planner
and Strategist   212

A MANAGER'S CHALLENGE
Sorenson Plans for Growth at Marriott   213

Overview   214

Chapter 9
Value Chain Management:
Functional Strategies
for Competitive
Advantage   244

A MANAGER'S CHALLENGE
Efficiency Frees Kraft Heinz to Innovate   245

Overview   246

Part Four | Organizing and Controlling

Chapter 10
Managing Organizational Structure and Culture 272

A MANAGER'S CHALLENGE

Chapter 11
Organizational Control and Change 308

A MANAGER'S CHALLENGE

Chapter 12
Human Resource Management   338

Part Five | Leading Individuals and Groups

Chapter 13
Motivation and Performance   372

Chapter 14
Leadership   404

Chapter 15
Effective Groups and Teams   434

Part Six | Managing Critical Organizational Processes

Chapter 16
Promoting Effective
Communication   466

Chapter 17
Managing Conflict, Politics,
and Negotiation   496

Chapter 18
Using Advanced
Information
Technology to Increase
Performance   522

CONTEMPORARY
Management

CHAPTER 1

Managers and Managing

©Sam Edwards/age fotostock

Learning Objectives

After studying this chapter, you should be able to:

LO1-1 Describe what management is, why management is important, what managers do, and how managers use organizational resources efficiently and effectively to achieve organizational goals.

LO1-2 Distinguish among planning, organizing, leading, and controlling (the four principal managerial tasks), and explain how managers' ability to handle each one affects organizational performance.

LO1-3 Differentiate among three levels of management, and understand the tasks and responsibilities of managers at different levels in the organizational hierarchy.

LO1-4 Distinguish among three kinds of managerial skill, and explain why managers are divided into different departments to perform their tasks more efficiently and effectively.

LO1-5 Discuss some major changes in management practices today that have occurred as a result of globalization and the use of advanced information technology (IT).

LO1-6 Discuss the principal challenges managers face in today's increasingly competitive global environment.

Satya Nadella Reboots Microsoft

What difference can a manager make?

After the success of its Windows operating system and Office software suite, Microsoft struggled to find a source of new growth. While earnings continued to rise, an unmoving stock price suggested that investors no longer saw a rosy future.[1] This changed when Microsoft made Satya Nadella its third chief executive officer (CEO).

Nadella brought a fresh vision. Microsoft had defined its mission as a personal computer on every desk and in every home, running Microsoft's software. By the end of the millennium in most of the world, that mission was accomplished. It no longer illuminated a way forward. Nadella introduced a new mission: to "create technology so that others can create more technology," enabling people and organizations to accomplish more.[2] This is a view of technology being beneficial—for example, opening ways for people with disabilities to participate in the world more fully.

Nadella brought Microsoft a new kind of leadership, based on empathy. Empathy includes listening carefully for customer needs—information essential for providing relevant products and services.[3] Nadella asks employees to use empathy with one another, too. Leading by example, he conducts town-hall meetings online, inviting employees to give live feedback by submitting anonymous emojis, which he reviews to gauge employee concerns.[4] He also is known for listening attentively to employees' ideas.

Nadella instructs employees to avoid a fixed mind-set, using existing skills to reach some endpoint and then staying put. He teaches a growth mind-set, based on learning and constantly improving. Nadella exemplifies this with his open mindedness toward his own performance. He has said that reflecting on

Microsoft CEO Satya Nadella has brought a new perspective and vision to the tech giant. His leadership and focus on empathy and diversity are a winning combination.
©Matt Winkelmeyer/Getty Images

his mistakes inspires him, as it motivates him to change.[5] He shares this spirit in each of the leadership team's weekly meetings by scheduling a presentation by employees who are working on something exciting. When employees try for growth but fall short, Nadella encourages them to push on and fix the problem.

Nadella values diversity. High-tech companies have been criticized as unfriendly to some employees, particularly women. In contrast, Nadella's drive for a culture of empathy fosters an environment that recognizes all employees' contributions. His goal is that Microsoft will not merely hire a diverse workforce, but enable employees to participate and thrive. Nadella is particularly committed to providing opportunities for persons with disabilities.

What prepared Nadella for all this? He knows the business well, having worked for Microsoft since age 25. Raised in Hyderabad, India, he earned a master's degree in computer science from the University of Wisconsin–Madison and joined Microsoft after a few years with Sun Microsystems. He accepted tough assignments and guidance from mentors, including a Netflix executive who took him to board meetings so Nadella could see that company's agile decision making. He reads widely and is skillful at making connections among ideas. Being the father of three children, two with disabilities, has taught him the value of empathy and a desire to empower people to make change.[6]

Under Nadella's leadership, Microsoft is exceeding expectations. It is getting involved in today's cutting-edge technology. Employee morale and product quality have risen, and the market value of its stock has soared.[7]

Overview

Managing today's organizations is a complex affair, and seasoned leaders like Satya Nadella face multiple challenges from within and outside their organizations. To make decisions and lead others successfully, managers must possess a complex set of skills, knowledge, and abilities that help them interpret cues from the environment and respond accordingly.

In this chapter we consider what managers do and the skills, knowledge, and abilities they must possess to lead their organizations effectively. We also identify the different kinds of managers that organizations rely on to help guide them. Finally, we consider some of the challenges that managers must overcome to help their organizations prosper.

What Is Management?

When you think of a manager, what kind of person comes to mind? Do you think of an executive like Satya Nadella, who helps direct his company? Or do you see a manager at a fast-food restaurant, who engages directly with employees and customers? Perhaps you think of a foreman at a manufacturing company? Regardless of how we view managers, they all share important characteristics. First, they all work in organizations. **Organizations** are collections of people who work together and coordinate their actions to achieve a wide variety of goals or desired future outcomes. Second, as managers, they are the people responsible for supervising and making the most of an organization's human and other resources to achieve its goals.

Management, then, is the planning, organizing, leading, and controlling of human and other resources to achieve organizational goals efficiently and effectively. An organization's *resources* include assets such as people and their skills, know-how, and experience; machinery; raw materials; computers and information technology; and patents, financial capital, and loyal customers and employees.

organizations Collections of people who work together and coordinate their actions to achieve a wide variety of goals or desired future outcomes.

management The planning, organizing, leading, and controlling of human and other resources to achieve organizational goals efficiently and effectively.

4

Achieving High Performance: A Manager's Goal

One of the key goals that organizations try to achieve is to provide goods and services that customers value and desire. Satya Nadella's principal goal is to manage Microsoft so that the company continues to leverage cutting edge technology and to innovate with new products and services for the global marketplace. Likewise, the principal goal of fast-food managers is to produce tasty and convenient food that customers enjoy and come back to buy. Finally, manufacturing managers must balance the quality needs of their consumers against the pressure to be cost-effective.

Organizational performance is a measure of how efficiently and effectively managers use available resources to satisfy customers and achieve organizational goals. Organizational performance increases in direct proportion to increases in efficiency and effectiveness, as Figure 1.1 shows. What are efficiency and effectiveness?

Efficiency is a measure of how productively resources are used to achieve a goal.[8] Organizations are efficient when managers minimize the amount of input resources (such as labor, raw materials, and component parts) or the amount of time needed to produce a given output of goods or services. For example, Burger King develops ever more efficient fat fryers that not only reduce the amount of oil used in cooking but also speed up the cooking of french fries. UPS develops new work routines to reduce delivery time, such as instructing drivers to leave their truck doors open when going short distances.

To encourage efficiency, CEO Nadella has led Microsoft in a comprehensive retooling of the company's products and services since he took the helm less than five years ago. He has eliminated unsuccessful product lines while expanding others and continues to foster a collaborative environment in which he encourages employees to be fearless in their efforts to help transform the company into a digital powerhouse.[9]

Effectiveness is a measure of the *appropriateness* of the goals that managers have selected for the organization to pursue and the degree to which the organization achieves those goals.

Figure 1.1
Efficiency, Effectiveness, and Performance in an Organization

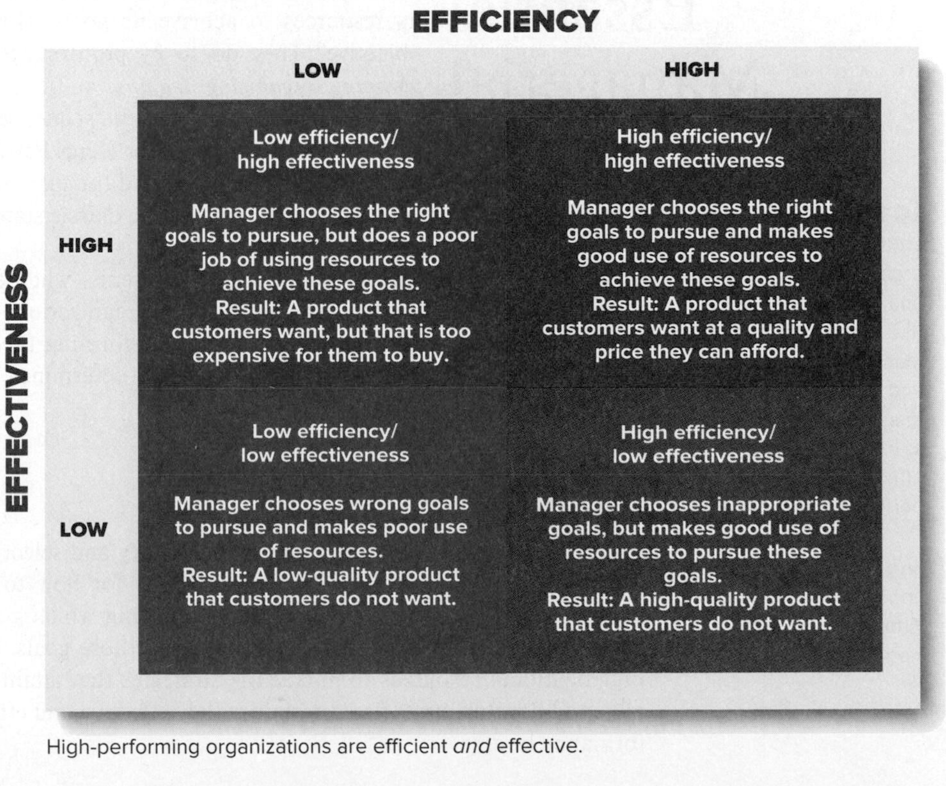

EFFICIENCY

	LOW	HIGH
HIGH (EFFECTIVENESS)	**Low efficiency/ high effectiveness** Manager chooses the right goals to pursue, but does a poor job of using resources to achieve these goals. Result: A product that customers want, but that is too expensive for them to buy.	**High efficiency/ high effectiveness** Manager chooses the right goals to pursue and makes good use of resources to achieve these goals. Result: A product that customers want at a quality and price they can afford.
LOW (EFFECTIVENESS)	**Low efficiency/ low effectiveness** Manager chooses wrong goals to pursue and makes poor use of resources. Result: A low-quality product that customers do not want.	**High efficiency/ low effectiveness** Manager chooses inappropriate goals, but makes good use of resources to pursue these goals. Result: A high-quality product that customers do not want.

High-performing organizations are efficient *and* effective.

Organizations are effective when managers choose appropriate goals and then achieve them. Some years ago, for example, managers at McDonald's decided on the goal of providing breakfast service to attract more customers. The choice of this goal proved smart: Sales of breakfast food accounted for more than one-third of company revenues over the years. In 2015, in an effort to increase overall sales, McDonald's management made the decision to serve breakfast all day long, a strategy that has been successful and well received by consumers.[10] High-performing organizations such as Apple, McDonald's, Walmart, Intel, Home Depot, Accenture, and Habitat for Humanity are simultaneously efficient and effective. Effective managers are those who choose the right organizational goals to pursue and have the skills to utilize resources efficiently.

Why Study Management?

The dynamic and complex nature of modern work means that managerial skills are in demand. Organizations need individuals like you, who can understand this complexity, respond to environmental contingencies, and make decisions that are ethical and effective. Studying management helps equip individuals to accomplish each of these tasks.

In a broader sense, individuals generally learn through personal experience (think the "school of hard knocks") or the experiences of others. By studying management in school, you are exposing yourself to the lessons others have learned. The advantage of such social learning is that you are not bound to repeat the mistakes others have made in the past. Furthermore, by studying and practicing the behaviors of good managers and high-performing companies, you will equip yourself to help your future employer succeed.

The economic benefits of becoming a good manager are also impressive. In the United States, general managers earn a median wage of $99,310, with a projected growth rate in job openings for 5% to 9% between now and 2026.[11]

Finally, learning management principles can help you make good decisions in nonwork contexts. If you're coaching a child's baseball team, organizing a charity 5K run, planning your financial budget, or starting a new business, good management principles will help you understand others, make quality decisions, and improve your personal success.

Essential Managerial Tasks

LO1-2 Distinguish among planning, organizing, leading, and controlling (the four principal managerial tasks), and explain how managers' ability to handle each one affects organizational performance.

planning Identifying and selecting appropriate goals; one of the four principal tasks of management.

The job of management is to help an organization make the best use of its resources to achieve its goals. How do managers accomplish this objective? They do so by performing four essential managerial tasks: *planning, organizing, leading,* and *controlling.* The arrows linking these tasks in Figure 1.2 suggest the sequence in which managers typically perform them. French manager Henri Fayol first outlined the nature of these managerial activities around the turn of the 20th century in *General and Industrial Management,* a book that remains the classic statement of what managers must do to create a high-performing organization.[12]

Managers at all levels and in all departments—whether in small or large companies, for-profit or not-for-profit organizations, or organizations that operate in one country or throughout the world—are responsible for performing these four tasks, which we look at next. How well managers perform these tasks determines how efficient and effective their organizations are.

Planning

To perform the planning task, managers identify and select appropriate organizational goals and courses of action; they develop *strategies* for how to achieve high performance. The three steps involved in planning are (1) deciding which goals the organization will pursue, (2) deciding what strategies to adopt to attain those goals, and (3) deciding how to allocate organizational resources to pursue the strategies that attain those goals. How well managers plan and develop strategies determines how effective and efficient the organization is—its performance level.[13]

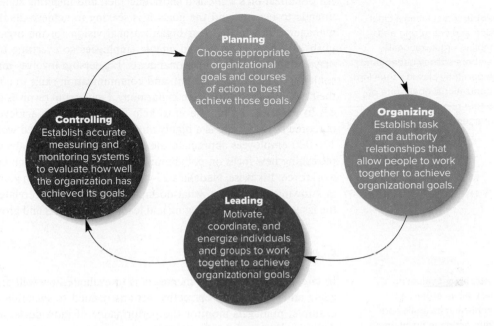

Figure 1.2

Four Tasks of Management

As an example of planning in action, consider Microsoft's recent innovation in artificial intelligence (AI) with its app, Seeing AI, which uses computer vision to audibly help blind and visually impaired people "see" the world around them through narration on an iOS device. Users can customize the voice it uses to verbalize observations and set how fast the voice talks. In addition, the app boasts currency recognition (e.g., U.S. dollars, British pounds, Euros), can detect the color of specific objects like clothing, recognizes handwriting, and includes a musical light detector to alert users with an audible tone to light in a specific environment. Microsoft says this last feature will save users from touching a hot bulb or LED battery to check if it's working. To date, the app has been downloaded more than 100,000 times since its release in 2017 and is now available in 35 countries.[14]

Organizing

organizing Structuring working relationships in a way that allows organizational members to work together to achieve organizational goals; one of the four principal tasks of management.

organizational structure A formal system of task and reporting relationships that coordinates and motivates organizational members so they work together to achieve organizational goals.

Organizing is structuring working relationships so organizational members interact and cooperate to achieve organizational goals. Organizing people into departments according to the kinds of job-specific tasks they perform lays out the lines of authority and responsibility between different individuals and groups. Managers must decide how best to organize resources, particularly human resources.

The outcome of organizing is the creation of an **organizational structure**, a formal system of task and reporting relationships that coordinates and motivates members so they work together to achieve organizational goals. Organizational structure determines how an organization's resources can be best used to create goods and services. As Microsoft shifts its focus from PCs and software to cloud services and other innovations, management continues to face the issue of how best to structure or reorganize different groups within the organization. For example, Microsoft recently announced a new model to help explain the restructuring of its sales force. For fiscal year 2018, Microsoft reorganized its commercial field sales team around two customer segments: enterprise customers and small, medium, and corporate (SMC) customers. According to executive vice president Judson Althoff, Microsoft's highest growth opportunities will be in the enterprise sector, with specialist sales teams focused on new business. Going forward, Microsoft will continue to target six high-priority vertical markets: manufacturing, financial services, retail, health, education, and government.[15] We examine the organizing process in detail in Chapters 10 through 12.

Leading

leading Articulating a clear vision and energizing and enabling organizational members so they understand the part they play in achieving organizational goals; one of the four principal tasks of management.

An organization's *vision* is a short, succinct, and inspiring statement of what the organization intends to become and the goals it is seeking to achieve—its desired future state. In leading, managers articulate a clear organizational vision for the organization's members to accomplish, and they energize and enable employees so everyone understands the part he or she plays in achieving organizational goals. Leadership involves managers using their power, personality, influence, persuasion, and communication skills to coordinate people and groups so their activities and efforts are in harmony. Leadership revolves around encouraging all employees to perform at a high level to help the organization achieve its vision and goals. Another outcome of leadership is a highly motivated and committed workforce. Microsoft's more than 120,000 employees appreciate the core values of their leadership, especially CEO Nadella's refreshing new focus on collaboration and innovation, which contributes to their success as a workforce. Likewise, Nadella's 25-year tenure with the tech giant gives him a competitive edge in knowing what works, what doesn't, and how better to relate to his employees. We discuss the issues involved in managing and leading individuals and groups in Chapters 13 through 16.

Controlling

controlling Evaluating how well an organization is achieving its goals and taking action to maintain or improve performance; one of the four principal tasks of management.

In controlling, the task of managers is to evaluate how well an organization has achieved its goals and to take any corrective actions needed to maintain or improve performance. For example, managers monitor the performance of individuals, departments, and the organization as a whole to see whether they are meeting desired performance standards. Satya Nadella learned early in his career about the importance of monitoring performance to ensure that his organization realized its profit objectives. When these goals fall short, Nadella and Microsoft's management team must find ways to improve performance.

The outcome of the control process is the ability to measure performance accurately and regulate organizational efficiency and effectiveness. To exercise control, managers must decide which goals to measure—perhaps goals pertaining to productivity, quality, or responsiveness to customers—and then they must design control systems that will provide the information necessary to assess performance—that is, determine to what degree the goals have been met. The controlling task also helps managers evaluate how well they themselves are performing the other three tasks of management—planning, organizing, and leading—and take corrective action. For an example of a manager who excels at controlling, see the "Manager as a Person" feature.

MANAGER AS A PERSON

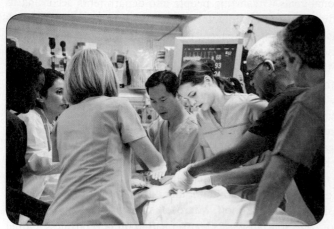

Working closely with employees can help managers control daily operations and increase efficiencies, even in a busy ER department.

©monkeybusinessimages/Getty Images

Making ER Visits as Painless as Possible

If you've ever had the misfortune of visiting a hospital's emergency room, you know the hardest part can be waiting for a doctor. And on the hospital's side, ERs have their own challenges from serving patients who are often in desperate situations. The best case, then, is to have a manager like Erin Daley, the ER director for Mercy Medical Center in Massachusetts.

Daley says that since her days as a nursing student, she has loved "everything" about working in an emergency room.[16] She sees an exciting challenge in the way each patient's arrival can require the staff to restructure all their activities to meet the most pressing need. Thriving in that environment, Daley spent a decade in Mercy's

ER, moving up from staff nurse to charge nurse to clinical nurse supervisor. The supervisory position gave her experience in hiring and scheduling. From there, she moved up to the nurse manager position, adding duties related to the productivity of the nursing staff.[17]

In her role as ER director, Daley focuses on improving the department's performance in meeting objectives for efficiency and quality of care. While keeping costs within her $65 million budget, she has found ways her staff can move patients through the system faster while improving survey scores for patient satisfaction. Under her watch, Mercy's ER has also cut the rate of patients who leave before they have been seen by a doctor. In a further measure of quality performance, Mercy has won awards for superior care of patients who experience strokes.[18]

Daley's approach involves working with her team to study exactly what steps occur to take a patient through the process of getting care. Team members look for any wasted steps they can cut to improve efficiency. They set up a process that sorts patients who have less severe conditions in which they don't need a bed from those with more serious conditions. Those in the first group are seen in one room and then discharged, while the others follow a separate process. Before this process was implemented, beds were too often filled with patients who didn't really need them. The team also set up systems for treating ER patients as a "whole person," not just a broken leg or a drug overdose. This means educating patients about their conditions, planning what will happen after their release, and following up to help manage their recovery.[19]

The four managerial tasks—planning, organizing, leading, and controlling—are essential parts of a manager's job. At all levels in the managerial hierarchy, and across all jobs and departments in an organization, effective management means performing these four activities successfully in ways that increase efficiency and effectiveness.

Performing Managerial Tasks: Mintzberg's Typology

So far, our discussion of management has presented it as an orderly process in which individuals carefully weigh information before making the best possible decision. Henry Mintzberg was one of the first to show that management is often chaotic, marked by quick decisions in a tense and sometimes emotional environment. Quick, immediate reactions to situations, rather than deliberate thought and reflection, are an important aspect of managerial action. Mintzberg, a professor at McGill University, has spent most of his life researching management in an attempt to help organizations better achieve their goals in an ethical manner. Some of his most important research examined the different roles that managers play in organizations and directly informs our discussion in this chapter. Often managers are overloaded with responsibilities and do not have time to analyze every nuance of a situation; they therefore make decisions in uncertain conditions, not knowing which outcomes will be best.[20] Moreover, top managers face constantly changing situations, and a decision that seems right today may prove to be wrong tomorrow. The range of problems that managers face is enormous; managers usually must handle many problems simultaneously; and they often must make snap decisions using the intuition and experience gained through their careers to perform their jobs to the best of their abilities.[21] Henry Mintzberg, by following managers and observing what they actually *do* hour by hour and day by day, identified 10 kinds of specific roles, or sets of job responsibilities, that capture the dynamic nature of managerial work.[22] He grouped these roles according to whether the responsibility is primarily decisional, interpersonal, or informational; they are described in Table 1.1.

Given the many complex, difficult job responsibilities managers have, it is no small wonder that many claim they are performing their jobs well if they are right just half of the time.[23] And it is understandable that many experienced managers accept their subordinates' failure as a normal part of the learning experience and a rite of passage to becoming an effective manager. Managers and their subordinates learn from both their successes and their failures.

Table 1.1

Managerial Roles Identified by Mintzberg

Type of Role	Specific Role	Examples of Role Activities
Decisional	Entrepreneur	Commit organizational resources to develop innovative goods and services; decide to expand internationally to obtain new customers for the organization's products.
	Disturbance handler	Move quickly to take corrective action to deal with unexpected problems facing the organization from the external environment, such as a crisis like an oil spill, or from the internal environment, such as producing faulty goods or services.
	Resource allocator	Allocate organizational resources among different tasks and departments of the organization; set budgets and salaries of middle and first-level managers.
	Negotiator	Work with suppliers, distributors, and labor unions to reach agreements about the quality and price of input, technical, and human resources; work with other organizations to establish agreements to pool resources to work on joint projects.
Interpersonal	Figurehead	Outline future organizational goals to employees at company meetings; open a new corporate headquarters building; state the organization's ethical guidelines and the principles of behavior employees are to follow in their dealings with customers and suppliers.
	Leader	Provide an example for employees to follow; give direct commands and orders to subordinates; make decisions concerning the use of human and technical resources; mobilize employee support for specific organizational goals.
	Liaison	Coordinate the work of managers in different departments; establish alliances between different organizations to share resources to produce new goods and services.
Informational	Monitor	Evaluate the performance of managers in different tasks and take corrective action to improve their performance; watch for changes occurring in the external and internal environments that may affect the organization in the future.
	Disseminator	Inform employees about changes taking place in the external and internal environments that will affect them and the organization; communicate to employees the organization's vision and purpose.
	Spokesperson	Launch a national advertising campaign to promote new goods and services; give a speech to inform the local community about the organization's future intentions.

Levels and Skills of Managers

To perform the four managerial tasks efficiently and effectively, organizations group or differentiate their managers in two main ways—by level in hierarchy and by type of skill. First, they differentiate managers according to their level or rank in the organization's hierarchy of authority. The three levels of managers are first-line managers, middle managers, and top managers—arranged in a hierarchy. Typically, first-line managers report to middle managers, and middle managers report to top managers.

Second, organizations group managers into different departments (or functions) according to their specific job-related skills, expertise, and experiences, such as a manager's engineering

department A group of people who work together and possess similar skills or use the same knowledge, tools, or techniques to perform their jobs.

skills, marketing expertise, or sales experience. A **department**, such as the manufacturing, accounting, engineering, or sales department, is a group of managers and employees who work together because they possess similar skills and experience or use the same kind of knowledge, tools, or techniques to perform their jobs. Within each department are all three levels of management. Next we examine why organizations use a hierarchy of managers and group them, by the jobs they perform, into departments.

Levels of Management

LO1-3 Differentiate among three levels of management, and understand the tasks and responsibilities of managers at different levels in the organizational hierarchy.

first-line manager A manager who is responsible for the daily supervision of nonmanagerial employees.

middle manager A manager who supervises first-line managers and is responsible for finding the best way to use resources to achieve organizational goals.

Organizations normally have three levels of management: first-line managers, middle managers, and top managers (see Figure 1.3). Managers at each level have different but related responsibilities for using organizational resources to increase efficiency and effectiveness.

At the base of the managerial hierarchy are **first-line managers**, often called *supervisors*. They are responsible for daily supervision of the nonmanagerial employees who perform the specific activities necessary to produce goods and services. First-line managers work in all departments or functions of an organization. Examples of first-line managers include the supervisor of a work team in the manufacturing department of a car plant, the head nurse in the obstetrics department of a hospital, and the chief mechanic overseeing a crew of mechanics in the service function of a new car dealership.

Supervising the first-line managers are **middle managers**, responsible for finding the best way to organize human and other resources to achieve organizational goals. To increase efficiency, middle managers find ways to help first-line managers and nonmanagerial employees better use resources to reduce manufacturing costs or improve customer service. To increase effectiveness, middle managers evaluate whether the organization's goals are appropriate and suggest to top managers how goals should be changed. Often the suggestions that middle managers make to top managers can dramatically increase organizational performance. A major part of the middle manager's job is developing and fine-tuning skills and know-how, such as manufacturing or marketing expertise, that allow the organization to be efficient and effective. Middle managers make thousands of specific decisions about the production of goods and services: Which first-line supervisors should be chosen for this particular project? Where can we find the highest-quality resources? How should employees be organized to allow them to make the best use of resources?

Figure 1.3
Levels of Managers

Behind a top-notch sales force, look for the middle managers responsible for training, motivating, and rewarding the salespeople. Behind a committed staff of high school teachers, look for the principal who energizes them to find ways to obtain the resources they need to do outstanding and innovative jobs in the classroom.

top manager A manager who establishes organizational goals, decides how departments should interact, and monitors the performance of middle managers.

In contrast to middle managers, **top managers** are responsible for the performance of *all* departments. They have *cross-departmental responsibility.* Top managers establish organizational goals, such as which goods and services the company should produce; they decide how the different departments should interact; and they monitor how well middle managers in each department use resources to achieve goals.[24] Top managers are ultimately responsible for the success or failure of an organization, and their performance is continually scrutinized by people inside and outside the organization, such as other employees and investors.[25]

The *chief executive officer (CEO)* is a company's most senior and important manager, the one all other top managers report to. Today the term *chief operating officer (COO)* often refers to top managers, who are being groomed to assume CEO responsibilities when the current CEO retires, leaves the company, or assumes other responsibilities. Together the CEO and COO are responsible for developing good working relationships among the top managers of various departments (manufacturing and marketing, for example); usually, these top managers have the title "vice president." A central concern of the CEO is the creation of a smoothly functioning **top management team**, a group composed of the CEO, the COO, and the vice presidents most responsible for achieving organizational goals.[26]

top management team A group composed of the CEO, the COO, and the vice presidents most responsible for achieving organizational goals.

The relative importance of planning, organizing, leading, and controlling—the four principal managerial tasks—to any manager depends on the manager's position in the managerial hierarchy.[27] The amount of time managers spend planning and organizing resources to maintain and improve organizational performance increases as they ascend the hierarchy (see Figure 1.4).[28] Top managers devote most of their time to planning and organizing, the tasks so crucial to determining an organization's long-term performance. The lower that managers' positions are in the hierarchy, the more time the managers spend leading and controlling first-line managers or nonmanagerial employees.

Figure 1.4

Relative Amount of Time Managers Spend on the Four Managerial Tasks

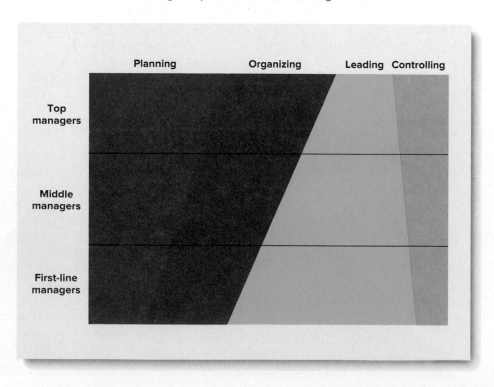

Managerial Skills

LO1-4 Distinguish among three kinds of managerial skill, and explain why managers are divided into different departments to perform their tasks more efficiently and effectively.

conceptual skills The ability to analyze and diagnose a situation and to distinguish between cause and effect.

Both education and experience enable managers to recognize and develop the personal skills they need to put organizational resources to their best use. Research has shown that education and experience help managers acquire and develop three types of skills: *conceptual, human,* and *technical.*[29]

Conceptual skills are demonstrated in the general ability to analyze and diagnose a situation and to distinguish between cause and effect. Top managers require the best conceptual skills because their primary responsibilities are planning and organizing.[30] Managers like Satya Nadella must constantly identify new opportunities and mobilize organizational resources to take advantage of those opportunities.

Formal education and training are important in helping managers develop conceptual skills. Business training at the undergraduate and graduate (MBA) levels provides many of the conceptual tools (theories and techniques in marketing, finance, and other areas) that managers need to perform their roles effectively. The study of management helps develop the skills that allow managers to understand the big picture confronting an organization. The ability to focus on the big picture lets managers see beyond the immediate situation and consider choices while keeping in mind the organization's long-term goals.

Today continuing management education and training, including training in advanced information technology (IT), are an integral part of building managerial skills because new theories and techniques are constantly being developed to improve organizational effectiveness, such as total quality management, global supply chain management, and cloud computing and virtual business-to-business (B2B) networks. A quick scan through a magazine such as *Bloomberg Businessweek* or *Fortune* reveals a host of seminars on topics such as advanced marketing, finance, leadership, and human resource management that are offered to managers at many levels in the organization, from the most senior corporate executives to middle managers. Microsoft, IBM, Oracle, and many other organizations designate a portion of each manager's personal budget to be used at the manager's discretion to attend management development programs.

In addition, organizations may wish to develop a particular manager's abilities in a specific skill area—perhaps to learn an advanced component of departmental skills, such as international bond trading, or to learn the skills necessary to implement a total quality management program. The organization thus pays for managers to attend specialized programs to develop these skills. Indeed, one signal that a manager is performing well is an organization's willingness to invest in that manager's skill development. Similarly, many nonmanagerial employees who are performing at a high level (because they have studied management) are often sent to intensive management training programs to develop their management skills and to prepare them for promotion to first-level management positions.

human skills The ability to understand, alter, lead, and control the behavior of other individuals and groups.

Human skills include the general ability to understand, alter, lead, and control the behavior of other individuals and groups. The ability to communicate, to coordinate, to motivate, and to mold individuals into a cohesive team distinguishes effective from ineffective managers. Skills such as these are especially significant for successful management in the public (government) sector, as described in the "Management Insight" feature. Like conceptual skills, human skills can be learned through education and training, as well as be developed through experience.[31] Organizations increasingly use advanced programs in leadership skills and team leadership as they seek to capitalize on the advantages of self-managed teams.[32] To manage personal interactions effectively, each person in an organization needs to learn how to empathize with other people—to understand their viewpoints and the problems they face. One way to help managers understand their personal strengths and weaknesses is to have their superiors, peers, and subordinates provide feedback about their job performance. Thorough and direct feedback allows managers to develop their human skills.

technical skills The job-specific knowledge and techniques required to perform an organizational role.

Technical skills are the *job-specific* skills required to perform a particular type of work or occupation at a high level. Examples include a manager's specific manufacturing, accounting, marketing, and IT skills. Managers need a range of technical skills to be effective. The array of technical skills managers need depends on their position in their organizations. The manager of a restaurant, for example, may need cooking skills to fill in for an absent cook, accounting and bookkeeping skills to keep track of receipts and costs and to administer the payroll, and aesthetic skills to keep the restaurant looking attractive for customers.

Succeeding as a City Manager

Businesses are not the only organizations that need people with management skills. Governments are an important sector of the economy that also employs managers. Many cities, for example, have a government structure in which an elected city council hires a manager to oversee the work of the city government.

A city manager faces the challenge of serving a diverse group of citizens while also maintaining productive relationships with the elected officials who hired him or her. Jim Schutz recalls that when he became city manager of San Rafael, California, he faced a steep learning curve.[33] On any given day, the issues he faced included personnel matters, budget shortfalls, emergencies involving the police and fire departments, and publicly aired complaints from unhappy residents. He has faced those with a vision of a service-oriented approach to providing government services and a growing appreciation of the community's many strengths. Keeping his approach positive has helped him succeed in the job.

As Schutz discovered, a key part of the city manager's necessary skills involves the ability to work with other people. The council members who hire and fire a city manager are necessarily concerned with the political impact of actions taken by the city government.[34] Therefore, the manager needs to plan for residents' and politicians' reactions to any new policy or new spending. The manager also has to build support from and cooperation with other members of the local government, such as judges and administrators of the public schools. And the city manager is usually the one to carry out personnel decisions, such as hiring and firing.

To bring these skills to the job, a city manager needs experience in working for a local government. Many managers seek education beyond a bachelor's degree, such as a master's in public administration.[35] A group of public managers in Massachusetts determined that city managers could bring more skills to the job if they had a training program. They pooled their experience to create a boot camp for new managers and administrators, which focuses on human skills such as working effectively with government colleagues, taking a leadership role in the community, and developing a network for career support.[36] City managers have found that sharing experiences at the boot camp is a valuable way to build skills for their complex jobs.

As noted earlier, managers and employees who possess the same kinds of technical skills typically become members of a specific department and are known as, for example, marketing managers or manufacturing managers.[37] Managers are grouped into different departments because a major part of a manager's responsibility is to monitor, train, and supervise employees so their job-specific skills and expertise increase. Obviously this is easier to do when employees with similar skills are grouped into the same department because they can learn from one another and become more skilled and productive at their particular jobs.

Figure 1.5 shows how an organization groups managers into departments on the basis of their job-specific skills. It also shows that inside each department, a managerial hierarchy of first-line, middle, and top managers emerges. These managers work together on similar tasks in departments. For example, middle and front-line managers may specialize in areas such as marketing and sales, human resource management, accounting, engineering, or production. When the head of manufacturing finds that she has no time to supervise computer assembly, she may recruit experienced manufacturing middle managers from other companies to assume this responsibility.

core competency The specific set of departmental skills, knowledge, and experience that allows one organization to outperform another.

Today the term **core competency** is often used to refer to the specific set of departmental skills, knowledge, and experience that allows one organization to outperform its competitors. In other words, departmental skills that create a core competency give an organization a

Figure 1.5

Types and Levels of Managers

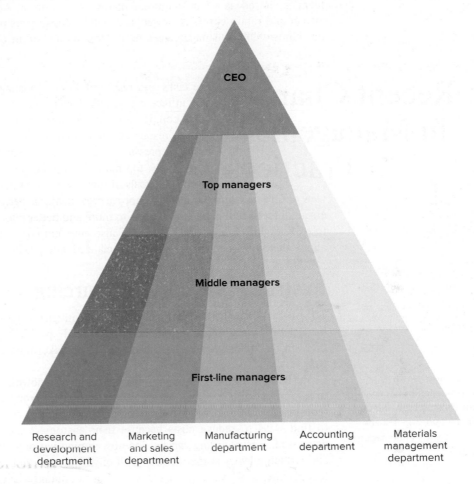

competitive advantage. Dell, for example, was the first PC maker to develop a core competency in materials management that allowed it to produce PCs at a much lower cost than its competitors—a major source of competitive advantage. Google is well known for its core competency in research and development (R&D) that allows it to innovate new products and services at a faster rate than its competitors. From computerized glasses to self-driving cars, Google has been pioneering the development of technology for the masses.

Effective managers need all three kinds of skills—conceptual, human, and technical—to help their organizations perform more efficiently and effectively. The absence of even one type of managerial skill can lead to failure. One of the biggest problems that people who start small businesses confront, for example, is their lack of appropriate conceptual and human skills. Someone who has the technical skills to start a new business does not necessarily know how to manage the venture successfully. Similarly, one of the biggest problems that scientists or engineers who switch careers from research to management confront is their lack of effective human skills. Ambitious managers or prospective managers are constantly in search of the latest educational contributions to help them develop the conceptual, human, and technical skills they need to perform at a high level in today's changing and increasingly competitive global environment.

Developing new and improved skills through education and training has become a priority for both aspiring managers and the organizations they work for. Many people are enrolling in advanced management courses, and many companies, such as Microsoft, GE, and IBM, have established their own colleges to train and develop their employees and managers at all levels. Every year these companies put thousands of their employees through management programs designed to identify the employees who the company believes have the competencies that can be developed to become its future top managers. Most organizations closely link promotion to a manager's ability to acquire the competencies a particular company believes are important.[38] At Apple and 3M, for example, the ability to successfully lead a new product development team is viewed as a vital requirement for promotion; at Accenture and IBM, the ability to attract and retain clients is viewed as a skill its consultants must possess. We discuss the various kinds of skills managers need to develop in most of the chapters of this book.

Recent Changes in Management Practices

The tasks and responsibilities of managers have been changing dramatically in recent years. Two major factors that have led to these changes are global competition and advances in information technology. Stiff competition for resources from organizations both at home and abroad has put increased pressure on all managers to improve efficiency and effectiveness. Increasingly, top managers are encouraging lower-level managers to look beyond the goals of their own departments and take a cross-departmental view to find new opportunities to improve organizational performance. Modern IT gives managers at all levels and in all areas access to more and better information and improves their ability to plan, organize, lead, and control. IT also gives employees more job-related information and allows them to become more skilled, specialized, and productive.[39]

Restructuring and Outsourcing

To utilize IT to increase efficiency and effectiveness, CEOs and top management teams have restructured organizations and outsourced specific organizational activities to reduce the number of employees on the payroll and make more productive use of the remaining workforce.

restructuring Downsizing an organization by eliminating the jobs of large numbers of top, middle, and first-line managers and nonmanagerial employees.

Restructuring involves simplifying, shrinking, or downsizing an organization's operations to lower operating costs, as Macy's, Microsoft, and Xerox have been forced to do. The global recession of 2008–2010 forced most companies—large and small, and profit and nonprofit—to find ways to reduce costs because their customers spent less money, so their revenues decreased. Restructuring can be done by eliminating product teams, shrinking departments, and reducing levels in the hierarchy, all of which result in the loss of large numbers of jobs of top, middle, or first-line managers, as well as nonmanagerial employees. Modern IT's ability to improve efficiency has increased the amount of downsizing in recent years because IT makes it possible for fewer employees to perform a given task. IT increases each person's ability to process information and make decisions more quickly and accurately, for example. In 2018, global spending on IT was projected to top $3.7 trillion, including enterprise software, devices, and communications services to improve efficiency and effectiveness.[40] We discuss the many effects of IT on management in Chapter 18 and throughout the book.

Restructuring, however, can produce some powerful negative outcomes. It can reduce the morale of remaining employees, who worry about their own job security. And top managers of many downsized organizations realize that they have downsized too far when their employees complain they are overworked and when increasing numbers of customers complain about poor service.[41]

outsourcing Contracting with another company, usually abroad, to have it perform an activity the organization previously performed itself.

Outsourcing involves contracting with another company, usually in a low-cost country abroad, to have it perform a work activity the organization previously performed itself, such as manufacturing, marketing, or customer service. Outsourcing increases efficiency because it lowers operating costs, freeing up money and resources that can be used in more effective ways—for example, to develop new products.

Low-cost global competition dramatically increased outsourcing in the early 2000s. In 2016, more than 1.4 million jobs were outsourced to other countries. India, Indonesia, and China were rated as the top outsourcing countries. Companies primarily sent jobs offshore to control costs and gain access to unavailable resources while freeing up internal ones. Thousands of high-paying IT jobs have also moved abroad, to countries such as India, Bulgaria, and the Philippines, where programmers work for one-third the salary of those in the United States.[42]

Large for-profit organizations today typically employ 10–20% fewer people than they did 10 years ago because of restructuring, outsourcing, and advances in new technologies. Ford, IBM, AT&T, and DuPont are among the thousands of organizations that have streamlined

Auto Production Thrives in Mexico

As quality issues continue to dominate and workers' wages increase in parts of Asia, most notably in China, global auto companies are looking for other locations to build new production facilities. While some U.S. companies tout their commitment to "Made in the USA" and promise to bring jobs back home, the reality is that production costs in this country, particularly jobs associated with union wages, continue to be prohibitive.

In recent years, many of the world's automakers have decided to build new production facilities in Mexico for several reasons. There are plenty of locations in Mexico that would be suitable to build new, state-of-the-art facilities—for a reasonable price. And in terms of logistics, most of the new facilities are within a few hours' drive of major shipping ports, which expedites the transportation process. Mexico has a large workforce, including college graduates with engineering degrees, who do not make anywhere near the annual salaries made by U.S. engineers. It is estimated that the starting salary of engineers in Mexico would be approximately one-quarter of the annual paycheck of their U.S. counterparts. In addition, average annual wages for Mexican workers are $15,000 compared to $60,000 for U.S. workers.[43]

Although some would argue that the North American Free Trade Agreement (NAFTA) has given Mexico unfair advantages when it comes to new manufacturing facilities, others—including Ford, Toyota, BMW, and Audi—believe that Mexico's close proximity to the U.S. border dramatically decreases shipping and transportation costs for cars made in Mexico, enabling the companies to maintain decent profit margins on vehicles built there.[44]

Despite fears that auto manufacturing in Mexico could be hurt by the possible renegotiation of NAFTA by the United States with trading partners Canada and Mexico in the coming year, Mexican auto production and exports hit a record high in 2017, with auto exports increasing by more than 12%.[45]

their operations to increase efficiency and effectiveness. The argument is that the managers and employees who have lost their jobs will find employment in new and growing U.S. companies where their skills and experience will be better utilized. For example, the millions of manufacturing jobs that have been lost overseas will be replaced by higher-paying U.S. jobs in the service sector, which are made possible because of the growth in global trade. At the same time, many companies continue to experience outsourcing problems in Asia, as well as increasing wages in that part of the world. Auto manufacturers, in particular, are looking for venues that offer both skilled workers and low wages. As discussed in the accompanying "Managing Globally" feature, automakers are setting up manufacturing facilities south of the border.

LO1-5 Discuss some major changes in management practices today that have occurred as a result of globalization and the use of advanced information technology (IT).

empowerment The expansion of employees' knowledge, tasks, and decision-making responsibilities.

Empowerment and Self-Managed Teams

The second principal way managers have sought to increase efficiency and effectiveness is by empowering lower-level employees and moving to self-managed teams. **Empowerment** is a management technique that involves giving employees more authority and responsibility over how they perform their work activities. Many companies, from start-ups to well-established organizations, have embraced empowerment as a key corporate strategy. One byproduct of fostering an empowered workforce may include a flatter organizational structure. For example, Valve Corporation, a billion-dollar company in Bellevue, Washington, does not believe in managers. Started more than 20 years ago, Valve is a video game developer that has gained a reputation for a dynamic organizational culture. At Valve, there is no hierarchy or top-down control, and innovation permeates the company environment. There is no "reporting" structure at Valve

At Valve Corporation in Bellevue, Washington, there are no managers and no reporting structure. Employees are encouraged to become the CEOs of their own work.
©Adam Hester/Blend Images

self-managed work team
A group of employees who assume responsibility for organizing, controlling, and supervising their own activities and monitoring the quality of the goods and services they provide.

and employees pick their own projects, which typically are high profile and complex. While this may seem daunting to some employees, others thrive in this environment in which they are empowered to be the CEOs of their own work. In addition, bonuses, hirings, and firings are all determined by peer review, not managers.[46]

IT is being increasingly used to empower employees because it expands employees' job knowledge and increases the scope of their job responsibilities. Frequently, IT allows one employee to perform a task that was previously performed by many employees. As a result, the employee has more autonomy and responsibility. IT also facilitates the use of a **self-managed work team**, a group of employees who assume collective responsibility for organizing, controlling, and supervising their own work activities. Using IT designed to give team members real-time information about each member's performance, a self-managed team can often find ways to accomplish a task more quickly and efficiently. Moreover, self-managed teams assume many tasks and responsibilities previously performed by first-line managers, so a company can better utilize its workforce.[47] First-line managers act as coaches or mentors whose job is not to tell employees what to do but to provide advice and guidance and help teams find new ways to perform their tasks more efficiently. Using the same IT, middle managers can easily monitor what is happening in these teams and make better resource allocation decisions as a result. We discuss self-managed teams in more detail in Chapters 2, 10, and 15.

Challenges for Management in a Global Environment

global organizations
Organizations that operate and compete in more than one country.

LO1-6 Discuss the principal challenges managers face in today's increasingly competitive global environment.

Because the world has been changing more rapidly than ever before, managers and other employees throughout an organization must perform at higher and higher levels. In the last 20 years, rivalry between organizations competing domestically (in the same country) and globally (in countries abroad) has increased dramatically. The rise of **global organizations**, organizations that operate and compete in more than one country, has pressured many organizations to identify better ways to use their resources and improve their performance. The successes of the German pharmaceutical conglomerate Bayer, Italian furniture manufacturer Natuzzi, Korean electronics companies Samsung and LG, Brazilian plane maker Embraer, and Europe's Airbus Industries are putting pressure on companies in other countries to raise their level of performance to compete successfully against these global organizations.

Even in the not-for-profit sector, global competition is spurring change. Schools, universities, police forces, and government agencies are reexamining their operations because looking at how activities are performed in other countries often reveals better ways to do them. For example, many curriculum and teaching changes in the United States have resulted from the study of methods that Japanese and European school systems use. Similarly, European and Asian hospital systems have learned much from the U.S. system—which may be the most effective, though not the most efficient, in the world.

Today managers who make no attempt to learn from and adapt to changes in the global environment find themselves reacting rather than innovating, and their organizations often become uncompetitive and fail. Five major challenges stand out for managers in today's world: building a competitive advantage, maintaining ethical standards, managing a diverse workforce, utilizing new information systems and technologies, and practicing global crisis management.

Building Competitive Advantage

competitive advantage The ability of one organization to outperform other organizations because it produces desired goods or services more efficiently and effectively than they do.

What are the most important lessons for managers and organizations to learn if they are to reach and remain at the top of the competitive environment of business? The answer relates to the use of organizational resources to build a competitive advantage. **Competitive advantage** is the ability of one organization to outperform other organizations because it produces desired goods or services more efficiently and effectively than its competitors. The four building blocks

Figure 1.6
Building Blocks of Competitive Advantage

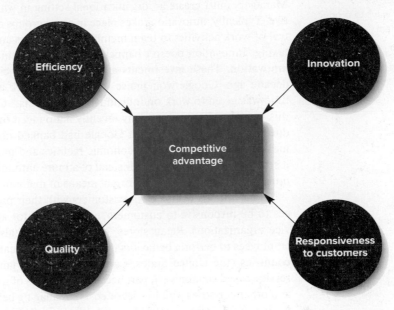

of competitive advantage are superior *efficiency; quality; speed, flexibility, and innovation;* and *responsiveness to customers,* as Figure 1.6 shows.

Organizations increase their efficiency when they reduce the quantity of resources (such as people and raw materials) they use to produce goods or services. In today's competitive environment, organizations continually search for new ways to use their resources to improve efficiency. Many organizations are training their workforces in the new skills and techniques needed to operate heavily computerized assembly plants. Similarly, cross-training gives employees the range of skills they need to perform many different tasks, and organizing employees in new ways, such as in self-managed teams, lets them make good use of their skills. These are important steps in the effort to improve productivity. Japanese and German companies invest far more in training employees than do American or Italian companies.

Managers must improve efficiency if their organizations are to compete successfully with companies operating in Mexico, Malaysia, and other countries where employees are paid comparatively low wages. New methods must be devised either to increase efficiency or to gain some other competitive advantage—higher-quality goods, for example—if outsourcing and the loss of jobs to low-cost countries are to be prevented.

The challenge from global organizations such as Korean electronics manufacturers, Mexican agricultural producers, and European design and financial companies also has increased pressure on companies to develop the skills and abilities of their workforces in order to improve the quality of their goods and services. One major thrust to improving quality has been to introduce the quality-enhancing techniques known as *total quality management (TQM)*. Employees involved in TQM are often organized into quality control teams and are responsible for finding new and better ways to perform their jobs; they also must monitor and evaluate the quality of the goods they produce. We discuss ways of managing TQM successfully in Chapter 9.

Today companies can win or lose the competitive race depending on their *speed*—how fast they can bring new products to market—or their *flexibility*—how easily they can change or alter the way they perform their activities to respond to actions of their competitors. Companies that have speed and flexibility are agile competitors: Their managers have superior planning and organizing abilities; they can think ahead, decide what to do, and then speedily mobilize their resources to respond to a changing environment. We examine how managers can build speed and flexibility in their organizations in later chapters. Agile companies are adept at responding to changes in their environments, including change from technological, regulatory, and economic sources. For example, companies like Microsoft are seeking ways to produce their products more economically amid tightening margins and increased competition. One way Microsoft is responding to this pressure is by expanding its portfolio of products and services and its business partnerships, which will help support the company's other endeavors.[48]

innovation The process of creating new or improved goods and services or developing better ways to produce or provide them.

Innovation, the process of creating new or improved goods and services that customers want or developing better ways to produce or provide goods and services, poses a special challenge. Managers must create an organizational setting in which people are encouraged to be innovative. Typically, innovation takes place in small groups or teams; management decentralizes control of work activities to team members and creates an organizational culture that rewards risk taking. Innovation doesn't happen by itself; companies have to devote resources that enable innovation. These investments are a delicate balancing act. Consider Google. More than a decade ago, Google won praise for its 80/20 work allocation, where 20% of an employee's time was given to work on individual "pet projects." Consumer hits such as Gmail came from this program. But the company recently announced that it was suspending the 80/20 program due to productivity concerns. Google had banked on the idea that slack time would enable individuals to innovate, but economic realities and productivity needs meant a change in how it structured employee work. Instead of a more autonomous approach to innovation, Google is now relying on its X lab as a formal means of maintaining a competitive edge.[49]

Organizations compete for customers with their products and services, so training employees to be responsive to customers' needs is vital for all organizations, but particularly for service organizations. Retail stores, banks, and hospitals, for example, depend entirely on their employees to perform behaviors that result in high-quality service at a reasonable cost. As many countries (the United States, Canada, and Switzerland are just a few) move toward a more service-based economy (in part because of the loss of manufacturing jobs to Vietnam, Malaysia, and other countries with low labor costs), managing behavior in service organizations is becoming increasingly important. Many organizations are empowering their customer service employees and giving them the authority to take the lead in providing high-quality customer service. As noted previously, empowering nonmanagerial employees and creating self-managed teams change the role of first-line managers and lead to more efficient use of organizational resources.

turnaround management The creation of a new vision for a struggling company based on a new approach to planning and organizing to make better use of a company's resources and allow it to survive and prosper.

Sometimes the best efforts of managers to revitalize their organizations' fortunes fail; faced with bankruptcy, the directors of these companies are forced to appoint a new CEO who has a history of success in rebuilding a company. **Turnaround management** is the creation of a new vision for a struggling company using a new approach to planning and organizing to make better use of a company's resources and allow it to survive and eventually prosper—something Apple's Steve Jobs excelled at. It involves developing radical new strategies, such as how to reduce the number of products sold or change how they are made and distributed, or closing corporate and manufacturing operations to reduce costs. Organizations that appoint turnaround CEOs are generally experiencing a crisis because they have become inefficient or ineffective; sometimes this is because of poor management over a continuing period, or sometimes it occurs because a competitor introduces a new product or technology that makes their own products unattractive to customers. For example, fast-casual food chain Chipotle was flying high until food safety scares in 2015 and 2017 caused the company to lose customers, market share, and consumers' confidence in the chain's reputation for quality. Founder and CEO Steve Ells, who ran the chain since its start in 1993, stepped aside as CEO in 2018 and was replaced by Brian Niccol, former CEO of Taco Bell.[50]

Achieving a competitive advantage requires that managers use all their skills and expertise, as well as their companies' other resources, to find new and better ways to improve efficiency, quality, innovation, and responsiveness to customers. We revisit this theme often as we examine the ways managers plan strategies, organize resources and activities, and lead and control people and groups to increase efficiency and effectiveness.

Maintaining Ethical and Socially Responsible Standards

Managers at all levels, especially after the recent recession, are under considerable pressure to make the best use of resources to increase the level at which their organizations perform.[51] For example, top managers feel pressure from shareholders to increase the performance of the entire organization to boost its stock price, improve profits, or raise dividends. In turn, top managers may pressure middle managers to find new ways to use organizational resources to increase efficiency or quality and, thus, attract new customers and earn more revenues—and then middle managers hit on their department's supervisors.

Pressure to increase performance can be healthy for an organization because it leads managers to question how the organization is working, and it encourages them to find new and better ways to plan, organize, lead, and control. However, too much pressure to perform can be harmful. It may induce managers to behave unethically, and even illegally, when dealing with people and groups inside and outside the organization.[52]

A purchasing manager for a nationwide retail chain, for example, might buy inferior clothing as a cost-cutting measure or ignore the working conditions under which products are made to obtain low-priced products. These issues faced the managers of companies that made footwear and clothing in the 1990s, when customers learned about the sweatshop conditions in which garment and shoe workers around the world labored. Today companies such as Nike, Walmart, and Apple are trying to stop sweatshop practices and prevent managers abroad from adopting work practices that harm their workers. They now employ hundreds of inspectors who police the overseas factories that make the products they sell and who can terminate contracts with suppliers when they behave in an unethical or illegal way.

Similarly, to secure a large foreign contract, a sales manager in a large company, such as in the defense or electronics industry, might offer bribes to foreign officials to obtain lucrative contracts—even though this is against the law. For example, cosmetics manufacturer Avon paid $135 million to settle a U.S. bribery probe into its development of new markets. Other companies like Siemens, Teva Pharmaceutical, and Brazil-based Odebrecht SA have paid billions in penalties to resolve international bribery charges.[53]

The issue of social responsibility, discussed in Chapter 4, centers on deciding what obligations a company has toward the people and groups affected by its activities—such as employees, customers, or the cities in which it operates. Some companies have strong views about social responsibility; their managers believe they should protect the interests of others. But some managers may decide to act in an unethical way and put their own interests first, hurting others in the process. A recent example showing why managers must always keep the need to act in an ethical and socially responsible way at the forefront of their decision making is described in the following "Ethics in Action" box.

ETHICS IN ACTION

Fallout Continues from Wells Fargo Scandal

Protesters outside Wells Fargo headquarters in New York City draw attention to some of the ethical missteps by the organization, including the firing of more than 5,000 employees pressured to engage in fraud against customers by opening more than 3.5 million fake accounts.
©Pacific Press/Getty Images

"Eight is great" was the mantra of former Wells Fargo CEO John Stumpf when it came to the bank's business strategy of cross-selling products to customers. Employees were encouraged to sign up customers for various products and services—checking accounts, credit cards, loans, mortgages, overdraft protection, and others—which would allow the bank to charge fees for each of the customer's accounts. And for several years, this cross-selling approach was seen as a solid business strategy that worked well for the banking giant, at one point helping to make Wells Fargo the world's most valuable bank.[54]

But continuing pressure and unrealistic sales quotas from management caused thousands of employees to open up more than 3.5 million fake checking and credit card accounts for Wells Fargo customers for almost five years to meet sales quotas and keep their jobs. Despite branch managers and other employees reaching out to top management to complain about the unrealistic sales quotas and to report unethical practices, cross-selling continued until a news article in the *Los Angeles Times* got the attention of the city's attorney, who filed a civil complaint against Wells Fargo in 2015.[55]

Soon after the civil lawsuit was filed, federal regulators got involved in the investigation, and Wells Fargo agreed to pay $185 million in state and federal fines and $142 million to customers to move beyond the scandal. Unfortunately, fallout continued for the bank, which said it dismissed some 5,300 workers for the illegal practices. In September 2016, members of Congress called for a hearing on the case, requesting that CEO Stumpf testify before Congress.[56]

In appearances before the House and the Senate, Stumpf apologized for the scandal, pledged to fix what went wrong, and denied there was an "orchestrated effort" to defraud customers. Congressional members were frustrated by Stumpf's responses and continued to put pressure on him and other top managers about their accountability for the fraudulent practices. Two weeks later, in October 2016, Wells Fargo announced that Stumpf would retire "effective immediately" and replaced him with 29-year company veteran, Timothy J. Sloan.[57]

Fallout from the scandal continues to take a toll on Wells Fargo's bottom line, not to mention its reputation with customers and the general public. CEO Sloan says the bank has spent millions of dollars as a result of the investigations and fraudulent sales practices. The company reported that new credit card applications and checking account openings continue to be down—even into 2018. As a result of the scandal, Wells Fargo announced it would eliminate sales goals for employees and strengthen its training programs, controls, and oversights within the organization.[58]

Adding insult to injury, departing Federal Reserve Chair Janet Yellen, who left her post in February 2018, issued new sanctions on Wells Fargo, imposing a "cease and desist" order that prohibits the bank from growing its assets and forces the bank to replace four of its board members in the coming year.[59]

Managing a Diverse Workforce

A major challenge for managers everywhere is to recognize the ethical need and legal requirement to treat human resources fairly and equitably. Today the age, gender, race, ethnicity, religion, sexual preference, and socioeconomic composition of the workforce presents new challenges for managers. To create a highly trained and motivated workforce, as well as to avoid lawsuits, managers must establish human resource management (HRM) procedures and practices that are legal and fair and do not discriminate against any organizational members.[60] Today most organizations understand that to motivate effectively and take advantage of the talents of a diverse workforce, they must make promotion opportunities available to every employee. Managers must recognize the performance-enhancing possibilities of a diverse workforce, such as the ability to take advantage of the skills and experiences of different kinds of people from different generations.[61]

Accenture provides a good example of a company that has utilized the potential of its diverse employees. Accenture is a global management consulting company that serves the needs of thousands of client companies in over 120 countries around the world. A major driving force behind Accenture's core organizational vision is to manage and promote diversity in order to improve employee performance and client satisfaction. At Accenture, managers at all levels realize consultants bring distinct experiences, talents, and values to their work, and a major management initiative is to take advantage of that diversity to encourage collaboration between consultants to improve the service Accenture provides each of its clients. Because Accenture's clients are also diverse by country, religion, ethnicity, and so forth, it tries to match its teams of consultants to the attributes of its diverse clients.

Accenture provides hundreds of diversity management training programs to its consultants each year. In 2016 Accenture became the first large consulting firm to publish its race and gender statistics in an effort to increase transparency when it comes to diversity and inclusion among its employees. Almost 40% of its workforce is composed of women, and a little more than half of its employees are white and a third Asian. Julie Sweet, CEO of Accenture, North America, believes the company needs to make progress in hiring more African Americans, Latinos, and military veterans. Accenture also works to accommodate individuals with disabilities, as well as promoting an inclusionary environment for lesbian, gay, bisexual, and

Global management consulting firm Accenture provides hundreds of diversity programs to its employees each year in an effort to promote individual and organizational performance.
©Lisette Le Bon/Purestock/Superstock

transgender employees.[62] The firm also provides diversity training programs to its suppliers and prospective suppliers around the world to show them how diversity can increase their efficiency and effectiveness. In all these ways, Accenture uses its expertise in managing diversity to promote individual and organizational performance—one reason it has become the most successful and fast-growing consultancy company in the world.

Managers who value their diverse employees not only invest in developing these employees' skills and capabilities, but also succeed best in promoting performance over the long run. Today more organizations are realizing that people are their most important resource and that developing and protecting human resources is the most important challenge for managers in a competitive global environment. For the first time ever in 2018, *Forbes* released a list of America's best employers for diversity, based on a survey of more than 30,000 U.S. employees working for firms or institutions with 1,000 or more employees. The top five employers on this inaugural list were Northern Trust, a banking and financial services firm in Chicago; the Smithsonian Institution in Washington, DC; Levy Restaurants, headquartered in Chicago; Intuit, an IT, Internet, and software services company located in Mountain View, California; and Harvard University in Cambridge, Massachusetts.[63] We discuss the many issues surrounding the management of a diverse workforce in Chapter 5.

Utilizing New Technologies

As we have discussed, another important challenge for managers is to continually utilize efficient and effective new IT that can link and enable managers and employees to better perform their jobs—whatever their level in the organization. One example of how IT has changed the jobs of people at all organizational levels comes from UPS, where the average UPS driver makes 120 deliveries a day, and figuring out the quickest way to navigate all of those stops is a problem with economic implications for the shipping company. UPS estimates that a driver with 25 packages could choose from 15 trillion different routes! To help it navigate these difficult roads, UPS relies on ORION—its On-Road Integrated Optimization and Navigation. ORION is designed to blend GPS navigation and learning to help drivers optimize their routes. Of course, UPS drivers must also balance promised delivery times, traffic, and other factors into their decisions, meaning ORION is a critical technological competency helping UPS work effectively and efficiently. According to the company, now that ORION has been fully implemented, the system helps reduce miles driven annually by 100 million and saves UPS upwards of $300 to $400 million each year.[64]

Increasingly, new kinds of IT enable not just individual employees, but also self-managed teams by giving them important information and allowing virtual interactions around the globe using the Internet. Increased global coordination helps improve quality and increase the pace of innovation. Microsoft, Hitachi, IBM, and most other companies now search for new IT that can help them build a competitive advantage. The importance of IT is discussed in detail in Chapters 16 and 18, and throughout the text you will find examples of how IT is changing the way companies operate.

Practicing Global Crisis Management

Today another challenge facing managers and organizations is global crisis management. The causes of global crises or disasters fall into two main categories: natural causes and human causes. Crises that arise because of natural causes include the hurricanes, wildfires, earthquakes, famines, and diseases that have devastated so many countries over the past few years. According to insurance data, losses from natural disasters worldwide in 2017 totaled more than $300 billion, of which only one-third was covered by insurance.[65]

Meanwhile, human-created crises result from factors such as industrial pollution, inattention to employee safety, the destruction of natural habitat or environment, and geopolitical tension and terrorism, including war. Human-created crises, such as global warming due to emissions of carbon dioxide and other gases, may intensify the effects of natural disasters.

For example, increasing global temperatures and acid rain may have increased the intensity of hurricanes, led to unusually strong rains, and contributed to lengthy droughts. Scientists believe that global warming is responsible for the rapid destruction of coral reefs, forests, animal species, and the natural habitat in many parts of the world. The shrinking polar ice caps are expected to raise the sea level by a few critical inches.

Increasing geopolitical tensions, which reflect increased globalization, have upset the balance of world power as nations have jockeyed to protect their economic and political interests. For example, global cyberattacks, tensions between the United States and North Korea, military conflicts in Syria, Russia's meddling in recent U.S. elections—all could play a part in global instability and result in the need for managers who can interpret and respond to often unpredictable situations in a global marketplace.[66]

Management has an important role to play in helping people, organizations, and countries respond to global crises; such crises provide lessons in how to plan, organize, lead, and control the resources needed to both forestall and respond effectively to a crisis. Crisis management involves making important choices about how to (1) create teams to facilitate rapid decision making and communication, (2) establish the organizational chain of command and reporting relationships necessary to mobilize a fast response, (3) recruit and select the right people to lead and work in such teams, and (4) develop bargaining and negotiating strategies to manage the conflicts that arise whenever people and groups have different interests and objectives. How well managers make such decisions determines how quickly an effective response to a crisis can be implemented, and it sometimes can prevent or reduce the severity of the crisis itself.

Summary and Review

LO1-1   **WHAT IS MANAGEMENT?**   A manager is a person responsible for supervising the use of an organization's resources to meet its goals. An organization is a collection of people who work together and coordinate their actions to achieve a wide variety of goals. Management is the process of using organizational resources to achieve organizational goals effectively and efficiently through planning, organizing, leading, and controlling. An efficient organization makes the most productive use of its resources. An effective organization pursues appropriate goals and achieves these goals by using its resources to create goods or services that customers want.

LO1-2   **ESSENTIAL MANAGERIAL TASKS**   The four principal managerial tasks are planning, organizing, leading, and controlling. Managers at all levels of the organization and in all departments perform these tasks. Effective management means managing these activities successfully.

LO1-3, 1-4   **LEVELS AND SKILLS OF MANAGERS**   Organizations typically have three levels of management. First-line managers are responsible for the day-to-day supervision of nonmanagerial employees. Middle managers are responsible for developing and utilizing organizational resources efficiently and effectively. Top managers have cross-departmental responsibility. Three main kinds of managerial skills are conceptual, human, and technical. The need to develop and build technical skills leads organizations to divide managers into departments according to their job-specific responsibilities. Top managers must establish appropriate goals for the entire organization and verify that department managers are using resources to achieve those goals.

LO1-5   **RECENT CHANGES IN MANAGEMENT PRACTICES**   To increase efficiency and effectiveness, many organizations have altered how they operate. Managers have restructured and downsized operations and outsourced activities to reduce costs. Companies are also empowering their workforces and using self-managed teams to increase efficiency and effectiveness. Managers are increasingly using IT to achieve these objectives.

LO1-6   **CHALLENGES FOR MANAGEMENT IN A GLOBAL ENVIRONMENT**   Today's competitive global environment presents many interesting challenges to managers. One of the main challenges is building a competitive advantage by increasing efficiency; quality; speed, flexibility, and innovation; and responsiveness to customers. Other challenges include behaving in an ethical and socially responsible way toward people inside and outside the organization, managing a diverse workforce, utilizing new technologies, and practicing global crisis management.

Management in Action

Topics for Discussion and Action

Discussion

1. Describe the difference between efficiency and effectiveness, and identify real organizations that you think are, or are not, efficient and effective. **[LO1-1]**

2. In what ways can managers at each of the three levels of management contribute to organizational efficiency and effectiveness? **[LO1-3]**

3. Identify an organization that you believe is high-performing and one that you believe is low-performing. Give five reasons you think the performance levels of the two organizations differ so much. **[LO1-2, 1-4]**

4. What are the building blocks of competitive advantage? Why is obtaining a competitive advantage important to managers? **[LO1-5]**

5. In what ways do you think managers' jobs have changed the most over the last 10 years? Why have these changes occurred? **[LO1-6]**

Action

6. Choose an organization such as a school or a bank; visit it; then list the different organizational resources it uses. How do managers use these resources to maintain and improve its performance? **[LO1-2, 1-4]**

7. Visit an organization, and talk to first-line, middle, and top managers about their respective management roles in the organization and what they do to help the organization be efficient and effective. **[LO1-3, 1-4]**

8. Ask a middle or top manager, perhaps someone you already know, to give examples of how he or she performs the managerial tasks of planning, organizing, leading, and controlling. How much time does he or she spend in performing each task? **[LO1-3]**

9. Like Mintzberg, try to find a cooperative manager who will allow you to follow him or her around for a day. List the roles the manager plays, and indicate how much time he or she spends performing them. **[LO1-3, 1-4]**

Building Management Skills

Thinking about Managers and Management [LO1-2, 1-3, 1-4]

Think of an organization that has provided you with work experience and the manager to whom you report (or talk to someone who has had extensive work experience); then answer these questions:

1. Think about your direct supervisor. Of what department is he or she a member, and at what level of management is this person?

2. How do you characterize your supervisor's approach to management? For example, which particular management tasks and roles does this person perform most often? What kinds of management skills does this manager have?

3. Are the tasks, roles, and skills of your supervisor appropriate for the particular job he or she performs? How could this manager improve his or her task performance? How can IT affect this?

4. How does your supervisor's approach to management affect your attitudes and behavior? For example, how well do you perform as a subordinate, and how motivated are you?

5. Think about the organization and its resources. Do its managers use organizational resources effectively? Which resources contribute most to the organization's performance?

6. Describe how the organization treats its human resources. How does this treatment affect the attitudes and behaviors of the workforce?

7. If you could give your manager one piece of advice or change one management practice in the organization, what would it be?

8. How attuned are the managers in the organization to the need to increase efficiency, quality, innovation, or responsiveness to customers? How well do you think the organization performs its prime goals of providing the goods or services that customers want or need the most?

Managing Ethically [LO1-1, 1-3]

Think about an example of unethical behavior that you observed recently. The incident could be something you experienced as an employee or a customer or something you observed informally.

Questions

1. Either by yourself or in a group, give three reasons you think the behavior was unethical. For example, what rules or norms were broken? Who benefited or was harmed by what took place? What was the outcome for the people involved?

2. What steps might you take to prevent such unethical behavior and encourage people to behave in an ethical way?

Small Group Breakout Exercise

Opening a New Restaurant [LO1-2, 1-3, 1-4]

Form groups of three or four people, and appoint one group member as the spokesperson who will communicate your findings to the entire class when called on by the instructor. Then discuss the following scenario:

You and your partners have decided to open a restaurant in your local community; it will be open from 7 a.m. to 3 p.m. daily to serve breakfast and lunch. Each of you is investing $50,000 in the venture, and together you have secured a bank loan for $300,000 to begin operations. You and your partners have little experience in managing a restaurant beyond serving meals or eating in restaurants, and you now face the task of deciding how you will manage the restaurant and what your respective roles will be.

1. Decide what each partner's managerial role in the restaurant will be. For example, who will be responsible for the necessary departments and specific activities? Describe your managerial hierarchy.

2. Which building blocks of competitive advantage do you need to establish to help your restaurant succeed? What criteria will you use to evaluate how successfully you are managing the restaurant?

3. Discuss the most important decisions that must be made about (a) planning, (b) organizing, (c) leading, and (d) controlling to allow you and your partners to use organizational resources effectively and build a competitive advantage.

4. For each managerial task, list the issues to solve, and decide which roles will contribute the most to your restaurant's success.

Be the Manager [LO1-2, 1-5]

Rapid Growth Causes Problems

You have just been called in to help managers at Achieva, a fast-growing Internet software company that specializes in business-to-business (B2B) network software. Your job is to help Achieva solve some management problems that have arisen because of its rapid growth.

Customer demand to license Achieva's software has boomed so much in just two years that more than 50 new software programmers have been added to help develop a new range of software products. Achieva's growth has been so swift that the company still operates informally, its organizational structure is loose and flexible, and programmers are encouraged to find solutions to problems as they go along. Although this structure worked well in the past, you have been told that problems are arising.

There have been increasing complaints from employees that good performance is not being recognized in the organization and that they do not feel equitably treated. Moreover, there have been complaints about getting managers to listen to their new ideas and to act on them. A bad atmosphere is developing in the company, and recently several talented employees left. Your job is to help Achieva's managers solve these problems quickly and keep the company on the fast track.

Questions

1. What kinds of organizing and controlling problems is Achieva suffering from?

2. What kinds of management changes need to be made to solve them?

Bloomberg Case in the News [LO 1-1, 1-2, 1-6]

"Amazon Effect" Is Hiking Pay and Fueling Land Rush in U.S.

On a recent weekday morning, a handful of job seekers were filling out applications at desktop computers in the Jefferson, Ga., office of Hire Dynamics, a staffing company with several locations across the South. All were there to tap the warehouse boom in Jackson County, about 50 miles northeast of Atlanta. Since 2015, at least 31 e-commerce fulfillment centers and other distribution depots have opened or are under development. The list of arrivals includes Amazon.com, Williams-Sonoma, and FedEx.

Larry Feinstein, chief executive officer of Hire Dynamics, says the local labor market was already tight when Amazon.com Inc. opened a 1,000-person fulfillment center in the county last year. "Amazon comes in and sucks up all the labor," says Feinstein, whose recruiters are scrambling to hire 40 people a day for a warehouse operated by Carter's Inc., a maker of baby and children's clothing. "Every one of our clients up there has raised their pay rates at least $2."

Forklift drivers are especially hard to find and now command at least $15 an hour, and up to $17.50 in parts of Georgia, according to the Randstad staffing agency. Meanwhile, general laborers have seen their wages bumped up a couple dollars to $12 or $13 an hour, which is at least a 30% premium over what most cashiers in the state earn and slightly more than what retail salespeople earn. Unemployment in Jackson County was 3.3% in December, almost 1 percentage point below the national average.

What's happening here is part of a nationwide boom in warehouse construction reshaping economies that once relied on farms or factories. Between 2013 and 2017, developers added about 848 million square feet of warehouse space, or more than double the roughly 300 million square feet built over the five previous years, according to real estate firm Cushman & Wakefield.

The number of stock clerks and order fillers—which is the Bureau of Labor Statistics' designation—expanded by almost 311,000 in the decade to 2016.

In Lehigh Valley, a metropolitan corridor that straddles Pennsylvania and New Jersey, employment in e-commerce and distribution centers has surged by 10,000 over the last five years and now trails the area's traditional manufacturing sector by just a few thousand jobs. "We almost don't have enough people with low skills to fill all the need in the fulfillment industry," says Don Cunningham, who heads the Lehigh Valley Economic Development Corporation.

It's not just workers who are in short supply. The vacancy rate for industrial space in the U.S. fell to 5.2% in the third quarter of last year, the lowest on record, real estate company Colliers International Group said in a recent report. The scarcity of 50- to 100-acre tracts close to major highways and with suitable access to utilities has caused industrial land prices to more than double in a few years. The price of an acre on the fringes of metro areas was about $50,000 in 2015 and has since climbed to more than $100,000, according to commercial real estate company CBRE Group and researcher CoStar Group. "There has been significant new construction in this sector, and all of it has gotten absorbed," says Barbara Denham, senior economist with researcher Reis Inc.

Companies have always put their distribution hubs on the edge of urban areas. What's changing is the "edge" keeps getting redefined outward as 500,000-square-foot facilities become million-square-foot ones, says David Egan, head of industrial and logistics research at CBRE.

Employees who used to drive from 25 miles out are now having to commute from as far away as 40 miles—a long haul for someone making $12 an hour. Amazon, which has 70 fulfillment centers in the U.S., runs shuttles for employees at some locations and hands out gift certificates to those willing to carpool, says spokeswoman Ashley Robinson.

Robert Connor, 22, one of the applicants who showed up at Hire Dynamics hoping to land a warehouse job, lives in Winder, Ga., outside Jackson County. "Just to drive here and back takes a half-tank," says Connor, who owns a 2000 Honda Accord. "Thank God I don't have one of those six-cylinder trucks."

Six of the new warehouses in Jackson exceed a million square feet, and a seventh is just shy of it, a county map shows. "Anything under a million square feet is considered small, which is kind of unbelievable to me," says Mike Buffington, publisher of the *Jackson Herald* and several small newspapers in the region. Coincidentally, a million square feet is about the size of a regional mall, many of which are struggling as more Americans go online to do their shopping. Large mall retailers other than department stores closed 2,468 stores last year, many quietly without announcement, according to researcher Green Street Advisors LLC.

Jackson County's residents have to contend with some unpleasant side effects from the warehouse boom. A traffic jam at Interstate 85's intersection with state Route 53 near Braselton stretched up to two miles during the past holiday season, recalls Ronnie Jones, owner of Stonewall's BBQ restaurant. Fewer customers seem to be coming by for barbecue in the late afternoon. He attributes the drop in business to people avoiding the area because of gridlock as the warehouses empty out around 4:30 p.m. Some locals have showed up at county meetings wearing red T-shirts to signal "no more warehouses" as they creep closer to residential areas.

Economic development officials are ambivalent: They'll put out the welcome mat if e-tailers come calling, but they generally don't seek them out, says Brian Hercules, a chamber of commerce executive in Murfreesboro, TN. The threat that many of the jobs they create could soon be lost to automation is one concern. The availability of affordable housing is another.

Murfreesboro, a 40-minute drive from Nashville, landed an Amazon facility five years ago, while a unit of Ebuys Inc., which sells footwear and accessories online, opened a warehouse in surrounding Rutherford County a year ago. "You get one or two of these businesses and it's great, because you have a certain percent of the population with those skills," says Hercules. Yet there's a limit to how much they help a local economy, he says: "At $25,000 a year, if you have a wife and two kids, are you going to be able to buy a house?"

Overall, Jackson County's warehouse boom is a net positive, even if it snarls traffic on occasion and puts pressure on the housing stock, says Jim Shaw of the Jackson County Area Chamber of Commerce. Residents who once depended on its now-shuttered textile mills or its still-active poultry processing industry are finding overnight shift work in warehouses. "We've filled a lot of jobs in the distribution centers over the past few years," Shaw says. "I often wonder if, as hard as that work may be, it seems a lot easier than working in a broiler house."

Questions for Discussion

1. What challenges do managers of these warehouses face when the unemployment rate is low? When the rate is high?

2. What strategies can managers employ to retain talented workers?

3. How does planning figure in to a manager's day-to-day responsibilities as competition for workers and real estate heats up in this area of the country?

Source: Michael Sasso and Steve Matthews, "'Amazon Effect' Is Hiking Pay and Fueling Land Rush in U.S.," *Bloomberg,* February 27, 2018, https://www.bloomberg.com/news/articles/2018-02-27/-amazon-effect-is-hiking-pay-and-fueling-land-rush-in-u-s. Used with permission of Bloomberg L.P. Copyright © 2017. All rights reserved.

Notes

1. K. Ryssdal and B. Bodnar, "CEO Satya Nadella on Why He's Hitting Refresh at Microsoft," *Marketplace,* www.marketplace.org, September 27, 2017; H. McCracken, "Satya Nadella Rewrites Microsoft's Code," *Fast Company,* www.fastcompany.com, September 18, 2017; "What Satya Nadella Did at Microsoft," *The Economist,* www.economist.com, March 16, 2017.

2. McCracken, "Satya Nadella Rewrites Microsoft's Code"; M. Murphy, "Satya Nadella on AI, Sexual Harassment, and Microsoft's Soul," *Bloomberg Businessweek,* www.bloomberg.com, December 21, 2017; K. Ryssdal and B. Bodnar, "CEO Satya Nadella Explains His Vision for Microsoft and the Future," *Marketplace,* www.marketplace.org, September 28, 2017.

3. Murphy, "Satya Nadella on AI, Sexual Harassment, and Microsoft's Soul"; McCracken, "Satya Nadella Rewrites Microsoft's Code."

4. Ryssdal and Bodnar, "CEO Satya Nadella Explains His Vision."

5. Ryssdal and Bodnar, "CEO Satya Nadella on Why He's Hitting Refresh"; Murphy, "Satya Nadella on AI, Sexual Harassment, and Microsoft's Soul."

6. J. Francisco, "Satya and Anu Nadella Open Up about Their Family Life," *Good Housekeeping,* www.goodhousekeeping.com, September 27, 2017.

7. McCracken, "Satya Nadella Rewrites Microsoft's Code"; *Economist,* "What Satya Nadella Did at Microsoft"; J. Fortt, "Microsoft's CEO Satya Nadella Broke Unspoken Rules on His Rise to CEO," *CNBC,* www.cnbc.com, October 2, 2017.

8. J.P. Campbell, "On the Nature of Organization Effectiveness," in P.S. Goodman, J.M. Pennings, et al., *New Perspectives on Organizational Effectiveness* (San Francisco: Jossey-Bass, 1977).

9. Bob Evans, "10 Powerful Examples of Microsoft CEO Satya Nadella's Transformative Vision," *Forbes,* www.forbes.com, July 26, 2017.

10. P. Wahba, "McDonald's All-Day Breakfast Helps Send Stock to All-Time High," *Fortune,* http://fortune.com, April 25, 2017.

11. "Summary Report: 11-1021.00—General and Operations Managers," *O*NET OnLine,* www.onetonline.org, accessed February 1, 2018.

12. H. Fayol, *General and Industrial Management* (New York: IEEE Press, 1984). Fayol actually identified five different managerial tasks, but most scholars today believe these four capture the essence of Fayol's ideas.

13. P.F. Drucker, *Management Tasks, Responsibilities, and Practices* (New York: Harper & Row, 1974).

14. S. Shah, "Microsoft's Seeing AI App for the Blind Now Reads Handwriting," *Engadget,* www.engadget.com, December 14, 2017; S. G. Carmichael, "Microsoft's CEO on Rediscovering the Company's Soul," *Harvard Business Review,* https://hbr.org, September 28, 2017.

15. M.J. Foley, "Microsoft Announces Internally Its New 'Commercial and Consumer' Sales Model," *ZDNet,* www.zdnet.com, July 3, 2017; D. Bass, "Microsoft Is Planning Sales Reorganization Focused on the Cloud," *Bloomberg Technology,* www.bloomberg.com, June 30, 2017.

16. G. O'Brien, "ER Manager Creates Efficiencies—and a True 'Front Door,'" *BusinessWest,* http://businesswest.com, September 5, 2017.

17. "New Responsibilities for Members of Mercy's Nursing Leadership," *SPHS Journal* (Sisters of Providence Health System), June 2015, 3.

18. A.G. Flynn, "Mercy Medical Center Earns Top Honors for Stroke Care," *MassLive,* www.masslive.com, July 11, 2017.

19. O'Brien, "ER Manager Creates Efficiencies"; "Mercy's Healthcare Heroes," *Journal* (Trinity Health of New England/Mercy Medical Center), www.mercycares.com, September 26, 2017.

20. L. Hill, *Becoming a Manager: Mastery of a New Identity* (Boston: Harvard Business School Press, 1992).

21. Ibid.

22. H. Mintzberg, "The Manager's Job: Folklore and Fact," *Harvard Business Review,* July-August 1975, 56–62.

23. H. Mintzberg, *The Nature of Managerial Work* (New York: Harper & Row, 1973).

24. A.I. Kraul, P.R. Pedigo, D.D. McKenna, and M.D. Dunnett, "The Role of the Manager: What's Really Important in Different Management Jobs," *Academy of Management Executive* (November 1989), 286–93; C.P. Hales, "What Do Managers Do? A Critical Review of the Evidence," *Journal of Management Studies* (January 1986), 88–115.

25. A.K. Gupta, "Contingency Perspectives on Strategic Leadership," in D.C. Hambrick, ed., *The Executive Effect: Concepts and Methods for Studying Top Managers* (Greenwich, CT: JAI Press, 1988), 147–78.

26. D.G. Ancona, "Top Management Teams: Preparing for the Revolution," in J.S. Carroll, ed., *Applied Social Psychology and Organizational Settings* (Hillsdale, NJ: Erlbaum, 1990); D.C. Hambrick and P.A. Mason, "Upper Echelons: The Organization as a Reflection of Its Top Managers," *Academy of Management Journal* 9 (1984), 193–206.

27. L. Gomez-Mejia, J. McCann, and R.C. Page, "The Structure of Managerial Behaviors and Rewards," *Industrial Relations* 24 (1985), 147–54.

28. W.R. Nord and M.J. Waller, "The Human Organization of Time: Temporal Realities and Experiences," *Academy of Management Review* 29 (January 2004), 137–40.

29. R.L. Katz, "Skills of an Effective Administrator," *Harvard Business Review,* September–October 1974, 90–102.

30. Ibid.

31. P. Tharenou, "Going Up? Do Traits and Informal Social Processes Predict Advancing in Management?" *Academy of Management Journal* 44 (October 2001), 1005–18.

32. C.J. Collins and K.D. Clark, "Strategic Human Resource Practices, Top Management Team Social Networks, and Firm Performance: The Role of Human Resource Practices in Creating Organizational Competitive Advantage," *Academy of Management Journal* 46 (December 2003), 740–52.

33. J. Schutz, "Tales from a City Manager's Freshman Year," *Public Management,* October 2017, 18–21.

34. M. Roberts, "Government Job Profile: City Manager," *The Balance,* www .thebalance.com, November 22, 2016.

35. Ibid.

36. K. Fitzpatrick, J. Nutting, and J. Petrin, "Massachusetts' Boot Camp for Managers," *Public Management,* December 2017, 10–13.

37. R. Stewart, "Middle Managers: Their Jobs and Behaviors," in J.W. Lorsch, ed., *Handbook of Organizational Behavior* (Englewood Cliffs, NJ: Prentice-Hall, 1987), 385–91.

38. S.C. de Janasz, S.E. Sullivan, and V. Whiting, "Mentor Networks and Career Success: Lessons for Turbulent Times," *Academy of Management Executive* 17 (November 2003), 78–92.

39. C. Massey, "New Technology Key to Employee Engagement, Employer Success," *Forbes,* www.forbes.com, accessed February 1, 2018.

40. "Gartner Says Global IT Spending to Reach $3.7 Trillion in 2018," *Business Wire,* www.businesswire.com, January 16, 2018.

41. B. Wysocki, "Some Companies Cut Costs Too Far, Suffer from Corporate Anorexia," *The Wall Street Journal,* July 5, 1995, A1.

42. "Job Overseas Outsourcing Statistics," *Statistic Brain,* www.statisticbrain.com, accessed February 1, 2018; A. Mohamed, "Top Five Outsourcing Destinations to Watch," *Computer Weekly,* www.computerweekly.com, accessed February 1, 2018.

43. T. Black, "American Jobs Are Headed to Mexico Once Again," *Bloomberg,* www .bloomberg.com, March 31, 2017; P. Gillespie, "$75 a Day vs. $75,000 a Year: How We Lost Jobs to Mexico," *CNN Money,* http://money.cnn.com, March 31, 2016.

44. C. Rogers, "Ford to More Than Double Mexico Production Capacity in 2018," *The Wall Street Journal,* www.wsj.com, February 8, 2016.

45. S. Angulo, "Mexican Auto Exports Surge in 2017 Despite NAFTA Fears," *Reuters,* www.reuters.com, January 8, 2018.

46. "Welcome to Valve," www.valvesoftware .com, accessed February 22, 2018; S. Wagreich, "A Billion Dollar Company with *No Bosses? Yes, It Exists,*" *Inc.,* www.inc.com, accessed February 22, 2018; E. Jansen, "What's Going On with Employee Empowerment?" https://shift.newco.co, March 2, 2017; R. Peters, "Success Through Self-Governing Teams," *LinkedIn,* www.linkedin.com, February 2, 2016.

47. C. Blakeman, "Why Self-Managed Teams Are the Future of Business," *Inc.,* www .inc.com, accessed February 22, 2018.

48. McCracken, "Satya Nadella Rewrites Microsoft's Code."

49. M. Karch, "Google X, the Secret Google Lab," *Lifewire,* www.lifewire.com, February 22, 2017.

50. A. Nusca, "Chipotle Names a New CEO. Here's What to Watch For," *Fortune,* http://fortune.com, February 14, 2018.

51. C. Manibog and S. Foley, "The Long and Winding Road to Economic Recovery," *Financial Times,* www.ft.com, August 9, 2017.

52. W.H. Shaw and V. Barry, *Moral Issues in Business,* 6th ed. (Belmont, CA: Wadsworth, 1995).

53. H. Whitehead, "Top Ten FCPA Fines," *International Compliance Association,* www .int-comp.org, May 17, 2017; P. Wahba, "Avon Settles Justice Department Charges of China Bribery for $135 Million," *Fortune,* http://fortune.com, December 17, 2014.

54. "The Wells Fargo Fake Account Scandal: A Timeline," *Forbes,* www.forbes.com, accessed February 20, 2018; J. Bukhari, "3 More Scandals That Will Have You Saying, 'WTF Wells Fargo,'" *Fortune,*

http://fortune.com, January 24, 2017; Z. Faux, L.J. Keller, and J. Surane, "Wells Fargo CEO Stumpf Quits in Fallout from Fake Accounts," *Bloomberg,* www .bloomberg.com, October 13, 2016.

55. J. Wattles, B. Geier, and M. Egan, "Wells Fargo's 17-Month Nightmare," *CNN Money,* http://money.com, February 5, 2018.

56. M. Corkery, "Wells Fargo Struggling in Aftermath of Fraud Scandal," *The New York Times,* www.nytimes.com, January 13, 2017; E. Scott Reckard, "L.A. Sues Wells Fargo, Alleging 'Unlawful and Fraudulent Conduct,'" *Los Angeles Times,* www.latimes.com, May 4, 2015.

57. R. Merle, "Wells Fargo Fired 5,300 Workers for Improper Sales Push. The Executive in Charge Is Retiring with $125 Million," *The Washington Post,* www .washingtonpost.com, September 13, 2016.

58. J. Wieczner, "Here's How Much Wells Fargo's Fake Accounts Scandal Is Hurting the Bank," *Fortune,* http://fortune.com, January 13, 2017.

59. J. Wieczner, "Janet Yellen's Last Act at the Federal Reserve: Punishing Wells Fargo," *Fortune,* http://fortune.com, February 3, 2018.

60. D. Meinert, "Creating an Ethical Workplace," www.shrm.org, accessed February 20, 2018.

61. D. Rock and H. Grant, "Why Diverse Teams Are Smarter," *Harvard Business Review,* https://hbr.org, November 4, 2016.

62. "Diversity Makes Us Stronger," www .accenture.com, accessed February 20, 2018; J. Burnett, "Accenture Aims at Ambitious Goal for 2025: A Workforce of Half Men, Half Women," *The Ladders,* www.theladders.com, June 14, 2017; K. Bellstrom, "Exclusive: Accenture Is the First Big Consulting Firm to Publish Race and Gender Stats," *Fortune,* http://fortune .com, February 8, 2016.

63. "Forbes Releases First-Ever List of America's Best Employers for Diversity," *Forbes,* www.forbes.com, January 23, 2018.

64. R.V. Zicari, "Big Data at UPS: Interview with Jack Levis," *ODBMS Industry Watch,* www.odbms.org, August 1, 2017; S. Clevenger, "UPS Routing Program ORION Helps Drivers Trim Miles, Reduce Costs," *Transport Topics,* www .ttnews.com, accessed January 26, 2017.

65. J. Daniels, "Global Disasters in 2017 Caused an Estimated $306 Billion in Economic Losses, Says Swiss Re," *CNBC,* www.cnbc.com, December 20, 2017.

66. "2018 Is Ripe for a 'Big Unexpected Crisis,' Eurasia Says," *Fortune,* http:// fortune.com, January 2, 2018.

CHAPTER 2

The Evolution of Management Thought

©Fuse/Getty Images

Learning Objectives

After studying this chapter, you should be able to:

LO2-1 Describe how the need to increase organizational efficiency and effectiveness has guided the evolution of management theory.

LO2-2 Explain the principle of job specialization and division of labor, and tell why the study of person–task relationships is central to the pursuit of increased efficiency.

LO2-3 Identify the principles of administration and organization that underlie effective organizations.

LO2-4 Trace the changes in theories about how managers should behave to motivate and control employees.

LO2-5 Explain the contributions of management science to the efficient use of organizational resources.

LO2-6 Explain why the study of the external environment and its impact on an organization has become a central issue in management thought.

Comcast Rethinks the Customer Experience

What is the best way to maintain a competitive edge? Cable companies know they can gain a competitive advantage by delivering a great customer experience, but getting there hasn't been easy. Comcast found in its product development group someone who could lead such an effort: Charlie Herrin, one of the executives who led the development of the Xfinity X1 entertainment platform.[1] Comcast made him executive vice president and chief customer experience officer of its cable division.

A basic question facing Herrin was *how* to improve performance. If he had been running a factory in the early 20th century, he might have directed workers in precisely how to assemble hardware efficiently. If he had been managing in the 1960s, he might have given customer service representatives more control over how they handle customer calls. In today's business environment, however, Herrin knew he needed a broader view of systems and processes that would take into account technology, workflow, and the needs of employees as well as customers. Efficiency and worker empowerment would be part of his plan.

Herrin's key insight was that product design and customer service are inseparable. He told a reporter, "If the product is working well, for the most part you don't have customer-service issues."[2] With Internet-connected systems such as X1, the potential for product design to ease service problems is especially great. Herrin focuses on giving customers useful information. Ideally, that would be a message that Comcast is already working on the problem or, second best, a menu customers step through to correct the problem or schedule a service call.

Herrin worked with his team to methodically redesign the experiences of starting up service and getting help with problems. They mapped out customers' points of interaction with the company and identified those seen as difficult or unpleasant in order to redesign them. A major frustration is waiting for service technicians, so Comcast upgraded its technology to send customers updates about when help will arrive. Messaging

Charlie Herrin, Comcast's chief customer experience officer, is charged with making sure customers are a key component of the company's business strategies.
©Tribune Content Agency LLC/Alamy Stock Photo

tools include follow-up texts to make sure the customer knows what to expect and is satisfied.[3]

Herrin has made customer experience a companywide focus. Customer experience was made a component of all executives' budgets and project reviews. One of Herrin's early successes was witnessing that teams throughout the company were talking about customer experience even when he wasn't leading the conversation. Throughout these changes, Herrin has addressed the impact on employees. He includes an HR staff member on his customer experience team. Together they ensure that all employees have training in what customer experience is and why it matters.[4]

The customer experience team is delivering results, according to Comcast. Even as more consumers are moving from cable to Internet-based entertainment, plugging in more devices, Comcast officials see complaints declining by some measures.[5] The customer satisfaction ratings collected for the American Customer Satisfaction Index show a marked improvement. And Herrin says the investment has begun showing a positive return.[6] Recognizing the successful impact of Herrin's systemwide approach, Comcast restructured its departments to make customer service and customer experience part of its technology and products division, rather than independent functions.[7]

Overview

When a company such as Comcast is facing a difficult problem, many factors are in play. Does the solution come from changes to people, processes, technology, or reporting relationships? Compared with managers a century ago, Charlie Herrin had a significant advantage: He could apply the knowledge gained by the researchers, consultants, and businesspeople who have studied management, constructing and testing theories about what gets results.

In this chapter we examine how management thought has evolved in modern times and the central concerns that have guided ongoing advances in management theory. First we examine the so-called classical management theories that emerged around the turn of the 20th century. These include scientific management, which focuses on matching people and tasks to maximize efficiency, and administrative management, which focuses on identifying the principles that will lead to the creation of the most efficient system of organization and management. Next we consider behavioral management theories, developed both before and after World War II; these focus on how managers should lead and control their workforces to increase performance. Then we discuss management science theory, which developed during World War II and has become increasingly important as researchers have developed rigorous analytical and quantitative techniques to help managers measure and control organizational performance. Finally, we discuss changes in management practices from the middle to the late 20th century and focus on the theories developed to help explain how the external environment affects the way organizations and managers operate.

By the end of this chapter you will understand how management thought and theory have evolved over time. You will also understand how economic, political, and cultural forces have affected the development of these theories and how managers and their organizations have changed their behavior as a result. In Figure 2.1 we summarize the chronology of the management theories discussed in this chapter.

Scientific Management Theory

The evolution of modern management began in the closing decades of the 19th century, after the industrial revolution had swept through Europe and America. In the new economic climate, managers of all types of organizations—political, educational, and economic—were trying to find better ways to satisfy customers' needs. Many major economic, technical, and cultural changes were taking place. The introduction of steam power and the development of sophisticated machinery and equipment

Figure 2.1

The Evolution of Management Theory

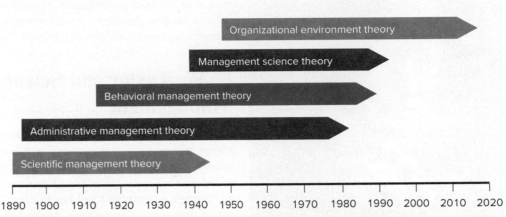

changed how goods were produced, particularly in the weaving and clothing industries. Small workshops run by skilled workers who produced hand-manufactured products (a system called *crafts production*) were being replaced by large factories in which sophisticated machines controlled by hundreds or even thousands of unskilled or semiskilled workers made products. For example, raw cotton and wool, which in the past had been spun into yarn by families or whole villages working together, were now shipped to factories, where workers operated machines that spun and wove large quantities of yarn into cloth.

Owners and managers of the new factories found themselves unprepared for the challenges accompanying the change from small-scale crafts production to large-scale, mechanized manufacturing. Moreover, many managers and supervisors in these workshops and factories were engineers who had only a technical orientation. They were unprepared for the social problems that occur when people work together in large groups in a factory or shop system. Managers began to search for new techniques to manage their organizations' resources, and soon they started focusing on ways to increase the efficiency of the worker-task mix.

Job Specialization and the Division of Labor

Initially, management theorists were interested in why the new machine shops and factory system were more efficient and produced greater quantities of goods and services than older, crafts-style production operations. Nearly 200 years before, Adam Smith had been one of the first writers to investigate the advantages associated with producing goods and services in factories. A famous economist, Smith journeyed around England in the 1700s, studying the effects of the industrial revolution.[8] In a study of factories that produced various pins or nails, Smith identified two different manufacturing methods. The first was similar to crafts-style production, in which each worker was responsible for all the 18 tasks involved in producing a pin. The other had each worker performing only one or a few of these 18 tasks.

Smith found that the performance of the factories in which workers specialized in only one or a few tasks was much greater than the performance of the factory in which each worker performed all 18 pin-making tasks. In fact, Smith found that 10 workers specializing in a particular task could make 48,000 pins a day, whereas those workers who performed all the tasks could make only a few thousand.[9] Smith reasoned that this performance difference occurred because the workers who specialized became much more skilled at their specific tasks and as a group were thus able to produce a product faster than the group of workers who each performed many tasks. Smith concluded that increasing the level of **job specialization**—the process by which a division of labor occurs as different workers specialize in tasks—improves efficiency and leads to higher organizational performance.[10]

LO2-1 Describe how the need to increase organizational efficiency and effectiveness has guided the evolution of management theory.

LO2-2 Explain the principle of job specialization and division of labor, and tell why the study of person–task relationships is central to the pursuit of increased efficiency.

job specialization The process by which a division of labor occurs as different workers specialize in different tasks over time.

Frederick W. Taylor, founder of scientific management and one of the first people to study the behavior and performance of people at work.
©Bettmann/Getty Images

scientific management The systematic study of relationships between people and tasks for the purpose of redesigning the work process to increase efficiency.

Armed with the insights gained from Adam Smith's observations, other managers and researchers began to investigate how to improve job specialization to increase performance. Management practitioners and theorists focused on how managers should organize and control the work process to maximize the advantages of job specialization and the division of labor.

F. W. Taylor and Scientific Management

Frederick W. Taylor (1856–1915) is best known for defining the techniques of **scientific management**, the systematic study of relationships between people and tasks for the purpose of redesigning the work process to increase efficiency. Taylor was a manufacturing manager who eventually became a consultant and taught other managers how to apply his scientific management techniques. Taylor believed that if the amount of time and effort that each worker expends to produce a unit of output (a finished good or service) can be reduced by increasing specialization and the division of labor, the production process will become more efficient. According to Taylor, the way to create the most efficient division of labor could best be determined by scientific management techniques rather than by intuitive or informal, rule-of-thumb knowledge. Based on his experiments and observations as a manufacturing manager in a variety of settings, he developed four principles to increase efficiency in the workplace:

- Principle 1: *Study the way workers perform their tasks, gather all the informal job knowledge that workers possess, and experiment with ways of improving how tasks are performed.*

To discover the most efficient method of performing specific tasks, Taylor studied in great detail and measured the ways different workers went about performing their tasks. One of the main tools he used was a time-and-motion study, which involves the careful timing and recording of the actions taken to perform a particular task. Once Taylor understood the existing method of performing a task, he then experimented to increase specialization. He tried different methods of dividing and coordinating the various tasks necessary to produce a finished product. Usually, this meant simplifying jobs and having each worker perform fewer, more routine tasks, as at a pin factory or on a car assembly line. Taylor also sought to find ways to improve each worker's ability to perform a particular task—for example, by reducing the number of motions workers made to complete the task, by changing the layout of the work area or the type of tools workers used, or by experimenting with tools of different sizes.

- Principle 2: *Codify the new methods of performing tasks into written rules and standard operating procedures.*

Once the best method of performing a particular task was determined, Taylor specified that it should be recorded so this procedure could be taught to all workers performing the same task. These new methods further standardized and simplified jobs—essentially making jobs even more routine. In this way efficiency could be increased throughout an organization.

- Principle 3: *Carefully select workers who possess skills and abilities that match the needs of the task, and train them to perform the task according to the established rules and procedures.*

To increase specialization, Taylor believed workers had to understand the tasks that were required and be thoroughly trained to perform the tasks at the required level. Workers who could not be trained to this level were to be transferred to a job where they were able to reach the minimum required level of proficiency.[11]

- Principle 4: *Establish a fair or acceptable level of performance for a task, and then develop a pay system that rewards performance above the acceptable level.*

To encourage workers to perform at a high level of efficiency, and to give them an incentive to reveal the most efficient techniques for performing a task, Taylor advocated that workers benefit from any gains in performance. They should be paid a bonus and receive some percentage of the performance gains achieved through the more efficient work process.[12]

By 1910 Taylor's system of scientific management had become nationally known and in many instances was faithfully and fully practiced.[13] However, managers in many organizations chose to implement the new principles of scientific management selectively. This decision ultimately resulted in problems. For example, some managers using scientific management obtained increases in performance, but rather than sharing performance gains with workers through bonuses, as Taylor had advocated, they simply increased the amount of work that each worker was expected to do. Many workers experiencing the reorganized work system found that as their performance increased, managers required that they do more work for the same pay. Workers also learned that performance increases often meant fewer jobs and a greater threat of layoffs, because fewer workers were needed. In addition, the specialized, simplified jobs were often monotonous and repetitive, and many workers became dissatisfied with their jobs.

Scientific management brought many workers more hardship than gain and a distrust of managers who did not seem to care about workers' well-being.[14] These dissatisfied workers resisted attempts to use the new scientific management techniques and at times even withheld their job knowledge from managers to protect their jobs and pay. It is not difficult for workers to conceal the true potential efficiency of a work system to protect their interests. Experienced machine operators, for example, can slow their machines in undetectable ways by adjusting the tension in the belts or misaligning the gears.

Unable to inspire workers to accept the new scientific management techniques for performing tasks, some organizations increased the mechanization of the work process. For example, one reason Henry Ford introduced moving conveyor belts in his factory was the realization that when a conveyor belt controls the pace of work (instead of workers setting their own pace), workers can be pushed to perform at higher levels—levels that they may have thought were beyond their reach. Charlie Chaplin captured this aspect of mass production in one of the opening scenes of his famous movie *Modern Times* (1936). In the film Chaplin caricatured a new factory employee fighting to work at the machine-imposed pace but losing the battle to the machine. Henry Ford also used the principles of scientific management to identify the tasks that each worker should perform on the production line and, thus, to determine the most effective division of labor to suit the needs of a mechanized production system.

From a performance perspective, the combination of the two management practices—(1) achieving the right worker–task specialization and (2) linking people and tasks by the speed of the production line—makes sense. It produces the huge cost savings and dramatic output increases that occur in large, organized work settings. For example, in 1908 managers at the Franklin Motor Company using scientific management principles redesigned the work process, and the output of cars increased from 100 cars a *month* to 45 cars a *day;* workers' wages, however, increased by only 90%.[15] From other perspectives, however, scientific management practices raise many concerns. Some companies, like McDonald's in the accompanying "Ethics in Action" feature, have codified management practices to protect workers.

ETHICS IN ACTION

Ensuring Workers' Rights

When most individuals think about McDonald's, they might think of a Big Mac, a McChicken Sandwich, or perhaps Ronald McDonald, the lovable clown. Workers' rights probably would be far down the list.

However, McDonald's, like other global companies, has faced increased scrutiny about the way its employees are treated. McDonald's estimates that one in eight Americans has worked for the fast-food giant. Celebrities such as Sharon Stone, Jay Leno, Shania Twain, Rachel McAdams, and Pink have all been employed at McDonald's.

Fast-food work is not well paid, and it sometimes places employees in uncomfortable and stressful situations. In one case, a McDonald's franchise owner in Virginia faced charges for subjecting employees to racial and sexual harassment on a regular basis.[16]

In response to the increased scrutiny, the McDonald's Corporation issued a report on the sustainability and corporate responsibility of its businesses. The McDonald's Corporation operates more than 36,000 restaurants worldwide. Of these, more than 80% are owned by independent businesses or franchisees. This means that McDonald's has only indirect control over the majority of its restaurants. Yet the company has put in place a number of managerial controls designed to help ensure that all McDonald's employees are treated humanely and fairly.[17]

For example, McDonald's has hired a global chief compliance officer to ensure that its businesses comply with local and international regulations regarding the treatment of employees. This officer maintains a staff that travels to stores throughout the world to interview employees and ensure that each restaurant is complying with the standards the company has developed. McDonald's also conducts training on the humane treatment of employees. Finally, McDonald's maintains a hotline for employees to report instances of mistreatment. To ensure that employees are not afraid to report violations, the company has a "nonretaliation policy" that protects employees from retaliation by management.[18]

Recently, however, the fast-food giant came under pressure in a case before the National Labor Relations Board (NLRB), which suggests that McDonald's should be considered a "joint-employer" of the workers employed by company franchisees. This case has far-reaching implications for McDonald's as well as its competitors in the fast-food industry, in which most workers are actually considered employees of individual franchisees, not McDonald's. A ruling against the Golden Arches could increase pressure on the company to boost wages and accept more responsibility for working conditions at franchise stores.[19]

Although the NLRB case has not been settled as of this writing, McDonald's continues to work with company-owned outlets and franchise owners to ensure that all employees are treated fairly, and that any rights' violations will be quickly reported and resolved.

The Gilbreths

Two prominent followers of Taylor were Frank Gilbreth (1868-1924) and Lillian Gilbreth (1878-1972), who refined Taylor's analysis of work movements and made many contributions to time-and-motion study.[20] Their aims were to (1) analyze every individual action necessary to perform a particular task and break it into each of its component actions, (2) find better ways to perform each component action, and (3) reorganize each of the component actions so that the action as a whole could be performed more efficiently—at less cost in time and effort.

This scene from the 2003 version of *Cheaper by the Dozen* illustrates how "efficient families" such as the Gilbreths use formal family courts to solve problems, such as assigning chores to different family members.
©Collection Christophel/Alamy Stock Photo

The Gilbreths often filmed a worker performing a particular task and then separated the task actions, frame by frame, into their component movements. Their goal was to maximize the efficiency with which each individual task was performed so that gains across tasks would add up to enormous savings of time and effort. Their attempts to develop improved management principles were captured—at times quite humorously—in the movie *Cheaper by the Dozen,* a new version of which appeared in 2003, which depicts how the Gilbreths (with their 12 children) tried to live their own lives according to these efficiency principles and apply them to daily actions such as shaving, cooking, and even raising a family.[21]

Eventually, the Gilbreths became increasingly interested in the study of fatigue. They studied how physical characteristics of the workplace contribute to job stress that often leads to fatigue and, thus, poor performance. They isolated factors that result in worker fatigue, such as lighting, heating, the color of walls, and the design of tools and machines. Their pioneering studies paved the way for new advances in management theory.

In workshops and factories, the work of the Gilbreths, Taylor, and many others had a major effect on the practice of management. In comparison with the old crafts system, jobs in the new system were more repetitive, boring, and monotonous as a result of the application of scientific management principles, and workers became increasingly dissatisfied. Frequently, the management of work settings became a game between workers and managers: Managers tried to initiate work practices to increase performance, and workers tried to hide the true potential efficiency of the work setting to protect their own well-being.

Administrative Management Theory

LO2-3 Identify the principles of administration and organization that underlie effective organizations.

administrative management The study of how to create an organizational structure and control system that leads to high efficiency and effectiveness.

bureaucracy A formal system of organization and administration designed to ensure efficiency and effectiveness.

authority The power to hold people accountable for their actions and to make decisions concerning the use of organizational resources.

While scientific managers were studying the person-technology mix to increase efficiency, other managers and researchers were focusing on **administrative management**, the study of how to create an organizational structure and control system that leads to high efficiency and effectiveness. *Organizational structure* is the system of task and authority relationships that controls how employees use resources to achieve the organization's goals. Two of the most influential early views regarding the creation of efficient systems of organizational administration were developed in Europe: Max Weber, a German sociology professor, developed one theory, and Henri Fayol, the French manager who developed the model of management introduced in Chapter 1, developed the other.

The Theory of Bureaucracy

Max Weber (1864–1920) wrote at the turn of the 20th century, when Germany was undergoing its industrial revolution.[22] To help Germany manage its growing industrial enterprises while it was striving to become a world power, Weber developed the principles of **bureaucracy**—a formal system of organization and administration designed to ensure efficiency and effectiveness. A bureaucratic system of administration is based on the five principles summarized in Figure 2.2:

- Principle 1: *In a bureaucracy, a manager's formal authority derives from the position he or she holds in the organization.*

Authority is the power to hold people accountable for their actions and to make decisions concerning the use of organizational resources. Authority gives managers the right to direct and control their subordinates' behavior to achieve organizational goals. In a bureaucratic

Figure 2.2

Weber's Principles of Bureaucracy

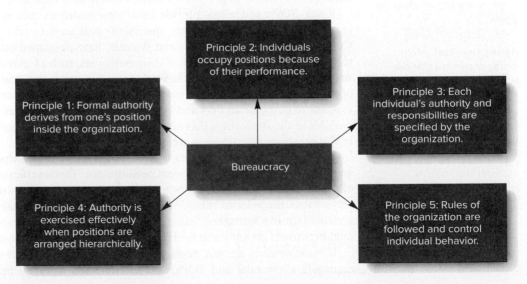

Principle 2: Individuals occupy positions because of their performance.

Principle 1: Formal authority derives from one's position inside the organization.

Principle 3: Each individual's authority and responsibilities are specified by the organization.

Bureaucracy

Principle 4: Authority is exercised effectively when positions are arranged hierarchically.

Principle 5: Rules of the organization are followed and control individual behavior.

Max Weber developed the principles of bureaucracy during Germany's burgeoning industrial revolution to help organizations increase their efficiency and effectiveness.
©akg-images/The Image Works

system of administration, obedience is owed to a manager not because of any personal qualities—such as personality, wealth, or social status—but because the manager occupies a position that is associated with a certain level of authority and responsibility.[23]

- **Principle 2:** *In a bureaucracy, people should occupy positions because of their performance, not because of their social standing or personal contacts.*

This principle was not always followed in Weber's time and is often ignored today. Some organizations and industries are still affected by social networks in which personal contacts and relations, not job-related skills, influence hiring and promotion decisions.

- **Principle 3:** *The extent of each position's formal authority and task responsibilities, and its relationship to other positions in an organization, should be clearly specified.*

When the tasks and authority associated with various positions in the organization are clearly specified, managers and workers know what is expected of them and what to expect from each other. Moreover, an organization can hold all its employees strictly accountable for their actions when they know their exact responsibilities.

- **Principle 4:** *Authority can be exercised effectively in an organization when positions are arranged hierarchically so employees know whom to report to and who reports to them.*

Managers must create an organizational hierarchy of authority that makes it clear who reports to whom and to whom managers and workers should go if conflicts or problems arise. This principle is especially important in the military, the FBI, the CIA, and other organizations that deal with sensitive issues involving possible major repercussions. It is vital that managers at high levels of the hierarchy be able to hold subordinates accountable for their actions.

- **Principle 5:** *Managers must create a well-defined system of rules, standard operating procedures, and norms so they can effectively control behavior within an organization.*

rules Formal, written instructions that specify actions to be taken under different circumstances to achieve specific goals.

standard operating procedures (SOPs) Specific sets of written instructions about how to perform a certain aspect of a task.

norms Unwritten, informal codes of conduct that prescribe how people should act in particular situations and are considered important by most members of a group or an organization.

Rules are formal, written instructions that specify actions to be taken under different circumstances to achieve specific goals (for example, if A happens, do B). **Standard operating procedures (SOPs)** are specific sets of written instructions about how to perform a certain aspect of a task. A rule might state that at the end of the workday employees are to leave their machines in good order, and a set of SOPs would specify exactly how they should do so, itemizing which machine parts must be oiled or replaced. **Norms** are unwritten, informal codes of conduct that prescribe how people should act in particular situations and are considered important by most members of a group or an organization. For example, an organizational norm in a restaurant might be that waiters should help each other if time permits.

Rules, SOPs, and norms provide behavioral guidelines that increase the performance of a bureaucratic system because they specify the best ways to accomplish organizational tasks. Companies such as McDonald's and Walmart have developed extensive rules and procedures to specify the behaviors required of their employees, such as "Always greet the customer with a smile." For example, Walmart, the world's largest retailer, automatically tracks inventory levels of products at its stores. When inventory is too low, the retailer sends an automatic request to a supplier to purchase an item and have it shipped. These items are then routed as efficiently as possible to the store where they are needed. Thus, Walmart incorporates bureaucratic controls in its operations to make employees as efficient as possible.[24]

Weber believed organizations that implement all five principles establish a bureaucratic system that improves organizational performance. The specification of positions and the use of rules and SOPs to regulate how tasks are performed make it easier for managers to organize and control the work of subordinates. Similarly, fair and equitable selection and promotion systems improve managers' feelings of security, reduce stress, and encourage organizational members to act ethically and further promote the interests of the organization.

If bureaucracies are not managed well, however, many problems can result. Sometimes managers allow rules and SOPs, "bureaucratic red tape," to become so cumbersome that decision making is slow and inefficient and organizations cannot change. When managers rely too much on rules to solve problems and not enough on their own skills and judgment, their behavior becomes inflexible. A key challenge for managers is to use bureaucratic principles to benefit, rather than harm, an organization.

Fayol's Principles of Management

Henri Fayol (1841–1925) was the CEO of Comambault Mining. Working at the same time as Weber, but independently, Fayol identified 14 principles (summarized in Table 2.1) that he believed essential to increasing the efficiency of the management process.[25] We discuss these principles in detail here because, although they were developed at the turn of the 20th century, they remain the bedrock on which much of recent management theory and research is based. In fact, as the "Management Insight" feature following this discussion suggests, modern writers, such as well-known management guru Jim Collins, continue to extol these principles.

DIVISION OF LABOR   A champion of job specialization and the division of labor for reasons already mentioned, Fayol was nevertheless among the first to point out the downside of too much specialization: boredom—a state of mind likely to diminish product quality, worker initiative, and flexibility. As a result, Fayol advocated that workers be given more job duties to perform or be encouraged to assume more responsibility for work outcomes—a principle increasingly applied today in organizations that empower their workers. Modern grocery stores, like Publix, use division of labor in their operations. For example, in the bakery and deli, employees focus on creating cakes, pies, and ready-to-eat meals. By using division of labor, Publix employees are able to develop expertise they might not otherwise gain.[26]

AUTHORITY AND RESPONSIBILITY   Like Weber, Fayol emphasized the importance of authority and responsibility. Fayol, however, went beyond Weber's formal authority, which derives from a manager's position in the hierarchy, to recognize the *informal* authority that

Table 2.1
Fayol's 14 Principles of Management

Division of labor Job specialization and the division of labor should increase efficiency, especially if managers take steps to lessen workers' boredom.

Authority and responsibility Managers have the right to give orders and the power to exhort subordinates for obedience.

Unity of command An employee should receive orders from only one superior.

Line of authority The length of the chain of command that extends from the top to the bottom of an organization should be limited.

Centralization Authority should not be concentrated at the top of the chain of command.

Unity of direction The organization should have a single plan of action to guide managers and workers.

Equity All organizational members are entitled to be treated with justice and respect.

Order The arrangement of organizational positions should maximize organizational efficiency and provide employees with satisfying career opportunities.

Initiative Managers should allow employees to be innovative and creative.

Discipline Managers need to create a workforce that strives to achieve organizational goals.

Remuneration of personnel The system that managers use to reward employees should be equitable for both employees and the organization.

Stability of tenure of personnel Long-term employees develop skills that can improve organizational efficiency.

Subordination of individual interests to the common interest Employees should understand how their performance affects the performance of the whole organization.

Esprit de corps Managers should encourage the development of shared feelings of comradeship, enthusiasm, or devotion to a common cause.

derives from personal expertise, technical knowledge, moral worth, and the ability to lead and to generate commitment from subordinates.

unity of command A reporting relationship in which an employee receives orders from, and reports to, only one superior.

UNITY OF COMMAND The principle of unity of command specifies that an employee should receive orders from, and report to, only one superior. Fayol believed that *dual command,* the reporting relationship that exists when two supervisors give orders to the same subordinate, should be avoided except in exceptional circumstances. Dual command confuses subordinates, undermines order and discipline, and creates havoc within the formal hierarchy of authority. For example, the U.S. Army maintains unity of command for its soldiers. Clearly defined ranks range from private to five-star general, and each soldier answers to a commanding officer with a higher rank. While operating in the field, it is critical that soldiers understand their objectives, and consistent unity of command enables each soldier to know exactly whom he or she should follow to get the job done.[27]

line of authority The chain of command extending from the top to the bottom of an organization.

LINE OF AUTHORITY The line of authority is the chain of command extending from the top to the bottom of an organization. Fayol was one of the first management theorists to point out the importance of limiting the length of the chain of command by controlling the number of levels in the managerial hierarchy. The more levels in the hierarchy, the longer communication takes between managers at the top and bottom and the slower the pace of planning and organizing. Restricting the number of hierarchical levels to lessen these communication problems lets an organization act quickly and flexibly.

Fayol also pointed out that when organizations are split into different departments or functions, each with its own hierarchy, it is important to allow middle and first-line managers in each department to interact with managers at similar levels in other departments. This interaction helps speed decision making because managers know each other and know whom to go to when problems arise. For cross-departmental integration to work, Fayol noted the importance of keeping one's superiors informed about what is taking place so that lower-level decisions do not harm activities taking place in other parts of the organization.

centralization The concentration of authority at the top of the managerial hierarchy.

CENTRALIZATION Fayol also was one of the first management writers to focus on centralization, the concentration of authority at the top of the managerial hierarchy. Fayol believed authority should not be concentrated at the top of the chain of command. One of the most significant issues that top managers face is how much authority to centralize at the top of the organization and what authority to decentralize to managers and workers at lower hierarchical levels. This important issue affects the behavior of people at all levels in the organization.

If authority is very centralized, only managers at the top make important decisions and subordinates simply follow orders. This arrangement gives top managers great control over organizational activities and helps ensure that the organization is pursuing its strategy, but it makes it difficult for the people who are closest to problems and issues to respond to them in a timely manner. It also can reduce the motivation of middle and first-line managers and make them less flexible and adaptable because they become reluctant to make decisions on their own, even when doing so is necessary. They get used to passing the buck. The pendulum is now swinging toward decentralization as organizations seek to empower middle managers and create self-managed teams that monitor and control their own activities, both to increase organizational flexibility and to reduce operating costs and increase efficiency.

unity of direction The singleness of purpose that makes possible the creation of one plan of action to guide managers and workers as they use organizational resources.

UNITY OF DIRECTION Just as there is a need for unity of command, there is also a need for unity of direction, the singleness of purpose that makes possible the creation of one plan of action to guide managers and workers as they use organizational resources. An organization without a single guiding plan becomes inefficient and ineffective; its activities become unfocused, and individuals and groups work at cross-purposes. Successful planning starts with top managers working as a team to craft the organization's strategy, which they communicate to middle managers, who decide how to use organizational resources to implement the strategy.

equity The justice, impartiality, and fairness to which all organizational members are entitled.

EQUITY As Fayol wrote, "For personnel to be encouraged to carry out their duties with all the devotion and loyalty of which they are capable, they must be treated with respect for their own sense of integrity, and equity results from the combination of respect and justice."[28] Equity—the justice, impartiality, and fairness to which all organizational members are entitled—is receiving much attention today; the desire to treat employees fairly is a primary concern of managers. (Equity theory is discussed in Chapter 13.)

ORDER   Like Taylor and the Gilbreths, Fayol was interested in analyzing jobs, positions, and individuals to ensure that the organization was using resources as efficiently as possible. To Fayol, **order** meant the methodical arrangement of positions to provide the organization with the greatest benefit and to provide employees with career opportunities that satisfy their needs. Thus Fayol recommended the use of organizational charts to show the position and duties of each employee and to indicate which positions an employee might move to or be promoted into in the future. He also advocated that managers engage in extensive career planning to help ensure orderly career paths.

order The methodical arrangement of positions to provide the organization with the greatest benefit and to provide employees with career opportunities.

INITIATIVE   Although order and equity are important means to fostering commitment and loyalty among employees, Fayol believed managers must also encourage employees to exercise **initiative**, the ability to act on their own without direction from a superior. Used properly, initiative can be a major source of strength for an organization because it leads to creativity and innovation. Managers need skill and tact to achieve the difficult balance between the organization's need for order and employees' desire for initiative. Fayol believed the ability to strike this balance was a key indicator of a superior manager.

initiative The ability to act on one's own without direction from a superior.

DISCIPLINE   In focusing on the importance of **discipline**—obedience, energy, application, and other outward marks of respect for a superior's authority—Fayol was addressing the concern of many early managers: how to create a workforce that was reliable and hardworking and would strive to achieve organizational goals. According to Fayol, discipline results in respectful relationships between organizational members and reflects the quality of an organization's leadership and a manager's ability to act fairly and equitably.

discipline Obedience, energy, application, and other outward marks of respect for a superior's authority.

REMUNERATION OF PERSONNEL   Fayol proposed reward systems including bonuses and profit-sharing plans, which are increasingly used today as organizations seek ways to motivate employees. Convinced from his own experience that an organization's payment system has important implications for organizational success, Fayol believed effective reward systems should be equitable for both employees and the organization, encourage productivity by rewarding well-directed effort, not be subject to abuse, and be uniformly applied to employees. PayScale is a company dedicated to helping its clients effectively compensate their employees. The company works with highly competitive customers to track employee performance and effectively reward talent, increasing employee morale and productivity while reducing employee turnover.[29]

STABILITY OF TENURE OF PERSONNEL   Fayol also recognized the importance of long-term employment, and this idea has been echoed by contemporary management gurus such as Tom Peters, Jeff Pfeffer, and Jim Collins. When employees stay with an organization for extended periods, they develop skills that improve the organization's ability to use its resources.

SUBORDINATION OF INDIVIDUAL INTERESTS TO THE COMMON INTEREST   The interests of the organization as a whole must take precedence over the interests of any individual or group if the organization is to survive. Equitable agreements must be established between the organization and its members to ensure that employees are treated fairly and rewarded for their performance and to maintain the disciplined organizational relationships so vital to an efficient system of administration.

ESPRIT DE CORPS   As this discussion of Fayol's ideas suggests, the appropriate design of an organization's hierarchy of authority and the right mix of order and discipline foster cooperation and commitment. Likewise, a key element in a successful organization is the development of **esprit de corps**, a French expression that refers to shared feelings of comradeship, enthusiasm, or devotion to a common cause among members of a group. (Today the term *organizational culture* is used to refer to these shared feelings; this concept is discussed at length in Chapter 3.)

esprit de corps Shared feelings of comradeship, enthusiasm, or devotion to a common cause among members of a group.

Some of the principles that Fayol outlined have faded from contemporary management practices, but most have endured. The characteristics of successful organizations that Jim Collins presents in his best-selling book *Good to Great* are discussed in the accompanying "Management Insight."

Getting from *Good to Great*

In his book *Good to Great,* Jim Collins, noted consultant and business coach, reports on a case study of firms with exemplary performance. He is seeking to shed light on the factors that contributed to these firms' rise to excellence.[30] Collins says that several principles predict a firm's success.

The first is that of Level 5 leadership. These leaders possess great humility but also an intense professional will. Although Level 5 leadership is applicable to all levels of the organization, Collins proposes that its application only by top managers is enough to raise an organization from mediocrity to greatness.

Second, Collins argues that having the right people in place is more important than establishing the values and strategy of the firm. Firms should focus on hiring the right people, and getting rid of the wrong people, to move firms in an upward trajectory.

Third, Collins says that confrontation and conflict are important drivers of decision success. Thus it is critical for managers to establish a climate of trust where information can be readily shared. Furthermore, Collins asserts that attempting to motivate others is wrong because the right employees will be self-motivated—rewards may actually be counterproductive.

Fourth, Collins argues for the Hedgehog Principle, which says that companies should stick to what they know; companies should do what they can excel at, make money at, and be passionate about. Fifth, Collins says that great companies are disciplined companies. Here *discipline* means adhering to only those opportunities that accommodate the Hedgehog Principle. Opportunities that violate the Hedgehog Principle should be avoided.

Finally, *Good to Great* proposes that great companies do not chase technological fads but, instead, seek incremental improvements in technology that complement core businesses. According to Collins, great companies pursue incremental change and improvement instead of radical change.[31]

LO2-4 Trace the changes in theories about how managers should behave to motivate and control employees.

As this insight into contemporary management suggests, the basic concerns that motivated Fayol continue to inspire management theorists.[32] The principles that Fayol and Weber set forth still provide clear and appropriate guidelines that managers can use to create a work setting that efficiently and effectively uses organizational resources. These principles remain the bedrock of modern management theory; recent researchers have refined or developed them to suit modern conditions. For example, Weber's and Fayol's concerns for equity and for establishing appropriate links between performance and reward are central themes in contemporary theories of motivation and leadership.

Behavioral Management Theory

Because the writings of Weber and Fayol were not translated into English and published in the United States until the late 1940s, American management theorists in the first half of the 20th century were unaware of the contributions of these European pioneers. American management theorists began where Taylor and his followers left off. Although their writings were different, these theorists all espoused a theme that focused on **behavioral management**, the study of how managers should personally behave to motivate employees and encourage them to perform at high levels and be committed to achieving organizational goals.

behavioral management The study of how managers should behave to motivate employees and encourage them to perform at high levels and be committed to the achievement of organizational goals.

The Work of Mary Parker Follett

If F. W. Taylor is considered the father of management thought, Mary Parker Follett (1868–1933) serves as its mother. Much of her writing about management and about the way managers should behave toward workers was a response to her concern that Taylor was

Mary Parker Follett, an early management thinker who advocated, "Authority should go with knowledge . . . whether it is up the line or down."

ignoring the human side of the organization. She pointed out that management often overlooks the multitude of ways in which employees can contribute to the organization when managers allow them to participate and exercise initiative in their everyday work lives.[33] Taylor, for example, never proposed that managers should involve workers in analyzing their jobs to identify better ways to perform tasks or should even ask workers how they felt about their jobs. Instead he used time-and-motion experts to analyze workers' jobs for them. Follett, in contrast, argued that because workers know the most about their jobs, they should be involved in job analysis and managers should allow them to participate in the work development process.

Follett proposed that "authority should go with knowledge . . . whether it is up the line or down." In other words, if workers have the relevant knowledge, then workers, rather than managers, should be in control of the work process itself, and managers should behave as coaches and facilitators—not as monitors and supervisors. In making this statement, Follett anticipated the current interest in self-managed teams and empowerment. She also recognized the importance of having managers in different departments communicate directly with each other to speed decision making. She advocated what she called "cross-functioning": members of different departments working together in cross-departmental teams to accomplish projects—an approach that is increasingly used today.[34]

Fayol also mentioned expertise and knowledge as important sources of managers' authority, but Follett went further. She proposed that knowledge and expertise, not managers' formal authority deriving from their position in the hierarchy, should decide who will lead at any particular moment. She believed, as do many management theorists today, that power is fluid and should flow to the person who can best help the organization achieve its goals. Follett took a horizontal view of power and authority, in contrast to Fayol, who saw the formal line of authority and vertical chain of command as being most essential to effective management. Follett's behavioral approach to management was very radical for its time.

The Hawthorne Studies and Human Relations

Probably because of its radical nature, Follett's work was unappreciated by managers and researchers until quite recently. Most continued to follow in the footsteps of Taylor and the Gilbreths. To increase efficiency, they studied ways to improve various characteristics of the work setting, such as job specialization or the kinds of tools workers used. One series of studies was conducted from 1924 to 1932 at the Hawthorne Works of the Western Electric Company.[35] This research, now known as the *Hawthorne studies,* began as an attempt to investigate how characteristics of the work setting—specifically, the level of lighting, or illumination—affect worker fatigue and performance. The researchers conducted an experiment in which they systematically measured worker productivity at various levels of illumination.

The experiment produced some unexpected results. The researchers found that regardless of whether they raised or lowered the level of illumination, productivity increased. In fact, productivity began to fall only when the level of illumination dropped to the level of moonlight—a level at which workers could presumably no longer see well enough to do their work efficiently.

The researchers found these results puzzling and invited a noted Harvard psychologist, Elton Mayo, to help them. Mayo proposed another series of experiments to solve the mystery. These experiments, known as the *relay assembly test experiments,* were designed to investigate the effects of other aspects of the work context on job performance, such as the effect of the number and length of rest periods and hours of work on fatigue and monotony.[36] The goal was to raise productivity.

During a two-year study of a small group of female workers, the researchers again observed that productivity increased over time, but the increases could not be solely attributed to the effects of changes in the work setting. Gradually, the researchers discovered that, to some degree, the results they were obtaining were influenced by the fact that the researchers themselves had become part of the experiment. In other words, the presence of the researchers was affecting the results because the workers enjoyed receiving attention and being the subject of study and were willing to cooperate with the researchers to produce the results they believed the researchers desired.

Subsequently, it was found that many other factors also influence worker behavior, and it was not clear what was actually influencing the Hawthorne workers' behavior. However, this particular effect—which became known as the Hawthorne effect—seemed to suggest that workers' attitudes toward their managers affect the level of workers' performance. In particular, the significant finding was that each manager's personal behavior or leadership approach can affect performance. This finding led many researchers to turn their attention to managerial behavior and leadership. If supervisors could be trained to behave in ways that would elicit cooperative behavior from their subordinates, productivity could be increased. From this view emerged the human relations movement, which advocates that supervisors be behaviorally trained to manage subordinates in ways that elicit their cooperation and increase their productivity.

The importance of behavioral, or human relations, training became even clearer to its supporters after another series of experiments—the *bank wiring room experiments*. In a study of workers making telephone switching equipment, researchers Elton Mayo and F. J. Roethlisberger discovered that the workers, as a group, had deliberately adopted a norm of output restriction to protect their jobs. Workers who violated this informal production norm were subjected to sanctions by other group members. Those who violated group performance norms and performed above the norm were called "ratebusters"; those who performed below the norm were called "chiselers."

The experimenters concluded that both types of workers threatened the group as a whole. Ratebusters threatened group members because they revealed to managers how fast the work could be done. Chiselers were looked down on because they were not doing their share of the work. Work group members disciplined both ratebusters and chiselers to create a pace of work that the workers (not the managers) thought was fair. Thus, a work group's influence over output can be as great as the supervisors' influence. Because the work group can influence the behavior of its members, some management theorists argue that supervisors should be trained to behave in ways that gain the goodwill and cooperation of workers so that supervisors, not workers, control the level of work group performance.

One implication of the Hawthorne studies was that the behavior of managers and workers in the work setting is as important in explaining the level of performance as the technical aspects of the task. Managers must understand the workings of the informal organization, the system of behavioral rules and norms that emerge in a group, when they try to manage or change behavior in organizations. Many studies have found that as time passes, groups often develop elaborate procedures and norms that bond members together, allowing unified action either to cooperate with management to raise performance or to restrict output and thwart the attainment of organizational goals. The Hawthorne studies demonstrated the importance of understanding how the feelings, thoughts, and behavior of work group members and managers affect performance. It was becoming increasingly clear to researchers that understanding behavior in organizations is a complex process that is critical to increasing performance.[37] Indeed, the increasing interest in the area of management known as organizational behavior, the study of the factors that have an impact on how individuals and groups respond to and act in organizations, dates from these early studies.

Theory X and Theory Y

Several studies after World War II revealed how assumptions about workers' attitudes and behavior affect managers' behavior. Perhaps the most influential approach was developed by Douglas McGregor. He proposed two sets of assumptions about how work attitudes and behaviors not only dominate the way managers think but also affect how they behave in organizations. McGregor named these two contrasting sets of assumptions *Theory X* and *Theory Y* (see Figure 2.3).[38]

THEORY X   According to the assumptions of Theory X, the average worker is lazy, dislikes work, and will try to do as little as possible. Moreover, workers have little ambition and wish to avoid responsibility. Thus, the manager's task is to counteract workers' natural tendencies

---

Hawthorne effect The finding that a manager's behavior or leadership approach can affect workers' level of performance.

human relations movement A management approach that advocates the idea that supervisors should receive behavioral training to manage subordinates in ways that elicit their cooperation and increase their productivity.

informal organization The system of behavioral rules and norms that emerge in a group.

organizational behavior The study of the factors that have an impact on how individuals and groups respond to and act in organizations.

Theory X A set of negative assumptions about workers that leads to the conclusion that a manager's task is to supervise workers closely and control their behavior.

Figure 2.3

Theory X versus Theory Y

THEORY X	THEORY Y
The average employee is lazy, dislikes work, and will try to do as little as possible.	Employees are not inherently lazy. Given the chance, employees will do what is good for the organization.
To ensure that employees work hard, managers should closely supervise employees.	To allow employees to work in the organization's interest, managers must create a work setting that provides opportunities for workers to exercise initiative and self-direction.
Managers should create strict work rules and implement a well-defined system of rewards and punishments to control employees.	Managers should decentralize authority to employees and make sure employees have the resources necessary to achieve organizational goals.

Source: D. McGregor, *The Human Side of Enterprise.* Copyright © McGraw-Hill Education. Reprinted with permission.

to avoid work. To keep workers' performance at a high level, the manager must supervise workers closely and control their behavior by means of "the carrot and stick"—rewards and punishments.

Managers who accept the assumptions of Theory X design and shape the work setting to maximize their control over workers' behaviors and minimize workers' control over the pace of work. These managers believe workers must be made to do what is necessary for the success of the organization, and they focus on developing rules, SOPs, and a well-defined system of rewards and punishments to control behavior. They see little point in giving workers autonomy to solve their own problems because they think the workforce neither expects nor desires cooperation. Theory X managers see their role as closely monitoring workers to ensure that they contribute to the production process and do not threaten product quality. Henry Ford, who closely supervised and managed his workforce, fits McGregor's description of a manager who holds Theory X assumptions.

THEORY Y In contrast, Theory Y assumes that workers are not inherently lazy, do not naturally dislike work, and, if given the opportunity, will do what is good for the organization. According to Theory Y, the characteristics of the work setting determine whether workers consider work to be a source of satisfaction or punishment, and managers do not need to closely control workers' behavior to make them perform at a high level because workers exercise self-control when they are committed to organizational goals. The implication of Theory Y, according to McGregor, is that "the limits of collaboration in the organizational setting are not limits of human nature but of management's ingenuity in discovering how to realize the potential represented by its human resources." It is the manager's task to create a work setting that encourages commitment to organizational goals and provides opportunities for workers to be imaginative and to exercise initiative and self-direction.

When managers design the organizational setting to reflect the assumptions about attitudes and behavior suggested by Theory Y, the characteristics of the organization are quite different from those of an organizational setting based on Theory X. Managers who believe workers are motivated to help the organization reach its goals can decentralize authority and give more control over the job to workers, both as individuals and in groups. In this setting, individuals and groups are still accountable for their activities; however, the manager's role is not to control employees but to provide support and advice, to make sure employees have the resources they need to perform their jobs, and to evaluate them on their ability to help the organization meet its goals. Henri Fayol's approach to administration more closely reflects the assumptions of Theory Y rather than Theory X. Companies such as 3M, Apple, and Google exemplify those that follow Theory Y.

Theory Y A set of positive assumptions about workers that leads to the conclusion that a manager's task is to create a work setting that encourages commitment to organizational goals and provides opportunities for workers to be imaginative and to exercise initiative and self-direction.

Herb Kelleher, co-founder and former CEO of Southwest Airlines, built a company known for customer service by following an open-door policy and giving employees flexible job descriptions and significant discretion in interacting with customers.
©Jon Freilich/Bloomberg/Getty Images

Southwest Airlines has long been the darling of the airline industry, and Southwest's leadership cites their Theory Y culture as a driving force. Inspired by co-founder and former CEO Herb Kelleher, Southwest Airlines emphasizes a culture of fun, creativity, and camaraderie.[39] Southwest employees note how Kelleher maintained an open-door policy of contact, which enabled him to stay in touch with problems facing the airline and find solutions faster.

Employees have highly flexible job descriptions that enable them to chip in and help where needed. Unlike many of its competitors, which use highly regimented and formalized employee roles, Southwest employees are encouraged to help solve problems where they see them. Thus, it's not uncommon to see a Southwest manager helping move passenger luggage into aircraft or check in passengers at a gate.

Southwest also gives its employees significant discretion, enabling them to solve problems quickly. In an industry dominated by tight schedules and narrow windows to resolve problems, these actions enable employees to serve customers better.

Finally, Southwest Airlines views its unions as partners rather than adversaries. It works with independent unions to ensure that employees are compensated and treated fairly, and it routinely solicits input from its employees on how to improve operations.[40] As a result of this innovative culture dominated by Theory Y thinking, Southwest Airlines has become the most consistently profitable company among its competitors.

Management Science Theory

LO2-5 Explain the contributions of management science to the efficient use of organizational resources.

management science theory An approach to management that uses rigorous quantitative techniques to help managers make maximum use of organizational resources.

Management science theory is a contemporary approach to management that focuses on the use of rigorous quantitative techniques to help managers make maximum use of organizational resources to produce goods and services. In essence, management science theory is a contemporary extension of scientific management, which, as developed by Taylor, also took a quantitative approach to measuring the worker–task mix to raise efficiency. There are many branches of management science, and IT, which has a significant impact on all kinds of management practices, continues to affect the tools managers use to make decisions.[41] Each branch of management science deals with a specific set of concerns:

- *Quantitative management* uses mathematical techniques—such as linear and nonlinear programming, modeling, simulation, queuing theory, and chaos theory—to help managers decide, for example, how much inventory to hold at different times of the year, where to locate a new factory, and how best to invest an organization's financial capital. IT offers managers new and improved ways of handling information so they can make more accurate assessments of the situation and better decisions.

- *Operations management* gives managers a set of techniques they can use to analyze any aspect of an organization's production system to increase efficiency. IT, through the Internet and through growing B2B networks, is transforming how managers acquire inputs and distribute finished products.

- *Management information systems (MISs)* give managers information about events occurring inside the organization as well as in its external environment—information that is vital for effective decision making. IT gives managers access to more and better information and allows more managers at all levels to participate in the decision-making process.

All these subfields of management science, enhanced by sophisticated IT, provide tools and techniques that managers can use to help improve the quality of their decision making and increase efficiency and effectiveness. For example, Toyota applied management science theory with its Toyota Production System (TPS). The TPS emphasizes continuous improvement in quality and the reduction of waste through learning. TPS was a major catalyst for the "lean revolution" in global manufacturing, and manufacturing companies worldwide have embraced this philosophy and adapted it for their own operations.[42] We discuss many important developments in management science theory in this book. In particular, Chapter 9 focuses on how to use operations management and the principle of total quality management (TQM) to improve quality, efficiency, and responsiveness to customers. And Chapter 18 describes the many ways managers use information systems and other technologies to improve their planning, organizing, and controlling functions.

Organizational Environment Theory

LO2-6 Explain why the study of the external environment and its impact on an organization has become a central issue in management thought.

organizational environment The set of forces and conditions that operate beyond an organization's boundaries but affect a manager's ability to acquire and utilize resources.

open system A system that takes in resources from its external environment and converts them into goods and services that are then sent back to that environment for purchase by customers.

closed system A system that is self-contained and thus not affected by changes occurring in its external environment.

entropy The tendency of a closed system to lose its ability to control itself and thus to dissolve and disintegrate.

synergy Performance gains that result when individuals and departments coordinate their actions.

An important milestone in the history of management thought occurred when researchers went beyond the study of how managers can influence behavior within organizations to consider how managers control the organization's relationship with its external environment, or **organizational environment**—the set of forces and conditions that operate beyond an organization's boundaries but affect a manager's ability to acquire and utilize resources. Resources in the organizational environment include the raw materials and skilled people that an organization requires to produce goods and services, as well as the support of groups, including customers who buy these goods and services and provide the organization with big data critical to the firm's overall financial success. One way of determining the relative success of an organization is to consider how effective its managers are at obtaining scarce and valuable resources.[43] The importance of studying the environment became clear after the development of open-systems theory and contingency theory during the 1960s and other more recent theories, including dynamic capabilities.

The Open-Systems View

One of the most influential views of how an organization is affected by its external environment was developed by Daniel Katz, Robert Kahn, and James Thompson in the 1960s.[44] These theorists viewed the organization as an **open system**—a system that takes in resources from its external environment and converts or transforms them into goods and services that are sent back to that environment, where they are bought by customers (see Figure 2.4).

At the *input stage* an organization acquires resources such as raw materials, money, and skilled workers to produce goods and services. Once the organization has gathered the necessary resources, conversion begins. At the *conversion stage* the organization's workforce, using appropriate tools, techniques, and machinery, transforms the inputs into outputs of finished goods and services such as cars, hamburgers, or flights to Hawaii. At the *output stage* the organization releases finished goods and services to its external environment, where customers purchase and use them to satisfy their needs. The money the organization obtains from the sales of its outputs allows the organization to acquire more resources so the cycle can begin again.

The system just described is said to be open because the organization draws from and interacts with the external environment in order to survive; in other words, the organization is open to its environment. A **closed system**, in contrast, is a self-contained system that is not affected by changes in its external environment. Organizations that operate as closed systems, that ignore the external environment, and that fail to acquire inputs are likely to experience **entropy**, which is the tendency of a closed system to lose its ability to control itself and thus to dissolve and disintegrate.

Management theorists can model the activities of most organizations by using the open-systems view. For example, manufacturing companies, like Ford and General Electric, buy inputs such as component parts, skilled and semiskilled labor, and robots and computer-controlled manufacturing equipment; then at the conversion stage they use their manufacturing skills to assemble inputs into outputs of cars and appliances. As we discuss in later chapters, competition between organizations for resources is one of several major challenges to managing the organizational environment.

Researchers using the open-systems view are also interested in how the various parts of a system work together to promote efficiency and effectiveness. Systems theorists like to argue that the whole is greater than the sum of its parts; they mean that an organization performs at a higher level when its departments work together rather than separately. **Synergy**, the

Figure 2.4

The Organization as an Open System

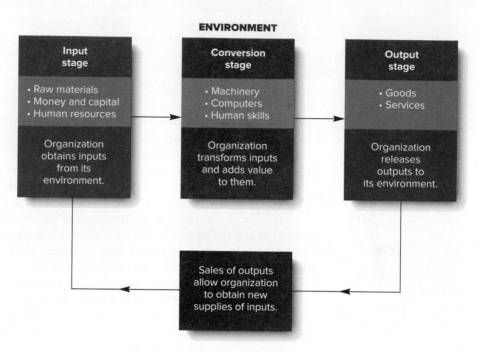

performance gains that result from the *combined* actions of individuals and departments, is possible only in an organized system. The strategy of using teams composed of people from different departments reflects systems theorists' interest in designing organizational systems to create synergy and thus increase efficiency and effectiveness.

Contingency Theory

contingency theory The idea that the organizational structures and control systems managers choose depend on (are contingent on) characteristics of the external environment in which the organization operates.

Another milestone in management theory was the development of **contingency theory** in the 1960s by Tom Burns and G. M. Stalker in Britain and Paul Lawrence and Jay Lorsch in the United States.[45] The crucial message of contingency theory is that *there is no one best way to organize:* The organizational structures and the control systems that managers choose depend on (are contingent on) characteristics of the external environment in which the organization operates. According to contingency theory, the characteristics of the environment affect an organization's ability to obtain resources; to maximize the likelihood of gaining access to resources, managers must allow an organization's departments to organize and control their activities in ways most likely to allow them to obtain resources, given the constraints of the environment they face. In other words, how managers design the organizational hierarchy, choose a control system, and lead and motivate their employees is contingent on the characteristics of the organizational environment (see Figure 2.5).

An important characteristic of the external environment that affects an organization's ability to obtain resources is the degree to which the environment is changing. Changes in the organizational environment include changes in technology, which can lead to the creation of new products (such as Amazon Echo) and result in the obsolescence of existing products (Blu-ray players); the entry of new competitors (such as foreign organizations that compete for available resources); and unstable economic conditions. In general, the more quickly the organizational environment is changing, the greater the problems are associated with gaining access to resources, and the greater is managers' need to find ways to coordinate the activities of people in different departments to respond to the environment quickly and effectively.

MECHANISTIC AND ORGANIC STRUCTURES   Drawing on Weber's and Fayol's principles of organization and management, Burns and Stalker proposed two basic ways in which managers can organize and control an organization's activities to respond to characteristics

Figure 2.5

Contingency Theory of Organizational Design

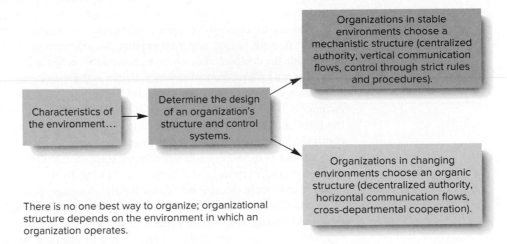

Characteristics of the environment... → Determine the design of an organization's structure and control systems.

Organizations in stable environments choose a mechanistic structure (centralized authority, vertical communication flows, control through strict rules and procedures).

Organizations in changing environments choose an organic structure (decentralized authority, horizontal communication flows, cross-departmental cooperation).

There is no one best way to organize; organizational structure depends on the environment in which an organization operates.

of its external environment: They can use a *mechanistic structure* or an *organic structure*.[46] As you will see, a mechanistic structure typically rests on Theory X assumptions, and an organic structure typically rests on Theory Y assumptions.

When the environment surrounding an organization is stable, managers tend to choose a mechanistic structure to organize and control activities and make employee behavior predictable. In a **mechanistic structure**, authority is centralized at the top of the managerial hierarchy, and the vertical hierarchy of authority is the main means used to control subordinates' behavior. Tasks and roles are clearly specified, subordinates are closely supervised, and the emphasis is on strict discipline and order. Everyone knows his or her place, and there is a place for everyone. A mechanistic structure provides the most efficient way to operate in a stable environment because it allows managers to obtain inputs at the lowest cost, giving an organization the most control over its conversion processes and enabling the most efficient production of goods and services with the smallest expenditure of resources. McDonald's restaurants operate with a mechanistic structure. Supervisors make all important decisions; employees are closely supervised and follow well-defined rules and standard operating procedures.

In contrast, when the environment is changing rapidly, it is difficult to obtain access to resources, and managers need to organize their activities in a way that allows them to cooperate, to act quickly to acquire resources (such as new types of inputs to produce new kinds of products), and to respond effectively to the unexpected. In an **organic structure**, authority is decentralized to middle and first-line managers to encourage them to take responsibility and act quickly to pursue scarce resources. Departments are encouraged to take a cross-departmental or functional perspective, and cross-functional teams composed of people from different departments are formed. As in Follett's model, the organization operates in an organic way because authority rests with the individuals, departments, and teams best positioned to control the current problems the organization is facing. As a result, managers in an organic structure can react more quickly to a changing environment than can managers in a mechanistic structure. However, an organic structure is generally more expensive to operate because it requires that more managerial time, money, and effort be spent on coordination. So it is used only when needed—when the organizational environment is unstable and changing rapidly.[47] Google, Apple, and 3M are examples of companies that operate with organic structures.

Dynamic Capabilities

Over the past few decades, other management theories have emerged, which have had a significant impact on how organizations function, including total quality management (discussed in Chapter 9), organizational learning (described in Chapter 7), and dynamic capabilities. David Teece, a professor at UC–Berkeley's Haas School of Business, came up with the theory of **dynamic capabilities** in the late 1990s to explain how companies must be stable enough to deliver value

mechanistic structure An organizational structure in which authority is centralized, tasks and rules are clearly specified, and employees are closely supervised.

organic structure An organizational structure in which authority is decentralized to middle and first-line managers and tasks and roles are left ambiguous to encourage employees to cooperate and respond quickly to the unexpected.

dynamic capabilities Theory that organizations have the ability to build, integrate, and reconfigure processes to address rapidly changing internal and external environments.

to customers yet resilient and flexible enough to shift focus when situations demand a different approach.[48] Unlike best practices, which typically are learned capabilities and activities undertaken by one or two companies that spread to an entire industry, dynamic capabilities are unique to each company and are more than likely rooted in the organization's past experiences.[49]

According to Teece, three types of managerial activities can help make a process or activity dynamic: sensing, seizing, and transforming. *Sensing* refers to identifying and assessing opportunities outside the company. For example, Steve Jobs recognized consumers wanted a smaller, more attractive mp3 player than what was available in the marketplace. *Seizing* describes the action of mobilizing company resources to capture value for the organization from these opportunities. Acting on its assessment of the competition, Apple seized the opportunity to design and produce the iPod, a sleek alternative to bulky mp3 devices. *Transforming* is an organization's ability to continue making changes as needed to maintain success. Once Apple created the iPod, the company shifted its focus from solely producing computers to expanding its product line to consumer electronics and, eventually, digital music streaming. In 2018, Apple topped the *Forbes* annual list of the world's most valuable brands for the eighth straight year, worth more than $182 billion.[50]

In addition, technological advances, such as social media and big data, among others, have prompted managers to devise processes and innovative tools to take advantage of opportunities while staying ahead of the competition. For example, big data, information gathered via social media and other digital platforms, can be analyzed and categorized into useful patterns and data sets, which companies use to change or refine internal processes, develop and introduce new products and services, and create efficiencies in managing customers and suppliers.[51] These technologies and dynamic capabilities can be tested, scaled, and adapted quickly, giving organizations tremendous competitive advantage.[52]

Summary and Review

In this chapter we examined the evolution of management theory and research over the last century. Much of the material in the rest of this book stems from developments and refinements of this work. Indeed, the rest of this book incorporates the results of the extensive research in management that has been conducted since the development of the theories discussed here.

LO2-1, 2-2 **SCIENTIFIC MANAGEMENT THEORY** The search for efficiency started with the study of how managers could improve person–task relationships to increase efficiency. The concept of job specialization and division of labor remains the basis for the design of work settings in modern organizations. New developments such as lean production and total quality management are often viewed as advances on the early scientific management principles developed by Taylor and the Gilbreths.

LO2-3 **ADMINISTRATIVE MANAGEMENT THEORY** Max Weber and Henri Fayol outlined principles of bureaucracy and administration that are as relevant to managers today as they were when developed at the turn of the 20th century. Much of modern management research refines these principles to suit contemporary conditions. For example, the use of cross-departmental teams and the empowerment of workers are issues that managers also faced a century ago.

LO2-4 **BEHAVIORAL MANAGEMENT THEORY** Researchers have described many different approaches to managerial behavior, including Theories X and Y. Often the managerial behavior that researchers suggest reflects the context of their own historical eras and cultures. Mary Parker Follett advocated managerial behaviors that did not reflect accepted modes of managerial behavior at the time, and her work was largely ignored until conditions changed.

LO2-5 **MANAGEMENT SCIENCE THEORY** The various branches of management science theory provide rigorous quantitative techniques that give managers more control over each organization's use of resources to produce goods and services.

LO2-6 **ORGANIZATIONAL ENVIRONMENT THEORY** A main focus of contemporary management research is to find methods to help managers improve how they use organizational resources and compete in the global environment. The importance of studying the organization's external environment became clear after the development of open-systems and contingency theories during the 1960s. More recent management approaches have emerged, including dynamic capabilities.

Management in Action

Topics for Discussion and Action

Discussion

1. Choose a fast-food restaurant, a fitness club, or some other organization with which you are familiar, and describe the division of labor and job specialization it uses to produce goods and services. How might this division of labor be improved? **[LO2-1, 2-2]**

2. Apply Taylor's principles of scientific management to improve the performance of the organization you chose in question 1. **[LO2-2]**

3. In what ways are Weber's and Fayol's ideas about bureaucracy and administration similar? How do they differ? **[LO2-3]**

4. Which of Weber's and Fayol's principles seem most relevant to the creation of an ethical organization? **[LO2-4, 2-6]**

5. How are companies using management science theory to improve their processes? Is this theory equally applicable for manufacturing and service companies? If so, how? **[LO2-4, 2-5]**

6. What is contingency theory? What kinds of organizations familiar to you have been successful or unsuccessful in dealing with contingencies from the external environment? **[LO2-6]**

7. Why are mechanistic and organic structures suited to different organizational environments? **[LO2-4, 2-6]**

Action

8. Question a manager about his or her views of the relative importance of Fayol's 14 principles of management. **[LO2-3, 2-4]**

9. Visit at least two organizations in your community, and identify those that seem to operate with a Theory X or a Theory Y approach to management. **[LO2-4]**

Building Management Skills

Managing Your Own Business [LO2-2, 2-4]

Now that you understand the concerns addressed by management thinkers over the last century, use this exercise to apply your knowledge to developing your management skills.

Imagine that you are the founder of a software company that specializes in developing games for mobile devices. Customer demand for your games has increased so much that over the last year your company has grown from a busy one-person operation to one with 16 employees. In addition to yourself, you employ six software developers to produce the software, three graphic artists, two computer technicians, two marketing and sales personnel, and two assistants. In the next year you expect to hire 30 new employees, and you are wondering how best to manage your growing company.

1. Use the principles of Weber and Fayol to decide on the system of organization and management that you think will be most effective for your growing organization. How many levels will the managerial hierarchy of your organization have? How much authority will you decentralize to your subordinates? How will you establish the division of labor between subordinates? Will your subordinates work alone and report to you or work in teams?

2. Which management approach (for example, Theory X or Y) do you propose to use to run your organization? In 50 or fewer words, write a statement describing the management approach you believe will motivate and coordinate your subordinates, and tell why you think this style will be best.

Managing Ethically [LO2-3, 2-4]

How Unethical Behavior Shut Down a Meatpacking Plant

By all appearances the Westland/Hallmark Meat Co. based in Chico, California, was considered to be an efficient and sanitary meatpacking plant. Under the control of its owner and CEO, Steven Mendell, the plant regularly passed inspections by the U.S. Dept. of Agriculture (USDA). Over 200 workers were employed to slaughter cattle and prepare the beef for shipment to fast-food restaurants such as Burger King and Taco Bell. Also, millions of pounds of meat the plant produced yearly were delivered under contract to one of the federal government's most coveted accounts: the National School Lunch Program.[53]

When the Humane Society turned over a videotape (secretly filmed by one of its investigators, who had taken a job as a plant employee) to the San Bernardino County district attorney, showing major violations of health procedures, an uproar followed. The videotape showed two workers dragging sick cows up the ramp that led to the slaughterhouse using metal chains and forklifts, and shocking them with electric prods and shooting streams of water in their noses and faces. Not only did the tape show inhumane treatment of animals, but it also provided evidence that the company was flouting the ban on allowing sick animals to enter the food supply chain—something that federal regulations explicitly outlaw because of concerns for human health and safety.

Once the USDA was informed that potentially contaminated beef products had entered the supply chain—especially the one to the nation's schools—it issued a notice for the recall of the 143 million pounds of beef processed in the plant over the last two years, the largest recall in history.

In addition, the plant was shut down as the investigation proceeded. CEO Steven Mendell was subpoenaed to appear before the House Panel on Energy and Commerce Committee. He denied that these violations had taken place and that diseased cows had entered the food chain. However, when panel members demanded that he view the videotape, which he claimed he had not seen, he was forced to acknowledge that inhumane treatment of animals had occurred.[54] Moreover, federal investigators turned up evidence that as early as 1996 the plant had been cited for overuse of electric prods to speed cattle through the plant and had been cited for other violations since, suggesting that these abuses had been going on for a long period.

Not only were consumers and schoolchildren harmed by these unethical actions, but the plant itself was permanently shut down and all 220 workers lost their jobs. In addition, the employees directly implicated in the video were prosecuted and one, who pleaded guilty to animal abuse, was convicted and sentenced to six months in prison.[55] Clearly, all the people and groups affected by the meatpacking plant have suffered from its unethical and inhumane organizational behaviors and practices.

Questions

1. Use the theories discussed in the chapter to debate the ethical issues involved in the way the Westland/Hallmark Meat Co. business operated.

2. Use the theories to discuss the ethical issues involved in the way the meatpacking business is being conducted today.

3. Search the web for changes occurring in the meatpacking industry.

Small Group Breakout Exercise

Modeling an Open System [LO2-6]

Form groups of three to five people, and appoint one group member as the spokesperson who will communicate your findings to the class when called on by the instructor. Then discuss the following scenario:

Think of an organization with which you are all familiar, such as a local restaurant, store, or bank. After choosing an organization, model it from an open-systems perspective. Identify its input, conversion, and output processes, and identify forces in the external environment that help or hurt the organization's ability to obtain resources and dispose of its goods or services.

Be the Manager [LO2-2, 2-4]

How to Manage a Luxury Hotel

You have been called in to advise the owners of an exclusive new luxury hotel. For the venture to succeed, hotel employees must focus on providing customers with the highest-quality service possible. The challenge is to devise a way of organizing and controlling employees that will promote high-quality service, that will encourage employees to be committed to the hotel, and that will reduce the level of employee turnover and absenteeism—which are typically high in the hotel business.

Questions

1. How do the various management theories discussed in this chapter offer clues for organizing and controlling hotel employees?

2. Which parts would be the most important for an effective system to organize and control employees?

Bloomberg Case in the News [LO 2-1, 2-4, 2-6]

The Retail Real Estate Glut Is Getting Worse

The fall of the Toys "R" Us chain, with more than 700 U.S. stores, shows how much retail real estate has changed in just the last decade. When KKR & Co., Bain Capital, and Vornado Realty Trust took over the company in 2005, the buyers justified the $7.5 billion price, in part, because of the supposedly valuable properties that came with the deal.

Real estate can put a floor under the value of a retailer and make it easier for the company to borrow. Maybe a particular store concept doesn't work out as consumers' tastes change, but in that case, investors can always sell the land and buildings to someone with a better plan. Long-term leases can be similarly valuable. But what if the problem isn't that a particular store is out of fashion, but that consumers are just shopping less at brick-and-mortar retailers in general? As more storefronts empty, the valuation floor will look wobblier.

The ultimate fate of Toys "R" Us locations will be sorted out as the company sells off its various parts; Isaac Larian, the founder of a toy company, announced on April 13 a last-minute bid to save part of the chain. But the stores wouldn't be the only vacancies hitting the retail market. While it's not going out of business like the toy seller, J.Crew Group Inc., which leases its locations, says it's closing a net of nine stores this fiscal year, after shuttering a net 41 in 2017. Walmart Inc.'s Sam's Club in January said it will close 63 locations, about 10 percent of its total. At last count, U.S. store closures announced this year reached a staggering 77 million square feet, according to data on national and regional chains compiled by CoStar Group Inc. That means retailers are well on their way to surpassing the record 105 million square feet announced for closure in all of 2017.

And with shifts to Internet shopping and retailer debt woes continuing, there's no indication the shakeout will end anytime soon. "A huge amount of retail real estate in the U.S. is going to meet its demise," says James Corl, managing director and head of real estate at private equity firm Siguler Guff & Co. Property owners will "try to re-let it as a gun range or a church—or it's going to go back to being a cornfield."

Even though retailers have been retreating for years, the country still has about 24 square feet of shopping space per person, many times more than any other developed nation, according to research firm Green Street Advisors. Consumers aren't spending enough offline to support such a generous amount. Vacancies are headaches for landlords, of course, but they also have a mushrooming effect. People may steer clear of a mall that has lost an anchor tenant or has an abundance of "for lease" signs in smaller spaces. Deserted big-box stores, their facades naked and parking lots barren, can spread a sense of blight for blocks around. Who wants to open a business next to a place that's gone out of business?

Shopping space isn't completely done for. Amazon.com Inc., blamed for the death of so many bookstores, has opened more than a dozen of its own and is betting on the grocery market with its purchase of Whole Foods. Apple Inc.'s stores are packed, and internet retailers such as Warby Parker and Blue Nile are trying out physical locations.

There's a silver lining of a sort in the dead real estate as some investors see other uses for it. "Certainly, lease values have come down," says Andy Graiser, co-president of A&G Realty Partners. But for owned property, "the range of interested parties has gotten a lot wider." Some retooling is under way. Simon Property Group Inc., the largest U.S. retail landlord, recently filed plans to redevelop an aging mall north of Seattle into a complex that includes offices and apartments. Reimagining retail real estate is also part of Brookfield Property Partners LP's agenda in its takeover of GGP Inc., the No. 2 mall owner.

But not every deserted retail property can be turned into a gym, theater, or boutique outlet of a tech company. That reality will weigh on any investor thinking about scooping up a struggling chain with real estate assets today—especially buyers in private equity, who borrow heavily to finance their deals. "Retailers cannot support large debt loads," says Perry Mandarino, head of restructuring at B. Riley FBR, an investment bank that's worked on retail liquidations. "Add to that the possibility of a decrease in the value of other collateral, such as real estate, and the successful execution of a retail-leveraged buyout may be almost impossible."

Questions for Discussion

1. In today's business environment, would using a Theory X approach help or hinder retailers faced with real estate and debt concerns? Explain your reasoning.

2. How could real estate managers apply contingency theory in transforming out-of-date retail spaces?

3. Describe how the theory of dynamic capabilities might be used by a brick-and-mortar retailer to gain competitive advantage.

Notes

1. Mike Farrell, "Customer Service Makeover Yields Results," *Multichannel News,* September 18–25, 2017, 12–15; Mike Farrell, "Comcast Names Herrin SVP Customer Experience," *Multichannel News,* www.multichannel.com, September 26, 2014.

2. Farrell, "Customer Service Makeover." See also Jeanne Bliss, "Comcast Customer Experience Improvement Plan, with Charlie Herrin," *The Chief Customer Officer Human Duct Tape Show,* episode 73, www.customerbliss.com, October 17, 2017.

3. Dan Gingiss, "How Comcast Customer Service Agents Are Following Issues All the Way to Resolution," *Forbes,* www.forbes.com, January 11, 2018.

4. Bliss, "Comcast Customer Experience Improvement Plan."

5. Bob Fernandez, "Comcast Customer Gripes about Internet Surpass Those for Cable TV," *Philadelphia Inquirer,* www.philly.com, August 3, 2017; Mike Rogoway, "Comcast Says Customer Service Overhaul Is Showing Results," *Oregonian,* www.oregonlive.com, April 23, 2017.

6. Bliss, "Comcast Customer Experience Improvement Plan."

7. Jeff Baumgartner, "Comcast Folds Customer Experience, Service Teams into Technology and Products Division," *Multichannel News,* www.multichannel.com, May 4, 2017.

8. A. Smith, *The Wealth of Nations* (London: Penguin, 1982).

9. Ibid., 110.

10. J.G. March and H.A. Simon, *Organizations* (New York: Wiley, 1958).

11. L.W. Fry, "The Maligned F.W. Taylor: A Reply to His Many Critics," *Academy of Management Review* 1 (1976), 124–29.

12. F.W. Taylor, *Shop Management* (New York: Harper, 1903); F.W. Taylor, *The Principles of Scientific Management* (New York: Harper, 1911).

13. J.A. Litterer, *The Emergence of Systematic Management as Shown by the Literature from 1870–1900* (New York: Garland, 1986).

14. H.R. Pollard, *Developments in Management Thought* (New York: Crane, 1974).

15. D. Wren, *The Evolution of Management Thought* (New York: Wiley, 1994), 134.

16. N. Resnikoff, "McDonald's Sued over Allegations of Discrimination," *America Aljazeera,* http://america.aljazeera.com, January 22, 2015.

17. "Our Business Model," http://corporate.mcdonalds.com, accessed February 28, 2018.

18. "Standards of Business Conduct," www.mcdonalds.com, accessed February 28, 2018.

19. S. Block and B. Sachs, "The Trump Administration Is Abandoning McDonald's Workers—and Everyone Else," *The Washington Post,* www.washingtonpost.com, February 9, 2018; C. Opfer and B. Penn, "Labor Board Looks to Settle McDonald's Joint Employer Case," *Bloomberg News,* www.bna.com, January 18, 2018.

20. F.B. Gilbreth, *Primer of Scientific Management* (New York: Van Nostrand Reinhold, 1912).

21. F.B. Gilbreth Jr. and E.G. Gilbreth, *Cheaper by the Dozen* (New York: Crowell, 1948).

22. M. Weber, *From Max Weber: Essays in Sociology,* ed. H.H. Gerth and C.W. Mills (New York: Oxford University Press, 1946); M. Weber, *Economy and Society,* ed. G. Roth and C. Wittich (Berkeley: University of California Press, 1978).

23. C. Perrow, *Complex Organizations,* 2nd ed. (Glenview, IL: Scott, Foresman, 1979).

24. E. Lopez, "Behind the Scenes of Walmart's New On-Time, In-Full Policy," *Supply Chain Dive,* www.supplychaindive.com, October 17, 2017.

25. H. Fayol, *General and Industrial Management* (New York: IEEE Press, 1984).

26. "Company Overview," http://corporate.publix.com, accessed February 28, 2018.

27. J. Jones, "Unity of Command and Unity of Effort in Complex Operations: Implications for Leadership," https://inssblog.wordpress.com, accessed February 28, 2018.

28. Fayol, *General and Industrial Management,* 79.

29. "About Us," www.payscale.com, accessed February 28, 2018.

30. J. Collins, "Good to Great," www.jimcollins.com, accessed February 28, 2018.

31. A. Hill, Straight from the Hedgehog's Mouth: Management Jim Collins," *Financial Times,* www.ft.com, April 28, 2017; K. Weisul, "Jim Collins: Good to Great in 10 Steps," *Inc.,* www.inc.com, May 7, 2012.

32. R.E. Eccles and N. Nohira, *Beyond the Hype: Rediscovering the Essence of Management* (Boston: Harvard Business School Press, 1992).

33. P. Graham, *M.P. Follett–Prophet of Management: A Celebration of Writings from the 1920s* (Boston: Harvard Business School Press, 1995).

34. M.P. Follett, *Creative Experience* (London: Longmans, 1924).

35. E. Mayo, *The Human Problems of Industrial Civilization* (New York: Macmillan, 1933); F.J. Roethlisberger and W.J. Dickson, *Management and the Worker* (Cambridge: Harvard University Press, 1947).

36. D.W. Organ, "Review of *Management and the Worker,* by F.J. Roethlisberger and W.J. Dickson," *Academy of Management Review* 13 (1986), 460–64.

37. For an analysis of the problems in distinguishing cause from effect in the Hawthorne studies and in social settings in general, see A. Carey, "The Hawthorne Studies: A Radical Criticism," *American Sociological Review* 33 (1967), 403–16.

38. D. McGregor, *The Human Side of Enterprise* (New York: McGraw-Hill, 1960).

39. "Southwest Citizenship," https://www.southwest.com, accessed February 28, 2018.

40. "Labor Relations: FAQs," http://swamedia.com, accessed February 28, 2018.

41. T. Dewett and G.R. Jones, "The Role of Information Technology in the Organization: A Review, Model, and Assessment," *Journal of Management* 27 (2001), 313–46.

42. Company website, "Toyota Production System," www.toyota-global.com, accessed February 28, 2018.

43. J.D. Thompson, *Organizations in Action* (New York: McGraw-Hill, 1967).

44. D. Katz and R.L. Kahn, *The Social Psychology of Organizations* (New York: Wiley, 1966); Thompson, *Organizations in Action.*

45. T. Burns and G.M. Stalker, *The Management of Innovation* (London: Tavistock, 1961); P.R. Lawrence and J.R. Lorsch, *Organization and Environment* (Boston: Graduate School of Business Administration, Harvard University, 1967).

46. Burns and Stalker, *The Management of Innovation.*

47. C.W.L. Hill and G.R. Jones, *Strategic Management: An Integrated Approach,* 8th ed. (Florence, KY: Cengage, 2010).

48. A. Kleiner, "The Dynamic Capabilities of David Teece," *Strategy + Business,* www.strategy-business.com, November 11, 2013.

49. D.J. Teece, "Explicating Dynamic Capabilities: The Nature and Microfoundations of (Sustainable) Enterprise Performance," *Strategic Management Journal* 28: 1319–1350, August 2007.

50. A. Wong, "The Key to Keeping Up: Dynamic Capabilities," *California Management Review,* http://cmr.berkeley.edu, August 22, 2016; K. Badenhausen, "The World's Most Valuable Brands 2018: By the Numbers," *Forbes*, www.forbes.com, May 23, 2018.

51. G. George, M.R. Haas, and A. Pentland, "Big Data and Management," *Academy of Management Journal,* 57 (2014), 321–26.

52. G. George and Y. Lin, "Analytics, Innovation, and Organizational Adaptation," *Innovation* 19(1): 16–22, 2017.

53. E. Werner, "Slaughterhouse Owner Acknowledges Abuse," www.pasadenastarnews.com, March 13, 2008.

54. D. Bunis and N. Luna, "Sick Cows Never Made Food Supply, Meat Plant Owner Says," www.ocregister.com, March 12, 2008.

55. "Owners of Infamous Calif. Slaughterhouse Pay Millions to Settle Government Fraud Case," *The Humane Society,* www.humanesociety.org, November 27, 2013; "Worker Sentenced in Slaughterhouse Abuse," www.yahoo.com, March 22, 2008.

CHAPTER 3

Values, Attitudes, Emotions, and Culture: The Manager as a Person

©Sam Edwards/age fotostock

Learning Objectives

After studying this chapter, you should be able to:

LO3-1 Describe the various personality traits that affect how managers think, feel, and behave.

LO3-2 Explain what values and attitudes are, and describe their impact on managerial action.

LO3-3 Appreciate how moods and emotions influence all members of an organization.

LO3-4 Describe the nature of emotional intelligence and its role in management.

LO3-5 Define organizational culture, and explain how managers both create and are influenced by organizational culture.

CEO Illuminates a New Path for PG&E

What qualities does a successful manager possess? Often, desirable qualities include those demonstrated by Geisha Williams, CEO of PG&E, one of the country's largest gas-and-electric utilities, serving northern and central California. Her appointment to that position made her the first Latina to run a *Fortune* 500 company.[1]

Since childhood, Williams has overcome challenges with an open mind, hard work, and determination. When she was five, her parents, dissidents in Cuba, got permission to immigrate to the United States, a change they had to plan and carry out over just a few days. Her parents labored hard at factory, restaurant, and sewing jobs to save enough money to buy a small grocery store, gradually acquiring larger stores as they made a success of the business. Following their example, Williams studied and worked hard. She was drawn to math, which she could understand even while learning English. After school, she worked in the family store until she headed to Wisconsin to earn an engineering degree. During college, she landed a summer job at Florida Power & Light, where she inspected customers' homes, identified ways to save energy, and sold customers on the benefits of making changes. She returned to FP&L after graduating and stayed almost 25 years, learning all aspects of the business.[2]

Williams has a visionary outlook, seeing opportunities where others might see only problems. At FP&L, a manager encouraged her by saying, "Somebody has to run this company; why not you?"[3] Though he offered similar advice to others, Williams seized on it and aimed for the top. When she made the move to PG&E, she embraced the need to create a new electric grid for a new era of energy distribution. As CEO, she gathered the leadership to craft a new vision statement centered on affordable, sustainable energy.[4] "You learn so much by doing a difficult job," she later told a *Fortune* reporter.[5]

Williams's attitudes are expressed in a positive mood, exuding strength and enthusiasm. Looking back at her childhood and youth, which some might have described as a time of hardship, Williams saw learning math as enjoyable, working in the store as a chance to feel useful, and the hot work of inspecting homes as a fun job. The manager who encouraged her at FP&L called her both "tough as nails" and "well liked"; similarly, a PG&E executive said she "can talk tough issues and simple issues—and all in this disarming way." Her current boss at PG&E, president Chris Johns, called her "a force for innovation and change."[6]

These qualities are a good match for an industry that demands transformation, especially in California. While utilities around the world are addressing the challenges associated with changing climates and advancing technology,

PG&E CEO Geisha Williams is up to the challenge of managing one of the country's largest gas-and-electric utility companies. The first Latina to run a *Fortune* 500 company, Williams fosters a culture of innovation and change, encouraging employees to make a difference.
©Paul Morigi/Stringer/Getty Images

California has ambitious goals—requiring, for example, that by 2030, utilities must generate 50% of their power from renewable sources. As customers install solar panels and other electricity sources, PG&E must be able to buy from them as well as sell to them. Furthermore, California's regulation of transportation is spurring use of electric cars, which will require a network of recharging stations. Typically, Williams defines these challenges as an opportunity to make a difference, and under her lead, PG&E is already exceeding the targets, ahead of schedule.[7]

Overview

LO3-1 Describe the various personality traits that affect how managers think, feel, and behave.

Like people everywhere, Geisha Williams has her own distinctive personality, values, ways of viewing things, and personal challenges and disappointments. In this chapter we focus on the manager as a feeling, thinking human being. We start by describing enduring characteristics that influence how managers work and how they view other people, their organizations, and the world around them. We also discuss how managers' values, attitudes, and moods play out in organizations, shaping organizational culture. By the end of this chapter you will appreciate how the personal characteristics of managers influence the process of management in general—and organizational culture in particular.

Enduring Characteristics: Personality Traits

personality traits Enduring tendencies to feel, think, and act in certain ways.

All people, including managers, have certain enduring characteristics that influence how they think, feel, and behave both on and off the job. These characteristics are **personality traits**: particular tendencies to feel, think, and act in certain ways that can be used to describe the personality of every individual. It is important to understand the personalities of managers because their personalities influence their behavior and their approach to managing people and resources.

Some managers are demanding, difficult to get along with, and highly critical of other people. Other managers may be as concerned about effectiveness and efficiency as highly critical managers but are easier to get along with, are likable, and frequently praise the people around them. Both management styles may produce excellent results, but their effects on employees are quite different. Do managers deliberately decide to adopt one of these approaches to management? Although they may do so part of the time, in all likelihood their personalities account for their different approaches. Indeed, research suggests that the way people react to different conditions depends, in part, on their personalities.[8]

The Big Five Personality Traits

We can think of an individual's personality as being composed of five general traits or characteristics: extraversion, negative affectivity, agreeableness, conscientiousness, and openness to experience. Researchers often consider these the Big Five personality traits.[9] Each of them can be viewed as a continuum along which every individual or, more specifically, every manager falls (see Figure 3.1).

Some managers may be at the high end of one trait continuum, others at the low end, and still others somewhere in between. An easy way to understand how these traits can affect a person's approach to management is to describe what people are like at the high and low ends of each trait continuum. As will become evident as you read about each trait, no single trait is right or wrong for being an effective manager. Rather, effectiveness is determined by a complex interaction between the characteristics of managers (including personality traits) and the nature of the job and organization in which they are working. Moreover, personality traits that enhance managerial effectiveness in one situation may impair it in another. Recent studies suggest that personality traits may even predict job performance in certain situations. For example, researchers found that extraversion better predicted performance in jobs requiring social skills, while agreeableness was less positively related to job performance in competitive environments.[10]

Figure 3.1

The Big Five Personality Traits

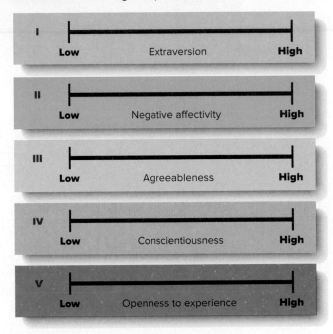

Managers' personalities can be described by determining which point on each of the following dimensions best characterizes the manager in question:

extraversion The tendency to experience positive emotions and moods and to feel good about oneself and the rest of the world.

EXTRAVERSION   Extraversion is the tendency to experience positive emotions and moods and to feel good about oneself and the rest of the world. Managers who are high on extraversion (often called *extraverts*) tend to be sociable, affectionate, outgoing, and friendly. Managers who are low on extraversion (often called *introverts*) tend to be less inclined toward social interactions and to have a less positive outlook. Being high on extraversion may be an asset for managers whose jobs entail especially high levels of social interaction. Managers who are low on extraversion may nevertheless be highly effective and efficient, especially when their jobs do not require much social interaction. Their quieter approach may enable them to accomplish quite a bit of work in limited time. See Figure 3.2 for an example of a scale that can be used to measure a person's level of extraversion.

negative affectivity The tendency to experience negative emotions and moods, to feel distressed, and to be critical of oneself and others.

NEGATIVE AFFECTIVITY   Negative affectivity is the tendency to experience negative emotions and moods, feel distressed, and be critical of oneself and others. Managers high on this trait may often feel angry and dissatisfied and complain about their own and others' lack of progress. Managers who are low on negative affectivity do not tend to experience many negative emotions and moods and are less pessimistic and critical of themselves and others. On the plus side, the critical approach of a manager high on negative affectivity may sometimes spur both the manager and others to improve their performance. Nevertheless, it is probably more pleasant to work with a manager who is low on negative affectivity; the better working relationships that such a manager is likely to cultivate also can be an important asset.

agreeableness The tendency to get along well with other people.

AGREEABLENESS   Agreeableness is the tendency to get along well with others. Managers who are high on the agreeableness continuum are likable, tend to be affectionate, and care about other people. Managers who are low on agreeableness may be somewhat distrustful of others, unsympathetic, uncooperative, and even at times antagonistic. Being high on agreeableness may be especially important for managers whose responsibilities require that they develop good, close relationships with others. Nevertheless, a low level of agreeableness may be an asset in managerial jobs that actually require that managers be antagonistic, such as drill sergeants and some other kinds of military managers. See Figure 3.2 for an example of a scale that measures a person's level of agreeableness.

Figure 3.2

Measures of Extraversion, Agreeableness, Conscientiousness, and Openness to Experience

Listed below are phrases describing people's behaviors. Please use the rating scale below to describe how accurately each statement describes *you*. Describe yourself as you generally are now, not as you wish to be in the future. Describe yourself as you honestly see yourself, in relation to other people you know of the same sex as you are and roughly your same age.

1	2	3	4	5
Very inaccurate	Moderately inaccurate	Neither inaccurate nor accurate	Moderately accurate	Very accurate

_____ **1.** Am interested in people.

_____ **2.** Have a rich vocabulary.

_____ **3.** Am always prepared.

_____ **4.** Am not really interested in others.*

_____ **5.** Leave my belongings around.*

_____ **6.** Am the life of the party.

_____ **7.** Have difficulty understanding abstract ideas.*

_____ **8.** Sympathize with others' feelings.

_____ **9.** Don't talk a lot.*

_____ **10.** Pay attention to details.

_____ **11.** Have a vivid imagination.

_____ **12.** Insult people.*

_____ **13.** Make a mess of things.*

_____ **14.** Feel comfortable around people.

_____ **15.** Am not interested in abstract ideas.*

_____ **16.** Have a soft heart.

_____ **17.** Get chores done right away.

_____ **18.** Keep in the background.*

_____ **19.** Have excellent ideas.

_____ **20.** Start conversations.

_____ **21.** Am not interested in other people's problems.*

_____ **22.** Often forget to put things back in their proper place.*

_____ **23.** Have little to say.*

_____ **24.** Do not have a good imagination.*

_____ **25.** Take time out for others.

_____ **26.** Like order.

_____ **27.** Talk to a lot of different people at parties.

_____ **28.** Am quick to understand things.

_____ **29.** Feel little concern for others.*

_____ **30.** Shirk my duties.*

_____ **31.** Don't like to draw attention to myself.*

_____ **32.** Use difficult words.

_____ **33.** Feel others' emotions.

_____ **34.** Follow a schedule.

_____ **35.** Spend time reflecting on things.

_____ **36.** Don't mind being the center of attention.

_____ **37.** Make people feel at ease.

_____ **38.** Am exacting in my work.

_____ **39.** Am quiet around strangers.*

_____ **40.** Am full of ideas.

* Item is reverse-scored: 1 = 5, 2 = 4, 4 = 2, 5 = 1
Scoring: Sum responses to items for an overall scale.
    Extraversion = sum of items 6, 9, 14, 18, 20, 23, 27, 31, 36, 39
    Agreeableness = sum of items 1, 4, 8, 12, 16, 21, 25, 29, 33, 37
    Conscientiousness = sum of items 3, 5, 10, 13, 17, 22, 26, 30, 34, 38
    Openness to experience = sum of items 2, 7, 11, 15, 19, 24, 28, 32, 35, 40

Source: L. R. Goldberg, Oregon Research Institute, http://ipip.ori.org/ipip/.

conscientiousness The tendency to be careful, scrupulous, and persevering.

openness to experience The tendency to be original, have broad interests, be open to a wide range of stimuli, be daring, and take risks.

CONSCIENTIOUSNESS Conscientiousness is the tendency to be careful, scrupulous, and persevering.[11] Managers who are high on the conscientiousness continuum are organized and self-disciplined; those who are low on this trait might sometimes appear to lack direction and self-discipline. Conscientiousness has been found to be a good predictor of performance in many kinds of jobs, including managerial jobs in a variety of organizations.[12] Entrepreneurs who found their own companies often are high on conscientiousness, and their persistence and determination help them overcome obstacles and turn their ideas into successful new ventures. Figure 3.2 provides an example of a scale that measures conscientiousness.

OPENNESS TO EXPERIENCE Openness to experience is the tendency to be original, have broad interests, be open to a wide range of stimuli, be daring, and take risks.[13] Managers who are high on this trait continuum may be especially likely to take risks and be innovative in their planning and decision making. Geisha Williams, discussed in this chapter's opening feature, continues to explore new ways for her company PG&E to grow, innovate, and succeed—a testament to her high level of openness to experience. Managers who are low on openness to experience may be less prone to take risks and more conservative in their planning and decision making. In certain organizations and positions, this tendency might be an asset. The manager of the fiscal office in a public university, for example, must ensure that all university departments and units follow the university's rules and regulations pertaining to budgets, spending accounts, and reimbursements of expenses. Figure 3.2 provides an example of a measure of openness to experience.

Some successful top managers in Silicon Valley are high on conscientiousness and openness to experience, which has contributed to their accomplishments in technology and management, as the following "Manager as a Person" feature describes.

MANAGER AS A PERSON

Openness to Experience Helps Lee Thrive

In her mid-thirties, Jess Lee has demonstrated her determination, persistence, originality, consciousness, and willingness to take risks as she has taken a path that is anything but ordinary.

Jess Lee's ambition, hard work, and persistence have repeatedly paid off in her success at Google, Polyvore, and now Sequoia Capital.
©Bryan Bedder/Getty Images

Growing up in Hong Kong, Lee loved to draw and thought she would like to be a comic book artist when she grew up. Her parents had other ideas, and as an entrepreneur who operated a translation business from home, her mother instilled in Lee a sense of the value of being in charge of what you do in life.[14]

Lee attended Stanford University, where she received a degree in computer science. She had planned on becoming an engineer and had a job lined up when she received a call from a Google recruiter, inviting her to interview for their associate product manager program. While interviewing at Google, Lee spoke with Marisa Mayer (a Google exec who later became Yahoo's CEO). Lee told Mayer she wasn't sure if she wanted to work at Google because she already had another offer and planned to be an engineer. Mayer advised Lee to choose the job she thought would be the most challenging. Lee joined Google and never looked back.[15]

As a product manager for Google Maps, Lee realized it was important for the engineers she worked with to hold her in high regard. While her computer science background certainly helped, so did her hard work, determination, and persistence. While at Google, one of her friends introduced her to Polyvore, a fashion and home decor website. With her love of art and fashion, Lee became hooked on site, which enables users to build collages of products from millions of images that combine clothing, fashion, and household items into artistic compilations.[16] Spending an hour or two on the site each evening, Lee decided to let Polyvore's founders know that she liked the site but also gave them suggestions for improvements and described the challenges she encountered while using the site. Her attention to detail and close connection to Polyvore and its users made an impression on the founders, who suggested she might want to join the company and fix the problems she had encountered as a consumer.[17]

Always open to new experiences, Lee undertook many different tasks to help Polyvore create a great user experience—from coding to management to sales. She also assumed many responsibilities at Polyvore that she had never done before, which provided her with challenges and opportunities for learning. In recognition of her dedication and contributions to Polyvore, company founders first made Lee a cofounder and then appointed her CEO.[18] Under Lee's unique style of leadership, Polyvore became profitable and was named one of the five best websites for online shopping on a single site.[19]

In 2015 Yahoo acquired Polyvore for $230 million, and the next year Lee and the company celebrated the site's ninth birthday. After Yahoo was acquired by Verizon in 2016, Lee decided to look for another business opportunity where she could make a difference. In 2017, Lee joined venture capital firm Sequoia Capital as the company's first female investing partner for its U.S. operations.[20]

Lee's ambition, hard work, determination, and persistence will continue to guide her in her position at Sequoia, where she says she's excited to help the next generation of entrepreneurs.

Successful managers occupy a variety of positions on the Big Five personality trait continuum. One highly effective manager may be high on extraversion and negative affectivity; another, equally effective manager may be low on both these traits; and still another may be somewhere in between. Members of an organization must understand these differences among managers because they can shed light on how managers behave and on their approach to planning, leading, organizing, or controlling. If subordinates realize, for example, that their manager is low on extraversion, they will not feel slighted when the manager seems to be aloof because they will realize that by nature he or she is simply not outgoing.

Managers themselves also need to be aware of their own personality traits and the traits of others, including those of their subordinates and fellow managers. A manager who knows that he has a tendency to be highly critical of other people might try to tone down his negative approach. Similarly, a manager who realizes that her chronically complaining subordinate tends to be so negative because of his personality may take all his complaints with a grain of salt and realize that things probably are not as bad as this subordinate says they are.

In order for all members of an organization to work well together and with people outside the organization, such as customers and suppliers, they must understand each other. Such understanding comes, in part, from an appreciation of some fundamental ways in which people differ from one another—that is, an appreciation of personality traits.

Other Personality Traits That Affect Managerial Behavior

Many other specific traits in addition to the Big Five describe people's personalities. Here we look at traits that are particularly important for understanding managerial effectiveness: locus of control; self-esteem; and the needs for achievement, affiliation, and power.

LOCUS OF CONTROL   People differ in their views about how much control they have over what happens to and around them. The locus of control trait captures these beliefs.[21] People with an **internal locus of control** believe they themselves are responsible for their own fate; they see their own actions and behaviors as being major and decisive determinants of important outcomes such as attaining levels of job performance, being promoted, or being turned down for a choice job assignment. Some managers with an internal locus of control see the success of a whole organization resting on their shoulders. One example is Geisha Williams, CEO

internal locus of control The tendency to locate responsibility for one's fate within oneself

of PG&E, described in "A Manager's Challenge." An internal locus of control also helps to ensure ethical behavior and decision making in an organization because people feel accountable and responsible for their own actions.

external locus of control The tendency to locate responsibility for one's fate in outside forces and to believe one's own behavior has little impact on outcomes.

People with an external locus of control believe that outside forces are responsible for what happens to and around them; they do not think their own actions make much of a difference. As such, they tend not to intervene to try to change a situation or solve a problem, leaving it to someone else.

Managers need an internal locus of control because they *are* responsible for what happens in organizations; they need to believe they can and do make a difference. Moreover, managers are responsible for ensuring that organizations and their members behave in an ethical fashion, and for this as well they need an internal locus of control—they need to know and feel they can make a difference.

self-esteem The degree to which individuals feel good about themselves and their capabilities.

SELF-ESTEEM Self-esteem is the degree to which individuals feel good about themselves and their capabilities. People with high self-esteem believe they are competent, deserving, and capable of handling most situations. People with low self-esteem have poor opinions of themselves, are unsure about their capabilities, and question their ability to succeed at different endeavors.[22] Research suggests that people tend to choose activities and goals consistent with their levels of self-esteem. High self-esteem is desirable for managers because it facilitates their setting and keeping high standards for themselves, pushes them ahead on difficult projects, and gives them the confidence they need to make and carry out important decisions.

need for achievement The extent to which an individual has a strong desire to perform challenging tasks well and to meet personal standards for excellence.

NEEDS FOR ACHIEVEMENT, AFFILIATION, AND POWER Psychologist David McClelland has extensively researched the needs for achievement, affiliation, and power.[23] The need for achievement is the extent to which an individual has a strong desire to perform challenging tasks well and to meet personal standards for excellence. People with a high need for achievement often set clear goals for themselves and like to receive performance feedback. The need for affiliation is the extent to which an individual is concerned about establishing and maintaining good interpersonal relations, being liked, and having the people around him or her get along with one another. The need for power is the extent to which an individual desires to control or influence others.[24]

need for affiliation The extent to which an individual is concerned about establishing and maintaining good interpersonal relations, being liked, and having other people get along.

need for power The extent to which an individual desires to control or influence others.

Research suggests that high needs for achievement and for power are assets for first-line and middle managers and that a high need for power is especially important for upper-level managers.[25] One study found that U.S. presidents with a relatively high need for power tended to be especially effective during their terms of office.[26] A high need for affiliation may not always be desirable in managers because it might lead them to try too hard to be liked by others (including subordinates) rather than doing all they can to ensure that performance is as high as it can and should be. Although most research on these needs has been done in the United States, some studies suggest that these findings may also apply to people in other countries such as India and New Zealand.[27]

Taken together, these desirable personality traits for managers—an internal locus of control, high self-esteem, and high needs for achievement and power—suggest that managers need to be take-charge people who not only believe their own actions are decisive in determining their own and their organizations' fates but also believe in their own capabilities. Such managers have a personal desire for accomplishment and influence over others.

Additional Personality Assessments

In addition to the Big Five personality factors discussed earlier, several other personality assessments can be effective in helping managers and others identify positive and negative behaviors demonstrated by individuals in the workplace.

The Myers-Briggs Type Indicator (MBTI) is the most widely used personality instrument around the world—an estimated 3.5 million assessments are administered annually. Based on the theories of psychologist Carl Jung, MBTI measures a person's preferences for introversion versus extroversion, sensation versus intuition, thinking versus feeling, and judging versus perceiving. Various combinations of these four preferences result in 16 unique personality types, which can be helpful to individuals who seek to understand not only how they make decisions, but also how they manage their time, solve problems, make decisions, and deal with stress. In addition, recent research suggests that the four personality dimensions can be linked to various job-related components including job satisfaction, job performance, motivation, and promotion. More than 80% of *Fortune* 100 companies use this type of assessment to build stronger and healthier organizations.[28]

Another personality measure that can be useful to individuals as well as managers and others in an organization is the DiSC Inventory Profile, which many companies use to assess the personality characteristics of their employees. DiSC is based on the work of William Marston, a psychologist who attempted to characterize normal behavior patterns. A person taking the DiSC inventory receives a profile describing his or her behavioral style, preferred environment, and strategies for effectiveness. Behavior style is described in terms of **d**ominance, **i**nfluence, **s**teadiness, and **c**onscientiousness (DiSC).[29]

Information from these types of assessments help companies better understand their employees' strengths and weaknesses and how people perceive and process information—all factors that contribute to the success of an organization.

Values, Attitudes, and Moods and Emotions

What are managers striving to achieve? How do they think they should behave? What do they think about their jobs and organizations? And how do they actually feel at work? We can find some answers to these questions by exploring managers' values, attitudes, and moods.

Values, attitudes, and moods and emotions capture how managers experience their jobs as individuals. *Values* describe what managers are trying to achieve through work and how they think they should behave. *Attitudes* capture their thoughts and feelings about their specific jobs and organizations. *Moods and emotions* encompass how managers actually feel when they are managing. Although these three aspects of managers' work experience are highly personal, they also have important implications for understanding how managers behave, how they treat and respond to others, and how, through their efforts, they help contribute to organizational effectiveness through planning, leading, organizing, and controlling.

LO3-2 Explain what values and attitudes are, and describe their impact on managerial action.

terminal value A lifelong goal or objective that an individual seeks to achieve.

instrumental value A mode of conduct that an individual seeks to follow.

norms Unwritten, informal codes of conduct that prescribe how people should act in particular situations and that are considered important by most members of a group or an organization.

value system The terminal and instrumental values that are guiding principles in an individual's life.

Values: Terminal and Instrumental

The two kinds of personal values are *terminal* and *instrumental*. A **terminal value** is a personal conviction about lifelong goals or objectives; an **instrumental value** is a personal conviction about desired modes of conduct or ways of behaving. Terminal values often lead to the formation of **norms**, which are unwritten, informal codes of conduct, such as behaving honestly or courteously, that prescribe how people should act in particular situations and that are considered important by most members of a group or an organization.

Milton Rokeach, a leading researcher in the area of human values, identified 18 terminal values and 18 instrumental values that describe each person's value system. By rank ordering the terminal values from "1 (most important as a guiding principle in one's life)" to "18 (least important as a guiding principle in one's life)" and then rank ordering the instrumental values from 1 to 18, people can give good pictures of their **value systems**—what they are striving to achieve in life and how they want to behave.[30]

Although Rokeach's research is more than 40 years old, some of his findings are still applicable today.[31] Several terminal values seem to be especially important for managers, such as a sense of accomplishment, equality, and self-esteem. For example, a manager who thinks a sense of accomplishment is particularly important might focus his or her energies on making a lasting contribution to an organization by developing a new product or by opening a new foreign subsidiary.

Several of Rokeach's instrumental values are also important modes of conduct for managers, such as being ambitious, open minded, competent, responsible, and self-disciplined.[32] A manager who considers being honest to be of paramount importance may be a driving force for taking steps to ensure that all members of an organization behave ethically, as described in the following "Ethics in Action" feature.

Promoting Ethical Values in the Hotel Industry

Hotels aim to operate at a profit, but actions that give an immediate boost to earnings may not serve a hotel's best interests in the long run. For example, overbooking might ensure that every room is occupied on any given night, but if the hotel is turning away guests, the practice can hurt the hotel's reputation. The problem is worse if the company tries to keep costs low by staffing the front desk with untrained employees who lack the skills and authority to handle unhappy guests. Managers with an eye on long-term success value not just efficiency, but also integrity, honesty, and empathy.[33]

Another ethical norm for working in a hotel is to be respectful in handling interactions with customers and coworkers. This includes staying calm and pleasant in difficult situations, as well as respecting privacy and keeping promises.[34] Experiencing such behavior turns first-time guests into loyal customers, and employees who are treated respectfully are more apt to be dedicated workers.

Judi Brownell, a professor at Cornell University, explored the challenges managers face in promoting ethical values among hotel employees. She found that many managers value ethical behavior, but they need to teach the values because they have a diverse workforce of people with a wide range of values concerning desirable behavior at work.[35] This calls for personal feedback and face-to-face discussions of ethical situations that arise. Brownell also has investigated the practice of listening, which plays an important role in respectful treatment of others. Brownell identified particular skills a person can learn in order to listen well; examples include focus, comprehension, and interpretation. But she found that training in these skills affects behavior only when people value listening.[36]

Scott Nadel, through his experience as a manager for DMC Hotels/Dhillon Management, has identified ways a manager can promote ethical values among hotel employees.[37] He values ethical behavior and makes it a part of hiring decisions and employee training. He connects ethical principles to employees' own lives and ambitions so that employees don't merely know ethical standards, but also embrace the value that ethics matters. To help employees work respectfully with others, he encourages patience and compassion, along with the use of deep-breathing techniques during difficult encounters. His experience has convinced Nadel that creating a climate of ethical conduct also creates a welcoming atmosphere for hotel customers.

Managers in the hotel industry can encourage ethical values by having face-to-face discussions with employees about situations that may arise and providing personal feedback about best how to handle the situation.
©Gabriel Georgescu/Shutterstock

All in all, managers' value systems signify what managers as individuals are trying to accomplish and become in their personal lives and at work. Thus, managers' value systems are fundamental guides to their behavior and efforts at planning, leading, organizing, and controlling.

Attitudes

attitude A collection of feelings and beliefs.

An **attitude** is a collection of feelings and beliefs. Like everyone else, managers have attitudes about their jobs and organizations, and these attitudes affect how they approach their jobs. Two of the most important attitudes in this context are job satisfaction and organizational commitment.

job satisfaction The collection of feelings and beliefs that managers have about their current jobs.

JOB SATISFACTION   Job satisfaction is the collection of feelings and beliefs that managers have about their current jobs. Managers who have high levels of job satisfaction generally like their jobs, feel they are fairly treated, and believe their jobs have many desirable features or characteristics (such as interesting work, good pay and job security, autonomy, or nice coworkers). Figure 3.3 shows sample items from two scales that managers can use to measure job satisfaction. Levels of job satisfaction tend to increase as one moves up the hierarchy in an organization. Upper managers, in general, tend to be more satisfied with their jobs than entry-level employees. Managers' levels of job satisfaction can range from very low to very high.

One might think that in tough economic times, when unemployment is high and layoffs are prevalent, people who have jobs might be relatively satisfied with them. However, this is not necessarily the case. For example, in 2009 in the middle of the global recession, the U.S. unemployment rate was 10%, thousands of jobs were lost from the economy, and the underemployment rate (which includes people who have given up looking for jobs and those who are working part-time because they can't find a full-time position) was 17.3%. During these recessionary conditions, job satisfaction levels in the United States fell to record lows.[38]

The Conference Board has been tracking levels of U.S. job satisfaction since 1987, when 61.1% of workers surveyed indicated that they were satisfied with their jobs. In 2009 only 45% of workers surveyed indicated that they were satisfied with their jobs, an all-time low for the survey.[39] In 2017, more than 50% of U.S. workers indicated they were satisfied with their jobs

Figure 3.3

Sample Items from Two Measures of Job Satisfaction

Sample items from the Minnesota Satisfaction Questionnaire:
People respond to each of the items in the scale by checking whether they are:

[ ] Very dissatisfied
[ ] Dissatisfied
[ ] Can't decide whether satisfied or not

[ ] Satisfied
[ ] Very satisfied

On my present job, this is how I feel about . . .

_____ **1.** Being able to do things that don't go against my conscience.

_____ **2.** The way my job provides for steady employment.

_____ **3.** The chance to do things for other people.

_____ **4.** The chance to do something that makes use of my abilities.

_____ **5.** The way company policies are put into practice.

_____ **6.** My pay and the amount of work I do.

_____ **7.** The chances for advancement on this job.

_____ **8.** The freedom to use my own judgment.

_____ **9.** The working conditions.

_____ **10.** The way my coworkers get along with each other.

_____ **11.** The praise I get for doing a good job.

_____ **12.** The feeling of accomplishment I get from the job.

The Faces Scale
Workers select the face which best expresses how they feel about their job in general.

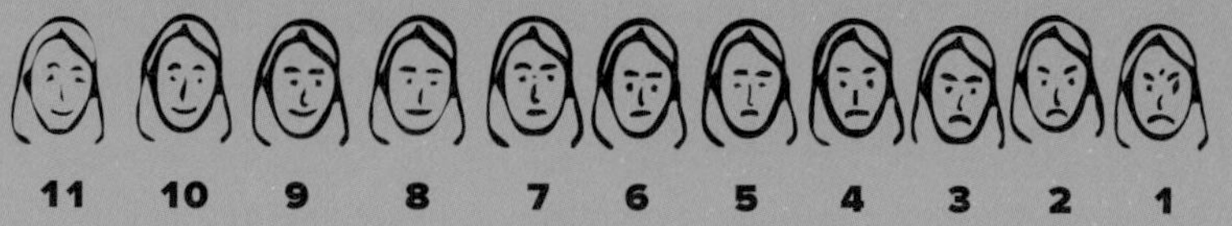

11   10   9   8   7   6   5   4   3   2   1

Source: Adapted from D. J. Weiss et al., *Manual for the Minnesota Satisfaction Questionnaire.* Copyrighted by the Vocational Psychology Research, University of Minnesota; copyright © 1975 by the American Psychological Association.

according to the Conference Board's annual survey. This was the sixth year in a row that job satisfaction among U.S. workers improved. The increase in job satisfaction is largely due to the improving labor market in which layoff rates were at an all-time low. In addition to overall job satisfaction, the survey also looks at other components that contribute to job satisfaction. The report suggests more than 62% of workers are satisfied with their colleagues at work. On the downside, workers are least satisfied with employee recognition (37%), the performance review process (32%), and educational/training programs available in their organizations (32%).[40]

Some organizations have combined a concern about protecting the environment with a concern about keeping workers happy and avoiding layoffs, as illustrated in the accompanying "Ethics in Action" feature.

ETHICS IN ACTION

Subaru Protects Jobs and the Environment

Subaru of Indiana Automotive (SIA) is located in Lafayette, Indiana, and is the home of North American Subaru production. Models built at the plant include the Subaru Legacy, Outback, and Impreza. SIA employs more than 5,600 associates, all of whom are committed to quality, safety, and the environment.[41] SIA employees receive annual raises, paid vacations and holidays, profit-sharing plan plus 401k feature with company match, health care insurance, tuition reimbursement, domestic partner benefits, and paid time off for volunteer time, among other benefits.[42] While Indiana has lost thousands of auto jobs over the past decade, SIA appears to be thriving.

In addition to exceptional employee benefits, SIA continues to be on an uncompromising mission to protect the environment and save money by eliminating waste. SIA was the first U.S. auto plant to achieve zero landfill—meaning no waste goes to a landfill for disposal. For example, scrap metal from the stamping plant is collected and sent off to become smaller car parts, glass from used light bulbs is turned into reflective road striping, and plastic packaging used to ship parts to SIA is sent back to the part suppliers to be used over again.[43]

SIA combines its minimal environmental impact philosophy with a commitment to reducing worker injuries and promoting worker health. For example, rather than inspecting the quality of welds by taking cars apart, as was customary, SIA now uses ultrasonic technology to check welds. This change reduced worker injuries from jackhammers and metals waste and results in a process that is more effective, quicker, and less expensive. SIA has a free on-site gym with wellness and weight loss programs. Workers receive bonuses for identifying unnecessary packaging and processes, which can cut costs and be a source of rebates from suppliers, with the top bonus being a brand new Subaru Legacy. All these cost savings are used for further plant investments and overtime pay.[44]

SIA's relentless quest for efficiency in terms of reducing waste/protecting the environment and increasing productivity on the assembly line puts a lot of pressure on employees, who are expected to work long hours. Nonetheless, they know that their jobs are secure, and they receive overtime pay and premium-free health insurance. When the Japanese earthquake in 2011 forced the plant to slow down because of disruptions in the supply of parts from Japan, SIA continued to pay all its employees their full wages to volunteer in the local community. Thus, it is not surprising that there are about 10 applicants for each open position at SIA. Clearly, SIA has demonstrated that it is possible to protect the environment and protect jobs to the benefit of all.[45]

Subaru of Indiana, unlike many auto manufacturers, is thriving, perhaps due to its environmental philosophy, combined with a commitment to reducing worker injuries and promoting worker health.
©Rick Bowmer/ASSOCIATED PRESS

organizational citizenship behaviors (OCBs) Behaviors that are not required of organizational members but that contribute to and are necessary for organizational efficiency, effectiveness, and competitive advantage.

In general, it is desirable for managers to be satisfied with their jobs, for at least two reasons. First, satisfied managers may be more likely to go the extra mile for their organizations or perform **organizational citizenship behaviors (OCBs)**—behaviors that are not required of organizational members but that contribute to and are necessary for organizational efficiency, effectiveness, and competitive advantage.[46] Managers who are satisfied with their jobs are more likely to perform these "above and beyond the call of duty" behaviors, which can include putting in long hours when needed to coming up with truly creative ideas and overcoming obstacles to implement them (even when doing so is not part of the manager's job) or going out of one's way to help a coworker, subordinate, or superior (even when doing so entails considerable personal sacrifice).[47]

A second reason it is desirable for managers to be satisfied with their jobs is that satisfied managers may be less likely to quit. A manager who is highly satisfied may never even think about looking for another position; a dissatisfied manager may always be on the lookout for new opportunities. Turnover can hurt an organization because it causes the loss of the experience and knowledge that managers have gained about the company, industry, and business environment.[48]

A growing source of dissatisfaction for many lower-level and middle managers, as well as for nonmanagerial employees, is the threat of unemployment and increased workloads from organizational restructurings, including layoffs. Organizations that try to improve their efficiency through restructuring and layoffs often eliminate a sizable number of first-line and middle management positions. This decision obviously hurts the managers who are laid off, and it can reduce the job satisfaction levels of managers who remain. They might fear being the next to be let go. In addition, the workloads of remaining employees often increase dramatically as a result of restructuring, and this can contribute to dissatisfaction.

How managers and organizations handle layoffs is of paramount importance, not only for the employees let go but also for employees who survive the layoff and keep their jobs. Showing compassion and empathy for layoff victims, giving them as much advance notice as possible about the layoff, providing clear information about severance benefits, and helping them in their job search efforts are a few of the ways in which managers can humanely manage a layoff.[49]

organizational commitment The collection of feelings and beliefs that managers have about their organization as a whole.

ORGANIZATIONAL COMMITMENT **Organizational commitment** is the collection of feelings and beliefs that managers have about their organization as a whole.[50] Managers who are committed to their organizations believe in what their organizations are doing, are proud of what these organizations stand for, and feel a high degree of loyalty toward their organizations. Committed managers are more likely to go above and beyond the call of duty to help their company and are less likely to quit.[51] Organizational commitment can be especially strong when employees and managers truly believe in organizational values; it also leads to a strong organizational culture.

Organizational commitment is likely to help managers perform some of their figurehead and spokesperson roles (see Chapter 1). It is much easier for a manager to persuade others, both inside and outside the organization, of the merits of what the organization has done and is seeking to accomplish if the manager truly believes in and is committed to the organization.

Do managers in different countries have similar or different attitudes? Differences in the levels of job satisfaction and organizational commitment among managers in different countries are likely because these managers have different kinds of opportunities and rewards and because they face different economic, political, and sociocultural forces in their organizations' general environments. Levels of organizational commitment from one country to another may depend on the extent to which countries have legislation affecting firings and layoffs and the extent to which citizens of a country are geographically mobile.

LO3-3 Appreciate how moods and emotions influence all members of an organization.

Moods and Emotions

mood A feeling or state of mind.

Just as you sometimes are in a bad mood and at other times are in a good mood, so are managers. A **mood** is a feeling or state of mind. When people are in a positive mood, they feel excited, enthusiastic, active, or elated. When people are in a negative mood, they feel distressed, fearful, scornful, hostile, jittery, or nervous.[52] People who are high on negative affectivity are especially likely to experience negative moods. People's situations or circumstances also determine their moods; however, receiving a raise is likely to put most people in a good mood regardless of their personality traits. People who are high on negative affectivity are not always in a bad mood, and people who are low on extraversion still experience positive moods.[53]

emotions Intense, relatively short-lived feelings.

Emotions are more intense feelings than moods, are often directly linked to whatever caused the emotion, and are more short-lived.[54] However, once whatever has triggered the emotion has been dealt with, the feelings may linger in the form of a less intense mood.[55] For example, a manager who gets very angry when a subordinate has engaged in an unethical behavior may find his anger decreasing in intensity once he has decided how to address the problem. Yet he continues to be in a bad mood the rest of the day, even though he is not directly thinking about the unfortunate incident.

Research has found that moods and emotions affect the behavior of managers and all members of an organization. For example, research suggests that the subordinates of managers who experience positive moods at work may perform at somewhat higher levels and be less likely to resign and leave the organization than the subordinates of managers who do not tend to be in a positive mood at work.[56] Other research suggests that under certain conditions creativity might be enhanced by positive moods, whereas under other conditions negative moods might push people to work harder to come up with truly creative ideas.[57] Recognizing that both mood states have the potential to contribute to creativity in different ways, recent research suggests that employees may be especially likely to be creative to the extent that they experience both mood states (at different times) on the job and to the extent that the work environment is supportive of creativity.[58]

Other research suggests that moods and emotions may play an important role in ethical decision making. For example, researchers at Princeton University found that when people are trying to solve difficult personal moral dilemmas, the parts of their brains that are responsible for emotions and moods are especially active.[59]

More generally, emotions and moods give managers and all employees important information and signals about what is going on in the workplace.[60] Positive emotions and moods signal that things are going well and thus can lead to more expansive, and even playful, thinking. Negative emotions and moods signal that there are problems in need of attention and areas for improvement. So when people are in negative moods, they tend to be more detail-oriented and focused on the facts at hand.[61] Some studies suggest that critical thinking and devil's advocacy may be promoted by a negative mood, and sometimes especially accurate judgments may be made by managers in negative moods.[62]

Managers and other members of an organization need to realize that how they feel affects how they treat others and how others respond to them, including their subordinates. For example, a subordinate may be more likely to approach a manager with a somewhat unusual but potentially useful idea if the subordinate thinks the manager is in a good mood. Likewise, when managers are in very bad moods, their subordinates might try to avoid them at all costs. Figure 3.4 is an example of a scale that can measure the extent to which a person experiences positive and negative moods at work.

Figure 3.4
A Measure of Positive and Negative Mood at Work

People respond to each item by indicating the extent to which the item describes how they felt at work during the past week on the following scale:

1 = Very slightly or not at all   4 = Quite a bit
2 = A little   5 = Very much
3 = Moderately

____ **1.** Active	____ **7.** Enthusiastic
____ **2.** Distressed	____ **8.** Fearful
____ **3.** Strong	____ **9.** Peppy
____ **4.** Excited	____ **10.** Nervous
____ **5.** Scornful	____ **11.** Elated
____ **6.** Hostile	____ **12.** Jittery

Scoring: Responses to items 1, 3, 4, 7, 9, and 11 are summed for a positive mood score; the higher the score, the more positive mood is experienced at work. Responses to items 2, 5, 6, 8, 10, and 12 are summed for a negative mood score; the higher the score, the more negative mood is experienced at work.

Sources: A. P. Brief, M. J. Burke, J. M. George, B. Robinson, and J. Webster, "Should Negative Affectivity Remain an Unmeasured Variable in the Study of Job Stress?" *Journal of Applied Psychology* 72 (1988), 193–98; M. J. Burke, A. P. Brief, J. M. George, L. Roberson, and J. Webster, "Measuring Affect at Work: Confirmatory Analyses of Competing Mood Structures with Conceptual Linkage in Cortical Regulatory Systems," *Journal of Personality and Social Psychology* 57 (1989), 1091–102.

Emotional Intelligence

LO3-4 Describe the nature of emotional intelligence and its role in management.

emotional intelligence The ability to understand and manage one's own moods and emotions and the moods and emotions of other people.

In understanding the effects of managers' and all employees' moods and emotions, it is important to take into account their levels of emotional intelligence. Emotional intelligence is the ability to understand and manage one's own moods and emotions and the moods and emotions of other people.[63] Managers with a high level of emotional intelligence are more likely to understand how they are feeling and why, and they are more able to effectively manage their feelings. When managers are experiencing stressful feelings and emotions such as fear or anxiety, emotional intelligence lets them understand why and manage these feelings so they do not get in the way of effective decision making.[64]

Emotional intelligence also can help managers perform their important roles such as their interpersonal roles (figurehead, leader, and liaison).[65] Understanding how your subordinates feel, why they feel that way, and how to manage these feelings is central to developing strong interpersonal bonds with them.[66] For work that involves encounters with people from different cultures, this effort is more complex but just as important, as described in the "Managing Globally" feature. Moreover, emotional intelligence has the potential to contribute to effective leadership in multiple ways[67] and can help managers make lasting contributions to society. For example, Bernard (Bernie) Goldhirsh founded *Inc.* magazine in 1979, a time when entrepreneurs received more notoriety than respect, if they were paid attention at all.[68] Goldhirsh was an entrepreneur himself at the time, with his own publishing company. He recognized the vast contributions entrepreneurs could make to society, creating something out of nothing, and he realized firsthand what a tough task entrepreneurs faced.[69] His emotional intelligence helped him understand the challenges and frustrations entrepreneurs like himself faced and their need for support.

MANAGING GLOBALLY

Emotional Intelligence across Borders

Although definitions of emotional intelligence are based on the work of U.S. researchers, the idea has attracted the interest of managers, psychologists, and educators around the world.[70] While managing and reading emotions is important globally, the specific emotional information tends to vary by culture.

For example, in the United States, people express enthusiasm openly; this is considered both normal and desirable. Hiring managers tend to look favorably on job candidates who express enthusiasm, and people who act excited about a new project or product are admired for being devoted to the company's vision. In other countries, this outward enthusiasm is seen as odd or even annoying or offensive. British businesspeople tend to tone down their emotions, and Chinese people might interpret enthusiastic behavior as showing off rather than fitting in.[71]

Smiling also differs by culture. In North America, people smile often to signal they are friendly and well intentioned. This looks odd in Northern Europe, where smiles have the more limited purpose of signaling happiness. In Japan, a smile is more often a way to cover up embarrassment or unhappiness.[72]

Evidence suggests that differences such as these are less about what people feel (feelings are similar across cultures) and more about what they learn to express around others. Those differences in expression are tied to cultural values.[73] For example, British people value mature self-control, so they don't broadcast enthusiasm. In the United States, enthusiasm is more compatible with the high value placed on individual success and happiness. In much of Asia, group harmony is valued over individuality, so open celebrations of personal success can seem inappropriate. Further, as people practice different culture-based behaviors, they tend to develop different areas of strength in emotional intelligence. Travis Bradberry, president of TalentSmart, compared test scores of U.S. and Chinese managers and found that the Chinese managers scored higher in aspects of emotional intelligence focused on the feelings of others.[74]

Recognizing that emotional expressions vary by culture can build emotional intelligence.[75] A starting point is to recognize that unexpected behavior might indicate that emotions are being expressed differently. For example, if a U.S. manager notices that a Chinese employee seems unenthusiastic about a new project, the manager should check the assumption that absence of enthusiastic behavior signals lack of interest. Follow-up questions can be an effective way to find out. Also, whenever situations involve interacting with people from different cultures, it's worthwhile to learn each culture's emotional norms.

When Goldhirsh founded *Inc.,* entrepreneurs had few sources to which they could turn for advice, guidance, and solutions to management problems. *Inc.* was born to fill this gap and give entrepreneurs information and support by profiling successful and unsuccessful entrepreneurial ventures, highlighting management techniques that work, and providing firsthand accounts of how successful entrepreneurs developed and managed their businesses.[76]

Goldhirsh's emotional intelligence helped him recognize the many barriers entrepreneurs face and the emotional roller coaster of staking all one has on an idea that may or may not work. Goldhirsh believed that helping society understand the entrepreneurial process through *Inc.* magazine not only helped entrepreneurs but also enlightened bankers, lawmakers, and the public at large about the role these visionaries play, the challenges they face, and the support their ventures depend on.[77]

Emotional intelligence helps managers understand and relate well to other people. It also helps managers maintain their enthusiasm and confidence and energize subordinates to help the organization attain its goals.[78] Recent theorizing and research suggest that emotional intelligence may be especially important in awakening employee creativity.[79] Managers themselves are increasingly recognizing the importance of emotional intelligence. An example of a scale that measures emotional intelligence is provided in Figure 3.5.

Organizational Culture

LO3-5 Define organizational culture, and explain how managers both create and are influenced by organizational culture.

organizational culture The shared set of beliefs, expectations, values, norms, and work routines that influence how individuals, groups, and teams interact with one another and cooperate to achieve organizational goals.

Personality is a way of understanding why all managers and employees, as individuals, characteristically think and behave in different ways. However, when people belong to the same organization, they tend to share certain beliefs and values that lead them to act in similar ways.[80] Organizational culture comprises the shared set of beliefs, expectations, values, norms, and work routines that influence how members of an organization relate to one another and work together to achieve organizational goals. In essence, organizational culture reflects the distinctive ways in which organizational members perform their jobs and relate to others inside and outside the organization. It may, for example, be how customers in a particular hotel chain are treated from the time they are greeted at check-in until they leave, or it may be the shared work routines that research teams use to guide new product development. When organizational members share an intense commitment to cultural values, beliefs, and routines and use them to achieve their goals, a *strong* organizational culture exists.[81] When organizational members are not strongly committed to a shared system of values, beliefs, and routines, organizational culture is weak.

The stronger the culture of an organization, the more one can think about it as being the "personality" of an organization because it influences the way its members behave.[82] Organizations that possess strong cultures may differ on a wide variety of dimensions that determine how their members behave toward one another and perform their jobs. For example, organizations differ in how members relate to each other (formally or informally), how important decisions are made (top-down or bottom-up), willingness to change (flexible or unyielding), innovation (creative or predictable), and playfulness (serious or serendipitous). In an innovative design firm like IDEO in Silicon Valley, employees are encouraged to adopt a playful attitude toward their work, look outside the organization to find inspiration, and adopt a flexible approach toward product design that uses multiple perspectives.[83] IDEO's culture is vastly different from that of companies such as Citibank and ExxonMobil, in which employees treat each other in a more formal or deferential way, employees are expected to adopt a serious approach to their work, and decision making is constrained by the hierarchy of authority.

Figure 3.5

A Measure of Emotional Intelligence

Please indicate the extent to which you agree or disagree with each of the following items using the 1–7 scale below:

1	2	3	4	5	6	7
Totally disagree	Disagree	Somewhat disagree	Neither agree nor disagree	Somewhat agree	Agree	Totally agree

_____ **1.** I have a good sense of why I have certain feelings most of the time.

_____ **2.** I always know my friends' emotions from their behavior.

_____ **3.** I always set goals for myself and then try my best to achieve them.

_____ **4.** I am able to control my temper so that I can handle difficulties rationally.

_____ **5.** I have a good understanding of my own emotions.

_____ **6.** I am a good observer of others' emotions.

_____ **7.** I always tell myself I am a competent person.

_____ **8.** I am quite capable of controlling my own emotions.

_____ **9.** I really understand what I feel.

_____ **10.** I am sensitive to the feelings and emotions of others.

_____ **11.** I am a self-motivating person.

_____ **12.** I can always calm down quickly when I am very angry.

_____ **13.** I always know whether or not I am happy.

_____ **14.** I have good understanding of the emotions of people around me.

_____ **15.** I would always encourage myself to try my best.

_____ **16.** I have good control of my own emotions.

Scoring: Self-emotions appraisal = sum of items 1, 5, 9, 13
Others-emotions appraisal = sum of items 2, 6, 10, 14
Use of emotion = sum of items 3, 7, 11, 15
Regulation of emotion = sum of items 4, 8, 12, 16

Sources: K. Law, C. Wong, and L. Song, "The Construct and Criterion Validity of Emotional Intelligence and Its Potential Utility for Management Studies," *Journal of Applied Psychology* 89, no. 3 (June 2004), 496; C. S. Wong and K. S. Law, "The Effects of Leader and Follower Emotional Intelligence on Performance and Attitude: An Exploratory Study," *Leadership Quarterly* 13 (2002), 243–74.

Managers and Organizational Culture

While all members of an organization can contribute to developing and maintaining organizational culture, managers play a particularly important part in influencing organizational culture[84] because of their multiple and important roles (see Chapter 1). How managers create culture is most vividly evident in start-ups of new companies. Entrepreneurs who start their own companies are typically also the start-ups' top managers until the companies grow and become profitable. Often referred to as the firms' founders, these managers literally create their organizations' cultures.

The founders' personal characteristics play an important role in the creation of organizational culture. Benjamin Schneider, a well-known management researcher, developed a model that helps explain the role that founders' personal characteristics play in determining organizational culture.[85] His model, called the **attraction–selection–attrition (ASA) framework**, posits

attraction–selection–attrition (ASA) framework A model that explains how personality may influence organizational culture.

IDEO employees brainstorming – informal communication, casual attire, and flexibility are all hallmarks of this organization.
©IDEO Corporation

that when founders hire employees for their new ventures, they tend to be attracted to and choose employees whose personalities are similar to their own.[86] These similar employees are more likely to stay with the organization. Although employees who are dissimilar in personality might be hired, they are more likely to leave the organization over time. As a result of these attraction, selection, and attrition processes, people in the organization tend to have similar personalities, and the typical or dominant personality profile of organizational members determines and shapes organizational culture.[87]

For example, when David Kelley became interested in engineering and product design challenges in the late 1970s, he realized that who he was as a person meant he would not be happy working in a typical corporate environment. Kelley is high on openness to experience, driven to go where his interests take him, and not content to follow others' directives. Kelley recognized that he needed to start his own business, and with the help of other Stanford-schooled engineers and design experts, IDEO was born.[88]

From the start, IDEO's culture has embodied Kelley's spirited, freewheeling approach to work and design—from colorful and informal workspaces to an emphasis on networking and communicating with as many people as possible to understand a design problem. No project or problem is too big or too small for IDEO; the company designed the Apple Lisa computer and mouse (the precursor of the Mac), the Palm, and more recently PillPack, a prescription home-delivery system for consumers.[89] Kelley hates rules, job titles, big corner offices, and all the other trappings of large, traditional organizations that stifle creativity. Employees who are attracted to, are selected by, and remain with IDEO value creativity and innovation and embrace one of IDEO's mottos: "Everyone is creative."[90]

Although ASA processes are most evident in small firms such as IDEO, they also can operate in large companies.[91] According to the ASA model, this is a naturally occurring phenomenon to the extent that managers and new hires are free to make the kinds of choices the model specifies. However, while people tend to get along well with others who are similar to themselves, too much similarity in an organization can impair organizational effectiveness. That is, similar people tend to view conditions and events in similar ways and thus can be resistant to change. Moreover, organizations benefit from a diversity of perspectives rather than similarity in perspectives (see Chapter 5). At IDEO, Kelley recognized early on how important it is to take advantage of the diverse talents and perspectives that people with different personalities, backgrounds, experiences, and education can bring to a design team. Hence, IDEO's design teams include not only engineers, but others who might have a unique insight into a problem, such as anthropologists, communications experts, doctors, and users of a product. When new employees are hired at IDEO, they meet many employees who have different backgrounds and characteristics; the focus is not on hiring someone who will fit in but, rather, on hiring someone who has something to offer and can "wow" different kinds of people with his or her insights.[92]

In addition to personality, other personal characteristics of managers shape organizational culture; these include managers' values, attitudes, moods and emotions, and emotional intelligence.[93] For example, both terminal and instrumental values of managers play a role in determining organizational culture. Managers who highly value freedom and equality, for example, might be likely to stress the importance of autonomy and empowerment in their organizations, as well as fair treatment for all. As another example, managers who highly value being helpful and forgiving might not only tolerate mistakes but also emphasize the importance of organizational members' being kind and helpful to one another.

Managers who are satisfied with their jobs, are committed to their organizations, and experience positive moods and emotions might also encourage these attitudes and feelings in others. The result would be an organizational culture emphasizing positive attitudes and feelings. Research suggests that attitudes like job satisfaction and organizational commitment can be affected by the influence of others. Managers are in a particularly strong position to engage in social influence, given their multiple roles. Moreover, research suggests that moods and emotions can be contagious and that spending time with people who are excited and enthusiastic can increase one's own levels of excitement and enthusiasm.

The Role of Values and Norms in Organizational Culture

Shared terminal and instrumental values play a particularly important role in organizational culture. *Terminal values* signify what an organization and its employees are trying to accomplish, and *instrumental values* guide how the organization and its members achieve organizational goals. In addition to values, shared norms also are a key aspect of organizational culture. Recall that norms are unwritten, informal rules or guidelines that prescribe appropriate behavior in particular situations. For example, norms at IDEO include not being critical of others' ideas, coming up with multiple ideas before settling on one, and developing prototypes of new products.[94]

Managers determine and shape organizational culture through the kinds of values and norms they promote in an organization. Some managers, like David Kelley of IDEO, cultivate values and norms that encourage risk taking, creative responses to problems and opportunities, experimentation, tolerance of failure in order to succeed, and autonomy.[95] Top managers at organizations such as Microsoft and Google encourage employees to adopt such values to support their commitment to innovation as a source of competitive advantage.

Other managers, however, might cultivate values and norms that tell employees they should be conservative and cautious in their dealings with others and should consult their superiors before making important decisions or any changes to the status quo. Accountability for actions and decisions is stressed, and detailed records are kept to ensure that policies and procedures are followed. In settings where caution is needed—nuclear power stations, oil refineries, chemical plants, financial institutions, insurance companies—a conservative, cautious approach to making decisions might be appropriate. In a nuclear power plant, for example, the catastrophic consequences of a mistake make a high level of supervision vital. Similarly, in a bank or mutual fund company, the risk of losing investors' money makes a cautious approach to investing appropriate.

Managers of different kinds of organizations deliberately cultivate and develop the organizational values and norms that are best suited to their task and general environments, strategy, or technology. Organizational culture is maintained and transmitted to organizational members through the values of the founder, the process of socialization, ceremonies and rites, and stories and language (see Figure 3.6).

VALUES OF THE FOUNDER   From the ASA model just discussed, it is clear that founders of an organization can have profound and long-lasting effects on organizational culture. Founders' values inspire the founders to start their own companies and, in turn, drive the nature of

Figure 3.6

Factors That Maintain and Transmit Organizational Culture

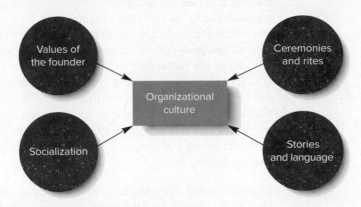

these new companies and their defining characteristics. Thus, an organization's founder and his or her terminal and instrumental values have a substantial influence on the values, norms, and standards of behavior that develop over time within the organization.[96] Founders set the scene for the way cultural values and norms develop because their own values guide the building of the company, and they hire other managers and employees who they believe will share these values and help the organization attain them. Moreover, new managers quickly learn from the founder what values and norms are appropriate in the organization and thus what is desired of them. Subordinates imitate the style of the founder and, in turn, transmit their values and norms to their subordinates. Gradually, over time, the founder's values and norms permeate the organization.[97]

A founder who requires a great display of respect from subordinates and insists on proprieties, such as formal job titles and formal dress, encourages subordinates to act in this way toward their subordinates. Often a founder's personal values affect an organization's competitive advantage. For example, McDonald's founder Ray Kroc insisted from the beginning on high standards of customer service and cleanliness at McDonald's restaurants; these became core sources of McDonald's competitive advantage. Similarly, Bill Gates, the cofounder of Microsoft, pioneered certain cultural values in Microsoft. Employees are expected to be creative and to work hard, but they are encouraged to dress informally and to personalize their offices. Gates also established a host of company events such as cookouts, picnics, and sports events to emphasize to employees the importance of being both an individual and a team player.

SOCIALIZATION   Over time, organizational members learn from each other which values are important in an organization and the norms that specify appropriate and inappropriate behaviors. Eventually, organizational members behave in accordance with the organization's values and norms—often without realizing they are doing so.

organizational socialization
The process by which newcomers learn an organization's values and norms and acquire the work behaviors necessary to perform jobs effectively.

Organizational socialization is the process by which newcomers learn an organization's values and norms and acquire the work behaviors necessary to perform jobs effectively.[98] As a result of their socialization experiences, organizational members internalize an organization's values and norms and behave in accordance with them, not only because they think they have to but because they think these values and norms describe the right and proper way to behave.[99]

At Texas A&M University, for example, all new students are encouraged to go to "Fish Camp" to learn how to be an "Aggie" (the traditional nickname of students at the university). They learn about the ceremonies that have developed over time to commemorate significant events or people in A&M's history. In addition, they learn how to behave at football games and in class and what it means to be an Aggie. As a result of this highly organized socialization program, by the time new students arrive on campus and start their first semester, they have been socialized into what a Texas A&M student is supposed to do, and they have relatively few problems adjusting to the college environment.

Most organizations have some kind of socialization program to help new employees learn the ropes—the values, norms, and culture of the organization. The military, for example, is well known for the rigorous socialization process it uses to turn raw recruits into trained soldiers. Organizations such as The Walt Disney Company also put new recruits through a rigorous training program to teach them to perform well in their jobs and play their parts in helping visitors have fun in the company's theme parks. New recruits at Disney are called "cast members" and attend Disney University to learn the Disney culture and their parts in it. Disney's culture emphasizes the values of safety, courtesy, entertainment, and efficiency, and these values are brought to life for newcomers at Disney University. Newcomers also learn about the attraction area they will be joining (such as Adventureland or Fantasyland) at Disney University and then receive on-the-job socialization in the area itself from experienced cast members.[100] Through organizational socialization, founders and managers of an organization transmit to employees the cultural values and norms that shape the behavior of organizational members. Thus, the values and norms of founder Walt Disney live on today as newcomers are socialized into the Disney way.

CEREMONIES AND RITES   Another way in which managers can create or influence organizational culture is by developing organizational ceremonies and rites—formal events that recognize incidents of importance to the organization as a whole and to specific employees.[101] The most common rites that organizations use to transmit cultural norms and values to their members are rites of passage, of integration, and of enhancement (see Table 3.1).[102]

Rites of passage determine how individuals enter, advance within, and leave the organization. The socialization programs developed by military organizations (such as the U.S. Army) or by large accountancy and law firms are rites of passage. Likewise, the ways in which an organization prepares people for promotion or retirement are rites of passage.

Rites of integration, such as shared announcements of organizational successes, office parties, and company cookouts, build and reinforce common bonds among organizational members. IDEO uses many rites of integration to make its employees feel connected to one another and special. In addition to having wild "end-of-year" celebratory bashes, groups of IDEO employees periodically take time off to go to a sporting event, movie, or meal or sometimes go on a long bike ride or for a sail. These kinds of shared activities not only reinforce IDEO's culture but also can be a source of inspiration on the job (for example, IDEO has been involved in making movies such as *The Abyss* and *Free Willy*). One 35-member design studio at IDEO led by Dennis Boyle has bimonthly lunch fests with no set agenda—anything goes. While enjoying great food, jokes, and camaraderie, studio members often end up sharing ideas for their latest great products, and the freely flowing conversation that results often leads to creative insights.[103]

A company's annual meeting also may be used as a ritual of integration, offering an opportunity to communicate organizational values to managers, other employees, and shareholders.[104] Walmart, for example, makes its annual stockholders' meeting an extravagant ceremony that celebrates the company's success. The company often flies thousands of its highest-performing employees to its annual meeting at its Bentonville, Arkansas, headquarters for a huge weekend entertainment festival complete with star musical performances. Walmart believes that rewarding its supporters with entertainment reinforces the company's high-performance values and culture. The proceedings are shown live over closed-circuit television in all Walmart stores so all employees can join in the rites celebrating the company's achievements.[105]

Rites of enhancement, such as awards dinners, press releases, and employee promotions, let organizations publicly recognize and reward employees' contributions and thus strengthen

Table 3.1

Organizational Rites

Type of Rite	Example of Rite	Purpose of Rite
Rite of passage	Induction and basic training	Learn and internalize norms and values
Rite of integration	Office holiday party	Build common norms and values
Rite of enhancement	Presentation of annual awards	Motivate commitment to norms and values

their commitment to organizational values. By bonding members within the organization, rites of enhancement reinforce an organization's values and norms.

Stories and language also communicate organizational culture. Stories (whether fact or fiction) about organizational heroes and villains and their actions provide important clues about values and norms. Such stories can reveal the kinds of behaviors that are valued by the organization and the kinds of practices that are frowned upon.[106] At the heart of the rich culture at McDonald's are hundreds of stories that organizational members tell about founder Ray Kroc. Most of these stories focus on how Kroc established the strict operating values and norms that are at the heart of McDonald's culture. Kroc was dedicated to achieving perfection in McDonald's quality, service, cleanliness, and value for money (QSC&V), and these four central values permeate McDonald's culture. For example, an often retold story describes what happened when Kroc and a group of managers from the Houston region were touring various restaurants. One of the restaurants was having a bad day operationally. Kroc was incensed about the long lines of customers, and he was furious when he realized that the products customers were receiving that day were not up to his high standards. To address the problem, he jumped up and stood on the front counter to get the attention of all customers and operating crew personnel. He introduced himself, apologized for the long wait and cold food, and told the customers they could have freshly cooked food or their money back—whichever they wanted. As a result, the customers left happy; and when Kroc checked on the restaurant later, he found that his message had gotten through to its managers and crew—performance had improved. Other stories describe Kroc scrubbing dirty toilets and picking up litter inside or outside a restaurant. These and similar stories are spread around the organization by McDonald's employees. They are the stories that have helped establish Kroc as McDonald's "hero."

Because spoken language is a principal medium of communication in organizations, the characteristic slang or jargon—that is, organization-specific words or phrases—that people use to frame and describe events provides important clues about norms and values. "McLanguage," for example, is prevalent at all levels of McDonald's. A McDonald's employee described as having "ketchup in his or her blood" is someone who is truly dedicated to the McDonald's way—someone who has been completely socialized to its culture. McDonald's has an extensive training program that teaches new employees "McDonald's speak," and new employees are welcomed into the family with a formal orientation that illustrates Kroc's dedication to QSC&V.

The concept of organizational language encompasses not only spoken language but how people dress, the offices they occupy, the cars they drive, and the degree of formality they use when they address one another. For example, casual dress reflects and reinforces IDEO's entrepreneurial culture and values. Formal business attire supports the conservative culture found in many banks, which emphasizes the importance of conforming to organizational norms such as respect for authority and staying within one's prescribed role. When employees speak and understand the language of their organization's culture, they know how to behave in the organization and what is expected of them.

At IDEO, language, dress, the physical work environment, and extreme informality all underscore a culture that is adventuresome, playful, risk-taking, egalitarian, and innovative. For example, when designing products at IDEO, employees refer to taking the consumers' perspective as "being left-handed." Employees dress in T-shirts and jeans, the physical work environment continually evolves and changes depending on how employees wish to personalize their workspace, no one "owns" a fancy office with a window, and rules are almost nonexistent.[107]

Culture and Managerial Action

While founders and managers play a critical role in developing, maintaining, and communicating organizational culture, the same culture shapes and controls the behavior of all employees, including managers themselves. For example, culture influences how managers perform their four main functions: planning, organizing, leading, and controlling. As we consider these functions, we continue to distinguish between top managers who create organizational values and norms that encourage creative, innovative behavior and top managers who encourage a conservative, cautious approach by their subordinates. We noted earlier that both kinds of values and norms can be appropriate depending on the situation and type of organization.

PLANNING   Top managers in an organization with an innovative culture are likely to encourage lower-level managers to participate in the planning process and develop a flexible approach to planning. They are likely to be willing to listen to new ideas and to take risks involving the development of new products. In contrast, top managers in an organization with conservative values are likely to emphasize formal top-down planning. Suggestions from lower-level managers are likely to be subjected to a formal review process, which can significantly slow decision making. Although this deliberate approach may improve the quality of decision making in a nuclear power plant, it can have unintended consequences. In the past, at conservative IBM, the planning process became so formalized that managers spent most of their time assembling complex slide shows and overheads to defend their current positions rather than thinking about what they should do to keep IBM abreast of the changes taking place in the computer industry. When former CEO Lou Gerstner took over, he used every means at his disposal to abolish this culture, even building a brand-new campus-style headquarters to change managers' mindsets. IBM's culture underwent further changes initiated by its next CEO, Samuel Palmisano. IBM's current CEO, Ginni Rometty, has changed the company's culture in her own way, including bringing back thousands of remote workers to IBM regional offices in an effort to improve collaboration and accelerate the pace of work and innovation at the tech giant.[108]

ORGANIZING   What kinds of organizing will managers in innovative and in conservative cultures encourage? Valuing creativity, managers in innovative cultures are likely to try to create an organic structure—one that is flat, with few levels in the hierarchy, and one in which authority is decentralized so employees are encouraged to work together to solve ongoing problems. A product team structure may be suitable for an organization with an innovative culture. In contrast, managers in a conservative culture are likely to create a well-defined hierarchy of authority and establish clear reporting relationships so employees know exactly whom to report to and how to react to any problems that arise.

LEADING   In an innovative culture, managers are likely to lead by example, encouraging employees to take risks and experiment. They are supportive regardless of whether employees succeed or fail. In contrast, managers in a conservative culture are likely to use management by objectives and to constantly monitor subordinates' progress toward goals, overseeing their every move. We examine leadership in detail in Chapter 14, when we consider the leadership styles that managers can adopt to influence and shape employee behavior.

CONTROLLING   The ways in which managers evaluate, and take actions to improve, performance differ depending on whether the organizational culture emphasizes formality and caution or innovation and change. Managers who want to encourage risk taking, creativity, and innovation recognize that there are multiple potential paths to success and that failure must be accepted for creativity to thrive. Thus, they are less concerned about employees' performing their jobs in a specific, predetermined manner and in strict adherence to preset goals and more concerned about employees' being flexible and taking the initiative to come up with ideas for improving performance. Managers in innovative cultures are also more concerned about long-term performance than short-term targets because they recognize that real innovation entails much uncertainty that necessitates flexibility. In contrast, managers in cultures that emphasize caution and maintenance of the status quo often set specific, difficult goals for employees, frequently monitor progress toward these goals, and develop a clear set of rules that employees are expected to adhere to.

The values and norms of an organization's culture strongly affect the way managers perform their management functions. The extent to which managers buy into the values and norms of their organization shapes their view of the world and their actions and decisions in particular circumstances. In turn, the actions that managers take can have an impact on the performance of the organization. Thus, organizational culture, managerial action, and organizational performance are all linked together.

While our earlier example of IDEO illustrates how organizational culture can give rise to managerial actions that ultimately benefit the organization, this is not always the case. The cultures of some organizations become dysfunctional, encouraging managerial actions that harm the organization and discouraging actions that might improve performance. Corporate scandals at large companies such as Enron, Tyco, and WorldCom show how damaging a dysfunctional culture can be to an organization and its members. For example, Enron's arrogant, "success at all costs" culture led to fraudulent behavior on the part of its top managers.[109] Unfortunately, hundreds of Enron employees paid a heavy price for the unethical behavior of these top managers and the dysfunctional organizational culture. Not only did these employees lose their jobs, but many also lost their life savings in Enron stock and pension funds, which became worth just a fraction of their value before the wrongdoing at Enron came to light. We discuss ethics and ethical cultures in depth in the next chapter.

Summary and Review

LO3-1 **ENDURING CHARACTERISTICS: PERSONALITY TRAITS** Personality traits are enduring tendencies to feel, think, and act in certain ways. The Big Five general traits are extraversion, negative affectivity, agreeableness, conscientiousness, and openness to experience. Other personality traits that affect managerial behavior include locus of control, self-esteem, and the needs for achievement, affiliation, and power. Several other personality assessments can be effective in helping managers and individuals identify positive and negative behaviors in themselves and others. These include the Myers-Briggs Type Indicator (MBTI) and the DiSC Inventory Profile.

LO3-2, 3-3, 3-4 **VALUES, ATTITUDES, AND MOODS AND EMOTIONS** A terminal value is a personal conviction about lifelong goals or objectives; an instrumental value is a personal conviction about modes of conduct. Terminal and instrumental values have an impact on what managers try to achieve in their organizations and the kinds of behaviors they engage in. An attitude is a collection of feelings and beliefs. Two attitudes important for understanding managerial behaviors include job satisfaction (the collection of feelings and beliefs that managers have about their jobs) and organizational commitment (the collection of feelings and beliefs that managers have about their organizations). A mood is a feeling or state of mind; emotions are intense feelings that are short-lived and directly linked to their causes. Managers' moods and emotions, or how they feel at work on a day-to-day basis, have the potential to impact not only their own behavior and effectiveness but also those of their subordinates. Emotional intelligence is the ability to understand and manage one's own and other people's moods and emotions.

LO3-5 **ORGANIZATIONAL CULTURE** Organizational culture is the shared set of beliefs, expectations, values, norms, and work routines that influence how members of an organization relate to one another and work together to achieve organizational goals. Founders of new organizations and managers play an important role in creating and maintaining organizational culture. Organizational socialization is the process by which newcomers learn an organization's values and norms and acquire the work behaviors necessary to perform jobs effectively.

Management in Action

Topics for Discussion and Action

Discussion

1. Discuss why managers who have different types of personalities can be equally effective and successful. **[LO3-1]**

2. Can managers be too satisfied with their jobs? Can they be too committed to their organizations? Why or why not? **[LO3-2]**

3. Assume that you are a manager of a restaurant. Describe what it is like to work for you when you are in a negative mood. **[LO3-3]**

4. Why might managers be disadvantaged by low levels of emotional intelligence? **[LO3-4]**

Action

5. Interview a manager in a local organization. Ask the manager to describe situations in which he or she is especially likely to act in accordance with his or her values. Ask the manager to describe situations in which he or she is less likely to act in accordance with his or her values. **[LO3-2]**

6. Watch a popular television show, and as you watch it, try to determine the emotional intelligence levels of the characters the actors in the show portray. Rank the characters from highest to lowest in terms of emotional intelligence. As you watched the show, what factors influenced your assessments of emotional intelligence levels? **[LO3-4]**

7. Go to an upscale store in your neighborhood, and go to a store that is definitely not upscale. Observe the behavior of employees in each store as well as the store's environment. In what ways are the organizational cultures in each store similar? In what ways are they different? **[LO3-5]**

Building Management Skills

Diagnosing Culture [LO3-5]

Think about the culture of the last organization you worked for, your current university, or another organization or club to which you belong. Then answer the following questions:

1. What values are emphasized in this culture?

2. What norms do members of this organization follow?

3. Who seems to have played an important role in creating the culture?

4. In what ways is the organizational culture communicated to organizational members?

Managing Ethically [LO3-1, 3-2]

Some organizations rely on personality and interest inventories to screen potential employees. Other organizations attempt to screen employees by using paper-and-pencil honesty tests.

Questions

1. Either individually or in a group, think about the ethical implications of using personality and interest inventories to screen potential employees. How might this practice be unfair to potential applicants? How might organizational members who are in charge of hiring misuse it?

2. Because of measurement error and validity problems, some relatively trustworthy people may "fail" an honesty test given by an employer. What are the ethical implications of trustworthy people "failing" honesty tests, and what obligations do you think employers should have when relying on honesty tests for screening?

Small Group Breakout Exercise

Making Difficult Decisions in Hard Times [LO3-2, 3-3, 3-4, 3-5]

Form groups of three or four people, and appoint one member as the spokesperson who will communicate your findings to the whole class when called on by the instructor. Then discuss the following scenario:

You are on the top management team of a medium-size company that manufactures cardboard boxes, containers, and other packaging materials. Your company is facing increasing levels of competition for major corporate customer accounts, and profits have declined significantly. You have tried everything you can to cut costs and remain competitive, with the exception of laying off employees. Your company has had a no-layoff policy for the past 20 years, and you believe it is an important part of the organization's culture. However, you are experiencing mounting pressure to increase your firm's performance, and your no-layoff policy has been questioned by shareholders. Even though you haven't decided whether to lay off employees and thus break with a 20-year tradition for your company, rumors are rampant in your organization that something is afoot, and

employees are worried. You are meeting today to address this problem.

1. Develop a list of options and potential courses of action to address the heightened competition and decline in profitability that your company has been experiencing.

2. Choose your preferred course of action, and justify why you will take this route.

3. Describe how you will communicate your decision to employees.

4. If your preferred option involves a layoff, justify why. If it doesn't involve a layoff, explain why.

Be the Manager [LO3-1, 3-2, 3-3, 3-4, 3-5]

You have recently been hired as the vice president for human resources in an advertising agency. One problem that has been brought to your attention is the fact that the creative departments at the agency have dysfunctionally high levels of conflict. You have spoken with members of each of these departments, and in each one it seems that a few members of the department are creating all the

problems. All these individuals are valued contributors who have many creative ad campaigns to their credit. The high levels of conflict are creating problems in the departments, and negative moods and emotions are much more prevalent than positive feelings. What are you going to do to both retain valued employees and alleviate the excessive conflict and negative feelings in these departments?

Bloomberg Businessweek Case in the News

The Undergrad Fixing Finance [LO 3-1, 3-4]

One morning last June, Angel Onuoha took a train from Connecticut, where he was staying with a friend, to New York City. His summer internship at C.L. King & Associates Inc., a small investment bank, was his first real taste of the finance world outside the student financial clubs he'd joined as a Harvard freshman. It was also a reality check. After a month on the job, he says, he had yet to meet another black employee.

Onuoha knew that Wall Street lacked diversity, but on the train that

morning he decided to do something about it. He remembered that his friend and fellow freshman Drew Tucker, whom he'd met through a campus organization for black men, was also interested in Wall Street—and that the two had discussed how the clubs did a poor job recruiting black students. So Onuoha texted Tucker with an idea: What if they started an investment fund that would give students hands-on experience and provide banks with a pool of talented black students to pull from?

Tucker, it turned out, had been pondering something similar. Within days the two began work on what would become BLK Capital Management Corp., a hedge fund that now has about 85 student members. They don't manage a lot of money—so far, just $92,000—and they haven't made any investments. But they've attracted funding from the likes of Goldman Sachs Group Inc. and JPMorgan Chase & Co. as part of an ambitious effort to reverse a dispiriting trend. For all the talk of increasing diversity on

Wall Street, finance hasn't welcomed people like Onuoha. According to a November report from the U.S. Government Accountability Office, the proportion of black financial managers was a paltry 6.3% in 2015, slightly fewer than when the government measured eight years earlier. "The lack of diversity is extraordinary," says John Rogers, chief executive officer of Ariel Investments LLC, one of the largest black-owned money managers in the U.S. "People have not thought about this problem in creative ways. That's why there's been so little progress."

Traditionally, banks recruit on college campuses to fill internships and entry-level jobs. But the finance clubs that produce top prospects can be exclusionary. For one group, Onuoha had to go through an application process that all but required him to have relevant experience: He had to complete a case study and sit through an interview that included probability analysis. For a lot of kids, those skills are hard to come by. Only 5,300 U.S. high schools offer an Advanced Placement course in macroeconomics. "That's a great opportunity that black students tend to miss out on," he says.

Onuoha favors button-down shirts and has a broad, inviting smile. He was born in Colorado and raised with two brothers and an adopted sister by his mother, Tina, who'd immigrated from Nigeria. Tina worked as a procurement manager, among other roles, for Hewlett-Packard Co. Money was tight. At one point, the five of them lived in a two-bedroom apartment in The Woodlands, a Houston suburb. Onuoha attended private school there thanks to financial aid. "My friends would always be going to the movies or going bowling, and I wouldn't be able to partake in any of those activities because we didn't have the money," he says.

Back then, Onuoha didn't know much about money, but he knew he wanted to make some. As a sophomore, he and a friend pooled $200 to start a sneaker-flipping business. On Saturdays, Onuoha would wake up early to scour online marketplaces

for Air Jordans or Yeezys, which they'd then resell at a steep markup. With his profits, Onuoha increased his personal collection to 15 pairs worth about $3,000—that is, until the day his mom strode into his bedroom and chucked the shoes, declaring them frivolous. "Thousands of dollars down the drain," he says. "It still doesn't make sense."

Onuoha moved on from sneakers, but he remained industrious. He applied to five Ivy League schools and was accepted to all of them. He wakes at 8 a.m. most days, the crack of dawn for an undergrad, to swim laps in Harvard's pool. There are no posters on his dorm room walls because he doesn't see the point—it's only temporary housing, so why spend the money? Earlier this spring, he deleted social media apps from his phone so he'd have more time to read *The Wall Street Journal*.

BLK would have been founded earlier, but when Onuoha called legal services provider LegalZoom to find out how to start a company, he was told to wait until he was 18. The day after his birthday, on July 5, he started the paperwork process. To reach students beyond Harvard, he and Tucker brought on another friend, Menelik Graham, a Princeton student Tucker knew through a leadership program for students from low-income backgrounds. (Tucker will be a market specialist intern with Bloomberg LP this summer.) In November, the trio went to the Black Ivy League Business Conference to fill their ranks.

BLK is a nonprofit 501(c)(3), so any earnings are rolled back into the fund. This means that contributors—in addition to JPMorgan and Goldman, others include Point72 Asset Management, Bank of America, Bridgewater Associates, and Dodge & Cox—can write off the donations as charity. For the inexperienced student investors, $92,000 is a decent amount to handle, but for Wall Street firms their share barely registers as an expense. Earlier this year, Bank of America gave more money to the Civil Rights Institute Inland Southern California than all sponsors combined have given to BLK.

Still, the money provides the students with a pipeline to recruiters and

an in-the-trenches financial education. Aside from a small leadership group, everyone in BLK is an equity analyst focusing on a different sector of the economy. When someone feels confident about a prospective investment, she submits a pitch to the executive board for vetting. Then Onuoha, the CEO, gets final say. Because he wanted the students to learn the fundamentals, he picked a simple long-short investing strategy. BLK takes a long position on stocks it thinks will appreciate, and short positions on equities it expects to lose value. BLK plans to invest in smaller firms that analysts cover less and therefore might be under- or overvalued, and returns will be judged using the Russell 2000 Index as a benchmark.

BLK got about 450 applicants; they accepted about one-fifth of them. Strangers messaged the co-founders on Instagram and Twitter asking to join. Serious candidates faced an intensive application process that included an interview and a case study that was adjusted for prior experience. BLK pulled heavily from the Ivies but also from schools such as Stanford and the University of Virginia. Being part of the fund takes commitment: Everyone in BLK is expected to join a two-hour conference call on Sundays. There's also about five to seven hours of homework a week, which might include practicing, say, a discounted cash flow analysis.

On a mid-April afternoon in a wood-paneled meeting room at Harvard, eight club members gathered to discuss why they'd joined. They wore blazers and cardigans, with one sporting a Harvard Business School vest. (Asked if they normally dressed this nicely, the answer was a resounding no—Onuoha had asked them to do so.) Naomi Vickers, a freshman, said that when she joined one of Harvard's finance clubs, she realized that out of more than 100 people at an intro meeting, she was the only black woman. It diminished her confidence: "I was like, OK, this is what I have to do. I'm going to learn finance. It's OK if it's a white world. I'll get through it. Two weeks in, I'm like, I have no motivation to do this." Now she's BLK's chief operating officer.

Recently, Steven Cohen's Point72 signed a seven-year partnership with BLK. Point72 wants internship and job candidates "who generally have been historically underrepresented in our industry," says Jonathan Jones, head of investment talent development. In the past, Point72 recruited almost exclusively from investment banks, which tend to be racially homogeneous. (The firm declined to disclose its employee diversity numbers.)

Point72 invited BLK members to its Manhattan office for an investment pitch competition in late April. Nine groups of students spent three hours trying to sell Point72 representatives on stocks they'd researched, such as Tractor Supply Co. and human resources service provider TriNet Group Inc. Afterward, the students sat quietly as a talent developer offered them feedback. The winners, three Harvard students who'd pitched the health-care cybersecurity company CynergisTek Inc., won new iPads. Onuoha says BLK will consider CynergisTek as a possible first investment, while Point72 will consider the winners for summer internships. That would be a big deal for any college student: Point72 accepts few undergrads for its investing internship every year.

The idea that you have to be a member of an Ivy League hedge fund just to get a look as a black student isn't lost on Onuoha. "Obviously, it's unfair," he says. "That's one of the biggest adds of our organization—to develop that preprofessional aspect." It seems to be working. This summer, Onuoha will intern at Goldman.

Questions for Discussion

1. Which Big Five personality traits have been instrumental in helping Onuoha manage the BLK Capital Management Corp.?

2. Describe how Onuoha's internal locus of control contributes to his managerial success.

3. What role has emotional intelligence played in Onuoha's ability to open up the world of financial management to minorities and women?

Notes

1. PG&E Corporation, "Our Team," http://www.pgecorp.com, accessed January 31, 2018; S. Gharib, "For This CEO, the Next Generation's Success Is Just as Important as Her Own," *Fortune,* http://fortune.com, January 8, 2018; A. Jones, "How PG&E Is Working to Power the Clean Energy Future," *Newsweek,* www.newsweek.com, December 11, 2017; V. Zarya, "A Bolt of Energy," *Fortune,* June 15, 2017, 160-64.

2. Zarya, "A Bolt of Energy."

3. Zarya, "A Bolt of Energy"; "Women in Industry: Geisha Williams, Pacific Gas & Electric Company (PG&E)," www.ey.com, accessed January 31, 2018.

4. Jones, "How PG&E Is Working."

5. Gharib, "For This CEO."

6. "Geisha Williams: PG&E's Top Electric Executive," *Hispanic Engineer,* http://hispanicengineer.com, November 22, 2017; Zarya, "A Bolt of Energy."

7. Zarya, "A Bolt of Energy"; "PG&E CEO Geisha Williams Highlights California's Clean Energy Progress and Key Challenge for the Future," *Yahoo Finance,* https://finance.yahoo.com, January 31, 2018; S. Gharib, "PG&E and CEO Geisha Williams Want to Lead the Charge in Clean Energy," *Fortune,* http://fortune.com, November 30, 2017.

8. E. Larson, "Here's How Your Personality Type Affects Your Decision Making at Work," *Forbes,* www.forbes.com, March 6, 2017.

9. J.M. George, "Personality, Five-Factor Model," in S. Clegg and J.R. Bailey, eds., *International Encyclopedia of Organization Studies* (Thousand Oaks, CA: Sage, 2007); J.M. Digman, "Personality Structure: Emergence of the Five-Factor Model," *Annual Review of Psychology* 41(1990), 417-40.

10. T.A. Judge and C.P. Zapata, "The Person-Situation Debate Revisited: Effect of Situation Strength and Trait Activation on the Validity of the Big Five Personality Traits in Predicting Job Performance," *Academy of Management Journal* 58, no. 4 (2015), 1149-79.

11. L.A. Witt and G.R. Ferris, "Social Skills as Moderator of Conscientiousness-Performance Relationship: Convergent Results across Four Studies," *Journal of Applied Psychology* 88, no. 5 (2003), 809-20; M.J. Simmering, J.A. Colquitte, R.A. Noe, and C.O.L.H. Porter, "Conscientiousness, Autonomy Fit, and Development: A Longitudinal Study," *Journal of Applied Psychology* 88, no. 5 (2003), 954-63.

12. M.R. Barrick and M.K. Mount, "The Big Five Personality Dimensions and Job Performance: A Meta-Analysis," *Personnel Psychology* 44 (1991), 1-26; S. Komar, D.J. Brown, J.A. Komar, and C. Robie, "Faking and the Validity of Conscientiousness: A Monte Carlo Investigation," *Journal of Applied Psychology* 93 (2008), 140-54.

13. Digman, "Personality Structure."

14. "Jess Lee," https://www.sequoiacap.com, accessed March 1, 2018.

15. C. Schubarth, "VC Jess Lee on Challenges Women Founders Face," *Silicon Valley Business Journal,* www.bizjournals.com, November 28, 2017.

16. D. Reich, "The $2.3 Billion Business Model—How Content, Community and Commerce Are Fueling These Companies," *Forbes,* www.forbes.com, July 29, 2014.

17. "15 Questions with Jess Lee," *CNN Tech,* http://money.cnn.com, accessed March 1, 2018.

18. T. Lien, "How I Made It: Jess Lee's Unlikely Path to Running Polyvore," *Los Angeles Times,* www.latimes.com, September 2, 2016.

19. L.K. Inamedinova, "Top 5 Fashion E-commerce Websites That Change the Way You Shop," *Forbes,* www.forbes.com, May 5, 2016.

20. L. Chapman and S. McBride, "Sequoia Capital Hires Yahoo's Jess Lee as First Woman U.S. Investing Partner," *Bloomberg Technology,* www.bloomberg.com, October 20, 2016.

21. J.B. Rotter, "Generalized Expectancies for Internal versus External Control of Reinforcement," *Psychological Monographs* 80 (1966), 1-28; P. Spector, "Behaviors in Organizations as a Function of Employees' Locus of Control," *Psychological Bulletin* 91 (1982), 482-97.

22. M. Ruderman, "How Low Self-Esteem at Work Can Kill Your Chances for Success," *Glassdoor,* www.glassdoor.com, February 21, 2017.

23. D.C. McClelland, *Human Motivation* (Glenview, IL: Scott, Foresman, 1985); D.C. McClelland, "How Motives, Skills, and Values Determine What People Do," *American Psychologist* 40 (1985), 812–25; D.C. McClelland, "Managing Motivation to Expand Human Freedom," *American Psychologist* 33 (1978), 201–10.

24. D.G. Winter, *The Power Motive* (New York: Free Press 1973).

25. M.J. Stahl, "Achievement, Power, and Managerial Motivation: Selecting Managerial Talent with the Job Choice Exercise," *Personnel Psychology* 36 (1983), 775–89; D.C. McClelland and D.H. Burnham, "Power Is the Great Motivator," *Harvard Business Review* 54 (1976), 100–10.

26. R.J. House, W.D. Spangler, and J. Woycke, "Personality and Charisma in the U.S. Presidency: A Psychological Theory of Leader Effectiveness," *Administrative Science Quarterly* 36 (1991), 364–96.

27. G.H. Hines, "Achievement, Motivation, Occupations and Labor Turnover in New Zealand," *Journal of Applied Psychology* 58 (1973), 313–17; P.S. Hundal, "A Study of Entrepreneurial Motivation: Comparison of Fast- and Slow-Progressing Small Scale Industrial Entrepreneurs in Punjab, India," *Journal of Applied Psychology* 55 (1971), 317–23.

28. "MBTI® Basics," www.myersbriggs.org, accessed March 1, 2018; Elena Bajic, "How the MBTI Can Help You Build a Stronger Company," *Forbes,* www.forbes.com, September 28, 2015; A. Furnham and J. Crump, "The Myers-Briggs Type Indicator (MBTI) and Promotion at Work," *Psychology* 6, no. 12 (September 2015) 1510–15.

29. "What Is DiSC?" http://discprofile.com, accessed March 1, 2018.

30. M. Rokeach, *The Nature of Human Values* (New York: Free Press 1973).

31. K. Tuulik, T. Ounapuu, K. Kuimet, and E. Titov, "Rokeach's Instrumental and Terminal Values as Descriptors of Modern Organisation Values," *International Journal of Organizational Leadership* 5 (2016), 151–61.

32. Rokeach, *The Nature of Human Values.*

33. J. Brownell, "Ethics from the Bottom Up," *Cornell Hospitality Report* 17 (April 3, 2017), 3–13; S. Nadel, "Increasing the Role of Ethics in the Hospitality Industry," *Hotel Business Review,* www.hotelexecutive.com, September 21, 2014.

34. Brownell, "Ethics from the Bottom Up"; Nadel, "Increasing the Role of Ethics."

35. Brownell, "Ethics from the Bottom Up"; Glenn Withiam, "A Strong Strategy Is Required When Talking about Ethics," *Hotel Management,* June 1, 2017, 30.

36. "Cornell's Judi Brownell: Listening to Women Business Travelers," GlassCeiling.com, accessed February 1, 2018.

37. Nadel, "Increasing the Role of Ethics."

38. B. Steverman, "Layoffs: Short-Term Profits, Long-Term Problems," *Bloomberg,* www.bloomberg.com, January 13, 2010; P.S. Goodman, "U.S. Job Losses in December Dim Hopes for Quick Upswing," *The New York Times,* www.nytimes.com, January 9, 2010.

39. Conference Board, "U.S. Job Satisfaction at Lowest Level in Two Decades," www.conference-board.org, January 5, 2010.

40. "Labor Day Survey: 51% of U.S. Employees Overall Satisfied with Their Job," www.conference-board.org, August 29, 2018; J. McGregor, "Job Satisfaction Is Up, But Still Well Below One-Time Highs," *The Washington Post,* www.washingtonpost.com, September 1, 2017.

41. "About Us," http://subaru-sia.wixsite.com, accessed March 1, 2018.

42. "Why Subaru?" www.subaru.com, accessed March 1, 2018

43. "We Work to Sustain," http://subaru-sia.wixsite.com, accessed March 1, 2018.

44. R. Farzad, "Subaru of Indiana, America's Scrappiest Carmaker," *Bloomberg Businessweek,* www.bloomberg.com, accessed March 1, 2018.

45. Ibid.

46. D.W. Organ, *Organizational Citizenship Behavior: The Good Soldier Syndrome* (Lexington, MA: Lexington Books, 1988).

47. J.M. George and A.P. Brief, "Feeling Good—Doing Good: A Conceptual Analysis of the Mood at Work—Organizational Spontaneity Relationship," *Psychological Bulletin* 112 (1992), 310–29.

48. A. Kopoulos, "How to Engage Your Managers," *Employee Connect,* www.employeeconnect.com, accessed March 1, 2018.

49. S. M. Heathfield, "Tips for Compassionate Layoffs," *The Balance,* www.thebalance.com, April 7, 2017; K.W. Freeman, "A Guide to Being Compassionate During Layoffs," *Harvard Business Review,* https://hbr.org, February 25, 2016.

50. N. Solinger, W. van Olffen, and R.A. Roe, "Beyond the Three-Component Model of Organizational Commitment," *Journal of Applied Psychology* 93 (2008), 70–83.

51. J.E. Mathieu and D.M. Zajac, "A Review and Meta-Analysis of the Antecedents, Correlates, and Consequences of Organizational Commitment," *Psychological Bulletin* 108 (1990), 171–94.

52. D. Watson and A. Tellegen, "Toward a Consensual Structure of Mood," *Psychological Bulletin* 98 (1985), 219–35.

53. J.M. George, "The Role of Personality in Organizational Life: Issues and Evidence," *Journal of Management* 18 (1992), 185–213.

54. H.A. Elfenbein, "Emotion in Organizations: A Review and Theoretical Integration," in J.P. Walsh and A.P. Brief, eds., *The Academy of Management Annals,* vol. 1 (New York: Erlbaum, 2008), 315–86.

55. J.P. Forgas, "Affect in Social Judgments and Decisions: A Multi-Process Model," in M. Zamma, ed., *Advances in Experimental and Social Psychology,* vol. 25 (San Diego, CA: Academic Press, 1992), 227–75; J.P. Forgas and J.M. George, "Affective Influences on Judgments and Behavior in Organizations: An Information Processing Perspective," *Organizational Behavior and Human Decision Processes* 86 (2001), 3–34; J.M. George, "Emotions and Leadership: The Role of Emotional Intelligence," *Human Relations* 53 (2000), 1027–55; W.N. Morris, *Mood: The Frame of Mind* (New York: Springer-Verlag, 1989).

56. J.M. George and K. Bettenhausen, "Understanding Prosocial Behavior, Sales Performance, and Turnover: A Group Level Analysis in a Service Context," *Journal of Applied Psychology* 75 (1990), 698–709.

57. George and Brief, "Feeling Good—Doing Good"; J.M. George and J. Zhou, "Understanding When Bad Moods Foster Creativity and Good Ones Don't: The Role of Context and Clarity of Feelings," paper presented at the Academy of Management Annual Meeting, 2001; A.M. Isen and R.A. Baron, "Positive Affect as a Factor in Organizational Behavior," in B.M. Staw and L.L. Cummings, eds., *Research in Organizational Behavior,* vol. 13 (Greenwich, CT: JAI Press, 1991), 1–53.

58. J.M. George and J. Zhou, "Dual Tuning in a Supportive Context: Joint Contributions of Positive Mood, Negative Mood, and Supervisory Behaviors to Employee Creativity," *Academy of Management Journal* 50 (2007), 605–22; J.M. George, "Creativity in Organizations," in J.P. Walsh and A.P. Brief, eds., *The Academy of Management Annals,* vol. 1 (New York: Erlbaum, 2008), 439–77.

59. J.D. Greene, R.B. Sommerville, L.E. Nystrom, J.M. Darley, and J.D. Cohen, "An FMRI Investigation of Emotional Engagement in Moral Judgment," *Science,* September 14, 2001, 2105–08; L. Neergaard, "Brain Scans Show Emotions Key to Resolving Ethical Dilemmas," *Houston Chronicle,* September 14, 2001, 13A.

60. George and Zhou, "Dual Tuning in a Supportive Context."

61. George and Zhou, "Dual Tuning in a Supportive Context;" J.M. George, "Dual Tuning: A Minimum Condition for

Understanding Affect in Organizations?" *Organizational Psychology Review.* 2 (2011), 147-64.

62. R.C. Sinclair, "Mood, Categorization Breadth, and Performance Appraisal: The Effects of Order of Information Acquisition and Affective State on Halo, Accuracy, Informational Retrieval, and Evaluations," *Organizational Behavior and Human Decision Processes* 42 (1988), 22-46.

63. D. Goleman, *Emotional Intelligence* (New York: Bantam Books, 1994); J.D. Mayer and P. Salovey, "The Intelligence of Emotional Intelligence," *Intelligence* 17 (1993), 433-42; J.D. Mayer and P. Salovey, "What Is Emotional Intelligence?" in P. Salovey and D. Sluyter, eds., *Emotional Development and Emotional Intelligence: Implications for Education* (New York: Basic Books, 1997); P. Salovey and J.D. Mayer, "Emotional Intelligence," *Imagination, Cognition, and Personality* 9 (1989-1990), 185-211.

64. S. Epstein, *Constructive Thinking* (Westport, CT: Praeger, 1998).

65. "Leading by Feel," *Inside the Mind of the Leader,* January 2004, 27-37.

66. P.C. Early and R.S. Peterson, "The Elusive Cultural Chameleon: Cultural Intelligence as a New Approach to Intercultural Training for the Global Manager," *Academy of Management Learning and Education* 3, no. 1 (2004), 100-15.

67. George, "Emotions and Leadership"; S. Begley, "The Boss Feels Your Pain," *Newsweek,* October 12, 1998, 74; D. Goleman, *Working with Emotional Intelligence* (New York: Bantam Books, 1998).

68. J. Bercovici, "Remembering Bernie Goldhirsh," www.medialifemagazine.com/news2003/jun03/jun30/4_thurs/news1thursday.html, April 15, 2004.

69. B. Burlingham, "Legacy: The Creative Spirit," *Inc.,* September 2003, 11-12.

70. See Daniel Goleman, "Emotional Intelligence," www.danielgoleman.info, accessed March 2, 2018.

71. A. Molinsky, "Emotional Intelligence Doesn't Translate across Borders," *Harvard Business Review,* https://hbr.org, April 20, 2015.

72. P. Surana, "Is Emotional Intelligence Culture Specific?" *LinkedIn,* www.linkedin.com, May 4, 2017.

73. Surana, "Is Emotional Intelligence Culture Specific?"; Molinsky, "Emotional Intelligence Doesn't Translate."

74. P.Gaul, "Travis Bradberry, *TD,* May 2017, 60-61.

75. Molinsky, "Emotional Intelligence Doesn't Translate"; Surana, "Is Emotional Intelligence Culture Specific?"

76. B. Burlingham, "Legacy: The Creative Spirit," *Inc.,* September 2003, 11-12.

77. Ibid.

78. "Leading by Feel"; George, "Emotions and Leadership."

79. J. Zhou and J.M. George, "Awakening Employee Creativity: The Role of Leader Emotional Intelligence," *Leadership Quarterly* 14 (2003), 545-68.

80. H.M. Trice and J.M. Beyer, *The Cultures of Work Organizations* (Englewood Cliffs, NJ: Prentice-Hall, 1993).

81. J.B. Sørensen, "The Strength of Corporate Culture and the Reliability of Firm Performance," *Administrative Science Quarterly* 47 (2002), 70-91.

82. "Personality and Organizational Culture," in B. Schneider and D.B. Smith, eds., *Personality and Organizations* (Mahway, NJ: Erlbaum, 2004), 347-69; J.E. Slaughter, M.J. Zickar, S. Highhouse, and D.C. Mohr, "Personality Trait Inferences about Organizations: Development of a Measure and Assessment of Construct Validity," *Journal of Applied Psychology* 89, no. 1 (2004), 85-103.

83. "About IDEO," www.ideo.com, accessed March 2, 2018; T. Kelley, *The Art of Innovation: Lessons in Creativity from IDEO, America's Leading Design Firm* (New York: Random House, 2001).

84. "Personality and Organizational Culture."

85. B. Schneider, "The People Make the Place," *Personnel Psychology* 40 (1987), 437-53.

86. "Personality and Organizational Culture."

87. B. Schneider, H.B. Goldstein, and D.B. Smith, "The ASA Framework: An Update," *Personnel Psychology* 48 (1995), 747-73; J. Schaubroeck, D.C. Ganster, and J.R. Jones, "Organizational and Occupational Influences in the Attraction-Selection-Attrition Process," *Journal of Applied Psychology* 83 (1998), 869-91.

88. Kelley, *The Art of Innovation.*

89. "Launching an Online Pharmacy Startup," www.ideo.com, accessed March 2, 2018.

90. "Who We Are," www.ideo.com, accessed March 2, 2018.

91. "Personality and Organizational Culture."

92. L. Lamb, "Inside the Creative Office Cultures at Facebook, IDEO, and Virgin America," *Fast Company,* www.fastcompany.com, accessed March 2, 2018.

93. George, "Emotions and Leadership."

94. Lamb, "Inside the Creative Office Cultures at Facebook, IDEO, and Virgin America."

95. Kelley, *The Art of Innovation.*

96. M. McClain, "How Corporate Culture Can Make (or Break) Your Organization," *Forbes,* www.forbes.com, November 6, 2017.

97. H. Schein, "The Role of the Founder in Creating Organizational Culture," *Organizational Dynamics* 12 (1983), 13-28.

98. J.M. George, "Personality, Affect, and Behavior in Groups," *Journal of Applied Psychology* 75 (1990), 107-16.

99. J. Van Maanen, "Police Socialization: A Longitudinal Examination of Job Attitudes in an Urban Police Department," *Administrative Science Quarterly* 20 (1975), 207-28.

100. Monet, "Disney University 101—What It Is and Why You'll Love It," *Disney Fanatic,* www.disneyfanatic.com, accessed March 2, 2018.

101. M. West and K. McCoubrey Judson, "Want to Strengthen Workplace Culture? Design a Ritual," *Huffington Post,* www.huffingtonpost.com, December 6, 2017.

102. H.M. Trice and J.M. Beyer, "Studying Organizational Culture through Rites and Ceremonies," *Academy of Management Review* 9 (1984), 653-69.

103. Kelley, *The Art of Innovation.*

104. H.M. Trice and J.M. Beyer, *The Cultures of Work Organizations* (Englewood Cliffs, NJ: Prentice-Hall, 1993).

105. R. Feloni, "How the Walmart Shareholders Meeting Went from a Few Guys in a Coffee Shop to a 14,000-Person, Star-Studded Celebration," *Business Insider,* www.businessinsider.com, June 2, 2017.

106. Trice and Beyer, "Studying Organizational Culture through Rites and Ceremonies."

107. Kelley, *The Art of Innovation.*

108. J. Simons, "IBM, a Pioneer of Remote Work, Calls Workers Back to the Office," *The Wall Street Journal,* www.wsj.com, May 18, 2017.

109. B. McLean and P. Elkind, *The Smartest Guys in the Room: The Amazing Rise and Scandalous Fall of Enron* (New York: Penguin Books, 2003); R. Smith and J.R. Emshwiller, *24 Days: How Two Wall Street Journal Reporters Uncovered the Lies That Destroyed Faith in Corporate America* (New York: HarperCollins, 2003); M. Swartz and S. Watkins, *Power Failure: The Inside Story of the Collapse of ENRON* (New York: Doubleday, 2003).

CHAPTER 4

Ethics and Social Responsibility

©Hero Images/Getty Images

Learning Objectives

After studying this chapter, you should be able to:

LO4-1 Explain the relationship between ethics and the law.

LO4-2 Differentiate between the claims of the different stakeholder groups affected by managers and their companies' actions.

LO4-3 Describe four rules that can help companies and their managers act in ethical ways.

LO4-4 Discuss why it is important for managers to behave ethically.

LO4-5 Identify the four main sources of managerial ethics.

LO4-6 Distinguish among the four main approaches toward social responsibility that a company can take.

Musk Steers Tesla Ahead while Helping Others

How can doing good help a company do well? For Elon Musk, the answer is to use technology to address big social issues like environmental quality and economic development. He launched Tesla Motors to make electric cars that would offer a cleaner-fuel alternative to gasoline-powered vehicles. That required developing better batteries, capable of storing more energy. Now Tesla is deploying its battery expertise to make electricity available in underserved areas that need help.

Tesla's approach to electricity distribution is to build microgrids, networks of solar panels and batteries large enough to collect and save energy from the sun, and distribute it as electric power to a local area. The method addresses the main shortcoming of solar power: It only works when the sun is shining. The batteries store energy during sunny periods and release it as needed. Tesla tested the idea on Ta'u, a 600-resident island in American Samoa, building a network of solar panels and batteries that almost fully meets the population's energy needs.[1] Tesla has built microgrids in Australia, including the Hornsdale Power Reserve, a huge system linking wind turbines to batteries for backup power in South Australia.[2] At Hornsdale, the backup system has beaten traditional power plants in restoring power during service interruptions. Causes of problems at power plants, including heat waves and big storms, are expected to increase in the future, so this type of service may grow in importance.

Following Hurricane Maria in 2017, Tesla then turned its attention to the dire situation in Puerto Rico, where months after the storm, many people and organizations still lacked power. Tesla built a microgrid linking batteries to solar panels at a children's hospital in San Juan.[3] The project serves the immediate humanitarian purpose of keeping a hospital operating after a disaster, but Musk intends it also to be a model for economic development in places that have been poorly served by traditional electric utilities. While investors have been hesitant to get involved with Puerto Rico's cash-strapped electrical utility, solar power companies see potential in launching their own projects there.

The microgrid projects are situated in areas that offer abundant sunshine and wind and tend to be far from fossil-fuel supplies. Providing oil and natural gas to an island, for example, is costly, so electricity from fossil fuels is more expensive in places like Puerto Rico and Hawaii than on the mainland United States. Microgrids, if they succeed, will not only bring a better standard of living to these areas, but also present a business opportunity.

After learning about the devastating hurricane that hit Puerto Rico recently, Tesla CEO Elon Musk offered the company's innovative battery technology to build a microgrid to help keep the power on at a children's hospital in San Juan when the island was without electricity.
© Rich Pedroncelli/AP Photo

Energy solutions are part of Musk's strategic vision for Tesla.[4] Musk, born in South Africa and educated in Canada and the United States, has a history of innovating with technology.[5] He founded X.com (later PayPal), Tesla Motors, and SpaceX, among other businesses. Tesla acquired SolarCity Corporation, a maker of solar panels, in 2016. While this wasn't a logical fit for Tesla as a carmaker, it seized on a new use for its battery storage technology. Musk sees "no scalability limit" on the use of microgrids; they can be set up wherever there is a source of renewable energy and a need to generate, store, and distribute electricity.[6]

Overview

As Tesla's work with microgrid technology illustrates, management decision making can have far-reaching implications when it comes to doing business in a socially responsible manner. Elon Musk's relentless drive to find solutions to energy challenges not only helps his company's bottom line, but also provides assistance to people in many areas around the world.

Globally, nations, companies, and managers differ enormously in their commitment to various *stakeholders*—groups of people who may benefit or be harmed by how managers make decisions that affect them. Managers of some companies make the need to behave ethically toward stakeholders their main priority. Managers of other companies pursue their own self-interest at the expense of their stakeholders and do harm to them—such as the harm done to the millions of people around the world who live and work in dangerous conditions.

In this chapter we examine the obligations and responsibilities of managers and the companies they work for toward the people and society that are affected by their actions. First we examine the nature of ethics and the sources of ethical problems. Next we discuss the major stakeholder groups that are affected by how companies operate. We also look at four rules or guidelines managers can use to decide whether a specific business decision is ethical or unethical. Finally, we consider the sources of managerial ethics and the reasons why it is important for a company to behave in a socially responsible manner. By the end of this chapter you will understand the central role of ethics in shaping the practice of management and the life of a people, society, and nation.

The Nature of Ethics

Suppose you see a person being mugged. Will you act in some way to help even though you risk being hurt? Will you walk away? Perhaps you might not intervene, but will you call the police? Does how you act depend on whether the person being mugged is a fit male, an elderly person, or a homeless person? Does it depend on whether other people are around so you can tell yourself, "Oh, well, someone else will help or call the police. I don't need to"?

Ethical Dilemmas

ethical dilemma The quandary people find themselves in when they have to decide if they should act in a way that might help another person or group even though doing so might go against their own self-interest.

ethics The inner guiding moral principles, values, and beliefs that people use to analyze or interpret a situation and then decide what is the right or appropriate way to behave.

The situation just described is an example of an ethical dilemma, the quandary people find themselves in when they have to decide if they should act in a way that might help another person or group and is the right thing to do even though doing so might go against their own self-interest.[7] A dilemma may also arise when a person has to choose between two different courses of action, knowing that whichever course he or she selects will harm one person or group even though it may benefit another. The ethical dilemma here is to decide which course of action is the lesser of two evils.

People often know they are confronting an ethical dilemma when their moral scruples come into play and cause them to hesitate, debate, and reflect upon the rightness or goodness of a course of action. Moral scruples are thoughts and feelings that tell a person what is right or wrong; they are a part of a person's ethics. Ethics are the inner guiding moral principles, values, and beliefs that people use to analyze or interpret a situation and then decide what is the right or appropriate way to behave. Ethics also indicate what is inappropriate behavior and how a person should behave to avoid harming another person.

The essential problem in dealing with ethical issues, and thus solving moral dilemmas, is that no absolute or indisputable rules or principles can be developed to decide whether an action is ethical or unethical. Put simply, different people or groups may dispute which actions are ethical or unethical depending on their personal self-interest and specific attitudes, beliefs, and values—concepts we discussed in Chapter 3. How are we and companies and their managers and employees to decide what is ethical and, so, act appropriately toward other people and groups?

Ethics and the Law

LO4-1 Explain the relationship between ethics and the law.

The first answer to this question is that society as a whole, using the political and legal process, can lobby for and pass laws that specify what people can and cannot do. Many different kinds of laws govern business—for example, laws against fraud and deception and laws governing how companies can treat their employees and customers. Laws also specify what sanctions or punishments will follow if those laws are broken. Different groups in society lobby for which laws should be passed based on their own personal interests and beliefs about right and wrong. The group that can summon the most support can pass laws that align with its interests and beliefs. Once a law is passed, a decision about what the appropriate behavior is with regard to a person or situation is taken from the personally determined ethical realm to the societally determined legal realm. If you do not conform to the law, you can be prosecuted; and if you are found guilty of breaking the law, you can be punished. You have little say in the matter; your fate is in the hands of the court and its lawyers.

In studying the relationship between ethics and law, it is important to understand that *neither laws nor ethics are fixed principles* that do not change over time. Ethical beliefs change as time passes; as they do so, laws change to reflect the changing ethical beliefs of a society. It was seen as ethical, and it was legal, for example, to acquire and possess slaves in ancient Rome and Greece and in the United States until the late 19th century. Ethical views regarding whether slavery was morally right or appropriate changed, however. Slavery was made illegal in the United States when those in power decided that slavery degraded the meaning of being human. Slavery makes a statement about the value or worth of human beings and about their right to life, liberty, and the pursuit of happiness. And if we deny these rights to other people, how can we claim to have any natural rights to these things?

Moreover, what is to stop any person or group that becomes powerful enough to take control of the political and legal process from enslaving us and denying us the right to be free and to own property? In denying freedom to others, one risks losing it oneself, just as stealing from others opens the door for them to steal from us in return. "Do unto others as you would have them do unto you" is a common ethical or moral rule that people apply in such situations to decide what is the right thing to do.

Changes in Ethics over Time

There are many types of behavior—such as murder, theft, slavery, rape, and driving while intoxicated—that most people currently believe are unacceptable and unethical and should therefore be illegal. However, the ethics of many other actions and behaviors are open to dispute. Some people might believe a particular behavior—for example, smoking tobacco or possessing guns—is unethical and, so, should be made illegal. Others might argue that it is up to the individual or group to decide if such behaviors are ethical and thus whether a particular behavior should remain legal.

As ethical beliefs change over time, some people may begin to question whether existing laws that make specific behaviors illegal are still appropriate. They might argue that although a specific behavior is deemed illegal, this does not make it unethical and thus the law should be changed. In 20 states, for example, it is illegal to possess or use marijuana (cannabis). To justify this law, it is commonly argued that smoking marijuana leads people to try more dangerous drugs. Once the habit of taking drugs has been acquired, people can get hooked on them.

Coldbath Fields Prison, London, circa 1810. The British criminal justice system around this time was severe: A person could be executed for 350 different crimes, including sheep stealing. As ethical beliefs change over time, so do laws.

©Hulton Archive/Getty Images

More powerful drugs such as heroin and other narcotics are addictive, and most people cannot stop using them without help. Thus, the use of marijuana, because it might lead to further harm, is an unethical practice.

It has been documented medically, however, that marijuana use can help people with certain illnesses. For example, for cancer sufferers who are undergoing chemotherapy and for those with AIDS who are on potent medications, marijuana offers relief from many treatment side effects, such as nausea and lack of appetite. Yet in the United States it is illegal in some states for doctors to prescribe marijuana for these patients, so their suffering continues. Since 1996, however, 30 states have made it legal to prescribe marijuana for medical purposes; nevertheless, the federal government has sought to stop such state legislation. The U.S. Supreme Court ruled in 2005 that only Congress or the states could decide whether medical marijuana use should be made legal, and people in many states are currently lobbying for a relaxation of state laws against its use for medical purposes.[8] While not making the drug legal, decriminalization removes the threat of prosecution even for uses that are not medically related and allows the drug to be taxed. Initiatives are under way in several states to decriminalize the possession of small amounts of marijuana for personal use as well as to make it more widely available to people legally for medical purposes. A major ethical debate is currently raging over this issue in many states and countries.

The important point to note is that while ethical beliefs lead to the development of laws and regulations to prevent certain behaviors or encourage others, laws themselves change or even disappear as ethical beliefs change. In Britain in 1830 a person could be executed for over 350 different crimes, including sheep stealing. Today the death penalty is no longer legal in Britain.

Thus, both ethical and legal rules are *relative:* No absolute or unvarying standards exist to determine how we should behave, and people are caught up in moral dilemmas all the time. Because of this, we have to make ethical choices.

The previous discussion highlights an important issue in understanding the relationship among ethics, law, and business. Throughout the 2010s many scandals plagued major companies such as JPMorgan Chase, HSBC, Standard Chartered Bank, ING, Barclays, and Wells Fargo. Managers at some of these companies engaged in risky trades, interest rate manipulation, illegal trade facilitation, drug money laundering, and deception of customers.

In other cases no laws were broken, yet outrage was expressed over perceptions of unethical actions. One example of this is the anti-gun movement, a protest that has been growing over the last several years as a result of multiple instances of gun violence. In February 2018, 14 students and 3 coaches and teachers were gunned down inside Marjory Stoneman Douglas High School in Parkland, Florida, by a former student who purchased an AR-15 assault rifle legally.[9] The friends and schoolmates of the slain students started the #marchforourlives protest, which included a national walk on Washington, DC. The ongoing protest, spearheaded by students on social media, has caused several major companies to end their business relationships with the National Rifle Association (NRA) and eliminate discounts to NRA members. In addition, major retailers such as Walmart, Dick's Sporting Goods, and Kroger have changed their policies with regard to gun sales.[10]

Stakeholders and Ethics

stakeholders The people and groups that supply a company with its productive resources and, so, have a claim on and a stake in the company.

Just as people have to work out the right and wrong ways to act, so do companies. When the law does not specify how companies should behave, their managers must decide the right or ethical way to behave toward the people and groups affected by their actions. Who are the people or groups that are affected by a company's business decisions? If a company behaves in an ethical way, how does this benefit people and society? Conversely, how are people harmed by a company's unethical actions?

The people and groups affected by how a company and its managers behave are called its stakeholders. Stakeholders supply a company with its productive resources; as a result, they have a claim on and a stake in the company.[11] Because stakeholders can directly benefit or be harmed by its actions, the ethics of a company and its managers are important to them. Who are a company's major stakeholders? What do they contribute to a company, and what do they claim in return? Here we examine the claims of these stakeholders—stockholders; managers; employees; suppliers and distributors; customers; and community, society, and nation-state as Figure 4.1 depicts.

Stockholders

LO4-2 Differentiate between the claims of the different stakeholder groups affected by managers and their companies' actions.

Stockholders have a claim on a company because when they buy its stock or shares they become its owners. When the founder of a company decides to publicly incorporate the business to raise capital, shares of the stock of that company are issued. This stock grants its buyers ownership of a certain percentage of the company and the right to receive any future stock dividends. For example, in 2005 Microsoft decided to pay the owners of its 5 billion shares a special dividend payout of $32 billion. Bill Gates received $3.3 billion in dividends based on his stockholding, and he donated this money to the Bill and Melinda Gates Foundation, to which he has reportedly donated over $50 billion to date, with the promise of much more to come. In 2017, for example, Gates gave the Foundation $4.6 billion worth of his Microsoft stock shares.[12] Gates' friend and fellow billionaire, Warren Buffett, committed to donate at least $30 billion of his fortune to the Gates Foundation over the next decade. Two of the richest people in the world have decided to give away a large part of their wealth to serve global ethical causes—in particular to address global concerns such as education, malnutrition, malaria, tuberculosis, and AIDS.

Stockholders are interested in how a company operates because they want to maximize the return on their investment. Thus, they watch the company and its managers closely to ensure that management is working diligently to increase the company's profitability.[13] Stockholders also want to ensure that managers are behaving ethically and not risking investors' capital by engaging in actions that could hurt the company's reputation. No company wants the reputation described by the #marchforourlives protesters, who allege that some business organizations value money over people. However, experts warn businesses not to ignore the movement. They warn the growing voice and influence of the gun violence movement may continue to single out politicians, companies, and other organizations that continue to associate or do business with the NRA and its millions of members.[14]

Figure 4.1

Types of Company Stakeholders

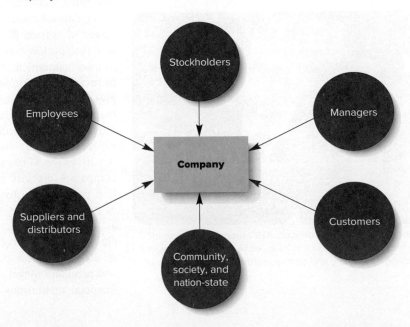

Managers

Managers are a vital stakeholder group because they are responsible for using a company's financial, capital, and human resources to increase its performance and thus its stock price.[15] Managers have a claim on an organization because they bring to it their skills, expertise, and experience. They have the right to expect a good return or reward by investing their human capital to improve a company's performance. Such rewards include good salaries and benefits, the prospect of promotion and a career, and stock options and bonuses tied to company performance.

Managers are the stakeholder group that bears the responsibility to decide which goals an organization should pursue to most benefit stakeholders and how to make the most efficient use of resources to achieve those goals. In making such decisions, managers frequently must juggle the interests of different stakeholders, including themselves.[16] These sometimes difficult decisions challenge managers to uphold ethical values because some decisions that benefit certain stakeholder groups (managers and stockholders) harm other groups (individual workers and local communities). For example, in economic downturns or when a company experiences performance shortfalls, layoffs may help cut costs (thus benefiting shareholders) at the expense of the employees laid off. Many U.S. managers have recently faced this difficult decision. Until the 2009 financial crisis sent unemployment soaring over 10%, on average about 1.6 million U.S. employees out of a total labor force of 140 million were affected by mass layoffs each year, and over 3 million jobs from the United States, Europe, and Japan have been outsourced to Asia since 2005. Layoff decisions are always difficult: They not only take a heavy toll on workers, their families, and local communities, but also mean the loss of the contributions of valued employees to an organization. In 2018, telecommunications giant AT&T announced plans to eliminate 4,600 jobs in its wireline telephone division in an effort to streamline company operations and shift resources to growing parts of its business such as wireless and TV.[17]

As we discussed in Chapter 1, managers must be motivated and given incentives to work hard in the interests of stockholders. Their behavior must also be scrutinized to ensure they do not behave illegally or unethically, pursuing goals that threaten stockholders and the company's interests. Unfortunately, we have seen in the 2010s how easy it is for top managers to find ways to ruthlessly pursue their self-interest at the expense of stockholders and employees because laws and regulations are not strong enough to force them to behave ethically.

In a nutshell, the problem has been that in many companies corrupt managers focus not on building the company's capital and stockholders' wealth, but on maximizing their own personal capital and wealth. In an effort to prevent future scandals, the Securities and Exchange Commission (SEC), the government's top business watchdog, has begun to rework the rules governing a company's relationship with its auditor, as well as regulations concerning stock options, and to increase the power of outside directors to scrutinize a CEO. The SEC's goal is to outlaw many actions that were previously classified as merely unethical. For example, companies are now forced to reveal to stockholders the value of the stock options they give their top executives and directors and when they give them these options; this shows how greatly such payments reduce company profits. Managers and directors can now be prosecuted if they disguise or try to hide these payments. In the 2010s the SEC announced many new rules requiring that companies disclose myriad details of executive compensation packages to investors; already the boards of directors of many companies have stopped giving CEOs perks such as free personal jet travel, membership in exclusive country clubs, and luxury accommodations on "business trips." Also, in 2010 Congress passed new laws preventing the many unethical and illegal actions of managers of banks and other financial institutions that led to the 2009 financial crisis.

Layoff decisions are always difficult. AT&T recently announced plans to reduce the workforce in its wireline telephone division to streamline operations and shift resources to growing parts of its business.

©asiseeit/Getty Images

One of these regulations, the "Volcker Rule," seeks to reduce the chances that banks will put depositors' money at risk. In 2018, however, Wall Street and U.S. banks asked federal regulators to revisit the Volcker Rule in an effort to loosen some of the stricter requirements of the legislation, which could lessen the financial burden put on banking institutions nationwide.[18]

Indeed, many experts argue that the rewards given to top managers, particularly the CEO and COO, grew out of control in the 2000s. Top managers are today's "elites," and through their ability to influence the board of directors and raise their own pay, they have amassed personal fortunes worth hundreds of millions of dollars. For example, according to a study by the Federal Reserve, U.S. CEOs now get paid about 270 times what the average worker earns, compared to about 40 times in 1980–a staggering increase. In 2017, the median CEO compensation was $11.5 million.[19] We noted in Chapter 1 that besides their salaries, top managers often receive tens of millions in stock bonuses and options—even when their companies perform poorly.

Is it ethical for top managers to receive such vast amounts of money from their companies? Do they earn it? Remember, this money could have gone to shareholders in the form of dividends. It could also have reduced the huge salary gap between those at the top and those at the bottom of the hierarchy. Many people argue that the growing disparity between the rewards given to CEOs and to other employees is unethical and should be regulated. CEO pay has skyrocketed because CEOs are the people who set and control one another's salaries and bonuses; they can do this because they sit on the boards of other companies as outside directors. Others argue that because top managers play an important role in building a company's capital and wealth, they deserve a significant share of its profits. Some recent research has suggested that the companies whose CEO compensation includes a large percentage of stock options tend to experience big share losses more often than big gains, and on average, company performance improves as stock option use declines.[20] The debate over how much money CEOs and other top managers should be paid is still raging, particularly because the financial crisis beginning in 2009 showed how much money the CEOs of troubled financial companies earned even as their companies' performance and stock prices collapsed.

Ethics and Nonprofit Organizations

The issue of what is fair compensation for top managers is not limited to for-profit companies; it is one of many issues facing nonprofits. The many ethics scandals that have plagued companies in the 2010s might suggest that the issue of ethics is important only for profit-seeking companies, but this is untrue. There are almost 2 million private nonprofit charitable and philanthropic organizations in the United States, and charges that their managers have acted in unethical and even illegal ways have grown in the 2010s. For example, many states and the federal government are investigating the huge salaries that the top executives of charitable institutions earn.

One impetus for this was the revelation that the NYSE, which used to be classified as a nonprofit, paid its disgraced top executive, Richard A. Grasso, over $187 million in pension benefits. According to recent research, more than 2,700 executives of nonprofit organizations (including hospitals, universities, and charities) each earn more than $1 million a year in salary, bonus, and other benefits, and the boards of trustees or directors of many of these organizations also enjoy lavish perks and compensation for attendance at board meetings.[21] And unlike for-profit companies, which are required by law to provide detailed reports of their operations to their shareholders, nonprofits do not have shareholders, so the laws governing disclosure are far weaker. As a result, the board and its top managers have considerable latitude to decide how they will spend a nonprofit's resources, and little oversight exists.

To remedy this situation, many states and the federal government are considering new laws that would subject nonprofits to strict Sarbanes-Oxley-type regulations that force the disclosure of issues related to managerial compensation and financial integrity. In fact, the tax reform legislation signed into law by President Trump in late 2017 includes a new 21% excise tax on nonprofit employers for salaries over $1 million.[22]

Experts hope that the introduction of new rules and regulations to monitor and oversee how nonprofits spend their funds will result in much more value being created from the funds given by donors. After all, every cent that is spent administering a nonprofit is a cent not being used to help the people or cause for which the money was intended. Ethical issues are involved because some badly run charities spend 70 cents of every dollar on administration costs. And charges have been leveled against charities such as the Red Cross for mishandling the hundreds of millions of dollars they received in donations after Hurricane Katrina struck; changes have been made in the Red Cross to address these issues. Clearly, the directors and managers of all organizations need to carefully consider the ethical issues involved in their decision making.

Employees

A company's employees are the hundreds of thousands of people who work in its various departments and functions, such as research, sales, and manufacturing. Employees expect to receive rewards consistent with their performance. One principal way that a company can act ethically toward employees and meet their expectations is by creating an occupational structure that fairly and equitably rewards employees for their contributions. Companies, for example, need to develop recruitment, training, performance appraisal, and reward systems that do not discriminate against employees and that employees believe are fair.

Suppliers and Distributors

No company operates alone. Every company is in a network of relationships with other companies that supply it with the inputs (such as raw materials, components, contract labor, and clients) that it needs to operate. It also depends on intermediaries such as wholesalers and retailers to distribute its products to the final customers. Suppliers expect to be paid fairly and promptly for their inputs; distributors expect to receive quality products at agreed-upon prices. Once again, many ethical issues arise in how companies contract and interact with their suppliers and distributors.

Many other issues depend on business ethics. For example, numerous products sold in U.S. stores have been outsourced to countries that do not have U.S.-style regulations and laws to protect the workers who make these products. All companies must take an ethical position on the way they obtain and make the products they sell. Commonly, this stance is published on a company's website. Table 4.1 presents part of the Gap's statement about its approach to global ethics (www.gapinc.com).

Customers

Customers are often regarded as the most critical stakeholder group because if a company cannot attract them to buy its products, it cannot stay in business. Thus, managers and employees must work to increase efficiency and effectiveness in order to create loyal customers and attract new ones. They do so by selling customers quality products at a fair price and providing good after-sales service. They can also strive to improve their products over time and provide guarantees to customers about the integrity of their products, like the Soap Dispensary, profiled in the accompanying "Management Insight" feature.

Community, Society, and Nation

The effects of the decisions made by companies and their managers permeate all aspects of the communities, societies, and nations in which they operate. *Community* refers to physical locations like towns or cities or to social milieus like ethnic neighborhoods in which companies are located. A community provides a company with the physical and social infrastructure that allows it to operate; its utilities and labor force; the homes in which its managers and employees live; the schools, colleges, and hospitals that serve their needs; and so on.

Table 4.1

Some Principles from the Gap's Code of Vendor Conduct

As a condition of doing business with Gap Inc., each and every factory must comply with this Code of Vendor Conduct. Gap Inc. will continue to develop monitoring systems to assess and ensure compliance. If Gap Inc. determines that any factory has violated this Code, Gap Inc. may either terminate its business relationship or require the factory to implement a corrective action plan. If corrective action is advised but not taken, Gap Inc. will suspend placement of future orders and may terminate current production.

I. General Principles

Factories that produce goods for Gap Inc. shall operate in full compliance with the laws of their respective countries and with all other applicable laws, rules, and regulations.

II. Environment

Factories must comply with all applicable environmental laws and regulations. Where such requirements are less stringent than Gap Inc.'s own, factories are encouraged to meet the standards outlined in Gap Inc.'s statement of environmental principles.

III. Discrimination

Factories shall employ workers on the basis of their ability to do the job, without regard to race, color, gender, nationality, religion, age, maternity, or marital status.

IV. Forced Labor

Factories shall not use any prison, indentured, or forced labor.

V. Child Labor

Factories shall employ only workers who meet the applicable minimum legal age requirement or are at least 15 years of age, whichever is greater. Factories must also comply with all other applicable child labor laws. Factories are encouraged to develop lawful workplace apprenticeship programs for the educational benefit of their workers, provided that all participants meet both Gap Inc.'s minimum age standard of 15 and the minimum legal age requirement.

VI. Wages & Hours

Factories shall set working hours, wages, and overtime premiums in compliance with all applicable laws. Workers shall be paid at least the minimum legal wage or a wage that meets local industry standards, whichever is greater. While it is understood that overtime is often required in garment production, factories shall carry out operations in ways that limit overtime to a level that ensures humane and productive working conditions.

MANAGEMENT INSIGHT

Keeping Things Clean and Green

Soap consumption is not as clean a business as you might think. First, soap is often packaged in plastic—dishwashing detergent, clothing detergent, shampoos, body washes, liquid hand soaps—they're all in plastic containers. Recent estimates suggest that worldwide, more than 4.9 billion metric tons of plastic find their way into landfills and natural environments such as oceans.[23]

Second, many soaps have chemicals that contain suspected cancer-causing agents, and many other household products emit hazardous chemicals via their fragrances.[24] One such chemical is triclosan, which is commonly found in soap products. Triclosan is toxic to aquatic plants and animals. When it reacts with chlorine in water, it can cause cancer, nerve disorders, and immune system disorders. It also contributes to antibiotic resistance in bacteria that cause infection in humans.

To combat the dirty residue of soap consumption and household products, stores like the Soap Dispensary in Vancouver, Canada, are popping up. The Soap Dispensary is a refill store specializing in soaps, household cleaners, and personal care products that are not harmful to humans or the environment. Instead of harsh

At the Soap Dispensary in Vancouver, owner Linh Truong sells biodegradable household and personal products free from fillers, dyes, and perfumes. Customers bring their own containers to refill over and over again, and Truong tracks the savings to the environment with each bottle refilled.

©Liang Sen Xinhua News Agency/Newscom

chemicals, the Soap Dispensary's products are selected to be as free as possible from fillers, dyes, and synthetic perfumes. The products are also biodegradable and animal cruelty-free, and some are vegan certified.

Customers take their own containers back to the store again and again to refill instead of throwing them away, or they can pay a small deposit fee to obtain a reusable container from the store. The store also sells ingredients customers can use to make their own soaps (as well as other products) and conducts classes to teach customers how to make them at home. Classes range from simple soap making to aromatherapy. Besides soap, the store sells nonplastic cleaning supplies, reusable razors, natural beeswax candles, repurposed fabric, and other environmentally friendly items.

Linh Truong and Stewart Lampe, owners of the Soap Dispensary, estimate that in the first two years of the store's existence, it kept more than 12,000 plastic containers from being thrown away.

The store also has provided a venue where customers can purchase locally made products. These locally made soaps and their locally acquired ingredients make a short supply chain that is easier on the environment than a national or international one. When locally owned businesses provide supplies for other locally owned businesses, less fuel and other energy is spent on transportation, creating less pollution in the environment.[25]

The Soap Dispensary tracks the savings to the environment of each bottle refilled, which Truong uses to inspire her customers to keep conserving. Stores like the Soap Dispensary make a difference by focusing on one feasible aspect of sustainability and by working with the local community to reduce its environmental footprint. Truong also achieves her mission of reducing waste by encouraging her suppliers to switch to more sustainable packaging and by washing out some delivery containers to return to suppliers for reuse.

In late 2017, the socially conscious owners took their commitment to the environment and local community to the next level by becoming Vancouver's first zero-waste food grocery store. The expanded store (now called the Soap Dispensary & Kitchen Staples) continues to refill soap and other household product containers for its customers, but it also sells groceries for purchase, such as berries, herbs, cheese, and dips—with no plastic packaging. According to Truong, the goal is to reduce and reuse materials—and only use recycling as a last resort.[26]

Through the salaries, wages, and taxes it pays, a company contributes to the economy of its town or region and often determines whether the community prospers or declines. Similarly, a company affects the prosperity of a society and a nation and, to the degree that a company is involved in global trade, all the countries it operates in and thus the prosperity of the global economy. We have already discussed the many issues surrounding global outsourcing and the loss of jobs in the United States, for example.

Although the individual effects of the way each McDonald's restaurant operates might be small, for instance, the combined effects of how all McDonald's and other fast-food companies do business are enormous. In the United States alone, more than 3.5 million people work in the fast-food industry, and many thousands of suppliers, like farmers, paper cup manufacturers, and builders, depend on it for their livelihood. Small wonder, then, that the ethics of the fast-food business are scrutinized closely. This industry was the major lobbyer against attempts to raise the national minimum wage (which was raised to $7.25 an hour in 2009, where it remains in 2018, up from $5.15—a figure that had not changed since 1997), for example, because a higher minimum wage would substantially increase its operating costs. However, responding to protests about chickens raised in cages where they cannot move, McDonald's—the largest egg buyer in the United States—issued new ethical guidelines concerning cage size and related matters that its egg suppliers must abide by if they are to retain its business. What ethical rules does McDonald's use to decide its stance toward minimum pay or minimum cage size?

Business ethics are also important because the failure of a company can have catastrophic effects on a community; a general decline in business activity affects a whole nation. The decision of a large company to pull out of a community, for example, can threaten the community's future. Some companies may attempt to improve their profits by engaging in actions that, although not illegal, can hurt communities and nations. One of these actions is pollution. For example, many U.S. companies reduce costs by trucking their waste to Mexico, where it is legal to dump waste in the Rio Grande. The dumping pollutes the river from the Mexican side, but the U.S. side of the river is increasingly experiencing pollution's negative effects.

Rules for Ethical Decision Making

LO4-3 Describe four rules that can help companies and their managers act in ethical ways.

When a stakeholder perspective is taken, questions on company ethics abound.[27] What is the appropriate way to manage the claims of all stakeholders? Company decisions that favor one group of stakeholders, for example, are likely to harm the interests of others.[28] High prices charged to customers may bring high returns to shareholders and high salaries to managers in the short run. If in the long run customers turn to companies that offer lower-cost products, however, the result may be declining sales, laid-off employees, and the decline of the communities that support the high-priced company's business activity.

When companies act ethically, their stakeholders support them. For example, banks are willing to supply them with new capital, they attract highly qualified job applicants, and new customers are drawn to their products. Thus, ethical companies grow and expand over time, and all their stakeholders benefit. The results of unethical behavior are loss of reputation and resources, shareholders selling their shares, skilled managers and employees leaving the company, and customers turning to the products of more reputable companies.

When making business decisions, managers must consider the claims of all stakeholders. To help themselves and employees make ethical decisions and behave in ways that benefit their stakeholders, managers can use four ethical rules or principles to analyze the effects of their business decisions on stakeholders: the *utilitarian, moral rights, justice,* and *practical* rules (Figure 4.2).[29] These rules are useful guidelines that help managers decide on the appropriate way to behave in

Figure 4.2

Four Ethical Rules

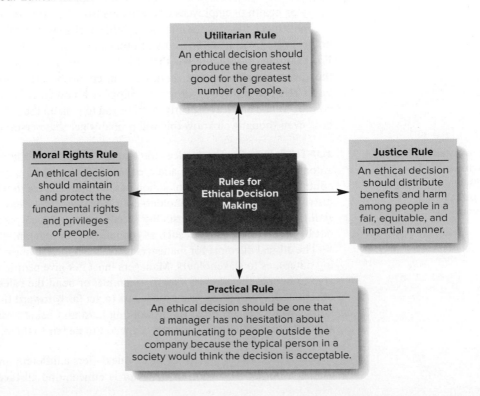

Utilitarian Rule

An ethical decision should produce the greatest good for the greatest number of people.

Moral Rights Rule

An ethical decision should maintain and protect the fundamental rights and privileges of people.

Rules for Ethical Decision Making

Justice Rule

An ethical decision should distribute benefits and harm among people in a fair, equitable, and impartial manner.

Practical Rule

An ethical decision should be one that a manager has no hesitation about communicating to people outside the company because the typical person in a society would think the decision is acceptable.

situations where it is necessary to balance a company's self-interest and the interests of its stake-holders. Remember, the right choices will lead resources to be used where they can create the most value. If all companies make the right choices, all stakeholders will benefit in the long run.

UTILITARIAN RULE

utilitarian rule An ethical decision is a decision that produces the greatest good for the greatest number of people.

The **utilitarian rule** is that an ethical decision is a decision that produces the greatest good for the greatest number of people. To decide which is the most ethical course of business action, managers should first consider how different possible courses of business action would benefit or harm different stakeholders. They should then choose the course of action that provides the most benefits, or, conversely, the one that does the least harm, to stakeholders.[30]

The ethical dilemma for managers is this: How do you measure the benefit and harm that will be done to each stakeholder group? Moreover, how do you evaluate the rights of different stakeholder groups, and the relative importance of each group, in coming to a decision? Because stockholders own the company, shouldn't their claims be held above those of employees? For example, managers might face a choice of using global outsourcing to reduce costs and lower prices or continuing with high-cost production at home. A decision to use global outsourcing benefits shareholders and customers but will result in major layoffs that will harm employees and the communities in which they live. Typically, in a capitalist society such as the United States, the interests of shareholders are put above those of employees, so production will move abroad. This is commonly regarded as being an ethical choice because in the long run the alternative, home production, might cause the business to collapse and go bankrupt, in which case greater harm will be done to all stakeholders.

MORAL RIGHTS RULE

moral rights rule An ethical decision is one that best maintains and protects the fundamental or inalienable rights and privileges of the people affected by it.

Under the **moral rights rule**, an ethical decision is one that best maintains and protects the fundamental or inalienable rights and privileges of the people affected by it. For example, ethical decisions protect people's rights to freedom, life and safety, property, privacy, free speech, and freedom of conscience. The adage "Do unto others as you would have them do unto you" is a moral rights principle that managers should use to decide which rights to uphold. Customers must also consider the rights of the companies and people who create the products they wish to consume.

From a moral rights perspective, managers should compare and contrast different courses of business action on the basis of how each course will affect the rights of the company's different stakeholders. Managers should then choose the course of action that best protects and upholds the rights of *all* stakeholders. For example, decisions that might significantly harm the safety or health of employees or customers would clearly be unethical choices.

The ethical dilemma for managers is that decisions that will protect the rights of some stakeholders often will hurt the rights of others. How should they choose which group to protect? For example, in deciding whether it is ethical to snoop on employees, or search them when they leave work to prevent theft, does an employee's right to privacy outweigh an organization's right to protect its property? Suppose a coworker is having personal problems and is coming in late and leaving early, forcing you to pick up the person's workload. Do you tell your boss even though you know this will probably get that person fired?

JUSTICE RULE

justice rule An ethical decision distributes benefits and harms among people and groups in a fair, equitable, or impartial way.

The **justice rule** is that an ethical decision distributes benefits and harms among people and groups in a fair, equitable, or impartial way. Managers should compare and contrast alternative courses of action based on the degree to which they will fairly or equitably distribute outcomes to stakeholders. For example, employees who are similar in their level of skill, performance, or responsibility should receive similar pay; allocation of outcomes should not be based on differences such as gender, race, or religion.

The ethical dilemma for managers is to determine the fair rules and procedures for distributing outcomes to stakeholders. Managers must not give people they like bigger raises than they give to people they do not like, for example, or bend the rules to help their favorites. On the other hand, if employees want managers to act fairly toward them, then employees need to act fairly toward their companies by working hard and being loyal. Similarly, customers need to act fairly toward a company if they expect it to be fair to them.

PRACTICAL RULE

Each of these rules offers a different and complementary way of determining whether a decision or behavior is ethical, and all three rules should be used to sort out the ethics of a particular course of action. Ethical issues, as we just discussed, are seldom clear-cut, however, because the rights, interests, goals, and incentives of different stakeholders often conflict. For this reason many experts on ethics add a fourth rule to determine whether a business decision is ethical: The **practical rule** is that an ethical decision is one that a manager has no hesitation or reluctance about communicating to people outside the company because the typical person in a society would think it is acceptable. A business decision is probably acceptable on ethical grounds if a manager can answer yes to each of these questions:

practical rule An ethical decision is one that a manager has no reluctance about communicating to people outside the company because the typical person in a society would think it is acceptable.

1. Does my decision fall within the accepted values or standards that typically apply in business activity today?
2. Am I willing to see the decision communicated to all people and groups affected by it—for example, by having it reported on TV or via social media?
3. Would the people with whom I have a significant personal relationship, such as family members, friends, or even managers in other organizations, approve of the decision?

Applying the practical rule to analyze a business decision ensures that managers are taking into account the interests of all stakeholders.[31] After applying this rule, managers can judge if they have chosen to act in an ethical or unethical way, and they must abide by the consequences.

Why Should Managers Behave Ethically?

LO4-4 Discuss why it is important for managers to behave ethically.

Why is it so important that managers, and people in general, act ethically and temper their pursuit of self-interest by considering the effects of their actions on others? The answer is that the relentless pursuit of self-interest can lead to a collective disaster when one or more people start to profit from being unethical because this encourages other people to act in the same way.[32] More and more people jump onto the bandwagon, and soon everybody is trying to manipulate the situation to serve their personal ends with no regard for the effects of their action on others. This is called the "tragedy of the commons."

Suppose that in an agricultural community there is common land that everybody has an equal right to use. Pursuing self-interest, each farmer acts to make the maximum use of the free resource by grazing his or her own cattle and sheep. Collectively, all the farmers overgraze the land, which quickly becomes worn out. Then a strong wind blows away the exposed topsoil, so the common land is destroyed. The pursuit of individual self-interest with no consideration of societal interests leads to disaster for each individual and for the whole society because scarce resources are destroyed.[33] Consider digital piracy: The tragedy that would result if all people were to steal digital media would be the disappearance of music, movie, and book companies as creative people decided there was no point in working hard to produce original songs, stories, and so on.

We can look at the effects of unethical behavior on business activity in another way. Suppose companies and their managers operate in an unethical society, meaning one in which stakeholders routinely try to cheat and defraud one another. If stakeholders expect each other to cheat, how long will it take them to negotiate the purchase and shipment of products? When they do not trust each other, stakeholders will probably spend hours bargaining over fair prices, and this is a largely unproductive activity that reduces efficiency and effectiveness.[34] The time and effort that could be spent improving product quality or customer service are lost to negotiating and bargaining. Thus, unethical behavior ruins business commerce, and society has a lower standard of living because fewer goods and services are produced, as Figure 4.3 illustrates.

On the other hand, suppose companies and their managers operate in an ethical society, meaning stakeholders believe they are dealing with others who are basically moral and honest. In this society stakeholders have a greater reason to trust others. **Trust** is the willingness of one person or group to have faith or confidence in the goodwill of another person, even though this puts them at risk (because the other might act in a deceitful way). When trust exists, stakeholders are likely to signal their good intentions by cooperating and providing information that makes it easier to exchange and price goods and services. When one person acts in a trustworthy way, this encourages others to act in the same way. Over time, as greater trust between stakeholders develops, they can work together more efficiently and effectively, which

trust The willingness of one person or group to have faith or confidence in the goodwill of another person, even though this puts them at risk.

Figure 4.3

Some Effects of Ethical and Unethical Behavior

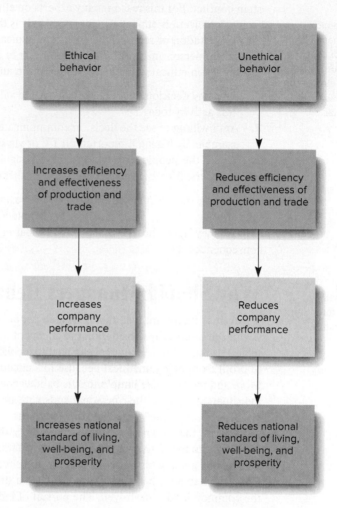

raises company performance (see Figure 4.3). As people see the positive results of acting in an honest way, ethical behavior becomes a valued social norm, and society in general becomes increasingly ethical.

As noted in Chapter 1, a major responsibility of managers is to protect and nurture the resources under their control. Any organizational stakeholders—managers, workers, stockholders, suppliers—who advance their own interests by behaving unethically toward other stakeholders, either by taking resources or by denying resources to others, waste collective resources. If other individuals or groups copy the behavior of the unethical stakeholder, the rate at which collective resources are misused increases, and eventually few resources are available to produce goods and services. Unethical behavior that goes unpunished creates incentives for people to put their unbridled self-interests above the rights of others.[35] When this happens, the benefits that people reap from joining together in organizations disappear quickly.

An important safeguard against unethical behavior is the potential for loss of reputation.[36] **Reputation**, the esteem or high repute that people or organizations gain when they behave ethically, is an important asset. Stakeholders have valuable reputations, which they must protect because their ability to earn a living and obtain resources in the long run depends on how they behave.

If a manager misuses resources and other parties regard that behavior as being at odds with acceptable standards, the manager's reputation will suffer. Behaving unethically in the short run can have serious long-term consequences. A manager who has a poor reputation will have difficulty finding employment with other companies. Stockholders who

reputation The esteem or high repute that individuals or organizations gain when they behave ethically.

see managers behaving unethically may refuse to invest in their companies, and this will decrease the stock price, undermine the companies' reputations, and ultimately put the managers' jobs at risk.[37]

All stakeholders have reputations to lose. Suppliers who provide shoddy inputs find that organizations learn over time not to deal with them, and eventually they go out of business. Powerful customers who demand ridiculously low prices find that their suppliers become less willing to deal with them, and resources ultimately become harder for them to obtain. Workers who shirk responsibilities on the job find it hard to get new jobs when they are fired. In general, if a manager or company is known for being unethical, other stakeholders are likely to view that individual or organization with suspicion and hostility, creating a poor reputation. But a manager or company known for ethical business practices will develop a good reputation.[38]

In summary, in a complex, diverse society, stakeholders, and people in general, need to recognize they are part of a larger social group. How they make decisions and act not only affects them personally but also affects the lives of many other people. Unfortunately, for some people, the daily struggle to survive and succeed or their total disregard for others' rights can lead them to lose that bigger connection to other people. We can see our relationships to our families and friends, school, church, and so on. But we must go further and keep in mind the effects of our actions on other people—people who will be judging our actions and whom we might harm by acting unethically. Our moral scruples are like those "other people" but are inside our heads.

Ethics and Social Responsibility

Some companies, like Starbucks, L'Oreal, Microsoft, Marriott International, and Aflac, are known for their ethical business practices.[39] Other companies such as Enron, which is out of business, or WorldCom, Tyco, and Siemens, which have been totally restructured, repeatedly engaged in unethical and illegal business activities. What explains such differences between the ethics of these companies and their managers?

There are four main determinants of differences in ethics among people, employees, companies, and countries: *societal* ethics, *occupational* ethics, *individual* ethics, and *organizational* ethics—especially the ethics of a company's top managers.[40] (See Figure 4.4.)

Figure 4.4
Sources of Ethics

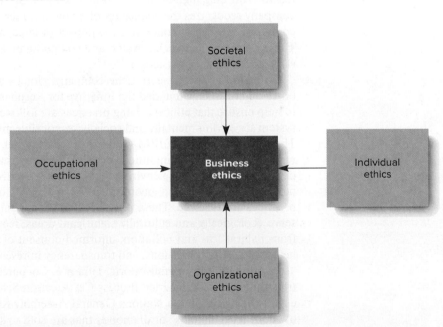

LO4-5 Identify the four main sources of managerial ethics.

societal ethics Standards that govern how members of a society should deal with one another in matters involving issues such as fairness, justice, poverty, and the rights of the individual.

Societal Ethics

Societal ethics are standards that govern how members of a society should deal with one another in matters involving issues such as fairness, justice, poverty, and the rights of the individual. Societal ethics emanate from a society's laws, customs, and practices and from the unwritten values and norms that influence how people interact with each other. People in a particular country may automatically behave ethically because they have *internalized* (made a part of their morals) certain values, beliefs, and norms that specify how they should behave when confronted with an ethical dilemma.

Societal ethics vary among societies. Countries like Germany, Japan, Sweden, and Switzerland are known as being some of the most ethical countries in the world, with strong values about social order and the need to create a society that protects the welfare of all their citizens. In other countries the situation is different. In many economically poor countries, bribery is standard practice to get things done—such as getting a telephone installed or a contract awarded. In the United States and other economically advanced countries, bribery is considered unethical and has been made illegal.

German engineering firm Siemens reported its involvement in a price-fixing cartel in Brazil so that it could build the Sao Paolo Metro.[41] Brazil ranks 96 out of 180 countries in the corruption perceptions index compiled by Transparency International.[42] Despite Brazilian laws put in place to thwart bribery and other unethical activities leading up to the 2016 Rio Olympic Games, government officials continued to face corruption charges months after the Games finished.[43]

Countries also differ widely in their beliefs about appropriate treatment for their employees. In general, the poorer a country is, the more likely employees are to be treated with little regard. One issue of concern is how an organization uses the resources of another country. The accompanying "Ethics in Action" feature discusses how the jewelry company Tiffany works to be ethical in its sourcing.

ETHICS IN ACTION

Sourcing Diamonds Responsibly

Tiffany & Co., a U.S. multinational luxury jewelry and specialty retailer, is committed to "sourcing high-quality diamonds with complete integrity." On its website the company recognizes the challenges of living up to that commitment. According to the company, the biggest concern is the impact of large, industrial-scale mining activities. These concerns include air, water, and soil contamination; the destruction of cultural sites; and human rights abuses.[44]

To address these concerns, the company, along with the Jewelers of America and other organizations, founded the Initiative for Responsible Mining Assurance (IRMA) to help ensure that ethical mining practices are followed. IRMA created a certification system for environmentally and socially responsible mining, which took effect in 2015. The vision statement of IRMA calls for practices that "respect human rights and aspirations of affected communities, provide safe, healthy and respectful workplaces, avoid or minimize harm to the environment and leave positive legacies." IRMA believes that most negative social and environmental impacts can be avoided if responsible mining practices are followed. These practices include careful choice of mine location to preserve ecologically and culturally significant areas, reduction of environmental impact from habitat loss and pollution, informed consent of indigenous peoples for mining, health and safety provisions, and transparency in revenue and corporate governance.[45]

In other ethical sourcing efforts, Tiffany & Co. purchases diamonds only from countries that use the Kimberley Process Certification Scheme (KPCS). This process was established by a United Nations General Assembly Resolution to stop the smuggling of "conflict diamonds" or diamonds that are sold to support violence, war efforts, or other malevolent activities. While the company believes the Kimberley Process has made a difference, it would like to see the definition of "conflict diamonds" expanded to include diamond-related human rights abuses.[46]

Michael J. Kowalski, Tiffany's chairman, reiterates the firm's commitment to social and environmental responsibility: "While we certainly have a deep moral commitment to act responsibly—a commitment which emanates not just from myself or the senior management group but from all our Tiffany colleagues around the world—we also believe we have a business imperative to act responsibly."[47]

Occupational Ethics

occupational ethics Standards that govern how members of a profession, trade, or craft should conduct themselves when performing work-related activities.

Occupational ethics are standards that govern how members of a profession, trade, or craft should conduct themselves when performing work-related activities.[48] For example, medical ethics govern how doctors and nurses should treat their patients. Doctors are expected to perform only necessary medical procedures and to act in the patient's interest, not their own self-interest. The ethics of scientific research require that scientists conduct their experiments and present their findings in ways that ensure the validity of their conclusions. Like society at large, most professional groups can impose punishments for violations of ethical standards.[49] Doctors and lawyers can be prevented from practicing their professions if they disregard professional ethics and put their own interests first.

Within an organization, occupational rules and norms often govern how employees such as lawyers, researchers, and accountants should make decisions to further stakeholder interests. Employees internalize the rules and norms of their occupational group (just as they do those of society) and often follow them automatically when deciding how to behave. Because most people tend to follow established rules of behavior, people frequently take ethics for granted. However, when occupational ethics are violated, such as when engineers alter software to disguise the harmful effects of products, ethical issues come to the forefront. For example, in 2017 Volkswagen was ordered to pay a $2.8 billion criminal penalty for its diesel emission scandal in which the company was caught rigging some of its diesel engines to pass U.S. emissions tests. As part of its settlement with the U.S. Justice Department, Volkswagen incurred costs of more than $30 billion, a figure that included the price of buying back nearly 500,000 diesel vehicles sold in the United States. In addition, seven current and former Volkswagen employees have been charged with crimes connected with the scandal. To date, this is the largest fine ever handed out to any automaker.[50] Table 4.2 lists some failures or lapses in professional ethics according to the type of functional manager.

Individual Ethics

individual ethics Personal standards and values that determine how people view their responsibilities to others and how they should act in situations when their own self-interests are at stake.

Individual ethics are personal standards and values that determine how people view their responsibilities to other people and groups and, thus, how they should act in situations when their own self-interests are at stake.[51] Sources of individual ethics include the influence of one's family, peers, and upbringing in general. The experiences gained over a lifetime—through membership in social institutions such as schools and religions, for example—also contribute to the development of the personal standards and values that a person uses to evaluate a situation and decide what is the morally right or wrong way to behave. However, suppose you are the son or daughter of a mobster, and your upbringing and education take place in an organized crime context; this affects how you evaluate a situation. You may come to believe that it is ethical to do anything and perform any act, up to and including murder, if it benefits your family or friends. These are your ethics. They are obviously not the ethics of the wider society and, so, are subject to sanction. In a similar way, managers and employees in an organization may come to believe that actions they take to promote or protect their organization are more important than any harm these actions may cause other stakeholders. So they behave unethically or illegally, and when this is discovered, they could be sanctioned.

Recently a federal class-action lawsuit was filed in New York against Uber in which UberX customers accused the ride-sharing company of charging them based on different less-efficient

Table 4.2

Some Failures in Professional Ethics

For manufacturing and materials management managers:
- Releasing products that are not of a consistent quality because of defective inputs
- Producing product batches that may be dangerous or defective and harm customers
- Compromising workplace health and safety to reduce costs (for example, to maximize output, employees are not given adequate training to maintain and service machinery and equipment)

For sales and marketing managers:
- Knowingly making unsubstantiated product claims
- Engaging in sales campaigns that use covert persuasive or subliminal advertising to create customer need for the product
- Marketing to target groups such as the elderly, minorities, or children to build demand for a product
- Sponsoring ongoing campaigns of unsolicited junk mail, spam, door-to-door, or telephone selling

For accounting and finance managers:
- Engaging in misleading financial analysis involving creative accounting or "cooking the books" to hide salient facts
- Authorizing excessive expenses and perks to managers, customers, and suppliers
- Hiding the level and amount of top management and director compensation

For human resource managers:
- Failing to act fairly, objectively, and in a consistent manner toward different employees or kinds of employees because of personal factors such as personality and beliefs
- Excessively encroaching on employee privacy through non-job-related surveillance or personality, ability, and drug testing
- Failing to respond to employee observations and concerns surrounding health and safety violations, hostile workplace issues, or inappropriate or even illegal behavior by managers or employees

routes than the ones it's basing driver pay on—resulting in higher fares for riders. The lawsuit pertains to Uber's "upfront" pricing model, which offers drivers a guaranteed rate based on miles and minutes driven. The complaint alleges Uber intentionally designed the pricing software to use a longer, less-efficient route than the route the company uses to populate the driver's Uber app, which charges the rider a higher fare and pays the driver a lower fare, when the two should be the same. According to the complaint, Uber is pocketing an additional $7.43 million per month due to the upfront pricing model. A similar lawsuit was filed on behalf of Uber drivers in California, which alleges drivers are being shortchanged. As of this writing, the lawsuits are still pending.[52]

In general, many decisions or behaviors that one person finds unethical, such as using animals for cosmetics testing, may be acceptable to another person. If decisions or behaviors are not illegal, individuals may agree to disagree about their ethical beliefs, or they may try to impose their own beliefs on other people and make those ethical beliefs the law. In all cases, however, people should develop and follow the ethical criteria described earlier to balance their self-interests against those of others when determining how they should behave in a particular situation.

Organizational Ethics

organizational ethics The guiding practices and beliefs through which a particular company and its managers view their responsibility toward their stakeholders.

Organizational ethics are the guiding practices and beliefs through which a particular company and its managers view their responsibility toward their stakeholders. The individual ethics of a company's founders and top managers are especially important in shaping the organization's code of ethics. Organizations whose founders had a vital role in creating a highly ethical code of organizational behavior include UPS, Procter & Gamble, Johnson & Johnson, and the Prudential Insurance Company. Johnson & Johnson's code of ethics—its credo—reflects a well-developed concern for its stakeholders (see Figure 4.5). Company credos, such as that of Johnson & Johnson, are meant to deter self-interested, unethical behavior; to demonstrate to managers and employees that a company will not tolerate people who, because of their own poor ethics, put their personal interests above the interests of other organizational stakeholders

Figure 4.5
Johnson & Johnson's Credo

Our Credo

We believe our first responsibility is to the doctors, nurses and patients, to mothers and fathers and all others who use our products and services. In meeting their needs everything we do must be of high quality. We must constantly strive to reduce our costs in order to maintain reasonable prices. Customers' orders must be serviced promptly and accurately. Our suppliers and distributors must have an opportunity to make a fair profit.

We are responsible to our employees, the men and women who work with us throughout the world. Everyone must be considered as an individual. We must respect their dignity and recognize their merit. They must have a sense of security in their jobs. Compensation must be fair and adequate, and working conditions clean, orderly and safe. We must be mindful of ways to help our employees fulfill their family responsibilities. Employees must feel free to make suggestions and complaints. There must be equal opportunity for employment, development and advancement for those qualified. We must provide competent management, and their actions must be just and ethical.

We are responsible to the communities in which we live and work and to the world community as well. We must be good citizens — support good works and charities and bear our fair share of taxes. We must encourage civic improvements and better health and education. We must maintain in good order the property we are privileged to use, protecting the environment and natural resources.

Our final responsibility is to our stockholders. Business must make a sound profit. We must experiment with new ideas. Research must be carried on, innovative programs developed and mistakes paid for. New equipment must be purchased, new facilities provided and new products launched. Reserves must be created to provide for adverse times. When we operate according to these principles, the stockholders should realize a fair return.

Johnson & Johnson

Source: ©Johnson & Johnson. Used with permission.

and ignore the harm they are inflicting on others; and to demonstrate that those who act unethically will be punished.

Managers or workers may behave unethically if they feel pressured to do so by the situation they are in and by unethical top managers. People typically confront ethical issues when weighing their personal interests against the effects of their actions on others. Suppose a manager knows that promotion to vice president is likely if she can secure a $100 million contract, but getting the contract requires bribing the contract giver with $1 million. The manager reasons that performing this act will ensure her career and future, and what harm would it do, anyway? Bribery is common and she knows that, even if she decides not to pay the bribe, someone else surely will. So what to do? Research seems to suggest that people who realize they have the most at stake in a career sense or a monetary sense are the ones most likely to act unethically.

And it is exactly in this situation that a strong code of organizational ethics can help people behave in the right or appropriate way. *The New York Times* detailed code of ethics, for example, was crafted by its editors to ensure the integrity and honesty of its journalists as they report sensitive information.

If a company's top managers consistently endorse the ethical principles in its corporate credo, they can prevent employees from going astray. Managers should model the behavior expected from their employees, as well as educate employees in the ethical behavior the organization expects. The "Ethics in Action" feature describes how management consulting firm Accenture helps employees apply its code of ethical conduct. Employees are much more likely to act unethically when a credo does not exist or is disregarded. Arthur Andersen, for example, did not follow its credo at all; its unscrupulous partners ordered middle managers to shred records that showed evidence of their wrongdoing. Although the middle managers knew this was wrong, they followed the orders because they responded to the personal power and status of the partners and not the company's code of ethics. They were afraid they would lose their jobs if they did not behave unethically, but their actions cost them their jobs anyway.

ETHICS IN ACTION

Chatbot Provides Ethical Guidance

Ethical, responsible employee conduct is a critical objective for Accenture, because a consulting firm relies on its reputation to open clients' doors. Furthermore, with 425,000 employees in more than 120 countries, Accenture must guide employees representing diverse cultures and languages.[53] The firm posted its code of ethics online and provided training programs. But the code runs to more than 50 pages, addressing values (respect, professionalism, nondiscrimination, and integrity), the importance of clients' best interests, social responsibility, and more.[54] Accenture's managers realized that asking employees to search through this document was no longer meeting the standards of how people get information today. As the firm is advising clients to do in other areas of business, Accenture wanted to create a way to interact with the information easily and naturally on computers and mobile devices. So Accenture developed a chatbot.

A chatbot combines a database with natural-language processing and artificial intelligence (AI).[55] Users text their questions, and the natural-language processing interprets the question to deliver a relevant answer from the database. The AI component helps the system improve the answers through experience with users. The use of chatbots is increasing as organizations realize that today's customers and employees prefer to share information by texting. With Accenture's chatbot, called COBE (for code of business ethics), the database is the code of conduct, and employees text questions about applying its contents.

To develop the COBE chatbot, Accenture turned to its digital-marketing service group, which had been developing chatbots for clients to use in improving customer service.[56] The team applied the technology to Accenture's own employees, treating them as the customers. They created a chatbot for employees only, keeping queries anonymous and offering options to converse in several languages and with accommodations for visual impairments. The effort was part of a larger overhaul of the code of business ethics, modernizing the content to address issues such as the use of social media and artificial intelligence.

The introduction of COBE has increased employees' use of the company's code of conduct. According to Chad Jerdee, Accenture's chief compliance officer, each week, 20 times as many employees look up information on the website now that they can text a question rather than clicking through a lengthy document.[57] Jerdee considers this visible commitment to ethical, responsible conduct as particularly appealing to the kinds of people Accenture recruits as employees.

Top managers play a crucial role in determining a company's ethics. It is clearly important, then, that when making appointment decisions, the board of directors should scrutinize the reputations and ethical records of top managers. It is the responsibility of the board to decide whether a prospective CEO has the maturity, experience, and integrity needed to head a company and be entrusted with the capital and wealth of the organization, on which the fate of all its stakeholders depends. Clearly, a track record of success is not enough to decide whether a top manager is capable of moral decision making; a manager might have achieved this success through unethical or illegal means. It is important to investigate prospective top managers and examine their credentials. Although the best predictor of future behavior is often past behavior, the board of directors needs to be on guard against unprincipled executives who use unethical means to rise to the top of the organizational hierarchy. For this reason it is necessary that a company's directors continuously monitor the behavior of top executives. In the 2000s this increased scrutiny led to the dismissal of many top executives for breaking ethical rules concerning issues such as excessive personal loans, stock options, inflated expense accounts, and even sexual misconduct.

Approaches to Social Responsibility

LO4-6 Distinguish among the four main approaches toward social responsibility that a company can take.

social responsibility The way a company's managers and employees view their duty or obligation to make decisions that protect, enhance, and promote the welfare and well-being of stakeholders and society as a whole.

A company's ethics are the result of differences in societal, organizational, occupational, and individual ethics. In turn, a company's ethics determine its stance on social responsibility. A company's stance on **social responsibility** is the way its managers and employees view their duty or obligation to make decisions that protect, enhance, and promote the welfare and well-being of stakeholders and society as a whole. As we noted earlier, when no laws specify how a company should act toward stakeholders, managers must decide the right, ethical, and socially responsible thing to do. Differences in business ethics can lead companies to diverse positions or views on their responsibility toward stakeholders.

Many kinds of decisions signal a company's beliefs about its obligations to make socially responsible business decisions (see Table 4.3). The decision to spend money on training and educating employees—investing in them—is one such decision, so is the decision to minimize or avoid layoffs whenever possible. The decision to act promptly and warn customers when a batch of defective merchandise has been accidentally sold is another one. Companies that try to hide such problems show little regard for social responsibility. In the past both GM and Ford tried to hide the fact that several of their vehicles had defects that made them dangerous to drive; the companies were penalized with hundreds of millions of dollars in damages for their unethical behavior, and today they move more quickly to recall vehicles to fix problems. Several years ago, General Motors CEO Mary Barra admitted that the automaker did not react fast enough when fault was found with an ignition switch that triggered the recall of eventually more than 10 million cars worldwide.[58] On the other side, Fitbit voluntarily recalled its activity

Table 4.3

Forms of Socially Responsible Behavior

Managers are being socially responsible and showing their support for their stakeholders when they
- Provide severance payments to help laid-off workers make ends meet until they can find another job.
- Give workers opportunities to enhance their skills and acquire additional education so they can remain productive and do not become obsolete because of changes in technology.
- Allow employees to take time off when they need to and provide health care and pension benefits for employees.
- Contribute to charities or support various civic-minded activities in the cities or towns in which they are located (Target and Levi Strauss both contribute 5% of their profits to support schools, charities, the arts, and other good works).
- Decide to keep open a factory whose closure would devastate the local community.
- Decide to keep a company's operations in the United States to protect the jobs of American workers rather than move abroad.
- Decide to spend money to improve a new factory so it will not pollute the environment.
- Decline to invest in countries that have poor human rights records.
- Choose to help poor countries develop an economic base to improve living standards.

tracking wrist band, the Fitbit Force, due to skin rash issues. The company offered to send consumers a return kit and promised a reimbursement check or exchange within two to six weeks of receipt.[59] The way a company announces business problems or admits its mistakes provides strong clues about its stance on social responsibility.

Four Different Approaches

obstructionist approach
Companies and their managers choose *not* to behave in a socially responsible way and instead behave unethically and illegally.

The strength of companies' commitment to social responsibility can range from low to high (see Figure 4.6). At the low end of the range is an obstructionist approach, in which companies and their managers choose *not* to behave in a socially responsible way. Instead they behave unethically and often illegally and do all they can to prevent knowledge of their behavior from reaching other organizational stakeholders and society at large. Managers at the Manville Corporation adopted this approach when they sought to hide evidence that asbestos causes lung damage; so, too, did tobacco companies when they sought to hide evidence that cigarette smoking causes lung cancer. In 2010 it was revealed that the managers of Lehman Brothers, whose bankruptcy helped propel the 2008–2009 financial crisis, used loopholes in U.K. law to hide billions of dollars of worthless assets on its balance sheet to disguise its poor financial condition.

Top managers at Enron also acted in an obstructionist way when they prevented employees from selling Enron shares in their pension funds while they sold hundreds of millions of dollars' worth of their own Enron stock. Most employees lost all their retirement savings. Senior partners at Arthur Andersen who instructed their subordinates to shred files chose an obstructionist approach that caused not only a loss of reputation but devastation for the organization and for all stakeholders involved. These companies are no longer in business.

defensive approach
Companies and their managers behave ethically to the degree that they stay within the law and strictly abide by legal requirements.

A defensive approach indicates at least some commitment to ethical behavior. Defensive companies and managers stay within the law and abide strictly by legal requirements but make no attempt to exercise social responsibility beyond what the law dictates; thus, they can and often do act unethically. These are the kinds of companies, like Computer Associates, World-Com, and Merrill Lynch, that gave their managers large stock options and bonuses even as company performance was declining rapidly. The managers are the kind who sell their stock in advance of other stockholders because they know their company's performance is about to fall. Although acting on inside information is illegal, it is often hard to prove because top managers have wide latitude regarding when they sell their shares. The founders of most dot-com companies took advantage of this legal loophole to sell billions of dollars of their dot-com shares before their stock prices collapsed. When making ethical decisions, such managers put their own interests first and commonly harm other stakeholders.

accommodative approach
Companies and their managers behave legally and ethically and try to balance the interests of different stakeholders as the need arises.

An accommodative approach acknowledges the need to support social responsibility. Accommodative companies and managers agree that organizational members ought to behave legally and ethically, and they try to balance the interests of different stakeholders so the claims of stockholders are seen in relation to the claims of other stakeholders. Managers adopting this approach want to make choices that are reasonable in the eyes of society and want to do the right thing.

This approach is the one taken by the typical large U.S. company, which has the most to lose from unethical or illegal behavior. Generally, the older and more reputable a company, the more likely its managers are to curb attempts by their subordinates to act unethically. Large companies, like GM, Intel, DuPont, and Dell, seek every way to build their companies' competitive advantage. Nevertheless, they rein in attempts by their managers to behave unethically or illegally, knowing the grave consequences such behavior can have on future profitability.

Figure 4.6
Four Approaches to Social Responsibility

Sometimes they fail, however, such as in 2013 when SAC Capital Advisors (among others) agreed to pay $1.8 billion and plead guilty to criminal insider trading charges. To date, this is the biggest insider trading settlement in history.[60]

proactive approach Companies and their managers actively embrace socially responsible behavior, going out of their way to learn about the needs of different stakeholder groups and using organizational resources to promote the interests of all stakeholders.

Companies and managers taking a **proactive approach** actively embrace the need to behave in socially responsible ways. They go out of their way to learn about the needs of different stakeholder groups and are willing to use organizational resources to promote the interests not only of stockholders, but also of the other stakeholders such as their employees and communities. U.S. steelmaker Nucor is one such company. In 1977 its visionary CEO Ken Iverson announced that throughout its history Nucor had never laid off one employee, and even though a major recession was raging, it did not plan to start now. In 2009 Nucor CEO Daniel R. DiMicco announced that Nucor again would not start layoffs despite the fact its steel mills were operating at only 50% of capacity (compared to 95% just months earlier) because customers had slashed orders due to the recession. While rivals laid off thousands of employees, Nucor remained loyal to its employees. However, even though there were no layoffs, both managers and employees took major cuts in pay and bonuses to weather the storm together, as they always had, and they searched for ways to reduce operating costs so they would all benefit when the economy recovered, and by 2012 their sacrifice had paid off: Nucor was doing well again. In 2018, Nucor paid out an increased cash dividend for the 45th year in a row.[61]

Proactive companies are often at the forefront of campaigns for causes such as a pollution-free environment; recycling and conservation of resources; the minimization or elimination of the use of animals in drug and cosmetics testing; and the reduction of crime, illiteracy, and poverty. For example, companies such as McDonald's, Google, REI, Whole Foods, and Target all have reputations for being proactive in the support of stakeholders such as their suppliers or the communities in which they operate. For a more detailed example of proactive companies in the fashion industry, see the "Managing Globally" feature.

MANAGING GLOBALLY

Protecting Home-Based Workers

Demand for handcrafted clothing is soaring. Especially when sourced from developing nations, these products deliver eye-catching beauty at low prices. With social media, sellers can attract attention to unique items from exotic locales. World trade in arts and crafts nearly doubled from 2002 to 2012, and almost 60% of production for the fashion industry is done by workers operating from home.[62] Most of them are women, and their pay, averaging $1.80 per day, is far below that of factory workers.

Home-based work is a complex economic sector. Workers are spread out in many locations and may be subcontractors of subcontractors, making the chain of responsibility difficult to follow.[63] Many labor part time, spending the rest of the day maintaining their home and caring for family members. This makes work more accessible to women dealing with physical dangers and gender-based role restrictions, but it obscures whether a daily pay rate translates to a fair hourly wage. Besides the impact on workers, there are environmental concerns. Apparel production is a high-polluting industry, for reasons including chemical use and the trend toward fast-changing, disposable fashions.[64]

Socially responsible clothing companies and retailers want to ensure that the workers who make their products are well treated, but monitoring home-based workers is difficult.[65] Businesses have tried applying their standards for factory work, but these typically are too rigid. With a factory, one visit may reveal working conditions and hours; with home-based work, every worker's home would require an inspection.

Nest, a nonprofit organization, is helping home-based artisans by partnering with them and fashion retailers to develop standards for protecting workers and providing them with fair compensation.
©Rodrigo Torres/Glow Images

Nest, a nonprofit organization, aims to help businesses overcome these hurdles. Nest is building a global network of artisans to explore the ethical challenges of home-based labor.[66] Nest also partnered with fashion retailers and producers, including Target, Patagonia, and Eileen Fisher, to develop standards for protecting workers and their communities in six areas: worker rights, transparent business records, child labor, fair compensation, worker health and safety, and environmental protection.[67] The Nest standards are flexible. Enforcement starts with training suppliers that use home-based workers and then lets them correct problems before undergoing an inspection. For example, Nest has designed low-cost methods to prevent water pollution. When sellers demonstrate that their production meets Nest standards, they can mark their goods with Nest's logo certifying compliance.

The businesses adopting Nest standards view them as a way to meet their goals for socially responsible conduct. The Nest logo informs customers that the sellers are socially responsible. And at prominent companies such as Target, managers also see a chance to be industry role models.[68]

Why Be Socially Responsible?

Several advantages result when companies and their managers behave in a socially responsible manner. First, demonstrating its social responsibility helps a company build a good reputation. Reputation is the trust, goodwill, and confidence others have in a company that lead them to want to do business with it. The rewards for a good company reputation are increased business and improved ability to obtain resources from stakeholders. Reputation thus can enhance profitability and build stockholder wealth, and behaving responsibly socially is the economically right thing to do because companies that do so benefit from increasing business and rising profits.

A second major reason for companies to act responsibly toward employees, customers, and society is that, in a capitalist system, companies as well as the government, have to bear the costs of protecting their stakeholders, providing health care and income, paying taxes, and so on. So if all companies in a society act responsibly, the quality of life as a whole increases.

Moreover, how companies behave toward their employees determines many of a society's values and norms and the ethics of its citizens, as already noted. It has been suggested that if all organizations adopted a caring approach and agreed that their responsibility is to promote the interests of their employees, a climate of caring would pervade the wider society. Experts point to Japan, Sweden, Germany, the Netherlands, and Switzerland as countries where organizations are highly socially responsible and where, as a result, crime, poverty, and unemployment rates are relatively low, literacy rates are relatively high, and sociocultural values promote harmony between different groups of people. Business activity affects all aspects of people's lives, so how business behaves toward stakeholders affects how stakeholders behave toward business. You "reap what you sow," as the adage goes.

The Role of Organizational Culture

Although an organization's code of ethics guides decision making when ethical questions arise, managers can go one step further by ensuring that important ethical values and norms are key features of an organization's culture. For example, Herb Kelleher and Coleen Barrett created Southwest Airlines's culture in which promoting employee well-being is a main company priority; this translates into organizational values and norms dictating that layoffs should be avoided and employees should share in the profits the company makes.[69] Google, UPS, and Toyota are among the many companies that espouse similar values. When ethical values and norms such as these are part of an organization's culture, they help organizational members resist self-interested action because they recognize that they are part of something bigger than themselves.[70]

Managers' roles in developing ethical values and standards in other employees are important. Employees naturally look to those in authority to provide leadership, just as a country's citizens look to its political leaders, and managers become ethical role models whose behavior is scrutinized by subordinates. If top managers are perceived as being self-interested and not ethical, their subordinates are not likely to behave in an ethical manner. Employees may think that if it's all right for a top manager to engage in dubious behavior, it's all right for them, too, and for employees this might mean slacking off, reducing customer support, and not taking supportive actions to help their company. The actions of top managers such as CEOs and the president of the United States are scrutinized so closely for ethical improprieties because their actions represent the values of their organizations and, in the case of the president, the values of the nation.

ethics ombudsperson A manager responsible for communicating and teaching ethical standards to all employees and monitoring their conformity to those standards.

Managers can also provide a visible means of support to develop an ethical culture. Increasingly, organizations are creating the role of ethics officer, or **ethics ombudsperson**, to monitor their ethical practices and procedures. The ethics ombudsperson is responsible for communicating ethical standards to all employees, designing systems to monitor employees' conformity to those standards, and teaching managers and employees at all levels of the organization how to respond to ethical dilemmas appropriately.[71] Because the ethics ombudsperson has organizationwide authority, organizational members in any department can communicate instances of unethical behavior by their managers or coworkers without fear of retribution. This arrangement makes it easier for everyone to behave ethically. In addition, ethics ombudspeople can provide guidance when organizational members are uncertain about whether an action is ethical. Some organizations have an organizationwide ethics committee to provide guidance on ethical issues and help write and update the company code of ethics.

Ethical organizational cultures encourage organizational members to behave in a socially responsible manner. As mentioned earlier in this chapter, one company epitomizing an ethical, socially responsible firm is Johnson & Johnson (J&J). The ethical values and norms in Johnson & Johnson's culture, along with its credo, have guided its managers to make the right decision in difficult situations for decades.

Summary and Review

THE NATURE OF ETHICS Ethical issues are central to how companies and their managers make decisions, and they affect not only the efficiency and effectiveness of company operations but also the prosperity of the nation. The result of ethical behavior is a general increase in company performance and in a nation's standard of living, well-being, and wealth.

LO4-1 An ethical dilemma is the quandary people find themselves in when they have to decide if they should act in a way that might help another person or group and is the right thing to do, even though it might go against their own self-interest. Ethics are the inner guiding moral principles, values, and beliefs that people use to analyze or interpret a situation and then decide what is the right or appropriate way to behave.

Ethical beliefs alter and change as time passes, and as they do so, laws change to reflect the changing ethical beliefs of a society.

LO4-2, 4-4 **STAKEHOLDERS AND ETHICS** Stakeholders are people and groups who have a claim on and a stake in a company. The main stakeholder groups are stockholders, managers, employees, suppliers and distributors, customers, and the community, society, and nation. Companies and their managers need to make ethical business decisions that promote the well-being of their stakeholders and avoid doing them harm.

LO4-3, 4-5 **ETHICS AND DECISION MAKING** To determine whether a business decision is ethical, managers can use four ethical rules to analyze it: the utilitarian, moral rights, justice, and practical rules. Managers should behave ethically because this avoids the tragedy of the commons and results in a general increase in efficiency, effectiveness, and company performance. The main determinants of differences in a manager's, company's, and country's business ethics are societal, occupational, individual, and organizational.

LO4-6 **ETHICS AND SOCIAL RESPONSIBILITY** A company's stance on social responsibility is the way its managers and employees view their duty or obligation to make decisions that protect, enhance, and promote the welfare and well-being of stakeholders and society as a whole. There are four main approaches to social responsibility: obstructionist, defensive, accommodative, and proactive. The rewards from behaving in a socially responsible way are a good reputation, the support of all organizational stakeholders, and thus superior company performance.

Management in Action

Topics for Discussion and Action

Discussion

1. What is the relationship between ethics and the law? [**LO4-1**]

2. Why do the claims and interests of stakeholders sometimes conflict? [**LO4-2**]

3. Why should managers use ethical criteria to guide their decision making? [**LO4-3**]

4. As an employee of a company, what are some of the most unethical business practices that you have encountered in its dealings with stakeholders? [**LO4-4**]

5. What are the main determinants of business ethics? [**LO4-5**]

Action

6. Find a manager and ask about the most important ethical rules he or she uses to make the right decisions. [**LO4-3**]

7. Find an example of (a) a company that has an obstructionist approach to social responsibility and (b) one that has an accommodative approach. [**LO4-6**]

Building Management Skills

Dealing with Ethical Dilemmas [LO4-1, 4-4]

Use the chapter material to decide how you, as a manager, should respond to each of the following ethical dilemmas:

1. You are planning to leave your job to go work for a competitor; your boss invites you to an important meeting where you will learn about new products your company will be bringing out next year. Do you go to the meeting? Explain your reasoning.

2. You're the manager of sales in an expensive sports car dealership. A young executive who has just received a promotion comes in and wants to buy a car that you know is out of her price range. Do you encourage the executive to buy it so you can receive a big commission on the sale or do you persuade her to buy a less-expensive model?

3. You sign a contract to manage a young rock band, and that group agrees to let you produce their next five records, for which they will receive royalties of 5%. Their first record is a smash hit and sells millions. Do you increase their royalty rate on future records? Why or why not?

Managing Ethically [LO4-3, 4-5]

Apple Juice or Sugar Water?

In the early 1980s Beech-Nut, a maker of baby foods, was in grave financial trouble as it tried to compete with Gerber Products, the market leader. Threatened with bankruptcy if it could not lower its operating costs, Beech-Nut entered an agreement with a low-cost supplier of apple juice concentrate. The agreement would save the company over $250,000 annually when every dollar counted. Soon one of Beech-Nut's food scientists became concerned about the quality of the concentrate. He believed it was not made from apples alone but contained large quantities of corn syrup and cane sugar.

He brought this information to the attention of top managers at Beech-Nut, but they were obsessed with the need to keep costs down and chose to ignore his concerns. The company continued to produce and sell its product as pure apple juice.[72]

Eventually, investigators from the U.S. Food and Drug Administration (FDA) confronted Beech-Nut with evidence that the concentrate was adulterated. The top managers issued denials and quickly shipped the remaining stock of apple juice to the market before their inventory could be seized. The scientist who had questioned the purity of the apple juice had resigned from Beech-Nut, but he decided to blow the whistle on the company. He told the FDA that

Beech-Nut's top management had known of the problem with the concentrate and had acted to maximize company profits rather than to inform customers about the additives in the apple juice. In 1987 the company pleaded guilty to charges that it had deliberately sold adulterated juice and was fined over $2 million. Its top managers were also found guilty and were sentenced to prison terms. The company's reputation was ruined, and it was eventually sold to Ralston Purina, which installed a new management team and a new ethical code of values to guide future business decisions.

Questions

1. Why is it that an organization's values and norms can become too strong and lead to unethical behavior?

2. What steps can a company take to prevent this problem—to stop its values and norms from becoming so inwardly focused that managers and employees lose sight of their responsibility to their stakeholders?

Small Group Breakout Exercise

Is Chewing Gum the "Right" Thing to Do? [LO4-1, 4-3]

Form groups of three or four people, and appoint one member as the spokesperson who will communicate your findings to the class when called on by the instructor. Then discuss the following scenario:

In the United States, the right to chew gum is taken for granted. Although it is often against the rules to chew gum in a classroom, church, and so on, it is legal to do so on the street. If you possess or chew gum on a street in Singapore, you can be arrested. Chewing gum has been made illegal in Singapore because those in power believe it creates a mess on pavements and feel that people cannot be trusted to dispose of their gum properly and, thus, should have no right to use it.

1. What makes chewing gum acceptable in the United States but unacceptable in Singapore?

2. Why can you chew gum on the street but not in a church?

3. How can you use ethical principles to decide when gum chewing is ethical or unethical and if and when it should be made illegal?

Be the Manager [LO4-3]

Creating an Ethical Code

You are an entrepreneur who has decided to go into business and open a steak and chicken restaurant. Your business plan requires that you hire at least 20 people as chefs, waiters, and so on. As the owner, you are drawing up a list of ethical principles that each of these people will receive and must agree to when he or she accepts a job

offer. These principles outline your view of what is right or acceptable behavior and what will be expected both from you and from your employees.

Create a list of the five main ethical rules or principles you will use to govern how your business operates. Be sure to spell out how these principles relate to your stakeholders; for example, state the rules you intend to follow in dealing with your employees and customers.

Bloomberg Businessweek Case in the News

The Greening of Throwaway Stuff [LO 4-2, 4-6]

In a factory the size of an airport terminal, laser cutters zip across long sheets of cotton, slicing out sleeves for Zara jackets. Until last year, the scraps that spill out into wire baskets were repurposed into stuffing for furniture or hauled off to a landfill near

the plant in the northern Spanish town of Arteixo. Now they're chemically reduced to cellulose, which is mixed with wood fibers and spun into a textile called Refibra that's used in more than a dozen items such as T-shirts, trousers, and tops.

The initiative by Inditex SA, the company that owns Zara and seven other brands, highlights a shift in an industry known for churning out supercheap stuff that fills closets for just a few months before being tossed into the used-clothing bin. Gap Inc. promises that by 2021 it will take cotton only from organic farms or other producers it deems sustainable. Japan's Fast Retailing Co., owner of Uniqlo Co., is experimenting with lasers to create distressed jeans using less water and chemicals. And Swedish retail giant Hennes & Mauritz AB is funding startups developing recycling technologies and fabrics made from unconventional materials such as mushroom roots. "One of the biggest challenges is how to continue to provide fashion for a growing population while improving the impact on the environment," says Karl-Johan Persson, chief executive officer of H&M. "We need to speed the shift toward waste-free models."

The $3 trillion fashion industry consumes vast amounts of cotton, water, and power to make 100 billion accessories and garments annually—three-fifths of which are thrown away within a year, according to McKinsey & Co. And less than 1% of that is recycled into new clothes, says Rob Opsomer, a researcher at the Ellen MacArthur Foundation, an environmental research group in England. "The equivalent of a dump truck filled with textiles gets landfilled or incinerated every single second," he says.

Inditex in 2016 made 1.4 billion garments, a scale that's helped its stock price almost quintuple over the past decade. But the industry's growth is slowing as millennials increasingly understand fast fashion's impact on the environment and exhibit a preference for spending on experiences rather than goods. Inditex and H&M have missed analysts' revenue expectations in recent quarters, and shares in both companies have lost about a third of their value since last summer. "Their business model is fundamentally unsustainable," says Edwin Keh, CEO of the Hong Kong Research Institute of Textiles and Apparel. "We all have enough stuff."

That creates an opening for companies to use sustainability to differentiate their brands. With growing concern over the waste, retailers have placed recycling bins prominently in many stores. Highlighting such initiatives in tandem with efforts to use greener materials can help win customers, says Jill Standish, a retailing consultant at Accenture Plc. A "bag that's made with grapes or a dress made of orange peels tells a story," she says.

To tap into this trend, H&M is seeking to make all its products from recycled and sustainable materials by 2030, up from 35% today. Since 2015 it's sponsored an annual contest in which startups developing technologies to make fashion greener compete for a piece of a €1 million ($1.2 million) grant. One of this year's five winners was Smart Stitch, a company that's developed a thread that dissolves at high temperatures, which could simplify recycling by making it easier to remove zippers and buttons. Another is Crop-A-Porter, which spins yarn out of field waste from flax, banana, and pineapple plantations. A third is working on separating fibers from blended fabrics, and others make textiles from mushrooms and algae. If any of those initiatives "succeed at a commercial scale, it would be pretty disruptive," says Vikram Widge, head of climate policy at International Finance Corp. and a former judge for H&M's competition. "Anything anyone can do is critical."

Inditex last winter started disassembling old clothing to spin into yarns for fashions it markets as "garments with a past." The company has grouped many of its sustainability efforts—clothes made from organic cotton, Refibra, and other repurposed fabrics—into a sub-brand called Join Life. While the line grew 50% last year, it still accounts for fewer than 1 in 10 garments Inditex sells. To boost the share of greener textiles in its mix, the company is funding research programs at the Massachusetts Institute of Technology and universities in Spain. One initiative is seeking to use 3D printing to make textiles using byproducts from timber operations. Another is looking for ways to separate cotton from polyester in blended fabrics. "We're trying to find a more sustainable version of all materials," says Germán García Ibáñez, who manages Inditex's push to reuse old clothing and textiles. Today's recycled jeans, he says, are typically only about 15% repurposed cotton, because the fiber "gets worn down and we have to mix with new."

Inditex and H&M say that for now they're absorbing the extra costs of using recycled or reconstituted textiles. The Join Life line is priced competitively with other items in Zara stores, with T-shirts going for less than $10 and some jeans under $40. H&M likewise says it plans to keep a lid on prices of its greener materials, expecting the cost to fall as production increases. "We take it as a long-term investment instead of charging it to our customers," says Anna Gedda, who oversees H&M's efforts to clean up its operations. "We believe sustainable fashion should be affordable for all."

Questions for Discussion

1. Which stakeholders benefit from companies' efforts to recycle clothing components? Which stakeholders lose as a result of this business strategy?

2. Do you think setting up recycling bins in retail stores encourages consumers to buy more items? Explain your reasoning.

3. Which approach to social responsibility do Inditex and other companies demonstrate when recycling/re-using clothing materials?

Source: Anna Hirtenstein, "The Greening of Throwaway Stuff," *Bloomberg Businessweek*, May 7, 2018, pp. 19–20. Used with permission of Bloomberg L.P. Copyright © 2017. All rights reserved.

Notes

1. Julian Turner, "Building Resilient US Grids after Maria, Harvey and Irma," *Power Technology,* www.power-technology.com, January 16, 2018; Brian Fung, "Tesla's Enormous Battery in Australia, Just Weeks Old, Is Already Responding to Outages in 'Record' Time," *The Washington Post,* https://www.washingtonpost.com, December 26, 2017.

2. "Tesla Solar Power Arrives in Puerto Rico," *BBC,* www.bbc.com, October 25, 2017.

3. Turner, "Building Resilient US Grids"; Adele Peters, "Can Puerto Rico Be the Model for a Renewables-Powered Energy System?" *Fast Company,* www.fastcompany.com, November 7, 2017.

4. Turner, "Building Resilient US Grids."

5. "Elon Musk," *Biography.com,* A&E Television Networks, www.biography.com, accessed January 23, 2018.

6. Turner, "Building Resilient US Grids."

7. T. Mann, "What Causes an Ethical Dilemma in Conducting Business?" *Houston Chronicle,* http://smallbusiness.chron.com, accessed March 8, 2018.

8. A. Smith, "The U.S. Legal Marijuana Industry Is Booming," *CNN Money,* http://money.cnn.com, January 31, 2018.

9. E. Levenson and J. Sterling, "These Are the Victims of the Florida School Shooting," *CNN,* www.cnn.com, February 21, 2018.

10. "March for Our Lives," https://marchforourlives.com, accessed March 9, 2018; M. Sheeran, "NRA Losing Corporate Ties Amid Calls for Boycott in Wake of Parkland Shooting," *ABC News,* http://abcnews.go.com, February 27, 2018.

11. R.E. Freeman, *Strategic Management: A Stakeholder Approach* (Marshfield, MA: Pitman, 1984).

12. K. Gilchrist, "Bill Gates Makes $4.6 Billion Pledge, His Largest Since 2000," *CNBC,* www.cnbc.com, August 16, 2017.

13. J.A. Pearce, "The Company Mission as a Strategic Tool," *Sloan Management Review,* Spring 1982, 15–24.

14. C. Ingraham, "Nobody Knows How Many Members the NRA Has, But Its Tax Returns Offer Some Clues," *The Washington Post,* www.washingtonpost.com, February 26, 2018.

15. C.I. Barnard, *The Functions of the Executive* (Cambridge, MA: Harvard University Press, 1948).

16. Freeman, *Strategic Management.*

17. "AT&T to Cut About 4,600 Jobs," *ABC News,* http://abcnews.go.com, accessed March 8, 2018.

18. Reuters, "US Regulators Are Examining Wall Street's 'Volcker Rule' Wish List: Sources," *CNBC,* www.cnbc.com, February 28, 2018.

19. "Equilar/Associated Press CEO Pay Study 2017," www.equilar.com, accessed March 8, 2018; G. Donnelley, "Top CEOs Make More in Two Days Than an Average Employee Does in One Year," *Fortune,* http://fortune.com, July 20, 2017.

20. S. Clifford, "How Companies Actually Decide What to Pay CEOs," *The Atlantic,* www.theatlantic.com, June 14, 2017.

21. J. Novak, "How Tax Reform Will End the Nonprofit Executive Pay Scam," *CNBC,* www.cnbc.com, December 20, 2017.

22. L. DePillis, "Tax Bill Makes Nonprofits Pay Up for Millionaire Execs," *CNN Money,* http://money.cnn.com, December 20, 2017.

23. "Humans Have Made 8.3 Billion Tons of Plastic. Where Does It All Go? *PBS News Hour,* www.pbs.org, July 19, 2017.

24. N. Kounang, "Dangerous Chemicals Hiding in Everyday Products," *CNN,* www.cnn.com, July 1, 2016.

25. "The Soap Dispensary & Kitchen Staples," www.thesoapdispensary.com, accessed March 8, 2018; "Refill Stores Keep Opening Around the World," www.fillgood.co, February 15, 2018.

26. "Vancouver's First Zero-Waste Grocery Store Open for Business," *CBC News,* www.cbc.ca, November 25, 2017.

27. T.L. Beauchamp and N.E. Bowie, eds., *Ethical Theory and Business* (Englewood Cliffs, NJ: Prentice-Hall, 1929); A. MacIntyre, *After Virtue* (South Bend, IN: University of Notre Dame Press, 1981).

28. R.E. Goodin, "How to Determine Who Should Get What," *Ethics,* July 1975, 310–21.

29. T.M. Jones, "Ethical Decision Making by Individuals in Organization: An Issue Contingent Model," *Academy of Management Journal* 16 (1991), 366–95; G.F. Cavanaugh, D.J. Moberg, and M. Velasquez, "The Ethics of Organizational Politics," *Academy of Management Review* 6 (1981), 363–74.

30. T.M. Jones, "Instrumental Stakeholder Theory: A Synthesis of Ethics and Economics," *Academy of Management Review* 20 (1995), 404–37.

31. B. Victor and J.B. Cullen, "The Organizational Bases of Ethical Work Climates," *Administrative Science Quarterly* 33 (1988), 101–25.

32. D. Collins, "Organizational Harm, Legal Consequences and Stakeholder Retaliation," *Journal of Business Ethics* 8 (1988), 1–13.

33. R.C. Solomon, *Ethics and Excellence* (New York: Oxford University Press, 1992).

34. T.E. Becker, "Integrity in Organizations: Beyond Honesty and Conscientiousness," *Academy of Management Review* 23 (January 1998), 154–62.

35. S.W. Gellerman, "Why Good Managers Make Bad Decisions," in K.R. Andrews, ed., *Ethics in Practice: Managing the Moral Corporation* (Boston: Harvard Business School Press, 1989).

36. J. Dobson, "Corporate Reputation: A Free Market Solution to Unethical Behavior," *Business and Society* 28 (1989), 1–5.

37. M.S. Baucus and J.P. Near, "Can Illegal Corporate Behavior Be Predicted? An Event History Analysis," *Academy of Management Journal* 34 (1991), 9–36.

38. L.K. Trevino, "Ethical Decision Making in Organizations: A Person–Situation Interactionist Model," *Academy of Management Review* 11, no. 3 (1986), 601–17.

39. "The World's Most Ethical Companies 2018 Honorees," Ethisphere Institute, https://www.worldsmostethicalcompanies.com, accessed March 9, 2018.

40. A.S. Waterman, "On the Uses of Psychological Theory and Research in the Process of Ethical Inquiry," *Psychological Bulletin* 103, no. 3 (1988), 283–98.

41. "Siemens, Brazilian Prosecutors Eyeing Settlement over Bribery Lawsuit: Newspaper," *Reuters,* www.reuters.com, December 4, 2017.

42. "2017 Corruption by Country/Territory: Brazil," Transparency International, www.transparency.org, accessed March 9, 2018.

43. J. Chade, "Stadium Deals, Corruption and Bribery: The Questions at the Heart of Brazil's Olympic and World Cup 'Miracle,'" *The Guardian,* www.theguardian.com, April 23, 2017.

44. "Responsible Mining and Tiffany Diamonds," www.tiffany.com, accessed March 9, 2018.

45. "About IRMA," www.responsiblemining.net, accessed March 9, 2018.

46. "About KP Basics," www.kimberleyprocess.com, accessed March 9, 2018.

47. P. Kanani, "CEO of Tiffany & Co. on Ethical Sourcing, Responsible Mining, and Leadership," *Forbes,* www.forbes.com, accessed March 9, 2018; W. Gabriel, "The Iconic Tiffany Blue Goes Green," *Recycle Nation,* http://recyclenation.com, October 5, 2017.

48. M.S. Frankel, "Professional Codes: Why, How, and with What Impact?" *Ethics* 8 (1989), 109–15.

49. J. Van Maanen and S.R. Barley, "Occupational Communities: Culture and Control in Organizations," in B. Staw and L. Cummings, eds., *Research in Organizational Behavior,* vol. 6 (Greenwich, CT: JAI Press, 1984), 287–365.

50. P.A. Eisenstein, "Volkswagen Slapped with Largest Ever Fine for Automakers," *NBC News,* www.nbcnews.com, April 21, 2017.

51. Jones, "Ethical Decision Making."

52. A. Bucher, "Uber Upfront Pricing Class Action Lawsuit Moves Forward," *Top Class* Actions, http://topclassactions.com, August 3, 2017; R. Reader, "Lawsuit Accuses Uber of Fare Fraud," *Fast Company,* www.fastcompany.com, May 24, 2017.

53. "Accenture Reimagines Its Code of Business Ethics through Intelligent Technology," news release, https://newsroom .accenture.com, December 20, 2017.

54. *Welcome to the Code of Business Ethics: Your Guide to Responsible Behavior, Every Day,* http://www.accenture.com, accessed March 9, 2018.

55. "Accenture Reimagines Its Code of Business Ethics"; "Embracing the Disruptive Power of Chatbots," https://www .accenture.com, accessed March 9, 2018; A. Kramer, "Intelligent Technology Can Give Ethical Guidance," *Technology, Telecom and Internet Blog* (Bloomberg Law), https://www.bna.com, December 20, 2017.

56. S. Rubenfeld, "Accenture Tries Chatbot for Code of Conduct," *The Wall Street Journal,* https://blogs.wsj.com, January 24, 2018; Kramer, "Intelligent Technology Can Give Ethical Guidance."

57. Rubenfeld, "Accenture Tries Chatbot."

58. "GM: Steps to a Recall Nightmare," *CNN Money,* http://money.cnn.com, accessed March 9, 2018.

59. M. Maslakovic, "Fitness Tracker Rash: How to Avoid Getting a Rash from Your Fitness Tracker," http://gadgetsandwearables.com, January 26, 2018; "Fitbit Force Skin Irritation FAQs," https://help.fitbit.com, February 26, 2014.

60. C. English: "Conviction Upheld in Biggest Insider-Trading Case in History," *New York Post,* https://nypost.com, August 23, 2017.

61. "Nucor Announces 180th Consecutive Dividend," http://www.nucor.com, accessed March 9, 2018.

62. Ben DiPietro, "Retailers, NGO Create Standards for Artisans, Home-Based Workers," *The Wall Street Journal,* https://blogs.wsj.com, February 5, 2018; "Eileen Fisher and Nest Team Up to Drive Transparency in Fashion," *Forbes,* www.forbes.com, December 18, 2017; Nest, "Compliance for Homes and Small Workshops," www.buildanest.org, accessed February 5, 2018; Emily Farra, "The United Nations to Discuss the New Handworker Economy and the Future of Ethical Fashion," *Vogue,* www.vogue.com, December 11, 2017.

63. DiPietro, "Retailers, NGO Create Standards"; "Eileen Fisher and Nest Team Up."

64. Farra, "The United Nations to Discuss the New Handworker Economy."

65. DiPietro, "Retailers, NGO Create Standards"; "Eileen Fisher and Nest Team Up."

66. "Eileen Fisher and Nest Team Up"; "Compliance for Homes and Small Workshops."

67. "New Code of Conduct for Artisans and Homeworkers," www.buildanest.org, accessed February 9, 2018; "Compliance for Homes and Small Workshops"; DiPietro, "Retailers, NGO Create Standards"; Tracey Greenstein, "Nest and Ecopsis Tackle Wastewater Solutions for Fashion Brands," *WWD,* http://www.wwd.com, December 12, 2017.

68. DiPietro, "Retailers, NGO Create Standards"; "Eileen Fisher and Nest Team Up."

69. "2016 Southwest Airlines One Report," www.southwest.com, accessed March 9, 2018.

70. G.R. Jones, *Organizational Theory: Text and Cases* (Englewood Cliffs, NJ: Prentice-Hall, 2008).

71. P.E. Murphy, "Creating Ethical Corporate Structure," *Sloan Management Review,* Winter 1989, 81–87.

72. R. Johnson, "Ralston to Buy Beechnut, Gambling It Can Overcome Apple Juice Scandal," *The Wall Street Journal,* September 18, 1989, B11.

CHAPTER 5

Managing Diverse Employees in a Multicultural Environment

©Sam Edwards/age fotostock

Learning Objectives

After studying this chapter, you should be able to:

LO5-1 Discuss the increasing diversity of the workforce and the organizational environment.

LO5-2 Explain the central role that managers play in the effective management of diversity.

LO5-3 Explain why the effective management of diversity is both an ethical and a business imperative.

LO5-4 Discuss how perception and the use of schemas can result in unfair treatment.

LO5-5 List the steps managers can take to manage diversity effectively.

LO5-6 Identify the two major forms of sexual harassment and how they can be eliminated.

What steps can an organization take to ensure diversity among its workforce? The U.S. high-tech industry has a reputation for being dominated by white (and sometimes Asian) males—and an often-unconscious expectation this is what computer experts look like. The numbers support this view: Women and people of color are under-represented in college computer programs and even more so in the big tech companies.[1] Companies tend to blame the problem on a shortage of women and minorities with technical skills, but some industry insiders observe companies limiting their recruiting to top-tier universities and managers failing to recognize the contributions of women and minorities.

Intel's former CEO, Brian Krzanich, realized this criticism could apply to his company. Of Intel's U.S. workforce, more than 6 in 10 were white and Asian males, with single-digit percentages of employees who were black, Hispanic, or Native American.[2] Krzanich doubted that such a workforce could fully identify with and serve the needs of its more diverse customers. He decided to make a public commitment to diversifying Intel's workforce. In 2015, he announced that the company would commit $300 million to a diversity initiative.[3] The goal: By 2020, the composition of Intel's workforce by race and sex would match these groups' percentages in the U.S. labor supply for Intel's job categories.

Krzanich appointed Danielle Brown to lead Intel's diversity initiative. As chief diversity and inclusion officer, she reported directly to the CEO, signaling that diversity was to become a companywide issue. She determined that to meet the 2020 targets, Intel needed to bring in 2,300 female and/or minority employees. She launched a program based on accountability, transparency, data-based decisions, and a holistic view of the issue.[4] Managers have goals for their group's diversity, and part of their pay depends on meeting those goals. Twice yearly, Intel publishes a report of its performance on the diversity goal, including data for hiring, pay levels, rate of employees leaving, and rate being promoted. To support decision making based on data, rather than comfort with similarity, managers receive data on their people's performance. As the program began delivering results, Google recruited Brown, and Intel promoted Barbara Whye to continue the effort in Brown's place.[5] As a black engineer with more than two decades at Intel in various roles, Whye has firsthand experience with the challenges involved.

So far, Brown's and Whye's efforts are bearing fruit. Intel is ahead of its timeline for hiring diverse workers. As of mid-2017, it was 800 employees shy of closing the gap in minority employees. One productive technique has been ensuring that each slate of candidates for a position includes at least two qualified

Senior management at Intel continues to work toward closing the gap when it comes to diversity and inclusion in its workforce.
©Robert Kneschke/Shutterstock

people who meet criteria for diverse hiring.[6] Intel expanded the pool of candidates by recruiting at a wider variety of schools and publicly posting all job openings. For interviews, it brings together a diverse group into a panel, rather than relying on one manager alone.

Retention has been a stickier problem, but Intel has reduced its exit rates for minority employees to near the rates for whites and Asians—and the rates for women are below the rates for men.[7] This progress came after Brown introduced

a program called WarmLine, a phone number employees can use to contact her team if they feel dissatisfied with conditions. The diversity and inclusion team provides a personal response to problems such as managers being "too busy" to help new employees develop a career path. The results yield data Intel uses in preventing such problems in the first place—for example, training managers to fully engage with all their employees. WarmLine has opened over 6,000 cases, and Whye reports a success rate above 90%.[8]

Overview

As described in "A Manager's Challenge," effective management of diversity means more than hiring diverse employees. It means learning to appreciate and respond appropriately to the needs, attitudes, beliefs, and values that diverse people bring to an organization. It also means correcting misconceptions about why and how various kinds of employee groups differ from one another and finding the most effective way to use the skills and talents of diverse employees.

LO5-1 Discuss the increasing diversity of the workforce and the organizational environment.

diversity Dissimilarities or differences among people due to age, gender, race, ethnicity, religion, sexual orientation, socioeconomic background, education, experience, physical appearance, capabilities/disabilities, and any other characteristic that is used to distinguish among people.

In this chapter we focus on the effective management of diversity in an environment that is becoming increasingly diverse in all respects. Not only are the diversity and integration of the global workforce increasing, but suppliers and customers are also becoming increasingly diverse. Managers need to manage diversity proactively to attract and retain the best employees and compete effectively in a global environment. For example, managers at the audit and consulting firm Deloitte have instituted a program to encourage minority suppliers to compete for its business, and the firm sponsors schools and colleges that supply a stream of well-trained recruits.[9]

Sometimes well-intentioned managers inadvertently treat various groups of employees differently, even though there are no performance-based differences between them. This chapter explores why differential treatment occurs and the steps managers and organizations can take to ensure that diversity, in all respects, is effectively managed for the good of all organizational stakeholders.

The Increasing Diversity of the Workforce and the Environment

One of the most important management issues to emerge over the last 40 years has been the increasing diversity of the workforce. Diversity is dissimilarities—differences—among people due to age, gender, race, ethnicity, religion, sexual orientation, socioeconomic background, education, experience, physical appearance, capabilities/disabilities, and any other characteristic that is used to distinguish among people (see Figure 5.1).

Diversity raises important ethical issues and social responsibility issues (see Chapter 4). It is also a critical issue for organizations—one that if not handled well can bring an organization to its knees, especially in our increasingly global environment. There are several reasons that diversity continues to be such a pressing concern and an issue, both in the popular press and for managers and organizations:

- There is a strong ethical imperative in many societies that diverse people must receive equal opportunities and be treated fairly and justly. Unfair treatment is also illegal.

- Effectively managing diversity can improve organizational effectiveness. When managers effectively manage diversity, they not only encourage other managers to treat diverse members of an organization fairly and justly but also realize that diversity is an important

Figure 5.1

Sources of Diversity in the Workplace

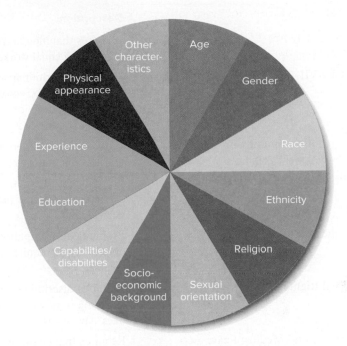

organizational resource that can help an organization gain a competitive advantage.[10] Current research suggests there are specific situations in which diversity can enhance performance, for example, in teams. However, simply having a diverse workforce may not guarantee higher performance.[11] This last point is important as managers continue to explore the impact of diversity on the workplace and the challenges of moving employees and organizations forward in an effective manner.

- There is substantial evidence that diverse individuals continue to experience unfair treatment in the workplace as a result of biases, stereotypes, and overt discrimination. In a recent review of multiple studies, evidence suggests that hiring discrimination against African Americans has not changed significantly over the past 25 years in the United States, and Latinos have experienced only a moderate drop in discrimination.[12] In addition, a recent survey of U.S. workers suggests that "pay secrecy" within companies in the private sector may contribute to reducing women's bargaining power when it comes to salaries and may also be a factor in the ongoing gender wage gap.[13]

- Finally, the **glass ceiling**—the invisible barrier that prevents women and minorities from being promoted to top corporate positions—is beginning to crack, though much work still needs to be done. For example, in January 2018, only 27 leaders of *Fortune* 500 companies were women (5.4%) and only 3 were African American men (0.6%). With the retirement of Xerox's Ursula Burns in 2016, there currently are no African American women running these top organizations.[14]

glass ceiling A metaphor alluding to the invisible barriers that prevent minorities and women from being promoted to top corporate positions.

Before we can discuss the multitude of issues surrounding the effective management of diversity, we must document just how diverse the U.S. workforce is becoming.

Age

According to data from the U.S. Census Bureau, the median age of a person in the United States is the highest it has ever been, at 37.9 years. Moreover, it is projected that by 2060, close to 24% of the U.S. population will be 65 or older. The Age Discrimination in Employment Act of 1967 prohibits age discrimination.[15] Although we discuss federal employment legislation in more depth in Chapter 12, major equal employment opportunity legislation that prohibits discrimination among diverse groups is summarized in Table 5.1.

Table 5.1

Major Equal Employment Opportunity Laws Affecting Human Resources Management

Year	Law	Description
1963	Equal Pay Act	Requires that men and women be paid equally if they are performing equal work.
1964	Title VII of the Civil Rights Act	Prohibits discrimination in employment decisions on the basis of race, religion, sex, color, or national origin; covers a wide range of employment decisions, including hiring, firing, pay, promotion, and working conditions.
1967	Age Discrimination in Employment Act	Prohibits discrimination against workers over the age of 40 and restricts mandatory retirement.
1978	Pregnancy Discrimination Act	Prohibits discrimination against women in employment decisions on the basis of pregnancy, childbirth, and related medical decisions.
1990	Americans with Disabilities Act	Prohibits discrimination against disabled individuals in employment decisions and requires that employers make accommodations for disabled workers to enable them to perform their jobs.
1991	Civil Rights Act	Prohibits discrimination (as does Title VII) and allows for the awarding of punitive and compensatory damages, in addition to back pay, in cases of intentional discrimination.
1993	Family and Medical Leave Act	Requires that employers provide 12 weeks of unpaid leave for medical and family reasons, including paternity and illness of a family member.
1994	Uniformed Services Employment and Reemployment Rights Act	Protects the civilian employment of active and reserve military personnel called to active duty; prohibits discrimination on the basis of military status and military service obligations; also provides certain reemployment rights following military service.

The aging of the population suggests that managers need to be vigilant to ensure that employees are not discriminated against because of age. Moreover, managers need to ensure that the policies and procedures they have in place treat all workers fairly, regardless of their ages. Additionally, effectively managing diversity means employees of diverse ages are able to learn from each other, work well together, and take advantage of the unique perspective each has to offer.

Gender

Women and men both have substantial participation rates in the U.S. workforce (approximately 45.8% women and 54.2% men), yet women's median weekly earnings are estimated to be $769 compared to $964 for men.[16] Although the gender wage gap has narrowed in recent years, it continues to be as an issue, just like the glass ceiling. According to Catalyst, a nonprofit organization that studies women in business, while women comprise about 44.7% of employees in managerial and professional positions, only around 26.5% of executive officers in S&P 500 companies are women, and only 11% of the top earners in these companies are women.[17] These women, such as Mary Barra of GM, Ginni Rometty of IBM, and Michele Buck of Hershey, stand out among their male peers and often receive a disparate amount of attention in the media. Women are also underrepresented on companies' boards of directors—they currently hold close to 21% of the board seats on S&P 500 companies.[18]

Additionally, research conducted by consulting firms suggests that female executives outperform their male colleagues in skills such as motivating others, promoting good communication, turning out high-quality work, and being good listeners. For example, the Hagberg Group performed in-depth evaluations of 425 top executives in a variety of industries, with

A female executive enjoying the company plane is not as rare a sight today as it used to be. Nevertheless, the glass ceiling remains a real barrier to women and minorities in the business workforce.
©ColorBlind Images/Blend Images LLC

each executive rated by approximately 25 people. Of the 52 skills assessed, women received higher ratings than men on 42 skills, although at times the differences were small.[19] Results of a study conducted by Catalyst found that organizations with higher proportions of women in top management positions had significantly better financial performance than organizations with lower proportions of female top managers.[20] Another study conducted by Credit Suisse found that companies with one or more women on their boards of directors performed better in terms of returns on equity, sales, and invested capital than companies with fewer or no women on their boards.[21] Studies such as these make one wonder why the glass ceiling continues to hamper the progress of women in business (a topic we address later in the chapter).

Race and Ethnicity

The U.S. Census Bureau distinguished among the following races in the 2010 census: American Indian or Alaska Native, Asian Indian, black or African American, Chinese, Filipino, Japanese, Korean, Vietnamese, other Asian, Native Hawaiian, Guamanian or Chamorro, Samoan, other Pacific Islander, white, and other races. Although *ethnicity* refers to a grouping of people based on some shared characteristic such as national origin, language, or culture, the U.S. Census Bureau treats ethnicity in terms of whether a person is Hispanic, Latino, or of Spanish origin or not.[22] For the 2020 Census, the government has conducted extensive research to fine-tune the various ethnic groups that will be tracked in the upcoming national census survey. More than ever before, many individuals see themselves as multiracial with various ethnicities.[23]

The racial and ethnic diversity of the U.S. population continues to change, as does the diversity of the workforce. According to the U.S. Census Bureau, approximately one of every three U.S. residents belongs to a minority group (is not a non-Hispanic white). More specifically, 17.8% of the population is Hispanic or Latino, 82.2% is not Hispanic or Latino, and 61.3% of the population is white alone (that is, white and not Hispanic or Latino).[24] For those individuals self-identifying one race in the 2010 census, approximately 76.9% are white, 13.3% are black or African American, 1.3% are American Indian or Alaska Native, 5.7% are Asian, 0.2% are Native Hawaiian and other Pacific Islander alone, and 2.6% of the population self-identifies as two or more races.[25] According to projections released by the U.S. Census Bureau, the composition of the U.S. population in 2060 will be quite different from its composition today: In 2060 the U.S. population is projected to be close to 56% minority.[26] And while this discussion focuses on diversity in the United States, managers anywhere in the world need to be aware of their region's pattern of ethnic diversity. The "Managing Globally" feature about SodaStream describes a company based in Israel that works diligently to address diversity.

The increasing racial and ethnic diversity of the workforce and the population as a whole underscores the importance of effectively managing diversity. Data compiled by the Bureau of Labor Statistics suggest that much needs to be done in terms of ensuring that diverse employees have equal opportunities. For example, median weekly earnings for black men are approximately 69.3% of median earnings for white men; median weekly earnings for black women are approximately 82.7% of median earnings for white women.[27] In the remainder of this chapter, we focus on the fair treatment of diverse employees and explore why this is such an important challenge and what managers can do to meet it. We begin by taking a broader perspective and considering how increasing racial and ethnic diversity in an organization's environment (such as customers and suppliers) affects decision making and organizational effectiveness.

At a general level, managers and organizations are increasingly being reminded that stakeholders are diverse and expect organizational decisions and actions to reflect this diversity. For example, many advocacy groups continue to lobby the entertainment industry to increase the diversity in TV programming, acting, writing, and producing.[28] The need for such increased diversity is more than apparent. For example, while Hispanics make up more than 17% of the U.S. population (more than 57 million potential TV viewers), less than 6% of the characters

SodaStream's Oasis of Diversity

Daniel Birnbaum is CEO of SodaStream International, which makes countertop devices that inject carbon dioxide into liquids to add bubbles. A reusable bottle offers an alternative to buying soda in disposable bottles. Birnbaum took the position so he could stay in Israel.[29] Born in New York, he grew up in Israel and left to earn an MBA at Harvard. After returning to Israel, he worked for Pillsbury and Nike until his next career move would involve relocating. The job offer from SodaStream came in 2007, when the company was struggling financially. Birnbaum revitalized the company by repositioning the product as eco-friendly.

SodaStream employs over 2,000 people of 30 different nationalities at its headquarters and manufacturing facilities in five countries.[30] Its main production facility is in Rahat, a city in the Negev, the desert region in southern Israel. Rahat's dominant ethnic group is Bedouin, desert dwellers of the region, traditionally nomads. The SodaStream workers include Bedouins, Palestinians, Druze (a religious sect living mainly in Syria, Lebanon, and Israel), and Jews whose families came to Israel from Russia and Ethiopia.[31]

Building this diverse workforce was not originally Birnbaum's vision; rather, it met business needs.[32] Rising demand required more workers at the SodaStream factory, then located in the Palestinian-governed West Bank. Israeli workers weren't interested, so he recruited Palestinians. He admits to being surprised at how productive they were and how well the Palestinians and Israelis got along. Later, however, political pressures forced him to close the West Bank facility and relocate. Working in the Negev location requires Palestinians to get permits and spend hours commuting through Israeli checkpoints. But for those who meet the requirements, a job at SodaStream can be worthwhile.

In the larger political sphere, the ethnic groups represented at the Rahat factory feel mistrust, even hostility. Birnbaum unifies the workforce by focusing everyone on the business and treating workers justly and respectfully.[33] In contrast to other Israeli companies, SodaStream pays equally regardless of workers' ethnicity. Working together teaches employees to see one another's shared humanity. SodaStream, recognizing that inclusiveness enhances its reputation as an employer, recently posted a recruiting video aimed at creative, socially conscious workers.

Under Birnbaum, SodaStream's diverse workforce has been delivering results.[34] As consumers learn they can make fizzy drinks with healthful ingredients and low impact on the environment, sales have been rising briskly. SodaStream's market capitalization (total value of stock shares) is 250 times greater than when Birnbaum took the helm.

in prime-time TV shows are Hispanics, according to a study conducted by USC's Annenberg School for Communication and Journalism.[35] Pressure continues to mount on networks and the media in general to increase diversity within their ranks to reflect the diversity of the population as a whole.[36]

Religion

Title VII of the Civil Rights Act prohibits discrimination based on religion (as well as based on race/ethnicity, country of origin, and sex; see Table 5.1 and Chapter 12). In addition to enacting Title VII, in 1997 the federal government issued "The White House Guidelines on Religious Exercise and Expression in the Federal Workplace."[37] These guidelines, while technically applicable only in federal offices, also are frequently relied on by large corporations. The guidelines require that employers make reasonable accommodations for religious practices, such as observances of holidays, as long as doing so does not entail major costs or hardships.[38]

A key issue for managers in religious diversity is recognizing and being aware of different religions and their beliefs, with particular attention being paid to when religious holidays fall. For example, critical meetings should not be scheduled during a holy day for members of a certain faith, and managers should be flexible in allowing people to have time off for religious observances. According to Lobna Ismail, director of a diversity training company in Silver Spring, Maryland, when managers acknowledge, respect, and make even small accommodations for religious diversity, employee loyalty is often enhanced. For example, allowing employees to leave work early on certain days instead of taking a lunch break or posting holidays for different religions on the company calendar can go a long way toward making individuals of diverse religions feel respected and valued as well as enabling them to practice their faith.[39] According to research conducted by the Tanenbaum Center for Interreligious Understanding in New York, while only about 23% of employees who feel they are victims of religious discrimination actually file complaints, about 45% of these employees start looking for other jobs.[40]

Capabilities/Disabilities

The Americans with Disabilities Act (ADA) of 1990 prohibits discrimination against persons with disabilities and requires that employers make reasonable accommodations to enable these people to effectively perform their jobs. On the surface, few would argue with the intent of this legislation. However, as managers attempt to implement policies and procedures to comply with the ADA, they face a number of interpretation and fairness challenges.

On one hand, some people with real disabilities warranting workplace accommodations are hesitant to reveal their disabilities to their employers and claim the accommodations they deserve.[41] On the other hand, some employees abuse the ADA by seeking unnecessary accommodations for disabilities that may or may not exist.[42] Thus, it is perhaps not surprising that the passage of the ADA does not appear to have increased employment rates significantly for those with disabilities.[43] A key challenge for managers is to promote an environment in which employees needing accommodations feel comfortable disclosing their need while ensuring that the accommodations not only enable those with disabilities to effectively perform their jobs, but also are perceived to be fair by those who are not disabled.[44]

In addressing this challenge, often managers must educate both themselves and their employees about the disabilities, as well as the real capabilities, of those who are disabled. According to recent statistics, the unemployment rate for disabled workers is twice that of workers without disabilities. However, many companies are committed to hiring workers with disabilities and recognize that diversity and inclusion are two strategies vital to their overall business success. In 2017, the American Association of People with Disabilities and the U.S. Business Leadership Network recognized more than 60 U.S. companies with their "best places to work for people with disabilities" award, including Starbucks, Northrop Grumman, AT&T, and EY (Ernst & Young). These companies scored 100% on the Disability Equality Index, a benchmarking tool that provides organizations with an objective score on their disability and inclusion policies and practices.[45]

The ADA also protects employees with acquired immune deficiency syndrome (AIDS) from being discriminated against in the workplace. AIDS is caused by the human immunodeficiency virus (HIV) and is transmitted through sexual contact, infected needles, and contaminated blood products. HIV is not spread through casual, nonsexual contact. Yet out of ignorance, fear, or prejudice, some people wish to avoid all contact with anyone infected with HIV. Infected individuals may not necessarily develop AIDS, and some individuals with HIV are able to remain effective performers of their jobs while not putting others at risk.[46]

AIDS awareness training can help people overcome their fears and give managers a tool to prevent illegal discrimination against HIV-infected employees. Such training focuses on educating employees about HIV and AIDS, dispelling myths, communicating relevant organizational policies, and emphasizing the rights of HIV-positive employees to privacy and an environment that allows them to be productive.[47] The need for AIDS awareness training is underscored by some of the problems HIV-positive employees may experience once others in their workplace become aware of their condition.[48] Moreover, organizations are required to make reasonable accommodations to enable people with AIDS to effectively perform their jobs.

Thus, managers have an obligation to educate employees about HIV and AIDS, dispel myths and the stigma of AIDS, and ensure that HIV-related discrimination is not occurring in the workplace. Moreover, significant advances in medication and treatment mean that more infected individuals are able to continue working or are able to return to work after their condition improves. Thus, managers need to ensure that these employees are fairly treated by all members of their organizations.[49] And managers and organizations that do not treat HIV-positive employees in a fair manner, as well as provide reasonable accommodations (such as allowing time off for doctor visits or to take medicine), risk costly lawsuits.

Socioeconomic Background

The term *socioeconomic background* typically refers to a combination of social class and income-related factors. From a management perspective, socioeconomic diversity (and, in particular, diversity in income levels) requires that managers be sensitive and responsive to the needs and concerns of individuals who might not be as well off as others. U.S. welfare reform in the middle to late 1990s emphasized the need for single mothers and others receiving public assistance to join or return to the workforce. In conjunction with a strong economy, this led to record declines in the number of families, households, and children living below the poverty level, according to the 2000 U.S. Census.[50] However, the economic downturns in the early and late 2000s suggest that some past gains that lifted families out of poverty have been reversed. In a strong economy, it is much easier for poor people with few skills to find jobs; in a weak economy, when companies lay off employees in hard times, people who need their incomes the most are unfortunately often the first to lose their jobs.[51] And in recessionary times, it is difficult for laid-off employees to find new positions. For example, in December 2009 there were an average of 6.1 unemployed workers for every open position.[52]

According to statistics released by the U.S. Census Bureau, the official poverty rate in the United States in 2016 was 12.7%, or 40.6 million people; in 2012 the poverty rate was 15.0%, or 46.5 million people.[53] The Census Bureau relies on predetermined threshold income figures, based on family size and composition, adjusted annually for inflation, to determine the poverty level. Families whose income falls below the threshold level are considered poor. For example, in 2017 a family of four was considered poor if their annual income fell below $24,858.[54] When workers earn less than $15 per hour, it is often difficult, if not impossible, for them to meet their families' needs.[55] Moreover, increasing numbers of families are facing the challenge of finding suitable child care arrangements that enable the adults to work long hours and/or through the night to maintain an adequate income level. New information technology has led to more businesses operating 24 hours a day, creating challenges for workers on the night shift, especially those with children.[56]

Hundreds of thousands of parents across the country are scrambling to find someone to care for their children while they are working the night shift, commuting several hours a day, working weekends and holidays, or putting in long hours on one or more jobs. This has led to the opening of day-care facilities that operate around the clock as well as to managers seeking ways to provide such care for children of their employees. For example, Yessika Magdaleno, an experienced, state-licensed child care provider in Garden Grove, California, offers early morning, evening, and overnight day-care services for parents with irregular work hours.[57]

Socioeconomic diversity suggests that managers need to be sensitive and responsive to the needs and concerns of workers who may be less fortunate than themselves in terms of income and financial resources, child care and elder care options, housing opportunities, and the existence of sources of social and family support. Moreover—and equally important—managers should try to give such individuals opportunities to learn, advance, and make meaningful contributions to their organizations while improving their economic well-being.

Sexual Orientation

According to research conducted by Gary Gates of the Williams Institute at the UCLA School of Law, approximately 4.1% of adults in the United States, or more than 10 million U.S. residents, self-identify as lesbian, gay, bisexual, or transgender (LGBT).[58] In 2015 the Equal

Macy's employees raise awareness about diversity and equality at Miami's annual Pride Parade. Corporate support can go a long way toward making sure the workplace environment is safe and respectful for everyone.
©Jeff Greenburg/Getty Images

Employment Opportunity Commission pronounced that workplace discrimination on the grounds of sexual orientation is illegal, according to federal law. In that same year, the U.S. Supreme Court declared same-sex marriage was legal in all 50 states.[59] More and more companies are recognizing the inclusion of LGBT employees, affirming their rights to fair and equal treatment and providing benefits to their partners and/or spouses. In 2017, Disney was recognized with a Diversity & Inclusion Award from the *Profiles in Diversity Journal* for its innovative solutions in the area of workforce diversity and inclusion. From providing benefits for same-sex partners to supporting community organizations and working to ensure a safe and welcoming environment for LGBT employees, the company has a long-standing and ongoing commitment to equality.[60]

Other Kinds of Diversity

Other kinds of diversity are important in organizations, are critical for managers to deal with effectively, and are potential sources of unfair treatment. For example, organizations and teams need members with diverse backgrounds and experiences. This is clearly illustrated by the prevalence of cross-functional teams in organizations whose members might come from various departments such as marketing, production, finance, and sales (teams are covered in depth in Chapter 15). A team responsible for developing and introducing a new product, for example, often needs the expertise of employees not only from research and design and engineering but also from marketing, sales, production, and finance.

Other types of diversity can affect how employees are treated in the workplace. For example, employees differ from each other in how attractive they are (based on the standards of the cultures in which an organization operates) and in body weight. Whether individuals are attractive, unattractive, thin, or overweight in most cases has no bearing on their job performance unless they have jobs in which physical appearance plays a role, such as modeling. Yet sometimes these physical sources of diversity affect advancement rates and salaries. According to a recent Vanderbilt University study, overweight women are more likely to work in lower-paying and more physically demanding jobs, they are less likely to get higher-wage jobs that include interacting with the public, and they make less money than average-size women and all men.[61] Clearly, managers need to ensure that all employees are treated fairly, regardless of their physical appearance.

Managers and the Effective Management of Diversity

The increasing diversity of the environment—which, in turn, increases the diversity of an organization's workforce—increases the challenges managers face in effectively managing diversity. Each of the kinds of diversity just discussed presents a particular set of issues managers need to appreciate before they can respond to them effectively. Understanding these issues is not always a simple matter, as many informed managers have discovered. Research on how different groups are currently treated and the unconscious biases that might adversely affect them is vital because it helps managers become aware of the many subtle and unobtrusive ways in which diverse employee groups can come to be treated unfairly over time. Managers can take many more steps to become sensitive to the ongoing effects of diversity in their organizations, take advantage of all the contributions diverse employees can make, and prevent employees from being unfairly treated.

LO5-2 Explain the central role that managers play in the effective management of diversity.

Critical Managerial Roles

In each of their managerial roles (see Chapter 1), managers can either promote the effective management of diversity or derail such efforts; thus, they are critical to this process. For example, in their interpersonal roles, managers can convey that the effective management of diversity is a valued goal

Table 5.2

Managerial Roles and the Effective Management of Diversity

Type of Role	Specific Role	Example
Interpersonal	Figurehead	Conveys that the effective management of diversity is a valued goal and objective.
	Leader	Serves as a role model and institutes policies and procedures to ensure that diverse members are treated fairly.
	Liaison	Enables diverse individuals to coordinate their efforts and cooperate with one another.
Informational	Monitor	Evaluates the extent to which all employees are treated fairly.
	Disseminator	Informs employees about diversity policies and initiatives and the intolerance of discrimination.
	Spokesperson	Supports diversity initiatives in the wider community and speaks to diverse groups to interest them in career opportunities.
Decisional	Entrepreneur	Commits resources to develop new ways to effectively manage diversity and eliminate biases and discrimination.
	Disturbance handler	Takes quick action to correct inequalities and curtail discriminatory behavior.
	Resource allocator	Allocates resources to support and encourage the effective management of diversity.
	Negotiator	Works with organizations (e.g., suppliers) and groups (e.g., labor unions) to support and encourage the effective management of diversity.

and objective (figurehead role), can serve as a role model and institute policies and procedures to ensure that all organizational members are treated fairly (leader role), and can enable diverse individuals and groups to coordinate their efforts and cooperate with each other both inside the organization and at the organization's boundaries (liaison role). Table 5.2 summarizes ways in which managers can ensure that diversity is effectively managed as they perform their different roles.

Given the formal authority that managers have in organizations, they typically have more influence than rank-and-file employees. When managers commit to supporting diversity, as is the case at Intel discussed in "A Manager's Challenge," their authority and positions of power and status influence other members of an organization to make a similar commitment. Research on social influence supports such a link: People are likely to be influenced and persuaded by others who have high status.[62]

Consider the steps that managers at PricewaterhouseCoopers (PwC) have taken to effectively manage diversity, as profiled in the accompanying "Focus on Diversity" feature.

FOCUS ON DIVERSITY

Managing Diversity Effectively at PwC

PricewaterhouseCoopers (PwC), one of the largest private companies in the United States with revenues over $37 billion and more than 236,000 employees, has taken multiple proactive steps to effectively manage diversity. The company provides audit and assurance, tax, legal, and consulting services to clients in 158 countries.[63] PwC's commitment to the effective management of diversity starts at the top and extends throughout the firm. Bob Moritz, global chairman of PwC, has long been an enthusiastic supporter and proponent of the effective management of diversity.[64] A long-tenured member of PwC, Moritz learned some valuable diversity lessons early in his career when he spent three years in PwC Tokyo assisting U.S. and European financial services firms doing business in Japan with audit and advisory services. Working in Japan opened Moritz's eyes to a host of diversity-related issues—what it felt like to be in the minority, to not speak the native language, and to experience discrimination. It also made him appreciate the value of cultural

PricewaterhouseCoopers, which provides audit and consulting services to clients, is committed to the effective management of diversity and inclusion in areas such as recruiting, retention, engagement, promotion, and cross-cultural mentoring.
©Radharc Images/Alamy Stock Photo

diversity, diversity of thought, and building trusting relationships with people who might be different from you on a number of dimensions.[65] As Moritz puts it, "Embracing diversity and inclusion makes business sense and more importantly is the right thing to do. By sharing experiences and ideas we can all learn from each other and drive the change we need."[66]

Moritz gets together with diversity resource groups on a regular basis to ensure that executives and partners are working toward diversity and inclusion goals in a variety of areas such as recruiting and retention, engagement, promotions, and cross-cultural mentoring.

Mike Dillon is PwC's chief diversity officer, leading the company's diversity strategies and initiatives.[67] He believes that effectively managing diversity includes providing all employees with the chance to have a successful career; he also believes that everyone needs to work to understand people who are different from themselves and help each other to thrive. Diverse employees also help PwC to innovatively meet the needs of diverse clients.

At PwC, multiple dimensions of diversity are valued and effectively managed, including ethnicity, gender, race, sexual orientation, religion, physical ability, and generation. A key focus of PwC's diversity initiatives is providing and maintaining an inclusive environment whereby diverse individuals not only feel welcome and supported, but also have the opportunity to succeed and thrive. Thus, initiatives focus on ensuring that PwC has a good pipeline for hiring diverse employees and that these employees can make valuable contributions and achieve early success in their careers with PwC. Providing ongoing opportunities for development and advancement is also key, along with having a diverse leadership base.[68]

Initiatives and resources are in place for a variety of minority and majority employees. For example, working parents are supported in numerous ways such as through paid parental leave, child care provisions (discounts for child care, a nanny resource/referral service, and backup child care for emergencies), adoption assistance and leave, parenting circles, and groups for working parents. As another example, LGBT professionals are supported in multiple ways and have social networking and networking circles as well as access to full domestic partner benefit coverage and tax equalization.

Over 35% of newly hired employees at PwC are minorities, and PwC actively strives to ensure that these valuable employees are retained and advance in the firm. Diversity circles are professional forums whereby members of these and other diversity groupings can make contact with each other and provide learning, development, and mentoring experiences. The circles also give employees role models as they seek to advance in their careers. In addition, the company recently established the Disability Caregivers Network, which seeks to provide a support group for professionals who have a disability or special need or have someone in their personal lives with a special need or disability.[69]

Recognizing that many employees, at some point in their careers and lives, need or want flexibility to balance professional demands with their personal lives, PwC has a variety of flexible work arrangements that employees can take advantage of. PwC also helps employees determine which type of flexible work arrangement might best meet their professional and personal needs.[70] This is just a sampling of the many diversity-related endeavors PwC has undertaken and continues to pursue. PwC continues to strive to effectively manage diversity in multiple ways for the good of its employees, its clients, the firm itself, and other stakeholders.

When managers commit to diversity, their commitment legitimizes the diversity management efforts of others.[71] In addition, resources are devoted to such efforts, and all members of an organization believe that their diversity-related efforts are supported and valued. Consistent with this reasoning, top management commitment and rewards for the support of diversity are often cited as critical ingredients in the success of diversity management initiatives.[72] Additionally, seeing managers express confidence in the abilities and talents of diverse employees causes other organizational members to be similarly confident and helps reduce any prejudice they have as a result of ignorance or stereotypes.[73]

Two other important factors emphasize why managers are so central to the effective management of diversity. The first factor is that women, African Americans, Hispanics, and other minorities often start out at a slight disadvantage due to how they are perceived by others in organizations, particularly in work settings where they are a numerical minority. As Virginia Valian, a psychologist at Hunter College who studies gender, indicates, "In most organizations women begin at a slight disadvantage. A woman does not walk into the room with the same status as an equivalent man, because she is less likely than a man to be viewed as a serious professional."[74]

The second factor is that research suggests that slight differences in treatment can accumulate and result in major disparities over time. Even small differences—such as a small favorable bias toward men for promotions—can lead to major differences in the number of male and female managers over time.[75] Thus, while women and other minorities are sometimes advised not to make "a mountain out of a molehill" when they perceive they have been unfairly treated, research conducted by Valian and others suggests that molehills (slight differences in treatment based on irrelevant distinctions such as race, gender, or ethnicity) can turn into mountains over time (major disparities in important outcomes such as promotions) if they are ignored.[76] Once again, managers have the obligation, from both an ethical and a business perspective, to prevent any disparities in treatment and outcomes due to irrelevant distinctions such as race or ethnicity.

LO5-3 Explain why the effective management of diversity is both an ethical and a business imperative.

The Ethical Imperative to Manage Diversity Effectively

Effectively managing diversity not only makes good business sense (which is discussed in the next section) but also is an ethical imperative in U.S. society. Two moral principles guide managers in their efforts to meet this imperative: distributive justice and procedural justice.

distributive justice A moral principle calling for fair distribution of pay, promotions, and other organizational resources based on meaningful contributions that individuals have made and not personal characteristics over which they have no control.

DISTRIBUTIVE JUSTICE   The principle of distributive justice dictates fair distribution of pay, promotions, job titles, interesting job assignments, office space, and other organizational resources among members of an organization. These outcomes should be distributed according to the meaningful contributions that individuals have made to the organization (such as time, effort, education, skills, abilities, and performance levels) and not irrelevant personal characteristics over which individuals have no control (such as gender, race, or age).[77] Managers have an obligation to ensure that distributive justice exists in their organizations. This does not mean that all members of an organization receive identical or similar outcomes; rather, it means that members who receive more favorable outcomes than others have made substantially higher or more significant contributions to the organization.

Is distributive justice common in organizations in corporate America? Probably the best way to answer this question is to say things are getting better. Fifty years ago, overt discrimination against women and minorities was common; today organizations are inching closer toward the ideal of distributive justice. Statistics comparing the treatment of women and minorities with the treatment of other employees suggest that most managers need to take a proactive approach to achieve distributive justice in their organizations.[78] For example, across occupations, women consistently earn less than men (see Table 5.3), according to data collected by the U.S. Bureau of Labor Statistics.[79] Even in occupations dominated by women, such as sales and office occupations, men tend to earn more than women.

In many countries, managers have not only an ethical obligation to strive to achieve distributive justice in their organizations but also a legal obligation to treat all employees fairly. They risk being sued by employees who believe they are not being fairly treated. That is precisely

Table 5.3

Median Weekly Earnings for Full-Time Workers by Sex and Occupation in 2017

Occupation	Men	Women	Women's Earnings as a Percentage of Men's
Management, professional, and related	$1,442	$1,052	73%
Service	608	501	82
Sales and office	834	672	81
Natural resources, construction, and maintenance	809	579	72
Production, transportation, and material moving	736	545	74

Source: "Household Data; Annual Averages; 39. Median Weekly Earnings of Full-Time Wage and Salary Workers by Detailed Occupation and Sex," www.bls.gov, accessed March 16, 2018.

what more than 30 female Ford workers did when they experienced racial bias and sexual discrimination.[80]

procedural justice A moral principle calling for the use of fair procedures to determine how to distribute outcomes to organizational members.

PROCEDURAL JUSTICE   The principle of **procedural justice** requires that managers use fair procedures to determine how to distribute outcomes to organizational members.[81] This principle applies to typical procedures such as appraising subordinates' performance, deciding who should receive a raise or a promotion, and deciding whom to lay off when an organization is forced to downsize. Procedural justice exists, for example, when managers (1) carefully appraise a subordinate's performance; (2) take into account any environmental obstacles to high performance beyond the subordinate's control, such as lack of supplies, machine breakdowns, or dwindling customer demand for a product, and (3) ignore irrelevant personal characteristics such as the subordinate's age or ethnicity. Like distributive justice, procedural justice is necessary not only to ensure ethical conduct but also to avoid costly lawsuits.

Effectively Managing Diversity Makes Good Business Sense

Diverse organizational members can be a source of competitive advantage, helping an organization provide customers with better goods and services.[82] The variety of points of view and approaches to problems and opportunities that diverse employees provide can improve managerial decision making. Suppose a frozen food company is trying to come up with creative ideas for new frozen meals that will appeal to health-conscious, time-conscious customers tired of the same old frozen fare. Which group do you think is likely to come up with the most creative ideas: a group of white women with marketing degrees from Yale University who grew up in upper-middle-class families in the Northeast or a racially mixed group of men and women who grew up in families with varying income levels in different parts of the country and attended a variety of geographically dispersed business schools? Most people would agree that the diverse group is likely to have a wider range of creative ideas. Although this example is simplistic, it underscores one way in which diversity can lead to a competitive advantage.

Just as the workforce is becoming increasingly diverse, so are the customers who buy an organization's goods or services. In an attempt to suit local customers' needs and tastes, organizations like Target often vary the selection of products available in stores in different cities and regions.[83]

Diverse members of an organization are likely to be attuned to what goods and services diverse segments of the market want and do not want. Automakers, for example, are increasingly assigning women to their design teams to ensure that the needs and desires of female customers are taken into account in new car design.

Another way that effective management of diversity can improve profitability is by increasing retention of valued employees, which decreases the costs of hiring replacements for those who quit as well as ensures that all employees are highly motivated. In terms of retention, given the current legal environment, more and more organizations are attuned to the need to emphasize the importance of diversity in hiring. Once hired, if diverse employees think they are being unfairly treated, however, they will be likely to seek opportunities elsewhere. Thus, recruiting diverse employees has to be followed with ongoing effective management of diversity to retain valued organizational members.

If diversity is not effectively managed and turnover rates are higher for members of groups who are not treated fairly, profitability will suffer on several counts. Not only are the future contributions of diverse employees lost when they quit, but the organization also has to bear the costs of hiring replacement workers. According to a recent report, it costs employers an average of 33% of a worker's annual salary to hire a replacement if that employee leaves the organization. In addition, the company experiences substantial indirect costs associated with the new hire, which can include knowledge lost when an experienced worker leaves, time spent finding a replacement, and time the new employee needs to get up to speed in the new job.[84]

Effectively managing diversity makes good business sense for another reason. More and more, managers and organizations concerned about diversity are insisting that their suppliers also support diversity.[85]

Finally, from both business and ethical perspectives, effective management of diversity is necessary to avoid costly lawsuits. In 2000 Coca-Cola settled a class-action suit brought by African American employees at a cost of $192 million. The damage such lawsuits cause goes beyond the monetary awards to the injured parties; it can tarnish a company's image. One positive outcome of Coca-Cola's 2000 settlement is the company's recognition of the need to commit additional resources to diversity management initiatives. Coca-Cola is increasing its use of minority suppliers, instituting a formal mentoring program, and instituting days to celebrate diversity with its workforce.[86] These efforts have paid off, and Coca-Cola has appeared on *DiversityInc.*'s list of the "Top 50 Companies for Diversity."

By now it should be clear that effectively managing diversity is a necessity on both ethical and business grounds. This brings us to the question of why diversity presents managers and all of us with so many challenges—a question we address in the next section, on perception.

Perception

LO5-4 Discuss how perception and the use of schemas can result in unfair treatment.

Most people tend to think that the decisions managers make in organizations and the actions they take are the result of objective determination of the issues involved and the surrounding situation. However, each manager's interpretation of a situation or even of another person is precisely that—an interpretation. Nowhere are the effects of perception more likely to lead to different interpretations than in the area of diversity. This is because each person's interpretation of a situation, and subsequent response to it, is affected by his or her own age, race, gender, religion, socioeconomic status, capabilities, and sexual orientation. For example, different managers may see the same 21-year-old black male, gay, gifted, and talented subordinate in different ways: One may see a creative maverick with a great future in the organization, while another may see a potential troublemaker who needs to be watched closely.

perception The process through which people select, organize, and interpret what they see, hear, touch, smell, and taste to give meaning and order to the world around them.

Perception is the process through which people select, organize, and interpret sensory input—what they see, hear, touch, smell, and taste—to give meaning and order to the world around them.[87] All decisions and actions of managers are based on their subjective perceptions. When these perceptions are relatively accurate—close to the true nature of what is actually being perceived—good decisions are likely to be made and appropriate actions taken. Managers of fast-food restaurant chains such as McDonald's, Pizza Hut, and Wendy's accurately perceived that their customers were becoming more health-conscious in the 1980s and 1990s and added salad bars and low-fat entries to their menus. Managers at Kentucky Fried Chicken, Jack-in-the-Box, and Burger King took much longer to perceive this change in what customers wanted.

One reason that McDonald's is so successful is that its managers go to great lengths to make sure their perceptions of what customers want are accurate. McDonald's has over 36,000 restaurants in over 100 nations that generate billions of dollars in annual revenues.[88] Key to McDonald's success in these diverse markets are managers' efforts to perceive accurately a country's culture and taste in food and then to act on these perceptions. For instance, McDonald's serves veggie pies in India and melon ice cream floats in Japan.[89]

When managers' perceptions are relatively inaccurate, managers are likely to make bad decisions and take inappropriate actions that hurt organizational effectiveness. Bad decisions concerning diversity for reasons of age, ethnicity, or sexual orientation include (1) not hiring qualified people, (2) failing to promote top-performing subordinates, who subsequently may take their skills to competing organizations, and (3) promoting poorly performing managers because they have the same "diversity profile" as the manager or managers making the decision.

Factors That Influence Managerial Perception

Several managers' perceptions of the same person, event, or situation are likely to differ because managers differ in personality, values, attitudes, and moods (see Chapter 3). Each of these factors can influence how someone perceives a person or situation. An older middle manager who is high on openness to experience is likely to perceive the recruitment of able young managers as a positive learning opportunity; a similar middle manager who is low on openness to experience may perceive able younger subordinates as a threat. A manager who has high levels of job satisfaction and organizational commitment may perceive a job transfer to another department or geographic location that has very different employees (age, ethnicity, and so on) as an opportunity to learn and develop new skills. A dissatisfied, uncommitted manager may perceive the same transfer as a demotion.

schema An abstract knowledge structure that is stored in memory and makes possible the interpretation and organization of information about a person, an event, or a situation.

Managers' and all organizational members' perceptions of one another also are affected by their past experiences with and acquired knowledge about people, events, and situations—information that is organized into preexisting schemas. Schemas are abstract knowledge structures stored in memory that allow people to organize and interpret information about a person, an event, or a situation.[90] Once a person develops a schema for a kind of person or event, any newly encountered person or situation that is related to the schema activates it, and information is processed in ways consistent with the information stored in the schema. Thus, people tend to perceive others by using the expectations or preconceived notions contained in their schemas.[91] Once again, these expectations are derived from past experience and knowledge.

People tend to pay attention to information that is consistent with their schemas and to ignore or discount inconsistent information. Thus, schemas tend to be reinforced and strengthened over time because the information attended to is seen as confirming the schemas. This also results in schemas being resistant to change.[92] This does not mean schemas never change; if that were the case, people could never adapt to changing conditions and learn from their mistakes. Rather, it suggests that schemas are slow to change and that for people to change their schemas, they need to encounter a considerable amount of contradictory information.

Schemas that accurately depict the true nature of a person or situation are functional because they help people make sense of the world around them. People typically confront so much information that it is not possible to make sense of it without relying on schemas. Schemas are dysfunctional when they are inaccurate because they cause managers and all members of an organization to perceive people and situations inaccurately and assume certain things that are not necessarily true.

gender schemas Preconceived beliefs or ideas about the nature of men and women and their traits, attitudes, behaviors, and preferences.

Psychologist Virginia Valian refers to inaccurate preconceived notions of men and women as gender schemas. Gender schemas are a person's preconceived notions about the nature of men and women and their traits, attitudes, behaviors, and preferences.[93] Research suggests that among white middle-class Americans, the following gender schemas are prevalent: Men are action-oriented, assertive, independent, and task-focused; women are expressive, nurturing, and oriented toward and caring of other people.[94] Any schemas such as these—which assume that a single visible characteristic such as gender causes a person to possess specific traits and tendencies—are bound to be inaccurate. For example, not all women are alike and not all men are alike, and many women are more independent and task-focused than men. Gender schemas can be learned in childhood and are reinforced in a number of ways in society. For instance, while young girls may be encouraged by their parents to play with toy trucks and tools (stereotypically masculine toys), boys generally are not encouraged to, and sometimes are actively discouraged from, playing with dolls (stereotypically feminine toys).[95] As children grow up, they learn that occupations dominated by men have higher status than occupations dominated by women.

Perception as a Determinant of Unfair Treatment

Even though most people would agree that distributive justice and procedural justice are desirable goals, diverse organizational members are sometimes treated unfairly, as previous examples illustrate. Why is this problem occurring? One important overarching reason is inaccurate perceptions. To the extent that managers and other members of an organization rely on inaccurate information, such as gender schemas, to guide their perceptions of each other, unfair treatment is likely to occur.

stereotype Simplistic and often inaccurate belief about the typical characteristics of particular groups of people.

Gender schemas are a kind of **stereotype**, which is composed of simplistic and often inaccurate beliefs about the typical characteristics of particular groups of people. Stereotypes are usually based on a visible characteristic such as a person's age, gender, or race.[96] Managers who allow stereotypes to influence their perceptions assume erroneously that a person possesses a whole host of characteristics simply because the person happens to be an Asian woman, a white man, or a lesbian, for example. African American men are often stereotyped as good athletes, Hispanic women as subservient.[97] Obviously, there is no reason to assume that every African American man is a good athlete or that every Hispanic woman is subservient. Stereotypes, however, lead people to make such erroneous assumptions. A manager who accepts stereotypes might, for example, decide not to promote a highly capable Hispanic woman into a management position because the manager thinks she will not be assertive enough to supervise others.

A recent study suggests that stereotypes might hamper the progress of mothers in their organizations when they are seeking to advance in positions that are traditionally held by men. According to the study, based on gender stereotypes, people tend to view mothers as less competent in terms of skills and capabilities related to advancing in such positions.[98]

People with disabilities might also be unfairly treated due to stereotypes.[99] Although the ADA requires (as mentioned previously) that organizations provide disabled employees with accommodations, employment rates of people with disabilities tend to be low. That is, around 18% of people with disabilities are employed compared to 65% of people without disabilities.[100] In a recent study, when fictitious cover letters and résumés were sent for thousands of accounting openings, letters disclosing a disability were 26% less likely to yield an expression of interest from employers (the cover letters and résumés were identical except for whether or not a disability was disclosed in the cover letter).[101] However, as profiled in the accompanying "Ethics in Action" feature, a number of organizations have not only provided employment opportunities for adults with disabilities but also have benefited from their valuable contributions.

ETHICS IN ACTION

Disabled Employees Make Valuable Contributions

Some large organizations, like McDonald's, Walmart, Home Depot, and Walgreens, actively recruit employees with disabilities to work in positions such as cashiers, maintenance workers, greeters, shelf stockers, and floor workers who help customers find items. Home Depot, for example, works with a nonprofit agency called Ken's Krew Inc., founded by parents of disabled adults, to recruit and place employees with disabilities in its stores. Thus far, working with Ken's Krew has enabled Home Depot to recruit and place disabled adults in over 110 of its stores.[102]

Often, when given the opportunity, employees with disabilities make valuable contributions to their organizations. Walgreens opened an automated distribution center in Anderson, South Carolina, in which more than 40% of its 264 employees have disabilities. For disabled employees like Harrison Mullinax, who has autism and checks in merchandise to be distributed to drugstores with a bar code scanner, having a regular job is a godsend. Randy Lewis, senior vice president of distribution and logistics at Walgreens, thought about hiring workers with disabilities when Walgreens was considering

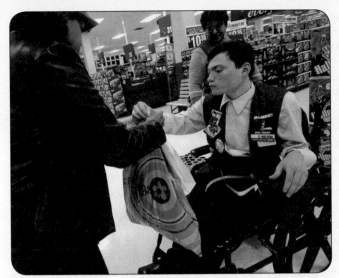

Working through his training as a greeter, Jamie Heal embraces his job at Walmart with gusto. His new-found independence became a catalyst for life changes (going by the name Cameron was one) as well as a deeper sense of self-respect.
©Tannis Toohey/Toronto Star via Getty Images

using technology to increase automation levels in a distribution center. Lewis, the father of a young adult son who has autism, was aware of how difficult it can be for young adults like his son to find employment. Various accommodations were made, such as redesigning workstations and computer displays to suit employees' needs, and employees received appropriate training in how to do their jobs. Some days, disabled employees are actually the most productive in the center. As Lewis puts it, "One thing we found is they can all do the job. . . . What surprised us is the environment that it's created. It's a building where everybody helps each other out."[103]

Walgreens is a large organization, but small organizations also have benefited from the valuable contributions of disabled employees. Habitat International Inc., founded by current CEO David Morris and his father, Saul, over 30 years ago, is a manufacturer and contractor of indoor–outdoor carpet and artificial grass and a supplier to home improvement companies, like Lowe's and Home Depot. Habitat's profits have steadily increased over the years, and the factory's defect rate is less than 0.5%.[104]

Morris attributes Habitat's success to its employees, 75% of whom have either a physical or a mental disability, or both. Habitat has consistently provided employment opportunities to people with disabilities such as Down syndrome, schizophrenia, or cerebral palsy.[105] The company has also hired the homeless, recovering alcoholics, and non-English-speaking refugees from other countries. And these employees were relied on by plant manager Connie Presnell when she needed to fill a rush order by assigning it to a team of her fastest workers. Habitat pays its employees regionally competitive wages and has low absence and turnover rates. Employees who need accommodations to perform their jobs are provided them, and Habitat has a highly motivated, satisfied, and committed workforce.[106]

While Habitat has actually gained some business from clients who applaud its commitment to diversity, Habitat's ethical values and social responsibility have also led the company to forgo a major account when stereotypes reared their ugly heads. Several years ago CEO Morris dropped the account of a distribution company because its representatives had made derogatory comments about his employees. Although it took Habitat two years to regain the lost revenues from this major account, Morris had no regrets. Habitat's commitment to diversity and fair treatment is a win–win situation; the company is thriving, and so are its employees.[107]

bias The systematic tendency to use information about others in ways that result in inaccurate perceptions.

Inaccurate perceptions leading to unfair treatment of diverse members of an organization also can be due to biases. **Biases** are systematic tendencies to use information about others in ways that result in inaccurate perceptions. Because of the way biases operate, people often are unaware that their perceptions of others are inaccurate.

Implicit bias is defined as the attitudes or stereotypes that affect our understanding, actions, and decisions in an unconscious manner. These tendencies are activated involuntarily and without awareness. Research into this type of bias suggests that it is pervasive in many areas of daily life, such as employment, education, and criminal justice, among others.[108] The concept of implicit bias is important to managers because it can lead to unfair treatment of diverse employees simply because they are different from the managers who are perceiving them, evaluating them, and making decisions that affect their future in the organization.[109] Some organizations are implementing hiring processes aimed at combating implicit bias in their hiring practices. For example, the NFL's Rooney Rule requires teams to interview at least one minority candidate when hiring a head coach or pay steep fines.[110]

Managers (particularly top managers) are likely to be white men. Although these managers may endorse the principles of distributive and procedural justice, they may unintentionally fall into the trap of perceiving other white men more positively than they perceive women and minorities. Being aware of this bias as well as using objective information about employees' capabilities and performance as much as possible in decision making about job assignments, pay raises, promotions, and other outcomes can help managers avoid implicit bias.

Social status—a person's real or perceived position in a society or an organization—can also be a source of implicit bias. This is the tendency to perceive individuals with high social status more positively than we perceive those with low social status. A high-status person may be perceived as smarter and more believable, capable, knowledgeable, and responsible than a low-status person, even in the absence of objective information about either person.

Imagine being introduced to two people at a company holiday party. Both are white men in their late thirties, and you learn that one is a member of the company's top management team and the other is a supervisor in the mailroom. From this information alone, you might assume that the top manager is smarter, more capable, more responsible, and even more interesting than the mailroom supervisor. Because women and minorities have traditionally had lower social status than white men, the social status effect may lead some people to perceive women and minorities less positively than they perceive white men.

Have you ever stood out in a crowd? Maybe you were the only man in a group of women, or maybe you were dressed formally for a social gathering but everyone else was in jeans. Salience (that is, conspicuousness) is another source of implicit bias. The *salience effect* is the tendency to focus attention on individuals who are conspicuously different from others in a group; the salience effect results in extra attention being focused on a person who stands out from the group mold. When people are salient, they often feel as though all eyes are watching them, and this perception is not far from the mark. Salient individuals are more often the object of attention than are other members of a work group, for example. A manager who has six white subordinates and one Hispanic subordinate reporting to her may inadvertently pay more attention to the Hispanic in group meetings because of the salience effect. Individuals who are salient are often perceived to be primarily responsible for outcomes and operations and are evaluated more extremely in either a positive or a negative direction.[111] Thus, when the Hispanic subordinate does a good job on a project, she receives excessive praise, and when she misses a deadline, she is excessively chastised. Part of being a good manager includes being aware of these sorts of tendencies and actively working against them.

Overt Discrimination

overt discrimination Knowingly and willingly denying diverse individuals access to opportunities and outcomes in an organization.

Inaccurate schemas and perceptual biases can lead well-meaning managers and organizational members to unintentionally discriminate against others. On the other hand, overt discrimination, or knowingly and willingly denying diverse individuals access to opportunities and outcomes in an organization, is intentional and deliberate. Overt discrimination is both unethical and illegal. Unfortunately, just as some managers steal from their organizations, others engage in overt discrimination.

Overt discrimination is a clear violation of the principles of distributive and procedural justice. Moreover, when managers are charged with overt discrimination, costly lawsuits can ensue. Organizations including Tesla, Fox News, Uber, Google, Oracle, and others have settled or face pending lawsuits alleging overt workplace discrimination.[112] Whereas in the past, lawsuits due to overt workplace discrimination focused on unfair treatment of women and minority group members, given the aging of the U.S. workforce, increasing numbers of discrimination cases are being brought by older workers who believe they were unfairly dismissed from their jobs due to their age.[113]

Despite all the advances that have been made, allegations of overt discrimination based on gender, race, age, and other forms of diversity continue to occur in the United States. For example, Nike settled a class-action lawsuit filed on behalf of 400 African American employees of its Chicago Niketown store. Employees claimed that managers used racial slurs when referring to African American employees and customers, gave African American employees lower-paying jobs, made unwarranted accusations of theft, and had security personnel monitor employees and customers based on race. Although Nike denied the allegations, as part of the settlement, Nike agreed to pay current and former employees $7.6 million and to promote effective management of diversity, partly by providing diversity training to all managers and supervisors in the store.[114]

Overt discrimination continues to be a problem in other countries as well. For example, although Japan passed its first Equal Employment Opportunity Law in 1985 and Japanese women are increasingly working in jobs once dominated by men, professional Japanese women have continued to find it difficult to advance in their careers and assume managerial positions. Women make up almost half of the Japanese workforce, but only around 8% of managerial positions in business and government are occupied by women.[115]

Overt discrimination also can be a potential problem when it comes to layoff decisions. Organizational restructurings, a weak economy, and the recession that began in December 2007 led to record numbers of U.S. employees being laid off from 2007 to 2010. Although it is always a challenge for managers to decide who should be let go when layoffs take place, some laid-off employees felt that factors that should be irrelevant to this tough decision played a role in the layoffs at their former employers. And while many workers who believe they were unfairly discriminated against do not pursue legal remedies, some filed lawsuits alleging discrimination in layoff decisions.

Age-related discrimination complaints have been at record highs over the last decade.[116] Although this might be due to the fact that there were more older employees in the workforce than in previous years, David Grinberg, speaking on behalf of the EEOC, suggests that the rise in age discrimination allegations could also be due to the fact that older workers tend to be paid more and have better benefits. For example, Joan Zawacki, in her late fifties, was laid off from her position as a vice president at the Cartus division of Realogy Corp. after having worked at the company for over 30 years. According to Zawacki, senior managers such as herself were told to talk discreetly with older workers in a friendly manner and suggest that they inquire with human resources about early retirement packages while protecting the jobs of younger workers. Zawacki indicates that she was laid off after not having convinced an older employee in her department to retire. A company spokesperson disputed the allegations in Zawacki's age discrimination lawsuit. In addition, over 90 employees at the Lawrence Livermore National Laboratory filed complaints alleging age discrimination in layoffs. Eddy Stappaerts, a 62-year-old senior scientist who had worked at the lab for 11 years and has a PhD from Stanford University, says, "A week before I was laid off, my boss said my contributions were essential." He alleges that some of the work he did was given to a younger employee.[117]

Some women laid off from their jobs in the financial industry filed lawsuits alleging gender discrimination. Laid-off female executives at Citigroup, Merrill Lynch, Bank of America, and Bank of Tokyo have claimed that gender played a role in their firings. In some cases, the women had done very well in their early years with the firms, were transferred to less desirable positions after becoming pregnant and taking maternity leaves, and ultimately were let go. Some of these women suggest that they were laid off even though they were just as qualified as men who were able to keep their jobs.[118]

How to Manage Diversity Effectively

Various kinds of barriers arise to managing diversity effectively in organizations. Some barriers originate in the person doing the perceiving; others are based on the information and schemas that have built up over time concerning the person being perceived. To overcome these barriers and effectively manage diversity, managers (and other organizational members) must possess or develop certain attitudes and values as well as the skills needed to change other people's attitudes and values.

Steps in Managing Diversity Effectively

LO5-5 List the steps managers can take to manage diversity effectively.

Managers can take a number of steps to change attitudes and values and promote the effective management of diversity. Here we describe these steps (listed in Table 5.4), some of which we have referred to previously.

SECURE TOP MANAGEMENT COMMITMENT As mentioned earlier in the chapter, top management's commitment to diversity is crucial for the success of any diversity-related

Table 5.4

Promoting the Effective Management of Diversity

- Secure top management commitment.
- Increase the accuracy of perceptions.
- Increase diversity awareness.
- Increase diversity skills.
- Encourage flexibility.
- Pay close attention to how employees are evaluated.
- Consider the numbers.
- Empower employees to challenge discriminatory behaviors, actions, and remarks.
- Reward employees for effectively managing diversity.
- Provide training, utilizing a multipronged, ongoing approach.
- Encourage mentoring of diverse employees.

initiatives. Top managers need to develop the correct ethical values and performance- or business-oriented attitudes that allow them to make appropriate use of their human resources.

STRIVE TO INCREASE THE ACCURACY OF PERCEPTIONS   One aspect of developing the appropriate values and attitudes is to take steps to increase the accuracy of perceptions. Managers should consciously attempt to be open to other points of view and perspectives, seek them out, and encourage their subordinates to do the same.[119] Organizational members who are open to other perspectives put their own beliefs and knowledge to an important reality test and will be more inclined to modify them when necessary. Managers should not be afraid to change their views about a person, an issue, or an event; moreover, they should encourage their subordinates to be open to changing their views in the light of disconfirming evidence. Additionally, managers and all other members of an organization should strive to avoid making snap judgments about people; rather, judgments should be made only when sufficient and relevant information has been gathered.[120]

INCREASE DIVERSITY AWARENESS   It is natural for managers and other members of an organization to view other people from their own perspective because their own feelings, thoughts, attitudes, and experiences guide their perceptions and interactions. The ability to appreciate diversity, however, requires that people become aware of other perspectives and the various attitudes and experiences of others. Many diversity awareness programs in organizations strive to increase managers' and workers' awareness of (1) their own attitudes, biases, and stereotypes and (2) the differing perspectives of diverse managers, subordinates, coworkers, and customers. Diversity awareness programs often have these goals:[121]

- Providing organizational members with accurate information about diversity
- Uncovering personal biases and stereotypes
- Assessing personal beliefs, attitudes, and values and learning about other points of view
- Overturning inaccurate stereotypes and beliefs about different groups
- Developing an atmosphere in which people feel free to share their differing perspectives and points of view
- Improving understanding of others who are different from oneself

Sometimes simply taking the time to interact with someone who is different in some way can increase awareness. Often when employees and managers are at social functions or just having lunch with a coworker, they interact with the people with whom they feel most comfortable. If all members of an organization make an effort to interact with people they ordinarily would not, mutual understanding is likely to be enhanced.

In large organizations, top managers are often far removed from entry-level employees—they may lack an understanding and appreciation for what these employees do day in and day out, the challenges and obstacles they face, and the steps that can be taken to improve effectiveness. Recognizing this fact, some managers have taken concrete steps to improve their understanding of the experiences, attitudes, and perspectives of frontline employees.

INCREASE DIVERSITY SKILLS Efforts to increase diversity skills focus on improving how managers and their subordinates interact with each other and improving their ability to work with different kinds of people.[122] An important issue here is being able to communicate with diverse employees. Diverse organizational members may have different communication styles, may differ in their language fluency, may use words differently, may differ in the nonverbal signals they send through facial expressions and body language, and may differ in how they perceive and interpret information. Managers and their subordinates must learn to communicate effectively with one another if an organization is to take advantage of the skills and abilities of its entire workforce. Educating organizational members about differences in ways of communicating is often a good starting point.

Diversity education can help managers and subordinates gain a better understanding of how people may interpret certain kinds of comments. Diversity education also can help employees learn how to resolve misunderstandings. Organizational members should feel comfortable enough to solve communication difficulties and misunderstandings as they occur rather than letting problems grow and fester without acknowledgment.

ENCOURAGE FLEXIBILITY Managers and their subordinates must learn how to be open to different approaches and ways of doing things. This does not mean organizational members have to suppress their personal styles. Rather, it means they must be open to, and not feel threatened by, different approaches and perspectives and must have the patience and flexibility to understand and appreciate diverse perspectives.[123]

To the extent feasible, managers should also be flexible enough to incorporate the differing needs of diverse employees. Earlier we mentioned that religious diversity suggests that people of certain religions might need time off for holidays that are traditionally workdays in the United States; managers need to anticipate and respond to such needs with flexibility (perhaps letting people skip the lunch hour so they can leave work early). Moreover, flexible work hours, the option to work from home, and cafeteria-style benefit plans (see Chapter 12) are just a few of the many ways in which managers can respond to the differing needs of diverse employees while enabling those employees to be effective contributors to an organization.

PAY CLOSE ATTENTION TO HOW ORGANIZATIONAL MEMBERS ARE EVALUATED Whenever feasible, it is desirable to rely on objective performance indicators (see Chapter 12) because they are less subject to bias. When objective indicators are not available or are inappropriate, managers should ensure that adequate time and attention are focused on the evaluation of employees' performance and that evaluators are held accountable for their evaluations.[124] Vague performance standards should be avoided.[125]

CONSIDER THE NUMBERS Looking at the numbers of members of different minority groups and women in various positions, at various levels in the hierarchy, in locations that differ in their desirability, and in any other relevant categorizations in an organization can tell managers important information about potential problems and ways to rectify them.[126] If members of certain groups are underrepresented in particular kinds of jobs or units, managers need to understand why this is the case and resolve any problems they uncover.

EMPOWER EMPLOYEES TO CHALLENGE DISCRIMINATORY BEHAVIORS, ACTIONS, AND REMARKS When managers or employees witness another organizational member being unfairly treated, they should be encouraged to speak up and rectify the situation. Top managers can make this happen by creating an organizational culture (see Chapter 3) that has zero tolerance for discrimination. As part of such a culture, organizational members should feel empowered to challenge discriminatory behavior, whether the behavior is directed at them or they witness it being directed at another employee.[127]

REWARD EMPLOYEES FOR EFFECTIVELY MANAGING DIVERSITY If effective management of diversity is a valued organizational objective, then employees should be rewarded for their contributions to this objective. For example, after settling a major race discrimination lawsuit, The Coca-Cola Company now ties managers' pay to their achievement of diversity goals. Examples of other organizations that do so include American Express and Bayer Corporation.[128]

PROVIDE TRAINING UTILIZING A MULTIPRONGED, ONGOING APPROACH   Many managers use a multipronged approach to increase diversity awareness and skills in their organizations; they use films and printed materials supplemented by experiential exercises to uncover hidden biases and stereotypes. Sometimes simply providing a forum for people to learn about and discuss their differing attitudes, values, and experiences can be a powerful means of increasing awareness. Also useful are role-plays that enact problems resulting from lack of awareness and show the increased understanding that comes from appreciating others' viewpoints. Accurate information and training experiences can debunk stereotypes. Group exercises, role-plays, and diversity-related experiences can help organizational members develop the skills they need to work effectively with a variety of people. Many organizations hire outside consultants to provide diversity training, in addition to utilizing their own in-house diversity experts.[129]

More than 50 years ago, UPS, a package delivery company, developed an innovative community internship program to increase the diversity awareness and skills of its managers and, at the same time, benefit the wider community. Upper and middle managers participating in the program take one month off the job to be community interns.[130] They work in community organizations helping people who, in many instances, are very different from themselves—such organizations include a detention center in McAllen, Texas, for Mexican immigrants; homeless shelters; AIDS centers; Head Start programs; migrant farmworker assistance groups; and groups aiming to halt the spread of drug abuse in inner cities.

Many managers who complete the UPS community internship program have superior diversity skills as a result of their experiences. During their internships, they learn about different cultures and approaches to work and life; they learn to interact effectively with people whom they ordinarily do not come into contact with; and they are forced to learn flexibility because of the dramatic differences between their roles at the internship sites and their roles as managers at UPS.

ENCOURAGE MENTORING OF DIVERSE EMPLOYEES   Unfortunately, African Americans and other minorities continue to be less likely to attain high-level positions in their organizations, and for those who do attain them, the climb up the corporate ladder typically takes longer than it does for white men. David Thomas, a professor at the Harvard Business School, has studied the careers of minorities in corporate America. One of his major conclusions is that mentoring is very important for minorities, most of whom have reached high levels in their organizations by having a solid network of mentors and contacts.[131] Mentoring is a process by which an experienced member of an organization (the mentor) provides advice and guidance to a less experienced member (the protégé) and helps the less experienced member learn how to advance in the organization and in his or her career.

According to Thomas, effective mentoring is more than providing instruction, offering advice, helping build skills, and sharing technical expertise. Of course, these aspects of mentoring are important and necessary. However, equally important is developing a high-quality, close, and supportive relationship with the protégé. Emotional bonds between a mentor and a protégé can enable a protégé, for example, to express fears and concerns, and sometimes even reluctance to follow a mentor's advice. The mentor can help the protégé build his or her confidence and feel comfortable engaging in unfamiliar work behaviors.[132]

mentoring A process by which an experienced member of an organization (the mentor) provides advice and guidance to a less experienced member (the protégé) and helps the less experienced member learn how to advance in the organization and in his or her career.

Sexual Harassment

Sexual harassment seriously damages both the people who are harassed and the reputation of the organization in which it occurs. It also can cost organizations billions. In late 2017, a new social movement called the #MeToo campaign began after Hollywood entertainment mogul Harvey Weinstein was accused of sexual harassment and assault by many women in the film industry over the last three decades.[133] Women were encouraged to tweet about

The #MeToo movement continues to help bring the issue of sexual harassment out of the shadows and into the mainstream and to increase public awareness about this serious topic.
©Sundry Photography/Shutterstock

their harassment experiences, and within the first 24 hours of the movement, the #MeToo hashtag was used more than 12 million times.[134] Other famous men accused of sexual harassment included Charlie Rose, Bill O'Reilly, Matt Lauer, Louis C.K., Kevin Spacey, and Al Franken.

But sexual harassment is not limited to the entertainment industry. According to a recent MSN poll, one in three (33%) people in the United States admits to being sexually harassed at work, with nearly 45% of women polled saying they have been sexually harassed in the workplace—this amounts to more than 33 million women.[135] In 2017, for example, Uber fired more than 20 employees after a company investigation into sexual harassment claims and workplace culture.[136] And over the past seven years, women at Microsoft filed more than 238 complaints with the company's HR department for sexual harassment and gender discrimination.[137]

Unfortunately, these are not isolated incidents. Sexual harassment victims can be women or men, and their harassers do not necessarily have to be of the opposite sex.[138] However, women are the most frequent victims of sexual harassment, particularly those in male-dominated occupations or those who occupy positions stereotypically associated with certain gender relationships, such as a female secretary reporting to a male boss. Sexual harassment is not only unethical, but also illegal. Managers have an ethical obligation to ensure that they, their coworkers, and their subordinates never engage in sexual harassment, even unintentionally.

Forms of Sexual Harassment

LO5-6 Identify the two major forms of sexual harassment and how they can be eliminated.

There are two basic forms of sexual harassment: quid pro quo sexual harassment and hostile work environment sexual harassment. **Quid pro quo sexual harassment** occurs when a harasser asks or forces an employee to perform sexual favors to keep a job, receive a promotion, receive a raise, obtain some other work-related opportunity, or avoid receiving negative consequences such as demotion or dismissal.[139] This "Sleep with me, honey, or you're fired" form of harassment is the more extreme type and leaves no doubt in anyone's mind that sexual harassment has taken place.[140]

quid pro quo sexual harassment Asking or forcing an employee to perform sexual favors in exchange for receiving some reward or avoiding negative consequences.

Hostile work environment sexual harassment is more subtle. It occurs when organizational members face an intimidating, hostile, or offensive work environment because of their sex.[141] Lewd jokes, sexually oriented comments or innuendos, vulgar language, displays of pornography, displays or distribution of sexually oriented objects, and sexually oriented remarks about one's physical appearance are examples of hostile work environment sexual harassment.[142] A hostile work environment interferes with organizational members' ability to perform their jobs effectively and has been deemed illegal by the courts. Managers who engage in hostile work environment harassment or allow others to do so risk costly lawsuits for their organizations. For example, a federal jury awarded Marion Schwab $3.24 million after deliberating on her sexual harassment case against FedEx. Schwab was the only female tractor-trailer driver at the FedEx facility serving the Harrisburg International Airport vicinity in Middletown, Pennsylvania, from 1997 to 2000. During that period she was the target of sexual innuendos, was given inferior work assignments, and was the brunt of derogatory comments about her appearance and the role of women in society. On five occasions the brakes on her truck were tampered with. The federal EEOC sued FedEx, and Schwab was part of the suit.[143]

hostile work environment sexual harassment Telling lewd jokes, displaying pornography, making sexually oriented remarks about someone's personal appearance, and other sex-related actions that make the work environment unpleasant.

The courts have recently recognized other forms of hostile work environment harassment in addition to sexual harassment. For example, a California jury awarded $61 million in punitive and compensatory damages to two FedEx Ground drivers. The drivers, of Lebanese descent, indicated that they had faced a hostile work environment and high levels of stress because a manager had harassed them with racial slurs for two years.[144]

Steps Managers Can Take to Eradicate Sexual Harassment

Managers have an ethical obligation to eradicate sexual harassment in their organizations. There are many ways to accomplish this objective. Here are four steps managers can take to deal with the problem:[145]

- *Develop and clearly communicate a sexual harassment policy endorsed by top management.* This policy should include prohibitions against both quid pro quo and hostile work environment sexual harassment. It should contain (1) examples of types of behavior that are unacceptable, (2) a procedure for employees to use to report instances of harassment, (3) a discussion of the disciplinary actions that will be taken when harassment has taken place, and (4) a commitment to educate and train organizational members about sexual harassment.

- *Use a fair complaint procedure to investigate charges of sexual harassment.* Such a procedure should (1) be managed by a neutral third party, (2) ensure that complaints are dealt with promptly and thoroughly, (3) protect and fairly treat victims, and (4) ensure that alleged harassers are fairly treated.

- *When it has been determined that sexual harassment has taken place, take corrective actions as soon as possible.* These actions can vary depending on the severity of the harassment. When harassment is extensive, prolonged, of a quid pro quo nature, or severely objectionable in some other manner, corrective action may include firing the harasser.

- *Provide sexual harassment education and training to all organizational members, including managers.* The majority of *Fortune* 500 firms currently provide this education and training for their employees. Managers at DuPont, for example, developed DuPont's "A Matter of Respect" program to help educate employees about sexual harassment and eliminate its occurrence. The program includes a four-hour workshop in which participants are given information that defines sexual harassment, sets forth the company's policy against it, and explains how to report complaints and access a 24-hour hotline. Participants watch video clips showing actual instances of harassment. One clip shows a saleswoman having dinner with a male client who, after much negotiating, seems about to give her company his business when he suddenly suggests that they continue their conversation in his hotel room. The saleswoman is confused about what to do. Will she be reprimanded if she says no and the deal is lost? After watching a video, participants discuss what they have seen, why the behavior is inappropriate, and what organizations can do to alleviate the problem.[146] Throughout the program, managers stress to employees that they do not have to tolerate sexual harassment or get involved in situations in which harassment is likely to occur. The "Management Insight" box provides tips for ensuring that the training is effective.

MANAGEMENT INSIGHT

Providing Effective Anti-Harassment Training

A swirl of sexual harassment charges in workplaces has made preventing such behavior a hot topic. The sight of prominent women speaking up about their experiences and of perpetrators being held accountable has given more employees hope that if they speak up, they may be taken seriously. The Equal Employment Opportunity Commission indicated that in the months after the Harvey Weinstein scandal, its website began receiving four times as many visits.[147] Companies including Fox News, NBC, and Uber announced new training in harassment prevention.

The problem, however, is that there is little evidence to support the effectiveness of anti-harassment training programs.[148] Typical programs were designed mainly to tell people what sexual harassment is and that it is illegal. Often, it involves a set of videos to watch and identify bad behavior. Few companies follow up to find out if attitudes or behavior have changed. When they do, they sometimes discover that knowledge is unchanged or they have simply reinforced stereotypes.

But the evidence does suggest some ideas for effective training to prevent sexual harassment. One helpful tactic is to set up training in small groups.[149] Face-to-face conversations and job-related examples are more powerful than generic presentations. Further, having everyone, especially leaders, participate in the training signals that respectful behavior is valued and necessary at all levels of the organization.

Another promising method is to focus the training on civil behavior.[150] Employees know they shouldn't grab a coworker, but some worry about what they *can* do. Civility training can promote behavior like respectful listening and affirmation of others' contributions, especially with regard to those who may feel marginalized. Managers can be trained in how to mentor employees in ways that empower rather than harass.

Another good practice is to recognize that harassment is more about exerting power than about expressing sexuality.[151] Therefore, one way to stop it is to equip bystanders to intervene. Training can offer options: A bystander can point out the behavior's inappropriateness, provide a disruption, or find an occasion to talk to the target so he or she isn't isolated.

Finally, training should be embedded in an ethical culture of respect and inclusion.[152] Organizations that are inclusive in hiring, training, and promotions will place more women and people of color in positions of power. This restrains the power dynamic that supports harassment. And as with any other kind of behavior, the behavior of the organization's leaders sets the tone for everyone else.

Barry S. Roberts and Richard A. Mann, experts on business law and authors of several books on the topic, suggest a number of additional factors that managers and all members of an organization need to keep in mind about sexual harassment:

- Every sexual harassment charge should be taken seriously.
- Employees who go along with unwanted sexual attention in the workplace can be sexual harassment victims.
- Employees sometimes wait before they file complaints of sexual harassment.
- An organization's sexual harassment policy should be communicated to each new employee and reviewed with current employees periodically.
- Suppliers and customers need to be familiar with an organization's sexual harassment policy.
- Managers should give employees alternative ways to report incidents of sexual harassment.
- Employees who report sexual harassment must have their rights protected; this includes being protected from any potential retaliation.
- Allegations of sexual harassment should be kept confidential; those accused of harassment should have their rights protected.
- Investigations of harassment charges and any resultant disciplinary actions need to proceed in a timely manner.
- Managers must protect employees from sexual harassment from third parties they may interact with while performing their jobs, such as suppliers or customers.[153]

Summary and Review

LO5-1 **THE INCREASING DIVERSITY OF THE WORKFORCE AND THE ENVIRONMENT** Diversity is dissimilarity or differences among people. Diversity is a pressing concern for managers and organizations for business and ethical reasons. There are multiple forms of diversity such as age, gender, race and ethnicity, religion, capabilities/disabilities, socioeconomic background, sexual orientation, and physical appearance.

LO5-2, 5-3 **MANAGERS AND THE EFFECTIVE MANAGEMENT OF DIVERSITY** Both the workforce and the organizational environment are increasingly diverse, and effectively managing this diversity is an essential component of management. In each of their managerial roles, managers can encourage the effective management of diversity, which is both an ethical and a business imperative.

LO5-4   PERCEPTION   Perception is the process through which people select, organize, and interpret sensory input to give meaning and order to the world around them. It is inherently subjective. Schemas guide perception; when schemas are based on a single visible characteristic such as race or gender, they are inaccurate stereotypes that lead to unfair treatment. Unfair treatment also can result from biases and overt discrimination.

LO5-5   HOW TO MANAGE DIVERSITY EFFECTIVELY   Managers can take many steps to manage diversity effectively, an ongoing process that requires frequent monitoring.

LO5-6   SEXUAL HARASSMENT   Two forms of sexual harassment are quid pro quo sexual harassment and hostile work environment sexual harassment. Steps that managers can take to eradicate sexual harassment include development and communication of a sexual harassment policy endorsed by top management, use of fair complaint procedures, prompt corrective action when harassment occurs, and sexual harassment training and education.

Management in Action

Topics for Discussion and Action

Discussion

1. Discuss why violations of the principles of distributive and procedural justice continue to occur in modern organizations. What can managers do to uphold these principles in their organizations? [LO5-2, 5-3, 5-4, 5-5]

2. Sometimes employees who test positive for HIV experience discrimination in the workplace. As a manager, what would you do to ensure such discrimination is eliminated? [LO5-1, 5-4]

3. Some workers might resent accommodations made for disabled employees. As a manager, what could you do to ensure all employees are treated fairly? [LO5-1, 5-4]

4. Discuss the ways in which schemas can be functional and dysfunctional. [LO5-4]

5. Discuss an occasion when you may have been treated unfairly because of stereotypical thinking. What stereotypes were applied to you? How did they result in your being treated unfairly? [LO5-4]

6. How does implicit bias influence your own behavior and decisions? [LO5-4]

7. Why is mentoring particularly important for minorities? [LO5-5]

8. Why is it important to consider the numbers of different groups of employees at various levels in an organization's hierarchy? [LO5-5]

9. Think about a situation in which you would have benefited from mentoring but a mentor was not available. What could you have done to try to get the help of a mentor in this situation? [LO5-5]

Action

10. Choose a *Fortune* 500 company not mentioned in the chapter. Conduct research to determine what steps this organization has taken to manage diversity effectively and eliminate sexual harassment. [LO5-2, 5-5, 5-6]

Building Management Skills

Solving Diversity-Related Problems [LO5-1, 5-2, 5-3, 5-4, 5-5, 5-6]

Think about the last time that you (1) were treated unfairly because you differed from a decision maker on a particular dimension of diversity or (2) observed someone else being treated unfairly because that person differed from a decision maker on a particular dimension of diversity. Then answer these questions:

1. Why do you think the decision maker acted unfairly in this situation?

2. In what ways, if any, were biases, stereotypes, or overt discrimination involved in this situation?

3. Was the decision maker aware that he or she was acting unfairly?

4. What could you or the person who was treated unfairly have done to improve matters and rectify the injustice on the spot?

5. Was any sexual harassment involved in this situation? If so, what kind was it?

6. If you had authority over the decision maker (that is, if you were his or her manager or supervisor), what steps would you take to ensure that the decision maker stops treating people unfairly?

Managing Ethically [LO5-1, 5-2, 5-3, 5-5]

Some companies require that their employees work long hours and travel extensively. Employees with young children, employees taking care of elderly relatives, and employees who have interests outside the workplace sometimes find that their careers are jeopardized if they try to work more reasonable hours or limit their work-related travel. Some of these employees feel that it is unethical for their managers to expect so much of them in the workplace and not understand their needs as parents and caregivers.

Questions

1. Either individually or in a group, think about the ethical implications of requiring long hours and extensive amounts of travel for some jobs.

2. What obligations do you think managers and companies have to enable employees to have balanced lives and meet nonwork needs and demands?

Small Group Breakout Exercise

Determining If a Problem Exists [LO5-1, 5-2, 5-3, 5-4, 5-5]

Form groups of three or four people, and appoint one member as the spokesperson who will communicate your findings to the whole class when called on by the instructor. Then discuss the following scenario:

You and your partners own and manage a local chain of restaurants, with moderate to expensive prices, that are open for lunch and dinner during the week and for dinner on weekends. Your staff is diverse, and you believe that you are managing diversity effectively. Yet on visits to the different restaurants, you have noticed that your African American employees tend to congregate together and communicate mainly with each other. The same is true for your Hispanic employees and your white employees. You are meeting with your partners today to discuss this observation.

1. Discuss why the patterns of communication that you observed might be occurring in your restaurants.

2. Discuss whether your observation reflects an underlying problem. If so, why? If not, why not?

3. Discuss whether you should address this issue with your staff and in your restaurants. If so, how and why? If not, why not?

Be the Manager [LO5-1, 5-2, 5-3, 5-4, 5-5]

You are Maria Herrera and have been recently promoted to the position of director of financial analysis for a medium-sized consumer goods firm. During your first few weeks on the job, you took the time to have lunch with each of your subordinates to try to get to know him or her better. You have 12 direct reports, junior and senior financial analysts who support different product lines. Susan Epstein, one of the female financial analysts you had lunch with, made the following statement: "I'm so glad we finally have a woman in charge. Now, hopefully, things will get better around here." You pressed Epstein to elaborate, but she clammed up. She indicated that she didn't want to unnecessarily bias you and

that the problems were pretty self-evident. In fact, Epstein was surprised that you didn't know what she was talking about and jokingly mentioned that perhaps you should spend some time undercover, observing her group and their interactions with others.

You spoke with your supervisor and the former director, who had been promoted and volunteered to be on call if you had any questions. Neither man knew of any diversity-related issues in your group. In fact, your supervisor's response was, "We've got a lot of problems, but fortunately that's not one of them."

What are you going to do to address this issue?

Bloomberg Businessweek Case in the News

New Kids on the Board [LO 5-1, 5-2, 5-3, 5-4, 5-5]

For most of the past decade, Cheryl Miller has spent her days trying to put more cars on America's roads—first as the treasurer and now as the chief financial officer of AutoNation Inc., the largest auto retailer in the U.S. And for the past year she's been working on behalf of another of the country's biggest companies, Tyson Foods Inc., as one of the newest members of its board of directors.

When she was appointed in late 2016, at age 44, Miller, one of several female directors in the meat and poultry company's 83-year history, had never served on a corporate

board. A growing number of companies, including Tyson, Republic Services, Foot Locker, and Best Buy, are eschewing traditional board candidates—retired chief executive officers, who are overwhelmingly older white men—and opting for diverse members, many of them first-timers with no experience.

In 2017, 45% of appointees to the boards of S&P 500 companies were novice directors, the most since recruiter Spencer Stuart started keeping tabs in 2006. Last year also was the first time a majority of the incoming directors were women or

minority candidates. "Two years ago, they would have said, 'Oh, it would be great to have diversity, but we really want a CEO,'" says Julie Daum, who leads Spencer Stuart's North American board practice. "Now it feels like the female will occasionally beat out the CEO."

Tyson's board started searching for new candidates about three years ago, after the company's $7.8 billion purchase of rival meat producer Hillshire Brands. Since then, two other younger first-time directors have joined the board, both white men: Jeff Schomburger, 56, global sales officer at Procter & Gamble Co., in late 2016, and Dean Banks, 44, who heads the X unit of Google parent Alphabet Inc., in late 2017. "I've seen a richer outcome from having a whole lot of voices around the table trying to have the best conversation possible," says John Tyson, chairman of the company.

Waste management company Republic Services Inc. has been looking for diverse directors since 2011, after a 2008 merger with Allied Waste Industries left it with an all-male board, including one black man. "Change meant bringing people into the waste business who had other experiences," says CEO Don Slager. "Prior to the merger, frankly, they were just a bunch of garbage men."

As part of this push, the company enacted some new policies, including a mandatory retirement age of 73 for directors. A variety of experience also was a priority, Slager says. Candidates ideally would bring expertise in areas not already represented, such as logistics and financial reporting. "When you drop a layer below the C-suite, it opens you up to a whole new group of people who are the future leaders of these organizations," he says.

Within five years, retirements created a few openings. Republic added Jennifer Kirk, 43, the controller at oil producer Occidental Petroleum Corp., in July 2016, and Sandra Volpe, 50, the senior vice president for strategic planning for FedEx Ground, in December of that year. Both had never been directors before. In 2017,

a third woman, Kim Pegula, 48, one of the principal owners of the NFL's Buffalo Bills and another novice, joined Republic's roster.

Changing a board's demographics and traditions comes with risks, says David Larcker, a professor at Stanford's Graduate School of Business. "We're really pro-diversity," he says. Still, the board needs to function well to perform its oversight. "It's not just a check box," he says. "It's going to take some give or take on both sides."

Less experienced directors often require more training and resources early in their tenure to better understand and fill their roles, says Bonnie Gwin, who heads the board management practice at executive recruiter Heidrick & Struggles. Often boards pair new members with experienced directors who serve as coaches during the transition.

For Miller, joining Tyson's board required regular one-on-one meetings with the other directors before her appointment, as well as a crash course in the meat company's business. She also was coached by AutoNation's lead director, Michael Larson, the chief investment officer of BMGI, which managers Bill Gates's non-Microsoft investments and those of the Bill & Melinda Gates Foundation Trust. (Larson also sits on Republic Services' board.)

Getting that first appointment is hard, says Stacy Brown-Philpot, 42, CEO of TaskRabbit Inc., which connects

consumers with home-improvement services. Many boards still are reluctant to appoint executives who don't have a track record, she says. It took her three years to land her first appointment, at HP Inc., in 2016. She says she felt she needed to bolster her application with recommendations from big names, such as Facebook Chief Operating Officer Sheryl Sandberg and HP CEO Meg Whitman.

Turnover remains slow. Fewer than 7% of directors' seats change hands in any given year, and the average age has risen to 63, from 61 two years ago, according to Spencer Stuart. As long as it takes, Miller says, she is committed to helping more candidates like herself. "Let's look at diversity not just because it's going to check a box," she says, "but because we think it's going to add value as a company in the marketplace."

Questions for Discussion

1. How does a diverse board of directors help increase organizational performance?

2. What are some advantages and disadvantages of implementing a mandatory retirement age for corporate directors?

3. What role could implicit bias play in nominating individuals to a company's board of directors?

Source: Jeff Green, "New Kids on the Board," *Bloomberg Businessweek,* April 23, 2018, pp. 19–20. Used with permission of Bloomberg L.P. Copyright © 2017. All rights reserved.

Notes

1. B. Ortutay, "Diversity in Tech: Lots of Attention, Little Progress," *Associated Press,* https://apnews.com, January 24, 2017, https://apnews.com.

2. M. R. Dickey, "Intel's Diversity Efforts Are Somewhat Paying Off," *TechCrunch,* https://techcrunch.com, February 28, 2107; Erin Carson, "Intel Diversity Report Shows Progress Is Tough to Measure," *CNET,* https://www.cnet.com, August 15, 2017; Grace Donnelly, "Intel CEO in New Diversity Report: 'Let's Turn This Tragedy into Action,'" *Fortune,* http://fortune.com, August 15, 2017.

3. S. G. Carmichael, "Making Intel More Diverse," interview with Danielle Brown, *Harvard Business Review,* https://hbr.org, March 10, 2017; Carson, "Intel Diversity Report Shows Progress Is Tough to Measure."

4. Carmichael, "Making Intel More Diverse"; Donnelly, "Intel CEO in New Diversity Report."

5. S. Lynn, "Meet Intel's Newest Executive, Barbara Whye," *Black Enterprise,* www.blackenterprise.com, April 13, 2017.

6. Carmichael, "Making Intel More Diverse"; Dickey, "Intel's Diversity Efforts Are

Somewhat Paying Off"; Carson, "Intel Diversity Report Shows Progress Is Tough to Measure."

7. Carmichael, "Making Intel More Diverse"; Dickey, "Intel's Diversity Efforts."

8. J. Michelson, "How a Diverse Team Drives Innovation—Insights from Intel," *Forbes,* www.forbes.com, June 27, 2018.

9. "Deloitte's Supplier Diversity Program," www.div2000.com, accessed March 16, 2018.

10. E. Larson, "New Research: Diversity + Inclusion = Better Decision Making at Work," *Forbes,* www.forbes.com, September 21, 2017.

11. S. Tasheva and A. Hillman, "Integrating Diversity at Different Levels: Multi-Level Human Capital, Social Capital, and Demographic Diversity and Their Implications for Team Effectiveness," *Academy of Management Review,* January 19, 2018.

12. E. Sherman, "Hiring Bias Blacks and Latinos Face Hasn't Improved in 25 Years," *Forbes,* www.forbes.com, September 16, 2017.

13. "Private Sector Workers Lack Transparency," Institute for Women's Policy Research, https://iwpr.org, December 2017.

14. J. Berman, "When a Woman or Person of Color Becomes CEO, White Men Have a Strange Reaction," *MarketWatch,* www.marketwatch.com, March 3, 2018.

15. "Fact Sheet: Aging in the United States," Population Reference Bureau, www.prb.org, accessed March 16, 2018; "Age Discrimination," www.eeoc.gov, accessed March 16, 2018; U.S. Census Bureau, "The Nation's Median Age Continues to Rise," www.census.gov, June 22, 2017.

16. Bureau of Labor Statistics, "Usual Weekly Earnings of Wage and Salary Workers, Q4 2017," www.bls.gov, January 17, 2018.

17. Catalyst, "Pyramid: Women in S&P 500 Companies," www.catalyst.org, February 5, 2018.

18. Ibid.

19. K. Daum, "7 Reasons Women Executives Make Better Leaders," *Inc.,* www.inc.com, accessed March 16, 2018; R. Sharpe, "As Leaders, Women Rule," *Businessweek,* November 20, 2000, 75–84.

20. "Catalyst Study Reveals Financial Performance Is Higher for Companies with More Women at the Top," www.catalyst.org, accessed March 16, 2018.

21. "100 Women: Do Women on Boards Increase Company Profits?" *BBC,* www.bbc.com, October 2, 2017.

22. "Race Data," www.census.org, accessed March 16, 2018.

23. U.S. Census Bureau, "Director's Blog: 2015 National Content Test Results Released This Week," www.census.gov, March 3, 2017.

24. U.S. Census Bureau, "Civilian Labor Force by Age, Sex, Race, and Ethnicity," www.census.gov, accessed March 16, 2018.

25. U.S. Census Bureau, "Quick Facts," www.census.gov, accessed March 16, 2018.

26. U.S. Census Bureau, "Table 11: Percent Distribution of the Projected Population by Hispanic Origin and Race for the United States, 2015 to 2060," www.census.gov, accessed March 16, 2018.

27. Bureau of Labor Statistics, "Usual Weekly Earnings of Wage and Salary Workers, Fourth Quarter 2017," www.bls.gov, accessed March 16, 2018.

28. K. Shattuck, "Alan Cumming Helps CBS Unfurl Its Rainbow Flag with *Instinct,*" *The New York Times,* www.nytimes.com, March 8, 2018; M. Berg, "Note to Networks: Diversity on TV Pays Off," *Forbes,* www.forbes.com, February 22, 2017.

29. "About SodaStream," www.sodastream.com, accessed March 17, 2018; D. Leonard and Y. Benmeleh, "How SodaStream Makes—and Markets—Peace," *Bloomberg Businessweek,* December 25, 2017, 60–65.

30. "About SodaStream."

31. Leonard and Benmeleh, "How SodaStream Makes—and Markets—Peace."

32. Ibid.

33. Jennifer O'Brien, "SodaStream Reveals Why 'Disruptive' Influencers Campaigns Are Vital to Reaching New Audiences," *CMO,* www.cmo.com.au, February 9, 2018; Jennifer Rooney, "The Future of Recruiting Talent? SodaStream Launches Commercial to Find 'Rainmakers,'" *Forbes,* www.forbes.com, February 2, 2018; Leonard and Benmeleh, "How SodaStream Makes—and Markets—Peace."

34. Leonard and Benmeleh, "How SodaStream Makes—and Markets—Peace."

35. B. Latimer, "Latinos in Hollywood: Few Roles, Frequent Stereotypes, New Study Finds," *NBC,* www.nbcnews.com, February 22, 2016.

36. T. Abbady, "The Modern Newsroom Is Stuck Behind the Gender and Color Line," *NPR,* www.npr.org, May 1, 2017.

37. J.H. Conlan, "Putting a Little Faith in Diversity," *BusinessWeek Online,* December 21, 2000.

38. K. Klenner, "Religious Expression in Today's Workplace Is a Thorny Issue," *Labor and Employment Blog,* www.bna.com, December 2, 2016.

39. Conlan, "Putting a Little Faith in Diversity."

40. K. Holland, "When Religious Needs Test Company Policy," *The New York Times,* www.nytimes.com, accessed March 17, 2018; K.K. Chang, "What Companies Can Do When Work and Religion Conflict," *Harvard Business Review,* https://hbr.org, March 15, 2016.

41. J.N. Cleveland, J. Barnes-Farrell, and J.M. Ratz, "Accommodation in the Workplace," *Human Resource Management Review* 7 (1997), 77–108; A. Colella, "Coworker Distributive Fairness Judgments of the Workplace Accommodations of Employees with Disabilities," *Academy of Management Review* 26 (2001), 100–16.

42. Colella, "Coworker Distributive Fairness Judgments of the Workplace Accommodations of Employees with Disabilities"; M.S. West and R.L. Cardy, "Accommodating Claims of Disability: The Potential Impact of Abuses," *Human Resource Management Review* 7 (1997), 233–46.

43. A. Bhattacharya and H. Long, "America Still Leaves the Disabled Behind," *CNN Money,* http://money.cnn.com, July 26, 2015.

44. Colella, "Coworker Distributive Fairness Judgments of the Workplace Accommodations of Employees with Disabilities."

45. "What We Do" and "The Disability Equality Index," www.usbln.org, accessed March 16, 2018; S. Blahovec, "Why Hire Disabled Workers? 4 Powerful (and Inclusive) Companies Answer," *The Huffington Post,* www.huffingtonpost.com, February 24, 2017.

46. J.M. George, "AIDS/AIDS-Related Complex," in L.H. Peters, C.R. Greer, and S.A. Youngblood, eds., *The Blackwell Encyclopedic Dictionary of Human Resource Management* (Oxford, UK: Blackwell, 1997), 6–7.

47. J.M. George, "AIDS Awareness Training," in L.H. Peters, C.R. Greer, and S.A. Youngblood, eds., *The Blackwell Encyclopedic Dictionary of Human Resource Management* (Oxford, UK: Blackwell, 1997), 6.

48. A. Smith, "EEOC Offers Guidance to Employees with HIV," *SHRM,* www.shrm.org, December 7, 2015.

49. A. Scaccia, "Stigma Drives Workplace Discrimination Against Workers Living with HIV," https://rewire.news, accessed March 16, 2018.

50. R. Brownstein, "Honoring Work Is Key to Ending Poverty," *Detroit News,* October 2, 2001, 9; G. Koretz, "How Welfare to Work Worked," *BusinessWeek,* September 24, 2001 (*BusinessWeek* Archives).

51. "As Ex-Welfare Recipients Lose Jobs, Offer Safety Net," *Atlanta Constitution,* October 10, 2001, A18.

52. C.S. Rugaber, "Job Openings in a Squeeze," *Houston Chronicle,* February 10, 2010, D1.

53. E. Sherman, "Poverty Rate Is Down to 12.7%, But Probably Not for Long," *Forbes,* www.forbes.com, September 12, 2017.

54. "Poverty Thresholds for 2017 by Size of Family and Number of Related Children under 18 Years," www.census.gov, accessed March 16, 2018.

55. G. Thompson, "This Is What $15 an Hour Looks Like," *The Nation,* www.thenation.com, January 7, 2016.

56. N. Scheiber, "The Perils of Ever-Changing Work Schedules Extend to Children's Well-Being," *The New York Times,* www.nytimes.com, August 12, 2015.

57. A. Chan, "Overnight Childcare Fills Void in 24/7 Economy," *Los Angeles Times,* www.latimes.com, April 20, 2017.

58. G.J. Gates, "In U.S., More Adults Identifying as LGBT," http://news.gallup.com, January 11, 2018.

59. D. Wiessner, "U.S. Appeals Court Says Title VII Covers Discrimination Based on Sexual Orientation," *Reuters,* www.reuters.com, February 26, 2018; B. Chappell,

"Supreme Court Declares Same-Sex Marriage Legal in All 50 States," *NPR,* www.npr.org, June 26, 2015.

60. "Disney Recognized for Innovation on Workplace Equality," https://thewaltdisneycompany.com, October 16, 2017.

61. J.B. Shinall, "Occupational Characteristics and the Obesity Wage Penalty," Vanderbilt University Law School, Public Law & Legal Theory Working Paper 16-23, accessed at http://ssrn.com, March 16, 2018; A. Wolf, "Overweight Women Lose in the Job Market: Vanderbilt Study," https://news.vanderbilt.edu, October 21, 2014.

62. V. Valian, *Why So Slow? The Advancement of Women* (Cambridge, MA: MIT Press, 2000); S.T. Fiske and S.E. Taylor, *Social Cognition,* 2nd ed. (New York: McGraw-Hill, 1991).

63. "PwC Revenues Grow by 7% to Record US$37.7 Billion," *Globe Newswire,* https://globenewswire.com, October 4, 2017.

64. "Robert E. Moritz, Chairman—PricewaterhouseCoopers International Limited," www.pwc.com, accessed March 16, 2018.

65. A. Bryant, "Bob Moritz, on How to Learn About Diversity," *The New York Times,* www.nytimes.com, accessed March 16, 2018.

66. "PwC Shares 10 Diversity and Inclusion Lessons," https://press.pwc.com, September 18, 2016.

67. B. Marcus, "What Happens When CEOs Take a Pledge to Improve Diversity and Inclusion?" *Forbes,* https://www.forbes.com, January 19, 2018.

68. "Leveraging the Power of Our Differences," www.pwc.com, accessed March 16, 2018.

69. "Our Circles," https://www.pwc.com, accessed March 16, 2018.

70. "Leveraging the Power of Our Differences."

71. Valian, *Why So Slow?*

72. S. Rynes and B. Rosen, "A Field Survey of Factors Affecting the Adoption and Perceived Success of Diversity Training," *Personnel Psychology* 48 (1995), 247–70; Valian, *Why So Slow?*

73. V. Brown and F.L. Geis, "Turning Lead into Gold: Leadership by Men and Women and the Alchemy of Social Consensus," *Journal of Personality and Social Psychology* 46 (1984), 811–24; Valian, *Why So Slow?*

74. Valian, *Why So Slow?*

75. J. Cole and B. Singer, "A Theory of Limited Differences: Explaining the Productivity Puzzle in Science," in H. Zuckerman, J.R. Cole, and J.T. Bruer, eds., *The Outer Circle: Women in the Scientific Community* (New York: Norton, 1991), 277–310; M.F. Fox, "Sex, Salary, and Achievement: Reward Dualism in Academia," *Sociology of Education* 54 (1981), 71–84; J.S. Long, "The Origins of Sex Differences in Science," *Social Forces* 68 (1990), 1297–315;

R.F. Martell, D.M. Lane, and C. Emrich, "Male–Female Differences: A Computer Simulation," *American Psychologist* 51 (1996), 157–58; Valian, *Why So Slow?*

76. Ibid.

77. R. Folger and M.A. Konovsky, "Effects of Procedural and Distributive Justice on Reactions to Pay Raise Decisions," *Academy of Management Journal* 32 (1989), 115–30; J. Greenberg, "Organizational Justice: Yesterday, Today, and Tomorrow," *Journal of Management* 16 (1990), 399–402; O. Janssen, "How Fairness Perceptions Make Innovative Behavior More or Less Stressful," *Journal of Organizational Behavior* 25 (2004), 201–15.

78. A. Krivkovich, K. Robinson, I. Starikova, R. Valentino, and L. Yee, "Women in the Workplace," *McKinsey & Company,* www.mckinsey.com, October 2017; J. Gordon, "3 Ways to Equalize the Treatment of Women in the Workplace," *Forbes,* www.forbes.com, April 3, 2017.

79. "Household Data; Annual Averages: 39. Median Weekly Earnings of Full-Time Wage and Salary Workers by Detailed Occupation and Sex," www.bls.gov, accessed March 16, 2018.

80. A. Elejalde-Ruiz, "Ford Settles Sexual, Racial Harassment Claims at Chicago Plants for $10 Million," *Chicago Tribune,* www.chicagotribune.com, August 17, 2017.

81. Greenberg, "Organizational Justice"; M.G. Ehrhart, "Leadership and Procedural Justice Climate as Antecedents of Unit-Level Organizational Citizenship Behavior," *Personnel Psychology* 57 (2004), 61–94; A. Colella, R.L. Paetzold, and M.A. Belliveau, "Factors Affecting Coworkers' Procedural Justice Inferences of the Workplace Accommodations of Employees with Disabilities," *Personnel Psychology* 57 (2004), 1–23.

82. G. Robinson and K. Dechant, "Building a Case for Business Diversity," *Academy of Management Executive* 3 (1997), 32–47.

83. D. Keyes, "Target Opens New Small-Format Stores," *Business Insider,* www.businessinsider.com, October 23, 2017.

84. V. Bolden-Barrett, "Study: Turnover Costs Employers $15,000 per Worker," *HR Dive,* www.hrdive.com, August 11, 2017.

85. J. Suarez, "What These Top Companies' Supplier Diversity Programs Share," https://blog.cvmsolutions.com, December 20, 2017.

86. G. Winter, "Coca-Cola Settles Racial Bias Case," *The New York Times,* www.nytimes.com, November 17, 2000.

87. H.R. Schiffmann, *Sensation and Perception: An Integrated Approach* (New York: Wiley, 1990).

88. "History," http://corporate.mcdonalds.com, accessed March 16, 2018.

89. R. Cardoza, "25 Craziest McDonald's Menu Items from Around the World,"

Eat This, Not That, www.eatthis.com, June 20, 2017.

90. S.T. Fiske and S.E. Taylor, *Social Cognition* (Reading, MA: Addison-Wesley, 1984).

91. J.S. Bruner, "Going beyond the Information Given," in H. Gruber, G. Terrell, and M. Wertheimer, eds., *Contemporary Approaches to Cognition* (Cambridge, MA: Harvard University Press, 1957); Fiske and Taylor, *Social Cognition.*

92. Fiske and Taylor, *Social Cognition.*

93. Valian, *Why So Slow?*

94. D. Bakan, *The Duality of Human Existence* (Chicago: Rand McNally, 1966); J.T. Spence and R.L. Helmreich, *Masculinity and Femininity: Their Psychological Dimensions, Correlates, and Antecedents* (Austin: University of Texas Press, 1978); J.T. Spence and L.L. Sawin, "Images of Masculinity and Femininity: A Reconceptualization," in V.E. O'Leary, R.K. Unger, and B.B. Wallston, eds., *Women, Gender, and Social Psychology* (Hillsdale, NJ: Erlbaum, 1985), 35–66; Valian, *Why So Slow?*

95. Valian, *Why So Slow?*

96. P.R. Sackett, C.M. Hardison, and M.J. Cullen, "On Interpreting Stereotype Threat as Accounting for African American–White Differences on Cognitive Tests," *American Psychologist* 59, no. 1 (January 2004), 7–13; C.M. Steele and J.A. Aronson, "Stereotype Threat Does Not Live by Steele and Aronson (1995) alone," *American Psychologist* 59, no. 1 (January 2004), 47–48; P.R. Sackett, C.M. Hardison, and M.J. Cullen, "On the Value of Correcting Mischaracterizations of Stereotype Threat Research," *American Psychologist* 59, no. 1 (January 2004), 48–49; D.M. Amodio, E. Harmon-Jones, P.G. Devine, J.J. Curtin, S.L. Hartley, and A.E. Covert, "Neural Signals for the Detection of Unintentional Race Bias," *Psychological Science* 15, no. 2 (2004), 88–93.

97. M. Loden and J.B. Rosener, *Workforce America! Managing Employee Diversity as a Vital Resource* (Burr Ridge, IL: Irwin, 1991).

98. M.E. Heilman and T.G. Okimoto, "Motherhood: A Potential Source of Bias in Employment Decisions," *Journal of Applied Psychology* 93, no. 1 (2008), 189–98.

99. L. Roberson, B.M. Galvin, and A.C. Charles, "Chapter 13, When Group Identities Matter: Bias in Performance Appraisal," in J.P. Walsh and A.P. Brief, eds., *The Academy of Management Annals* vol. 1 (New York: Erlbaum, 2008), 617–50.

100. "Persons with a Disability: Labor Force Characteristics Summary," www.bls.gov, June 21, 2017.

101. N. Scheiber, "Study Using Fake Job Letters Exposes Bias against Disabled," *The New York Times,* November 2, 2015, B1, B2.

102. "Ken's Krew Fast Facts," www.kenskrew .org, accessed September 12, 2018.

103. A. Merrick, "Erasing 'Un' from 'Unemployable,'" *The Wall Street Journal,* August 2, 2007, B6.

104. Habitat International, "Home Page" and "Our Products," www.habitatint.com, accessed March 16, 2018; A. Stein Wellner, "The Disability Advantage," *Inc.,* www.inc.com, October 2005, 29–31.

105. Habitat International, "Our People" www .habitatint.com, accessed March 16, 2018; Wellner, "The Disability Advantage."

106. Ibid.

107. Ibid.

108. Kirwan Institute for the Study of Race and Ethnicity, "Implicit Bias Review: 2017," http://kirwaninstitute.osu.edu, accessed March 16, 2018.

109. I. Bohnet, A. van Geen, and M. Bazerman, "When Performance Trumps Gender Bias: Joint vs. Separate Evaluation," *Management Science* 62, no. 5 (2015), 1225–34.

110. A. Stites, "NFL's Rooney Rule: What Is It and How Does It Work?" *SBNation,* www .sbnation.com, January 6, 2018; B. W. Collins, "Tackling Unconscious Bias in Hiring Practices: The Plight of the Rooney Rule," *New York University Law Review* 82, no. 3, June 2007.

111. Fiske and Taylor, *Social Cognition.*

112. D. Hull, "Tesla Slams Racial Bias Lawsuit as a 'Hotbed of Misinformation,'" *Bloomberg Technology,* www.bloomberg.com, November 15, 2017; S. Ember, "11 Sue Fox News, Citing 'Intolerable' Racial Bias," *The New York Times,* www.nytimes .com, April 25, 2017; T. Jan, "How Racial Bias Could Be Hurting Silicon Valley's Bottom Line," *The Washington Post,* www .washingtonpost.com, February 2, 2017.

113. K. Terrell, "3 Lawsuits That Could Stop Age Discrimination," *AARP,* www.aarp .org, November 21, 2017.

114. "Nike Settles Discrimination Suit for $7.6 Million," *The Wall Street Journal,* July 31, 2007, B9.

115. S. Yan, "Why Japan Is Failing Its Women," *CNN Money,* http://money.cnn .com, October 16, 2016.

116. C. Farrell, "The Age Discrimination Law at 50: A Mixed Bag," *Forbes,* www.forbes .com, February 14, 2017.

117. J. Levitz, "More Workers Cite Age Bias During Layoffs," *The Wall Street Journal,* March 11, 2009, D1–2.

118. A. Raghavan, "Terminated: Why the Women of Wall Street Are Disappearing," Forbes.com—Magazine Article, *ForbesWoman,* http://forbes. com/forbes/2009/0316-072_t-erminated_ women_print.html, March 16, 2009, accessed February 10, 2010.

119. A.G. Greenwald and M. Banaji, "Implicit Social Cognition: Attitudes, Self-Esteem, and Stereotypes," *Psychological Review* 102 (1995), 4–27.

120. "How to Increase Workplace Diversity," *The Wall Street Journal,* http://guides.wsj .com, accessed March 16, 2018.

121. A.P. Carnevale and S.C. Stone, "Diversity: Beyond the Golden Rule," *Training & Development,* October 1994, 22–39.

122. B.A. Battaglia, "Skills for Managing Multicultural Teams," *Cultural Diversity at Work* 4 (1992); Carnevale and Stone, "Diversity."

123. W.B. Swann Jr., J.T. Polzer, D.C. Seyle, and S.J. Ko, "Finding Value in Diversity: Verification of Personal and Social Self-Views in Diverse Groups," *Academy of Management Review* 29, no. 1 (2004), 9–27.

124. Valian, *Why So Slow?*

125. A.P. Brief, R.T. Buttram, R.M. Reizenstein, S.D. Pugh, J.D. Callahan, R.L. McCline, and J.B. Vaslow, "Beyond Good Intentions: The Next Steps toward Racial Equality in the American Workplace," *Academy of Management Executive,* November 1997, 59–72.

126. Ibid.

127. Ibid.

128. J. Lindzon, "Is It Time for Investors to Tie Executive Compensation to Diversity Goals?" Fast Company, www.fastcompany .com, February 9, 2017; Y. Cole, "Linking Diversity to Executive Compensation," *DiversityInc.,* August–September 2003, 58–62.

129. B. Mandell and S. Kohler-Gray, "Management Development That Values Diversity," *Personnel,* March 1990, 41–47.

130. "Community Internship Program," https://sustainability.ups.com, accessed March 16, 2018; B. Leak, "Online Extra: UPS Delivers an Eye-Opener," *BusinessWeek,* www.businessweek.com, accessed February 11, 2010.

131. D.A. Thomas, "Race Matters: The Truth about Mentoring Minorities," *Harvard Business Review,* April 2001, 99–107.

132. Ibid.

133. J. Kantor and M. Twohey, "Harvey Weinstein Paid Off Sexual Harassment Accusers for Decades," *The New York Times,* www .nytimes.com, October 5, 2017.

134. N. Smartt, "Sexual Harassment in the Workplace in a #MeToo World," *Forbes,* www.forbes.com, December 20, 2017.

135. R. Gillett, "Sexual Harassment Isn't a Hollywood, Tech, or Media Issue—It Affects Everyone," *Business Insider,* www .businessinsider.com, November 30, 2017.

136. O. Solon, "Uber Fires More than 20 Employees After Sexual Harassment Investigation," *The Guardian,* www .theguardian.com, June 6, 2017.

137. S. Fiegerman, "Microsoft Received 238 Gender Discrimination and Harassment Complaints," *CNNMoney,* http://money .cnn.com, March 13, 2018.

138. R. DiGiacomo, "More Men Report Sexual Harassment at Work," *Monster,* www.monster.com, accessed March 16, 2018.

139. R.L. Paetzold and A.M. O'Leary-Kelly, "Organizational Communication and the Legal Dimensions of Hostile Work Environment Sexual Harassment," in G.L. Kreps, ed., *Sexual Harassment: Communication Implications* (Cresskill, NJ: Hampton Press, 1993).

140. B. Zoller, "Harvey Weinstein and Top Sexual Harassment Mistakes Employers Make," *Xpert HR Blog,* www.xperthr.com, October 18, 2017.

141. A.M. O'Leary-Kelly, R.L. Paetzold, and R.W. Griffin, "Sexual Harassment as Aggressive Action: A Framework for Understanding Sexual Harassment," paper presented at the annual meeting of the Academy of Management, Vancouver, August 1995.

142. B.S. Roberts and R.A. Mann, "Sexual Harassment in the Workplace: A Primer," www3.uakron.edu/lawrev/robert1.html, May 1, 2004.

143. "Former FedEx Driver Wins EEOC Lawsuit," *Houston Chronicle,* February 26, 2004, 9B.

144. J. Robertson, "California Jury Awards $61M for Harassment," http://news .Yahoo.com, June 4, 2006.

145. C. Zillman, "From #MeToo to Now What? Actions That Could Actually Stop Sexual Harassment," *Fortune,* http:// fortune.com, October 20, 2017.

146. "Du Pont's Solution," *Training,* March 1992, 29.

147. R. Natour, "Does Sexual Harassment Training Work?" *PBS NewsHour,* www .pbs.org, January 8, 2018.

148. Natour, "Does Sexual Harassment Training Work?"; C.C. Miller, "Sexual Harassment Training Doesn't Work, but Some Things Do," *The New York Times,* www.nytimes.com, December 11, 2017; V.J. Magley and J. L. Grossman, "Do Sexual Harassment Prevention Trainings Really Work?" *Scientific American,* https:// blogs.scientificamerican.com, November 10, 2017; M. Rhodan, "Does Sexual Harassment Training Work? Here's What the Research Shows," *Time,* http://time .com, November 21, 2017.

149. Natour, "Does Sexual Harassment Training Work?"; Rhodan, "Does Sexual Harassment Training Work?"

150. Natour, "Does Sexual Harassment Training Work?"

151. Natour, "Does Sexual Harassment Training Work?"; Miller, "Sexual Harassment Training Doesn't Work."

152. Natour, "Does Sexual Harassment Training Work?"; Rhodan, "Does Sexual Harassment Training Work?"

153. "Du Pont's Solution."

CHAPTER 6

Managing in the Global Environment

©Polka Dot Images/Jupiterimages

Learning Objectives

After studying this chapter, you should be able to:

LO6-1 Explain why the ability to perceive, interpret, and respond appropriately to the global environment is crucial for managerial success.

LO6-2 Differentiate between the global task and global general environments.

LO6-3 Identify the main forces in the global task and general environments, and describe the challenges that each force presents to managers.

LO6-4 Explain why the global environment is becoming more open and competitive, and identify the forces behind the process of globalization that increase the opportunities, complexities, challenges, and threats managers face.

LO6-5 Discuss why national cultures differ and why it is important that managers be sensitive to the effects of falling trade barriers and regional trade associations on the political and social systems of nations around the world.

Amazon Primed for Success in India

Which factors should managers consider when going global? As technology continues to make the world smaller at a feverish pace, e-commerce giant Amazon has expanded its business to many countries, including Japan, the United Kingdom, Spain, France, and Italy. Starting out as an online bookstore in 1994, Amazon has grown dramatically, particularly over the last decade, after it created its Amazon Prime service for customers.[1]

Doing business in the United States is not the same as doing business in other countries, even though technology continues to dissolve national borders. Amazon, like other global businesses, has learned this difficult lesson while trying to expand its operations around the globe. For example, Amazon all but abandoned business in China several years ago because it tried to follow the business model it used in other countries, which proved unsuccessful in China. According to Amazon CEO Jeff Bezos, the company should have paid more attention to local customs and culture when scaling up its e-commerce business in China.[2] Learning from its mistakes in China, Amazon expanded its business to India in 2013, but this time the company was committed to learning about local customs and the way business is conducted in the world's second most populous country.

India poses several challenges for global companies such as Amazon. Although it is a largely untapped e-commerce market with a young population that loves technology and mobile phones, close to 70% of the population lives in rural areas where infrastructure (including roads and Internet) is underdeveloped. India is also blanketed with "mom and pop" convenience stores, which are the lifeline of most local communities, selling goods and services to customers typically via cash transactions. To protect these small businesses, the Indian government has implemented strict regulations that prevent foreign retailers from selling directly to consumers online. Foreign companies must partner with Indian businesses and basically become a third-party seller for Indian-made products. Rather than trying to shift this culture

Amazon founder and CEO Jeff Bezos celebrates the company's recent expansion of operations in India. Understanding the local culture and the way Indian consumers shop has helped the e-commerce giant grow its business there.
©MANJUNATH KIRAN/Getty Images

to conform to its way of doing business in other countries, the company sought out small Indian companies that produce goods made locally which could act as suppliers to Amazon on a local as well as global basis.[3]

To help expand its business, the company developed a program called Amazon Chai Cart, mobile carts that traveled through the streets serving tea and other refreshments to small business owners while teaching them about e-commerce. The chai team traveled thousands of miles across more than 30 Indian cities interacting with thousands of vendors. To help these businesses get online quickly, Amazon set up mobile "studios" that provide website launch services to thousands of business owners, including registration, guidelines for posting images, and sales training.[4]

Amazon also had to "think local" when it came to fulfillment operations in India. Using a service called "Easy Ship," Amazon couriers pick up goods from a seller's place of business and deliver them directly to consumers. With a program called "Seller Flex," vendors designate a section of their own warehouses for products sold on the Indian Amazon website (Amazon.in) and Amazon then coordinates delivery. This local approach is convenient for sellers and benefits Amazon because it can speed up delivery times.[5]

In addition, Amazon engaged with local store owners to become partners in its delivery operations. In remote areas where residents have little or no Internet access, they can go to the local store, use the owner's Internet connection to browse, and select goods from the Amazon website. Store owners record orders; collect cash payments for the purchases; alert customers when products will be delivered to the store; and after taking out a handling fee for their services, pass along the money to Amazon. This process allows e-commerce transactions to occur in a mostly cash economy.[6]

More than five years into e-commerce operations in India, Amazon recently announced an additional $3 billion investment there, betting that the country will become a major online-shopping market for the company. According to recent data, shopping on the web in India is on target to reach $48 billion by 2020.[7] The company also introduced "Amazon Launchpad," a program that will help Indian start-up companies launch, market, and sell their products to Amazon customers across India and around the world through a dedicated online store.[8] Now that the e-commerce retailer has demonstrated successful local solutions for the Indian market, Amazon recently announced it would re-enter the Chinese marketplace and offer Prime services to consumers in China.[9]

Overview

Top managers of a global company like Amazon operate in an environment where they compete with other companies for scarce and valuable resources. Managers of companies large and small have found that to survive and prosper in the 21st century, most organizations must become **global organizations** that operate and compete not only domestically, at home, but also globally, in countries around the world. Operating in the global environment is uncertain and unpredictable because it is complex and changes constantly.

If organizations are to adapt successfully to this changing environment, their managers must learn to understand the forces that operate in it and how these forces give rise to opportunities and threats. In this chapter we examine why the environment, both domestically and globally, has become more open, vibrant, and competitive. We examine how forces in the task and general environments affect global organizations and their managers. By the end of this chapter, you will appreciate the changes that are taking place in the environment and understand why it is important for managers to develop a global perspective as they strive to increase organizational efficiency and effectiveness.

global organizations Organizations that operate and compete in more than one country.

LO6-1 Explain why the ability to perceive, interpret, and respond appropriately to the global environment is crucial for managerial success.

What Is the Global Environment?

LO6-2 Differentiate between the global task and global general environments.

global environment The set of global forces and conditions that operates beyond an organization's boundaries but affects a manager's ability to acquire and utilize resources.

task environment The set of forces and conditions that originates with suppliers, distributors, customers, and competitors and affects an organization's ability to obtain inputs and dispose of its outputs. These forces and conditions influence managers daily.

The **global environment** is a set of forces and conditions in the world outside an organization's boundary that affects how it operates and shapes its behavior.[10] These forces change over time and thus present managers with *opportunities* and *threats.* Some changes in the global environment, such as the development of efficient new production technology, the availability of lower-cost components, or the opening of new global markets, create opportunities for managers to make and sell more products, obtain more resources and capital, and thereby strengthen their organization. In contrast, the rise of new global competitors, a global economic recession, or an oil shortage poses threats that can devastate an organization if managers are unable to sell its products. The quality of managers' understanding of forces in the global environment and their ability to respond appropriately to those forces, such as Samsung's managers' ability to make and sell the electronic products that customers around the world want to buy, are critical factors affecting organizational performance.

In this chapter we explore the nature of these forces and consider how managers can respond to them. To identify opportunities and threats caused by forces in the environment, it is helpful for managers to distinguish between the *task environment* and the more encompassing *general environment* (see Figure 6.1).

The **task environment** is the set of forces and conditions that originates with global suppliers, distributors, customers, and competitors; these forces and conditions affect an organization's ability to obtain inputs and dispose of its outputs. The task environment contains the forces that have the most *immediate* and *direct* effect on managers because they pressure and influence managers daily. When managers turn on the radio or television, arrive at their offices in the morning, open their mail, or look at their computer screens, they are likely to learn about problems facing them because of changing conditions in their organization's task environment.

Figure 6.1
Forces in the Global Environment

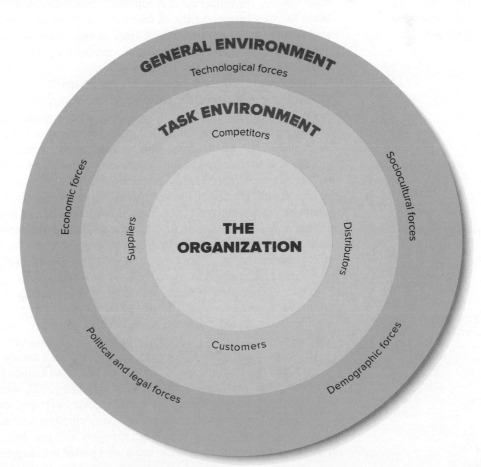

general environment The wide-ranging global, economic, technological, sociocultural, demographic, political, and legal forces that affect an organization and its task environment.

The **general environment** includes the wide-ranging global, economic, technological, sociocultural, demographic, political, and legal forces that affect the organization and its task environment. For the individual manager, opportunities and threats resulting from changes in the general environment are often more difficult to identify and respond to than are events in the task environment. However, changes in these forces can have major impacts on managers and their organizations.

The Task Environment

Forces in the task environment result from the actions of suppliers, distributors, customers, and competitors both at home and abroad (see Figure 6.1). These four groups affect a manager's ability to obtain resources and dispose of outputs daily, weekly, and monthly and thus have a significant impact on short-term decision making.

Suppliers

suppliers Individuals and organizations that provide an organization with the input resources it needs to produce goods and services.

LO6-3 Identify the main forces in the global task and general environments, and describe the challenges that each force presents to managers.

Suppliers are the individuals and companies that provide an organization with the input resources (such as raw materials, component parts, or employees) it needs to produce goods and services. In return, the suppliers receive payment for those goods and services. An important aspect of a manager's job is to ensure a reliable supply of input resources.

Consider Dell Technologies—a leading PC and information technology company—as an example. Dell has many suppliers of component parts such as microprocessors (Intel) and disk drives (Nvidia and Intel). It also has suppliers of pre-installed software, including the operating systems and specific application software (Microsoft, Chrome, and Adobe). Dell's providers of capital, such as banks and other financial institutions, are also key suppliers.

Dell has several suppliers of labor. One source is the educational institutions that train future Dell employees and therefore provide the company with skilled workers. Another is trade unions, organizations that represent employee interests and can control the supply of labor by exercising the right of unionized workers to strike. Unions also can influence the terms and conditions under which labor is employed. In organizations and industries where unions are strong, an important part of a manager's job is negotiating and administering agreements with unions and their representatives.

Changes in the nature, number, or type of suppliers produce opportunities and threats to which managers must respond if their organizations are to prosper. For example, a major supplier-related threat that confronts managers arises when suppliers' bargaining positions are so strong that they can raise the prices of the inputs they supply to the organization. A supplier's bargaining position is especially strong when (1) the supplier is the sole source of an input and (2) the input is vital to the organization.[11] For example, for 17 years G. D. Searle was the sole supplier of NutraSweet, the artificial sweetener used in most diet soft drinks. Not only was NutraSweet an important ingredient in diet soft drinks, but it also was one for which there was no acceptable substitute (saccharin and other artificial sweeteners raised health concerns). Searle earned its privileged position because it invented and held the patent for NutraSweet, and patents prohibit other organizations from introducing competing products for 17 years. As a result, Searle was able to demand a high price for NutraSweet, charging twice the price of an equivalent amount of sugar; paying that price raised the costs of soft drink manufacturers such as Coca-Cola and PepsiCo. When Searle's patent expired, many other companies introduced products similar to NutraSweet, and prices fell.[12] In the 2000s Splenda, which was made by McNeil Nutritionals, replaced NutraSweet as the artificial sweetener of choice, and NutraSweet's price fell further; Splenda began to command a high price from soft drink companies.[13]

However, a natural sweetener introduced less than a decade ago has gained market share on Splenda and other sweeteners. A zero-calorie sweetener extracted from the stevia plant is expected to have a global market of more than $720 million by 2022, according to recent research, replacing many artificial sweeteners in soft drinks, other beverages, and food products.[14]

In contrast, when an organization has many suppliers for a particular input, it is in a relatively strong bargaining position with those suppliers and can demand low-cost, high-quality inputs from them. Often an organization can use its power with suppliers to force them to reduce their prices, as Dell frequently does. Dell, for example, is constantly searching for low-cost suppliers abroad to keep its prices competitive. At a global level, organizations can buy products from suppliers overseas or become their own suppliers by manufacturing their products abroad.

It is important that managers recognize the opportunities and threats associated with managing the global supply chain. On one hand, gaining access to low-cost products made abroad represents an opportunity for U.S. companies to lower their input costs.[15] On the other hand, they have less control over production processes carried out by contractors located far away. This poses a threat to the brand if the suppliers deliver poor quality. Buying from low-wage countries also involves a threat related to social responsibility: if stakeholders determine that suppliers aren't meeting minimum standards for ethical treatment of their workers, the company's reputation may be damaged. To see how Levi Strauss has addressed this issue, read the "Ethics in Action" feature.

ETHICS IN ACTION

Levi Strauss Motivates Global Suppliers to Treat Workers Well

When Levi Strauss & Company began sourcing work from low-wage countries in the 1990s, it was concerned about poor working conditions. In response, the global retailer prepared a code of conduct—its Terms of Engagement, requiring measures to meet workers' basic needs and protect their rights and the environment.[16] A supplier wanting to sell to Levi's had to meet those terms. Eventually, this innovation became the norm in the clothing industry. But despite efforts to enforce the terms with suppliers, violations continued. CEO Chip Bergh decided that lasting change required a shift in managers' attitudes.

Levi's launched an initiative it calls Worker Well-Being.[17] Its goal is to improve the experience of workers at Levi's suppliers, leading to greater efficiency and reliability, thereby creating a stronger supply network. Caring for workers' interests thus generates a win for all. Levi's provides funds and guidance, but each supplier plans how to achieve worker well-being. The basic approach is to survey workers; learn what they need to be healthy, productive, and engaged at work; identify the company's labor-related areas of improvement; and work with nonprofit partners to meet those needs. Because "well-being" is a broad objective, Levi's partnered with Harvard's Center for Health and the Global Environment to develop success measures that connect worker well-being with business performance.[18] Ultimately, the measures should demonstrate to factory managers why worker well-being matters to the company.

Early participants in the well-being initiative included the 1,200-worker Apparel International factory in Nazareno, Mexico.[19] AI's president, Oscar González Franch, and CEO Tomas Bello Garza were uncertain how to start, but they already had a track record of innovating to improve the factory's environmental impact. After a company-provided survey didn't illuminate worker needs, they partnered with a nongovernment organization, which created tools more appropriate for the community. They learned that the key issues were lack of access to health care and poor communication between managers and workers. AI trained its supervisors in communicating respectfully and creating a healthier work environment. As attitudes and productivity improved, González Franch and Bello Garza began using company resources to improve health conditions in the community.

In the first five years, Levi's rolled out the program to facilities in 12 countries with 100,000 workers.[20] In Egypt, health education reduced absenteeism and turnover among female employees, and in Turkey, changes to the work schedule did the same. Levi's set a timetable for the program to cover the factories producing 80% of its products by 2020 and to cover all suppliers' workers by 2025.

The purchasing activities of global companies have become increasingly complicated. Hundreds of suppliers around the world produce parts for Boeing's 787 Dreamliner.
©Thor Jorgen Udvang/Shutterstock

A common problem facing managers of large, global companies such as Ford, Sony, and Dell is managing the development of a global supplier network that will allow their companies to keep costs down and quality high. For example, Boeing's 777 jet was originally built using many components from over 500 global suppliers. Boeing chose these suppliers because they were the best in the world at performing their particular activities, and Boeing's goal was to produce a high-quality final product.[21] Pleased with the outcome, Boeing decided to outsource a greater percentage of components to global suppliers when it designed the new Boeing 787 Dreamliner; however, many serious problems delayed the introduction of the new aircraft for several years.[22]

The purchasing activities of global companies have become increasingly complicated as a result of the development of a whole range of skills and competencies in different countries around the world. It is clearly in companies' interests to search out the lowest-cost, best-quality suppliers. Advances in technology and the global reach of the Internet continue to make it easier for companies to coordinate complicated long-distance exchanges involving the purchasing of inputs and the disposal of outputs—something many global companies have taken advantage of as they consolidate the number of suppliers to reduce costs.

global outsourcing The purchase or production of inputs or final products from overseas suppliers to lower costs and improve product quality or design.

Global outsourcing occurs when a company contracts with suppliers in other countries to make the various inputs or components that go into its products or to assemble the final products to reduce costs. For example, Apple contracts with companies in Taiwan and China to make inputs such as the chips, batteries, and LCD displays that power its digital devices; then it contracts with outsourcers such as Foxconn to assemble its final products—such as iPhones and iPads. Apple also outsources the distribution of its products around the world by contracting with companies such as FedEx or UPS.

Global outsourcing has grown enormously to take advantage of national differences in the cost and quality of resources such as labor or raw materials that can significantly reduce manufacturing costs or increase product quality or reliability. Today such global exchanges are becoming so complex that some companies specialize in managing other companies' global supply chains. Global companies use the services of overseas intermediaries or brokers, which are located close to potential suppliers, to find the suppliers that can best meet the needs of a particular company. They can design the most efficient supply chain for a company to outsource the component and assembly operations required to produce its final products. Because these suppliers are located in thousands of cities in many countries, finding them is difficult. Li & Fung, based in Hong Kong, is one broker that has helped hundreds of major U.S. companies to outsource their component or assembly operations to suitable overseas suppliers, especially suppliers in mainland China.[23]

Although outsourcing to take advantage of low labor costs has helped many companies perform better, in the 2010s its risks have also become apparent, especially when issues such as reliability, quality, and speed are important. Consequently, some companies have decided to bring jobs back to the United States. For example, Trans-Lux, a New York–based manufacturer of LCD and LED displays, including the large digital screens (that is, the "Big Board") that run the tickers at the New York Stock Exchange, recently announced it would bring back the remaining 40% of its production from China over the next year. Company officials explained increasing labor and shipping costs accelerated their decision to move jobs back home.[24]

On the other hand, some companies do not outsource manufacturing; they prefer to establish their own assembly operations and factories in countries around the world to protect their proprietary technology. For example, most global automakers own their production operations in China to retain control over their global decision making and keep their operations secret.

Distributors

distributors Organizations that help other organizations sell their goods or services to customers.

Distributors are organizations that help other organizations sell their goods or services to customers. The decisions managers make about how to distribute products to customers can have important effects on organizational performance. For example, package delivery companies such as FedEx, UPS, and the U.S. Postal Service have become vital distributors for the millions of items bought online and shipped to customers by Internet companies, both at home and abroad.

The changing nature of distributors and distribution methods can bring opportunities and threats for managers. If distributors become so large and powerful that they can control customers' access to a particular organization's goods and services, they can threaten the organization by demanding that it reduce the prices of its goods and services.[25] For example, the huge retail distributor Walmart controls its suppliers' access to millions of customers and, thus, can demand that its suppliers reduce their prices to keep its business. If an organization such as Procter & Gamble refuses to reduce its prices, Walmart might respond by buying products only from Procter & Gamble's competitors—companies such as Unilever and Colgate. Walmart used its power as a distributor recently to demand additional fees from U.S. suppliers for using Walmart distribution centers and warehouses. The retail giant has also changed the frequency of payments to some vendors—tying payment to how quickly a supplier's inventory moves off the shelves at Walmart stores.[26]

Recently Germany's Deutsche Bank agreed to pay $38 million to settle lawsuits over allegations it conspired with other global banks to fix silver prices at the expense of investors and other financial institutions. In the lawsuits, plaintiffs claimed that Deutsche Bank, Bank of Nova Scotia, and HSBC Holdings rigged worldwide silver prices from 2007 through 2013 via a secret daily meeting called the Silver Fix.[27]

Customers

customers Individuals and groups that buy the goods and services an organization produces.

Customers are the individuals and groups that buy the goods and services an organization produces. For example, Dell's customers can be segmented into several distinct groups: (1) individuals who purchase PCs for home use, (2) small companies, (3) large companies, and (4) government agencies and educational institutions. Changes in the number and types of customers or in customers' tastes and needs create opportunities and threats. An organization's success depends on its responsiveness to customers—whether it can satisfy their needs. In the PC industry, customers are demanding smaller computers, longer battery life, new apps, and lower prices—and PC makers must respond to the changing types and needs of customers, such as by introducing tablets and other mobile devices. A school, too, must adapt to the changing needs of its customers. For example, if more Spanish-speaking students enroll, additional classes in English as a second language may need to be scheduled. A manager's ability to identify an organization's main customer groups, and make the products that best satisfy their particular needs, is a crucial factor affecting organizational and managerial success.

The most obvious opportunity associated with expanding into the global environment is the prospect of selling goods and services to millions or billions of new customers, as Amazon .com's CEO, Jeff Bezos, discovered when he expanded his company's operations in many countries. Similarly, Accenture and Capgemini, two large consulting companies, established regional operating centers around the globe, and they recruit and train thousands of overseas consultants to serve the needs of customers in their respective world regions.

Today many products have gained global customer acceptance. This consolidation is occurring both for consumer goods and for business products and has created enormous opportunities for managers. The worldwide acceptance of Coca-Cola, Apple iPads, McDonald's hamburgers, and Samsung smartphones is a sign that the tastes and preferences of customers in different countries may not be so different after all. Likewise, large, global markets exist for business products such as telecommunications equipment, electronic components, and computer and financial services. Thus, Cisco and Siemens sell their telecommunications equipment; Intel, its microprocessors; and Oracle and SAP, their business systems management software, to customers all over the world.

Competitors

competitors Organizations that produce goods and services that are similar to a particular organization's goods and services.

One of the most important forces an organization confronts in its task environment is competitors. Competitors are organizations that produce goods and services similar and comparable to a particular organization's goods and services. In other words, competitors are organizations trying to attract the same customers. Dell's competitors include other domestic PC makers (such as Apple and HP) as well as overseas competitors (such as Sony and Toshiba in Japan,

Lenovo in China, and Acer in Taiwan). Similarly, online stockbroker E*Trade has other competitors such as TD Ameritrade and Charles Schwab.

Rivalry between competitors is potentially the most threatening force managers must deal with. A high level of rivalry typically results in price competition, and falling prices reduce customer revenues and profits. In the early 2000s competition in the PC industry became intense because Dell was aggressively cutting costs and prices to increase its global market share. IBM had to exit the PC business after it lost billions in its battle against low-cost rivals, and HP also suffered losses while Dell's profits soared. By 2006, however, HP's fortunes had recovered because it had found ways to lower its costs and offer stylish new PCs, and Apple was growing rapidly, so Dell's profit margins continued to shrink. In 2009 HP overtook Dell to become the largest global PC maker. After a long and harsh battle with investors over the future of Dell, founder Michael Dell took the company private and shifted its focus to becoming more of an all-around technology company with less reliance on PC sales. In 2017, HP took the top spot as the world's largest PC maker, followed by Lenovo and Dell, although the overall PC market continues to shrink worldwide.[28]

potential competitors Organizations that presently are not in a task environment but can enter if they so choose.

Although extensive rivalry between existing competitors is a major threat to profitability, so is the potential for new competitors to enter the task environment. **Potential competitors** are organizations that are not presently in a task environment but have the resources to enter if they so choose. In 2010 Amazon.com, for example, was not in the furniture or large appliance business, but it could enter these businesses if its managers decided it could profitably sell such products online—and today, the e-commerce giant sells furniture and appliances. When new competitors enter an industry, competition increases and prices and profits decrease—as furniture and electronics stores such as Best Buy have discovered as they battle Amazon.com. Another industry where competition has become fierce is the music-streaming business. Major players in this sector include Daniel Ek and his company, Spotify, highlighted in the "Manager as a Person" feature.

MANAGER AS A PERSON

Spotify's CEO Outplays the Competition

Daniel Ek is a 30-something musician and avid technology user from Sweden who started writing basic computer code at age 7 and designing commercial websites at 14. Ek has always been a disrupter, someone who is not afraid of asking questions, taking risks, or changing the way music is played or listened to by consumers around the world.

At the age of 23, he cofounded Spotify, an on-demand music-streaming platform, with Swedish tech entrepreneur Martin Lorentzon. A decade later, Spotify has become a serious business competing with the likes of Apple Music, Pandora, Amazon Music, Tidal, and others.[29]

Acknowledging that Steve Jobs' iTunes idea probably started the competition to reinvent the music industry and perhaps resurrect its popularity, Ek believes Spotify has taken the music industry one step further than iTunes because people don't pay to download individual songs on Spotify like they do on iTunes. Spotify provides music fans with two options: streaming music free with an occasional advertisement heard in the playlist and a limited number of skipping songs per hour or paying a monthly fee (currently $9.99 per month in the United States) for a premium service that offers unlimited streaming with no ad interruptions; offline listening; and

Daniel Ek, CEO and cofounder of Spotify, believes the local approach to online music streaming gives the company business advantages over its competitors.
©Akio Kon/Bloomberg/Getty Images

the Spotify Connect app—the ability to listen to music remotely on supported devices such as speakers, TVs, smart watches, and game consoles like PlayStation.[30]

Unlike competitor Pandora, Spotify allows listeners to set up their own playlists from the 35+ million songs that the service offers, share or swap their favorite tunes with friends via Facebook and Twitter on any number of mobile devices, and listen to personalized music selections determined by data analytics and individuals' listening habits. The other advantage of using Spotify is that the service is "localized" to more than 65 countries where the music-streaming service is available.[31]

Ek says he started Spotify when he lived in Sweden because the streaming service was a "viable alternative to music piracy," which was rampant in the Scandinavian country at the time. Paying music companies and their artists as part of the business plan is costly: Recent figures suggest Spotify pays more than 50% of its annual sales in licensing fees. The company paid nearly $10 billion in royalties through 2017. Ek orchestrated several rounds of funding from various investors and is poised to take the company public in 2018.[32]

In the meantime, Ek and his management team are streamlining the organizational structure, working to renegotiate licensing agreements with music companies in an effort to reduce costs, increasing the paying subscriber base (now more than 83 million paying users), adding more countries to the "locals" list, and acquiring several companies known for their data analytics, artificial intelligence, and social media expertise.[33] Ek knows paying artists and music companies for licensing fees will always be part of the music-streaming business. However, by acquiring other companies that can help enhance the Spotify experience and generate additional revenues, Ek hopes to expand the company's global reach.

barriers to entry Factors that make it difficult and costly for an organization to enter a particular task environment or industry.

BARRIERS TO ENTRY In general, the potential for new competitors to enter a task environment (and thus increase competition) is a function of barriers to entry. **Barriers to entry** are factors that make it difficult and costly for a company to enter a particular task environment or industry.[34] In other words, the more difficult and costly it is to enter the task environment, the higher are the barriers to entry. The higher the barriers to entry, the fewer the competitors in an organization's task environment and, thus, the lower the threat of competition. With fewer competitors, it is easier to obtain customers and keep prices high.

economies of scale Cost advantages associated with large operations.

Barriers to entry result from three main sources: economies of scale, brand loyalty, and government regulations that impede entry (see Figure 6.2). **Economies of scale** are the cost advantages associated with large operations. Economies of scale result from factors such as manufacturing products in very large quantities, buying inputs in bulk, or making more effective use of organizational resources than do competitors by fully utilizing employees' skills and knowledge. If organizations already in the task environment are large and enjoy significant

Figure 6.2
Barriers to Entry and Competition

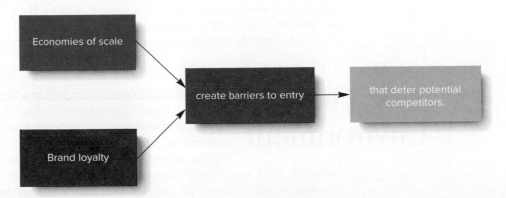

Now that Japan imports rice from other countries, including the United States, Japanese rice farmers, who cannot compete against lower-priced imports, have been forced to leave fields idle or grow less profitable crops.
©travelgame/Getty Images

brand loyalty Customers' preference for the products of organizations currently existing in the task environment.

economies of scale, their costs are lower than the costs that potential entrants will face, and newcomers will find it expensive to enter the industry. Amazon, for example, enjoys significant economies of scale relative to most other Internet companies because of its highly efficient distribution system.[35]

Brand loyalty is customers' preference for the products of organizations currently in the task environment. If established organizations enjoy significant brand loyalty, a new entrant will find it difficult and costly to obtain a share of the market. Newcomers must bear huge marketing costs to build customer awareness of the goods or services they intend to provide. Today Apple, Google, Samsung, and Amazon enjoy a high level of brand loyalty and have some of the highest website hit rates, which allows them to increase their marketing revenues.

In some cases, *government regulations* function as a barrier to entry at both the industry and the country levels. Many industries that were deregulated, such as air transport, trucking, utilities, and telecommunications, experienced a high level of new entry after deregulation; this forced existing companies in those industries to operate more efficiently or risk being put out of business. At the national and global levels, administrative barriers are government policies that create barriers to entry and limit imports of goods by overseas companies. Japan is well known for the many ways in which it attempts to restrict the entry of overseas competitors or lessen their impact on Japanese firms. Japan has come under intense pressure to relax and abolish regulations such as those governing the import of rice, for example.

The Japanese rice market, like many other Japanese markets, was closed to overseas competitors until 1993 to protect Japan's thousands of high-cost, low-output rice farmers. Rice cultivation is expensive in Japan because of the country's mountainous terrain, and Japanese consumers have always paid high prices for rice. Under overseas pressure, the Japanese government opened the market, but overseas competitors were allowed to export to Japan only 8% of its annual rice consumption, to protect its farmers.

In the 2000s, however, an alliance between organic rice grower Lundberg Family Farms of California and the Nippon Restaurant Enterprise Co. found a new way to break into the Japanese rice market. Because there is no tariff on rice used in processed foods, Nippon converts the U.S. organic rice into "O-bento," an organic hot boxed lunch packed with rice, vegetables, chicken, beef, and salmon, all imported from the United States. The lunches, which cost about $4 compared to a Japanese rice bento that costs about $9, are sold at railway stations and other outlets throughout Japan and have become very popular. A storm of protest from Japanese rice farmers arose because the entry of U.S. rice growers forced them to leave their rice fields idle or grow less profitable crops. Recently Japan experienced a serious shortage of reasonably priced rice for its food service sector due to the country's strict policy on growing rice for animal feed. This resulted in a higher demand for U.S. rice, which accounted for 49% of Japan's rice imports in 2017.[36]

In summary, intense rivalry among competitors creates a task environment that is highly threatening and makes it increasingly difficult for managers to gain access to the resources an organization needs to make goods and services. Conversely, low rivalry results in a task environment where competitive pressures are more moderate and managers have greater opportunities to acquire the resources they need to make their organizations effective.

The General Environment

Economic, technological, sociocultural, demographic, political, and legal forces in the general environment often have important effects on forces in the task environment that determine an organization's ability to obtain resources—effects that managers may not be aware of. For example, the sudden, dramatic upheavals in the mortgage and banking industry that started in 2007 were brought about by a combination of the development of complex new financial lending instruments called derivatives; a speculative boom in commodities and housing prices; and lax government regulation that allowed unethical bankers and financial managers to exploit the derivatives to make immense short-term profits. These events triggered the economic crisis that peaked in 2008 but continued to ripple through the world economy for years, causing stock markets around the world to plummet, devastating the retirement savings of hundreds of millions of ordinary people, and causing layoffs of millions of employees as companies slashed their workforces because customers reduced their spending. Fortunately, sound economic policies put in place during the recession helped the economy recover over the past several years.

The implication is clear: Managers must continuously analyze forces in the general environment because these forces affect ongoing decision making and planning. How well managers can perform this task determines how quickly an organization can respond to the changes taking place. Next we discuss the major forces in the general environment and examine their impact on an organization's task environment.

Economic Forces

economic forces Interest rates, inflation, unemployment, economic growth, and other factors that affect the general health and well-being of a nation or the regional economy of an organization.

Economic forces affect the general health and well-being of a country or world region. They include interest rates, inflation, unemployment, and economic growth. Economic forces produce many opportunities and threats for managers. Low levels of unemployment and falling interest rates give people more money to spend, and as a result organizations can sell more goods and services. Good economic times affect the supply of resources that become easier or more inexpensive to acquire, and organizations have an opportunity to flourish. High-tech companies enjoyed this throughout the 1990s when computer and electronics companies, like Sony, made record profits as the global economy boomed because of advances in IT and growing global trade.

In contrast, worsening macroeconomic conditions, like those in the early 2010s, posed a major threat because they reduced managers' ability to gain access to the resources their organizations needed to survive and prosper. Profit-seeking organizations such as hotels and retail stores have fewer customers during economic downturns; hotel rates dropped by 14% in 2009 compared to 2008, for example, just as retail sales plunged. Nonprofits such as charities and colleges also saw donations decline by more than 20% because of the economic downturn.

Poor economic conditions make the environment more complex and managers' jobs more difficult and demanding. Companies often need to reduce the number of their managers and employees, streamline their operations, and identify ways to acquire and use resources more efficiently and effectively. Successful managers realize the important effects that economic forces have on their organizations, and they pay close attention to what is occurring in the economy at the national and regional levels to respond appropriately.

Technological Forces

technology The combination of skills and equipment that managers use in designing, producing, and distributing goods and services.

technological forces Outcomes of changes in the technology managers use to design, produce, or distribute goods and services.

Technology is the combination of tools, machines, computers, skills, information, and knowledge that managers use to design, produce, and distribute goods and services; **technological forces** are outcomes of changes in that technology. The overall pace of technological change has accelerated greatly in the last decades because technological advances in microprocessors and computer hardware and software have spurred technological advances in most businesses and industries. The effects of changing technological forces are still increasing in magnitude.

Technological forces can have profound implications for managers and organizations. Technological change can make established products obsolete—for example, cathode-ray tube (CRT) computer monitors and televisions, bound sets of encyclopedias, and newspapers and magazines—forcing managers to find new ways to satisfy customer needs. Although technological change can threaten an organization, it also can create a host of new opportunities for designing, making, or distributing new and better kinds of goods and services. In 2017 AMD launched a new generation of Ryzen desktop processors with more speed, built-in graphics, and a new algorithm that improves overall performance. Innovations like these continue to push IT boundaries and spur demand for all kinds of new digital computing devices and services, which affect the competitive position of technology companies.[37]

Changes in technology are altering the nature of work itself within organizations, including that of the manager's job. Today telecommuting, videoconferencing, and cloud computing are everyday activities that let managers supervise and coordinate geographically dispersed employees. Salespeople in many companies work from home offices and commute electronically to work. They communicate with other employees through companywide electronic communication networks using smartphones and other mobile devices to orchestrate "face-to-face" meetings with coworkers across the country or globe.

Sociocultural Forces

sociocultural forces
Pressures emanating from the social structure of a country or society or from the national culture.

social structure The traditional system of relationships established between people and groups in a society.

Sociocultural forces are pressures emanating from the social structure of a country or society or from the national culture, such as the concern for diversity, discussed in the previous chapter. Pressures from both sources can either constrain or facilitate the way organizations operate and managers behave. **Social structure** is the traditional system of relationships established between people and groups in a society. Societies differ substantially in social structure. In societies that have a high degree of social stratification, there are many distinctions among individuals and groups. Caste systems in India and Tibet and the recognition of numerous social classes in Great Britain and France produce a multilayered social structure in each of those countries. In contrast, social stratification is lower in relatively egalitarian New Zealand and in the United States, where the social structure reveals few distinctions among people. Most top managers in France come from the upper classes of French society, but top managers in the United States come from all strata of American society.

Societies also differ in the extent to which they emphasize the individual over the group. Such differences may dictate how managers need to motivate and lead employees.

national culture The set of values that a society considers important and the norms of behavior that are approved or sanctioned in that society.

National culture is the set of values that a society considers important and the norms of behavior that are approved or sanctioned in that society. Societies differ substantially in the values and norms they emphasize. For example, in the United States, individualism is highly valued, but in Korea and Japan individuals are expected to conform to group expectations.[38] National culture, discussed at length later in this chapter, also affects how managers motivate and coordinate employees and how organizations do business. Ethics, an important aspect of national culture, were discussed in detail in Chapter 4.

Social structure and national culture not only differ across societies but also change within societies over time. In the United States, attitudes toward the roles of women, sex, marriage, and gays and lesbians changed in each past decade. Many people in Asian countries such as Hong Kong, Singapore, Korea, and even China think the younger generation is far more individualistic and "American-like" than previous generations. Currently, throughout much of Eastern Europe, new values that emphasize individualism and entrepreneurship are replacing communist values based on collectivism and obedience to the state. The pace of change is accelerating.

Individual managers and organizations must be responsive to changes in, and differences among, the social structures and national cultures of all the countries in which they operate. In today's increasingly integrated global economy, managers are likely to interact with people from several countries, and many managers live and work abroad. Effective managers are sensitive to differences between societies and adjust their behavior accordingly.

Managers and organizations also must respond to social changes within a society. In the last decades, for example, Americans have become increasingly interested in their personal health and fitness. Managers who recognized this trend early and took advantage of the opportunities that resulted from it were able to reap significant gains for their organizations, such as organic food delivery services. The organic produce industry has been growing for the past decade, even during the recession, due to people's interest in chemical-free food.[39] Many organizations have begun to

The organic produce industry has taken advantage of U.S. consumers' push for chemical-free food by offering home delivery of organic fruits, vegetables, and other products.
©kritchanut/123RF

offer weekly home delivery to customers. PepsiCo used the opportunity presented by the fitness trend and took market share from archrival Coca-Cola by being the first to introduce diet colas and fruit-based soft drinks. Then Quaker Oats made Gatorade the most popular energy drink, and now others, like Red Bull, Monster, and Rockstar, are increasing in popularity. The health trend, however, did not offer opportunities to all companies; to some it posed a threat. Tobacco companies came under intense pressure due to consumers' greater awareness of negative health impacts from smoking. The rage for "low-carb" foods in the 2000s increased demand for meat and protein, and bread and doughnut companies such as Kraft and Krispy Kreme suffered. Today U.S. consumers are looking for healthier, "cleaner" foods, which are being promoted by grocery chains, fast-casual restaurants, and home meal delivery services.[40]

Demographic Forces

demographic forces
Outcomes of changes in, or changing attitudes toward, the characteristics of a population, such as age, gender, ethnic origin, race, sexual orientation, and social class.

Demographic forces are outcomes of changes in, or changing attitudes toward, the characteristics of a population, such as age, gender, ethnic origin, race, sexual orientation, and social class. Like the other forces in the general environment, demographic forces present managers with opportunities and threats and can have major implications for organizations. We examined the nature of these challenges in depth in our discussion of diversity in Chapter 5.

Today most industrialized nations are experiencing the aging of their populations as a consequence of falling birth and death rates and the aging of the baby boom generation. Consequently, the absolute number of older people has increased substantially, which has generated opportunities for organizations that cater to older people, such as the home health care, recreation, and medical industries, which have seen an upswing in demand for their services. The aging of the population also has several implications for the workplace. Most significant are a relative decline in the number of young people joining the workforce and an increase in the number of active employees who are postponing retirement beyond the traditional age of 65. Indeed, the financial crisis in the late 2000s made it impossible for millions of older people to retire because their savings have been destroyed. These changes suggest that organizations need to find ways to motivate older employees and use their skills and knowledge—an issue that many Western societies continue to tackle.

Political and Legal Forces

political and legal forces
Outcomes of changes in laws and regulations, such as deregulation of industries, privatization of organizations, and increased emphasis on environmental protection.

Political and legal forces are outcomes of changes in laws and regulations. They result from political and legal developments that take place within a nation, within a world region, or across the world and significantly affect managers and organizations everywhere. Political processes shape a nation's laws and the international laws that govern the relationships between nations. Laws constrain the operations of organizations and managers and thus create both opportunities and threats.[41] For example, throughout much of the industrialized world there has been a strong trend toward deregulation of industries previously controlled by the state and privatization of organizations once owned by the state such as airlines, railways, and utility companies.

Another important political and legal force affecting managers and organizations is the political integration of countries that has been taking place during the last decades. Increasingly, nations are forming political unions that allow free exchange of resources and capital. The growth of the European Union (EU) is one example: Common laws govern trade and commerce between EU member countries, and the European Commission has the right to examine the business of any global organization and to approve any proposed mergers between overseas companies that operate inside the EU. For example, in 2018, Apple's proposed acquisition of Shazam, a UK-based app, is now being reviewed by the European Commission because of its potential threat to competition among music-sharing platforms in Europe. The Shazam app uses a microphone on a smartphone or computer to identify almost any song playing nearby and then directs users to places where they can listen to the music, such as Apple Music or Spotify. Acquiring Shazam would help Apple embed that capability deeper into its

LO6-4 Explain why the global environment is becoming more open and competitive, and identify the forces behind the process of globalization that increase the opportunities, complexities, challenges, and threats managers face.

music offerings, which might push more consumers to sign on with Apple Music. The Commission took up the review at the request of several EU members, including Austria, Italy, and Sweden.[42] In addition, the impending departure of the United Kingdom from the EU may have a significant impact on political and legal forces worldwide. The start of "Brexit" is expected to commence in March 2019; the process could take several years.[43]

Indeed, international agreements to abolish laws and regulations that restrict and reduce trade between countries have been having profound effects on global organizations. The falling legal trade barriers create enormous opportunities for companies to sell goods and services internationally. But by allowing overseas companies to compete in a nation's domestic market for customers, falling trade barriers also pose a serious threat because they increase competition in the task environment. For example, the Obama administration negotiated for several years for the United States to join the Trans-Pacific Partnership (TPP), a trade agreement between the United States and 11 other countries. In 2017, however, in the early days of his presidency, Donald Trump issued an executive order pulling the country out of the TPP, taking a stand against foreign competitors as part of his "America First" strategy.[44]

Deregulation, privatization, and the removal of legal barriers to trade are just a few of the many ways in which changing political and legal forces can challenge organizations and managers. Others include increased emphasis on environmental protection and the preservation of endangered species, increased emphasis on workplace safety, and legal constraints against discrimination on the basis of race, gender, or age. Managers face major challenges when they seek to take advantage of the opportunities created by changing political, legal, and economic forces.

The Changing Global Environment

The 21st century has banished the idea that the world is composed of distinct national countries and markets that are separated physically, economically, and culturally. Managers need to recognize that companies compete in a truly global marketplace, which is the source of the opportunities and threats they must respond to. Managers continually confront the challenges of global competition such as establishing operations in a country abroad, obtaining inputs from suppliers abroad, or managing in a different national culture.[45]

In essence, as a result of falling trade barriers, managers view the global environment as open—that is, as an environment in which companies are free to buy goods and services from, and sell goods and services to, whichever companies and countries they choose. They also are free to compete against each other to attract customers around the world. All large companies must establish an international network of operations and subsidiaries to build global competitive advantage. Coca-Cola and PepsiCo, for example, have competed aggressively for decades to develop the strongest global beverage empire, just as Toyota and Honda have built hundreds of car plants around the world to provide the vehicles that global customers like.

In this section we first explain how this open global environment is the result of globalization and the flow of capital around the world. Next we examine how specific economic, political, and legal changes, such as the lowering of barriers to trade and investment, have increased globalization and led to greater interaction and exchanges between organizations and countries. Then we discuss how declining barriers of distance and culture have also increased the pace of globalization, and we consider the specific implications of these changes for managers and organizations. Finally, we note that nations still differ widely from each other because they have distinct cultural values and norms and that managers must appreciate these differences to compete successfully across countries.

Despite recent economic headwinds due to lower commodity prices and other factors, Africa's overall economy is still strong. According to analysts at African Development Bank, Africa was the second fastest-growing continent in the world in 2016 just behind Asia. African countries face economic, political, and environmental challenges as the process of globalization accelerates changes to business and everyday life in cities such as Lagos, Nigeria, pictured here.
©Getty Images

The Process of Globalization

globalization The set of specific and general forces that work together to integrate and connect economic, political, and social systems *across* countries, cultures, or geographic regions so that nations become increasingly interdependent and similar.

Perhaps the most important reason the global environment has become more open and competitive is the increase in globalization. Globalization is the set of specific and general forces that work together to integrate and connect economic, political, and social systems across countries, cultures, or geographic regions. The result of globalization is that nations and peoples become increasingly interdependent because the same forces affect them in similar ways. The fates of peoples in different countries become interlinked as the world's markets and businesses become increasingly interconnected. And as nations become more interdependent, they become more similar to one another in the sense that people develop a similar liking for products as diverse as cell phones, iPads, blue jeans, soft drinks, sports teams, hybrid cars, and foods such as curry, green tea, and Colombian coffee.

But what drives or spurs globalization? What makes companies like IKEA, Toyota, or Microsoft want to venture into an uncertain global environment? The answer is that the path of globalization is shaped by the ebb and flow of *capital*—valuable wealth-generating assets or resources that people move through companies, countries, and world regions to seek their greatest returns or profits. Managers, employees, and companies like IKEA and Samsung are motivated to try to profit or benefit by using their skills to make products customers around the world want to buy. The four principal forms of capital that flow between countries are these:

- *Human capital:* the flow of people around the world through immigration, migration, and emigration
- *Financial capital:* the flow of money capital across world markets through overseas investment, credit, lending, and aid
- *Resource capital:* the flow of natural resources, parts, and components between companies and countries, such as metals, minerals, lumber, energy, food products, microprocessors, and auto parts
- *Political capital:* the flow of power and influence around the world using diplomacy, persuasion, aggression, and force of arms to protect the right or access of a country, world region, or political bloc to the other forms of capital

Most of the economic advances associated with globalization are the result of these four capital flows and the interactions between them, as nations compete on the world stage to protect and increase their standards of living and to further the political goals and social causes that are espoused by their societies' cultures. The next sections look at the factors that have increased the rate at which capital flows between companies and countries. In a positive sense, the faster the flow, the more capital is being utilized where it can create the most value, such as people moving to where their skills earn more money, or investors switching to the stocks or bonds that give higher dividends or interest, or companies finding lower-cost sources of inputs. In a negative sense, however, a fast flow of capital also means that individual countries or world regions can find themselves in trouble when companies and investors move their capital to invest it in more productive ways in other countries or world regions—often those with lower labor costs or rapidly expanding markets. When capital leaves a country, the results are higher unemployment, recession, and a lower standard of living for its people.

Declining Barriers to Trade and Investment

tariff A tax that a government imposes on imported or, occasionally, exported goods.

One of the main factors that has speeded globalization by freeing the movement of capital has been the decline in barriers to trade and investment, discussed earlier. During the 1920s and 1930s many countries erected formidable barriers to international trade and investment in the belief that this was the best way to promote their economic well-being. Many of these barriers were high tariffs on imports of manufactured goods. A tariff is a tax that a government imposes on goods imported into one country from another. The aim of import tariffs is to protect domestic industries and jobs, such as those in the auto or steel industry, from overseas competition by raising the price of these products from abroad. For example, in May 2018, President Trump announced a 25% tariff on imported steel and 10% tariff on imported aluminum, which caused a global outcry from other countries and received mixed reviews from U.S. business leaders. In addition, the president is also planning to penalize China for its theft of American intellectual property with heavy tariffs on U.S. imports and restrictions on U.S. investments.[46]

The reason for removing tariffs is that, very often, when one country imposes an import tariff, others follow suit and the result is a series of retaliatory moves as countries progressively raise tariff barriers against each other. In the 1920s this behavior depressed world demand and helped usher in the Great Depression of the 1930s and massive unemployment. Beginning with the 2009 economic crisis, the governments of most countries have worked hard in the 2010s not to fall into the trap of raising tariffs to protect jobs and industries in the short run because they know the long-term consequences of this would be the loss of even more jobs. Governments of countries that resort to raising tariff barriers ultimately reduce employment and undermine the economic growth of their countries because capital and resources will always move to their most highly valued use—wherever that is in the world.

GATT AND THE RISE OF FREE TRADE   After World War II, advanced Western industrial countries, having learned from the Great Depression, committed themselves to the goal of removing barriers to the free flow of resources and capital between countries. This commitment was reinforced by acceptance of the principle that free trade, rather than tariff barriers, was the best way to foster a healthy domestic economy and low unemployment.[47]

free-trade doctrine The idea that if each country specializes in the production of the goods and services that it can produce most efficiently, this will make the best use of global resources.

The free-trade doctrine predicts that if each country agrees to specialize in the production of the goods and services that it can produce most efficiently, this will make the best use of global capital resources and will result in lower prices.[48] For example, if Indian companies are highly efficient in the production of textiles and U.S. companies are highly efficient in the production of computer software, then, under a free-trade agreement, capital would move to India and be invested there to produce textiles, while capital from around the world would flow to the United States and be invested in its innovative software companies. Consequently, prices of both textiles and software should fall because each product is being produced where it can be made at the lowest cost, benefiting consumers and making the best use of scarce capital. This doctrine is also responsible for the increase in global outsourcing and the loss of millions of U.S. jobs in textiles and manufacturing as capital has been invested in factories in Asian countries such as China and Malaysia. However, millions of U.S. jobs have also been created because of new capital investments in the high-tech, IT, and service sectors, which in theory should offset manufacturing job losses in the long run.

Historically, countries that accepted this free-trade doctrine set as their goal the removal of barriers to the free flow of goods, services, and capital between countries. They attempted to achieve this through an international treaty known as the General Agreement on Tariffs and Trade (GATT). In the years since World War II, there have been eight rounds of GATT negotiations aimed at lowering tariff barriers. The last round, the Uruguay Round, involved 117 countries and succeeded in lowering tariffs by over 30% from the previous level. It also led to the dissolving of GATT and its replacement by the World Trade Organization (WTO), which continues the struggle to reduce tariffs and has more power to sanction countries that break global agreements. On average, the tariff barriers among the governments of developed countries declined from over 40% in 1948 to about 3% today, causing a dramatic increase in world trade.[49]

Declining Barriers of Distance and Culture

Historically, barriers of distance and culture also closed the global environment and kept managers focused on their domestic market. The management problems Unilever, the huge, British-based soap and detergent maker, experienced at the turn of the 20th century illustrate the effect of these barriers.

Founded in London during the 1880s by William Lever, a Quaker, Unilever had a worldwide reach by the early 1900s and operated subsidiaries in most major countries of the British Empire, including India, Canada, and Australia. Lever had a very hands-on, autocratic management style and found his far-flung business empire difficult to control. The reason for Lever's control problems was that communication over great distances was difficult. It took six weeks to reach India by ship from England, and international telephone and telegraph services were unreliable.

Another problem Unilever encountered was the difficulty of doing business in societies that were separated from Britain by barriers of language and culture. Different countries have different sets of national beliefs, values, and norms, and Lever found that a management approach that worked in Britain did not necessarily work in India or Persia (now Iran). As a result, management practices had to be tailored to suit each unique national culture. After Lever's death in 1925, top management at Unilever lowered or *decentralized* (see Chapter 10) decision-making authority to the managers of the various national subsidiaries so they could develop a management approach that suited the country in which they were operating. One result of this strategy was that the subsidiaries grew distant and remote from one another, which reduced Unilever's performance.[50]

Since the end of World War II, a continuing stream of advances in communications and transportation technology has worked to reduce the barriers of distance and culture that affected Unilever and all global organizations. Over the last decades, global communication has been revolutionized by developments in satellites, digital technology, the Internet and global computer networks, and video teleconferencing that allow transmission of vast amounts of information and make reliable, secure, and instantaneous communication possible between people and companies anywhere in the world.[51] This revolution has made it possible for a global organization—a tiny garment factory in Li & Fung's network or a huge company such as IKEA or Unilever—to do business anywhere, anytime and to search for customers and suppliers around the world.

One of the most important innovations in transportation technology that has opened the global environment has been the growth of commercial jet travel. New York is now closer in travel time to Tokyo than it was to Philadelphia in the days of the 13 colonies—a fact that makes control of far-flung international businesses much easier today than in William Lever's era. In addition to speeding travel, modern communications and transportation technologies have also helped reduce the cultural distance between countries. The Internet and its millions of websites facilitate the development of global communications networks and media that are helping to create a worldwide culture that, in some cases, has diluted unique national cultures. Moreover, television networks such as CNN, MTV, ESPN, BBC, and HBO can now be received in many countries, and Hollywood films and other original content are streamed via the Internet across the globe.

Effects of Free Trade on Managers

The lowering of barriers to trade and investment and the decline of distance and culture barriers have created enormous opportunities for companies to expand the market for their goods and services through exports and investments in overseas countries. The shift toward a more open global economy has created not only more opportunities to sell goods and services in markets abroad but also the opportunity to buy more from other countries. A manager's job is more challenging in a dynamic global environment because of the increased intensity of competition that goes hand in hand with the lowering of barriers to trade and investment.

REGIONAL TRADE AGREEMENTS The growth of regional trade agreements, such as the North American Free Trade Agreement (NAFTA), and more recently the Central American Free Trade Agreement (CAFTA), also presents opportunities and threats for managers and their organizations. In North America, NAFTA, which became effective in 1994, had the aim of abolishing the tariffs on 99% of the goods traded between Mexico, Canada, and the United States by 2004. Although it did not achieve this lofty goal, NAFTA has removed most barriers on the cross-border flow of resources, giving, for example, financial institutions and retail businesses in Canada and the United States unrestricted access to the Mexican marketplace. After NAFTA was signed, there was a flood of investment into Mexico from the United States, as well as many other countries such as Japan. Walmart, Costco, Ford, and many major U.S. retail chains expanded their operations in Mexico; Walmart, for example, is stocking many more products from Mexico in its U.S. stores, and its Mexican store chain is also expanding rapidly.

The establishment of free-trade areas creates an opportunity for manufacturing organizations because it lets them reduce their costs. They can do this either by shifting production to the lowest-cost location within the free-trade area (for example, U.S. auto and textile companies shifting production to Mexico) or by serving the whole region from one location rather than establishing separate operations in each country. Some managers, however, view regional free-trade agreements as a threat because they expose a company based in one member country to increased competition from companies based in the other member countries. NAFTA has had this effect; today Mexican managers in some industries face the threat of head-to-head competition against efficient U.S. and Canadian companies. But the opposite is true as well: U.S. and Canadian managers are experiencing threats in labor-intensive industries, such as the flooring tile, roofing, and textile industries, where Mexican businesses have a cost advantage. As of this writing, negotiating teams from the United States, Mexico, and Canada have been through seven rounds of meetings to "renegotiate and modernize" NAFTA; however, final details and revisions are far from finalized.[52]

There are many regional trade agreements around the world. For example, founded in 1999, the African Union's purpose is both political and economic. Its goals include removing any remnants of colonization and apartheid, as well as creating cooperation for development. Complementing the role of the African Union is the Southern African Development Community, a 15-country group whose goals include socioeconomic development and poverty eradication. Another trade agreement is the Cooperation Council for the Arab States of the Gulf, which is made up of several countries, including Qatar, Oman, Bahrain, the United Arab Emirates, Kuwait, and Saudi Arabia. As part of the agreement, countries work on regional cooperation and economic relations.[53] These trade agreements are designed to allow managers to take advantage of opportunities that other members of the agreements can provide.

The Role of National Culture

Despite evidence that countries are becoming more similar because of globalization and that the world may become "a global village," the cultures of different countries still vary widely because of vital differences in their values, norms, and attitudes. As noted earlier, national culture includes the values, norms, knowledge, beliefs, moral principles, laws, customs, and other practices that unite the citizens of a country. National culture shapes individual behavior by specifying appropriate and inappropriate behavior and interaction with others. People learn national culture in their everyday lives by interacting with those around them. This learning starts at an early age and continues throughout their lives.

Cultural Values and Norms

values Ideas about what a society believes to be good, right, desirable, or beautiful.

The basic building blocks of national culture are values and norms. **Values** are beliefs about what a society considers to be good, right, desirable, or beautiful—or their opposites. They provide the basic underpinnings for notions of individual freedom, democracy, truth, justice, honesty, loyalty, social obligation, collective responsibility, the appropriate roles for men and women, love, sex, marriage, and so on. Values are more than merely abstract concepts; they are invested with considerable emotional significance. People argue, fight, and even die over values such as freedom or dignity.

Although deeply embedded in society, values are not static; they change over time, but change is often the result of a slow and painful process. For example, the value systems of many former communist states such as Georgia, Hungary, and Romania have undergone significant changes as these countries have moved away from values that emphasize state control toward values that emphasize individual freedoms. Social turmoil often results when countries undergo major changes in their values, as is happening today in Asia, South America, and the Middle East.

norms Unwritten, informal codes of conduct that prescribe how people should act in particular situations and are considered important by most members of a group or organization.

Norms are unwritten, informal codes of conduct that prescribe appropriate behavior in particular situations and are considered important by most members of a group or organization. They shape the behavior of people toward one another. Two types of norms play a major role in national culture: mores and folkways. **Mores** are norms that are considered to be of central importance to the functioning of society and to social life. Accordingly, the violation of mores brings serious retribution. Mores include proscriptions against murder, theft, adultery, and incest. In many societies mores have been enacted into law. Thus, all advanced societies have laws against murder and theft. However, there are many differences in mores from one society

mores Norms that are considered to be central to the functioning of society and to social life.

to another. In the United States, for example, drinking alcohol is widely accepted, but in Saudi Arabia consumption of alcohol is viewed as a serious violation of social mores and is punishable by imprisonment or even death.

folkways The routine social conventions of everyday life.

Folkways are the routine social conventions of everyday life. They concern customs and practices such as dressing appropriately for particular situations, having good social manners, eating with the correct utensils, and engaging in neighborly behavior. Although folkways define how people are expected to behave, violation of folkways is not a serious or moral matter. People who violate folkways are often thought to be eccentric or ill-mannered, but they are not usually considered immoral or wicked. In many countries, strangers are usually excused for violating folkways because they are unaccustomed to local behavior, but if they repeat the violation, they are censured because they are expected to learn appropriate behavior—hence the importance of managers working in countries abroad to gain wide experience.

Hofstede's Model of National Culture

LO6-5 Discuss why national cultures differ and why it is important that managers be sensitive to the effects of falling trade barriers and regional trade associations on the political and social systems of nations around the world.

Researchers have spent considerable time and effort identifying similarities and differences in the values and norms of different countries. One model of national culture was developed by Geert Hofstede.[54] As a psychologist for IBM, Hofstede collected data on employee values and norms from more than 100,000 IBM employees in 64 countries. Based on his research, Hofstede developed five dimensions along which national cultures can be placed.[55]

INDIVIDUALISM VERSUS COLLECTIVISM   The first dimension, which Hofstede labeled "individualism versus collectivism," has a long history in human thought. **Individualism** is a worldview that values individual freedom and self-expression and adherence to the principle that people should be judged by their individual achievements rather than by their social background. In Western countries, individualism usually includes admiration for personal success, a strong belief in individual rights, and high regard for individual entrepreneurs.[56]

individualism A worldview that values individual freedom and self-expression and adherence to the principle that people should be judged by their individual achievements rather than by their social background.

In contrast, **collectivism** is a worldview that values subordination of the individual to the goals of the group and adherence to the principle that people should be judged by their contribution to the group. Collectivism was widespread in communist countries but has become less prevalent since the collapse of communism in most of those countries. Japan is a noncommunist country where collectivism is highly valued.

Managers must realize that organizations and organizational members reflect their national culture's emphasis on individualism or collectivism. Indeed, one of the major reasons Japanese and American management practices differ is that Japanese culture values collectivism and U.S. culture values individualism.[57]

collectivism A worldview that values subordination of the individual to the goals of the group and adherence to the principle that people should be judged by their contribution to the group.

POWER DISTANCE   By **power distance,** Hofstede meant the degree to which societies accept the idea that inequalities in the power and well-being of their citizens are due to differences in individuals' physical and intellectual capabilities and heritage. This concept also encompasses the degree to which societies accept the economic and social differences in wealth, status, and well-being that result from differences in individual capabilities.

power distance The degree to which societies accept the idea that inequalities in the power and well-being of their citizens are due to differences in individuals' physical and intellectual capabilities and heritage.

Societies in which inequalities are allowed to persist or grow over time have *high power distance.* In high-power-distance societies, workers who are professionally successful amass wealth and pass it on to their children, and, as a result, inequalities may grow over time. In such societies, the gap between rich and poor, with all the attendant political and social consequences, grows very large. In contrast, in societies with *low power distance,* large inequalities between citizens are not allowed to develop. In low-power-distance countries, the government uses taxation and social welfare programs to reduce inequality and improve the welfare of the least fortunate. These societies are more attuned to preventing a large gap between rich and poor and minimizing discord between different classes of citizens.

Advanced Western countries such as the United States, Germany, the Netherlands, and the United Kingdom have relatively low power distance and high individualism. Economically poor Latin American countries such as Guatemala and Panama, and Asian countries such as Malaysia and the Philippines, have high power distance and low individualism.[58] These findings suggest that the cultural values of richer countries emphasize protecting the rights of individuals and, at the same time, provide a fair chance of success to every member of society.

achievement orientation
A worldview that values assertiveness, performance, success, and competition.

nurturing orientation
A worldview that values the quality of life, warm personal friendships, and services and care for the weak.

uncertainty avoidance The degree to which societies are willing to tolerate uncertainty and risk.

long-term orientation
A worldview that values thrift and persistence in achieving goals.

short-term orientation A worldview that values personal stability or happiness and living for the present.

ACHIEVEMENT VERSUS NURTURING ORIENTATION Societies that have an **achievement orientation** value assertiveness, performance, success, competition, and results. Societies that have a **nurturing orientation** value the quality of life, warm personal relationships, and services and care for the weak. Japan and the United States tend to be achievement-oriented; the Netherlands, Sweden, and Denmark are more nurturing-oriented.

UNCERTAINTY AVOIDANCE Societies as well as individuals differ in their tolerance for uncertainty and risk. Societies low on **uncertainty avoidance** (such as the United States and Hong Kong) are easygoing, value diversity, and tolerate differences in personal beliefs and actions. Societies high on uncertainty avoidance (such as Japan and France) are more rigid and skeptical about people whose behaviors or beliefs differ from the norm. In these societies, conformity to the values of the social and work groups to which a person belongs is the norm, and structured situations are preferred because they provide a sense of security.

LONG-TERM VERSUS SHORT-TERM ORIENTATION The last dimension that Hofstede described is orientation toward life and work.[59] A national culture with a **long-term orientation** rests on values such as thrift (saving) and persistence in achieving goals. A national culture with a **short-term orientation** is concerned with maintaining personal stability or happiness and living for the present. Societies with a long-term orientation include Taiwan and Hong Kong, well known for their high rate of per capita savings. The United States and France have a short-term orientation, and their citizens tend to spend more and save less.

The GLOBE Project

Hofstede's research has inspired other major international research projects, including the GLOBE Project, which extends Hofstede's work by looking at additional cultural dimensions. Conceived in the early 1990s by Professor Robert J. House of the University of Pennsylvania, the GLOBE (Global Leadership and Organizational Behavior Effectiveness) Project is an ongoing international research endeavor involving more than 200 researchers who have collected data from more than 17,000 managers in 62 countries.[60] The GLOBE Project looks at nine cultural dimensions:

1. *Performance orientation:* The degree to which individuals in a society are rewarded for performance improvement and excellence.
2. *Assertiveness:* The degree to which members of organizations are confrontational and aggressive in their relationships with others.
3. *Future orientation:* The extent to which individuals engage in behaviors such as planning, investing in the future, and delaying gratification.
4. *Humane orientation:* The degree to which an organization encourages and rewards individuals for being fair, altruistic, generous, caring, and kind to others.
5. *Institutional collectivism:* The degree to which organizational and societal practices encourage and reward collective distribution of resources and collective action.
6. *In-group collectivism:* The degree to which individuals express pride, loyalty, and cohesiveness in their organizations or families.
7. *Gender egalitarianism:* The degree to which an organization minimizes gender inequality.
8. *Power distance:* The extent to which the community accepts and endorses authority, unequal distribution of power, and status privileges.
9. *Uncertainty avoidance:* The extent to which a society or organization uses rules, regulations, and procedures to alleviate the unpredictability of future events.[61]

Based on the data, countries receive an average score on the nine cultural dimensions. For example, Russia scores high on power distance, Singapore scored low on humane orientation, and China scored high on gender differentiation. Managers can also use GLOBE data to cluster countries based on similar cultural values, which would give people working in foreign countries a research-based starting point on how individuals from these cultural clusters are likely to behave.[62]

In Asian countries such as Japan where collectivism is highly valued, coworkers identify strongly with being part of a group, rather than being recognized as an individual.
©IMAGEMORE Co, Ltd./Getty Images

National Culture and Global Management

Differences among national cultures have important implications for managers. First, because of cultural differences, management practices that are effective in one country might be troublesome in another. General Electric's managers learned this while trying to manage Tungsram, a Hungarian lighting products company GE acquired for $150 million. GE was attracted to Tungsram, widely regarded as one of Hungary's best companies, because of Hungary's low wage rates and the possibility of using the company as a base from which to export lighting products to Western Europe. GE transferred some of its best managers to Tungsram and hoped it would soon become a leader in Europe. Unfortunately, many problems arose.

One problem resulted from major misunderstandings between the American managers and the Hungarian workers. The Americans complained that the Hungarians were lazy; the Hungarians thought the Americans were pushy. The Americans wanted strong sales and marketing functions that would pamper customers. In the prior command economy, sales and marketing activities were unnecessary. In addition, Hungarians expected GE to deliver Western-style wages, but GE went to Hungary to take advantage of the country's low wage structure.[63] As Tungsram's losses mounted, GE managers had to admit that because of differences in basic attitudes between countries, they had underestimated the difficulties they would face in turning Tungsram around. Nevertheless, these problems were eventually solved, and the increased efficiency of GE's Hungarian operations made General Electric a major player in the European lighting market for more than a decade. Recently GE sold its lighting operations in Europe, the Middle East, Africa, and Turkey to a company now headed by the former CEO of GE Hungary.[64]

Often management practices must be tailored to suit the cultural contexts within which an organization operates. An approach effective in the United States might not work in Japan, Hungary, or Mexico because of differences in national culture. For example, U.S.-style pay-for-performance systems that emphasize the performance of individuals might not work well in Japan, where individual performance in pursuit of group goals is the value that receives emphasis.

Managers doing business with individuals from another country must be sensitive to the value systems and norms of that country and behave accordingly. For example, Friday is the Islamic Sabbath. Thus, it would be impolite and inappropriate for a U.S. manager to schedule a busy day of activities for Saudi Arabian managers on a Friday.

A culturally diverse management team can be a source of strength for an organization participating in the global marketplace. Compared to organizations with culturally homogeneous management teams, organizations that employ managers from a variety of cultures have a better appreciation of how national cultures differ, and they tailor their management systems and behaviors to the differences.[65] Indeed, one advantage that many Western companies have over their Japanese competitors is greater willingness to create global teams composed of employees from different countries around the world who can draw on and share their different cultural experiences and knowledge to provide service that is customized to the needs of companies in different countries. For example, because IT services account for more than half of IBM's annual revenues, it has been searching for ways to better use its talented workforce to both lower costs and offer customers unique, specialized kinds of services that its competitors cannot. IBM has developed several kinds of techniques to accomplish this.[66]

In the 2000s, IBM created "competency centers" around the world, staffed by employees who share the same specific IT skill. Most of IBM's employees are concentrated in competency centers located in the countries in which IBM has the most clients and does the most business. These employees have a wide variety of skills, developed from their previous work experience, and the challenge facing IBM is to use

IBM's competency centers customize teams of workers who have just the right mix of skills to address a specific client's business needs.
©ColorBlind Images/Blend Images LLC

these experts efficiently. To accomplish this, IBM used its own IT expertise to develop sophisticated software that allows it to create self-managed teams composed of IBM experts who have the optimum mix of skills to solve a client's particular problems. First, IBM programmers analyze the skills and experience of its 80,000 global employees and enter the results into the software program. Then they analyze and code the nature of a client's specific problem and input that information. IBM's program matches each specific client problem to the skills of IBM's experts and identifies a list of "best fit" employees. One of IBM's senior managers narrows this list and decides on the actual composition of the self-managed team.

Once selected, team members, from wherever they happen to be in the world, assemble as quickly as possible and go to work analyzing the client's problem. Together, team members use their authority. This new IT lets IBM create an ever-changing set of global self-managed teams that form to develop the software and service packages necessary to solve the problems of IBM's global clients. At the same time, IBM's IT also optimizes the use of its whole talented workforce because each employee is placed in his or her "most highly valued use"—that is, in the team where the employee's skills can best increase efficiency and effectiveness. A lot of factors are involved in working for a global organization. The accompanying "Management Insight" feature describes how managers might educate themselves about some of the issues.

MANAGEMENT INSIGHT

Challenges Faced by Expats

Where in the world would you like to work? The annual Expat Explorer Survey by HSBC Bank International could help you decide. The survey ranks the best and worst places in the world to be an expat. The results are available on the company's website (https://expatexplorer.hsbc.com) and can help people understand what it would be like to be an expatriate in different countries.[67]

The HSBC site also allows users to submit tips based on their expatriate experiences. Regardless of the countries where expats are working, they seem to echo some of the same advice:

- Learn to work with the culture and the people rather than try to get them to do things your way.

- Join any group activity that interests you (fitness classes, cooking classes, etc.) so you can meet and make friends.

- Make an effort to learn the local language and take an interest in local culture and customs.

- Don't get stuck in the local expat community—go out and meet other people.[68]

Other information on the site is general in nature. In the 2017 survey, for example, Norway, Singapore, New Zealand, Switzerland, and Germany are highly rated for raising children and gaining access to health care. And when it comes to earning disposable income, Taiwan, Norway, Singapore, Australia, and New Zealand top the list.

The HSBC survey ranks countries based on experience, economics, and family. The economics factor includes income, disposable income, and host economic satisfaction. The experience factor includes a long list of issues from entertainment and work–life balance to local culture and making local friends to local weather and learning the local language. The family factor also includes a long list of issues from closeness with partner to quality of child care and schools.

While the factors in the survey can be chosen to tailor a list of the best countries for an individual expatriate, the survey does rank the countries from best to worst. Among the "best" countries are Singapore, Norway, and New Zealand. The "worst" countries for expats include Egypt, Peru, and Argentina. The United States ranked 27 out of 46 countries due to poor scores on work–life balance, health care, and childcare quality.

There are several tips from foreign workers on how to adapt to life in the United States, including

- Plan on living in a place with a good public school system.
- Make sure you have a good health insurance plan.
- Have a fair amount of savings on hand just in case things take longer than expected (for example, immigration papers, finding a place to live).
- Travel across country—there is much to see and do.
- Understand U.S. culture, sports, and public holidays as well as important facts Americans treasure about the history of their country.[69]

The website contains a disclaimer that content on the site is the opinion of users and not verified by HSBC. Nevertheless, the information is invaluable to expats and their families as they undertake employment opportunities in countries across the globe.

Summary and Review

LO6-1   **WHAT IS THE GLOBAL ENVIRONMENT?**   The global environment is the set of forces and conditions that operates beyond an organization's boundaries but affects a manager's ability to acquire and use resources. The global environment has two components: the task environment and the general environment.

LO6-2, 6-3   **THE TASK ENVIRONMENT**   The task environment is the set of forces and conditions that originates with global suppliers, distributors, customers, and competitors and influences managers daily. The opportunities and threats associated with forces in the task environment become more complex as a company expands globally.

LO6-2, 6-3   **THE GENERAL ENVIRONMENT**   The general environment comprises wide-ranging global economic, technological, sociocultural, demographic, political, and legal forces that affect an organization and its task environment.

LO6-4, 6-5   **THE CHANGING GLOBAL ENVIRONMENT**   In recent years there has been a marked shift toward a more open global environment in which capital flows more freely as people and companies search for new opportunities to create profit and wealth. This has hastened the process of globalization. Globalization is the set of specific and general forces that work together to integrate and connect economic, political, and social systems across countries, cultures, or geographic regions so that nations become increasingly interdependent and similar. The process of globalization has been furthered by declining barriers to international trade and investment and declining barriers of distance and culture.

Management in Action

Topics for Discussion and Action

Discussion

1. Why is it important for managers to understand the forces in the global environment that are acting on them and their organizations? **[LO6-1]**

2. Which organization is likely to face the most complex task environment—a biotechnology company trying to develop a cure for cancer or a large retailer such as The Gap or Macy's? Why? **[LO6-2, 6-3]**

3. The population is aging because of declining birth rates, declining death rates, and the aging of the Baby Boomer generation. What might some of the implications of this demographic trend be for (a) a pharmaceutical company and (b) the home construction industry? **[LO6-1, 6-2, 6-3]**

4. How do political, legal, and economic forces shape national culture? What characteristics of national culture do you think have the most important effect on how successful a country is in doing business abroad? **[LO6-3, 6-5]**

5. After the passage of NAFTA, many U.S. companies shifted production operations to Mexico to take advantage of lower labor costs and lower standards for environmental and worker protection. As a result, they cut their costs and were better able to survive in an increasingly competitive global environment. Was their behavior ethical—that is, did the ends justify the means? **[LO6-4]**

Action

6. Choose an organization, and ask a manager in that organization to list the number and strengths of forces in the organization's task environment. Ask the manager to pay particular attention to identifying opportunities and threats that result from pressures and changes in customers, competitors, and suppliers. **[LO6-1, 6-2, 6-3]**

Building Management Skills

Analyzing an Organization's Environment [LO6-1, 6-2, 6-3]

Pick an organization with which you are familiar. It can be an organization in which you have worked or currently work or one that you interact with regularly as a customer (such as the college you are attending). For this organization, do the following:

1. Describe the main forces in the global task environment that are affecting the organization.

2. Describe the main forces in the global general environment that are affecting the organization.

3. Explain how environmental forces affect the job of an individual manager within this organization. How do they determine the opportunities and threats that its managers must confront?

Managing Ethically [LO6-4, 6-5]

Home Depot misjudged the Chinese market for its products and services. The world's largest home improvement chain entered China in 2006 and left six years later. The company was unable to sell its do-it-yourself brand to Chinese consumers. Cheap labor in China means many people can hire someone else to do home improvement work for them, so Chinese consumers are not very interested in DIY projects. In addition, apartment or high-rise living is prevalent in China, which means demand for extensive DIY projects is not extensive among Chinese consumers.[70]

Questions

1. What could Home Depot have done to avoid its mistake?

2. In what cultures might Home Depot find better success?

Small Group Breakout Exercise

How to Enter the Copying Business [LO6-1, 6-2]

Form groups of three to five people, and appoint one group member as the spokesperson who will communicate your findings to the whole class when called on by the instructor. Then discuss the following scenario:

You and your partners have decided to open a small printing and copying business in a college town of 100,000 people. Your business will compete with companies like FedEx Office. You know that over 50% of small businesses fail in their first year, so to increase your chances of success, you have decided to perform a detailed analysis of the task environment of the copying business to discover what opportunities and threats you will encounter.

1. Decide what you must know about (a) your future customers, (b) your future competitors, and (c) other critical forces in the task environment if you are to be successful.

2. Evaluate the main barriers to entry into the copying business.

3. Based on this analysis, list some steps you would take to help your new copying business succeed.

Be the Manager [LO6-1, 6-2]

The Changing Environment of Retailing

You are the new manager of a major clothing store that is facing a crisis. This clothing store has been the leader in its market for the last 15 years. In the last 3 years, however, two other major clothing store chains have opened, and they have steadily been attracting customers away from your store—your sales are down 30%. To find out why, your store surveyed former customers and learned that they perceive your store as not keeping up with changing fashion trends and new forms of customer service. In examining how the store operates, you found out that the 10 purchasing managers who buy the clothing and accessories for the store have been buying from the same clothing suppliers and have become reluctant to try new ones. Moreover, salespeople rarely, if ever, make suggestions for changing how the store operates, and they don't respond to customer requests; the culture of the store has become conservative and risk-averse.

Questions

1. Analyze the major forces in the task environment of a retail clothing store.

2. Devise a program that will help other managers and employees to better understand and respond to their store's task environment.

Bloomberg Businessweek Case in the News

Europe's Magic Bus Is California Dreaming [LO 6-1, 6-2, 6-3, 6-4]

With their reputation for skid row stations, grueling rides, and stinking toilets, intercity buses have long been the travel option of last resort. But in Europe, a startup called FlixBus has given buses a trendier, eco-friendly, sharing-economy vibe. Now it's aiming to take on Greyhound Lines Inc. in the U.S.

Since introducing a handful of routes in Bavaria when Germany liberalized its long-distance bus market five years ago, Flix has become Europe's biggest network, serving 1,700 destinations in 27 countries. More than 100,000 people board one of the company's 1,500 bright-green coaches every day, embarking for destinations as far-flung as Kiev, Lisbon, and Oslo. With backing from private equity companies General Atlantic LLC and Silver Lake Management LLC, Flix in March added train travel in Germany and is experimenting with long-distance electric buses—an escalating ambition reflected in the change of its name to FlixMobility in 2016. "We didn't win because we had the most money, and we're not always the cheapest," says André Schwämmlein, the company's co-chief executive officer and one of three founders. "We focused on the customer, the brand, and the technology."

By that, Schwämmlein means Flix has stayed out of the messy and capital-intensive business of owning and operating buses, instead adopting a model akin to that of Uber Technologies Inc. The company leaves the driving to 300 partners—mostly small, family-owned companies that keep 75% of ticket receipts—allowing Flix to focus on scheduling, customer service, and online ticket sales. "They're a marketing machine," Nico Schoenecker, managing director of partner Autobus Oberbayern GmbH, says in his Munich depot brimming with dozens of coaches, including two with FlixBus branding. Like all others in the Flix fleet, they feature Wi-Fi, electric outlets, and aisle seats that can slide over for a little more personal space—paid for by the operators. Before teaming up with FlixBus,

Autobus Oberbayern was squeaking by on its route between Munich and Prague. Since handing the line over, the service has grown more than sixfold. "They're closer to the customer" than traditional bus companies, Schoenecker says.

Schwämmlein and his partners aim to replicate their model in the U.S., with plans to roll out across the Southwest this summer, linking destinations such as Los Angeles, Las Vegas, and Phoenix. In taking on the market, Flix follows Britain's Stagecoach Group Plc, which in 2006 introduced its Megabus brand in the U.S. After an initial splash, Megabus retrenched as low fuel prices made driving a cheaper alternative. "This isn't our first rodeo," says Andy Kaplinsky, chief commercial officer at Greyhound. "The chatter and buzz of an upstart helps build awareness." Greyhound, owned by British bus operator FirstGroup Plc since 2007, introduced its own hipper, bargain alternative, Bolt-Bus, in 2008, and it has since added Wi-Fi and electric outlets on all its buses.

Flix is confident it can transfer its success from Europe to the U.S. It has,

after all, managed to thrive—turning a profit last year for the first time—in an environment where there are ample alternatives to the bus: an extensive train network and plenty of low-cost flights. Schwämmlein likens the U.S. to Europe five years ago, with untapped demand and an array of local operators ready to make buses available. "At the beginning, you're driven by pain. You grow because you have to," says Schwämmlein, who went to school with fellow founder and technology chief Daniel Krauss and met co-CEO Jochen Engert when both worked for Boston Consulting Group. "Now we're more opportunity-driven. We think we can create a market in the U.S."

Key to that will be prices, and by almost any standard, FlixBus is cheap: just €25 to €50 ($30–$60) gets you from Berlin to Amsterdam, vs. €40 to €150 by train. Flix also takes a targeted approach to setting up routes, going where customers are rather than making them trudge to the bus station. In Berlin the company has 16 stops and frequently revamps timetables and routes to fine-tune the network. That helps keep the buses full—and

persuades operators to hire drivers and invest the $350,000-plus that each new coach costs. "FlixBus isn't a classic bus company but a highly professional sales platform," says Christoph Gipp, managing director of IGES Institute in Berlin, which tracks infrastructure trends in Europe. "They've managed to get away from the stigma associated with bus travel."

Questions for Discussion

1. Do you think the "Uber-like" structure of FlixBus will be an advantage to setting up U.S. operations? Why or why not?

2. What task environment factors could be a challenge to FlixBus in doing business in the United States?

3. How will American culture impact FlixBus' decision to expand its business to the United States?

Source: Chris Reiter, "Europe's Magic Bus Is California Dreaming," *Bloomberg Businessweek,* April 30, 2018, pp. 17–18. Used with permission of Bloomberg L.P. Copyright © 2017. All rights reserved.

Notes

1. V. Govindarajan and A. Warren, "How Amazon Adapted Its Business Model to India," *Harvard Business Review,* http://hbr.org, accessed March 17, 2018.

2. J. Russell, "Jeff Bezos Says Amazon Will 'Keep Investing' in India as Rivals Raise New War Chests," *Tech Crunch,* https://techcrunch.com, June 26, 2017.

3. "How Amazon Adapted Its Business Model to India."

4. Ibid.

5. "Jeff Bezos Says Amazon Will 'Keep Investing' in India."

6. S. Brady, "From Chai to Buy: 5 Questions with Amazon India's Gopal Pillai," *Brand Channel,* http://brandchannel.com, September 12, 2016.

7. P. Ganguly, "Demonetization Hits Ecommerce Growth, Forrester Slashes Projections by Over a Third," *Economic Times,* https://economictimes.indiatimes.com, February 10, 2017.

8. Amazon.in Introduces Global Program 'Amazon Launchpad' to Support Indian Startups," www.amazon.in, accessed March 17, 2018.

9. L.Y. Chen, "Amazon Starts Prime Service in China to Compete with Alibaba," *Bloomberg,* www.bloomberg.com, October 28, 2016.

10. L.J. Bourgeois, "Strategy and Environment: A Conceptual Integration," *Academy of Management Review* 5 (1985), 25–39.

11. M.E. Porter, *Competitive Strategy* (New York: Free Press, 1980).

12. "Coca-Cola versus Pepsi-Cola and the Soft Drink Industry," Harvard Business School Case 9-391-179.

13. www.spenda.com, accessed March 17, 2018.

14. Industry ARC, "Natural Sweetener Stevia Market to Reach 720 Million USD by 2022," *PR Newswire,* www.prnewswire.com, October 26, 2017.

15. A.K. Gupta and V. Govindarajan, "Cultivating a Global Mind-Set," *Academy of Management Executive* 16 (February 2002), 116–27.

16. Levi Strauss & Co., "Sustainability: People," www.levistrauss.com, accessed March 17, 2018; Erika Fry, "The Ties That Bind at Levi's," *Fortune,* September 15, 2017, 104–10; Adele Peters, "How Levi's Is Building Well-Being Programs Where They Matter Most: In Its Factories," *Fast Company,* www.fastcompany.com, October 13, 2016.

17. Ibid.

18. Harvard School of Public Health, Center for Health and the Global Environment,

"Worker Health and Well-Being in the Supply Chain," https://chge.hsph.harvard.edu, accessed March 17, 2018.

19. Fry, "The Ties That Bind at Levi's."

20. Levi Strauss & Co., "Sustainability: People"; Peters, "How Levi's Is Building."

21. "Boeing's Worldwide Supplier Network," *Seattle Post-Intelligencer,* April 9, 1994, 13; I. Metthee, "Playing a Larger Part," *Seattle Post-Intelligencer,* April 9, 1994, 13.

22. J. Johnsson, "Boeing Falls as Analyst Deems 787 Cost Recoup 'Unachievable,'" *Bloomberg,* www.bloomberg.com, April 20, 2016.

23. "What We Do," www.lifung.com, accessed March 17, 2018.

24. J. Thornton-O'Connell, "7 Companies That Have Reinvested in America Following Trump's Election," *Go Banking Rates,* www.gobankingrates.com, March 15, 2017.

25. M.E. Porter, *Competitive Advantage* (New York: Free Press, 1985).

26. "Walmart Greatly Extending Payment Terms, Asking Some Vendors to Pay DC Handling Fee," *Supply Chain Digest,* www.scdigest.com, accessed March 17, 2018; S. Sit, "Wal-Mart Squeezes Suppliers in Price War," *Supply Management,* www.cips.org, March 31, 2017.

27. Reuters, "Deutsche Bank to Pay $38 Million in U.S. Silver Price-Fixing Case," *CNBC*, www.cnbc.com, October 18, 2016.

28. Y. Heisler, "Apple Outperformed Nearly Every PC Maker in 2017 as Mac Sales Remain Steady," *BGR*, http://bgr.com, January 14, 2018.

29. S. Bertoni, "Spotify's Daniel Ek: The Most Important Man in Music," *Forbes*, www.forbes.com, accessed March 17, 2018; R. Molla and P. Kafka, "Here's Why the Music Industry Is Celebrating Again—and Here's Why the Music Industry Is Still in Mourning," *Recode*, www.recode.net, January 27, 2018.

30. "Help: Premium and Spotify on PlayStation," https://support.spotify.com, accessed March 17, 2018; "Spotify's Daniel Ek: The Most Important Man in Music."

31. "About Spotify: Fast Facts," https://press.spotify.com, accessed September 14, 2018.

32. "About Spotify: Fast Facts"; P. Hall, "Apple Music Is Growing Fast, But It Will Be a While Before World Domination," *Digital Trends*, www.digitaltrends.com, February 5, 2018.

33. "Music Streaming Is Booming . . . So What Happens Next?" *Musically*, http://musically.com, accessed March 17, 2018; L. Nguyen and L. Shaw, "Apple, Spotify, YouTube Lose as Court Raises Streaming Music Royalty Rates," *The Mercury News*, www.mercurynews.com, January 29, 2018; T. Ingham, "Spotify Acquires 4th Company in Past 3 Months—and Looks Set to Buy More," *Music Business Worldwide*, www.musicbusinessworldwide.com, May 21, 2017.

34. For views on barriers to entry from an economics perspective, see Porter, *Competitive Strategy*. For the sociological perspective, see J. Pfeffer and G. R. Salancik, *The External Control of Organization: A Resource Dependence Perspective* (New York: Harper & Row, 1978).

35. S. Soper, "Amazon Building Global Delivery Business to Take on Alibaba," *Bloomberg Technology*, www.bloomberg.com, February 9, 2016.

36. B. Cummings, "Rice: U.S. Enjoying Strong Demand in Japan," *Agfax*, https://agfax.com, August 24, 2017.

37. R. Hallock, "10 Facts about the New AMD Ryzen™ Desktop Processor with Radeon™ Vega Graphics," https://community.amd.com, accessed March 17, 2018; M. Chiappetta, "AMD Second-Generation Ryzen Processors: Five Reasons Why They're Going to Rock," *Forbes*, www.forbes.com, February 26, 2018; J. Martindale, "The Best AMD CPUs on Any Budget," *Digital Trends*, www.digitaltrends.com, February 12, 2018.

38. N. Goodman, *An Introduction to Sociology* (New York: HarperCollins 1991); C. Nakane, *Japanese Society* (Berkeley: University of California Press, 1970).

39. E. Monaco, "The 9 Organic and Sustainable Food Trends Taking Over 2018," *Organic Authority*, www.organicauthority.com, January 16, 2018.

40. A. Smith, "Walmart Is Bringing Meal Kits to Thousands of Stores," *CNN Money*, http://money.cnn.com, March 5, 2018; C. Siegner, "6 Major Food Trends to Watch in 2018," *Food Dive*, www.fooddive.com, January 23, 2018.

41. For a detailed discussion of the importance of the structure of law as a factor explaining economic change and growth, see D.C. North, *Institutions, Institutional Change, and Economic Performance* (Cambridge: Cambridge University Press, 1990).

42. D. Meyer, "Why the EU Is Holding Up Apple's Shazam Takeover," *Fortune*, http://fortune.com, February 7, 2018; A. White, "Apple-Shazam Deal May Hurt Competition in Europe, EU Says," *Bloomberg Technology*, www.bloomberg.com, February 6 2018.

43. A. Hunt and B. Wheeler, "Brexit: All You Need to Know about the UK Leaving the EU," *BBC News*, www.bbc.com, March 3, 2018.

44. P. Baker, "Trump Abandons Trans-Pacific Partnership, Obama's Signature Trade Deal," *The New York Times*, www.nytimes.com, January 23, 2017.

45. M.A. Carpenter and J.W. Fredrickson, "Top Management Teams, Global Strategic Posture, and the Moderating Role of Uncertainty," *Academy of Management Journal* 44 (June 2001), 533–46.

46. D. J. Lynch, J. Dawsey, and D. Paletta, "Trump Imposes Steel and Aluminum Tariffs on the E.U., Canada and Mexico," *The Washington Post*, www.washingtonpost.com, May 31, 2018; A. Swanson, "Trump Readies Sweeping Tariffs and Investment Restrictions on China," *The New York Times*, www.nytimes.com, March 15, 2018.

47. For a summary of these theories, see P. Krugman and M. Obstfeld, *International Economics: Theory and Policy* (New York: HarperCollins, 1991). Also see C.W.L. Hill, *International Business* (New York: McGraw-Hill, 1997), chap. 4.

48. A.M. Rugman, "The Quest for Global Dominance," *Academy of Management Executive* 16 (August 2002), 157–60.

49. "Understanding the WTO: The Agreements," www.wto.org, accessed March 17, 2018.

50. C.A. Bartlett and S. Ghoshal, *Managing across Borders* (Boston: Harvard Business School Press, 1989).

51. C. Arnst and G. Edmondson, "The Global Free-for-All," *BusinessWeek*, September 26, 1994, 118–26.

52. U.S. Trade Representative, "Trilateral Statement on the Conclusion of the Fifth Round of NAFTA Negotiations," https://ustr.gov, accessed March 17, 2018; P. Gillespie, "A Year Later, NAFTA Is Still Alive," *CNNMoney*, http://money.cnn.com, February 26, 2018.

53. Organization website, "AU in a Nutshell," www.au.int, accessed March 18, 2018; organization website, "SADC Facts & Figures," www.sadc.int, accessed March 18, 2018; organization website, "Areas of Cooperation Achievements," www.gcc-sg.gov, accessed March 18, 2018.

54. G. Hofstede, B. Neuijen, D.D. Ohayv, and G. Sanders, "Measuring Organizational Cultures: A Qualitative and Quantitative Study Across Twenty Cases," *Administrative Science Quarterly* 35 (1990), 286–316.

55. M.H. Hoppe, "Introduction: Geert Hofstedes Culture's Consequences: International Difference in Work-Related Values," *Academy of Management Executive* 19 (February 2004), 73–75.

56. R. Bellah, *Habits of the Heart: Individualism and Commitment in American Life* (Berkeley: University of California Press, 1985).

57. C. Nakane, *Japanese Society*. University of California Press, 1970.

58. G. Hofstede, "The Cultural Relativity of Organizational Practices and Theories," *Journal of International Business Studies*, (Fall 1983), 75–89.

59. Hofstede et al., "Measuring Organizational Cultures."

60. R. House, M. Javidan, P. Hanges, and P. Dorfman, "Understanding Cultures and Implicit Leadership Theories Across the Globe: An Introduction to Project GLOBE," *Journal of World Business*, no. 37(2002), 3–10.

61. R.J. House et al, *Culture, Leadership, and Organizations: The GLOBE Studies of 62 Societies* (Los Angeles: Sage Publishing, 2004).

62. M. Javidan and A. Dastmalchian, "Managerial Implications of the GLOBE Project: A Study of 62 Societies," *Asia Pacific Journal of Human Resources* 47, no. 1(2009), 41–58.

63. J. Perlez, "GE Finds Tough Going in Hungary," *The New York Times*, July 25, 1994, C1, C3.

64. T. Gryta, "GE Begins to Sell Off One of Its Oldest Businesses: Lights," *The Wall Street Journal*, www.wsj.com, February 15, 2018.

65. J.P. Fernandez and M. Barr, *The Diversity Advantage* (New York: Lexington Books, 1994).

66. "IBM Centers of Competency," www.ibm.com, accessed March 18, 2018.

67. "2017 Expat Explorer Survey," https://expatexplorer.hsbc.com, accessed March 18, 2018.

68. "Expat Hints & Tips," https://expatexplorer.hsbc.com, accessed March 18, 2018.

69. "Tips about Living in the United States," https://expatexplorer, accessed March 18, 2018.

70. L. Burkitt, "Home Depot Learns Chinese Prefer 'Do-It-for-Me,'" *The Wall Street Journal*, www.wsj.com, accessed March 18, 2018; "University Study Concludes Why Home Depot Failed in China: It Ignored Women," *Fierce Retail*, www.fierceretail.com, April 29, 2013.

CHAPTER 7

Decision Making, Learning, Creativity, and Entrepreneurship

©Robert Nicholas/age fotostock

Learning Objectives

After studying this chapter, you should be able to:

LO7-1 Understand the nature of managerial decision making, differentiate between programmed and nonprogrammed decisions, and explain why nonprogrammed decision making is a complex, uncertain process.

LO7-2 Describe the six steps managers should take to make the best decisions, and explain how cognitive biases can lead managers to make poor decisions.

LO7-3 Identify the advantages and disadvantages of group decision making, and describe techniques that can improve it.

LO7-4 Explain the role that organizational learning and creativity play in helping managers to improve their decisions.

LO7-5 Describe how managers can encourage and promote entrepreneurship to create a learning organization, and differentiate between entrepreneurs and intrapreneurs.

Creativity and Ability to Learn Keep 23andMe Strong

How do managers make decisions that add value? Anne Wojcicki, cofounder and CEO of 23andMe, applies a creative mind-set with adaptability in the face of change. These qualities propelled decisions to launch the company she helped start in 2006 and to identify ways forward when the company ran into trouble.

Wojcicki's business idea would have been unimaginable 15 years ago. Scientists were developing ways to interpret human DNA, and as techniques advanced, their cost was falling. Wojcicki, who had studied biology in college and worked in the financial industry as a biotech analyst, saw an opportunity to put health information into the hands of individuals. The product would be a test kit: a tube in which a person spits some saliva to mail in for a genetic analysis.[1] Wojcicki developed a business plan that was cautious on spending for office supplies but ambitious in terms of the product. Her company, 23andMe, was the first to offer genetic screening to the general public. Besides selling a technologically advanced product, 23andMe overturned a business model by competing with the medical facilities that had provided this service to patients. Within a few years, 23andMe offered customers more than 250 possible reports.[2]

In 2013, however, 23andMe hit a roadblock. The Food and Drug Administration determined that the test kit was a medical device because it provided information that patients would use for making medical decisions.[3] The company had not sought, much less obtained, the required FDA approval to sell such a device. Managers had assumed the test kit was a diagnostic test carried out in a single lab, and that is what they obtained approval to sell it to consumers. The FDA investigated when doctors and geneticists expressed concern that the test provided insufficient information for making informed decisions.

The agency ruled that 23andMe could continue selling the test kit if the results addressed customers' ancestry only, not their health risks. This restriction destroyed the company's fundamental

23andMe CEO Anne Wojcicki learned an valuable lesson about decision making and being flexible when it came to a viable business model for the company.
©Kimberly White/Getty Images

business model, but Wojcicki decided it was a challenge that perseverance could solve, not a death blow to 23andMe.[4]

Wojcicki and her staff began working with the FDA to address its concerns.[5] They began meeting with FDA staff every couple of months and sending frequent messages as they prepared an application for approval. After rejecting the first application, the FDA considered a second. Wojcicki saw the situation as a learning opportunity. She identified a key problem: 23andMe had originally lacked the right people for navigating the complex process of meeting regulatory requirements. She hired an expert in regulatory affairs, and they divided the desired tests into chunks, focusing first on tests they thought would most easily win approval. Finally, four years later, the Food and Drug Administration began allowing 23andMe to report results indicating risk factors for certain diseases, including Parkinson's and Alzheimer's.

In the meantime, Wojcicki had recognized an even more significant way forward. Consumers—more than a million—kept buying tests, even just to learn about their ancestry, and most agreed to allow their data to be used in scientific research.[6] These customers filled out surveys, creating a massive and growing database about their health, genetics, and behaviors. Managers at 23andMe realized they were building a product more valuable than the test kits: the data. They decided to identify ethical ways to use the data as an asset. They began selling data sets (without patients' names) to drug companies and makers of health-related products. For Wojcicki, the process was like starting up a company all over again.[7] And this time, she already had the added advantage of experience.

Overview

"A Manager's Challenge" illustrates how decision making can have a profound influence on organizational effectiveness. The decisions managers make at all levels in companies large and small can change the growth and prosperity of these companies and the well-being of their employees, customers, and other stakeholders. Yet such decisions can be difficult to make because they are fraught with uncertainty.

LO7-1 Understand the nature of managerial decision making, differentiate between programmed and nonprogrammed decisions, and explain why nonprogrammed decision making is a complex, uncertain process.

In this chapter we examine how managers make decisions, and we explore how individual, group, and organizational factors affect the quality of the decisions they make and ultimately determine organizational performance. We discuss the nature of managerial decision making and examine some models of the decision-making process that help reveal the complexities of successful decision making. Then we outline the main steps of the decision-making process; in addition, we explore the biases that may cause capable managers to make poor decisions, both as individuals and as members of a group. Next we examine how managers can promote organizational learning and creativity and improve the quality of decision making throughout an organization. Finally, we discuss the important role of entrepreneurship in promoting organizational creativity, and we differentiate between entrepreneurs and intrapreneurs. By the end of this chapter you will appreciate the critical role of management decision making in creating a high-performing organization.

The Nature of Managerial Decision Making

Every time managers plan, organize, direct, or control organizational activities, they make a stream of decisions. In opening a new restaurant, for example, managers have to decide where to locate it, what kinds of food to provide, which people to employ, and so on. Decision making is a basic part of every task managers perform. In this chapter we study how these decisions are made.

decision making The process by which managers respond to opportunities and threats by analyzing options and making determinations about specific organizational goals and courses of action.

As we discussed in the last three chapters, one of the main tasks facing a manager is to manage the organizational environment. Forces in the external environment give rise to many opportunities and threats for managers and their organizations. In addition, inside an organization, managers must address many opportunities and threats that may arise as organizational resources are used. To deal with these opportunities and threats, managers must make decisions—that is, they must select one solution from a set of alternatives. **Decision making** is the process by which managers respond to opportunities and threats by analyzing the options and making determinations, or *decisions,* about specific organizational goals and courses of action.

Good decisions result in the selection of appropriate goals and courses of action that increase organizational performance; bad decisions lower performance.

Decision making in response to opportunities occurs when managers search for ways to improve organizational performance to benefit customers, employees, and other stakeholder groups. As described in "A Manager's Challenge," Anne Wojcicki seized the opportunity to develop new products that capitalize on 23andMe's strengths. *Decision making in response to threats* occurs when events inside or outside the organization adversely affect organizational performance and managers search for ways to increase performance.[8] Wojcicki responded to the FDA's complaint that the 23andMe product was actually a medical device by hiring experts experienced in navigating the maze of regulatory requirements and by working closely with FDA staff every step of the way during the approval process. Decision making is central to being a manager, and whenever managers engage in planning, organizing, leading, and controlling—their four principal tasks—they are constantly making decisions.

Managers are always searching for ways to make better decisions to improve organizational performance. At the same time, they do their best to avoid costly mistakes that will hurt organizational performance. Examples of spectacularly good decisions include Martin Cooper's decision to develop the first cell phone at Motorola and Apple's decision to develop the iPod.[9] Examples of spectacularly bad decisions include the decision by managers at NASA and Morton Thiokol to launch the *Challenger* space shuttle—a decision that killed six astronauts in 1986—and the decision by NASA to launch the *Columbia* space shuttle in 2003, which killed seven astronauts.

Programmed and Nonprogrammed Decision Making

Regardless of the specific decisions a manager makes, the decision-making process is either programmed or nonprogrammed.[10]

programmed decision making Routine, virtually automatic decision making that follows established rules or guidelines.

PROGRAMMED DECISION MAKING   Programmed decision making is a *routine,* virtually automatic process. Programmed decisions are decisions that have been made so many times in the past that managers have developed rules or guidelines to be applied when certain situations inevitably occur. Programmed decision making takes place when a school principal asks the school board to hire a new teacher whenever student enrollment increases by 40 students; when a manufacturing supervisor hires new workers whenever existing workers' overtime increases by more than 10%; and when an office manager orders basic office supplies, such as paper and pens, whenever the inventory of supplies drops below a certain level. Furthermore, in the last example, the office manager probably orders the same amount of supplies each time.

This decision making is called *programmed* because office managers, for example, do not need to repeatedly make new judgments about what should be done. They can rely on long-established decision rules such as these:

- *Rule 1:* When the storage shelves are three-quarters empty, order more copy paper.
- *Rule 2:* When ordering paper, order enough to fill the shelves.

Managers can develop rules and guidelines to regulate all routine organizational activities. For example, rules can specify how a worker should perform a certain task, and rules can specify the quality standards that raw materials must meet to be acceptable. Most decision making that relates to the day-to-day running of an organization is programmed decision making. Examples include deciding how much inventory to hold, when to pay bills, when to bill customers, and when to order materials and supplies. Programmed decision making occurs when managers have the information they need to create rules that will guide decision making. There is little ambiguity involved in assessing when the stockroom is empty or counting the number of new students in class.

nonprogrammed decision making Nonroutine decision making that occurs in response to unusual, unpredictable opportunities and threats.

NONPROGRAMMED DECISION MAKING   Suppose, however, that managers are not certain that a course of action will lead to a desired outcome. Or in even more ambiguous terms, suppose managers are not even sure what they are trying to achieve. Obviously, rules cannot be developed to predict uncertain events.

Nonprogrammed decision making is required for these *nonroutine* decisions. Nonprogrammed decisions are made in response to unusual or novel opportunities and threats. Nonprogrammed decision making occurs when there are no ready-made decision rules that managers can apply to a situation. Rules do not exist because the situation is unexpected or uncertain and managers lack the information they would need to develop rules to cover it. Examples of nonprogrammed decision making include decisions to invest in a new technology, develop a new kind of product, launch a new promotional campaign, enter a new market, expand internationally, start a new business, or invest in research and development like Anne Wojcicki and 23andMe did, as discussed in the chapter's opening story.

How do managers make decisions in the absence of decision rules? They may rely on their **intuition**—feelings, beliefs, and hunches that come readily to mind, require little effort and information gathering, and result in on-the-spot decisions.[11] Or they may make **reasoned judgments**—decisions that require time and effort and result from careful information gathering, generation of alternatives, and evaluation of alternatives. "Exercising" one's judgment is a more rational process than "going with" one's intuition. For reasons that we examine later in this chapter, both intuition and judgment often are flawed and can result in poor decision making. Thus, the likelihood of error is much greater in nonprogrammed decision making than in programmed decision making.[12] In the remainder of this chapter, when we talk about decision making, we are referring to *nonprogrammed* decision making because it causes the most problems for managers and is inherently challenging.

Sometimes managers have to make rapid decisions and don't have time to carefully consider the issues involved. They must rely on their intuition to respond quickly to a pressing concern. For example, when fire chiefs, captains, and lieutenants manage firefighters battling dangerous, out-of-control fires, they often need to rely on their expert intuition to make on-the-spot decisions that will protect the lives of the firefighters and save the lives of others, contain the fires, and preserve property—decisions made in emergency situations entailing high uncertainty, high risk, and rapidly changing conditions.[13] In other cases managers do have time to make reasoned judgments, but there are no established rules to guide their decisions, such as when deciding whether to proceed with a proposed merger.

Regardless of the circumstances, making nonprogrammed decisions can result in effective or ineffective decision making. As indicated in the accompanying "Management Insight" feature, managers have to be on their guard to avoid being overconfident in decisions that result from either intuition or reasoned judgment.

The classical and administrative decision-making models reveal many of the assumptions, complexities, and pitfalls that affect decision making. These models help reveal the factors that managers and other decision makers must be aware of to improve the quality of their decision making. Keep in mind, however, that the classical and administrative models are just guides that can help managers understand the decision-making process. In real life the process is typically not cut-and-dried, but these models can help guide a manager through it.

intuition Feelings, beliefs, and hunches that come readily to mind, require little effort and information gathering, and result in on-the-spot decisions.

reasoned judgment A decision that requires time and effort and results from careful information gathering, generation of alternatives, and evaluation of alternatives.

Nonprogrammed decision making covers areas with no previous benchmarks or rubrics, such as making expert chess moves.
©Blend Images/Shutterstock

classical model A prescriptive approach to decision making based on the assumption that the decision maker can identify and evaluate all possible alternatives and their consequences and rationally choose the most appropriate course of action.

optimum decision The most appropriate decision in light of what managers believe to be the most desirable consequences for the organization.

The Classical Model

One of the earliest models of decision making, the **classical model**, is *prescriptive,* which means it specifies how decisions *should* be made. Managers using the classical model make a series of simplifying assumptions about the nature of the decision-making process (see Figure 7.1). The premise of the classical model is that once managers recognize the need to make a decision, they should be able to generate a complete list of *all* alternatives and consequences and make the best choice. In other words, the classical model assumes managers have access to *all* the information they need to make the **optimum decision**, which is the most appropriate decision possible in light of what they believe to be the most desirable consequences for the organization. Furthermore, the classical model assumes managers can easily list their own preferences for each alternative and rank them from least to most preferred to make the optimum decision.

Curbing Overconfidence in Decision Making

Should managers be confident in their intuition and reasoned judgments? Decades of research by Nobel Prize winner Daniel Kahneman; his longtime collaborator, the late Amos Tversky; and other researchers suggest that managers (like all people) tend to be overconfident in the decisions they make, whether based on intuition or reasoned judgment.[14] And with overconfidence comes failure to evaluate and rethink the wisdom of the decisions one makes and failure to learn from mistakes.[15]

Kahneman distinguishes between the intuition of managers who are truly expert in the content domain of a decision and the intuition of managers who have some knowledge and experience but are not true experts.[16] Although the intuition of both types can be faulty, that of experts is less likely to be flawed. This is why fire captains can make good decisions and why expert chess players can make good moves, in both cases without spending much time or deliberating carefully on what, for non-experts, is a complicated set of circumstances. What distinguishes expert managers from those with limited expertise is that the experts have extensive experience under conditions in which they receive quick and clear feedback about the outcomes of their decisions.[17]

Unfortunately, managers who have some experience in a content area but are not true experts tend to be overly confident in their intuition and judgments.[18] As Kahneman puts it, "People jump to statistical conclusions on the basis of very weak evidence. We form powerful intuitions about trends and about the replicability of results on the basis of information that is truly inadequate."[19] Not only do managers, and all people, tend to be overconfident about their intuition and judgments, but they also tend not to learn from mistakes. Compounding this undue optimism is the human tendency to be overconfident in one's own abilities and influence over unpredictable events. Surveys have found that the majority of people think they are above average, make better decisions, and are less prone to making bad decisions than others (of course, it is impossible for most people to be above average on any dimension).[20]

Examples of managerial overconfidence abound. Research has consistently found that mergers tend to turn out poorly—postmerger profitability declines, stock prices drop, and so forth. For example, Chrysler had the biggest profits of the three largest automakers in the United States when it merged with Daimler; the merger was a failure and both Chrysler and Daimler would have been better off if it never had happened.[21] One would imagine that top executives and boards of directors would learn from this research and from articles in the business press about the woes of merged companies (such as the AOL–Time Warner merger, the Kmart–Sears merger, and the eBay–Skype merger).[22] Evidently not. Top managers seem to overconfidently believe they can succeed where others have failed.[23] Similarly, whereas less than half of new ventures succeed as viable businesses for more than five years, entrepreneurs, on average, tend to think that they have a 6 out of 10 chance of being successful.[24]

Jeffrey Pfeffer, a professor at Stanford University's Graduate School of Business, suggests that managers can avoid the perils of overconfidence by critically evaluating the decisions they have made and the outcomes of those decisions. They should admit to themselves when they have made a mistake and really learn from their mistakes (rather than dismissing them as flukes or situations out of their control). In addition, managers should be leery of too much agreement at the top. As Pfeffer puts it, "If two people agree all the time, one of them is redundant."[25]

Figure 7.1

The Classical Model of Decision Making

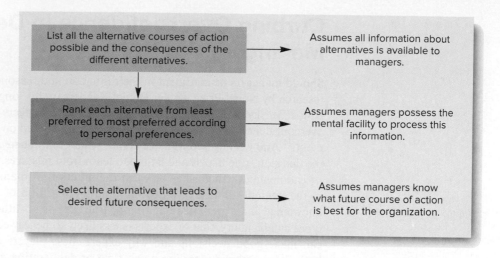

The Administrative Model

James March and Herbert Simon disagreed with the underlying assumptions of the classical model of decision making. In contrast, they proposed that managers in the real world do *not* have access to all the information they need to make a decision. Moreover, they pointed out that even if all information were readily available, many managers would lack the mental or psychological ability to absorb and evaluate it correctly. As a result, March and Simon developed the **administrative model** of decision making to explain why decision making is always an inherently uncertain and risky process—and why managers can rarely make decisions in the manner prescribed by the classical model. The administrative model is based on three important concepts: *bounded rationality, incomplete information,* and *satisficing.*

administrative model An approach to decision making that explains why decision making is inherently uncertain and risky and why managers usually make satisfactory rather than optimum decisions.

BOUNDED RATIONALITY   March and Simon pointed out that human decision-making capabilities are bounded by people's cognitive limitations—that is, limitations in their ability to interpret, process, and act on information.[26] They argued that the limitations of human intelligence constrain the ability of decision makers to determine the optimum decision. March and Simon coined the term **bounded rationality** to describe the situation in which the number of alternatives a manager must identify is so great and the amount of information so vast that it is difficult for the manager to even come close to evaluating it all before making a decision.[27]

bounded rationality Cognitive limitations that constrain one's ability to interpret, process, and act on information.

INCOMPLETE INFORMATION   Even if managers had unlimited ability to evaluate information, they still would not be able to arrive at the optimum decision because they would have incomplete information. Information is incomplete because the full range of decision-making alternatives is unknowable in most situations, and the consequences associated with known alternatives are uncertain.[28] In other words, information is incomplete because of risk and uncertainty, ambiguity, and time constraints (see Figure 7.2).

RISK AND UNCERTAINTY   As we saw in Chapter 6, forces in the organizational environment are constantly changing. **Risk** is present when managers know the possible outcomes of a particular course of action and can assign probabilities to them. For example, managers in the biotechnology industry know that new drugs have a 10% probability of successfully passing advanced clinical trials and a 90% probability of failing. These probabilities reflect the experiences of thousands of drugs that have gone through advanced clinical trials. Thus, when managers in the biotechnology industry decide to submit a drug for testing, they know that there is only a 10% chance that the drug will succeed, but at least they have some information on which to base their decision.

risk The degree of probability that the possible outcomes of a particular course of action will occur.

When **uncertainty** exists, the probabilities of alternative outcomes *cannot* be determined and future outcomes are *unknown.* Managers are working blind. Because the probability of a given

uncertainty Unpredictability.

Figure 7.2

Why Information Is Incomplete

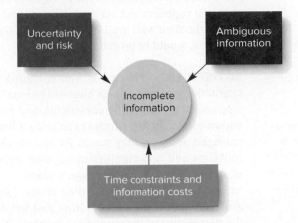

outcome occurring is not known, managers have little information to use in making a decision. For example, in 1993, when Apple Computer introduced the Newton, its personal digital assistant (PDA), managers had no idea what the probability of a successful product launch for a PDA might be. Because Apple was the first to market this totally new product, there was no body of well-known data that Apple's managers could draw on to calculate the probability of a successful launch. Uncertainty plagues most managerial decision making.[29] Although Apple's initial launch of its PDA was a disaster due to technical problems, an improved version was more successful.

AMBIGUOUS INFORMATION A second reason information is incomplete is that much of the information managers have at their disposal is ambiguous information. Its meaning is not clear—it can be interpreted in multiple and often conflicting ways.[30] Take a look at Figure 7.3. Do you see a young woman or an old woman? In a similar fashion, managers often interpret the same piece of information differently and make decisions based on their own interpretations.

ambiguous information Information that can be interpreted in multiple and often conflicting ways.

TIME CONSTRAINTS AND INFORMATION COSTS The third reason information is incomplete is that managers have neither the time nor the money to search for all possible alternative solutions and evaluate all the potential consequences of those alternatives. Consider

Figure 7.3

Ambiguous Information: Young Woman or Old Woman?

the situation confronting a Ford Motor Company purchasing manager who has one month to choose a supplier for a small engine part. There are 20,000 potential suppliers for this part in the United States alone. Given the time available, the purchasing manager cannot contact all potential suppliers and ask each for its terms (price, delivery schedules, and so on). Moreover, even if the time were available, the costs of obtaining the information, including the manager's own time, would be prohibitive.

satisficing Searching for and choosing an acceptable, or satisfactory, response to problems and opportunities, rather than trying to make the best decision.

SATISFICING   March and Simon argued that managers do not attempt to discover every alternative when faced with bounded rationality, an uncertain future, unquantifiable risks, considerable ambiguity, time constraints, and high information costs. Rather, they use a strategy known as satisficing, which is exploring a limited sample of all potential alternatives.[31] When managers satisfice, they search for and choose acceptable, or satisfactory, ways to respond to problems and opportunities rather than trying to make the optimum decision.[32] In the case of the Ford purchasing manager's search, for example, satisficing may involve asking a limited number of suppliers for their terms, trusting that they are representative of suppliers in general, and making a choice from that set. Although this course of action is reasonable from the perspective of the purchasing manager, it may mean that a potentially superior supplier is overlooked.

March and Simon pointed out that managerial decision making is often more art than science. In the real world, managers must rely on their intuition and judgment to make what seems to them to be the best decision in the face of uncertainty and ambiguity.[33] Moreover, managerial decision making is often fast-paced; managers use their experience and judgment to make crucial decisions under conditions of incomplete information. Although there is nothing wrong with this approach, decision makers should be aware that human judgment is often flawed. As a result, even the best managers sometimes make poor decisions.[34]

Steps in the Decision-Making Process

LO7-2 Describe the six steps managers should take to make the best decisions, and explain how cognitive biases can lead managers to make poor decisions.

Using the work of March and Simon as a basis, researchers have developed a step-by-step model of the decision-making process and the issues and problems that managers confront at each step. Perhaps the best way to introduce this model is to examine the real-world nonprogrammed decision making of Scott McNealy at a crucial point in Sun Microsystems's history. McNealy was a founder of Sun Microsystems and was the chairman of the board of directors until Sun was acquired by Oracle in 2010.[35]

In early August 1985, Scott McNealy, then CEO of Sun Microsystems[36] (a hardware and software computer workstation manufacturer focused on network solutions), had to decide whether to go ahead with the launch of the new Carrera workstation computer, scheduled for September 10. Sun's managers had chosen the date nine months earlier when the development plan for the Carrera was first proposed. McNealy knew it would take at least a month to prepare for the September 10 launch, and the decision could not be put off.

Customers were waiting for the new machine, and McNealy wanted to be the first to provide a workstation that took advantage of Motorola's powerful 16-megahertz 68020 microprocessor. Capitalizing on this opportunity would give Sun a significant edge over Apollo, its main competitor in the workstation market. McNealy knew, however, that committing to the September 10 launch date was risky. Motorola was having production problems with the 16-megahertz 68020 microprocessor and could not guarantee Sun a steady supply of these chips. Moreover, the operating system software was not completely free of bugs.

If Sun launched the Carrera on September 10, the company might have to ship some machines with software that was not fully operational, was likely to crash the system, and utilized Motorola's less powerful 12-megahertz 68020 microprocessor instead of the 16-megahertz version.[37] Of course, Sun could later upgrade the microprocessor and operating system software in any machines purchased by early customers, but the company's reputation would suffer. If Sun did not go ahead with the September launch, the company would miss an important opportunity.[38] Rumors were circulating in the industry that Apollo would be launching a new machine of its own in December.

McNealy clearly had a difficult decision to make. He had to decide quickly whether to launch the Carrera, but he did not have all the facts. He did not know, for example, whether

Figure 7.4

Six Steps in Decision Making

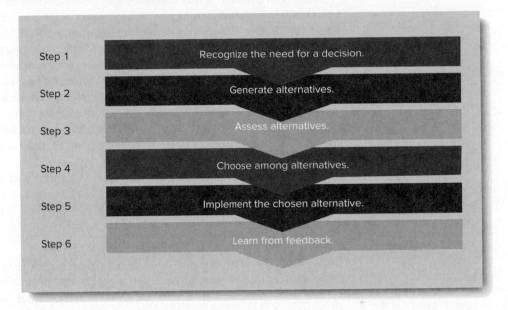

Step 1 — Recognize the need for a decision.

Step 2 — Generate alternatives.

Step 3 — Assess alternatives.

Step 4 — Choose among alternatives.

Step 5 — Implement the chosen alternative.

Step 6 — Learn from feedback.

the microprocessor or operating system problems could be resolved by September 10; nor did he know whether Apollo was going to launch a competing machine in December. But he could not wait to find these things out—he had to make a decision. We'll see what he decided later in the chapter.

Many managers who must make important decisions with incomplete information face dilemmas similar to McNealy's. Managers should consciously follow six steps to make a good decision (see Figure 7.4).[39] We review these steps in the remainder of this section.

Recognize the Need for a Decision

The first step in the decision-making process is to recognize the need for a decision. Scott McNealy recognized this need, and he realized a decision had to be made quickly.

Some stimuli usually spark the realization that a decision must be made. These stimuli often become apparent because changes in the organizational environment result in new kinds of opportunities and threats. This happened at Sun Microsystems. The September 10 launch date had been set when it seemed that Motorola chips would be readily available. Later, with the supply of chips in doubt and bugs remaining in the system software, Sun was in danger of failing to meet its launch date.

The stimuli that spark decision making are as likely to result from the actions of managers inside an organization as they are from changes in the external environment.[40] An organization possesses a set of skills, competencies, and resources in its employees and in departments such as marketing, manufacturing, and research and development. Managers who actively pursue opportunities to use these competencies create the need to make decisions. Managers thus can be proactive or reactive in recognizing the need to make a decision, but the important issue is that they must recognize this need and respond in a timely and appropriate way.[41]

Generate Alternatives

Having recognized the need to make a decision, a manager must generate a set of feasible alternative courses of action to take in response to the opportunity or threat. Management experts cite failure to properly generate and consider different alternatives as one reason that managers sometimes make bad decisions.[42] In the Sun Microsystems decision, the alternatives seemed clear: go ahead with the September 10 launch or delay the launch until the Carrera was 100%

ready for market introduction. Often, however, the alternatives are not so obvious or so clearly specified.

One major problem is that managers may find it difficult to come up with creative alternative solutions to specific problems. Perhaps some of them are used to seeing the world from a single perspective—they have a certain "managerial mind-set." Many managers find it difficult to view problems from a fresh perspective. According to best-selling management author Peter Senge, we all are trapped within our personal mental models of the world—our ideas about what is important and how the world works.[43] Generating creative alternatives to solve problems and take advantage of opportunities may require that we abandon our existing mind-sets and develop new ones—something that usually is difficult to do.

The importance of getting managers to set aside their mental models of the world and generate creative alternatives is reflected in the growth of interest in the work of authors such as Peter Senge and Edward de Bono, who have popularized techniques for stimulating problem solving and creative thinking among managers.[44] Later in this chapter, we discuss the important issues of organizational learning and creativity in detail.

Assess Alternatives

Once managers have generated a set of alternatives, they must evaluate the advantages and disadvantages of each one.[45] The key to a good assessment of the alternatives is to define the opportunity or threat exactly and then specify the criteria that *should* influence the selection of alternatives for responding to the problem or opportunity. One reason for bad decisions is that managers often fail to specify the criteria that are important in reaching a decision.[46] In general, successful managers use four criteria to evaluate the pros and cons of alternative courses of action (see Figure 7.5):

1. *Legality:* Managers must ensure that a possible course of action will not violate any domestic or international laws or government regulations.
2. *Ethicalness:* Managers must ensure that a possible course of action is ethical and will not unnecessarily harm any stakeholder group. Many decisions managers make may help some organizational stakeholders and harm others (see Chapter 4). When examining alternative courses of action, managers need to be clear about the potential effects of their decisions.

Figure 7.5

General Criteria for Evaluating Possible Courses of Action

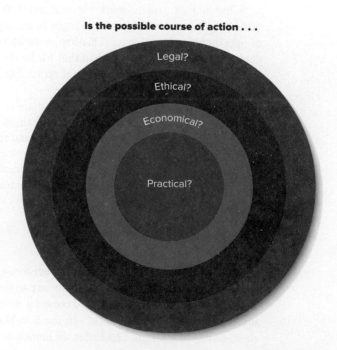

Is the possible course of action . . .

Legal?

Ethical?

Economical?

Practical?

3. *Economic feasibility:* Managers must decide whether the alternatives are economically feasible—that is, whether they can be accomplished, given the organization's performance goals. Typically, managers perform a cost-benefit analysis of the various alternatives to determine which one will have the best net financial payoff.

4. *Practicality:* Managers must decide whether they have the capabilities and resources required to implement the alternative, and they must be sure the alternative will not threaten the attainment of other organizational goals. At first glance an alternative might seem economically superior to other alternatives, but if managers realize it is likely to threaten other important projects, they might decide it is not practical after all.

Often a manager must consider these four criteria simultaneously. Scott McNealy framed the problem at hand at Sun Microsystems quite well. The key question was whether to go ahead with the September 10 launch date. Two main criteria were influencing McNealy's choice: the need to ship a machine that was as "complete" as possible (the *practicality* criterion) and the need to beat Apollo to market with a new workstation (the *economic feasibility* criterion). These two criteria conflicted. The first suggested that the launch should be delayed; the second, that the launch should go ahead. McNealy's actual choice was based on the relative importance that he assigned to these two criteria. In fact, Sun Microsystems went ahead with the September 10 launch, which suggests that McNealy thought the need to beat Apollo to market was the more important criterion.

Some of the worst managerial decisions can be traced to poor assessment of the alternatives, such as the decision to launch the *Challenger* space shuttle, mentioned earlier. In that case, the desire of NASA and Morton Thiokol managers to demonstrate to the public the success of the U.S. space program in order to ensure future funding (*economic feasibility*) conflicted with the need to ensure the safety of the astronauts (*ethicalness*). Managers deemed the economic criterion more important and decided to launch the space shuttle even though there were unanswered questions about safety. Tragically, some of the same decision-making problems that resulted in the *Challenger* tragedy led to the demise of the *Columbia* space shuttle 17 years later, killing all seven astronauts on board.[47] In both the *Challenger* and the *Columbia* disasters, safety questions were raised before the shuttles were launched; safety concerns took second place to budgets, economic feasibility, and schedules; top decision makers seemed to ignore or downplay the inputs of those with relevant technical expertise; and speaking up was discouraged.[48] Rather than making safety a top priority, decision makers seemed overly concerned with keeping on schedule and within budget.[49]

As indicated in the accompanying "Ethics in Action" feature, to help ensure that decisions meet the *ethicalness* criteria, some organizations have created the position of chief sustainability officer.

ETHICS IN ACTION

Ensuring Decisions Contribute to Sustainability

Some large organizations have added the position of chief sustainability officer to their ranks of top managers reporting to the chief executive officer or chief operating officer. Chief sustainability officers (CSOs) are typically concerned with helping to ensure that decisions that are made in organizations conserve energy and protect the environment.[50] For example, Scott Wicker was the first chief sustainability officer for UPS. Wicker effectively led a team that presided over a sustainability directors committee and a sustainability working committee focused on developing performance indicators and goals pertaining to sustainability to guide decision making.[51] Tamara Barker is the current chief sustainability officer for UPS.[52]

Krysta Harden is vice president of public policy and chief sustainability officer at DuPont, replacing Linda Fisher, who was the first CSO ever named at a publicly traded company back in 2004. Before joining DuPont in 2016, Harden most recently served as deputy secretary of the U.S. Department of Agriculture. Harden leads efforts at DuPont to make decisions that help reduce energy consumption, toxins and carcinogens in the air, and greenhouse emissions. In addition, she spearheads the company's efforts to help customers reduce their own environmental footprints.[53]

Beatriz Perez has been in charge of sustainability at The Coca-Cola Company for almost a decade. In her current role of senior vice president and chief public affairs, communications, and sustainability officer, Perez leads a companywide initiative centered around major goals and initiatives with a focus on water stewardship and women's economic empowerment. She and her team have implemented a global sustainability strategy designed to help grow the company's business while making lasting positive differences for consumers, communities, and the environment.[54] Clearly, ensuring that decisions contribute to sustainability means much more than simply complying with legal requirements. Having chief sustainability officers with dedicated teams and offices focused on sustainability might be a step in the right direction.

Choose among Alternatives

Once the set of alternative solutions has been carefully evaluated, the next task is to rank the various alternatives (using the criteria discussed in the previous section) and make a decision. When ranking alternatives, managers must be sure *all* the information available is brought to bear on the problem or issue at hand. As the Sun Microsystems case indicates, however, identifying all *relevant* information for a decision does not mean the manager has *complete* information; in most instances, information is incomplete.

Perhaps more serious than the existence of incomplete information is the often documented tendency of managers to ignore critical information, even when it is available. We discuss this tendency in detail later when we examine the operation of cognitive biases and groupthink.

Implement the Chosen Alternative

Once a decision has been made and an alternative has been selected, it must be implemented, and many subsequent and related decisions must be made. After a course of action has been decided—say, to develop a new line of women's clothing—thousands of subsequent decisions are necessary to implement it. These decisions would involve recruiting dress designers, obtaining fabrics, finding high-quality manufacturers, and signing contracts with clothing stores to sell the new line.

Although the need to make subsequent decisions to implement the chosen course of action may seem obvious, many managers make a decision and then fail to act on it. This is the same as not making a decision at all. To ensure that a decision is implemented, top managers must assign to middle managers the responsibility for making the follow-up decisions necessary to achieve the goal. They must give middle managers sufficient resources to achieve the goal, and they must hold the middle managers accountable for their performance. If the middle managers succeed in implementing the decision, they should be rewarded; if they fail, they should be subject to sanctions.

Learn from Feedback

The final step in the decision-making process is learning from feedback. Effective managers always conduct a retrospective analysis to see what they can learn from past successes or failures. Managers who do not evaluate the results of their decisions do not learn from experience; instead they stagnate and are likely to make the same mistakes again and again.[55] To avoid this problem, managers must establish a formal procedure with which they can learn from the results of past decisions. The procedure should include these steps:

1. Compare what actually happened to what was expected to happen as a result of the decision.
2. Explore why any expectations for the decision were not met.
3. Derive guidelines that will help in future decision making.

Managers who always strive to learn from past mistakes and successes are likely to continuously improve the decisions they make. A significant amount of learning can take place when the outcomes of decisions are evaluated, and this assessment can produce enormous benefits.

Cognitive Biases and Decision Making

heuristics Rules of thumb that simplify decision making.

systematic errors Errors that people make over and over and that result in poor decision making.

In the 1970s psychologists Daniel Kahneman and the late Amos Tversky suggested that because all decision makers are subject to bounded rationality, they tend to use **heuristics**, which are rules of thumb that simplify the process of making decisions.[56] Kahneman and Tversky argued that rules of thumb are often useful because they help decision makers make sense of complex, uncertain, and ambiguous information. Sometimes, however, the use of heuristics can lead to systematic errors in the way decision makers process information about alternatives and make decisions. **Systematic errors** are errors that people make over and over and that result in poor decision making. Because of cognitive biases, which are caused by systematic errors, otherwise capable managers may end up making bad decisions.[57] Four sources of bias that can adversely affect the way managers make decisions are confirmation, representativeness, the illusion of control, and escalating commitment (see Figure 7.6).

Confirmation Bias

confirmation bias A cognitive bias resulting from the tendency to base decisions on one's existing beliefs even if evidence shows that those beliefs are wrong.

Decision makers who have strong existing beliefs about the relationship between two variables tend to make decisions based on those beliefs *even when presented with evidence that those initial beliefs may be wrong*. In doing so, they fall victim to **confirmation bias**.[58] In addition, decision makers tend to seek and use information consistent with those existing beliefs and to ignore information that contradicts those beliefs. Research suggests that confirmation bias is particularly strong when information is presented sequentially and the individual is asked to revisit his or her decision in light of new information.[59]

Representativeness Bias

representativeness bias A cognitive bias resulting from the tendency to generalize inappropriately from a small sample or from a single vivid event or episode.

Many decision makers inappropriately generalize from a small sample or even from a single vivid case or episode; these are instances of the **representativeness bias**. Consider the case of a bookstore manager in the Southeast United States who decided to partner with a local independent school for a "Book Day": Students and parents from the school would be encouraged to buy books at the bookstore as a fund-raiser for the school, and the bookstore would share a small portion of proceeds from these sales with the school. After quite a bit of planning, the Book Day generated lackluster sales and publicity for the store. When other public and independent schools approached the bookstore manager with similar proposals for fund-raising

Figure 7.6

Sources of Cognitive Bias at the Individual and Group Levels

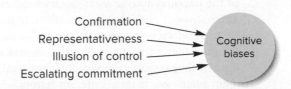

and Book Days, the manager declined based on her initial bad experience. As a result, she lost opportunities to expand sales and gain word-of-mouth advertising and publicity for her store. Her initial bad experience was the result of a scheduling snafu at the school, an important lacrosse game was scheduled the same day as the Book Day.

Illusion of Control

illusion of control A source of cognitive bias resulting from the tendency to overestimate one's own ability to control activities and events.

Other errors in decision making result from the illusion of control, which is the tendency of decision makers to overestimate their ability to control activities and events. Top managers seem particularly prone to this bias. Having worked their way to the top of an organization, they tend to have an exaggerated sense of their own worth and are overconfident about their ability to succeed and to control events.[60] The illusion of control causes managers to overestimate the odds of a favorable outcome and, consequently, to make inappropriate decisions. As mentioned earlier, most mergers turn out unfavorably, yet time and time again, top managers overestimate their abilities to combine companies with vastly different cultures in a successful merger.[61]

Escalating Commitment

escalating commitment A source of cognitive bias resulting from the tendency to commit additional resources to a project even if evidence shows that the project is failing.

Having already committed significant resources to a course of action, some managers commit more resources to the project *even if they receive feedback that the project is failing*.[62] Feelings of personal responsibility for a project apparently bias the analysis of decision makers and lead to this escalating commitment. The managers decide to increase their investment of time and money in a course of action and even ignore evidence that it is illegal, unethical, uneconomical, or impractical (see Figure 7.5). Often the more appropriate decision would be to cut their losses and run.

Consider the case of Mark Gracin, who owns a landscape company in the Southwest United States. Gracin had a profitable business doing general landscape work (such as mowing grass, picking up leaves, and fertilizing) for home owners in a large city. To expand his business into landscape design, he hired a landscape designer, advertised landscape design services in local newspapers, and gave his existing customers free design proposals for their front and back yards. After a few months, Gracin had no landscape design customers. Still convinced that landscape design was a great way to expand his business despite this negative feedback, he decided he needed to do more. He rented a small office for his landscape designer (who used to work from her own home office) to meet with clients, hired an assistant for the designer, had a public relations firm create promotional materials, and started advertising on local TV. These efforts also did not generate sufficient interest in his landscape design services to offset their costs. Yet Gracin's escalating commitment caused him to continue to pour money into trying to drum up business in landscape design. In fact, Gracin reluctantly decided to abandon his landscape design services only when he realized he could no longer afford their mounting costs.

Be Aware of Your Biases

How can managers avoid the negative effects of cognitive biases and improve their decision-making and problem-solving abilities? Managers must become aware of biases and their effects, and they must identify their own personal style of making decisions. One useful way for managers to analyze their decision-making style is to review two decisions that they made recently—one decision that turned out well and one that turned out poorly. Problem-solving experts recommend that managers start by determining how much time to spend on each of the decision-making steps, such as gathering information to identify the pros and cons of alternatives or ranking the alternatives, to make sure they spend sufficient time on each step.[63]

Another recommended technique for examining decision-making style is for managers to list the criteria they typically use to assess and evaluate alternatives—the heuristics (rules of thumb) they typically employ, their personal biases, and so on—and then critically evaluate the appropriateness of these different factors.

Many individual managers are likely to have difficulty identifying their own biases, so it is often advisable for managers to scrutinize their own assumptions by working with other managers to help expose weaknesses in their decision-making style. In this context, the issue of group decision making becomes important.

Group Decision Making

LO7-3 Identify the advantages and disadvantages of group decision making, and describe techniques that can improve it.

Many (or perhaps most) important organizational decisions are made by groups or teams of managers rather than by individuals. Group decision making is superior to individual decision making in several respects. When managers work as a team to make decisions and solve problems, their choices of alternatives are less likely to fall victim to the biases and errors discussed previously. They are able to draw on the combined skills, competencies, and accumulated knowledge of group members and thereby improve their ability to generate feasible alternatives and make good decisions. Group decision making also allows managers to process more information and to correct one another's errors. And in the implementation phase, all managers affected by the decisions agree to cooperate. When a group of managers makes a decision (as opposed to one top manager making a decision and imposing it on subordinate managers), the probability that the decision will be implemented successfully increases. (We discuss how to encourage employee participation in decision making in Chapter 14.) To see how group decision making helped a beauty products startup, read the "Manager as a Person" feature.

MANAGER AS A PERSON

Glossier Shines Because Founder Won't Go It Alone

Emily Weiss's success as a business founder comes from following her passions and working hard. As a teen attracted to fashion, she worked as a model and talked her way into an internship with Ralph Lauren.[64] Impressed with her dedication and enthusiasm, a design director introduced her to the editor-in-chief of *Teen Vogue,* resulting in a part-time internship while she attended college. After graduating, Weiss returned to the fashion business as an assistant at *W* and *Vogue.*

For her next step, starting a business, Weiss applied her people skills and industry knowledge.[65] Working around fashion designers and models at *Vogue,* she demonstrated interest, asking about beauty regimens and listening attentively to hear their insecurities and needs as well as their best ideas. She then applied her knowledge about magazine design and content to publish her own blog, *Into the Gloss.* Tapping her network of contacts, she interviewed industry insiders and landed advertisers for the blog. As the blog began getting 10 million page views per month, she realized that in today's beauty industry, opinions about products are shared and formed through social media. Weiss decided to use this insight as the basis for a bigger business, called Glossier (pronounced gloss-ee-ay). To

Glossier CEO Emily Weiss learned the importance of enlisting others to help make effective decisions about her e-commerce beauty products business.
©Vivien Killilea/Getty Images

achieve her goal of building a beauty company focused on positive body messages and social media, she began seeking investors.

Seasoned investors immediately saw the limits of Weiss's decision making.[66] She listened and communicated effectively; she knew about skin care and makeup. But she lacked training in how to run a business. She didn't know how to write a business plan or even formulate products. Even after 11 rejections for financing, Weiss never gave up. She met venture capitalist Kirsten Green, who was impressed with Weiss's ability to turn an idea into a successful blogging venture and with her broad vision of the industry's potential. Green invested enough for Weiss to build a team of decision makers, including a creative director and a chief operating officer, to organize her vision into projects. They started with four products, priced affordably. Within a few years, they built a $34 million company selling two dozen beauty products and posting an annual sales increase of 600%.[67]

Weiss's team continues to build on her responsiveness to consumers' needs. As Glossier grew, the team invested early in collecting data from social media to identify what customers loved and hated about the products.[68] When customers offer feedback, Weiss or other employees reply, and when customers have ideas, Glossier quickly adapts. Every few weeks, another product launches.

Some potential disadvantages are associated with group decision making. Groups often take much longer than individuals to make decisions. Getting two or more managers to agree to the same solution can be difficult because managers' interests and preferences are often different. In addition, just like decision making by individual managers, group decision making can be undermined by biases. A major source of group bias is *groupthink*.

The Perils of Groupthink

groupthink A pattern of faulty and biased decision making that occurs in groups whose members strive for agreement among themselves at the expense of accurately assessing information relevant to a decision.

Groupthink is a pattern of faulty and biased decision making that occurs in groups whose members strive for agreement among themselves at the expense of accurately assessing information relevant to a decision.[69] When managers are subject to groupthink, they collectively embark on a course of action without developing appropriate criteria to evaluate alternatives. Typically, a group rallies around one central manager, such as the CEO, and the course of action that manager supports. Group members become blindly committed to that course of action without evaluating its merits. Commitment is often based on an emotional, rather than an objective, assessment of the optimal course of action.

The decision President Kennedy and his advisers made to launch the unfortunate Bay of Pigs invasion in Cuba in 1962, the decisions made by President Johnson and his advisers from 1964 to 1967 to escalate the war in Vietnam, the decision made by President Nixon and his advisers in 1972 to cover up the Watergate break-in, and the decision made by NASA and Morton Thiokol in 1986 to launch the ill-fated *Challenger* shuttle—all were likely influenced by groupthink. After the fact, decision makers such as these who may fall victim to groupthink are often surprised that their decision-making process and outcomes were so flawed.

When groupthink occurs, pressures for agreement and harmony within a group have the unintended effect of discouraging individuals from raising issues that run counter to majority opinion. For example, when managers at NASA and Morton Thiokol fell victim to groupthink, they convinced each other that all was well and that there was no need to delay the launch of the *Challenger* space shuttle.

Devil's Advocacy and Dialectical Inquiry

The existence of cognitive biases and groupthink raises the question of how to improve the quality of group and individual decision making so managers make decisions that are realistic

Figure 7.7

Devil's Advocacy and Dialectical Inquiry

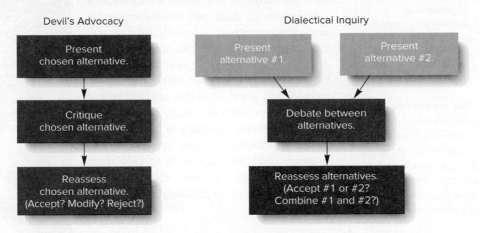

and are based on thorough evaluation of alternatives. Two techniques known to counteract groupthink and cognitive biases are devil's advocacy and dialectical inquiry (see Figure 7.7).[70]

devil's advocacy Critical analysis of a preferred alternative, made in response to challenges raised by a group member who, playing the role of devil's advocate, defends unpopular or opposing alternatives for the sake of argument.

Devil's advocacy is a critical analysis of a preferred alternative to ascertain its strengths and weaknesses before it is implemented.[71] Typically, one member of the decision-making group plays the role of devil's advocate. The devil's advocate critiques and challenges the way the group evaluated alternatives and chose one over the others. The purpose of devil's advocacy is to identify all the reasons that might make the preferred alternative unacceptable. In this way, decision makers can be made aware of the possible perils of recommended courses of action.

Dialectical inquiry goes one step further. Two groups of managers are assigned to a problem, and each group is responsible for evaluating alternatives and selecting one of them.[72] Top managers hear each group present its preferred alternative, and then each group critiques the other's position. During this debate, top managers challenge both groups' positions to uncover potential problems and perils associated with their solutions. The goal is to find an even better alternative course of action for the organization to adopt.

dialectical inquiry Critical analysis of two preferred alternatives in order to find an even better alternative for the organization to adopt.

Both devil's advocacy and dialectical inquiry can help counter the effects of cognitive biases and groupthink.[73] In practice, devil's advocacy is probably easier to implement because it involves less managerial time and effort than does dialectical inquiry.

Diversity among Decision Makers

Another way to improve group decision making is to promote diversity in decision-making groups (see Chapter 5).[74] Bringing together managers of both genders from various ethnic, national, and functional backgrounds broadens the range of life experiences and opinions that group members can draw on as they generate, assess, and choose among alternatives. Moreover, diverse groups are sometimes less prone to groupthink because group members already differ from each other and thus are less subject to pressures for uniformity.

organizational learning The process through which managers seek to improve employees' desire and ability to understand and manage the organization and its task environment.

Organizational Learning and Creativity

The quality of managerial decision making ultimately depends on innovative responses to opportunities and threats. How can managers increase their ability to make nonprogrammed decisions that will allow them to adapt to, modify, and even drastically alter their task environments so they can continually increase organizational performance? The answer is by encouraging organizational learning.[75]

Organizational learning is the process through which managers seek to improve employees' desire and ability to understand and manage the organization and its task environment so employees can make decisions that continuously increase organizational

LO7-4 Explain the role that organizational learning and creativity play in helping managers to improve their decisions.

learning organization An organization in which managers try to maximize the ability of individuals and groups to think and behave creatively and thus maximize the potential for organizational learning to take place.

creativity A decision maker's ability to discover original and novel ideas that lead to feasible alternative courses of action.

personal mastery Process by which individuals develop a desire for personal learning that may continue indefinitely in the person's daily life, including work activities.

effectiveness.[76] A **learning organization** is one in which managers do everything possible to maximize the ability of individuals and groups to think and behave creatively and thus maximize the potential for organizational learning to take place. At the heart of organizational learning is **creativity**, which is the ability of a decision maker to discover original and novel ideas that lead to feasible alternative courses of action. Encouraging creativity among managers is such a pressing organizational concern that many organizations hire outside experts to help them develop programs to train their managers in the art of creative thinking and problem solving.

Creating a Learning Organization

How can managers foster a learning organization? Learning theorist Peter Senge identified five principles for creating a learning organization (see Figure 7.8):[77]

1. For organizational learning to occur, top managers must allow every person in the organization to develop a sense of **personal mastery**, which is the process by which an individual develops the desire for personal learning that will continue throughout the person's life. Managers must understand this process and empower each employee to experiment, create, and explore their own ideas of personal learning, which can have a positive effect on the overall organization.[78]

2. As part of attaining personal mastery, individuals should think about some of the assumptions they have about how the world works and develop ideas about these so-called *mental models*. Often, however, individuals are unaware of the mental models or assumptions they hold and must look within to understand how they see the world. Once individuals gain perspective on how they view the world, they can use this information to expand their way of thinking not only on a personal level, but also at work. Developing complex mental models—sophisticated ways of thinking that challenge them to find new or better ways of performing a task—can assist individuals and managers in expanding the way an

Get off email and lose the desk! Giving yourself and your employees the time and space to know that contributions off the beaten track are valued increases the ability to think outside the box.
©D. Hurst/Alamy Stock Photo

Figure 7.8
Senge's Principles for Creating a Learning Organization

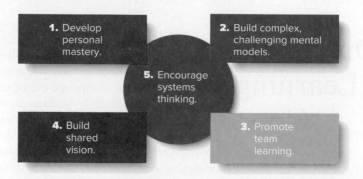

organization thinks about how they perform work. To expand thinking in this way requires experimentation, taking risks, and thinking outside the lines, which can help reshape how an organization performs at all levels.[79]

3. Managers must do everything they can to promote creativity within groups. Team members must be encouraged to learn together through exchanging ideas, listening to one another, and working together to solve problems. Ongoing dialog between group members is very important. Senge thought that *team learning* is more important than individual learning as a way to increase organizational learning. He pointed out that most important decisions are made within organization subunits such as groups, functions, and divisions.

4. Managers must emphasize the importance of building a shared vision—meaning that employees share their vision for the future of the organization. Once this shared vision is identified, members of the organization can frame problems and opportunities with the shared vision in mind and work together to achieve common goals that correspond to the vision.

5. Managers must encourage *systems thinking* (a concept drawn from systems theory discussed earlier in Chapter 2). This concept is a way of seeing the whole picture. It is a framework for seeing interrelationships and patterns rather than static "snapshots" within an organization. Systems thinking can be thought of as a conceptual cornerstone that pulls together the other four principles for creating a learning organization.[80]

Building a learning organization requires that managers change their management assumptions radically. Developing a learning organization is neither a quick nor an easy process. Senge worked with Ford Motor Company to help managers make Ford a learning organization. Why would Ford want this? Top management believed that to compete successfully Ford must improve its members' ability to be creative and make the right decisions.

Increasingly, managers are being called on to promote global organizational learning. The "Managing Globally" feature provides one example of such an effort. Likewise, managers at Walmart have used the lessons derived from its failures and successes in one country to promote global organizational learning across the many countries in which it now operates. When Walmart entered Malaysia, it was convinced customers there would respond to its one-stop shopping format. It found, however, that Malaysians enjoy the social experience of shopping in a lively market or bazaar and thus did not like the impersonal efficiency of the typical Walmart store. As a result, Walmart learned the importance of designing store layouts to appeal specifically to the customers of each country in which it operates. Clearly, global organizational learning is essential for companies such as Walmart that have significant operations in multiple countries.

MANAGING GLOBALLY

Constant Learning Keeps Western Union Relevant

Western Union (WU) offers a financial lifeline worldwide, sending 130 currencies to recipients in 200-plus countries.[81] When a customer pays, a code is sent to the recipient, who presents it to an agent, who hands over cash minus a processing fee. WU later reimburses the agent. Currency transfers could include support from emigrants to family members back home, help to a stranded traveler overseas, or tuition payments for a child studying abroad.

WU outlasted competitors by learning to embrace industry transformations.[82] It started as a telegraph operator, transmitting information to newspapers, banks, brokerages, and even betting parlors. After stumbling by turning down a chance to buy the patent for the telephone, WU learned it must commit to technological advances. It kept communication services up-to-date with teleprinters, faxes, and satellites until anyone could deliver messages from home or work. By then, however, the company had built its money transfer business. Profits accelerated along with immigration into the United States.

WU's CEO is Hikmet Ersek, son of a Turkish father and Austrian mother, who was raised in Istanbul, studied economics in Vienna, and worked in Europe.[83] Hired by WU to run its southeastern European operations, Ersek noticed rising international migration there as in the United States, and he expanded operations. Ersek maintains that a multicultural mind-set is a competitive strength. Every international transaction requires knowledge of customer needs and legal requirements in the sending and receiving countries. Learning these facts is easier with local experience and open-mindedness. Thus, when WU launched a project to create a mobile app, Ersek chose a leader with a multicultural-customer focus: the head of WU's Africa business.

The next front for learning will be technological. Digital and mobile devices enable easy, low-cost, methods of money transfer for Western Union—and new competitors.[84] WU's size is an advantage because millions of daily digital transactions provide valuable data. WU monitors patterns in money flows to quickly identify changing needs. In mid-2014, managers saw a spike in money transfers from North America and Northern Europe to the Mediterranean region. Soon the Greek government was calling, asking for locations of WU's facilities. Such data showed WU knew before others about the flood of refugees into Europe. Monitoring patterns of increased traffic, managers opened facilities accordingly.

As Western Union continues navigating global trends, it has adopted WU Way, a program in which everyone learns to provide better service more efficiently.[85] Top leaders assigned to champion the change meet with managers for informal learning. As employees make processes more efficient and as more consumers use WU's app to make transfers themselves, the company can maintain its strength with competitive fees.

Promoting Individual Creativity

Research suggests that when certain conditions are met, managers are more likely to be creative. People must be given the opportunity and freedom to generate new ideas.[86] Creativity declines when managers look over the shoulders of talented employees and try to "hurry up" a creative solution. How would you feel if your boss said you had one week to come up with a new product idea to beat the competition? Creativity results when employees have an opportunity to experiment, to take risks, and to make mistakes and learn from them. And employees must not fear that they will be looked down on or penalized for ideas that might at first seem outlandish; sometimes those ideas yield truly innovative products and services.[87] Highly innovative companies such as Google, Apple, and Facebook are well known for the wide degree of freedom they give their managers and employees to experiment and develop innovative goods and services.[88]

Once managers have generated alternatives, creativity can be fostered by giving them constructive feedback so they know how well they are doing. Ideas that seem to be going nowhere can be eliminated and creative energies refocused in other directions. Ideas that seem promising can be promoted, and help from other managers can be obtained.[89]

Top managers must stress the importance of looking for alternative solutions and should visibly reward employees who come up with creative ideas. Being creative can be demanding and stressful. Employees who believe they are working on important, vital issues are motivated to put forth the high levels of effort that creativity demands. Creative people like to receive the acclaim of others, and innovative organizations have many kinds of ceremonies and rewards to recognize creative employees.

Employees on the front line are often in a good position to come up with creative ideas for improvements but may be reluctant to speak up or share their ideas. To encourage frontline employees to come up with creative ideas and share them, some managers have used contests and rewards.[90] Contests and rewards signal the importance of coming up with creative ideas and encouraging employees to share them.

Promoting Group Creativity

To encourage creativity at the group level, organizations can use group problem-solving techniques that promote creative ideas and innovative solutions. These techniques can also prevent groupthink and help managers uncover biases. Here we look at three group decision-making techniques: *brainstorming,* the *nominal group technique,* and the *Delphi technique.*

BRAINSTORMING   *Brainstorming* is a group problem-solving technique in which managers meet face-to-face to generate and debate a wide variety of alternatives from which to make a decision.[91] Generally, from 5 to 15 managers meet in a closed-door session and proceed like this:

- One manager describes in broad outline the problem the group is to address.

- Group members share their ideas and generate alternative courses of action.

- As each alternative is described, group members are not allowed to criticize it; everyone withholds judgment until all alternatives have been heard. One member of the group records the alternatives on a flip chart.

- Group members are encouraged to be as innovative and radical as possible. Anything goes; and the greater the number of ideas put forth, the better. Moreover, group members are encouraged to "piggyback," or build on, each other's suggestions.

- When all alternatives have been generated, group members debate the pros and cons of each and develop a short list of the best alternatives.

Brainstorming is useful in some problem-solving situations—for example, when managers are trying to find a name for a new perfume or car model. But sometimes individuals working alone can generate more alternatives. The main reason for the loss of productivity in brainstorming appears to be **production blocking**, which occurs because group members cannot always simultaneously make sense of all the alternatives being generated, think up additional alternatives, and remember what they were thinking.[92]

production blocking A loss of productivity in brainstorming sessions due to the unstructured nature of brainstorming.

nominal group technique A decision-making technique in which group members write down ideas and solutions, read their suggestions to the whole group, and discuss and then rank the alternatives.

NOMINAL GROUP TECHNIQUE   To avoid production blocking, the **nominal group technique** is often used. It provides a more structured way of generating alternatives in writing and gives each manager more time and opportunity to come up with potential solutions. The nominal group technique is especially useful when an issue is controversial and when different managers might be expected to champion different courses of action. Generally, a small group of managers meets in a closed-door session and adopts the following procedures:

- One manager outlines the problem to be addressed, and 30 or 40 minutes are allocated for group members, working individually, to write down their ideas and solutions. Group members are encouraged to be innovative.

- Managers take turns reading their suggestions to the group. One manager writes all the alternatives on a flip chart. No criticism or evaluation of alternatives is allowed until all alternatives have been read.

- The alternatives are then discussed, one by one, in the sequence in which they were proposed. Group members can ask for clarifying information and critique each alternative to identify its pros and cons.

- When all alternatives have been discussed, each group member ranks all the alternatives from most preferred to least preferred, and the alternative that receives the highest ranking is chosen.[93]

Brainstorming is one example of a group problem-solving technique that helps promote creative ideas and innovation solutions within an organization.
©Jacob Lund/Shutterstock

DELPHI TECHNIQUE   Both the nominal group technique and brainstorming require that managers meet to generate creative ideas and engage in joint problem solving. What happens if managers are in different cities or in different parts of the world and cannot meet face-to-face? Videoconferencing is one way to bring distant managers together to brainstorm. Another way is to use the Delphi technique, which is a written approach to creative problem solving.[94] The Delphi technique works like this:

- The group leader writes a statement of the problem and a series of questions to which participating managers are to respond.

- The questionnaire is sent to the managers and departmental experts who are most knowledgeable about the problem. They are asked to generate solutions and mail the questionnaire back to the group leader.

- A team of top managers records and summarizes the responses. The results are then sent back to the participants, with additional questions to be answered before a decision can be made.

- The process is repeated until a consensus is reached and the most suitable course of action is apparent.

Entrepreneurship and Creativity

Entrepreneurs are individuals who notice opportunities and decide how to mobilize the resources necessary to produce new and improved goods and services. Entrepreneurs make all of the planning, organizing, leading, and controlling decisions necessary to start new business ventures. Thus, entrepreneurs are an important source of creativity in the organizational world. These people, such as Ben Silbermann and Evan Sharp (founders of Pinterest), make vast fortunes when their businesses succeed. Or they are among the millions of people who start new business ventures only to lose their money when they fail. Despite the fact that many small businesses fail in the first three to five years, many men and women in today's workforce want to start their own companies.[95]

Social entrepreneurs are individuals who pursue initiatives and opportunities to address social problems and needs to improve society and well-being, such as reducing poverty, increasing literacy, protecting the natural environment, or reducing substance abuse. Social entrepreneurs seek to mobilize resources to solve social problems through creative solutions.[96]

Many managers, scientists, and researchers employed by companies engage in entrepreneurial activity, and they are an important source of organizational creativity. They are involved in innovation, developing new and improved products and ways to make them, which we describe in detail in Chapter 9. Such employees notice opportunities for either quantum or incremental product improvements and are responsible for managing the product development process. These individuals are known as **intrapreneurs** to distinguish them from entrepreneurs, who start their own businesses. But in general, entrepreneurship involves creative decision making that gives customers new or improved goods and services.

There is an interesting relationship between entrepreneurs and intrapreneurs. Many managers with intrapreneurial talents become dissatisfied if their superiors decide neither to support nor to fund new product ideas and development efforts that the managers think will succeed. What do intrapreneurial managers who feel they are getting nowhere do? Often they decide to leave their current organizations and start their own companies to take advantage of their new product ideas! In other words, intrapreneurs become entrepreneurs and found companies that often compete with the companies they left. To avoid losing these individuals, top managers must find ways to facilitate the entrepreneurial spirit of their most creative employees. In the remainder of this section we consider issues involved in promoting successful entrepreneurship in both new and existing organizations.

Entrepreneurship and New Ventures

The fact that a significant number of entrepreneurs were frustrated intrapreneurs provides a clue about the personal characteristics of people who are likely to start a new venture and bear all the uncertainty and risk associated with being an entrepreneur.

CHARACTERISTICS OF ENTREPRENEURS Entrepreneurs are likely to possess a particular set of the personality characteristics we discussed in Chapter 3. First, they are likely to be high on the personality trait of *openness to experience,* meaning they are predisposed to be original, to be open to a wide range of stimuli, to be daring, and to take risks. Entrepreneurs also are likely to have an *internal locus of control,* believing that they are responsible for what happens to them and that their own actions determine important outcomes such as the success or failure of a new business. People with an external locus of control, in contrast, would be unlikely to leave a secure job in an organization and assume the risk associated with a new venture.

Entrepreneurs are likely to have a high level of *self-esteem* and feel competent and capable of handling most situations—including the stress and uncertainty surrounding a plunge into a risky new venture. Entrepreneurs are also likely to have a high *need for achievement* and have a strong desire to perform challenging tasks and meet high personal standards of excellence.

ENTREPRENEURSHIP AND MANAGEMENT Given that entrepreneurs are predisposed to activities that are somewhat adventurous and risky, in what ways can people become involved in entrepreneurial ventures? One way is to start a business from scratch. Taking advantage of modern IT, some people start solo ventures or partnerships.

When people who go it alone succeed, they frequently need to hire other people to help them run the business. Michael Dell, for example, began his computer business as a college student and within weeks had hired several people to help him assemble computers from the components he bought from suppliers. From his solo venture grew Dell Computer.

Some entrepreneurs who start a new business have difficulty deciding how to manage the organization as it grows; **entrepreneurship** is *not* the same as management. Management encompasses all the decisions involved in planning, organizing, leading, and controlling resources. Entrepreneurship is noticing an opportunity to satisfy a customer need and then deciding how to find and use resources to make a product that satisfies that need. When an entrepreneur has produced something customers want, entrepreneurship gives way to management because the pressing need becomes providing the product both efficiently and effectively. Frequently, a founding entrepreneur lacks the skills, patience, and experience to engage in the difficult and challenging work of management. Some entrepreneurs find it hard to delegate authority because they are afraid to risk their company by letting others manage it. As a result, they become overloaded and the quality of their decision making declines. Other entrepreneurs lack the detailed knowledge necessary to establish state-of-the-art information systems and technology or to create the operations management procedures that are vital to increase the efficiency of their organizations' production systems. Thus, to succeed, it is necessary to do more than create a new product; an entrepreneur must hire managers who can create an operating system that will let a new venture survive and prosper.

entrepreneurship The mobilization of resources to take advantage of an opportunity to provide customers with new or improved goods and services.

Intrapreneurship and Organizational Learning

The intensity of competition today, particularly from agile, small companies, has made it increasingly important for large, established organizations to promote and encourage intrapreneurship to raise their level of innovation and organizational learning. As we discussed earlier, a learning organization encourages all employees to identify opportunities and solve problems, thus enabling the organization to continuously experiment, improve, and increase its ability to provide customers with new and improved goods and services. The higher the level of intrapreneurship, the higher will be the level of learning and innovation. How can organizations promote organizational learning and intrapreneurship?

product champion A manager who takes "ownership" of a project and provides the leadership and vision that take a product from the idea stage to the final customer.

PRODUCT CHAMPIONS One way to promote intrapreneurship is to encourage individuals to assume the role of **product champion**, a manager who takes "ownership" of a project and provides the leadership and vision that take a product from the idea stage to the final customer. 3M, a company well known for its attempts to promote intrapreneurship, encourages all its managers to become product champions and identify new product ideas. A product champion becomes responsible for developing a business plan for the product. Armed with this business plan, the champion appears before 3M's product development committee, a team of senior

3M managers who probe the strengths and weaknesses of the plan to decide whether it should be funded. If the plan is accepted, the product champion assumes responsibility for product development.

SKUNKWORKS   The idea behind the product champion role is that employees who feel ownership for a project are inclined to act as outside entrepreneurs and go to great lengths to make the project succeed. Using skunkworks and new venture divisions can also strengthen this feeling of ownership. A **skunkworks** is a group of intrapreneurs who are deliberately separated from the normal operation of an organization—for example, from the normal chain of command—to encourage them to devote all their attention to developing new products. The idea is that if these people are isolated, they will become so intensely involved in a project that development time will be relatively brief and the quality of the final product will be enhanced. The term *skunkworks* was coined at the Lockheed Corporation, which formed a team of design engineers to develop special aircraft such as the U2 spy plane. The secrecy with which this unit functioned and speculation about its goals led others to refer to it as "the skunkworks."

REWARDS FOR INNOVATION   To encourage managers to bear the uncertainty and risk associated with the hard work of entrepreneurship, it is necessary to link performance to rewards. Increasingly companies are rewarding intrapreneurs on the basis of the outcome of the product development process. Intrapreneurs are paid large bonuses if their projects succeed, or they are granted stock options that can make them millionaires if their products sell well. Both Microsoft and Google, for example, have made hundreds of their employees multimillionaires as a result of the stock options they were granted as part of their reward packages. In addition to receiving money, successful intrapreneurs can expect to receive promotion to the ranks of top management. Most of 3M's top managers, for example, reached the executive suite because they had a track record of successful intrapreneurship. Organizations must reward intrapreneurs equitably if they wish to prevent them from leaving and becoming outside entrepreneurs who might form a competitive new venture. Nevertheless, intrapreneurs frequently do so.

skunkworks A group of intrapreneurs who are deliberately separated from the normal operation of an organization to encourage them to devote all their attention to developing new products.

Summary and Review

LO7-1   **THE NATURE OF MANAGERIAL DECISION MAKING**   Programmed decisions are routine decisions made so often that managers have developed decision rules to be followed automatically. Nonprogrammed decisions are made in response to situations that are unusual or novel; they are nonroutine decisions. The classical model of decision making assumes that decision makers have complete information; are able to process that information in an objective, rational manner; and make optimum decisions. March and Simon argued that managers exhibit bounded rationality, rarely have access to all the information they need to make optimum decisions, and consequently satisfice and rely on their intuition and judgment when making decisions.

LO7-2   **STEPS IN THE DECISION-MAKING PROCESS**   When making decisions, managers should take these six steps: recognize the need for a decision, generate alternatives, assess alternatives, choose among alternatives, implement the chosen alternative, and learn from feedback.

LO7-2   **COGNITIVE BIASES AND DECISION MAKING**   Most of the time, managers are fairly good decision makers. On occasion, however, problems can result because human judgment can be adversely affected by the operation of cognitive biases that result in poor decisions. Cognitive biases are caused by systematic errors in the way decision makers process information and make decisions. Sources of these errors include confirmation bias, representativeness bias, the illusion of control, and escalating commitment. Managers should undertake a personal decision audit to become aware of their biases and thus improve their decision making.

LO7-3   **GROUP DECISION MAKING**   Many advantages are associated with group decision making, but there are also several disadvantages. One major source of poor decision making is groupthink. Afflicted decision makers collectively embark on a dubious course of action without questioning the assumptions that underlie their decision. Managers can improve the quality of group decision making by using techniques such as devil's advocacy and dialectical inquiry and by increasing diversity in the decision-making group.

LO7-4 **ORGANIZATIONAL LEARNING AND CREATIVITY** Organizational learning is the process through which managers seek to improve employees' desire and ability to understand and manage the organization and its task environment so employees can make decisions that continuously raise organizational effectiveness. Managers must take steps to promote organizational learning and creativity at the individual and group levels to improve the quality of decision making.

LO7-5 **ENTREPRENEURSHIP AND CREATIVITY** Entrepreneurship is the mobilization of resources to take advantage of an opportunity to provide customers with new or improved goods and services. Entrepreneurs start new ventures of their own. Intrapreneurs work inside organizations and manage the product development process. Organizations need to encourage intrapreneurship because it leads to organizational learning and innovation.

Management in Action

Topics for Discussion and Action

Discussion

1. What are the main differences between programmed decision making and nonprogrammed decision making? **[LO7-1]**

2. In what ways do the classical and administrative models of decision making help managers appreciate the complexities of real-world decision making? **[LO7-1]**

3. Why do capable managers sometimes make bad decisions? What can individual managers do to improve their decision-making skills? **[LO7-1, 7-2]**

4. In what kinds of groups is groupthink most likely to be a problem? When is it least likely to be a problem? What steps can group members take to ward off groupthink? **[LO7-3]**

5. What is organizational learning, and how can managers promote it? **[LO7-4]**

6. What is the difference between entrepreneurship and intrapreneurship? **[LO7-5]**

Action

7. Ask a manager to recall the best and the worst decisions he or she ever made. Try to determine why these decisions were so good or so bad. **[LO7-1, 7-2, 7-3]**

8. Think about an organization in your local community or your university, or an organization that you are familiar with, that is doing poorly. Now think of questions managers in the organization should ask stakeholders to elicit creative ideas for turning around the organization's fortunes. **[LO7-4]**

Building Management Skills

How Do You Make Decisions? [LO7-1, 7-2, 7-4]

Pick a decision you made recently that has had important consequences for you. It may be your decision about which college to attend, which major to select, whether to take a part-time job, or which part-time job to take. Using the material in this chapter, analyze how you made the decision:

1. Identify the criteria you used, either consciously or unconsciously, to guide your decision making.

2. List the alternatives you considered. Were they all possible alternatives? Did you unconsciously (or consciously) ignore some important alternatives?

3. How much information did you have about each alternative? Were you making the decision on the basis of complete or incomplete information?

4. Try to remember how you reached the decision. Did you sit down and consciously think through the implications of each alternative, or did you make the decision on the basis of intuition? Did you use any rules of thumb to help you make the decision?

5. In retrospect, do you think your choice of alternative was shaped by any of the cognitive biases discussed in this chapter?

6. Having answered the previous five questions, do you think in retrospect that you made a reasonable decision? What, if anything, might you do to improve your ability to make good decisions in the future?

Managing Ethically [LO7-3]

Sometimes groups make extreme decisions—decisions that are either more risky or more conservative than they would have been if individuals acting alone had made them. One explanation for the tendency of groups to make extreme decisions is diffusion of responsibility. In a group, responsibility for the outcomes of a decision is spread among group members, so each person feels less than fully accountable. The group's decision is extreme because no individual has taken full responsibility for it.

Questions

1. Either alone or in a group, think about the ethical implications of extreme decision making by groups.

2. When group decision making takes place, should each member of a group feel fully accountable for the outcomes of the decision? Why or why not?

Small Group Breakout Exercise

Brainstorming [LO7-3, 7-4]

Form groups of three or four people, and appoint one member as the spokesperson who will communicate your findings to the class when called on by the instructor. Then discuss the following scenario:

You and your partners are trying to decide which kind of restaurant to open in a centrally located shopping center that has just been built in your city. The problem confronting you is that the city already has many restaurants that provide different kinds of food at all price ranges. You have the resources to open any type of restaurant. Your challenge is to decide which type is most likely to succeed.

Use brainstorming to decide which type of restaurant to open. Follow these steps:

1. As a group, spend 5–10 minutes generating ideas about the alternative restaurants that the members think will be most likely to succeed. Each group member should be as innovative and creative as possible, and no suggestions should be criticized.

2. Appoint one group member to write down the alternatives as they are identified.

3. Spend the next 10–15 minutes debating the pros and cons of the alternatives. As a group, try to reach a consensus on which alternative is most likely to succeed.

After making your decision, discuss the pros and cons of the brainstorming method, and decide whether any production blocking occurred.

When called on by the instructor, the spokesperson should be prepared to share your group's decision with the class, as well as the reasons for the group's decision.

Be the Manager [LO7-1, 7-2, 7-3, 7-4, 7-5]

You are a top manager who was recently hired by an oil field services company in Oklahoma to help it respond more quickly and proactively to potential opportunities in its market. You report to the chief operating officer (COO), who reports to the CEO, and you have been on the job for eight months. Thus far, you have come up with three initiatives you carefully studied, thought were noteworthy, and proposed and justified to the COO. The COO seemed cautiously interested when you presented the proposals, and each time he indicated he would think about them and discuss them with the CEO because considerable resources were involved. Each time you never heard back from the COO, and after a few weeks elapsed, you casually asked the COO if there was any news on the proposal in question. For the first proposal, the COO said, "We think it's a good idea, but the timing is off. Let's shelve it for the time being and reconsider it next year." For the second proposal, the COO said, "Mike

[the CEO] reminded me that we tried that two years ago and it wasn't well received in the market. I am surprised I didn't remember it myself when you first described the proposal, but it came right back to me once Mike mentioned it." For the third proposal, the COO simply said, "We're not convinced it will work."

You believe your three proposed initiatives are viable ways to seize opportunities in the marketplace, yet you cannot proceed with any of them. Moreover, for each proposal, you invested considerable time and even worked to bring others on board to support the proposal, only to have it shot down by the CEO. When you interviewed for the position, both the COO and the CEO claimed they wanted "an outsider to help them step out of the box and innovate." However, your experience to date has been just the opposite. What are you going to do?

Bloomberg Businessweek Case in the News

Taylor Swift Wants Her Money Back [LO 7-1, 7-3, 7-5]

Taylor Swift's most recent tour was a success by every measure. Named after the best-selling album of her career, *1989,* it grossed more than $250 million worldwide, the top tour of 2015. Critics raved about the production, with one going so far as to say it was "engineered to be the best night of your life." Yet Swift felt something was missing—about $85 million in revenue that went to scalpers.

Some 30% to 40% of tickets to the world's top concerts are resold on secondary websites such as StubHub and SeatGeek. Many of those sales are by scalpers who believe people are willing to pay far more than the initial price to see stars of Swift's magnitude; they double and sometimes triple the ticket price. Thousands of Swift's die-hard fans, Swifties, spent huge sums the singer never saw. That didn't sit well with Swift, who is as much an entrepreneur as she is an artist.

As she prepared to hit the road to support her latest album, *Reputation,* Swift and Ticketmaster Entertainment Inc. concocted a strategy to neuter the scalpers. They used Ticketmaster's Verified Fan program, which utilizes in-house technology to identify actual fans and determine which of them should have access to fan-only presale tickets, based on their devotion to Swift as measured by their willingness to buy albums, sign up for a newsletter, and watch her music videos. While prices in the presale were fairly low for most people, Swift and promoter AEG Presents raised the cost of all the tickets in the later general sale to make them less attractive to scalpers.

The success of this latest attempt to combat scalping remains uncertain. Most major tours, including Swift's most recent, sell out in minutes. But her upcoming *Reputation* tour hasn't sold out a single date in the past month and a half, prompting the *New York Post* to dub it a disaster. Yet Ticketmaster says Swift will get the last laugh. Most tours sell out right away because prices are too low, and scalpers buy up all the inventory. Instead, Ticketmaster expects Swift's tour will sell out closer to when she takes the stage on May 8 in Glendale, Ariz., the first of more than 40 dates scheduled through October. It also expects the artist and promoters to collect more of the cash—and provide the music industry with a new model to boost North American concert ticket sales, which collectively hit $8 billion last year.

"It's so easy for people to take shots at Taylor," says David Marcus, head of music at Ticketmaster. But, he says, "we were successful beyond my expectations and were able to drive the biggest registration we've ever seen for Verified Fan."

Ticketmaster has used the Verified Fan program to block scalpers from concerts, festivals, and Broadway shows such as *Springsteen on Broadway* and the upcoming *Harry Potter and the Cursed Child.* The company requires fans seeking tickets to register online in advance and identify the show they want to attend, hoping to weed out bots. It then uses artificial intelligence to determine which fans are most likely to attend and verifies a certain number for a presale.

Swift's use of Verified Fan added tweaks not tried before, Marcus says. Fans who wanted access to the first tickets on sale took part in a program called Taylor Swift Tix where they earned boosts in the virtual line by buying her album and merchandise, watching music videos, or spreading the word to friends. Javier Benavente, a 25-year-old Swiftie who's seen the pop star more than a dozen times, bought three albums and scored floor seats for $180 a pop. The new regular-price tickets can run as much as 10 times that.

What's more, Benavente says he loved being able to take his time deciding on his seat, because of the Swift tour's unusual assigned purchase windows—spread across a week and giving purchasers several minutes to view different available seats before making a decision. "She somehow found this weird happy medium where you benefit both the fans and their pockets," he says.

Some critics have called Swift greedy, panning her system as giving the best presale slots to fans who spend the most on her other goods. Ticketmaster says most of the fans who participated in the presale spent no money apart from the ticket purchase and noted those early sales started at $49.50—cheap for a star of Swift's stature. While tickets in the general sale can climb to near $2,000 for some shows, the prices aren't so different from those of male acts such as Justin Timberlake or U2. If some higher prices are what's needed to combat scalping, the Swift camp is unapologetic. Says Marcus: "Taylor is trying to take control of her tour."

Questions for Discussion

1. To what extent is Swift's strategy to outsmart the ticket bots a nonprogrammed decision?

2. Playing devil's advocate, do you think Swift's decision was greedy or creative? Explain your reasoning.

3. Provide three reasons Taylor Swift could be considered an entrepreneur.

Source: Lucas Shaw, "Taylor Swift Wants Her Money Back," *Bloomberg Businessweek,* February 5, 2018, pp. 17–18. Used with permission of Bloomberg L.P. Copyright © 2017. All rights reserved.

Notes

1. A. Regalado, "23andMe," *MIT Technology Review,* July/August 2016, 68–69; J. Bercovici, "The DNA Whisperer," *Inc.,* October 2015, 62–64, 148.

2. A. Bluestein, "After a Comeback, 23andMe Faces Its Next Test," *Fast Company,* www.fastcompany.com, August 9, 2017.

3. Bluestein, "After a Comeback"; Regalado, "23andMe."

4. Bercovici, "The DNA Whisperer."

5. Bluestein, "After a Comeback"; Bercovici, "The DNA Whisperer."

6. Bluestein, "After a Comeback"; Regalado, "23andMe"; Bercovici, "The DNA Whisperer"; K. Ryssdal and R. Garrova, "Why 23andMe Wants Your Genetic Data" (interview with Anne Wojcicki), *Marketplace,* www.marketplace.org, April 19, 2017.

7. Ryssdal and Garrova, "Why 23andMe Wants Your Genetic Data."

8. G.P. Huber, *Managerial Decision Making* (Glenview, IL: Scott, Foresman, 1993).

9. L. Kahney, "An Illustrated History of the iPod and Its Massive Impact," *Cult of Mac,* www.cultofmac.com, accessed March 22, 2018; T. Anjarwalla, "Inventor of Cell Phone: We Knew Someday Everybody

Would Have One," *CNN,* www.cnn.com, accessed March 22, 2018.

10. H.A. Simon, *The New Science of Management* (Englewood Cliffs, NJ: Prentice-Hall, 1977).

11. D. Kahneman, "Maps of Bounded Rationality: A Perspective on Intuitive Judgment and Choice," *Prize Lecture,* December 8, 2002; E. Jaffe, "What Was I Thinking? Kahneman Explains How Intuition Leads Us Astray," *American Psychological Society* 17, no. 5 (May 2004), 23–26; E. Dane and M. Pratt, "Exploring Intuition and Its Role in Managerial Decision Making," *Academy of Management Review* 32 (2007), 33–54.

12. One should be careful not to generalize too much here, however, for as Peter Senge has shown, programmed decisions rely on the implicit assumption that the environment is in a steady state. If environmental conditions change, sticking to a routine decision rule can produce disastrous results. See P. Senge, *The Fifth Discipline: The Art and Practice of the Learning Organization* (New York: Doubleday, 1990).

13. Kahneman, "Maps of Bounded Rationality"; Jaffe, "What Was I Thinking?"

14. Woodrow Wilson School of Public and International Affairs, "Daniel Kahneman," www.princeton.edu, accessed March 22, 2018; J. Lehrer, "The Science of Irrationality," *The Wall Street Journal,* October 15, 2011, C18.

15. D. Shariatmadari, "Daniel Kahneman: 'What Would I Eliminate If I Had a Magic Wand? Overconfidence,'" *The Guardian,* www.theguardian.com, July 18, 2015.

16. Kahneman, "Maps of Bounded Rationality"; Jaffe, "What Was I Thinking?"

17. Ibid.

18. Shariatmadari, "Daniel Kahneman"; J. Pfeffer, "Curbing the Urge to Merge," *Business 2.0,* July 2003, 58.

19. Kahneman, "Maps of Bounded Rationality"; Jaffe, "What Was I Thinking?"

20. Shariatmadari, "Daniel Kahneman"; Pfeffer, "Curbing the Urge to Merge."

21. N.E. Boudette, "DaimlerChrysler: Poster Child of Failed Mergers," *Automotive News,* www.autonews.com, accessed March 22, 2018; R.D. Lewis, "Cross-Cultural Issues Relating to DaimlerChrysler Merge—Case Study," *Cross Culture,* www.crossculture.com, April 27, 2016.

22. "9 Mergers That Epically Failed," *Huffington Post,* www.huffingtonpost.com, accessed March 22, 2018.

23. Pfeffer, "Curbing the Urge to Merge."

24. S. Patel, "9 Ways Entrepreneurs Think Differently Than Employees," *Inc.,* www.inc.com, accessed March 22, 2018; Pfeffer, "Curbing the Urge to Merge."

25. Pfeffer, "Curbing the Urge to Merge."

26. H.A. Simon, *Administrative Behavior* (New York: Macmillan, 1947), 79.

27. H.A. Simon, *Models of Man* (New York: Wiley, 1957).

28. K.J. Arrow, *Aspects of the Theory of Risk Bearing* (Helsinki: Yrjo Johnssonis Saatio, 1965).

29. Ibid.

30. R.L. Daft and R.H. Lengel, "Organizational Information Requirements, Media Richness and Structural Design," *Management Science* 32 (1986), 554–71.

31. R. Cyert and J. March, *Behavioral Theory of the Firm* (Englewood Cliffs, NJ: Prentice-Hall, 1963).

32. J.G. March and H.A. Simon, *Organizations* (New York: Wiley, 1958).

33. H.A. Simon, "Making Management Decisions: The Role of Intuition and Emotion," *Academy of Management Executive* 1 (1987), 57–64.

34. M.H. Bazerman, *Judgment in Managerial Decision Making* (New York: Wiley, 1986). Also see Simon, *Administrative Behavior.*

35. "Scott G. McNealy Profile," Forbes.com, http://people.forbes.com/profile/scott-g-mcnealy/75347, February 16, 2010; Sun Oracle, "Overview and Frequently Asked Questions," www.oracle.com, February 16, 2010.

36. "Sun Microsystems—Investor Relations: Officers and Directors," www.sun.com/aboutsun/investor/sun_facts/officers_directors.html, June 1, 2004; "How Sun Delivers Value to Customers," *Sun Microsystems—Investor Relations: Support & Training,* www.sun.com/aboutsun/investor/sun_facts/core_strategies.html, June 1, 2004; "Sun at a Glance," *Sun Microsystems—Investor Relations: Sun Facts,* www.sun.com/aboutsun/investor/sun_facts/index.html, June 1, 2004; "Plug In the System, and Everything Just Works," *Sun Microsystems—Investor Relations: Product Portfolio,* www.sun.com/aboutsun/investor/sun_facts/portfolio/html, June 1, 2004.

37. N.J. Langowitz and S.C. Wheelright, "Sun Microsystems, Inc. (A)," Harvard Business School Case, 686-133.

38. R.D. Hof, "How to Kick the Mainframe Habit," *BusinessWeek,* June 26, 1995, 102–4.

39. Bazerman, *Judgment in Managerial Decision Making;* Huber, *Managerial Decision Making;* J.E. Russo and P.J. Schoemaker, *Decision Traps* (New York: Simon & Schuster, 1989).

40. M.D. Cohen, J.G. March, and J.P. Olsen, "A Garbage Can Model of Organizational Choice," *Administrative Science Quarterly* 17 (1972), 1–25.

41. Ibid.

42. Bazerman, *Judgment in Managerial Decision Making.*

43. Senge, *The Fifth Discipline.*

44. E. de Bono, *Lateral Thinking* (London: Penguin, 1968); Senge, *The Fifth Discipline.*

45. Russo and Schoemaker, *Decision Traps.*

46. Bazerman, *Judgment in Managerial Decision Making.*

47. B. Berger, "NASA: One Year after *Columbia*—Bush's New Vision Changes Agency's Course Midstream," *Space News Business Report,* www.space.com/spacenews/businessmonday_040126.html, January 26, 2004.

48. J. Glanz and J. Schwartz, "Dogged Engineer's Effort to Assess Shuttle Damage," *The New York Times,* September 26, 2003, A1.

49. M.L. Wald and J. Schwartz, "NASA Chief Promises a Shift in Attitude," *The New York Times,* August 28, 2003, A23.

50. C. Bader, "What Do Chief Sustainability Officers Actually Do?" *The Atlantic,* www.theatlantic.com, May 6, 2015.

51. Bader, "What Do Chief Sustainability Officers Actually Do?"; "Executive Statement—Scott Wicker, Chief Sustainability Officer," https://pressroom.ups.com, April 17, 2014.

52. "UPS Names Tamara Barker New Chief Sustainability Officer," https://pressroom.ups.com, April 13, 2016.

53. "DuPont Names Krysta Harden as Vice President of Public Policy and Chief Sustainability Officer," www.dupont.com, March 2, 2016.

54. "Senior Leadership: Beatriz Perez," www.coca-colacompany.com, accessed March 22, 2018; M. Albanese, "How She Leads: Coca-Cola's Beatriz Perez," *Green Biz,* www.greenbiz.com, April 18, 2012.

55. Russo and Schoemaker, *Decision Traps.*

56. D. Kahneman and A. Tversky, "Judgment under Uncertainty: Heuristics and Biases," *Science* 185 (1974), 1124–31.

57. C.R. Schwenk, "Cognitive Simplification Processes in Strategic Decision Making," *Strategic Management Journal* 5 (1984), 111–28.

58. R.S. Nickerson, "Confirmation Bias: A Ubiquitous Phenomenon in Many Guises," *Review of General Psychology* 2, no. 2 (1998), 175–220.

59. E. Jonas, S. Schulz-Hardt, D. Frey, and N. Thelen, "Confirmation Bias in Sequential Information Search after Preliminary Decisions: An Expansion of Dissonance Theoretical Research on Selective Exposure to Information," *Journal of Personality and Social Psychology* 80, no. 4 (2001), 557–71.

60. An interesting example of the illusion of control is Richard Roll's hubris hypothesis of takeovers. See R. Roll, "The Hubris Hypothesis of Corporate Takeovers," *Journal of Business* 59 (1986), 197–216.

61. J. Pfeffer and R.I. Sutton, *Hard Facts, Dangerous Half-Truths, and Total Nonsense: Profiting from Evidence-Based Management* (Boston: Harvard Business School Press, 2006).

62. B.M. Staw, "The Escalation of Commitment to a Course of Action," *Academy of Management Review* 6 (1981), 577–87.

63. Russo and Schoemaker, *Decision Traps.*

64. A. Larocca, "The Magic Skin of Glossier's Emily Weiss," *New York,* www.thecut.com, January 9, 2018; A. Giacobbe, "The People's Gloss," *Entrepreneur,* September 2017, 36–42.

65. Larocca, "The Magic Skin of Glossier's Emily Weiss"; Giacobbe, "The People's Gloss"; E. Canal, "How This Beauty Blogger Created a Cult Brand (and Raised $34 Million)," *Inc.,* www.inc.com, December 5, 2017.

66. Giacobbe, "The People's Gloss"; Larocca, "The Magic Skin of Glossier's Emily Weiss"; L. Fessler, "Glossier CEO Emily Weiss Doesn't Have Time for Excuses: 'Just Do Your Job,'" *Quartz,* https://work.qz.com, February 6, 2018.

67. Giacobbe, "The People's Gloss"; Larocca, "The Magic Skin of Glossier's Emily Weiss"; Canal, "How This Beauty Blogger Created a Cult Brand"; Fessler, "Glossier CEO Emily Weiss Doesn't Have Time for Excuses: 'Just Do Your Job.'"

68. Giacobbe, "The People's Gloss"; Canal, "How This Beauty Blogger Created a Cult Brand."

69. I.L. Janis, *Groupthink: Psychological Studies of Policy Decisions and Disasters,* 2nd ed. (Boston: Houghton Mifflin, 1982).

70. C.R. Schwenk, *The Essence of Strategic Decision Making* (Lexington, MA: Lexington Books, 1988).

71. See R.O. Mason, "A Dialectic Approach to Strategic Planning," *Management Science* 13 (1969), 403–14; R.A. Cosier and J.C. Aplin, "A Critical View of Dialectic Inquiry in Strategic Planning," *Strategic Management Journal* 1 (1980), 343–56; I.I. Mitroff and R.O. Mason, "Structuring III—Structured Policy Issues: Further Explorations in a Methodology for Messy Problems," *Strategic Management Journal* 1 (1980), 331–42.

72. Mason, "A Dialectic Approach to Strategic Planning."

73. D.M. Schweiger and P.A. Finger, "The Comparative Effectiveness of Dialectic Inquiry and Devil's Advocacy," *Strategic Management Journal* 5 (1984), 335–50.

74. E. Larson, "New Research: Diversity + Inclusion = Better Decision Making at Work," *Forbes,* www.forbes.com, September 21, 2017; M.C. Gentile, *Differences That Work: Organizational Excellence through Diversity* (Boston: Harvard Business School Press: 1994).

75. B. Hedberg, "How Organizations Learn and Unlearn," in W.H. Starbuck and P.C. Nystrom, eds., *Handbook of Organizational Design,* vol. 1 (New York: Oxford University Press, 1981), 1–27.

76. Senge, *The Fifth Discipline.*

77. Ibid.

78. P.M. Senge, "The Leader's New Work: Building Learning Organizations," *Sloan Management Review,* Fall 1990, 7–23.

79. Ibid.

80. Senge, "The Leader's New Work," 12, 23.

81. D. Bennett and L. Etter, "Give Us Your Tired, Your Poor, Your Huddled Masses Yearning to Send Cash," *Bloomberg Businessweek,* https://bloomberg.com, June 16, 2017; L. Davison and K. Rajgopal, "Working across Many Cultures at Western Union" (interview with Hikmet Ersek), *McKinsey Quarterly,* www.mckinsey.com, January 2018.

82. Bennett and Etter, "Give Us Your Tired"; Davison and Rajgopal, "Working across Many Cultures at Western Union."

83. Bennett and Etter, "Give Us Your Tired."

84. Bennett and Etter, "Give Us Your Tired."

85. "The Western Union (WU) Q3 2017 Results—Earnings Call Transcript," *Seeking Alpha,* www.msn.com, November 3, 2017; P. Harris, "The Relentless Pursuit of Better," *TD,* October 2017, 28–30; Bennett and Etter, "Give Us Your Tired"; Davison and Rajgopal, "Working across Many Cultures at Western Union."

86. J.M George, "Creativity in Organizations," in J.P. Walsh and A.P. Brief, eds., *The Academy of Management Annals,* vol. 1 (New York: Erlbaum, 2008), 439–77.

87. George, "Creativity in Organizations."

88. "The World's 50 Most Innovative Companies," *Fast Company,* www.fastcompany.com, accessed March 25, 2018.

89. R.W. Woodman, J.E. Sawyer, and R.W. Griffin, "Towards a Theory of Organizational Creativity," *Academy of Management Review* 18 (1993), 293–321.

90. J. Haden, "25 Rewards That Great Employees Actually Love to Receive," *Inc.,* www.inc.com, December 21, 2017.

91. T.J. Bouchard Jr., J. Barsaloux, and G. Drauden, "Brainstorming Procedure, Group Size, and Sex as Determinants of Problem Solving Effectiveness of Individuals and Groups," *Journal of Applied Psychology* 59 (1974), 135–38.

92. M. Diehl and W. Stroebe, "Productivity Loss in Brainstorming Groups: Towards the Solution of a Riddle," *Journal of Personality and Social Psychology* 53 (1987), 497–509.

93. D.H. Gustafson, R.K. Shulka, A. Delbecq, and W.G. Walster, "A Comparative Study of Differences in Subjective Likelihood Estimates Made by Individuals, Interacting Groups, Delphi Groups, and Nominal Groups," *Organizational Behavior and Human Performance* 9 (1973), 280–91.

94. N. Dalkey, *The Delphi Method: An Experimental Study of Group Decision Making* (Santa Monica, CA: Rand Corp., 1989).

95. D. Pridham, "Entrepreneurs: Here's Good News for 2018," *Forbes,* www.forbes.com, January 10, 2018.

96. A. Wilson, "Meet the 30 Under 30 Social Entrepreneurs Making an Impact in 2018," *Forbes,* www.forbes.com, November 14, 2017.

CHAPTER 8

The Manager as a Planner and Strategist

©Tom Merton/age fotostock

Learning Objectives

After studying this chapter, you should be able to:

LO8.1 Identify the three main steps of the planning process, and explain the relationship between planning and strategy.

LO8.2 Describe some techniques managers can use to improve the planning process so they can better predict the future and mobilize organizational resources to meet future contingencies.

LO8.3 Differentiate among the main types of business-level strategies, and explain how they give an organization a competitive advantage that may lead to superior performance.

LO8.4 Differentiate among the main types of corporate-level strategies, and explain how they are used to strengthen a company's business-level strategy and competitive advantage.

LO8.5 Describe the vital role managers play in implementing strategies to achieve an organization's mission and goals.

Sorenson Plans for Growth at Marriott

What do successful managers consider when they plan a way forward? Marriott's CEO is a good example. Marriott International is the world's largest hotel chain, with 226,500 employees at over 6,500 properties and the company's headquarters in Bethesda, Maryland.[1] Its 2016 acquisition of Starwood Hotels & Resorts gave it a huge lead over its next-largest competitor, Hilton. That deal closed under the leadership of Arne Sorenson, the company's third CEO. Before joining Marriott, he was a lawyer handling cases related to mergers and acquisitions. Sorenson loves exploring the world; he grew up in Japan as the child of missionaries and continues to enjoy travels with his wife and children.

Sorenson intends for Marriott to accelerate its growth. His three-year plan is to add about 100,000 rooms per year, up from 76,000 added in 2017.[2] He is optimistic but grounds his plans in observations about the environment for the travel business. A key opportunity is growing demand for travel-related services; more than a billion people travel internationally, a number expected to grow 50% by 2030.[3] The major threat Sorenson identifies is online travel agencies (OTAs). Travelers, especially tourists, increasingly seek low-priced flights and hotel stays on websites like Expedia, Priceline, and Travelocity. Given their price-consciousness, OTAs pressure the hotels they represent to offer discounts. A second challenge is home-sharing businesses, especially Airbnb, which is offering new competition, especially at the low end of the price range. Finally, in the United States, businesses have recently reported a decline in tourism from overseas, despite the growth worldwide. On this last problem, competitors have a common interest, so industry organizations are trying to present a more favorable face of the United States to the world.[4]

In facing these challenges, Marriott benefits from its size and international presence.[5] Controlling a major share of the hotel rooms in the United States and a growing share abroad gives Marriott greater clout when negotiating with OTAs. The acquisition of Starwood brought Marriott Starwood's very successful customer-loyalty rewards program. Customers who belong to a rewards program are likelier to book directly with a hotel, rather than through an OTA, which takes a share of the price as its fee. Starwood also had more experience with distinctive hotel properties that draw customers looking for a fun experience. Marriott has a further advantage in its business model. Rather than focusing on building and owning hotel properties, it staffs and manages hotels that others own. This has allowed Marriott to focus on delivering a great experience to guests without the expense, risk, and time of construction and other real estate projects.

Marriott's growth strategy includes adding distinctive properties to its chain, which

According to Marriott CEO Arne Sorenson, the company's growth strategies include international expansion, particularly in China, as more and more Chinese consumers want to travel.
©Bloomberg/Getty Images

includes hotel brands Aloft, Courtyard, Fairfield Inn, Ritz-Carlton, and more.[6] Sorenson sees features such as entertainment lounges and comfortable lobbies as a way to lure travelers away from Airbnb. Even a low-priced hotel can offer fun amenities that a traveler is unlikely to find in a spare bedroom or apartment for rent. At the new Moxy Times Square in New York, for example, guests can play miniature golf at a rooftop bar.

A key part of Marriott's growth plan involves international expansion, particularly in China. In the United States, years of business expansion have pushed the supply of hotel rooms ahead of demand. China, in contrast, is a dramatic growth story: The population is huge, accelerating numbers are moving up into the middle class, and many want to travel. Serving the Chinese domestically develops brand loyalty these travelers pack with them when they go abroad.[7]

Overview

In a fast-changing, competitive environment, managers must continually evaluate how well their products are meeting customer needs, and they must engage in thorough, systematic planning to find new strategies to tailor their products to better meet those needs. This chapter explores the manager's role both as planner and as strategist. First, we discuss the nature and importance of planning, the kinds of plans managers develop, and the levels at which planning takes place. Second, we discuss the three major steps in the planning process: (1) determining an organization's mission and major goals, (2) choosing or formulating strategies to realize the mission and goals, and (3) selecting the most effective ways to implement and put these strategies into action. We also examine several techniques, such as scenario planning and SWOT analysis, that can help managers improve the quality of their planning; and we discuss a range of strategies managers can use to give their companies a competitive advantage over their rivals. By the end of this chapter, you will understand the vital role managers carry out when they plan, develop, and implement strategies to create a high-performing organization.

LO8-1 Identify the three main steps of the planning process, and explain the relationship between planning and strategy.

Planning and Strategy

planning Identifying and selecting appropriate goals and courses of action; one of the four principal tasks of management.

strategy A cluster of decisions about what goals to pursue, what actions to take, and how to use resources to achieve goals.

mission statement A broad declaration of an organization's purpose that identifies the organization's products and customers and distinguishes the organization from its competitors.

Planning, as we noted in Chapter 1, is a process managers use to identify and select appropriate goals and courses of action for an organization.[8] The organizational plan that results from the planning process details the goals of the organization and the specific strategies managers will implement to attain those goals. Recall from Chapter 1 that a **strategy** is a cluster of related managerial decisions and actions to help an organization attain one of its goals. Thus, planning is both a goal-making and a strategy-making process.

In most organizations, planning is a three-step activity (see Figure 8.1). The first step is determining the organization's mission and goals. A **mission statement** is a broad declaration of an organization's overriding purpose, what it is seeking to achieve from its activities; this statement also identifies what is *unique or important* about its products to its employees and customers; finally, it *distinguishes or differentiates* the organization in some ways from its competitors. (For example, the mission statement of Nike is "to bring inspiration and innovation to every athlete in the world."[9])

The second step is formulating strategy. Managers analyze the organization's current situation and then conceive and develop the strategies necessary to attain the organization's mission and goals. The third step is implementing strategy. Managers decide how to allocate the resources and responsibilities required to implement the strategies among people and groups within the organization.[10] In subsequent sections of this chapter we look in detail at the specifics of these steps. But first we examine the general nature and purpose of planning.

Figure 8.1

Three Steps in Planning

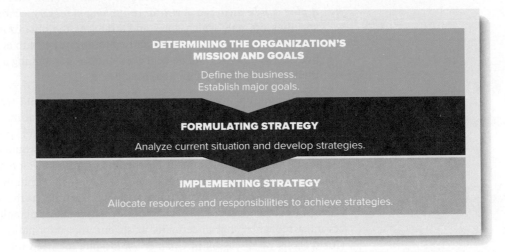

DETERMINING THE ORGANIZATION'S
MISSION AND GOALS

Define the business.
Establish major goals.

FORMULATING STRATEGY

Analyze current situation and develop strategies.

IMPLEMENTING STRATEGY

Allocate resources and responsibilities to achieve strategies.

The Nature of the Planning Process

Essentially, to perform the planning task, managers (1) establish and discover where an organization is at the *present time;* (2) determine where it should be in the future, its *desired future state;* and (3) decide how to *move it forward* to reach that future state. When managers plan, they must forecast what may happen in the future to decide what to do in the present. The better their predictions, the more effective will be the strategies they formulate to take advantage of future opportunities and counter emerging competitive threats in the environment. As previous chapters noted, however, the external environment is uncertain and complex, and managers typically must deal with incomplete information and "limitations on time, cognitive capacity, and data." This is why planning and strategy making are so difficult and risky, and if managers' predictions are wrong and strategies fail, organizational performance falls.

Why Planning Is Important

Almost all managers participate in some kind of planning because they must try to predict future opportunities and threats and develop a plan and strategies that will result in a high-performing organization. Moreover, the absence of a plan often results in hesitations, false steps, and mistaken changes of direction that can hurt an organization or even lead to disaster. Planning is important for four main reasons:

1. *Planning is necessary to give the organization a sense of direction and purpose.*[11] A plan states what goals an organization is trying to achieve and what strategies it intends to use to achieve them. Without the sense of direction and purpose that a formal plan provides, managers may interpret their own specific tasks and jobs in ways that best suit themselves. The result will be an organization that is pursuing multiple and often conflicting goals and a set of managers who do not cooperate and work well together. By stating which organizational goals and strategies are important, a plan keeps managers on track so they use the resources under their control efficiently and effectively.

2. *Planning is a useful way of getting managers to participate in decision making about the appropriate goals and strategies for an organization.* Effective planning gives all managers the opportunity to participate in decision making. At Intel, for example, top managers, as part of their annual planning process, regularly request input from lower-level managers to determine what the organization's goals and strategies should be.

3. *A plan helps coordinate managers of the different functions and divisions of an organization to ensure that they all pull in the same direction and work to achieve its desired future state.* Without a well-thought-out plan, for example, it is possible that the manufacturing function will make more products than the sales function can sell, resulting in a mass of unsold

inventory. In fact, this happened on the East Coast in 2018 when harsh winter storms slowed car sales and left carmakers with unsold inventory. To sell the extra cars, many carmakers had to offer deep discounts to sell off their excess stock.

4. *A plan can be used as a device for controlling managers within an organization.* A good plan specifies not only which goals and strategies the organization is committed to but also *who* bears the responsibility for putting the strategies into action to attain the goals. When managers know they will be held accountable for attaining a goal, they are motivated to do their best to make sure the goal is achieved.

Henri Fayol, the originator of the model of management we discussed in Chapter 1, said that effective plans should have four qualities: unity, continuity, accuracy, and flexibility.[12] *Unity* means that at any time only one central, guiding plan is put into operation to achieve an organizational goal; more than one plan to achieve a goal would cause confusion and disorder. *Continuity* means that planning is an ongoing process in which managers build and refine previous plans and continually modify plans at all levels—corporate, business, and functional—so they fit together into one broad framework. *Accuracy* means that managers need to make every attempt to collect and use all available information in the planning process. Of course, managers must recognize that uncertainty exists and that information is almost always incomplete (for reasons we discussed in Chapter 7). Despite the need for continuity and accuracy, however, Fayol emphasized that the planning process should be *flexible* enough so plans can be altered if the situation changes; managers must not be bound to a static plan.

Levels of Planning

In large organizations, planning usually takes place at three levels of management: corporate, business or division, and department or functional. Consider how General Mills operates. The Minneapolis-based global consumer food company has been in business for more than 150 years and has experienced both growth and headwinds over the past several years. Its current CEO, Jeff Harmening, is a company veteran with nearly 25 years of experience and took over the top job in 2017.[13] Like many large organizations, General Mills has three main levels of management: corporate level, business or divisional level, and functional level (see Figure 8.2). At the corporate level are CEO Harmening, his top management team, and their corporate support staff. Together they are responsible for planning and strategy making for the organization as a whole.

Below the corporate level is the business level. At the business level are the different *divisions* or *business units* of the company. Each division or business unit has its own set of *divisional managers* who control planning and strategy for their division or unit. For example, the managers in General Mill's North America Retail division plan how to operate efficiently and keep costs in check while still meeting the shifting tastes of consumers in the United States and Canada. In 2017, General Mills revised its organizational structure in an effort to increase operational agility and scale global operations efficiently. Each of the four business units includes five global platforms: cereal, snacks, yogurts, convenient meals, and super-premium ice cream. More than 75% of the company's global sales are concentrated in these five areas.[14]

Going down one more level, each division has its own set of *functions* or *departments,* such as manufacturing, marketing, human resources, and research and development (R&D). Each division's *functional managers* are responsible for the planning and strategy making necessary to increase the efficiency and effectiveness of their particular function. For example, the sales managers in General Mills' Convenience Stores & Foodservice division would be responsible for working with marketing colleagues to ensure various advertising and sales campaigns targeted potential customers in supermarket bakeries.

Levels and Types of Planning

As just discussed, planning at General Mills, as at all other large organizations, takes place at each level. Figure 8.3 shows the link between these three levels and the three steps in the planning and strategy-making process illustrated in Figure 8.1.

Figure 8.2

Levels of Planning at General Mills

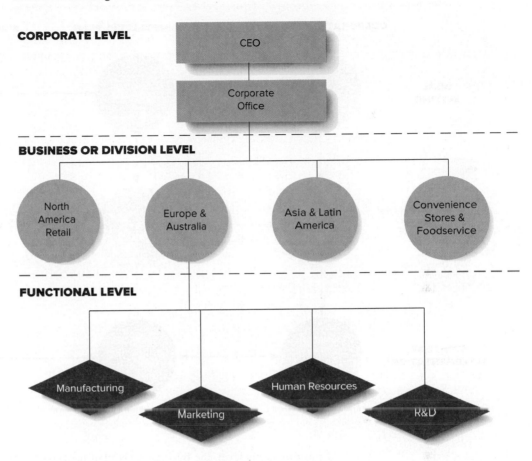

corporate-level plan Top management's decisions pertaining to the organization's mission, overall strategy, and structure.

corporate-level strategy A plan that indicates in which industries and national markets an organization intends to compete.

business-level plan Divisional managers' decisions pertaining to divisions' long-term goals, overall strategy, and structure.

business-level strategy A plan that indicates how a division intends to compete against its rivals in an industry.

The **corporate-level plan** contains top management's decisions concerning the organization's mission and goals, overall (corporate-level) strategy, and structure (see Figure 8.3). **Corporate-level strategy** specifies in which industries and national markets an organization intends to compete and why. One of the goals stated in General Mills' corporate-level plan is that the company is seeking to increase its market share in the organic/natural food sector. Already this portfolio generates more than $1 billion in sales for the company in North America alone. In 2018, the company announced plans to purchase Blue Buffalo Pet Products, an acquisition that would cost more than $8 billion. Company management believes that adding Blue Buffalo to its other organic products (Annie's Homegrown and Epic Provisions) will help General Mills open up new opportunities in the lucrative pet food industry.[15]

In general, corporate-level planning and strategy are the primary responsibility of top or corporate managers.[16] The corporate-level goal of General Mills is to be the market leader in every business sector in which it competes. Jeff Harmening and his top management team decide which food product sectors General Mills should compete in to achieve this goal. The corporate-level plan provides the framework within which divisional managers create their business-level plans. At the business level, the managers of each division create a **business-level plan** that details (1) the long-term divisional goals that will allow the division to meet corporate goals and (2) the division's business-level strategy and structure necessary to achieve divisional goals. **Business-level strategy** outlines the specific methods a division, a business unit, or an organization will use to compete effectively against its rivals in an industry. For example, managers in General Mills' Asia and Latin America division continue to develop strategies for growth of its Yoplait yogurt brand in the Chinese market, which is roughly twice the size of the U.S. yogurt market.[17]

Figure 8.3

Levels and Types of Planning

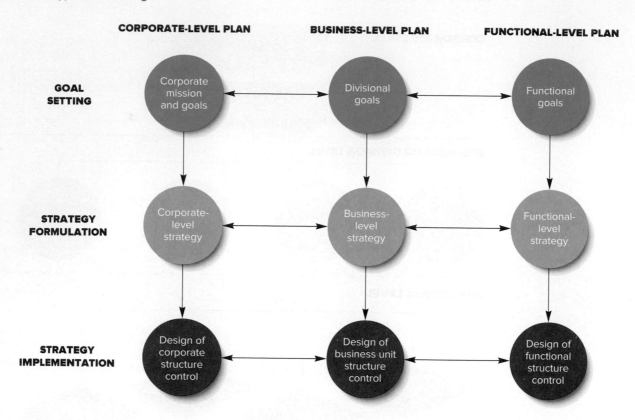

At the functional level, the business-level plan provides the framework within which functional managers devise their plans. A **functional-level plan** states the goals that the managers of each function will pursue to help their division attain its business-level goals, which, in turn, will allow the entire company to achieve its corporate goals. **Functional-level strategy** is a plan of action that managers of individual functions (such as manufacturing or marketing) can follow to improve the ability of each function to perform its task-specific activities in ways that add value to an organization's goods and services and thereby increase the value customers receive. Thus, for example, consistent with the strategy of increasing Yoplait sales in China, General Mills might adopt the goal "To increase production by 20% over the next three years," and functional strategies to achieve this goal might include (1) investing in state-of-the-art manufacturing facilities and (2) developing a global supply chain that will increase efficiencies and reduce shipping costs. The many ways in which managers can use functional-level strategy to strengthen business-level strategy are discussed in detail in Chapter 9.

In the planning process, it is important to ensure that planning across the three different levels is *consistent*—functional goals and strategies should be consistent with divisional goals and strategies—which, in turn, should be consistent with corporate goals and strategies, and vice versa. When consistency is achieved, the whole company operates in harmony; activities at one level reinforce and strengthen those at the other levels, increasing efficiency and effectiveness. To help accomplish this, each function's plan is linked to its division's business-level plan, which is linked to the corporate plan. With a renewed vigor and detailed business strategies in place at each level of the organization, General Mills continues to review and revise its plans to ensure they are an effective guide to managerial decision making.[18]

functional-level plan Functional managers' decisions pertaining to the goals that they propose to pursue to help the division attain its business-level goals.

functional-level strategy A plan of action to improve the ability of each of an organization's functions to perform its task-specific activities in ways that add value to an organization's goods and services.

Time Horizons of Plans

time horizon The intended duration of a plan.

Plans differ in their **time horizons**, the periods of time over which they are intended to apply or endure. Managers usually distinguish among *long-term plans,* with a time horizon of five years or more; *intermediate-term plans,* with a horizon between one and five years; and *short-term plans,* with a horizon of one year or less.[19] Typically, corporate- and business-level goals and strategies require long- and intermediate-term plans, and functional-level goals and strategies require intermediate- and short-term plans.

Although most companies operate with planning horizons of five years or more, this does not mean that managers undertake major planning exercises only once every five years and then "lock in" a specific set of goals and strategies for that period. Most organizations have an annual planning cycle that is usually linked to the annual financial budget (although a major planning effort may be undertaken only every few years). So a corporate- or business-level plan that extends over several years is typically treated as a *rolling plan*—a plan that is updated and amended every year to take account of changing conditions in the external environment. Thus, the time horizon for an organization's 2020 corporate-level plan might be 2025; for the 2021 plan, it might be 2026; and so on. The use of rolling plans is essential because of the high rate of change in the environment and the difficulty of predicting competitive conditions five years in the future. Rolling plans enable managers to make midcourse corrections if environmental changes warrant or to change the thrust of the plan altogether if it no longer seems appropriate. The use of rolling plans allows managers to plan flexibly without losing sight of the need to plan for the long term.

Standing Plans and Single-Use Plans

LO8-2 Describe some techniques managers can use to improve the planning process so they can better predict the future and mobilize organizational resources to meet future contingencies.

Another distinction often made between plans is whether they are standing plans or single-use plans. Managers create standing and single-use plans to help achieve an organization's specific goals. *Standing plans* are used in situations in which programmed decision making is appropriate. When the same situations occur repeatedly, managers develop policies, rules, and standard operating procedures (SOPs) to control the way employees perform their tasks. A policy is a general guide to action; a rule is a formal, written guide to action; and a standard operating procedure is a written instruction describing the exact series of actions that should be followed in a specific situation. For example, an organization may have a standing plan about ethical behavior by employees. This plan includes a policy that all employees are expected to behave ethically in their dealings with suppliers and customers, a rule that requires any employee who receives from a supplier or customer a gift worth more than $50 to report the gift, and an SOP that obliges the recipient of the gift to make the disclosure in writing within 30 days.

scenario planning The generation of multiple forecasts of future conditions followed by an analysis of how to respond effectively to each of those conditions.

In contrast, *single-use plans* are developed to handle nonprogrammed decision making in unusual or one-of-a-kind situations. Examples of single-use plans include *programs,* which are integrated sets of plans for achieving certain goals, and *projects,* which are specific action plans created to complete various aspects of a program. For instance, NASA is working on a major program to launch a rover in 2020 to investigate a specific environment on the surface of Mars. One project in this program is to develop the scientific instruments to bring samples back from Mars.[20] To learn more about the role of projects in planning at Los Angeles World Airports, read the "Manager as a Person" feature.

As we know all too well, oil and gas prices are unpredictable. Oil industry managers therefore sometimes use scenario planning to deal with this chaotic market.
©Justin Sullivan/Getty Images

Scenario Planning

Earlier we noted that effective plans have four qualities: unity, continuity, accuracy, and flexibility. One of the most widely used planning methods or techniques that can help managers create plans that have these qualities is scenario planning. **Scenario planning** (also known as *contingency planning*) is the generation of multiple forecasts of future conditions followed by an analysis of how to respond effectively to each of those conditions.

MANAGER AS A PERSON

With CEO's Guidance, LAX Projects Take Flight

As CEO of Los Angeles World Airports, Deborah Ale Flint is responsible for running Los Angeles International (LAX), Van Nuys, and Ontario International Airports.[21] It's a job she prepared for as director of aviation for the Port of Oakland, in Northern California. Flint is enthusiastic about airports. She relishes mingling with travelers in the terminals because it's "where the magic happens for the passenger."[22]

Flint knew projects would be a major part of her work in Los Angeles. LAX, the nation's second-busiest airport and the world's fourth-busiest, is her biggest responsibility. When she arrived, LAX was already undergoing a multibillion-dollar renovation.[23] The terminals are being upgraded to prepare for technological advances and the expected further growth in passenger traffic. The entire effort consists of dozens of projects that must be planned, funded, and implemented. Flint arrived after completion of the international terminal and in time to lead work on additional terminals and connecting spaces. The plans aim to reduce congestion, lower energy consumption, and update technology with, for example, flight information displays that travelers can scan with a smartphone to get personalized maps.

A key project under Flint's guidance is the Landside Access Modernization Program (LAMP).[24] Besides lounges, baggage claim areas, and walkways between terminals, LAMP includes a consolidated facility for car rental agencies and a people-mover system to transport travelers swiftly from terminals to garages and public transit. Funding for LAMP was recently authorized by the airport commissioners, triggering the start of the design process. The plan calls for completion in three years.

Running an airport poses special planning challenges because U.S. airports are managed by the cities they serve. Unlike a business selling tickets or charging admission, LAX assesses fees from the airlines using terminals and collects passenger facility charges from passengers when they pay for flights.[25] The city also can borrow for projects by issuing bonds. Therefore, to get the go-ahead for projects, Flint has to win the backing of the local community, including the government. Her enthusiasm for her city surely helps. Flint's vision for LAX is that it represents a vibrant, creative city to local and world travelers, so it should be as creative and forward-thinking as the city. As Flint describes the renovation, it's not merely a construction project, but a means of "creating an experience" for travelers, giving them a "great first and last impression of Los Angeles."[26]

As noted previously, planning is about trying to forecast the future in order to be able to anticipate future opportunities and threats. The future, however, is inherently unpredictable. How can managers best deal with this unpredictability? This question preoccupied managers at Royal Dutch Shell, the third largest global oil company, in the 1980s. In 1984 oil was $30 a barrel, and most analysts and managers, including Shell's, believed it would hit $50 per barrel by 1990. Although these high prices guaranteed high profits, Shell's top managers decided to conduct a scenario-planning exercise. Shell's corporate and divisional managers were told to use scenario planning to generate different future scenarios of conditions in the oil market and then to develop a set of plans that detailed how they would respond to these opportunities and threats if any such scenario occurred.

One scenario assumed that oil prices would fall to $15 per barrel, and managers had to decide what they should do to remain profitable in such a case. Managers went to work with the goal of creating a plan consisting of a series of recommendations. The final plan included proposals to cut oil exploration costs by investing in new technologies, to accelerate investments in cost-efficient oil-refining facilities, and to weed out unprofitable gas stations.[27] In reviewing these proposals, top management came to the conclusion that even if oil prices continued to rise, all of these actions would benefit Shell and increase its profit margin. So they decided to put the cost-cutting plan into action. As it happened, in the mid-1980s oil prices did not rise; they collapsed to $15 a barrel, but Shell, unlike its competitors, had already taken steps to be profitable in a low-oil-price world. Consequently, by 1990 the company was twice as profitable as its major competitors.

As this example suggests, because the future is unpredictable—the $30-a-barrel oil level was not reached again until the early 2000s, for example—the best way to improve planning is first to generate "multiple futures," or scenarios of the future, based on different assumptions about conditions that *might prevail* in the future and then to develop different plans that detail what a company should do if one of these scenarios occurs. Scenario planning is a learning tool that raises the quality of the planning process and can bring benefits to an organization.[28] Over the years Shell scenario planners have generated more than 30 rounds of scenarios, including one that involved exploring the critical role energy plays in dealing with climate change.[29] A major advantage of scenario planning is its ability not only to anticipate the challenges of an uncertain future but also to educate managers to think about the future—*to think strategically.*

Determining the Organization's Mission and Goals

As we discussed earlier, determining the organization's mission and goals is the first step of the planning process. Once the mission and goals are agreed upon and formally stated in the corporate plan, they guide the next steps by defining which strategies are appropriate.[30] Figure 8.4 presents the mission statements of three Internet-based companies.

Defining the Business

To determine an organization's *mission*—the overriding reason it exists to provide customers with goods or services they value—managers must first *define its business* so they can identify what kinds of value customers are receiving. To define the business, managers must ask three related questions about a company's products: (1) *Who* are our customers? (2) *What* customer needs are being satisfied? (3) *How* are we satisfying customer needs?[31] Managers ask these questions to identify the customer needs that the organization satisfies and how the organization satisfies those needs. Answering these questions helps managers identify not only the customer needs they are satisfying now but also the needs they should try to satisfy in the future and who their true competitors are. All this information helps managers plan and establish appropriate goals.

Figure 8.4

Mission Statements for Three Internet Companies

COMPANY	MISSION STATEMENT
Facebook:	"To give people the power to build community and bring the world closer together."
Twitter:	"To give everyone the power to create and share ideas and information instantly, without barriers."
Google:	"To organize the world's information and make it universally accessible and useful."

Sources: Facebook's mission: https://newsroom.fb.com; Twitter's mission: https://abouttwitter.com; Google's mission: https://google.com, accessed March 24, 2018.

Establishing Major Goals

Once the business is defined, managers must establish a set of primary goals to which the organization is committed. Developing these goals gives the organization a sense of direction or purpose. In most organizations, articulating major goals is the job of the CEO, although other managers have input into the process. Thus, at General Mills, CEO Harmening's primary goal is still to be one of the top performers in every market in which the company competes, even though this is highly challenging. However, the best statements of organizational goals are ambitious—that is, they *stretch* the organization and require that each of its members work to improve company performance.[32] The role of **strategic leadership**, the ability of the CEO and top managers to convey to their subordinates a compelling vision of what they want to achieve, is important here. If subordinates buy into the vision and model their behaviors on their leaders, they develop a willingness to undertake the hard, stressful work that is necessary for creative, risk-taking strategy making.[33]

strategic leadership The ability of the CEO and top managers to convey to their subordinates a compelling vision of what they want the organization to achieve.

Although goals should be challenging, they should also be realistic. Challenging goals give managers at all levels an incentive to look for ways to improve organizational performance, but a goal that is clearly unrealistic and impossible to attain may prompt managers to give up.[34] For example, General Mills' CEO has to be careful not to set unrealistic sales targets for the company's business units that might discourage their top managers.

Finally, the time period in which a goal is expected to be achieved should be stated. Time constraints are important because they emphasize that a goal must be attained within a reasonable period; they inject a sense of urgency into goal attainment and act as a motivator. General Mills recently announced its global sustainability goals that include reducing greenhouse gas emissions across the entire value chain by 28% from 2010 levels by 2025, developing water stewardship plans for the most at-risk watersheds in its global supply chain by 2025, and sustainably sourcing 100% of its 10 priority ingredients by 2020—which represents more than 40% of its annual raw material purchases on a global basis.[35]

Formulating Strategy

strategy formulation The development of a set of corporate, business, and functional strategies that allow an organization to accomplish its mission and achieve its goals.

Once the mission and goals of the organization have been set, a strategy to achieve them needs to be formulated. In **strategy formulation**, managers work to develop the set of strategies (corporate, divisional, and functional) that will allow an organization to accomplish its mission and achieve its goals.[36] Strategy formulation begins with managers' systematically analyzing the factors or forces inside an organization and outside in the global environment that affect the organization's ability to meet its goals now and in the future. SWOT analysis and the five forces model are two handy techniques managers can use to analyze these factors.

SWOT Analysis

SWOT analysis A planning exercise in which managers identify organizational strengths (S) and weaknesses (W) and environmental opportunities (O) and threats (T).

SWOT analysis is a planning exercise in which managers identify *internal* organizational strengths (S) and weaknesses (W) and *external* environmental opportunities (O) and threats (T). Based on a SWOT analysis, managers at the different levels of the organization select the corporate, business, and functional strategies to best position the organization to achieve its mission and goals (see Figure 8.5). In Chapter 6 we discussed forces in the task and general environments that have the potential to affect an organization. We noted that changes in these forces can produce opportunities that an organization might take advantage of and threats that may harm its current situation.

The first step in SWOT analysis is to identify an organization's strengths and weaknesses. Table 8.1 lists many important strengths (such as high-quality skills in marketing and in research and development) and weaknesses (such as rising manufacturing costs and outdated technology). The task facing managers is to identify the strengths and weaknesses that characterize the present state of their organization.

The second step in SWOT analysis begins when managers embark on a full-scale SWOT planning exercise to identify potential opportunities and threats in the environment that affect the organization now or may affect it in the future. Examples of possible opportunities and

Figure 8.5

Planning and Strategy Formulation

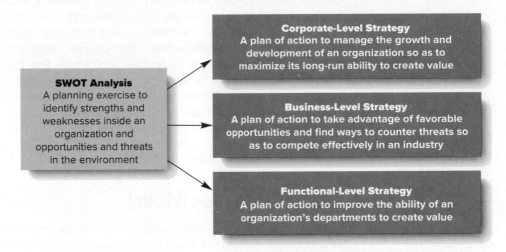

threats that must be anticipated (many of which were discussed in Chapter 6) are listed in Table 8.1. Scenario planning is often used to strengthen this analysis.

With the SWOT analysis completed, and strengths, weaknesses, opportunities, and threats identified, managers can continue the planning process and determine specific strategies for achieving the organization's mission and goals. The resulting strategies should enable

Table 8.1

Questions for SWOT Analysis

Potential Strengths	Potential Opportunities	Potential Weaknesses	Potential Threats
Well-developed strategy?	Expand core business(es)?	Poorly developed strategy?	Attacks on core business(es)?
Strong product lines?	Exploit new market segments?	Obsolete, narrow product lines?	Increase in domestic competition?
Broad market coverage?	Widen product range?	Rising manufacturing costs?	Increase in foreign competition?
Manufacturing competence?	Extend cost or differentiation advantage?	Decline in R&D innovations?	Change in consumer tastes?
Good marketing skills?		Poor marketing plan?	
Good materials management systems?	Diversify into new growth businesses?	Poor materials management systems?	Fall in barriers to entry?
R&D skills and leadership?	Expand into foreign markets?	Loss of customer goodwill?	Rise in new or substitute products?
Human resource competencies?	Apply R&D skills in new areas?	Inadequate human resources?	Increase in industry rivalry?
Brand-name reputation?	Enter new related businesses?	Loss of brand name?	New forms of industry competition?
Cost of differentiation advantage?	Vertically integrate forward?	Growth without direction?	Potential for takeover?
Appropriate management style?	Vertically integrate backward?	Loss of corporate direction?	
Appropriate organizational structure?	Overcome barriers to entry?	Infighting among divisions?	Changes in demographic factors?
		Loss of corporate control?	Changes in economic factors?
Appropriate control systems?	Reduce rivalry among competitors?	Inappropriate organizational structure and control systems?	Downturn in economy?
Ability to manage strategic change?	Apply brand-name capital in new areas?	High conflict and politics?	Rising labor costs?
Other strengths?	Seek fast market growth?	Other weaknesses?	Slower market growth?
	Other opportunities?		Other threats?

the organization to attain its goals by taking advantage of opportunities, countering threats, building strengths, and correcting organizational weaknesses. To appreciate how managers can use SWOT analysis to formulate strategy, consider a recent SWOT analysis comparison between e-tailer Amazon.com and clicks-and-mortar retailer Walmart. Although each company has differing strengths and weaknesses, they both face similar threats and opportunities in the expanding e-commerce market.[37] For example, Walmart's recent acquisition of several e-commerce companies such as Jet.com, Mod Cloth, ShoeBuy, and Bonobos provides some interesting opportunities for the world's largest retailer to gain market share in the online retail space—as well as some threats to Amazon's position as a top online apparel retailer. In addition, Amazon's recent acquisition of Whole Food Markets specialty grocery chain provides some interesting opportunities for Amazon in the home meal-kit delivery market sector as it provides a viable threat to Walmart and other food retailers that sell grocery items such as organic fruits and vegetables.[38]

The Five Forces Model

A well-known model that helps managers focus on the five most important competitive forces, or potential threats, in the external environment is Michael Porter's five forces model.[39] We discussed the first four forces in the following list in Chapter 6. Porter identified these five factors as major threats because they affect how much profit organizations competing within the same industry can expect to make:

- *The level of rivalry among organizations in an industry:* The more that companies compete against one another for customers—for example, by lowering the prices of their products or by increasing advertising—the lower is the level of industry profits (low prices mean less profit).

- *The potential for entry into an industry:* The easier it is for companies to enter an industry—because, for example, barriers to entry, such as brand loyalty, are low—the more likely it is for industry prices and therefore industry profits to be low.

- *The power of large suppliers:* If there are only a few large suppliers of an important input, then suppliers can drive up the price of that input, and expensive inputs result in lower profits for companies in an industry.

- *The power of large customers:* If only a few large customers are available to buy an industry's output, they can bargain to drive down the price of that output. As a result, industry producers make lower profits.

- *The threat of substitute products:* Often the output of one industry is a substitute for the output of another industry (plastic may be a substitute for steel in some applications, for example; similarly, bottled water is a substitute for cola). When a substitute for their product exists, companies cannot demand high prices for it or customers will switch to the substitute, and this constraint keeps their profits low.

Porter argued that when managers analyze opportunities and threats, they should pay particular attention to these five forces because they are the major threats an organization will encounter. It is the job of managers at the corporate, business, and functional levels to formulate strategies to counter these threats so an organization can manage its task and general environments, perform at a high level, and generate high profits.

Sometimes, however, management's review of competitive forces or potential threats cannot keep a company from filing bankruptcy or liquidating its stores. Consider what recently happened to toy retailer Toys "R" Us (TRU). The past decade or so have been quite challenging for the retailer—with holiday sales unable to provide the turnaround the company needed to regain profitability. Looking at Porter's framework, TRU experienced a high level of rivalry from other retailers selling the same toys, which pushed down prices when TRU could least likely afford to reduce its margins. By 1998, Walmart began selling more toys than TRU. The potential for entry into the retail toy industry was high and devastating for TRU because there were few barriers to entry—very little brand loyalty for TRU itself from consumers who could buy toys and other items cheaper and more conveniently from discount retailers and e-commerce websites.

Reviewing competitive forces or potential threats didn't help Toys "R" Us stay in business. Saddled with insurmountable debt, the toy retailer could not get financing or support from its creditors and was forced to liquidate its inventory and close its stores in 2018.

©photocritical/Shutterstock

hypercompetition Permanent, ongoing, intense competition brought about in an industry by advancing technology or changing customer tastes.

With regard to the power of large suppliers and customers, economies of scale could have played to TRU's advantage; however, the company had been highly leveraged with almost insurmountable debt, and many of its suppliers refused to give the company additional financing or extended credit to purchase the inventory it desperately needed for the all-important holiday season.[40] Lastly, the threat of substitute products was high in the case of TRU, especially if one considers alternative forms of entertainment (such as video games and streaming content) that met the same consumer needs as toys. Analyzing TRU's recent plight using the five forces model, it shows the company was vulnerable in several areas, which caused it to reduce its prices to attract shoppers, while trying to pay back enormous amounts of debt. TRU first filed for bankruptcy protection from creditors, and then, in March 2018, started liquidating and closing stores in the United States and abroad.[41]

Today competition is tough in most industries, whether companies make cars, soup, computers, or dolls. The term **hypercompetition** applies to industries that are characterized by permanent, ongoing, intense competition brought about by advancing technology or changing customer tastes and fads and fashions.[42] Clearly, planning and strategy formulation are much more difficult and risky when hypercompetition prevails in an industry.

Formulating Business-Level Strategies

Michael Porter, the researcher who developed the five forces model, also developed a theory of how managers can select a business-level strategy—a plan to gain a competitive advantage in a particular market or industry.[43] Porter argued that business-level strategy creates a competitive advantage because it allows an organization (or a division of a company) to *counter and reduce* the threat of the five industry forces. That is, successful business-level strategy reduces rivalry, prevents new competitors from entering the industry, reduces the power of suppliers or buyers, and lowers the threat of substitutes—and this raises prices and profits.

According to Porter, to obtain these higher profits managers must choose between two basic ways of increasing the value of an organization's products: *differentiating the product* to increase its value to customers or *lowering the costs* of making the product. Porter also argues that managers must choose between serving the whole market or serving just one segment of a market. Based on those choices, managers choose to pursue one of four business-level strategies: low-cost, differentiation, focused low-cost, or focused differentiation (see Table 8.2).

Table 8.2

Porter's Business-Level Strategies

	Number of Market Segments Served	
Strategy	**Many**	**Few**
Low-cost	√	
Focused low-cost		√
Differentiation	√	
Focused differentiation		√

Low-Cost Strategy

With a low-cost strategy, managers try to gain a competitive advantage by focusing the energy of all the organization's departments or functions on driving the company's costs down below the costs of its industry rivals. This strategy, for example, would require that manufacturing managers search for new ways to reduce production costs, R&D managers focus on developing new products that can be manufactured more cheaply, and marketing managers find ways to lower the costs of attracting customers. According to Porter, companies pursuing a low-cost strategy can sell a product for less than their rivals sell it and yet still make a good profit because of their lower costs. Thus, such organizations enjoy a competitive advantage based on their low prices. For example, BIC pursues a low-cost strategy: It offers customers razor blades priced lower than Gillette's and ballpoint pens less expensive than those offered by Cross or Waterman. Also, when existing companies have low costs and can charge low prices, it is difficult for new companies to enter the industry because entering is always an expensive process.

Differentiation Strategy

With a differentiation strategy, managers try to gain a competitive advantage by focusing all the energies of the organization's departments or functions on *distinguishing* the organization's products from those of competitors on one or more important dimensions, such as product design, quality, or after-sales service and support. Often the process of making products unique and different is expensive. This strategy, for example, frequently requires that managers increase spending on product design or R&D to differentiate products, and costs rise as a result. Organizations that successfully pursue a differentiation strategy may be able to charge a *premium price* for their products; the premium price lets organizations pursuing a differentiation strategy recoup their higher costs. Coca-Cola, PepsiCo, and Procter & Gamble are some of the many well-known companies that pursue a strategy of differentiation. They spend enormous amounts of money on advertising to differentiate, and create a unique image for, their products. Also, differentiation makes industry entry difficult because new companies have no brand name to help them compete and customers don't perceive other products to be close substitutes, so this also allows premium pricing and results in high profits.

According to Porter's theory, managers cannot simultaneously pursue both a low-cost strategy and a differentiation strategy. Porter identified a simple correlation: Differentiation raises costs and thus necessitates premium pricing to recoup those high costs. For example, if BIC suddenly began to advertise heavily to try to build a strong global brand image for its products, BIC's costs would rise. BIC then could no longer make a profit simply by pricing its blades or pens lower than Gillette or Cross. According to Porter, managers must choose between a low-cost strategy and a differentiation strategy.

More and more, however, exceptions to Porter's ideas about the "either/or" approach to gaining competitive advantage by low cost or differentiation can be found in today's business environment. For example, Southwest Airlines has written its mission statement to say "dedication to the highest quality of customer service delivered with a sense of warmth, friendliness, individual pride, and company spirit."[44] Based on this statement, the company seems to be pursuing a differentiation strategy based on customer service. Yet the average price of a one-way ticket on a Southwest flight continues to be among the lowest, which suggests a cost leadership strategy. Likewise, Apple has a story that mixes cost leadership with differentiation. Apple CEO Tim Cook emphasizes that Apple's strategy is to focus on making great products—a differentiation strategy. He said the company never had the goal of selling a low-cost phone.[45] However, he said, the company did find a way to reach its goal of providing a great experience with a phone while reducing its cost. Cook emphasizes that differentiation was the goal, but low cost also became possible. These examples suggest that although Porter's ideas may be valid in most cases, very well-managed companies such as Southwest Airlines and Apple may pursue both low costs and differentiated products.

Focused Low-Cost and Focused Differentiation Strategies

focused low-cost strategy Serving only one segment of the overall market and trying to be the lowest-cost organization serving that segment.

Both the differentiation strategy and the low-cost strategy are aimed at serving many or most segments of a particular market, such as for cars, toys, foods, or computers. Porter identified two other business-level strategies that aim to serve the needs of customers in only one or a few market segments.[46] Managers pursuing a focused low-cost strategy serve one or a few segments of the overall market and aim to make their organization the lowest-cost company serving that segment. By contrast, managers pursuing a focused differentiation strategy serve just one or a few segments of the market and aim to make their organization the most differentiated company serving that segment.

focused differentiation strategy Serving only one segment of the overall market and trying to be the most differentiated organization serving that segment.

Companies pursuing either of these strategies have chosen to *specialize* in some way by directing their efforts at a particular kind of customer (such as serving the needs of babies or affluent customers) or even the needs of customers in a specific geographic region (customers on the East or West Coast). BMW, for example, pursues a focused differentiation strategy, producing cars exclusively for higher-income customers. By contrast, Toyota pursues a differentiation strategy and produces cars that appeal to consumers in almost all segments of the car market, from basic transportation (Toyota Corolla) through the middle of the market (Toyota Camry) to the high-income end of the market (Lexus).

Increasingly, smaller companies are finding it easier to pursue a focused strategy and compete successfully against large, powerful low-cost and differentiated companies because of advances in technology (IT) that lower costs and enable them to reach and attract customers. By establishing a storefront on the web, thousands of small, specialized companies have been able to carve out a profitable niche against large bricks-and-mortar and virtual competitors.

Zara is a flagship brand for Spanish global retailer Iditex, whose sales have soared in recent years, and provides an excellent example of the way even a bricks-and-mortar company can use IT to pursue a focused strategy and compete globally.[47] Zara has managed to position itself as the low-price, low-cost leader in the fashion segment of the clothing market, against differentiators like Gucci and H&M, because it has applied IT to its specific needs. Zara has created IT that allows it to manage its design and manufacturing process in a way that minimizes the inventory it has to carry—the major cost borne by a clothing retailer. However, its IT also gives its designers instantaneous feedback on which clothes are selling well and in which countries, and this gives Zara a competitive advantage from differentiation. Specifically, Zara can manufacture more of a particular kind of dress or suit to meet high customer demand, decide which clothing should be sold in its rapidly expanding network of global stores, and constantly change the mix of clothes it offers customers to keep up with fashion—at low cost.

Zara's approach to technology also lets it efficiently manage the interface between its design and manufacturing operations, which work side by side in its corporate headquarters in Arteixo, Spain. Zara sometimes takes only two weeks to design, manufacture, and ship new clothing items to stores across the globe. By contrast, H&M, the trendy Swedish retailer, takes several months to get its advanced orders into hands of customers.[48] This short time to market gives Zara great flexibility and allows the company to respond quickly to the rapidly changing fashion market, in which fashions can change several times a year. Because of the quick manufacturing-to-sales cycle and just-in-time fashion, Zara offers clothes collections at relatively low prices and still makes profits that are the envy of the fashion apparel industry.

Zara has been able to pursue a focused strategy that is simultaneously low cost and differentiated because it has developed many strengths in functions such as clothing design, marketing, and IT that have given it a competitive advantage. Developing functional-level strategies that strengthen business-level strategy and increase competitive advantage is a vital managerial task. Discussion of this important issue is left until the next chapter. First, we need to go up one planning level and examine how corporate strategy helps an organization achieve its mission and goals.

Zara's ongoing retail success is based on a focused strategy that identifies fashion trends quickly and turns out new products in record time.
©Markel Redondo/Bloomberg via Getty Images

Formulating Corporate-Level Strategies

LO8-4 Differentiate among the main types of corporate-level strategies, and explain how they are used to strengthen a company's business-level strategy and competitive advantage.

Once managers have formulated the business-level strategies that will best position a company, or a division of a company, to compete in an industry and outperform its rivals, they must look to the future. If their planning has been successful, the company will be generating high profits, and their task now is to plan how to invest these profits to increase performance over time.

Recall that *corporate-level strategy* is a plan of action that involves choosing in which industries and countries a company should invest its resources to achieve its mission and goals. In choosing a corporate-level strategy, managers ask, How should the growth and development of our company be managed to increase its ability to create value for customers (and thus increase its performance) over the long run? Managers of effective organizations actively seek new opportunities to use a company's resources to create new and improved goods and services for customers. Examples of organizations whose product lines are growing rapidly are Google, Intel, Apple, and Toyota, whose managers pursue any feasible opportunity to use their companies' skills to provide customers with new products.

In addition, some managers must help their organizations respond to threats due to changing forces in the task or general environment that have made their business-level strategies less effective and reduced profits. For example, customers may no longer be buying the kinds of goods and services a company is producing (high-salt soup, bulky CRT televisions, or gas-guzzling SUVs), or other organizations may have entered the market and attracted away customers (this happened to Sony in the 2000s after Apple and Samsung began to produce better MP3 players, laptops, and smartphones). Top managers aim to find corporate strategies that can help the organization strengthen its business-level strategies and thus respond to these changes and improve performance.

The principal corporate-level strategies that managers use to help a company grow and keep it at the top of its industry, or to help it retrench and reorganize to stop its decline, are (1) concentration on a single industry, (2) vertical integration, (3) diversification, and (4) international expansion. An organization will benefit from pursuing any of these strategies only when the strategy helps further increase the value of the organization's goods and services so that more customers buy them. Specifically, to increase the value of goods and services, a corporate-level strategy must help a company, or one of its divisions, either (1) lower the costs of developing and making products or (2) increase product differentiation so that more customers want to buy the products even at high or premium prices. Both of these outcomes strengthen a company's competitive advantage and increase its performance.

Concentration on a Single Industry

Most growing companies reinvest their profits to strengthen their competitive position in the industry in which they are currently operating; in doing so, they pursue the corporate-level strategy of concentration on a single industry. Most commonly, an organization uses its functional skills to develop new kinds of products, or it expands the number of locations in which it uses those skills. For example, Apple continuously introduces improved mobile wireless digital devices such as the iPhone and iPad, whereas McDonald's, which began as one restaurant in California, focused all its efforts on using its resources to quickly expand across the globe to become the biggest and most profitable U.S. fast-food company. The way Michelin focuses on the tire business is discussed in the following "Management Insight" feature.

concentration on a single industry Reinvesting a company's profits to strengthen its competitive position in its current industry.

On the other hand, when organizations are performing effectively, they often decide to enter *new industries* in which they can use their growing profits to establish new operating divisions to create and make a wider range of more valuable products. Thus, they begin to pursue vertical integration or diversification—such as Coca-Cola, PepsiCo, and Campbell's Soup.

Vertical Integration

When an organization is performing well in its industry, managers often see new opportunities to create additional value either by producing the inputs it uses to make products or by distributing and selling its products to customers. This process is called vertical integration.

MANAGEMENT INSIGHT

Innovation Drives Michelin

More than a hundred years ago, two French brothers, André and Edouard Michelin, revolutionized the tire industry by inventing a detachable steel wheel with a bicycle inner tube to replace the wooden wheels previously used on vehicles. A century later, Michelin continues to innovate in a single industry: making tires for cars, trucks, recreational vehicles, earthmovers, farm equipment, airplanes, motorcycles, and bicycles.[49] Michelin's North American subsidiary is a $10 billion company with 19 plants in 16 locations, employing more than 22,000 people. Headquartered in Greenville, South Carolina, the company manufactures tires in six states as well as in Canada and Mexico.[50]

Innovation continues to be a key component of the company's success. Considered the world's top tire manufacturer, Michelin invented the steel-belted radial tire in the 1950s and brought the technology to the United States in the mid-1960s when Ford chose the French tire maker to supply radial tires for its Lincoln Continental. Not long after, Sears chose Michelin as its tire supplier because of the company's technical expertise. Today, Michelin's North America R&D Center, which employs more than 900 people, has developed many key products, including the first 80,000-mile passenger tire for American-made vehicles. And its testing facility in Laurens, South Carolina, maintains numerous special tracks of varying lengths and surfaces for testing tires and suspension systems, as well as for training drivers.[51]

As the global demand for radial tires increased in the 1970s, Michelin North America continued to expand, building plants to manufacture both car and truck tires. Under the guidance of François Michelin (grandson of one of the founders), the company moved its stateside headquarters from New York to South Carolina, a state that had lost its flourishing textile industry to overseas competitors.[52]

Innovation continues to drive the corporate strategies at Michelin, the global tire manufacturer with more than 125 years in business. The company's Michelin Man mascot is considered one of the world's oldest and most recognized trademarks.
©Getty Images

Concentrating business in a single industry can be challenging; however, Michelin took several steps to expand its product line, including the acquisition of one of its top U.S. competitors, Uniroyal–Goodrich Tire Company, in 1989. This acquisition allows the company to offer tires at several price points while maintaining the quality Michelin is known for around the world.[53]

Michelin is still going strong after more than 125 years in business. Its iconic round Michelin Man (whose name is Bibendum) is one of the world's oldest trademarks, introduced in France at the Lyon Exhibition in 1894.[54] And the Michelin brothers, ever the marketers, created the *Michelin Guide* back in 1926 as a guide to restaurants in France to encourage consumers to travel—and eventually buy more tires for their vehicles. Today, the well-respected restaurant and travel guide and its coveted three-star rating system cover more than 30 countries worldwide.[55]

vertical integration Expanding a company's operations either backward into an industry that produces inputs for its products or forward into an industry that uses, distributes, or sells its products.

Vertical integration is a corporate-level strategy in which a company expands its business operations either backward into a new industry that produces inputs for the company's products (*backward vertical integration*) or forward into a new industry that uses, distributes, or sells the company's products (*forward vertical integration*).[56] For example, as Tesla Motors works toward its goal of mass-producing an electric car that will sell for close to $35,000, it recognizes it will need batteries for the vehicles. To meet that need, Tesla has become its own battery supplier, building the $5 billion Gigafactory outside Sparks, Nevada, which went on line in 2017. This

Figure 8.6

Stages in a Vertical Value Chain

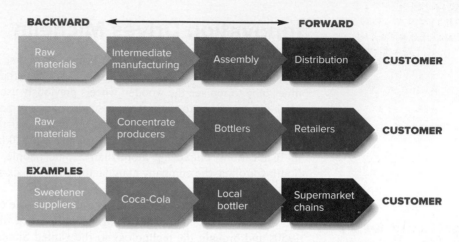

backward vertical integration not only supplies Tesla's need for inputs to make the new electric car model, it is also expected to help lower the cost of the batteries.[57]

Figure 8.6 illustrates the four main stages in a typical raw material to customer value chain; value is added to the product at each stage by the activities involved in each industry. For a company based in the assembly stage, backward integration would involve establishing a new division in the intermediate manufacturing or raw material production industries, and forward integration would involve establishing a new division to distribute its products to wholesalers or a retail division to sell directly to customers. A division at one stage or one industry receives the product produced by the division in the previous stage or industry, transforms it in some way—adding value, and then transfers the output at a higher price to the division at the next stage in the chain.

As an example of how this industry value chain works, consider the cola segment of the soft drink industry. In the raw material industry, suppliers include sugar companies and manufacturers of artificial sweeteners such as NutraSweet and Splenda, which are used in diet colas. These companies sell their products to companies in the soft drink industry that make concentrate—such as Coca-Cola and PepsiCo—which mix these inputs with others to produce the cola concentrate. In the process, they add value to these inputs. The concentrate producers then sell the concentrate to companies in the bottling and distribution industry, which add carbonated water to the concentrate and package the resulting drinks—again adding value to the concentrate. Next the bottlers distribute and sell the soft drinks to retailers, including stores such as Costco and Walmart and fast-food chains such as McDonald's. Companies in the retail industry add value by making the product accessible to customers, and they profit from direct sales to customers. Thus, value and profit are added by companies at each stage in the raw material to consumer chain.

Managers pursue vertical integration because it allows them either to add value to their products by making them special or unique or to lower the costs of making and selling them. An example of using forward vertical integration to increase differentiation is Apple's decision to open its own stores to make its unique products more accessible to customers who could try them out before they bought them. So, too, is PepsiCo's decision to buy its bottlers so they can better differentiate their products and lower costs in the future.

Although vertical integration can strengthen an organization's competitive advantage and increase its performance, it can also reduce its flexibility to respond to changing environmental conditions and create threats that must be countered by changing the organization's strategy. For example, P&G acquired the Gillette Company in 2005. Duracell batteries, a vertical integration for Gillette, came with it. However, Duracell stood out as an oddball among other products in P&G's portfolio, and the company was sold to Warren Buffett's Berkshire Hathaway in 2016.[58]

Thus, when considering vertical integration as a strategy to add value, managers must be careful because sometimes it may *reduce* a company's ability to create value when the environment changes. This is why so many companies have divested themselves of units that draw attention and resources away from an organization's primary purpose.

Diversification

diversification Expanding a company's business operations into a new industry in order to produce new kinds of valuable goods or services.

related diversification Entering a new business or industry to create a competitive advantage in one or more of an organization's existing divisions or businesses.

synergy Performance gains that result when individuals and departments coordinate their actions.

Diversification is the corporate-level strategy of expanding a company's business operations into a new industry in order to produce new kinds of valuable goods or services.[59] Examples include PepsiCo's diversification into the snack food business with the purchase of Frito Lay and Cisco's diversification into consumer electronics when it purchased Linksys. There are two main kinds of diversification: related and unrelated.

RELATED DIVERSIFICATION **Related diversification** is the strategy of entering a new business or industry to create a competitive advantage in one or more of an organization's existing divisions or businesses. Related diversification can add value to an organization's products if managers can find ways for its various divisions or business units to share their valuable skills or resources so that synergy is created.[60] **Synergy** is obtained when the value created by two divisions cooperating is greater than the value that would be created if the two divisions operated separately and independently. For example, suppose two or more divisions of a diversified company can use the same manufacturing facilities, distribution channels, or advertising campaigns—that is, share functional activities. Each division has to invest fewer resources in a shared functional activity than it would have to invest if it performed the functional activity by itself. Related diversification can be a major source of cost savings when divisions share the costs of performing a functional activity.[61] Similarly, if one division's R&D skills can improve another division's products and increase their differentiated appeal, this synergy can give the second division an important competitive advantage over its industry rivals—so the company as a whole benefits from diversification.

The way Procter & Gamble's disposable diaper and paper towel divisions cooperate is a good example of the successful production of synergies. These divisions share the costs of procuring inputs such as paper and packaging; a joint sales force sells both products to retail outlets; and both products are shipped using the same distribution system. This resource sharing has enabled both divisions to reduce their costs, and as a result, they can charge lower prices than their competitors and so attract more customers.[62] In addition, the divisions can share the research costs of developing new and improved products, such as finding more absorbent material, that increase both products' differentiated appeal. This is something that is also at the heart of 3M's corporate strategy. From the beginning, 3M has pursued related diversification and created new businesses by leveraging its skills in research and development. Today the company has five business groups that share resources such as technology and marketing. The five groups are industrial, consumer, safety and graphics, health care, and electronics and energy. The company spends about 5.8% of its annual sales on research and development, which helps produce more than 3,000 new patents each year and a steady stream of unique products for consumers and businesses alike.[63]

How does 3M do it? First, the company is a science-based enterprise with a strong tradition of innovation and risk taking. Risk taking is encouraged, and failure is not punished but is seen as a natural part of the process of creating new products and businesses.[64] Second, 3M's management is relentlessly focused on the company's customers and the problems they face. Many of 3M's products have come from helping customers to solve difficult problems. Third, managers set stretch goals that require the company to create new products and businesses at a rapid rate. Fourth, employees are given considerable autonomy to pursue their own ideas; indeed, 15% of employees' time can be spent working on projects of their own choosing without management approval. Many products have resulted from this autonomy, including the ubiquitous Post-it Notes. Fifth, while products

How did we ever survive without Post-it Notes? 3M's intense focus on solving customer problems results in new products that sell well, including countless variations of the original sticky note.
©Kuznetsov Alexey/Shutterstock

belong to business units and business units are responsible for generating profits, the technologies belong to every unit within the company. Anyone at 3M is free to try to develop new applications for a technology developed by its business units. Finally, 3M organizes many companywide meetings where researchers from its different divisions are brought together to share the results of their work.

In sum, to pursue related diversification successfully, managers search for new businesses where they can use the existing skills and resources in their departments and divisions to create synergies, add value to new products and businesses, and improve their competitive position and that of the entire company. In addition, managers may try to acquire a company in a new industry because they believe it possesses skills and resources that will improve the performance of one or more of their existing divisions. If successful, such skill transfers can help an organization to lower its costs or better differentiate its products because they create synergies between divisions.

UNRELATED DIVERSIFICATION Managers pursue **unrelated diversification** when they establish divisions or buy companies in new industries that are *not* linked in any way to their current businesses or industries. One main reason for pursuing unrelated diversification is that sometimes managers can buy a poorly performing company, transfer their management skills to that company, turn around its business, and increase its performance—all of which create value.

Another reason for pursuing unrelated diversification is that purchasing businesses in different industries lets managers engage in *portfolio strategy,* which is apportioning financial resources among divisions to increase financial returns or spread risks among different businesses, much as individual investors do with their own portfolios. For example, managers may transfer funds from a rich division (a "cash cow") to a new and promising division (a "star") and, by appropriately allocating money between divisions, create value. Though used as a popular explanation in the 1980s for unrelated diversification, portfolio strategy ran into increasing criticism in the 1990s because it simply does not work.[65] Why? As managers expand the scope of their organization's operations and enter more and more industries, it becomes increasingly difficult for top managers to be knowledgeable about all of the organization's diverse businesses. Managers do not have the time to process all of the information required to adequately assess the strategy and performance of each division, so the performance of the entire company often falls.

Thus, although unrelated diversification can create value for a company, research evidence suggests that *too much* diversification can cause managers to lose control of their organization's core business. As a result, diversification can reduce value rather than create it.[66] Because of this, during the last decade there has been an increasing trend for diversified companies to divest many of their unrelated, and sometimes related, divisions. Managers in companies like Novartis, Nestlé, and Textron have sold off numerous divisions and focused on increasing performance of the businesses that remained—in other words, they went back to a strategy of concentrating on a limited number of industries. In 2016, for example, Honeywell International sold its technology development and engineering unit to KBR, an engineering and construction conglomerate, in an effort to streamline its business portfolio and concentrate on the aerospace industry.[67]

International Expansion

As if planning whether to vertically integrate, diversify, or concentrate on the core business were not a difficult enough task, corporate-level managers also must decide on the appropriate way to compete internationally. A basic question confronts the managers of any organization that needs to sell its products abroad and compete in more than one national market: To what extent should the organization customize features of its products and marketing campaign to different national conditions?

If managers decide that their organization should sell the same standardized product in each national market in which it competes, and use the same basic marketing approach, they adopt a **global strategy**. Such companies undertake little, if any, customization to suit the specific needs of customers in different countries. But if managers decide to customize products and marketing strategies to specific national conditions, they adopt a **multidomestic strategy**. Panasonic has traditionally pursued a global strategy, selling the same basic TVs, camcorders, and DVD and MP3 players in every country in which it does business and often using the same basic marketing

unrelated diversification Entering a new industry or buying a company in a new industry that is not related in any way to an organization's current businesses or industries.

global strategy Selling the same standardized product and using the same basic marketing approach in each national market.

multidomestic strategy Customizing products and marketing strategies to specific national conditions.

approach. Unilever, the European food and household products company, has pursued a multidomestic strategy. Thus, to appeal to German customers, Unilever's German division sells a different range of food products and uses a different marketing approach than its North American division.

Both global and multidomestic strategies have advantages and disadvantages. The major advantage of a global strategy is the significant cost savings associated with not having to customize products and marketing approaches to different national conditions. For example, Rolex watches, Ralph Lauren or Tommy Hilfiger clothing, Chanel or Armani clothing or accessories or perfume, Apple computers, Chinese-made plastic toys, and U.S.-grown rice and wheat are all products that can be sold using the same marketing across many countries by simply changing the language. Thus, companies can save a significant amount of money. Organizations that serve business customers often adopt a global strategy because customer needs such as improving quality and lowering costs are consistent from place to place. For an example of such a company, see the "Managing Globally" feature.

MANAGING GLOBALLY

Early U.S. Wins Help FourKites Fly Overseas

The founders of FourKites met in engineering school in Chennai, India, and then embarked on careers with U.S.-based companies.[68] Arun Chandrasekaran worked for Cognizant, Microsoft, and Groupon. Mathew Elenjickal continued his studies in engineering and management at Northwestern University before taking jobs at Oracle and i2 Technologies/JDA. The two friends encountered a widespread business problem: When will deliveries arrive? Having kept in touch, they decided to form a company that would provide reliable answers.

FourKites gathers data from trucks' onboard computers, along with weather and traffic updates, to recalculate each truck's expected arrival time at a given location.[69] Even without FourKites, an individual driver can use a smartphone app or global positioning system (GPS) to get an arrival estimate. But big companies await deliveries from thousands of trucks run by independent contractors using different devices. FourKites combines data from all those sources and provides updates for any truck in the fleet. Further, the analytical software identifies information changes that will affect arrival time, so the system sends only relevant notifications. For example, a storm or traffic jam likely to delay delivery would trigger an alert. Since launching, FourKites has added tracking of ships and trains, as well as tracking of temperature in refrigerated trucks, which is essential for transporting perishable foods.

FourKites delivers alerts in real time, as problems arise. When customers recognize problems right away, they often can make corrections. FourKites' customers report measurable improvements in the percentage of on-time deliveries. For example, Smithfield Foods says on-time deliveries rose from 87% to 94%, and Kraft Heinz improved on-time deliveries from around 50% to better than 75%.[70]

On-time deliveries translate into efficient operations and satisfied customers. The salespeople at FourKites say business clients are eager to discuss this solution to a vexing problem.[71] Those who signed a deal include Best Buy, Kraft Heinz, Nokia, and Procter & Gamble.[72] They report less time wasted waiting for deliveries at warehouses and declines in stock shortages.

FourKites started with two headquarters, in Chicago and Chennai.[73] The Chennai office focuses on developing new software, while the Chicago office started by building sales in the United States, later signing up a trucking firm that also operates in Mexico. As FourKites grows, it has raised funds for global expansion. The company hired Dave Walker to serve as chief revenue officer, in charge of building a global sales force. Initial wins include Unilever in Europe and Anheuser-Busch InBev in South Africa.

The offices of Hindustan Unilever Limited in Mumbai, India. Unilever uses a multidomestic strategy to market its products globally.
©INDRANIL MUKHERJEE/Getty images

The major disadvantage of pursuing a global strategy is that by ignoring national differences, managers may leave themselves vulnerable to local competitors that differentiate their products to suit local tastes. Global food makers Kellogg's and Nestlé learned this when they entered the Indian processed food market, which is worth over $100 billion a year. These companies did not understand how to customize their products to the tastes of the Indian market and initially suffered large losses. When Kellogg's launched its breakfast cereals in India, for example, it failed to understand that most Indians eat cooked breakfasts because milk is normally not pasteurized. Today, with the growing availability of pasteurized or canned milk, it offers exotic cereals made from basmati rice and flavored with mango to appeal to customers. Similarly, Nestlé's Maggi noodles failed to please Indian customers until it gave them a "marsala" or mixed curry spice flavor; today its noodles have become a staple in Indian diets.[74]

The advantages and disadvantages of a multidomestic strategy are the opposite of those of a global strategy. The major advantage of a multidomestic strategy is that by customizing product offerings and marketing approaches to local conditions, managers may be able to gain market share or charge higher prices for their products. The major disadvantage is that customization raises production costs and puts the multidomestic company at a price disadvantage because it often has to charge prices higher than the prices charged by competitors pursuing a global strategy. Obviously, the choice between these two strategies calls for trade-offs.

CHOOSING A WAY TO EXPAND INTERNATIONALLY
As we have discussed, a more competitive global environment has proved to be both an opportunity and a threat for organizations and managers. The opportunity is that organizations that expand globally can open new markets, reach more customers, and gain access to new sources of raw materials and to low-cost suppliers of inputs. The threat is that organizations that expand globally are likely to encounter new competitors in the foreign countries they enter and must respond to new political, economic, and cultural conditions.

Before setting up foreign operations, managers of companies such as Amazon.com, Lands' End, GE, P&G, and Boeing needed to analyze the forces in the environment of a particular country (such as Korea or Brazil) to choose the right method to expand and respond to those forces in the most appropriate way. In general, four basic ways to operate in the global environment are exporting and importing, licensing and franchising, strategic alliances, and wholly owned foreign subsidiaries. We briefly discuss each one, moving from the lowest level of foreign involvement and investment required of a global organization and its managers, and the least amount of risk, to the high end of the spectrum (see Figure 8.7).[75]

EXPORTING AND IMPORTING
The least complex global operations are exporting and importing. A company engaged in **exporting** makes products at home and sells them abroad. An organization might sell its own products abroad or allow a local organization in the foreign country to distribute its products. Few risks are associated with exporting because a company does not have to invest in developing manufacturing facilities abroad. It can further reduce its investment abroad if it allows a local company to distribute its products.

A company engaged in **importing** sells products at home that are made abroad (products it makes itself or buys from other companies). For example, most of the products that Pier 1 Imports sells to its customers are made abroad. In many cases the appeal of a product—Irish crystal, French wine, Italian furniture, or Indian silk—is that it is made abroad. The Internet has made it much easier for companies to tell potential foreign buyers about their products; detailed product specifications and features are available online, and informed buyers can communicate easily with prospective sellers.

LICENSING AND FRANCHISING
In **licensing**, a company (the licenser) allows a foreign organization (the licensee) to take charge of both manufacturing and distributing one or more of its products in the licensee's country or world region in return for a negotiated fee. Chemical

exporting Making products at home and selling them abroad.

importing Selling products at home that are made abroad.

licensing Allowing a foreign organization to take charge of manufacturing and distributing a product in its country or world region in return for a negotiated fee.

Figure 8.7

Four Ways to Expand Internationally

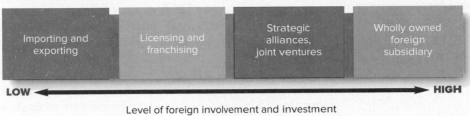

Importing and exporting | Licensing and franchising | Strategic alliances, joint ventures | Wholly owned foreign subsidiary

LOW ◄─────────────────────► **HIGH**

Level of foreign involvement and investment
and degree of risk

maker DuPont might license a local factory in India to produce nylon or Teflon. The advantage of licensing is that the licenser does not have to bear the development costs associated with opening up in a foreign country; the licensee bears the costs. The risks associated with this strategy are that the company granting the license has to give its foreign partner access to its technological know-how and, so, risks losing control of its secrets.

Whereas licensing is pursued primarily by manufacturing companies, franchising is pursued primarily by service organizations. In **franchising**, a company (the franchiser) sells to a foreign organization (the franchisee) the rights to use its brand name and operating know-how in return for a lump-sum payment and share of the franchiser's profits. Hilton Hotels might sell a franchise to a local company in Chile to operate hotels under the Hilton name in return for a franchise payment. The advantage of franchising is that the franchiser does not have to bear the development costs of overseas expansion and avoids the many problems associated with setting up foreign operations. The downside is that the organization that grants the franchise may lose control over how the franchisee operates, and product quality may fall. In this way franchisers, such as Hilton, Avis, and McDonald's, risk losing their good names. American customers who buy McDonald's hamburgers in Korea may reasonably expect those burgers to be as good as the ones they get at home. If they are not, McDonald's reputation will suffer over time. Once again, the Internet facilitates communication between partners and allows them to better meet each other's expectations.

STRATEGIC ALLIANCES One way to overcome the loss-of-control problems associated with exporting, licensing, and franchising is to expand globally by means of a strategic alliance. In a **strategic alliance**, managers pool or share their organization's resources and know-how with those of a foreign company, and the two organizations share the rewards or risks of starting a new venture in a foreign country. Sharing resources allows a U.S. company, for example, to take advantage of the high-quality skills of foreign manufacturers and the specialized knowledge of foreign managers about the needs of local customers and to reduce the risks involved in a venture. At the same time, the terms of the alliance give the U.S. company more control over how the good or service is produced or sold in the foreign country than it would have as a franchiser or licenser.

A strategic alliance can take the form of a written contract between two or more companies to exchange resources, or it can result in the creation of a new organization. A **joint venture** is a strategic alliance between two or more companies that agree to jointly establish and share the ownership of a new business.[76] An organization's level of involvement abroad increases in a joint venture because the alliance normally involves a capital investment in production facilities abroad in order to produce goods or services outside the home country. Risk, however, is reduced. The Internet and global teleconferencing provide the increased communication and coordination necessary for global partners to work together. For example, General Mills participates in two international joint ventures. Cereal Partners Worldwide (CPW) is a 50–50 joint venture between General Mills and Nestlé, which markets breakfast cereals in more than 130 countries. CPW combines the expertise of General Mills—the second-largest cereal manufacturer in North America—with the worldwide presence and distribution strength of global giant Nestlé. General Mills' other joint venture is Häagen-Dazs shops. In 2017, these joint ventures accounted for $1 billion of revenue for General Mills.[77]

---

franchising Selling to a foreign organization the rights to use a brand name and operating know-how in return for a lump-sum payment and a share of the profits.

strategic alliance An agreement in which managers pool or share their organization's resources and know-how with a foreign company, and the two organizations share the rewards and risks of starting a new venture.

joint venture A strategic alliance among two or more companies that agree to jointly establish and share the ownership of a new business.

wholly owned foreign subsidiary Production operations established in a foreign country independent of any local direct involvement.

WHOLLY OWNED FOREIGN SUBSIDIARIES When managers decide to establish a **wholly owned foreign subsidiary**, they invest in establishing production operations in a foreign country independent of any local direct involvement. Many Japanese car component companies, for example, have established their own operations in the United States to supply U.S.-based Japanese carmakers such as Toyota and Honda with high-quality car components.

Operating alone, without any direct involvement from foreign companies, an organization receives all of the rewards and bears all of the risks associated with operating abroad.[78] This method of international expansion is much more expensive than the others because it requires a higher level of foreign investment and presents managers with many more threats. However, investment in a foreign subsidiary or division offers significant advantages: It gives an organization high potential returns because the organization does not have to share its profits with a foreign organization, and it reduces the level of risk because the organization's managers have full control over all aspects of their foreign subsidiary's operations. Moreover, this type of investment allows managers to protect their technology and know-how from foreign organizations. Large, well-known companies like DuPont, GM, and P&G, which have plenty of resources, make extensive use of wholly owned subsidiaries.

Planning and Implementing Strategy

LO8-5 Describe the vital role managers play in implementing strategies to achieve an organization's mission and goals.

After identifying appropriate business and corporate strategies to attain an organization's mission and goals, managers confront the challenge of putting those strategies into action. Strategy implementation is a five-step process:

1. Allocating responsibility for implementation to the appropriate individuals or groups
2. Drafting detailed action plans that specify how a strategy is to be implemented
3. Establishing a timetable for implementation that includes precise, measurable goals linked to the attainment of the action plan
4. Allocating appropriate resources to the responsible individuals or groups
5. Holding specific individuals or groups responsible for the attainment of corporate, divisional, and functional goals

The planning process goes beyond just identifying effective strategies; it also includes plans to ensure that these strategies are put into action. Normally, the plan for implementing a new strategy requires the development of new functional strategies, the redesign of an organization's structure, and the development of new control systems; it might also require a new program to change an organization's culture. These are issues we address in the next three chapters.

Summary and Review

LO8-1, 8-2

PLANNING Planning is a three-step process: (1) determining an organization's mission and goals, (2) formulating strategy, and (3) implementing strategy. Managers use planning to identify and select appropriate goals and courses of action for an organization and to decide how to allocate the resources they need to attain those goals and carry out those actions. A good plan builds commitment for the organization's goals, gives the organization a sense of direction and purpose, coordinates the different functions and divisions of the organization, and controls managers by making them accountable for specific goals. In large organizations, planning takes place at three levels: corporate, business or divisional, and functional or departmental. Long-term plans have a time horizon of five years or more; intermediate-term plans, between one and five years; and short-term plans, one year or less.

LO8-1, 8-2, 8-3, 8-4

DETERMINING MISSION AND GOALS AND FORMULATING STRATEGY Determining the organization's mission requires that managers define the business of the organization and establish major goals. Strategy formulation requires that managers perform a SWOT analysis and then choose appropriate strategies at the corporate, business, and functional levels. At the business level, managers are responsible for developing a successful low-cost and/or differentiation strategy, either for the whole market or a particular segment of it. At the functional level, departmental managers develop strategies to help the organization either add value to its products by differentiating them or lower the costs of value creation. At the corporate level, organizations use strategies such as concentration on a single industry, vertical integration, related and unrelated diversification, and international expansion to strengthen their competitive advantage by increasing the value of the goods and services provided to customers.

LO8-5 **IMPLEMENTING STRATEGY** Strategy implementation requires that managers allocate responsibilities to appropriate individuals or groups; draft detailed action plans that specify how a strategy is to be implemented; establish a timetable for implementation that includes precise, measurable goals linked to the attainment of the action plan; allocate appropriate resources to the responsible individuals or groups; and hold individuals or groups accountable for the attainment of goals.

Management in Action

Topics for Discussion and Action

Discussion

1. Describe the three steps of planning. Explain how they are related. [LO8-1]

2. How can scenario planning help managers predict the future? [LO8-2]

3. What is the relationship among corporate-, business-, and functional-level strategies, and how do they create value for an organization? [LO8-3, 8-4]

4. Pick an industry and identify four companies in the industry that pursue one of the four main business-level strategies (low-cost, focused low-cost, and so on). [LO8-2, 8-3]

5. What is the difference between vertical integration and related diversification? [LO8-4]

Action

5. Ask a manager about the kinds of planning exercises he or she regularly uses. What are the purposes of these exercises, and what are their advantages or disadvantages? [LO8-1, 8-2]

7. Ask a manager to identify the corporate- and business-level strategies used by his or her organization. [LO8-3, 8-4]

Building Management Skills

How to Analyze a Company's Strategy [LO8-3, 8-4]

Pick a well-known business organization that has received recent press coverage and that provides annual reports on its website. From the information in the articles and annual reports, answer these questions:

1. What is (are) the main industry(ies) in which the company competes?

2. What business-level strategy does the company seem to be pursuing in this industry? Why?

3. What corporate-level strategies is the company pursuing? Why?

4. Have there been any major changes in its strategy recently? Why?

Managing Ethically [LO8-2, 8-5]

A few years ago, IBM announced that it had fired the three top managers of its Argentine division because of their involvement in a scheme to secure a $250 million contract for IBM to provide and service the computers of one of Argentina's largest state-owned banks. The three executives paid $14 million of the contract money to a third company, CCR, which paid nearly $6 million to phantom companies. This $6 million was then used to bribe the bank executives, who agreed to give IBM the contract.

These bribes are not necessarily illegal under Argentine law. Moreover, the three managers argued that all companies have to pay bribes to get new business contracts, and they were not doing anything that managers in other companies were not.

Questions

1. Either by yourself or in a group, decide if the business practice of paying bribes is ethical or unethical.

2. Should IBM allow its foreign divisions to pay bribes if all other companies are doing so?

3. If bribery is common in a particular country, what effect does this likely have on the nation's economy and culture?

Small Group Breakout Exercise

Low-Cost or Differentiation? [LO8-2, 8-3]

Form groups of three or four people, and appoint one member as the spokesperson who will communicate your findings to the class when called on by the instructor. Then discuss the following scenario:

You are a team of managers of a major national clothing chain, and you have been charged with finding a way to restore your organization's competitive advantage. Recently, your organization has been experiencing increasing competition from two sources. First, discount stores such as Walmart and Target have been undercutting your prices because they buy their clothes from low-cost foreign manufacturers, whereas you buy most of yours from high-quality domestic suppliers. Discount stores have been attracting your customers who buy at the low end of the price range. Second, small boutiques opening in malls provide high-price designer clothing and are attracting your customers at the high end of the market. Your company has become stuck in the middle, and you have to decide what to do: Should you start to buy abroad so you can lower your prices and pursue a low-cost strategy? Should you focus on the high end of the market and become more of a differentiator? Or should you try to pursue both a low-cost strategy and a differentiation strategy?

1. Using scenario planning, analyze the pros and cons of each alternative.

2. Think about the various clothing retailers in your local malls and city, and analyze the choices they have made about how to compete along the low-cost and differentiation dimensions.

Be the Manager [LO8-2, 8-3]

A group of investors in your city is considering opening a new upscale supermarket to compete with the major supermarket chains that are currently dominating the city's marketplace. They have called you in to help them determine what kind of upscale supermarket they should open. In other words, how can they best develop a competitive advantage against existing supermarket chains?

Questions

1. List the supermarket chains in your city, and identify their strengths and weaknesses.

2. What business-level strategies are these supermarkets currently pursuing?

3. What kind of supermarket would do best against the competition? What kind of business-level strategy should it pursue?

Bloomberg Case in the News

The Tiny Ikea of the Future, Without Meatballs or Showroom Mazes [LO 8-1, 8-2]

Whether in San Diego, Novosibirsk, or Tokyo, the Ikea experience is almost as standardized as its flat packs. The blue-and-yellow big box, the vast showroom maze, the Swedish meatballs in the cafeteria—this formula propelled Ikea of Sweden AB to global No. 1 in furniture retailing, with €38.3 billion ($45.7 billion) in sales and more than 400 stores in 49 countries.

There are no meatballs in Ikea's newest London outlet, part of a shopping mall in a redeveloped urban neighborhood near the 2012 Summer Olympics complex. One of two dozen small-scale stores that Ikea has opened since 2015, it measures only 900 square meters (about 9,700 square feet), while the typical suburban Ikea sprawls across more than 25,000 square meters. It has a few model rooms fitted out with furniture and accessories, but hardly anything can be purchased and taken home immediately. Instead, shoppers use touchscreen computers to place orders and arrange for delivery or pickup later.

Even the do-it-yourself ritual is optional: Customers can request assembly help from TaskRabbit Inc., a San Francisco-based startup that Ikea recently acquired. Task-Rabbit will dispatch someone to their homes to assemble that Billy bookcase.

Ikea is trying to future-proof its global dominance with these smaller outlets and with other initiatives including pop-up stores and expansion of its e-commerce footprint. "We will test and try to develop a new world of Ikea," says Ikea Chief Executive Officer Jesper Brodin. "It's a revolutionary speed that we're taking on right now."

Ikea can't afford to move slowly. Foot traffic at its traditional stores has been stagnant for most of the past five years, as young people—long its core customers—move into big cities, drive less frequently, and do more of their shopping online. Young couples who might earlier have spent a weekend afternoon at Ikea are more likely now to do their browsing online.

"The entire premise that Ikea developed was that consumers would be willing to drive their cars 50 kilometers to save some money on something that looks amazing," says Ray Gaul, an analyst at Kantar Retail in London. "Young people like Ikea, but they can't or don't want to drive to Ikea," he says. "Ikea has no choice but to invest in better services."

Ikea also is scrambling to catch up in e-commerce. Online sales of furniture and appliances worldwide are expected to grow almost 12% annually over the next three years, outpacing better-established categories such as consumer electronics, according to research by data analytics group Statista Inc. Yet Ikea offers online sales in only half of the markets where it operates, according to Bloomberg Intelligence.

The company is battling aggressive competitors such as Wayfair Inc., a Boston-based home-furnishing e-tailer founded in 2011 that now does more than $4 billion in sales across the U.S. and Europe. Amazon.com Inc. last fall launched its own furniture lines,

including a midcentury-modern brand called Rivet aimed at cost-conscious millennials. Ikea says it plans to offer online sales globally by the end of 2018 and will soon begin selling goods on third-party sites such as Amazon and Alibaba Group Holding Ltd.'s Tmall, although details haven't been disclosed.

The 24 smaller-footprint outlets that Ikea has opened are in Canada, China, Japan, and countries in Europe; so far there are none in the U.S. Each is slightly different, allowing the company to test various alternatives: downtown streets vs. shopping malls, with or without cafes, which are in stores ranging from London's diminutive size to about 4,000 square meters.

At the London store, the only refreshment offered is from a coffee machine. Instead of a supervised kids' play area, another staple of the Ikea experience, there are a couple of tablet computers loaded with *Candy Crush*. Still, with as many as 20 staff members on duty at peak times, customers can expect "more of a personal shopping experience" than at a traditional Ikea, says London store manager Mirco Righetto. Employees help customers plan larger projects such as kitchen renovations with the aid of virtual-reality software.

To try out new formats, Ikea recently opened a pop-up in central Madrid that offers only bedroom furnishings. Another, in Stockholm, specializes in kitchens and invites shoppers to cook on the premises.

The company is also rolling out new technologies. An augmented-reality app launched last fall, called Ikea Place, lets customers visualize how their purchases will look inside their homes. Part of the digital expansion includes an overhaul of logistics capabilities to speed the process of ordering, pickup, and delivery. "It's a huge investment to make sure we transform into a multichannel company," CEO Brodin says.

The payoff from these initiatives isn't yet clear. Visits to the ikea.com website have grown about 10% annually over the past two years, but brick-and-mortar stores still account for well over 90% of sales.

Some customers aren't sold on the smaller stores. "The showroom isn't extensive enough," says Bora Assumani, a fitness instructor shopping at the London store. "I like to be able to touch and see everything before I buy." Another shopper, Susan Davies, says she wanted "a bigger selection of little things to buy now."

Still, Ikea says its efforts are attracting customers who might otherwise never have shopped there. In Madrid, for example, 70% of people visiting the bedroom pop-up store had never been to an Ikea big-box store, says Stefan Sjostrand, the company's global commercial manager. What's more, he says, e-commerce sales in Madrid have risen more than 50% since the shop opened. In Canada, sales at new, smaller outlets in Quebec City and London, Ont., have been so strong that Ikea now plans to open full-size suburban stores nearby.

"We are surprising the customer," Sjostrand says. "They are getting an emotional connection to the brand."

Questions for Discussion

1. Are the functional-level strategies the same for managers of both types of Ikea stores? Explain your reasoning.

2. How would Ikea managers utilize scenario planning when it comes to expanding the company's e-commerce footprint? Provide some examples.

3. Provide a SWOT analysis for the smaller Ikea stores.

Source: Carol Matlack, "The Tiny Ikea of the Future, Without Meatballs or Showroom Mazes," *Bloomberg,* January 10, 2018, https://www.bloomberg.com/news/articles/2018-01-10/the-tiny-ikea-of-the-future-without-meatballs-or-showroom-mazes. Used with permission of Bloomberg L.P. Copyright © 2017. All rights reserved.

Notes

1. Marriott International, "Marriott International Reports Strong Fourth Quarter 2017 Results," news release, February 14, 2018, accessed at www.prnewswire.com; K. Ryssdal and R. Garrova, "How the World's Largest Hotel Company Adapts to a Changing Economy," *Marketplace,* www.marketplace.org, October 4, 2017; S. Tully, "Marriott Goes All In," *Fortune,* June 15, 2017, 200-208.

2. Tully, "Marriott Goes All In"; Marriott International, "Marriott International Reports Strong Fourth Quarter 2017."

3. Tully, "Marriott Goes All In"; Ryssdal and Garrova, "How the World's Largest Hotel Company Adapts."

4. J. T. Fox, "At Davos, U.S. Hospitality Industry Responds to International Visitor Downturn," *Hotel Management,* www.hotelmanagement.net, January 26, 2018; L. Gallagher, "Marriott's Latest New York Hotel Is for the Airbnb Generation," *Fortune,* http://fortune.com, November 11, 2017.

5. Tully, "Marriott Goes All In"; Ryssdal and Garrova, "How the World's Largest Hotel Company Adapts."

6. Tully, "Marriott Goes All In"; Gallagher, "Marriott's Latest New York Hotel."

7. Tully, "Marriott Goes All In"; Gallagher, "Marriott's Latest New York Hotel"; Fox, "At Davos, U.S. Hospitality Industry Responds."

8. A. Chandler, *Strategy and Structure: Chapters In the History of the American Enterprise* (Cambridge, MA: MIT Press, 1962).

9. "Our Mission," http://about.nike.com, accessed March 24, 2018.

10. Chandler, *Strategy and Structure.*

11. H. Fayol, *General and Industrial Management* (1884; New York: IEEE Press, 1984).

12. Ibid., 18.

13. K. L. Painter, "General Mills Says Jeffrey Harmening Will Become CEO on June 1," *Star Tribune,* www.startribune.com, May 3, 2017.

14. "Businesses," www.generalmills.com, accessed March 24, 2018; "General Mills Announces New Organizational Structure to Maximize Global Scale," www.prnewswire, December 5, 2016.

15. "Global Growth and Returns: General Mills 2017 Annual Report," www.generalmills.com, accessed March 24, 2018; A. Smith, "General Mills to Buy Blue Buffalo Pet Food for $8 Billion," *CNNMoney,* http://money.cnn.com, February 23, 2018.

16. L. Chevreux, J. Lopez, and X. Mesnard, "The Best Companies Know How to Balance Strategy and Purpose," *Harvard Business Review,* https://hbr.org, November 2, 2017.

17. M. E. Shoup, "General Mills Optimistic on Yogurt Business as It Eyes More Markets," *Dairy Reporter,* www.dairyreporter.com, February 22, 2018.

18. "Global Growth and Returns: General Mills 2017 Annual Report."

19. C.W. Hofer and D. Schendel, *Strategy Formulation: Analytical Concepts* (St. Paul, MN: West, 1978).

20. J. Bennett, "NASA's Next Great Mars Rover Will Search for Martians and Prepare for Humans to Follow," *Popular Mechanics,* www.popularmechanics.com, January 17, 2018.

21. K. Ryssdal and B. Bodnar, "CEO Deborah Flint Is at the Helm of LAX and Its Multibillion Dollar Makeover," *Marketplace,* www.marketplace.org, June 9, 2017; "Ale Flint Confirmed as New Head of Los Angeles Airports Authority," KPCC, www.scpr.org, June 23, 2015.

22. Ryssdal and Bodnar, "CEO Deborah Flint Is at the Helm."

23. Ryssdal and Bodnar, "CEO Deborah Flint Is At the Helm"; J. Bates, "LA Story," *Airport World,* www.airport-world.com, May 11, 2017; "Here's a Look into LAX's $14 Billion Facelift," *CBS Los Angeles,* http://losangeles.cbslocal.com, November 15, 2017; J. Bates, "Airport Carbon Accreditation Success for LAX and Van Nuys," *Airport World,* www.airport-world.com, September 19, 2017.

24. Bates, "LA Story"; D. Symonds, "LAX Board Authorizes Contract for LAMP Infrastructure," *Passenger Terminal Today,* www.passengerterminaltoday.com, January 25, 2018.

25. Ryssdal and Bodnar, "CEO Deborah Flint Is at the Helm."

26. Bates, "LA Story"; Ryssdal and Bodnar, "CEO Deborah Flint Is At the Helm."

27. "What Are Shell Scenarios?" www.shell.com, accessed March 24, 2018.

28. P. Wack, "Scenarios: Shooting the Rapids," *Harvard Business Review,* November-December 1985, 139-50.

29. "New Lens Scenario: A Better Life with a Healthy Planet," www.shell.com, accessed March 24, 2018.

30. J. A. Pearce, "The Company Mission as a Strategic Tool," *Sloan Management Review,* Spring 1992, 15-24.

31. D.F. Abell, *Defining the Business: The Starting Point of Strategic Planning* (Englewood Cliffs, NJ: Prentice-Hall, 1980).

32. G. Hamel and C.K. Prahalad, "Strategic Intent," *Harvard Business Review,* May-June 1989, 63-73.

33. D.I. Jung and B.J. Avolio, "Opening the Black Box: An Experimental Investigation of the Mediating Effects of Trust and Value Congruence on Transformational and Transactional Leadership," *Journal of Organizational Behavior,* December 2000, 949-64; B.M. Bass and B.J. Avolio, "Transformational and Transactional Leadership: 1992 and Beyond," *Journal of European Industrial Training,* January 1990, 20-35.

34. E.A. Locke, G.P. Latham, and M. Erez, "The Determinants of Goal Commitment," *Academy of Management Review* 13 (1988), 23-39.

35. "Global Growth and Returns: General Mills 2017 Annual Report."

36. K.R. Andrews, *The Concept of Corporate Strategy* (Homewood, IL: Irwin, 1971).

37. S. Kumar, J. Eiden, and D. N. Perdomo, "Clash of the e-Commerce Titans: A New Paradigm for Consumer Purchase Process Improvement," *International Journal of Productivity and Performance Management* 61, no.7 (2012), 805-30.

38. Y. Chen, "What You Need to Know about Walmart's e-Commerce Acquisition Spree," *Digiday,* https://digiday.com, August 11, 2017; G. Petro, "Amazon's Acquisition of Whole Foods Is About Two Things: Data and Product," *Forbes,* www.forbes.com, August 2, 2017.

39. M.E. Porter, "How Competititve Forces Shape Strategy," *Harvard Business Review,* March-April 1979.

40. M. Segarra, "Toys R Us and Why the Retail Downturn Is All About Debt," *Marketplace,* www.marketplace.org, March 14, 2018.

41. D. Green, "Toys R Us Is Closing or Selling All of Its US Stores—Here's Why the Company Couldn't Be Saved," *Business Insider,* www.businessinsider.com, March 15, 2018.

42. R.D. Aveni, *Hypercompetition* (New York: Free Press, 1994).

43. M.E. Porter, *Competitive Strategy* (New York: Free Press, 1980).

44. "About Southwest," https://www.southwest.com, accessed March 24, 2018.

45. S. Grobart, "Tim Cook: The Complete Interview," *Bloomberg Businessweek,* www.bloomberg.com, accessed March 24, 2018.

46. Porter, *Competitive Strategy.*

47. S. Chaudhuri and P. Kowsmann, "Zara Owner Inditex Stays Ahead of the

Competition," *The Wall Street Journal,* www.wsj.com, June 15, 2016.

48. P. Kowsmann, "Fast Fashion: How a Zara Coat Went from Design to Fifth Avenue in 25 Days," *The Wall Street Journal,* www.wsj.com, accessed March 24, 2018.

49. "Innovation in Tires," www.michelin.com, accessed March 25, 2018.

50. "About Michelin North America," www.michelinman.com, accessed March 25, 2018.

51. Ibid.

52. Pete Selleck, "The Michelin Man Who Helped Transform South Carolina," *The State,* www.thestate.com, accessed March 25, 2018.

53. M. Bartiromo, "Bartiromo Talks Tires with USA's Michelin Man, *USA Today,* www.usatoday.com, accessed March 25, 2018.

54. "The Birth of the Michelin Man," *Logo/Design/Love,* www.logodesignlove.com, accessed March 25, 2018.

55. "Michelin Guide," https://guide.michelin.com, accessed March 25, 2018. B. Krystal, "What You Need to Know About the Michelin Guide Before It's Released in Washington," *The Washington Post,* https://www.washingtonpost.com, accessed March 25, 2018.

56. M.K. Perry, "Vertical Integration: Determinants and Effects," in R. Schmalensee and R.D. Willig, eds., *Handbook of Industrial Organization,* vol. 1 (New York: Elsevier Science, 1989).

57. "Model 3," www.tesla.com, accessed March 25, 2018; F. Lambert, "Tesla Increases Hiring Effort at Gigafactory 1 to Reach Goal of 35 GWh of Battery Production," https://electrek.co, January 3, 2018; M. DeBord, "Tesla Is Investing $350 Million in Its Giant Gigafactory and Hiring Hundreds of Workers," *Business Insider,* www.businessinsider.com, January 18, 2017; A. Mamiit, "Tesla Motors' $5 Billion Gigafactory Now Online: World's Biggest Factory Starts Battery Production,"

Tech Times, www.techtimes.com, January 4, 2017.

58. A. Coolidge, "Duracell Leaves P&G Fold," *Cincinnati Enquirer,* www.cincinnati.com, March 1, 2016.

59. E. Penrose, *The Theory of the Growth of the Firm* (Oxford: Oxford University Press, 1959).

60. M.E. Porter, "From Competitive Advantage to Corporate Strategy," *Harvard Business Review* 65 (1987), 43–59.

61. D.J. Teece, "Economies of Scope and the Scope of the Enterprise," *Journal of Economic Behavior and Organization* 3 (1980), 223–47.

62. M.E. Porter, *Competitive Advantage: Creating and Sustaining Superior Performance* (New York: Free Press, 1985).

63. "3M Research & Development," www.3m.com, accessed March 25, 2018.

64. D. Schiff, "How 3M Drives Innovation through Empathy and Collaboration," *Forbes,* www.forbes.com, March 31, 2016.

65. For a review of the evidence, see C.W.L. Hill and G.R. Jones, *Strategic Management: An Integrated Approach,* 5th ed. (Boston: Houghton Mifflin, 2011), chap.10.

66. "Global Corporate Divestment Study 2018," http://cdn.ey.com, accessed March 25, 2018.

67. "KBR Closes HTSI Buyout, Fortifies Government Services Unit," www.zacks.com, September 20, 2016; D. Diakantonis, "Honeywell Sheds Cybersecurity Division, Following Plans to Spin Off Resins Business," *Mergers & Acquisitions,* www.themiddlemarket.com, August 12, 2016.

68. M. Siva, "A View from the Top on Supply Chain Process," *Hindu Business Line,* www.hindubusinessline.com, October 30, 2017.

69. Siva, "A View from the Top"; R. Starr, "Is FourKites Tracking Technology a Game Changer for Small Trucking Companies?" *Small Business Trends,* https://smallbiztrends.com, June 21, 2017;

C. Loizos, "FourKites Raises $13 Million to Track Trucks on the Road for Customers Like Staples," *TechCrunch,* https://techcrunch.com, October 12, 2016; J. Smith, "'Amazon Effect' Sparks Deals for Software-Tracking Firms," *The Wall Street Journal,* www.wsj.com, August 29, 2017.

70. Siva, "A View from the Top"; J. Smith, "Startup FourKites Raises $35 Million to Expand Abroad, Improve Shipping-Time Prediction," *The Wall Street Journal,* www.wsj.com, February 20, 2018; Starr, "Is FourKites Tracking Technology a Game Changer?"; Smith, "'Amazon Effect' Sparks Deals."

71. A. Rekdal, "'I've Got to Be Part of This': How This Sales Team Pitches Big Data to an Old-School Industry," *Built in Chicago,* www.builtinchicago.org, March 21, 2017; Loizos, "FourKites Raises $13 Million."

72. Siva, "A View from the Top"; Smith, "Startup FourKites Raises $35 Million."

73. Siva, "A View from the Top"; Smith, "Startup FourKites Raises $35 Million"; "FourKites Hires Industry Veteran Dave Walker as the Chief Revenue Officer," news release, March 23, 2016, accessed at https://www.prnewswire.com.

74. S. Tandon, "Nestle's Maggi Noodle Is India's Favorite Instant Noodle Again," *Quartz,* http://qz.com, April 19, 2016.

75. R.E. Caves, *Multinational Enterprise and Economic Analysis* (Cambridge: Cambridge University Press, 1982).

76. B. Kogut, "Joint Ventures: Theoretical and Empirical Perspectives," *Strategic Management Journal* 9 (1988), 319–33.

77. "Cereal Partners Worldwide," www.nestle.com, accessed March 25, 2018; "Global Growth and Returns: General Mills 2017 Annual Report," accessed March 25, 2018.

78. N. Hood and S. Young, *The Economics of the Multinational Enterprise* (London: Longman, 1979).

CHAPTER 9

Value Chain Management: Functional Strategies for Competitive Advantage

©Tom Merton/age fotostock

Learning Objectives

After studying this chapter, you should be able to:

LO9-1 Explain the role of functional strategy and value chain management in achieving superior quality, efficiency, innovation, and responsiveness to customers.

LO9-2 Describe what customers want, and explain why it is so important for managers to be responsive to their needs.

LO9-3 Explain why achieving superior quality is so important, and understand the challenges facing managers and organizations that seek to implement total quality management.

LO9-4 Explain why achieving superior efficiency is so important, and understand the different kinds of techniques that need to be employed to increase efficiency.

LO9-5 Differentiate between two forms of innovation, and explain why innovation and product development are crucial components of the search for competitive advantage.

Efficiency Frees Kraft Heinz to Innovate

How do managers ensure that their group's activities add value to the company? For Bernardo Hees, chief executive of Kraft Heinz, the answer includes making sure the company operates efficiently and grows by adding new products that appeal to changing consumer tastes.

Kraft Heinz was formed in the 2015 merger of Pittsburgh-based Heinz with Kraft, headquartered near Chicago.[1] Its famous brands, along with Kraft cheese and Heinz ketchup, include Jell-O, Oscar Mayer, and Velveeta. While these are widely known and loved, they are attached to processed foods at a time when consumers are increasingly asking for freshness. The largest shareholder of the combined company is 3G Capital Partners, which appointed Hees to run the company.

When the merger was complete, Hees embarked on an effort to drive down any spending that wasn't contributing to the company's overall success.[2] This continued a pre-merger focus of Hees, who had led Heinz before the merger. He closed facilities located far from suppliers and customers, moving work to more centrally located facilities. He let executives know they would have more control over decision making but would do without offices and expensive perks. Such efforts have enabled the company to increase its profit margin, a measure of revenues relative to costs. While some see 3G's focus on efficiency as ruthless cost cutting, Hees insists that it is primarily a way to build value by freeing up resources "to invest in our brands [and] . . . people."[3]

Indeed, the company has been pursuing ideas for new products. For example, observing that sales of Oscar Mayer hot dogs have been flat, management launched an investigation of whether the brand could become associated with healthy eating. The company developed an "all-natural" hot dog, which launched to a favorable response.[4] To build on its existing brands with a new breakfast food, the company developed Just Crack an Egg, a microwaveable serving-size cup containing a mixture of Kraft cheese, Ore-Ida potatoes, vegetables, and Oscar Mayer breakfast meat. The consumer stirs in an egg (for a fresh-food experience) and zaps the contents for a quick, protein-rich breakfast.[5]

These new product ideas are the result of responsiveness to customer wants and needs. Product managers at Kraft Heinz conduct research into what challenges consumers are facing related to their eating habits. They found that consumers want to do more of their shopping in the produce, meat, and dairy sections of the store to get fresh, healthful options. But even as they want to eat well, they are pressed for time. A product such as Just Crack an Egg addresses all of these wishes, and for that

Implementing operational efficiencies has allowed Kraft Heinz CEO Bernardo Hees to invest in new products that address consumers' changing tastes.
©Bloomberg/Getty Images

reason, it was intentionally developed to contain no artificial colors or flavors.[6]

To keep up with changing tastes, Kraft Heinz cannot merely tweak its existing products; it needs to get involved with what is new and exciting. The company recently launched a business unit devoted to identifying opportunities and backing them financially.[7] The unit, called Springboard, focuses on natural, organic, craft, and specialty foods, looking for business ideas that could open up whole new categories. Start-up companies apply to Springboard for backing, and the ones selected will get coaching as well as access to Kraft Heinz's R&D facilities. If Springboard lives up to its name, it should launch Kraft Heinz on to a new growth trajectory.

Overview

As "A Manager's Challenge" suggests, organizations must constantly evaluate their business practices in an effort to remain successful. Some organizations may adopt the latest research and methods, while others find different ways to stay competitive.

In this chapter we focus on the functional-level strategies managers can use to achieve superior efficiency, quality, innovation, and responsiveness to customers and, so, build competitive advantage. We also examine the nature of an organization's value chain and discuss how the combined, or cooperative, efforts of managers across the value chain are required if an organization is to achieve its mission and goal of maximizing the amount of value its products provide customers. By the end of this chapter, you will understand the vital role value chain management plays in creating competitive advantage and a high-performing organization.

Functional Strategies, the Value Chain, and Competitive Advantage

As we noted in Chapter 8, managers can use two basic business-level strategies to add value to an organization's products and achieve a competitive advantage over industry rivals. First, managers can pursue a *low-cost strategy* and lower the costs of creating value to attract customers by keeping product prices as low as or lower than competitors' prices. Second, managers can pursue a *differentiation strategy* and add value to a product by finding ways to make it superior in some way to the products of other companies. If they are successful and customers see greater value in the product, then, like Apple, they can charge a premium or higher price for the product. The four specific ways in which managers can lower costs and/or increase differentiation to obtain a competitive advantage were mentioned in Chapter 1 and are reviewed here; how organizations seek to achieve them is the topic of this chapter. (See Figure 9.1.)

LO9-1 Explain the role of functional strategy and value chain management in achieving superior quality, efficiency, innovation, and responsiveness to customers.

1. *Achieve superior efficiency.* Efficiency is a measure of the amount of inputs required to produce a given amount of outputs. The fewer the inputs required to produce a given output, the higher is efficiency and the lower the cost of outputs. For example, Apple has been recognized by Gartner, a U.S. research firm, in the Masters category of its annual rankings for sustained supply chain leadership over the last 10 years. The question remains whether Apple can continue its supply chain leadership, as new innovations will be needed from the global tech giant to match its colossal success during the last decade.[8]

2. *Achieve superior quality.* Quality means producing goods and services that have attributes—such as design, styling, performance, and reliability—that customers perceive as being superior to those found in competing products.[9] Providing high-quality products creates a brand-name reputation for an organization's products, and this enhanced reputation allows it to charge higher prices. In the car industry, for example, Toyota's reputation for making reliable vehicles allows it to outperform rival carmakers and gives it a competitive advantage.

3. *Achieve superior innovation, speed, and flexibility.* Anything new or better about the way an organization operates or the goods and services it produces is the result of innovation.

Figure 9.1

Four Ways to Create a Competitive Advantage

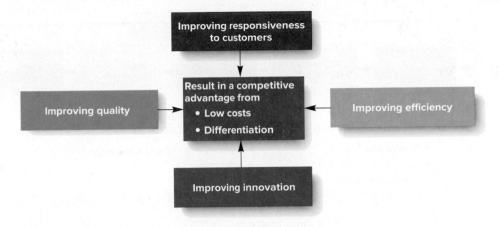

Successful innovation gives an organization something *unique* or different about its products that rivals lack—more attractive, useful, sophisticated products or superior production processes that strengthen its competitive advantage. Innovation adds value to products and allows the organization to further differentiate itself from rivals and attract customers who are often willing to pay a premium price for unique products. For example, Nintendo's competitive advantage in handheld video game devices has completely eroded, now that games are available on smartphones and tablets. The company recently entered the movie industry in an effort to strengthen its overall video content business, announcing that a new film featuring its iconic character Mario is under development with Illumination Entertainment, the U.S. animation studio behind the *Despicable Me* film series.[10]

4. *Attain superior responsiveness to customers.* An organization that is responsive to customers tries to satisfy their needs and give them *exactly* what they want. An organization that treats customers better than its rivals do also provides a valuable service some customers may be willing to pay a higher price for. Managers can increase responsiveness by providing excellent after-sales service and support and by working to provide improved products or services to customers in the future. Today smartphone companies such as Samsung, Apple, and HTC are searching for ways to better satisfy changing customer needs for higher-quality video, sound, and Internet connection speed.

Functional Strategies and Value Chain Management

functional-level strategy A plan of action to improve the ability of each of an organization's functions to perform its task-specific activities in ways that add value to an organization's goods and services.

value chain The coordinated series or sequence of functional activities necessary to transform inputs such as new product concepts, raw materials, component parts, or professional skills into the finished goods or services customers value and want to buy.

value chain management The development of a set of functional-level strategies that support a company's business-level strategy and strengthen its competitive advantage.

Functional-level strategy is a plan of action to improve the ability of each of an organization's functions or departments (such as manufacturing or marketing) to perform its task-specific activities in ways that add value to an organization's goods and services. A company's **value chain** is the coordinated series or sequence of functional activities necessary to transform inputs such as new product concepts, raw materials, component parts, or professional skills into the finished goods or services customers value and want to buy (see Figure 9.2). Each functional activity along the chain *adds value* to the product when it lowers costs or gives the product differentiated qualities that increase the price a company can charge for it.

Value chain management is the development of a set of functional-level strategies that support a company's business-level strategy and strengthen its competitive advantage. Functional managers develop the strategies that increase efficiency, quality, innovation, and/or responsiveness to customers and, thus, strengthen an organization's competitive advantage. So the better the fit between functional- and business-level strategies, the greater is the organization's competitive advantage, and the better able the organization is to achieve its mission and goal of maximizing the amount of value it gives customers. Each function along the value chain has an important role to play in value creation.

Figure 9.2

Functional Activities and the Value Chain

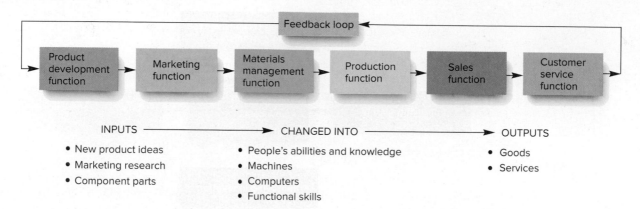

As Figure 9.2 suggests, the starting point of the value chain is often the search for new and improved products that will better appeal to customers, so the activities of the product development and marketing functions become important. *Product development* is the engineering and scientific research activities involved in innovating new or improved products that add value to a product. For example, Apple has been a leader in developing new kinds of mobile digital devices that have become so popular among buyers that its products are rapidly imitated by its competitors. Once a new product has been developed, the *marketing function's* task is to persuade customers that the product meets their needs and convince them to buy it. Marketing can help create value through brand positioning and advertising that increase customer perceptions of the utility of a company's product. For example, moviegoers appear willing to pay more to watch a movie in 3D. In 2018 more than 33 films were slated to be released in 3D.[11]

Even the best-designed product can fail if the marketing function hasn't devised a careful plan to persuade people to buy it and try it out—or to make sure customers really want it. For this reason, marketing often conducts consumer research to discover unmet customer product needs and to find better ways to tailor existing products to satisfy customer needs. Marketing then presents its suggestions to product development, which performs its own research to discover how best to design and make the new or improved products.

At the next stage of the value chain, the *materials management function* controls the movement of physical materials from the procurement of inputs through production and to distribution and delivery to the customer. The efficiency with which this is carried out can significantly lower costs and create more value. Walmart has the most efficient materials management function in the retail industry. By tightly controlling the flow of goods from its suppliers through its stores and into the hands of customers, Walmart has eliminated the need to hold large inventories of goods. Lower inventories mean lower costs and hence greater value creation.

The *production function* is responsible for creating, assembling, or providing a good or service—for transforming inputs into outputs. For physical products, when we talk about production, we generally mean manufacturing and assembly. For services such as banking or retailing, production takes place when the service is actually provided or delivered to the customer (for example, when a bank originates a loan for a customer, it is engaged in "production" of the loan). By performing its activities efficiently, the production function helps to lower costs. For example, the efficient production operations of Honda and Toyota have made them more profitable than competitors such as Renault, Volkswagen, and Chrysler. The production function can also perform its activities in a way that is consistent with high product quality, which leads to differentiation (and higher value) and to lower costs.

At the next stage in the value chain, the *sales function* plays a crucial role in locating customers and then informing and persuading them to buy the company's products. Personal selling—that is, direct face-to-face communication by salespeople with existing and potential customers to promote a company's products—is a crucial value chain activity. Which products retailers choose to stock, for example, or which drugs doctors choose to prescribe often depends on the salesperson's ability to inform and persuade customers that his or her company's product is superior and, thus, the best choice.

Finally, the role of the *customer service function* is to provide after-sales service and support. This function can create a perception of superior value in the minds of customers by solving customer problems and supporting customers after they have purchased the product. For example, FedEx can get its customers' parcels to any point in the world within 24 hours, creating value and support for customers' businesses. Customer service controls the electronic systems for tracking sales and inventory, pricing products, selling products, dealing with customer inquiries, and so on, all of which can greatly increase responsiveness to customers. Indeed, an important activity of sales and customer service is to tell product development and marketing why a product is meeting or not meeting customers' needs so the product can be redesigned or improved. Hence, a feedback loop links the end of the value chain to its beginning (see Figure 9.2).

Value Chain Analysis

After identifying the components of its value chain, a company needs to analyze how the value chain is working to meet overall business goals. In his 1985 book, *Competitive Advantage,* management expert Michael Porter described the various components of a company or business, how they are organized, and how they form a value chain. Porter theorized that companies should set up their value chains and link them to the achievement of strategic objectives. In addition, Porter broke down the value chain into primary and support activities. Primary activities directly contribute to the making of a product or service—for example, logistics, operations, marketing, sales, and service. He defined support activities as factors that contribute to creating value but are not directly linked to a product or service—for example, company infrastructure, evolving technology, and human resource management. Porter suggested that once these activities were identified and categorized as primary or support factors, a company could determine which activities provided the most value to the organization and which ones needed to be modified to help meet company objectives.[12]

Using its value chain as a diagnostic tool can provide several benefits to an organization, including increased efficiency, reduced costs, and strengthened collaboration between various functional activities, creating even greater value for the firm.[13] As smart technologies continue to evolve and impact business operations, some researchers suggest that companies must rethink and retool their value chains to maintain competitive advantage in their respective industries.[14]

In the rest of this chapter, we examine the functional strategies used to manage the value chain to improve quality, efficiency, innovation, and responsiveness to customers. Notice, however, that achieving superior quality, efficiency, and innovation is *part* of attaining superior responsiveness to customers. Customers want value for their money, and managers who develop functional strategies that result in a value chain capable of creating innovative, high-quality, low-cost products best deliver this value to customers. For this reason, we begin by discussing how functional managers can increase responsiveness to customers.

Improving Responsiveness to Customers

All organizations produce outputs—goods or services—that are consumed by customers, who, in buying these products, provide the monetary resources most organizations need to survive. Because customers are vital to organizational survival, managers must correctly identify their customers and pursue strategies that result in products that best meet their needs. This is why the marketing function plays such an important part in the value chain, and good value chain management requires that marketing managers focus on defining their company's business in terms of the customer *needs* it is satisfying, not by the *type of products* it makes—or the result can be disaster.[15] For example, Kodak's managers said "no thanks" when the company was offered the rights to "instant photography," which was later marketed by Polaroid. Why did they make this mistake? Because the managers adopted a product-oriented approach to their business that didn't put the needs of customers first. Kodak's managers believed their job was to sell high-quality glossy photographs to people. Why would they want to become involved in instant photography, which results in inferior-quality photographs? In reality, Kodak was not satisfying people's needs for high-quality photographs; it was satisfying the need customers had to *capture and record the images of their lives*—their birthday parties, weddings, graduations, and so on. And people wanted those images quickly so they could share them right away with other people—which is why today digital photography has taken off and Kodak filed for bankruptcy in 2012.

What Do Customers Want?

LO9-2 Describe what customers want, and explain why it is so important for managers to be responsive to their needs.

Given that satisfying customer demand is central to the survival of an organization, an important question is, "What do customers want?" Although specifying *exactly* what customers want is not possible because their needs vary from product to product, most customers prefer

1. A lower price to a higher price.
2. High-quality products to low-quality products.
3. Quick service and good after-sales service to slow service and poor after-sales support.
4. Products with many useful or valuable features to products with few features.
5. Products that are, as far as possible, customized to their unique needs.

To meet those preferences, managers seek data about customers' definitions of high quality and good service, so they can correct any problems and offer what is most valued. The "Managing Globally" feature tells how a company based in Finland is meeting that need for customers around the world.

MANAGING GLOBALLY

HappyOrNot Helps Customers Keep *Their* Customers Happy

A frustrated teenager in Finland saw the need for HappyOrNot while trying to get help locating computer supplies in a store (during the 1990s, when computer users went to stores to buy disks). The shopper, Heikki Väänänen, wished he could easily send feedback to someone who cared about the store's performance. In college, he started a coding company; when a client bought it, he looked for a new business idea. No one had ever solved his shopping problem, so he and a colleague decided to try.[16]

Their solution was a terminal with a screen and four bright buttons labeled with four faces, happy to sad, green to red.[17] The screen invited customers to rate their experience. The first terminal, installed in a local grocery store, obtained more than 120 customer ratings in the first day. Besides giving shoppers a voice, the terminal solved a business problem: how to get feedback from large numbers of customers at an affordable cost. Survey responses are delayed and too time-consuming for many customers, and a sophisticated marketing research program is expensive. A set of HappyOrNot terminals delivers the right combination of features and price.

HappyOrNot had a strong launch in Finland, with government grants and a highly skilled labor force. But the founders needed help to spread the concept internationally. They hired a manager experienced in international sales, who introduced the terminals to London's heavily traveled Heathrow Airport in time for the 2012 Summer Olympics. Travelers saw the concept and became curious. They learned that the systems aren't just an easy-to-use gimmick but provide time-stamped data electronically in real time, so managers can pinpoint problems. A surge in complaints above a defined threshold triggers an alert, enabling a rapid response; for example, a spike in complaints around a restroom could signal a maintenance issue.[18]

As awareness has grown, Avis, McDonald's, UPS Stores, and other customers in more than 120 countries have installed HappyOrNot terminals. The company,

Companies around the world have installed HappyOrNot terminals in their business locations to gather consumer feedback about their products and services.
©HappyOrNot Ltd.

now operating at a profit, has seen several years of doubling revenues. Besides the original terminals, it offers a touch-screen version for gathering comments along with ratings and an online tool to collect feedback from customers of web-based businesses.[19]

One satisfied customer is the San Francisco 49ers, which installed HappyOrNot terminals around Levi's Stadium, linked to an app that lets managers monitor data within seconds of its entry. They can see, for example, which concession stands are performing well at which hours, displayed on a colorful map.[20]

Managers know that the more desired product attributes a company's value chain builds into its products, the higher the price that must be charged to cover the costs of developing and making the product. So what do managers of a customer-responsive organization do? They try to develop functional strategies that allow the organization's value chain to deliver to customers either *more* desired product attributes for the *same price* or the *same* product attributes for a *lower price*.[21] For example, in 2014 Walmart announced that it had made a deal to be the only national retailer to sell the Wild Oats brand organic foods and that it would do so at prices lower than those usually charged for organic products. Unfortunately, Walmart's strategy was short lived; the global retailer decided to phase out the Wild Oats food brand in 2016, saying the brand didn't catch on with Walmart shoppers.[22]

Managing the Value Chain to Increase Responsiveness to Customers

Because satisfying customers is so important, managers try to design and improve the way their value chains operate so they can supply products that have the desired attributes—quality, cost, and features. For example, the need to respond to customer demand for competitively priced, quality cars drove U.S. carmakers like Ford and GM to imitate Japanese companies and copy how Toyota and Honda perform their value chain activities. Today the imperative of satisfying customer needs shapes the activities of U.S. carmakers' materials management and manufacturing functions. As an example of the link between responsiveness to customers and an organization's value chain, consider how Southwest Airlines, the most profitable U.S. airline, operates.[23]

The major reason for Southwest's success is that it has pursued functional strategies that improve how its value chain operates to give customers what they want. Southwest commands high customer loyalty precisely because it can deliver products, such as flights from Houston to Dallas, that have all the desired attributes: reliability, convenience, and low price. In each of its functions, Southwest's strategies revolve around finding ways to lower costs. For example, Southwest offers a no-frills approach to in-flight customer service: No meals are served onboard, and there are no first-class seats. Southwest does not subscribe to the big reservation computers used by travel agents because the booking fees are too costly. Also, the airline flies only one aircraft, the fuel-efficient Boeing 737, which keeps training and maintenance costs down. All this translates into low prices for customers. Additionally, Southwest is one of the few airlines that does not charge baggage fees. Passengers can check two bags for free.[24]

Southwest's reliability derives from the fact that it has the quickest aircraft turnaround time in the industry. A Southwest ground crew needs only 15 minutes to turn around an incoming aircraft and prepare it for departure. This speedy operation helps keep flights on time. Southwest has such a quick turnaround because it has a flexible workforce that has been cross-trained to perform multiple tasks. Thus, the person who checks tickets might also help with baggage loading if time is short.

A Southwest ticket agent may assist a customer and then turn around to load his or her baggage as part of the organization's emphasis on cross-training workers for multiple tasks. Southwest's operating system is geared toward satisfying customer demand for low-priced, reliable, and convenient air travel, making it one of the most consistently successful airlines in recent years.
©Joseph Kaczmarek/AP Images

Southwest's convenience comes from its scheduling multiple flights every day between its popular locations, such as Dallas and Houston, and its use of airports that are close to downtown areas (Hobby at Houston and Love Field at Dallas) instead of using more distant major airports.[25] In sum, Southwest's excellent value chain management has given it a competitive advantage in the airline industry. Another company that has found a way to be responsive to customers by offering them faster service is Panera, which is profiled in the accompanying "Management Insight" feature.

MANAGEMENT INSIGHT

Need for Speed Pays Off for Panera

Panera is a bakery-café chain with more than 2,300 stores in the United States and Canada. Until recently, the stores had been operating successfully with a traditional model of offerings and services. That's until founder and now chairman Ron Shaich had a revelation. Always running late when driving his son to school in the morning, Shaich would call ahead to a local Panera and order breakfast and lunch for his son. When Shaich arrived at the store, his son would run in with his dad's credit card, skip the line, and pick up the food. While the system worked for Shaich and his family, it was not available to other Panera customers.[26]

That's what gave Shaich the idea for what he called Panera 2.0. After several years of testing, the new ordering system is in place in all of the stores. Customers can now place orders via computer or mobile app. When the customer arrives at the restaurant, he or she can skip the line, pay for the ordered food via mobile app or credit card, and dine in or carry out. There are also touch-screen kiosks at each restaurant for customers who didn't order ahead but who want to get through the line faster. And, of course, customers can still go to the register and place an order.[27]

One advantage of the ordering system is that is syncs with the My Panera rewards program. The program remembers all orders that the customer places. If a customer ordered a custom sandwich at one visit, the system remembers it and offers to place the same order at the next visit. The company's loyalty program now has more than 29 million members, which is more than half of all Panera transactions. The company currently processes more than 28% of its orders digitally, with digital sales reaching close to $1.2 billion in 2017.[28]

The system has also improved accuracy rates when it comes to customer orders. The industry average is one in seven orders filled incorrectly, with many of the errors occurring during input at the register. Now that many customers enter their orders into the system, employees have time to double-check each order before it leaves the store.

Implementing the ordering system has meant changes for Panera employees, too. For instance, the company's IT staff has doubled in size. In addition, when customers place orders online or at an in-store kiosk, the process allows employees at the register to be redeployed to the kitchen area to help keep up with the demand of incoming orders, which helps productivity. Shaich's vision for Panera 2.0 continues to pay dividends for the fast-casual chain. In addition to landing on Technomic's and *QSR* magazine's annual lists of top chain restaurants, Panera's same-store sales continue to grow. Shaich was recently honored by *Restaurant Business* magazine as its 2018 Restaurant Leader of the Year.[29]

After Ron Shaich got the idea for Panera 2.0, customers can now place orders online, skip the in-store ordering line, and pay via mobile app. The ordering system allows Panera to improve efficiencies and increase customer service satisfaction.
©Alexey Rotanov/Shutterstock

Although managers must seek to improve their responsiveness to customers by improving how the value chain operates, they should not offer a level of responsiveness to customers that results in costs becoming *too high*—something that threatens an organization's future performance and survival. For example, a company that customizes every product to the unique demands of individual customers is likely to see its costs grow out of control.

Customer Relationship Management

One functional strategy managers can use to get close to customers and understand their needs is **customer relationship management (CRM)**. CRM is a technique that uses IT to develop an ongoing relationship with customers to maximize the value an organization can deliver to them over time. By the 2000s most large companies had installed sophisticated CRM IT to track customers' changing demands for a company's products; this became a vital tool to maximize responsiveness to customers. CRM IT monitors, controls, and links each of the functional activities involved in marketing, selling, and delivering products to customers, such as monitoring the delivery of products through the distribution channel, monitoring salespeople's selling activities, setting product pricing, and coordinating after-sales service. CRM systems have three interconnected components: sales and selling, after-sales service and support, and marketing.

Suppose a sales manager has access only to sales data that show the total sales revenue each salesperson generated in the last 30 days. This information does not break down how much revenue came from sales to existing customers versus sales to new customers. What important knowledge is being lost? First, if most revenues are earned from sales to existing customers, this suggests that the money being spent by a company to advertise and promote its products is not attracting new customers and, so, is being wasted. Second, important dimensions involved in sales are pricing, financing, and order processing. In many companies, to close a deal, a salesperson has to send the paperwork to a central sales office, which handles matters such as approving the customer for special financing and determining specific shipping and delivery dates. In some companies, different departments handle these activities, and it can take a long time to get a response from them; this keeps customers waiting—something that often leads to lost sales. Until CRM systems were introduced, these kinds of problems were widespread and resulted in missed sales and higher operating costs. Today the sales and selling CRM software contains *best sales practices* that analyze this information and then recommend ways to improve how the sales process operates.

One company that has improved its sales and customer service practices by implementing CRM is global athletic retailer, Adidas. The CRM system has enabled Adidas to transform its sales and customer service approach from a slower, brick-and-mortar focus to an agile online platform customized for the consumer experience. Through the Adidas website, the global brand now offers premium, connected, and personalized experiences delivered by more than 1,100 Adidas "care agents," in a variety of formats—via phone, email, web, or social—all from a single CRM application. The system allows the care agents to have one view of each Adidas customer and his or her preferences, tastes, and shopping experience, which allows for agility, speed, and a customized connection to each consumer. In addition, the customer service process becomes more efficient because all customer service agents have access to the same information. The principal benefit of using this CRM approach is that it takes all the guesswork out of accessing key consumer information and data points, allowing customer service agents to focus more on creating a brand experience that will have consumers making more Adidas purchases because of their experience with the company and its front-facing staff.[30]

When a company implements after-sales service and support CRM software, salespeople are required to input detailed information about their follow-up visits to customers. Because the system tracks and documents every customer's case history, salespeople have instant access to a record of everything that occurred during previous phone calls or visits. They are in a much better position to respond to customers' needs and build customer loyalty, so a company's after-sales service improves. For example, cellular service companies, like T-Mobile and Sprint, require that telephone sales reps collect information about all customers' inquiries, complaints, and requests, and this is recorded electronically in customer logs. The CRM module can analyze the information in these logs to evaluate whether the customer service reps are meeting or exceeding the company's required service standards.

customer relationship management (CRM)
A technique that uses IT to develop an ongoing relationship with customers to maximize the value an organization can deliver to them over time.

A CRM system can also identify the top 10 reasons for customer complaints. Sales managers can then work to eliminate the sources of these problems and improve after-sales support procedures. The CRM system also identifies the top 10 best service and support practices, which can then be taught to all sales reps.

Finally, as a CRM system processes information about changing customer needs, this improves marketing in many ways. Marketing managers, for example, have access to detailed customer profiles, including data about purchases and the reasons individuals were or were not attracted to a company's products. Armed with this knowledge, marketing can better identify customers and the specific product attributes they desire. Traditional CRM systems were organized by having salespeople input customer information. Now social CRM systems can track customers on social media and put them on a company's radar. For example, if a Twitter user posts frequently about a topic relevant to the company or about the company's product, a CRM system can bring the user to the attention of the company as an important connection or a potential customer.[31] In sum, a CRM system is a comprehensive method of gathering crucial information about how customers respond to a company's products. It is a powerful functional strategy used to align a company's products with customer needs.

Improving Quality

As noted earlier, high-quality products possess attributes such as superior design, features, reliability, and after-sales support; these products are designed to better meet customer requirements.[32] Quality is a concept that can be applied to the products of both manufacturing and service organizations—goods such as an Apple computer or services such as customer service in a Citibank branch. Why do managers seek to control and improve the quality of their organizations' products?[33] There are two reasons (see Figure 9.3).

LO9-3 Explain why achieving superior quality is so important, and understand the challenges facing managers and organizations that seek to implement total quality management.

First, customers usually prefer a higher-quality product to a lower-quality product. So an organization able to provide, *for the same price,* a product of higher quality than a competitor's product is serving its customers better—it is being more responsive to its customers. Often providing high-quality products creates a brand-name reputation for an organization's products. This enhanced reputation may allow the organization to charge more for its products than its competitors can charge, and thus it makes greater profits. For example, in 2018 Lexus ranked first on the J.D. Power list of the 10 most reliable carmakers for the seventh consecutive year.[34] The high quality of Lexus vehicles enables the company to charge higher prices for its cars than the prices charged by rival carmakers.

The second reason for trying to boost product quality is that higher product quality can increase efficiency and thereby lower operating costs and boost profits. Achieving high product quality lowers operating costs because of the effect of quality on employee productivity: Higher product quality means less employee time is wasted in making defective products that must be discarded or in providing substandard services; thus, less time has to be spent fixing mistakes. This translates into higher employee productivity, which also means lower costs.

Figure 9.3

The Impact of Increased Quality on Organizational Performance

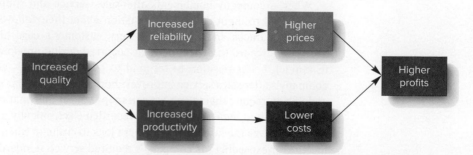

Total Quality Management

total quality management (TQM) A management technique that focuses on improving the quality of an organization's products and services.

At the forefront of the drive to improve product quality is a functional strategy known as total quality management.[35] **Total quality management (TQM)** focuses on improving the quality of an organization's products and stresses that *all* of an organization's value chain activities should be directed toward this goal. TQM requires the cooperation of managers in every function of an organization and across functions.[36] To show how TQM works, we next describe the way that Citibank used the technique. Then, using Citibank as an example, we look at the 10 steps that are necessary for managers to implement a successful TQM program.

In the 2000s Citibank's top managers decided the bank could retain and expand its customer base only if it could increase customer loyalty, so they decided to implement a TQM program to better satisfy customer needs. As the first step in its TQM effort, Citibank identified the factors that dissatisfy its customers. When analyzing the complaints, it found that most concerned the time it took to complete a customer's request, such as responding to an account problem or getting a loan. So Citibank's managers began to examine how they handled each kind of customer request. For each distinct request, they formed a cross-functional team that broke down the request into the steps required, between people and departments, to complete the response. In analyzing the steps, teams found that many of them were unnecessary and could be replaced by using the right information systems. They also found that delays often occurred because employees did not know how to handle a request. They were not being given the right kind of training, and when they couldn't handle a request, they simply put it aside until a supervisor could deal with it.

Citibank's second step to increase its responsiveness was to implement an organizationwide TQM program. Managers and supervisors were charged with reducing the complexity of the work process and finding the most effective way to process each particular request, such as a request for a loan. Managers were also charged with training employees to answer each specific request. The results were remarkable. For example, in the loan department the TQM program reduced by 75% the number of handoffs necessary to process a request. The department's average response time dropped from several hours to 30 minutes. What are the 10 steps in TQM that made this possible?

1. *Build organizational commitment to quality.* TQM will do little to improve the performance of an organization unless all employees embrace it, and this often requires a change in an organization's culture.[37] At Citibank the process of changing culture began at the top. First a group of top managers, including the CEO, received training in TQM from consultants from Motorola, where Six Sigma was founded (Six Sigma is trademarked by Motorola).[38] Each member of the top management group was then given the responsibility of training a group at the next level in the hierarchy, and so on down through the organization until all 100,000 employees had received basic TQM training.

2. *Focus on the customer.* TQM practitioners see a focus on the customer as the starting point.[39] According to TQM philosophy, the customer, not managers in quality control or engineering, defines what quality is. The challenge is fourfold: (1) to identify what customers want from the good or service that the company provides, (2) to identify what the company actually provides to customers, (3) to identify any gap between what customers want and what they actually get (the quality gap), and (4) to formulate a plan for closing the quality gap. The efforts of Citibank managers to increase responsiveness to customers illustrate this aspect of TQM well.

3. *Find ways to measure quality.* Another crucial element of TQM is the development of a measuring system that managers can use to evaluate quality. Devising appropriate measures is relatively easy in manufacturing companies, where quality can be measured by criteria such as defects per million parts. It is more difficult in service companies, where outputs are less tangible. However, with a little creativity, suitable quality measures can be devised as they were by managers at Citibank. Citibank used customer satisfaction surveys as quality measures and defined a defect as any rating below the two highest ratings.[40]

4. *Set goals and create incentives.* Once a measure has been devised, managers' next step is to set a challenging quality goal and to create incentives for reaching that goal. At Citibank the CEO set an initial goal of reducing customer complaints by 50%. One way of creating incentives to attain a goal is to link rewards, such as bonus pay and promotional opportunities, to the goal.

5. *Solicit input from employees.* Employees are a major source of information about the causes of poor quality, so it is important that managers establish a system for soliciting employee suggestions about improvements that can be made. At most companies, like Citibank, this is an ongoing endeavor—the process never stops.

6. *Identify defects and trace them to their source.* A major source of product defects is the production system; a major source of service defects is poor customer service procedures. TQM preaches the need for managers to identify defects in the work process, trace those defects back to their source, find out why they occurred, and make corrections so they do not occur again. Today IT makes quality measurement much easier.

7. *Introduce just-in-time inventory systems.* Inventory is the stock of raw materials, inputs, and component parts that an organization has on hand at a particular time. When the materials management function designs a just-in-time (JIT) inventory system, parts or supplies arrive at the organization when they are needed, not before. Also, under a JIT inventory system, defective parts enter an organization's operating system immediately; they are not warehoused for months before use. This means defective inputs can be quickly spotted. JIT is discussed more later in the chapter.

8. *Work closely with suppliers.* A major cause of poor-quality finished goods is poor-quality component parts. To decrease product defects, materials managers must work closely with suppliers to improve the quality of the parts they supply. Managers at Xerox worked closely with suppliers to get them to adopt TQM programs, and the result was a huge reduction in the defect rate of component parts. Managers also need to work closely with suppliers to get them to adopt a JIT inventory system, also required for high quality.

9. *Design for ease of production.* The more steps required to assemble a product or provide a service, the more opportunities there are for making a mistake. It follows that designing products that have fewer parts or finding ways to simplify providing a service should be linked to fewer defects or customer complaints. For example, Apple continually redesigns the way it assembles its mobile digital devices to reduce the number of assembly steps required, and it constantly searches for new ways to reduce the number of components that have to be linked together. The consequence of these redesign efforts was a continuous fall in assembly costs and marked improvement in product quality during the 2000s. At Citibank, defect detection and resolution lead to better performance in process time, cash management, and customer satisfaction.[41]

10. *Break down barriers between functions.* Successful implementation of TQM requires substantial cooperation between the different value chain functions. Materials managers have to cooperate with manufacturing managers to find high-quality inputs that reduce manufacturing costs; marketing managers have to cooperate with manufacturing so that customer problems identified by marketing can be acted on; information systems have to cooperate with all other functions of the company to devise suitable IT training programs; and so on. At Citibank, a cross-functional process mapping method was used to describe the functions involved in each step of a process flow.[42]

In essence, to increase quality, all functional managers need to cooperate to develop goals and spell out exactly how they will be achieved. Managers should embrace the philosophy that mistakes, defects, and poor-quality materials are not acceptable and should be eliminated. Functional managers should spend more time working with employees and providing them with the tools they need to do the job. Managers should create an environment in which employees will not be afraid to report problems or recommend improvements. Output goals and targets need to include not only numbers or quotas but also some indicators of quality to promote the production of defect-free output. Functional managers also need to train employees in new skills to keep pace with changes in the workplace. Finally, achieving better quality requires that managers develop organizational values and norms centered on improving quality.

SIX SIGMA   One TQM technique called Six Sigma has gained increasing popularity in the last decade, particularly because of the well-publicized success GE enjoyed as a result of implementing it across its operating divisions. The goal of Six Sigma is to improve a company's quality to only three defects per million by systematically altering the way all the processes involved in value chain activities are performed, and then carefully measuring how much improvement has been made using statistical methods. Six Sigma shares with TQM its focus

---

inventory The stock of raw materials, inputs, and component parts that an organization has on hand at a particular time.

just-in-time (JIT) inventory system A system in which parts or supplies arrive at an organization when they are needed, not before.

Six Sigma A technique used to improve quality by systematically improving how value chain activities are performed and then using statistical methods to measure the improvement.

on improving value chain processes to increase quality; but it differs because TQM emphasizes top-down organizationwide employee involvement, whereas the Six Sigma approach is to create teams of expert change agents, known as "green belts and black belts," to take control of the problem-finding and problem-solving process and then to train other employees in implementing solutions. The accompanying "Manager as a Person" feature shows how Six Sigma works for a Massachusetts accounting firm.

MANAGER AS A PERSON

Using Six Sigma to Buy Time

Melyssa Brown is a senior manager in the auditing department of Meyers Brothers Kalicka (MBK), the largest independent accounting firm in western Massachusetts.[43] MBK's services include accounting, auditing, tax preparation, and business advice. Its name signifies its formation as the merger of two firms—Meyers Brothers and Joseph D. Kalicka and Company—that had long served the region. MBK maintains a commitment to fostering clients' success by recruiting, retaining, and developing high-caliber professionals, of which Brown is one.

MBK values continuous learning,[44] and this laid a foundation for involvement with Six Sigma. Seeking greater efficiency, the firm had tried some techniques unsuccessfully. Brown and some colleagues attended a presentation on Six Sigma as a way to improve the delivery of services. They decided to try it. Brown agreed to take on this quality improvement project as her own. She underwent the first level of training, earning a "green belt" certification.[45]

As an auditor, Brown possesses analytical skills and used them in a process that was often troublesome for clients and MBK alike: client interaction to obtain necessary data. Brown picked apart the process of requesting data from clients, receiving the data, and making it accessible to the client's team at MBK. The process sounded simple: Mail or email a list of needed information and then receive documents by email or on a portable computer drive. In practice, though, MBK personnel often were asking around to see if one item or another had arrived. So Brown set up a process for automatically sharing information: an online portal for each client, accessible by everyone working on that client's matters. Clients post to their portal, and everyone involved, including the client, can see what MBK has received.[46]

Brown expected the Six Sigma process to be intense but also beneficial, and she was right on both counts. MBK's time sheets demonstrate that partners, associates, and staff members are spending less time handling each matter. The reduction in hours needed to serve each client opens up time to schedule work more effectively and cultivate new clients. In sum, Brown notes that MBK's "interaction with the client is better, and our delivery of services to the client is better."[47] With these improvements under her (green) belt, Brown is looking at new Six Sigma projects to streamline billing and administrative work.

Improving Efficiency

The third goal of value chain management is to increase the efficiency of the various functional activities. The fewer the input resources required to produce a given volume of output, the higher will be the efficiency of the operating system. So efficiency is a useful measure of how well an organization uses all its resources—such as labor, capital, materials, or energy—to produce its outputs, or goods and services. Developing functional strategies to improve efficiency is an extremely important issue for managers because increased efficiency lowers production costs, which lets an organization make a greater profit or attract more customers by lowering its price. Several important functional strategies are discussed here.

Facilities Layout, Flexible Manufacturing, and Efficiency

The strategies managers use to lay out or design an organization's physical work facilities also determine its efficiency. First, the way in which machines and workers are organized or grouped together into workstations affects the efficiency of the operating system. Second, a major determinant of efficiency is the cost associated with setting up the equipment needed to make a particular product. **Facilities layout** is the strategy of designing the machine–worker interface to increase operating system efficiency. **Flexible manufacturing** is a strategy based on the use of IT to reduce the costs associated with the product assembly process or the way services are delivered to customers. For example, this might be how computers are made on a production line or how patients are routed through a hospital.

FACILITIES LAYOUT   The way in which machines, robots, and people are grouped together affects how productive they can be. Figure 9.4 shows three basic ways of arranging workstations: product layout, process layout, and fixed-position layout.

In a *product layout,* machines are organized so that each operation needed to manufacture a product or process a patient is performed at workstations arranged in a fixed sequence. In manufacturing, workers are stationary in this arrangement, and a moving conveyor belt takes the product being worked on to the next workstation so that it is progressively assembled. Mass production is the familiar name for this layout; car assembly lines are probably the best-known example. It used to be that product layout was efficient only when products were created in large quantities; however, the introduction of modular assembly lines controlled by computers is making it efficient to make products in small batches.

In a *process layout,* workstations are not organized in a fixed sequence. Rather, each workstation is relatively self-contained, and a product goes to whichever workstation is needed to perform the next operation to complete the product. Process layout is often suited to manufacturing settings that produce a variety of custom-made products, each tailored to the needs of a different kind of customer. For example, a custom furniture manufacturer might use a process layout so different teams of workers can produce different styles of chairs or tables made from different kinds of woods and finishes. Such a layout also describes how a patient might go through a hospital from emergency room to X-ray room, to operating room, and so

Figure 9.4

Three Facilities Layouts

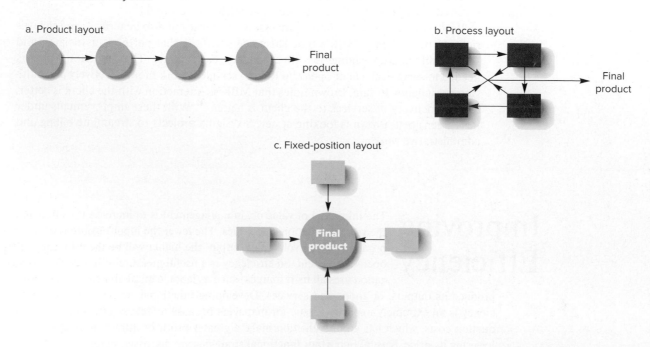

a. Product layout

Final product

b. Process layout

Final product

c. Fixed-position layout

Final product

on. A process layout provides the flexibility needed to change a product, whether it is a PC or a patient's treatment. Such flexibility, however, often reduces efficiency because it is expensive.

In a *fixed-position layout,* the product stays in a fixed position. Its component parts are produced in remote workstations and brought to the production area for final assembly. Increasingly, self-managed teams are using fixed-position layouts. Different teams assemble each component part and then send the parts to the final assembly team, which makes the final product. A fixed-position layout is commonly used for products such as jet airliners, mainframe computers, and gas turbines—products that are complex and difficult to assemble or so large that moving them from one workstation to another would be difficult. Regardless of the layout, facilities need to be designed with efficiency in mind. Unfortunately, the same cannot be said for boarding an airplane, as discussed in the accompanying "Management Insight" feature.

MANAGEMENT INSIGHT

Boarding a Plane Shouldn't Be This Difficult

Is it faster to board the back of the plane first? Or should airlines board passengers with window seats first, followed by middle seat fliers, and then those with aisle seats? What about assigning passengers to random boarding groups? Or how about not assigning seats and letting flyers sit wherever they want? Believe it or not, two recent studies found that random boarding does work more quickly than other options.

American Airlines spent several years studying ways to speed up the boarding process and decided on randomized group boarding for most passengers. As part of the study, observers watched thousands of boarding processes to see where things bogged down—and, no surprise, carry-on bags were a big problem. To avoid paying baggage fees, passengers brought on large bags. When the plane was boarded back to front, those waiting in the aisles to get to their seats would put their bags in overhead bins at the front of the plane, leaving no space for the bags of passengers who boarded later in the process.

Using computer simulations, American found that back-to-front boarding was slower than the window-middle-aisle seat method and, surprisingly, putting passengers into random boarding groups allowed the plane to fill up faster. Also, passengers were more likely to stow their bags in overhead bins closer to their seats than at the front of the plane. In 2017, American Airlines tried yet another boarding process—dividing passengers into nine groups—as a way of "simplifying" the overall boarding experience.[48]

MythBusters, the Discovery Channel TV show that applies scientific methods to test various accepted ideas, confirmed in its study, "when boarding a plane, boarding back to front is the slowest method." Using a plane replica complete with seats and overhead bins, volunteers tested various boarding methods. To further simulate reality, 5% of the volunteers were told to disrupt the boarding process by sitting in the wrong seat or standing in the aisle for longer than needed. It turns out the method with the highest satisfaction was the "reverse pyramid" in which elite passengers boarded first, followed by a complex set of zones that began with rear window seats. The method that allowed the fastest boarding was the one with no assigned seats; however, this method also had the lowest satisfaction rating of all the methods tested.[49]

Airlines continue to search for the fastest way to board passengers. What holds up the process? People who jump the line or pay to board early and too many carry-ons.
©Sergio Azenha/Alamy Stock Photo

What slows down boarding? Industry analysts cite several reasons. First, many passengers board before their boarding group is called, which makes the system less efficient. Second, some passengers pay for early boarding or get on earlier as part of a frequent flier reward program, which has the same effect as those who jump the line and board earlier than they are supposed to.[50]

Southwest Airlines avoids some of these boarding roadblocks by using the unassigned seat method of boarding—passengers line up in groups and numerical order and select a seat once on the plane—and this method seems to works well for the airline.[51]

Probably the biggest culprit for slow boarding is carry-on baggage. Most airlines have charged for checked bags since 2008 when fuel prices skyrocketed. To avoid fees, more passengers began using carry-on luggage, which slows down the boarding process. As a result, when the overhead bins are full, many bags have to be taken off the plane and checked at the last minute, causing more delays.

Why is the speed of boarding an airplane important? Airlines save about $40 for every minute shaved off boarding times. However, airlines appear to be making back some of this money in the various fees they now charge passengers. For example, in 2017, U.S. airlines charged more than $3.4 billion in baggage fees according to the U.S. Department of Transportation.[52]

FLEXIBLE MANUFACTURING   In a manufacturing company, a major source of costs is setting up the equipment needed to make a particular product. One of these costs is that of production forgone because nothing is produced while the equipment is being set up. For example, components manufacturers often need as much as half a day to set up automated production equipment when switching from production of one component part (such as a washer ring for the steering column of a car) to another (such as a washer ring for the steering column of a truck). During this half-day, a manufacturing plant is not producing anything, but employees are paid for this "nonproductive" time.

It follows that if setup times for complex production equipment can be reduced, so can setup costs, and efficiency will rise; that is, the time that plant and employees spend in actually producing something will increase. This simple insight has been the driving force behind the development of flexible manufacturing techniques.

Flexible manufacturing aims to reduce the time required to set up production equipment.[53] By redesigning the manufacturing process so production equipment geared for manufacturing one product can be quickly replaced with equipment geared to make another product, setup times and costs can be reduced dramatically. Another favorable outcome from flexible manufacturing is that a company can produce many more varieties of a product than before in the same amount of time. Thus flexible manufacturing increases a company's ability to be responsive to its customers.

To realize the benefits of flexible manufacturing, General Motors built a plant in Lansing, Michigan, back in 2001 that can expand to meet demand. When it was first built, the company's Grand River Assembly plant was already more flexible than GM's other plants and was modeled after the company's innovative facilities overseas.[54] While some GM executives expressed concern that the site was too small to work efficiently, the plant has received praise for its ability to produce a variety of car models, as well as for its collaborative team management style and automation capabilities. In 2017, the company announced a multimillion-dollar investment in the Grand River plant for new tooling and equipment, as well as a major expansion of the facility's body shop.[55]

Just-in-Time Inventory and Efficiency

As noted earlier, a just-in-time inventory system gets components to the assembly line just as they are needed and thus drives down costs. In a JIT inventory system, component parts travel from suppliers to the assembly line in a small wheeled container known as a *kanban.* Assembly-line workers empty the kanbans, which are sent back to the suppliers as the signal to produce another small batch of component parts, and so the process repeats itself. This system can be contrasted with a just-in-case view of inventory, which leads an organization to stockpile excess inputs in a warehouse in case it needs them to meet sudden upturns in demand.

JIT inventory systems have major implications for efficiency. Great cost savings can result from increasing inventory turnover and reducing inventory holding costs, such as warehousing and storage costs and the cost of capital tied up in inventory. Although companies that manufacture and assemble products can obviously use JIT to great advantage, so can service organizations.[56] Walmart, the largest retailer in the world, recently modified its JIT process to one the company calls OTIF (on-time, in full). A recognized concept in supply chain management, OTIF simply means suppliers should deliver their products when and how the buyer needs them. Announcing the new policy in 2017, Walmart expects food and consumable suppliers to deliver goods within a one-day window, while general merchandise or soft line suppliers must comply with a two-day period. If a delivery arrives early, late, or improperly packaged, a supplier could be fined a 3% penalty against invoice charges.[57]

By all measures of performance, JIT systems have been successful—inventory holding costs have fallen sharply and products are being delivered to customers on time. In addition, the design-to-product cycles for new products have dropped almost in half because suppliers are involved much earlier in the design process so they can supply new inputs as needed. Finally, as Walmart's OTIF process suggests, companies must continue to look for innovative ways to streamline global supply chains, especially because of the time pressures of e-commerce sales and deliveries.[58]

Self-Managed Work Teams and Efficiency

Another functional strategy to increase efficiency is the use of self-managed work teams. A typical self-managed team consists of 5 to 15 employees who produce an entire product instead of just parts of it.[59] Team members learn all team tasks and move from job to job. The result is a flexible workforce because team members can fill in for absent coworkers. The members of each team also assume responsibility for scheduling work and vacations, ordering materials, and hiring new members—previously all responsibilities of first-line managers. Because people often respond well to greater autonomy and responsibility, the use of empowered self-managed teams can increase productivity and efficiency. Moreover, cost savings arise from eliminating supervisors and creating a flatter organizational hierarchy, which further increase efficiency.

The effect of introducing self-managed teams is often an increase in efficiency of 30% or sometimes much more. The introduction of self-managed teams at a GE aviation plant in Durham, North Carolina, has produced year-over-year productivity growth, first-time yield quality, and successful on-time delivery rates.[60]

Process Reengineering and Efficiency

process reengineering The fundamental rethinking and radical redesign of business processes to achieve dramatic improvement in critical measures of performance such as cost, quality, service, and speed.

The value chain is a collection of functional activities or business processes that transforms one or more kinds of inputs to create an output that is of value to the customer. **Process reengineering** involves the fundamental rethinking and radical redesign of business processes (and thus the *value chain*) to achieve dramatic improvements in critical measures of performance such as cost, quality, service, and speed.[61] Order fulfillment, for example, can be thought of as a business process: When a customer's order is received (the input), many different functional tasks must be performed as necessary to process the order, and then the ordered goods are delivered to the customer (the output). Process reengineering boosts efficiency when it reduces the number of order fulfillment tasks that must be performed, or reduces the time they take, and so reduces operating costs.

For an example of process reengineering in practice, consider how Ford used it. One day a manager from Ford was working at its Japanese partner Mazda and discovered that Mazda had only five people in its accounts payable department. The Ford manager was shocked because Ford's U.S. operation had 500 employees in accounts payable. He reported his discovery to Ford's U.S. managers, who decided to form a task force to study this difference.

Ford managers discovered that procurement began when the purchasing department sent a purchase order to a supplier and sent a copy of the purchase order to Ford's accounts payable department. When the supplier shipped the goods and they arrived at Ford, a clerk at

Managers at Ford Motor Company have used process reengineering to improve the efficiency of the company's procurement process. By simplifying the process, Ford has significantly reduced the time spent by accounts payable staff to rectify complex vehicle orders that contain conflicting information.
©Robert Clay/Alamy Stock Photo

the receiving dock completed a form describing the goods and sent the form to accounts payable. The supplier, meanwhile, sent accounts payable an invoice. Thus accounts payable received three documents relating to these goods: a copy of the original purchase order, the receiving document, and the invoice. If the information in all three was in agreement (most of the time it was), a clerk in accounts payable issued payment. Occasionally, however, all three documents did not agree. And Ford discovered that accounts payable clerks spent most of their time straightening out the 1% of instances in which the purchase order, receiving document, and invoice contained conflicting information.[62]

Ford managers decided to reengineer the procurement process to simplify it. Now when a buyer in the purchasing department issues a purchase order to a supplier, that buyer also enters the order into an online database. As before, suppliers send goods to the receiving dock. When the goods arrive, the clerk at the receiving dock checks a computer terminal to see whether the received shipment matches the description on the purchase order. If it does, the clerk accepts the goods and pushes a button on the terminal keyboard that tells the database the goods have arrived. Receipt of the goods is recorded in the database, and a computer automatically issues and sends a check to the supplier. If the goods do not correspond to the description on the purchase order in the database, the clerk at the dock refuses the shipment and sends it back to the supplier.

Payment authorization, which used to be performed by accounts payable, is now accomplished at the receiving dock. The new process has come close to eliminating the need for an accounts payable department. In some parts of Ford, the size of the accounts payable department has been cut by 95%. By reducing the head count in accounts payable, the reengineering effort reduced the amount of time wasted on unproductive activities, thereby increasing the efficiency of the total organization.

Information Systems, the Internet, and Efficiency

With the rapid spread of computers, the explosive growth of the Internet and corporate intranets, and high-speed digital technology, the information systems function is moving to center stage in the quest for operating efficiencies and a lower cost structure. The impact of information systems on productivity is wide-ranging and potentially affects all other activities of a company. For example, Cisco Systems has been able to realize significant cost savings by moving its ordering and customer service functions online. Cisco Systems designs, manufactures, and sells networking equipment. The company has just 300 service agents handling all its customer accounts, compared to the 900 it would need if sales were not handled online. The difference represents an annual savings of $30 million a year. Moreover, without automated customer service functions, Cisco calculates that it would need at least 1,000 additional service engineers, which would cost around $100 million.

All large companies today use the Internet to manage the value chain, feeding real-time information about order flow to suppliers, which use this information to schedule their own production to provide components on a just-in-time basis. This approach reduces the costs of coordination both between the company and its customers and between the company and its suppliers. Using the Internet to automate customer and supplier interactions substantially reduces the number of employees required to manage these interfaces, which significantly reduces costs. This trend extends beyond high-tech companies. Banks and financial service companies are finding that they can substantially reduce costs by moving customer accounts and support functions online. Such a move reduces the need for customer service representatives, bank tellers, stockbrokers, insurance agents, and others. For example, it costs about $1 when a customer executes a transaction at a bank, such as shifting money from one account to another; over the Internet the same transaction costs about $0.01.

Improving Innovation

As discussed in Chapter 6, *technology* comprises the skills, know-how, experience, body of scientific knowledge, tools, machines, computers, and equipment used in the design, production, and distribution of goods and services. Technology is involved in all functional activities, and the rapid advance of technology today is a significant factor in managers' attempts to improve how their value chains innovate new kinds of goods and services or ways to provide them.

LO9-5 Differentiate between two forms of innovation, and explain why innovation and product development are crucial components of the search for competitive advantage.

Two Kinds of Innovation

Two principal kinds of innovation can be identified based on the nature of the technological change that brings them about. **Quantum product innovation** results in the development of new, often radically different, kinds of goods and services because of fundamental shifts in technology brought about by pioneering discoveries. Examples are the creation of the Internet and the World Wide Web that have revolutionized the computer, cell phone, and media/music industries, and biotechnology, which has transformed the treatment of illness by creating new, genetically engineered medicines. In addition, Panera, Shake Shack, and Chipotle started a restaurant trend in the early 2010s called "fast-casual," which offers rapidly prepared, high-quality food in an upscale dining environment and prices that are typically higher than fast-food chains.[63]

quantum product innovation The development of new, often radically different, kinds of goods and services because of fundamental shifts in technology brought about by pioneering discoveries.

Incremental product innovation results in gradual improvements and refinements of products over time as existing technologies are perfected and functional managers, like those at Apple, Toyota, and McDonald's, learn how to perform value chain activities in better ways—ways that add more value to products. For example, since their debut, Google's staffers have made thousands of incremental improvements to the company's search engine, Chrome Internet browser, and Android operating system—changes that have enhanced their capabilities enormously such as giving them the ability to work on all kinds of mobile devices and making them available in many different languages.

incremental product innovation The gradual improvement and refinement of existing products that occur over time as existing technologies are perfected.

Quantum product innovations are relatively rare; most managers' activities focus on incremental product innovations that result from ongoing technological advances. For example, every time Dell or HP puts a new, faster Intel or AMD chip into a PC, or Google improves its search engine's capability, the company is making incremental product innovations. Similarly, every time car engineers redesign a car model, and every time McDonald's managers work to improve the flavor and texture of burgers, fries, and salads, their product development efforts are intended to lead to incremental product innovations. Incremental innovation is frequently as important as—or even more important than—quantum innovation in raising a company's performance. Indeed, as discussed next, it is often managers' ability to successfully manage incremental product development that results in success or failure in an industry.

The need to speed innovation and quickly develop new and improved products becomes especially important when the technology behind the product is advancing rapidly. This is because the first companies in an industry to adopt the new technology will be able to develop products that better meet customer needs and gain a "first-mover" advantage over their rivals. Indeed, managers who do not quickly adopt and apply new technologies to innovate products may soon find they have no customers for their products—and destroy their organizations. In sum, the greater the rate of technological change in an industry, the more important it is for managers to innovate.

Strategies to Promote Innovation and Speed Product Development

product development The management of the value chain activities involved in bringing new or improved goods and services to the market.

There are several ways in which managers can promote innovation and encourage the development of new products. **Product development** is the management of the value chain activities involved in bringing new or improved goods and services to the market. The steps that Monte Peterson, former CEO of Thermos, took to develop a new barbecue grill show how good product development should proceed. Peterson had no doubt about how to increase Thermos's sales of barbecue grills: motivate Thermos's functional managers to create new and improved models. So Peterson assembled a cross-functional product development team of five functional managers (from marketing, engineering, manufacturing, sales, and finance) and told them to develop a new barbecue grill within 18 months. To ensure that they were not spread too thin, he assigned them to this team only. Peterson also arranged for leadership of the team to rotate. Initially, to focus on what customers wanted, the marketing manager would take the lead; then, when technical developments became the main consideration, leadership would switch to engineering; and so on.

Team members christened the group the "lifestyle team." To find out what people really wanted in a grill, the marketing manager and nine subordinates spent a month on the road, visiting customers. What they found surprised them. The stereotype of Dad slaving over a smoky barbecue grill was wrong—more women were barbecuing. Many cooks were tired of messy charcoal, and many homeowners did not like rusty grills that spoiled the appearance of their decks. Moreover, environmental and safety issues were increasing in importance. In California charcoal starter fluid is considered a pollutant and is banned; in New Jersey the use of charcoal and gas grills on the balconies of condos and apartments has been prohibited to avoid fires. Based on these findings, the team decided Thermos had to produce a barbecue grill that not only made the food taste good, but also looked attractive, used no pollutants, and was safe for balcony use (which meant it had to be electric).

Within one year the basic attributes of the product were defined, and leadership of the team moved to engineering. The critical task for engineering was to design a grill that gave food the cookout taste that conventional electric grills could not provide because they did not get hot enough. To raise the cooking temperature, Thermos's engineers designed a domed vacuum top that trapped heat inside the grill, and they built electric heat rods directly into the surface of the grill. These features made the grill hot enough to sear meat and give it brown barbecue lines and a barbecue taste.

Manufacturing had been active from the early days of the development process, making sure any proposed design could be produced economically. Because manufacturing was involved from the beginning, the team avoided some costly mistakes. At one critical team meeting the engineers said they wanted tapered legs on the grill. Manufacturing explained that tapered legs would have to be custom-made—and would raise manufacturing costs—and persuaded the team to go with straight legs.

When the new grill was introduced on schedule, it was an immediate success. The study of many product development successes, such as that of Thermos's lifestyle team, suggests three strategies managers can implement to increase the likelihood that their product development efforts will result in innovative and successful new products.

INVOLVE BOTH CUSTOMERS AND SUPPLIERS   Many new products fail when they reach the marketplace because they were designed with scant attention to customer needs. Successful product development requires inputs from more than just an organization's members; also needed are inputs from customers and suppliers. Thermos team members spent a month on the road, visiting customers to identify their needs. The revolutionary electric barbecue grill was a direct result of this process. In other cases companies have found it worthwhile to include customer representatives as peripheral members of their product development teams. Boeing, for example, included its customers, the major airlines, in the design of its most recent commercial jet aircraft, the 787 Dreamliner. Boeing built a mockup of the aircraft's cabin and then, over a period of months, allowed each airline's representatives to experiment with repositioning the galleys, seating, aisles, and bathrooms to best meet the needs of their particular airline. Boeing learned a great deal from this process.

ESTABLISH A STAGE–GATE DEVELOPMENT FUNNEL   One of the most common mistakes managers make in product development is trying to fund too many new projects at any one time. This approach spreads the activities of the different value chain functions too thinly over too many different projects. As a consequence, no single project is given the functional resources and attention required.

One strategy for solving this problem is for managers to develop a structured process for evaluating product development proposals and deciding which to support and which to reject. A common solution is to establish a **stage–gate development funnel**, a technique that forces managers to choose among competing projects so functional resources are not spread thinly over too many projects. The funnel gives functional managers control over product development and allows them to intervene and take corrective action quickly and appropriately (see Figure 9.5).

stage–gate development funnel A planning model that forces managers to choose among competing projects so organizational resources are not spread thinly over too many projects.

Figure 9.5

A Stage–Gate Development Funnel

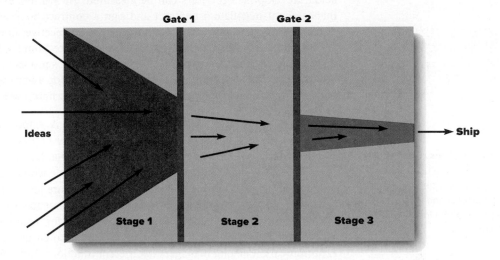

At stage 1 the development funnel has a wide mouth, so top managers initially can encourage employees to come up with as many new product ideas as possible. Managers can create incentives for employees to come up with ideas. Many organizations run "bright-idea programs" that reward employees whose ideas eventually make it through the development process. Other organizations allow research scientists to devote a certain amount of work time to their own projects. Top managers at 3M, for example, have a 15% rule: They expect a research scientist to spend 15% of the workweek working on a project of his or her own choosing. Ideas may be submitted by individuals or by groups. Brainstorming (see Chapter 7) is a technique that managers frequently use to encourage new ideas.

New product ideas are written up as brief proposals. The proposals are submitted to a cross-functional team of managers, who evaluate each proposal at gate 1. The cross-functional team considers a proposal's fit with the organization's strategy and its technical feasibility. Proposals that are consistent with the strategy of the organization and are judged technically feasible pass through gate 1 and into stage 2. Other proposals are turned down (although the door is often left open for reconsidering a proposal later).

product development plan A plan that specifies all of the relevant information that managers need in order to decide whether to proceed with a full-blown product development effort.

The primary goal in stage 2 is to draft a detailed product development plan. The **product development plan** specifies all of the relevant information that managers need to decide whether to go ahead with a full-blown product development effort. The product development plan should include strategic and financial objectives, an analysis of the product's market potential, a list of desired product features, a list of technological requirements, a list of financial and human resource requirements, a detailed development budget, and a time line that contains specific milestones (for example, dates for prototype completion and final launch).

A cross-functional team of managers normally drafts this plan. Good planning requires a good strategic analysis (see Chapter 8), and team members must be prepared to spend considerable time in the field with customers, trying to understand their needs. Drafting a product development plan generally takes about three months. Once completed, the plan is reviewed by a senior management committee at gate 2 (see Figure 9.5). These managers focus on the details of the plan to see whether the proposal is attractive (given its market potential) and viable (given the technological, financial, and human resources that would be needed to develop the product). Senior managers making this review keep in mind all other product development efforts currently being undertaken by the organization. One goal at this point is to ensure that limited organizational resources are used to their maximum effect.

contract book A written agreement that details product development factors such as responsibilities, resource commitments, budgets, time lines, and development milestones.

At gate 2 projects are rejected, sent back for revision, or allowed to pass through to stage 3, the development phase. Product development starts with the formation of a cross-functional team that is given primary responsibility for developing the product. In some companies, at the beginning of stage 3 top managers and cross-functional team members sign a **contract book**, a written agreement that details factors such as responsibilities, resource commitments, budgets, time lines, and development milestones. Signing the contract book is viewed as the symbolic launch of a product development effort. The contract book is also a document against which actual development progress can be measured. At 3M, for example, team members and top management negotiate a contract and sign a contract book at the launch of a development effort, thereby signaling their commitment to the objectives contained in the contract.

The stage 3 development effort can last anywhere from six months to 10 years, depending on the industry and type of product. Some electronics products have development cycles of six months, but it takes from three to five years to develop a new car, about five years to develop a new jet aircraft, and as long as 10 years to develop a new medical drug.

ESTABLISH CROSS-FUNCTIONAL TEAMS   A smooth-running cross-functional team also seems to be a critical component of successful product development, as the experience of Thermos suggests. Marketing, engineering, and manufacturing personnel are **core members** of a successful product development team—the people who have primary responsibility for the product development effort. Other people besides core members work on the project when the need arises, but the core members (generally from three to six individuals) stay with the project from inception to completion of the development effort (see Figure 9.6).

The reason for using a cross-functional team is to ensure a high level of coordination and communication among managers in different functions. Input from both marketing and manufacturing members of Thermos's lifestyle team determined the characteristics of the barbecue that the engineers on the team ended up designing.

If a cross-functional team is to succeed, it must have the right kind of leadership and it must be managed effectively. To be successful, a product development team needs a team leader who can rise above a functional background and take a cross-functional view. In addition to having effective leadership, successful cross-functional product development teams have several other key characteristics. Often core members of successful teams are located close to one another, in the same office space, to foster a sense of shared mission and commitment to a development program. Successful teams develop a clear sense of their objectives and how they will be achieved, the purpose again being to create a sense of shared mission. Thermos eventually sold its grill business to the Char-Broil Division of W.C. Bradley Co. But its story demonstrates the three strategies that help ventures succeed: involving customers and suppliers, establishing a stage-gate development funnel, and establishing cross-functional teams.

core members The members of a team who bear primary responsibility for the success of a project and who stay with a project from inception to completion.

Figure 9.6

Members of a Cross-Functional Product Development Team

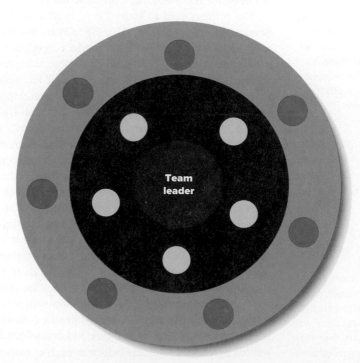

Managing innovation is an increasingly important aspect of a manager's job in an era of dramatic changes in advanced IT. Promoting successful new product development is difficult and challenging, and some product development efforts are much more successful than others. In sum, managers need to recognize that successful innovation and product development cut across roles and functions and require a high level of cooperation. They should recognize the importance of common values and norms in promoting the high levels of cooperation and cohesiveness necessary to build a culture for innovation. They also should reward successful innovators and make heroes of the employees and teams who develop successful new products. Finally, managers should fully utilize the product development techniques just discussed to guide the process.

Summary and Review

VALUE CHAIN MANAGEMENT AND COMPETITIVE ADVANTAGE To achieve high performance, managers try to improve their responsiveness to customers, the quality of their products, and the efficiency of their organization. To achieve these goals, managers can use a number of value chain management techniques to improve the way an organization operates.

LO9-1 ates. In addition, analysis of an organization's value chain can provide several benefits, including increased efficiency, reduced costs, and strengthened collaboration between various functional activities.

LO9-2 **IMPROVING RESPONSIVENESS TO CUSTOMERS** To achieve high performance in a competitive environment, it is imperative that the organization's value chain be managed to produce outputs that have the attributes customers desire. A central task of value chain management is to develop new and improved operating systems that enhance the ability of the organization to economically deliver more of the product attributes that customers desire for the same price. Techniques such as CRM and TQM, JIT, flexible manufacturing, and process reengineering are popular because they promise to do this. As important as responsiveness to customers is, however, managers need to recognize that there are limits to how responsive an organization can be and still cover its costs.

LO9-3 **IMPROVING QUALITY** Managers seek to improve the quality of their organization's output because doing so enables them to better serve customers, to raise prices, and to lower production costs. Total quality management focuses on improving the quality of an organization's products and services and stresses that all of an organization's operations should be directed toward this goal. Putting TQM into practice requires having an organizationwide commitment to TQM, having a strong customer focus, finding ways to measure quality, setting quality improvement goals, soliciting input from employees about how to improve product quality, identifying defects and tracing them to their source, introducing just-in-time inventory systems, getting suppliers to adopt TQM practices, designing products for ease of manufacture, and breaking down barriers between functional departments.

LO9-4 **IMPROVING EFFICIENCY** Improving efficiency requires one or more of the following: the introduction of a TQM program, the adoption of flexible manufacturing technologies, the introduction of just-in-time inventory systems, the establishment of self-managed work teams, and the application of process reengineering. Top management is responsible for setting the context within which efficiency improvements can take place by, for example, emphasizing the need for continuous improvement. Functional-level managers bear prime responsibility for identifying and implementing efficiency-enhancing improvements in operating systems.

LO9-5 **IMPROVING PRODUCT INNOVATION** When technology is changing, managers must quickly innovate new and improved products to protect their competitive advantage. Some value chain strategies managers can use to achieve this are (1) involving both customers and suppliers in the development process; (2) establishing a stage–gate development funnel for evaluating and controlling different product development efforts; and (3) establishing cross-functional teams composed of individuals from different functional departments, and giving each team a leader who can rise above his or her functional background.

Management in Action

Topics for Discussion and Action

Discussion

1. Why is it important for managers to pay close attention to value chain management if they wish to be responsive to their customers? [**LO9-1, 9-2**]

2. What is CRM, and how can it help improve responsiveness to customers? [**LO9-2**]

3. What are the main challenges in implementing a successful total quality management program? [**LO9-3**]

4. What is efficiency, and what are some strategies managers can use to increase it? [**LO9-4**]

5. What is innovation, and what are some strategies managers can use to develop successful new products? [**LO9-5**]

Action

6. Ask a manager how responsiveness to customers, quality, efficiency, and innovation are defined and measured in his or her organization. [**LO9-1, 9-2**]

7. Go to a local store, restaurant, or supermarket; observe how customers are treated; and list the ways in which you think the organization is being responsive or unresponsive to the needs of its customers. How could this business improve its responsiveness to customers? [**LO9-1, 9-2**]

Building Management Skills

Managing the Value Chain [LO9-1, 9-2]

Choose an organization with which you are familiar—one that you have worked in or patronized or one that has received extensive coverage in the popular press. The organization should be involved in only one industry or business. Answer these questions about the organization:

1. What is the output of the organization?
2. Describe the value chain activities that the organization uses to produce this output.

3. What product attributes do customers of the organization desire?

4. Try to identify improvements that might be made to the organization's value chain to boost its responsiveness to customers, quality, efficiency, and innovation.

Managing Ethically [LO9-1, 9-4]

After implementing efficiency-improving techniques, many companies commonly lay off hundreds or thousands of employees whose services are no longer required. And frequently remaining employees must perform more tasks more quickly—a situation that can generate employee stress and other work-related problems. Also, these employees may experience guilt because they stayed while many of their colleagues and friends were fired.

Questions

1. Either by yourself or in a group, think through the ethical implications of using a new functional strategy to improve organizational performance.

2. What criteria would you use to decide which kind of strategy is ethical to adopt and how far to push employees to raise the level of their performance?

3. How big a layoff, if any, is acceptable? If layoffs are acceptable, what could be done to reduce their harm to employees?

Small Group Breakout Exercise

How to Compete in the Sandwich Business [LO9-1, 9-2]

Form groups of three or four people, and appoint one member as the spokesperson who will communicate your findings to the class when called on by the instructor. Then discuss the following scenario:

You and your partners are thinking about opening a new kind of sandwich shop that will compete head-to-head with Subway and Jimmy John's. Because these chains have good brand-name recognition, it is vital that you find some source of competitive advantage for your new sandwich shop, and you are meeting to brainstorm ways of obtaining one.

1. Identify the product attributes that a typical sandwich shop customer wants the most.

2. In what ways do you think you will be able to improve on the operations and processes of existing sandwich shops and increase responsiveness to customers through better product quality, efficiency, or innovation?

Be the Manager [LO9-1, 9-3, 9-4, 9-5]

How to Build Flatscreen Displays

You are the top manager of a start-up company that will produce innovative new flatscreen displays for PC makers like Apple and HP. The flatscreen display market is highly competitive, so there is considerable pressure to reduce costs. Also, PC makers are demanding ever-higher quality and better features to please customers. In addition, they demand that delivery of your product meets their production schedule needs. Functional managers want your advice on how to best meet these requirements, especially because

they are in the process of recruiting new workers and building a production facility.

Questions

1. What kinds of techniques discussed in the chapter can help your functional managers to increase efficiency?

2. In what ways can these managers develop a program to increase quality and innovation?

3. What critical lessons do these managers need to learn about value chain management?

Bloomberg Businessweek Case in the News

At KFC, a Bucketful of Trouble [LO 9-1, 9-2, 9-3]

Ruari Lee didn't care about supply chains, distribution centers, logistics, or any of the finer points of the globalized economy. All he wanted was his regular chicken fillet burger meal at KFC. But the restaurant operator's shop in Kendal, a town in northern England, had been closed four days that week in mid-February, like many of the other U.K. restaurants belonging to the chain formerly known as Kentucky Fried Chicken. The reason for the shutdown: There was no chicken.

"It's ridiculous," says Lee, who dropped by the reopened store on Feb. 23 after work. It's also a telling sign of the need for reliable supply chains, the often overlooked systems that can make—or break—a business's ability to operate smoothly.

In a global economy where fewer and fewer goods are made near where they're sold, managing the movement of those goods from manufacturers to shops and customers has become more essential—and risky—to any business. That's the case not only for major manufacturers (Airbus SE shuttles airplane parts between 14 plants across a half-dozen countries) but also for the restaurant chain that serves up a 14-piece "bargain bucket" of Original Recipe chicken with fries for £16.99 ($24) to hungry patrons in England.

When things go right, companies can manage with less inventory on hand, reducing costs. "Everyone's trying to save money in logistics," says Malory Davies, editor of *Logistics Manager* magazine. "Everyone's trying to become

more efficient." When the supply chain goes awry, bottlenecks may develop that not only make a business operate less efficiently but can also wreak havoc on products that are particularly time-sensitive. That's what happened at KFC, which pared back its logistics network to cut expenses and ended up leaving about two-thirds of its 900 outlets across the U.K. without chicken for several days.

KFC, which says 3% of its U.K. restaurants remain closed, on Feb. 28 was also hit by a gravy shortage. "Since we deliver hundreds of items, including fresh and temperature-controlled, to our 900 restaurants, it brings an incredible amount of complexity to the process," says a spokesman.

The epicenter of the so-called #KFCCrisis was in Rugby in central

England at a KFC distribution center, which suffered a breakdown in its first week as the hub of the chain's new cost-cutting strategy. Before getting anywhere near Colonel Sanders's 11 herbs and spices, tons of chicken spoiled there or in the backs of trucks that idled for hours as drivers awaited instructions that never came. Yum! Brands Inc., the U.S.-based fast-food giant that owns KFC, is now tallying millions of dollars in lost sales.

In February prior to the shutdown, KFC dropped its longtime food-delivery partner, Bidvest, and switched to a pair of German outfits, DHL and QSL. In announcing the deal, they'd promised "a new benchmark" in food supply, consolidating from five regional distribution sites to just the one in Rugby. Changing long-standing supply practices can be risky. That's especially true with chicken. KFC delivers fresh meat to its stores to be breaded and fried on-site. Because chicken is prone to contamination from campylobacter and salmonella, it's subject to strict regulations on the conditions of transport, which must be done in refrigerated trucks. Many other fast-food chains, including McDonald's and Taco Bell, use frozen chicken, which is easier to handle.

KFC's U.K. restaurants get most of their chicken from two huge suppliers. One of them, 2 Sisters Food Group, is owned by Ranjit Singh Boparan, an entrepreneur known as the Chicken King. The company produces one-third of the poultry products eaten in the U.K., according to its website, processing 6 million birds a week. The other, Moy Park, is based in Northern Ireland and has processing plants across the U.K. It works with more than 800 poultry farms, including independents.

From those suppliers, the meat is sent via truck to the distribution center, and that's where things went awry. DHL, a division of Germany's Deutsche Post AG that's better known for delivering parcels to online shoppers' front doors, provides trucks and warehousing, while QSL is responsible for stock management, using an information system it says is state-of-the-art for the food-delivery sector.

Under the previous deal with Bidvest, part of South Africa's Bid Corp., chicken was sent from the regional distribution sites to KFC stores. With the new system, all meat is dispatched from the Rugby hub to satellite depots, then moved to smaller vehicles for the last leg of the journey, says Mick Rix, national officer at the GMB trade union, whose members were among 255 employees who lost jobs when one of the old distribution sites was shut.

That's a tried-and-true model for delivery of auto parts or express parcels. "But chicken and car parts are not the same," Rix says. "DHL's model is completely different to that of the specialist food-distribution companies who do nothing but temperature-controlled deliveries." DHL and QSL didn't respond to requests for comment.

KFC initially downplayed the chicken shortage as a result of "a couple of teething problems" in the new supply setup. By the end of the first week of the snafu, with dozens of stores still shut, the chain changed its tune, taking out full-page newspaper ads to apologize and sending lighthearted tweets that rearranged the chain's brand letters to FCK.

KFC needs to reassure consumers fast for a simple reason: They have plenty of other options. Says longtime patron Lee, munching on a chicken burger in Kendal: "There's always a McDonald's down the road."

Questions for Discussion

1. How did KFC's decision to cut costs impact its competitive advantage?

2. What should KFC had done differently to address customer complaints?

3. Cite steps KFC could have taken to maintain the quality of its chicken supply chain.

Source: Christopher Jasper and Eric Pfanner, "At KFC, a Bucketful of Trouble," *Bloomberg Businessweek,* March 5, 2018, pp. 20–21. Used with permission of Bloomberg L.P. Copyright © 2017. All rights reserved.

Notes

1. A. Gasparro, "Kraft Heinz's CEO on Cost-Cutting, Dealmaking and Oprah," *The Wall Street Journal,* www.wsj.com, May 16, 2017; B. Sweeney, "Kraft Heinz CEO: It's All about Long-Term Perspective, Not Ruthless Cost-Cutting," *Crain's Chicago Business,* www.chicagobusiness.com, September 12, 2017.

2. Gasparro, "Kraft Heinz's CEO on Cost-Cutting"; Sweeney, "Kraft Heinz CEO"; A. Gasparro, "Tightfisted New Owners Put Heinz on Diet," *The Wall Street Journal,* www.wsj.com, February 10, 2014.

3. Sweeney, "Kraft Heinz CEO; see also Gasparro, "Tightfisted New Owners Put Heinz on Diet."

4. Sweeney, "Kraft Heinz CEO."

5. B. Kowitt, "Why Kraft Heinz Is Betting Big on Eggs," *Fortune,* http://fortune.com, February 26, 2018; D. Buss, "Customer-Led Innovation: Five Questions with Kraft Heinz's Greg Guidotti," *Brandchannel,* www.brandchannel.com, March 5, 2018.

6. Kowitt, "Why Kraft Heinz Is Betting Big on Eggs"; Buss, "Customer-Led Innovation."

7. S. Bomkamp, "Processed-Food Stalwart Kraft Heinz Creates Unit to Go after Health-Conscious Consumers," *Chicago Tribune,* www.chicagotribune.com, March 7, 2018.

8. "Gartner Announces Rankings of the 2017 Supply Chain Top 25," www.gartner.com, May 25, 2017.

9. See D. Garvin, "What Does Product Quality Really Mean?" *Sloan Management Review* 26 (Fall 1984), 25–44; P.B. Crosby, *Quality Is Free* (New York: Mentor Books, 1980); A. Gabor, *The Man Who Discovered Quality* (New York: Times Books, 1990).

10. K. MacDonald, "Nintendo Announces New Mario Film with Minions Studio," *The Guardian,* www.theguardian.com, February 1, 2018.

11. M. Reyes, "2018 3D Movie Scheduled: The Full List of Titles and Release Dates," *Cinema Blend,* www.cinemablend.com, accessed March 30, 2018.

12. Michael E. Porter, *Competitive Advantage: Creating and Sustaining Superior Performance* (New York: Free Press, 1985).

13. K. Robson, *Service-ability: Create a Customer Centric Culture and Achieve*

Competitive Advantage (New York: Wiley, 2013).

14. M.E. Porter and J.E. Heppelmann, "How Smart, Connected Products Are Transforming Competition," *Harvard Business Review,* https://hbr.org, accessed March 31, 2018.

15. D.F. Abell, *Defining the Business: The Starting Point of Strategic Planning* (Englewood Cliffs, NJ: Prentice-Hall, 1980).

16. D. Owen, "Customer Satisfaction at the Push of a Button," *The New Yorker,* www.newyorker.com, February 5, 2018; G. Dickinson, "The Smiley Feedback Buttons at Airports Do Actually Work—and They Are Changing the Way We Travel," *(London) Telegraph,* www.telegraph.co.uk, February 16, 2018.

17. Owen, "Customer Satisfaction at the Push of a Button"; D. Eisen, "Customer Satisfaction Surveys Are Getting It All Wrong: There's a Better Way," *Hotel Management,* www.hotelmanagement.net, February 26, 2018.

18. Owen, "Customer Satisfaction at the Push of a Button"; Eisen, "Customer Satisfaction Surveys Are Getting It All Wrong."

19. Owen, "Customer Satisfaction at the Push of a Button"; HappyOrNot home page, https://www.happy-or-not.com, accessed March 9, 2018.

20. Owen, "Customer Satisfaction at the Push of a Button."

21. According to Richard D'Aveni, the process of pushing price-attribute curves to the right is a characteristic of the competitive process. See R. D'Aveni, *Hypercompetition* (New York: Free Press, 1994).

22. S. Nassauer, "Wal-Mart to Drop Wild Oats Organic Food Brand," *The Wall Street Journal,* www.wsj.com, April 25, 2016.

23. "Southwest Airlines Reports Record Fourth Quarter and Annual Profit; 45th Consecutive Year of Profitability," http://investors.southwest.com, January 25, 2018.

24. "Bags Fly Free®," www.southwest.com, accessed March 30, 2018.

25. J. Schleckser, "The Secret to the Success of Southwest Airlines, Google, and Ritz Carlton: It's Not What You Think," *Inc.,* www.inc.com, October 17, 2017.

26. "Management Bios: Ronald M. Shaich," www.panerabread.com, accessed March 30, 2018.

27. J. Kell, "Panera Bread Says It Hit $1 Billion Digital Sales Target," *Fortune,* http://fortune.com, June 14, 2017.

28. "Management Bios: Blaine E. Hurst," www.panerabread.com, accessed March 30, 2018.

29. "The 2017 QSR 50," *QSR,* www.qsr.com, accessed March 30, 2018; "Restaurant Business Names Panera Bread's Ron Shaich 2018 Restaurant Leader of the Year," *Restaurant Business,* www.restaurantbusinessonline.com, February 14, 2018.

30. "Adidas Is a Trailblazer," www.salesforce.com, accessed March 30, 2018;

N. Gilliland, "How Adidas Uses Digital to Enable Powerful Experiences," https://econsultancy.com, May 16, 2017.

31. "Buyer's Guide to Social CRM Software," https://technologyadvice.com, accessed May 30, 2018.

32. The view of quality as reliability goes back to the work of Deming and Juran; see Gabor, *The Man Who Discovered Quality.*

33. See Garvin, "What Does Product Quality Really Mean?"; Crosby, *Quality Is Free;* Gabor, *The Man Who Discovered Quality.*

34. "Most Owners Still in Love with Their Three-Year-Old Vehicles, J.D. Power Finds," www.jdpower.com, February 14, 2018.

35. See J.W. Dean and D.E. Bowen, "Management Theory and Total Quality: Improving Research and Practice through Theory Development," *Academy of Management Review* 19 (1994), 392–418.

36. For general background information, see J.C. Anderson, M. Rungtusanatham, and R.G. Schroeder, "A Theory of Quality Management Underlying the Deming Management Method," *Academy of Management Review* 19 (1994), 472–509; "How to Build Quality," *The Economist,* September 23, 1989, 91–92; Gabor, *The Man Who Discovered Quality;* Crosby, *Quality Is Free.*

37. Bowles, "Is American Management Really Committed to Quality?" *Management Review,* April 1992, 42–46.

38. "The History of Six Sigma," https://www.isixsigma.com, accessed March 31, 2018.

39. Gabor, *The Man Who Discovered Quality.*

40. J. Biolos, "Six Sigma Meets the Service Economy—Six Sigma: It's Not Just for Manufacturing," *Harvard Business School: Working Knowledge Archive,* hbswk.hbs.edu/archive/3278.html, January 27, 2003.

41. S. Kumar, "Six Sigma at Citibank," Sigma Way, www.gosigmaway.com/index.php/easyblog/entry/six-sigma-at-citibank#sthash.15OXtwLH.dpuf, April 2, 2014.

42. R. Rucker, "Six Sigma at Citibank," Quality Digest, www.qualitydigest.com/dec99/html/citibank.html.

43. Meyers Brothers Kalicka, "MBK Advantage," https://www.mbkcpa.com, accessed March 9, 2018; G. O'Brien, "A Different Kind of Number Crunching," *BusinessWest,* June 26, 2017, 34–37; Cori Urban, "Reader Raves: Meyers Brothers Kalicka Gets Award for Best Accountant," *MassLive,* www.masslive.com, January 21, 2013.

44. Meyers Brothers Kalicka, "MBK Advantage."

45. O'Brien, "A Different Kind of Number Crunching,"

46. Ibid.

47. Ibid., 35.

48. S. McCartney, "It Can't Be This Hard to Board a Plane," *The Wall Street Journal,* www.wsj.com, March 1, 2017; K. Paul, "American Airlines' 'Simplified' New Boarding Process

Has Nine Groups," *Market Watch,* www.marketwatch.com, February 25, 2017.

49. "Episode 197: Airplane Boarding," *MythBusters Results,* http://mythbustersresults.com, December 16, 2012.

50. C. Morran, "4 Things That Make Airline Boarding a Complete Mess," *Consumerist,* https://consumerist.com, November 18, 2018.

51. "Boarding the Plane," www.southwest.com, accessed March 30, 2018; B. Sumers, "Why the Airline Boarding Process Is All Wrong," *Condé Nast Traveler,* www.cntraveler.com, February 17, 2016.

52. "Baggage Fees by Airline 2017," www.bts.gov, accessed March 30, 2018.

53. P. Nemetz and L. Fry, "Flexible Manufacturing Organization: Implication for Strategy Formulation," *Academy of Management Review* 13 (1988), 627–38; N. Greenwood, *Implementing Flexible Manufacturing Systems* (New York: Halstead Press, 1986).

54. L. VanHulle, "Lansing Grand River Plant's Milestone 'Means Confidence,'" *Lansing State Journal,* http://archive.lansingstatejournal.com, accessed March 30, 2018.

55. "Lansing Grand River Assembly Plant: Recent Major Investments," http://media.gm.com, accessed March 30, 2018.

56. For an interesting discussion of some other drawbacks of JIT and other "Japanese" manufacturing techniques, see S.M. Young, "A Framework for Successful Adoption and Performance of Japanese Manufacturing Practices in the United States," *Academy of Management Review* 17 (1992), 677–701.

57. E. Lopez, "Behind the Scenes of Walmart's New On-Time, In-Full Policy," *Supply Chain Dive,* www.supplychaindive.com, October 17, 2017.

58. "The E-commerce Threat: CPG Supply Chains Need to Up Their Game," *Food Ingredients First,* www.foodingredientsfirst.com, January 26, 2018.

59. See C.W.L. Hill, "Transaction Cost Economizing as a Source of National Competitive Advantage: The Case of Japan," *Organization Science* 2 (1994); M. Aoki, *Information, Incentives, and Bargaining in the Japanese Economy* (Cambridge: Cambridge University Press, 1989).

60. S. Kessler, "GE Has a Version of Self-Management That Is Much Like Zappos' Holacracy—and It Works," *Quartz,* https://qz.com, June 6, 2017; D.N. Paula, "Are Self-Managed Teams Right for Your Organization?" *LinkedIn,* www.linkedin.com, May 24, 2017.

61. M. Hammer and J. Champy, *Reengineering the Corporation* (New York: HarperBusiness, 1993), 35.

62. Ibid.

63. T. Carman, "Fast Casual Nation: The Movement That Has Changed How America Eats," *The Washington Post,* www.washingtonpost.com, August 29, 2017.

CHAPTER 10

Managing Organizational Structure and Culture

©Patrick Heagney/Getty Images

Learning Objectives

After studying this chapter, you should be able to:

LO10-1 Identify the factors that influence managers' choice of an organizational structure.

LO10-2 Explain how managers group tasks into jobs that are motivating and satisfying for employees.

LO10-3 Describe the types of organizational structures managers can design, and explain why they choose one structure over another.

LO10-4 Explain why managers must coordinate jobs, functions, and divisions using the hierarchy of authority and integrating mechanisms.

LO10-5 List the four sources of organizational culture, and explain why and how a company's culture can lead to competitive advantage.

How can organizational culture influence employee performance and customer service? For close to 50 years, McDonald's corporate headquarters has resided on a 150-acre campus of beautiful trees and walking trails in Oak Brook, Illinois, a western suburb of Chicago. Operating from a Chicago office back in the mid-1950s, the company decided to move to Oak Brook in 1972 to be near its customers, many of whom had moved out of the city to work and raise their families in the suburbs.[1]

In 2018, McDonald's returned to its urban roots. Its corporate headquarters (and well-known Hamburger University) moved to the West Loop neighborhood of Chicago, building a new corporate location on the former site of Oprah Winfrey's Harpo Studios, not far from the urban offices of Google, LinkedIn, and Glassdoor.[2] The decision to move into the city was a dramatic one, made by Steve Easterbrook, McDonald's president and CEO since 2015.

Easterbrook took these drastic measures to try and shift the culture and bureaucratic mind-set of the fast-food giant, and the changes haven't been easy. Relocating to the city is only part of Easterbrook's strategy. In a surprising move, several senior executives who spent most of their professional careers at McDonald's recently announced their retirement. And contrary to McDonald's typical corporate moves, Easterbrook promoted a relative newcomer to the company to become the new president of the USA division. Chris Kempczinski, who joined McDonald's in 2015 as head of strategy and business development from Kraft Foods, has since been promoted to U.S. president of McDonald's.[3]

In addition, more than 400 long-time employees at the corporate headquarters in Oak Brook were offered voluntary buyouts in 2016, which included severance pay commensurate with salary and length of service. The buyouts were part of the company's plan to cut more than $500 million in general and administrative costs by reorganizing and simplifying the company's structure in an effort to modernize its business, streamline operations, and attract new customers.[4]

The global fast-food industry has suffered over the past few years as many consumers, particularly Millennials, have moved away from McDonald's and other chains in search of fresher ingredients that can be customized and ordered via mobile device.[5] Currently there are more than 74 million Millennials in the United States, and this generation has recently surpassed Baby Boomers to become the largest generation in the country. Easterbrook and his executive team realize they cannot ignore this group of consumers, especially as they enter their highest spending years.[6]

Some of the steps McDonald's has taken to attract new customers include removing artificial preservatives from Chicken McNuggets and eliminating high fructose corn syrup from its sandwich buns. In addition, the company recently

Changing the culture and structure at a global giant like McDonald's is never easy. But that hasn't stopped CEO Steve Easterbrook from shaking things up. From moving corporate headquarters to an urban setting in Chicago to introducing digital self-order kiosks in some stores, Easterbrook is on a mission to transform the fast-food chain.
©Hannelore Foerster/Getty Images

announced it would use fresh (not frozen) beef patties for its Quarter Pounder, as it faces stiff competition from fast-casual chains Shake Shack and Smashburger. McDonald's also plans to roll out table service and digital self-order kiosks to 2,500 stores in five major metro areas, including Chicago. And mobile ordering via app is now available for customers on the go across 14,000 U.S. locations.[7] These innovations have received high praise from customers and Wall Street alike, as McDonald's stock price hit an all-time high recently.[8]

And Millennial customers might want to take another look at the Golden Arches and its corporate headquarters in Chicago as a possible new workplace. As Easterbrook acknowledges, the 50+ years in a suburban setting are a proud part of McDonald's heritage, but he thinks it's time to drive a change in organizational culture and bring in people with a fresh perspective. He hopes the move downtown will help McDonald's get closer to customers, the competition, and the trends happening in society. He asks, "Why do you want to be on the edge of one of the most vibrant cities in the world when you can be at the heart of one of the most vibrant cities in the world?"[9]

Overview

As the opening story suggests, organizational structure and culture are powerful influences on how employees work. The way an organization's structure is designed also affects employee behavior and how well the organization functions. In a quickly changing business environment, managers at all levels of an organization must identify the best way to organize people and resources to increase efficiency and effectiveness.

In Part 4 of this book, we examine how managers can organize and control human and other resources to create high-performing organizations. To organize and control (two of the four tasks of management identified in Chapter 1), managers must design an organizational architecture that makes the best use of resources to produce the goods and services customers want. **Organizational architecture** is the combination of organizational structure, culture, control systems, and human resource management (HRM) systems that determines how efficiently and effectively organizational resources are used.

By the end of this chapter, you will be familiar not only with various forms of organizational structures and cultures but also with various factors that determine the organizational design choices that managers make. Then, in Chapters 11 and 12, we examine issues surrounding the design of an organization's control systems and HRM systems.

organizational architecture
The organizational structure, control systems, culture, and human resource management systems that together determine how efficiently and effectively organizational resources are used.

Designing Organizational Structure

LO10-1 Identify the factors that influence managers' choice of an organizational structure.

organizational structure
A formal system of task and reporting relationships that coordinates and motivates organizational members so they work together to achieve an organization's goals.

Organizing is the process by which managers establish the structure of working relationships among employees to allow them to achieve an organization's goals efficiently and effectively. **Organizational structure** is the formal system of task and job reporting relationships that determines how employees use resources to achieve an organization's goals.[10] *Organizational culture,* discussed in Chapter 3, is the shared set of beliefs, values, and norms that influence how people and groups work together to achieve an organization's goals. **Organizational design** is the process by which managers create a specific type of organizational structure and culture so a company can operate in the most efficient and effective way.[11]

Once a company decides what kind of work attitudes and behaviors it wants from its employees, managers create a particular arrangement of task and authority relationships, and promote specific cultural values and norms, to obtain these desired attitudes and behaviors. The challenge facing all companies is to design a structure and a culture that (1) *motivate* managers and employees to work hard and to develop supportive job behaviors and attitudes and (2) *coordinate* the actions of employees, groups, functions, and divisions to ensure they work together efficiently and effectively.

As noted in Chapter 2, according to contingency theory, managers design organizational structures to fit the factors or circumstances that are affecting the company the most and causing the most uncertainty.[12] Thus, there is no one best way to design an organization:

Figure 10.1
Factors Affecting Organizational Structure

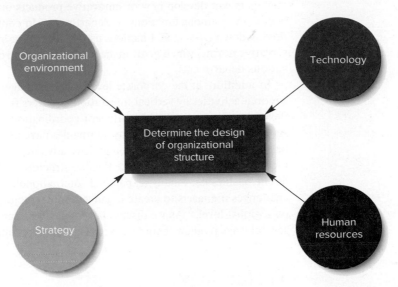

organizational design
The process by which managers make specific organizing choices that result in a particular kind of organizational structure.

Design reflects each organization's specific situation, and researchers have argued that stable, mechanistic structures may be most appropriate in some situations, whereas in others flexible, organic structures might be the most effective. Four factors are important determinants of the type of organizational structure or culture managers select: the nature of the organizational environment, the type of strategy the organization pursues, the technology (and particularly information technology) the organization uses, and the characteristics of the organization's human resources (see Figure 10.1).[13]

The Organizational Environment

In general, the more quickly the external environment is changing and the greater the uncertainty within it, the greater are the problems managers face in trying to gain access to scarce resources. In this situation, to speed decision making and communication and make it easier to obtain resources, managers typically make organizing choices that result in more flexible structures and entrepreneurial cultures.[14] They are likely to decentralize authority, empower lower-level employees to make important operating decisions, and encourage values and norms that emphasize change and innovation—a more organic form of organizing.

In contrast, if the external environment is stable, resources are readily available, and uncertainty is low, then less coordination and communication among people and functions are needed to obtain resources. Managers can make organizing choices that bring more stability or formality to the organizational structure and can establish values and norms that emphasize obedience and being a team player. Managers in this situation prefer to make decisions within a clearly defined hierarchy of authority and to use detailed rules, standard operating procedures (SOPs), and restrictive norms to guide and govern employees' activities—a more mechanistic form of organizing.

As we discussed in Chapter 6, change is rapid in today's marketplace, and increasing competition both at home and abroad is putting greater pressure on managers to attract customers and increase efficiency and effectiveness. Consequently, interest in finding ways to structure organizations—such as through empowerment and self-managed teams—to allow people and departments to behave flexibly has been increasing.

Strategy

Chapter 8 suggests that once managers decide on a strategy, they must choose the right means to implement it. Different strategies often call for the use of different organizational structures and cultures. For example, a differentiation strategy aimed at increasing the value customers perceive in an organization's goods and services usually succeeds best in a flexible structure with a culture that values innovation; flexibility facilitates a differentiation strategy because managers can develop new or innovative products quickly—an activity that requires extensive cooperation among functions or departments. In contrast, a low-cost strategy that is aimed at driving down costs in all functions usually fares best in a more formal structure with more conservative norms, which gives managers greater control over the activities of an organization's various departments.[15]

In addition, at the corporate level, when managers decide to expand the scope of organizational activities by vertical integration or diversification, for example, they need to design a flexible structure to provide sufficient coordination among the different business divisions.[16] As discussed in Chapter 8, many companies have been divesting businesses because managers have been unable to create a competitive advantage to keep them up to speed in fast-changing industries. By moving to a more flexible structure, managers gain more control over their different businesses. Finally, expanding internationally—operating in many different countries— challenges managers to create organizational structures that allow organizations to be flexible on a global level.[17] As we discuss later, managers can group their departments or divisions in several ways to allow them to effectively pursue an international strategy.

Technology

Recall that technology is the combination of skills, knowledge, machines, and computers that are used to design, make, and distribute goods and services. As a rule, the more complicated the technology that an organization uses, the more difficult it is to regulate or control it because more unexpected events can arise. Thus, the more complicated the technology, the greater is the need for a flexible structure and progressive culture to enhance managers' ability to respond to unexpected situations—and give them the freedom and desire to work out new solutions to the problems they encounter. In contrast, the more routine the technology, the more appropriate is a formal structure because tasks are simple and the steps needed to produce goods and services have been worked out in advance.

What makes a technology routine or complicated? One researcher who investigated this issue, Charles Perrow, argued that two factors determine how complicated or nonroutine technology is: task variety and task analyzability.[18] *Task variety* is the number of new or unexpected problems or situations that a person or function encounters in performing tasks or jobs. *Task analyzability* is the degree to which programmed solutions are available to people or functions to solve the problems they encounter. Nonroutine or complicated technologies are characterized by high task variety and low task analyzability; this means many varied problems occur and solving these problems requires significant nonprogrammed decision making. In contrast, routine technologies are characterized by low task variety and high task analyzability; this means the problems encountered do not vary much and are easily resolved through programmed decision making.

Examples of nonroutine technology are found in the work of scientists in an R&D laboratory who develop new products or discover new drugs, and they are seen in the planning exercises an organization's top management team uses to chart future strategy. Examples of routine technology include typical mass production or assembly operations, where workers perform the same task repeatedly and where managers have already identified the programmed solutions necessary to perform a task efficiently. Similarly, in service organizations such as fast-food restaurants, the tasks that crew members perform in making and serving fast food are routine.

Human Resources

LO10-2 Explain how managers group tasks into jobs that are motivating and satisfying for employees.

Final important factors affecting an organization's choice of structure and culture are the characteristics of the human resources it employs. In general, the more highly skilled its workforce, and the greater the number of employees who work together in groups or teams, the more likely an organization is to use a flexible, decentralized structure and a professional culture based on values and norms that foster employee autonomy and self-control. Highly skilled employees, or employees who have internalized strong professional values and norms of behavior as part of their training, usually desire greater freedom and autonomy and dislike close supervision.

Flexible structures, characterized by decentralized authority and empowered employees, are well suited to the needs of highly skilled people. Similarly, when people work in teams, they must be allowed to interact freely and develop norms to guide their own work interactions, which also is possible in a flexible organizational structure. Thus, when designing organizational structure and culture, managers must pay close attention to the needs of the workforce and to the complexity and kind of work employees perform.

In summary, an organization's external environment, strategy, technology, and human resources are the factors to be considered by managers seeking to design the best structure and culture for an organization. The greater the level of uncertainty in the organization's environment, the more complex its strategy and technologies, and the more highly qualified and skilled its workforce, the more likely managers are to design a structure and a culture that are flexible, can change quickly, and allow employees to be innovative in their responses to problems, customer needs, and so on. The more stable the organization's environment, the less complex and more well understood its strategy or technology, and the less skilled its workforce, the more likely managers are to design an organizational structure that is formal and controlling and a culture whose values and norms prescribe how employees should act in particular situations.

Later in the chapter we discuss how managers can create different kinds of organizational cultures. First, however, we discuss how managers can design flexible or formal organizational structures. The way an organization's structure works depends on the organizing choices managers make about three issues:

1. How to group tasks into individual jobs.
2. How to group jobs into functions and divisions.
3. How to allocate authority and coordinate or integrate functions and divisions.

Grouping Tasks into Jobs: Job Design

job design The process by which managers decide how to divide tasks into specific jobs.

The first step in organizational design is **job design**, the process by which managers decide how to divide into specific jobs the tasks that have to be performed to provide customers with goods and services. Managers at McDonald's, for example, have decided how best to divide the tasks required to provide customers with fast, cheap food in each McDonald's restaurant. After experimenting with different job arrangements, McDonald's managers decided on a basic division of labor among chefs and food servers. Managers allocated all the tasks involved in actually cooking the food (putting oil in the fryers, opening packages of frozen french fries, putting beef patties on the grill, making salads, and so on) to the job of chef. They allocated all the tasks involved in giving the food to customers (such as greeting customers, taking orders, putting fries and burgers into bags, and taking money) to food servers. In addition, they created other jobs—the job of dealing with drive-through customers, the job of keeping the restaurant clean, and the job of overseeing employees and responding to unexpected events. The result of the job design process is a *division of labor* among employees, one that McDonald's managers have discovered through experience is most efficient.

Establishing an appropriate division of labor among employees is a critical part of the organizing process, one that is vital to increasing efficiency and effectiveness. At McDonald's, the tasks associated with chef and food server were split into different jobs because managers found that, for the kind of food McDonald's serves, this approach was most efficient. It is efficient because when each employee is given fewer tasks to perform (so that each job becomes more specialized), employees become more productive at performing the tasks that constitute each job.

At Subway sandwich shops, however, managers chose a different kind of job design. At Subway there is no division of labor among the people who make the sandwiches, wrap the sandwiches, give them to customers, and take the money. The roles of chef and food server are combined into one. This different division of tasks and jobs is efficient for Subway and not for McDonald's because Subway serves a limited menu of mostly submarine-style sandwiches that are prepared to order. Subway's production system is far simpler than McDonald's; McDonald's menu is much more varied, and its chefs must cook many different kinds of foods.

job simplification The process of reducing the number of tasks that each worker performs.

Managers of every organization must analyze the range of tasks to be performed and then create jobs that best allow the organization to give customers the goods and services they want. In deciding how to assign tasks to individual jobs, however, managers must be careful not to take **job simplification**, the process of reducing the number of tasks that each worker performs, too far.[19] Too much job simplification may reduce efficiency rather than increase it if workers find their simplified jobs boring and monotonous, become demotivated and unhappy, and as a result, perform at a low level.

Job Enlargement and Job Enrichment

In an attempt to create a division of labor and design individual jobs to encourage workers to perform at a higher level and be more satisfied with their work, several researchers have proposed ways other than job simplification to group tasks into jobs: job enlargement and job enrichment.

job enlargement Increasing the number of different tasks in a given job by changing the division of labor.

Job enlargement is increasing the number of different tasks in a given job by changing the division of labor.[20] For example, because Subway food servers make the food as well as serve it, their jobs are "larger" than the jobs of McDonald's food servers. The idea behind job enlargement is that increasing the range of tasks performed by a worker will reduce boredom and fatigue and may increase motivation to perform at a high level—increasing both the quantity and the quality of goods and services provided. The accompanying "Management Insight" feature describes how a regional fast-food chain has made a commitment to enlisting managers and employees to deliver accurate orders at lightning speed to the delight of its customers.

MANAGEMENT INSIGHT

Pal's Sudden Service Takes Training Seriously

More than 60 years ago, Fred "Pal" Barger started a fast-food restaurant that focused on the usual fare of burgers, fries, hot dogs, and shakes. Headquartered in Kingsport, Tennessee, Pal's Sudden Service has 29 locations in and around the Kingsport area and other towns in southwest Virginia.[21]

What makes Pal's Sudden Service unique is its devotion to speed, accuracy, hiring, and training. The fast-food chain is not your typical eatery. There is no sit-down service at its restaurants. Customers drive up to a window, place their orders face-to-face with an employee, pull around to the other side of the building, take their food, and drive off—in an average of 30 seconds, which is four times faster than the *second-fastest* quick-serve restaurant chain in the country.[22] Not only is Pal's fast, but its pinpoint accuracy is astounding. According to the company, Pal's employees make only 1 mistake in every 3,600 orders.[23]

One reason for the company's success is its hiring and training process. Pal's employs approximately 1,100 workers, 90% of whom work part time and 40% of whom are teenagers between the ages of 16 and 18. The company has created and fine-tuned a screening system to evaluate candidates, which is a survey of agree/disagree statements based on the attitudes and attributes of Pal's top performers.[24]

Once employees have been hired, they are immersed in more than 120 hours of training before they are allowed to work on their own, and they must be certified in each of the jobs they perform. But that's not enough.

Employee training is a big part of the success story at Pal's Sudden Service. The drive-thru eatery is known for its quick, accurate service, with customer order and pickup experiences lasting an average of 30 seconds. Employees undergo more than 120 hours of training before they are allowed to work on their own.
©Carol M. Highsmith/Buyenlarge/Getty Images

Every day on every work shift in every restaurant, the Training Tracker software system randomly generates the names of two to four employees to be recertified in their job tasks, much like taking a pop quiz as part of your work. If an employee fails the test, he or she gets retrained before doing the job again. According to the company, the average employee gets tested two or three times a month. Thom Crosby, Pal's president–CEO, believes that managers are educators and responsible for coaching and training employees as part of their daily routine. In fact, it is Pal's policy that every manager (including the CEO) must identify a coaching and training target they engage with every day to discuss a relevant topic.[25]

Pal's Sudden Service was the first restaurant company of any size to win the prestigious Malcolm Baldrige National Quality Award, which recognizes business excellence, innovation, and leadership. As a result of this award in 2001, the company created its Business Excellence Institute as a way to share its best practices with other companies, including 3M, The Coca-Cola Company, Boston Market, YMCA, and Siemens.[26] Quick and accurate orders, exceptional customer service, and intensive training for all employees continue to be the recipe for success at Pal's Sudden Service.

job enrichment Increasing the degree of responsibility a worker has over his or her job.

Job enrichment is increasing the degree of responsibility a worker has over a job by, for example, (1) empowering workers to experiment to find new or better ways of doing the job, (2) encouraging workers to develop new skills, (3) allowing workers to decide how to do the work and giving them the responsibility for deciding how to respond to unexpected situations, and (4) allowing workers to monitor and measure their own performance.[27] The idea behind job enrichment is that increasing workers' responsibility increases their involvement in their jobs and, thus, improves their interest in the quality of the goods they make or the services they provide.

In general, managers who make design choices that increase job enrichment and job enlargement are likely to increase the degree to which people behave flexibly rather than rigidly or mechanically. Narrow, specialized jobs are likely to lead people to behave in predictable ways; workers who perform a variety of tasks and who are allowed and encouraged to discover new and better ways to perform their jobs are likely to act flexibly and creatively. Thus, managers who enlarge and enrich jobs create a flexible organizational structure, and those who simplify jobs create a more formal structure. If workers are grouped into self-managed work teams, the organization is likely to be flexible because team members provide support for each other and can learn from one another.

The Job Characteristics Model

J. R. Hackman and G. R. Oldham's job characteristics model is an influential model of job design that explains in detail how managers can make jobs more interesting and motivating.[28] Hackman and Oldham's model also describes the likely personal and organizational outcomes that will result from enriched and enlarged jobs.

According to Hackman and Oldham, every job has five characteristics that determine how motivating the job is. These characteristics determine how employees react to their work and lead to outcomes such as high performance and satisfaction and low absenteeism and turnover:

- *Skill variety:* The extent to which a job requires that an employee use a wide range of different skills, abilities, or knowledge. Example: The skill variety required by the job of a research scientist is higher than that called for by the job of a Burger King food server.

- *Task identity:* The extent to which a job requires that a worker perform all the tasks necessary to complete the job, from the beginning to the end of the production process. Example: A craftsworker who takes a piece of wood and transforms it into a custom-made desk has higher task identity than does a worker who performs only one of the numerous operations required to assemble a flat-screen TV.

- *Task significance:* The degree to which a worker feels his or her job is meaningful because of its effect on people inside the organization, such as coworkers, or on people outside the organization, such as customers. Example: A teacher who sees the effect of his or her efforts in a well-educated and well-adjusted student enjoys high task significance compared to a dishwasher who monotonously washes dishes as they come to the kitchen.

- *Autonomy:* The degree to which a job gives an employee the freedom and discretion needed to schedule different tasks and decide how to carry them out. Example: Salespeople who have to plan their schedules and decide how to allocate their time among different customers have relatively high autonomy compared to assembly-line workers, whose actions are determined by the speed of the production line.

- *Feedback:* The extent to which actually doing a job provides a worker with clear and direct information about how well he or she has performed the job. Example: An air traffic controller whose mistakes may result in a midair collision receives immediate feedback on job performance; a person who compiles statistics for a business magazine often has little idea of when he makes a mistake or does a particularly good job.

Hackman and Oldham argue that these five job characteristics affect an employee's motivation because they affect three critical psychological states. The more that employees feel that their work is *meaningful* and that they are *responsible for work outcomes* and *responsible for knowing how those outcomes affect others,* the more motivating work becomes and the more likely employees are to be satisfied and to perform at a high level. Moreover, employees who have jobs that are highly motivating are called on to use their skills more and to perform more tasks, and they are given more responsibility for doing the job. All of the foregoing are characteristic of jobs and employees in flexible structures where authority is decentralized and where employees commonly work with others and must learn new skills to complete the range of tasks for which their group is responsible.

Grouping Jobs into Functions and Divisions: Designing Organizational Structure

Once managers have decided which tasks to allocate to which jobs, they face the next organizing decision: how to group jobs together to best match the needs of the organization's environment, strategy, technology, and human resources. Typically, managers first decide to group jobs into departments and then design a *functional structure* to use organizational resources effectively. As an organization grows and becomes more difficult to control, managers must choose a more complex organizational design, such as a divisional structure or a matrix or product team structure. The different ways in which managers can design organizational structure are discussed next. Selecting and designing an organizational structure to increase efficiency and effectiveness is a significant challenge. As noted in Chapter 8, managers reap the rewards of a well-thought-out strategy only if they choose the right type of structure to implement the strategy. The ability to make the right kinds of organizing choices is often what differentiates effective from ineffective managers and creates a high-performing organization.

Functional Structure

LO10-3 Describe the types of organizational structures managers can design, and explain why they choose one structure over another.

functional structure An organizational structure composed of all the departments that an organization requires to produce its goods or services.

A *function* is a group of people, working together, who possess similar skills or use the same kind of knowledge, tools, or techniques to perform their jobs. Manufacturing, sales, and research and development are often organized into functional departments. A **functional structure** is an organizational structure composed of all the departments that an organization requires to produce its goods or services. Figure 10.2 shows the functional structure that Pier 1 Imports, a home furnishings company, uses to supply its customers with a range of goods from around the world to satisfy their desires for new and innovative products.[29]

Within Pier 1's organizational structure, the main functions include finance and administration, merchandising (purchasing the goods), global sourcing (managing the vendors who supply the goods), marketing and sales, planning and allocations (managing credit and product distribution), and human resources. Each job inside a function exists because it helps the function perform the activities necessary for high organizational performance. Thus, within the marketing function are all the jobs necessary to efficiently advertise Pier 1's products to increase their appeal to customers (such as promotion, digital media, and visual communication).

Figure 10.2

The Functional Structure of Pier 1 Imports

There are several advantages to grouping jobs according to function. First, when people who perform similar jobs are grouped together, they can learn from observing one another and thus become more specialized and can perform at a higher level. The tasks associated with one job often are related to the tasks associated with another job, which encourages cooperation within a function. In Pier 1's marketing department, for example, the person designing the graphics for an ad campaign works closely with the person responsible for designing store layouts and with visual communication experts. As a result, Pier 1 can develop a strong, focused marketing campaign to differentiate its products.

Second, when people who perform similar jobs are grouped together, it is easier for managers to monitor and evaluate their performance.[30] Imagine if marketing experts, purchasing experts, and real estate experts were grouped together in one function and supervised by a manager from merchandising. Obviously, the merchandising manager would not have the expertise to evaluate all these different people appropriately. A functional structure allows workers to evaluate how well coworkers are performing their jobs, and if some workers are performing poorly, more experienced workers can help them develop new skills.

Finally, managers appreciate functional structure because it lets them create the set of functions they need to scan and monitor the competitive environment and obtain information about how it is changing.[31] With the right set of functions in place, managers are in a good position to develop a strategy that allows the organization to respond to its changing situation. Employees in the marketing group can specialize in monitoring new marketing developments that will allow Pier 1 to better target its customers. Employees in merchandising can monitor all potential suppliers of home furnishings, both at home and abroad, to find the goods most likely to appeal to Pier 1's customers.

As an organization grows, and particularly as its task environment and strategy change because it is beginning to produce a wider range of goods and services for different kinds of customers, several problems can make a functional structure less efficient and effective.[32] First, managers in different functions may find it more difficult to communicate and coordinate with one another when they are responsible for several different kinds of products, especially as the organization grows both domestically and internationally. Second, functional managers may become so preoccupied with supervising their own specific departments and achieving their departmental goals that they lose sight of the organization's goals. If that happens, organizational effectiveness will suffer because managers will be viewing issues and problems facing the organization only from their own, relatively narrow departmental perspectives.[33] Both of these problems can reduce efficiency and effectiveness.

Divisional Structures: Product, Market, and Geographic

divisional structure An organizational structure composed of separate business units, within which are the functions that work together to produce a specific kind of product for a specific kind of customer.

As the problems associated with growth and diversification increase over time, managers must search for new ways to organize their activities to overcome the problems associated with a functional structure. Most managers of large organizations choose a **divisional structure** and create a series of business units to produce a specific kind of product for a specific kind of customer. Each *division* is a collection of functions or departments that work together to

Pier 1 organizes its operations by function, which means that employees can more easily learn from one another and improve the service they provide to customers.
©Marlin Levison/ZUMAPRESS/Newscom

produce the product. The goal behind the change to a divisional structure is to create smaller, more manageable units within the organization. There are three forms of divisional structure (see Figure 10.3).[34] When managers organize divisions according to the *type of good or service* they provide, they adopt a product structure. When managers organize divisions according to the *area of the country or world* they operate in, they adopt a geographic structure. When managers organize divisions according to *the type of customer* they focus on, they adopt a market structure.

PRODUCT STRUCTURE   Imagine the problems that managers at Pier 1 would encounter if they decided to diversify into producing and selling cars, fast food, and health insurance—in addition to home furnishings—and tried to use their existing set of functional managers to oversee the production of all four kinds of products. No manager would have the necessary skills or abilities to oversee those four products. No individual marketing manager, for example, could effectively market cars, fast food, health insurance, and home furnishings at the same time. To perform a functional activity successfully, managers must have experience in specific markets or industries. Consequently, if managers decide to diversify into new industries or to expand their range of products, they commonly design a product structure to organize their operations (see Figure 10.3A).

Using a **product structure**, managers place each distinct product line or business in its own, self-contained division and give divisional managers the responsibility for devising an appropriate business-level strategy to allow the division to compete effectively in its industry or market.[35] Each division is self-contained because it has a complete set of all the functions— marketing, R&D, finance, and so on—that it needs to produce or provide goods or services efficiently and effectively. Functional managers report to divisional managers, and divisional managers report to top or corporate managers.

Grouping functions into divisions focused on particular products has several advantages for managers at all levels in the organization. First, a product structure allows functional managers to specialize in only one product area, so they can build expertise and fine-tune their skills in this particular area. Second, each division's managers can become experts in their industry; this expertise helps them choose and develop a business-level strategy to differentiate their products or lower their costs while meeting the needs of customers. Third, a product structure frees corporate managers from the need to supervise directly each division's day-to-day operations; this latitude lets corporate managers create the best corporate-level strategy to maximize

product structure An organizational structure in which each product line or business is handled by a self-contained division.

Figure 10.3

Product, Geographic, and Market Structures

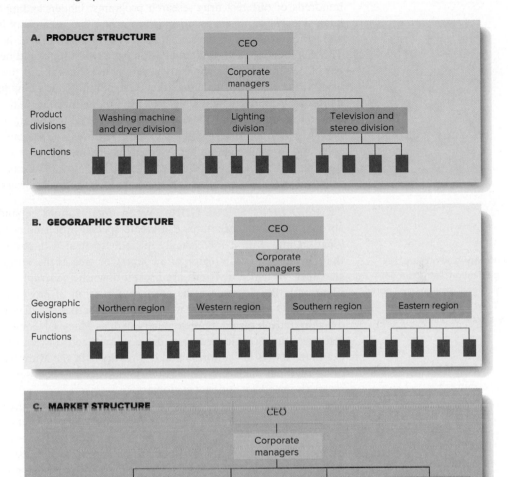

the organization's future growth and ability to create value. Corporate managers are likely to make fewer mistakes about which businesses to diversify into or how to best expand internationally, for example, because they can take an organizationwide view.[36] Corporate managers also are likely to evaluate better how well divisional managers are doing, and they can intervene and take corrective action as needed.

The extra layer of management, the divisional management layer, can improve the use of organizational resources. Moreover, a product structure puts divisional managers close to their customers and lets them respond quickly and appropriately to the changing task environment. One pharmaceutical company that successfully adopted a new product structure to better organize its activities is GlaxoSmithKline (GSK). The need to innovate new kinds of prescription drugs to boost performance is a continual battle for pharmaceutical companies. In the 2000s many of these companies merged to try to increase their research productivity, and one of them, GlaxoSmithKline, was created from the merger between Glaxo Wellcome and Smith-Kline Beecham.[37] Prior to the merger, both companies experienced a steep decline in the number of new prescription drugs their scientists were able to invent. The problem facing the new company's top managers was how to best use and combine the talents of the scientists and researchers from both of the former companies to allow them to quickly innovate exciting new drugs.

Top managers realized that after the merger there would be enormous problems associated with coordinating the activities of the thousands of research scientists who were working on hundreds of different drug research programs. Understanding the problems associated with large size, the top managers decided to group the researchers into eight product divisions to allow them to focus on particular clusters of diseases such as heart disease or viral infections. The members of each product division were told they would be rewarded based on the number of new prescription drugs they were able to invent and the speed with which they could bring these new drugs to the market. GlaxoSmithKline's new product structure worked well; its research productivity doubled after the reorganization, and a record number of new drugs moved into clinical trials.[38] Several years ago, GSK teamed up with Swiss pharmaceutical firm Novartis in a consumer health care joint venture, which focused on products such as toothpaste and over-the-counter flu and cough medicines. Although the joint venture reaped benefits for both companies, GSK recently agreed to buy Novartis's stake in the venture for $13 billion, as Novartis focuses corporate efforts on re-invigorating its drug-discovery pipeline.[39]

geographic structure An organizational structure in which each region of a country or area of the world is served by a self-contained division.

GEOGRAPHIC STRUCTURE   When organizations expand rapidly both at home and abroad, functional structures can create special problems because managers in one central location may find it increasingly difficult to deal with the different problems and issues that may arise in each region of a country or area of the world. In these cases, a geographic structure, in which divisions are broken down by geographic location, is often chosen (see Figure 10.3B). To achieve the corporate mission of providing next-day mail service, Fred Smith, CEO of FedEx, chose a geographic structure and divided up operations by creating a division in each region. Large retailers such as Macy's, Neiman Marcus, and Brooks Brothers also use a geographic structure. Because the needs of retail customers differ by region—for example, shorts in California and down parkas in the Midwest—a geographic structure gives retail regional managers the flexibility they need to choose the range of products that best meets the needs of regional customers.

In adopting a *global geographic structure,* as shown in Figure 10.4A, managers locate different divisions in each of the world regions where the organization operates. Managers are most likely to do this when they pursue a multidomestic strategy because customer needs vary widely by country or world region. If products that appeal to U.S. customers do not sell in Europe, the Pacific Rim, or South America, managers must customize the products to meet the needs of customers in those different world regions; a global geographic structure with global divisions will allow them to do this. For example, food and beverage companies need to customize the taste of their products to closely match the desires of customers in different countries and world regions.

In contrast, to the degree that customers abroad are willing to buy the same kind of product or slight variations thereof, managers are more likely to pursue a global strategy. In this case, they are more likely to use a global product structure. In a *global product structure,* each product division, not the country and regional managers, takes responsibility for deciding where to manufacture its products and how to market them in countries worldwide (see Figure 10.4B). Product division managers manage their own global value chains and decide where to establish foreign subsidiaries to distribute and sell their products to customers in foreign countries.

market structure An organizational structure in which each kind of customer is served by a self-contained division; also called *customer structure.*

MARKET STRUCTURE   Sometimes the pressing issue facing managers is to group functions according to the type of customer buying the product in order to tailor the products the organization offers to each customer's unique demands. A PC maker such as Dell, for example, has several kinds of customers, including large businesses (which might demand networks of computers linked to a mainframe computer), small companies (which may need just a few PCs linked together), educational users in schools and universities (which might want thousands of independent PCs for their students), and individual users (who may want a high-quality multimedia PC so they can play the latest video games).

To satisfy the needs of diverse customers, a company might adopt a market structure, which groups divisions according to the particular kinds of customers they serve (see Figure 10.3C). A market structure lets managers respond to the needs of their customers and allows them to act flexibly in making decisions in response to customers' changing needs. To spearhead its turnaround in the PC business, for example, Dell created four streamlined market divisions that each focus on being responsive to one particular type of customer: individual consumers, small businesses, large companies, and government and state agencies.

Figure 10.4

Global Geographic and Global Product Structures

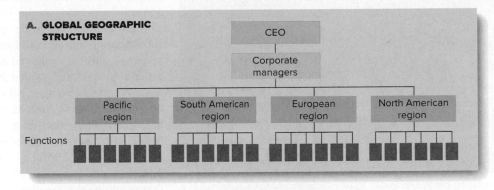

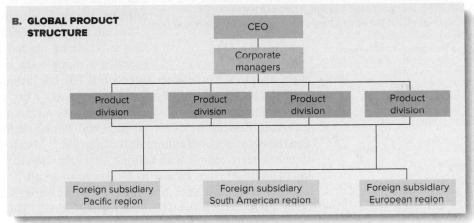

Organizations and their management need to continually evaluate structure and culture to ensure that operations are working according to plan. The accompanying "Manager as a Person" feature describes how one manager led the culture changes at a sports organization to improve its chances at overall success.

MANAGER AS A PERSON

Theo Epstein Changes Cubs Culture and Wins Big

108 years is a long time to wait for a World Series victory, just ask the millions of Chicago Cubs fans around the country. The "Lovable Losers" in Chicago are no more, thanks to a 2016 World Series win and an organization that believes in putting the team first. This approach has been embraced by the Ricketts family, who bought the Cubs in 2009, and by the management team the owners tapped to help break the championship curse.

Theo Epstein became the Cubs president of operations in late 2011, coming from his success in Boston where he remade the Red Sox and guided them to World Series wins in 2004 and 2007—more than 86 years after the team had last won the coveted baseball title.[40] When Epstein took over the Cubs top job, he asked for patience, warning fans it could take a while to put the key ingredients together to make the Cubs a World Series contender. And fans were patient, having to wait only five years to bask in championship glory.[41]

Hoisting the World Series trophy to celebrate the Chicago Cubs' 2016 championship season, Theo Epstein knows a thing or two about the key ingredients needed for a winning organizational culture.
©PictureGroup/Sipa USA/Newscom

As part of the team's makeover, and shortly after he took over the Cubs, Epstein called a meeting with every manager, coach, scout, instructor, trainer, and baseball operations person in the organization. This four-day summit focused on hitting, pitching, defense and base running, and character (an unusual topic for a baseball meeting). Epstein explained his reasoning for discussing a player's character: "What types of human beings we wanted and what our expectations would be for players, how we want them to behave." As a result of the summit, Epstein put together a spiral-bound book of more than 250 pages that defined the organization's doctrine and managerial philosophy. Epstein titled the book, *The Cubs Way,* and it became a "living, breathing document" that would be the foundation for the organization's culture and mission to win the World Series.[42]

In addition to drafting young talented players, Epstein knew he needed a manager who could bring together a young team and make them a family that cared about each other—not an easy task. He got his man in Joe Maddon, a journeyman ball player and well-respected bench coach. After taking the Tampa Bay Rays to the World Series in 2008, Maddon caught the attention of many baseball executives, including Epstein. By 2015, Maddon had signed on to become the Cubs manager, and the organizational culture shift continued.[43] Maddon's quirky, low-key managerial style has been credited with keeping his young Cubs team loose and focused and making them believe they have what it takes to win it all.[44]

After more than a century without a World Series win, the Chicago Cubs seem to be on their way to a new winning tradition. Credit Theo Epstein (named the world's greatest leader in 2017 by *Fortune* magazine) and his managers for changing the organizational culture and embracing an atmosphere that values the importance of a team approach.

Matrix and Product Team Designs

Moving to a product, market, or geographic divisional structure allows managers to respond more quickly and flexibly to the particular circumstances they confront. However, when information technology or customer needs are changing rapidly and the environment is uncertain, even a divisional structure may not give managers enough flexibility to respond to the environment quickly. To operate effectively under these conditions, managers must design the most flexible kinds of organizational structure available: a matrix structure or a product team structure (see Figure 10.5).

matrix structure An organizational structure that simultaneously groups people and resources by function and by product.

MATRIX STRUCTURE   In a matrix structure, managers group people and resources in two ways simultaneously: by function and by product.[45] Employees are grouped by *functions* to allow them to learn from one another and become more skilled and productive. In addition, employees are grouped into *product teams* in which members of different functions work together to develop a specific product. The result is a complex network of reporting relationships among product teams and functions that makes the matrix structure very flexible (see Figure 10.5A). Each person in a product team reports to two managers: (1) a functional boss, who assigns individuals to a team and evaluates their performance from a functional perspective, and (2) the boss of the product team, who evaluates their performance on the team. Thus, team members are known as *two-boss employees.* The functional employees assigned to product teams change over time as the specific skills that the team needs change. At the beginning of the product development process, for example, engineers and R&D specialists are assigned to

Figure 10.5

Matrix and Product Team Structures

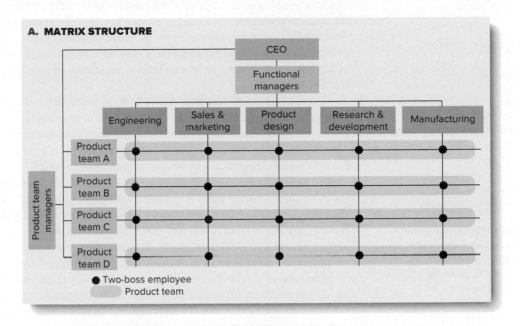

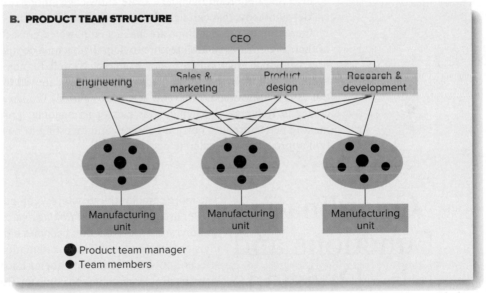

a product team because their skills are needed to develop new products. When a provisional design has been established, marketing experts are assigned to the team to gauge how customers will respond to the new product. Manufacturing personnel join when it is time to find the most efficient way to produce the product. As their specific jobs are completed, team members leave and are reassigned to new teams. In this way the matrix structure makes the most use of human resources.

To keep the matrix structure flexible, product teams are empowered and team members are responsible for making most of the important decisions involved in product development.[46] The product team manager acts as a facilitator, controlling the financial resources and trying to keep the project on time and within budget. The functional managers try to ensure that the product is the best it can be to maximize its differentiated appeal.

High-tech companies that operate in environments where new product development takes place monthly or yearly have used matrix structures successfully for many years, and the need to innovate quickly is vital to the organization's survival. The flexibility afforded by a matrix structure lets managers keep pace with a changing and increasingly complex environment.[47]

PRODUCT TEAM STRUCTURE   The dual reporting relationships that are at the heart of a matrix structure have always been difficult for managers and employees to deal with. Often the functional boss and the product boss make conflicting demands on team members, who do not know which boss to satisfy first. Also, functional and product team bosses may come into conflict over precisely who is in charge of which team members and for how long. To avoid these problems, managers have devised a way of organizing people and resources that still allows an organization to be flexible but makes its structure easier to operate: a product team structure.

product team structure An organizational structure in which employees are permanently assigned to a cross-functional team and report only to the product team manager or to one of his or her direct subordinates.

The product team structure differs from a matrix structure in two ways: (1) It does away with dual reporting relationships and two-boss employees, and (2) functional employees are permanently assigned to a cross-functional team that is empowered to bring a new or redesigned product to market. A cross-functional team is a group of managers brought together from different departments to perform organizational tasks. When managers are grouped into cross-functional teams, the artificial boundaries between departments disappear, and a narrow focus on departmental goals is replaced with a general interest in working together to achieve the organization's goals. For example, when mattress company Sealy saw its sales slipping, it pulled together a cross-functional team that was allowed to work outside the organization's hierarchy and quickly design a new mattress. With everyone focused on the goal, team members created a mattress that broke previous sales records.[48]

cross-functional team A group of managers brought together from different departments to perform organizational tasks.

Members of a cross-functional team report only to the product team manager or to one of his or her direct subordinates. The heads of the functions have only an informal advisory relationship with members of the product teams—the role of functional managers is only to counsel and help team members, share knowledge among teams, and provide new technological developments that can help improve each team's performance (see Figure 10.5B).[49]

Increasingly, organizations are making empowered cross-functional teams an essential part of their organizational architecture to help them gain a competitive advantage in fast-changing organizational environments. For example, Newell Brands, the well-known maker of such products as Rubbermaid, Calphalon, and Sharpies, moved to a product structure to speed up the rate of innovation.[50] Several years ago, Newell Brands opened a design and innovation center in Kalamazoo, Michigan, as part of its ongoing "growth game plan," which involves making better product portfolio choices and investing in new marketing, design, and innovation approaches to accelerate performance.[51]

Coordinating Functions and Divisions

LO10-4 Explain why managers must coordinate jobs, functions, and divisions using the hierarchy of authority and integrating mechanisms.

The more complex the structure a company uses to group its activities, the greater are the problems of *linking and coordinating* its different functions and divisions. Coordination becomes a problem because each function or division develops a different orientation toward the other groups that affects how it interacts with them. Each function or division comes to view the problems facing the company from its own perspective; for example, it may develop different views about the major goals, problems, or issues facing a company.

At the functional level, the manufacturing function typically has a short-term view; its major goal is to keep costs under control and get the product out the factory door on time. By contrast, the product development function has a long-term viewpoint because developing a new product is a relatively slow process, and high product quality is seen as more important than low costs. Such differences in viewpoint may make manufacturing and product development managers reluctant to cooperate and coordinate their activities to meet company goals. At the divisional level, in a company with a product structure, employees may become concerned more with making *their* division's products a success than with the profitability of the entire company. They may refuse, or simply not see the need, to cooperate and share information or knowledge with other divisions.

The problem of linking and coordinating the activities of different functions and divisions becomes more acute as the number of functions and divisions increases. We look first at how managers design the hierarchy of authority to coordinate functions and divisions so that they work together effectively. Then we focus on integration and examine the integrating mechanisms managers can use to coordinate functions and divisions.

Allocating Authority

As organizations grow and produce a wider range of goods and services, the size and number of their functions and divisions increase. To coordinate the activities of people, functions, and divisions and to allow them to work together effectively, managers must develop a clear hierarchy of authority.[52] Authority is the power vested in a manager to make decisions and use resources to achieve the organization's goals by virtue of his or her position in an organization. The hierarchy of authority is an organization's *chain of command*—the relative authority that each manager has—extending from the CEO at the top, down through the middle managers and first-line managers, to the nonmanagerial employees who actually make goods or provide services. Every manager, at every level of the hierarchy, supervises one or more subordinates. The term span of control refers to the number of subordinates who report directly to a manager.

Figure 10.6 shows a simplified picture of the hierarchy of authority at McDonald's Corporation as of March 2018. As described in this chapter's opening feature, the fast-food giant's president and CEO, Steve Easterbrook, has taken bold steps to revise the company's organizational structure in an effort to revitalize the business and change the organization's corporate culture. Easterbrook, who has been CEO since March 2015, is the manager who has the ultimate responsibility for the company's overall performance, and he has the authority to decide how to use organizational resources to benefit McDonald's stakeholders. McDonald's four divisions focus on markets with similar needs, challenges, and opportunities for growth rather than a geographic approach to operations. Also in the top management hierarchy is Robert Gibbs, executive vice president and chief communications officer. Unlike other managers, Gibbs is not a line manager, someone in the direct line or chain of command who has formal authority over people and resources. Rather, Gibbs is a staff manager, responsible for one of McDonald's specialist functions—communications. He reports directly to Easterbrook.[53]

Managers at each level of the hierarchy confer with managers at the next level down the authority hierarchy to decide how to use organizational resources. Accepting this authority, those lower-level managers are accountable for how well they make those decisions. Managers who make the right decisions are typically promoted, and organizations motivate managers with the prospects of promotion and increased responsibility within the chain of command.

Below Kempczinski are the other main levels, or layers, in the McDonald's USA chain of command—presidents of its Northeast, South, Central, and West regions; zone managers; regional managers; and supervisors. A hierarchy is also evident in each company-owned McDonald's restaurant. At the top is the store manager; at lower levels are the first assistant, shift managers, and crew personnel. McDonald's managers have decided that this hierarchy of authority best allows the company to pursue its business-level strategy of providing fast food at reasonable prices.

TALL AND FLAT ORGANIZATIONS As an organization grows in size (normally measured by the number of its managers and employees), its hierarchy of authority normally lengthens, making the organizational structure taller. A *tall* organization has many levels of authority relative to company size; a *flat* organization has fewer levels relative to company size (see Figure 10.7).[54] As a hierarchy becomes taller, problems that make the organization's

authority The power to hold people accountable for their actions and to make decisions concerning the use of organizational resources.

hierarchy of authority An organization's chain of command, specifying the relative authority of each manager.

span of control The number of subordinates who report directly to a manager.

line manager Someone in the direct line or chain of command who has formal authority over people and resources at lower levels.

staff manager Someone responsible for managing a specialist function, such as finance or marketing.

Figure 10.6

The Hierarchy of Authority and Span of Control at McDonald's Corporation

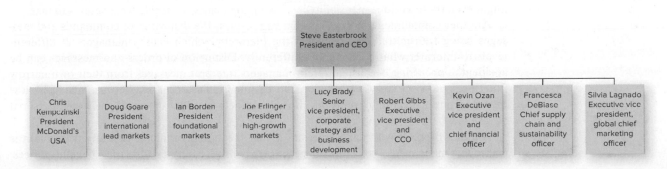

Figure 10.7

Tall and Flat Organizations

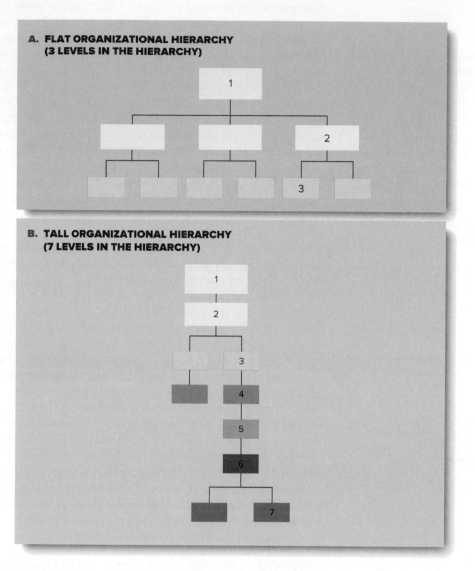

**A. FLAT ORGANIZATIONAL HIERARCHY
(3 LEVELS IN THE HIERARCHY)**

**B. TALL ORGANIZATIONAL HIERARCHY
(7 LEVELS IN THE HIERARCHY)**

structure less flexible and slow managers' response to changes in the organizational environment may result.

Communication problems may arise when an organization has many levels in the hierarchy. It can take a long time for the decisions and orders of upper-level managers to reach managers further down in the hierarchy, and it can take a long time for top managers to learn how well their decisions worked. Feeling out of touch, top managers may want to verify that lower-level managers are following orders and may require written confirmation from them. Middle managers, who know they will be held strictly accountable for their actions, start devoting too much time to the process of making decisions to improve their chances of being right. They might even try to avoid responsibility by making top managers decide what actions to take.

Another communication problem that can result is the distortion of commands and messages being transmitted up and down the hierarchy, which causes managers at different levels to interpret what is happening differently. Distortion of orders and messages can be accidental, occurring because different managers interpret messages from their own narrow functional perspectives. Or distortion can be intentional, occurring because managers low in the hierarchy decide to interpret information in a way that increases their own personal advantage.

Another problem with tall hierarchies is that they usually indicate that an organization is employing many managers, and managers are expensive. Managerial salaries, benefits, offices, and support staff are a huge expense for organizations. Large companies such as IBM and GM pay their managers millions of dollars a year. During the global recession, hundreds of thousands of managers lost their jobs as companies restructured and downsized their workforces to reduce costs. Today, however, a strong economic recovery seems to be under way, with the U.S. economy experiencing robust hiring gains among workers and managers.[55]

THE MINIMUM CHAIN OF COMMAND   To ward off the problems that result when an organization becomes too tall and employs too many managers, top managers need to ascertain whether they are employing the right number of middle and first-line managers and whether they can redesign their organizational architecture to reduce the number of managers. Top managers might well follow a basic organizing principle—the principle of the minimum chain of command—which states that top managers should always construct a hierarchy with the fewest levels of authority necessary to efficiently and effectively use organizational resources.

Effective managers constantly scrutinize their hierarchies to see whether the number of levels can be reduced—for example, by eliminating one level and giving the responsibilities of managers at that level to managers above and by empowering employees below. One manager who has worked to empower employees is David Novak, former executive chairman and CEO of Yum Brands. Instead of dictating what the company's Taco Bell, KFC, and Pizza Hut brands should do, Novak turned Yum's corporate headquarters into a support center for worldwide operations. Also a best-selling author, Novak recently launched a digital leadership platform called "oGOLead," which provides online training programs in effective leadership, as well as other resources to help individuals develop leadership skills that can be important tools in today's workplace environment.[56]

Plexus Corp. uses empowered work teams to help it utilize a "low–high" manufacturing technology that can help produce low volumes of many different kinds of products.
©Maskot/Getty Images

In the United States over 7 million manufacturing jobs have been lost to factories in low-cost countries abroad in the 2000s. While many large U.S. manufacturing companies have given up the battle, some small companies such as electronics maker Plexus Corp. have been able to find ways of organizing that allow them to survive and prosper in a low-cost manufacturing world. They have done this by creating empowered work teams. U.S. companies cannot match the efficiency of manufacturers abroad in producing high volumes of a single product, such as millions of a particular circuit board used in a laptop computer. So Plexus's managers decided to focus their efforts on developing a manufacturing technology, called "low–high," that could efficiently produce low volumes of many different kinds of products. Plexus's managers formed a team to design an organizational structure based on creating four "focused factories" in which control over production decisions is given to the workers, whose managers cross-train them so they can perform all the operations involved in making a product in their "factory." Now, when work slows down at any point in the production of a particular product, a worker further along the production process can move back to help solve the problem that has arisen at the earlier stage.[57]

Furthermore, managers organized workers into self-managed teams that are empowered to make all the decisions necessary to make a particular product in one of the four factories. Because each product is different, the ability of the teams to make rapid decisions and respond to unexpected contingencies is vital on a production line, where time is money. At Plexus, managers, by allowing teams to experiment, have reduced changeover time from hours to as little as 30 minutes so the line is making products over 80% of the time.[58] The flexibility brought about by self-managed teams is why Plexus is so efficient and can compete against low-cost manufacturers abroad.

decentralizing authority
Giving lower-level managers
and nonmanagerial employees
the right to make important
decisions about how to use
organizational resources.

CENTRALIZATION AND DECENTRALIZATION OF AUTHORITY Another way in which managers can keep the organizational hierarchy flat is by **decentralizing authority**—that is, by giving lower-level managers and nonmanagerial employees the right to make important decisions about how to use organizational resources.[59] If managers at higher levels give lower-level employees the responsibility of making important decisions and only *manage by exception,* then the problems of slow and distorted communication noted previously are kept to a minimum. Moreover, fewer managers are needed because their role is not to make decisions but to act as coach and facilitator and to help other employees make the best decisions. In addition, when decision-making authority is low in the organization and near the customer, employees are better able to recognize and respond to customer needs.

Decentralizing authority allows an organization and its employees to behave in a flexible way even as the organization grows and becomes taller. This is why managers are so interested in empowering employees, creating self-managed work teams, establishing cross-functional teams, and even moving to a product team structure. These design innovations help keep the organizational architecture flexible and responsive to complex task and general environments, complex technologies, and complex strategies.

Although more and more organizations are taking steps to decentralize authority, *too much* decentralization has certain disadvantages. If divisions, functions, or teams are given too much decision-making authority, they may begin to pursue their own goals at the expense of the organization's goals. Managers in engineering design or R&D, for example, may become so focused on making the best possible product that they fail to realize that the best product may be so expensive few people are willing or able to buy it. Also, too much decentralization can cause lack of communication among functions or divisions; this prevents the synergies of cooperation from ever materializing, and organizational performance suffers.

Top managers must seek the balance between centralization and decentralization of authority that best meets the four major contingencies an organization faces (see Figure 10.1). If managers are in a stable environment, are using well-understood technology, and are producing stable kinds of products (such as cereal, canned soup, or books), there is no pressing need to decentralize authority, and managers at the top can maintain control of much of organizational decision making.[60] However, in uncertain, changing environments where high-tech companies are producing state-of-the-art products, top managers must often empower employees and allow teams to make important strategic decisions so the organization can keep up with the changes taking place. No matter what its environment, a company that fails to control the balance between centralization and decentralization will find its performance suffering.

Integrating and Coordinating Mechanisms

Much coordination takes place through the hierarchy of authority. However, several problems are associated with establishing contact among managers in different functions or divisions. As discussed earlier, managers from different functions and divisions may have different views about what must be done to achieve the organization's goals. But if the managers have equal authority (as functional managers typically do), the only manager who can tell them what to do is the CEO, who has the ultimate authority to resolve conflicts. The need to solve everyday conflicts, however, wastes top management time and slows strategic decision making; indeed, one sign of a poorly performing structure is the number of problems sent up the hierarchy for top managers to solve.

integrating mechanisms
Organizing tools that managers can use to increase communication and coordination among functions and divisions.

To increase communication and coordination among functions or between divisions and to prevent these problems from emerging, top managers incorporate various **integrating mechanisms** into their organizational architecture. The greater the complexity of an organization's structure, the greater is the need for coordination among people, functions, and divisions to make the organizational structure work efficiently and effectively. Thus when managers adopt a divisional, matrix, or product team structure, they must use complex integrating mechanisms to achieve the organization's goals. Several integrating mechanisms are available to managers to increase communication and coordination.[61] Figure 10.8 lists these mechanisms, as well as examples of the individuals or groups who might use them.

LIAISON ROLES Managers can increase coordination among functions and divisions by establishing liaison roles. When the volume of contacts between two functions increases, one

Figure 10.8

Types and Examples of Integrating Mechanisms

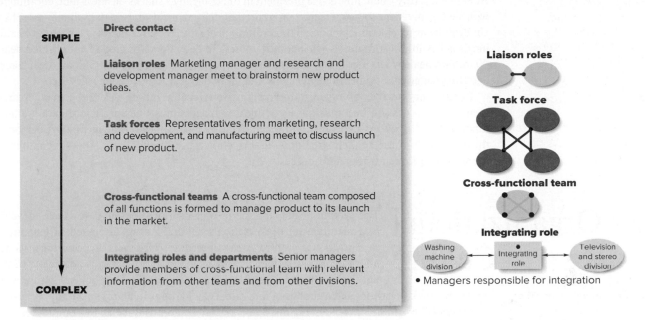

SIMPLE

Direct contact

Liaison roles Marketing manager and research and development manager meet to brainstorm new product ideas.

Task forces Representatives from marketing, research and development, and manufacturing meet to discuss launch of new product.

Cross-functional teams A cross-functional team composed of all functions is formed to manage product to its launch in the market.

Integrating roles and departments Senior managers provide members of cross-functional team with relevant information from other teams and from other divisions.

COMPLEX

Liaison roles

Task force

Cross-functional team

Integrating role

Washing machine division   Integrating role   Television and stereo division

• Managers responsible for integration

---

way to improve coordination is to give one manager in each function or division the responsibility for coordinating with the other. These managers may meet daily, weekly, monthly, or as needed. A liaison role is illustrated in Figure 10.8; the small dot represents the person within a function who has responsibility for coordinating with the other function. Coordinating is part of the liaison's full-time job, and usually an informal relationship develops between the people involved, greatly easing strains between functions. Furthermore, liaison roles provide a way of transmitting information across an organization, which is important in large organizations whose employees may know no one outside their immediate function or division.

TASK FORCES   When more than two functions or divisions share many common problems, direct contact and liaison roles may not provide sufficient coordination. In these cases, a more complex integrating mechanism, a task force, may be appropriate (see Figure 10.8). One manager from each relevant function or division is assigned to a task force that meets to solve a specific, mutual problem; members are responsible for reporting to their departments on the issues addressed and the solutions recommended. Task forces are often called *ad hoc committees* because they are temporary; they may meet on a regular basis or only a few times. When the problem or issue is solved, the task force is no longer needed; members return to their normal roles in their departments or are assigned to other task forces. Typically, task force members also perform many of their normal duties while serving on the task force.

CROSS-FUNCTIONAL TEAMS   In many cases the issues addressed by a task force are recurring problems, such as the need to develop new products or find new kinds of customers. To address recurring problems effectively, managers are increasingly using permanent integrating mechanisms such as cross-functional teams. An example of a cross-functional team is a new product development committee that is responsible for the choice, design, manufacturing, and marketing of a new product. Such an activity obviously requires a great deal of integration among functions if new products are to be successfully introduced, and using a complex integrating mechanism such as a cross-functional team accomplishes this. As discussed earlier, in a product team structure people and resources are grouped into permanent cross-functional teams to speed products to market. These teams assume long-term responsibility for all aspects of development and making the product.

INTEGRATING ROLES   An integrating role is a role whose only function is to increase coordination and integration among functions or divisions to achieve performance gains from

task force A committee of managers from various functions or divisions who meet to solve a specific, mutual problem; also called *ad hoc committee*.

synergies. Usually, managers who perform integrating roles are experienced senior managers who can envisage how to use the resources of the functions or divisions to obtain new synergies. At PepsiCo, Amy Chen, now a vice president in the company's snacks business unit, coordinated with several divisions to help create a program that delivers meals during the summer months to children from low-income families. The resulting program, Food for Good, now makes healthy meals accessible year round to low-income families. To date, Food for Good has delivered nearly 40 million healthy servings to low-income families in need.[62] The more complex an organization and the greater the number of its divisions, the more important integrating roles are.

In summary, to keep an organization responsive to changes in its task and general environments as it grows and becomes more complex, managers must increase coordination among functions and divisions by using complex integrating mechanisms. Managers must decide on the best way to organize their structures—that is, choose the structure that allows them to make the best use of organizational resources.

Organizational Culture

organizational culture The shared set of beliefs, expectations, values, and norms that influence how members of an organization relate to one another and cooperate to achieve the organization's goals.

The second principal issue in organizational design is to create, develop, and maintain an organization's culture. As we discussed in Chapter 3, organizational culture is the shared set of beliefs, expectations, values, and norms that influence how members of an organization relate to one another and cooperate to achieve the organization's goals. Culture influences the work behaviors and attitudes of individuals and groups in an organization because its members adhere to shared values, norms, and expected standards of behavior. Employees *internalize* organizational values and norms and then let these values and norms guide their decisions and actions.[63]

A company's culture is a result of its pivotal or guiding values and norms. A company's *values* are the shared standards that its members use to evaluate whether they have helped the company achieve its vision and goals. The values a company might adopt include any or all of the following standards: excellence, stability, predictability, profitability, economy, creativity, morality, and usefulness. A company's *norms* specify or prescribe the kinds of shared beliefs, attitudes, and behaviors that its members should observe and follow. Norms are informal, but powerful, rules about how employees should behave or conduct themselves in a company if they are to be accepted and help it to achieve its goals. Norms can be equally as constraining as the formal written rules contained in a company's handbook. Companies might encourage workers to adopt norms such as working hard, respecting traditions and authority, and being courteous to others; being conservative, cautious, and a "team player"; being creative and courageous and taking risks; or being honest and frugal and maintaining high personal standards. Norms may also prescribe certain specific behaviors such as keeping one's desk tidy, cleaning up at the end of the day, taking one's turn to bring doughnuts, and even wearing jeans on Fridays.

Ideally, a company's norms help the company achieve its values. For example, a new computer company whose culture is based on values of excellence and innovation may try to attain this high standard by encouraging workers to adopt norms about being creative, taking risks, and working hard now and looking long-term for rewards (this combination of values and norms leads to an *entrepreneurial* culture in a company). On the other hand, a bank or an insurance company that has values of stability and predictability may emphasize norms of cautiousness and obedience to authority (the result of adopting these values and norms would be a *stable, conservative* culture in a company).

Over time, members of a company learn from one another how to perceive and interpret various events that happen in the work setting and to respond to them in ways that reflect the company's guiding values and norms. This is why organizational culture is so important: When a strong and cohesive set of organizational values and norms is in place, employees focus on what is best for the organization in the long run—all their decisions and actions become oriented toward helping the organization perform well. For example, a teacher spends personal time after school, coaching and counseling students; an R&D scientist works 80 hours a week, evenings, and weekends to help speed up a late project; or a salesclerk at a department store runs after a customer who left a credit card at the cash register. A notable example of a company where cultural values have become a driver of success is Sodexo, described in the "Focus on Diversity" feature.

Sodexo Serves Up a Culture of Diversity

Sodexo, based in Paris, is one of the world's largest employers. The company, which provides food services and manages facilities for schools, hospitals, businesses, and other organizations, employs 425,000 people in 80 countries. Its chief executive is Michel Landel, a Frenchman born in Morocco. Its chief diversity officer is Rohini Anand, an Indian woman who earned her doctorate in the United States, where she works now.[64]

With diversity evident in the company's scope and leadership, a culture that values diversity might seem inevitable. In fact, although such a culture reflects a personal commitment of Landel's, creating and maintaining it requires constant effort. Landel started with the belief that equitable treatment of men and women is "the right thing to do" as part of an employer's responsibility for employees' well-being and development.[65] Anand, a consultant when she met Landel, was attracted by the chance to have a major impact, guided by a mentor who encouraged her to apply her expertise in culture and organizations.[66]

Anand started by taking the perspective of Sodexo's managers. She gathered performance data from more than 100 Sodexo business entities with over 50,000 managers. Initial results—which have held up over five years of follow-up studies—show that the best performance occurs in groups where 40% to 60% of the managers are women. Managers saw gender balance bringing superior customer satisfaction, client retention, safety, and profits. Those who initially doubted the value of gender balance began advocating for it.[67]

The evidence of business benefits smoothed a path for making gender balance a norm. Sodexo set measurable targets and linked part of managers' pay to achieving them. It offered flexible work arrangements and required that job titles be gender-neutral. As these practices began to deliver results, Landel keeps them relevant by urging managers to avoid letting other business objectives crowd out the diversity-related goals. Anand reminds Sodexo's people that "when women do better, we all do better."[68]

So far, the diversity effort has focused on gender equity, reflecting the urgency of this issue as a first step in many countries where Sodexo operates. The ultimate goal is for the entire workforce to have gender-balanced management by 2025; so far, 59% of employees do. In addition, half the board members and roughly one-third of senior managers are female. As the company moves toward gender balance, Landel and Anand aim to extend the diversity culture to other categories, including age, religion, ethnic groups, and disability status.[69]

Sodexo's commitment to cultural diversity and gender equity within the organization continues to pay dividends in terms of employee engagement and overall business success.
©Monkey Business Images/Shutterstock

LO10-5 List the four sources of organizational culture, and explain why and how a company's culture can lead to competitive advantage.

Where Does Organizational Culture Come From?

In managing organizational architecture, some important questions arise: Where does organizational culture come from? Why do different companies have different cultures? Why might a culture that for many years helped an organization achieve its goals suddenly harm the organization?

Figure 10.9
Sources of an Organization's Culture

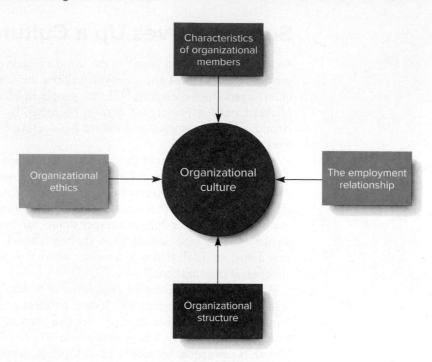

Organizational culture is shaped by the interaction of four main factors: the personal and professional characteristics of people within the organization, organizational ethics, the nature of the employment relationship, and the design of its organizational structure (see Figure 10.9). These factors work together to produce different cultures in different organizations and cause changes in culture over time.

CHARACTERISTICS OF ORGANIZATIONAL MEMBERS   The ultimate source of organizational culture is the people who make up the organization. If you want to know why organizational cultures differ, look at how the characteristics of their members differ. Organizations A, B, and C develop distinctly different cultures because they attract, select, and retain people who have different values, personalities, and ethics.[70] Recall the attraction–selection–attrition model from Chapter 3. People may be attracted to an organization whose values match theirs; similarly, an organization selects people who share its values. Over time, people who do not fit in leave. The result is that people inside the organization become more similar, the values of the organization become more pronounced and clear-cut, and the culture becomes distinct from those of similar organizations.[71] The unique organizational culture of Warby Parker is described in the accompanying "Management Insight" feature.

MANAGEMENT INSIGHT

Warby Parker Keeps an Eye on Its Culture

How does organizational culture influence employee performance? If you ask the four friends who started Warby Parker, the influence is eye opening. A decade ago, Neil Blumenthal, Dave Gilboa, Andy Hunt, and Jeff Raider were MBA students at the Wharton School. Between classes, they got into a conversation about why glasses cost so much and why they weren't sold online. Later that day, actually in the middle of the night, Blumenthal emailed his three friends and proposed they start an online eyewear company.[72]

Neil Blumenthal, left, and Dave Gilboa, right, are the visionaries behind Warby Parker, the online retailer that has successfully disrupted the eyewear industry and created a unique organizational culture.

©Carolyn Cole/Los Angeles Times via Getty Images

While researching the eyewear industry, the founders discovered a few large companies controlled the business, a fact that kept prices artificially high, reaping huge profits from consumers who had few options. By designing frames under their own brand, working closely with suppliers, and dealing directly with customers, Warby Parker could avoid the middleman and provide high-quality, stylish prescription eyewear for $95 a frame—including lenses. As part of its innovative business model, the company also lets prospective customers pick five frames to be shipped to their homes so they can try them on for size and style—and return shipping is free.[73]

Since the beginning, Warby Parker has put organizational culture at the forefront of its business. Within the company, there is a "culture team" responsible for planning company outings and themed luncheons. The team also plays a part in screening job candidates, ensuring Warby Parker culture is evident from the start of any potential employee's tenure with the company. To encourage a cohesive workforce, the company implemented weekly episodes of lunch roulette—where four randomly selected employees are sent out to lunch together so they get to know each other away from their desks.[74]

The company has grown dramatically from its early days in Blumenthal's apartment to a workforce of more than 1,000 employees and 64-plus brick-and-mortar stores. As part of that quick expansion, Warby Parker management knows its employees need to be agile and ready to jump in at a moment's notice. To underscore the need for agility, employees at Warby Parker spend a week training on the Customer Experience team—just in case they are called on to wait on customers in the retail stores or answer questions via the website.[75]

Disrupting the eyewear industry with its innovative business model, Warby Parker continues to stay true to its vision of leading the way with a strong organizational culture and the ability to stay comfortable in an ever-changing business environment.

The fact that an organization's members become similar over time and come to share the same values may actually hinder their ability to adapt and respond to changes in the environment.[76] This happens when the organization's values and norms become so strong and promote so much cohesiveness in members' attitudes that the members begin to misperceive the environment.[77] Companies such as Ford, Google, Apple, and Microsoft need a strong set of values that emphasize innovation and hard work; they also need to be careful their success doesn't lead members to believe their company is the best in the business. Companies frequently make this mistake. One famous example is the CEO of Digital Equipment, who in the 1990s laughed off the potential threat posed by PCs to his powerful minicomputers, claiming, "Personal computers are just toys." This company no longer exists.

organizational ethics The moral values, beliefs, and rules that establish the appropriate way for an organization and its members to deal with each other and with people outside the organization.

ORGANIZATIONAL ETHICS   The managers of an organization can set out purposefully to develop specific cultural values and norms to control how its members behave. One important class of values in this category stems from **organizational ethics**, which are the moral values, beliefs, and rules that establish the appropriate way for an organization and its members to deal with each other and with people outside the organization. Recall from Chapter 4 that ethical values rest on principles stressing the importance of treating organizational stakeholders fairly and equitably. Managers and employees are constantly making choices about the right, or ethical, thing to do; to help them make ethical decisions, top managers purposefully implant ethical values into an organization's culture.[78] Consequently, ethical values, and the rules and norms that embody them, become an integral part of an organization's culture and determine how its members will manage situations and make decisions.

THE EMPLOYMENT RELATIONSHIP   A third factor shaping organizational culture is the nature of the employment relationship a company establishes with its employees via its human resource policies and practices. Recall from Chapter 1 our discussion of the changing relationship between organizations and their employees due to the growth of outsourcing and employment of contingent workers. Like a company's hiring, promotion, and layoff policies, human resource policies, along with pay and benefits, can influence how hard employees will work to achieve the organization's goals, how attached they will be to the organization, and whether they will buy into its values and norms.[79] As we discuss in Chapter 12, an organization's human resource policies are a good indicator of the values in its culture concerning its responsibilities to employees. Consider the effects of a company's promotion policy, for example: A company with a policy of promoting from within will fill higher-level positions with employees who already work for the organization. On the other hand, a company with a policy of promotion from without will fill its open positions with qualified outsiders. What does this say about each organization's culture?

Promoting from within will bolster strong values and norms that build loyalty, align employees' goals with the organization, and encourage employees to work hard to advance within the organization. If employees see no prospect of being promoted from within, they are likely to look for better opportunities elsewhere, cultural values and norms result in self-interested behavior, and cooperation and cohesiveness fall. The tech sector has gone through great turmoil in recent years, and over 2 million U.S. tech employees lost their jobs during the 2000s because of outsourcing and the recession. Apple, HP, and IBM—known for their strong employee-oriented values that emphasized long-term employment and respect for employees—were among the many companies forced to lay off employees, and their cultures have changed as a result. To rebuild their cultures and make their remaining employees feel like "owners," many companies have HRM pay policies that reward superior performance with bonuses and stock options.[80] For example, Southwest Airlines and Google established companywide stock option systems that encourage their employees to be innovative and responsive to customers. Other companies offer different perks, such as Airbnb's $2,000 annual stipend for each employee to travel and stay in an Airbnb listing anywhere in the world and PwC's $1,200 per year student loan debt reimbursement.[81]

ORGANIZATIONAL STRUCTURE   We have seen how the values and norms that shape employee work attitudes and behaviors derive from an organization's people, ethics, and HRM policies. A fourth source of cultural values comes from the organization's structure. *Different kinds of structure give rise to different kinds of culture;* thus, to create a certain culture, managers often need to design a particular type of structure. Tall and highly centralized structures give rise to totally different sets of norms, rules, and cultural values than do structures that are flat and decentralized. In a tall, centralized organization, people have little personal autonomy, and norms that focus on being cautious, obeying authority, and respecting traditions emerge because predictability and stability are desired goals. In a flat, decentralized structure, people have more freedom to choose and control their own activities, and norms that focus on being creative and courageous and taking risks appear, giving rise to a culture in which innovation and flexibility are desired goals.

Whether a company is centralized or decentralized also leads to the development of different kinds of cultural values. By decentralizing authority and empowering employees, an organization can establish values that encourage and reward creativity or innovation. In doing this, an organization signals employees that it's okay to be innovative and do things their own way—as long as their actions are consistent with the good of the organization. Conversely, in some organizations it is important that employees do not make decisions on their own and that their actions be open to the scrutiny of superiors. In cases like this, centralization can be used to create cultural values that reinforce obedience and accountability. For example, in nuclear power plants, values that promote stability, predictability, and obedience to authority are deliberately fostered to prevent disasters.[82] Through norms and rules, employees are taught the importance of behaving consistently and honestly, and they learn that sharing information with supervisors, especially information about mistakes or errors, is the only acceptable form of behavior.[83]

An organization that seeks to manage and change its culture must take a hard look at all four factors that shape culture: the characteristics of its members, its ethical values, its human resource policies, and its organizational structure. However, changing a culture can be difficult because of the way these factors interact and affect one another.[84] Often a major reorganization is necessary for a cultural change to occur, as we discuss in the next chapter.

Strong, Adaptive Cultures versus Weak, Inert Cultures

Many researchers and managers believe that employees of some organizations go out of their way to help the organization because it has a strong and cohesive organizational culture—an adaptive culture that controls employee attitudes and behaviors. *Adaptive cultures* are those whose values and norms help an organization to build momentum and to grow and change as needed to achieve its goals and be effective. By contrast, *inert cultures* are those whose values and norms fail to motivate or inspire employees; they lead to stagnation and, often, failure over time. What leads to a strong adaptive culture or one that is inert and hard to change?

Researchers have found that organizations with strong adaptive cultures, like 3M, UPS, Microsoft, and IBM, invest in their employees. They demonstrate their commitment to their members by, for example, emphasizing the long-term nature of the employment relationship and trying to avoid layoffs. These companies develop long-term career paths for their employees and spend a lot of money on training and development to increase employees' value to the organization. In these ways, terminal and instrumental values pertaining to the worth of human resources encourage the development of supportive work attitudes and behaviors.

In adaptive cultures employees often receive rewards linked directly to their performance and to the performance of the company as a whole. Sometimes employee stock ownership plans (ESOPs) are developed in which workers as a group are allowed to buy a significant percentage of their company's stock. Workers who are owners of the company have additional incentive to develop skills that allow them to perform highly and search actively for ways to improve quality, efficiency, and performance.

Some organizations, however, develop cultures with values that do not include protecting and increasing the worth of their human resources as a major goal. Their employment practices are based on short-term employment according to the needs of the organization and on minimal investment in employees who perform simple, routine tasks. Moreover, employees are not often rewarded on the basis of their performance and, thus, have little incentive to improve their skills or otherwise invest in the organization to help it achieve goals. If a company has an inert culture, poor working relationships frequently develop between the organization and its employees and instrumental values of noncooperation, laziness, and loafing and work norms of output restriction are common.

Moreover, an adaptive culture develops an emphasis on entrepreneurship and respect for the employee and allows the use of organizational structures, such as the cross-functional team structure, that empower employees to make decisions and motivate them to succeed. By contrast, in an inert culture, employees are content to be told what to do and have little incentive or motivation to perform beyond minimum work requirements. As you might expect, the emphasis is on close supervision and hierarchical authority, which result in a culture that makes it difficult to adapt to a changing environment.

Google is a good example of a company in which managers strive to create an adaptive culture that is based on values that emphasize creativity and innovation and where decision making is pushed right down to the bottom line to teams of employees who take up the challenge of developing the advanced software and hardware for which the company is known. Bureaucracy is kept to a minimum at Google; its adaptive culture is based on informal and personal relationships and norms of cooperation and teamwork. To help strengthen its culture, Google built a futuristic open-plan campus (called the Googleplex) in which its employees can work together to innovate advanced products and business solutions such as Google Maps, Google Drive, and Chrome.[85] Google's cultural values and norms can't be written down but are present in the work routines that cement people together and in the language and stories its members use to orient themselves to the company.

Another company with an adaptive culture is GlaxoSmithKline. Much of GSK's success can be attributed to its ability to recruit the best research scientists because its adaptive culture nurtures scientists and emphasizes values and norms of innovation. Scientists are given great freedom to pursue intriguing ideas even if the commercial payoff is questionable. Moreover, researchers are inspired to think of their work as a quest to alleviate human disease and suffering worldwide, and GSK has a reputation as an ethical company whose values put people above profits.

Although the experience of Google and GSK suggests that organizational culture can give rise to managerial actions that ultimately benefit the organization, this is not always the case. The cultures of some organizations become dysfunctional, encouraging managerial actions that harm the organization and discouraging actions that might improve performance.[86] For example, when Marissa Mayer left Google to become Yahoo CEO in 2012, she jumped into a difficult situation. The company was already in decline, and several of her CEO predecessors at the company had failed to make inroads into a dysfunctional culture or crystallize a solid business plan. Undaunted, Mayer tried to change the company's culture while acquiring several innovative start-up companies to help Yahoo get back on track—with mixed results. Several activist investors joined Yahoo's board to demand change at the company, which culminated in Yahoo selling itself to Verizon for nearly $4.5 billion and Mayer leaving the company in 2017.[87]

Summary and Review

LO10-1   **DESIGNING ORGANIZATIONAL STRUCTURE** The four main determinants of organizational structure are the external environment, strategy, technology, and human resources. In general, the higher the level of uncertainty associated with these factors, the more appropriate is a flexible, adaptable structure as opposed to a formal, rigid one.

LO10-2   **GROUPING TASKS INTO JOBS** Job design is the process by which managers group tasks into jobs. To create more interesting jobs, and to get workers to act flexibly, managers can enlarge and enrich jobs. The job characteristics model is a tool that managers can use to measure how motivating or satisfying a particular job is.

LO10-3   **ORGANIZATIONAL STRUCTURE: GROUPING JOBS INTO FUNCTIONS AND DIVISIONS** Managers can choose from many kinds of organizational structures to make the best use of organizational resources. Depending on the specific organizing problems they face, managers can choose from functional, product, geographic, market, matrix, product team, and hybrid structures.

LO10-4   **COORDINATING FUNCTIONS AND DIVISIONS** No matter which structure managers choose, they must decide how to distribute authority in the organization, how many levels to have in the hierarchy of authority, and what balance to strike between centralization and decentralization to keep the number of levels in the hierarchy to a minimum. As organizations grow, managers must increase integration and coordination among functions and divisions. Four integrating mechanisms that facilitate this are liaison roles, task forces, cross-functional teams, and integrating roles.

LO10-5   **ORGANIZATIONAL CULTURE** Organizational culture is the set of values, norms, and standards of behavior that control how individuals and groups in an organization interact with one another and work to achieve the organization's goals. The four main sources of organizational culture are member characteristics, organizational ethics, the nature of the employment relationship, and the design of organizational structure. How managers work to influence these four factors determines whether an organization's culture is strong and adaptive or inert and difficult to change.

Management in Action

Topics for Discussion and Action

Discussion

1. Would a flexible or a more formal structure be appropriate for these organizations? (a) a large department store, (b) a Big Four accounting firm, (c) a biotechnology company. Explain your reasoning. [LO10-1, 10-2]

2. Using the job characteristics model as a guide, discuss how a manager can enrich or enlarge subordinates' jobs. [LO10-2]

3. How might a salesperson's job or an administrative assistant's job be enlarged or enriched to make it more motivating? [LO10-2, 10-3]

4. When and under what conditions might managers change from a functional to (a) a product, (b) a geographic, or (c) a market structure? [LO10-1, 10-3]

5. How do matrix structure and product team structure differ? Why is product team structure more widely used? [LO10-1, 10-3, 10-4]

6. What is organizational culture, and how does it affect the way employees behave? [LO10-5]

Action

7. Find and interview a manager, and identify the kind of organizational structure that his or her organization uses to coordinate its people and resources. Why is the organization using that structure? Do you think a different structure would be more appropriate? Which one? [LO10-1, 10-3, 10-4]

8. With the same or another manager, discuss the distribution of authority in the organization. Does the manager think that decentralizing authority and empowering employees are appropriate? [LO10-1, 10-3]

9. Interview some employees of an organization, and ask them about the organization's values and norms, the typical characteristics of employees, and the organization's ethical values and socialization practices. Using this information, try to describe the organization's culture and the way it affects how people and groups behave. [LO10-1, 10-5]

Building Management Skills

Understanding Organizing [LO10-1, 10-2, 10-3]

Think of an organization with which you are familiar—perhaps one you have worked for, such as a store, a restaurant, an office, a church, or a school. Then answer the following questions:

1. Which contingencies are most important in explaining how the organization is organized? Do you think it is organized in the best way? Why or why not?

2. Using the job characteristics model, how motivating do you think the job of a typical employee is in this organization?

3. Provide examples of how a typical job could be enlarged or enriched in this organization.

4. What kind of organizational structure does the organization use? If it is part of a chain, what kind of structure does the entire organization use? What other structures discussed in the chapter might allow the organization to operate more effectively? For

example, would the move to a product team structure lead to greater efficiency or effectiveness? Why or why not?

5. How many levels are in the organization's hierarchy? Is authority centralized or decentralized? Describe the span of control of the top manager and of middle or first-line managers.

6. Is the distribution of authority appropriate for the organization and its activities? Would it be possible to flatten the hierarchy by decentralizing authority and empowering employees?

7. What are the principal integrating mechanisms used in the organization? Do they provide sufficient coordination among individuals and functions? How might they be improved?

8. Now that you have analyzed the way this organization is structured, what advice would you give its managers to help them improve how it operates?

Managing Ethically [LO10-1, 10-3, 10-5]

Suppose an organization is downsizing and laying off many of its middle managers. Some top managers charged with deciding whom to terminate might decide to keep the subordinates they like and who are obedient to them, rather than the ones who are difficult or the best performers. They might also decide to lay off the most highly paid subordinates even if they are high performers. Think of the ethical issues involved in designing a hierarchy, and discuss the following issues.

Questions

1. What ethical rules (see Chapter 4) should managers use to decide which employees to terminate when redesigning their hierarchy?

2. Some people argue that employees who have worked for an organization for many years have a claim on the organization at least as strong as that of its shareholders. What do you think of the ethics of this position—can employees claim to "own" their jobs if they have contributed significantly to the organization's past success? How does a socially responsible organization behave in this situation?

Small Group Breakout Exercise

Bob's Appliances [LO10-1, 10-3]

Form groups of three or four people, and appoint one member as the spokesperson who will communicate your findings to the class when called on by the instructor. Then discuss the following scenario:

Bob's Appliances sells and services household appliances such as washing machines, dishwashers, ranges, and refrigerators. Over the years, the company has developed a good reputation for the quality of its customer service, and many local builders patronize the store. However, large retailers such as Home Depot, Walmart, and Costco are also providing an increasing range of appliances. Moreover, to attract more customers, these stores also carry a complete range of consumer electronics products—TVs, computers, and digital devices. Bob Lange, the owner of Bob's Appliances, has decided that if he is to stay in business, he must widen his product range and compete directly with the chains.

In 2018 he decided to build a 20,000-square-foot store and service center, and he is now hiring new employees to sell and service the new line of consumer electronics. Because of his company's increased size, Lange is not sure of the best way to organize the employees. Currently, he uses a functional structure; employees are divided into sales, purchasing and accounting, and repair. Bob is wondering whether selling and servicing consumer electronics is so different from selling and servicing appliances that he should move to a product structure (see the accompanying figure) and create separate sets of functions for each of his two lines of business.[88]

You are a team of local consultants whom Bob has called in to advise him as he makes this crucial choice. Which structure do you recommend? Why?

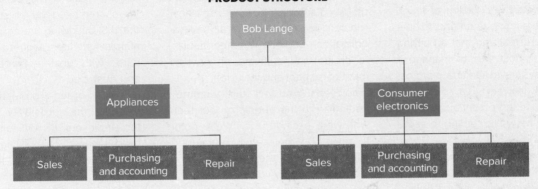

FUNCTIONAL STRUCTURE

Bob Lange

Sales | Purchasing and accounting | Repair

PRODUCT STRUCTURE

Bob Lange

Appliances | Consumer electronics

Sales | Purchasing and accounting | Repair

Sales | Purchasing and accounting | Repair

Be the Manager [LO10-1, 10-3, 10-5]

Speeding Up Website Design

You have been hired by a website design, production, and hosting company whose new animated website designs are attracting a lot of attention and many customers. Currently, employees are organized into different functions such as hardware, software design, graphic art, and website hosting, as well as functions such as marketing and human resources. Each function takes its turn to work on a new project from initial customer request to final online website hosting.

The problem the company is experiencing is that it typically takes one year from the initial idea stage to the time a website is up and running; the company wants to shorten this time by half to protect and expand its market niche. In talking to other managers, you discover that they believe the company's current functional structure is the source of the problem—it is not allowing employees to develop websites fast enough to satisfy customers' demands. They want you to design a better structure.

Questions

1. Discuss how you can improve the way the current functional structure operates so it speeds website development.

2. Discuss the pros and cons of moving to a (a) multidivisional, (b) matrix, and (c) product team structure to reduce website development time.

3. Which of these structures do you think is most appropriate, and why?

4. What kind of culture would you help create to make the company's structure work more effectively?

Bloomberg Case in the News [LO 10-1, 10-2, 10-4, 10-5]

Companies Have an Aha! Moment: Bullies Don't Make the Best Managers

After Nike Inc. ousted a handful of male executives for behavior issues over the past few months, some media reports tied the departures to the #MeToo movement and its revelations of sexual harassment and assault. Interviews with more than a dozen former Nike employees, including senior executives, however, paint a picture of a workplace contaminated by a different behavior: corporate bullying. The workers say the sneaker giant could be a bruising place for both men and women, and that females did bullying, too. On May 8, Nike signaled as much when it

303

confirmed four more exits stemming from an internal misconduct inquiry, including the departure of a woman with more than 20 years at the company.

The surprise announcement in March that 55-year-old Nike brand president Trevor Edwards—who had a reputation for humiliating subordinates in meetings—would leave following an internal investigation about workplace behavior issues suggests the coddling of tough guys may have come to an end. "Some companies are realizing that a bullying boss isn't the best way to manage a company," says David Yamada, a professor at Suffolk University Law School in Boston who's authored antibullying legislation. "Maybe we're starting to see a tipping point."

Gary Namie, co-founder of the Workplace Bullying Institute, who consults with businesses on workplace issues, says one reason some companies have long tolerated or even encouraged such behavior is that many American managers believe the workplace is by nature rough around the edges. "Bullying is inextricably interwoven with capitalism," he says. "It creates a zero-sum, competitive work environment where people feel they need to obliterate their competitors."

Some former employees say that was the case at Nike, particularly among managers who used abusive tactics to safeguard their own position or authority. "There are a lot of very talented people deeper in the organization who have been marginalized both by senior and middle management trying to protect their domain," says Shaz Kahng, who was a senior executive at Nike for six years through 2010. "People are often promoted based on relationships, not on results."

In response to complaints, including from departing female executives, Nike ousted Edwards, who'd been a favorite to become the company's next chief executive officer. Edwards, according to some of the former employees, at times bullied workers through insults and disparaging comments. More important, once he set the tone, other people mirrored his

behavior, they say. A handful of executives who worked for Edwards have since left Nike.

"I've been disturbed to hear from some employees of behavior inconsistent with our values," CEO Mark Parker said in an emailed statement. "When we discover issues, we take action."

Nike also provided Bloomberg with the transcript of a town hall Parker held on May 3, in which he vowed the environment will change. "We all have an obligation—and it's non-negotiable—to create and cultivate an environment of respect and inclusion," he told employees. "And that starts with me. I apologize to the people on our team who were excluded. . . . We're going to move from a place where the loudest voices carry the conversation to [one where] every voice is heard."

The company declined to make Edwards available for an interview. He's acting as an adviser to Parker until he retires in August, when he'll receive a $525,000 payout, according to public filings.

Nike says it's reviewing how it deals with complaints, redesigning management training, and beginning unconscious bias awareness education for employees this year. It's also vowed to promote more women and minorities into leadership roles. Currently, managers are 38% women and 23% nonwhite.

Workplace bullying is often defined as behavior—including verbal abuse, derogatory remarks, humiliation, and undermining work performance—that results in physical or mental harm. About 1 in 5 Americans say they've been the target of it, according to a 2017 survey by Zogby Analytics that was commissioned by the Workplace Bullying Institute. Men make up 70% of the perpetrators and 34% of the targets. "It's a significant and still underreported problem," Yamada says. Surveys have shown such behavior is four times more prevalent than legally actionable sexual harassment, he says. "Bullying looms large."

Ironically, Nike is one of the minority of companies that has a formal anti-

harassment policy that calls out bullying behavior such as verbal abuse, intimidation, humiliation, and retaliation, according to a copy obtained by Bloomberg. It also notes that harassment not based on a legally protected characteristic, such as gender or race, can still violate company rules.

One reason few companies have specific antibullying policies is that there aren't federal or state laws in the U.S. outlawing the behavior, which makes America a laggard when compared with Western Europe, Canada, and Australia.

A lack of legal protections greatly reduces the possibility of liability for employers. It's difficult to bring a lawsuit based on bullying, and businesses have worked to keep it that way. Over the past decade, antibullying bills were introduced in about 30 states, but they've all been defeated after opposition from corporate lobbying groups, Yamada says. A workplace bullying bill is gaining sponsors in Massachusetts' legislature, but its future is uncertain. If there were antibullying laws, companies would be liable and do more to deter the practice, according to Namie. "It's the only form of abuse that hasn't been addressed by law," he says. "It goes beyond gender to 'I'm powerful, I can do any damn thing I want.'"

When executives feel entitled or untouchable, that often leads to bullying and then to other inappropriate behavior, Yamada says. In many of the workplace environments that resulted in some of the high-profile #MeToo moments, such as that at Weinstein Co., an "undercurrent" of bullying created a belief that mistreatment would go unpunished, he says. "It's that bullying atmosphere that helps to enable and empower sexual harassment."

According to the former Nike employees, the lack of a fear of reprisal created an environment where male executives, many married, could pursue and have sexual relationships with subordinates and assistants—behavior Nike says it tries to prevent but doesn't prohibit. Many times the careers of those involved were unaffected, which only normalized the behavior, they say. And when there were repercussions, the men received little if any punishment, while women often faced consequences. In one instance several years ago, they say, an executive was caught having sex with his assistant on a conference table. He wasn't disciplined, some of the people say, but the woman was reassigned.

Several former female employees describe similar experiences of encountering several slights and offenses—not one egregious incident—that increased as they moved up the ladder. One woman says her boss, a senior director, had derogatory nicknames for female staffers and would

overtly favor men on the team with better opportunities. A former female manager says a male colleague had multiple complaints of bullying made against him to human resources, but the only punishment meted out was a delayed promotion. Eventually, frustration with Nike's handling of such incidents persuaded several women to leave the company, they say.

The situation was particularly galling to employees who'd been drawn to Nike because of its cool and progressive reputation, burnished by such advertising slogans as "If You Let Me Play" and its T-shirts adorned simply with the word "equality." "We always wished the company would live up to its marketing," says one former female executive. "But it didn't."

Questions for Discussion

1. Do you think misbehavior on the part of managers is affected by organizational structure? Why or why not?

2. Do you think authority was misused on the part of bullying managers? Explain your reasoning.

3. Going forward, how can Nike revise or re-invent its organizational culture to attract and retain top talent?

Source: Matthew Townsend and Esmé E. Deprez, "Companies Have an Aha! Moment: Bullies Don't Make the Best Managers," *Bloomberg*, May 9, 2018, https://www.bloomberg.com/news/articles/2018-05-09/nike-s-executive-exodus-shows-bullies-don t-make-good-bosses. Used with permission of Bloomberg L.P. Copyright © 2017. All rights reserved.

Notes

1. W. Gay, "Is McDonald's Moving to Attract Millennial Talent?" *Forbes,* www.forbes.com, accessed March 30, 2018.

2. B. Mikel, "Want to Attract Top Talent? Follow the Lead of McDonald's and Do This," *Inc.,* www.inc.com, accessed March 30, 2018.

3. Reuters, "McDonald's Already Found Its Next U.S. President," *Forbes,* www.forbes.com, September 1, 2016; P. Rosenthal, "Innovate or Not, McDonald's New President Will Find It's Harder to Hit a Home Run in the Hot Seat," *Chicago Tribune,* www.chicagotribune.com, August 31, 2016.

4. P. Frost, "McDonald's Offers Buyouts to Hundreds of Headquarters Staffers," *Crain's Chicago Business,* www.chicagobusiness.com, June 3, 2016.

5. J. Jargon, "McDonald's to See More Executives Announcing Exits This Week," *The Wall Street Journal,* www.wsj.com, October 17, 2016.

6. Trefis Team, "Here's How McDonald's Is Seeking to Attract Millennials," *Forbes,* www.forbes.com, November 17, 2016.

7. P. McGroarty, "McDonald's Puts Fresh Beef on the Menu," *The Wall Street Journal,* www.wsj.com, March 6, 2018; P. Frost, "Easterbrook on McD's Turnaround, Its Move to Chicago and More," *Crain's Chicago Business,* www.chicagobusiness.com, November 22, 2016.

8. T. Kim, "McDonald's Hits All-Time High as Wall Street Cheers Replacement of

Cashiers with Kiosks," *CNBC,* www.cnbc.com, June 22, 2017.

9. Frost, "Easterbrook on McD's Turnaround, Its Move to Chicago, and More."

10. G. R. Jones, *Organizational Theory, Design, and Change: Text and Cases* (Upper Saddle River: Prentice-Hall, 2011).

11. J. Child, *Organization: A Guide for Managers and Administrators* (New York: Harper & Row, 1977).

12. P.R. Lawrence and J.W. Lorsch, *Organization and Environment* (Boston: Graduate School of Business Administration, Harvard University, 1967).

13. R. Duncan, "What Is the Right Organizational Design?" *Organizational Dynamics* (Winter 1979), 59–80.

14. T. Burns and G.R. Stalker, *The Management of Innovation* (London: Tavistock, 1966).

15. D. Miller, "Strategy Making and Structure: Analysis and Implications for Performance," *Academy of Management Journal* 30 (1987), 7–32.

16. A.D. Chandler, *Strategy and Structure* (Cambridge, MA: MIT Press, 1962).

17. J. Stopford and L. Wells, *Managing the Multinational Enterprise* (London: Longman, 1972).

18. C. Perrow, *Organizational Analysis: A Sociological View* (Belmont, CA: Wadsworth, 1970).

19. F.W. Taylor, *The Principles of Scientific Management* (New York: Harper, 1911).

20. R.W. Griffin, *Task Design: An Integrative Approach* (Glenview, IL: Scott, Foresman, 1982).

21. "Company Info," http://palsweb.com, accessed March 30, 2018.

22. "Pal's Sudden Service: Taking Fast Food to the Next Level," *Working Knowledge,* https://hbswk.hbs.edu, August 10, 2017; B. Taylor, "How One Fast-Food Chain Keeps Its Turnover Rates Absurdly Low," *Harvard Business Review,* https://hbr.org, January 26, 2016.

23. "Pal's: America's Least-Known Well-Run Burger Chain," *Burger Business,* http://burgerbusiness.com, accessed March 30, 2018.

24. L. Buchanan, "Training the Best Damn Fry Cooks (and Future Leaders) in the U.S.," *Inc.,* www.inc.com, accessed March 30, 2017.

25. "How One Fast-Food Chain Keeps Its Turnover Rates Absurdly Low"; "Pal's: America's Least-Known Well-Run Burger Chain."

26. "About Us," https://www.palsbei.com, accessed March 30, 2018.

27. Griffin, *Task Design: An Integrative Approach.*

28. J.R. Hackman and G.R. Oldham, *Work Redesign* (Reading, MA: Addison-Wesley, 1980).

29. "Executive Management," https://investors.pier1.com, accessed March 30, 2018.

30. J.R. Galbraith and R.K. Kazanjian, *Strategy Implementation: Structure, System, and

Process, 2nd ed. (St. Paul, MN: West, 1986).

31. Lawrence and Lorsch, *Organization and Environment*.

32. Jones, *Organizational Theory*.

33. Lawrence and Lorsch, *Organization and Environment*.

34. R.H. Hall, *Organizations: Structure and Process* (Englewood Cliffs, NJ: Prentice-Hall, 1972); R. Miles, *Macro Organizational Behavior* (Santa Monica, CA: Goodyear, 1980).

35. Chandler, *Strategy and Structure*.

36. G.R. Jones and C.W.L. Hill, "Transaction Cost Analysis of Strategy-Structure Choice," *Strategic Management Journal* 9 (1988), 159–72.

37. "Our History," www.gsk.com, accessed March 30, 2018.

38. Ibid.

39. N. Allen and N. Bisserbe, "GSK Buys Novartis's Stake in Health-Care Unit for $13 Billion," *The Wall Street Journal*, March 27, 2018.

40. E. Schaal, "5 MLB Teams with the Most World Series Titles," *Sports Cheat Sheet*, www.cheatsheet.com, November 4, 2016; S. Gregory, "How the Chicago Cubs Made World Series History," *TIME*, http://time.com, November 3, 2016.

41. N. Scott, "Theo Epstein Is the Greatest Baseball Executive of the Modern Era," *USA Today*, http://ftw.usatoday.com, November 3, 2016.

42. T. Verducci, "Why Theo Epstein and the Cubs Are Fortune's MVPs This Year," *Fortune*, http://fortune.com, March 23, 2017; T. Verducci, "The Rainmaker: How Cubs Boss Theo Epstein Ended a Second Epic Title Drought," *Sports Illustrated*, www.si.com, December 14, 2016.

43. T. Berg, "Joe Maddon Explains How Philly Fans Conspired Against the Rays in His Last World Series," *USA Today*, http://ftw.usatoday.com, October 26, 2016.

44. J. Arguello, "Is Corny the New Cool? Cubs Focus on Culture That Cares Puts Them on the Cutting Edge," *Chicago Now*, www.chicagonow.com, accessed March 30, 2018; D. Yaeger, "Embrace High Expectations: Lessons from Joe Maddon and the Chicago Cubs," *Forbes*, www.forbes.com, October 7, 2016.

45. S.M. Davis and P.R. Lawrence, *Matrix* (Reading, MA: Addison-Wesley, 1977); J.R. Galbraith, "Matrix Organization Designs: How to Combine Functional and Project Forms," *Business Horizons* 14 (1971), 29–40.

46. L.R. Burns, "Matrix Management in Hospitals: Testing Theories of Matrix Structure and Development," *Administrative Science Quarterly* 34 (1989), 349–68.

47. C.W.L. Hill, *International Business* (Homewood, IL: Irwin, 2003).

48. Kotter International, "5 Innovation Secrets from Sealy," *Forbes*, www.forbes.com/sites/johnkotter/2012/10/10/5-innovation-secrets-from-sealy/, October 10, 2012.

49. Jones, *Organizational Theory*.

50. "Newell Brands: Fast Facts," http://design.newellbrands.com, accessed March 30, 2018.

51. "Leading Through Design and Innovation to Connect with Consumers," http://design.newellbrands.com, accessed March 30, 2018; A. Jones, "Newell Brands Will Expand in Kalamazoo with $1.48M from State," *Michigan Live*, www.mlive.com, September 26, 2017.

52. P. Blau, "A Formal Theory of Differentiation in Organizations," *American Sociological Review* 35 (1970), 684–95.

53. "Executive Team," http://news.mcdonalds.com, accessed March 30, 2018.

54. Child, *Organization*.

55. C. Rugaber, "Big Pay Gains for US Workers Contribute to Wall St. Sell-Off," *The Mercury News*, www.mercurynews.com, February 2, 2018.

56. "Heartwiring and Hardwiring Your Leadership," https://ogolead.com, accessed March 30, 2018; Here's the Best Way to Cure Toxic Leadership, Says Former YUM Brands CEO," *CNBC.com*, www.cnbc.com, February 22, 2018.

57. "About Us," www.plexus.com, accessed March 30, 2018.

58. Ibid

59. P.M. Blau and R.A. Schoenherr, *The Structure of Organizations* (New York: Basic Books, 1971).

60. Jones, *Organizational Theory*.

61. J.R. Galbraith, *Designing Complex Organizations* (Reading, MA: Addison-Wesley, 1977), chap. 1; Galbraith and Kazanjian, *Strategy Implementation*, chap. 7.

62. "Food for Good Fact Sheet," www.pepsicofoodforgood.com, accessed March 30, 2018.

63. S.D.N. Cook and D. Yanow, "Culture and Organizational Learning." *Journal of Management Inquiry* 2 (1993), 373–90.

64. J. J. Moses, "When Women Do Better, We All Do Better: Dr. Rohini Anand," *People Matters*, www.peoplematters.in, March 22, 2018; B. Shah, "Meet the Woman Who Has Made Sodexo One of the World's Most Women-Friendly Companies," *Your Story*, https://yourstory.com, March 15, 2018; S. Karabell, "Surrounded by Women: Sodexo CEO Michel Landel on Leadership," *Forbes*, www.forbes.com, January 4, 2017.

65. Karabell, "Surrounded by Women."

66. Moses, "When Women Do Better"; Shah, "Meet the Woman."

67. Karabell, "Surrounded by Women"; Shah, "Meet the Woman"; S. O'Beirne, "Sodexo Study Finds Teams with Gender Diversity Achieve Better Results," *Facilities Management Journal*, www.fjm.co.uk, March 7, 2018.

68. Moses, "When Women Do Better"; Karabell, "Surrounded by Women."

69. O'Beirne, "Sodexo Study"; Shah, "Meet the Woman."

70. B. Schneider, "The People Make the Place," *Personnel Psychology* 40 (1987), 437–53.

71. J.E. Sheriden, "Organizational Culture and Employee Retention," *Academy of Management Journal* 35 (1992), 657–92.

72. G. Winfrey, "The Mistake That Turned Warby Parker into an Overnight Legend," *Inc.*, www.inc.com, accessed March 31, 2018.

73. D. Zax, "Fast Talk: How Warby Parker's Cofounders Disrupted the Eyewear Industry and Stayed Friends," *Inc.*, www.inc.com, accessed March 31, 2018.

74. L. Kane, "Why Every New Employee at a Billion-Dollar Glasses Brand Gets Kerouac and Pretzels as a Welcome Gift," *Business Insider*, www.businessinsider.com, April 14, 2017; "We Have a Culture Crush on Warby Parker," *Big Spaceship*, www.bigspaceship.com, accessed March 31, 2018; K. Burke, "Inside Warby Parker: How Vision, Mission & Culture Helped Build a Billion Dollar Business," *Hub Spot*, https://blog.hubspot.com, accessed March 31, 2018.

75. L. Thomas, "Warby Parker Aims to Run Nearly 100 Stores This Year, As Other Web Shops Follow," *CNBC*, www.cnbc.com, February 16, 2018; T. Novellino, "7 Warby Parker Secrets for a Talented, Happy Workforce," *New York Business Journal*, www.bizjournals.com, September 29, 2015.

76. M. Hannan and J. Freeman, "Structural Inertia and Organizational Change," *American Sociological Review* 49 (1984), 149–64.

77. C.A. O'Reilly, J. Chatman, and D.F. Caldwell, "People and Organizational Culture: Assessing Person-Organizational Fit," *Academy of Management Journal* 34 (1991), 487–517.

78. T.L. Beauchamp and N.E. Bowie, eds., *Ethical Theory and Business* (Englewood Cliffs, NJ: Prentice-Hall, 1979); A. MacIntyre, *After Virtue* (Notre Dame, IN: University of Notre Dame Press, 1981).

79. A. Sagie and D. Elizur, "Work Values: A Theoretical Overview and a Model of Their Effects," *Journal of Organizational Behavior* 17 (1996), 503–14.

80. G.R. Jones, "Transaction Costs, Property Rights, and Organizational Culture: An

Exchange Perspective," *Administrative Science Quarterly* 28 (1983), 454–67.

81. W. Morrow, "10 Benefits and Perks for Attracting and Keeping the Best Employee," *Entrepreneur,* www .entrepreneur.com, October 31, 2017; K. Lobosco, "New Employee Perk: $100 a Month for Student Loans," *CNN Money,* http://money.cnn.com, October 19, 2017.

82. S. L. Morrow, G. K. Koves, and V.E. Barnes, "Exploring the Relationship between Safety Culture and Safety Performance in U.S. Nuclear Power Operations," *Safety Science* 69: 37–47, November 2014.

83. H. Mintzberg, *The Structuring of Organizational Structures* (Englewood Cliffs, NJ: Prentice-Hall, 1979).

84. G. Kunda, *Engineering Culture* (Philadelphia: Temple University Press, 1992).

85. "Google Careers: Mountain View (Global HQ)," https://careers.google.com, accessed March 30, 2018.

86. K.E. Weick, *The Social Psychology of Organization* (Reading, MA: Addison-Wesley, 1979).

87. I. Lunden, "Verizon Closes $4.5B Acquisition of Yahoo, Marissa Mayer Resigns," *Tech Crunch,* https://techcrunch.com, June 13, 2017; A. Kharpal, "Verizon Completes Its $4.48 Billion Acquisition of Yahoo; Marissa Mayer Leaves with $23 Million," *CNBC,* www.cnbc.com, June 13, 2017.

88. Copyright © 2006, Gareth R. Jones.

CHAPTER 11

Organizational Control and Change

©Image Source/Getty Images

Learning Objectives

After studying this chapter, you should be able to:

LO11-1 Define organizational control, and explain how it increases organizational effectiveness.

LO11-2 Describe the four steps in the control process and the way it operates over time.

LO11-3 Identify the main output controls, and discuss their advantages and disadvantages as means of coordinating and motivating employees.

LO11-4 Identify the main behavior controls, and discuss their advantages and disadvantages as a means of coordinating and motivating employees.

LO11-5 Discuss the relationship between organizational control and change, and explain why managing change is a vital management task.

Procter & Gamble Takes a Hard Look at Digital Ads

What controls can managers use to ensure organizational success? Procter & Gamble, the seller of dozens of major consumer brands, including Bounty, Crest, Pampers, and Tide, spends more on advertising than any other company in the world.[1] As a marketing leader, P&G was early to direct many of its billions of advertising dollars to the Internet. Eventually, online ad spending reached about one-third of its total budget for advertising.

Advertising must fulfill a business purpose, of course. P&G, like other organizations, wants to know how many people are receiving its ad messages and whether the messages produce an increase in sales. Ineffective ads are a wasted expense, while effective ads increase sales. Further, P&G wants to spend ad dollars efficiently in order to increase profits along with sales. These are all considerations of Chief Brand Officer Marc Pritchard, while CEO David Taylor keeps an eye on the company's overall performance.

As Pritchard and Taylor reviewed the company's marketing performance, they became increasingly dissatisfied with what they were learning about the performance of digital media. More consumers have been installing ad blockers, a sign that they felt overwhelmed by ads. The more consumers who used ad blockers, the more P&G was paying for ads that would go unseen because they were blocked. Furthermore, ads sometimes appeared next to controversial content. A famous example occurred on YouTube, which for a time was running ads for Tide next to videos of the Tide Pod challenge in which people tried eating the laundry detergent. Even the number of clicks on an ad was becoming a questionable performance measure: sites were counting clicks by software bots that had been created just to click on links in order to drive up results. Pritchard and Taylor expressed their concerns publicly, and media companies took note. If they didn't satisfy P&G's concerns, they risked losing a major source of revenues. In particular, Google and Facebook agreed to let the Media Rating Council audit their performance data.[2]

Over the months that followed, Pritchard and Taylor analyzed the audit results and other data. Much of what they learned was not favorable to digital media. For example, they learned that, on average, consumers looked at an online ad for just 17 seconds. P&G tried cutting digital-marketing expenses by more than $100 million and saw little measurable impact on sales—suggesting that those ads had not delivered the most important kind of results.[3]

Pritchard responded to the information by making changes in P&G's advertising budgets.

Evaluating poor digital media results caused Procter & Gamble's senior executives (including Chief Brand Officer Marc Pritchard, pictured here) to redirect spending to other forms of advertising for P&G's products.
©Neil Hall/Reuters Pictures

The company directed hundreds of millions of dollars away from digital, especially from sites that had not placed ads next to appropriate content or generated much response from consumers. Of the money still spent on Internet media, more now goes to retail sites, such as Amazon and Walmart, where shoppers can see P&G's brands while looking for related products. Along with these changes, Pritchard continues to look for cost savings that keep the overall marketing program operating as efficiently as possible.[4]

One immediate outcome of P&G's pressure and changes in spending is that online media companies have scrambled to create a more favorable environment for P&G and other advertisers. These changes include rewriting algorithms for what content is featured and what ads are displayed. Furthermore, as P&G cut online ad spending, it posted stronger profits.[5]

Overview

As we discussed in Chapter 10, the first task facing managers is to establish a structure of task and job reporting relationships that allows organizational members to use resources most efficiently and effectively. Structure alone, however, does not provide the incentive or motivation for people to behave in ways that help achieve organizational goals. When managers choose how to influence, shape, and regulate the activities of organizational divisions, functions, and employees to achieve the organization's mission and goals, they establish the second foundation of organizational architecture: organizational control. An organization's structure provides the organization with a skeleton, but its control systems give it the muscles, sinews, nerves, and sensations that allow managers to regulate and govern its activities. The control systems also give managers specific feedback on how well the organization and its members are performing. As underscored in the opening story about Procter & Gamble, the managerial functions of organizing and controlling are inseparable, and effective managers must learn to make them work together in a harmonious way.

In this chapter we look in detail at the nature of organizational control and describe the main steps in the control process. We also discuss the different types of control systems that are available to managers to shape and influence organizational activities—*output control, behavior control,* and *clan control.*[6] Finally, we discuss the important issue of organizational change, which is possible only when managers have put in place a control system that allows them to adjust the way people and groups behave and alter, or transform, the way the organization operates. Control is the essential ingredient needed to bring about and manage organizational change efficiently and effectively. By the end of this chapter, you will appreciate the different forms of control available to managers and understand why developing an appropriate control system is vital to increasing organizational performance.

What Is Organizational Control?

As noted in Chapter 1, *controlling* is the process whereby managers monitor and regulate how efficiently and effectively an organization and its members are performing the activities necessary to achieve organizational goals. As discussed in previous chapters, when planning and organizing, managers develop the organizational strategy and structure that they hope will allow the organization to use resources most effectively to create value for customers. In controlling, managers monitor and evaluate whether the organization's strategy and structure are working as intended, how they can be improved, and how they might be changed if they are not working.

Control, however, does not mean just reacting to events after they have occurred. It also means keeping an organization on track, anticipating events that might occur, and then changing the organization to respond to whatever opportunities or threats have been identified. Control is concerned with keeping employees motivated, focused on the important problems confronting the organization, and working together to make the changes that will help an organization improve its performance over time.

LO11-1 Define organizational control, and explain how it increases organizational effectiveness.

The Importance of Organizational Control

To understand the importance of organizational control, consider how it helps managers obtain superior efficiency, quality, responsiveness to customers, and innovation—the four building blocks of competitive advantage.

To determine how efficiently they are using their resources, managers must be able to accurately measure how many units of inputs (raw materials, human resources, and so on) are being used to produce a unit of output, such as a Toyota vehicle. Managers also must be able to measure how many units of outputs (goods and services) are being produced. A control system contains the measures, or yardsticks, that let managers assess how efficiently the organization is producing goods and services. Moreover, if managers experiment with changing how the organization produces goods and services to find a more efficient way of producing them, these measures tell managers how successful they have been. For example, when Kimberly-Clark, maker of Kleenex and other products, outsourced logistics at a U.K. plant to a leading lean organization, it reduced long shifts and overtime for its workers. Absenteeism dropped and productivity improved as staff morale went up. Without a control system in place, managers have no idea how well their organization is performing and how its performance can be improved—information that is becoming increasingly important in today's highly competitive environment.

Today much of the competition among organizations centers on increasing the quality of goods and services. In the car industry, for example, cars within each price range compete in features, design, and reliability. Thus, whether a customer buys a Ford Focus, Toyota Avalon, or Honda CRV depends significantly on the design and quality of each car. Organizational control is important in determining the quality of goods and services because it gives managers feedback on product quality. If the managers of carmakers consistently measure the number of customer complaints and the number of new cars returned for repairs, or if school principals measure how many students drop out of school or how achievement scores on nationally based tests vary over time, they have a good indication of how much quality they have built into their product—whether it is an educated student or a car that does not break down. Effective managers create a control system that consistently monitors the quality of goods and services so they can continuously improve quality—an approach to change that gives them a competitive advantage.

Effective organizational control can also increase responsiveness to customers. Managers can help make their organizations more responsive to customers, for example, if they develop a control system, such as a CRM system, that allows them to evaluate how well customer-contact employees perform their jobs. Monitoring employee behavior can help managers find ways to increase employees' performance levels, perhaps by revealing areas in which skill training or new procedures can allow employees to perform their jobs better. Also, when employees know their behaviors are being monitored, they have more incentive to be helpful and consistent in how they act toward customers. For example, Caterpillar has a lean initiative to bring employees closer to customers so the employees can provide products and services that match customers' needs. Before Caterpillar introduced its lean manufacturing principle at its Aurora, Illinois, facility in 2013, discovering defects on its medium wheel loader value stream was considered normal. Because the defects were discovered, they were fixed before being passed on to the customer. However, the defects were still costing the company lost time and other costs. After the company introduced its lean program at the plant and made it clear that the company was dedicated to eliminating defects, average internal defects fell by 60%.[7]

Finally, controlling can raise the level of innovation in an organization. Successful innovation takes place when managers create an organizational setting in which employees feel empowered to be creative and in which authority is decentralized to employees so they feel free to experiment and take control of their work activities. Deciding on the appropriate control systems to encourage risk taking is an important management challenge; organizational culture is vital in this regard. At Caterpillar the lean initiative extends beyond manufacturing to all functional areas including engineering, purchasing, accounting, and human resources. With its lean initiative well under way across the organization, in 2016 Caterpillar reduced its variable manufacturing costs by $675 million.[8]

Sometimes, however, organizational control systems, including email, can lead to challenges, frustrations, and lost productivity. As the "Management Insight" feature suggests, implementing email policies throughout an organization may help employee productivity and morale.

Controlling Your Office Inbox

In terms of challenges in today's workplace, managing email may be at the top of the list. Overuse of this communication method and problems surrounding it continue to hinder employee effectiveness and efficiency.[9] Research suggests that the average worker spends more than 13 hours a week on email—and those hours are not limited to time spent in the office.[10] In this 24/7 world, with people connected to multiple devices simultaneously, how can managers implement controls that help employees handle email so that the quality of their work and their work-life balance don't suffer? Philadelphia-based Vynamic may have the answer: a Zmail policy.

Vynamic is a health care consulting firm that prides itself on a strong and healthy organizational culture. Several years ago, employees started to complain about the stress of constant email contact at all hours. Founder and CEO Dan Calista describes a common scenario that many professionals experience in this digital world. An employee checks email before going to sleep. Next thing the person knows, he or she is now thinking about the email instead of getting a restful stretch of "ZZZs." Thus, the Zmail policy was born. Vynamic employees

Implementing company controls such as email policies may help improve employee productivity and morale.
©Rawpixel.com/Shutterstock

(including managers) are requested not to send emails between 10 p.m. and 6 a.m. during the week and all day Saturday and Sunday.[11]

The company recognizes that some employees like to spend a few hours over the weekend reviewing pertinent emails and sending communications to clients and colleagues when no one is distracting them. For some people, there are benefits to this type of work habit. However, Calista recommends saving the email as a draft and sending it off first thing Monday morning. He asks, "Why is it so important to you that the other person join your weekend time?"[12]

Despite Vynamic's ban on late-night and weekend emails, employees are expected to communicate with clients and colleagues as necessary to keep business moving forward.[13] Calista says that unplugging from email and mentally disconnecting from work is not only liberating, it might also help employees become more productive after a good night's sleep. Vynamic employees see the Zmail policy as an important benefit to working for the company: Over the past five years, less than 10% of its consultants have left the organization.[14]

Not all companies have the tools or the time to implement organizational controls like the one initiated by Vynamic. However, there are ways that managers and employees alike can get a handle on managing the email challenge. The following tips can be useful to professionals at all levels of an organization:

- Turn off notifications so you're not distracted by every message received in your inbox.

- Don't check email more than three times a day, and select specific times in the workday to check for messages.

- If you need information from a colleague in less than three hours, use a mode of communication other than email—how about picking up the phone and asking for the information? This allows coworkers to work on other tasks without dreading one more email notification.

- Respond to simple and urgent messages, file those that do not require a reply, and flag any that require more thought and follow-up before sending a response.
- Empty the email trash at the end of the day. Sometimes you will need to retrieve an email that you mistakenly trashed, so make this the last thing you do at the end of the workday.[15]

Control Systems and IT

control systems Formal target-setting, monitoring, evaluation, and feedback systems that provide managers with information about how well the organization's strategy and structure are working.

Control systems are formal target-setting, monitoring, evaluation, and feedback systems that provide managers with information about whether the organization's strategy and structure are working efficiently and effectively.[16] Effective control systems alert managers when something is going wrong and give them time to respond to opportunities and threats. An effective control system has three characteristics: It is flexible enough to allow managers to respond as necessary to unexpected events; it provides accurate information about organizational performance; and it gives managers information in a timely manner because making decisions on the basis of outdated information is a recipe for failure.

New forms of IT have revolutionized control systems because they facilitate the flow of accurate and timely information up and down the organizational hierarchy and between functions and divisions. Today employees at all levels of the organization routinely feed information into a company's information system or network and start the chain of events that affect decision making in some other part of the organization. This could be the department store clerk whose scanning of purchased clothing tells merchandise managers what kinds of clothing need to be reordered or the salesperson in the field who feeds into a tablet computer the CRM information necessary to inform marketing about customers' changing needs.

feedforward control Control that allows managers to anticipate problems before they arise.

Control and information systems are developed to measure performance at each stage in the process of transforming inputs into finished goods and services (see Figure 11.1). At the input stage, managers use **feedforward control** to anticipate problems before they arise so problems do not occur later during the conversion process.[17] For example, by giving stringent product specifications to suppliers in advance (a form of performance target), an organization can control the quality of the inputs it receives from its suppliers and, thus, avoid potential problems during the conversion process. Also, IT can be used to keep in contact with suppliers and to monitor their progress. Similarly, by screening job applicants, often by viewing their résumés electronically and using several interviews to select the most highly skilled people, managers can lessen the chance that they will hire people who lack the necessary skills or experience to perform effectively. In general, the development of management information systems promotes feedforward control that gives managers timely information about changes in the

Figure 11.1

Three Types of Control

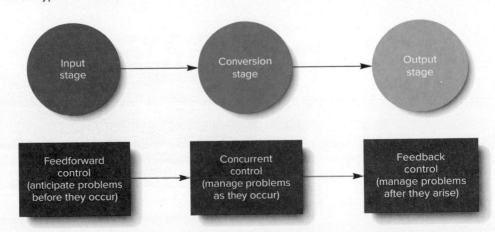

task and general environments that may impact their organization later on. Effective managers always monitor trends and changes in the external environment to try to anticipate problems. (We discuss management information systems in detail in Chapter 18.)

At the conversion stage, **concurrent control** gives managers immediate feedback on how efficiently inputs are being transformed into outputs so managers can correct problems as they arise. Concurrent control through IT alerts managers to the need to react quickly to whatever is the source of the problem, whether it is a defective batch of inputs, a machine that is out of alignment, or a worker who lacks the skills necessary to perform a task efficiently. Concurrent control is at the heart of total quality management programs (discussed in Chapter 9), in which workers are expected to constantly monitor the quality of the goods or services they provide at every step of the production process and inform managers as soon as they discover problems. For example, United Technologies Corporation uses a system called Achieving Competitive Excellence (ACE) to get employees involved in identifying and solving design and quality problems and finding better ways to assemble its products to increase quality and reduce costs. When problems are corrected on an ongoing basis, the result is finished products that are more valuable to customers and command higher prices.

At the output stage, managers use **feedback control** to provide information about customers' reactions to goods and services so corrective action can be taken if necessary. For example, a feedback control system that monitors the number of customer returns alerts managers when defective products are being produced, and a management information system (MIS) that measures increases or decreases in relative sales of different products alerts managers to changes in customer tastes so they can increase or reduce the production of specific products.

concurrent control Control that gives managers immediate feedback on how efficiently inputs are being transformed into outputs so managers can correct problems as they arise.

feedback control Control that gives managers information about customers' reactions to goods and services so corrective action can be taken if necessary.

The Control Process

The control process, whether at the input, conversion, or output stage, can be broken down into four steps: establishing standards of performance and then measuring, comparing, and evaluating actual performance (see Figure 11.2).[18]

LO11-2 Describe the four steps in the control process and the way it operates over time.

- Step 1: *Establish the standards of performance, goals, or targets against which performance is to be evaluated.*

At step 1 in the control process, managers decide on the standards of performance, goals, or targets that they will use in the future to evaluate the performance of the entire organization or part of it (such as a division, a function, or an individual). The standards of performance that managers select measure efficiency, quality, responsiveness to customers, and innovation.[19] If managers decide to pursue a low-cost strategy, for example, they need to measure efficiency at all levels in the organization.

Figure 11.2

Four Steps in Organizational Control

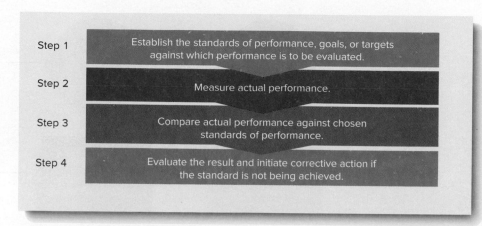

Step 1	Establish the standards of performance, goals, or targets against which performance is to be evaluated.
Step 2	Measure actual performance.
Step 3	Compare actual performance against chosen standards of performance.
Step 4	Evaluate the result and initiate corrective action if the standard is not being achieved.

At the corporate level, a standard of performance that measures efficiency is operating costs, the actual costs associated with producing goods and services, including all employee-related costs. Top managers might set a corporate goal of "reducing operating costs by 10% for the next three years" to increase efficiency. Corporate managers might then evaluate divisional managers for their ability to reduce operating costs within their respective divisions, and divisional managers might set cost-saving targets for functional managers. Thus, performance standards selected at one level affect those at the other levels, and ultimately the performance of individual managers is evaluated in terms of their ability to reduce costs.

The number of standards or indicators of performance that an organization's managers use to evaluate efficiency, quality, and so on can run into the thousands or hundreds of thousands. Managers at each level are responsible for selecting standards that will best allow them to evaluate how well the part of the organization they are responsible for is performing.[20] Managers must be careful to choose standards of performance that let them assess how well they are doing with all four building blocks of competitive advantage. If managers focus on just one standard (such as efficiency) and ignore others (such as determining what customers really want and innovating a new line of products to satisfy them), managers may end up hurting their organization's performance.

- Step 2: *Measure actual performance.*

Once managers have decided which standards or targets they will use to evaluate performance, the next step in the control process is to measure actual performance. In practice, managers can measure or evaluate two things: (1) the actual *outputs* that result from the behavior of their members and (2) the *behaviors* themselves (hence the terms *output control* and *behavior control* used in this chapter).[21]

Sometimes both outputs and behaviors can be easily measured. Measuring outputs and evaluating behavior is relatively easy in a fast-food restaurant, for example, because employees are performing routine tasks. Managers at Home Depot are rigorous in using output control to measure how fast inventory flows through stores. Similarly, managers of a fast-food restaurant can easily measure outputs by counting how many customers their employees serve, the time each transaction takes, and how much money each customer spends. Managers can easily observe each employee's behavior and quickly take action to solve any problems that may arise.

When an organization and its members perform complex, nonroutine activities that are intrinsically hard to measure, it is more challenging for managers to measure outputs or behavior.[22] For example, it might be simple for a manager at Amazon to measure a customer service representative's effectiveness by examining sales figures and customer satisfaction reports. However, it would be difficult for the managers at the companies that supply Amazon with products to measure a product designer's creativity just by watching the designer's actions.

In general, the more nonroutine or complex organizational activities are, the harder it is for managers to measure outputs or behaviors.[23] Outputs, however, are usually easier to measure than behaviors because they are more tangible and objective. Therefore, the first kind of performance measures that managers tend to use is those that measure outputs. Then managers develop performance measures or standards that allow them to evaluate behaviors to determine whether employees at all levels are working toward organizational goals. Some simple behavior measures are (1) whether employees come to work on time and (2) whether employees consistently follow the established rules for greeting and serving customers. The various types of output and behavior control and how they are used at the different organizational levels—corporate, divisional, functional, and individual—are discussed in detail subsequently.

- Step 3: *Compare actual performance against chosen standards of performance.*

During step 3, managers evaluate whether—and to what extent—performance deviates from the standards of performance chosen in step 1. If performance is higher than expected, managers might decide they set performance standards too low and may raise them for the next period to challenge their subordinates.[24] Managers at successful companies are well known for the way they try to improve performance in manufacturing settings by constantly raising performance standards to motivate managers and workers to find new ways to reduce costs or increase quality.

However, if performance is too low and standards were not reached, or if standards were set so high that employees could not achieve them, managers must decide whether to take corrective action.[25] It is easy to take corrective action when the reasons for poor performance can be identified—for instance, high labor costs. To reduce costs, managers can search for low-cost overseas suppliers, invest more in technology, or implement cross-functional teams. More often, however, the reasons for poor performance are hard to identify. Changes in the environment, such as the emergence of a new global competitor, a recession, or an increase in interest rates, might be the source of the problem. Within an organization, perhaps the R&D function underestimated the problems it would encounter in developing a new product or the extra costs of doing unforeseen research or perhaps the faulty design of just one component in thousands slipped through the cracks. If managers are to take any form of corrective action, step 4 is necessary.

- Step 4: *Evaluate the result and initiate corrective action (that is, make changes) if the standard is not being achieved.*

The final step in the control process is to evaluate the results and bring about change as appropriate. Whether or not performance standards have been met, managers can learn a great deal during this step. If managers decide the level of performance is unacceptable, they must try to change how work activities are performed to solve the problem. Sometimes performance problems occur because the work standard was too high—for example, a sales target was too optimistic and impossible to achieve. In this case, adopting more realistic standards can reduce the gap between actual performance and desired performance.

However, if managers determine that something in the situation is causing the problem, then to raise performance they will need to change how resources are being utilized or shared.[26] Perhaps the latest technology is not being used; perhaps workers lack the advanced training needed to perform at a higher level; perhaps the organization needs to buy its inputs or assemble its products abroad to compete against low-cost rivals; perhaps it needs to restructure itself or reengineer its work processes using Six Sigma to increase efficiency.

The simplest example of a control system is the thermostat in a home. By setting the thermostat, you establish the standard of performance with which actual temperature is to be compared. The thermostat contains a sensing or monitoring device that measures the actual temperature against the desired temperature. Whenever there is a difference between them, the furnace or air-conditioning unit is activated to bring the temperature back to the standard. In other words, corrective action is initiated. This is a simple control system: It is entirely self-contained and the target (temperature) is easy to measure.

Establishing targets and designing measurement systems are much more difficult for managers because the high level of uncertainty in the organizational environment means managers rarely know what might happen in the future. Thus, it is vital for managers to design control systems to alert them to problems quickly so they can be dealt with before they become threatening. Another issue is that managers are not just concerned about bringing the organization's performance up to some predetermined standard; they want to push that standard forward to encourage employees at all levels to find new ways to raise performance. In 2015 the U.S. Justice Department fined General Motors $935 million for an ignition switch defect that killed 124 people. In addition, GM paid out more than $575 million to settle civil lawsuits, as well as additional monies to fix millions of cars that still contained the defective switch. The financial toll of company employees covering up the defect for more than a decade now exceeds $2.3 billion.[27]

In the following sections, we consider three important types of control systems that managers use to coordinate and motivate employees to ensure that they pursue superior efficiency, quality, innovation, and responsiveness to customers: output control, behavior control, and clan control (see Figure 11.3). Managers use all three to shape, regulate, and govern organizational activities, no matter what specific organizational structure is in place. However, as Figure 11.3 suggests, an important element of control is embedded in organizational culture, which is discussed later.

Figure 11.3

Three Organizational Control Systems

Type of Control	Mechanisms of Control
Output control	Financial measures of performance Organizational goals Operating budgets
Behavior control	Direct supervision Management by objectives Rules and standard operating procedures
Clan control	Values Norms Socialization

Output Control

LO11-3 Identify the main output controls, and discuss their advantages and disadvantages as means of coordinating and motivating employees.

All managers develop a system of output control for their organizations. First they choose the goals or output performance standards or targets that they think will best measure efficiency, quality, innovation, and responsiveness to customers. Then they measure to see whether the performance goals and standards are being achieved at the corporate, divisional, functional, and individual employee levels of the organization. The three main mechanisms that managers use to assess output or performance are financial measures, organizational goals, and operating budgets.

Financial Measures of Performance

Top managers are most concerned with overall organizational performance and use various financial measures to evaluate it. The most common are profit ratios, liquidity ratios, leverage ratios, and activity ratios. They are discussed here and summarized in Table 11.1.[28]

- *Profit ratios* measure how efficiently managers are using the organization's resources to generate profits. *Return on investment (ROI),* an organization's net income before taxes divided by its total assets, is the most commonly used financial performance measure because it allows managers of one organization to compare performance with that of other organizations. ROI lets managers assess an organization's competitive advantage. *Operating margin* is calculated by dividing a company's operating profit (the amount it has left after all the costs of making the product and running the business have been deducted) by sales revenues. This measure tells managers how efficiently an organization is using its resources; every successful attempt to reduce costs will be reflected in increased operating profit, for example. Also, operating margin is a means of comparing one year's performance to another; for example, if managers discover operating margin has improved by 5% from one year to the next, they know their organization is building a competitive advantage.

- *Liquidity ratios* measure how well managers have protected organizational resources to be able to meet short-term obligations. The *current ratio* (current assets divided by current liabilities) tells managers whether they have the resources available to meet the claims of short-term creditors. The *quick ratio* shows whether they can pay these claims without selling inventory.

- *Leverage ratios,* such as the *debt-to-assets ratio* and the *times-covered ratio,* measure the degree to which managers use debt (borrow money) or equity (issue new shares) to finance ongoing operations. An organization is highly leveraged if it uses more debt than

Table 11.1

Four Measures of Financial Performance

Profit Ratios

Return on investment	$=$	$\dfrac{\text{Net profit before taxes}}{\text{Total assets}}$	Measures how well managers are using the organization's resources to generate profits.
Operating margin	$=$	$\dfrac{\text{Total operating profit}}{\text{Sales revenues}}$	Measures how much percentage profit a company is earning on sales; the higher the percentage, the better a company is using its resources to make and sell the product.

Liquidity Ratios

Current ratio	$=$	$\dfrac{\text{Current assets}}{\text{Current liabilities}}$	Measures the availability of resources to meet claims of short-term creditors.
Quick ratio	$=$	$\dfrac{\text{Current assets} - \text{Inventory}}{\text{Current liabilities}}$	Measures ability to pay off claims of short-term creditors without selling inventory.

Leverage Ratios

Debt-to-assets ratio	$=$	$\dfrac{\text{Total debt}}{\text{Total assets}}$	Measures the extent to which managers have used borrowed funds to finance investments.
Times-covered ratio	$=$	$\dfrac{\text{Profit before interest and taxes}}{\text{Total interest charges}}$	Measures how far profits can decline before managers cannot meet interest charges. If this ratio declines to less than 1, the organization is technically insolvent.

Activity Ratios

Inventory turnover	$=$	$\dfrac{\text{Cost of good sold}}{\text{Inventory}}$	Measures how efficiently managers are turning inventory over so that excess inventory is not carried.
Days sales outstanding	$=$	$\dfrac{\text{Current accounts receivable}}{\text{Sales for period divided by days in period}}$	Measures how efficiently managers are collecting revenues from customers to pay expenses.

equity. Debt can be risky when net income or profit fails to cover the interest on the debt—as some people learn too late when their paychecks do not allow them to pay off their credit cards.

- *Activity ratios* show how well managers are creating value from organizational assets. *Inventory turnover* measures how efficiently managers are turning inventory over so excess inventory is not carried. *Days sales outstanding* reveals how efficiently managers are collecting revenue from customers to pay expenses.

The objectivity of financial measures of performance is the reason why so many managers use them to assess the efficiency and effectiveness of their organizations. When an organization fails to meet performance standards such as ROI, revenue, or stock price targets, managers know they must take corrective action. Thus, financial controls tell managers when a corporate reorganization might be necessary, when they should sell off divisions and exit businesses, or when they should rethink their corporate-level strategies.[29] In addition to quantitative skills, job candidates need problem-solving skills and teamwork abilities in today's job market, as described in the accompanying "Management Insight" feature.

Although financial information is an important output control, financial information by itself does not tell managers all they need to know about the four building blocks of competitive advantage. Financial results inform managers about the results of decisions they have already made; they do not tell managers how to find new opportunities to build competitive advantage in the future. To encourage a future-oriented approach, top managers must establish organizational goals that encourage middle and first-line managers to achieve superior efficiency, quality, innovation, and responsiveness to customers.

MANAGEMENT INSIGHT

Wanted: Problem Solvers & Team Players

Looking to land your first real job? Research suggests that work experience as an intern gets high marks from company executives looking to hire recent grads.

©Click_and_Photo/Getty Images

In today's competitive job market, problem-solving skills and the ability to work in a team are the top attributes employers are looking for on a candidate's résumé. According to the *Job Outlook 2018 Survey* by the National Association of Colleges and Employers (NACE), close to 83% of respondents cite problem-solving skills and teamwork abilities as the most important attributes for job candidates. This is the second consecutive year that the largest percentage of employers will look for these attributes on students' résumés. In addition to a strong GPA, other desirable attributes include written communication skills, leadership traits, and a strong work ethic.[30]

While past NACE research found a student's major the deciding factor between two otherwise qualified candidates, the 2018 survey results suggest that the most influential factor is whether the candidate has internship experience either within the hiring organization or within the organization's industry. On a scale of 1 to 5, with 1 being no influence at all and 5 being extreme influence, completing an internship with the hiring organization or within the same industry rated scores of 4.6 and 4.4, respectively.[31] This finding underscores employer sentiment that internships provide students with professional experience and opportunities to fine-tune communications and problem-solving skills, as well as learn basic office etiquette, which will help them hit the ground running on the first day of their new job.[32]

Although hiring forecasts lag slightly for 2018 grads, NACE estimates that employers plan to hire 4% more new graduates for their U.S. operations than they did in 2017.[33] Among employers planning to increase their new hires, company growth, impending retirements, and the need for entry-level talent were cited as primary reasons behind the hiring plans. Some of the top companies looking for entry-level employees in 2018 include Enterprise, EY (Ernst & Young), the FBI, Bank of America, and Amazon.[34]

Organizational Goals

Once top managers consult with lower-level managers and set the organization's overall goals, they establish performance standards for the divisions and functions. These standards specify for divisional and functional managers the level at which their units must perform if the organization is to achieve its overall goals.[35] Each division is given a set of specific goals to achieve (see Figure 11.4). For example, Jeff Harmening, CEO of General Mills, has established the goal of having each of the company's divisions be first or second in its industry in profit. Divisional managers then develop a business-level strategy (based on achieving superior efficiency or innovation) that they hope will allow them to achieve that goal.[36] In consultation with functional managers, they specify the functional goals that the managers of different functions need to achieve to allow the division to achieve its goals. For example, sales managers might be evaluated for their ability to increase sales; materials management managers, for their ability to increase the quality of inputs or lower their costs; R&D managers, for the number of products they innovate or the number of patents they receive. In turn, functional managers establish goals that first-line managers and nonmanagerial employees need to achieve to allow the function to achieve its goals.

Figure 11.4

Organizationwide Goal Setting

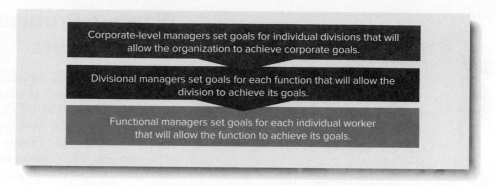

Corporate-level managers set goals for individual divisions that will allow the organization to achieve corporate goals.

Divisional managers set goals for each function that will allow the division to achieve its goals.

Functional managers set goals for each individual worker that will allow the function to achieve its goals.

Output control is used at every level of the organization, and it is vital that the goals set at each level harmonize with the goals set at other levels so managers and other employees through-out the organization work together to attain the corporate goals that top managers have set.[37] It is also important that goals be set appropriately so managers are motivated to accomplish them. If goals are set at an impossibly high level, managers might work only half-heartedly to achieve them because they are certain they will fail. In contrast, if goals are set so low that they are too easy to achieve, managers will not be motivated to use all their resources as efficiently and effec-tively as possible. Research suggests that the best goals are specific, difficult goals—goals that challenge and stretch managers' ability but are not out of reach and do not require an impossibly high expenditure of managerial time and energy. Such goals are often called *stretch goals.*

Deciding what is a specific, difficult goal and what is a goal that is too difficult or too easy is a skill that managers must develop. Based on their own judgment and work experience, manag-ers at all levels must assess how difficult a certain task is, and they must assess the ability of a particular subordinate manager to achieve the goal. If they do so successfully, challenging, interrelated goals—goals that reinforce one another and focus on achieving overall corporate objectives—will energize the organization.

Operating Budgets

operating budget A budget that states how managers intend to use organizational resources to achieve organiza-tional goals.

Once managers at each level have been given a goal or target to achieve, the next step in devel-oping an output control system is to establish operating budgets that regulate how managers and workers attain their goals. An **operating budget** is a blueprint that states how managers intend to use organizational resources to achieve organizational goals efficiently. Typically, managers at one level allocate to subordinate managers a specific amount of resources to pro-duce goods and services. Once they have been given a budget, these lower-level managers must decide how to allocate money for different organizational activities. They are then evaluated for their ability to stay within the budget and to make the best use of available resources. For example, managers in General Mills' cereal business might have a budget of $25 million to spend on developing and selling a new line of organic cereal bars in Europe and Southeast Asia. They must decide how much money to allocate to the various functions, such as finance, R&D, production, and sales, so the business unit generates the most customer revenue and makes the biggest profit. The "Managing Globally" feature describes a budgeting method that is helping international companies reduce their expenses.

Large organizations often treat each division as a singular, or stand-alone, responsibility center. Corporate managers then evaluate each division's contribution to corporate perfor-mance. Managers of a division may be given a fixed budget for resources and be evaluated on the amount of goods or services they can produce using those resources (this is a cost or expense budget approach). Alternatively, managers may be asked to maximize the revenues from the sales of goods and services produced (a revenue budget approach). Or managers may be evaluated on the difference between the revenues generated by the sales of goods and services and the budgeted cost of making those goods and services (a profit budget approach).

Zero-Based Budgeting Spreads around the World

More and more global businesses are telling investors or researchers that they have adopted a budgeting practice called zero-based budgeting (ZBB). With ZBB, the manager of each group or business division creates each year's budget from a blank worksheet. Every amount for every line item is established based on what is necessary for carrying out the year's work to accomplish the year's goals. This may sound basic, but in practice, most managers have saved both time and effort by starting with the previous year's budget and adjusting it upward (or downward) to reflect any changes in goals or circumstances. This tends to leave in place spending done out of habit or provided as a cushion for managers confronting unexpected needs. Creating a budget from scratch is harder, but today's information systems are making the use of ZBB more practical because they can quickly deliver detailed data about spending almost in real time.[38]

A study by Accenture of large global companies found that the percentage of companies using ZBB has been rising 57% per year during this decade. Among the organizations adopting the method are the Anglo-Dutch company Unilever, the United Kingdom's Tesco supermarket chain, and the U.S.-based food giants Kraft Heinz and Mondelez International.[39]

A chief reason for using ZBB is to cut unnecessary spending in the face of international competition for resources and customers. Unilever, for example, announced expected savings greater than $6 billion in marketing and logistics expenses. In the Accenture survey, the companies using ZBB saved an average of $280 million per year, representing reductions of 15% on average. To be effective, cost cutting should be linked to organizational strategy. Most companies in the Accenture study did this by using savings from ZBB to increase profitability; about half used the savings to free up funds for growth. At Kraft Heinz, the chief information officer used ZBB strategically by emphasizing robotics and artificial-intelligence projects, because they could help the company the most in its cost-reduction efforts. The annual routine of ZBB also helps to embed cost consciousness into an organization's culture.[40]

Consultants at Accenture see a bigger future for the principles of ZBB. They believe that the annual process—ground-up planning followed by performance measurement and control—applies to more than budgets. With this mind-set, organizations can look anew at all their processes to see where performance data can help them create a system that does the essentials and does them well.[41]

Japanese companies' use of operating budgets and challenging goals to increase efficiency is instructive in this context.

In summary, three components—objective financial measures, challenging goals and performance standards, and appropriate operating budgets—are the essence of effective output control. Most organizations develop sophisticated output control systems to allow managers at all levels to keep accurate account of the organization so they can move quickly to take corrective action as needed.[42] Output control is an essential part of management.

Problems with Output Control

When designing an output control system, managers must be careful to avoid some pitfalls. For example, they must be sure the output standards they create motivate managers at all levels and do not cause managers to behave in inappropriate ways to achieve organizational goals.

Suppose top managers give divisional managers the goal of doubling profits over a three-year period. This goal seems challenging and reachable when it is jointly agreed upon, and in the first two years profits go up by 70%. In the third year, however, an economic recession hits and sales plummet. Divisional managers think it is increasingly unlikely that they will meet their profit goal. Failure will mean losing the substantial monetary bonus tied to achieving the goal. How might managers behave to try to preserve their bonuses?

Perhaps they might find ways to reduce costs because profit can be increased either by raising sales revenues or reducing costs. Thus, divisional managers might cut back on expensive research activities, delay machinery maintenance, reduce marketing expenditures, and lay off middle managers and workers to reduce costs so that at the end of the year they will make their target of doubling profits and receive their bonuses. This tactic might help them achieve a short-run goal—doubling profits—but such actions could hurt long-term profitability or ROI (because a cutback in R&D can reduce the rate of product innovation, a cutback in marketing will lead to the loss of customers, and so on).

The message is clear: Although output control is a useful tool for keeping managers and employees at all levels motivated and the organization on track, it is only a guide to appropriate action. Managers must be sensitive in how they use output control and must constantly monitor its effects at all levels in the organization—and on customers and other stakeholders.

Behavior Control

LO11-4 Identify the main behavior controls, and discuss their advantages and disadvantages as a means of coordinating and motivating employees.

Organizational structure by itself does not provide any mechanism that motivates managers and nonmanagerial employees to behave in ways that make the structure work—or even improve how it works, hence the need for control. Put another way, managers can develop an organizational structure that has the right grouping of divisions and functions, and an effective chain of command, but it will work as designed *only* if managers also establish control systems that motivate and shape employee behavior in ways that *match* this structure.[43] Output control is one method of motivating employees; behavior control is another method. This section examines three mechanisms of behavior control that managers can use to keep subordinates on track and make organizational structures work as they are designed to work: direct supervision, management by objectives, and rules and bureaucratic control via standard operating procedures (see Figure 11.3).

Direct Supervision

The most immediate and potent form of behavior control is direct supervision by managers who actively monitor and observe the behavior of their subordinates, teach subordinates the behaviors that are appropriate and inappropriate, and intervene to take corrective action as needed. Moreover, when managers personally supervise subordinates, they lead by example and in this way can help subordinates develop and increase their own skill levels. (Leadership is the subject of Chapter 14.)

Direct supervision allows managers at all levels to become personally involved with their subordinates and allows them to mentor subordinates and develop their management skills. Thus, control through personal supervision can be an effective way of motivating employees and promoting behaviors that increase efficiency and effectiveness.[44]

Nevertheless, certain problems are associated with direct supervision. First, it is expensive because a manager can personally manage only a relatively small number of subordinates effectively. Therefore, if direct supervision is the main kind of control being used in an organization, a lot of managers will be needed and costs will increase. For this reason, output control is usually preferred to behavior control; indeed, output control tends to be the first type of control that managers at all levels use to evaluate performance. Second, direct supervision can *demotivate* subordinates. This occurs if employees feel they are under such close scrutiny that they are not free to make their own decisions or if they feel they are not being evaluated in an accurate and impartial way. Team members and other employees may start to pass the buck, avoid responsibility, and cease to cooperate with other team members if they feel their manager is not accurately evaluating their performance and is favoring some people over others.

Third, as noted previously, for many jobs personal control through direct supervision is simply not feasible. The more complex a job is, the more difficult it is for a manager to evaluate how well a subordinate is performing. The performance of divisional and functional managers, for example, can be evaluated only over relatively long periods (this is why an output control system is developed), so it makes little sense for top managers to continually monitor their performance. However, managers can still communicate the organization's mission and goals to their subordinates and reinforce the values and norms in the organization's culture through their own personal style.

Management by Objectives

management by objectives (MBO) A goal-setting process in which a manager and each of his or her subordinates negotiate specific goals and objectives for the subordinate to achieve and then periodically evaluate the extent to which the subordinate is achieving those goals.

To provide a framework within which to evaluate subordinates' behavior and, in particular, to allow managers to monitor progress toward achieving goals, many organizations implement some version of management by objectives. **Management by objectives (MBO)** is a formal system of evaluating subordinates on their ability to achieve specific organizational goals or performance standards and to meet operating budgets.[45] Most organizations use some form of MBO system because it is pointless to establish goals and then fail to evaluate whether they are being achieved. Management by objectives involves three specific steps:

- Step 1: *Specific goals and objectives are established at each level of the organization.*

MBO starts when top managers establish overall organizational objectives, such as specific financial performance goals or targets. Then, objective setting cascades down throughout the organization as managers at the divisional and functional levels set their goals to achieve corporate objectives.[46] Finally, first-level managers and employees jointly set goals that will contribute to achieving functional objectives.

- Step 2: *Managers and their subordinates together determine the subordinates' goals.*

An important characteristic of management by objectives is its participatory nature. Managers at every level sit down with each of the subordinate managers who report directly to them, and together they determine appropriate and feasible goals for the subordinate and bargain over the budget that the subordinate will need to achieve his or her goals. The participation of subordinates in the objective-setting process is a way of strengthening their commitment to achieving their goals and meeting their budgets.[47] Another reason it is so important for subordinates (both individuals and teams) to participate in goal setting is that doing so enables them to tell managers what they think they can realistically achieve.[48]

- Step 3: *Managers and their subordinates periodically review the subordinates' progress toward meeting goals.*

Once specific objectives have been agreed on for managers at each level, managers are accountable for meeting those objectives. Periodically, they sit down with their subordinates to evaluate their progress. Normally, salary raises and promotions are linked to the goal-setting process, and managers who achieve their goals receive greater rewards than those who fall short. (The issue of how to design reward systems to motivate managers and other organizational employees is discussed in Chapter 13.)

In companies that have decentralized responsibility for the production of goods and services to empowered teams and cross-functional teams, management by objectives works somewhat differently. Managers ask each team to develop a set of goals and performance targets that the team hopes to achieve—goals consistent with organizational objectives. Managers then negotiate with each team to establish its final goals and the budget the team will need to achieve them. The reward system is linked to team performance, not to the performance of any one team member.

Cypress Semiconductor offers an interesting example of how IT can be used to manage the MBO process quickly and effectively. In the fast-moving semiconductor business, a premium is placed on organizational adaptability. At Cypress, founder and former CEO T. J. Rodgers was facing a problem: How could he control his growing 1,500-employee organization without developing a bureaucratic management hierarchy? Rodgers believed that a tall hierarchy hinders the ability of an organization to adapt to changing conditions. He was committed to maintaining a flat and decentralized organizational structure with a minimum of management layers. At the same time, he needed to control his employees to ensure that they performed in a manner consistent with the goals of the company. How could he achieve this without resorting to direct supervision and the lengthy management hierarchy that it implies?

To solve this problem, Rodgers implemented an online information system through which he could monitor what every employee and team was doing in his fast-moving and decentralized organization. Each employee maintained a list of 10 to 15 goals, such as "Meet with marketing for new product launch" or "Make sure to check with customer X." Noted next to each goal were when it was agreed upon, when it was due to be finished, and whether it had finished. All this information was stored on a centralized system. Rodgers claimed he could review the goals of all employees in about four hours and did so on a weekly basis. How was this possible? Rodgers used the strategy of *managing by exception,* the process of looking only for employees who were falling behind. When this occurred, Rodgers called employees—not to scold them but to ask whether there was anything he could do to help them get the job done. This system allowed Rodgers to exercise control over the organization without resorting to expensive layers of a management hierarchy and direct supervision.[49]

MBO does not always work out as planned, however. Managers and their subordinates at all levels must believe that performance evaluations are accurate and fair. Any suggestion that personal biases and political objectives play a part in the evaluation process can lower or even destroy MBO's effectiveness as a control system. This is why many organizations work so hard to protect the integrity of their systems.

Also, when people work in teams, each member's contribution to the team and each team's contribution to the goals of the organization must be fairly evaluated. This is not easy to do. It depends on managers' ability to create an organizational control system that measures performance accurately and fairly and links performance evaluations to rewards so that employees stay motivated and coordinate their activities to achieve the organization's mission and goals.

Bureaucratic Control

bureaucratic control Control of behavior by means of a comprehensive system of rules and standard operating procedures.

When direct supervision is too expensive and management by objectives is inappropriate, managers might turn to another mechanism to shape and motivate employee behavior: bureaucratic control. **Bureaucratic control** is control by means of a comprehensive system of rules and standard operating procedures (SOPs) that shapes and regulates the behavior of divisions, functions, and individuals. In Chapter 2 we discussed Weber's theory of bureaucracy and noted that all organizations use bureaucratic rules and procedures but some use them more than others. Recall that rules and SOPs are formal, written instructions that specify a series of actions that employees should follow to achieve a given end; in other words, if *A* happens, then do *B* and *C.* For example, a supervisor of custodial workers at a health care facility might insist that employees call by a specific time before their shift starts to notify her of their absence or lateness—or face disciplinary action.

Rules and SOPs guide behavior and specify what employees are to do when they confront a problem that needs a solution. It is the responsibility of a manager to develop rules that allow employees to perform their activities efficiently and effectively. Rules and SOPs also clarify people's expectations about one another and prevent misunderstandings over responsibility or the use of power. Such guidelines can prevent a supervisor from arbitrarily increasing a subordinate's workload and prevent a subordinate from ignoring tasks that are a legitimate part of the job.

When employees follow the rules that managers have developed, their behavior is *standardized*—actions are performed the same way time and time again—and the outcomes of their work are predictable. And to the degree that managers can make employees' behavior predictable, there is no

Employees demonstrate standardized behavior when they follow the rules that management has developed—actions that are performed the same way time and time again—such as tasks performed on an automobile manufacturing assembly line. This type of bureaucratic control helps maintain quality and increase efficiency.
©Monty Rakusen/Getty Images

need to monitor the outputs of behavior because *standardized behavior leads to standardized outputs,* such as goods and services of the same uniform quality. Suppose a worker at Honda comes up with a way to attach exhaust pipes that reduces the number of steps in the assembly process and increases efficiency. Always on the lookout for ways to standardize and improve procedures, managers make this idea the basis of a new rule that says, "From now on, the procedure for attaching the exhaust pipe to the car is as follows." If all workers follow the rule to the letter, every car will come off the assembly line with its exhaust pipe attached in the new way, and there will be no need to check exhaust pipes at the end of the line.

In practice, mistakes and lapses of attention happen, so output control is used at the end of the line, and each car's exhaust system is given a routine inspection. However, the number of quality problems with the exhaust system is minimized because the rule (bureaucratic control) is being followed. Service organizations such as retail stores, fast-food restaurants, and home improvement stores also attempt to standardize employee behavior, such as customer service quality, by instructing employees in the correct way to greet customers or the appropriate way to serve and bag food. Employees are trained to follow the rules that have proved to be most effective in a particular situation, and the better trained the employees are, the more standardized is their behavior and the more trust managers can have that outputs (such as food quality) will be consistent.

The goal is simple: Use the rules to achieve a quick resolution of a complex issue. If the existing rules don't work, employees must experiment; when they find a solution, it is turned into a new rule to be included in the procedures book to aid the future decision making of all employees in the organization.

Problems with Bureaucratic Control

All organizations make extensive use of bureaucratic control because rules and SOPs effectively control routine organizational activities. With a bureaucratic control system in place, managers can manage by exception, intervening and taking corrective action only when necessary. However, managers need to be aware of a number of problems associated with bureaucratic control because such problems can reduce organizational effectiveness.[50]

First, establishing rules is always easier than discarding them. Organizations tend to become overly bureaucratic over time as managers do everything according to the rule book. If the amount of red tape becomes too great, decision making slows and managers react sluggishly to changing conditions. This can imperil an organization's survival if agile new competitors emerge.

Second, because rules constrain and standardize behavior and lead people to behave in predictable ways, people might become so used to automatically following rules that they stop thinking for themselves. Thus, too much standardization can actually *reduce* the level of learning taking place in an organization and get the organization off track if managers and workers focus on the wrong issues. An organization thrives when its members are constantly thinking of new ways to increase efficiency, quality, and customer responsiveness. By definition, new ideas do not come from blindly following standardized procedures. Similarly, the pursuit of innovation implies a commitment by managers to discover new ways of doing things; innovation, however, is incompatible with extensive bureaucratic control.

Consider, for example, what happened at The Walt Disney Company when Bob Iger became CEO of the troubled company. Bob Iger had been COO of Disney under CEO Michael Eisner, and he noticed that Disney was plagued by slow decision making that had led to many mistakes in putting its new strategies into action. Its Disney stores were losing money; its Internet properties were flops; and even its theme parks seemed to have lost their luster as few new rides or attractions were introduced. Iger believed one of the main reasons for Disney's declining performance was that it had become too tall and bureaucratic and its top managers were following financial rules that did not lead to innovative strategies.

Eliminating unnecessary layers in Disney's management hierarchy has helped CEO Bob Iger foster an environment of innovation and creativity.
©VCG/VCG via Getty Images

One of Iger's first moves to turn around performance was to dismantle Disney's central strategic planning office. In this office, several levels of managers were responsible for sifting through all the new ideas and innovations sent up by Disney's different business divisions, such as theme parks, movies, and gaming, and then deciding which ones to present to the CEO. Iger saw the strategic planning office as a bureaucratic bottleneck that reduced the number of ideas coming from below. So he dissolved the office and reassigned its managers back to the different business units.[51]

The result of cutting this unnecessary layer in Disney's hierarchy has been that more new ideas are generated by its different business units. The level of innovation has increased because managers are more willing to speak out and champion their ideas when they know they are dealing directly with the CEO and a top management team searching for innovative ways to improve performance—rather than a layer of strategic planning bureaucrats concerned only with the bottom line.[52] Disney continues to do well in several sectors, including movies and theme parks. Its recent superhero film, Marvel Studio's *Black Panther*, which features a mostly African American cast, shattered box office records in 2018. And the company's theme park and hotel resort in Shanghai, China, continues to draw enthusiastic crowds.[53]

Managers must always be sensitive about the way they use bureaucratic control. It is most useful when organizational activities are routine and well understood and when employees are making programmed decisions—for example, in mass-production settings such as Ford or in routine service settings such as stores like Target or Midas Muffler. Bureaucratic control is much less useful in situations where nonprogrammed decisions have to be made and managers have to react quickly to changes in the task environment.

To use output control and behavior control, managers must be able to identify the outcomes they want to achieve and the behaviors they want employees to perform to achieve those outcomes. For many of the most important and significant organizational activities, however, output control and behavior control are inappropriate for several reasons:

- A manager cannot evaluate the performance of workers such as doctors, research scientists, or engineers by observing their daily behavior.

- Rules and SOPs are of little use in telling a doctor how to respond to an emergency situation or a scientist how to discover something new.

- Output controls such as the amount of time a surgeon takes for each operation or the costs of making a discovery are crude measures of the quality of performance.

How can managers attempt to control and regulate the behavior of their subordinates when personal supervision is of little use, when rules cannot be developed to tell employees what to do, and when outputs and goals cannot be measured at all or can be measured usefully only over long periods? One solution might be the use of clan control in an organization.

Clan Control

clan control The control exerted on individuals and groups in an organization by shared values, norms, standards of behavior, and expectations.

Increasingly, organizations are using **clan control**, which takes advantage of the power of internalized values and norms to guide and constrain employee attitudes and behavior in ways that increase organizational performance.[54] The first function of a control system is to shape the behavior of organizational members to ensure that they are working toward organizational goals and to take corrective action if those goals are not being met. The second function of control, however, is to keep organizational members focused on thinking about what is best for their organization in the future and to keep them looking for new opportunities to use organizational resources to create value. Clan control serves this dual function of keeping organizational members goal-directed while open to new opportunities because it takes advantage of the power of organizational culture, discussed in the previous chapter.

Organizational culture functions as a kind of control system because managers can deliberately try to influence the kind of values and norms that develop in an organization—values and norms that specify appropriate and inappropriate behaviors and, so, determine the way its members behave.[55] We discussed the sources of organizational culture and the way managers can help create different kinds of cultures in Chapter 10.

Organizational Change

organizational change The movement of an organization away from its present state and toward some preferred future state to increase its efficiency and effectiveness.

As we have discussed, many problems can arise if an organization's control systems are not designed correctly. One of these problems is that an organization cannot change or adapt in response to a changing environment unless it has effective control over its activities. Companies can lose this control over time, or they can change in ways that make them more effective. Organizational change is the movement of an organization away from its present state toward some preferred future state to increase its efficiency and effectiveness.

Interestingly enough, there is a fundamental tension or need to balance two opposing forces in the control process that influences how organizations change. As just noted, organizations and their managers need to be able to control their activities and make their operations routine and predictable. At the same time, however, organizations have to be responsive to the need to change, and managers and employees have to "think on their feet" and realize when they need to depart from routines to be responsive to unpredictable events. In other words, even though adopting the right set of output and behavior controls is essential for improving efficiency, because the environment is dynamic and uncertain, employees also need to feel that they have the autonomy to depart from routines as necessary to increase effectiveness. (See Figure 11.5.)

LO11-5 Discuss the relationship between organizational control and change, and explain why managing change is a vital management task.

For this reason, many researchers believe that the highest-performing organizations are those that are constantly changing—and thus become experienced at doing so—in their search to become more efficient and effective. Companies like UPS, Toyota, and Walmart are constantly changing the mix of their activities to move forward even as they seek to make their existing operations more efficient. For example, UPS entered the air express parcel market, bought a chain of mailbox stores, and began offering a consulting service. At the same time, the company's ORION on-board technology system, which has increased the efficiency of its delivery process in the United States, is expected to save the company between $300 million and $400 million a year while reducing the average driving route of a UPS driver by close to eight miles.[56]

Lewin's Force-Field Theory of Change

Researcher Kurt Lewin developed a theory about organizational change. According to his *force-field theory,* a wide variety of forces arise from the way an organization operates—from its structure, culture, and control systems—that make organizations resistant to change. At the same time, a wide variety of forces arise from changing task and general environments that push organizations toward change. These two sets of forces are always in opposition in an organization.[57] When the forces are evenly balanced, the organization is in a state of inertia and does not change. To get an organization to change, managers must find a way to *increase* the forces for change, *reduce* resistance to change, or do *both* simultaneously. Any of these strategies will overcome inertia and cause an organization to change.

Figure 11.5
Organizational Control and Change

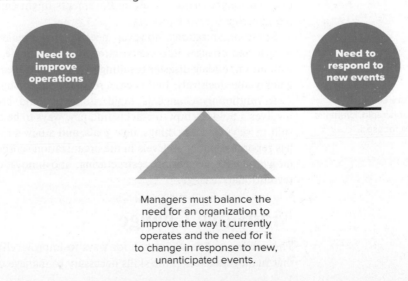

Need to improve operations

Need to respond to new events

Managers must balance the need for an organization to improve the way it currently operates and the need for it to change in response to new, unanticipated events.

Figure 11.6

Lewin's Force-Field Model of Change

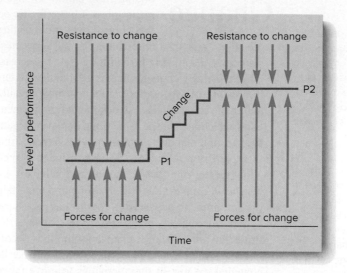

Figure 11.6 illustrates Lewin's theory. An organization at performance level P1 is in balance: Forces for change and resistance to change are equal. Management, however, decides that the organization should strive to achieve performance level P2. To get to level P2, managers must *increase* the forces for change (the increase is represented by the lengthening of the up arrows), *reduce* resistance to change (the reduction is represented by the shortening of the down arrows), or both. If managers pursue any of the three strategies successfully, the organization will change and reach performance level P2. Before we look in more detail at the techniques managers can use to overcome resistance and facilitate change, we need to look at the types of change they can implement to increase organizational effectiveness.

Evolutionary and Revolutionary Change

Managers continually face choices about how best to respond to the forces for change. There are several types of change that managers can adopt to help their organizations achieve desired future states.[58] In general, types of change fall into two broad categories: evolutionary change and revolutionary change.[59]

evolutionary change Change that is gradual, incremental, and narrowly focused.

Evolutionary change is gradual, incremental, and narrowly focused. Evolutionary change is not drastic or sudden but, rather, is a constant attempt to improve, adapt, and adjust strategy and structure incrementally to accommodate changes taking place in the environment.[60] Sociotechnical systems theory and total quality management, or kaizen, are two instruments of evolutionary change. Such improvements might entail using technology in a better way or reorganizing the work process.

Some organizations, however, need to make major changes quickly. Faced with drastic, unexpected changes in the environment (for example, a new technological breakthrough) or with an impending disaster resulting from mismanagement, an organization might need to act quickly and decisively. In this case, revolutionary change is called for.

revolutionary change Change that is rapid, dramatic, and broadly focused.

Revolutionary change is rapid, dramatic, and broadly focused. Revolutionary change involves a bold attempt to quickly find new ways to be effective. It is likely to result in a radical shift in ways of doing things, new goals, and a new structure for the organization. The process has repercussions at all levels in the organization—corporate, divisional, functional, group, and individual. Reengineering, restructuring, and innovation are three important instruments of revolutionary change.

Managing Change

The need to constantly search for ways to improve efficiency and effectiveness makes it vital that managers develop the skills necessary to manage change effectively. Several experts have

Figure 11.7

Four Steps in the Organizational Change Process

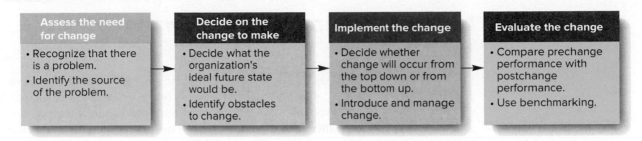

Assess the need for change	Decide on the change to make	Implement the change	Evaluate the change
• Recognize that there is a problem. • Identify the source of the problem.	• Decide what the organization's ideal future state would be. • Identify obstacles to change.	• Decide whether change will occur from the top down or from the bottom up. • Introduce and manage change.	• Compare prechange performance with postchange performance. • Use benchmarking.

proposed a model of change that managers can follow to implement change successfully—that is, to move an organization away from its present state and toward some desired future state to increase its efficiency and effectiveness.[61] Figure 11.7 outlines the steps in this process. In the rest of this section, we examine each one.

ASSESSING THE NEED FOR CHANGE   Organizational change can affect practically all aspects of organizational functioning, including organizational structure, culture, strategies, control systems, and groups and teams, as well as the human resource management system and critical organizational processes such as communication, motivation, and leadership. Organizational change can alter how managers carry out the critical tasks of planning, organizing, leading, and controlling and the ways they perform their managerial roles.

Deciding how to change an organization is a complex matter because change disrupts the status quo and poses a threat, prompting employees to resist attempts to alter work relationships and procedures. Organizational learning—the process through which managers try to increase organizational members' abilities to understand and appropriately respond to changing conditions—can be an important impetus for change and can help all members of an organization, including managers, effectively make decisions about needed changes.

Assessing the need for change calls for two important activities: recognizing that there is a problem and identifying its source. Sometimes the need for change is obvious, such as when an organization's performance is suffering. Often, however, managers have trouble determining that something is going wrong because problems develop gradually; organizational performance may slip for a number of years before a problem becomes obvious. Thus, during the first step in the change process, managers need to recognize that there is a problem that requires change.

Often the problems that managers detect have produced a gap between desired performance and actual performance. To detect such a gap, managers need to look at performance measures—such as falling market share or profits, rising costs, or employees' failure to meet their established goals or stay within budgets—that indicate whether change is needed. These measures are provided by organizational control systems, discussed earlier in the chapter.

To discover the source of the problem, managers need to look both inside and outside the organization. Outside the organization, they must examine how changing environmental forces may be creating opportunities and threats that are affecting internal work relationships. Perhaps the emergence of low-cost competitors abroad has led to conflict among different departments that are trying to find new ways to gain a competitive advantage. Managers also need to look within the organization to see whether its structure is causing problems between departments. Perhaps a company does not have integrating mechanisms in place to allow different departments to respond to low-cost competition. The "Manager as a Person" feature describes how members of the Nordstrom family are looking inside and outside their retail business to recognize the forces compelling change.

DECIDING ON THE CHANGE TO MAKE   Once managers have identified the source of the problem, they must decide what they think the organization's ideal future state would be. In other words, they must decide where they would like their organization to be in the future— what kinds of goods and services it should be making, what its business-level strategy should

Nordstrom Family Makes Changes to Stay Afloat

In retailing, the winds of change are blowing at hurricane strength. Department stores gave way to big-box stores, which gave way to online retailing. Fashions constantly change, and young people would rather purchase travel and entertainment than clothes and accessories. Many retailers have closed down, but one that remains standing is the Nordstrom department store chain, started by John Nordstrom and a partner in 1901.

Nordstrom survives because the company's leaders are open to new ideas. The company has three copresidents, brothers Blake, Pete, and Erik Nordstrom; the president of stores is their cousin Jamie Nordstrom. As great-grandsons of the founder, the four have a long-term view, which makes them willing to take risks. They also extend themselves because, as Pete told a reporter, they "don't want to be known as the generation of Nordstroms that screwed this thing up."[62] Pete determined two decades ago that the company could increase profits by selling more luxury goods, and he wound up being the one who frequently visits Europe to attend fashion shows and make deals with designers.

In today's turbulent environment, the Nordstrom leaders keep their stores relevant. They determined that a store selling fashion needs a presence in New York City (where the company has the greatest online sales). They opened a men's store, featuring natural lighting and a bar where shoppers can purchase drinks to sip as they shop. In California, the company is trying a concept called Nordstrom Local, which stocks a full line of merchandise—one in every size, so shoppers can try on items but not take them. When shoppers find something to buy, an employee orders it.[63]

The managers also plan ways to merge the benefits of online and in-store shopping. Online shoppers can reserve items to be waiting in the store to try on in dressing rooms conveniently located near the doors. Furthermore, two-thirds of online shoppers making returns do so in a store. They often stay to shop, so Nordstrom also locates return desks near entrances. Tailors work in the stores, including Nordstrom Local, and a new policy allows shoppers to bring in any clothes to have them altered—again with the hope they will shop. Finally, through acquisitions, the company is investing in digital technologies for selling, including the BevyUp platform for communication among sales associates and the MessageYes app, which provides an easy way for consumers to respond to texts from Nordstrom.[64]

Unlike some of their competition, the Nordstrom brothers seem determined to keep moving ahead by thinking outside the box and remaining flexible in their approach to customers' tastes and shopping habits. Managing change is never easy; however, Nordstrom family members and their employees are determined to keep navigating the choppy retail waters.

be, how the organizational structure should be changed, and so on. During this step, managers also must plan how to attain the organization's ideal future state.

This step in the change process also includes identifying obstacles or sources of resistance to change. Managers must analyze the factors that may prevent the company from reaching its ideal future state. Obstacles to change are found at the corporate, divisional, departmental, and individual levels of the organization.

Corporate-level changes in an organization's strategy or structure, even seemingly trivial changes, may significantly affect how divisional and departmental managers behave. Suppose that to compete with low-cost foreign competitors, top managers decide to increase the

Organizational change can be a slow and painful process for both managers and employees. Resistance to new processes and other changes can be overcome by improving communication from leadership as to why and how such changes need to be made.
©fizkes/Shutterstock

resources spent on state-of-the-art machinery and reduce the resources spent on marketing or R&D. The power of manufacturing managers would increase, and the power of marketing and R&D managers would fall. This decision would alter the balance of power among departments and might increase conflict as departments fight to retain their status in the organization. An organization's present strategy and structure are powerful obstacles to change.[65]

Whether a company's culture is adaptive or inert facilitates or obstructs change. Organizations with entrepreneurial, flexible cultures, such as high-tech companies, are much easier to change than are organizations with more rigid cultures, such as those sometimes found in large, bureaucratic organizations like the military or GM.

The same obstacles to change exist at the divisional and departmental levels. Division managers may differ in their attitudes toward the changes that top managers propose and, if their interests and power seem threatened, will resist those changes. Managers at all levels usually fight to protect their power and control over resources.[66] Because departments have different goals and time horizons, they may also react differently to the changes other managers propose. When top managers are trying to reduce costs, for example, sales managers may resist attempts to cut back on sales expenditures if they believe that problems stem from manufacturing managers' inefficiencies.

At the individual level, too, people often resist change because it brings uncertainty and stress. For example, individuals may resist the introduction of a new technology because they are uncertain about their abilities to learn it and effectively use it. Or, by their very nature, other individuals may take comfort in the status quo and believe any type of change will require more work on their part, so they resist.[67]

All of these obstacles make organizational change a slow and sometimes painful process. Managers at all levels of the organization must recognize the potential obstacles to change and take them into consideration. Some obstacles can be overcome by improving communication from leadership so all organizational members are aware of the need for change and the nature of the changes being implemented. Empowering employees and inviting them to participate in planning for change may overcome some resistance and allay employees' fears. However, it is also important for managers to listen to employees' sentiment about possible changes, especially when the employees believe they have rational reasons why the change could prove detrimental to the organization. Considering this alternate view of resistance allows organizations to engage in better decision making regarding which changes to undertake.[68]

IMPLEMENTING THE CHANGE   Generally, managers implement—that is, introduce and manage—change from the top down or from the bottom up.[69] **Top-down change** is implemented quickly: Top managers identify the need for change, decide what to do, and then move quickly to implement the changes throughout the organization. For example, top managers may decide to restructure and downsize the organization and then give divisional and departmental managers specific goals to achieve. With top-down change, the emphasis is on making the changes quickly and dealing with problems as they arise; it is revolutionary in nature.

Bottom-up change is typically more gradual or evolutionary. Top managers consult with middle and first-line managers about the need for change. Then, over time, managers at all levels work to develop a detailed plan for change. A major advantage of bottom-up change is that it can co-opt resistance to change from employees. Because the emphasis in bottom-up change is on participation and on keeping people informed about what is going on, uncertainty and resistance are minimized.

EVALUATING THE CHANGE   The last step in the change process is to evaluate how successful the change effort has been in improving organizational performance.[70] Using measures such as changes in market share, profits, or the ability of scientists to innovate new drugs,

top-down change A fast, revolutionary approach to change in which top managers identify what needs to be changed and then move quickly to implement the changes throughout the organization.

bottom-up change A gradual or evolutionary approach to change in which managers at all levels work together to develop a detailed plan for change.

benchmarking The process of comparing one company's performance on specific dimensions with the performance of high-performing organizations.

managers compare how well an organization is performing after the change with how well it was performing before. Managers also can use **benchmarking**, comparing their performance on specific dimensions with the performance of high-performing organizations to decide how successful a change effort has been. For example, when Xerox was performing poorly in the 1980s, it benchmarked the efficiency of its distribution operations against that of L.L.Bean, the efficiency of its central computer operations against that of John Deere, and the efficiency of its marketing abilities against that of Procter & Gamble. Those three companies are renowned for their skills in these different areas, and by studying how they performed, Xerox was able to dramatically increase its own performance. Benchmarking is a key tool in total quality management, an important change program discussed in Chapter 9.

In summary, organizational control and change are closely linked because organizations operate in environments that are constantly changing, so managers must be alert to the need to change their strategies and structures. Managers of high-performing organizations are attuned to the need to continually modify the way they operate, and they adopt techniques such as empowered work groups and teams, benchmarking, and global outsourcing to remain competitive in a global world.

Summary and Review

LO11-1, 11-2

WHAT IS ORGANIZATIONAL CONTROL? Controlling is the process whereby managers monitor and regulate how efficiently and effectively an organization and its members are performing the activities necessary to achieve organizational goals. Controlling is a four-step process: (1) establishing performance standards, (2) measuring actual performance, (3) comparing actual performance against performance standards, and (4) evaluating the results and initiating corrective action if needed.

LO11-3 **OUTPUT CONTROL** To monitor output or performance, managers choose goals or performance standards that they think will best measure efficiency, quality, innovation, and responsiveness to customers at the corporate, divisional, departmental or functional, and individual levels. The main mechanisms that managers use to monitor output are financial measures of performance, organizational goals, and operating budgets.

LO11-4 **BEHAVIOR CONTROL** In an attempt to shape behavior and induce employees to work toward achieving organizational goals, managers use direct supervision, management by objectives, and bureaucratic control by means of rules and standard operating procedures.

CLAN CONTROL Clan control is the control exerted on individuals and groups by shared values, norms, and prescribed standards of behavior. An organization's culture is deliberately fashioned to emphasize the values and norms top managers believe will lead to high performance.

LO11-5 **ORGANIZATIONAL CHANGE** There is a need to balance two opposing forces in the control process that influences the way organizations change. On one hand, managers need to be able to control organizational activities and make their operations routine and predictable. On the other hand, organizations have to be responsive to the need to change, and managers must understand when they need to depart from routines to be responsive to unpredictable events. The four steps in managing change are (1) assessing the need for change, (2) deciding on the changes to make (including identification of possible sources of resistance to change), (3) implementing change, and (4) evaluating the results of change.

Management in Action

Topics for Discussion and Action

Discussion

1. What is the relationship between organizing and controlling? [LO11-1]

2. How do output control and behavior control differ? [LO11-2, 11-3]

3. Why is it important for managers to involve subordinates in the control process? [LO11-3, 11-4]

4. What kind of controls would you expect to find most used in (a) a hospital, (b) the U.S. Navy, and (c) a city police force? Why? [LO11-2, 11-3, 11-4]

5. What are the main obstacles to organizational change? What techniques can managers use to overcome these obstacles? [LO11-1, 11-5]

Action

6. Ask a manager to list the main performance measures that he or she uses to evaluate how well the organization is achieving its goals. [LO11-1, 11-3, 11-4]

7. Ask the same or a different manager to list the main forms of output control and behavior control that he or she uses to monitor and evaluate employee behavior. [LO11-3, 11-4]

Building Management Skills

Understanding Controlling [LO11-1, 11-3, 11-4]

For this exercise you will analyze the control systems used by a real organization such as a department store, restaurant, hospital, police department, or small business. It can be the organization that you investigated in Chapter 10 or a different one. Your objective is to uncover all the different ways in which managers monitor and evaluate the performance of the organization and employees.

1. At what levels does control take place in this organization?

2. Which output performance standards (such as financial measures and organizational goals) do managers use most often to evaluate performance at each level?

3. Does the organization have a management by objectives system in place? If it does, describe it. If it does not, speculate about why not.

4. How important is behavior control in this organization? For example, how much of managers' time is spent directly supervising employees? How formalized is the organization? Do employees receive a book of rules to teach them how to perform their jobs?

5. What kind of culture does the organization have? What are the values and norms? What effect does the organizational culture have on the way employees behave or treat customers?

6. Based on this analysis, do you think there is a fit between the organization's control systems and its culture? What is the nature of this fit? How could it be improved?

Managing Ethically [LO11-1, 11-5]

Some managers and organizations go to great lengths to monitor their employees' behavior, and they keep extensive records about employees' behavior and performance. Some organizations also seem to possess norms and values that cause their employees to behave in certain ways.

Questions

1. Either by yourself or in a group, think about the ethical implications of organizations' monitoring and collecting information about their employees. What kinds of

information is it ethical or unethical to collect? Why? Should managers and organizations tell subordinates they are collecting such information? Explain your reasoning.

2. Similarly, some organizations' cultures seem to develop norms and values that cause their members to behave in unethical ways. When and why does a strong norm that encourages high performance become one that can cause people to act unethically? How can organizations keep their values and norms from becoming "too strong"?

Small Group Breakout Exercise

How Best to Control the Sales Force? [LO11-1, 11-3, 11-5]

Form groups of three or four people, and appoint one member as the spokesperson who will communicate your findings to the class when called on by the instructor. Then discuss the following scenario:

You are the regional sales managers of an organization that supplies high-quality windows and doors to building supply centers nationwide. Over the last three years, the rate of sales growth has decreased. There is increasing evidence that, to make their jobs easier, salespeople are primarily servicing large customer accounts and ignoring small accounts. In addition, the salespeople are not dealing promptly with customer questions and complaints, and this inattention has resulted in poor after-sales service. You have talked about these problems, and you are meeting to design a control system to increase both the amount of sales and the quality of customer service.

1. Design a control system that you think will best motivate salespeople to achieve these goals.

2. What relative importance do you put on (a) output control, (b) behavior control, and (c) organizational culture in this design?

Be the Manager

You have been asked by your company's CEO to find a way to improve the performance of its teams of web design and web hosting specialists and programmers. Each team works on a different aspect of website production; although each is responsible for the quality of its own performance, its performance also depends on how well the other teams perform. Your task is to create a control system that will help to increase the performance of each team separately and facilitate cooperation among the teams. This is necessary because the various projects are interlinked and affect one another, just as the different parts of a car must fit together. Because competition in the website production market is intense, it is imperative that each website be up and running as quickly as possible and incorporate all the latest advances in website software technology.

Questions

1. What kind of output controls will best facilitate positive interactions both within the teams and among the teams?

2. What kind of behavior controls will best facilitate positive interactions both within the teams and among the teams?

3. How would you help managers develop a culture to promote high team performance?

Bloomberg Case in the News [LO11-1, 11-2, 11-5]

Beloved Guitar Maker Gibson Faces Crushing $560 Million Debt

Like the blues giant Robert Johnson, whose mastery of a Gibson guitar was said to be the result of a deal with the Devil, the company has come to a crossroads.

After 116 years, the Devil's knocking on Gibson's door. Debt of as much as $560 million is due this summer, and investors are whispering that Chief Executive Officer Henry Juszkiewicz has got to go.

Juszkiewicz traded a slice of Gibson's soul in an attempt to become more than just the maker of the world's most beloved guitar. He bought pieces of consumer electronics companies to relaunch Gibson Guitars as Gibson Brands Inc., a "music lifestyle" company. It didn't work out as planned.

"My dream was to be the Nike of music lifestyle," Juszkiewicz said in an interview. "At this point, I have to cut back on that ambition, frankly."

Elvis Presley changed history on a Gibson J200. Eric Clapton's famous solo on the Beatles' "While My Guitar Gently Weeps" was played on a Gibson, and when young B.B. King fled a burning building and realized he'd left his Gibson behind, he risked his life by going back inside to retrieve it. The fire had been accidentally started by two men fighting over a woman, and King gave his hollow-body guitar her name—Lucille.

But pop cares little for legend. Gibson says sales are strong, but guitars don't have the mystique they did in King's day.

Consumer Electronics

"We have a younger generation coming in with tastes toward a different type of music," said Al Di Meola, a Grammy-winning jazz guitarist.

Juszkiewicz tried diversification. He bought a line of consumer electronics from Japanese company Onkyo Corp., and in 2014 he added Royal Philips NV's audio and home entertainment business, WOOX Innovations, for $135 million.

The purchases fit into Juszkiewicz's vision for the company's future. Not everyone was pleased.

"Gibson has chosen to go into that market where they're competing with the really big dogs," said Pat Foley, who leads artist relations at Orange Amplifiers. He ran Gibson's entertainment relations worldwide before being fired in 2014. "In the guitar market, we were the big dogs."

Cash Drain

There appears to be no going back. The closely held company skipped January's National Association of Music Merchants show, the music industry's leading trade event. Instead, executives attended the International Consumer Electronics Show alongside tech behemoths like Sony Corp.

The transition has drained more cash than expected, with a particular downhill turn after the Philips deal.

"We got sort of a grab bag full of stuff, and some of it really did make sense, but some of it was very unprofitable," Juszkiewicz said.

A looming $375 million bond maturity means he's running out of time for a turnaround, according to Moody's Investors Service senior analyst Kevin Cassidy. On top of the Aug. 1 payment, the company has a "springing lien" that will cause $185 million of debt to become current in July if Gibson falls behind on payments, according to S&P Global Ratings. Gibson is also facing tighter credit terms from its suppliers and growing pressure from new import regulations on rosewood, a crucial material for Gibson's high-end instruments, according to S&P.

Nashville, Memphis

The company has expressed pride that its Gibson guitars are made in the U.S. Acoustic instruments come out of a factory in Bozeman, Montana, and solid-body electric guitars are made in Nashville, Tennessee. Hollow bodies, like King's Lucille, are crafted at its Memphis plant.

The Memphis factory sits near B.B. King's Blues Club and not far from the old Sun Records studio, where Presley cut his first album. The guitars are shaped, sanded, painted and polished by hand. Wood chips fly, sending the scent of cut rosewood into the air. It takes up to a month to make each instrument into a work of art. Only 60 are completed each day.

"We're preserving the artistry," Juszkiewicz said. "That's what Gibson is, and that's what people want from Gibson."

To raise cash, Gibson Brands sold the Memphis factory in December to private equity firms Somera Road and Tricera Capital for $14.1 million. It continues work there, for now.

Reduce Leverage

"Their hope is that the capital structure is refinanceable if they can reduce leverage," said Cassidy of Moody's. "We think the likelihood of a default or some type of financial restructuring is pretty high."

Another obstacle to the company's resurgence is its broken relationship with some retailers. A number of them have stopped selling the brand, citing unmanageable demands that range from annual credit checks to upfront orders for a year's merchandise.

"You have to eat so much garbage in order to be a Gibson dealer that it's not worth it," said George Gruhn, who owns Gruhn Guitars in Nashville.

Other vendors echoed that sentiment, including Frank Glionna, who says he'd been a Gibson dealer since the 1970s and called his decision to cut ties last year "bittersweet."

"Everybody Bailed"

"In the last couple of years, everybody bailed," said Glionna, owner of The Music Gallery in Highland Park, Illinois. "The company is in the worst place I've ever seen it in my decades as a dealer."

Juszkiewicz said that lightening Gibson's debt load and integrating the consumer electronics operations are difficult tasks, but ones that he thinks he can do.

If the creditors have their way, though, Juszkiewicz, after 30-plus years with the company, won't be leading Gibson much longer. An organized group of bondholders is pushing for a restructuring that would hand them ownership of the company and let them install new leadership. Juszkiewicz has pushed back publicly.

Gibson is "a company that's lost focus," said Laurence Juber, Grammy-winning former lead guitarist of Paul McCartney's 1970s band Wings, who owns seven Gibsons. "It's one of the iconic brands. I can't imagine that it would go away."

Questions for Discussion

1. How did Gibson's management lose organizational control? Cite some examples.

2. Which step(s) in the control process did Gibson's CEO ignore?

3. What can Gibson management do to repair its strained relationship with some of its dealers in an effort to turn around the company?

Source: Emma Orr and Austin Weinstein, "Beloved Guitar Maker Gibson Faces Crushing $560 Million Debt," *Bloomberg,* March 20, 2018, https://www.bloomberg.com/news/articles/2018-03-20/gibson-beloved-guitar-maker-faces-crushing-560-million-debt. Used with permission of Bloomberg L.P. Copyright © 2017. All rights reserved.

Notes

1. S. Vranica, "P&G Contends Too Much Digital Ad Spending Is a Waste," *The Wall Street Journal,* https://www.wsj.com, March 1, 2018; J. Neff, "Procter & Gamble Gets Smarter at Ad Tech," *AdAge,* http://adage.com, February 8, 2018; A. Bruell, "P&G's Marc Pritchard Doubles Down on Demands of Digital Ad Giants," *The Wall Street Journal,* https://www.wsj.com, March 2, 2017.

2. Vranica, "P&G Contends"; Bruell, "P&G's Marc Pritchard Doubles Down."

3. Vranica, "P&G Contends"; A. Bruell and S. Terlep, "P&G Cuts More than $100 Million in 'Largely Ineffective' Digital Ads," *The Wall Street Journal,* https://www.wsj.com, July 27, 2017.

4. Vranica, "P&G Contends"; Bruell, "P&G's Marc Pritchard Doubles Down"; Bruell and Terlep, "P&G Cuts More than $100 Million"; J. Neff, "P&G Will Cut Another $400 Million in Agency, Production Costs," *AdAge,* http://adage.com, February 22, 2018.

5. Vranica, "P&G Contends"; Bruell and Sharon Terlep, "P&G Cuts More than $100 Million."

6. W. G. Ouchi, "Markets, Bureaucracies, and Clans," *Administrative Science Quarterly* 25 (1980), 129–41.

7. "2015 Executive Summary," www.caterpillar.com, accessed April 3, 2018; "Caterpillar Enterprise System Group: Lean: A Journey That Delivers Significant Results,' http://reports.caterpillars.com, accessed April 3, 2018.

8. Caterpillar 2016 Annual Report, "Building Leaner," http://reports.caterpillar.com, accessed April 6, 2018.

9. A. LaFrance, "Is Email Evil?" *The Atlantic,* www.theatlantic.com, November 12, 2015.

10. D. Burkus, "Some Companies Are Banning Email and Getting More Done," *Harvard Business Review,* https://hbr.org, accessed April 6, 2018; D. Bates, "You've Got (More) Mail: The Average Office Worker Now Spends over a Quarter of Their Day Dealing with Email," *Daily Mail,* www.dailymail.co.uk, accessed April 3, 2018.

11. A. Peters, "One Trick to Make Employees Happy: Ban Emails on Nights and Weekends," *Fast Company,* www.fastcoexist.com, June 1, 2016.

12. L. Vanderkam, "Should Your Company Use 'Zmail'? The Case for Inbox Curfews," *Fast Company,* www.fastcompany.com, accessed July 20, 2016.

13. D. Calista, "CEO's Goal: Build the Happiest, Healthiest Company in Philly," *BizPhilly,* www.phillymag.com, October 28, 2015.

14. "The Five Most Outrageous Company Perks in the World," *Bloomberg Businessweek,* www.bloomberg.com, accessed July 20, 2016.

15. M. Steen, "Take Control of Your Email at Work," https://www.monster.com, accessed April 6, 2018; L. Kolowich, "How to Spend Less Time on Email: 12 Tips for Keeping Your Inbox Under Control," https://blog.hubspot.com, accessed April 6, 2018.

16. P. Lorange, M. Morton, and S. Ghoshal, *Strategic Control* (St. Paul, MN: West, 1986).

17. H. Koontz and R.W. Bradspies, "Managing through Feedforward Control," *Business Horizons,* June 1972, 25–36.

18. E.E. Lawler III and J.G. Rhode, *Information and Control in Organizations* (Pacific Palisades, CA: Goodyear, 1976).

19. C.W.L. Hill and G.R. Jones, *Strategic Management: An Integrated Approach,* 6th ed. (Boston: Houghton Mifflin, 2011).

20. E. Flamholtz, "Organizational Control Systems as a Management Tool," *California Management Review,* Winter 1979, 50–58.

21. W.G. Ouchi, "The Transmission of Control through Organizational Hierarchy," *Academy of Management Journal* 21 (1978), 173–92.

22. W.G. Ouchi, "The Relationship between Organizational Structure and Organizational Control," *Administrative Science Quarterly* 22 (1977), 95–113.

23. Ouchi, "Markets, Bureaucracies, and Clans."

24. W.H. Newman, *Constructive Control* (Englewood Cliffs, NJ: Prentice-Hall, 1975).

25. J.D. Thompson, *Organizations in Action* (New York: McGraw-Hill, 1967).

26. R.N. Anthony, *The Management Control Function* (Boston: Harvard Business School Press, 1988).

27. N. Bunkley, "After GM Settlement, an Unsettled Feeling," *Automotive News,* www.autonews.com, accessed April 6, 2018.

28. Ouchi, "Markets, Bureaucracies, and Clans."

29. Hill and Jones, *Strategic Management.*

30. National Association of Colleges and Employers (NACE), "The Key Attributes Employers Seek on Students' Resumes," www.naceweb.org, accessed April 6, 2018.

31. Ibid.

32. "Top 10 Skills Employers Want in an Intern," https://www.wayup.com, accessed April 6, 2018.

33. "Job Outlook 2018: College Hiring to Increase by 4%," www.naceweb.org, November 15, 2017.

34. "Robust Job Market for Grads Continues in 2018," *PRNewswire,* www.prnewswire.com, January 29, 2018.

35. R. Simons, "Strategic Orientation and Top Management Attention to Control Systems," *Strategic Management Journal* 12 (1991), 49–62.

36. G. Schreyogg and H. Steinmann, "Strategic Control: A New Perspective," *Academy of Management Review* 12 (1987), 91–103.

37. B. Woolridge and S.W. Floyd, "The Strategy Process, Middle Management Involvement, and Organizational Performance," *Strategic Management Journal* 11 (1990), 231–41.

38. N. Trentmann, "Global Companies Extend Use of Zero-Based Budgeting to Slash Costs," *The Wall Street Journal,* https://blogs.wsj.com, February 27, 2018; K. Timmermans and R. Abdalla, *Beyond the ZBB Buzz,* Accenture, 2018, www.accenture.com; N. Trentmann, "European Companies Use Old-School Budget Tactic to Cut Costs," *The Wall Street Journal,* www.wsj.com, April 7, 2017; A. Loten, "Kraft Heinz CIO Spends on AI, Robots to Cut Costs," *The Wall Street Journal,* https://blogs.wsj.com, October 3, 2017.

39. Trentmann, "Global Companies Extend Use"; Timmermans and Abdalla, *Beyond the ZBB Buzz;* Trentmann, "European Companies Use Old-School Budget Tactic."

40. Trentmann, "Global Companies Extend Use"; Timmermans and Abdalla, *Beyond the ZBB Buzz;* Trentmann, "European Companies Use Old-School Budget Tactic."

41. Timmermans and Abdalla, *Beyond the ZBB Buzz.*

42. J.A. Alexander, "Adaptive Changes in Corporate Control Practices," *Academy of Management Journal* 34 (1991), 162–93.

43. Hill and Jones, *Strategic Management.*

44. G.H.B. Ross, "Revolution in Management Control," *Management Accounting* 72 (1992), 23–27.

45. P.F. Drucker, *The Practice of Management* (New York: Harper & Row, 1954).

46. S.J. Carroll and H.L. Tosi, *Management by Objectives: Applications and Research* (New York: Macmillan, 1973).

47. R. Rodgers and J.E. Hunter, "Impact of Management by Objectives on Organizational Productivity," *Journal of Applied Psychology* 76 (1991), 322–26.

48. M.B. Gavin, S.G. Green, and G.T. Fairhurst, "Managerial Control—Strategies for Poor Performance over Time and the Impact on Subordinate Reactions," *Organizational Behavior and Human Decision Processes* 63 (1995), 207–21.

49. D. Clark, "Cypress Semi Says CEO to Step Down; Buying Broadcom Business,"

The Wall Street Journal, www.wsj.com, April 29, 2016. B. Dumaine, "The Bureaucracy Busters," *Fortune,* June 17, 1991, 46.

50. P.M. Blau, *The Dynamics of Bureaucracy* (Chicago: University of Chicago Press, 1955).

51. J. McGregor, "The World's Most Innovative Companies," www.businessweek.com, May 4, 2007.

52. www.waltdisney.com, 2010, 2012.

53. B. Barnes, "With $218 Million Haul, 'Black Panther' Smashes Box Office Records," *The New York Times,* www.nytimes.com, February 18, 2018; E. Yoon, "Shanghai Disneyland Visitors Top 11 Million in Its First Year, Blowing Past Expectations, CEO Iger Says," *CNBC,* www.cnbc.com, June 16, 2017.

54. Ouchi, "Markets, Bureaucracies, and Clans."

55. Ibid.

56. "ORION Backgrounder," https://pressroom.ups.com, accessed April 6, 2018; S. Rosenbush and L. Stevens, "At UPS, the Algorithm Is the Driver," *The Wall Street Journal,* www.wsj.com, February 15, 2015.

57. This section draws heavily on K. Lewin, *Field Theory in Social Science* (New York: Harper & Row, 1951).

58. L. Chung-Ming and R.W. Woodman, "Understanding Organizational Change: A Schematic Perspective," *Academy of Management Journal* 38, no. 2 (1995), 537-55.

59. D. Miller, "Evolution and Revolution: A Quantum View of Structural Change in Organizations," *Journal of Management Studies* 19 (1982), 131-151; D. Miller, "Momentum and Revolution in Organizational Adaptation," *Academy of Management Journal* 2 (1980), 591-614.

60. C.E. Lindblom, "The Science of Muddling Through," *Public Administration Review* 19 (1959), 79-88; P.C. Nystrom and W.H. Starbuck, "To Avoid Organizational Crises, Unlearn," *Organizational Dynamics* 12 (1984), 53-65.

61. L. Brown, "Research Action: Organizational Feedback, Understanding, and Change," *Journal of Applied Behavioral Research* 8 (1972), 697-711; P.A. Clark, *Action Research and Organizational Change* (New York: Harper & Row, 1972); N. Margulies and A.P. Raia, eds., *Conceptual Foundations of Organizational Development* (New York: McGraw-Hill, 1978).

62. C. Binkley, "Nordstrom's Biggest Bet Ever," *The Wall Street Journal,* March 1, 2018, https://www.wsj.com; S. Kapner, "Can the Nordstrom Family Outrun Retail's Woes?" *The Wall Street Journal,* February 14, 2018, https://www.wsj.com.

63. Binkley, "Nordstrom's Biggest Bet Ever"; S. Kapner, "Nordstrom Tries on a New Look: Stores without Merchandise," *The Wall Street Journal,* September 10, 2017, https://www.wsj.com; Kapner, "Can the Nordstrom Family Outrun Retail's Woes?"

64. Binkley, "Nordstrom's Biggest Bet Ever"; Kapner, "Nordstrom Tries on a New Look"; Deena M. Amato-McCoy, "Nordstrom Acquires Two Start-Ups Focused on Digital Experience," *Chain Store Age,* March 8, 2018, https://www.chainstoreage.com.

65. M. Choi and W. E. A. Ruona, "Individual Readiness for Organizational Change and Its Implications for Human Resource and Organization Development," *Human Resource Development Review* 10, no. 1 (2011), 46-73.

66. M. Peiperl, "Resistance to Change," in N. Nicholson, P.G. Audia, and M.M. Pillutla (eds.), *The Blackwell Encyclopedia of Management,* Volume 11: *Organizational Behavior,* 2nd ed., (New York: Wiley, 2005), 348.

67. Choi and Ruona, "Individual Readiness for Organizational Change."

68. S. K. Piderit, "Rethinking Resistance and Recognizing Ambivalence: A Multidimensional View of Attitudes Toward an Organizational Change," *Academy of Management Review* 25, no. 4 (2000), 783-94.

69. W.L. French and C.H. Bell, *Organizational Development* (Englewood Cliffs, NJ: Prentice-Hall, 1990).

70. W.L. French, "A Checklist for Organizing and Implementing an OD Effort," in W.L. French, C.H. Bell, and R.A. Zawacki, eds., *Organizational Development and Transformation* (Homewood, IL: Irwin, 1994), 484-95.

CHAPTER 12

Human Resource Management

©David Lees/Getty Images

Learning Objectives

After studying this chapter, you should be able to:

LO12-1 Explain why strategic human resource management can help an organization gain a competitive advantage.

LO12-2 Describe the steps managers take to recruit and select organizational members.

LO12-3 Discuss the training and development options that ensure organizational members can effectively perform their jobs.

LO12-4 Explain why performance appraisal and feedback are such crucial activities, and list the choices managers must make in designing effective performance appraisal and feedback procedures.

LO12-5 Explain the issues managers face in determining levels of pay and benefits.

LO12-6 Understand the role that labor relations play in the effective management of human resources.

Strategic HR Management Helps Build a Strong Future

How can managers retain top workers in a competitive labor market? For Home Depot, which operates home improvement stores and the fourth-largest e-commerce business in the United States, the trends shaping the retail and construction industries are bringing tremendous challenges and opportunities.[1] The popularity of online shopping has led many other retailers to scale back and close stores. The construction industry feels the swings of the business cycle. During downturns, for example, homeowners put off remodeling old homes or having new ones built, so demand for building supplies tumbles. More recently, construction is booming, generating sales increases. Home Depot, like the construction businesses it serves, is facing heavy competition for workers, with unemployment rates at their lowest levels in more than 15 years. Further complicating the picture, demand for workers in much of the country is seasonal, picking up in the spring and slowing as the weather turns cold.

With these challenges in mind, Home Depot's CEO, Craig Menear, has been following a strategy of using recessions as a time for investing in efficiency and growth to reap the benefits of delivering better service. During the last recession, Home Depot directed investments to improving the online shopping experience, renovating stores, and training workers, with the result that its stores were outselling Lowe's, a key competitor. A shorter-term challenge is to hire in a highly competitive labor market, where many workers are wary of retail jobs. For the past few years, Home Depot has set a hiring target of more than 80,000 seasonal workers.[2]

To compete in a tough labor market, Home Depot has tried to stand out as a superior employer. Like many employers after years of economic expansion, Home Depot has increased wages, and it recently announced one-time employee bonuses of $200 to $1,000, depending on years of service. Another way it does this is by simplifying the application process. The company offers an app that lets job seekers apply from their mobile devices, as well as a text-to-apply option. It reported that these options made applying faster and increased the number of applications by 50% over previous years. More recently, it has enhanced its job application app with a tool that lets the applicant schedule an

Home Depot CEO Craig Menear understands the importance of hiring, training, and retaining a top-notch workforce during both successful business cycles and economic downturns.
©Chris Kleponis/Polaris/Newscom

interview at a store or distribution center. In the first few months after the self-scheduling tool was launched, more than three-quarters of applicants used it to set up an interview.[3]

Besides making job applications more accessible, Home Depot has made training more convenient for employees. It introduced what it calls its "PocketGuide," a training app for use on mobile devices. The employee uses the app to look up product information and complete training activities. An early use of the app was to bring seasonal workers in the garden department up to speed quickly, which helps them succeed on the job and deliver better customer service.[4]

Looking further into the future, Home Depot's charitable foundation has committed to supporting training programs for construction workers.[5] Partnering with the Home Builders Institute, the foundation has donated funds to train 20,000 construction workers over 10 years, preparing them for careers as carpenters, electricians, and plumbers. The program is available to veterans and to high school students in underserved communities. Support for preparing the next generation of construction workers not only boosts Home Depot's reputation as a business that cares about the community, but also builds a customer base for the years ahead.

Overview

Managers are responsible for acquiring, developing, protecting, and utilizing the resources an organization needs to be efficient and effective. One of the most important resources in all organizations is human resources—the people involved in producing and distributing goods and services. Human resources include all members of an organization, ranging from top managers to entry-level employees. Effective managers, like Craig Menear in "A Manager's Challenge," realize how valuable human resources are and take active steps to make sure their organizations build and fully utilize their human resources to gain a competitive advantage.

This chapter examines how managers can tailor their human resource management system to their organization's strategy and structure. We discuss in particular the major components of human resource management: recruitment and selection, training and development, performance appraisal, pay and benefits, and labor relations. By the end of this chapter you will understand the central role human resource management plays in creating a high-performing organization.

LO12-1 Explain why strategic human resource management can help an organization gain a competitive advantage.

Strategic Human Resource Management

human resource management (HRM) Activities that managers engage in to attract and retain employees and to ensure that they perform at a high level and contribute to the accomplishment of organizational goals.

Organizational architecture (see Chapter 10) is the combination of organizational structure, control systems, culture, and a human resource management system that managers develop to use resources efficiently and effectively. **Human resource management (HRM)** includes all the activities managers engage in to attract and retain employees and to ensure that they perform at a high level and contribute to the accomplishment of organizational goals. These activities make up an organization's human resource management system, which has five major components: recruitment and selection, training and development, performance appraisal and feedback, pay and benefits, and labor relations (see Figure 12.1).

Strategic human resource management is the process by which managers design the components of an HRM system to be consistent with each other, with other elements of organizational architecture, and with the organization's strategy and goals.[6] The objective of strategic HRM is the development of an HRM system that enhances an organization's efficiency, quality, innovation, and responsiveness to customers—the four building blocks of competitive advantage.

As part of strategic human resource management, some managers have adopted Six Sigma quality improvement plans. These plans ensure that an organization's products and services are as free of errors or defects as possible through a variety of human resource–related initiatives.

Figure 12.1

Components of a Human Resource Management System

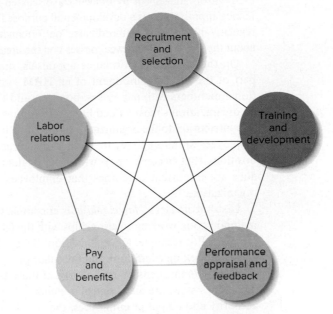

Each component of an HRM system influences
the others, and all five must fit together.

Jack Welch, former CEO of General Electric Company (GE), indicated that these initiatives
saved GE millions of dollars; and other companies, such as Whirlpool and Motorola, also have
implemented Six Sigma initiatives. For such initiatives to be effective, however, top managers
have to be committed to Six Sigma, employees must be motivated, and there must be demand
for the products or services of the organization in the first place. For example, if top managers are not committed to the quality initiative, they may not devote the necessary time and
resources to make it work and may lose interest in it prematurely.[7]

Overview of the Components of HRM

Managers use *recruitment and selection,* the first component of an HRM system, to attract and
hire new employees who have the abilities, skills, and experiences that will help an organization achieve its goals. Microsoft, for example, has the goal of becoming one of the top cloud-
computing tech giants in the world. To achieve this goal, managers at Microsoft realize the
importance of hiring only the best computer systems engineers: Hundreds of highly qualified
candidates are interviewed and rigorously tested. Microsoft has little trouble recruiting top
computer engineering talent because candidates know they will be at the forefront of the cloud-
computing industry if they work for Microsoft.[8]

After recruiting and selecting employees, managers use the second component, *training and
development,* to ensure that organizational members develop the skills and abilities that will
enable them to perform their jobs effectively in the present and the future. Training and development are an ongoing process, as is true at Home Depot in "A Manager's Challenge"; changes
in technology and the environment, as well as in an organization's goals and strategies, often
require that organizational members learn new techniques and ways of working. At Microsoft,
newly hired systems engineers receive on-the-job training by joining small teams that include
experienced employees who serve as mentors or advisers. New recruits learn firsthand from
colleagues how to develop cloud-computing services that are responsive to customers' needs.[9]

The third component, *performance appraisal and feedback,* serves two purposes in HRM.
First, performance appraisal can give managers the information they need to make good human

resources decisions—decisions about how to train, motivate, and reward organizational members.[10] Thus, the performance appraisal and feedback component is a kind of *control system* that can be used with management by objectives (discussed in Chapter 11). Second, feedback from performance appraisal serves a developmental purpose for members of an organization. When managers regularly evaluate their subordinates' performance, they can give employees valuable information about their strengths and weaknesses and the areas in which they need to concentrate.

On the basis of performance appraisals, managers distribute *pay* to employees, which is part of the fourth component of an HRM system. By rewarding high-performing organizational members with pay raises, bonuses, and the like, managers increase the likelihood that an organization's most valued human resources will be motivated to continue their high levels of contribution to the organization. Moreover, if pay is linked to performance, high-performing employees are more likely to stay with the organization, and managers are more likely to fill positions that become open with highly talented individuals. *Benefits* such as health insurance are important outcomes that employees receive by virtue of their membership in an organization.

Last but not least, *labor relations* encompass the steps that managers take to develop and maintain good working relationships with the labor unions that may represent their employees' interests. For example, an organization's labor relations component can help managers establish safe working conditions and fair labor practices in their offices and plants.

Managers must ensure that all five of these components fit together and complement their company's structure and control systems.[11] For example, if managers decide to decentralize authority and empower employees, they need to invest in training and development to ensure that lower-level employees have the knowledge and expertise they need to make the decisions that top managers would make in a more centralized structure.

Each of the five components of HRM influences the others (see Figure 12.1).[12] The kinds of people the organization attracts and hires through recruitment and selection, for example, determine (1) the kinds of training and development that are necessary, (2) the way performance is appraised, and (3) the appropriate levels of pay and benefits. Managers at Microsoft ensure that their organization has highly qualified systems engineers by (1) recruiting and selecting the best candidates, (2) guiding new hires with experienced team members, (3) appraising performance in terms of individual contributions and team performance, and (4) basing pay on individual and team performance.

The Legal Environment of HRM

In the rest of this chapter we focus in detail on the choices managers must make in strategically managing human resources to attain organizational goals and gain a competitive advantage. Effectively managing human resources is a complex undertaking for managers, and we provide an overview of some major issues they face. First, however, we need to look at how the legal environment affects human resource management.

The local, state, and national laws and regulations that managers and organizations must abide by add to the complexity of HRM. For example, the U.S. government's commitment to **equal employment opportunity (EEO)** has resulted in the creation and enforcement of a number of laws that managers must abide by. The goal of EEO is to ensure that all citizens have an equal opportunity to obtain employment regardless of their gender, race, country of origin, religion, age, or disabilities. Table 12.1 summarizes some of the major EEO laws affecting HRM. Other laws, such as the Occupational Safety and Health Act of 1970, require that managers ensure that employees are protected from workplace hazards and that safety standards are met.

In Chapter 5 we explained how effectively managing diversity is an ethical and business imperative, and we discussed the many issues surrounding diversity. EEO laws and their enforcement make the effective management of diversity a legal imperative as well. The Equal Employment Opportunity Commission (EEOC) is the division of the Department of Justice that enforces most EEO laws and handles discrimination complaints. In addition, the EEOC issues guidelines for managers to follow to ensure that they are abiding by EEO laws. For example, the Uniform Guidelines on Employee Selection Procedures issued by the EEOC

equal employment opportunity (EEO) The equal right of all citizens to the opportunity to obtain employment regardless of their gender, age, race, country of origin, religion, or disabilities.

Table 12.1

Major Equal Employment Opportunity Laws Affecting HRM

Year	Law	Description
1963	Equal Pay Act	Requires that men and women be paid equally if they are performing equal work.
1964	Title VII of the Civil Rights Act	Prohibits employment discrimination on the basis of race, religion, sex, color, or national origin; covers a wide range of employment decisions, including hiring, firing, pay, promotion, and working conditions.
1967	Age Discrimination in Employment Act	Prohibits discrimination against workers over the age of 40 and restricts mandatory retirement.
1978	Pregnancy Discrimination Act	Prohibits employment discrimination against women on the basis of pregnancy, childbirth, and related medical decisions.
1990	Americans with Disabilities Act	Prohibits employment discrimination against individuals with disabilities and requires that employers make accommodations for such workers to enable them to perform their jobs.
1991	Civil Rights Act	Prohibits discrimination (as does Title VII) and allows the awarding of punitive and compensatory damages, in addition to back pay, in cases of intentional discrimination.
1993	Family and Medical Leave Act	Requires that employers provide 12 weeks of unpaid leave for medical and family reasons, including paternity and illness of a family member.

(in conjunction with the Departments of Labor and Justice and the Civil Service Commission) guide managers on how to ensure that the recruitment and selection component of human resource management complies with Title VII of the Civil Rights Act (which prohibits discrimination based on gender, race, color, religion, and national origin).[13]

Contemporary challenges that managers face related to the legal environment include how to eliminate sexual harassment (see Chapter 5 for an in-depth discussion of sexual harassment), how to accommodate employees with disabilities, how to ensure LGBT (lesbian, gay, bisexual, transgender) employees are treated equally, how to address religious rights, how to minimize the wage gap between women and men, how to deal with employees who have substance abuse problems, and how to manage HIV-positive employees and employees with AIDS.[14] HIV-positive employees are infected with the virus that causes AIDS but may show no AIDS symptoms and may not develop AIDS in the near future. Often such employees are able to perform their jobs effectively, and managers must take steps to ensure that they are allowed to do so and are not discriminated against in the workplace. Employees with AIDS may or may not be able to perform their jobs effectively, and, once again, managers need to ensure that they are not unfairly discriminated against. Many organizations have instituted AIDS awareness training programs to educate organizational members about HIV and AIDS, dispel myths about how HIV is spread, and ensure that individuals infected with the HIV virus are treated fairly and are able to be productive as long as they can be while not putting others at risk.[15]

recruitment Activities that managers engage in to develop a pool of qualified candidates for open positions.

selection The process that managers use to determine the relative qualifications of job applicants and their potential for performing well in a particular job.

Recruitment and Selection

LO12-2 Describe the steps managers take to recruit and select organizational members.

Recruitment includes all the activities managers engage in to develop a pool of qualified candidates for open positions.[16] Selection is the process by which managers determine the relative qualifications of job applicants and their potential for performing well in a particular job. Before actually recruiting and selecting employees, managers need to engage in two important activities: human resource planning and job analysis (see Figure 12.2).

Figure 12.2

The Recruitment and Selection System

Human Resource Planning

Human resource planning includes all the activities managers engage in to forecast their current and future human resource needs. Current human resources are the employees an organization needs today to provide high-quality goods and services to customers. Future human resource needs are the employees the organization will need at some later date to achieve its longer-term goals.

As part of human resource planning, managers must make both demand forecasts and supply forecasts. *Demand forecasts* estimate the qualifications and numbers of employees an organization will need, given its goals and strategies. *Supply forecasts* estimate the availability and qualifications of current employees now and in the future, as well as the supply of qualified workers in the external labor market.

As a result of their human resource planning, managers sometimes decide to **outsource** to fill some of their human resource needs. Instead of recruiting and selecting employees to produce goods and services, managers contract with people who are not members of their organization to produce goods and services. Managers in publishing companies, for example, frequently contract with freelance editors to copyedit books that they intend to publish. Kelly Services is an organization that provides the services of technical and professional employees to managers who want to use outsourcing to fill some of their human resource requirements in these areas.[17]

Two reasons human resource planning sometimes leads managers to outsource are flexibility and cost. First, outsourcing can give managers increased flexibility, especially when accurately forecasting human resource needs is difficult, human resource needs fluctuate over time, or finding skilled workers in a particular area is difficult. Second, outsourcing can sometimes allow managers to use human resources at a lower cost. When work is outsourced, costs can be lower for a number of reasons: The organization does not have to provide benefits to workers; managers can contract for work only when the work is needed; and managers do not have to invest in training. Outsourcing can be used for functional activities such as payroll, bookkeeping and accounting, and the management of information systems.[18]

Outsourcing has disadvantages, however. When work is outsourced, managers may lose some control over the quality of goods and services. Also, individuals performing outsourced work may have less knowledge of organizational practices, procedures, and goals and less commitment to an organization than regular employees. In addition, unions resist outsourcing because it has the potential to eliminate the jobs of some of their members. To gain some of the flexibility and cost savings of outsourcing and avoid some of its disadvantages, a number of organizations, such as Microsoft and IBM, rely on a pool of temporary employees to, for example, oversee cybersecurity threats.

A major trend reflecting the increasing globalization of business is the outsourcing of office work, computer programming, and technical jobs from the United States and countries in Western Europe, with high labor costs, to countries such as India and Malaysia, with low labor costs.[19] For example, computer programmers in India earn a fraction of what their U.S. counterparts earn. Outsourcing (or *offshoring,* as it is also called when work is outsourced to other countries) has also expanded into knowledge-intensive work such as engineering, research and development, and the development of computer software. According to a study conducted by The Conference Board and Duke University's Offshoring Research Network, more than half of U.S. companies surveyed have some kind of offshoring strategy related to knowledge-intensive work and innovation.[20] Why are so many companies engaged in offshoring, and why are companies that already offshore work planning to increase the extent of offshoring? While cost savings continue to be a major motivation for offshoring, managers also want to take advantage of an increasingly talented global workforce and be closer to the growing global marketplace for goods and services.[21]

Major U.S. companies often earn a substantial portion of their revenues overseas. For example, Hewlett-Packard, Caterpillar, and IBM earn over 50% of their revenues from overseas markets. And many large companies employ thousands of workers overseas. For example, Caterpillar has more than 52,000 workers in foreign countries; IBM employs over 130,000 workers in India.[22] Key challenges for managers who offshore are retaining sufficient managerial control over activities and employee turnover.[23]

As the application to outsourcing indicates, HR planning is about more than simply numbers of employees. Managers also have to consider the value that various combinations of human resources can deliver. Effective managers plan ways to develop and allocate that talent so the value of human resources increases. To see how this applies to consumer products maker Unilever, read the following "Manager as a Person" feature.

MANAGER AS A PERSON

Unilever's chief HR officer, Leena Nair, believes the company's flexible approach to planning, organizing, and talent development has helped put decision-making authority in the hands of front-facing employees who can respond faster and better to customer needs.

©Ritam Banerjee/Stringer/Getty Images

Unilever Makes Talent Development Count

Leena Nair is the chief human resource officer (CHRO) of Unilever, which markets consumer products including popular brands such as Axe, Dove, and Lipton. She is responsible for planning the human resource needs of a 170,000-employee organization in about 190 countries. After joining Unilever as a management trainee in 1992, she worked her way up through a variety of HR positions before becoming the company's youngest and first female, first Asian CHRO.[24]

According to Nair, these are challenging times for managing human resources. The trend toward replacing labor and decision making with robots and artificial intelligence has raised questions about the future value of people in organizations. For Nair, this just increases the importance of her role. HR functions can no longer be content to create long-term career paths, but instead need to equip people to contribute what humans uniquely can offer—a spirit of curiosity, a drive to innovate, and empathy for others both inside and outside the organization.[25]

Nair's response to the challenge is Unilever's highly flexible approach to planning and operations. The initiative, called Connected for Growth, involves rewriting job descriptions and organizational structure to push decision making down to the employees closest to products and customers. Giving employees greater decision-making authority enables them to respond faster to customer needs using a flexible approach.[26]

Nair recognizes that employees can take on these responsibilities only if the company has properly identified the necessary skills, put people in positions they are prepared for, and created a system to develop the right kinds of talent. As CHRO, Nair takes a high-level view, looking at the key positions that influence business performance and ensuring the right skills are in place. For this fast-changing environment, training must be flexible and continuous. Getting a college degree is a starting point, not the end of learning. Unilever offers learning programs that Nair calls "snackable," meaning employees dip into learning resources often, adding skills as time and opportunity permit.[27]

Finally, planning must be paired with measurement of results, so plans can be reinforced or changed. Nair uses metrics associated with business performance. For example, she wants Unilever to be "the number one employer of choice" among workers in the markets where the company operates. Where Unilever meets that objective, the company acquires better employees despite spending less on recruitment. Nair's track record includes taking Unilever's employer brand to new heights—good news for the company's bottom line.[28]

Job Analysis

job analysis Identifying the tasks, duties, and responsibilities that make up a job and the knowledge, skills, and abilities needed to perform the job.

Job analysis is a second important activity that managers need to undertake prior to recruitment and selection.[29] **Job analysis** is the process of identifying (1) the tasks, duties, and responsibilities that make up a job (the *job description*) and (2) the knowledge, skills, and abilities needed to perform the job (the *job specifications*).[30] For each job in an organization, a job analysis needs to be done.

Job analysis can be done in a number of ways, including observing current employees as they perform the job or interviewing them. Often managers rely on questionnaires compiled by jobholders and their managers. The questionnaires ask about the skills and abilities needed to perform the job, job tasks and the amount of time spent on them, responsibilities, supervisory activities, equipment used, reports prepared, and decisions made. The Position Analysis Questionnaire (PAQ) is a comprehensive, standardized questionnaire that many managers rely on to conduct job analyses.[31] It focuses on behaviors jobholders perform, working conditions, and job characteristics and can be used for a variety of jobs. The PAQ contains 194 items organized into six divisions: (1) information input (where and how the jobholder acquires information to perform the job), (2) mental processes (reasoning, decision making, planning, and information processing activities that are part of the job), (3) work output (physical activities performed on the job and machines and devices used), (4) relationships with others (interactions with other people that are necessary to perform the job), (5) job context (the physical and social environment of the job), and (6) other job characteristics (such as work pace).[32] A trend, in some organizations, is toward more flexible jobs in which tasks and responsibilities change and cannot be clearly specified in advance. For these kinds of jobs, job analysis focuses more on determining the skills and knowledge workers need to be effective and less on specific duties.

After managers have completed human resource planning and job analyses for all jobs in an organization, they will know their human resource needs and the jobs they need to fill. They will also know what knowledge, skills, and abilities potential employees need to perform those jobs. At this point, recruitment and selection can begin.

External and Internal Recruitment

As noted earlier, recruitment is what managers do to develop a pool of qualified candidates for open positions. They traditionally have used two main types of recruiting, external and internal, which are now supplemented by recruiting over the Internet.

EXTERNAL RECRUITING   When managers recruit externally to fill open positions, they look outside the organization for people who have not worked for the organization previously. There are multiple means through which managers can recruit externally: job postings on career websites, such as Indeed or Monster; job fairs in the community; career fairs at colleges; open houses for students and career counselors at high schools and on site at the organization; recruitment meetings with groups in the local community; and advertising in local newspapers.

Many large organizations send teams of interviewers to college campuses to recruit new employees. External recruitment can also take place through informal networks, as occurs when current employees inform friends about open positions in their companies or recommend people they know to fill vacant spots. Some organizations use employment agencies for external recruitment, and some external recruitment takes place simply through walk-ins—job hunters going to an organization and inquiring about employment possibilities.

External recruiting has both advantages and disadvantages for managers. Advantages include having access to a potentially large applicant pool; being able to attract people who have the skills, knowledge, and abilities that an organization needs to achieve its goals; and being able to bring in newcomers who may have a fresh approach to problems and are up to date on the latest technology. These advantages have to be weighed against the disadvantages, including the relatively high costs of external recruitment. Employees recruited externally lack knowledge about the inner workings of the organization and may need to receive more training than those recruited internally. Finally, when employees are recruited externally, there is always uncertainty concerning whether they will actually be good performers. Nonetheless, managers can take steps to reduce some of the uncertainty surrounding external recruitment with methods such as tests, temporary jobs, and internships.

INTERNAL RECRUITING   When recruiting is internal, managers turn to existing employees to fill open positions. Employees recruited internally are either seeking **lateral moves** (job changes that entail no major changes in responsibility or authority levels) or promotions. Internal recruiting has several advantages. First, internal applicants are already familiar with the organization (including its goals, structure, culture, rules, and norms). Second, managers already know the candidates; they have considerable information about their skills, abilities, and actual behavior on the job. Third, internal recruiting can help boost levels of employee motivation and morale, both for the employee who gets the job and for other workers. Those who are not seeking a promotion or who may not be ready for one can see that promotion is a possibility in the future; or a lateral move can alleviate boredom once a job has been fully mastered and can be a useful way to learn new skills. Finally, internal recruiting is normally less time-consuming and expensive than external recruiting.

Given the advantages of internal recruiting, why do managers rely on external recruiting as much as they do? The answer lies in the disadvantages of internal recruiting—among them, a limited pool of candidates and a tendency among those candidates to be set in the organization's ways. Often the organization simply does not have suitable internal candidates. Sometimes even when suitable internal applicants are available, managers may rely on external recruiting to find the very best candidate or to help bring new ideas and approaches into their organization. When organizations are in trouble and performing poorly, external recruiting is often relied on to bring in managerial talent with a fresh approach.

HONESTY IN RECRUITING   At times, when trying to recruit the most qualified applicants, managers may be tempted to paint rosy pictures of both the open positions and the organization as a whole. They may worry that if they are honest about advantages and disadvantages, they either will not be able to fill positions or will have fewer or less qualified applicants. A manager trying to fill an administrative position, for example, may emphasize the high level of pay and benefits the job offers and fail to mention the fact that the position is usually a dead-end job offering few opportunities for promotion.

Research suggests that painting a rosy picture of a job and the organization is not a wise recruiting strategy. Recruitment is more likely to be effective when managers give potential applicants an honest assessment of both the advantages and the disadvantages of the job and organization. Such an assessment is called a **realistic job preview (RJP)**.[33] RJPs can reduce the number of new hires who quit when their jobs and organizations fail to meet their unrealistic expectations, and they help applicants decide for themselves whether a job is right for them.

Take the earlier example of the manager trying to recruit an administrative assistant. The manager who paints a rosy picture of the job might have an easy time filling it but might hire a person who expects to be promoted quickly to an executive assistant position. After a few weeks on the job, the individual may realize that a promotion is unlikely no matter how good his or her performance, become dissatisfied, and look for and accept another job. The manager then has to recruit, select, and train another new administrative assistant. The manager could

---

lateral moves Job changes that entail no major changes in responsibility or authority levels.

realistic job preview (RJP) An honest assessment of the advantages and disadvantages of a job and an organization.

have avoided this waste of valuable organizational resources by using a realistic job preview. The RJP would have increased the likelihood of hiring a person who was comfortable with few promotional opportunities and subsequently would have been satisfied to remain on the job.

The Selection Process

Ideally, the recruiting efforts have been broad enough and equitable enough to meet the standard of equal opportunity and provide a pool of applicants who meet basic qualifications. (For a discussion on seeking diverse candidates, see the following "Focus on Diversity" feature.) Managers then need to find out whether each applicant is qualified for the position and likely to be a good performer. If more than one applicant meets these two conditions, managers must further determine which applicants are likely to be better performers than others. They have several selection tools to help them sort out the relative qualifications of job applicants and appraise their potential for being good performers in a particular job. These tools include background information, interviews, paper-and-pencil tests, physical ability tests, performance tests, and references (see Figure 12.3).[34]

FOCUS ON DIVERSITY

Recruiting Practices That Promote Diversity

Many organizations have a policy of valuing diversity. Managers see advantages to including different perspectives, especially when employees reflect the diverse perspectives of the employer's customers and communities. Furthermore, a commitment to diversity widens the pool of potential talent, offering more ways to find the best people.[35]

A basic step is to review recruiting sources and messages. Recruiting in schools where many students are the same race or gender narrows the pool of candidates in terms of racial and gender diversity. Language also matters. Diversity-strategy consultant Joelle Emerson finds that women are less likely to respond to an ad looking for top performers described as "rock stars" than to an ad looking for someone who "seeks challenges." Daphne Wotherspoon, who helps companies find tech workers, makes a similar observation about the masculine appeal of a position described as "JavaScript ninja."[36]

Employers also should consider the image their recruiters and interviewers project. A survey of tax and accounting professionals found that most high-level managers in their organizations were white males. A person of color interviewed by these managers might doubt that the company values diversity. Conversely, Jessica Akue recalls that when she was the first black woman at a Canadian law firm, minority students would gravitate toward her at recruiting events, curious to know what it was like to work there. Employers also can set up panels of diverse interviewers. One interviewer may see and correct unintentional biases that a homogeneous panel would have overlooked.[37]

For the selection process, a useful control is to double-check one's opinions. Suppose the manager making a hiring decision likes a certain characteristic of a candidate. The manager can think, "Is this a preference, a tradition, or a job requirement?" Job requirements are essentials; preferences and traditions may be a plus, but they could limit selections to people who are so much alike that new ideas rarely surface.[38]

Similar issues arise with regard to physical or mental disabilities. Sean Casey, executive director of the Georgia Vocational Rehabilitation Agency, points out "everyone does things in life differently."[39] His point is that it is illogical as well as unjust to assume someone with a disability is less capable because he or she performs a task with accommodations. Casey adds that the disabled person, simply by figuring out a way to adapt to the disability, has already demonstrated problem-solving skills.

Figure 12.3
Selection Tools

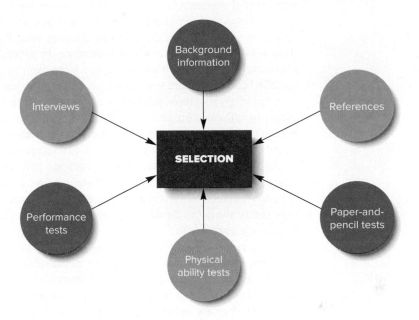

BACKGROUND INFORMATION To aid in the selection process, managers obtain background information from job applications and from résumés. Such information might include the highest levels of education obtained, college majors and minors, type of college or university attended, years and type of work experience, and mastery of foreign languages. Background information can be helpful both to screen out applicants who are lacking key qualifications (such as a college degree) and to determine which qualified applicants are more promising than others. For example, applicants with a BS may be acceptable, but those who also have an MBA may be preferable.

Increasing numbers of organizations are performing background checks to verify the background information prospective employees provide (and to uncover any negative information such as crime convictions). In a recent study, nearly 96% of employers surveyed said their organization conducts one or more types of employment background screening.[40] According to Automatic Data Processing Inc. (ADP), an outsourcing company that performs payroll and human resource functions for organizations, more and more companies are performing background checks on prospective employees and are uncovering inaccuracies, inconsistencies, and negative information not reported on applications. According to ADP, about 44% of applicants provide some form of false information about their employment history.[41]

INTERVIEWS Virtually all organizations use interviews during the selection process, as is true at Home Depot in "A Manager's Challenge." Interviews may be structured or unstructured. In a *structured interview,* managers ask each applicant the same standard questions (such as "What are your unique qualifications for this position?" and "What characteristics of a job are most important to you?"). Particularly informative questions may be those that prompt an interviewee to demonstrate skills and abilities needed for the job by answering the question. Sometimes called *situational interview questions,* these often present interviewees with a scenario they would likely encounter on the job and ask them to indicate how they would handle it.[42] For example,

Some managers find situational interview questions helpful in determining the right candidate for a specific job opening.
©Ariel Skelley/Getty Images

applicants for a sales job may be asked to indicate how they would respond to a customer who complained about waiting too long for service, a customer who was indecisive, and a customer whose order was lost.

An *unstructured interview* proceeds more like an ordinary conversation. The interviewer feels free to ask probing questions to discover what the applicant is like and does not ask a fixed set of questions determined in advance. In general, structured interviews are superior to unstructured interviews because they are more likely to yield information that will help identify qualified candidates, are less subjective, and may be less influenced by the interviewer's biases.

Even when structured interviews are used, however, the potential exists for the interviewer's biases to influence his or her judgment. Recall from Chapter 5 how implicit bias can cause people to perceive others who are similar to themselves more positively than those who are different and how stereotypes can result in inaccurate perceptions. Interviewers must be trained to avoid these biases and sources of inaccurate perceptions as much as possible. Many of the approaches to increasing diversity awareness and diversity skills described in Chapter 5 are used to train interviewers to avoid the effects of biases and stereotypes. In addition, using multiple interviewers can be advantageous because their individual biases and idiosyncrasies may cancel one another out.[43]

When conducting interviews, managers cannot ask questions that are irrelevant to the job in question; otherwise, their organizations run the risk of costly lawsuits. It is inappropriate and illegal, for example, to inquire about an interviewee's spouse or to ask questions about whether an interviewee plans to have children. Because questions such as these are irrelevant to job performance, they are discriminatory and violate EEO laws (see Table 12.1). Thus, interviewers need to be instructed in EEO laws and informed about questions that may violate those laws.

Managers can use interviews at various stages in the selection process. Some use interviews as initial screening devices; others use them as a final hurdle that applicants must jump. Regardless of when they are used, managers typically use other selection tools in conjunction with interviews because of the potential for bias and for inaccurate assessments of interviewees. Even though training and structured interviews can eliminate the effects of some biases, interviewers can still come to erroneous conclusions about interviewees' qualifications. Interviewees, for example, who make a bad initial impression or are overly nervous in the first minute or two of an interview tend to be judged more harshly than less nervous candidates, even if the rest of the interview goes well.

PAPER-AND-PENCIL TESTS   The two main kinds of paper-and-pencil tests used for selection purposes are ability tests and personality tests; both kinds of tests can be administered in hard copy or electronic form. *Ability tests* assess the extent to which applicants possess the skills necessary for job performance, such as verbal comprehension or numerical skills. Autoworkers hired by General Motors, Chrysler, and Ford, for example, are typically tested for their ability to read and to do mathematics.[44]

Personality tests measure personality traits and characteristics relevant to job performance. Some retail organizations, for example, give job applicants honesty tests to determine how trustworthy they are. The use of personality tests (including honesty tests) for hiring purposes is controversial. Some critics maintain that honesty tests do not really measure honesty (that is, they are not valid) and can be faked by job applicants. Before using any paper-and-pencil tests for selection purposes, managers must have sound evidence that the tests are actually good predictors of performance on the job in question. Managers who use tests without such evidence may be subject to costly discrimination lawsuits.

PHYSICAL ABILITY TESTS   For jobs requiring physical abilities, such as firefighting, garbage collecting, and package delivery, managers use physical ability tests that measure physical strength and stamina as selection tools. Autoworkers are typically tested for mechanical dexterity because this physical ability is an important skill for high job performance in many auto plants.[45]

PERFORMANCE TESTS   *Performance tests* measure job applicants' performance on actual job tasks. Applicants for secretarial positions, for example, typically are required to complete a keyboarding test that measures how quickly and accurately they type. Applicants for middle and top management positions are sometimes given short-term projects to complete—projects that mirror the kinds of situations that arise in the job being filled—to assess their knowledge and problem-solving capabilities.[46]

Assessment centers, first used by AT&T, take performance tests one step further. In a typical assessment center, about 10 to 15 candidates for managerial positions participate in a variety of activities over a few days. During this time they are assessed for the skills an effective manager needs—problem-solving, organizational, communication, and conflict resolution skills. Some of the activities are performed individually; others are performed in groups. Throughout the process, current managers observe the candidates' behavior and measure performance. Summary evaluations are then used as a selection tool.

REFERENCES Applicants for many jobs are required to provide references from former employers or other knowledgeable sources (such as a college instructor or adviser) who know the applicants' skills, abilities, and other personal characteristics. These individuals are asked to provide candid information about the applicant. References are often used at the end of the selection process to confirm a decision to hire. Yet the fact that many former employers are reluctant to provide negative information in references sometimes makes it difficult to interpret what a reference is really saying about an applicant.

In fact, several recent lawsuits filed by applicants who felt that they were unfairly denigrated or had their privacy invaded by unfavorable references from former employers have caused managers to be increasingly wary of providing any negative information in a reference, even if it is accurate. For jobs in which the jobholder is responsible for the safety and lives of other people, however, failing to provide accurate negative information in a reference does not just mean that the wrong person might get hired; it may also mean that other people's lives will be at stake.

THE IMPORTANCE OF RELIABILITY AND VALIDITY Whatever selection tools a manager uses need to be both reliable and valid. Reliability is the degree to which a tool or test measures the same thing each time it is administered. Scores on a selection test should be similar if the same person is assessed with the same tool on two different days; if there is quite a bit of variability, the tool is unreliable. For interviews, determining reliability is more complex because the dynamic is personal interpretation. That is why the reliability of interviews can be increased if two or more qualified interviewers interview the same candidate. If the interviews are reliable, the interviewers should come to similar conclusions about the interviewee's qualifications.

Validity is the degree to which a tool measures what it purports to measure—for selection tools, it is the degree to which the test predicts performance on the tasks or job in question. Does a physical ability test used to select firefighters, for example, actually predict on-the-job performance? Do assessment center ratings actually predict managerial performance? Do keyboarding tests predict secretarial performance? These are all questions of validity. Honesty tests, for example, are controversial because it is not clear that they validly predict honesty in such jobs as retailing and banking.

Managers have an ethical and legal obligation to use reliable and valid selection tools. Yet reliability and validity are matters of degree rather than all-or-nothing characteristics. Thus, managers should strive to use selection tools in such a way that they can achieve the greatest degree of reliability and validity. For ability tests of a particular skill, managers should keep up to date on the latest advances in the development of valid paper-and-pencil tests and use the test with the highest reliability and validity ratings for their purposes. Regarding interviews, managers can improve reliability by having more than one person interview job candidates.

reliability The degree to which a tool or test measures the same thing each time it is used.

validity The degree to which a tool or test measures what it purports to measure.

LO12-3 Discuss the training and development options that ensure organizational members can effectively perform their jobs.

Training and Development

Training and development help to ensure that organizational members have the knowledge and skills needed to perform jobs effectively, take on new responsibilities, and adapt to changing conditions, as is the case at Home Depot in "A Manager's Challenge." Training focuses primarily on teaching organizational members how to perform their current jobs and helping them acquire the knowledge and skills they need to be effective performers. Development focuses on building the knowledge and skills of organizational members so they are prepared to take on new responsibilities and challenges. Training tends to be used more frequently at lower levels of an organization; development tends to be used more frequently with professionals and managers.

training Teaching organizational members how to perform their current jobs and helping them acquire the knowledge and skills they need to be effective performers.

development Building the knowledge and skills of organizational members so they are prepared to take on new responsibilities and challenges.

needs assessment An assessment of which employees need training or development and what type of skills or knowledge they need to acquire.

Before creating training and development programs, managers should perform a **needs assessment** to determine which employees need training or development and what type of skills or knowledge they need to acquire (see Figure 12.4).[47]

Types of Training

There are two types of training: classroom instruction and on-the-job training.

CLASSROOM INSTRUCTION   Through classroom instruction, employees acquire knowledge and skills in a classroom setting. This instruction may take place within the organization or outside it, such as through courses at local colleges and universities or through online classes. Many organizations establish their own formal instructional divisions—some are even called "colleges"—to provide needed classroom instruction. For example, at Disney, classroom instruction and other forms of training and development are provided to employees at Disney University.[48]

Classroom instruction frequently uses videos and role-playing in addition to traditional written materials, lectures, and group discussions. *Videos* can demonstrate appropriate and inappropriate job behaviors. For example, by watching an experienced salesperson effectively deal with a loud and angry customer, inexperienced salespeople can develop skills in handling similar situations. During *role-playing,* trainees either directly participate in or watch others perform actual job activities in a simulated setting. At McDonald's Hamburger University, for example, role-playing helps franchisees acquire the knowledge and skills they need to manage their restaurants.

Simulations also can be part of classroom instruction, particularly for complicated jobs that require an extensive amount of learning and in which errors carry a high cost. In a simulation, key aspects of the work situation and job tasks are duplicated as closely as possible in an artificial setting. For example, air traffic controllers are trained by simulations because of the complicated nature of the work, the extensive amount of learning involved, and the very high costs of air traffic control errors.

Technology continues to expand the concept of classroom instruction to include classes of trainees scattered in various locations. With *distance learning,* trainees at different locations attend training programs online using computers to view lectures, participate in discussions, and share documents and other information. Technology applications in distant learning may include videoconferencing, email, instant messaging, document-sharing software, and web cameras.

Figure 12.4
Training and Development

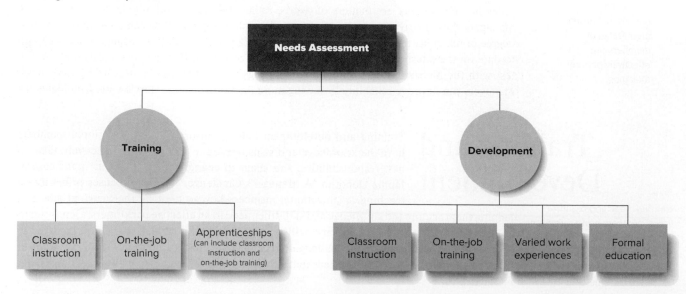

on-the-job training Training that takes place in the work setting as employees perform their job tasks.

ON-THE-JOB TRAINING   In **on-the-job training**, learning occurs in the work setting as employees perform their job tasks. On-the-job training can be provided by coworkers or supervisors or can occur simply as jobholders gain experience and knowledge from doing the work. Newly hired waiters and waitresses in chains such as Red Lobster or the Olive Garden often receive on-the-job training from experienced employees. The supervisor of a new bus driver for a campus bus system may ride the bus for a week to ensure that the driver has learned the routes and follows safety procedures. Chefs learn to create new and innovative dishes by experimenting with different combinations of ingredients and cooking techniques. For all on-the-job training, employees learn by doing.

Managers often use on-the-job training on a continuing basis to ensure that their subordinates keep up to date with changes in goals, technology, products, or customer needs and desires. For example, Leading Real Estate Companies of the World (LeadingRE), a Chicago-based firm, earned the top spot on *Training* magazine's 2018 list of the best training programs in the country. The company offers more than 350 online courses for managers, sales associates, and other staff, which are available 24/7 to accommodate busy schedules, can be used on mobile devices, and provide graphic-rich video and interactions to reinforce learning.[49]

Types of Development

Although both classroom instruction and on-the-job training can be used for development as well as training, development often includes additional activities such as varied work experiences and formal education.

VARIED WORK EXPERIENCES   Top managers need to develop an understanding of, and expertise in, a variety of functions, products and services, and markets. To develop executives who will have this expertise, managers frequently make sure that employees with high potential have a wide variety of job experiences, some in line positions and some in staff positions. Varied work experiences broaden employees' horizons and help them think about the big picture. For example, one- to three-year stints overseas are being used increasingly to provide managers with international work experiences. With organizations becoming more global, managers need to understand the different values, beliefs, cultures, regions, and ways of doing business in different countries.

Another development approach is mentoring. (Recall from Chapter 5 that a *mentor* is an experienced member of an organization who provides advice and guidance to a less experienced member, called a *protégé*.) Having a mentor can help managers seek out work experiences and assignments that will contribute to their development and can enable them to gain the most possible from varied work experiences.[50] Although some mentors and protégés create relationships informally, organizations have found that formal mentoring programs can be valuable ways to contribute to the development of managers and all employees. For example, Goldman Sachs, Deloitte, and Time Inc. all have formal (and mandatory) mentoring programs.[51]

Formal mentoring programs ensure that mentoring takes place in an organization and structure the process. Participants receive training, efforts are focused on matching mentors and protégés so meaningful developmental relationships ensue, and organizations can track reactions and assess the potential benefits of mentoring. Formal mentoring programs can also ensure that diverse members of an organization receive the benefits of mentoring. A study conducted by David A. Thomas, a professor at the Harvard Business School, found that members of racial minority groups at three large corporations who were very successful in their careers had the benefit of mentors. Formal mentoring programs help organizations make this valuable development tool available to all employees.[52]

When diverse members of an organization lack mentors, their progress in the organization and advancement to

At many restaurants, new employees receive on-the-job training by shadowing more experienced waiters and waitresses as they go about their work.

©Reza Estakhrian/Photographer's Choice/Getty Images

high-level positions can be hampered. Ida Abott, a lawyer and consultant on work-related issues, presented a paper to the Minority Corporate Counsel Association in which she concluded, "The lack of adequate mentoring has held women and minority lawyers back from achieving professional success and has led to high rates of career dissatisfaction and attrition."[53]

Mentoring can benefit all kinds of employees in all kinds of work.[54] John Washko, a manager at the Four Seasons hotel chain, benefited from the mentoring he received from Stan Bromley on interpersonal relations and how to deal with employees; mentor Bromley, in turn, found that participating in the Four Seasons mentoring program helped him develop his own management style.[55] More generally, development is an ongoing process for all managers, and mentors often find that mentoring contributes to their own personal development.

FORMAL EDUCATION   Many large corporations reimburse employees for tuition expenses they incur while taking college courses and obtaining advanced degrees. This is not just benevolence on the part of the employer or even a simple reward given to the employee; it is an effective way to develop employees who can take on new responsibilities and more challenging positions. For similar reasons, corporations spend thousands of dollars sending managers to executive development programs such as executive MBA programs. In these programs, experts teach managers the latest in business and management techniques and practices.

To save time and travel costs, some managers also rely on distance learning to formally educate and develop employees. Using videoconferencing technologies, business schools such as the Harvard Business School, the University of Michigan, and Babson College teach courses on video screens in corporate conference rooms. Business schools also customize courses and degrees to fit the development needs of employees in a particular company and/or a particular geographic region. Moreover, some employees and managers seek to advance their education through online degree programs.[56]

Transfer of Training and Development

Whenever training and development take place off the job or in a classroom setting, it is vital for managers to promote the transfer of the knowledge and skills acquired *to the actual work situation*. Trainees should be encouraged and expected to use their newfound expertise on the job.

Performance Appraisal and Feedback

LO12-4 Explain why performance appraisal and feedback are such crucial activities, and list the choices managers must make in designing effective performance appraisal and feedback procedures.

performance appraisal The evaluation of employees' job performance and contributions to their organization.

The recruitment/selection and training/development components of a human resource management system ensure that employees have the knowledge and skills needed to be effective now and in the future. Performance appraisal and feedback complement recruitment, selection, training, and development. **Performance appraisal** is the evaluation of employees' job performance and contributions to the organization. **Performance feedback** is the process through which managers share performance appraisal information with their subordinates, give subordinates an opportunity to reflect on their own performance, and develop, with subordinates, plans for the future. Before performance feedback, performance appraisal must take place. Performance appraisal could take place without providing performance feedback, but wise managers are careful to provide feedback because it can contribute to employee motivation and performance.

Performance appraisal and feedback contribute to the effective management of human resources in several ways. Performance appraisal gives managers important information on which to base human resource decisions. Decisions about pay raises, bonuses, promotions, and job moves all hinge on the accurate appraisal of performance. Performance appraisal can also help managers determine which workers are candidates for training and development and in what areas. Performance feedback encourages high levels of employee motivation and performance. It lets good performers know that their efforts are valued and appreciated. It also lets poor performers know that their lackluster performance needs improvement. Performance feedback can give both good and poor performers insight into their strengths and weaknesses and the ways in which they can improve their performance in the future.

Types of Performance Appraisal

Performance appraisal focuses on the evaluation of traits, behaviors, and results.[57]

TRAIT APPRAISALS   When trait appraisals are used, managers assess subordinates on personal characteristics that are relevant to job performance, such as skills, abilities, or personality. A factory worker, for example, may be evaluated based on her ability to use computerized equipment and perform numerical calculations. A social worker may be appraised based on his empathy and communication skills.

Three disadvantages of trait appraisals often lead managers to rely on other appraisal methods. First, possessing a certain personal characteristic does not ensure that the personal characteristic will actually be used on the job and result in high performance. For example, a factory worker may possess superior computer and numerical skills but be a poor performer due to low motivation. The second disadvantage of trait appraisals is linked to the first. Because traits do not always show a direct association with performance, workers and courts of law may view them as unfair and potentially discriminatory. The third disadvantage of trait appraisals is that they often do not enable managers to give employees feedback they can use to improve performance. Because trait appraisals focus on relatively enduring human characteristics that change only over the long term, employees can do little to change their behavior in response to performance feedback from a trait appraisal. Telling a social worker that he lacks empathy says little about how he can improve his interactions with clients, for example. These disadvantages suggest that managers should use trait appraisals only when they can demonstrate that the assessed traits are accurate and important indicators of job performance.

BEHAVIOR APPRAISALS   Through behavior appraisals, managers assess how workers perform their jobs—the actual actions and behaviors that workers exhibit on the job. Whereas trait appraisals assess what workers *are like,* behavior appraisals assess what workers *do.* For example, with a behavior appraisal, a manager might evaluate a social worker on the extent to which he looks clients in the eye when talking with them, expresses sympathy when they are upset, and refers them to community counseling and support groups geared toward the specific problems they are encountering. Behavior appraisals are especially useful when *how* workers perform their jobs is important. In educational organizations such as high schools, for example, the numbers of classes and students taught are important, but also important is how they are taught or the methods teachers use to ensure that learning takes place.

Behavior appraisals have the advantage of giving employees clear information about what they are doing right and wrong and how they can improve their performance. And because behaviors are much easier for employees to change than traits, performance feedback from behavior appraisals is more likely to lead to improved performance.

RESULTS APPRAISALS   For some jobs, *how* people perform the job is not as important as *what* they accomplish or the results they obtain. With results appraisals, managers appraise performance by the results or the actual outcomes of work behaviors. Take the case of two new car salespeople. One salesperson strives to develop personal relationships with her customers. She spends hours talking to them and frequently calls them to see how their decision-making process is going. The other salesperson has a much more hands-off approach. He is very knowledgeable, answers customers' questions, and then waits for them to come to him. Both salespersons sell, on average, the same number of cars, and the customers of both are satisfied with the service they receive, according to postcards the dealership mails to customers, asking for an assessment of their satisfaction. The manager of the dealership appropriately uses results appraisals (sales and customer satisfaction) to evaluate the salespeople's performance because it does not matter which behavior salespeople use to sell cars as long as they sell the desired number and satisfy customers. If one salesperson sells too few cars, however, the manager can give that person performance feedback about his or her low sales.

OBJECTIVE AND SUBJECTIVE APPRAISALS   Whether managers appraise performance in terms of traits, behaviors, or results, the information they assess is either *objective* or *subjective.* Objective appraisals are based on facts and are likely to be numerical—the number of cars sold, the number of meals prepared, the number of times late, the number of audits completed. Managers often use objective appraisals when results are being appraised because results tend

subjective appraisal An appraisal that is based on perceptions of traits, behaviors, or results.

to be easier to quantify than traits or behaviors. When *how* workers perform their jobs is important, however, subjective behavior appraisals are more appropriate than results appraisals.

Subjective appraisals are based on managers' perceptions of traits, behaviors, or results. Because subjective appraisals rest on managers' perceptions, there is always the chance that they are inaccurate (see Chapter 5). This is why both researchers and managers have spent considerable time and effort on determining the best way to develop reliable and valid subjective measures of performance.

Some of the more popular subjective measures such as the graphic rating scale, the behaviorally anchored rating scale (BARS), and the behavior observation scale (BOS) are illustrated in Figure 12.5.[58] When graphic rating scales are used, performance is assessed along a continuum with specified intervals. With a BARS, performance is assessed along a scale with clearly defined scale points containing examples of specific behaviors. A BOS assesses performance by how often specific behaviors are performed. Many managers may use both objective and

Figure 12.5
Subjective Measures of Performance

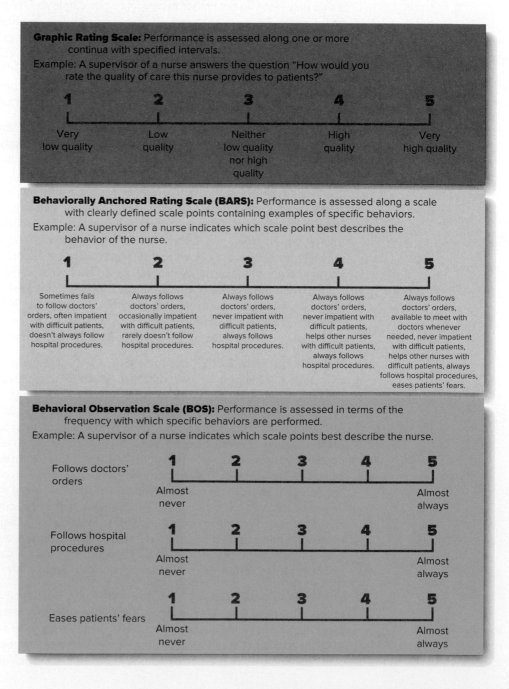

subjective appraisals. For example, a salesperson may be appraised both on the dollar value of sales (objective) and the quality of customer service (subjective).

In addition to subjective appraisals, some organizations employ *forced rankings,* whereby supervisors must rank their subordinates and assign them to different categories according to their performance (which is subjectively appraised). For example, at LendingTree, managers and employees are ranked by their superiors as a "1" (top 15% based on individual performance and goals), "2" (middle 75%), or "3" (bottom 10%).[59] Although the forced ranking system was originally adopted at LendingTree to reward high performers and make it less likely that they would seek positions elsewhere, in tough times when housing and mortgage sales are down, the "3's" are the ones mostly likely to be laid off if layoffs take place.[60]

Some managers are proponents of forced rankings, but others strongly oppose the practice. Proponents believe that forced rankings help ensure that human resource decisions are made based on merit, top performers are recognized, and all employees know where they stand relative to others. Opponents of forced ranking believe that forced rankings can be demoralizing, lead to a competitive environment unsupportive of cooperation and teamwork, and result in favoritism. And forced ranking schemes that force managers to group percentages of employees in certain predetermined categories might not make sense if the predetermined categories do not match the distribution of performance across the employees. For example, a forced ranking system might require a manager to "force" 20% of his or her subordinates into the bottom ranking designation when, in fact, most of the subordinates' performance is average or above average and only 5 to 10% of employees are poor performers. When forced rankings are applied on a regional basis, they can cause conflict and political maneuvering among managers, each of whom wants to ensure that his or her subordinates are ranked in the better categories. Interestingly enough, while forced rankings were popularized, in part, by their use at General Electric under the leadership of Jack Welch, GE no longer uses a forced ranking system. In fact, in 2016, GE did away with annual performance appraisals all together. More on this recent trend later in the chapter.

Who Appraises Performance?

We have been assuming that managers or the supervisors of employees evaluate performance. This is a reasonable assumption: Supervisors are the most common appraisers of performance. Performance appraisal is an important part of most managers' job duties. Managers are responsible for not only motivating their subordinates to perform at a high level but also making many decisions hinging on performance appraisals, such as pay raises or promotions. Appraisals by managers can be usefully augmented by appraisals from other sources (see Figure 12.6).

Figure 12.6
Who Appraises Performance?

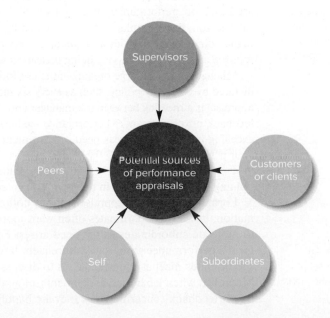

SELF, PEERS, SUBORDINATES, AND CLIENTS   When self-appraisals are used, managers supplement their evaluations with an employee's assessment of his or her own performance. Peer appraisals are provided by an employee's coworkers. Especially when subordinates work in groups or teams, feedback from peer appraisals can motivate team members while giving managers important information for decision making. A growing number of companies are having subordinates appraise their managers' performance and leadership as well. And sometimes customers or clients assess employee performance in terms of responsiveness to customers and quality of service. Although appraisals from these sources can be useful, managers need to be aware of issues that may arise when they are used. Subordinates may be inclined to inflate self-appraisals, especially if organizations are downsizing and they are worried about job security. Managers who are appraised by their subordinates may fail to take needed but unpopular actions out of fear that their subordinates will appraise them negatively. Some of these potential issues can be mitigated to the extent that there are high levels of trust in an organization.

360-DEGREE PERFORMANCE APPRAISALS   To improve motivation and performance, some organizations include 360-degree appraisals and feedback in their performance appraisal systems, especially for managers. In a 360-degree appraisal a variety of people, beginning with the manager and including peers or coworkers, subordinates, superiors, and sometimes even customers or clients, appraise a manager's performance. The manager receives feedback based on evaluations from these multiple sources.

Companies in a variety of industries rely on 360-degree appraisals and feedback.[61] For 360-degree appraisals and feedback to be effective, there has to be trust throughout an organization. More generally, trust is a critical ingredient in any performance appraisal and feedback procedure. In addition, research suggests that 360-degree appraisals should focus on behaviors rather than traits or results and that managers need to carefully select appropriate raters. Moreover, appraisals tend to be more honest when made anonymously and when raters have been trained in how to use 360-degree appraisal forms.[62] Additionally, managers need to think carefully about the extent to which 360-degree appraisals are appropriate for certain jobs and be willing to modify any appraisal system they implement if they become aware of unintended problems it creates, such as comments that seem too subjective on the part of the person rating the individual manager or employee.[63]

Effective Performance Feedback

For the appraisal and feedback component of a human resource management system to encourage and motivate high performance, managers must give their subordinates feedback. To generate useful information to feed back to their subordinates, managers can use both formal and informal appraisals. Formal appraisals are conducted at set times during the year and are based on performance dimensions and measures that have been specified in advance. A salesperson, for example, may be evaluated by his or her manager twice a year on the performance dimensions of sales and customer service, sales being objectively measured from sales reports, and customer service being measured with a BARS (see Figure 12.5).

Managers in most large organizations use formal performance appraisals on a fixed schedule dictated by company policy, such as every six months or every year. An integral part of a formal appraisal is a meeting between the manager and the subordinate in which the subordinate is given feedback on performance. Performance feedback lets subordinates know which areas they are excelling in and which areas need improvement; it should also tell them *how* they can improve their performance. Realizing the value of formal appraisals, managers in many large corporations have committed substantial resources to updating their performance appraisal procedures and training low-level managers in how to use them and provide accurate feedback to employees.[64]

Formal performance appraisals supply both managers and subordinates with valuable information; however, subordinates often want more frequent feedback, and managers often want to motivate subordinates as the need arises. For these reasons many companies supplement formal performance appraisal with frequent informal appraisals, for which managers and their subordinates meet as the need arises to discuss ongoing progress and areas for improvement. Moreover, when job duties, assignments, or goals change, informal appraisals can give workers timely feedback concerning how they are handling their new responsibilities.

360-degree appraisal A performance appraisal by peers, subordinates, superiors, and sometimes clients who are in a position to evaluate a manager's performance.

formal appraisal An appraisal conducted at a set time during the year and based on performance dimensions and measures that were specified in advance.

informal appraisal An unscheduled appraisal of ongoing progress and areas for improvement.

Managers often dislike providing performance feedback, especially when the feedback is negative, but doing so is an important managerial activity.[65] Here are some guidelines for giving effective performance feedback that contributes to employee motivation and performance:

- *Be specific and focus on behaviors or outcomes that are correctable and within a worker's ability to improve.* Example: Telling a salesperson that he is too shy when interacting with customers is likely to lower his self-confidence and prompt him to become defensive. A more effective approach would be to give the salesperson feedback about specific behaviors to engage in—greeting customers as soon as they enter the department, asking customers whether they need help, and volunteering to help customers find items.

- *Approach performance appraisal as an exercise in problem solving and solution finding, not criticizing.* Example: Rather than criticizing a financial analyst for turning in reports late, the manager helps the analyst determine why the reports are late and identify ways to better manage her time.

- *Express confidence in a subordinate's ability to improve.* Example: Instead of being skeptical, a first-level manager tells a subordinate that he is confident that the subordinate can increase quality levels.

- *Provide performance feedback both formally and informally.* Example: The staff of a preschool receives feedback from formal performance appraisals twice a year. The school director also provides frequent informal feedback such as complimenting staff members on creative ideas for special projects, noticing when they do a particularly good job handling a difficult child, and pointing out when they provide inadequate supervision.

- *Praise instances of high performance and areas of a job in which a worker excels.* Example: Rather than focusing on just the negative, a manager discusses the areas her subordinate excels in as well as the areas in need of improvement.

- *Avoid personal criticisms and treat subordinates with respect.* Example: An engineering manager acknowledges her subordinates' expertise and treats them as professionals. Even when the manager points out performance problems to subordinates, she refrains from criticizing them personally.

- *Agree to a timetable for performance improvements.* Example: A first-level manager and his subordinate decide to meet again in one month to determine whether quality levels have improved.

Recent Trends in Performance Appraisal

Performance reviews have always been a source of stress for both managers and employees. It's difficult to look back on an entire year's performance and come up with constructive feedback when situations or behaviors happened so far in the past.[66] When performance reviews take place on an annual basis, some employees are surprised and dismayed at some of the less-than-positive feedback they receive from supervisors, which may not have a positive impact on future employee performance.[67] In a recent Gallup survey, only 29% of employees strongly agreed that the annual evaluations they received were fair.[68]

Over the last several years, major organizations, such as GE, Microsoft, Adobe Systems, Netflix, and Accenture, have changed the way they evaluate employee performance—by doing away with annual performance reviews.[69] Instead, these organizations have adopted a more informal and ongoing dialogue between manager and employee as a way of discussing performance and providing feedback that can help shape future behavior.[70]

For example, Adobe's "Check-in" program requires managers and employees to meet at least once a quarter to discuss expectations, feedback, and growth and development.

Some companies have eliminated the annual performance review process all together, deciding instead that managers and their direct reports should discuss performance on an ongoing and informal basis.

©Production Perig/Shutterstock

The discussion is informal (with no script) and there is no paperwork to fill out. Now in its third year, the Check-in program is working well: Morale has increased significantly among both employees and managers, 30% fewer employees are leaving the company to take another job, and involuntary departures (people not meeting expectations) have increased by 50%.[71]

Regardless of the approach they use, managers need to remember *why* they are giving performance feedback: to encourage high levels of motivation and performance. Moreover, the information that managers gather through performance appraisal and feedback helps them determine how to distribute pay raises and bonuses.

Pay and Benefits

LO12-5 Explain the issues managers face in determining levels of pay and benefits.

Pay includes employees' base salaries, pay raises, and bonuses and is determined by a number of factors such as the characteristics of the organization and the job and levels of performance. Employee *benefits* are based on membership in an organization (not necessarily on the particular job held) and include sick days, vacation days, and medical and life insurance. In Chapter 13 we discuss how pay can motivate organizational members to perform at a high level, as well as the different kinds of pay plans managers can use to help an organization achieve its goals and gain a competitive advantage. As you will learn, it is important to link pay to behaviors or results that contribute to organizational effectiveness. Next we focus on establishing an organization's pay level and pay structure.

Pay Level

pay level The relative position of an organization's pay incentives in comparison with those of other organizations in the same industry employing similar kinds of workers.

Pay level is a broad, comparative concept that refers to how an organization's pay incentives compare, in general, to those of other organizations in the same industry employing similar kinds of workers. Managers must decide if they want to offer relatively high wages, average wages, or relatively low wages. High wages help ensure that an organization is going to be able to recruit, select, and retain high performers, but high wages also raise costs. Low wages give an organization a cost advantage but may undermine the organization's ability to select and recruit high performers and to motivate current employees to perform at a high level. Either of these situations may lead to inferior quality or inadequate customer service.

In determining pay levels, managers should take into account their organization's strategy. A high pay level may prohibit managers from effectively pursuing a low-cost strategy. But a high pay level may be worth the added costs in an organization whose competitive advantage lies in superior quality and excellent customer service. As one might expect, hotel and motel chains with a low-cost strategy, such as Days Inn and Hampton Inns, have lower pay levels than chains striving to provide high-quality rooms and services, such as the Four Seasons. In fact, the Four Seasons treats and pays its employees very well, as profiled in the accompanying "Management Insight" feature.

MANAGEMENT INSIGHT

Treating Employees Well Leads to Satisfied Customers

Four Seasons Hotels and Resorts is one of only around a dozen companies to be ranked one of the "100 Best Companies to Work For" every year since *Fortune* magazine started this annual ranking of companies (from 1998 to 2018).[72] And Four Seasons often receives other awards and recognition such as having some of its properties included on the *Condé Nast Traveler* Gold List, the *Travel + Leisure* It List, and TripAdvisor's Travelers' Choice Awards.[73] In an industry in which annual turnover rates are relatively high, the Four Season's turnover rate is among the lowest in the hospitality sector.[74] Evidently, employees and customers alike are satisfied with how they are treated at the Four Seasons. Understanding that the two are causally linked is perhaps the key to the Four Seasons' success. As the Four Seasons' founder and chairman of the board Isadore Sharp suggested, "How you treat your employees is how you expect them to treat the customer."[75]

The Four Seasons was founded by Sharp in 1961 when he opened his first hotel, called the Four Seasons Motor Hotel, in a less-than-desirable area outside downtown Toronto. Whereas his first hotel had 125 inexpensively priced rooms appealing to the individual traveler, his fourth hotel was built to appeal to business travelers and conventions with 1,600 rooms, conference facilities, several restaurants, banquet halls, and shops in an arcade. Both these hotels were successful, but Sharp decided he could provide customers with a different kind of hotel experience by combining the best features of both kinds of hotel experiences—the sense of closeness and personal attention that a small hotel brings with the amenities of a big hotel to suit the needs of business travelers.[76]

Sharp sought to provide the kind of personal service that would really help business travelers on the road—giving them the amenities they have at home and in the office and miss when traveling on business. Thus, the Four Seasons was the first hotel chain to provide bathrobes, shampoo, round-the-clock room service, laundry and dry cleaning services, large desks in every room, two-line phones, and round-the-clock secretarial assistance. While these are relatively concrete ways of personalizing the hotel experience, Sharp realized that how employees treat customers is just as, or perhaps even more, important. When employees view each customer as an individual with his or her own needs and desires, and empathetically try to meet these needs and desires and help customers both overcome any problems or challenges they face and truly enjoy their hotel experience, a hotel can indeed serve the purposes of a home away from home (and an office away from the office), and customers are likely to be both loyal and highly satisfied.[77]

Sharp always realized that for employees to treat customers well, the Four Seasons needs to treat its employees well. Salaries are relatively high by industry standards, and the company pays 79% of employees' health care coverage (for full-time as well as part-time workers and their dependents). In addition, Four Seasons matches 100% of employees' contributions to the company's 401(k) plan, up to 4% of their salaries.[78] All employees get free meals in the hotel cafeteria, have access to staff showers and a locker room, and receive an additional highly attractive perk—complementary stays at any Four Seasons hotel or resort in the world depending on their years of service.[79]

The Four Seasons also tends to promote from within. For example, while recent college graduates may start out as assistant managers, those who do well and have high aspirations could become general managers in less than 15 years. This helps to ensure that managers have empathy and respect for those in lower-level positions as well as the ingrained ethos of treating others (employees, subordinates, coworkers, and customers) as they would like to be treated. All in all, treating employees well leads to satisfied customers at the Four Seasons.[80]

Pay Structure

pay structure The arrangement of jobs into categories, reflecting their relative importance to the organization and its goals, levels of skill required, and other characteristics.

After deciding on a pay level, managers have to establish a pay structure for the different jobs in the organization. A pay structure clusters jobs into categories, reflecting their relative importance to the organization and its goals, levels of skill required, and other characteristics managers consider important. Pay ranges are established for each job category. Individual jobholders' pay within job categories is then determined by factors such as performance, seniority, and skill levels.

There are some interesting global differences in pay structures. Large corporations based in the United States tend to pay their CEOs and top managers higher salaries than do their European or Japanese counterparts. Also, the pay differential between employees at the bottom of the corporate hierarchy and those higher up is much greater in U.S. companies than in European or Japanese companies.[81]

Concerns have been raised over whether it is equitable or fair for CEOs of large companies in the United States to be making millions of dollars in years when their companies are restructuring and laying off a large portion of their workforces.[82] Additionally, the average

CEO in the United States typically earns over 271 times what the average hourly worker earns.[83] Is a pay structure with such a huge pay differential ethical? Shareholders and the public are increasingly asking this very question as well as asking large corporations to rethink their pay structures. Also troubling are the millions of dollars in severance packages that some CEOs receive when they leave their organizations. When many workers are struggling to make ends meet, people are questioning whether it is ethical for some top managers to be making so much money.[84]

Benefits

Organizations are legally required to provide certain benefits to their employees, including workers' compensation, Social Security, and unemployment insurance. Workers' compensation helps employees financially if they become unable to work due to a work-related injury or illness. Social Security provides financial assistance to retirees and disabled former employees. Unemployment insurance provides financial assistance to workers who lose their jobs due to no fault of their own. The legal system in the United States views these three benefits as ethical requirements for organizations and thus mandates that they be provided.

Other benefits such as health insurance, dental insurance, vacation time, pension plans, life insurance, flexible working hours, company-provided day care, and employee assistance and wellness programs have traditionally been provided at the option of employers. The Affordable Care Act signed into law by President Obama in 2010 now requires employers with 50 or more employees to provide their employees with health care coverage or face fines.[85] Benefits enabling workers to balance the demands of their jobs and of their lives away from the office or factory are of growing importance for many workers who have competing demands on their scarce time and energy.

cafeteria-style benefit plan A plan from which employees can choose the benefits they want.

In some organizations, top managers determine which benefits might best suit the employees and organization and offer the same benefit package to all employees. Other organizations, realizing that employees' needs and desires might differ, offer cafeteria-style benefit plans that let employees choose the benefits they want. Cafeteria-style benefit plans sometimes help managers deal with employees who feel unfairly treated because they are unable to take advantage of certain benefits available to other employees who, for example, have children. Some organizations have success with cafeteria-style benefit plans; others find them difficult to manage.

As health care costs escalate and overstretched employees find it hard to take time to exercise and take care of their health, more companies are providing benefits and incentives to promote employee wellness. According to a survey conducted by Fidelity Investments and the National Business Group on Health, close to 90% of organizations provide some kind of incentive, prize, or reward to employees who take steps to improve their health.[86] For working parents, family-friendly benefits are especially attractive. For example, access to on-site child care, the ability to telecommute and take time off to care for sick children, and provisions for emergency back-up child care can be valued benefits for working parents with young children.

Same-sex domestic partner benefits are also being used to attract and retain valued employees. Gay and lesbian workers are reluctant to work for companies that do not provide the same kinds of benefits for their partners as those provided for partners of the opposite sex.[87]

Labor Relations

Labor relations are the activities managers engage in to ensure that they have effective working relationships with the labor unions that represent their employees' interests. Although the U.S. government has responded to the potential for unethical and unfair treatment of workers by creating and enforcing laws regulating employment (including the EEO laws listed in Table 12.1), some workers believe a union will ensure that their interests are fairly represented in their organizations.

LO12-6 Understand the role that labor relations play in the effective management of human resources.

Before we describe unions in more detail, let's take a look at some examples of important employment legislation. In 1938 the government passed the Fair Labor Standards Act, which prohibited child labor and provided for minimum wages, overtime pay, and maximum working hours to protect workers' rights. In 1963 the Equal Pay Act mandated that men and

labor relations The activities managers engage in to ensure that they have effective working relationships with the labor unions that represent their employees' interests.

women performing equal work (work requiring the same levels of skill, responsibility, and effort performed in the same kind of working conditions) receive equal pay (see Table 12.1). In 1970 the Occupational Safety and Health Act mandated procedures for managers to follow to ensure workplace safety. These are just a few of the U.S. government's efforts to protect workers' rights. State legislatures also have been active in promoting safe, ethical, and fair workplaces.

Unions

Unions exist to represent workers' interests in organizations. Given that managers have more power than rank-and-file workers and that organizations have multiple stakeholders, there is always the potential for managers to take steps that benefit one set of stakeholders, such as shareholders, while hurting another, such as employees. For example, managers may decide to speed up a production line to lower costs and increase production in the hopes of increasing returns to shareholders. Speeding up the line, however, could hurt employees forced to work at a rapid pace and may increase the risk of injuries. Also, employees receive no additional pay for the extra work they are performing. Unions would represent workers' interests in a scenario such as this one.

Congress acknowledged the role that unions could play in ensuring safe and fair workplaces when it passed the National Labor Relations Act of 1935. This act made it legal for workers to organize into unions to protect their rights and interests and declared certain unfair or unethical organizational practices to be illegal. The act also established the National Labor Relations Board (NLRB) to oversee union activity. Currently, the NLRB conducts certification elections, which are held among the employees of an organization to determine whether they want a union to represent their interests. The NLRB also makes judgments concerning unfair labor practices and specifies practices that managers must refrain from.

Employees might vote to have a union represent them for any number of reasons.[88] They may think their wages and working conditions need improvement. They may believe managers are not treating them with respect. They may think their working hours are unfair or they need more job security or a safer work environment. Or they may be dissatisfied with management and find it difficult to communicate their concerns to their bosses. Regardless of the specific reason, one overriding reason is power: A united group inevitably wields more power than an individual, and this type of power may be especially helpful to employees in some organizations.

Although these would seem to be potent forces for unionization, some workers are reluctant to join unions. Sometimes this reluctance is due to the perception that union leaders are corrupt. Some workers may simply believe that belonging to a union might not do them much good while costing them money in membership dues. Employees also might not want to be forced into doing something they do not want to, such as striking because the union thinks it is in their best interest. Moreover, although unions can be a positive force in organizations, sometimes they also can be a negative force, impairing organizational effectiveness. For example, when union leaders resist needed changes in an organization or are corrupt, organizational performance can suffer.

The percentage of U.S. workers represented by unions today is smaller than it was in the 1950s, an era when unions were especially strong. In the 1950s, around 35% of U.S. workers were union members; in 2017, 10.7% of workers were members of unions.[89] The American Federation of Labor–Congress of Industrial Organizations (AFL–CIO) includes 69 voluntary member unions representing 12.5 million workers.[90] Overall, approximately 14.8 million workers in the United States belong to unions.[91] Union influence in manufacturing and heavy industries has been on the decline; more generally, approximately 6.5% of private-sector workers are union members, and 34.4% of government workers belong to unions.[92] Unions have made inroads in other segments of the workforce. In 2018, media employees of the *Los Angeles Times* and graduate students at Columbia, Yale, Tufts, and Brandeis all voted to join unions.[93]

Union membership and leadership, traditionally dominated by white men, are becoming increasingly diverse. For example, Linda Chavez-Thompson was the executive vice president of the AFL–CIO from 1995 to 2007 and was the first woman and Hispanic to hold a top management position in the federation.[94] Labor officials in Washington, DC, also are becoming increasingly diverse. Elaine L. Chao, the 24th Secretary of Labor, was the first Asian American woman to hold an appointment in a U.S. president's cabinet. Chao is currently the Secretary of Transportation in President Trump's administration.[95] In terms of union membership, women now make up over 48% of unionized workers.[96]

Collective Bargaining

collective bargaining Negotiation between labor unions and managers to resolve conflicts and disputes about issues such as working hours, wages, benefits, working conditions, and job security.

Collective bargaining is negotiation between labor unions and managers to resolve conflicts and disputes about important issues such as working hours, wages, working conditions, and job security. Sometimes union members go on strike to drive home their concerns to managers. Once an agreement that union members support has been reached (sometimes with the help of a neutral third party called a *mediator*), union leaders and managers sign a contract spelling out the terms of the collective bargaining agreement. We discuss conflict and negotiation in depth in Chapter 17, but some brief observations are in order here because collective bargaining is an ongoing consideration in labor relations.

The signing of a contract, for example, does not finish the collective bargaining process. Disagreement and conflicts can arise over the interpretation of the contract. In such cases, a neutral third party called an *arbitrator* is usually called in to resolve the conflict. An important component of a collective bargaining agreement is a *grievance procedure* through which workers who believe they are not being fairly treated are allowed to voice their concerns and have their interests represented by the union. Workers who think they were unjustly fired in violation of a union contract, for example, may file a grievance, have the union represent them, and get their jobs back if an arbitrator agrees with them. Union members sometimes go on strike when managers make decisions that the members think will hurt them and are not in their best interests.

Summary and Review

LO12-1

STRATEGIC HUMAN RESOURCE MANAGEMENT Human resource management (HRM) includes all the activities managers engage in to ensure that their organizations can attract, retain, and effectively use human resources. Strategic HRM is the process by which managers design the components of a human resource management system to be consistent with each other, with other elements of organizational architecture, and with the organization's strategies and goals.

LO12-2

RECRUITMENT AND SELECTION Before recruiting and selecting employees, managers must engage in human resource planning and job analysis. Human resource planning includes all the activities managers engage in to forecast their current and future needs for human resources. Job analysis is the process of identifying (1) the tasks, duties, and responsibilities that make up a job and (2) the knowledge, skills, and abilities needed to perform the job. Recruitment includes all the activities managers engage in to develop a pool of qualified applicants for open positions. Selection is the process by which managers determine the relative qualifications of job applicants and their potential for performing well in a particular job.

LO12-3

TRAINING AND DEVELOPMENT Training focuses on teaching organizational members how to perform effectively in their current jobs. Development focuses on broadening organizational members' knowledge and skills so they are prepared to take on new responsibilities and challenges.

LO12-4

PERFORMANCE APPRAISAL AND FEEDBACK Performance appraisal is the evaluation of employees' job performance and contributions to the organization. Performance feedback is the process through which managers share performance appraisal information with their subordinates, give them an opportunity to reflect on their own performance, and develop with them plans for the future. Performance appraisal gives managers useful information for decision making. Performance feedback can encourage high levels of motivation and performance.

Recent trends suggest that some organizations are moving away from the annual performance review for employees, instead taking a more informal approach to evaluating workers with ongoing conversations between manager and employee on a regular basis to discuss expectations, feedback, and plans for growth and development.

LO12-5   PAY AND BENEFITS   Pay level is the relative position of an organization's pay incentives in comparison with those of other organizations in the same industry employing similar workers. A pay structure clusters jobs into categories according to their relative importance to the organization and its goals, the levels of skill required, and other characteristics. Pay ranges are then established for each job category. Organizations are legally required to provide certain benefits to their employees; other benefits are provided at the discretion of employers.

LO12-6   LABOR RELATIONS   Labor relations include all the activities managers engage in to ensure that they have effective working relationships with the labor unions that represent their employees' interests. The National Labor Relations Board oversees union activity. Collective bargaining is the process through which labor unions and managers resolve conflicts and disputes and negotiate agreements.

Management in Action

Topics for Discussion and Action

Discussion

1. Discuss why it is important for human resource management systems to be in sync with an organization's strategy and goals and with each other. **[LO12-1]**

2. Discuss why training and development are ongoing activities for all organizations. **[LO12-3]**

3. Describe the type of development activities you think middle managers are most in need of. **[LO12-3]**

4. Evaluate the pros and cons of 360-degree performance appraisals and feedback. Would you like your performance to be appraised in this manner? Why or why not? **[LO12-4]**

5. Discuss why two restaurants in the same community might have different pay levels. **[LO12-5]**

6. Explain why union membership is becoming more diverse. **[LO12-6]**

Action

7. Interview a manager in a local organization to determine how that organization recruits and selects employees. **[LO12-2]**

Building Management Skills

Analyzing Human Resource Management Systems [LO12-1, 12-2, 12-3, 12-4, 12-5]

Think about your current job or a job you have had in the past. If you have never had a job, interview a friend or family member who is currently working. Answer the following questions about the job you have chosen:

1. How are people recruited and selected for this job? Are the recruitment and selection procedures the organization uses effective or ineffective? Why?

2. What training and development do people who hold this job receive? Are the training and development appropriate? Why or why not?

3. How is performance of this job appraised? Does performance feedback contribute to motivation and high performance on this job?

4. What levels of pay and benefits are provided on this job? Are these levels appropriate? Why or why not?

Managing Ethically [LO12-4, 12-5]

Some managers do not want to become overly friendly with their subordinates because they are afraid that doing so will impair their objectivity in conducting performance appraisals and making decisions about pay raises and promotions. Some subordinates resent it when they see one or more of their coworkers being very friendly with the boss; they are concerned about the potential for favoritism. Their reasoning runs something like this: If two subordinates are equally qualified for a promotion and one is a good friend of the boss and the other is a mere acquaintance, who is more likely to receive the promotion?

Questions

1. Either individually or in a group, think about the ethical implications of managers' becoming friendly with their subordinates.

2. Do you think managers should feel free to socialize and become good friends with their subordinates outside the workplace if they so desire? Why or why not?

Small Group Breakout Exercise

Building a Human Resource Management System [LO12-1, 12-2, 12-3, 12-4, 12-5]

Form groups of three or four people, and appoint one member as the spokesperson who will communicate your findings to the class when called on by the instructor. Then discuss the following scenario:

You and your three partners are engineers who minored in business at college and have decided to start a consulting business. Your goal is to provide manufacturing process engineering and other engineering services to large and small organizations. You forecast that there will be an increased use of outsourcing for these activities. You discussed with managers in several large organizations the services you plan to offer, and they expressed considerable interest. You have secured funding to start your business and now are building the HRM system. Your human resource planning suggests that you need to hire between five and eight experienced engineers with good communication skills, two clerical/secretarial workers, and two MBAs who between them have financial, accounting, and human resource skills. You are striving to develop your human resources in a way that will enable your new business to prosper.

1. Describe the steps you will take to recruit and select (a) the engineers, (b) the clerical/secretarial workers, and (c) the MBAs.

2. Describe the training and development the engineers, the clerical/secretarial workers, and the MBAs will receive.

3. Describe how you will appraise the performance of each group of employees and how you will provide feedback.

4. Describe the pay level and pay structure of your consulting firm.

Be the Manager [LO12-4]

You are Walter Michaels and have just received some disturbing feedback. You are the director of human resources for Maxi Vision Inc., a medium-size window and glass door manufacturer. You recently initiated a 360-degree performance appraisal system for all middle and upper managers at Maxi Vision, including yourself, but excluding the most senior executives and the top management team.

You were eagerly awaiting the feedback you would receive from the managers who report to you; you had recently implemented several important initiatives that affected them and their subordinates, including a complete overhaul of the organization's performance appraisal system. While the managers who report to you were evaluated based on 360-degree appraisals, their subordinates were evaluated using a 20-question BARS scale you recently created that focuses on behaviors. Conducted annually, appraisals are an important input into pay raise and bonus decisions.

You were so convinced that the new performance appraisal procedures were highly effective that you hoped your own subordinates would mention them in their feedback to you. And, boy, did they! You were amazed to learn that the managers and their subordinates thought the new BARS scales were unfair, inappropriate, and a waste of time. In fact, the managers' feedback to you was that their own performance was suffering, based on the 360-degree appraisals they received, because their subordinates hated the new appraisal system and partially blamed their bosses, who were part of management. Some managers even admitted giving all their subordinates approximately the same scores on the scales so their pay raises and bonuses would not be affected by their performance appraisals.

You couldn't believe your eyes when you read these comments. You spent so much time developing what you thought was the ideal rating scale for this group of employees. Evidently, for some unknown reason, they wouldn't give it a chance. Your own supervisor is aware of these complaints and said that it was a top priority for you to fix "this mess" (with the implication that you were responsible for creating it). What are you going to do?

Bloomberg Businessweek Case in the News

Why Pay Equality Is Still Out of Reach [LO 12-1, 12-5]

There's an essential, frustrating truth about the gender pay gap. You can size it up or down depending on what you'd like to measure—and what you'd like to measure depends on what you think the pay gap is. Are you talking about all women across the economy? In a specific industry? A specific company? In certain jobs? "You can whittle the pay gap down when you control for more and more variables," says Henry Farber, an economics professor at Princeton University. "But you can never make it go away."

This year, Britain is forcing companies to report their pay gaps as they actually exist, no whittling allowed. By April 4, all businesses with at least 250 employees working in the U.K. will have to disclose any discrepancies in pay between their male and female workers. Ultimately about 9,000 companies representing 15 million employees will be forced to report, although only about two-thirds had done so by March 28. Those that don't will be subject to unspecified fines and sanctions by the government's Equalities and Human Rights Commission.

The law—enacted in 2017, after a 2010 measure encouraging voluntary reports failed—is very clear about just what numbers British companies must report: unadjusted mean and median hourly wage and bonus pay for all men and all women, as well as percentages of men and women in each pay quartile. The rigid approach leaves companies nowhere to hide, no statistical mechanism to cover up their failure to mentor women, no rhetorical way around the fact that their higher-paid divisions are largely male. While the requirement is confined to companies' U.K. workforces, the numbers provide an insight into the structure of companies around the world. "The picture in the U.K. isn't that much different from the U.S.," says Farber. "Women earn less than men."

A lot less it turns out. Take HSBC Bank Plc. The average woman working there in the U.K. makes 59% less than the average man. More than half of the bank's workforce is female (54%), but most of the women are in lower-paying, junior roles: Women account for 71% of its lowest-tier employees and only 23% of its senior executives. About as many women as men earned bonuses at HSBC in U.K. last year, but because women are in lower-paid positions those bonuses were 86% smaller than those earned by men.

At Goldman Sachs International, women in the U.K. collectively make 55% less than men; at Barclays Plc, it's 48%; at Deloitte, 43%. Outside the financial sector, based on companies reporting so far, the gap isn't quite so bad. Women at the oil and gas company BP Plc make 23% less than men; at 3M Co., it's 14%; at Amnesty International, 11%. The gap at the latter two is smaller than the U.K. average, according to the Office for National Statistics, which has identified a national mean pay gap of 17.4%, roughly on par with the U.S.

"For most companies, this is the first time they've analyzed numbers like this," says Charles Cotton, a compensation adviser with Chartered Institute of Personnel and Development (CIPD), an association for human resource professionals. These figures can't tell you whether women and men holding the same jobs at a particular company are compensated equally. But they do describe what working women have known for decades: that their careers move slower than men's, peak at a lower level, and ultimately pay a lot less. "If men are doing all the top jobs and the women are making the tea, then there's something wrong," says Vince Cable, leader of the U.K. Liberal Democrat party, which led the law's passage. "The gap is

actually a lot worse than I think anybody anticipated."

That may be because most companies would prefer to analyze their salary data within very narrow parameters, if at all. In April 2016, Microsoft Corp. announced that it had run an internal analysis of its salary data and found that women at the company were paid 99.8% of what men working at the company working in the same roles at the same level received. That number becomes less impressive when you learn that each of Microsoft's dozens of pay grades at the time came with a set of salary ranges—it doesn't reflect whether women were assigned to the correct job levels in the first place or whether they were promoted as often as men. The company was essentially saying that men and women making roughly the same amount of money were, yes, making roughly the same amount of money. "If I'm doing the exact same job but am at a different level," one woman wrote in an email to Microsoft's head of HR, "that's not pay equality." Her email was released publicly in March as part of a pay disparity lawsuit filed in 2015 by three former Microsoft employees. Microsoft declined to comment, but said in a 2016 blog post that it was "encouraged" by its pay findings.

No law in the U.S. compels companies to analyze their salary data in the British way—or any way. An Obama-era rule, which would have required government contractors to report their salary data broken down by race and gender, was scrapped by the Trump Administration last year. Instead, companies such as Facebook, Amazon, Citigroup—and, yes, Microsoft—have come forward with pay gap figures largely in response to shareholder proposals put forward by Natasha Lamb, managing partner of the Boston investment firm Arjuna Capital. So far, Lamb has pushed only for job-for-job figures like the ones Microsoft reported, not the big aggregate gaps. "We see the equal-pay-for-equal-work number as a critical first step for companies," says Lamb. "The structural gap, like what you're seeing in the U.K., is the next step. So far we've had no takers on releasing that."

British companies haven't been thrilled about releasing their data. "We follow what we're asked to do, and we've done that," says Heidi Ashley, an HSBC spokeswoman. "We don't want to provide further information than is in the pay report." Several accounting and law firms have come under fire for excluding partners from the pay data, arguing that partners co-own the companies and therefore aren't employees. The accounting firm EY, for example, first reported a 20% gap, then later revised it to 38% when partners were included.

The law's supporters hold that the pain is necessary to achieve the kind of sweeping social changes that will close the pay gap for good. "There's an element of realism" to the very public nature of the reporting process, says CIPD's Cotton. "Companies can do a lot about how they promote and pay people. But they can't change cultural norms." When Goldman Sachs announced its 55% gap in March, Chief Executive Officer Lloyd Blankfein and President David Solomon issued a joint statement claiming that "the

real issue for our firm and many corporations is the underrepresentation of women." The company promised to have women account for half of its recruiting class by 2021 and 30% of its vice presidents (and above) by 2023. But it also called itself a "meritocracy" and said that gender wasn't a factor in how employees were paid. If that's true, then it follows that, until now, women haven't been rising through Goldman's ranks because they didn't deserve to.

"The pushback we hear is, 'We want a meritocracy, don't we?'" says Denise Wilson-White, CEO of the Hampton-Alexander Review, an organization that works with the U.K. government to lobby for more women on company boards. "We have to start questioning whether business is built on a foundation of meritocracy when consistently we're appointing senior white men into all of our leadership jobs. That doesn't feel like it is a meritocracy, does it? That feels like a highly biased selection process." In 2010 several former Goldman Sachs employees sued the company for what they alleged was widespread gender discrimination, claiming that women weren't given the same opportunities for promotions and advancement, were treated differently by their managers, and were sometimes paid less than male colleagues. Goldman denied the allegations and is still

fighting the case in court. The company declined to comment.

The numbers coming out of Britain reflect a globalized society structured so that men hold certain types of jobs and women others. Even if you accept that as true, the problem remains of how to apply knowledge of how all women get paid to how a specific woman gets paid. "If you say, 'Oh, we've got a gender pay gap because we've got more men in higher-paid roles,' that's an explanation, not a justification," says Cotton. "Really, what we're seeing is that we have 750 years of history and progress in Britain, and we've still got a pay gap of 18%."

Questions for Discussion

1. How can a company's HRM process take steps to close the pay gap? Cite some examples.

2. What can companies do to ensure that they provide equal pay for equal work?

3. You are an experienced female manager looking for a position with a different employer. Describe how you would research potential companies to learn about their pay policies and track record when it comes to women and other minorities.

Source: Claire Suddath, "Why Pay Equality Is Still Out of Reach," *Bloomberg Businessweek,* April 2, 2018, pp. 21–24. Used with permission of Bloomberg L.P. Copyright © 2017. All rights reserved.

Notes

1. L. Thomas, "Home Depot, Lowe's Embark on Spring Hiring Sprees as Labor Market Stiffens," *CNBC,* www.cnbc.com, February 14, 2018; P. Wahba, "Why Home Depot Is Spending an Extra $5.4 Billion on Stores and E-commerce in Next Three Years," *Fortune,* http://fortune.com, December 6, 2017.

2. Thomas, "Home Depot, Lowe's Embark"; Wahba, "Why Home Depot Is Spending an Extra $5.4 Billion."

3. Thomas, "Home Depot, Lowe's Embark"; "Home Depot Re-tools Interview Process in Latest Attempt to Attract New Hires," *Atlanta Business Chronicle,* https://www.bizjournals.com/atlanta, February 14, 2018.

4. *Atlanta Business Chronicle,* "Home Depot Re-tools."

5. S. McFarland, "Home Depot Giving $50M to Help Shore Up U.S. Labor Gap," *UPI,* www.upi.com, March 8, 2018.

6. J.E. Butler, G.R. Ferris, and N.K. Napier, *Strategy and Human Resource Management* (Cincinnati: Southwestern, 1991); P.M. Wright and G.C. McMahan, "Theoretical Perspectives for Strategic Human Resource Management," *Journal of Management* 18 (1992), 295–320.

7. J. LoPresti, "What Is the Biggest Drawback to Six Sigma?" *Six Sigma Daily,* www.sixsigmadaily.com, February 20, 2018.

8. A. Pressman, "Why Microsoft CEO Satya Nadella Is Tearing Up the Windows Business," *Fortune,* http://fortune.com, March 29, 2018.

9. "Empowering Our Employees: Training and Development," www.microsoft.com, accessed April 7, 2018.

10. C.D. Fisher, L.F. Schoenfeldt, and J.B. Shaw, *Human Resource Management* (Boston: Houghton Mifflin, 1990).

11. Wright and McMahan, "Theoretical Perspectives for Strategic Human Resource Management."

12. L. Baird and I. Meshoulam, "Managing Two Fits for Strategic Human Resource

Management," *Academy of Management Review* 13, no. 1 (1988), 116–28; J. Milliman, M. Von Glinow, and M. Nathan, "Organizational Life Cycles and Strategic International Human Resource Management in Multinational Companies: Implications for Congruence Theory," *Academy of Management Review* 16 (1991), 318–39; R.S. Schuler and S.E. Jackson, "Linking Competitive Strategies with Human Resource Management Practices," *Academy of Management Executive* 1 (1987), 207–19; P.M. Wright and S.A. Snell, "Toward an Integrative View of Strategic Human Resource Management," *Human Resource Management Review* 1 (1991), 203–25.

13. Equal Employment Opportunity Commission, "Uniform Guidelines on Employee Selection Procedures," *Federal Register* 43 (1978), 38290–315.

14. L. Wirthman, "Hot Topics in HR and Employment Law in 2018," *Forbes,* www.forbes.com, accessed April 7, 2018; A. Smith, "Religious and LGBT Rights: Find Solutions That Work for Everyone," www.shrm.org, March 14, 2017.

15. J.M. George, "AIDS/AIDS-Related Complex," in L. Peters, B. Greer, and S. Youngblood, eds., *The Blackwell Encyclopedic Dictionary of Human Resource Management* (Oxford, England: Blackwell, 1997).

16. S.L. Rynes, "Recruitment, Job Choice, and Post-Hire Consequences: A Call for New Research Directions," in M.D. Dunnette and L.M. Hough, eds., *Handbook of Industrial and Organizational Psychology,* vol. 2 (Palo Alto, CA: Consulting Psychologists Press, 1991), 399–444.

17. "Company Overview," www.kellyservices.us, accessed April 7, 2018.

18. "What Should Your Business Outsource in 2018?" *Paychex,* www.paychex.com, March 20, 2018.

19. "ISG Research Identifies Top Markets for Outsourcing Growth and Service Delivery in 2018," *PRNewswire,* www.prnewswire.com, January 31, 2018.

20. "Report: Offshoring Evolving at Rapid Pace," https://today.duke.edu, accessed April 7, 2018; S. Minter, "Offshoring by US Companies Doubles," *Industry Week,* www.industryweek.com, accessed April 7, 2018.

21. D.Z. Morris, "How Outsourcing Tech Jobs Could Deepen Income Inequality in America," *Fortune,* http://fortune.com, September 3, 2017.

22. "Average Number of Caterpillar Employees Worldwide from FY 2006 to FY 2017," *Statista,* www.statista.com, accessed April 7, 2018; V. Goel, "IBM Now Has More Employees in India Than in the U.S.," *The New York Times,* www.nytimes.com, September 28, 2017.

23. Deloitte, "The Risk Intelligent Approach to Outsourcing and Offshoring," www2.deloitte.com, accessed April 7, 2018.

24. Unilever, "About Us," https://www.unilever.com, accessed April 5, 2018; Rik Kirkland, "Talent Management as a Business Discipline: A Conversation with Unilever CHRO Leena Nair," McKinsey & Company, www.mckinsey.com, March 2018; WorkdayVoice, "Unilever CHRO Leena Nair: How to Thrive in an Upside-Down World," *Forbes,* www.forbes.com, December 4, 2017; "Most Influential 2017: Leena Nair, Chief HR Officer, Unilever," *HR* (United Kingdom), http://www.hrmagazine.co.uk, September 23, 2017.

25. WorkdayVoice, "Unilever CHRO Leena Nair."

26. WorkdayVoice, "Unilever CHRO Leena Nair"; Alison Eyring, "Connected for Growth at Unilever" (Interview with Leena Nair), *People + Strategy,* Fall 2017, 49–50.

27. WorkdayVoice, "Unilever CHRO Leena Nair"; Kirkland, "Talent Management as a Business Discipline"; *HR,* "Most Influential 2017."

28. Unilever, "About Us"; Kirkland, "Talent Management as a Business Discipline."

29. R.J. Harvey, "Job Analysis," in M.D. Dunnette and L.M. Hough, eds., *Handbook of Industrial and Organizational Psychology,* vol. 2 (Palo Alto, CA: Consulting Psychologists Press, 1991), 71–163.

30. E.L. Levine, *Everything You Always Wanted to Know about Job Analysis: A Job Analysis Primer* (Tampa, FL: Mariner, 1983).

31. E.J. McCormick, P.R. Jeanneret, and R.C. Mecham, *Position Analysis Questionnaire* (West Lafayette, IN: Occupational Research Center, Department of Psychological Sciences, Purdue University, 1969).

32. E.J. McCormick, *Job Analysis: Methods and Applications* (New York: American Management Association, 1979); E.J. McCormick and P.R. Jeanneret, "The Position Analysis Questionnaire," in S. Gael, ed., *The Job Analysis Handbook for Business, Industry, and Government* (New York: Wiley, 1988).

33. S.L. Premack and J.P. Wanous, "A Meta-Analysis of Realistic Job Preview Experiments," *Journal of Applied Psychology* 70 (1985), 706–19; J.P. Wanous, "Realistic Job Previews: Can a Procedure to Reduce Turnover also Influence the Relationship between Abilities and Performance?" *Personnel Psychology* 31 (1978), 249–58; J.P. Wanous, *Organizational Entry: Recruitment, Selection, and Socialization of Newcomers* (Reading, MA: Addison-Wesley, 1980).

34. R.M. Guion, "Personnel Assessment, Selection, and Placement," in M.D. Dunnette and L.M. Hough, eds., *Handbook of Industrial and Organizational Psychology,* vol. 2 (Palo Alto, CA: Consulting Psychologists Press, 1991), 327–97.

35. C. Vargas, "Diversifying Tax Workforce Could Start with Hiring Practices," *Bloomberg BNA,* www.bna.com, March 22, 2018.

36. L. Stevens, "Small Changes Can Increase Corporate Diversity," *The Wall Street Journal,* www.wsj.com, March 13, 2018; Danielle Westermann King, "Unconscious Bias: Inside the Underbelly of Hiring," *Recruiting Trends,* www.recruitingtrends.com, April 2, 2018.

37. Vargas, "Diversifying Tax Workforce"; King, "Unconscious Bias."

38. King, "Unconscious Bias."

39. S. T. Casey, "From an Employer's View, Hiring Jobseekers with Disabilities," *Atlanta Business Chronicle,* www.bizjournals.com/atlanta, April 1, 2018.

40. J. Loffredi, "Before You Run an Employee Background Check You Need to Know These 6 Things," *Inc.,* www.inc.com, January 19, 2018.

41. "Employee Background Checks," www.adp.com, accessed April 7, 2018.

42. R.A. Noe, J. R. Hollenbeck, B. Gerhart, and P.M. Wright, *Human Resource Management: Gaining a Competitive Advantage,* 11th ed. (Burr Ridge, IL: McGraw-Hill, 2019).

43. Noe et al, *Human Resource Management.*

44. "What Is the Hiring Process in the Automotive Industry?" www.jobtestprep.com, accessed April 7, 2018.

45. D. Lechner, "Pre-Employment Physical Testing: What Skills Are You Looking For?" *Ergo Science,* http://info.ergoscience.com, accessed April 7, 2018.

46. "Wanted: Middle Managers, Audition Required, *The Wall Street Journal,* December 28, 1995, A1.

47. I.L. Goldstein, "Training in Work Organizations," in M.D. Dunnette and L.M. Hough, eds., *Handbook of Industrial and Organizational Psychology,* vol. 2 (Palo Alto, CA: Consulting Psychologists Press, 1991), 507–619.

48. B. Capodagli and L. Jackson, "Training Lessons Learned from Disney," *Training,* https://trainingmag.com, accessed April 7, 2018; "Disney University 101—What It Is and Why You'll Love It," www.disneyfanatic.com, accessed April 7, 2018.

49. "Top 125 Award Winners," *Training,* www.trainingmag.com, January/February 2018, pp. 50–51.

50. T.D. Allen, L.T. Eby, M.L. Poteet, E. Lentz, and L. Lima, "Career Benefits Associated with Mentoring for Protégés: A Meta-Analysis," *Journal of Applied Psychology* 89, no. 1 (2004), 127–36.

51. M. Khidekel, "The Misery of Mentoring Millennials," *Bloomberg Businessweek,* http://www.businessweek.com/printer/articles/102262-the-misery-of-mentoring-millennials, April 24, 2014.

52. P. Garfinkel, "Putting a Formal Stamp on Mentoring," *The New York Times,* January 18, 2004, BU10.

53. Ibid.

54. Allen et al., "Career Benefits Associated with Mentoring"; L. Levin, "Lesson Learned: Know Your Limits. Get Outside Help Sooner Rather Than Later," *BusinessWeek Online,* www.businessweek.com, July 5, 2004; "Family, Inc.," *BusinessWeek Online,* www.businessweek.com, November 10, 2003; J. Salamon, "A Year with a Mentor. Now Comes the Test," *The New York Times,* September 30, 2003, B1, B5; E. White, "Making Mentorships Work," *The Wall Street Journal,* October 23, 2007, B11.

55. Garfinkel, "Putting a Formal Stamp on Mentoring."

56. "Executive Education," https://michiganross.umich.edu, accessed April 7, 2018; E. Brooks and R. Morse, "Methodology: Best Online MBA Programs Rankings," *US News,* www.usnews.com, January 8, 2018; J. A. Byrne, "Virtual B-Schools,"*BusinessWeek,* October 23, 1995, 64–68.

57. G.P. Latham and K.N. Wexley, *Increasing Productivity through Performance Appraisal* (Reading, MA: Addison-Wesley, 1982).

58. T.A. DeCotiis, "An Analysis of the External Validity and Applied Relevance of Three Rating Formats," *Organizational Behavior and Human Performance* 19 (1977), 247–66.

59. L. Kwoh, "Rank and Yank," *The Wall Street Journal,* January 31, 2012, B6.

60. Ibid.

61. J.S. Lublin, "Turning the Tables: Underlings Evaluate Bosses," *The Wall Street Journal,* October 4, 1994, B1, B14; S. Shellenbarger, "Reviews from Peers Instruct—and Sting," *The Wall Street Journal,* October 4, 1994, B1, B4.

62. C. Borman and D.W. Bracken, "360 Degree Appraisals," in C.L. Cooper and C. Argyris, eds., *The Concise Blackwell Encyclopedia of Management* (Oxford, England: Blackwell, 1998), 17; D.W. Bracken, "Straight Talk about Multi-Rater Feedback," *Training and Development* 48 (1994), 44–51; M.R. Edwards, W.C. Borman, and J.R. Sproul, "Solving the Double Bind in Performance Appraisal: A Saga of Solves, Sloths, and Eagles," *Business Horizons* 85 (1985), 59–68.

63. M. Buckingham, "The Fatal Flaw with 360 Surveys," *Harvard Business Review,* https://hbr.org, October 17, 2011.

64. S. C. Twohill, "Make Performance Reviews Effective Again," *Workforce,* www.workforce.com, January 31, 2017.

65. S.E. Moss and J.I. Sanchez, "Are Your Employees Avoiding You? Managerial Strategies for Closing the Feedback Gap," *Academy of Management Executive* 18, no. 1 (2004), 32–46.

66. B. Wigert and A. Mann, "Give Performance Reviews That Actually Inspire Employees," *Gallup Blog,* http://news.gallup.com, September 25, 2017.

67. A. Sarkar, "Is It Time to Do Away with Annual Performance Appraisal System? Benefits and Challenges Ahead," *Human Resource Management International Digest* 24, no. 3 (2016), 7–10.

68. Wigert and Mann, "Give Performance Reviews That Actually Inspire Employees."

69. K. Duggan, "Six Companies That Are Redefining Performance Management," *Fast Company,* www.fastcompany.com, December 15, 2015; K. Duggan, "Why the Annual Performance Review Is Going Extinct," *Fast Company,* www.fastcompany.com, October 20, 2015.

70. Sarkar, "Is It Time to Do Away with Annual Performance Appraisal System?"

71. "The Story of Check-in," www.adobe.com, accessed April 7, 2018; D. Burkus, "How Adobe Scrapped Its Performance Review System and Why It Worked," *Forbes,* www.forbes.com, June 1, 2016.

72. "Fortune 100 Best Companies to Work For®: Four Seasons Hotels & Resorts," http://fortune.com, April 7, 2018.

73. "2018 Awards and Accolades," https://press.fourseasons.com, accessed April 7, 2018.

74. M. Solomon, "Four Seasons Leader Isadore Sharp: Treat Employees Right So They Treat Customers Right," *Forbes,* www.forbes.com, August 17, 2015.

75. Ibid.

76. "About Us: Four Seasons History," www.fourseasons.com, accessed April 7, 2018.

77. M. Solomon, "Five-Star Customer Service Depends on Treating Employees Well, Say Ritz-Carlton, Four Seasons," *Forbes,* www.forbes.com, January 2, 2017.

78. "Four Seasons Hotels & Resorts: Perks and Programs," http://reviews.greatplacetowork.com, accessed April 7, 2018.

79. "Benefits," http://jobs.fourseasons.com, accessed April 7, 2018.

80. "Supervisory and Management Training," and "Benefits," http://jobs.fourseasons.com, accessed April 7, 2018.

81. Rob Du Boff, "What Is Just When It Comes to CEO-to-Average Worker Pay?" *Forbes,* www.forbes.com, October 10, 2017.

82. Ibid.

83. G. Donnelley, "Top CEOs Make More in Two Days Than an Average Employee Does in One Year," *Fortune,* http://fortune.com, July 20, 2017.

84. F. J. Reh, "Take a Look at the Issues with CEO Compensation," *The Balance,* www.thebalance.com, August 14, 2017.

85. S. Fishman, "What Are Employers' Healthcare Insurance Requirements under the Affordable Care Act (ACA) in 2018?" www.nolo.com, accessed April 7, 2018.

86. J. Wieczner, "Your Company Wants to Make You Healthy," *The Wall Street Journal,* www.wsj.com, April 8, 2013.

87. J. Green, "Gay Couples Still Miss Out on Corporate Benefits, Group Says," *Bloomberg,* www.bloomberg.com, November 9, 2017.

88. S. Premack and J.E. Hunter, "Individual Unionization Decisions," *Psychological Bulletin* 103 (1988), 223–34.

89. Bureau of Labor Statistics, "Union Members—2017," www.bls.gov, January 19, 2018.

90. "Quick Facts (AFL-CIO)," www.unionfacts.com, accessed April 7, 2018.

91. Bureau of Labor Statistics, "Union Members—2017."

92. Ibid.

93. A. Semuels, "Organized Labor's Growing Class Divide," *The Atlantic,* www.theatlantic.com, January 26, 2018.

94. "Chavez-Thompson to Retire as Executive Vice President," *AFL-CIO blog,* http://blog.aflcio, March 6, 2008.

95. "Secretary Elaine L. Chao," www.transportation.gov, accessed April 7, 2018; "Elaine Chao: Biography," www.elainelchao.com, accessed April 7, 2018.

96. "Table 1. Union Affiliation of Employed Wage and Salary Workers by Selected Characteristics—2017 Data," www.bls.gov, accessed April 7, 2018.

CHAPTER 13

Motivation and Performance

©Yuri Arcurs/Cutcaster

Learning Objectives

After studying this chapter, you should be able to:

LO13-1 Explain what motivation is and why managers need to be concerned about it.

LO13-2 Describe from the perspectives of expectancy theory and equity theory what managers should do to have a highly motivated workforce.

LO13-3 Explain how goals and needs motivate people and what kinds of goals are especially likely to result in high performance.

LO13-4 Identify the motivation lessons that managers can learn from operant conditioning theory and social learning theory.

LO13-5 Explain why and how managers can use pay as a major motivation tool.

Martha Firestone Ford Is a Motivating Force for Her Detroit Lions

How to get a losing team to aim higher and win? After years of humiliation, Detroit Lions fans are pinning their hopes on a tiny woman in her 90s—Martha Firestone Ford, the team's owner. Since their 1957 championship, the team has won just a single playoff game, and it has never played in a Super Bowl. Furthermore, frustrated fans have been less likely to attend games. The team's future looked bleak until control shifted to Ford, who has deep roots in the Detroit area. The granddaughter of the founder of Firestone Tire and Rubber, she married the grandson of Henry Ford and moved to Detroit, where she was active in the community. When her husband, the Lions' owner, died in 2014, Ford surprised observers by stepping up boldly to take an active role in team operations.[1]

What gives hope to fans and players alike is Ford's commitment to high performance. The team started the first season under Ford with a 1–7 record, and she swiftly decided that leadership changes were overdue. She fired the team's president, Tom Lewand, and its general manager, Martin Mayhew. Before long, other executives also were on their way out. She hired the well-respected Bob Quinn to be the new general manager. On the business side, she brought in the family's long-time financial adviser, Rod Wood, to serve as president. Wood has focused on listening to fans about their experience at games in order to address day-to-day issues with stadium cleanliness, safety, and lines at concession stands. Every aspect of the franchise is to excel, not just play on the field.[2]

Ford quickly signaled that the Lions would be driven by loftier goals, and everyone would be held accountable for achieving those goals. Immediately after the firings, she held a news conference to explain her goals and then met with the team to explain her actions. She answered their questions and emphasized the need to make changes in order to build a team that wins—which is, after all, exactly what players hope to do when they sign with a professional sports franchise. She wrote to season-ticket holders, telling them, "You deserve better."[3] Further demonstrating that she cares, she attends every game and greets all the players by name.[4]

The impact on the players—after surprise—was to rekindle their enthusiasm. Receiver Calvin Johnson remarked Ford's management changes represented "the look of an owner who wants to win."[5] Kicker Matt Prater concluded that Ford was demonstrating "she's willing to do whatever it takes to win, which is what you want from your owner."[6]

The more motivated players haven't yet won a championship as of this writing, but the team's record has improved. Out of six seasons, they have played in the postseason three times. With more wins to see, fans are returning to the games, with every game sold out since October

Detroit Lions' owner Martha Firestone Ford, pictured here with team executives, is not afraid to make organizational changes to help motivate employees as well as the NFL players who work for her.
©Paul Sancya/AP Images

2010.[7] And still the pressure to do better continues. After a 9–7 record in 2017, the Lions fired coach Jim Caldwell and replaced him with someone Bob Quinn said could "take the team to the next level": Matt Patricia, who had been defensive coordinator with the New England Patriots through that franchise's participation in the most recent Super Bowl. Perhaps some of that Super Bowl glory will yet rub off on the Lions and their highly motivated owner.[8]

Overview

Even with the best strategy in place and an appropriate organizational architecture, an organization will be effective only if its members are motivated to perform at a high level. Martha Firestone Ford and her Detroit Lions' management team, described in "A Manager's Challenge," clearly realize this. One reason that leading is such an important managerial activity is that it entails ensuring that each member of an organization is motivated to perform highly and help the organization achieve its goals. When managers are effective, the outcome of the leading process is a highly motivated workforce. A key challenge for managers of organizations both large and small is to encourage employees to perform at a high level.

In this chapter we describe what motivation is, where it comes from, and why managers need to promote high levels of it for an organization to be effective and achieve its goals. We examine important theories of motivation: expectancy theory, need theories, equity theory, goal-setting theory, and learning theories. Each gives managers important insights into how to motivate organizational members. The theories are complementary in that each focuses on a different aspect of motivation. Considering all the theories together helps managers gain a rich understanding of the many issues and problems involved in encouraging high levels of motivation throughout an organization. Last, we consider the use of pay as a motivation tool. By the end of this chapter you will understand what it takes to have a highly motivated workforce.

The Nature of Motivation

LO13-1 Explain what motivation is and why managers need to be concerned about it.

motivation Psychological forces that determine the direction of a person's behavior in an organization, a person's level of effort, and a person's level of persistence.

intrinsically motivated behavior Behavior that is performed for its own sake.

Motivation may be defined as psychological forces that determine the direction of a person's behavior in an organization, a person's level of effort, and a person's level of persistence in the face of obstacles.[9] The *direction of a person's behavior* refers to the many possible behaviors a person can engage in. For example, employees of the Detroit Lions know they should do whatever is required to provide high-quality customer service, such as providing top-notch food items at stadium concession stands or clean and safe restroom facilities at each home game. *Effort* refers to how hard people work. Detroit Lions' employees—players as well as managers—exert high levels of effort to make sure they continue their winning ways and provide an exceptional experience for their fans. *Persistence* refers to whether, when faced with roadblocks or other obstacles, people keep trying or give up. Managers with the Detroit Lions persistently seek to improve the profitability of the team's operations while maintaining high levels of customer service.

Motivation is central to management because it explains *why* people behave the way they do in organizations.[10] Motivation also explains why a waiter is polite or rude and why a kindergarten teacher really tries to get children to enjoy learning or just goes through the motions. It explains why some managers truly put their organizations' best interests first, whereas others are more concerned with maximizing their salaries and why—more generally—some workers put forth twice as much effort as others.

Motivation can come from either *intrinsic* or *extrinsic* sources. **Intrinsically motivated behavior** is behavior that is performed for its own sake; the source of motivation is actually performing the behavior, and motivation comes from doing the work itself. Many managers are intrinsically motivated; they derive a sense of accomplishment and achievement from helping the organization achieve its goals and gain competitive advantages. Jobs that are interesting and challenging or high on the five characteristics described by the job characteristics model (see Chapter 10) are more likely to lead to intrinsic motivation than are jobs that are boring or do not use a person's skills and abilities. An elementary school teacher who really enjoys teaching children, a software engineer who loves solving programming problems, and a commercial photographer who relishes taking creative photographs are all intrinsically motivated. For these individuals, motivation comes from performing their jobs—teaching children, finding bugs in computer programs, and taking pictures.

A lack of intrinsic motivation at work sometimes propels people to make major changes in their lives, as illustrated in the accompanying "Managing Globally" feature.

MANAGING GLOBALLY

Seeking Intrinsic Motivation in Far-Flung Places

Dom Jackman and Rob Symington, then in their late twenties, were doing financial consulting work for Ernst & Young in London when they were both struck by how lacking their jobs felt in terms of intrinsic motivation. As Symington put it, "It felt like the work we did, crunching spreadsheets, just didn't matter to anyone, including to our customers or employers."[11] Realizing that they were probably not the only young workers in the finance field who didn't enjoy the work they were doing, Jackman and Symington decided to do something about it. They quit their jobs and created Escape the City, a website devoted to helping bankers, financiers, and other professionals find interesting and exciting work in far-flung places.[12] "The City" refers to the financial district in London, and hence Escape the City is a fitting name for a website oriented toward "escaping unfulfilling corporate jobs."[13]

Employers pay to list positions on the site that entail initiative and adventure, while job seekers can sign up for free.[14] Weekly email messages inform job seekers of interesting opportunities they might want to pursue, ranging from African charity work and employment with venture capital firms in Mongolia to microfinance work in India and surf camps in Morocco. Escape the City earned profits its first year in operation and has expanded to the United States with a New York office.[15]

Asia Pacific Investment Partners hired an operations manager and a communications manager from posting listings on the site.[16] Will Tindall landed the latter position, and as chief communications officer for Asia Pacific, he worked out of Hong Kong, Ulan Bator, and London. Harry Minter found a position as the manager of Guludo Beach Lodge in Mozambique—he used to work in the hedge fund field at Headstart Advisers.[17] He has since moved on to another opportunity.[18] Of course, not all professionals in the corporate world find their work to be uninteresting and demotivating; some are intrinsically motivated by the work they do. Nonetheless, for those who are not motivated and desire more exciting, interesting, and meaningful work, Escape the City expands the set of options they might want to consider.

extrinsically motivated behavior Behavior that is performed to acquire material or social rewards or to avoid punishment.

Extrinsically motivated behavior is behavior that is performed to acquire material or social rewards or to avoid punishment; the source of motivation is the consequences of the behavior, not the behavior itself. A car salesperson who is motivated by receiving a commission on all cars sold, a lawyer who is motivated by the high salary and status that go along with the job, and a factory worker who is motivated by the opportunity to earn a secure income are all extrinsically motivated. Their motivation comes from the consequences they receive as a result of their work behaviors.

People can be intrinsically motivated, extrinsically motivated, or both intrinsically and extrinsically motivated.[19] A top manager who derives a sense of accomplishment and achievement

Where are you more likely to find prosocial motivation? Here in the classroom as a teacher walks her student through that tricky math problem. Getting companies to foster this type of motivation is a bit trickier!
©LWA/Dann Tardif/Blend Images/Corbis

from managing a large corporation and strives to reach year-end targets to obtain a hefty bonus is both intrinsically and extrinsically motivated. Similarly, a nurse who enjoys helping and taking care of patients and is motivated by having a secure job with good benefits is both intrinsically and extrinsically motivated. Within the Detroit Lions organization, employees are both extrinsically motivated because of opportunities for promotions and having their pay linked to the team's overall performance and intrinsically motivated because they get a sense of satisfaction out of serving customers and learning new things. Whether workers are intrinsically motivated, extrinsically motivated, or both depends on a wide variety of factors: (1) workers' own personal characteristics (such as their personalities, abilities, values, attitudes, and needs), (2) the nature of their jobs (such as whether they have been enriched or where they are on the five core characteristics of the job characteristics model), and (3) the nature of the organization (such as its structure, its culture, its control systems, its human resource management system, and the ways in which rewards such as pay are distributed to employees).

In addition to being intrinsically or extrinsically motivated, some people are prosocially motivated by their work.[20] **Prosocially motivated behavior** is behavior that is performed to benefit or help others.[21] Behavior can be prosocially motivated in addition to being extrinsically and/or intrinsically motivated. An elementary school teacher who not only enjoys the process of teaching young children (has high intrinsic motivation) but also has a strong desire to give children the best learning experience possible and help those with learning disabilities overcome their challenges, and who keeps up with the latest research on child development and teaching methods in an effort to continually improve the effectiveness of his teaching, has high prosocial motivation in addition to high intrinsic motivation. A surgeon who specializes in organ transplants, enjoys the challenge of performing complex operations, has a strong desire to help her patients regain their health and extend their lives through successful organ transplants, and is motivated by the relatively high income she earns has high intrinsic, prosocial, and extrinsic motivation. Recent preliminary research suggests that when workers have high prosocial motivation, also having high intrinsic motivation can be especially beneficial for job performance.[22]

Regardless of whether people are intrinsically, extrinsically, or prosocially motivated, they join and are motivated to work in organizations to obtain certain outcomes. An **outcome** is anything a person gets from a job or an organization. Some outcomes, such as autonomy, responsibility, a feeling of accomplishment, and the pleasure of doing interesting or enjoyable work, result in intrinsically motivated behavior. Outcomes such as improving the lives or well-being of other people and doing good by helping others result in prosocially motivated behavior. Other outcomes, such as pay, job security, benefits, and vacation time, result in extrinsically motivated behavior.

Organizations hire people to obtain important inputs. An **input** is anything a person contributes to the job or organization, such as time, effort, education, experience, skills, knowledge, and actual work behaviors. Inputs such as these are necessary for an organization to achieve its goals. Managers strive to motivate members of an organization to contribute inputs—through their behavior, effort, and persistence—that help the organization achieve its goals. How do managers do this? They ensure that members of an organization obtain the outcomes they desire when they make valuable contributions to the organization. Managers use outcomes to motivate people to contribute their inputs to the organization. Giving people outcomes when they contribute inputs and perform well aligns the interests of employees with the goals of the organization as a whole because when employees do what is good for the organization, they personally benefit.

This alignment between employees and organizational goals as a whole can be described by the motivation equation depicted in Figure 13.1. Managers seek to ensure that people are motivated to contribute important inputs to the organization, that these inputs are put to good use or focused in the direction of high performance, and that high performance results in workers' obtaining the outcomes they desire.

prosocially motivated behavior Behavior that is performed to benefit or help others.

outcome Anything a person gets from a job or an organization.

input Anything a person contributes to his or her job or organization.

Figure 13.1

The Motivation Equation

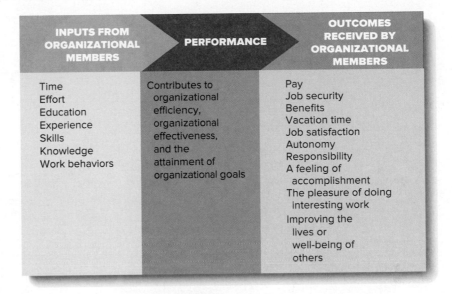

Each of the theories of motivation discussed in this chapter focuses on one or more aspects of this equation. Each theory focuses on a different set of issues that managers need to address to have a highly motivated workforce. Together the theories provide a comprehensive set of guidelines for managers to follow to promote high levels of employee motivation. Effective managers tend to follow many of these guidelines, whereas ineffective managers often fail to follow them and seem to have trouble motivating organizational members.

Expectancy Theory

Expectancy theory, formulated by Victor H. Vroom in the 1960s, posits that motivation is high when workers believe high levels of effort lead to high performance and high performance leads to the attainment of desired outcomes. Expectancy theory is one of the most popular theories of work motivation because it focuses on all three parts of the motivation equation: inputs, performance, and outcomes. Expectancy theory identifies three major factors that determine a person's motivation: *expectancy, instrumentality,* and *valence* (see Figure 13.2).[23]

Expectancy

Expectancy is a person's perception about the extent to which effort (an input) results in a certain level of performance. A person's level of expectancy determines whether he or she believes that a high level of effort results in a high level of performance. People are motivated to put forth a lot of effort on their jobs only if they think that their effort will pay off in high performance—that is, if they have high expectancy. Think about how motivated you would be to study for a test if you thought that no matter how hard you tried, you would get a D. Think about how motivated a marketing manager would be who thought that no matter how hard he or she worked, there was no way to increase sales of an unpopular product. In these cases, expectancy is low, so overall motivation is also low.

Members of an organization are motivated to put forth a high level of effort only if they think that doing so leads to high performance.[24] In other words, in order for people's motivation to be high, expectancy must be high. Thus, in attempting to influence motivation, managers need to make sure their subordinates believe that if they do try hard, they can actually succeed. One way managers can boost expectancies is through expressing confidence in their subordinates' capabilities. Managers at The Container Store, for example, express high levels of confidence

Figure 13.2

Expectancy, Instrumentality, and Valence

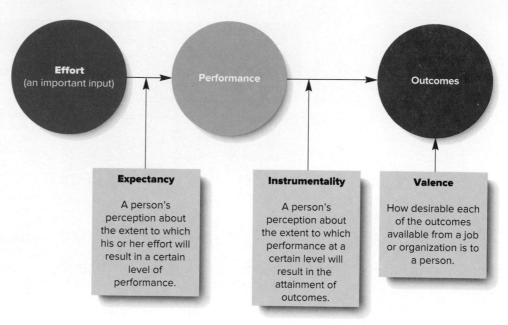

in their subordinates. As Container Store cofounder Garrett Boone put it, "Everybody we hire, we hire as a leader. Anybody in our store can take an action that you might think of typically being a manager's action."[25]

In addition to expressing confidence in subordinates, other ways for managers to boost subordinates' expectancy levels and motivation are by providing training so people have the expertise needed for high performance and increasing their levels of autonomy and responsibility as they gain experience so they have the freedom to do what it takes to perform at a high level. For example, the Best Buy chain of stores, selling electronics, computers, music and movies, and gadgets of all sorts, boosts salespeople's expectancies by giving them extensive training in on-site meetings and online. Electronic learning terminals in each department not only help salespeople learn how different systems work and can be sold as an integrated package but also enable them to keep up with the latest advances in technology and products. Salespeople also receive extensive training in how to determine customers' needs.[26]

Instrumentality

instrumentality In expectancy theory, a perception about the extent to which performance results in the attainment of outcomes.

Expectancy captures a person's perceptions about the relationship between effort and performance. Instrumentality, the second major concept in expectancy theory, is a person's perception about the extent to which performance at a certain level results in the attainment of outcomes (see Figure 13.2). According to expectancy theory, employees are motivated to perform at a high level only if they think high performance will lead to (or is *instrumental* in attaining) outcomes such as pay, job security, interesting job assignments, bonuses, or a feeling of accomplishment. In other words, instrumentalities must be high for motivation to be high—people must perceive that because of their high performance they will receive outcomes.[27]

Managers promote high levels of instrumentality when they link performance to desired outcomes. In addition, managers must clearly communicate this linkage to subordinates. By making sure that outcomes available in an organization are distributed to organizational members on the basis of their performance, managers promote high instrumentality and motivation. When outcomes are linked to performance in this way, high performers receive more outcomes than low performers. In "A Manager's Challenge," managers raise levels of instrumentality and motivation for Detroit Lions employees by linking opportunities for promotion and pay to performance.

Almost all entry-level employees participate in Enterprise's management training program, which allows new hires to learn all aspects of the company business, including how to provide excellent customer service and prepare for possible promotion opportunities. This strategy has helped Enterprise develop a highly motivated workforce.

©Carlos Osorio/AP Images

valence In expectancy theory, how desirable each of the outcomes available from a job or an organization is to a person.

Another example of high instrumentality contributing to high motivation can be found in the Cambodian immigrants who own, manage, and work in more than 80% of the doughnut shops in the Los Angeles area of California.[28] These immigrants see high performance as leading to many important outcomes such as income, a comfortable existence, family security, and the autonomy provided by working in a small business. Their high instrumentality contributes to their high motivation to succeed.

Valence

Although all members of an organization must have high expectancies and instrumentalities, expectancy theory acknowledges that people differ in their preferences for outcomes. For many people, pay is the most important outcome of working. For others, a feeling of accomplishment or enjoying one's work is more important than pay. The term **valence** refers to how desirable each of the outcomes available from a job or an organization is to a person. To motivate organizational members, managers need to determine which outcomes have high valence for them—are highly desired—and make sure that those outcomes are provided when members perform at a high level. For example, at Enterprise Holdings, the largest car rental company in the world, autonomy, responsibility, and opportunities for promotion are highly valent outcomes for many employees. The company's management training program is touted not only for promoting a strong "promote-from-within" culture, but also for developing new hires into the next generation of business leaders. According to the company, more than 15,000 employees were promoted in a recent year.[29]

Bringing It All Together

According to expectancy theory, high motivation results from high levels of expectancy, instrumentality, and valence (see Figure 13.3). If any one of these factors is low, motivation is likely

Figure 13.3
Expectancy Theory

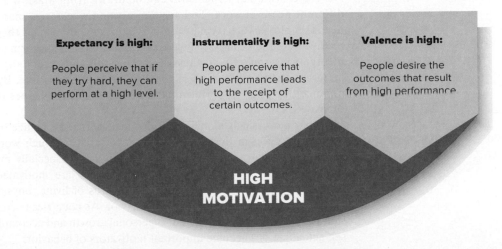

Expectancy is high:
People perceive that if they try hard, they can perform at a high level.

Instrumentality is high:
People perceive that high performance leads to the receipt of certain outcomes.

Valence is high:
People desire the outcomes that result from high performance.

HIGH MOTIVATION

to be low. No matter how tightly desired outcomes are linked to performance, if a person thinks it is practically impossible to perform at a high level, motivation to perform at a high level will be low. Similarly, if a person does not think outcomes are linked to high performance, or if a person does not desire the outcomes that are linked to high performance, motivation to perform at a high level will be low. Effective managers realize the importance of high levels of expectancy, instrumentality, and valence and take concrete steps to ensure that their employees are highly motivated.

Need Theories

LO13-3 Explain how goals and needs motivate people and what kinds of goals are especially likely to result in high performance.

need A requirement or necessity for survival and well-being.

need theories Theories of motivation that focus on what needs people are trying to satisfy at work and what outcomes will satisfy those needs.

Maslow's hierarchy of needs An arrangement of five basic needs that, according to Maslow, motivate behavior. Maslow proposed that the lowest level of unmet needs is the prime motivator and that only one level of needs is motivational at a time.

A **need** is a requirement or necessity for survival and well-being. The basic premise of **need theories** is that people are motivated to obtain outcomes at work that will satisfy their needs. Need theory complements expectancy theory by exploring in depth which outcomes motivate people to perform at a high level. Need theories suggest that to motivate a person to contribute valuable inputs to a job and perform at a high level, a manager must determine what needs the person is trying to satisfy at work and ensure that the person receives outcomes that help satisfy those needs when the person performs at a high level and helps the organization achieve its goals.

There are several need theories. Here we discuss Abraham Maslow's hierarchy of needs, Clayton Alderfer's ERG theory, Frederick Herzberg's motivator-hygiene theory, and David McClelland's needs for achievement, affiliation, and power. These theories describe needs that people try to satisfy at work. In doing so, they give managers insights into what outcomes motivate members of an organization to perform at a high level and contribute inputs to help the organization achieve its goals.

Maslow's Hierarchy of Needs

Psychologist Abraham Maslow proposed that all people seek to satisfy five basic kinds of needs: physiological needs, safety needs, belongingness needs, esteem needs, and self-actualization needs (see Table 13.1).[30] He suggested that these needs constitute a **hierarchy of needs**, with the most basic or compelling needs—physiological and safety needs—at the bottom. Maslow argued that these lowest-level needs must be met before a person strives to satisfy needs higher up in the hierarchy, such as self-esteem needs. Once a need is satisfied, Maslow proposed, it ceases to operate as a source of motivation. The lowest level of *unmet* needs in the hierarchy is the prime motivator of behavior; if and when this level is satisfied, needs at the next highest level in the hierarchy motivate behavior.

Although this theory identifies needs that are likely to be important sources of motivation for many people, research does not support Maslow's contention that there is a need hierarchy or his notion that only one level of needs is motivational at a time.[31] Nevertheless, a key conclusion can be drawn from Maslow's theory: People try to satisfy different needs at work. To have a motivated workforce, managers must determine which needs employees are trying to satisfy in organizations and then make sure that individuals receive outcomes that satisfy their needs when they perform at a high level and contribute to organizational effectiveness. By doing this, managers align the interests of individual members with the interests of the organization as a whole. By doing what is good for the organization (that is, performing at a high level), employees receive outcomes that satisfy their needs.

In our increasingly global economy, managers must realize that citizens of different countries might differ in the needs they seek to satisfy through work.[32] Some research suggests, for example, that people in Greece and Japan are especially motivated by safety needs and that people in Sweden, Norway, and Denmark are motivated by belongingness needs.[33] In less developed countries with low standards of living, physiological and safety needs are likely to be the prime motivators of behavior. As countries become wealthier and have higher standards of living, needs related to personal growth and accomplishment (such as esteem and self-actualization) become important motivators of behavior.

Table 13.1

Maslow's Hierarchy of Needs

	Needs	Description	Examples of How Managers Can Help People Satisfy These Needs at Work
Highest-Level Needs	**Self-actualization needs**	The needs to realize one's full potential as a human being.	Giving people the opportunity to use their skills and abilities to the fullest extent possible.
	Esteem needs	The needs to feel good about oneself and one's capabilities, to be respected by others, and to receive recognition and appreciation.	Granting promotions and recognizing accomplishments.
	Belongingness needs	Needs for social interaction, friendship, affection, and love.	Promoting good interpersonal relations and organizing social functions such as company picnics and holiday parties.
	Safety needs	Needs for security, stability, and a safe environment.	Providing job security, adequate health care benefits, and safe working conditions.
Lowest-Level Needs (Most Basic or Compelling)	**Physiological needs**	Basic needs for things such as food, water, and shelter that must be met in order for a person to survive.	Providing a level of pay that enables a person to buy food and clothing and have adequate housing.

The lowest level of unsatisfied needs motivates behavior; once this level of needs is satisfied, a person tries to satisfy the needs at the next level.

No one pumps their fist over their laptop unless it's for a good reason! Clearly, whipping an obnoxious spreadsheet into shape and sending out a calmly worded press release makes for satisfied self-actualization needs.
©Jim Esposito/Getty Images

Alderfer's ERG theory The theory that three universal needs—for existence, relatedness, and growth—constitute a hierarchy of needs and motivate behavior. Alderfer proposed that needs at more than one level can be motivational at the same time.

Alderfer's ERG Theory

Clayton **Alderfer's ERG theory** collapsed the five categories of needs in Maslow's hierarchy into three universal categories—existence, relatedness, and growth—also arranged in a hierarchy (see Table 13.2). Alderfer agreed with Maslow that as lower-level needs become satisfied, a person seeks to satisfy higher-level needs. Unlike Maslow, however, Alderfer believed that a person can be motivated by needs at more than one level at the same time. A cashier in a supermarket, for example, may be motivated by both existence needs and relatedness needs. The existence needs motivate the cashier to go to work regularly and not make mistakes so his job will be secure and he will be able to pay his rent and buy food. The relatedness needs motivate the cashier to become friends with some of the other cashiers and have a good relationship with the store manager. Alderfer also suggested that when people experience *need frustration* or are unable to satisfy needs at a certain level, they will focus more intently on satisfying the needs at the next lowest level in the hierarchy.[34]

As with Maslow's theory, research does not support some of the specific ideas outlined in ERG theory, such as the existence of the three-level need hierarchy that Alderfer proposed.[35] However, for managers, the important message from ERG theory is the same as that from Maslow's theory: Determine what needs your subordinates are trying to satisfy at work, and make sure they receive outcomes that satisfy these needs when they perform at a high level to help the organization achieve its goals.

Table 13.2

Alderfer's ERG Theory

	Needs	Description	Examples of How Managers Can Help People Satisfy These Needs at Work
Highest-Level Needs	**Growth needs**	The needs for self-development and creative and productive work.	Allowing people to continually improve their skills and abilities and engage in meaningful work.
	Relatedness needs	The needs to have good interpersonal relations, to share thoughts and feelings, and to have open two-way communication.	Promoting good interpersonal relations and providing accurate feedback.
Lowest-Level Needs	**Existence needs**	Basic needs for food, water, clothing, shelter, and a secure and safe environment.	Providing enough pay for the basic necessities of life and safe working conditions.

**As lower-level needs are satisfied, a person is motivated to satisfy higher-level needs.
When a person is unable to satisfy higher-level needs (or is frustrated),
motivation to satisfy lower-level needs increases.**

Herzberg's Motivator-Hygiene Theory

Herzberg's motivator-hygiene theory A need theory that distinguishes between motivator needs (related to the nature of the work itself) and hygiene needs (related to the physical and psychological context in which the work is performed) and proposes that motivator needs must be met for motivation and job satisfaction to be high.

Adopting an approach different from Maslow's and Alderfer's, Frederick Herzberg focused on two factors: (1) outcomes that can lead to high levels of motivation and job satisfaction and (2) outcomes that can prevent people from being dissatisfied. According to **Herzberg's motivator-hygiene theory**, people have two sets of needs or requirements: motivator needs and hygiene needs.[36] *Motivator needs* are related to the nature of the work itself and how challenging it is. Outcomes such as interesting work, autonomy, responsibility, the ability to grow and develop on the job, and a sense of accomplishment and achievement help to satisfy motivator needs. To have a highly motivated and satisfied workforce, Herzberg suggested, managers should take steps to ensure that employees' motivator needs are being met.

Hygiene needs are related to the physical and psychological context in which the work is performed. Hygiene needs are satisfied by outcomes such as pleasant and comfortable working conditions, pay, job security, good relationships with coworkers, and effective supervision. According to Herzberg, when hygiene needs are not met, workers are dissatisfied, and when hygiene needs are met, workers are not dissatisfied. Satisfying hygiene needs, however, does not result in high levels of motivation or even high levels of job satisfaction. For motivation and job satisfaction to be high, motivator needs must be met. Many research studies have tested Herzberg's propositions, and, by and large, the theory fails to receive support.[37] Nevertheless, Herzberg's formulations have contributed to our understanding of motivation in at least two ways. First, Herzberg helped to focus researchers' and managers' attention on the important distinction between intrinsic motivation (related to motivator needs) and extrinsic motivation (related to hygiene needs), covered earlier in the chapter. Second, his theory prompted researchers and managers to study how jobs could be designed or redesigned to be intrinsically motivating.

need for achievement The extent to which an individual has a strong desire to perform challenging tasks well and to meet personal standards for excellence.

need for affiliation The extent to which an individual is concerned about establishing and maintaining good interpersonal relations, being liked, and having the people around him or her get along with each other.

McClelland's Needs for Achievement, Affiliation, and Power

Psychologist David McClelland extensively researched the needs for achievement, affiliation, and power.[38] The **need for achievement** is the extent to which an individual has a strong desire to perform challenging tasks well and to meet personal standards for excellence. People with a high need for achievement often set clear goals for themselves and like to receive performance feedback. The **need for affiliation** is the extent to which an individual is concerned about establishing and maintaining good interpersonal relations, being liked, and having the

need for power The extent to which an individual desires to control or influence others.

people around him or her get along with each other. The **need for power** is the extent to which an individual desires to control or influence others.[39]

Although each of these needs is present in each of us to some degree, their importance in the workplace depends on the position one occupies. For example, research suggests that high needs for achievement and for power are assets for first-line and middle managers and that a high need for power is especially important for upper managers.[40] One study found that U.S. presidents with a relatively high need for power tended to be especially effective during their terms of office.[41] A high need for affiliation may not always be desirable in managers and other leaders because it might lead them to try too hard to be liked by others (including subordinates) rather than doing all they can to ensure that performance is as high as it can and should be. Although most research on these needs has been done in the United States, some studies suggest that the findings may be applicable to people in other countries as well, such as India and New Zealand.[42]

Other Needs

Clearly, more needs motivate workers than the needs described by these four theories. For example, more and more workers are feeling the need for work-life balance and time to take care of their loved ones while being highly motivated at work. Interestingly enough, recent research suggests that being exposed to nature (even just being able to see some trees from an office window) has many valuable effects, and a lack of such exposure can impair well-being and performance.[43] Thus, having some time during the day when one can at least see nature may be another important need.

Equity Theory

LO13-2 Describe from the perspectives of expectancy theory and equity theory what managers should do to have a highly motivated workforce.

equity theory A theory of motivation that focuses on people's perceptions of the fairness of their work outcomes relative to their work inputs.

equity The justice, impartiality, and fairness to which all organizational members are entitled.

Equity theory is a theory of motivation that concentrates on people's perceptions of the fairness of their work *outcomes* relative to, or in proportion to, their work *inputs*. Equity theory complements expectancy and need theories by focusing on how people perceive the relationship between the outcomes they receive from their jobs and organizations and the inputs they contribute. Equity theory was formulated in the 1960s by J. Stacy Adams, who stressed that what is important in determining motivation is the *relative* rather than the *absolute* levels of outcomes a person receives and inputs a person contributes. Specifically, motivation is influenced by the comparison of one's own outcome–input ratio with the outcome–input ratio of a referent.[44] The *referent* might be another person or a group of people who are perceived to be similar to oneself; the referent also might be oneself in a previous job or one's expectations about what outcome–input ratios should be. In a comparison of one's own outcome–input ratio to a referent's ratio, one's *perceptions* of outcomes and inputs (not any objective indicator of them) are key.

Equity

Equity exists when a person perceives his or her own outcome–input ratio to be equal to a referent's outcome–input ratio. Under conditions of equity (see Table 13.3), if a referent receives more outcomes than you receive, the referent contributes proportionally more inputs to the organization, so his or her outcome–input ratio still equals your ratio. Maria Sanchez and Claudia King, for example, both work in a shoe store in a large mall. Sanchez is paid more per hour than King but also contributes more inputs, including being responsible for some of the store's bookkeeping, closing the store, and periodically depositing cash in the bank. When King compares her outcome–input ratio to Sanchez's (her referent's), she perceives the ratios to be equitable because Sanchez's higher level of pay (an outcome) is proportional to her higher level of inputs (bookkeeping, closing the store, and going to the bank).

Similarly, under conditions of equity, if you receive more outcomes than a referent, your inputs are perceived to be proportionally higher. Continuing with our example, when Sanchez compares her outcome–input ratio to King's (her referent's) ratio, she perceives them to be equitable because her higher level of pay is proportional to her higher level of inputs. When equity exists, people are motivated to continue contributing their current levels of inputs to

Table 13.3

Equity Theory

Condition	Person		Referent	Example
Equity	$\dfrac{\text{Outcomes}}{\text{Inputs}}$	=	$\dfrac{\text{Outcomes}}{\text{Inputs}}$	An engineer perceives that he contributes more inputs (time and effort) and receives proportionally more outcomes (a higher salary and choice job assignments) than his referent.
Underpayment inequity	$\dfrac{\text{Outcomes}}{\text{Inputs}}$	< (less than)	$\dfrac{\text{Outcomes}}{\text{Inputs}}$	An engineer perceives that he contributes more inputs but receives the same outcomes as his referent.
Overpayment inequity	$\dfrac{\text{Outcomes}}{\text{Inputs}}$	> (greater than)	$\dfrac{\text{Outcomes}}{\text{Inputs}}$	An engineer perceives that he contributes the same inputs but receives more outcomes than his referent.

their organizations to receive their current levels of outcomes. If people wish to increase their outcomes under conditions of equity, they are motivated to increase their inputs.

Inequity

inequity Lack of fairness.

underpayment inequity The inequity that exists when a person perceives that his or her own outcome–input ratio is less than the ratio of a referent.

overpayment inequity The inequity that exists when a person perceives that his or her own outcome–input ratio is greater than the ratio of a referent.

Inequity, or lack of fairness, exists when a person's outcome–input ratio is not perceived to be equal to a referent's. Inequity creates pressure or tension inside people and motivates them to restore equity by bringing the two ratios back into balance.

There are two types of inequity: underpayment inequity and overpayment inequity (see Table 13.3). **Underpayment inequity** exists when a person's own outcome–input ratio is perceived to be *less* than that of a referent. In comparing yourself to a referent, you think you are *not* receiving the outcomes you should be, given your inputs. **Overpayment inequity** exists when a person perceives that his or her own outcome–input ratio is *greater* than that of a referent. In comparing yourself to a referent, you think you are receiving *more* outcomes than you should be, given your inputs.

Ways to Restore Equity

According to equity theory, both underpayment inequity and overpayment inequity create tension that motivates most people to restore equity by bringing the ratios back into balance.[45] When people experience *underpayment* inequity, they may be motivated to lower their inputs by reducing their working hours, putting forth less effort on the job, or being absent; or they may be motivated to increase their outcomes by asking for a raise or a promotion. Susan Richie, a financial analyst at a large corporation, noticed that she was working longer hours and getting more work accomplished than a coworker who had the same position, yet they both received exactly the same pay and other outcomes. To restore equity, Richie decided to stop going in early and staying late. Alternatively, she could have tried to restore equity by trying to increase her outcomes, perhaps by asking her boss for a raise.

When people experience underpayment inequity and other means of equity restoration fail, they can change their perceptions of their own or the referent's inputs or outcomes. For example, they may realize that their referent is really working on more difficult projects than they are or that they really take more time off from work than their referent does. Alternatively, if people who feel they are underpaid have other employment options, they may leave the organization. As an example, John Steinberg, an assistant principal in a high school, experienced underpayment inequity when he realized all the other assistant principals of high schools in his school district had received promotions to the position of principal even though they had been in their jobs for a shorter time than he had. Steinberg's performance had always been appraised as being high, so after his repeated requests for a promotion went unheeded, he found a job as a principal in a different school district.

When people experience *overpayment* inequity, they may try to restore equity by changing their perceptions of their own or their referent's inputs or outcomes. Equity can be restored when people realize they are contributing more inputs than they originally thought. Equity also can be restored by perceiving the referent's inputs to be lower or the referent's outcomes to be higher than one originally thought. When equity is restored in this way, actual inputs and outcomes are unchanged, and the person being overpaid takes no real action. What is changed is how people think about or view their or the referent's inputs and outcomes. For instance, Mary McMann experienced overpayment inequity when she realized she was being paid $2 an hour more than a coworker who had the same job as she did in a health food store and who contributed the same amount of inputs. McMann restored equity by changing her perceptions of her inputs. She realized she worked harder than her coworker and solved more problems that came up in the store.

Experiencing either overpayment or underpayment inequity, you might decide that your referent is not appropriate because, for example, the referent is too different from yourself. Choosing a more appropriate referent may bring the ratios back into balance. Angela Martinez, a middle manager in the engineering department of a chemical company, experienced overpayment inequity when she realized she was being paid quite a bit more than her friend, who was a middle manager in the marketing department of the same company. After thinking about the discrepancy for a while, Martinez decided that engineering and marketing were so different that she should not be comparing her job to her friend's job even though they were both middle managers. Martinez restored equity by changing her referent; she picked a middle manager in the engineering department as a new referent.

Motivation is highest when as many people as possible in an organization perceive that they are being equitably treated—their outcomes and inputs are in balance. Top contributors and performers are motivated to continue contributing a high level of inputs because they are receiving the outcomes they deserve. Mediocre contributors and performers realize that if they want to increase their outcomes, they have to increase their inputs. Managers of effective organizations realize the importance of equity for motivation and performance and continually strive to ensure that employees believe they are being equitably treated.

The dot-com boom, its subsequent bust, and two recessions, along with increased global competition, have resulted in some workers putting in longer and longer working hours (increasing their inputs) without any increase in their outcomes. For those whose referents are not experiencing a similar change, perceptions of inequity are likely. According to Jill Andresky Fraser, author of *White Collar Sweatshop,* over 25 million U.S. workers work more than 49 hours per week in the office, almost 11 million work more than 60 hours per week in the office, and many also put in additional work hours at home. Moreover, advances in information technology, such as email and mobile devices, have resulted in work intruding on home time, vacation time, and even special occasions.[46] For another example of an issue related to equity, see the "Focus on Diversity" feature.

FOCUS ON DIVERSITY

For Diversity to Motivate, It Must Come with Equity

Many organizations have sought to hire a diverse workforce in order to bring more points of view to their decision making and build stronger relationships with their different customers. Some are then surprised when people who differ from the majority group—say, women in a male-dominated workplace or blacks in a white-dominated workplace—are quick to leave. One cause of the turnover may be that these employees are experiencing inequity. Quitting is one way to restore the equity balance.

This is a widely reported problem in the high-tech industry. Although some observers assume that women aren't particularly interested in programming and would prefer

Equitable treatment of all employees helps empower individuals and retain a company's workforce, which is a good business strategy.

©monkeybusinessimages/Getty Images

jobs that are more "social," the women themselves are more apt to report that they felt uncomfortable at work and were often overlooked when they offered ideas or sought mentors. In fact, some have left their employer and started their own technology companies.[47]

Microsoft, for example, has made efforts to hire women and track their pay to make sure it is equitable. Even so, women there have reported pressure to act more like stereotypical college men in order to fit in with the culture. Aggression and criticism characterized the communication style, some have said. When everyone is expected to adopt a similar tone, the benefits of diversity get lost in the efforts at sameness, and some people are unable to contribute fully and receive the intrinsic and extrinsic rewards associated with valuable contributions.[48]

Like Microsoft, other companies also have focused on pay when considering their treatment of a diverse workforce. Starbucks, for example, spent 10 years adjusting pay to reach the point where pay for equal work in the United States is equal regardless of an employee's race or gender. The company continues to pursue pay equity for employees outside the United States. Intel measured its own achievement of pay equity one year earlier. The microchip maker also seeks to ensure equity in promoting and retaining workers. Lyft recently started annual audits of employee compensation, aiming to ensure that pay is equitable across race and gender. The ride-sharing company also hired a vice president of talent and inclusion, charged with ensuring the company welcomes diverse employees, so they can contribute fully.[49] Equitable treatment, because it empowers and retains an organization's workforce, is not only ethical, but also good for business.

Equity and Justice in Organizations

distributive justice A moral principle calling for the use of fair procedures to determine how to distribute outcomes to organizational members.

procedural justice A moral principle calling for the use of fair procedures to determine how to distribute outcomes to organizational members.

interpersonal justice A person's perception of the fairness of the interpersonal treatment he or she receives from whoever distributes outcomes to him or her.

informational justice A person's perception of the extent to which his or her manager provides explanations for decisions and the procedures used to arrive at them.

Equity theory, given its focus on the fair distribution of outcomes in organizations to foster high motivation, is often labeled a theory of distributive justice.[50] **Distributive justice** refers to an employee's perception of the fairness of the distribution of outcomes (such as promotions, pay, job assignments, and working conditions) in an organization.[51] Employees are more likely to be highly motivated when they perceive distributive justice to be high rather than low.

Three other forms of justice are important for high motivation. **Procedural justice** refers to an employee's perception of the fairness of the procedures used to determine how to distribute outcomes in an organization.[52] For example, if important outcomes such as pay and promotions are distributed based on performance appraisals (see Chapter 12) and an employee perceives that the procedure that is used (i.e., the performance appraisal system) is unfair, then procedural justice is low and motivation is likely to suffer. More generally, motivation is higher when procedural justice is high rather than low.[53] **Interpersonal justice** refers to an employee's perception of the fairness of the interpersonal treatment he or she receives from whoever distributes outcomes to him or her (typically his or her manager).[54] Interpersonal justice is high when managers treat subordinates with dignity and respect and are polite and courteous.[55] Motivation is higher when interpersonal justice is high rather than low. **Informational justice** refers to an employee's perception of the extent to which his or her manager provides explanations for decisions and the procedures used to arrive at them.[56] For example, if a manager explains how performance is appraised and how decisions about the distribution of outcomes are made, informational justice (and motivation) are more likely to be high than if the manager does not do this.[57] All in all, it is most advantageous for distributive, procedural, interpersonal, and informational justice all to be high.

Goal-Setting Theory

Goal-setting theory focuses on motivating workers to contribute their inputs to their jobs and organizations; in this way it is similar to expectancy theory and equity theory. But goal-setting theory takes this focus a step further by considering as well how managers can ensure that organizational members focus their inputs in the direction of high performance and the achievement of organizational goals.

Ed Locke and Gary Latham, the leading researchers for goal-setting theory, suggested that the goals organizational members strive to attain are prime determinants of their motivation and subsequent performance. A *goal* is what a person is trying to accomplish through his or her efforts and behaviors.[58] Just as you may have a goal to get a good grade in this course, so do members of an organization have goals they strive to meet. For example, salespeople at Nordstrom retail stores strive to meet sales goals, while top managers pursue market share and profitability goals.

Goal-setting theory suggests that to stimulate high motivation and performance, goals must be *specific* and *difficult*.[59] Specific goals are often quantitative—a salesperson's goal to sell $500 worth of merchandise per day, a scientist's goal to finish a project in one year, a CEO's goal to reduce debt by 40% and increase revenues by 20%, a restaurant manager's goal to serve 150 customers per evening. In contrast to specific goals, vague goals such as "doing your best" or "selling as much as you can" do not have much motivational impact.

Difficult goals are hard but not impossible to attain. In contrast to difficult goals, easy goals are those that practically everyone can attain, and moderate goals are goals that about one-half of the people can attain. Both easy and moderate goals have less motivational power than difficult goals.

Regardless of whether specific, difficult goals are set by managers, workers, or teams of managers and workers, they lead to high levels of motivation and performance. When managers set goals for their subordinates, their subordinates must accept the goals or agree to work toward them; also, they should be committed to them or really want to attain them. Some managers find that having subordinates participate in the actual setting of goals boosts their acceptance of and commitment to the goals. In addition, organizational members need to receive *feedback* about how they are doing; feedback can often be provided by the performance appraisal and feedback component of an organization's human resource management system (see Chapter 12). More generally, goals and feedback are integral components of performance management systems such as management by objectives (see Chapter 11).

Specific, difficult goals affect motivation in two ways. First, they motivate people to contribute more inputs to their jobs. Specific, difficult goals cause people to put forth high levels of effort, for example. Just as you would study harder if you were trying to get an A in a course instead of a C, so will a salesperson work harder to reach a $500 sales goal instead of a $200 sales goal. Specific, difficult goals also cause people to be more persistent when they run into difficulties than do easy, moderate, or vague goals. Salespeople who are told to sell as much as possible might stop trying on a slow day, whereas having a specific, difficult goal to reach causes them to keep trying.

A second way in which specific, difficult goals affect motivation is by helping people focus their inputs in the right direction. These goals let people know what they should be focusing their attention on, whether it is increasing the quality of customer service or sales or lowering new product development times. The fact that the goals are specific and difficult also frequently causes people to develop *action plans* for reaching them.[60] Action plans can include the strategies to attain the goals and timetables or schedules for the completion of different activities crucial to goal attainment. Like the goals themselves, action plans also help ensure that efforts are focused in the right direction and that people do not get sidetracked along the way.

Although specific, difficult goals have been found to increase motivation and performance in a wide variety of jobs and organizations both in the United States and abroad, recent research suggests that they may detract from performance under certain conditions. When people are performing complicated and challenging tasks that require them to

Specific, difficult goals can encourage people to exert high levels of effort and to focus efforts in the right direction.
©Stockbyte/Getty Images

focus on a considerable amount of learning, specific, difficult goals may actually impair performance.[61] Striving to reach such goals may direct some of a person's attention away from learning about the task and toward trying to figure out how to achieve the goal. Once a person has learned the task and it no longer seems complicated or difficult, then the assignment of specific, difficult goals is likely to have its usual effects. Additionally, for work that is very creative and uncertain, specific, difficult goals may be detrimental.

Learning Theories

The basic premise of learning theories as applied to organizations is that managers can increase employee motivation and performance by how they link the outcomes that employees receive to the performance of desired behaviors and the attainment of goals. Thus, learning theory focuses on the linkage between performance and outcomes in the motivation equation (see Figure 13.1).

Learning can be defined as a relatively permanent change in a person's knowledge or behavior that results from practice or experience.[62] Learning takes place in organizations when people learn to perform certain behaviors to receive certain outcomes. For example, a person learns to perform at a higher level than in the past or to come to work earlier because he or she is motivated to obtain the outcomes that result from these behaviors, such as a pay raise or praise from a supervisor. As mentioned earlier, Enterprise's emphasis on training ensures that new hires learn how to provide excellent customer service and perform all the activities necessary for successful branch operations.

Of the different learning theories, operant conditioning theory and social learning theory provide the most guidance to managers in their efforts to have a highly motivated workforce.

Operant Conditioning Theory

According to operant conditioning theory, developed by psychologist B. F. Skinner, people learn to perform behaviors that lead to desired consequences and learn not to perform behaviors that lead to undesired consequences.[63] Translated into motivation terms, Skinner's theory means that people will be motivated to perform at a high level and attain their work goals to the extent that high performance and goal attainment allow them to obtain outcomes they desire. Similarly, people avoid performing behaviors that lead to outcomes they do not desire. By linking the performance of *specific behaviors* to the attainment of *specific outcomes,* managers can motivate organizational members to perform in ways that help an organization achieve its goals.

Operant conditioning theory provides four tools that managers can use to motivate high performance and prevent workers from engaging in absenteeism and other behaviors that detract from organizational effectiveness. These tools are positive reinforcement, negative reinforcement, extinction, and punishment.[64]

POSITIVE REINFORCEMENT Positive reinforcement gives people outcomes they desire when they perform organizationally functional behaviors. These desired outcomes, called *positive reinforcers,* include any outcomes that a person desires, such as pay, praise, or a promotion. Organizationally functional behaviors are behaviors that contribute to organizational effectiveness; they can include producing high-quality goods and services, providing high-quality customer service, and meeting deadlines. By linking positive reinforcers to the performance of functional behaviors, managers motivate people to perform the desired behaviors.

NEGATIVE REINFORCEMENT Negative reinforcement also can encourage members of an organization to perform desired or organizationally functional behaviors. Managers using negative reinforcement actually eliminate or remove undesired outcomes once the functional behavior is performed. These undesired outcomes, called *negative reinforcers,* can range from a manager's constant nagging or criticism to unpleasant assignments or the ever present threat of losing one's job. When negative reinforcement is used, people are motivated to perform behaviors because they want to stop receiving or want to avoid undesired outcomes. Managers who try to encourage salespeople to sell more by threatening them with being fired are using negative reinforcement. In this case, the negative reinforcer is the threat of job loss, which is removed once the functional behavior is performed.

LO13-4 Identify the motivation lessons that managers can learn from operant conditioning theory and social learning theory.

learning theories Theories that focus on increasing employee motivation and performance by linking the outcomes that employees receive to the performance of desired behaviors and the attainment of goals.

learning A relatively permanent change in knowledge or behavior that results from practice or experience.

operant conditioning theory The theory that people learn to perform behaviors that lead to desired consequences and learn not to perform behaviors that lead to undesired consequences.

positive reinforcement Giving people outcomes they desire when they perform organizationally functional behaviors.

negative reinforcement Eliminating or removing undesired outcomes when people perform organizationally functional behaviors.

Whenever possible, managers should try to use positive reinforcement. Negative reinforcement can create a very unpleasant work environment and even a negative culture in an organization. No one likes to be nagged, threatened, or exposed to other kinds of negative outcomes. The use of negative reinforcement sometimes causes subordinates to resent managers and try to get back at them.

IDENTIFYING THE RIGHT BEHAVIORS FOR REINFORCEMENT Even managers who use positive reinforcement (and refrain from using negative reinforcement) can get into trouble if they are not careful to identify the right behaviors to reinforce—behaviors that are truly functional for the organization. Doing this is not always as straightforward as it might seem. First, it is crucial for managers to choose behaviors over which subordinates have control; in other words, subordinates must have the freedom and opportunity to perform the behaviors that are being reinforced. Second, it is crucial that these behaviors contribute to organizational effectiveness.

EXTINCTION Sometimes members of an organization are motivated to perform behaviors that detract from organizational effectiveness. According to operant conditioning theory, all behavior is controlled or determined by its consequences; one way for managers to curtail the performance of dysfunctional behaviors is to eliminate whatever is reinforcing the behaviors. This process is called **extinction**.

extinction Curtailing the performance of dysfunctional behaviors by eliminating whatever is reinforcing them.

Suppose a manager has a subordinate who frequently stops by his office to chat—sometimes about work-related matters but at other times about various topics ranging from politics to last night's football game. The manager and the subordinate share certain interests and views, so these conversations can get quite involved, and both seem to enjoy them. The manager, however, realizes that these frequent and sometimes lengthy conversations are causing him to stay at work later in the evenings to make up for the time he loses during the day. The manager also realizes that he is reinforcing his subordinate's behavior by acting interested in the topics the subordinate brings up and responding at length to them. To extinguish this behavior, the manager stops acting interested in these non-work-related conversations and keeps his responses polite and friendly but brief. No longer being reinforced with a pleasurable conversation, the subordinate eventually ceases to be motivated to interrupt the manager during working hours to discuss non-work-related issues.

punishment Administering an undesired or negative consequence when dysfunctional behavior occurs.

PUNISHMENT Sometimes managers cannot rely on extinction to eliminate dysfunctional behaviors because they do not have control over whatever is reinforcing the behavior or because they cannot afford the time needed for extinction to work. When employees are performing dangerous behaviors or behaviors that are illegal or unethical, the behaviors need to be eliminated immediately. Sexual harassment, for example, is an organizationally dysfunctional behavior that cannot be tolerated. In such cases managers often rely on **punishment**, which is administering an undesired or negative consequence to subordinates when they perform the dysfunctional behavior. Punishments used by organizations include verbal reprimands, pay cuts, temporary suspensions, demotions, and firings. Punishment, however, can have some unintended side effects—resentment, loss of self-respect, a desire for retaliation—and should be used only when necessary.

To avoid the unintended side effects of punishment, managers should keep in mind these guidelines:

- Downplay the emotional element involved in punishment. Make it clear that you are punishing a person's performance of a dysfunctional behavior, not the person himself or herself.

- Try to punish dysfunctional behaviors as soon as possible after they occur, and make sure the negative consequence is a source of punishment for the individuals involved. Be certain that organizational members know exactly why they are being punished.

- Try to avoid punishing someone in front of others because this can hurt a person's self-respect and lower esteem in the eyes of coworkers, as well as make coworkers feel uncomfortable.[65] Even so, making organizational members aware that an individual who has committed a serious infraction has been punished can sometimes be effective in preventing future infractions and in teaching all members of the organization that certain behaviors are unacceptable. For example, when organizational members are informed that a manager who has sexually harassed subordinates has been punished, they learn or are reminded of the fact that sexual harassment is not tolerated in the organization.

Managers and students alike often confuse negative reinforcement and punishment. To avoid such confusion, keep in mind the two major differences between them. First, negative reinforcement is used to promote the performance of functional behaviors in organizations; punishment is used to stop the performance of dysfunctional behaviors. Second, negative reinforcement entails the *removal* of a negative consequence when functional behaviors are performed; punishment entails the *administration* of negative consequences when dysfunctional behaviors are performed.

ORGANIZATIONAL BEHAVIOR MODIFICATION   When managers systematically apply operant conditioning techniques to promote the performance of organizationally functional behaviors and discourage the performance of dysfunctional behaviors, they are engaging in **organizational behavior modification (OB MOD).**[66] OB MOD has been successfully used to improve productivity, efficiency, attendance, punctuality, safe work practices, customer service, and other important behaviors in a wide variety of organizations such as banks, department stores, factories, hospitals, and construction sites.[67] The five basic steps in OB MOD are described in Figure 13.4.

OB MOD works best for behaviors that are specific, objective, and countable, such as attendance and punctuality, making sales, or putting telephones together, all of which lend themselves to careful scrutiny and control. OB MOD may be questioned because of its lack of relevance to certain work behaviors (for example, the many work behaviors that are not specific, objective, and countable). Some people also have questioned it on ethical grounds.

organizational behavior modification (OB MOD) The systematic application of operant conditioning techniques to promote the performance of organizationally functional behaviors and discourage the performance of dysfunctional behaviors.

Figure 13.4

Five Steps in OB MOD

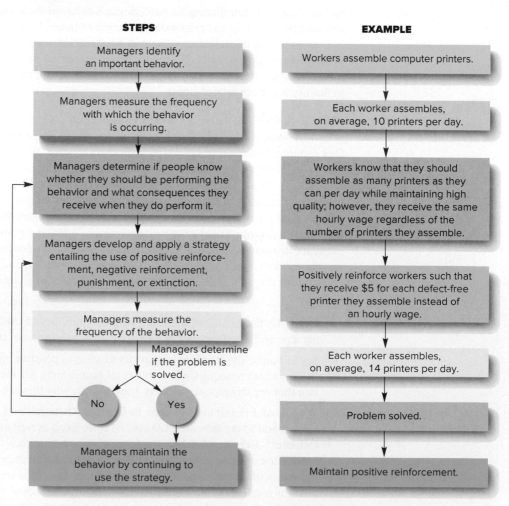

Source: Adapted from F. Luthans and R. Kreitner, *Organizational Behavior Modification and Beyond*, Scott Foresman, 1985. Copyright © 1985.

Critics of OB MOD suggest that it is overly controlling and robs workers of their dignity, individuality, freedom of choice, and even creativity. Supporters counter that OB MOD is a highly effective means of promoting organizational efficiency. There is some merit to both sides of this argument. What is clear, however, is that when used appropriately, OB MOD gives managers a technique to motivate the performance of at least some organizationally functional behaviors.[68]

Social Learning Theory

social learning theory A theory that takes into account how learning and motivation are influenced by people's thoughts and beliefs and their observations of other people's behavior.

Social learning theory proposes that motivation results not only from direct experience of rewards and punishments but also from a person's thoughts and beliefs. Social learning theory extends operant conditioning's contribution to managers' understanding of motivation by explaining (1) how people can be motivated by observing other people performing a behavior and being reinforced for doing so (*vicarious learning*), (2) how people can be motivated to control their behavior themselves (*self-reinforcement*), and (3) how people's beliefs about their ability to successfully perform a behavior affect motivation (*self-efficacy*).[69] We look briefly at each of these motivators.

vicarious learning Learning that occurs when the learner becomes motivated to perform a behavior by watching another person performing it and being reinforced for doing so; also called observational learning.

VICARIOUS LEARNING Vicarious learning, often called *observational learning*, occurs when a person (the learner) becomes motivated to perform a behavior by watching another person (the model) performing the behavior and being positively reinforced for doing so. Vicarious learning is a powerful source of motivation on many jobs in which people learn to perform functional behaviors by watching others. Salespeople learn how to help customers, medical school students learn how to treat patients, law clerks learn how to practice law, and nonmanagers learn how to be managers, in part, by observing experienced members of an organization perform these behaviors properly and be reinforced for them. In general, people are more likely to be motivated to imitate the behavior of models who are highly competent, are (to some extent) experts in the behavior, have high status, receive attractive reinforcers, and are friendly or approachable.[70]

To promote vicarious learning, managers should strive to have the learner meet the following conditions:

- The learner observes the model performing the behavior.
- The learner accurately perceives the model's behavior.
- The learner remembers the behavior.
- The learner has the skills and abilities needed to perform the behavior.
- The learner sees or knows that the model is positively reinforced for the behavior.[71]

self-reinforcer Any desired or attractive outcome or reward that a person gives to himself or herself for good performance.

SELF-REINFORCEMENT Although managers are often the providers of reinforcement in organizations, sometimes people motivate themselves through self-reinforcement. People can control their own behavior by setting goals for themselves and then reinforcing themselves when they achieve the goals.[72] **Self-reinforcers** are any desired or attractive outcomes or rewards that people can give to themselves for good performance, such as a feeling of accomplishment, going to a movie, having dinner out, or taking time out for a golf game. When members of an organization control their own behavior through self-reinforcement, managers do not need to spend as much time as they ordinarily would trying to motivate and control behavior through the administration of consequences because subordinates are controlling and motivating themselves. In fact, this self-control is often referred to as the *self-management of behavior.*

When employees are highly skilled and are responsible for creating new goods and services, managers typically rely on self-control and self-management of behavior, as is the case at Google.

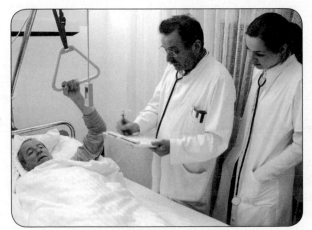

How do you treat that? When medical students enter residency, they learn vicariously by shadowing a full physician on his or her rounds.
©vario images GmbH & Co.KG/Alamy Stock Photo

Employees at Google are given the flexibility and autonomy to experiment, take risks, and sometimes fail as they work on new projects. They are encouraged to learn from their failures and apply what they learn to subsequent projects.[73]

self-efficacy A person's belief about his or her ability to perform a behavior successfully.

SELF-EFFICACY **Self-efficacy** is a person's belief about his or her ability to perform a behavior successfully.[74] Even with all the most attractive consequences or reinforcers hinging on high performance, people are not going to be motivated if they do not think they can actually perform at a high level. Similarly, when people control their own behavior, they are likely to set for themselves difficult goals that will lead to outstanding accomplishments only if they think they can reach those goals. Thus, self-efficacy influences motivation both when managers provide reinforcement and when workers themselves provide it.[75] The greater the self-efficacy, the greater the motivation and performance.

Pay and Motivation

In Chapter 12 we discussed how managers establish a pay level and structure for an organization as a whole. Here we focus on how, once a pay level and structure are in place, managers can use pay to motivate employees to perform at a high level and attain their work goals. Pay is used to motivate entry-level workers, first-line and middle managers, and even top managers such as CEOs. Pay can motivate people to perform behaviors that help an organization achieve its goals, and it can motivate people to join and remain with an organization.

LO13-5 Explain why and how managers can use pay as a major motivation tool.

Each of the theories described in this chapter alludes to the importance of pay and suggests that pay should be based on performance:

- *Expectancy theory:* Instrumentality, the association between performance and outcomes such as pay, must be high for motivation to be high. In addition, pay is an outcome that has high valence for many people.

- *Need theories:* People should be able to satisfy their needs by performing at a high level; pay can be used to satisfy several kinds of needs.

- *Equity theory:* Outcomes such as pay should be distributed in proportion to inputs (including performance levels).

- *Goal-setting theory:* Outcomes such as pay should be linked to the attainment of goals.

- *Learning theories:* The distribution of outcomes, such as pay, should be contingent on the performance of organizationally functional behaviors.

merit pay plan A compensation plan that bases pay on performance.

As these theories suggest, to promote high motivation, managers should base the distribution of pay to organizational members on performance levels so that high performers receive more pay than low performers (other things being equal).[76] This approach also addresses ethical issues related to motivation, as discussed earlier in the chapter in the context of equity theory and in the "Ethics in Action" feature. A compensation plan basing pay on performance is often called a **merit pay plan**.

ETHICS IN ACTION

The Fairness of Merit Pay

A recent attempt by United Airlines to make merit pay more motivating backfired. The company had been setting quarterly goals and paying a bonus of up to $300 per employee if the company met the goals. Managers thought the bonuses were too small to have much impact on employees' total pay and therefore not significant enough as a motivator. (In terms of expectancy theory, they saw the quarterly bonuses as having a low valence.) They decided to roll out a system they believed employees would consider exciting: Bonus spending would be pooled to create major prizes, from $2,000 cash to vacations and fancy cars. Each quarter, there would be a lottery in which several employees would receive one of these prizes, and one employee would receive the grand prize of $100,000.[77]

To the planners' surprise, the employees were not motivated, but upset. They saw the new plan as inequitable. Most employees would work hard to meet the quarterly goals yet receive no bonus (underpayment inequity). A few employees would receive big prizes regardless of how much they did to help the company achieve its goals (possible overpayment inequity). Employees began gathering signatures on a public petition, and management, realizing its mistake, discontinued the planned change.[78]

A more widespread, if less dramatic, example of employees perceiving merit pay as unfair and therefore unmotivating is pay that differs according to the employee's sex, race, or other personal characteristic, rather than his or her contribution to the company. In Britain, employers have been reporting their gender pay gaps to meet government regulations. In comparing salaries, the telecommunications company Sky reported pay gaps between about 5% and 11%, but the difference was more dramatic for merit pay: the gender gap for bonuses was 40%.[79] This identifies an area where the company, to be equitable, will need to investigate its process of setting goals and pay systems to reward performance. For example, are women at Sky being assigned to high-value projects at the same rate as their male counterparts?

In general, an employer should consider basic motivational issues to make merit pay equitable.[80] At a minimum, fairness requires defining the performance measures and goals ahead of time, so employees know what their incentive pay depends on. Also, employees need to see a link between what they do and what they can earn—the problem area with United's bonus lottery.

In tough economic times, when organizations lay off employees and pay levels and benefits of those who are at least able to keep their jobs may be cut while their responsibilities are often increased,[81] managers are often limited in the extent to which they can use merit pay, if at all. Nonetheless, in such times, managers can still try to recognize top performers. Jenny Miller, manager of 170 engineers in the commercial systems engineering department at Rockwell Collins, an aerospace electronics company in Cedar Rapids, Iowa, experienced firsthand the challenge of not being able to recognize top performers with merit pay during tough economic times. Rockwell Collins laid off 8% of its workforce, and the workloads for the engineers Miller managed increased by about 15%. The engineers were working longer hours without receiving any additional pay; there was a salary freeze, so they knew raises were not in store. With a deadline approaching for flight deck software for a customer, she needed some engineers to work over the Thanksgiving holiday and so sent out an email request for volunteers. Approximately 20 employees volunteered. In recognition of their contributions, Miller gave them each a $100 gift card.[82]

A $100 gift card might not seem like much for an employee who is already working long hours to work over the Thanksgiving holiday for no additional pay or time off. However, Steve Nieuwsma, division vice president at Rockwell Collins, indicates that the gift cards at least signaled that managers recognized and appreciated employees' efforts and sought to thank them for it. Not being able to give his employees raises at that time, Nieuwsma also gave gift cards to recognize contributions and top performers in amounts varying between $25 and $500.[83]

Once managers have decided to use a merit pay plan, they face two important choices: whether to base pay on individual, group, or organizational performance and whether to use salary increases or bonuses.

Basing Merit Pay on Individual, Group, or Organizational Performance

Managers can base merit pay on individual, group, or organizational performance. When individual performance (such as the dollar value of merchandise a salesperson sells, the number of loudspeakers a factory worker assembles, or a lawyer's billable hours) can be accurately determined, individual motivation is likely to be highest when pay is based on individual performance.[84] When members of an organization work closely together and individual performance cannot be accurately determined (as in a team of computer programmers developing a single software package), pay cannot be based on individual performance, and a group- or organization-based plan must be used. When the attainment of organizational goals hinges on members' working closely together and cooperating with each other (as in a small construction company that builds custom homes), group- or organization-based plans may be more appropriate than individual-based plans.[85]

It is possible to combine elements of an individual-based plan with a group- or organization-based plan to motivate each individual to perform highly and, at the same time, motivate all individuals to work well together, cooperate with one another, and help one another as needed. Lincoln Electric, a very successful company and a leading manufacturer of welding machines, uses a combination individual- and organization-based plan.[86] Pay is based on individual performance. In addition, each year the size of a bonus fund depends on organizational performance. Money from the bonus fund is distributed to people on the basis of their contributions to the organization, attendance, levels of cooperation, and other indications of performance. Employees of Lincoln Electric are motivated to cooperate and help one another because when the firm as a whole performs well, everybody benefits by having a larger bonus fund. Employees also are motivated to contribute their inputs to the organization because their contributions determine their share of the bonus fund.

Salary Increase or Bonus?

Managers can distribute merit pay to people in the form of a salary increase or a bonus on top of regular salaries. Although the dollar amounts of a salary increase and of a bonus might be identical, bonuses tend to have more motivational impact for at least three reasons. First, salary levels are typically based on performance levels, cost-of-living increases, and so forth from the day people start working in an organization, which means the absolute level of the salary is based largely on factors unrelated to *current* performance. A 5% merit increase in salary, for example, may seem relatively small in comparison to one's total salary. Second, a current salary increase may be affected by other factors in addition to performance, such as cost-of-living increases or across-the-board market adjustments. Third, because organizations rarely reduce salaries, salary levels tend to vary less than performance levels do. Related to this point is the fact that bonuses give managers more flexibility in distributing outcomes. If an organization is doing well, bonuses can be relatively high to reward employees for their contributions. However, unlike salary increases, bonus levels can be reduced when an organization's performance lags. All in all, bonus plans have more motivational impact than salary increases because the amount of the bonus can be directly and exclusively based on performance.[87]

Consistent with the lessons from motivation theories, bonuses can be linked directly to performance and vary from year to year and employee to employee, as at Gradient Corporation, a Cambridge, Massachusetts, environmental consulting firm.[88] Another organization that successfully uses bonuses is Nucor Corporation. Steelworkers at Nucor tend to be much more productive than steelworkers in other companies—probably because they can receive bonuses tied to performance and quality that can range from 130% to 150% of their regular base pay.[89] During the economic downturn in 2007–2009, Nucor struggled, as did many other companies, and bonus pay for steelworkers dropped considerably. However, managers at Nucor avoided having to lay off employees by finding ways to cut costs and having employees work on maintenance activities and safety manuals, along with taking on tasks that used to be performed by independent contractors, such as producing specialty parts and mowing the grass.[90]

In addition to receiving pay raises and bonuses, high-level managers and executives are sometimes granted employee stock options. Employee stock options are financial instruments that entitle the bearer to buy shares of an organization's stock at a certain price during a certain period or under certain conditions.[91] For example, in addition to salaries, stock options are sometimes used to attract high-level managers. The exercise price is the stock price at which the bearer can buy the stock, and the vesting conditions specify when the bearer can actually buy the stock at the exercise price. The option's exercise price is generally set equal to the market price of the stock on the date it is granted, and the vesting conditions might specify

employee stock option A financial instrument that entitles the bearer to buy shares of an organization's stock at a certain price during a certain period or under certain conditions.

that the manager has to have worked at the organization for 12 months or perhaps met some performance target (perhaps an increase in profits) before being able to exercise the option. In technology firms and start-ups, options are sometimes used in a similar fashion for employees at various levels in the organization.[92]

From a motivation standpoint, stock options are used not so much to reward past individual performance but, rather, to motivate employees to work in the future for the good of the company as a whole. This is true because stock options issued at current stock prices have value in the future only if an organization does well and its stock price appreciates; thus, giving employees stock options should encourage them to help the organization improve its performance over time.[93] At technology start-ups and dot-coms, stock options have often motivated potential employees to leave promising jobs in larger companies and work for the start-ups. In the late 1990s and early 2000s, many dot-commers were devastated to learn not only that their stock options were worthless, because their companies went out of business or were doing poorly, but also that they were unemployed. Unfortunately, stock options have also led to unethical behavior; for example, sometimes individuals seek to artificially inflate the value of a company's stock to increase the value of stock options.

Examples of Merit Pay Plans

Managers can choose among several merit pay plans, depending on the work that employees perform and other considerations. Using *piece-rate pay,* an individual-based merit plan, managers base employees' pay on the number of units each employee produces, whether televisions, computer components, or welded auto parts. Managers at Lincoln Electric use piece-rate pay to determine individual pay levels. Advances in information technology have dramatically simplified the administration of piece-rate pay in a variety of industries.

Using *commission pay,* another individual-based merit pay plan, managers base pay on a percentage of sales. Managers at the successful real estate company Re/Max International Inc. use commission pay for their agents, who are paid a percentage of their sales. Some department stores, such as Nordstrom, use commission pay for their salespeople.

Examples of organizational-based merit pay plans include the Scanlon plan and profit sharing. The *Scanlon plan* (developed by Joseph Scanlon, a union leader in a steel and tin plant in the 1920s) focuses on reducing expenses or cutting costs; members of an organization are motivated to propose and implement cost-cutting strategies because a percentage of the cost savings achieved during a specified time is distributed to the employees.[94] Under *profit sharing,* employees receive a share of an organization's profits. Regardless of the specific kind of plan that is used, managers should always strive to link pay to the performance of behaviors that help an organization achieve its goals.

Japanese managers in large corporations have long shunned merit pay plans in favor of plans that reward seniority. However, more and more Japanese companies are adopting merit-based pay due to its motivational benefits; among such companies are Toyota, Hitachi, and Panasonic.[95]

Summary and Review

THE NATURE OF MOTIVATION Motivation encompasses the psychological forces within a person that determine the direction of the person's behavior in an organization, the person's level of effort, and the person's level of persistence in the face of obstacles. Managers strive to motivate people to contribute their inputs to an organization, to focus

LO13-1 these inputs in the direction of high performance, and to ensure that people receive the outcomes they desire when they perform at a high level.

LO13-2 **EXPECTANCY THEORY** According to expectancy theory, managers can promote high levels of motivation in their organizations by taking steps to ensure that expectancy is high (people think that if they try, they can perform at a high level), instrumentality is high (people think that if they perform at a high level, they will receive certain outcomes), and valence is high (people desire these outcomes).

LO13-3 **NEED THEORIES**   Need theories suggest that to motivate their workforces, managers should determine what needs people are trying to satisfy in organizations and then ensure that people receive outcomes that satisfy these needs when they perform at a high level and contribute to organizational effectiveness.

LO13-2 **EQUITY THEORY**   According to equity theory, managers can promote high levels of motivation by ensuring that people perceive that there is equity in the organization or that outcomes are distributed in proportion to inputs. Equity exists when a person perceives that his or her own outcome–input ratio equals the outcome–input ratio of a referent. Inequity motivates people to try to restore equity. Equity theory is a theory of distributive justice. It is most advantageous for distributive, procedural, interpersonal, and informational justice all to be high.

LO13-3 **GOAL-SETTING THEORY**   Goal-setting theory suggests that managers can promote high motivation and performance by ensuring that people are striving to achieve specific, difficult goals. It is important for people to accept the goals, be committed to them, and receive feedback about how they are doing.

LO13-4 **LEARNING THEORIES**   Operant conditioning theory suggests that managers can motivate people to perform highly by using positive reinforcement or negative reinforcement (positive reinforcement being the preferred strategy). Managers can motivate people to avoid performing dysfunctional behaviors by using extinction or punishment. Social learning theory suggests that people can also be motivated by observing how others perform behaviors and receive rewards, by engaging in self-reinforcement, and by having high levels of self-efficacy.

LO13-5 **PAY AND MOTIVATION**   Each of the motivation theories discussed in this chapter alludes to the importance of pay and suggests that pay should be based on performance. Merit pay plans can be individual-, group-, or organization-based and can entail the use of salary increases or bonuses.

Management in Action

Topics for Discussion and Action

Discussion

1. Discuss why two people with similar abilities may have very different expectancies for performing at a high level. [LO13-2]

2. Describe why some people have low instrumentalities even when their managers distribute outcomes based on performance. [LO13-2]

3. Analyze how professors try to promote equity to motivate students. [LO13-2]

4. Describe three techniques or procedures that managers can use to determine whether a goal is difficult. [LO13-3]

5. Discuss why managers should always try to use positive reinforcement instead of negative reinforcement. [LO13-4]

Action

6. Interview three people who have the same kind of job (such as salesperson, waiter/waitress, or teacher), and determine what kinds of needs each is trying to satisfy at work. [LO13-3]

7. Interview a manager in an organization in your community to determine the extent to which the manager takes advantage of vicarious learning to promote high motivation among subordinates. [LO13-3]

Building Management Skills

Diagnosing Motivation [LO13-1, 13-2, 13-3, 13-4]

Think about the ideal job that you would like to obtain after graduation. Describe this job, the kind of manager you would like to report to, and the kind of organization you would be working in. Then answer the following questions:

1. What would be your levels of expectancy and instrumentality on this job? Which outcomes would have high valence for you on this job? What steps would your manager take to influence your levels of expectancy, instrumentality, and valence?

2. Whom would you choose as a referent on this job? What steps would your manager take to make you feel that you were being equitably treated? What would you do if, after a year on the job, you experienced underpayment inequity?

3. What goals would you strive to achieve on this job? Why? What role would your manager play in determining your goals?

4. What needs would you strive to satisfy on this job? Why? What role would your manager play in helping you satisfy these needs?

5. What behaviors would your manager positively reinforce on this job? Why? What positive reinforcers would your manager use?

6. Would there be any vicarious learning on this job? Why or why not?

7. To what extent would you be motivated by self-control on this job? Why?

8. What would be your level of self-efficacy on this job? Why would your self-efficacy be at this level? Should your manager take steps to boost your self-efficacy? If not, why not? If so, what would these steps be?

Managing Ethically [LO13-5]

Sometimes pay is so contingent upon performance that it creates stress for employees. Imagine a salesperson who knows that if sales targets are not met, he or she will not be able to make a house mortgage payment or pay the rent.

Questions

1. Either individually or in a group, think about the ethical implications of closely linking pay to performance.

2. Under what conditions might contingent pay be most stressful, and what steps can managers take to try to help their subordinates perform effectively and not experience excessive amounts of stress?

Small Group Breakout Exercise

Increasing Motivation [LO13-1, 13-2, 13-3, 13-4, 13-5]

Form groups of three or four people, and appoint one member as the spokesperson who will communicate your findings to the class when called on by the instructor. Then discuss the following scenario:

You and your partners own a chain of 15 dry-cleaning stores in a medium-size town. All of you are concerned about a problem in customer service that has surfaced recently. When any one of you spends the day, or even part of the day, in a particular store, clerks seem to provide excellent customer service, spotters make sure all stains are removed from garments, and pressers do a good job of pressing difficult items such as silk blouses. Yet during those same visits, customers complain to you about such things as stains not being removed and items being poorly pressed in some of their previous orders; indeed, several customers have brought garments in to be redone. Customers also sometimes comment on having waited too long for service on previous visits. You and your partners are meeting today to address this problem.

1. Discuss the extent to which you believe that you have a motivation problem in your stores.

2. Given what you have learned in this chapter, design a plan to increase the motivation of clerks to provide prompt service to customers even when they are not being watched by a partner.

3. Design a plan to increase the motivation of spotters to remove as many stains as possible even when they are not being watched by a partner.

4. Design a plan to increase the motivation of pressers to do a top-notch job on all clothes they press, no matter how difficult.

Be the Manager [LO13-1, 13-2, 13-3, 13-4, 13-5]

You supervise a team of marketing analysts who work on different snack products in a large food products company. The marketing analysts have recently received undergraduate degrees in business or liberal arts and have been on the job between one and three years. Their responsibilities include analyzing the market for their respective products, including competitors; tracking current marketing initiatives; and planning future marketing campaigns. They also need to prepare quarterly sales and expense reports for their products and estimated budgets for the next three quarters; to prepare these reports, they need to obtain data from financial and accounting analysts assigned to their products.

When they first started on the job, you took each marketing analyst through the reporting cycle, explaining what needs to be done and how to accomplish it and emphasizing the need for timely reports. Although preparing the reports can be tedious, you think the task is pretty straightforward and easily accomplished if the analysts plan ahead and allocate sufficient time for it. When reporting time approaches, you remind the analysts through email messages and emphasize the need for accurate and timely reports in team meetings.

You believe this element of the analysts' jobs couldn't be more straightforward. However, at the end of each quarter, the majority of the analysts submit their reports a day or two late, and, worse yet, your own supervisor (to whom the reports are eventually given) has indicated that information is often missing and sometimes the reports contain errors. Once you started getting flak from your supervisor about this problem, you decided you had better fix things quickly. You met with the marketing analysts, explained the problem, told them to submit the reports to you a day or two early so you could look them over, and more generally emphasized that they really needed to get their act together. Unfortunately, things have not improved much and you are spending more and more of your own time doing the reports. What are you going to do?

The Quest for Experienced Talent [LO 13-1, 13-2, 13-3]

Christopher Petermann, a partner at PKF O'Connor Davies LLP, has found a valuable source of talent for the accounting and advisory services company: partners of the largest accounting firms who typically are expected to retire by their early 60s. "We don't have mandatory retirement, and the older people we're hiring are vibrant, with expertise in areas that can help us grow—plus they're helping train younger employees," says Petermann, co-director of the New York-based company's foundation practice.

At a time of low unemployment, it's tough for many companies to find and keep the best talent. Competition is especially steep for accountants and consultants with financial and information technology know-how, as increased financial regulations, tax law changes, and the growth of Big Data and global trade spur demand for specialists. Restless veterans of big accounting firms such as KPMG LLP and Deloitte LLP provide a solution for small and midsize business service companies—among them PKF, Marcum, and WithumSmith+Brown.

Mandatory retirement policies were put in place decades ago when life expectancies were shorter and as a way to make room for younger employees to become partners. Today many accountants and other professionals aren't ready to stop working at 60, at least not entirely. Many want part-time or flexible schedules and are willing to take a salary cut.

"These older partners that large firms are ushering out the door are a talent gift to smaller companies," says Ruth Finkelstein, executive director of the Brookdale Center for Healthy Aging at Hunter College, who's studied older workers. "They don't need to be trained. They have experience and contacts that can bring in new business and important knowledge to pass

to younger employees." That includes experience in international business and governance, expertise that small and midsize client companies need and can get from the seniors at lower rates than if they hired big accounting firms.

It's an employment model that companies in many industries could use and benefit from, says Peter Gudmundsson, founder of Dallas-based Hire Maturity LLC, which produces career fairs and runs a job board for what he calls "mature talent." "If you've done tax or audit for decades—or marketing or finance or any business specialty—you have professional networks that are hugely valuable to employers and a willingness to help people coming up the ranks because you're no longer competing for promotions," he says.

Lawrence Baye felt at loose ends when he had to retire in 2015 from a 34-year career at Grant Thornton LLP, where he was a principal. So he was receptive when two years ago a recruiter connected him with PKF, which wanted his expertise in governance, risk, and compliance matters, as well as IT and business operations. "I don't have hobbies and was bored at home—and they welcome veterans here," says Baye, who's working as a consultant at the firm three days a week.

PKF's almost 800 employees range in age from 22 to 82, and many, regardless of how old they are, have flexible schedules aimed at helping them balance work and families. Those at traditional retirement age, such as Baye, can work part-time as consultants.

"I don't want to be promoted, so I'm not clogging the path for younger employees" says Baye, who likes working in smaller teams and informally mentoring younger colleagues. "I tell them what I'm doing and why and to try to envision the

end result they want on an assignment, but I also want them to critique me and do their own original work," he says.

The advice that veterans can offer is especially important to MarcumBP, a Marcum LLP unit that works primarily with clients that do business in or with China. The unit has about 90 employees in the country and about 25 in New York. It employs retirees from big companies, each with extensive knowledge about a particular industry such as health care. The veteran hires are training MarcumBP's Chinese staff, who are mostly in their 20s and 30s and, in many cases, studying to become U.S. certified public accountants.

"We're a small company that's working in an emerging market and can't afford to make a mistake," says Drew Bernstein, MarcumBP's co-managing partner. "The retiring partners we get from big firms are at the top of their game, with expertise that's very hard to obtain—and they're fantastic mentors."

Instead of recruiting from outside, other talent-hungry companies encourage veterans to keep working. New York-based WithumSmith+Brown PC, an accounting and consulting company with about 800 employees ranging in age from their early 20s to 91, requires veterans to step down as partners when they turn 65. But it invites them to become emeritus partners and to keep working as long as they're productive.

"There's a benefit to having five generations in the workplace, because everyone brings something to the table," says Joan Kampo, director of human resources. "It's not about age. It's about keeping talent in this tight labor market. You can have a 22-year-old who's wise beyond his years and someone in his 70s who's motivated and willing to embrace changes."

Questions for Discussion

1. What competitive advantages do these motivated veteran accountants bring to their new employers? Cite several examples.

2. List three specific outcomes received by organizational members who have moved to these smaller accounting firms from senior positions in larger organizations.

3. At which level of Maslow's hierarchy of needs would you place these veteran accountants? Explain your reasoning.

Source: Carol Hymowitz, "The Quest for Experienced Talent," *Bloomberg Businessweek,* April 16, 2018, pp. 46–47. Used with permission of Bloomberg L.P. Copyright © 2017. All rights reserved.

Notes

1. B. Shea, "How to Change a Culture, Detroit Lions Edition," *Crain's Detroit Business,* www.crainsdetroitbusiness.com, November 12, 2017; T. Foster, "Martha Ford Attempts to Tame the Detroit Lions," *Detroit Metro Times,* www.metrotimes.com, September 6, 2017; Johnette Howard, "Why Martha Ford, 90, Has Been Exactly the Owner the Lions Need," *ESPN,* www.espn.com, December 30, 2015; J. Vrentas, "Martha Firestone Ford's Patience Has Run Out," *Sports Illustrated,* www.si.com, December 2, 2015.

2. Shea, "How to Change a Culture"; Foster, "Martha Ford Attempts to Tame"; Howard, "Why Martha Ford, 90, Has Been Exactly the Owner the Lions Need"; Vrentas, "Martha Firestone Ford's Patience."

3. Howard, "Why Martha Ford, 90, Has Been Exactly the Owner the Lions Need."

4. Shea, "How to Change a Culture; Vrentas, "Martha Firestone Ford's Patience"; Howard, "Why Martha Ford, 90, Has Been Exactly the Owner the Lions Need."

5. Vrentas, "Martha Firestone Ford's Patience."

6. Howard, "Why Martha Ford, 90, Has Been Exactly the Owner the Lions Need"; Shea, "How to Change a Culture."

7. Shea, "How to Change a Culture."

8. M.Rothstein, "Lions Officially Name Matt Patricia as Head Coach," *ESPN,* www.espn.com, February 5, 2018; L. Lage, "Lions Fire Coach Jim Caldwell after Missing Playoffs," *Associated Press,* www.apnews.com, January 1, 2018.

9. R. Kanfer, "Motivation Theory and Industrial and Organizational Psychology," in M.D. Dunnette and L.M. Hough, eds., *Handbook of Industrial and Organizational Psychology,* 2nd ed., vol. 1 (Palo Alto, CA: Consulting Psychologists Press, 1990), 75-170.

10. G.P. Latham and M.H. Budworth, "The Study of Work Motivation in the 20th Century," in L.L. Koppes, ed., *Historical Perspectives in Industrial and Organizational Psychology* (Hillsdale, NJ: Erlbaum, 2006).

11. S. Clark, "Finding Daring Jobs for Bored Bankers," *Bloomberg Businessweek,* June 6-12, 2011, 53-54.

12. Clark, "Finding Daring Jobs for Bored Bankers"; "About Us," www.escapethecity.org, accessed April 13, 2018; S. Clark, "Ex-Banker Wants You to Trade Wall Street 'Misery' for Mongolia," *Bloomberg,* www.bloomberg.com, accessed April 13, 2018.

13. "We Create Careers That Matter to You," www.escapethecity.org, accessed April 13, 2018.

14. Clark, "Finding Daring Jobs for Bored Bankers."

15. Ibid.; "The Team—Escape the City," www.escapethecity.org, accessed April 13, 2018.

16. Clark, "Finding Daring Jobs for Bored Bankers."

17. Ibid.

18. "Harry Minter," *LinkedIn,* www.linkedin.com, May 1, 2014.

19. M.C. Bolino and A.C. Klotz, "How to Motivate Employees to Go Beyond Their Jobs," *Harvard Business Review,* https://hbr.org, September 15, 2017.

20. A.M. Grant, "Does Intrinsic Motivation Fuel the Prosocial Fire? Motivational Synergy in Predicting Persistence, Performance, and Productivity," *Journal of Applied Psychology* 93, no. 1 (2008), 48-58.

21. Grant, "Does Intrinsic Motivation Fuel the Prosocial Fire?"; C.D. Batson, "Prosocial Motivation: Is It Ever Truly Altruistic?" in L. Berkowitz, ed., *Advances in Experimental Social Psychology,* vol. 20 (New York: Academic Press, 1987), 65-122.

22. Grant, "Does Intrinsic Motivation Fuel the Prosocial Fire?"; Batson, "Prosocial Motivation."

23. J.P. Campbell and R.D. Pritchard, "Motivation Theory in Industrial and Organizational Psychology," in M.D. Dunnette, ed., *Handbook of Industrial and Organizational Psychology* (Chicago: Rand McNally, 1976), 63-130; T.R. Mitchell, "Expectancy Value Models in Organizational Psychology," in N.T. Feather, ed., *Expectations and Actions: Expectancy Value Models in Psychology* (Hillsdale, NJ: Erlbaum, 1982), 293-312; V.H. Vroom, *Work and Motivation* (New York: Wiley, 1964).

24. N. Shope Griffin, "Personalize Your Management Development," *Harvard Business Review* 8, no. 10 (2003), 113-19.

25. T.A. Stewart, "Just Think: No Permission Needed," *Fortune,* www.fortune.com, January 8, 2001, accessed June 26, 2001.

26. K. Roose, "Best Buy's Secrets for Thriving in the Amazon Age," *The New York Times,* www.nytimes.com, September 18, 2017; J. Wieczner, "Best Buy CEO on How to Lead a Corporate Turnaround (Without Making Employees Hate You)," *Fortune,* http://fortune.com, October 29, 2015; M. Copeland, "Best Buy's Selling Machine," *Business 2.0,* July 2004, 91-102.

27. T.J. Maurer, E.M. Weiss, and F.G. Barbeite, "A Model of Involvement in Work-Related Learning and Development Activity: The Effects of Individual, Situational, Motivational, and Age Variables," *Journal of Applied Psychology* 88, no. 4 (2003), 707-24.

28. D. Pierson, "Why Are Doughnut Boxes Pink? The Answer Could Only Come Out of Southern California," *Los Angeles Times,* www.latimes.com, May 25, 2017; E. Navales, "The Back Story Behind Cambodian-Owned Donut Shops," *Kore Asian Media,* http://kore.am, November 5, 2015; J. Kaufman, "How Cambodians Came to Control California Doughnuts," *The Wall Street Journal,* February 22, 1995, A1, A8.

29. "Training Program Drives Promote-from-Within Philosophy at Car Rental Company," *HR Daily,* https://hrdailyadvisor.blr.com, January 26, 2017.

30. A.H. Maslow, *Motivation and Personality* (New York: Harper & Row, 1954); Campbell and Pritchard, "Motivation Theory in Industrial and Organizational Psychology."

31. Kanfer, "Motivation Theory and Industrial and Organizational Psychology."

32. S. Ronen, "An Underlying Structure of Motivational Need Taxonomies: A Cross-Cultural

Confirmation," in H.C. Triandis, M.D. Dunnette, and L.M. Hough, eds., *Handbook of Industrial and Organizational Psychology,* vol. 4 (Palo Alto, CA: Consulting Psychologists Press, 1994), 241–69.

33. N.J. Adler, *International Dimensions of Organizational Behavior,* 2nd ed. (Boston: P.W.S. Kent, 1991); G. Hofstede, "Motivation, Leadership, and Organization: Do American Theories Apply Abroad?" *Organizational Dynamics,* Summer 1980, 42–63.

34. C.P. Alderfer, "An Empirical Test of a New Theory of Human Needs," *Organizational Behavior and Human Performance* 4 (1969), 142–75; C.P. Alderfer, *Existence, Relatedness, and Growth: Human Needs in Organizational Settings* (New York: Free Press, 1972); Campbell and Pritchard, "Motivation Theory in Industrial and Organizational Psychology."

35. Kanfer, "Motivation Theory and Industrial and Organizational Psychology."

36. F. Herzberg, *Work and the Nature of Man* (Cleveland: World, 1966).

37. N. King, "Clarification and Evaluation of the Two-Factor Theory of Job Satisfaction," *Psychological Bulletin* 74 (1970), 18–31; E.A. Locke, "The Nature and Causes of Job Satisfaction," in M.D. Dunnette, ed., *Handbook of Industrial and Organizational Psychology* (Cleveland: Rand McNally, 1976), 1297–349.

38. D.C. McClelland, *Human Motivation* (Glenview, IL: Scott, Foresman, 1985); D.C. McClelland, "How Motives, Skills, and Values Determine What People Do," *American Psychologist* 40 (1985), 812–25; D.C. McClelland, "Managing Motivation to Expand Human Freedom," *American Psychologist* 33 (1978), 201–10.

39. D.G. Winter, *The Power Motive* (New York: Free Press, 1973).

40. M.J. Stahl, "Achievement, Power, and Managerial Motivation: Selecting Managerial Talent with the Job Choice Exercise," *Personnel Psychology* 36 (1983), 775–89; D.C. McClelland and D.H. Burnham, "Power Is the Great Motivator," *Harvard Business Review* 54 (1976), 100–10.

41. R.J. House, W.D. Spangler, and J. Woycke, "Personality and Charisma in the U.S. Presidency: A Psychological Theory of Leader Effectiveness," *Administrative Science Quarterly* 36 (1991), 364–96.

42. G.H. Hines, "Achievement, Motivation, Occupations, and Labor Turnover in New Zealand," *Journal of Applied Psychology* 58 (1973), 313–17; P.S. Hundal, "A Study of Entrepreneurial Motivation: Comparison of Fast- and Slow-Progressing Small Scale Industrial Entrepreneurs in Punjab, India," *Journal of Applied Psychology* 55 (1971), 317–23.

43. C. Mooney, "Just Looking at Nature Can Help Your Brain Work Better, Study Finds," *The Washington Post,* www.washingtonpost.com, May 26, 2015; K.E. Lee et al., "40-Second Green Roof Views Sustain Attention," *Journal of Environmental Psychology* 42(2015): 182–89.

44. J.S. Adams, "Toward an Understanding of Inequity," *Journal of Abnormal and Social Psychology* 67 (1963), 422–36.

45. Adams, "Toward an Understanding of Inequity"; J. Greenberg, "Approaching Equity and Avoiding Inequity in Groups and Organizations," in J. Greenberg and R.L. Cohen, eds., *Equity and Justice in Social Behavior* (New York: Academic Press, 1982), 389–435; J. Greenberg, "Equity and Workplace Status: A Field Experiment," *Journal of Applied Psychology* 73 (1988), 606–13; R.T. Mowday, "Equity Theory Predictions of Behavior in Organizations," in R.M. Steers and L.W. Porter, eds., *Motivation and Work Behavior* (New York: McGraw-Hill, 1987), 89–110.

46. N. Ismail, "5 Ways Mobility Is Impacting the Workplace Today," *Information Age,* www.information-age.com, October 17, 2017.

47. P. B. Salgado, "Reframing Diversity to Achieve Equity in the Tech Industry," *Phys.org,* https://phys.org, March 15, 2018; Matt Day, "'I Felt So Alone': What Women at Microsoft Face, and Why Many Leave," *Seattle Times,* www.seattletimes.com, April 12, 2018.

48. Day, "'I Felt So Alone.'"

49. D. Kerr, "Lyft Pledges Equal Pay for Women, Men, People of Color," *CNET,* www.cnet.com, March 27, 2018; C. Connley, "Starbucks Has Closed Its Pay Gap in the US; Here Are 4 Other Companies That Have Done the Same," *CNBC,* www.cnbc.com, March 23, 2018.

50. L.J. Skitka and F.J. Crosby, "Trends in the Social Psychological Study of Justice," *Personality and Social Psychology Review* 7 (April 2003), 282–85.

51. J.A. Colquitt, J. Greenberg, and C.P. Zapata-Phelan, "What Is Organizational Justice? A Historical Overview," in J. Greenberg and J.A. Colquitt, eds., *Handbook of Organizational Justice* (Mahwah, NJ: Erlbaum, 2005), 12–45; J.A. Colquitt, "On the Dimensionality of Organizational Justice: A Construct Validation of a Measure," *Journal of Applied Psychology* 86 (March 2001), 386–400.

52. R. Folger and M.A. Konovsky, "Effects of Procedural and Distributive Justice on Reactions to Pay Raise Decisions," *Academy of Management Journal* 32 (1989), 115–30; J. Greenberg, "Organizational Justice: Yesterday, Today, and Tomorrow," *Journal of Management* 16 (1990),

339–432; M.L. Ambrose and A. Arnaud, "Are Procedural Justice and Distributive Justice Conceptually Distinct?" in J. Greenberg and J.A. Colquitt, eds., *Handbook of Organizational Justice* (Mahwah, NJ: Erlbaum, 2005), 60–78.

53. M.L. Ambrose and M. Schminke, "Organization Structure as a Moderator of the Relationship between Procedural Justice, Interactional Justice, Perceived Organizational Support, and Supervisory Trust," *Journal of Applied Psychology* 88 (February 2003), 295–305.

54. J.A. Colquitt, "On the Dimensionality of Organizational Justice: A Construct Validation of a Measure," *Journal of Applied Psychology* 86 (March 2001), 386–400.

55. Greenberg, "Organizational Justice"; E.A. Lind and T. Tyler, *The Social Psychology of Procedural Justice* (New York: Plenum, 1988).

56. R.J. Bies, "The Predicament of Injustice: The Management of Moral Outrage," in L.L. Cummings and B.M. Staw, eds., *Research in Organizational Behavior,* vol. 9 (Greenwich, CT: JAI Press, 1987), 289–319; R.J. Bies and D.L. Shapiro, "Interactional Fairness Judgments: The Influence of Casual Accounts," *Social Justice Research* 1 (1987), 199–218; J. Greenberg, "Looking Fair vs. Being Fair: Managing Impression of Organizational Justice," in B.M. Staw and L.L. Cummings, eds., *Research in Organizational Behavior,* vol. 12 (Greenwich, CT: JAI Press, 1990), 111–57; T.R. Tyler and R. J. Bies, "Beyond Formal Procedures: The Interpersonal Context of Procedural Justice," in J. Carroll, ed., *Advances in Applied Social Psychology: Business Settings* (Hillsdale, NJ: Erlbaum, 1989), 77–98; Colquitt, "On the Dimensionality of Organizational Justice."

57. Colquitt, "On the Dimensionality of Organizational Justice"; J.A. Colquitt and J.C. Shaw, "How Should Organizational Justice Be Measured?" in J. Greenberg and J.A. Colquitt, eds., *Handbook of Organizational Justice* (Mahwah, NJ: Erlbaum, 2005), 115–41.

58. E.A. Locke and G.P. Latham, *A Theory of Goal Setting and Task Performance* (Englewood Cliffs, NJ: Prentice-Hall, 1990).

59. Locke and Latham, *A Theory of Goal Setting and Task Performance;* J.J. Donovan and D.J. Radosevich, "The Moderating Role of Goal Commitment on the Goal Difficulty–Performance Relationship: A Meta-Analytic Review and Critical Analysis," *Journal of Applied Psychology* 83 (1998), 308–15; M.E. Tubbs, "Goal Setting: A Meta Analytic Examination of the Empirical Evidence," *Journal of Applied Psychology* 71 (1986), 474–83.

60. E.A. Locke, K.N. Shaw, L.M. Saari, and G.P. Latham, "Goal Setting and Task Performance: 1969-1980," *Psychological Bulletin* 90 (1981), 125-52.

61. P.C. Earley, T. Connolly, and G. Ekegren, "Goals, Strategy Development, and Task Performance: Some Limits on the Efficacy of Goal Setting," *Journal of Applied Psychology* 74 (1989), 24-33; R. Kanfer and P.L. Ackerman, "Motivation and Cognitive Abilities: An Integrative/Aptitude-Treatment Interaction Approach to Skill Acquisition," *Journal of Applied Psychology* 74 (1989), 657-90.

62. W.C. Hamner, "Reinforcement Theory and Contingency Management in Organizational Settings," in H. Tosi and W.C. Hamner, eds., *Organizational Behavior and Management: A Contingency Approach* (Chicago: St. Clair Press, 1974).

63. B.F. Skinner, *Contingencies of Reinforcement* (New York: Appleton-Century-Crofts, 1969).

64. H.W. Weiss, "Learning Theory and Industrial and Organizational Psychology," in M.D. Dunnette and L.M. Hough, eds., *Handbook of Industrial and Organizational Psychology* (Palo Alto, CA: Consulting Psychologists Press, 1991), 171-221.

65. Hamner, "Reinforcement Theory and Contingency Management."

66. F. Luthans and R. Kreitner, *Organizational Behavior Modification and Beyond* (Glenview, IL: Scott, Foresman, 1985); A.D. Stajkovic and F. Luthans, "A Meta-Analysis of the Effects of Organizational Behavior Modification on Task Performance, 1975-95," *Academy of Management Journal* 40 (1997), 1122-49.

67. A.D. Stajkovic and F. Luthans, "Behavioral Management and Task Performance in Organizations: Conceptual Background, Meta Analysis, and Test of Alternative Models," *Personnel Psychology* 56 (2003), 155-94.

68. Ibid.; F. Luthans and A.D. Stajkovic, "Reinforce for Performance: The Need to Go beyond Pay and Even Rewards," *Academy of Management Executive* 13, no. 2 (1999), 49-56; G. Billikopf and M.V. Norton, "Pay Method Affects Vineyard Pruner Performance," *California Agriculture,* September-October 1992, 12-13.

69. A. Bandura, *Principles of Behavior Modification* (New York: Holt, Rinehart and Winston, 1969); A. Bandura, *Social Learning Theory* (Englewood Cliffs, NJ: Prentice-Hall, 1977); T.R.V. Davis and F. Luthans, "A Social Learning Approach to Organizational Behavior," *Academy of Management Review* 5 (1980), 281-90.

70. A.P. Goldstein and M. Sorcher, *Changing Supervisor Behaviors* (New York: Pergamon Press, 1974); Luthans and Kreitner, *Organizational Behavior Modification and Beyond.*

71. Bandura, *Social Learning Theory;* Davis and Luthans, "A Social Learning Approach to Organizational Behavior"; Luthans and Kreitner, *Organizational Behavior Modification and Beyond.*

72. A. Bandura, "Self-Reinforcement: Theoretical and Methodological Considerations," *Behaviorism* 4 (1976), 135-55.

73. S. Vozza, "Why Employees at Apple and Google Are More Productive," *Fast Company,* www.fastcompany.com, March 13, 2017.

74. A. Bandura, *Self-Efficacy: The Exercise of Control* (New York: W.H. Freeman, 1997); J.B. Vancouver, K.M. More, and R.J. Yoder, "Self-Efficacy and Resource Allocation: Support for a Nonmonotonic, Discontinuous Model," *Journal of Applied Psychology* 93, no. 1 (2008), 35-47.

75. A. Bandura, "Self-Efficacy Mechanism in Human Agency," *American Psychologist* 37 (1982), 122-27; M.E. Gist and T.R. Mitchell, "Self-Efficacy: A Theoretical Analysis of Its Determinants and Malleability," *Academy of Management Review* 17 (1992), 183-211.

76. E.E. Lawler III, *Pay and Organization Development* (Reading, MA: Addison-Wesley, 1981).

77. S. Bomkamp and L. Zumbach, "United Walks Back New Bonus Lottery System That Angered Employees," *Chicago Tribune,* www.chicagotribune.com, March 5, 2018.

78. Ibid.

79. C. Tobitt, "Sky Reports Overall Gender Pay Gap of 11.5% but Figure Much Lower among Broadcasters," *Press Gazette (London),* http://pressgazette.co.uk, March 21, 2018. http://pressgazette.co.uk.

80. S. Waters, "Questioning the Power of Money," *HR Magazine,* November 2017, p. 58.

81. P. Dvorak and S. Thurm, "Slump Prods Firms to Seek New Compact with Workers," *The Wall Street Journal,* October 19, 2009, A1, A18.

82. D. Mattioli, "Rewards for Extra Work Come Cheap in Lean Times," *The Wall Street Journal,* January 4, 2010, B7.

83. Ibid.

84. Lawler, *Pay and Organization Development.*

85. Ibid.

86. "Why Lincoln Electric," www.lincolnelectric.com, accessed April 13, 2018; J.F. Lincoln, *Incentive Management* (Cleveland: Lincoln Electric Company, 1951); R. Zager, "Managing Guaranteed Employment," *Harvard Business Review* 56 (1978), 103-15.

87. Lawler, *Pay and Organization Development.*

88. "Benefits," https://gradientcorp.com, accessed April 13, 2018; M. Gendron, "Gradient Named 'Small Business of Year,'" *Boston Herald,* May 11, 1994, p. 35.

89. "Paying for Performance," www.nucor.com, accessed April 13, 2018; W. Zeller, R.D. Hof, R. Brandt, S. Baker, and D. Greising, "Go-Go Goliaths," *BusinessWeek,* February 13, 1995, 64-70.

90. R.G. Brewer, "7 Fascinating Things You Probably Didn't Know about Nucor Corp.," *Motley Fool,* www.fool.com, August 20, 2017; N. Byrnes, "A Steely Resolve," *BusinessWeek,* April 6, 2009, 54.

91. "Stock Option," *Encarta World English Dictionary,* www.dictionary.msn.com, June 28, 2001; personal interview with Professor Bala Dharan, Jones Graduate School of Business, Rice University, June 28, 2001.

92. Personal interview with Professor Bala Dharan.

93. Ibid.

94. C.D. Fisher, L.F. Schoenfeldt, and J.B. Shaw, *Human Resource Management* (Boston: Houghton Mifflin, 1990); B.E. Graham-Moore and T.L. Ross, *Productivity Gainsharing* (Englewood Cliffs, NJ: Prentice-Hall, 1983); A.J. Geare, "Productivity from Scanlon Type Plans," *Academy of Management Review* 1 (1976), 99-108.

95. K. Inagaki, "Japan Inc Shuns Seniority in Favour of Merit-Based Pay," *Financial Times,* www.ft.com, January 27, 2015.

CHAPTER 14

Leadership

©Joshua Hodge Photography/Getty Images

Learning Objectives

After studying this chapter, you should be able to:

LO14-1 Explain what leadership is, when leaders are effective and ineffective, and the sources of power that enable managers to be effective leaders.

LO14-2 Identify the traits that show the strongest relationship to leadership, the behaviors leaders engage in, and the limitations of the trait and behavior models of leadership.

LO14-3 Explain how contingency models of leadership enhance our understanding of effective leadership and management in organizations.

LO14-4 Describe what transformational leadership is, and explain how managers can engage in it.

LO14-5 Characterize the relationship between gender and leadership, and explain how emotional intelligence may contribute to leadership effectiveness.

Dana-Farber CEOs Provide the Right Leadership

What does effective leadership look like? The answer depends partly on the situation. The two most recent CEOs of the Dana-Farber Cancer Institute provide an example of leadership that matches the organization's needs.

Based in Boston, the Dana-Farber Cancer Institute is affiliated with Harvard Medical School. It offers cancer treatment to adults and children and has research facilities for advancing knowledge of cancer and the best ways to treat it. The organization's vision is "the eradication of cancer, AIDS, and related diseases and the fear that they engender."[1]

When Edward Benz was CEO, he observed that Dana-Farber was excellent at doing research in the usual way, but he also envisioned a new way that would lead to even better results. The usual practice for a research institution is to bring in top scientists and let them pursue their passions. As long as they can win grants and get results published in prestigious journals, this research advances knowledge and makes the institute a desirable place for scientists to work. This approach was generating a lot of good research at Dana-Farber, but the research was not always related to the institution's mission. Also, new knowledge about cancer was showing that cancer is not a single illness but takes many forms, and finding the best treatments increasingly requires a multidisciplinary approach. Consequently, the practice of funding research by individual scientists with narrow specialties was creating a competition for resources when the organization would benefit more from collaboration across different medical fields.[2]

Benz worked with the institute's chief scientific officer, Barrett Rollins, to transform Dana-Farber into an organization built on collaboration. They knew they would need the support of the top scientists, whose knowledge and reputation gave them significant power. Scientists would be reluctant to give that up. Benz brought them together to develop a research strategy for the institution as a whole. The scientists reviewed cancer research to identify 10 areas with the most potential to advance cancer treatment. Then the institute began creating what it calls Integrative Research Centers to oversee research in these areas. While individual labs would continue their work, scientists could take positions running the research centers, which would receive significant additional funding. In exchange, the centers required a business plan with financial as well as scientific objectives. The job of managing a center offers great visibility and potential to contribute important scientific advances, but the business aspects of the job were unfamiliar to most of the scientists. Rollins therefore held frequent one-on-one meetings to help scientists learn their new roles.[3]

Laurie Glimcher, CEO of the Dana-Farber Cancer Institute, is an effective leader who empowers employees to do their best while making sure the organization stays at the forefront of innovation in cancer research.
©Michael Blanchard/Metro Corp

As the collaborative programs began delivering breakthroughs, they increasingly attracted new talent and more funding. The projects hired scientists drawn to the interdisciplinary work. The organization's culture began shifting to one that highly values collaboration.[4]

Following this transformation, Benz retired as chief executive, and the institution brought in a respected researcher and medical school dean, Laurie Glimcher, to serve as CEO. By hiring a noted physician and immunologist, Dana-Farber makes the leader someone who understands and is respected by the professionals who work there. She does not need to transform the organization, as Benz did, but she must keep it moving forward. Glimcher has empowered employees and maintained the drive for innovation and collaboration. She does not hesitate to hire enough staff to enable researchers to balance work and family needs, and she is assertive about ensuring that women are represented. One of her female appointees is the institute's first chief innovation officer, who brings together scientists, clinicians, and hospital administrators to apply information technology to improving patient care.[5]

Overview

Laurie Glimcher and Edward Benz both exemplify the many facets of effective leadership. In Chapter 1 we explained that one of the four primary tasks of managers is leading. Thus, it should come as no surprise that leadership is a key ingredient in effective management. When leaders are effective, their subordinates or followers are highly motivated, committed, and high-performing. When leaders are ineffective, chances are good that their subordinates do not perform up to their capabilities, are demotivated, and may be dissatisfied as well. Laurie Glimcher is a leader at the top of an organization, but leadership is an important ingredient for managerial success at all levels of organizations: top management, middle management, and first-line management. Moreover, leadership is a key ingredient of managerial success for organizations large and small.

In this chapter we describe what leadership is and examine the major leadership models that shed light on the factors that contribute to a manager being an effective leader. We look at trait and behavior models, which focus on what leaders are like and what they do, and contingency models—Fiedler's contingency model, path–goal theory, and the leader substitutes model—each of which takes into account the complexity surrounding leadership and the role of the situation in leader effectiveness. We also describe how managers can use transformational leadership to dramatically affect their organizations. By the end of this chapter, you will appreciate the many factors and issues that managers face in their quest to be effective leaders.

LO14-1 Explain what leadership is, when leaders are effective and ineffective, and the sources of power that enable managers to be effective leaders.

The Nature of Leadership

Leadership is the process by which a person exerts influence over other people and inspires, motivates, and directs their activities to help achieve group or organizational goals.[6] The person who exerts such influence is a **leader**. When leaders are effective, the influence they exert over others helps a group or an organization achieve its performance goals. When leaders are ineffective, their influence does not contribute to, and often detracts from, goal attainment. As "A Manager's Challenge" makes clear, both Dana-Farber CEOs took multiple steps to inspire and motivate employees at all levels of the medical facility so they can help the organization achieve its goals.

Beyond facilitating the attainment of performance goals, effective leadership increases an organization's ability to meet all the contemporary challenges discussed throughout this book, including the need to obtain a competitive advantage, the need to foster ethical behavior, and the need to manage a diverse workforce fairly and equitably. Leaders who exert influence over organizational members to help meet these goals increase their organizations' chances of success.

leadership The process by which an individual exerts influence over other people and inspires, motivates, and directs their activities to help achieve group or organizational goals.

leader An individual who is able to exert influence over other people to help achieve group or organizational goals.

In considering the nature of leadership, we first look at leadership styles and how they affect managerial tasks and at the influence of culture on leadership styles. We then focus on the key to leadership, *power,* which can come from a variety of sources. Finally, we consider the contemporary dynamic of empowerment and how it relates to effective leadership.

Personal Leadership Style and Managerial Tasks

A manager's *personal leadership style*—that is, the specific ways in which a manager chooses to influence other people—shapes how that manager approaches planning, organizing, and controlling (the other principal tasks of managing). Consider Laurie Glimcher's personal leadership style as described in "A Manager's Challenge." She empowers employees, emphasizes doing what's best for patients, and fosters an environment for collaboration among the organization's varied medical specialties.

Managers at all levels and in all kinds of organizations have their own personal leadership styles, which determine not only how they lead their subordinates, but also how they perform the other management tasks. Michael Kraus, owner and manager of a dry cleaning store in the northeastern United States, for example, takes a hands-on approach to leadership. He has the sole authority for determining work schedules and job assignments for the 15 employees in his store (an organizing task), makes all important decisions by himself (a planning task), and closely monitors his employees' performance and rewards top performers with pay increases (a control task). Kraus's personal leadership style is effective in his organization. His employees generally are motivated, perform highly, and are satisfied—and his store is highly profitable.

Developing an effective personal leadership style often is a challenge for managers at all levels in an organization. This challenge is often exacerbated when times are tough, due, for example, to an economic downturn or a decline in customer demand. The recession in the late 2000s provided many managers with just such a challenge.

Although leading is one of the four principal tasks of managing, a distinction is often made between managers and leaders. When this distinction is made, managers are thought of as those organizational members who establish and implement procedures and processes to ensure smooth functioning and are accountable for goal accomplishment.[7] Leaders look to the future, chart the course for the organization, and attract, retain, motivate, inspire, and develop relationships with employees based on trust and mutual respect. They also provide meaning and purpose, seek innovation rather than stability, and impassion employees to work together to achieve the leaders' vision.[8]

Servant Leadership

As part of their personal leadership style, some leaders strive to serve others. Robert Greenleaf—who was director of management research at AT&T and upon his retirement embarked on a second career focused on writing, speaking, and consulting—came up with the term *servant leadership* to describe these leaders.[9] **Servant leaders**, above all else, have a strong desire to work for the benefit of others. Servant leaders share power with followers and strive to ensure that followers' most important needs are met, that they are able to develop as individuals, that their well-being is enhanced, and that attention is paid to those who are least well-off in a society.[10] Servant leadership is unique as a leadership approach because the leader views his or her role more as a motivator and listener, someone who empowers followers to act as collaborators and innovators within the organization.[11] Greenleaf founded a nonprofit organization called the Greenleaf Center for Servant Leadership (formerly called the Center for Applied Ethics) to foster leadership focused on service to others, power sharing, and a sense of community between organizations and their multiple stakeholders.[12] Some entrepreneurs strive to incorporate servant leadership into their personal leadership styles, as profiled in the accompanying "Ethics in Action" feature.

servant leader A leader who has a strong desire to serve and work for the benefit of others.

Servant Leadership at Zingerman's

Ari Weinzweig and Paul Saginaw founded Zingerman's Delicatessen in Ann Arbor, Michigan, in 1982.[13] Food lovers at heart, Weinzweig and Saginaw delighted in finding both traditional and exotic foods from around the world; making delicious sandwiches to order; and having extensive selections of food items ranging from olives, oils, and vinegars to cheeses, smoked fish, and salami. As their business grew, and to maintain an intimate atmosphere with excellent customer service, Weinzweig and Saginaw expanded from their original deli into a community of related businesses called Zingerman's Community of Businesses. In addition to the original deli, Zingerman's Community of Businesses now includes a mail-order business, a bakery, a catering business, a creamery, a restaurant, a wholesale coffee business, and a training business and has combined annual sales of around $58 million.[14] From the start, Weinzweig and Saginaw have been devoted to excellent customer service, great food, and a commitment to people and community.[15]

As part of their commitment to people and community, Weinzweig and Saginaw have incorporated servant leadership into their personal leadership styles. As their business has grown and prospered, they have realized that increasing success means greater responsibility to serve others. They strive to treat their employees as well as they treat their customers and give their employees opportunities for growth and development on the job. They have also realized that when their own needs or desires differ from what is best for their company, they should do what is best for the company.[16]

To this day, the cofounders encourage their employees to let them know how they can help them and what they can do for them. And given Zingerman's culture of mutual respect and trust, employees do not hesitate to communicate how their leaders can serve them in many and varied ways. For example, when Weinzweig visits the Zingerman's Roadhouse restaurant and the staff is very busy, they may ask him to

Paul Saginaw (left) and Ari Weinzweig have incorporated servant leadership into their personal leadership styles at Zingerman's.

©Courtesy of Zingerman's Community of Businesses

help out by serving customers or cleaning off tables. As he indicates, "People give me assignments all the time. Sometimes I'm the note-taker. Sometimes I'm the cleaner-upper. . . . Sometimes I'm on my hands and knees wiping up what people spilled."[17]

Weinzweig and Saginaw also have a strong sense of commitment to serving the local community; Zingerman's founded the nonprofit organization Food Gatherers to eliminate hunger and distribute food to the needy, and Food Gatherers is now an independent nonprofit responsible for the Washtenaw County Food Bank, with over 7,000 volunteers and a 30-member staff.[18] On Zingerman's 20th anniversary, 13 non-profit community organizations in Ann Arbor erected a plaque next to Zingerman's Delicatessen with a dedication that read "Thank you for feeding, sheltering, educating, uplifting, and inspiring an entire community."[19] Clearly, for Weinzweig and Saginaw, leadership entails being of service to others.[20]

Leadership Styles across Cultures

Some evidence suggests that leadership styles vary not only among individuals, but also among countries or cultures. Some research indicates that European managers tend to be more humanistic, or people-oriented, than both Japanese and American managers. The collectivistic culture in Japan places prime emphasis on the group rather than the individual, so the importance of individuals' own personalities, needs, and desires is minimized. Organizations in the United States tend to be very profit-oriented and thus tend to downplay the importance of individual employees' needs and desires. Many countries in Europe have a more individualistic perspective than Japan and a more humanistic perspective than the United States, and this may result in some European managers' being more people-oriented than their Japanese or American counterparts. European managers, for example, tend to be reluctant to lay off employees, and when a layoff is absolutely necessary, they take careful steps to make it as painless as possible.[21]

Another cross-cultural difference occurs in time horizons. While managers in any one country often differ in their time horizons, there are also national differences. For example, U.S. organizations tend to have a short-term profit orientation; thus, U.S. managers' personal leadership styles emphasize short-term performance. Japanese organizations tend to have a long-term growth orientation, so Japanese managers' personal leadership styles emphasize long-term performance. Justus Mische, a personnel manager at the European organization Hoechst, suggested that "Europe, at least the big international firms in Europe, have a philosophy between the Japanese, long term, and the United States, short term."[22] Research on these and other global aspects of leadership is ongoing; as it continues, more cultural differences in managers' personal leadership styles may be discovered.

Power: The Key to Leadership

No matter what one's leadership style, a key component of effective leadership is found in the *power* the leader has to affect other people's behavior and to get them to act in certain ways.[23] There are several types of power: legitimate, reward, coercive, expert, and referent power (see Figure 14.1).[24] Effective leaders take steps to ensure that they have sufficient levels of each type and that they use their power in beneficial ways.

legitimate power The authority that a manager has by virtue of his or her position in an organization's hierarchy.

LEGITIMATE POWER   Legitimate power is the authority a manager has by virtue of his or her position in an organization's hierarchy. Personal leadership style often influences how a manager exercises legitimate power. Take the case of Carol Loray, who is a first-line manager in a greeting card company and leads a group of 15 artists and designers. Loray has the legitimate power to hire new employees, assign projects to the artists and designers, monitor their work, and appraise their performance. She uses this power effectively. She always makes sure her project assignments match the interests of her subordinates as much as possible so they will enjoy their work. She monitors their work to make sure they are on track but does not engage

Figure 14.1

Sources of Managerial Power

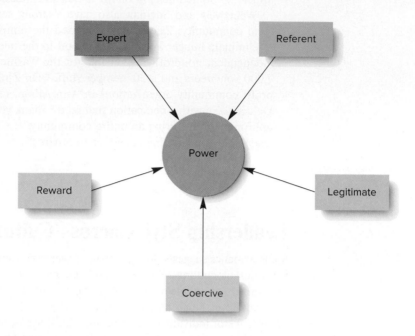

in close supervision, which can hamper creativity. She makes sure her performance appraisals are developmental, providing concrete advice for areas where improvements could be made. Recently, Loray negotiated with her manager to increase her legitimate power so she can now initiate and develop proposals for new card lines.

reward power The ability of a manager to give or withhold tangible and intangible rewards.

REWARD POWER   Reward power is the ability of a manager to give or withhold tangible rewards (pay raises, bonuses, choice job assignments) and intangible rewards (verbal praise, a pat on the back, respect). As you learned in Chapter 13, members of an organization are motivated to perform at a high level by a variety of rewards. Being able to give or withhold rewards based on performance is a major source of power, which allows managers to have a highly motivated workforce. Managers of salespeople in retail organizations, like Neiman Marcus, Nordstrom, and Macy's,[25] and in car dealerships such as Mazda, Ford, and Volvo often use their reward power to motivate their subordinates. Subordinates in organizations such as these often receive commissions on whatever they sell and rewards for the quality of their customer service, which motivate them to do the best they can.

Effective managers use their reward power to show appreciation for subordinates' good work and efforts. Ineffective managers use rewards in a more controlling manner (wielding the "stick" instead of offering the "carrot") that signals to subordinates that the manager has the upper hand. Managers also can take steps to increase their reward power. Carol Loray had the legitimate power to appraise her subordinates' performance, but she lacked the reward power to distribute raises and end-of-year bonuses until she discussed with her own manager why this would be a valuable motivational tool for her to use. Loray now receives a pool of money each year for salary increases and bonuses and has the reward power to distribute them as she sees fit.

coercive power The ability of a manager to punish others.

COERCIVE POWER   Coercive power is the ability of a manager to punish others. Punishment can range from verbal reprimands to reductions in pay or working hours to actual dismissal. In the previous chapter we discussed how punishment can have negative side effects, such as resentment and retaliation, and should be used only when necessary (for example, to curtail a dangerous behavior). Managers who rely heavily on coercive power tend to be ineffective as leaders and sometimes even get fired themselves. William J. Fife is one example; he was fired from his position as CEO of Giddings and Lewis Inc., a manufacturer of factory equipment, because of his overreliance on coercive power. In meetings Fife often verbally criticized,

The Chrysler Jefferson North Assembly plant in Detroit. Empowered employees make some decisions that managers or other leaders used to make.
©Paul Sancya/AP Images

attacked, and embarrassed top managers. Realizing how destructive Fife's use of punishment was for them and the company, these managers complained to the board of directors, who, after careful consideration of the issues, asked Fife to resign.[26]

Excessive use of coercive power seldom produces high performance and is questionable ethically. Sometimes it amounts to a form of mental abuse, robbing workers of their dignity and causing excessive levels of stress. Overuse of coercive power can even result in dangerous working conditions. Better results and, importantly, an ethical workplace that respects employee dignity can be obtained by using reward power.

EXPERT POWER   Expert power is based on the special knowledge, skills, and expertise that a leader possesses. The nature of expert power varies, depending on the leader's level in the hierarchy. First-level and middle managers often have technical expertise relevant to the tasks their subordinates perform. Their expert power gives them considerable influence over subordinates. Carol Loray has expert power: She is an artist herself and has drawn and designed some of her company's top-selling greeting cards. The two Dana-Farber CEOs highlighted in "A Manager's Challenge" have expert power from their knowledge and expertise in the health care industry, acquired over many years.

expert power Power that is based on the special knowledge, skills, and expertise that a leader possesses.

Some top managers derive expert power from their technical expertise. Other top-level managers lack technical expertise and derive their expert power from their abilities as decision makers, planners, and strategists. Jack Welch, the former leader and CEO of General Electric, summed it up this way: "The basic thing that we at the top of the company know is that we don't know the business. What we have, I hope, is the ability to allocate resources, people, and dollars."[27]

Effective leaders take steps to ensure that they have an adequate amount of expert power to perform their leadership roles. They may obtain additional training or education in their fields, make sure they keep up with the latest developments and changes in technology, stay abreast of changes in their fields through involvement in professional associations, and read widely to be aware of momentous changes in the organization's task and general environments. Expert power tends to be best used in a guiding or coaching manner rather than in an arrogant, high-handed way.

referent power Power that comes from subordinates' and coworkers' respect, admiration, and loyalty.

REFERENT POWER   Referent power is more informal than the other kinds of power. Referent power is a function of the personal characteristics of a leader; it is the power that comes from subordinates' and coworkers' respect, admiration, and loyalty. Leaders who are likable and whom subordinates wish to use as a role model are especially likely to possess referent power.

In addition to being a valuable asset for top managers, referent power can help first-line and middle managers be effective leaders as well. Sally Carruthers, for example, is the first-level manager of a group of secretaries in the finance department of a large state university. Carruthers's secretaries are known to be among the best in the university. Much of their willingness to go above and beyond the call of duty has been attributed to Carruthers's warm and caring nature, which makes each of them feel important and valued. Managers can take steps to increase their referent power, such as taking time to get to know their subordinates and showing interest in and concern for them.

Empowerment: An Ingredient in Modern Management

empowerment The expansion of employees' knowledge, tasks, and decision-making responsibilities.

More and more managers today are incorporating into their personal leadership styles an aspect that at first glance seems to be the opposite of being a leader. In Chapter 1 we described how empowerment—the process of giving employees at all levels the authority to make decisions, be responsible for their outcomes, improve quality, and cut costs—is becoming increasingly popular in organizations. When leaders empower their subordinates, the subordinates typically take over some responsibilities and authority that used to reside with the leader or manager, such as the right to reject parts that do not meet quality standards, the right to check one's own work, and the right to schedule work activities. Empowered subordinates are given the power to make some decisions that their leaders or supervisors used to make.

Empowerment might seem to be the opposite of effective leadership because managers are allowing subordinates to take a more active role in leading themselves. In actuality, however, empowerment can contribute to effective leadership for several reasons:

- Empowerment increases a manager's ability to get things done because the manager has the support and help of subordinates who may have special knowledge of work tasks.

- Empowerment often increases workers' involvement, motivation, and commitment; and this helps ensure that they are working toward organizational goals.

- Empowerment gives managers more time to concentrate on their pressing concerns because they spend less time on day-to-day supervision.

Effective managers, like Dana-Farber's Laurie Glimcher, realize the benefits of empowerment. The personal leadership style of managers who empower subordinates often entails developing subordinates' ability to make good decisions as well as being their guide, coach, and source of inspiration. Empowerment is a popular trend in the United States and is a part of servant leadership. Empowerment is also taking off around the world.[28] For instance, companies in South Korea (such as Samsung and Hyundai), in which decision making typically was centralized with the founding families, are now empowering managers at lower levels to make decisions.[29]

Trait and Behavior Models of Leadership

Leading is such an important process in all organizations—nonprofit organizations, government agencies, and schools, as well as for-profit corporations—that it has been researched for decades. Early approaches to leadership, called the *trait model* and the *behavior model*, sought to determine what effective leaders are like as people and what they do that makes them so effective.

The Trait Model

LO14-2 Identify the traits that show the strongest relationship to leadership, the behaviors leaders engage in, and the limitations of the trait and behavior models of leadership.

The trait model of leadership focused on identifying the personal characteristics that cause effective leadership. Researchers thought effective leaders must have certain personal qualities that set them apart from ineffective leaders and from people who never become leaders. Decades of research (beginning in the 1930s) and hundreds of studies indicate that certain personal characteristics do appear to be associated with effective leadership. (See Table 14.1 for a list of these.[30]) Notice that although this model is called the "trait" model, some of the personal characteristics that it identifies are not personality traits per se but, rather, are concerned with a leader's skills, abilities, knowledge, and expertise. As "A Manager's Challenge" shows, Dana-Farber's Laurie Glimcher appears to possess many of these characteristics (such as intelligence, knowledge and expertise, self-confidence, high energy, and integrity and honesty). Leaders who do not possess these traits may be ineffective.

Traits alone are not the key to understanding leader effectiveness, however. Some effective leaders do not possess all these traits, and some leaders who possess them are not effective in their leadership roles. This lack of a consistent relationship between leader traits and leader effectiveness led researchers to shift their attention away from traits and to search for new explanations for effective leadership. Rather than focusing on what leaders are like (the traits they possess), researchers began looking at what effective leaders actually do—in other words, at the behaviors that allow effective leaders to influence their subordinates to achieve group and organizational goals.

Table 14.1

Traits Related to Effective Leadership

Trait	Description
Intelligence	Helps managers understand complex issues and solve problems.
Knowledge and expertise	Help managers make good decisions and discover ways to increase efficiency and effectiveness.
Dominance	Helps managers influence their subordinates to achieve organizational goals.
Self-confidence	Contributes to managers' effectively influencing subordinates and persisting when faced with obstacles or difficulties.
High energy	Helps managers deal with the many demands they face.
Tolerance for stress	Helps managers deal with uncertainty and make difficult decisions.
Integrity and honesty	Help managers behave ethically and earn their subordinates' trust and confidence.
Maturity	Helps managers avoid acting selfishly, control their feelings, and admit when they have made a mistake.

The Behavior Model

After extensive study in the 1940s and 1950s, researchers at The Ohio State University identified two basic kinds of leader behaviors that many leaders in the United States, Germany, and other countries engaged in to influence their subordinates: *consideration* and *initiating structure*.[31]

consideration Behavior indicating that a manager trusts, respects, and cares about subordinates.

CONSIDERATION Leaders engage in **consideration** when they show their subordinates that they trust, respect, and care about them. Managers who truly look out for the well-being of their subordinates, and do what they can to help subordinates feel good and enjoy their work, perform consideration behaviors.

At Costco Wholesale Corporation, cofounder Jim Senegal believes that consideration not only is an ethical imperative, but also makes good business sense,[32] as indicated in the accompanying "Management Insight" feature.

MANAGEMENT INSIGHT

Consideration at Costco

Managers at Costco, including cofounder Jim Senegal and president, CEO, and director Craig Jelinek, believe consideration is so important that one of the principles in Costco's code of ethics is "Take Care of Our Employees."[33] Costco Wholesale Corporation is the third largest retailer and the top warehouse retailer in the United States.[34] Wages at Costco average $17 per hour—over 40% higher than the average hourly wage at Walmart, Costco's major competitor.[35] In March 2016, Costco announced that it was going to raise the minimum wage it pays workers to at least $13–$13.50 per hour. The company also announced that it was going to raise the highest hourly pay rate of $22.50 per hour by around 2.5%.[36] Costco pays the majority of health insurance costs for its employees (employees pay around 8% of health insurance costs compared

Loyal Costco customers like these know that their bargains don't come at the expense of employees' paychecks and benefits.
©Tim Boyle/Getty Images

to an industry average of around 25%), and part-time employees receive health insurance after they have been with the company six months. Overall, about 85% of Costco employees are covered by health insurance, compared with fewer than 45% of employees at Target and Walmart.[37]

Jim Senegal and Craig Jelinek believe that caring about the well-being of employees is a win–win proposition because Costco's employees are satisfied, committed, loyal, and motivated. Additionally, turnover and employee theft rates at Costco are much lower than industry averages.[38] In the retail industry, turnover tends to be high and costly because for every employee who quits, a new hire needs to be recruited, tested, interviewed, and trained. Even though pay and benefits are higher at Costco than at rival Walmart, Costco actually has lower labor costs as a percentage of sales and higher sales per square foot of store space than Walmart.[39]

Additionally, treating employees well helps build customer loyalty at Costco. Surely customers enjoy the bargains and low prices that come from shopping in a warehouse store, the relatively high quality of the goods Costco stocks, and Costco's policy of not marking up prices by more than 14–15% (relatively low markups for retail) even if the goods would sell with higher markups. However, customers are also loyal to Costco because they know the company treats its employees well and their bargains are not coming at the expense of employees' paychecks and benefits.[40]

Costco started out as a single warehouse store in Seattle, Washington, in 1983. Now the company has 749 stores (including stores in Puerto Rico, South Korea, Taiwan, Japan, Australia, Mexico, Canada, and Britain) and tens of millions of members who pay an annual fee to shop at Costco stores.[41] Costco's growth and financial performance are enviable.[42] For example, net sales for the 2017 fiscal year were $126 billion.[43] Clearly, consideration has paid off for Costco and for its employees.

True to caring for the well-being of employees, Costco did not lay off any employees during the recession in the late 2000s.[44] However, some female employees filed a class action lawsuit alleging gender discrimination at Costco.[45] The lawsuit started when Shirley Ellis filed a discrimination complaint and a later lawsuit in the early 2000s.[46] In December 2013 the lawsuit was tentatively settled for $8 million to compensate women who were inappropriately blocked from promotions to positions of assistant general manager and general manager.[47] The settlement also entails Costco having its promotion procedures for assistant general managers and general managers reviewed by an industrial organizational psychologist. Additionally, Costco will post assistant general manager openings and have a system for employees to indicate their interest in general manager positions. In terms of the settlement, Ellis indicated, "I believe this to be a fair settlement to both parties. . . . Even though this process has taken much longer than anticipated initially, I'm encouraged by Costco's efforts to welcome women and all they have to offer in the ranks of GM and AGM companywide."[48]

initiating structure Behavior that managers engage in to ensure that work gets done, subordinates perform their jobs acceptably, and the organization is efficient and effective.

INITIATING STRUCTURE   Leaders engage in **initiating structure** when they take steps to make sure that work gets done, subordinates perform their jobs acceptably, and the organization is efficient and effective. Assigning tasks to individuals or work groups, letting subordinates know what is expected of them, deciding how work should be done, making schedules, encouraging adherence to rules and regulations, and motivating subordinates to do a good job are all examples of initiating structure.[49]

Michael Teckel, the manager of an upscale store selling imported men's and women's shoes in a midwestern city, engages in initiating structure when he establishes weekly work, lunch, and break schedules to ensure that the store has enough salespeople on the floor. Teckel also initiates structure when he discusses the latest shoe designs with his subordinates so they are knowledgeable with customers, when he encourages adherence to the store's refund and exchange policies, and when he encourages his staff to provide high-quality customer service and to avoid a hard-sell approach.

Initiating structure and consideration are independent leader behaviors. Leaders can be high on both, low on both, or high on one and low on the other. Many effective leaders, like Laurie Glimcher of Dana-Farber Cancer Institute, engage in both of these behaviors.

Leadership researchers have identified leader behaviors similar to consideration and initiating structure. Researchers at the University of Michigan, for example, identified two categories of leadership behaviors, *employee-centered behaviors* and *job-oriented behaviors,* that correspond roughly to consideration and initiating structure, respectively.[50] Models of leadership popular with consultants also tend to zero in on these two kinds of behaviors. For example, Robert Blake and Jane Mouton's Managerial Grid focuses on *concern for people* (similar to consideration) and *concern for production* (similar to initiating structure). Blake and Mouton advise that effective leadership often requires both a high level of concern for people and a high level of concern for production.[51] As another example, Paul Hersey and Kenneth Blanchard's model focuses on *supportive behaviors* (similar to consideration) and *task-oriented behaviors* (similar to initiating structure). According to Hersey and Blanchard, leaders need to consider the nature of their subordinates when trying to determine the extent to which they should perform these two behaviors.[52]

You might expect that effective leaders and managers would perform both kinds of behaviors, but research has found that this is not necessarily the case. The relationship between performance of consideration and initiating-structure behaviors and leader effectiveness is not clear-cut. Some leaders are effective even when they do not perform consideration or initiating-structure behaviors, and some leaders are ineffective even when they perform both kinds of behaviors. Like the trait model of leadership, the behavior model alone cannot explain leader effectiveness. Realizing this, researchers began building more complicated models of leadership, focused not only on the leader and what he or she does, but also on the situation or context in which leadership occurs.

Contingency Models of Leadership

LO14-3 Explain how contingency models of leadership enhance our understanding of effective leadership and management in organizations.

Simply possessing certain traits or performing certain behaviors does not ensure that a manager will be an effective leader in all situations calling for leadership. Some managers who seem to possess the right traits and perform the right behaviors turn out to be ineffective leaders. Managers lead in a wide variety of situations and organizations and have various kinds of subordinates performing diverse tasks in a multiplicity of environmental contexts. Given the wide variety of situations in which leadership occurs, what makes a manager an effective leader in one situation (such as certain traits or behaviors) is not necessarily what that manager needs to be equally effective in a different situation. An effective army general might not be an effective university president; an effective restaurant manager might not be an effective clothing store manager; an effective football team coach might not be an effective fitness center manager; an effective first-line manager in a manufacturing company might not be an effective middle manager. The traits or behaviors that may contribute to a manager's being an effective leader in one situation might actually result in the same manager being an ineffective leader in another situation.

Contingency models of leadership take into account the situation, or context, within which leadership occurs. According to contingency models, whether or not a manager is an effective leader is the result of the interplay among what the manager is like, what he or she does, and the situation in which leadership takes place. Contingency models propose that whether a leader who possesses certain traits or performs certain behaviors is effective depends on, or is contingent on, the situation, or context. In this section we discuss three prominent contingency models developed to shed light on what makes managers effective leaders: Fred Fiedler's contingency model, Robert House's path–goal theory, and the leader substitutes model. As you will see, these leadership models are complementary; each focuses on a somewhat different aspect of effective leadership in organizations.

Fiedler's Contingency Model

Fred E. Fiedler was among the first leadership researchers to acknowledge that effective leadership is contingent on, or depends on, the characteristics of the leader *and* of the situation. Fiedler's contingency model helps explain why a manager may be an effective leader in one situation and ineffective in another; it also suggests which kinds of managers are likely to be most effective in which situations.[53]

LEADER STYLE   As with the trait approach, Fiedler hypothesized that personal characteristics can influence leader effectiveness. He used the term *leader style* to refer to a manager's characteristic approach to leadership and identified two basic leader styles: *relationship-oriented* and *task-oriented*. All managers can be described as having one of these styles.

relationship-oriented leaders Leaders whose primary concern is to develop good relationships with their subordinates and to be liked by them.

Relationship-oriented leaders are primarily concerned with developing good relationships with their subordinates and being liked by them. Relationship-oriented managers focus on having high-quality interpersonal relationships with subordinates. This does not mean, however, that the job does not get done when such leaders are at the helm. But it does mean that the quality of interpersonal relationships with subordinates is a prime concern for relationship-oriented leaders.

Task-oriented leaders are primarily concerned with ensuring that subordinates perform at a high level and focus on task accomplishment. While task-oriented leaders also may be concerned about having good interpersonal relationships with their subordinates, task accomplishment is their prime concern.

task-oriented leaders Leaders whose primary concern is to ensure that subordinates perform at a high level.

In his research, Fiedler measured leader style by asking leaders to rate the coworker with whom they have had the most difficulty working (called the least preferred coworker, or LPC) on a number of dimensions, such as whether the person is boring or interesting, gloomy or cheerful, enthusiastic or unenthusiastic, cooperative or uncooperative. Relationship-oriented leaders tend to describe the LPC in relatively positive terms; their concern for good relationships leads them to think well of others. Task-oriented leaders tend to describe the LPC in negative terms; their concern for task accomplishment causes them to think badly about others who make getting the job done difficult. Thus, relationship-oriented and task-oriented leaders are sometimes referred to as high-LPC and low-LPC leaders, respectively.

SITUATIONAL CHARACTERISTICS   According to Fiedler, leadership style is an enduring characteristic; managers cannot change their style, nor can they adopt different styles in different kinds of situations. With this in mind, Fiedler identified three situational characteristics that are important determinants of how favorable a situation is for leading: leader–member relations, task structure, and position power. When a situation is favorable for leading, it is relatively easy for a manager to influence subordinates so they perform at a high level and contribute to organizational efficiency and effectiveness. In a situation unfavorable for leading, it is much more difficult for a manager to exert influence.

leader–member relations The extent to which followers like, trust, and are loyal to their leader; a determinant of how favorable a situation is for leading.

LEADER–MEMBER RELATIONS   The first situational characteristic Fiedler described, leader–member relations, is the extent to which followers like, trust, and are loyal to their leader. Situations are more favorable for leading when leader–member relations are good.

task structure The extent to which the work to be performed is clear-cut so that a leader's subordinates know what needs to be accomplished and how to go about doing it; a determinant of how favorable a situation is for leading.

TASK STRUCTURE   The second situational characteristic Fiedler described, task structure, is the extent to which the work to be performed is clear-cut so that a leader's subordinates know what needs to be accomplished and how to go about doing it. When task structure is high, the situation is favorable for leading. When task structure is low, goals may be vague, subordinates may be unsure of what they should be doing or how they should do it, and the situation is unfavorable for leading.

Task structure was low for Geraldine Laybourne when she was a top manager at Nickelodeon, the children's television network. It was never precisely clear what would appeal to her young viewers, whose tastes can change dramatically, or how to motivate her subordinates to come up with creative and novel ideas.[54] In contrast, Herman Mashaba, founder of Black Like Me, a hair care products company based in South Africa, seemed to have relatively high task structure when he started his company. His company's goals were to produce and sell inexpensive hair care products to native Africans, and managers accomplished these goals by using simple yet appealing packaging and distributing the products through neighborhood beauty salons.[55]

position power The amount of legitimate, reward, and coercive power that a leader has by virtue of his or her position in an organization; a determinant of how favorable a situation is for leading.

POSITION POWER   The third situational characteristic Fiedler described, **position power**, is the amount of legitimate, reward, and coercive power a leader has by virtue of his or her position in an organization. Leadership situations are more favorable for leading when position power is strong.

COMBINING LEADER STYLE AND THE SITUATION   By considering all possible combinations of good and poor leader–member relations, high and low task structure, and strong and weak position power, Fiedler identified eight leadership situations, which vary in their favorability for leading (see Figure 14.2). After extensive research, he determined that relationship-oriented leaders are most effective in moderately favorable situations (IV, V, VI, and VII in Figure 14.2), and task-oriented leaders are most effective in situations that are either very favorable (I, II, and III) or very unfavorable (VIII).

PUTTING THE CONTINGENCY MODEL INTO PRACTICE   Recall that according to Fiedler, leader style is an enduring characteristic that managers cannot change. This suggests that for managers to be effective, either managers need to be placed in leadership situations that fit their style or situations need to be changed to suit the managers. Situations can be changed, for example, by giving a manager more position power or by taking steps to increase task structure, such as by clarifying goals.

Take the case of Mark Compton, a relationship-oriented leader employed by a small construction company. Compton was in a very unfavorable situation and was having a rough time leading his construction crew. His subordinates did not trust him to look out for their well-being (poor leader–member relations), the construction jobs he supervised tended to be novel and complex (low task structure), and he had no control over the rewards and disciplinary actions his subordinates received (weak position power). Recognizing the need to improve matters, Compton's supervisor gave him the power to reward crew members with bonuses and overtime work as he saw fit and to discipline crew members for poor-quality work and unsafe on-the-job behavior. As his leadership situation improved to moderately favorable, so did Compton's effectiveness as a leader and the performance of his crew.

Research studies tend to support some aspects of Fiedler's model but also suggest that, like most theories, it needs some modifications.[56] Some researchers have questioned what the LPC scale really measures. Others find fault with the model's premise that leaders cannot alter their styles. That is, it is likely that at least some leaders can diagnose the situation they are in and, when their style is inappropriate for the situation, modify their style so that it is more in line with what the leadership situation calls for. The ability to modify one's leadership style is especially important in today's global business environment because the expectations of leaders and followers differ from one culture to another (see the "Managing Globally" feature).

Figure 14.2
Fiedler's Contingency Theory of Leadership

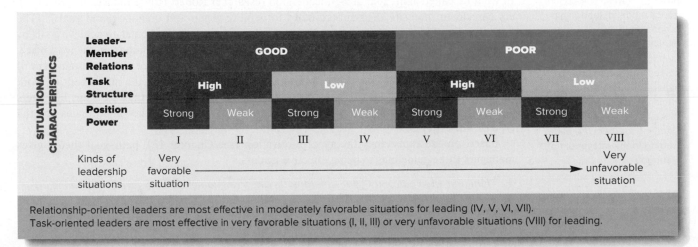

Relationship-oriented leaders are most effective in moderately favorable situations for leading (IV, V, VI, VII).
Task-oriented leaders are most effective in very favorable situations (I, II, III) or very unfavorable situations (VIII) for leading.

International Differences in Leadership

Erin Meyer, a professor of international management, has observed that expectations of a leader differ from one country to another. If employees perceive that a manager is not acting like their idea of a leader, they may feel confused or upset. Meyer has seen misunderstandings related to cultural ideas of authority, decision making, and the interactions between them. Authority has to do with how much importance people place on rank and how much they show respect based on rank. Decision making refers to whether leaders issue decisions or the group arrives at a consensus.[57]

These differences become more complex when combined. For example, in China and Indonesia, hierarchy is important, and leaders make top-down decisions. The Scandinavian countries downplay hierarchy, and decisions are reached through consensus. But in the United States and Great Britain, which also are egalitarian, a leader is typically expected to listen to views and then decide. And in Japan, although hierarchy is important, employees at lower levels of the organization confer, reach a consensus, and present their proposal to the next level up. The process can be slow, but once an idea has worked its way up through the hierarchy, it already has buy-in, the decision is firm, and the people are committed to implementing it.[58]

How can leaders navigate these differences? An important start is to learn about the cultures of followers' countries. A culturally agile leader can recognize and name those differences in order to identify which cultural style will be effective for particular decisions. Then the leader should clarify expectations—for example, by saying, "I want to hear three ideas from the team before I express my views" or "Here's our decision, but it's not firm until we get approval from the finance department." In addition to learning general cultural patterns, leaders should gather information from the group being led, according to Jo Owen, who has led international business and nonprofit groups. Owen advises that the best way to observe cultural norms and personal differences is to engage with people face-to-face. Like Meyer, Owen advises talking about norms, so people understand their group's dynamics. Leadership coach Amir Ghannad takes Owen's thinking one step further, urging leaders to see their followers first as unique individuals, rather than generic members of a culture. This prepares leaders to expect differences while seeing the other person's shared humanity.[59]

House's Path–Goal Theory

path–goal theory A contingency model of leadership proposing that leaders can motivate subordinates by identifying their desired outcomes, rewarding them for high performance and the attainment of work goals with these desired outcomes, and clarifying for them the paths leading to the attainment of work goals.

In what he called **path–goal theory**, leadership researcher Robert House focused on what leaders can do to motivate their subordinates to achieve group and organizational goals.[60] The premise of path–goal theory is that effective leaders motivate subordinates to achieve goals by (1) clearly identifying the outcomes that subordinates are trying to obtain from the workplace, (2) rewarding subordinates with these outcomes for high performance and the attainment of work goals, and (3) clarifying for subordinates the *paths* leading to the attainment of work *goals*. Path–goal theory is a contingency model because it proposes that the steps managers should take to motivate subordinates depend on both the nature of the subordinates and the type of work they do.

Based on the expectancy theory of motivation (see Chapter 13), path–goal theory gives managers three guidelines to being effective leaders:

1. *Find out what outcomes your subordinates are trying to obtain from their jobs and the organization.* These outcomes can range from satisfactory pay and job security to reasonable working hours and interesting and challenging job assignments. After identifying these outcomes, the manager should have the *reward power* needed to distribute or withhold the

outcomes. Mark Crane, for example, is the vice principal of a large elementary school. Crane determined that the teachers he leads are trying to obtain the following outcomes from their jobs: pay raises, autonomy in the classroom, and the choice of which grades they teach. Crane had reward power for the last two outcomes, but the school's principal determined how the pool of money for raises was to be distributed each year. Because Crane was the first-line manager who led the teachers and was most familiar with their performance, he asked the principal (his boss) to give him some say in determining pay raises. Realizing that this made a lot of sense, his principal gave Crane full power to distribute raises and requested only that Crane review his decisions with him before informing the teachers about them.

2. *Reward subordinates for high performance and goal attainment with the outcomes they desire.* The teachers and administrators at Crane's school considered several dimensions of teacher performance to be critical to achieving their goal of providing high-quality education: excellent in-class instruction, special programs to enhance student interest and learning (such as science and computer projects), and availability for meetings with parents to discuss their children's progress and special needs. Crane distributed pay raises to the teachers based on the extent to which they performed highly on each of these dimensions. The top-performing teachers were given first choice of grade assignments and had practically complete autonomy in their classrooms.

3. *Clarify the paths to goal attainment for subordinates, remove any obstacles to high performance, and express confidence in subordinates' capabilities.* This does not mean that a manager needs to tell subordinates what to do. Rather, it means that a manager needs to make sure subordinates are clear about what they should be trying to accomplish and have the capabilities, resources, and confidence levels needed to be successful. Crane made sure all the teachers understood the importance of the three targeted goals and asked them whether, to reach them, they needed any special resources or supplies for their classes. Crane also gave additional coaching and guidance to teachers who seemed to be struggling. For example, Patrick Conolly, in his first year of teaching after graduate school, was unsure how to use special projects in a third grade class and how to react to parents who were critical. Conolly's teaching was excellent, but he felt insecure about how he was doing on this dimension. To help build Conolly's confidence, Crane told Conolly that he thought he could be one of the school's top teachers (which was true). He gave Conolly some ideas about special projects that worked particularly well with the third grade, such as a writing project. Crane also role-played teacher-parent interactions with Conolly. Conolly played the role of a particularly dissatisfied or troubled parent, while Crane played the role of a teacher trying to solve the underlying problem while making the parent feel that his or her child's needs were being met. Crane's efforts to clarify the paths to goal attainment for Conolly paid off: Within two years the local PTS voted Conolly teacher of the year.

Path–goal theory identifies four kinds of leadership behaviors that motivate subordinates:

- *Directive behaviors* are similar to initiating structure and include setting goals, assigning tasks, showing subordinates how to complete tasks, and taking concrete steps to improve performance.

- *Supportive behaviors* are similar to consideration and include expressing concern for subordinates and looking out for their best interests.

- *Participative behaviors* give subordinates a say in matters and decisions that affect them.

- *Achievement-oriented behaviors* motivate subordinates to perform at the highest level possible by, for example, setting challenging goals, expecting that they be met, and believing in subordinates' capabilities.

Which of these behaviors should managers use to lead effectively? The answer to this question depends, or is contingent, on the nature of the subordinates and the kind of work they do.

Directive behaviors may be beneficial when subordinates are having difficulty completing assigned tasks, but they might be detrimental when subordinates are independent thinkers who work best when left alone. *Supportive* behaviors are often advisable when subordinates are experiencing high levels of stress. *Participative* behaviors can be particularly effective when subordinates'

You could stand over your subordinate and berate him or you could empower him to find the solution by working to see where the issue developed. Supportive managers make a world of difference in retaining and motivating employees.
©Stockbyte/Getty Images

leadership substitute A characteristic of a subordinate or of a situation, or context, that acts in place of the influence of a leader and makes leadership unnecessary.

support of a decision is required. *Achievement-oriented* behaviors may increase motivation levels of highly capable subordinates who are bored from having too few challenges, but they might backfire if used with subordinates who are already pushed to their limit.

The Leader Substitutes Model

The leader substitutes model suggests that leadership is sometimes unnecessary because substitutes for leadership are present. A **leadership substitute** is something that acts in place of the influence of a leader and makes leadership unnecessary. This model suggests that under certain conditions managers do not have to play a leadership role—members of an organization sometimes can perform at a high level without a manager exerting influence over them.[61] The leader substitutes model is a contingency model because it suggests that in some situations leadership is unnecessary.

Take the case of David Cotsonas, who teaches English at a foreign language school in Cyprus, an island in the Mediterranean Sea. Cotsonas is fluent in Greek, English, and French; is an excellent teacher; and is highly motivated. Many of his students are businesspeople who have some rudimentary English skills and wish to increase their fluency to be able to conduct more of their business in English. He enjoys not only teaching them English, but also learning about the work they do, and he often keeps in touch with his students after they finish his classes. Cotsonas meets with the director of the school twice a year to discuss semiannual class schedules and enrollments.

With practically no influence from a leader, Cotsonas is a highly motivated top performer at the school. In his situation, leadership is unnecessary because substitutes for leadership are present. Cotsonas's teaching expertise, his motivation, and his enjoyment of his work are substitutes for the influence of a leader—in this case, the school's director. If the school's director were to try to influence how Cotsonas performs his job, Cotsonas would probably resent this infringement on his autonomy, and it is unlikely that his performance would improve because he is already one of the school's best teachers.

As in Cotsonas's case, *characteristics of subordinates*—such as their skills, abilities, experience, knowledge, and motivation—can be substitutes for leadership.[62] *Characteristics of the situation, or context*—such as the extent to which the work is interesting and enjoyable—also can be substitutes. When work is interesting and enjoyable, as it is for Cotsonas, jobholders do not need to be coaxed into performing because performing is rewarding in its own right. Similarly, when managers *empower* their subordinates or use *self-managed work teams* (discussed in detail in Chapter 15), the need for leadership influence from a manager is decreased because team members manage themselves.

The concept of shared leadership is an effective example of a leadership substitute. In this situation, leadership is distributed among team members rather than being exhibited by one single leader. Research suggests teams that successfully share the leadership role among members may provide higher-quality outcomes to their customers.[63] Substitutes for leadership can increase organizational efficiency and effectiveness because they free up some of managers' valuable time and allow managers to focus their efforts on discovering new ways to improve organizational effectiveness. The director of the language school, for example, was able to spend much of his time making arrangements to open a second school in Rhodes, an island in the Aegean Sea, because of the presence of leadership substitutes, not only for Cotsonas but for most other teachers at the school as well.

Bringing It All Together

Effective leadership in organizations occurs when managers take steps to lead in a way that is appropriate for the situation, or context, in which leadership occurs and for the subordinates who are being led. The three contingency models of leadership just discussed help managers focus on the necessary ingredients for effective leadership. They are complementary in that each

Table 14.2

Contingency Models of Leadership

Model	Focus	Key Contingencies
Fiedler's contingency model	Describes two leader styles, relationship-oriented and task-oriented, and the kinds of situations in which each kind of leader will be most effective.	Whether a relationship-oriented or a task-oriented leader is effective is contingent on the situation.
House's path–goal theory	Describes how effective leaders motivate their followers.	The behaviors that managers should engage in to be effective leaders are contingent on the nature of the subordinates and the work they do.
Leader substitutes model	Describes when leadership is unnecessary.	Whether leadership is necessary for subordinates to perform highly is contingent on characteristics of the subordinates and the situation.

one looks at the leadership question from a different angle. Fiedler's contingency model explores how a manager's leadership style needs to be matched to that person's leadership situation for maximum effectiveness. House's path–goal theory focuses on how managers should motivate subordinates and describes the specific kinds of behaviors managers can engage in to have a highly motivated workforce. The leadership substitutes model alerts managers to the fact that sometimes they do not need to exert influence over subordinates and thus can free up their time for other important activities. Table 14.2 recaps these three contingency models of leadership.

Transformational Leadership

LO14-4 Describe what transformational leadership is, and explain how managers can engage in it.

Time and time again, throughout business history, certain leaders seem to transform their organizations, making sweeping changes to revitalize and renew operations. For example, when Sue Nokes became senior vice president of sales and customer service at T-Mobile USA in 2002, the quality of T-Mobile's customer service was lower than that of its major competitors; on average, 12% of employees were absent on any day; and annual employee turnover was over 100%.[64] When Nokes arrived at T-Mobile, valuable employees were quitting their jobs and customers weren't receiving high-quality service; neither employees nor customers were satisfied with their experience with the company.[65] However, by the late 2000s T-Mobile was regularly receiving highest rankings for customer care and satisfaction in the wireless category by J. D. Power and Associates, absence and turnover rates substantially declined, and around 80% of employees indicated that they were satisfied with their jobs.[66] In fact, when Nokes visited call centers, it was not uncommon for employees to greet her with cheers and accolades.[67]

Nokes transformed T-Mobile into a company in which satisfied employees provide excellent service to customers. When managers have such dramatic effects on their subordinates and on an organization as a whole, they are engaging in transformational leadership. **Transformational leadership** occurs when managers change (or transform) their subordinates in three important ways:[68]

transformational leadership Leadership that makes subordinates aware of the importance of their jobs and performance to the organization and aware of their own needs for personal growth and that motivates subordinates to work for the good of the organization.

1. *Transformational managers make subordinates aware of how important their jobs are for the organization and how necessary it is for them to perform those jobs as best they can so the organization can attain its goals.* At T-Mobile, Nokes visited call centers, conducted focus groups, and had town hall meetings to find out what employees and customers were unhappy with and what steps she could take to improve matters. Her philosophy was that when employees are satisfied with their jobs and view their work as important, they are much more likely to provide high-quality customer service. She made employees aware of how important their jobs were by the many steps she took to improve their working conditions, ranging from providing them with their own workspaces to substantially raising their salaries. She emphasized the importance of providing excellent customer service by periodically asking employees what was working well and what was not working well, asking

Sue Nokes exhibited transformational leadership at T-Mobile.
©IPON-BONESS/SIPA/Newscom

them what steps could be taken to improve problem areas, and taking actions to ensure that employees were able to provide excellent customer service. Nokes also instituted a performance measurement system to track performance in key areas such as quality of service and speed of problem resolution. She sincerely told employees, "You are No. 1, and the customer is why."[69]

2. *Transformational managers make their subordinates aware of the subordinates' own needs for personal growth, development, and accomplishment.* Nokes made T-Mobile's employees aware of their own needs in this regard by transforming training and development at T-Mobile and increasing opportunities for promotions to more responsible positions. Employees now spend over 130 hours per year in training and development programs and team meetings. Nokes also instituted a promote-from-within policy, and around 80% of promotions are given to current employees.

3. *Transformational managers motivate their subordinates to work for the good of the organization as a whole, not just for their own personal gain or benefit.* Nokes emphasized that employees should focus on what matters to customers, coworkers, and T-Mobile as a whole. She let employees know that when they were unnecessarily absent from their jobs, they were not doing right by their coworkers. And she emphasized the need to try to resolve customer problems in a single phone call so customers can get on with their busy lives.[70]

When managers transform their subordinates in these three ways, subordinates trust the managers, are highly motivated, and help the organization achieve its goals. How do managers such as Nokes transform subordinates and produce dramatic effects in their organizations? There are at least three ways in which transformational leaders can influence their followers: by being a charismatic leader, by intellectually stimulating subordinates, and by engaging in developmental consideration (see Table 14.3).

Being a Charismatic Leader

charismatic leader An enthusiastic, self-confident leader who is able to clearly communicate his or her vision of how good things could be.

Transformational managers such as Nokes are **charismatic leaders**. They have a vision of how good things could be in their work groups and organizations that is in contrast with the status quo. Their vision usually entails dramatic improvements in group and organizational performance as a result of changes in the organization's structure, culture, strategy, decision making, and other critical processes and factors. This vision paves the way for gaining a competitive advantage.

Charismatic leaders are excited and enthusiastic about their vision and clearly communicate it to their subordinates. The excitement, enthusiasm, and self-confidence of a charismatic leader contribute to the leader's being able to inspire followers to enthusiastically support his or her vision.[71] People often think of charismatic leaders or managers as being "larger than life." The essence of charisma, however, is having a vision and enthusiastically communicating it to others. Thus, managers who appear to be quiet and earnest can also be charismatic.

Stimulating Subordinates Intellectually

Transformational managers openly share information with their subordinates so they are aware of problems and the need for change. The manager causes subordinates to view problems in

Table 14.3
Transformational Leadership

Transformational managers
- Are charismatic.
- Intellectually stimulate subordinates.
- Engage in developmental consideration.

Subordinates of transformational managers
- Have increased awareness of the importance of their jobs and high performance.
- Are aware of their own needs for growth, development, and accomplishment.
- Work for the good of the organization and not just their own personal benefit.

their groups and throughout the organization from a different perspective, consistent with the manager's vision. Whereas in the past subordinates might not have been aware of some problems, may have viewed problems as a "management issue" beyond their concern, or may have viewed problems as insurmountable, the transformational manager's **intellectual stimulation** leads subordinates to view problems as challenges that they can and will meet and conquer. The manager engages and empowers subordinates to take personal responsibility for helping to solve problems, as did Nokes at T-Mobile.[72]

intellectual stimulation
Behavior a leader engages in to make followers aware of problems and view these problems in new ways, consistent with the leader's vision.

Engaging in Developmental Consideration

When managers engage in **developmental consideration**, they not only perform the consideration behaviors described earlier, such as demonstrating true concern for the well-being of subordinates, but also go one step further. The manager goes out of his or her way to support and encourage subordinates, giving them opportunities to enhance their skills and capabilities and to grow and excel on the job.[73] As mentioned earlier, Nokes did this in numerous ways. In fact, after she first met with employees in a call center in Albuquerque, New Mexico, Karen Viola, the manager of the call center, said, "Everyone came out crying. The people said that they had never felt so inspired in their lives, and that they had never met with any leader at that level who [they felt] cared."[74]

developmental consideration
Behavior a leader engages in to support and encourage followers and help them develop and grow on the job.

All organizations, no matter how large or small, successful or unsuccessful, can benefit when their managers engage in transformational leadership. Moreover, while the benefits of transformational leadership are often most apparent when an organization is in trouble, transformational leadership can be an enduring approach to leadership, leading to long-term organizational effectiveness.

The Distinction between Transformational and Transactional Leadership

Transformational leadership is often contrasted with transactional leadership. In **transactional leadership**, managers use their reward and coercive powers to encourage high performance. When managers reward high performers, reprimand or otherwise punish low performers, and motivate subordinates by reinforcing desired behaviors and extinguishing or punishing undesired ones, they are engaging in transactional leadership.[75] Managers who effectively influence their subordinates to achieve goals, yet do not seem to be making the kind of dramatic changes that are part of transformational leadership, are engaging in transactional leadership.

transactional leadership
Leadership that motivates subordinates by rewarding them for high performance and reprimanding them for low performance.

Many transformational leaders engage in transactional leadership. They reward subordinates for a job well done and notice and respond to substandard performance. But they also have their eyes on the bigger picture of how much better things could be in their organizations, how much more their subordinates are capable of achieving, and how important it is to treat their subordinates with respect and help them reach their full potential.

Research has found that when leaders engage in transformational leadership, their subordinates tend to have higher levels of job satisfaction and performance.[76] Additionally, subordinates of transformational leaders may be more likely to trust their leaders and their organizations and feel that they are being fairly treated, and this in turn may positively influence their work motivation (see Chapter 13).[77]

Gender and Leadership

The increasing number of women entering the ranks of management, as well as the problems some women face in their efforts to be hired as managers or promoted into management positions, has prompted researchers to explore the relationship between gender and leadership. Although there are relatively more women in management positions today than there were 10 years ago, there are still relatively few women in top management and, in some organizations, even in middle management.

When women do advance to top management positions, special attention often is focused on them and the fact that they are women. For example, women CEOs of large companies are still rare; those who make it to the top post, such as Michele Buck of Hershey and Mary Barra of General Motors, are scarce.[78] Although women have made inroads into leadership

LO14-5 Characterize the relationship between gender and leadership, and explain how emotional intelligence may contribute to leadership effectiveness.

positions in many organizations, they continue to be underrepresented in top leadership posts. As indicated in Chapter 5, for example, while almost 45% of the employees in managerial and professional jobs are women, only 26.5% of corporate officers in the *Fortune* 500 are women, and only 11% of the top earners are women.[79]

A widespread stereotype of women is that they are nurturing, supportive, and concerned with interpersonal relations. Men are stereotypically viewed as being directive and focused on task accomplishment. Such stereotypes suggest that women tend to be more relationship-oriented as managers and engage in more consideration behaviors, whereas men are more task-oriented and engage in more initiating-structure behaviors. Does the behavior of actual male and female managers bear out these stereotypes? Do women managers lead in different ways than men do? Are male or female managers more effective as leaders?

Research suggests that male and female managers who have leadership positions in organizations behave in similar ways.[80] Women do not engage in more consideration than men, and men do not engage in more initiating structure than women. Research does suggest, however, that leadership style may vary between women and men. Women tend to be somewhat more participative as leaders than are men, involving subordinates in decision making and seeking their input.[81] Male managers tend to be less participative than are female managers, making more decisions on their own and wanting to do things their own way.

There are at least two reasons that female managers may be more participative as leaders than are male managers.[82] First, subordinates may try to resist the influence of female managers more than they do the influence of male managers. Some subordinates may never have reported to a woman before, some may incorrectly see a management role as being more appropriate for a man than for a woman, and some may just resist being led by a woman. To overcome this resistance and encourage subordinates' trust and respect, women managers may adopt a participative approach.

A second reason that female managers may be more participative is that they sometimes have better interpersonal skills than male managers.[83] A participative approach to leadership requires high levels of interaction and involvement between a manager and his or her subordinates, sensitivity to subordinates' feelings, and the ability to make decisions that may be unpopular with subordinates but necessary for goal attainment. Good interpersonal skills may help female managers have the effective interactions with their subordinates that are crucial to a participative approach.[84] To the extent that male managers have more difficulty managing interpersonal relationships, they may shy away from the high levels of interaction with subordinates necessary for true participation.

The key finding from research on leader behaviors, however, is that male and female managers do *not* differ significantly in their propensities to perform different leader behaviors. Even though they may be more participative, female managers do not engage in more consideration or less initiating structure than male managers.

Perhaps a question even more important than whether male and female managers differ in the leadership behaviors they perform is whether they differ in effectiveness. Consistent with the findings for leader behaviors, research suggests that across different kinds of organizational settings, male and female managers tend to be *equally effective* as leaders.[85] Thus, there is no logical basis for stereotypes favoring male managers and leaders or for the existence of the "glass ceiling" (an invisible barrier that seems to prevent women from advancing as far as they should in some organizations). Because women and men are equally effective as leaders, the increasing number of women in the workforce should result in a larger pool of highly qualified candidates for management positions in organizations, ultimately enhancing organizational effectiveness.[86]

Emotional Intelligence and Leadership

Do the moods and emotions leaders experience on the job influence their behavior and effectiveness as leaders? Research suggests this is likely to be the case. For example, one study found that when store managers experienced positive moods at work, salespeople in their stores provided high-quality customer service and were less likely to quit.[87] Another study found that groups whose leaders experienced positive moods had better coordination, whereas groups whose leaders experienced negative moods exerted more effort; members of groups with leaders in positive moods also tended to experience more positive moods themselves; and members of groups with leaders in negative moods tended to experience more negative moods.[88]

A leader's level of emotional intelligence (see Chapter 3) may play a particularly important role in leadership effectiveness.[89] For example, emotional intelligence may help leaders develop a vision for their organizations, motivate their subordinates to commit to this vision, and energize them to enthusiastically work to achieve this vision. Moreover, emotional intelligence may enable leaders to develop a significant identity for their organization and instill high levels of trust and cooperation throughout the organization while maintaining the flexibility needed to respond to changing conditions.[90]

Emotional intelligence also plays a crucial role in how leaders relate to and deal with their followers, particularly when it comes to encouraging followers to be creative.[91] Creativity in organizations is an emotion-laden process; it often entails challenging the status quo, being willing to take risks and accept and learn from failures, and doing much hard work to bring creative ideas to fruition in terms of new products, services, or procedures and processes when uncertainty is bound to be high.[92] Leaders who are high on emotional intelligence are more likely to understand all the emotions surrounding creative endeavors, to be able to awaken and support the creative pursuits of their followers, and to provide the kind of support that enables creativity to flourish in organizations.[93]

The "Management Insight" feature provides some guidelines for applying the concept of emotional intelligence to the practice of leadership.

MANAGEMENT INSIGHT

Being a High-EQ Leader

What behaviors should a manager practice in order to lead with emotional intelligence (EQ)? A good starting point is to become aware of one's emotions. When someone puts forth an idea different from what you were advocating, what do you feel? Are you curious to learn more or defensive of an idea you were proud of? Or when you hear a critical remark, do you feel hurt, angry, or interested you might have information that will help you do better in the future? Defining these feelings can help you evaluate your options for action more accurately and fully.[94]

Another essential behavior to practice is empathy. The objective is to understand how people feel, not to encourage negative behavior or even necessarily to agree. To practice empathy, when you observe others, try to imagine yourself in their place. If you aren't sure how another person feels, ask and try to understand the answer. Even when you cannot—or do not think it is appropriate to—solve another person's problem, you demonstrate respect when you try to understand.[95]

Empathy increases when you practice listening. Communication skills are a mark of a high-EQ leader, and listening is among the most important of those skills. While listening, practice focusing on understanding rather than judging what the person says. Jumping to a judgment makes it harder to get the full message. Listening to learn about others, in contrast, is motivational as well as informative. When Tom Gartland became president of Avis Budget Group, he spent weeks on a bus tour to meet the company's employees face-to-face. Focusing on others and learning how he could help them resulted in the employees being highly committed to the company.[96]

Finally, emotionally intelligent leaders manage their emotions. The other practices can help with this. For example, anger at an employee is easier to manage if you have listened and practiced empathy, so that you have some understanding of what behavior to expect and why it is occurring. Learning to recognize your emotions alerts you to situations in which self-control will help you. For example, if conflict erupts during a meeting, awareness of one's own and others' feelings can put you on guard to keep your own anger or dismay under control. Then you can explore the ideas in play and perhaps even steer the group to a creative solution built on a variety of perspectives.[97]

Summary and Review

LO14-1

THE NATURE OF LEADERSHIP Leadership is the process by which a person exerts influence over other people and inspires, motivates, and directs their activities to help achieve group or organizational goals. Leaders can influence others because they possess power. The five types of power available to managers are legitimate power, reward power, coercive power, expert power, and referent power. Many managers are using empowerment as a tool to increase their effectiveness as leaders.

LO14-2

TRAIT AND BEHAVIOR MODELS OF LEADERSHIP The trait model of leadership describes personal characteristics, or traits, that contribute to effective leadership. However, some managers who possess these traits are not effective leaders, and some managers who do not possess all the traits are nevertheless effective leaders. The behavior model of leadership describes two kinds of behavior that most leaders engage in: consideration and initiating structure.

LO14-3

CONTINGENCY MODELS OF LEADERSHIP Contingency models take into account the complexity surrounding leadership and the role of the situation in determining whether a manager is an effective leader. Fiedler's contingency model explains why managers may be effective leaders in one situation and ineffective in another. According to Fiedler's model, relationship-oriented leaders are most effective in situations that are moderately favorable for leading, and task-oriented leaders are most effective in situations that are very favorable or very unfavorable for leading. House's path–goal theory describes how effective managers motivate their subordinates by determining what outcomes their subordinates want, rewarding subordinates with these outcomes when they achieve their goals and perform at a high level, and clarifying the paths to goal attainment. Managers can engage in four kinds of behaviors to motivate subordinates: directive, supportive, participative, and achievement-oriented behaviors. The leader substitutes model suggests that sometimes managers do not have to play a leadership role because their subordinates perform at a high level without the manager's having to exert influence over them.

LO14-4

TRANSFORMATIONAL LEADERSHIP Transformational leadership occurs when managers have dramatic effects on their subordinates and on the organization as a whole and they inspire and energize subordinates to solve problems and improve performance. These effects include making subordinates aware of the importance of their own jobs and high performance; making subordinates aware of their own needs for personal growth, development, and accomplishment; and motivating subordinates to work for the good of the organization and not just their own personal gain. Managers can engage in transformational leadership by being charismatic leaders, by intellectually stimulating subordinates, and by engaging in developmental consideration. Transformational managers also often engage in transactional leadership by using their reward and coercive powers to encourage high performance.

LO14-5

GENDER AND LEADERSHIP Female and male managers do not differ in the leadership behaviors they perform, contrary to stereotypes suggesting that women are more relationship-oriented and men more task-oriented. Female managers sometimes are more participative than male managers, however. Research has found that women and men are equally effective as managers and leaders.

LO14-5

EMOTIONAL INTELLIGENCE AND LEADERSHIP The moods and emotions leaders experience on the job, and their ability to effectively manage these feelings, can influence their effectiveness as leaders. Moreover, emotional intelligence can contribute to leadership effectiveness in multiple ways, including encouraging and supporting creativity among followers.

Management in Action

Topics for Discussion and Action

Discussion

1. Describe the steps managers can take to increase their power and ability to be effective leaders. **[LO14-1]**

2. Think of specific situations in which it might be especially important for a manager to engage in consideration and in initiating structure. **[LO14-2]**

3. For your current job or for a future job you expect to hold, describe what your supervisor could do to strongly motivate you to be a top performer. **[LO14-3]**

4. Discuss why managers might want to change the behaviors they engage in, given their situation, their subordinates, and the nature of the work being done. Do you think managers can readily change their leadership behaviors? Why or why not? **[LO14-3]**

5. Discuss why substitutes for leadership can contribute to organizational effectiveness. **[LO14-3]**

6. Describe what transformational leadership is, and explain how managers can engage in it. **[LO14-4]**

7. Discuss why some people still think men make better managers than women, even though research indicates that men and women are equally effective as managers and leaders. **[LO14-5]**

8. Imagine that you are working in an organization in an entry-level position after graduation and have come up with what you think is a great idea for improving a critical process in the organization that relates to your job. In what ways might your supervisor encourage you to implement your idea? How might your supervisor discourage you from even sharing your idea with others? **[LO14-4, 14-5]**

Action

9. Interview a manager to find out how the three situational characteristics that Fiedler identified affect his or her ability to provide leadership. **[LO14-3]**

10. Find a company that has dramatically turned around its fortunes and improved its performance. Determine whether a transformational manager was behind the turnaround and, if one was, what this manager did. **[LO14-4]**

Building Management Skills

Analyzing Failures of Leadership [LO14-1, 14-2, 14-3, 14-4]

Think about a situation you are familiar with in which a leader was very ineffective. Then answer the following questions:

1. What sources of power did this leader have? Did the leader have enough power to influence his or her followers?

2. What kinds of behaviors did this leader engage in? Were they appropriate for the situation? Why or why not?

3. From what you know, do you think this leader was a task-oriented leader or a relationship-oriented leader? How favorable was this leader's situation for leading?

4. What steps did this leader take to motivate his or her followers? Were these steps appropriate or inappropriate? Why?

5. What signs, if any, did this leader show of being a transformational leader?

Managing Ethically [LO14-1]

Managers who verbally criticize their subordinates, put them down in front of their coworkers, or use the threat of job loss to influence behavior are exercising coercive power. Some employees subject to coercive power believe that using it is unethical.

Questions

1. Either alone or in a group, think about the ethical implications of the use of coercive power.

2. To what extent do managers and organizations have an ethical obligation to put limits on the amount of coercive power that is exercised?

Small Group Breakout Exercise

Improving Leadership Effectiveness [LO14-1, 14-2, 14-3, 14-4]

Form groups of three to five people, and appoint one member as the spokesperson who will communicate your findings and conclusions to the class when called on by the instructor. Then discuss the following scenario:

You are a team of human resource consultants who have been hired by Carla Caruso, an entrepreneur who has started her own interior decorating business. A highly competent and creative interior decorator, Caruso has established a working relationship with most of the major home builders in her community. At first she worked on her own as an independent contractor. Then because of a dramatic increase in the number of new homes being built, she became swamped with requests for her services and decided to start her own company.

She hired a secretary–bookkeeper and four interior decorators, all of whom are highly competent. Caruso still does decorating jobs herself and has adopted a hands-off approach to leading the four decorators who report to her because she feels that interior design is a very personal, creative endeavor. Rather than pay the decorators on some kind of commission basis (such as a percentage of their customers' total billings), she pays them a premium salary, higher than average, so they are motivated to do what's best for a customer's needs and not what will result in higher billings and commissions.

Caruso thought everything was going smoothly until customer complaints started coming in. The complaints ranged from the decorators' being hard to reach, promising unrealistic delivery times, and being late for or failing to keep appointments to their being impatient and rude when customers had trouble making up their minds. Caruso knows her decorators are competent and is concerned that she is not effectively leading and managing them. She wonders, in particular, if her hands-off approach is to blame and if she should change the manner in which she rewards or pays her decorators. She has asked for your advice.

1. Analyze the sources of power that Caruso has available to her to influence the decorators. What advice can you give her to either increase her power base or use her existing power more effectively?

2. Given what you have learned in this chapter (for example, from the behavior model and path–goal theory), does Caruso seem to be performing appropriate leader behaviors in this situation? What advice can you give her about the kinds of behaviors she should perform?

3. What steps would you advise Caruso to take to increase the decorators' motivation to deliver high-quality customer service?

4. Would you advise Caruso to try to engage in transformational leadership in this situation? If not, why not? If so, what steps would you advise her to take?

Be the Manager [LO14-1, 14-2, 14-3, 14-4, 14-5]

You are the CEO of a medium-size company that makes window coverings such as blinds and shutters. Your company has a cost advantage in terms of being able to make custom window coverings at costs that are relatively low in the industry. However, the performance of your company has been lackluster. To make needed changes and improve performance, you met with the eight other top managers in your company and charged them with identifying problems and missed opportunities in each of their areas and coming up with an action plan to address the problems and take advantage of opportunities.

Once you gave the managers the okay, they were charged with implementing their action plans in a timely fashion and monitoring the effects of their initiatives monthly for the next 8 to 12 months.

You approved each of the managers' action plans, and a year later most of the managers were reporting that their initiatives had been successful in addressing the problems and opportunities they had identified a year ago. However, overall company performance continues to be lackluster and shows no signs of improvement. You are confused and starting to question your leadership capabilities and approach to change. What are you going to do to improve the performance and effectiveness of your company?

Bloomberg Case in the News

Amazon's Other Jeff Steps into the Spotlight [LO14-1, 14-2, 14-4]

Donald Trump has hammered Amazon .com Inc.'s share price in recent weeks by trying to pick fights online with Chief Executive Officer Jeff Bezos. But the actual object of his Twitter onslaught is the domain of Jeff Wilke, Bezos' right-hand man for most of the past 18 years. Wilke runs Amazon's worldwide consumer division, meaning he's in charge of both selling people stuff and figuring out how to deliver the items as efficiently as possible. Often, the company uses the U.S. Postal Service. That's an arrangement Trump has repeatedly threatened to hamper, arguing that it's ruinously unprofitable for taxpayers.

In Amazon's first public response to the president's criticism, Wilke says the business has been a win-win. "We've been around through four presidents and leadership changes all over the world," he says. "For more than two decades, we've worked with the post office to invent and deliver for customers and business all over the U.S. profitably, creating a bunch of jobs in the process. It's been a terrific partnership, and I hope it will remain so."

Amazon relies on the Postal Service for the so-called last mile (delivery from warehouses to customers' homes) on as many as 40% of all U.S. orders, according to analyst estimates. While the relationship is mutually beneficial—the mail carriers are getting paid for otherwise unused capacity—it saves Amazon an estimated $2.6 billion a year vs. the rates at independent couriers such as United Parcel Service Inc. and FedEx Corp. Trump recently ordered a review of the Postal Service's finances and suggested on Twitter that it might start charging Amazon higher delivery rates. Wilke says the company has other options, including UPS, FedEx, and its own couriers. "There are a bunch of ways to get product to the last mile all over the country," he says.

At 51, Wilke is just beginning to take a more public role in shaping Amazon's agenda, which includes advancing its technological ambitions as well as playing defense against presidential tweets. When he started at Amazon, the company was struggling to figure out how to profitably build warehouses that could deliver packages to customers' homes. Wilke took over North American retail in 2007 and, despite the Great Recession, built Amazon Prime memberships into a gargantuan sales machine. He added music and video streaming, narrowed delivery times to as little as an hour for certain products in dozens of cities, and watched the company's revenue grow more than tenfold, to $178 billion.

The downsides have been well-publicized. In 2011 news reports of its brutal warehouse working conditions led Amazon to publicly commit to reforms, including $50 million in new air conditioning across its U.S. facilities. And the company has taken various steps to soften its corporate image after a 2015 *New York Times* report described a cutthroat atmosphere where backstabbing flourished. Through it all, Wilke thrived. In 2016, Bezos named him CEO of the global consumer business, overseeing everything from the website and customer service to selling the Kindle and the Echo.

Wilke is a Pittsburgh native with, at least by Bezos standards, a relatively easygoing vibe. (Colleagues refer to him by his initials, JAW, to avoid confusing him with the other Jeff.) With degrees from Princeton and MIT, he came to Amazon from Allied Signal (now Honeywell International Inc.), where he ran a division that made pharmaceutical chemicals. He wears a ton of flannel during the holiday season and still dreams of being able to throw a 100 mph fastball. But former Amazon execs say he shares with Bezos a propensity for grand (and risky) experiments. "Wilke is a big supporter of crazy ideas," says Neil Ackerman, a former colleague who once proposed that Amazon use the empty space aboard returning delivery trucks to get into the recycling business.

These days, Wilke is focused largely on advancing Amazon's artificial intelligence and machine learning tools, technologies also being pursued by rivals including Google parent Alphabet, Apple, and Facebook. All the tech giants are competing to prove their AI bona fides, hire the top researchers and computer scientists, and pioneer the next generation of smart, intuitive computing services.

Google is the undisputed leader in the research community—making headlines with AI that can, say, beat top human players at the complex Chinese game Go. But Amazon may have the lead in applying machine learning to things you can buy. Amazon basically invented the smart speaker category with the Echo. In the past four years, it has sold tens of millions of Echo speakers and other devices carrying the company's digital assistant, Alexa. "I don't think they want to be the people who beat the world champion in Go," says Oren Etzioni, CEO of the Allen Institute for Artificial Intelligence and a computer science professor at the University of Washington. "They want to be the people who roll out very successful AI-based products."

Although Amazon's product recommendations and search engines now benefit from some of its AI advances, other, more visible, efforts clearly need more work. That includes the Echo; Wilke acknowledges that it's often difficult to get the devices to respond well in long conversations. "Sometimes it takes four or five questions to zero in on what somebody wants," he says. The company also has yet to add cashierless Amazon stores beyond a test model in Seattle, which opened to employees in late 2016 and to the public earlier this year. The store, called Amazon Go, uses AI algorithms and dozens of video cameras affixed to the ceiling to track when people take sandwiches, snacks, and drinks from shelves, charging them as they walk out.

Wilke says that while the store's testing phase is over, there are bugs to work out. "We want to reduce those as much as we can, which will make it more cost-effective," he says. He wouldn't discuss expansion plans beyond saying the no-cashiers model is unlikely to extend to Amazon's 470 Whole Foods Market stores.

Amazon's most significant use of AI, in its network of about 240 warehouses, is less visible. It does, however, play into anxieties that the technology could one day replace human labor. The company is using some 130,000 Kiva robots, conveyors that look like jumbo Roombas and move whole shelves around warehouse floors, sparing workers from having to walk miles each day to retrieve items. Amazon's researchers are working to train robots to identify and grab products from shelves, too, though the company has canceled an annual "pick challenge" in which

teams of researchers competed to build the best grasping robot.

While that sounds like it can't help but eliminate human workers, Wilke says automation will just shift Amazon warehouse staffers to higher-order tasks. "That's going to continue for as long as we have the ability to provide training and skills to people," he says. Amazon added 130,000 employees worldwide last year, mostly in its warehouses.

Despite its size, Amazon's retail business remains inherently low-margin. Investors are much happier with Amazon Web Services, its fast-growing, mega-profitable cloud computing arm. That's where the other big Bezos deputy, Andy Jassy, resides. When Bezos tapped Wilke as consumer CEO, he also made Jassy CEO of the cloud.

The consumer business is more mature, but Wilke isn't ready to concede that AWS will one day be the bigger business, as Bezos has occasionally suggested. He's especially

focused on expanding the U.S.-centric retailer into India, Australia, and Brazil. "We think the worldwide retail market is $25 trillion," Wilke says. "We round to less than 1% of that."

Questions for Discussion

1. How would you describe Jeff Wilke's personal leadership style and what sources of power does he possess?

2. What traits do you think Wilke is high on, and to what extent does he engage in considerations and initiating structure?

3. Do you think Wilke is a transformational leader? Explain your reasoning.

Source: Brad Stone and Spencer Soper, "Amazon's Other Jeff Steps into the Spotlight," *Bloomberg,* April 19, 2018, https://www.bloomberg.com/news/articles/2018-04-19/amazon-s-jeff-wilke-talks-about-ai-ambitions-robots-and-trump. Used with permission of Bloomberg L.P. Copyright © 2017. All rights reserved.

Notes

1. Dana-Farber Cancer Institute, "About Us," www.dana-farber.org, accessed April 13, 2018.

2. H. K. Gardner, "Getting Your Stars to Collaborate," *Harvard Business Review,* January–February 2017, pp. 100–108.

3. Gardner, "Getting Your Stars to Collaborate."

4. Gardner, "Getting Your Stars to Collaborate."

5. "Dana-Farber Cancer Institute Names Lesley Solomon SVP, Chief Innovation Officer," news release, May 31, 2017, www.newswise.com; P. D. McCluskey, "Five Things You Should Know about Laurie Glimcher," *Boston Globe,* www.bostonglobe.com, April 28, 2017; M. Bailey, "Recruited to Lead Harvard Med, 'Fearless' Scientist Chose Dana-Farber," *Stat,* www.statnews.com, March 1, 2016.

6. G. Yukl, *Leadership in Organizations,* 2nd ed. (New York: Academic Press, 1989); R.M. Stogdill, *Handbook of Leadership: A Survey of the Literature* (New York: Free Press, 1974).

7. W.D. Spangler, R.J. House, and R. Palrecha, "Personality and Leadership," in B. Schneider and D.B. Smith, eds., *Personality and Organizations* (Mahwah, NJ: Erlbaum, 2004), 251–90.

8. Spangler, House, and Palrecha, "Personality and Leadership"; L. Ryan, "Management vs. Leadership: Five Ways They Are Different," *Forbes,* www.forbes.com, March 27, 2016; V. Nayar, "Three Differences Between Managers and Leaders," *Harvard Business Review,* https://hbr.org, August 2, 2013.

9. Greenleaf Center for Servant Leadership, "Our History," www.greenleaf.org, accessed April 13, 2018.

10. Greenleaf Center for Servant Leadership, "What Is Servant Leadership?"; Review by F. Hamilton of L. Spears and M. Lawrence, *Practicing Servant Leadership: Succeeding through Trust, Bravery, and Forgiveness* (San Francisco: Jossey-Bass, 2004), in *Academy of Management Review* 30 (October 2005), 875–87; R.R. Washington, "Empirical Relationships between Theories of Servant, Transformational, and Transactional Leadership," *Academy of Management,* Best Paper Proceedings, 2007, 1–6.

11. M. Schwantes, "To Inspire and Influence Others, Make Sure to Do These 3 Things in 2018," *Inc.,* www.inc.com, January 3, 2018; J.E. Hoch, W. H. Bommer, J.H. Dulebohn, and D. Wu, "Do Ethical, Authentic, and Servant Leadership Explain Variance Above and Beyond Transformational Leadership? A Meta-Analysis," *Journal of Management,* http://journals.sagepub.com, August 31, 2016.

12. "What Is Servant Leadership?" www.greenleaf.org, accessed April 13, 2018.

13. B. Burlingham, "The Coolest Company in America," *Inc.,* www.inc.com, accessed April 17, 2018; "Zingerman's Community—Frequently Asked Questions," www.zingermanscommunity.com, accessed April 17, 2018; A. Weinzweig, "Step into the Future," *Inc.,* February 2011, 85–91.

14. B. Burlingham, "Decades Later, the Owners of Ann Arbor's Iconic Zingerman's Are Still at Odds over Expansion," *Forbes,* www.forbes.com, October 20, 2016.

15. Burlingham, "The Coolest Small Company in America"; Zingerman's Community of Businesses"; L. Buchanan, "In Praise of Selflessness," *Inc.,* May 2007, 33–35.

16. Buchanan, "In Praise of Selflessness."

17. Ibid.

18. Burlingham, "The Coolest Small Company in America"; Food Gatherers, "Mission & History," www.foodgatherers.org, accessed April 17, 2018.

19. Ibid.

20. Buchanan, "In Praise of Selflessness."

21. R. Calori and B. Dufour, "Management European Style," *Academy of Management Executive* 9, no. 3 (1995), 61-70.

22. Ibid.

23. H. Mintzberg, *Power in and around Organizations* (Englewood Cliffs, NJ: Prentice-Hall, 1983); J. Pfeffer, *Power in Organizations* (Marshfield, MA: Pitman, 1981).

24. R.P. French, Jr., and B. Raven, "The Bases of Social Power," in D. Cartwright and A.F. Zander, eds., *Group Dynamics* (Evanston, IL: Row, Peterson, 1960), 607-23.

25. D.J. Chung, "How to Really Motivate Salespeople," *Harvard Business Review,* https://hbr.org, April 2015 issue.

26. R.L. Rose, "After Turning Around Giddings and Lewis, Fife Is Turned Out Himself," *The Wall Street Journal,* June 22, 1993, A1.

27. M. Loeb, "Jack Welch Lets Fly on Budgets, Bonuses, and Buddy Boards," *Fortune,* May 29, 1995, 146.

28. A. Lee, S. Willis, and A.W. Tian, "When Empowering Employees Works, and When It Doesn't," *Harvard Business Review,* https://hbr.org, March 2, 2018.

29. L. Nakarmi, "A Flying Leap toward the 21st Century? Pressure from Competitors and Seoul May Transform the Chaebol," *BusinessWeek,* March 20, 1995, 78-80.

30. B.M. Bass, *Bass and Stogdill's Handbook of Leadership: Theory, Research, and Managerial Applications,* 3rd ed. (New York: Free Press, 1990); R.J. House and M.L. Baetz, "Leadership: Some Empirical Generalizations and New Research Directions," in B.M. Staw and L.L. Cummings, eds., *Research in Organizational Behavior,* vol. 1 (Greenwich, CT: JAI Press, 1979), 341-423; S. A. Kirpatrick and E.A. Locke, "Leadership: Do Traits Matter?" *Academy of Management Executive* 5, no. 2 (1991), 48-60; Yukl, *Leadership in Organizations;* G. Yukl and D.D. Van Fleet, "Theory and Research on Leadership in Organizations," in M.D. Dunnette and L.M. Hough, eds., *Handbook of Industrial and Organizational Psychology,* 2nd ed., vol. 3 (Palo Alto, CA: Consulting Psychologists Press, 1992), 147-97.

31. E.A. Fleishman, "Performance Assessment Based on an Empirically Derived Task Taxonomy," *Human Factors* 9 (1967), 349-66; E.A. Fleishman, "The Description of Supervisory Behavior," *Personnel Psychology* 37 (1953), 1-6; A.W. Halpin and B.J. Winer, "A Factorial Study of the Leader Behavior Descriptions," in R.M. Stogdill and A.I. Coons, eds., *Leader Behavior: Its Description and Measurement* (Columbus Bureau of Business Research, Ohio State University, 1957); D. Tscheulin, "Leader Behavior Measurement in German Industry," *Journal of Applied Psychology* 56 (1971), 28-31.

32. S. Greenhouse, "How Costco Became the Anti-Wal-Mart," *The New York Times,* July 17, 2005, BU1, BU8; "Costco Wholesale Corporation: Company Profile," http://phx.corporate-ir.net, accessed April 17, 2018.

33. "Corporate Governance," *Costco Wholesale, Investor Relations,* http://phx.corporate-ir.net/phoenix.zhtml?c583830&p5irol-govhighlights, April 28, 2006; J. Wohl, "Costco CEO's Legacy Continues as He Steps Down," Business & Financial News, Breaking US & International News, Reuters.com, http://www.reuters.com/assets/print?aid5USTRE7805VW20110901, September 1, 2011, accessed May 10, 2012; A. Gonzalez, "Costco Cofounder Sinegal Honored with Top Retail Award," *Seattle Times,* January 8, 2014, http://seattletimes.com/html/-businesstechnology/2022616694_costcoawardxml.html, May 14, 2014; Costco—Biography," http://phx.corporate-ir.net/phoenix.zhtml?c583830&p5irol-govBio&ID5202690, May 14, 2014; "Costco Wholesale Corporation—Investor Relations—Board of Directors," http://phx.corporate-ir.net/phoenix.zhtml?c=83830&p=irol-govboard, March 23, 2016.

34. "Top 100 Retailers: 2017," *Stores,* https://stores.org, accessed April 17, 2018.

35. Greenhouse, "How Costco Became the Anti-Wal-Mart."

36. S. Pettypiece, "Costco Will Raise Minimum Wage as Competition for Workers Grows," *Bloomberg Business,* http://www.bloomberg.com/news/articles/2016-03-03/costco-raising-minimum-wage-as-competition-for-workers-grows, March 23, 2016.

37. Greenhouse, "How Costco Became the Anti-Wal-Mart."

38. Ibid.; S. Clifford, "Because Who Knew a Big-Box Chain Could Have a Generous Soul," *Inc.,* April 2005, 88.

39. S. Holmes and W. Zellner, "Commentary: The Costco Way," *BusinessWeek Online,* www.businessweek.com/print/magazine/content/04_15/b3878084_mz021.htm? chan . . ., April 12, 2004; M. Herbst, "The Costco Challenge: An Alternative to Wal-Martization?" *LRA Online,* www.laborresearch.org/print.php?id5391, July 5, 2005.

40. Greenhouse, "How Costco Became the Anti-Wal-Mart."

41. Ibid.; "Costco Wholesale Corporate: Company Profile," http://phx.corporate-ir.net, accessed April 17, 2018.

42. A. Martinez and M. Allison, "Costco, Other Warehouse Clubs Holding Their Own during Recession," *Seattle Times,* http://seattletimes.nwsource.com/cgi-bin/PrintStory.pl?document_id52010922094&zsection . . ., February 1, 2010, accessed March 3, 2010; S. Skidmore, "Wholesale Clubs' Profit Grows as Grocery Supermarkets Slide," *USA TODAY,* http://www.usatoday.com/-cleanprint/?1267669249262, March 3, 2010.

43. "Costco Wholesale Corporation Reports Fourth Quarter and Fiscal Year 2017 Operating Results," https://globenewswire.com, October 5, 2017.

44. Martinez and Allison, "Costco, Other Warehouse Clubs Holding Their Own"; Allison, "Costco's Colorful CEO, Co-Founder Jim Sinegal to Retire."

45. "Costco Class Action Discrimination Lawsuit: Women Sue Costco," http://genderclassactionagainstcostco.com/costco94.pl, March 3, 2010; M.C. Fisk and K. Gullo, "Costco Ignored Sex Bias Warnings, Employees Say," http://www.seattlepi.com/business/284317_costcobias08.html, March 3, 2010; "Costco Job-Bias Lawsuit Advances," *Los Angeles Times,* http://articles.latimes.com/2007/jan/12/business/fi-costco12, January 12, 2007, accessed March 3, 2010.

46. A. Gonzalez, "Costco Settles Promotion Lawsuit for $8M, Vows Reforms," *Seattle Times,* http://seattletimes.com/html/businesstechnology/2022479586_costcosettlementxml.html, December 18, 2013, accessed May 14, 2014.

47. Gonzalez, "Costco Settles Promotion Lawsuit for $8M, Vows Reforms."

48. Ibid.

49. E.A. Fleishman and E.F. Harris, "Patterns of Leadership Behavior Related to Employee Grievances and Turnover," *Personnel Psychology* 15 (1962), 43-56.

50. R. Likert, *New Patterns of Management* (New York: McGraw-Hill, 1961); N.C. Morse and E. Reimer, "The Experimental Change of a Major Organizational Variable," *Journal of Abnormal and Social Psychology* 52 (1956), 120-29.

51. R.R. Blake and J.S. Mouton, *The New Managerial Grid* (Houston: Gulf, 1978).

52. P. Hersey and K. Blanchard, *Management of Organizational Behavior: Utilizing Human Resources* (Englewood Cliffs, NJ: Prentice-Hall, 1982).

53. F.E. Fiedler, *A Theory of Leadership Effectiveness* (New York: McGraw-Hill, 1967); F.E. Fiedler, "The Contingency Model and the Dynamics of the Leadership Process," in L. Berkowitz, ed., *Advances in Experimental Social Psychology* (New York: Academic Press, 1978).

54. J. Fierman, "Winning Ideas from Maverick Managers," *Fortune,* February 6, 1995, 66-80; "Geraldine Laybourne," https://allwomeninmedia.org, accessed April 13, 2018.

55. M. Schuman, "Free to Be," *Forbes,* May 8, 1995, 78-80; "Who Is Herman Mashaba?," https://www.enca.com, accessed April 13, 2018.

56. House and Baetz, "Leadership"; L.H. Peters, D.D. Hartke, and J.T. Pohlmann, "Fiedler's Contingency Theory of Leadership: An Application of the Meta-Analysis

Procedures of Schmidt and Hunter," *Psychological Bulletin* 97 (1985), 274-85; C.A. Schriesheim, B.J. Tepper, and L.A. Tetrault, "Least Preferred Co-Worker Score, Situational Control, and Leadership Effectiveness: A Meta-Analysis of Contingency Model Performance Predictions," *Journal of Applied Psychology* 79 (1994), 561-73.

57. E. Meyer, "Being the Boss in Brussels, Boston, and Beijing," *Harvard Business Review,* July-August 2017, 70-77.

58. Ibid., 75-77.

59. Ibid., 77; J. Owen, "How to Be a Global Leader," *Director,* November 2017, 56-57; A. Ghannad, "The Simple Key to Cross-Cultural Leadership," Association for Talent Development blog, www.td.org, February 5, 2018.

60. M.G. Evans, "The Effects of Supervisory Behavior on the Path-Goal Relationship," *Organizational Behavior and Human Performance* 5 (1970), 277-98; R.J. House, "A Path-Goal Theory of Leader Effectiveness," *Administrative Science Quarterly* 16 (1971), 321-38; J.C. Wofford and L.Z. Liska, "Path-Goal Theories of Leadership: A Meta-Analysis," *Journal of Management* 19 (1993), 857-76.

61. S. Kerr and J.M. Jermier, "Substitutes for Leadership: Their Meaning and Measurement," *Organizational Behavior and Human Performance* 22 (1978), 375-403; P. M. Podsakoff, B.P. Niehoff, S.B. MacKenzie, and M.L. Williams, "Do Substitutes for Leadership Really Substitute for Leadership? An Empirical Examination of Kerr and Jermier's Situational Leadership Model," *Organizational Behavior and Human Decision Processes* 54 (1993), 1-44.

62. Kerr and Jermier, "Substitutes for Leadership"; Podsakoff et al., "Do Substitutes for Leadership Really Substitute for Leadership?"

63. J. B. Carson, P.E. Tesluk, and J.A. Marrone, "Shared Leadership in Teams: An Investigation of Antecedent Conditions and Performance," *Academy of Management Journal* 50, no. 5 (2007), 1217-34.

64. J. Reingold, "You Got Served," *Fortune,* October 1, 2007, 55-58; J. Luce, "Lessons Learned by Customer Service Expert Sue Nokes," https://medium.com, November 20, 2017.

65. Reingold, "You Got Served."

66. Ibid.; "Company Information"; "Highest Customer Satisfaction & Wireless Call Quality—J.D. Power Awards," http://www.t-mobile.com/Company/CompanyInfo.aspx?tp5Abt_Tab_Awards, April 8, 2008.

67. Reingold, "You Got Served."

68. B.M. Bass, *Leadership and Performance beyond Expectations* (New York: Free Press, 1985); Bass, *Bass and Stogdill's Handbook of Leadership;* Yukl and Van Fleet, "Theory and Research on Leadership."

69. Reingold, "You Got Served."

70. Ibid.

71. J.A. Conger and R.N. Kanungo, "Behavioral Dimensions of Charismatic Leadership," in J.A. Conger, R.N. Kanungo, and Associates, eds., *Charismatic Leadership* (San Francisco: Jossey-Bass, 1988).

72. Bass, *Leadership and Performance beyond Expectations;* Bass, *Bass and Stogdill's Handbook of Leadership;* Yukl and Van Fleet, "Theory and Research on Leadership"; Reingold, "You Got Served."

73. Ibid.

74. Reingold, "You Got Served."

75. Bass, *Leadership and Performance beyond Expectations.*

76. Bass, *Bass and Stogdill's Handbook of Leadership;* B.M. Bass and B.J. Avolio,"Transformational Leadership: A Response to Critiques," in M.M. Chemers and R. Ayman, eds., *Leadership Theory and Research: Perspectives and Directions* (San Diego: Academic Press, 1993), 49-80; B.M. Bass, B.J. Avolio, and L. Goodheim, "Biography and the Assessment of Transformational Leadership at the World Class Level," *Journal of Management* 13 (1987), 7-20; J.J. Hater and B.M. Bass, "Supervisors' Evaluations and Subordinates' Perceptions of Transformational and Transactional Leadership," *Journal of Applied Psychology* 73 (1988), 695-702; R. Pillai, "Crisis and Emergence of Charismatic Leadership in Groups: An Experimental Investigation," *Journal of Applied Psychology* 26 (1996), 543-62; J. Seltzer and B.M. Bass, "Transformational Leadership: Beyond Initiation and Consideration," *Journal of Management* 16 (1990), 693-703; D.A. Waldman, B.M. Bass, and W.O. Einstein, "Effort, Performance, Transformational Leadership in Industrial and Military Service," *Journal of Occupation Psychology* 60 (1987), 1-10.

77. W. Jiang, X. Zhao, and J. Ni, "The Impact of Transformational Leadership on Employee Sustainable Performance: The Mediating Role of Organizational Citizenship Behavior," *Sustainability* 9 (2017), 1567-83; R. Pillai, C.A. Schriesheim, and E.S. Williams, "Fairness Perceptions and Trust as Mediators of Transformational and Transactional Leadership: A Two-Sample Study," *Journal of Management* 25 (1999), 897-933.

78. Catalyst, "Women CEOs of the S&P 500," https://www.catalyst.org, August 6, 2018; J. Carpenter, "This Is What Women Have to Do to Become CEO," *CNNMoney,* http://money.cnn.com, February 1, 2018.

79. Catalyst, "Pyramid: Women in S&P 500 Companies," www.catalyst.org, February 5, 2018.

80. A.H. Eagly and B.T. Johnson, "Gender and Leadership Style: A Meta-Analysis," *Psychological Bulletin* 108 (1990), 233-56.

81. Eagly and Johnson, "Gender and Leadership Style."

82. V. Lipman, "Are Women Better Managers Than Men?" *Psychology Today,* www.psychologytoday.com, April 23, 2015.

83. J. Baldoni, "Few Executives Are Self-Aware, But Women Have the Edge," *Harvard Business Review,* https://hbr.org, May 9, 2013.

84. Ibid.

85. A.H. Eagly, S.J. Karau, and M.G. Makhijani, "Gender and the Effectiveness of Leaders: A Meta-Analysis," *Psychological Bulletin* 117 (1995), 125-45.

86. Eagly, Karau, and Makhijani, "Gender and the Effectiveness of Leaders."

87. J.M. George and K. Bettenhausen, "Understanding Prosocial Behavior, Sales Performance, and Turnover: A Group-Level Analysis in a Service Context," *Journal of Applied Psychology* 75 (1990), 698-709.

88. T. Sy, S. Cote, and R. Saavedra, "The Contagious Leader: Impact of the Leader's Mood on the Mood of Group Members, Group Affective Tone, and Group Processes," *Journal of Applied Psychology* 90, no. 2, (2005), 295-305.

89. J.M. George, "Emotions and Leadership: The Role of Emotional Intelligence," *Human Relations* 53 (2000), 1027-55.

90. George, "Emotions and Leadership."

91. J. Zhou and J.M. George, "Awakening Employee Creativity: The Role of Leader Emotional Intelligence," *The Leadership Quarterly* 14, no. 45 (August-October 2003), 545-68.

92. Zhou and George, "Awakening Employee Creativity."

93. Ibid.

94. J. Garfinkle, "Five Qualities of Emotionally Intelligent Leaders," *Smart Brief,* www.smartbrief.com, January 15, 2018; B. Tracy, "Why Emotional Intelligence Is Indispensable for Leaders," *Forbes,* October 30, 2017, www.forbes.com; S.T.A. Phipps, "Why Emotional Intelligence Is Necessary for Effective Leadership," *Leadership Excellence Essentials,* June 2017, 56-57.

95. Garfinkle, "Five Qualities"; S. Bawany, "The Art and Practice of Servant Leadership," *Leadership Excellence Essentials,* November 2017, 34-35.

96. Tracy, "Why Emotional Intelligence Is Indispensable"; M. Prokopeak, "Building the Leader of the Future," *Chief Learning Officer,* www.clomedia.com, March 22, 2018.

97. S. Goldstein, "EQ Is Massively More Important Than IQ for Leaders. Here's Why," *Inc.,* www.inc.com, September 26, 2017.

432

CHAPTER 15

Effective Groups and Teams

©Flying Colours Ltd/Getty Images

Learning Objectives

After studying this chapter, you should be able to:

LO15-1 Explain why groups and teams are key contributors to organizational effectiveness.

LO15-2 Identify the different types of groups and teams that help managers and organizations achieve their goals.

LO15-3 Explain how different elements of group dynamics influence the functioning and effectiveness of groups and teams.

LO15-4 Explain why it is important for groups and teams to have a balance of conformity and deviance and a moderate level of cohesiveness.

LO15-5 Describe how managers can motivate group members to achieve organizational goals and reduce social loafing in groups and teams.

How can managers use teams to enhance performance? When it comes to technology and the development of new weapons, the worst enemy of the U.S. Army is its slow-moving layers of bureaucracy. When the army identifies a need, the process of creating specifications and designing a new product can take several years—so long that by the time the product is available, it is no longer considered advanced technology. The edge the army wants to maintain over any adversaries is all but wiped out.[1]

The army's leadership identified a solution involving teamwork. Specifically, it set up a Futures Command that identified eight areas in which development is crucial: long-range precision fires, a next-generation combat vehicle, improvement in lift capacity for aircraft, a data and communications network, air and missile defenses, and advances in soldier performance. For each, the command set up a team bringing together members from different functions, including planning, science and technology, finance, program management, testing, and materials. Each team is led by a one- or two-star officer with combat experience. The teams collectively report to Under Secretary of the Army Ryan D. McCarthy and Army Vice Chief of Staff Gen. James C. McConville, whose positions give them authority to allocate major resources.[2]

The team process benefits from accelerated learning from experimentation, prototyping, and adaptation. Instead of trying to design a perfect project with requirements for all possible features, the team develops an idea, perhaps using off-the-shelf systems, and goes straight to the prototype stage. This involves bringing in soldiers to test the prototype, which increases their support and gives them an opportunity to deliver feedback from a user's perspective. Through all of this, the team is learning and adapting the idea, based on test results and the soldiers' feedback. In some cases, it might begin producing a less-than-full-featured product as a best option while it continues the development process to improve requirements for the final version.[3]

For example, the cross-function team responsible for tactical networks is working to bring out a system that will survive modern-day threats like cyberattacks. The team is pressing for faster purchases of prototypes and more frequent feedback from soldiers, so the system design can be improved faster. This enables the team to create better requirements than if designers worked on their own. Another team, charged with updating the system for position, navigation, and timing, is working on several areas for improvement. It is rolling out upgrades to

Under Secretary of the U.S. Army, Ryan D. McCarthy, believes effective teamwork within the military spurs innovation and reduces bureaucracy.
Source: United States Army

solve urgent needs as the system moves forward, rather than waiting to deploy a system that would theoretically be perfect.[4]

Early results suggest that teamwork is a success. Among the most dramatic results is acceleration of the pace of work. McCarthy sees evidence that the kinds of decisions that used to wend their way up and down the hierarchy over a period of months now get done in a few days. In addition, he notes, years are being shaved off the overall process, which in the past could take a decade to complete. New night-vision goggles are ready for distribution just one year after being proposed. Development of a long-range precision artillery missile is advancing at a pace that could lead to completion five years ahead of schedule. Further, McCarthy notes that the more extensive prototyping and testing are yielding better decisions about where to spend money and how to improve products.[5]

Overview

LO15-1 Explain why groups and teams are key contributors to organizational effectiveness.

The U.S. Army is not alone in using groups and teams to innovate and improve organizational effectiveness. Managers in companies large and small are using groups and teams to enhance performance, increase responsiveness to customers, spur innovation, and motivate employees. In this chapter we look in detail at how groups and teams can contribute to organizational effectiveness and the types of groups and teams used in organizations. We discuss how different elements of group dynamics influence the functioning and effectiveness of groups, and we describe how managers can motivate group members to achieve organizational goals and reduce social loafing in groups and teams. By the end of this chapter you will appreciate why the effective management of groups and teams is a key ingredient in organizational performance and effectiveness.

Groups, Teams, and Organizational Effectiveness

group Two or more people who interact with each other to accomplish certain goals or meet certain needs.

team A group whose members work intensely with one another to achieve a specific common goal or objective.

A **group** may be defined as two or more people who interact with each other to accomplish certain goals or meet certain needs.[6] A **team** is a group whose members work *intensely* with one another to achieve a specific common goal or objective. As these definitions imply, all teams are groups, but not all groups are teams. The two characteristics that distinguish teams from groups are the *intensity* with which team members work together and the presence of a *specific, overriding team goal or objective.*

Recall some of the goals of the teams highlighted in "A Manager's Challenge." In contrast, the accountants who work in a small CPA firm are a group: They may interact with one another to achieve goals such as keeping up-to-date on the latest changes in accounting rules and regulations, maintaining a smoothly functioning office, satisfying clients, and attracting new clients, but they are not a team because they do not work intensely with one another. Each accountant concentrates on serving the needs of his or her own clients.

Because all teams are also groups, whenever we use the term *group* in this chapter, we are referring to both groups *and* teams. As you might imagine, because members of teams work intensely together, teams can sometimes be difficult to form, and it may take time for members to learn how to work effectively together. Under these conditions, for team development and performance to succeed, team members need "soft" skills, as described in the "Management Insight" feature.

Groups and teams can help an organization gain a competitive advantage because they can (1) enhance its performance, (2) increase its responsiveness to customers, (3) increase innovation, and (4) increase employees' motivation and satisfaction (see Figure 15.1). In this section we look at each of these contributions in turn.

Team Members Need Soft Skills

Teams are often formed for challenging activities: developing products, rolling out software systems, or planning a marketing campaign. These require the expertise of engineers, software developers, marketing researchers, finance professionals, and others. Besides this technical expertise, all teams require "soft" skills. These are the people-related skills that get team members connected with each other and aligned on carrying out a shared purpose. Soft skills include organizing, collaborating, solving interpersonal problems, and communicating (speaking, writing, and above all, listening).[7]

On teams with soft skills, members share ideas, pool their knowledge to solve problems, and keep each other updated on their progress. People are unafraid to make mistakes, are open to learning from one another, and listen to one another's ideas. Team members with soft skills benefit the team by connecting with the rest of the organization to gather information and other resources. These individuals bring out other members' ideas and get them motivated.[8]

However, soft skills are hard to measure, so it is difficult to select job candidates with soft skills. Furthermore, employers struggle to teach these skills. Annie Healy, recruiting manager for the Motley Fool, a media company focused on investing, recalls interviewing a candidate whose technical skills were so impressive that she did not fully explore the candidate's soft skills. The company made the hire but has since needed to intervene a great deal to make up for the person's lack of focus on teamwork.[9]

The first and most important way to form teams with soft skills is to hire people who have those skills or at least have shown potential to develop them. This requires identifying which soft skills will contribute to the team's success and developing questions that ask job candidates to describe situations in which they have used or would use the particular skills. Commercially available tests can screen for particular qualities such as empathy or emotional intelligence. Other tests measure individual differences such as problem-solving styles. Team leaders can be taught to use information from these tests to ensure that each person is contributing effectively according to his or her style.[10]

In addition, training should address development of soft skills. It should extend beyond classroom or coaching sessions by assigning behaviors to practice and situations in which to practice them. Along with training, the employee should have measurable goals, such as giving presentations or restructuring meetings to ensure all voices are heard.[11]

Figure 15.1

Groups' and Teams' Contributions to Organizational Effectiveness

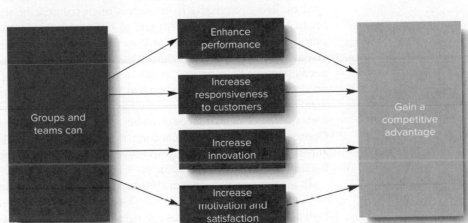

Groups and Teams as Performance Enhancers

synergy Performance gains that result when individuals and departments coordinate their actions.

One of the main advantages of using groups is the opportunity to obtain a type of **synergy**: People working in a group can produce more or higher-quality outputs than would have been produced if each person had worked separately and all their individual efforts were later combined. The essence of synergy is captured in the saying "The whole is more than the sum of its parts." Factors that can contribute to synergy in groups include the abilities of group members to bounce ideas off one another, to correct one another's mistakes, to solve problems immediately as they arise, to bring a diverse knowledge base to bear on a problem or goal, and to accomplish work that is too vast or all-encompassing for any individual to achieve alone.

To take advantage of the potential for synergy in groups, managers need to make sure that groups are composed of members who have complementary skills and knowledge relevant to the group's work. For example, at Hallmark Cards, synergies are created by bringing together all the different functions needed to create and produce a greeting card in a cross-functional team (a team composed of members from different departments or functions) (see Chapter 10). For instance, artists, writers, designers, and marketing experts work together as team members to develop new cards.[12]

At Hallmark the skills and expertise of the artists complement the contributions of the writers and vice versa. Managers also need to give groups enough autonomy so that the groups, rather than the manager, are solving problems and determining how to achieve goals and objectives, as is true in the cross-functional teams at Hallmark. To promote synergy, managers need to empower their subordinates and to be coaches, guides, and resources for groups while refraining from playing a more directive or supervisory role. The potential for synergy in groups may be the reason more and more managers are incorporating empowerment into their personal leadership styles (see Chapter 14).

When tasks are complex and involve highly sophisticated and rapidly changing technologies, achieving synergies in teams often hinges on having the appropriate mix of backgrounds and areas of expertise represented on the team. In large organizations with operations in many states and countries, managers can rely on databases and software applications to determine which employees might have the expertise needed on a particular team or for a certain project.

Groups, Teams, and Responsiveness to Customers

Being responsive to customers is not always easy. In manufacturing organizations, for example, customers' needs and desires for new and improved products have to be balanced against engineering constraints, production costs and feasibilities, government safety regulations, and marketing challenges. In service organizations such as health care organizations, being responsive to patients' needs and desires for prompt, high-quality medical care and treatment has to be balanced against meeting physicians' needs and desires and keeping health care costs under control. Being responsive to customers often requires the wide variety of skills and expertise found in different departments and at different levels in an organization's hierarchy. Sometimes, for example, employees at lower levels in an organization's hierarchy, such as sales representatives for a computer company, are closest to its customers and the most attuned to their needs. However, lower-level employees, like salespeople, often lack the technical expertise needed for new product ideas; such expertise is found in the research and development department. Bringing salespeople, research and development experts, and members of other departments together in a group or cross-functional team can enhance responsiveness to customers. Consequently, when managers form a team, they must make sure the diversity of expertise and knowledge needed to be responsive to customers exists within the team; this is why cross-functional teams are so popular.

In a cross-functional team, the expertise and knowledge in different organizational departments are brought together in the skills and knowledge of the team members. Managers of high-performing organizations are careful to determine which types of expertise and knowledge are required for teams to be responsive to customers, and they use this information in forming teams.

Teams and Innovation

Innovation—the creative development of new products, new technologies, new services, or even new organizational structures—is a topic we introduced in Chapter 1. Often an individual working alone does not possess the extensive and diverse skills, knowledge, and expertise required for successful innovation. Managers can better encourage innovation by creating teams of diverse individuals who together have the knowledge relevant to a particular type of innovation—as is the case with the U.S. Army's new Futures Command teams profiled in "A Manager's Challenge"—rather than by relying on individuals working alone.

Using teams to innovate has other advantages. First, team members can often uncover one another's errors or false assumptions; an individual acting alone would not be able to do this. Second, team members can critique one another's approaches and build off one another's strengths while compensating for weaknesses—an advantage of devil's advocacy and dialectical inquiry, discussed in Chapter 7.

To further promote innovation, managers can empower teams and make their members fully responsible and accountable for the innovation process. The manager's role is to provide guidance, assistance, coaching, and the resources that team members need, *not* to closely direct or supervise their activities. To speed innovation, managers also need to form teams in which each member brings a unique resource to the team, such as engineering prowess, knowledge of production, marketing expertise, or financial savvy. Successful innovation sometimes requires that managers form teams with members from different countries and cultures.

Groups and Teams as Motivators

Managers often form groups and teams to accomplish organizational goals and then find that using groups and teams brings additional benefits. Members of groups, and especially members of teams (because of the higher intensity of interaction in teams), are likely to be more satisfied than they would have been if they had been on their own. The experience of working alongside other highly charged and motivated people can be stimulating and motivating: Team members can see how their efforts and expertise directly contribute to the achievement of team and organizational goals, and they feel personally responsible for the outcomes or results of their work. This has been the case at Hallmark Cards.

The increased motivation and satisfaction that can accompany the use of teams can also lead to other outcomes, such as lower turnover. This has been Frank B. Day's experience as founder of Rock Bottom Restaurants Inc.[13] To provide high-quality customer service, Day organized the restaurants' employees into waitstaff teams, whose members work together to refill beers, take orders, take hot chicken enchiladas to the tables, or clear off the tables. Team members share the burden of undesirable activities and unpopular shift times, and customers no longer have to wait until a particular waitress or waiter is available. Motivation and satisfaction levels in Rock Bottom restaurants seem to be higher than in other restaurants, and turnover has been much less than experienced in other U.S. restaurant chains.[14]

Working in a group or team can also satisfy organizational members' needs for engaging in social interaction and feeling connected to other people. For workers who perform highly stressful jobs, such as hospital emergency and operating room staff, group membership can be an important source of social support and motivation. Family members or friends may not be able to fully understand or appreciate some sources of work stress that these group members experience firsthand. Moreover, group members may cope better with work stressors when they can share them with other members of their group. In addition, groups often devise techniques to relieve stress, such as the telling of jokes among hospital operating room staff.

Why do managers in all kinds of organizations rely so heavily on groups and teams? Effectively managed groups and teams can help managers in their quest for high performance, responsiveness to customers, and employee motivation. Before explaining how managers can effectively manage groups, however, we will describe the types of groups that are formed in organizations.

Types of Groups and Teams

LO15-2 Identify the different types of groups and teams that help managers and organizations achieve their goals.

formal groups Groups that managers establish to achieve organizational goals.

informal groups Groups that managers or nonmanagerial employees form to help them achieve their own goals or meet their own needs.

top management team A group composed of the CEO, the president, and the heads of the most important departments.

To achieve their goals of high performance, responsiveness to customers, innovation, and employee motivation, managers can form various types of groups and teams (see Figure 15.2). **Formal groups** are those that managers establish to achieve organizational goals. The formal work groups are *cross-functional* teams composed of members from different departments, such as those at Hallmark Cards, and *cross-cultural* teams composed of members from different cultures or countries, such as the teams at global carmakers. As you will see, some of the groups discussed in this section also can be considered to be cross-functional (if they are composed of members from different departments) or cross-cultural (if they are composed of members from different countries or cultures).

Sometimes organizational members, managers or nonmanagers, form groups because they feel that groups will help them achieve their own goals or meet their own needs (for example, the need for social interaction). Groups formed in this way are **informal groups**. Four nurses who work in a hospital and have lunch together twice a week constitute an informal group.

The Top Management Team

A central concern of the CEO and president of a company is to form a **top management team** to help the organization achieve its mission and goals. Top management teams are responsible for developing the strategies that result in an organization's competitive advantage; most have between five and seven members. In forming their top management teams, CEOs are well advised to stress diversity in expertise, skills, knowledge, and experience. Thus, many top management teams are also cross-functional teams: They are composed of members from different departments, such as finance, marketing, production, and engineering. Diversity helps ensure that the top management team will have all the background and resources it needs to make good decisions. Diversity also helps guard against *groupthink*—faulty group decision making that results when group members strive for agreement at the expense of an accurate assessment of the situation (see Chapter 7).

Research and Development Teams

research and development teams Teams whose members have the expertise and experience needed to develop new products.

Managers in pharmaceuticals, computers, electronics, electronic imaging, and other high-tech industries often create **research and development teams** to develop new products. Managers select research and development (R&D) team members on the basis of their expertise and experience in a certain area. Sometimes R&D teams are cross-functional, with members from departments such as engineering, marketing, and production in addition to members from the research and development department.

Figure 15.2

Types of Groups and Teams in Organizations

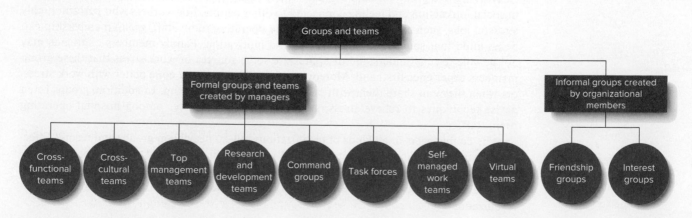

Command Groups

command group A group composed of subordinates who report to the same supervisor; also called *department* or *unit.*

Subordinates who report to the same supervisor compose a **command group.** When top managers design an organization's structure and establish reporting relationships and a chain of command, they are essentially creating command groups. Command groups, often called *departments* or *units,* perform a significant amount of the work in many organizations. In order to have command groups that help an organization gain a competitive advantage, managers not only need to motivate group members to perform at a high level, but also must be effective leaders. Examples of command groups include the salespeople in a large department store in New York who report to the same supervisor, the employees of a small swimming pool sales and maintenance company in Florida who report to a general manager, the customer service representatives at the MetLife insurance company who report to the same supervisor, and workers on an automobile assembly line in the Ford Motor Company who report to the same first-line manager.

Task Forces

task forces Committees of managers or nonmanagerial employees from various departments or divisions who meet to solve a specific, mutual problem; also called *ad hoc committees.*

Managers form **task forces** to accomplish specific goals or solve problems in a certain time period; task forces are sometimes called *ad hoc committees.* For example, Michael Rider, owner and top manager of a chain of six gyms and fitness centers in the Midwest, created a task force composed of the general managers of the six gyms to determine whether the fitness centers should institute a separate fee schedule for customers who wanted to use the centers only for aerobics classes (and not use other facilities such as weights, steps, tracks, and swimming pools). The task force was given three months to prepare a report summarizing the pros and cons of the proposed change in fee schedules. After the task force completed its report and reached the conclusion that the change in fee structure probably would reduce revenues rather than increase them and thus should not be implemented, the task force was disbanded. As in Rider's case, task forces can be a valuable tool for busy managers who do not have the time to personally explore an important issue in depth.

Sometimes managers need to form task forces whose work, so to speak, is never done. The task force may be addressing a long-term or enduring problem or issue facing an organization, such as how to most usefully contribute to the local community or how to make sure the organization provides opportunities for potential employees with disabilities. Task forces that are relatively permanent are often referred to as *standing committees.* Membership in standing committees changes over time. Members may have, for example, a two- or three-year term on the committee, and memberships expire at varying times so there are always some members with experience on the committee. Managers often form and maintain standing committees to make sure important issues continue to be addressed.

Self-Managed Work Teams

self-managed work teams Groups of employees who supervise their own activities and monitor the quality of the goods and services they provide.

Self-managed work teams are teams in which members are empowered and have the responsibility and autonomy to complete identifiable pieces of work. On a day-to-day basis, team members decide what the team will do, how it will do it, and which members will perform which specific tasks.[15] Managers can assign self-managed work teams' overall goals (such as assembling defect-free computer keyboards) but let team members decide how to meet those goals. Managers usually form self-managed work teams to improve quality, increase motivation and satisfaction, and lower costs. Often, by creating self-managed work teams, they combine tasks that individuals working separately used to perform, so the team is responsible for the whole set of tasks that yields an identifiable output or end product.

Managers can take a number of steps to ensure that self-managed work teams are effective and help an organization achieve its goals:[16]

- Give teams enough responsibility and autonomy to be truly self-managing. Refrain from telling team members what to do or solving problems for them, even if you (as a manager) know what should be done.

- Make sure a team's work is sufficiently complex so that it entails a number of different steps or procedures that must be performed and results in some kind of finished end product.

- Carefully select members of self-managed work teams. Team members should have the diversity of skills needed to complete the team's work, have the ability to work with others, and want to be part of a team.

- As a manager, realize that your role with self-managed work teams calls for guidance, coaching, and supporting, not supervising. You are a resource for teams to turn to when needed.

- Analyze what type of training team members need, and provide it. Working in a self-managed work team often requires that employees have more extensive technical and interpersonal skills.

Managers in a wide variety of organizations have found that self-managed work teams help the organization achieve its goals,[17] as illustrated in the accompanying "Management Insight" feature.

MANAGEMENT INSIGHT

Self-Managed Teams at W. L. Gore

W. L. Gore & Associates was founded by Wilbert ("Bill") Gore and his wife, Genevieve ("Vieve"), in the basement of their house in 1958, and the rest has literally been history.[18] Widely recognized for its diverse and innovative products, Gore has over $3 billion in annual revenues and over 9,500 employees (who are called associates) worldwide. Headquartered in Newark, Delaware, Gore's most widely recognized product is the waterproof fabric Gore-Tex. Gore makes a wide array of products, including fabrics for outerwear, medical products used in surgeries, fibers for astronauts' space suits, and Elixir strings for acoustic guitars. While Gore has thousands of products and over 2,000 worldwide patents, most of Gore's products are based on a very adaptable material, expanded polytetrafluoroethylene (ePTFE), a polymer invented by the Gores' son in 1969.[19] A key ingredient of Gore's enduring success is its use of teams to innovate and motivate rather than reliance on a hierarchy of managers.[20]

The Gores were 45 years old and the parents of five children when they took the plunge. Prior to starting his own company, Bill Gore worked at DuPont, which helped him realize how teams can be powerful sources of innovation and high performance. As a member of small R&D teams at DuPont, Gore experienced firsthand how inspiring and motivating it can be to work on a self-managed team with the objective to create and innovate and to have high levels of autonomy to do so. He reasoned that innovation and high motivation and performance would likely result when as many people as possible in an organization were members of self-managed teams tasked to be innovative and given high levels of autonomy. And that is what he set out to accomplish by founding W. L. Gore. Thus, many teams at Gore have the goal of developing innovative new products.[21]

While Gore has a CEO (Jason Field) and four divisions (electronics, fabrics, industrial, and medical), there are few managers, and associates do not have supervisors. Gore is structured around a lattice of self-managed teams in which associates and their teams communicate directly with each other whenever the need or desire arises and their the mission is to innovate, to perform highly, and to enjoy their work.[22] Personal initiative and

Gore uses teams to develop new products rather than a hierarchy of managers. Its best-known product is the waterproof fabric Gore-Tex.
©ZUMA Press, Inc./Alamy Stock Photo

high motivation are greatly valued at Gore, and working in self-managed teams with high levels of autonomy fuels new product innovations.[23]

Associates working in manufacturing are also empowered to work in self-managed teams. For example, a team of manufacturing associates realized that new manufacturing equipment was needed to produce work in the United States that had been produced overseas, leading to inefficiencies. The team gathered information from other teams to develop the specifications for the machinery. Teams of associates negotiated to have an outside supplier build the $2 million machinery. And all went well when the equipment was installed and used.[24]

At Gore, associates recognize leaders who are especially proficient at building great teams and accomplishing goals, and the associates willingly become their followers.[25] New hires at Gore are assigned into broad areas—such as R&D, engineering, sales and marketing, information technology, operations management, and human resources— and assigned a sponsor.[26] Sponsors are experienced associates who help newcomers learn the ropes, meet other associates, and acclimatize to Gore's unique culture and values centered around high trust and motivation. Ultimately, sponsors help newcomers find a team for which they are a good fit. Teams are truly self-managing, so it is up to the team members to decide if they want to have newcomers join them, and the newcomers are responsible to the teams they join. Experienced associates are typically members of multiple self-managed teams.[27]

One of the largest 200 privately held companies in the United States, Gore is owned by the associates as well as the Gore family.[28] Associates are awarded a percentage of their salary in shares of the company and participate in a profit-sharing program. The shares become vested after a certain time period, and associates who leave the company can sell their shares back for cash payouts.[29]

At Gore, associates are accountable to each other and the teams they are members of. Thus, perhaps it is not surprising that associates are reviewed by their peers. Each year information is gathered from around 20 colleagues of each associate and given to a compensation committee in their work unit that determines relative contributions and compensation levels for members of the unit.[30]

Associates thrive in Gore's collaborative and team-based structure. Thus, it is not surprising that Gore has received recognition for being a top employer. Gore has been on *Fortune* magazine's list of the "100 Best Companies to Work For" for 20 consecutive years—along with only 11 other companies.[31]

Sometimes employees have individual jobs but also are part of a self-managed team that is formed to accomplish a specific goal or work on an important project. Employees need to perform their own individual job tasks as well as actively contribute to the self-managed team so that the team achieves its goal.

Sometimes self-managed work teams run into trouble. Members may be reluctant to discipline one another by firing members or withholding bonuses from members who are not performing up to par.[32] Buster Jarrell, a manager who oversaw self-managed work teams in AES Corporation's Houston plant, found that although the self-managed work teams were highly effective, they had a difficult time firing team members who were performing poorly.[33]

The Dallas office of the New York Life Insurance Company experimented with having members of self-managed teams evaluate one another's performance and determine pay levels. Team members did not feel comfortable assuming this role, however, and managers ended up handling these tasks.[34] One reason for team members' discomfort may be the close personal relationships they sometimes develop with one another. In addition, members of self-managed work teams may sometimes take longer to accomplish tasks, such as when team members have difficulties coordinating their efforts.

virtual teams Teams whose members rarely or never meet face-to-face but, rather, interact by using various forms of information technology such as email, cloud computing, videoconferences, and various meeting and management apps.

Virtual Teams

Virtual teams are teams whose members rarely or never meet face-to-face but, rather, interact by using various forms of information technology such as email, text messaging, cloud computing, videoconferences, and various meeting and management apps. As organizations become increasingly global, and as the need for specialized knowledge increases due to advances in technology, managers can create virtual teams to solve problems or explore opportunities without being limited by team members' needing to work in the same geographic location.[35]

Take the case of an organization that has manufacturing facilities in Australia, Canada, the United States, and Mexico and is encountering a quality problem in a complex manufacturing process. Each of its facilities has a quality control team headed by a quality control manager. The vice president for production does not try to solve the problem by forming and leading a team at one of the four manufacturing facilities; instead, she forms and leads a virtual team composed of the quality control managers of the four plants and the plants' general managers. When these team members communicate via email, the company's networking site, and videoconferencing, a wide array of knowledge and experience is brought to solve the problem.

The principal advantage of virtual teams is that they enable managers to disregard geographic distances and form teams whose members have the knowledge, expertise, and experience to tackle a particular problem or take advantage of a specific opportunity.[36] Virtual teams also can include members who are not actually employees of the organization itself; a virtual team might include members of a company that is used for outsourcing. More and more companies, including Ultimate Software, General Electric, and SAP, are using virtual teams.[37]

Increasing globalization is likely to result in more organizations relying on virtual teams to a greater extent. One challenge that members of virtual teams face is building a sense of camaraderie and trust among team members who rarely, if ever, meet face-to-face. In fact, recent research suggests that the link between trust and team effectiveness was even stronger for virtual teams than for teams that work in the same location. This finding underscores the need for managers of virtual teams to focus on building trust among team members.[38] To address this challenge, some organizations schedule recreational activities, such as ski trips, so virtual team members can get together. Other organizations make sure virtual team members have a chance to meet in person soon after the team is formed and then schedule periodic face-to-face meetings to promote trust, understanding, and cooperation in the teams.[39] The need for such meetings is underscored by research suggesting that while some virtual teams can be as effective as teams that meet face-to-face, virtual team members might be less satisfied with teamwork efforts and have fewer feelings of camaraderie or cohesion. (Group cohesiveness is discussed in more detail later in the chapter.)[40]

Not surprisingly, members of successful virtual teams exhibit certain skills and abilities that help make these long-distance groups so effective. Researchers point out that leadership behaviors such as taking personal initiative and working independently are more beneficial to virtual teams than to teams that work face-to-face on a daily basis. In addition, studies point out that members' strong analytical and written communication skills provide competitive advantage to a company's virtual teams. These findings suggest that managers hiring employees for virtual teams might focus on some of these specific skills that have proved successful.[41]

Research also suggests that it is important for managers to keep track of virtual teams and intervene when necessary by, for example, encouraging members of teams who do not communicate often enough to monitor their team's progress and making sure team members actually have the time, and are recognized, for their virtual teamwork. Additionally, when virtual teams are experiencing downtime or rough spots, managers might try to schedule face-to-face team time to bring team members together and help them focus on their goals.[42]

Researchers at the London Business School, including Professor Lynda Gratton, studied global virtual teams to try to identify factors that might help such teams be effective. Based on their research, Gratton suggests that when forming virtual teams, it is helpful to include a few members who already know each other, other members who are well connected to people outside the team, and when possible, members who have volunteered to be a part of the team. It is also advantageous for companies to have some kind of online site where team members can learn more about each other and the kinds of work they are engaged in and, in particular, a shared online workspace that team members can access around the clock. Frequent communication is beneficial. Additionally, virtual team members should perceive their projects as meaningful, interesting, and important to promote and sustain their motivation.[43]

Today, members of virtual teams rely on many different technology tools to help them with their work activities, including Slack (a team chat app), Zoom (a videoconferencing/screen-sharing tool), World Time Buddy (a tool that allows workers to find optimum times to schedule calls and collaboration meetings with remote team members), and Google Drive (an online collaborative, document-sharing program).[44]

Friendship Groups

friendship groups Informal groups of employees who enjoy one another's company and socialize with one another.

The groups described so far are formal groups created by managers. **Friendship groups** are informal groups of employees who enjoy one another's company and socialize with one another. Members of friendship groups may have lunch together, take breaks together, or meet after work for meals, sports, or other activities. Friendship groups help satisfy employees' needs for interpersonal interaction, can provide needed social support in times of stress, and can contribute to people's feeling good at work and being satisfied with their jobs. Managers themselves often form friendship groups. The informal relationships that managers build in friendship groups can often help them solve work-related problems, because members of these groups typically discuss work-related matters and offer advice.

Interest Groups

interest groups Informal groups of employees seeking to achieve a common goal related to their membership in an organization.

Employees form informal **interest groups** when they seek to achieve a common goal related to their membership in an organization. Employees may form interest groups, for example, to encourage managers to consider instituting flexible working hours, providing on-site child care, improving working conditions, or more proactively supporting environmental protection. Interest groups can give managers valuable insights into the issues and concerns that are foremost in employees' minds. They also can signal the need for change.

Group Dynamics

How groups function and, ultimately, their effectiveness hinge on group characteristics and processes known collectively as *group dynamics*. In this section we discuss five key elements of group dynamics: group size, tasks, and roles; group leadership; group development; group norms; and group cohesiveness.

LO15-3 Explain how different elements of group dynamics influence the functioning and effectiveness of groups and teams.

Group Size, Tasks, and Roles

Managers need to take group size, group tasks, and group roles into account as they create and maintain high-performing groups and teams.

GROUP SIZE   The number of members in a group can be an important determinant of members' motivation and commitment and group performance. There are several advantages to keeping a group relatively small—between two and nine members. Compared with members of large groups, members of small groups tend to (1) interact more with each other and find it easier to coordinate their efforts, (2) be more motivated, satisfied, and committed, (3) find it easier to share information, and (4) be better able to see the importance of their personal contributions for group success. A disadvantage of small rather than large groups is that members of small groups have fewer resources available to accomplish their goals.

Large groups—with 10 or more members—also offer some advantages. They have more resources at their disposal to achieve group goals than small groups do. These resources include the knowledge, experience, skills, and abilities of group members as well as their actual time and effort. Large groups also let managers obtain the advantages stemming from the **division of labor**—splitting the work to be performed into particular tasks and assigning tasks to individual workers. Workers who specialize in particular tasks are likely to become skilled at performing those tasks and contribute significantly to high group performance.

division of labor Splitting the work to be performed into particular tasks and assigning tasks to individual workers.

The disadvantages of large groups include the problems of communication and coordination and the lower levels of motivation, satisfaction, and commitment that members of large groups sometimes experience. It is clearly more difficult to share information with, and coordinate the activities of, 16 people rather than 8 people. Moreover, members of large groups might not think their efforts are really needed and sometimes might not even feel a part of the group.

In deciding on the appropriate size for any group, managers attempt to gain the advantages of small group size and, at the same time, form groups with sufficient resources to accomplish their goals and have a well-developed division of labor. As a general rule of thumb, groups should have no more members than necessary to achieve a division of labor and provide the resources needed to achieve group goals. In R&D teams, for example, group size is too large when (1) members spend more time communicating what they know to others than applying what they know to solve problems and create new products, (2) individual productivity decreases, and (3) group performance suffers.[45]

GROUP TASKS   The appropriate size of a high-performing group is affected by the kind of tasks the group is to perform. An important characteristic of group tasks that affects performance is task interdependence—the degree to which the work performed by one member of a group influences the work performed by other members.[46] As task interdependence increases, group members need to interact more frequently and intensely with one another, and their efforts have to be more closely coordinated if they are to perform at a high level. Recent research underscores this point. Findings suggest that frequent and repeated interaction among team members results in greater familiarity, which in turn results in higher levels of information sharing, work coordination, and joint decision making. In addition, teams with higher levels of task interdependence should focus their interactions toward planning and orchestrating how tasks get done.[47] Management expert James D. Thompson identified three types of task interdependence: pooled, sequential, and reciprocal (see Figure 15.3).[48]

Pooled task interdependence exists when group members make separate and independent contributions to group performance; overall group performance is the sum of the performance of the individual members (see Figure 15.3A). Examples of groups that have pooled task interdependence include a group of teachers in an elementary school, a group of salespeople in a

task interdependence The degree to which the work performed by one member of a group influences the work performed by other members.

pooled task interdependence The task interdependence that exists when group members make separate and independent contributions to group performance.

Figure 15.3

Types of Task Interdependence

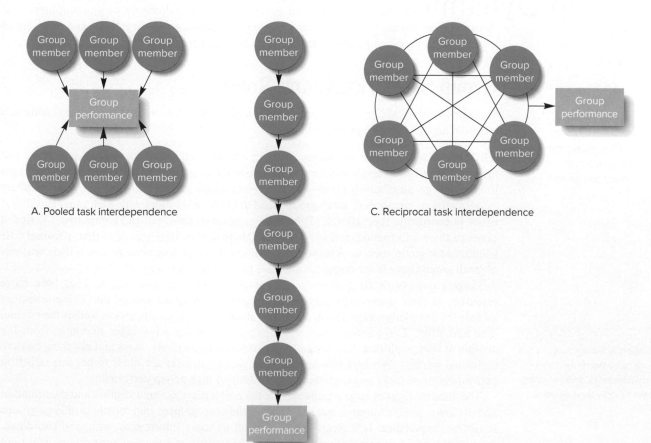

A. Pooled task interdependence

B. Sequential task interdependence

C. Reciprocal task interdependence

department store, a group of administrative assistants in an office, and a group of custodians in an office building. In these examples, group performance, whether it is the number of children who are taught and the quality of their education, the dollar value of sales, the amount of work completed, or the number of offices cleaned, is determined by summing the individual contributions of group members.

For groups with pooled interdependence, managers should determine the appropriate group size primarily from the amount of work to be accomplished. Large groups can be effective because group members work independently and do not have to interact frequently with one another. Motivation in groups with pooled interdependence will be highest when managers reward group members based on individual performance.

sequential task interdependence The task interdependence that exists when group members must perform specific tasks in a predetermined order.

Sequential task interdependence exists when group members must perform specific tasks in a predetermined order; certain tasks have to be performed before others, and what one worker does affects the work of others (see Figure 15.3B). Assembly lines and mass-production processes are characterized by sequential task interdependence.

When group members are sequentially interdependent, group size is usually dictated by the needs of the production process—for example, the number of steps needed in an assembly line to efficiently produce a DVD player. With sequential interdependence, it is difficult to identify individual performance, because one group member's performance depends on how well others perform their tasks. A slow worker at the start of an assembly line, for example, causes all workers farther down to work slowly. Thus, managers are often advised to reward group members for group performance. Group members will be motivated to perform at a high level because if the group performs well, each member will benefit. In addition, group members may put pressure on poor performers to improve so that group performance and rewards do not suffer.

reciprocal task interdependence The task interdependence that exists when the work performed by each group member is fully dependent on the work performed by other group members.

Reciprocal task interdependence exists when the work performed by each group member is fully dependent on the work performed by other group members; group members have to share information, intensely interact with one another, and coordinate their efforts in order for the group to achieve its goals (see Figure 15.3C). In general, reciprocal task interdependence characterizes the operation of teams, rather than other kinds of groups. The task interdependence of R&D teams, top management teams, and many self-managed work teams is reciprocal.

When group members are reciprocally interdependent, managers are advised to keep group size relatively small because of the necessity of coordinating team members' activities. Communication difficulties can arise in teams with reciprocally interdependent tasks because team members need to interact frequently with one another and be available when needed. As group size increases, communication difficulties increase and can impair team performance.

When a group's members are reciprocally interdependent, managers also are advised to reward group members on the basis of group performance. Individual levels of performance are often difficult for managers to identify, and group-based rewards help ensure that group members will be motivated to perform at a high level and make valuable contributions to the group. Of course, if a manager can identify instances of individual performance in such groups, they, too, can be rewarded to maintain high levels of motivation. Microsoft and many other companies reward group members for their individual performance as well as for the performance of their group.

Goal interdependence is another important aspect of group dynamics. This concept refers to the interconnection among group members as it pertains to the type of goal (individual or group) that guides the team's overall performance.[49] Research suggests collective goals can foster the development of effective strategies and team processes while implementation of individual goals does not encourage cooperative team processes.[50] In addition, research has shown that teams with higher task interdependence can achieve better performance when they also incorporate higher goal interdependence—which serves to encourage increased social activity among team members.[51]

First the steak, then the asparagus, then the carefully drizzled béarnaise; gourmet kitchens where the presentation is an integral part of the experience exemplify sequential task interdependence.

©Digital Vision/Getty Images

group role A set of behaviors and tasks that a member of a group is expected to perform because of his or her position in the group.

role making Taking the initiative to modify an assigned role by assuming additional responsibilities.

GROUP ROLES   A **group role** is a set of behaviors and tasks that a member of a group is expected to perform because of his or her position in the group. Members of cross-functional teams, for example, are expected to perform roles relevant to their special areas of expertise. In our earlier example of cross-functional teams at Hallmark Cards, it is the role of writers on the teams to create verses for new cards, the role of artists to draw illustrations, and the role of designers to put verse and artwork together in an attractive and appealing card design. The roles of members of top management teams are shaped primarily by their areas of expertise—production, marketing, finance, research and development—but members of top management teams also typically draw on their broad expertise as planners and strategists.

In forming groups and teams, managers need to clearly communicate to group members the expectations for their roles in the group, what is required of them, and how the different roles in the group fit together to accomplish group goals. Managers also need to realize that group roles often change and evolve as a group's tasks and goals change and as group members gain experience and knowledge. Thus, to get the performance gains that come from experience, or "learning by doing," managers should encourage group members to take the initiative to assume additional responsibilities as they see fit and modify their assigned roles. This process, called **role making**, can enhance individual and group performance.

In self-managed work teams and some other groups, group members themselves are responsible for creating and assigning roles. Many self-managed work teams also pick their own team leaders. When group members create their own roles, managers should be available to group members in an advisory capacity, helping them effectively settle conflicts and disagreements. At Johnsonville Foods, for example, the position titles of first-line managers were changed to "advisory coach" to reflect the managers' role with the self-managed work teams they oversaw.[52]

Group Leadership

All groups and teams need leadership. Indeed, as we discussed in detail in Chapter 14, effective leadership is a key ingredient in high-performing groups, teams, and organizations. Sometimes managers assume the leadership role in groups and teams, as is the case in many command groups and top management teams. Or a manager may appoint a member of a group who is not a manager to be group leader or chairperson, as is the case in a task force or standing committee. In other cases, group or team members may choose their own leaders, or a leader may emerge naturally as group members work together to achieve group goals. When managers empower members of self-managed work teams, they often let group members choose their own leaders. Some self-managed work teams find it effective to rotate the leadership role among their members. Whether or not leaders of groups and teams are managers, and whether they are appointed by managers (often referred to as *formal leaders*) or emerge naturally in a group (often referred to as *informal leaders*), they play an important role in ensuring that groups and teams perform up to their potential.

When teams do not live up to their promise, sometimes the problem is a lack of team leadership, as illustrated in the accompanying "Ethics in Action" feature.

ETHICS IN ACTION

Leadership in Teams at ICU Medical

Dr. George Lopez, an internal medicine physician, founded ICU Medical in San Clemente, California, in 1984 after a patient of his accidentally died when an intravenous (IV) line became inadvertently disconnected. Lopez thought there must be a better way to design components of IV lines so that these kinds of tragic accidents don't happen. He developed a product called the Click Lock, which has both a locking mechanism for IV systems and a protected needle so that health care workers are protected from accidental needle pricks.[53] Today ICU Medical has over 6,800 employees and revenues over \$1.2 billion, thanks to recent acquisitions.[54] Lopez is a member of the board of directors, and ICU Medical has made *Forbes* magazine's list of "The 200 Best Small Companies."[55] ICU Medical continues to focus on the development and manufacture of products that improve the functioning of IV lines and systems while protecting health care workers from accidental needle pricks. For example, the CLAVE NeedleFree Connector for IV lines is one of ICU Medical's top-selling products.[56]

In the early 1990s Lopez experienced something not uncommon to successful entrepreneurs as their businesses grow. As the entrepreneur–CEO, he continued to make the majority of important decisions himself, yet he had close to 100 employees, demand for the CLAVE was very high, and he was starting to feel overloaded to the point that he would often sleep at nights in the office. After watching one of his son's hockey games, he realized that a well-functioning team could work wonders; in the case of the hockey game, although the opposing team had an outstanding player, his son's team really pulled together as a team and was able to win the game despite the rival team's outstanding member. Lopez decided to empower employees to form teams to work on a pressing goal for ICU Medical: increasing production. While employees did form teams and spent a lot of time in team interactions, the teams did not seem to come up with any tangible results, perhaps because there were no team leaders in place and the teams had no guidelines to help them accomplish their goals.[57]

In an effort to improve team effectiveness, Lopez told employees that teams should elect team leaders. And together with Jim Reitz, ICU Medical's director of human resources at the time, Lopez came up with rules or guidelines teams should follow, such as "challenge the issue, not the person" and "stand up for your position, but never argue against the facts."[58] ICU Medical also started to reward team members for their team's contributions to organizational effectiveness. With these changes, Reitz and Lopez were striving to ensure that teams had leaders, had some guidelines for team member behavior, and were rewarded for their contributions to organizational effectiveness but, at the same time, were not bogged down by unnecessary constraints and structures and were truly self-managing.[59]

With these changes in place, teams at ICU Medical began to live up to their promise. Today any ICU Medical employee can create a team to address a problem, seize an opportunity, or work on a project ranging from developing a new product to making improvements in the physical work environment.[60] The teams have leaders and are self-managing.

Recognizing that self-managed teams still need rules, guidelines, leadership, and structure, a team of employees developed a 25-page guidebook for effective team functioning. And to ensure that teams learn from each other as well as get feedback, teams are required to put up notes from each of their meetings on ICU Medical's intranet, and any employee can provide feedback to any of the teams.[61] All in all, effectively led teams have helped ICU Medical prosper in its efforts to develop and manufacture products that protect the safety of both patients and health care workers.

Group Development over Time

As many managers overseeing self-managed teams have learned, it sometimes takes a self-managed work team two or three years to perform up to its capabilities.[62] As their experience suggests, what a group is capable of achieving depends in part on its stage of development. Knowing that it takes considerable time for self-managed work teams to get up and running has helped managers to have realistic expectations for new teams and to know that they need to give new team members considerable training and guidance.

Although every group's development over time is unique, researchers have identified five stages of group development that many groups seem to pass through (see Figure 15.4).[63] In the first stage, *forming,* members try to get to know one another and reach a common understanding of what the group is trying to accomplish and how group members should behave. During this stage, managers should strive to make each member feel that he or she is a valued part of the group.

Figure 15.4

Five Stages of Group Development

In the second stage, *storming,* group members experience conflict and disagreements because some members do not wish to submit to the demands of other group members. Disputes may arise over who should lead the group. Self-managed work teams can be particularly vulnerable during the storming stage. Managers need to keep an eye on groups at this stage to make sure conflict does not get out of hand.

During the third stage, *norming,* close ties between group members develop, and feelings of friendship and camaraderie emerge. Group members arrive at a consensus about what goals they should seek to achieve and how group members should behave toward one another. In the fourth stage, *performing,* the real work of the group is accomplished. Depending on the type of group in question, managers need to take different steps at this stage to help ensure that groups are effective. Managers of command groups need to make sure that group members are motivated and that they are effectively leading group members. Managers overseeing self-managed work teams have to empower team members and make sure teams are given enough responsibility and autonomy at the performing stage.

The last stage, *adjourning,* applies only to groups that eventually are disbanded, such as task forces. During adjourning, a group is dispersed. Sometimes adjourning takes place when a group completes a finished product, such as when a task force evaluating the pros and cons of providing on-site child care produces a report supporting its recommendation.

Managers should have a flexible approach to group development and should keep attuned to the different needs and requirements of groups at the various stages.[64] Above all else, and regardless of the stage of development, managers need to think of themselves as *resources* for groups. Thus, managers always should strive to find ways to help groups and teams function more effectively.

Group Norms

LO15-4 Explain why it is important for groups and teams to have a balance of conformity and deviance and a moderate level of cohesiveness.

All groups, whether top management teams, self-managed work teams, or command groups, need to control their members' behaviors to ensure that the group performs at a high level and meets its goals. Assigning roles to each group member is one way to control behavior in groups. Another important way in which groups influence members' behavior is through the development and enforcement of group norms.[65] **Group norms** are shared guidelines or rules for behavior that most group members follow. Groups develop norms concerning a wide variety of behaviors, including working hours, the sharing of information among group members, how certain group tasks should be performed, and even how members of a group should dress.

Managers should encourage members of a group to develop norms that contribute to group performance and the attainment of group goals. For example, group norms dictating that each member of a cross-functional team should always be available for the rest of the team when his or her input is needed, return phone calls as soon as possible, inform other team members of travel plans, and give team members a phone number at which he or she can be reached when traveling on business help to ensure that the team is efficient, performs at a high level, and achieves its goals. A norm in a command group of secretaries that dictates that secretaries who happen to have a light workload in any given week should help out secretaries with heavier workloads helps to ensure that the group completes all assignments in a timely and efficient manner. And a norm in a top management team that dictates that team members should always consult with one another before making major decisions helps to ensure that good decisions are made with a minimum of errors.

group norms Shared guidelines or rules for behavior that most group members follow.

CONFORMITY AND DEVIANCE   Group members conform to norms for three reasons: (1) They want to obtain rewards and avoid punishments. (2) They want to imitate group members whom they like and admire. (3) They have internalized the norms and believe they are the right and proper ways to behave.[66] Consider the case of Robert King, who conformed to his department's norm of attending a fund-raiser for a community food bank. King's conformity could be due to (1) his desire to be a member of the group in good standing and to have friendly relationships with other group members (rewards), (2) his copying the behavior of other members of the department whom he respects and who always attend the fund-raiser (imitating other group members), or (3) his belief in the merits of supporting the activities of the food bank (believing that is the right and proper way to behave).

Failure to conform, or deviance, occurs when a member of a group violates a group norm. Deviance signals that a group is not controlling one of its member's behaviors. Groups generally respond to members who behave deviantly in one of three ways:[67]

1. The group might try to get the member to change his or her deviant ways and conform to the norm. Group members might try to convince the member of the need to conform, or they might ignore or even punish the deviant. For example, in a Jacksonville Foods plant, Liz Senkbiel, a member of a self-managed work team responsible for weighing sausages, failed to conform to a group norm dictating that group members should periodically clean up an untidy interview room. Because Senkbiel refused to take part in the team's cleanup efforts, team members reduced her monthly bonus by about $225 for a two-month period.[68] Senkbiel clearly learned the costs of deviant behavior in her team.

2. The group might expel the member.

3. The group might change the norm to be consistent with the member's behavior.

This last alternative suggests that some deviant behavior can be functional for groups. Deviance is functional when it causes group members to evaluate norms that may be dysfunctional but are taken for granted by the group. Often group members do not think about why they behave in a certain way or why they follow certain norms. Deviance can cause group members to reflect on their norms and change them when appropriate.

Consider a group of receptionists in a beauty salon who followed the norm that all appointments would be handwritten in an appointment book and, at the end of each day, the receptionist on duty would enter the appointments into the salon's computer system, which printed out the hairdressers' daily schedules. One day a receptionist decided to enter appointments directly into the computer system when they were being made, bypassing the appointment book. This deviant behavior caused the other receptionists to think about why they were using the appointment book at all. After consulting with the owner of the salon, the group changed its norm. Now appointments are entered directly into the computer, which saves time and reduces scheduling errors.

ENCOURAGING A BALANCE OF CONFORMITY AND DEVIANCE   To effectively help an organization gain a competitive advantage, groups and teams need the right balance of conformity and deviance (see Figure 15.5). A group needs a certain level of conformity to ensure that it can control members' behavior and channel it in the direction of high performance and group goal accomplishment. A group also needs a certain level of deviance to ensure that dysfunctional norms are discarded and replaced with functional ones. Balancing conformity and deviance is a pressing concern for all groups, whether they are top management teams, R&D teams, command groups, or self-managed work teams.

The extent of conformity and reactions to deviance within groups are determined by group members themselves. The three bases for conformity just described are powerful forces that more often than not result in group members' conforming to norms. Sometimes these forces are so strong that deviance rarely occurs in groups, and when it does, it is stamped out.

Managers can take several steps to ensure adequate tolerance of deviance in groups so that group members are willing to deviate from dysfunctional norms and, when deviance occurs in their group, reflect on the appropriateness of the violated norm and change the norm if necessary. First, managers can be role models for the groups and teams they oversee. When managers encourage and accept employees' suggestions for changes in procedures, do not rigidly insist that tasks be accomplished in a certain way, and admit when a norm they once supported is no longer functional, they signal to group members that conformity should not come

Figure 15.5
Balancing Conformity and Deviance in Groups

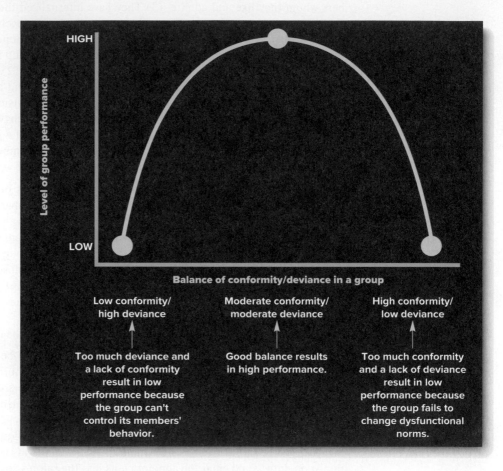

at the expense of needed changes and improvements. Second, managers should let employees know that there are always ways to improve group processes and performance levels and, thus, opportunities to replace existing norms with norms that will better enable a group to achieve its goals and perform at a high level. Third, managers should encourage members of groups and teams to periodically assess the appropriateness of their norms.

Group Cohesiveness

group cohesiveness The degree to which members are attracted to or loyal to their group.

Another important element of group dynamics that affects group performance and effectiveness is **group cohesiveness**, which is the degree to which members are attracted to or loyal to their group or team.[69] When group cohesiveness is high, individuals strongly value their group membership, find the group appealing, and have strong desires to remain a part of the group. When group cohesiveness is low, group members do not find their group particularly appealing and have little desire to retain their group membership. Research suggests that managers should strive to have a moderate level of cohesiveness in the groups and teams they manage because that is most likely to contribute to an organization's competitive advantage.

CONSEQUENCES OF GROUP COHESIVENESS   There are three major consequences of group cohesiveness: level of participation within a group, level of conformity to group norms, and emphasis on group goal accomplishment (see Figure 15.6).[70]

LEVEL OF PARTICIPATION WITHIN A GROUP   As group cohesiveness increases, the extent of group members' participation within the group increases. Participation contributes to group effectiveness because group members are actively involved in the group, ensure that group

Figure 15.6

Sources and Consequences of Group Cohesiveness

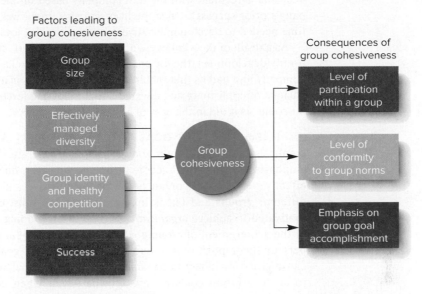

tasks get accomplished, readily share information with each other, and have frequent and open communication (the important topic of communication is covered in depth in Chapter 16).

A moderate level of group cohesiveness helps ensure that group members actively participate in the group and communicate effectively with one another. The reason that managers may not want to encourage high levels of cohesiveness is illustrated by the example of two cross-functional teams responsible for developing new toys. Members of the highly cohesive Team Alpha often have lengthy meetings that usually start with nonwork-related conversations and jokes, meet more often than most of the other cross-functional teams in the company, and spend a good portion of their time communicating the ins and outs of their department's contribution to toy development to other team members. Members of the moderately cohesive Team Beta generally have efficient meetings in which ideas are communicated and discussed as needed, do not meet more often than necessary, and share the ins and outs of their expertise with one another to the extent needed for the development process. Teams Alpha and Beta have both developed some top-selling toys. However, it generally takes Team Alpha 30% longer to do so than Team Beta. This is why too much cohesiveness can be too much of a good thing.

LEVEL OF CONFORMITY TO GROUP NORMS   Increasing levels of group cohesiveness result in increasing levels of conformity to group norms, and when cohesiveness becomes high, there may be so little deviance in groups that group members conform to norms even when they are dysfunctional. In contrast, low cohesiveness can result in too much deviance and undermine the ability of a group to control its members' behaviors to get things done.

Teams Alpha and Beta in the toy company both had the same norm for toy development. It dictated that members of each team would discuss potential ideas for new toys, decide on a line of toys to pursue, and then have the team member from R&D design a prototype. Recently, a new animated movie featuring a family of rabbits produced by a small film company was an unexpected hit, and major toy companies were scrambling to reach licensing agreements to produce toy lines featuring the rabbits. The top management team in the toy company assigned Teams Alpha and Beta to develop the new toy lines quickly to beat the competition.

Members of Team Alpha followed their usual toy development norm, even though the marketing expert on the team believed the process could have been streamlined to save time. The marketing expert on Team Beta urged the team to deviate from its

How much cohesiveness is too much? You can answer that question when you evaluate whether a group actually gets something done in its meetings or whether most of the conversation drifting out of the room consists of jokes, life experiences, or comparisons of the last company dinner's entrees.

©Glow Images/Getty Images

toy development norm. She suggested that the team not have R&D develop prototypes but, instead, modify top-selling toys the company already made to feature rabbits and then reach a licensing agreement with the film company based on the high sales potential (given the company's prior success). Once the licensing agreement was signed, the company could take the time needed to develop innovative and unique rabbit toys with more input from R&D.

As a result of the willingness of the marketing expert on Team Beta to deviate from the norm for toy development, the toy company obtained an exclusive licensing agreement with the film company and had its first rabbit toys on store shelves in a record three months. Groups need a balance of conformity and deviance, so a moderate level of cohesiveness often yields the best outcome, as it did in the case of Team Beta.

EMPHASIS ON GROUP GOAL ACCOMPLISHMENT   As group cohesiveness increases, the emphasis placed on group goal accomplishment also increases within a group. A strong emphasis on group goal accomplishment, however, does not always lead to organizational effectiveness. For an organization to be effective and gain a competitive advantage, the different groups and teams in the organization must cooperate with one another and be motivated to achieve *organizational goals,* even if doing so sometimes comes at the expense of the achievement of group goals. A moderate level of cohesiveness motivates group members to accomplish both group and organizational goals. High levels of cohesiveness can cause group members to be so focused on group goal accomplishment that they may strive to achieve group goals no matter what—even when doing so jeopardizes organizational performance.

At the toy company, the major goal of the cross-functional teams was to develop new toy lines that were truly innovative, that utilized the latest in technology, and that were in some way fundamentally distinct from other toys on the market. When it came to the rabbit project, Team Alpha's high level of cohesiveness contributed to its continued emphasis on its group goal of developing an innovative line of toys; thus, the team stuck with its usual design process. Team Beta, in contrast, realized that developing the new line of toys quickly was an important organizational goal that should take precedence over the group's goal of developing groundbreaking new toys, at least in the short term. Team Beta's moderate level of cohesiveness contributed to team members' doing what was best for the toy company in this case.

FACTORS LEADING TO GROUP COHESIVENESS   Four factors contribute to the level of group cohesiveness (see Figure 15.6).[71] By influencing these *determinants of group cohesiveness,* managers can raise or lower the level of cohesiveness to promote moderate levels of cohesiveness in groups and teams.

GROUP SIZE   As we mentioned earlier, members of small groups tend to be more motivated and committed than members of large groups. Thus, to promote cohesiveness in groups, when feasible, managers should form groups that are small to medium in size (about 2 to 15 members). If a group is low in cohesiveness and large in size, managers might want to consider dividing the group in half and assigning different tasks and goals to the two newly formed groups.

EFFECTIVELY MANAGED DIVERSITY   In general, people tend to like and get along with others who are similar to themselves. It is easier to communicate with someone, for example, who shares your values, has a similar background, and has had similar experiences. However, as discussed in Chapter 5, diversity in groups, teams, and organizations can help an organization gain a competitive advantage. Diverse groups often come up with more innovative and creative ideas. One reason cross-functional teams are so popular in organizations such as Hallmark Cards is that the diverse expertise represented in the teams results in higher levels of team performance.

In forming groups and teams, managers need to make sure the diversity in knowledge, experience, expertise, and other characteristics necessary for group goal accomplishment is represented in the new groups. Managers then have to make sure this diversity in group membership is effectively managed so groups will be cohesive (see Chapter 5). The "Focus on Diversity" feature describes how an assessment tool developed by Deloitte is helping organizations do this with regard to diverse work styles.

Tapping into Team Members' Diversity

Management consulting firm Deloitte developed a profile of four different ways people work: Pioneers, Guardians, Drivers, and Integrators. Which profile do you fit, and how can you use this style to work more effectively in a team setting?
©Adam Hester/Blend Images

Anyone with teamwork experience has at times noticed another team member focus on what seems unimportant or seen a few team members dominate a meeting. In these situations, the team is not fully drawing upon every team member, so the organization is not fully benefiting from the team. Consultants at Deloitte wanted to address this problem. They believed they were seeing a failure to consider different work styles and perspectives. If team members could readily understand this diversity, they could treat it as a resource rather than an obstacle to cooperation.[72]

Deloitte built on research about brain chemistry to develop and test profiles of four primary ways that people work. The resulting system, named Business Chemistry, defines four styles: *Pioneers* inspire creativity; they look at the big picture and are open to new ideas, willing to take risks, and comfortable basing decisions on intuition. *Guardians* are cautious about risk and value stability; they want to learn from experience and look for detailed data to back decisions. *Drivers* care about results and winning; they get the team moving and want data so they can solve problems and tackle challenges. *Integrators* focus on relationships; they seek consensus and try to strengthen the team. This model assumes that teams need all of these perspectives at various times.[73]

Teams with diverse profiles should be creative, and their decisions should be well thought out. In practice, diversity poses challenges. For example, if a Driver opens the floor to debate an issue, an Integrator might hesitate to speak up and provoke an argument. If Guardians raise concerns about an idea, a Driver might feel frustrated about being slowed down, even though the concerns might be valid and significant. Team members who are unaware of these differences might work ineffectively. A Guardian might come prepared with pages of data that won't capture the imaginations of the team's Pioneers.[74]

Business Chemistry can help team members address these issues constructively. They can be aware of the strengths and limitations of their view and the other views. They can practice imagining how people in other categories would think about situations. Also, team leaders can notice which kinds of perspectives aren't being addressed by the team and then seek out those perspectives. For example, if everyone is immediately excited about an idea, perhaps everyone is thinking like a Pioneer. The leader should pause and invite the team to consider what a Guardian-style team member would say about the idea.[75]

GROUP IDENTITY AND HEALTHY COMPETITION   When group cohesiveness is low, managers can often increase it by encouraging groups to develop their own identities or personalities and engage in healthy competition. This is precisely what managers at Eaton Corporation's manufacturing facility in Lincoln, Illinois, did. Eaton's employees manufacture products such as engine valves, gears, truck axles, and circuit breakers. Managers at Eaton created self-managed work teams to cut costs and improve performance. They realized, however, that the teams would have to be cohesive to ensure that they would strive to achieve their goals. Managers promoted group identity by having the teams give themselves names such as "The Hoods," "The Worms," and "Scrap Attack" (a team striving to reduce costly scrap metal waste by 50%). Healthy competition among groups was promoted by displaying measures of each team's performance and the extent to which teams met their goals on a large TV screen in the cafeteria and by rewarding team members for team performance.[76]

If groups are too cohesive, managers can try to decrease cohesiveness by promoting organizational (rather than group) identity and making the organization as a whole the focus of the group's efforts. Organizational identity can be promoted by making group members feel that they are valued members of the organization and by stressing cooperation across groups to promote the achievement of organizational goals. Excessive levels of cohesiveness also can be reduced by reducing or eliminating competition among groups and rewarding cooperation.

SUCCESS   When it comes to promoting group cohesiveness, there is more than a grain of truth to the saying "Nothing succeeds like success." As groups become more successful, they become increasingly attractive to their members, and their cohesiveness tends to increase. When cohesiveness is low, managers can increase cohesiveness by making sure a group can achieve some noticeable and visible successes.

Consider a group of salespeople in the housewares department of a medium-size department store. The housewares department had recently been moved to a corner of the store's basement. Its remote location resulted in low sales because of infrequent customer traffic in that part of the store. The salespeople, who were generally evaluated favorably by their supervisors and were valued members of the store, tried various initiatives to boost sales, but to no avail. As a result of this lack of success and the poor performance of their department, their cohesiveness started to plummet. To increase and preserve the cohesiveness of the group, the store manager implemented a group-based incentive across the store. In any month, members of the group with the best attendance and punctuality records would have their names and pictures posted on a bulletin board in the cafeteria and would each receive a $50 gift certificate. The housewares group frequently had the best records, and their success on this dimension helped to build and maintain their cohesiveness. Moreover, this initiative boosted attendance and discouraged lateness throughout the store.

Managing Groups and Teams for High Performance

LO15-5 Describe how managers can motivate group members to achieve organizational goals and reduce social loafing in groups and teams.

Now that you understand why groups and teams are so important for organizations, the types of groups managers create, and group dynamics, we consider some additional steps managers can take to make sure groups and teams perform at a high level and contribute to organizational effectiveness. Before discussing these strategies, however, we highlight some of the traits and characteristics associated with high-performing work groups.

The concept of high-performing work teams is not new; it has been used by successful organizations for more than 20 years. High-performing work teams can be defined as groups that consistently satisfy the needs of customers, employees, investors, and other stakeholders and that frequently outperform other teams that produce similar products or services.[77] Recent research into what constitutes a high-performing work group identifies several key factors that may contribute to the team's success, including a highly developed team culture; clearly defined norms that encourage effective behavior and high performance; and results-oriented meetings that include information sharing, problem solving, and decision making.[78] Understanding what it takes to assemble and manage such top-performing groups is an ongoing challenge for any organization. Ways to create such high performance begins with three key strategies: (1) motivating group members to work toward the achievement of organizational goals, (2) reducing social loafing, and (3) helping groups manage conflict effectively.

Motivating Group Members to Achieve Organizational Goals

When work is difficult, is tedious, or requires a high level of commitment and energy, managers cannot assume group members will always be motivated to work toward the achievement of organizational goals. Consider a group of house painters who paint the interiors and exteriors of new homes for a construction company and are paid on an hourly basis. Why should they strive to complete painting jobs quickly and efficiently if doing so will just make them feel more tired at the end of the day and they will not receive any tangible benefits? It makes more sense for the painters to adopt a relaxed approach, to take frequent breaks, and to work at a leisurely pace. This relaxed approach, however, impairs the construction company's ability to gain a competitive advantage because it raises costs and increases the time needed to complete a new home.

Managers can motivate members of groups and teams to achieve organizational goals by making sure the members themselves benefit when the group or team performs highly. For example, if members of a self-managed work team know they will receive a weekly bonus based on team performance, they will be motivated to perform at a high level.

Managers often rely on some combination of individual and group-based incentives to motivate members of groups and teams to work toward the achievement of organizational goals. When individual performance within a group can be assessed, pay is often determined by individual performance or by both individual and group performance. When individual performance within a group cannot be accurately assessed, group performance should be the key determinant of pay levels. Many companies that use self-managed work teams base team members' pay in part on team performance.[79] A major challenge for managers is to develop a fair pay system that will lead to both high individual motivation and high group or team performance.

Other benefits managers can make available to high-performing group members—in addition to monetary rewards—include extra resources such as equipment and computer software, awards and other forms of recognition, and choice of future work assignments. For example, members of self-managed work teams that develop new software at companies such as Microsoft often value working on interesting and important projects; members of teams that have performed at a high level are rewarded by being assigned to interesting and important new projects.

Reducing Social Loafing in Groups

social loafing The tendency of individuals to put forth less effort when they work in groups than when they work alone.

We have been focusing on the steps managers can take to encourage high levels of performance in groups. Managers, however, need to be aware of an important downside to group and team work: the potential for social loafing, which reduces group performance. Social loafing is the tendency of individuals to put forth less effort when they work in groups than when they work alone.[80] Have you ever worked on a group project in which one or two group members never seemed to be pulling their weight? Have you ever worked in a student club or committee in which some members always seemed to be missing meetings and never volunteered for activities? Have you ever had a job in which one or two of your coworkers seemed to be slacking off because they knew you or other members of your work group would make up for their low levels of effort? If so, you have witnessed social loafing in action.

Social loafing can occur in all kinds of groups and teams and in all kinds of organizations. It can result in lower group performance and may even prevent a group from attaining its goals. Fortunately, managers can take steps to reduce social loafing and sometimes completely eliminate it; we will look at three (see Figure 15.7).

1. *Make individual contributions to a group identifiable.* Some people may engage in social loafing when they work in groups because they think they can hide in the crowd—no one will notice if they put forth less effort than they should. Other people may think that if they put forth high levels of effort and make substantial contributions to the group, their contributions will not be noticed and they will receive no rewards for their work—so why bother?[81]

One way that managers can effectively eliminate social loafing is by making individual contributions to a group identifiable so that group members perceive that low and high levels of effort will be noticed and individual contributions evaluated.[82] Managers can accomplish this by assigning specific tasks to group members and holding them accountable for their completion. Take the case of a group of eight employees responsible for reshelving returned books in a large public library in New York. The head librarian was concerned that there was always a backlog of seven or eight carts of books to be reshelved, even though the employees never seemed to be particularly busy and some even found time to sit down and read newspapers and magazines. The librarian decided to try to eliminate the apparent social loafing by assigning each employee sole responsibility for reshelving a particular section of the library. Because the library's front desk employees sorted the books by section on the carts as they were returned,

Figure 15.7

Three Ways to Reduce Social Loafing

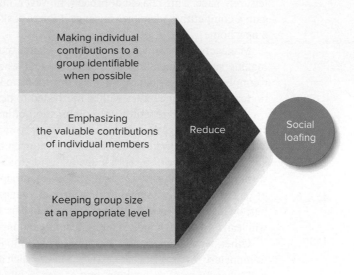

Making individual contributions to a group identifiable when possible

Emphasizing the valuable contributions of individual members

Keeping group size at an appropriate level

Reduce

Social loafing

holding the shelvers responsible for particular sections was easily accomplished. Once the shelvers knew the librarian could identify their effort or lack thereof, there were rarely any backlogs of books to be reshelved.

Sometimes the members of a group can cooperate to eliminate social loafing by making individual contributions identifiable. For example, in a small security company, members of a self-managed work team who assemble control boxes for home alarm systems start each day by deciding who will perform which tasks that day and how much work each member and the group as a whole should strive to accomplish. Each team member knows that, at the end of the day, the other team members will know exactly how much he or she has accomplished. With this system in place, social loafing never occurs in the team. Remember, however, that in some teams, individual contributions cannot be made identifiable, as in teams whose members are reciprocally interdependent.

2. *Emphasize the valuable contributions of individual members.* Another reason social loafing may occur is that people sometimes think their efforts are unnecessary or unimportant when they work in a group. They feel the group will accomplish its goals and perform at an acceptable level whether or not they personally perform at a high level. To counteract this belief, when managers form groups, they should assign individuals to a group on the basis of the valuable contributions that *each* person can make to the group as a whole. Clearly communicating to group members why each person's contributions are valuable to the group is an effective means by which managers and group members themselves can reduce or eliminate social loafing.[83] This is most clearly illustrated in cross-functional teams, where each member's valuable contribution to the team derives from a personal area of expertise. By emphasizing why each member's skills are important, managers can reduce social loafing in such teams.

3. *Keep group size at an appropriate level.* Group size is related to the causes of social loafing we just described. As size increases, identifying individual contributions becomes increasingly difficult, and members are increasingly likely to think their individual contributions are not important. To overcome this, managers should form groups with no more members than are needed to accomplish group goals and perform at a high level.[84]

Helping Groups to Manage Conflict Effectively

At some point, practically all groups experience conflict either within the group (*intragroup* conflict) or with other groups (*intergroup* conflict). In Chapter 17 we discuss conflict in depth and explore ways to manage it effectively. As you will learn, managers can take several steps to help groups manage conflict and disagreements.

Summary and Review

GROUPS, TEAMS, AND ORGANIZATIONAL EFFECTIVENESS   A group consists of two or more people who interact with each other to accomplish certain goals or meet certain needs. A team is a group whose members work intensely with one another to achieve a specific common goal or objective. Groups and teams can contribute to organizational

LO15-1   effectiveness by enhancing performance, increasing responsiveness to customers, increasing innovation, and being a source of motivation for their members.

LO15-2   **TYPES OF GROUPS AND TEAMS**   Formal groups are groups that managers establish to achieve organizational goals; they include cross-functional teams, cross-cultural teams, top management teams, research and development teams, command groups, task forces, self-managed work teams, and virtual teams. Informal groups are groups that employees form because they believe the groups will help them achieve their own goals or meet their needs; they include friendship groups and interest groups.

LO15-3, 15-4   **GROUP DYNAMICS**   Key elements of group dynamics are group size, tasks, and roles; group leadership; group development; group norms; and group cohesiveness. The advantages and disadvantages of large and small groups suggest that managers should form groups with no more members than are needed to provide the group with the human resources it needs to achieve its goals and use a division of labor. The type of task interdependence that characterizes a group's work gives managers a clue about the appropriate size of the group. A group role is a set of behaviors and tasks that a member of a group is expected to perform because of his or her position in the group. All groups and teams need leadership.

Five stages of development that many groups pass through are forming, storming, norming, performing, and adjourning. Group norms are shared rules for behavior that most group members follow. To be effective, groups need a balance of conformity and deviance. Conformity allows a group to control its members' behavior to achieve group goals; deviance provides the impetus for needed change.

Group cohesiveness is the attractiveness of a group or team to its members. As group cohesiveness increases, so do the level of participation and communication within a group, the level of conformity to group norms, and the emphasis on group goal accomplishment. Managers should strive to achieve a moderate level of group cohesiveness in the groups and teams they manage.

LO15-5   **MANAGING GROUPS AND TEAMS FOR HIGH PERFORMANCE**   To make sure groups and teams perform at a high level, managers need to motivate group members to work toward the achievement of organizational goals, reduce social loafing, and help groups to effectively manage conflict. Managers can motivate members of groups and teams to work toward the achievement of organizational goals by making sure members personally benefit when the group or team performs at a high level.

Management in Action

Topics for Discussion and Action

Discussion

1. Why do all organizations need to rely on groups and teams to achieve their goals and gain a competitive advantage? **[LO15-1]**

2. What kinds of employees would prefer to work in a virtual team? What kinds of employees would prefer to work in a team that meets face-to-face? **[LO15-2]**

3. Think about a group that you are a member of, and describe that group's current stage of development. Does the development of this group seem to be following the forming, storming, norming, performing, and adjourning stages described in the chapter? **[LO15-3]**

4. Think about a group of employees who work in a McDonald's restaurant. What type of task interdependence characterizes this group? What potential problems in the group should the restaurant manager be aware of and take steps to avoid? **[LO15-3]**

5. Discuss the reasons that too much conformity can hurt groups and their organizations. **[LO15-4]**

6. Why do some groups have very low levels of cohesiveness? **[LO15-4]**

7. Imagine that you are the manager of a hotel. What steps will you take to reduce social loafing by members of the cleaning staff who are responsible for keeping all common areas and guest rooms spotless? **[LO15-5]**

Action

8. Interview one or more managers in an organization in your local community to identify the types of groups and teams that the organization uses to achieve its goals. What challenges do these groups and teams face? **[LO15-2]**

Building Management Skills

Diagnosing Group Failures [LO15-1, 15-2, 15-3, 15-4, 15-5]

Think about the last dissatisfying or discouraging experience you had as a member of a group or team. Perhaps the group did not accomplish its goals, perhaps group members could agree about nothing, or perhaps there was too much social loafing. Now answer the following questions:

1. What type of group was this?

2. Were group members motivated to achieve group goals? Why or why not?

3. How large was the group, what type of task interdependence existed in the group, and what group roles did members play?

4. What were the group's norms? How much conformity and deviance existed in the group?

5. How cohesive was the group? Why do you think the group's cohesiveness was at this level? What consequences did this level of group cohesiveness have for the group and its members?

6. Was social loafing a problem in this group? Why or why not?

7. What could the group's leader or manager have done differently to increase group effectiveness?

8. What could group members have done differently to increase group effectiveness?

Managing Ethically [LO15-1, 15-2, 15-3, 15-4, 15-5]

Some self-managed teams encounter a vexing problem: One or more members engage in social loafing, and other members are reluctant to try to rectify the situation. Social loafing can be especially troubling if team members' pay is based on team performance and social loafing reduces the team's performance and, thus, the pay of all members (even the highest performers). Even if managers are aware of the problem, they may be reluctant to take action because the team is supposedly self-managing.

Questions

1. Either individually or in a group, think about the ethical implications of social loafing in a self-managed team.

2. Do managers have an ethical obligation to step in when they are aware of social loafing in a self-managed team? Why or why not? Do other team members have an obligation to try to curtail the social loafing? Why or why not?

Small Group Breakout Exercise

Creating a Cross-Functional Team [LO15-1, 15-2, 15-3, 15-4, 15-5]

Form groups of three or four people, and appoint one member as the spokesperson who will communicate your findings to the class when called on by the instructor. Then discuss the following scenario:

You are a group of managers in charge of food services for a large state university in the Midwest. Recently, a survey of students, faculty, and staff was conducted to evaluate customer satisfaction with the food services provided by the university's eight cafeterias. The results were disappointing, to put it mildly. Complaints ranged from dissatisfaction with the type and range of meals and snacks provided, operating hours, and food temperature to frustration about unresponsiveness to current concerns about healthful diets and the needs of vegetarians. You have decided to form a cross-functional team that will further evaluate reactions to

the food services and will develop a proposal for changes to be made to increase customer satisfaction.

1. Indicate who should be on this important cross-functional team, and explain why.

2. Describe the goals the team should strive to achieve.

3. Describe the different roles that will need to be performed on this team.

4. Describe the steps you will take to help ensure that the team has a good balance between conformity and deviance and has a moderate level of cohesiveness.

Be the Manager [LO15-1, 15-2, 15-3, 15-4, 15-5]

You were recently hired in a boundary-spanning role for the global unit of an educational and professional publishing company. The company is headquartered in New York (where you work) and has divisions in multiple countries. Each division is responsible for translating, manufacturing, marketing, and selling a set of books in its country. Your responsibilities include interfacing with managers in each of the divisions in your region (Central and South America), overseeing their budgeting and financial reporting to headquarters, and leading a virtual team consisting of the top managers in charge of each of the divisions in your region. The virtual team's mission is to promote global learning, explore new potential opportunities and markets, and address ongoing problems. You communicate directly with division managers via telephone and email, as well as written reports and memos. When virtual team meetings are convened, videoconferencing is often used.

After your first few virtual team meetings, you noticed that the managers seemed to be reticent about speaking up. Interestingly enough, when each manager communicates with you individually, primarily in telephone conversations and emails, he or she tends to be forthcoming and frank, and you feel you have a good rapport with each of them. However, getting the managers to communicate with one another as a virtual team has been a challenge. At the last meeting, you tried to prompt some of the managers to raise issues relevant to the agenda that you knew were on their minds from your individual conversations with them. Surprisingly, the managers skillfully avoided informing their teammates about the heart of the issues in question. You are confused and troubled. Although you feel your other responsibilities are going well, you know your virtual team is not operating like a team at all; and no matter what you try, discussions in virtual team meetings are forced and generally unproductive. What are you going to do to address this problem?

The Power of Play [LO 15-1, 15-2, 15-3, 15-4]

The rattle of dice is syncopated but constant.

A dozen or so men sit at different tables, each littered with an elaborate assortment of board game pieces—plastic figures, cards, and tokens. A bowl filled with candy-colored dice sits on one table like a giant assortment of the worst-ever M&M's.

Although these guys are playing to win, there's an atmosphere of camaraderie more than combat—no money is wagered—and they walk one another through each round, thinking aloud and discussing strategies. No wonder, given how complex many of the games are. "I could memorize the Torah, or this," says one man, laughing as he brandishes the brick of a rulebook for Advanced Squad Leader.

The group meets once a week in a gaming den in Manhattan's Chelsea neighborhood. Every surface in the wood-paneled room is piled with bright boxes. They're stacked precariously on the floor and windowsills and loaded onto shelves amid leatherbound books. The games display an array of styles: A Roman Empire-themed game is called Trajan; another one, Churchill, honors wartime politics; Star Wars: Rebellion lets you play on the side of the rebels or the Empire. There's even one based on Ken Follett's epic *The Pillars of the Earth*.

When J.R. Tracy bought this loft several years ago, he carved it in two—one half became the family home, the other a dedicated gaming lab. Tracy works in finance, and most of his fellow gamers are fortysomething bankers or lawyers or executives in other highly paid, highly stressful fields. "These guys come from taking depositions all day in a suit and tie. Then they look so happy to leave that all behind for a few hours," Tracy says, sipping a beer.

Tracy and his crew are not outliers. They're part of a quiet network that's more Snakes & Ladders than Skull & Bones, where groups of mostly white white-collar types come together to decompress with dice. "I used to be this weird freak, who had this odd hobby that I didn't share with anyone," says financier Jim Doughan, another regular gamer. "You would do it on the downlow. Now more people are doing it than I ever knew. In the finance industry, you don't have to play golf anymore—you can play games." He marvels at how wide-reaching his once-niche hobby is becoming. "My neighbor showed up the other day at a gaming event. He's a doctor. I had no idea."

One demographic that's underrepresented is women. "The hobby as a whole is nowhere near parity, so it's a very male group," Tracy says of his club. "But there are two women who come at least two or three times a year."

He pegs the gender divide to the hobby's war-gaming heritage, and Mindy Kyrkos, a corporate travel agent and avid gamer, agrees on its lingering impact. "Very often I'm the only woman at the table," she says. "It's not that women don't enjoy conflict, but not that type."

As with fraternal groups since time immemorial, this network provides other advantages beyond the chance to unwind. "When I was changing jobs, one of the best career decisions I've ever made, it came directly through a gaming contact, and I've certainly recommended people that way," Tracy says. "And I've hired people I'd never have known without gaming."

There are no formal statistics on the number of such groups, but the trend has caught hold enough that some companies have opted to include gameplay in their hiring process. Recruiters for Pennsylvania-based Susquehanna International Group [SIG] stage game nights at colleges and universities to seek out potential hires, looking for the strategic thinking such a hobby engenders. SIG also hosts regular play evenings for employees; multiple groups will play the same game, stress-testing it to see if it leads to good team-building.

"We approach it the same way we approach trading," says Todd Simkin, a 20-year veteran of the company who co-heads its education team. "We look for ways to play the game, the different nuances, and we stop and discuss strategies. Then we have a debriefing afterwards." A favorite, Avalon, divides players into good and bad guys, then tasks them with deducing who is on each side. SIG operates a standalone, company-run website, raiseyourgame.com, maintained by employees who share their observations, tips, and theories on all kinds of gaming, from sports to board games to cards.

It's this type of collaboration that makes board games different from the every-man-for-himself mentality of poker, says Benjamin Hoffstein, who works on the tech side of finance. He runs Compass, a scavenger hunt and puzzle competition where "New York City is the game board." Every year it attracts almost two dozen teams from Goldman Sachs Group, Bridgewater Associates, Barclays, BlackRock, JPMorgan Chase, and other companies to compete in live-action puzzles at various locations across the city—and raise money for charity along the way. Winning in business is rarely a solo endeavor, and Hoffstein says his successful players have a group mindset. "You might work on a trading desk for a firm," he says, "where you're trying to get a team of people to quote-unquote win."

According to NPD Group Inc., U.S. sales of board games in 2017 were $1.1 billion, up 7% from the previous year. Travis Parker, who runs Game Crafter LLC, a custom game business, estimates that more than 3,000 games are released annually. Their producers range from big companies such as Hasbro Inc. to individual creators using crowdsourcing platforms like

Kickstarter. Crowdfunding has been crucial to the board game boom: In 2017, for instance, Kickstarter saw 400 more successful campaigns for tabletop games than in the previous year, and revenue was up 30%. Not all titles become household names—the jury's still out on Advanced Squad Leader, for sure—but some have become bestsellers: Pandemic, Carcassonne, and Ticket to Ride, though none comes close to the sales of Catan (originally known as Settlers of Catan), a game in which players trade commodities to build an empire on a fictional island.

Launched in 1995, Catan has sold more than 20 million copies worldwide. It drummed up new enthusiasm for board games in a world of Nintendo consoles and was therefore pivotal in the emergence of networking groups such as Tracy's. Reid Hoffman of LinkedIn Corp. has called Catan "the board game of entrepreneurship." He's described board games in general as a kind of off-duty MBA course that can exercise the brain to think strategically. Hoffman and Zynga Inc.'s Mark Pincus were among the Silicon Valley execs who began making game nights popular among the tech set about a decade ago.

Not long after, East Coast legal and finance types began playing the same way. Spencer Sloe is in a weekly game group in Brooklyn, N.Y., whose ringmaster is a health-care lawyer. Ranged around the table are hedge funders and wealth managers. Sloe himself is an executive with media company Oath. "I've helped people network—like, 'Hey, my niece wants an internship, do you know XYZ person?'" he says. "It's like getting people into a cult."

Justin Carroll is a bankruptcy lawyer and fervent board gamer. The crowd at Carroll's games is a mix of gay and straight and largely white. Most players didn't know one another before showing up and were drawn by word-of-mouth. Indeed, that's how he met a lawyer who specializes in pro bono programs, who in turn helped Carroll begin a similar project at his own employer.

Wall Street insiders have been monitoring the rise of board gaming as a low-pressure networking device, according to executive coach Roy Cohen. He says playing such games has become more popular in the last three or four years. Gaming cabals can prove so useful, Cohen actively encourages many clients to seek them out to get ahead. One Scrabble-loving financier ended up joining a group after a chance conversation in a café in East Hampton, N.Y., and later found work through its members. "It's for obvious reasons," Cohen says. "They can blow off steam, decompress, and network all at the same time."

British journalist Tristan Donovan, the author of *It's All a Game,* which explores the history and enduring appeal of board games, suggests their current popularity derives from a newly time-pressed culture. Those who might once have spent an entire Saturday golfing together see an evening of board gaming as far more efficient. Networking at a table is also simpler than on the links: The structure of the evening makes conversation easier and erases the hierarchies of the 9 to 5. "You're sitting around pieces of cardboard, leaning in close, and it all feels a little more intimate," Donovan says. Unlike poker, which

relies on bluffing and concealing your true self, board games can act as inadvertent personality tests. These nights can provide a preview of how someone might behave as a colleague—those sore losers at Catan are likely to throw the same tantrum when a deal doesn't go as planned.

Of course, the surge in popularity of Catan and other games came hand in hand with the rise of nerd obsessions in general; video games, fantasy books such as the Harry Potter series, and films based on comics have become so pervasive that geekery is no longer a subculture, it's *the* culture.

Back at Tracy's group, the conversation grows noisier as the evening (and dice) rolls on, and wine glasses and beer cans begin cluttering the few empty surfaces. "I like the tactile nature of it, the social aspect of it," Tracy says, before leaping into a Japanese history game called Rising Sun to help steer a clan leader from making a losing mistake.

Questions for Discussion

1. How does game playing help managers in dealing with teams and groups within an organization?

2. Do you think game playing constitutes a form of teamwork that translates to a performance enhancer? Explain your reasoning.

3. To what extent do group norms play a significant role in these game-playing groups? Cite several examples.

Source: Mark Ellwood, "The Power of Play," *Bloomberg Businessweek,* April 30, 2018, pp. 63–65. Used with permission of Bloomberg L.P. Copyright © 2017. All rights reserved.

Notes

1. R. Maze and G. Cavallaro, "Battling Bureaucracy: The Way Forward Requires Modernizing the Modernization Process," Association of the United States Army, February 22, 2018, www.ausa.org.
2. Maze and Cavallaro, "Battling Bureaucracy"; M. Myers, "Abrams: Army Units Will Be Tasked to Work on Each of Futures Command's Priorities," *Army Times,* March 27, 2018, www.armytimes.com; N. Martin, "Mark Esper: Army Forms Cross-Functional Teams to Support Tech Requirements Devt Process," *Executive Gov,* December 11, 2017, www.executivegov.com.
3. Maze and Cavallaro, "Battling Bureaucracy"; Myers, "Abrams: Army Units Will Be Tasked"; M. Pomerleau, "How a New Army Team Plans to Modernize the Network," *C4ISRNET,* March 30, 2018, www.c4isrnet.com.
4. Pomerleau, "How a New Army Team Plans to Modernize"; J. Garamone, "Service Members Seeing First Fruits of Army Acquisition Changes," *DoD News*

(*Department of Defense*), April 18, 2018, www.defense.gov; M. Pomerleau, "In: Fast Solutions; Out: Drawn Out Development," *C4ISRNET,* March 29, 2018, www.c4isrnet.com.

5. Maze and Cavallaro, "Battling Bureaucracy"; Myers, "Abrams: Army Units Will Be Tasked"; Pomerleau, "How a New Army Team Plans to Modernize"; Garamone, "Service Members Seeing First Fruits"; D. Parsons, "Army Speeds Up Fielding Artillery Missile by Five Years," *Defense Daily,* March 27, 2018, www .defensedaily.com.

6. T.M. Mills, *The Sociology of Small Groups* (Englewood Cliffs, NJ: Prentice-Hall, 1967); M.E. Shaw, *Group Dynamics* (New York: McGraw-Hill, 1981).

7. K. Casey, "How to Cultivate Soft Skills in Your IT Team," The Enterprisers Project, February 12, 2018, https://enterprisers project.com; T. Rahschulte, "Investing for Soft Skills: Build, Buy or Both," *Chief Learning Officer,* January 3, 2018, www .clomedia.com; M. Fouts, "Improve Team Collaboration with These Key Skills," *Forbes,* June 22, 2017, www.forbes.com; M. Feffer, "HR's Hard Challenge: When Employees Lack Soft Skills," Society for Human Resource Management, April 1, 2016, www.shrm.org.

8. Ibid.

9. Feffer, "HR's Hard Challenge."

10. Casey, "How to Cultivate Soft Skills"; Feffer, "HR's Hard Challenge"; Fouts, "Improve Team Collaboration"; Rahschulte, "Investing for Soft Skills."

11. Feffer, "HR's Hard Challenge"; Rahschulte, "Investing for Soft Skills."

12. "Hallmark Fact Sheet," https://corporate .hallmark.com, accessed April 20, 2018; R.S. Buday, "Reengineering One Firm's Product Development and Another's Service Delivery," *Planning Review,* March–April 1993, 14–19; J.M. Burcke, "Hallmark's Quest for Quality Is a Job Never Done," *Business Insurance,* April 26, 1993, 122; M. Hammer and J. Champy, *Reengineering the Corporation* (New York: HarperBusiness, 1993); T.A. Stewart, "The Search for the Organization of Tomorrow," *Fortune,* May 18, 1992, 92–98.

13. "CraftWorks Restaurants & Breweries," www.craftworkrestaurants.com, accessed April 20, 2018; A. Wallace, "Rock Bottom Founder Calls Decision to Sell 'Bittersweet,'" *Daily Camera,* www.dailycamera .com, accessed April 20, 2018.

14. S. Dallas, "Rock Bottom Restaurants: Brewing Up Solid Profits," *BusinessWeek,* May 22, 1995, 74.

15. J.A. Pearce II and E.C. Ravlin, "The Design and Activation of Self-Regulating Work Groups," *Human Relations* 11 (1987), 751–82.

16. B. Dumaine, "Who Needs a Boss?" *Fortune,* May 7, 1990, 52–60; Pearce and Ravlin, "The Design and Activation of Self-Regulating Work Groups."

17. Dumaine, "Who Needs a Boss?"; A.R. Montebello and V.R. Buzzotta, "Work Teams That Work," *Training and Development,* March 1993, 59–64.

18. G. Hamel, *The Future of Management* (Boston: Harvard Business School Press, 2007); "The Gore Story," www.gore.com, accessed April 24, 2018.

19. Hamel, *The Future of Management;* "The Gore Story"; "W.L. Gore & Associates Financials and News—100 Best Companies to Work For," http://fortune.com/ best-companies/w-l-gore-associates-12/, April 1, 2016.

20. Hamel, The Future of Management; "The Gore Story."

21. Ibid.

22. "Our Beliefs & Principles," www.gore .com, accessed April 24, 2018.

23. Hamel, The Future of Management; "The Gore Story."

24. R.E. Silverman, "Who's the Boss? There Isn't One," *The Wall Street Journal,* June 20, 2012, B1, B8.

25. Hamel, The Future of Management; "The Gore Story."

26. Ibid; "What We Offer," www.gore.com, accessed April 24, 2018.

27. Hamel, The Future of Management.

28. "What We Offer."

29. "The Gore Story."

30. Hamel, The Future of Management.

31. C. Zillman, "Secrets from Best Companies All Stars," *Fortune,* http://fortune.com, March 9, 2017.

32. T.D. Wall, N.J. Kemp, P.R. Jackson, and C.W. Clegg, "Outcomes of Autonomous Work Groups: A Long-Term Field Experiment," *Academy of Management Journal* 29 (1986), 280–304.

33. A. Markels, "A Power Producer Is Intent on Giving Power to Its People," *The Wall Street Journal,* July 3, 1995, A1, A12; "AES Corporation/The Power of Being Global," www.aes.com/aes/ index?page5home, April 15, 2008.

34. J.S. Lublin, "My Colleague, My Boss," *The Wall Street Journal,* April 12, 1995, R4, R12.

35. W.R. Pape, "Group Insurance," *Inc.* (Technology Supplement), June 17, 1997, 29–31; A.M. Townsend, S.M. DeMarie, and A.R. Hendrickson, "Are You Ready for Virtual Teams?" *HR Magazine,* September 1996, 122–26; A.M. Townsend, S.M. DeMarie, and A.M. Hendrickson, "Virtual Teams: Technology and the Workplace of the Future," *Academy of Management Executive* 12, no. 3 (1998), 17–29.

36. Townsend et al., "Virtual Teams."

37. V. Maza, "Are Your Remote Workers Happy? How to Keep Teams Connected from Afar," *Forbes,* www.forbes.com, January 30, 2018; D. DeRosa, "3 Companies with High-Performing Virtual Teams," www .onpointconsultingllc.com, October 5, 2017.

38. C. Breuer, J. Hüffmeier, and G. Hertel, "Does Trust Matter More in Virtual Teams? A Meta-Analysis of Trust and Team Effectiveness Considering Virtuality and Documentation as Moderators," *Journal of Applied Psychology* 101, no. 8 (2016), 1151–77.

39. Maza, "Are Your Remote Workers Happy?"

40. E.J. Hill, B.C. Miller, S.P. Weiner, and J. Colihan, "Influences of the Virtual Office on Aspects of Work and Work/Life Balance," *Personnel Psychology* 31 (1998), 667–83; S.G. Strauss, "Technology, Group Process, and Group Outcomes: Testing the Connections in Computer-Mediated and Face-to-Face Groups," *Human Computer Interaction,* 12 (1997), 227–66; M.E. Warkentin, L. Sayeed, and R. Hightower, "Virtual Teams versus Face-to-Face Teams: An Exploratory Study of a Web-Based Conference System," *Decision Sciences* 28, no. 4 (Fall 1997), 975–96.

41. S. Krumm, J. Kanthak, K. Hartmann, and G. Hertel, "What Does It Take to Be a Virtual Team Player? The Knowledge, Skills, Abilities, and Other Characteristics Required in Virtual Teams," *Human Performance* 29, no. 2 (2016), 123–42.

42. S.A. Furst, M. Reeves, B. Rosen, and R.S. Blackburn, "Managing the Life Cycle of Virtual Teams," *Academy of Management Executive* 18, no. 2 (May 2004), 6–20.

43. L. Gratton, "Work Together. . . When Apart," *The Wall Street Journal,* June 16–17, 2007, R4.

44. A. S. Hirsch, "How to Use Technology to Support Remote Teams," www.shrm.org, September 22, 2017.

45. A. Deutschman, "The Managing Wisdom of High-Tech Superstars," *Fortune,* October 17, 1994, 197–206.

46. J.D. Thompson, *Organizations in Action* (New York: McGraw-Hill, 1967).

47. S.H. Courtright, G.R. Thurgood, G.L. Stewart, and A. J. Pierotti, "Structural Interdependence in Teams: An Integrative Framework and Meta-Analysis," *Journal of Applied Psychology* 100, no. 6 (2015), 1825–46.

48. Thompson, *Organizations in Action.*

49. R. Saavedra, P.C. Earley, and L. Van Dyne, "Complex Interdependence in Task-Performing Groups," *Journal of Applied Psychology* 78, no. 1 (1993), 61–72.

50. S.M. Gully, K.A. Incalcaterra, A. Joshi, and J.M. Beaubien, "A Meta-Analysis of Team-Efficacy, Potency, and Performance:

Interdependence and Level of Analysis as Moderators of Observed Relationships," *Journal of Applied Psychology* 87, no. 5 (2002), 819–32.

51. Courtright et al, "Structural Interdependence in Teams."

52. Lublin, "My Colleague, My Boss."

53. "About ICU Medical, Inc.," www.icumed .com, accessed April 24, 2018.

54. "2017 Annual Report to Shareholders and Form 10K," https://ir.icumed.com, accessed April 24, 2018.

55. "The 200 Best Small Companies #80 ICU Medical," *Forbes,* www.forbes.com, October 14, 2009.

56. "About ICU Medical, Inc."; "Clave Connector," www.icumed.com, accessed April 24, 2018.

57. E. White, "How a Company Made Everyone a Team Player," *The Wall Street Journal,* August 13, 2007, B1, B7.

58. Ibid.

59. Ibid.

60. Ibid.

61. Ibid.

62. R.G. LeFauve and A.C. Hax, "Managerial and Technological Innovations at Saturn Corporation," *MIT Management,* Spring 1992, 8–19.

63. B.W. Tuckman, "Developmental Sequences in Small Groups," *Psychological Bulletin* 63 (1965), 384–99; B.W. Tuckman and M.C. Jensen, "Stages of Small Group Development," *Group and Organizational Studies* 2 (1977), 419–27.

64. C.J.G. Gersick, "Time and Transition in Work Teams: Toward a New Model of Group Development," *Academy of Management Journal* 31 (1988), 9–41; C.J.G. Gersick, "Marking Time: Predictable Transitions in Task Groups," *Academy of Management Journal* 32 (1989), 274–309.

65. J.R. Hackman, "Group Influences on Individuals in Organizations," in M.D. Dunnette and L.M. Hough, eds., *Handbook of Industrial and Organizational Psychology,* 2nd ed., vol. 3 (Palo Alto, CA: Consulting Psychologists Press, 1992), 199–267.

66. Hackman, "Group Influences on Individuals."

67. Ibid.

68. Lublin, "My Colleague, My Boss."

69. L. Festinger, "Informal Social Communication," *Psychological Review* 57 (1950), 271–82; Shaw, *Group Dynamics.*

70. Hackman, "Group Influences on Individuals in Organizations"; Shaw, *Group Dynamics.*

71. D. Cartwright, "The Nature of Group Cohesiveness," in D. Cartwright and A. Zander, eds., *Group Dynamics,* 3rd ed. (New York: Harper & Row, 1968); L. Festinger, S. Schacter, and K. Black, *Social Pressures in Informal Groups* (New York: Harper & Row, 1950); Shaw, *Group Dynamics.*

72. K. Christfort, "The Power of Business Chemistry," Deloitte, www2.deloitte.com, accessed April 23, 2018; K. Christfort and S. Vickberg, "Business Chemistry in the C-Suite," *The Wall Street Journal,* November 2, 2017, http://deloitte.wsj .com; S.M. Johnson Vickberg and K. Christfort, "Pioneers, Drivers, Integrators, and Guardians," *Harvard Business Review,* March–April 2017, 50–57.

73. Vickberg and Christfort, "Pioneers, Drivers, Integrators, and Guardians"; T. Williams, "Business Chemistry: Are You a Driver, Guardian, Integrator, or Pioneer," *Economist,* https://exceed.economist.com, accessed April 23, 2018; Christfort and Vickberg, "Business Chemistry in the C-Suite."

74. Vickberg and Christfort, "Pioneers, Drivers, Integrators, and Guardians"; Christfort and Vickberg, "Business Chemistry in the C-Suite"; Christfort, "The Power of Business Chemistry."

75. Vickberg and Christfort, "Pioneers, Drivers, Integrators, and Guardians"; Christfort and Vickberg, "Business Chemistry in the C-Suite"; A. Beard, "How Work Styles Inform," *Harvard Business Review,* March–April 2017, 58–59; Christfort, "The Power of Business Chemistry."

76. T.F. O'Boyle, "A Manufacturer Grows Efficient by Soliciting Ideas from Employees," *The Wall Street Journal,* June 5, 1992, A1, A5.

77. E. Kur, "The Faces Model of High Performing Team Management," *Leadership & Organizational Development Journal* 17, no. 1 (1996), 32–41.

78. D. D. Warrick, "What Leaders Can Learn about Teamwork and Developing High Performance Teams from Organization Development Practitioners," *Performance Improvement* 55(3): 13–21, 2016.

79. Lublin, "My Colleague, My Boss."

80. P.C. Earley, "Social Loafing and Collectivism: A Comparison of the United States and the People's Republic of China," *Administrative Science Quarterly* 34 (1989), 565–81; J.M. George, "Extrinsic and Intrinsic Origins of Perceived Social Loafing in Organizations," *Academy of Management Journal* 35 (1992), 191–202; S.G. Harkins, B. Latane, and K. Williams, "Social Loafing: Allocating Effort or Taking It Easy," *Journal of Experimental Social Psychology* 16 (1980), 457–65; B. Latane, K.D. Williams, and S. Harkins, "Many Hands Make Light the Work: The Causes and Consequences of Social Loafing," *Journal of Personality and Social Psychology* 37 (1979), 822–32; J.A. Shepperd, "Productivity Loss in Performance Groups: A Motivation Analysis," *Psychological Bulletin* 113 (1993), 67–81.

81. George, "Extrinsic and Intrinsic Origins of Perceived Social Loafing in Organizations"; G.R. Jones, "Task Visibility, Free Riding, and Shirking: Explaining the Effect of Structure and Technology on Employee Behavior," *Academy of Management Review* 9 (1984), 684–95; K. Williams, S. Harkins, and B. Latane, "Identifiability as a Deterrent to Social Loafing: Two Cheering Experiments," *Journal of Personality and Social Psychology* 40 (1981), 303–11.

82. S. Harkins and J. Jackson, "The Role of Evaluation in Eliminating Social Loafing," *Personality and Social Psychology Bulletin* 11 (1985), 457–65; N.L. Kerr and S.E. Bruun, "Ringelman Revisited: Alternative Explanations for the Social Loafing Effect," *Personality and Social Psychology Bulletin* 7 (1981), 224–31; Williams et al., "Identifiability as a Deterrent to Social Loafing"; Harkins and Jackson, "The Role of Evaluation in Eliminating Social Loafing."

83. M.A. Brickner, S.G. Harkins, and T.M. Ostrom, "Effects of Personal Involvement: Thought-Provoking Implications for Social Loafing," *Journal of Personality and Social Psychology* 51 (1986), 763–69; S.G. Harkins and R.E. Petty, "The Effects of Task Difficulty and Task Uniqueness on Social Loafing," *Journal of Personality and Social Psychology* 43 (1982), 1214–29.

84. B. Latane, "Responsibility and Effort in Organizations," in P.S. Goodman, ed., *Designing Effective Work Groups* (San Francisco: Jossey-Bass, 1986); Latane et al., "Many Hands Make Light the Work"; I.D. Steiner, *Group Process and Productivity* (New York: Academic Press, 1972).

CHAPTER 16

Promoting Effective Communication

©Tom Merton/age fotostock

Learning Objectives

After studying this chapter, you should be able to:

LO16-1 Explain why effective communication helps an organization gain a competitive advantage.

LO16-2 Describe the communication process, and explain the role of perception in communication.

LO16-3 Define information richness, and describe the information richness of communication media available to managers.

LO16-4 Describe the communication networks that exist in groups and teams.

LO16-5 Explain how advances in technology have given managers new options for managing communication.

LO16-6 Describe important communication skills that managers need as senders and as receivers of messages and why it is important to understand differences in linguistic styles.

How Boston Consulting Group Promotes Better Communication

How can managers encourage effective communication? As a leading consulting firm focused on business strategy, Boston Consulting Group (BCG) has a culture that values learning. Its natural response to a problem or challenge is to investigate the situation, advance knowledge, and lead change. In recent years, BCG has used that approach to tackle two challenges related to communication within the organization.[1]

One challenge was triggered by plans to relocate BCG's New York office. Managing partner Ross Love was placed in charge of investigating what type of facilities would promote the kinds of interactions that promote innovation and problem solving. To find out what communication behaviors were already occurring, Love constructed an experiment. He signed up 115 employees to participate by wearing ID badges with sensors that tracked their locations and made a record of when and to whom the individual spoke (excluding the content of what they said) throughout the day over a four-month period. The initial data, which were anonymous, showed that people who engaged in more short, informal interactions spent less time in meetings—probably because they resolved more issues outside the meetings. This research guided plans to design facilities that would attract people into shared spaces, where they would be likely to informally connect throughout the day.[2]

In the new location, BCG again measured traffic patterns and communications. It found that "collisions"—interactions of 15 minutes or less—occurred almost 20% more often in the new location. This was good news because of the association with shorter time in meetings, especially because the interactions often crossed team boundaries, thereby promoting

more sharing of knowledge across the organization. In addition, more collisions at the new location crossed levels of the company's hierarchy, which for the junior employees is associated with feeling highly engaged. The greater variety of who is connecting with whom also is contributing to greater cohesion within teams and a move away from overreliance on a few individuals to convey information.[3]

Another communication challenge BCG addressed relates to the experience of women. The firm found that women were leaving at an unacceptable rate and were more likely than their male colleagues to have low job satisfaction. Research showed that the problem was not the usual suspects, such as work–life balance. Rather, the women were less likely to feel supported and encouraged. With regard to communication, career development tended to involve mentors criticizing the women's communication style because it didn't match assumptions about how successful men communicate. In particular, mentors urged female employees to be more

Boston Consulting Group found that employees who engage in short, informal interactions with their colleagues spent less time in meetings because they were able to communicate effectively and resolve issues quickly, particularly in a shared office environment.
©Gary Burchell/Getty Images

aggressive, on the assumption that this would strengthen their messages. Instead, the coaching was frustrating to hear and seldom was possible to implement. As one manager admitted, urging a female manager to "take up space" in the room felt like "encouraging her to grow 6 inches."[4]

BCG's talent development team reevaluated the program and determined that it would be more helpful to view effective communication as a broader set of skills that include not only asserting a point, but also building rapport with the audience and interpreting feedback. With the revised training, mentors and mentees alike were pleased to see communication become more effective as people chose methods that suited their own strengths.[5]

Overview

Even with all the advances in information technology that are available to managers, ineffective communication continues to take place in organizations. Ineffective communication is detrimental for managers, employees, and organizations; it can lead to poor performance, strained interpersonal relations, poor service, and dissatisfied customers. For an organization to be effective and gain a competitive advantage, managers at all levels need to be good communicators.

LO16-1 Explain why effective communication helps an organization gain a competitive advantage.

In this chapter we describe the nature of communication and the communication process and explain why all managers and their subordinates need to be effective communicators. We describe the communication media available to managers and the factors they need to consider in selecting a communication medium for each message they send. We consider the communication networks organizational members rely on, and we explore how advances in information technology have expanded managers' range of communication options. We describe the communication skills that help managers to be effective senders and receivers of messages. By the end of this chapter you will appreciate the nature of communication and the steps managers can take to ensure that they are effective communicators.

Communication and Management

communication The sharing of information between two or more individuals or groups to reach a common understanding.

Communication is the sharing of information between two or more individuals or groups to reach a common understanding.[6] First and foremost, no matter how electronically based, communication is a human endeavor and involves individuals and groups. Second, communication does not take place unless a common understanding is reached. Thus, when you call a business to speak to a person in customer service or billing and are bounced between endless automated messages and menu options and eventually hang up in frustration, communication has not taken place.

The Importance of Good Communication

In Chapter 1 we described how an organization can gain a competitive advantage when managers strive to increase efficiency, quality, responsiveness to customers, and innovation. Good communication is essential for attaining each of these four goals and, thus, is a necessity for gaining a competitive advantage.

Managers can *increase efficiency* by updating the production process to take advantage of new and more efficient technologies and by training workers to operate the new technologies and to expand their skills. Good communication is necessary for managers to learn about new technologies, implement them in their organizations, and train workers in how to use them. Similarly, *improving quality* hinges on effective communication. Managers need to communicate to all members of an organization the meaning and importance of high quality and the routes to attaining it. Subordinates need to communicate quality problems and suggestions for increasing quality to their superiors, and members of self-managed work teams need to share their ideas on improving quality.

Good communication can also help increase *responsiveness to customers*. When the organizational members who are closest to customers, such as department store salespeople and bank tellers, are empowered to communicate customers' needs and desires to managers, managers can better respond to these needs. Managers, in turn, must communicate with other organizational members to determine how best to respond to changing customer preferences.

Innovation, which often takes place in cross-functional teams, also requires effective communication. Members of a cross-functional team developing a new electronic game, for example, must effectively communicate with one another to develop a game that customers will want to play; that will be engaging, interesting, and fun; and that can lead to sequels. Members of the team also must communicate with managers to secure the resources they need for developing the game and to keep managers informed of progress on the project. Innovation, whether in products or processes, is likeliest in a culture where employees share ideas, rather than merely waiting for direction from above. To learn about a company that promotes this kind of communication, read the "Manager as a Person" feature.

MANAGER AS A PERSON

Hyphen's Goal for Employees: Be Heard at Work

For Ranjit Jose and Arnaud Grunwald, the impetus to start their business came from their experiences as employees and managers. The two were friends and coworkers at the same company, which had grown rapidly. The two men noted that as teams grew larger and the corporate structure more complex, people found it harder to point out problems and share ideas. For many, the lack of a voice was frustrating—and came with fear that if employees were bold enough to complain, there could be consequences. Jose and Grunwald proposed that their HR department conduct a survey of team members, but the department assured them they could wait for the annual survey, due in six more months.[7]

As the two men discussed the situation, they agreed that communication from employees to management was essential to business success. They also agreed that an annual survey in this age of Internet communication and computer analysis was sadly inadequate. And finally, they agreed that other growing businesses must have the same challenges, which suggested a need for a new business. Together, they planned the start-up of Hyphen. India-born Jose, who studied electrical and computer engineering in the United States, and Grunwald, who was born in France, attended the University of California, Berkeley, and managed global analytics, set up Hyphen with two headquarters, one in San Francisco and the other in Bangalore, India.[8]

Hyphen provides businesses with a technology platform that lets businesses gather and analyze anonymous communications from their employees. The purpose is to communicate to employees that their opinions matter and to make those opinions available quickly and easily, through a variety of methods. Employees can use mobile devices to reply to quick or more in-depth surveys. They can answer quick Pulse Polls containing weekly questions. And they can make anonymous comments using the Employee Voice tool. The computer system gathers the responses, analyzes them, and submits reports and alerts to management. For example, managers can gauge concerns about a new program or follow trends in employee satisfaction, both companywide and by division or team. The founders see the enterprise as distinctive in the way it combines ease of use on mobile devices with powerful analysis to support decision making.[9]

While technology enables the product, the company's tag line best expresses the founders' vision for its customers' employees: "Be Heard at Work."[10]

LO16-2 Describe the communication process, and explain the role of perception in communication.

Effective communication is necessary for managers and all members of an organization such as Boston Consulting Group, profiled in "A Manager's Challenge," to increase efficiency, quality, responsiveness to customers, and innovation and, thus, gain a competitive advantage for the organization. Managers therefore must understand the communication process well if they are to perform effectively.

The Communication Process

sender The person or group wishing to share information.

message The information that a sender wants to share.

encoding Translating a message into understandable symbols or language.

noise Anything that hampers any stage of the communication process.

receiver The person or group for whom a message is intended.

medium The pathway through which an encoded message is transmitted to a receiver.

decoding Interpreting and trying to make sense of a message.

verbal communication The encoding of messages into words, either written or spoken.

nonverbal communication The encoding of messages by means of facial expressions, body language, and style of dress.

The communication process consists of two phases. In the *transmission phase,* information is shared between two or more individuals or groups. In the *feedback phase,* a common understanding is ensured. In both phases, a number of distinct stages must occur for communication to take place (see Figure 16.1).[11]

Starting the transmission phase, the **sender,** the person or group wishing to share information with some other person or group, decides on the **message,** what information to communicate. Then the sender translates the message into symbols or language, a process called **encoding;** often messages are encoded into words. **Noise** is a general term that refers to anything that hampers any stage of the communication process.

Once encoded, a message is transmitted through a medium to the **receiver,** the person or group for whom the message is intended. A **medium** is simply the pathway, such as a phone call, a letter, a memo, or face-to-face communication in a meeting, through which an encoded message is transmitted to a receiver. At the next stage, the receiver interprets and tries to make sense of the message, a process called **decoding.** This is a critical point in communication.

The feedback phase is initiated by the receiver (who becomes a sender). The receiver decides what message to send to the original sender (who becomes a receiver), encodes it, and transmits it through a chosen medium (see Figure 16.1). The message might contain a confirmation that the original message-was received and understood, a restatement of the original message to make sure it has been correctly interpreted, or a request for more information. The original sender decodes the message and makes sure a common understanding has been reached. If the original sender determines that a common understanding has not been reached, sender and receiver cycle through the whole process as many times as needed to reach a common understanding. Feedback eliminates misunderstandings, ensures that messages are correctly interpreted, and enables senders and receivers to reach a common understanding.

The encoding of messages into words, written or spoken, is **verbal communication.** We can also encode messages without using written or spoken language.

Nonverbal communication shares information by means of facial expressions (smiling, raising an eyebrow, frowning, dropping one's jaw), body language (posture, gestures, nods, and shrugs), and even style of dress (casual, formal, conservative, trendy). The trend toward increasing empowerment of the workforce has led some managers to dress informally to communicate that all employees of an organization are team members, working together to create value for customers.

Figure 16.1
The Communication Process

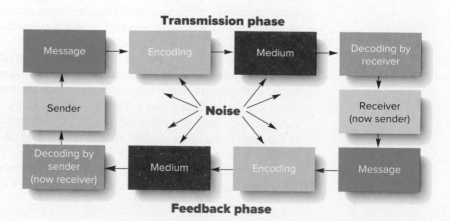

If a picture is worth a thousand words, so too is nonverbal communication. Facial expressions, body language, posture, and eye contact all send powerful messages.
©Christopher Robbins/Getty Images

Nonverbal communication can be used to reinforce verbal communication. Just as a warm and genuine smile can back up words of appreciation for a job well done, a concerned facial expression can back up words of sympathy for a personal problem. In such cases, the congruence between the verbal and the nonverbal communication helps to ensure that a common understanding is reached.

Sometimes when members of an organization decide not to express a message verbally, they inadvertently do so nonverbally. People tend to have less control over nonverbal communication, and often a verbal message that is withheld gets expressed through body language or facial expressions. A manager who agrees to a proposal that he or she actually does not like may unintentionally communicate disfavor by grimacing.

Sometimes nonverbal communication is used to send messages that cannot be sent through verbal channels. Many lawyers are well aware of this communication tactic. Lawyers are often schooled in techniques of nonverbal communication, such as choosing where to stand in the courtroom for maximum effect and using eye contact during different stages of a trial. Lawyers sometimes get into trouble for using inappropriate nonverbal communication in an attempt to influence juries.[12]

The Role of Perception in Communication

Perception plays a central role in communication and affects both transmission and feedback. In Chapter 5 we defined *perception* as the process through which people select, organize, and interpret sensory input to give meaning and order to the world around them. We mentioned that perception is inherently subjective and is influenced by people's personalities, values, attitudes, and moods as well as by their experience and knowledge. When senders and receivers communicate with each other, they do so based on their subjective perceptions. The encoding and decoding of messages and even the choice of a medium hinge on the perceptions of senders and receivers.

In addition, perceptual biases can hamper effective communication. Recall from Chapter 5 that *biases* are systematic tendencies to use information about others in ways that result in inaccurate perceptions. In Chapter 5 we described a number of biases that can cause unfair treatment of diverse members of an organization. The same biases also can lead to ineffective communication. For example, *stereotypes*—simplified and often inaccurate beliefs about the characteristics of particular groups of people—can interfere with the encoding and decoding of messages.

Suppose a manager stereotypes older workers as being fearful of change. When this manager encodes a message to an older worker about an upcoming change in the organization, she may downplay the extent of the change so as not to make the older worker feel stressed. The older worker, however, fears change no more than do his younger colleagues and, thus, decodes the message to mean that only a minor change is going to be made. The older worker fails to prepare adequately for the change, and his performance subsequently suffers because of his lack of preparation. Clearly, this ineffective communication was due to the manager's inaccurate assumptions about older workers. Instead of relying on stereotypes, effective managers strive to perceive other people accurately by focusing on their actual behaviors, knowledge, skills, and abilities. Accurate perceptions, in turn, contribute to effective communication.

The Dangers of Ineffective Communication

Because managers must communicate with others to perform their various roles and tasks, managers spend most of their time communicating, whether in meetings, in telephone conversations, through email, or in face-to-face interactions. Indeed, some experts estimate that managers spend approximately 80% of their time engaged in some form of communication.[13]

Effective communication is so important that managers cannot just be concerned that they themselves are effective communicators; they also have to help their subordinates be effective communicators. When all members of an organization can communicate effectively with one another and with people outside the organization, the organization is much more likely to perform highly and gain a competitive advantage.

When managers and other members of an organization are ineffective communicators, organizational performance suffers, and any competitive advantage the organization might have is likely to be lost. Moreover, poor communication can be downright dangerous and even lead to tragic and unnecessary loss of human life. For example, a recent study by Harvard University researchers found that changing how doctors communicate during shift changes reduced the risk of adverse events in patients by 30%. In addition, researchers found that improving communication methods could also reduce the rate of medical errors by almost 25%.[14]

Communication problems in airplane cockpits and between flying crews and air traffic controllers are all too common, sometimes with deadly consequences. In the late 1970s two jets collided in Tenerife (one of the Canary Islands) because of miscommunication between a pilot and the control tower, and 600 people were killed. The tower radioed to the pilot, "Clipper 1736 report clear of runway." The pilot mistakenly interpreted this message to mean that he was cleared for takeoff.[15] Unfortunately, communication problems persist in the airline industry. In 2009 a Northwest Airlines Airbus A320 flew 150 miles past its Minneapolis destination while the crew of the airplane was out of contact with air traffic controllers for over an hour.[16] A safety group at NASA tracked more than 6,000 unsafe flying incidents and found that communication difficulties had caused approximately 529 of them.[17] And NASA has its own communication difficulties.[18] In 2004 NASA released a report detailing communication problems at the International Space Station, jointly managed and staffed by NASA and the Russian space agency; the problems included inadequate record keeping, missing information, and failure to keep data current.[19]

Information Richness and Communication Media

LO16-3 Define information richness, and describe the information richness of communication media available to managers.

information richness The amount of information that a communication medium can carry and the extent to which the medium enables the sender and receiver to reach a common understanding.

To be effective communicators, managers (and other members of an organization) need to select an appropriate communication medium for each message they send. Should a change in procedures be communicated to subordinates in an email? Should a congratulatory message about a major accomplishment be communicated in a letter, in a phone call, or over lunch? Should a layoff announcement be made in a memo or at a plant meeting? Should the members of a purchasing team travel to Europe to cement a major agreement with a new supplier, or should they do so through conference calls and email messages? Managers deal with these questions day in and day out.

There is no one best communication medium for managers to rely on. In choosing a medium for any message, managers need to consider three factors. The first and most important is the level of information richness that is needed. **Information richness** is the amount of information a communication medium can carry and the extent to which the medium enables the sender and receiver to reach a common understanding.[20] The communication media that managers use vary in their information richness (see Figure 16.2).[21] Media high in information richness can carry an extensive amount of information and generally enable receivers and senders to come to a common understanding.

The second factor that managers need to take into account in selecting a communication medium is the *time* needed for communication, because managers' and other organizational members' time is valuable. Managers at AXA, a global financial services company, drastically reduced the amount of time they spent in meetings by using videoconferencing instead of traveling to foreign destinations to engage in communications with colleagues and clients.[22]

The third factor that affects the choice of a communication medium is the *need for a paper or electronic trail* or some kind of written documentation that a message was sent and received. A manager may wish to document in writing, for example, that a subordinate was given a formal warning about excessive lateness.

In the remainder of this section we examine four types of communication media that vary along these three dimensions (information richness, time, and paper or electronic trail).[23]

Figure 16.2

The Information Richness of Communication Media

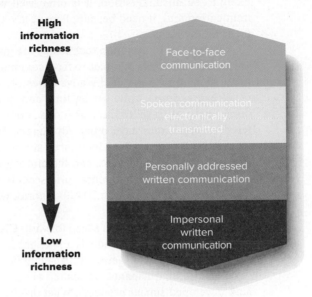

High information richness

Low information richness

Face-to-face communication

Spoken communication electronically transmitted

Personally addressed written communication

Impersonal written communication

Face-to-Face Communication

Face-to-face communication is the medium that is highest in information richness. When managers communicate face-to-face, they not only can take advantage of verbal communication, but also can interpret each other's nonverbal signals such as facial expressions and body language. A look of concern or puzzlement can sometimes say more than a thousand words, and managers can respond to such nonverbal signals on the spot. Face-to-face communication also enables managers to receive instant feedback. Points of confusion, ambiguity, or misunderstanding can be resolved, and managers can cycle through the communication process as many times as needed to reach a common understanding.

management by wandering around A face-to-face communication technique in which a manager walks around a work area and talks informally with employees about issues and concerns.

With the growing proliferation of electronic forms of communication, such as email, some managers fear that face-to-face communication is being shortchanged to the detriment of building common understandings and rapport.[24] Moreover, some messages that should be communicated face-to-face or at least in a phone conversation, and messages that are more efficiently communicated in this manner, are nonetheless sent electronically.[25]

Allowing opportunities for face-to-face communication can be especially important when trying to communicate effectively with employees located in other countries. For example, ProQuest, an information technology company, has remote teams scattered in cities around the world that communicate daily via various forms of media. However, the teams come together face-to-face every four months to plan the projects they will carry out in the coming year.[26]

Management by wandering around is a face-to-face communication technique that is effective for many managers at all levels in an organization. Rather than scheduling formal meetings with subordinates, managers walk around work areas and talk informally with employees about issues and concerns that both employees and managers may have. These informal conversations give managers and subordinates important information while fostering the development of positive relationships. With technology changing at breakneck speed and more employees working out of their homes or in remote locations, some experts suggest that in recent years, management by wandering around has evolved into management by weekly check-in, which makes effective communication critical to an organization's success.[27]

Because face-to-face communication is highest in information richness, you might think it should always be the medium of choice for managers.

Despite the popularity of electronic communication, face-to-face communication is still the medium that is highest in information richness.

©Digital Vision/Getty Images

This is not the case, however, because of the amount of time it can take and the lack of a paper or electronic trail resulting from it. For messages that are important, personal, or likely to be misunderstood, it is often well worth managers' time to use face-to-face communication and, if need be, supplement it with some form of written communication documenting the message.

Advances in information technology are giving managers new communication media that are close substitutes for face-to-face communication. Many organizations use *videoconferences* to capture some of the advantages of face-to-face communication (such as access to facial expressions) while saving time and money, because managers in different locations do not have to travel to meet with one another. In addition to saving travel costs, videoconferences sometimes have other advantages. Managers have found that decisions get made more quickly when videoconferences are used, because more managers can be involved in the decision-making process, and therefore, fewer managers have to be consulted outside the meeting itself. Videoconferences also seem to lead to more efficient meetings. Some managers have found meetings are 20–30% shorter when videoconferences are used instead of face-to-face meetings.

Taking videoconferences a leap forward, Cisco Systems has developed its TelePresence line of products, enabling individuals and teams in different locations to communicate live and in real time over the Internet with high-definition, life-size video and excellent audio that make it feel as if all participants, no matter where they are, in the same room.[28] Other companies have developed similar products. What distinguishes these products from older systems is the fact there are no delays in transmission; the video quality is sharp, clear, and in real time; and videoconferencing can be accessed routinely via smartphones or tablets.

Spoken Communication Electronically Transmitted

After face-to-face communication, spoken communication electronically transmitted over phone lines or via the Internet is second highest in information richness (see Figure 16.2). Although managers communicating over the telephone do not see body language and facial expressions, they do have access to the tone of voice in which a message is delivered, the parts of the message the sender emphasizes, and the general manner in which the message is spoken, in addition to the words themselves. Thus, telephone conversations can convey extensive amounts of information. Managers can ensure mutual understanding because they can get quick feedback over the phone and answer questions.

Video calling apps such as Skype and FaceTime enable people to communicate using voice and video over the Internet. They provide access to nonverbal forms of communication between sender and receiver as well as enable individuals and businesses to conduct conference calls and interviews quickly and inexpensively. More and more companies are using Skype or FaceTime to interview potential candidates for job openings.[29]

Personally Addressed Written Communication

Lower in information richness than electronically transmitted verbal communication is personally addressed written communication (see Figure 16.2). One advantage of face-to-face communication and electronically transmitted verbal communication is that they both tend to demand attention, which helps ensure that receivers pay attention. Personally addressed written communications, such as memos and letters, also have this advantage. Because they are addressed to a particular person, the chances are good that the person will pay attention to (and read) them. Moreover, the sender can write the message in a way that the receiver is most likely to

Video calling apps such as Skype and FaceTime enable individuals and businesses to communicate quickly and inexpensively. More and more companies are also using these apps to interview potential job candidates or to allow employees who work from home or other remote locations to communicate in real time with their colleagues in the office.
©Andriy Popov/123RF

understand. However, unlike spoken communication electronically transmitted, receivers of personally addressed written communication do not have access to the sender's tone of voice, parts of the message the sender emphasizes, and the general manner in which the message is spoken. Additionally, like voice mail, written communication does not enable a receiver to have his or her questions answered immediately; however, when messages are clearly written and feedback is provided, common understandings can still be reached.

Even if managers use face-to-face communication, sending a follow-up in writing is often necessary for messages that are important or complicated and need to be referred to later on. This is precisely what Karen Stracker, a hospital administrator, did when she needed to tell one of her subordinates about an important change in how the hospital would be handling denials of insurance benefits. Stracker met with the subordinate and described the changes face-to-face. Once she was sure the subordinate understood them, she handed her a sheet of instructions to follow, which essentially summarized the information they had discussed.

Email and text messages also fit into this category of communication media, because senders and receivers are communicating through personally addressed written words. The words, however, appear on their computer screens, laptops, or mobile devices rather than on paper. Email is so widespread in the business world that some managers find they have to deliberately take time out from managing their email to get their work done, including taking action on business strategies and coming up with new and innovative ideas. According to the Radicati Group, a technology marketing research firm, by 2022 worldwide email traffic will reach 333 *billion* emails every day—including both business and consumer users.[30] To help employees manage their email effectively, many organizations provide in-house training programs or other guidance to help workers (and managers) use email as part of their daily work activities.[31]

The use of email has also enabled many workers and managers to become telecommuters, people employed by organizations who work out of their homes at least one day a week. According to recent statistics, close to 40% of the U.S. workforce telecommutes with some frequency. Many who work out of their homes indicate the flexibility of working at home enables them to be more productive while giving them a chance to be closer to their families and not waste time traveling to and from the office.[32]

Today email continues to be the most used form of business communication in the workplace. Managers need to develop a clear, written policy specifying what company email can and should be used for—and what is out of bounds. Managers should clearly communicate this policy to all members of the organization, as well as tell them what procedures will be used when email abuse is suspected and what consequences will result if abuse is confirmed.[33]

In addition, email policies should specify how much personal email is appropriate and when those bounds have been overstepped. Just as employees make personal phone calls while on the job, so, too, do they send and receive personal email. Clearly banning all personal email is impractical and likely to have negative consequences for employees and their organizations (such as lower levels of job satisfaction and increased personal phone conversations). Some companies urge employees to use other web-based systems such as Gmail for personal communications rather than the corporate email system.[34]

What about surfing the Internet on company time? Results vary, but recent studies suggest that employees spend one to three hours a day doing personal business at work via the Internet. Over the past few years, a growing number of companies have banned Internet access for their employees at work or installed monitoring software for company computers, which can include information for accessing private sites like Facebook or personal email accounts.[35] As indicated in the accompanying "Ethics in Action" feature, personal email and Internet surfing at work present managers with some challenging ethical dilemmas.

Impersonal Written Communication

Impersonal written communication is lowest in information richness but is well suited for messages that need to reach many receivers. Because such messages are not addressed to particular receivers, feedback is unlikely, so managers must make sure messages sent by this medium are written clearly in language that all receivers will understand.

Managers often find company newsletters useful vehicles for reaching large numbers of employees. Many managers give their newsletters catchy names to spark employee interest

Tracking Email and Internet Use

A growing number of companies provide managers and organizations with tools to track the websites their employees visit and the email and social media messages they send. For example, network forensic software enables managers to record and replay everything that takes place on employees' computer monitors and can also track keystrokes. Many organizations, both large and small, track employees' activities in many different ways in an effort to become more efficient and productive.[36]

Monitoring employees raises concerns about privacy. Most employees would not like to have their bosses listening to their phone conversations; similarly, some believe that monitoring email and tracking Internet use are an invasion of privacy.[37] Given the increasingly long working hours of many employees, should personal email and Internet use be closely scrutinized? Clearly, when illegal and unethical email use is suspected, such as sexually harassing coworkers or divulging confidential company information, monitoring may be called for. But should it be a normal part of organizational life, even when there are no indications of a problem?

Essentially, this dilemma involves issues of trust. And given that there is no federal legislation to protect employees from having their companies monitor company-supplied machines such as computers, laptops, and cell phones, employees themselves can take steps to protect their own privacy.[38] Lewis Maltby, founder of the National Workrights Institute, which is devoted to safeguarding privacy at work, suggests that when sending sensitive or personal information, employees can use their own equipment (e.g., private cell phone or laptop) and an outside Wi-Fi provider so that their employing organization cannot access the information.[39] Employees also need to be careful about what email messages they send and avoid sending private and sensitive email on workplace systems. Once email messages are sent, they live on in the recipients' computers and systems and can come back to haunt senders or be subpoenaed in a court of law.[40]

Intrusive monitoring policies may have unintended negative consequences in organizations.
©pixinoo/Shuttetstock

and to inject a bit of humor into the workplace. Increasing numbers of companies distribute their newsletters online. For example, IBM's employee communications typically are available through the company's intranet, known internally as W3, and it has led a transformation from professional to user-generated content within the company.[41]

Managers can use impersonal written communication for various messages, including announcements of rules, regulations, policies, newsworthy information, changes in procedures, and the arrival of new organizational members. Impersonal written communication also can convey instructions about how to use machinery or how to process work orders or customer requests. For these kinds of messages, the paper or electronic trail left by this communication medium can be valuable for employees.

Just as with personal written communication, impersonal written communication can be delivered and retrieved electronically, and this is increasingly the case in companies large and small. Unfortunately, the ease with which electronic messages can spread has led to their proliferation. Many managers' and workers' electronic inboxes are so backlogged that often they do not have time to read all the electronic work-related information available to them.

information overload The potential for important information to be ignored or overlooked while tangential information receives attention.

blog A website on which an individual, a group, or an organization posts information, commentary, and opinions and to which readers can often respond with their own commentary and opinions.

social networking site A website that enables people to communicate with others with whom they have some common interest or connection.

The problem with such information overload is the potential for important information to be ignored or overlooked (even that which is personally addressed) while tangential information receives attention. Moreover, information overload can result in thousands of hours and millions of dollars in lost productivity.

Some managers and organizations use blogs to communicate with employees, investors, customers, and the general public. A blog is a website on which an individual, a group, or an organization posts information, commentary, and opinions and to which readers can often respond with their own commentary and opinions. Some top managers write their own blogs, and some companies such as JPMorgan Chase, American Express, and Casper, the mattress e-commerce company, have corporate blogs.[42] Just as organizations have rules and guidelines about employee email and Internet use, a growing number of organizations are instituting employee guidelines for blogs.[43]

A social networking site such as Instagram, Facebook, Twitter, YouTube, or LinkedIn enables people to communicate with others with whom they might have some common personal or professional interest or connection. Billions of people in the United States and around the world create custom profiles and communicate with networks of other participants through these sites. While communication through social networks may be work related, some managers are concerned that employees are wasting time at work communicating with their personal group of acquaintances through these sites. A recent study by Pew Research Center found that 27% of employees surveyed said they use social media at work to connect with family and friends.[44]

Communication Networks

LO16-4 Describe the communication networks that exist in groups and teams.

communication networks The pathways along which information flows in groups and teams and throughout the organization.

Although various communication media are used, communication in organizations tends to flow in certain patterns. The pathways along which information flows in groups and teams and throughout an organization are called communication networks. The type of communication network that exists in a group depends on the nature of the group's tasks and the extent to which group members need to communicate with one another to achieve group goals.

Communication Networks in Groups and Teams

As you learned in Chapter 15, groups and teams, whether they are cross-functional teams, top management teams, command groups, self-managed work teams, or task forces, are the building blocks of organizations. Four kinds of communication networks can develop in groups and teams: the wheel, the chain, the circle, and the all-channel network (see Figure 16.3).

WHEEL NETWORK In a wheel network, information flows to and from one central member of the group. Other group members do not need to communicate with one another to perform at a high level, so the group can accomplish its goals by directing all communication to and from the central member. Wheel networks are often found in command groups with pooled task interdependence. Picture a group of taxi drivers who report to the same dispatcher, who is also their supervisor. Each driver needs to communicate with the dispatcher, but the drivers do not need to communicate with one another. In groups such as this, the wheel network results in efficient communication, saving time without compromising performance. Although found in groups, wheel networks are not found in teams because they do not allow the intense interactions characteristic of teamwork.

CHAIN NETWORK In a chain network, members communicate with one another in a predetermined sequence. Chain networks are found in groups with sequential task interdependence, such as assembly-line groups. When group work has to be performed in a predetermined order, the chain network is often found because group members need to communicate with those whose work directly precedes and follows their own. Like wheel networks, chain networks tend not to exist in teams because of the limited amount of interaction among group members.

Figure 16.3
Communication Networks in Groups and Teams

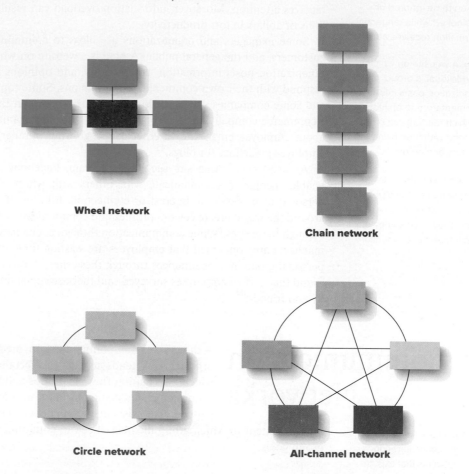

Wheel network

Chain network

Circle network

All-channel network

CIRCLE NETWORK In a circle network, group members communicate with others who are similar to them in experiences, beliefs, areas of expertise, background, office location, or even where they sit when the group meets. Members of task forces and standing committees, for example, tend to communicate with others who have similar experiences or backgrounds. People also tend to communicate with those whose offices are next to their own. Like wheel and chain networks, circle networks are most often found in groups that are not teams.

ALL-CHANNEL NETWORK An all-channel network is found in teams. It is characterized by high levels of communication: Every team member communicates with every other team member. Top management teams, cross-functional teams, and self-managed work teams frequently have all-channel networks. The reciprocal task interdependence often found in such teams requires that information flows in all directions. Computer software designed for use by work groups can help maintain effective communication in teams with all-channel networks, because it gives team members an efficient way to share information.

Organizational Communication Networks

An organization chart may seem to be a good summary of an organization's communication network, but often it is not. An organization chart summarizes the *formal* reporting relationships in an organization and the formal pathways along which communication takes place. Often, however, communication is *informal* and flows around issues, goals, projects, and ideas instead of moving up and down the organizational hierarchy in an orderly fashion. Thus, an organization's communication network includes not only the formal communication pathways summarized in an organization chart, but also informal communication pathways along which a great deal of communication takes place (see Figure 16.4).

Figure 16.4

Formal and Informal Communication Networks in an Organization

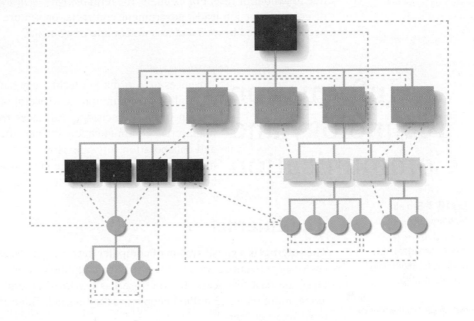

——— Formal pathways of communication summarized in an organization chart.

----- Informal pathways along which a great deal of communication takes place.

Communication can and should occur across departments and groups as well as within them and up and down and sideways in the corporate hierarchy. Communication up and down the corporate hierarchy is often called *vertical* communication. Communication among employees at the same level in the hierarchy, or sideways, is called *horizontal* communication. Managers obviously cannot determine in advance what an organization's communication network will be, nor should they try to. Instead, to accomplish goals and perform at a high level, organizational members should be free to communicate with whomever they need to contact. Because organizational goals change over time, so do organizational communication networks. Informal communication networks can contribute to an organization's competitive advantage, because they help ensure that organizational members have the information they need when they need it to accomplish their goals.

grapevine An informal communication network along which unofficial information flows.

The grapevine is an informal organizational communication network along which unofficial information flows quickly, if not always accurately.[45] People in an organization who seem to know everything about everyone are prominent in the grapevine. Information spread over the grapevine can be about issues of either a business nature (such as an impending takeover) or a personal nature (such as the CEO's separation from his wife).

External Networks

In addition to participating in networks within an organization, managers, professional employees, and those with work-related ties outside their employing organization often are part of external networks whose members span a variety of companies. For example, scientists working in universities and corporations often communicate in networks formed around common underlying interests in a particular topic or subfield. As another example, physicians working throughout the country belong to specialty professional associations that help them keep up-to-date on the latest advances in their fields. For some managers and professionals, participation in such interest-oriented networks is as important as, or even more important than, participation in internal company networks. Networks of contacts who are working in the same discipline or field or who have similar expertise and knowledge can be very helpful, for example, when an individual wants to change jobs or find a job after a layoff. Unfortunately, as a result of discrimination and stereotypes, some of these networks are off-limits to certain individuals due to gender or race. For example, the term *old boys' network* alludes to the fact that networks of contacts for job leads, government contracts, or venture capital funding have sometimes been dominated by men and less welcoming of women.[46]

Information Technology and Communication

Advances in information technology have dramatically increased managers' abilities to communicate with others as well as to quickly access information to make decisions. Advances that are having major impacts on managerial communication include the Internet, intranets, groupware, and collaboration software. However, managers must not forget that communication is essentially a human endeavor, no matter how much it may be facilitated by information technology.

LO16-5 Explain how advances in technology have given managers new options for managing communication.

Internet A global system of computer networks.

The Internet

The **Internet** is a global system of computer networks that is easy to join and is used by employees of organizations around the world to communicate inside and outside their companies. Over the past few years, Internet use has exploded around the world. In the United States alone, more than 312 million people use the Internet. Table 16.1 lists the 10 countries with the most Internet users.[47]

On the Internet, the World Wide Web is the "business district," with multimedia capabilities. Companies' home pages on the web are like offices that potential customers can visit. In attractive graphic displays on home pages, managers communicate information about the goods and services they offer, why customers should want to purchase them, how to purchase them, and where to purchase them. By surfing the web and visiting competitors' home pages, managers can see what their competitors are doing. Each day hundreds of new companies add themselves to the growing number of organizations on the World Wide Web. According to one study, the top countries in terms of competitiveness in the digital era are Norway, Sweden, Switzerland, Denmark, and Finland.[48] By all counts, use of the Internet for communication continues to expand.

Intranets

Growing numbers of managers are finding that the technology on which the World Wide Web and the Internet are based has enabled them to improve communication within their own

Table 16.1

Top 10 Countries in Internet Usage, as of December 31, 2017

Country	Internet Users
China	772,000,000
India	462,124,989
United States	312,322,257
Brazil	149,057,625
Indonesia	143,260,000
Japan	118,626,672
Russia	109,552,842
Nigeria	98,391,456
Mexico	85,000,000
Bangladesh	80,483,000

Source: Internet World Stats, "Top 20 Countries in Internet Users vs. Rest of the World—December 31, 2017," www.internetworldstats.com, accessed on April 23, 2018.

companies. These managers use this technology to share information within their own companies through company networks called **intranets**.

intranet A companywide system of computer networks.

Intranets allow employees to have many kinds of information at their fingertips. Directories, manuals, inventory figures, product specifications, information about customers, biographies of top managers and the board of directors, global sales figures, meeting minutes, annual reports, delivery schedules, and up-to-the-minute revenue, cost, and profit figures are just a few examples of the information that can be shared through intranets. Intranets can be accessed with different kinds of computers so that all members of an organization can be linked together. Intranets are protected from unwanted intrusions, by hackers or by competitors, by firewall security systems that ask users to provide passwords and other identification before they are allowed access.

The advantage of intranets lies in their versatility as a communication medium. They can be used for a number of different purposes by people who may have little expertise in computer software and programming. While some managers complain that the Internet is too crowded and the World Wide Web too glitzy, informed managers are realizing that using the Internet's technology to create their own computer networks may be one of the Internet's biggest contributions to organizational effectiveness.

Groupware and Collaboration Software

groupware Computer software that enables members of groups and teams to share information with one another.

Groupware is computer software that enables members of groups and teams to share information with one another to improve their communication and performance. In some organizations, such as the Bank of Montreal, managers have had success in introducing groupware into the organization; in other organizations, such as the advertising agency Young & Rubicam, managers have encountered considerable resistance to groupware.[49] Even in companies where the introduction of groupware has been successful, some employees resist using it. Some clerical and secretarial workers at the Bank of Montreal, for example, were dismayed to find that their neat and accurate files were being consolidated into computer files that would be accessible to many of their coworkers.

Groupware as a communication medium is likely to be most successful under these conditions:[50]

1. The work is group- or team-based and members are rewarded, at least in part, for group performance.
2. Groupware has the full support of top management.
3. The culture of the organization stresses flexibility and knowledge sharing, and the organization does not have a rigid hierarchy of authority.
4. Groupware is used for a specific purpose and is viewed as a tool that enables group or team members to work more effectively together, not as a personal source of power or advantage.
5. Employees receive adequate training in the use of computers and groupware.

Employees are likely to resist using groupware, and managers are likely to have a difficult time implementing it, when people are working primarily on their own and are rewarded for individual performance.[51] Under these circumstances, information is often viewed as a source of power, and people are reluctant to share information with others by means of groupware.

Consider three salespeople who sell insurance policies in the same geographic area; each is paid based on the number of policies he or she sells and on his or her retention of customers. Their supervisor invested in groupware and encouraged them to use it to share information about their sales, sales tactics, customers, insurance providers, and claim histories. The supervisor told the salespeople that having all this information at their fingertips would allow them to be more efficient as well as sell more policies and provide better service to customers.

Even though they received extensive training in how to use the groupware, the salespeople never got around to using it. Why? They all were afraid that giving away their secrets to their coworkers might reduce their own commissions. In this situation, the salespeople were essentially competing with one another and, thus, had no incentive to share information. Under such circumstances, a groupware system may not be a wise choice of communication medium. Conversely, had the salespeople been working as a team and had they received bonuses based on team performance, groupware might have been an effective communication medium.

For an organization to gain a competitive advantage, managers need to keep up-to-date on advances in information technology such as groupware. But managers should not adopt these or other advances without first considering carefully how the advance in question might improve communication and performance in their particular groups, teams, or whole organizations. Moreover, managers need to keep in mind that all of these advances in IT are tools for people to use to facilitate effective communication; they are not replacements for face-to-face communication.

Collaboration software is groupware that aims to promote collaborative, highly interdependent interactions among members of a team and to provide the team with an electronic meeting site for communication. Collaboration software gives team members an online work site where they can post, share, and save data, reports, sketches, and other documents; keep calendars; have team-based online conferences; and send and receive messages. The software can also keep and update progress reports, survey team members about various issues, forward documents to managers, and let users know which of their team members are also online and at the site. Having an integrated online work area can help organize and centralize the work of a team, help ensure that information is readily available as needed, and help team members make sure important information is not overlooked. Collaboration software can be much more efficient than email or instant messaging for managing ongoing team collaboration and interaction that is not face-to-face. Moreover, when a team does meet face-to-face, all documents the team might need in the meeting are just a click away. For work that is truly team-based, that entails a number of highly interdependent yet distinct components, and that involves team members with distinct areas of expertise who need to closely coordinate their efforts, collaboration software can be a powerful communication tool. *Wikis,* a result of the open-source software movement, are a free or very low-cost form of collaboration software that a growing number of organizations are using. Wikis enable the organizations not only to promote collaboration and better communication, but also to cut back on the use of email.

collaboration software
Groupware that promotes and facilitates collaborative, highly interdependent interactions and provides an electronic meeting site for communication among team members.

Communication Skills for Managers

LO16-6 Describe important communication skills that managers need as senders and as receivers of messages and why it is important to understand differences in linguistic styles.

Some of the barriers to effective communication in organizations have their origins in senders. Communication suffers when messages are unclear, incomplete, or difficult to understand; when they are sent over an inappropriate medium; or when no provision for feedback is made. Other communication barriers have their origins in receivers. When receivers pay no attention to or do not listen to messages or when they make no effort to understand the meaning of a message, communication is likely to be ineffective. Sometimes advanced information technology, such as automated phone systems, can hamper effective communication to the extent that the human element is missing.

To overcome these barriers and effectively communicate with others, managers (as well as other organizational members) must possess or develop certain communication skills. Some of these skills are particularly important when managers *send* messages; others are critical when managers *receive* messages. These skills help ensure that managers will be able to share information, will have the information they need to make good decisions and take action, and will be able to reach a common understanding with others.

Communication Skills for Managers as Senders

Organizational effectiveness depends on the ability of managers (as well as other organizational members) to effectively send messages to people both inside and outside the organization. Table 16.2 summarizes seven communication skills that help ensure that when managers send messages, they are properly understood and the transmission phase of the communication process is effective. Let's see what each skill entails.

SEND CLEAR AND COMPLETE MESSAGES Managers need to learn how to send a message that is clear and complete. A message is clear when it is easy for the receiver to understand and interpret, and it is complete when it contains all the information the sender and receiver need to reach a common understanding. In striving to send messages that are both clear and complete, managers must learn to anticipate how receivers will interpret messages and must adjust them to eliminate sources of misunderstanding or confusion.

Table 16.2

Seven Communication Skills for Managers as Senders of Messages

- Send messages that are clear and complete.
- Encode messages in symbols that the receiver understands.
- Select a medium that is appropriate for the message.
- Select a medium that the receiver monitors.
- Avoid filtering and information distortion.
- Ensure that a feedback mechanism is built into messages.
- Provide accurate information to ensure that misleading rumors are not spread.

Clear and complete messages include any nonverbal components. Messages are unclear if the tone of voice does not match the content of the words. Likewise, as described in the "Management Insight" feature, a person's nonverbal cues are very important when the manager is first meeting the person he or she is communicating with.

MANAGEMENT INSIGHT

Making a Positive First Impression

Many business and daily life situations involve introducing yourself to others. Some examples are job interviews, first meetings with customers or clients, and presentations to a group including strangers. In these contexts, a first impression carries a great deal of weight. What the other person first observes in the first few seconds will shape how the person interprets the communicator and the message.[52]

Managers cannot control every aspect of a first impression. They cannot overcome prejudices by changing their sex, race, or age, and they cannot change their facial features. But there are other ways to communicate a message of being trustworthy and agreeable.[53]

Facial expressions matter. A relaxed and smiling face is appealing. However, it is important to be consistent and sincere, not just flashing a smile when making eye contact. As for eye contact, it is necessary for building trust in a business context. Some experts suggest looking in the other person's eyes during 60–70% of the interaction. Those who are not used to making eye contact can practice by looking at the other person's eyebrows or space between the eyes until eye contact feels more natural.[54]

Posture and gestures make a difference as well. People tend to respond well to erect but not stiff posture, with hands visible and arms uncrossed. Taking a minute to slow one's breathing, stand firmly, and think confident thoughts can help. Then, while talking, the speaker can increase trust by leaning in a little toward the other person. Also, researchers have found greater appeal in presentations where the presenters used more hand gestures to emphasize points. In the same vein, shaking hands firmly is a gesture that builds rapport.[55]

Clothing also plays a role. Those seeking to make a good first impression should, within their means, seek clothes that fit well in a flattering style and are suitable for the context. At a minimum, it is essential to be clean and neat.[56]

First impressions include verbal communication, too. One way to make a positive and lasting impression is to greet people with questions that demonstrate a genuine interest. For example, if appropriate for the situation, a person might ask, "What has been the highlight of your day so far?" or "Has anything exciting been happening in your life?"[57] And then, of course, the questioner should listen carefully to the answer.

ENCODE MESSAGES IN SYMBOLS THE RECEIVER UNDERSTANDS Managers need to appreciate that when they encode messages, they should use symbols or language that the receiver understands. When sending messages in English to receivers whose native language is not English, for example, it is important to use common vocabulary and to avoid clichés that, when translated, may make little sense or are either comical or insulting. **Jargon**, specialized language that members of an occupation, a group, or an organization develop to facilitate communication among themselves, should never be used when communicating with people outside the occupation, group, or organization.

jargon Specialized language that members of an occupation, group, or organization develop to facilitate communication among themselves.

SELECT A MEDIUM APPROPRIATE FOR THE MESSAGE As you have learned, when relying on verbal communication, managers can choose from a variety of communication media, including face-to-face communication in person, written letters, memos, newsletters, phone conversations, email, voice mail, faxes, and videoconferences. When choosing among these media, managers need to take into account the level of information richness required, the time constraints, and the need for a paper or electronic trail. A primary concern in choosing an appropriate medium is the nature of the message. Is it personal, important, nonroutine, or likely to be misunderstood and in need of further clarification? If it is, face-to-face communication is likely to be in order.

SELECT A MEDIUM THE RECEIVER MONITORS Another factor that managers need to take into account when selecting a communication medium is whether the medium is one that the receiver monitors. Managers differ in the communication media they pay attention to. Many managers simply select the medium they themselves use the most and are most comfortable with, but doing this can lead to ineffective communication. Managers who dislike telephone conversations and too many face-to-face interactions may prefer to use email, send many email messages per day, and check their own email often. Managers who prefer to communicate with people in person or over the phone may have email addresses but are less likely to respond to email messages. No matter how much a manager likes email, sending email to someone who does not respond to email is futile. Learning which managers like things in writing and which prefer face-to-face interactions and then using the appropriate medium enhances the chance that receivers will actually receive and pay attention to messages.

A related consideration is whether receivers have disabilities that hamper their ability to decode certain messages. A blind receiver, for example, cannot read a written message. Managers should ensure that employees with disabilities have resources available to communicate effectively with others.[58]

filtering Withholding part of a message because of the mistaken belief that the receiver does not need or will not want the information.

AVOID FILTERING AND INFORMATION DISTORTION Filtering occurs when a sender withholds part of a message because he or she mistakenly thinks the receiver does not need the information or will not want to receive it. Filtering can occur at all levels in an organization and in both vertical and horizontal communication. Rank-and-file workers may filter messages they send to first-line managers, first-line managers may filter messages to middle managers, and middle managers may filter messages to top managers. Such filtering is most likely to take place when messages contain bad news or problems that subordinates are afraid they will be blamed for. Managers need to hear bad news and be aware of problems as soon as they occur so they can take swift steps to rectify the problem and limit the damage it may have caused.

Some filtering takes place because of internal competition in organizations or because organizational members fear their power and influence will be diminished if others have access to some of their specialized knowledge. By increasing levels of trust in an organization, taking steps to motivate all employees (and the groups and teams they belong to) to work together to achieve organizational goals, and ensuring that employees realize that when the organization reaches its goals and performs effectively, they will benefit as well, this kind of filtering can be reduced.

information distortion Changes in the meaning of a message as the message passes through a series of senders and receivers.

Information distortion occurs when the meaning of a message changes as the message passes through a series of senders and receivers. Some information distortion is accidental—due to faulty encoding and decoding or to a lack of feedback. Other information distortion is deliberate. Senders may alter a message to make themselves or their groups look good and to receive special treatment.

Managers themselves should avoid filtering and distorting information. But how can they eliminate these barriers to effective communication throughout their organizations? They need to establish trust throughout the organization. Subordinates who trust their managers believe they will not be blamed for things beyond their control and will be treated fairly. Managers who trust their subordinates give them clear and complete information and do not hold things back.

INCLUDE A FEEDBACK MECHANISM IN MESSAGES   Because feedback is essential for effective communication, managers should build a feedback mechanism into the messages they send. They should either include a request for feedback or indicate when and how they will follow up on the message to make sure it was received and understood. When managers write letters and memos or send faxes, they can request that the receiver respond with comments and suggestions in a letter, memo, or fax; schedule a meeting to discuss the issue; or follow up with a phone call. By building feedback mechanisms such as these into their messages, managers ensure that they have been heard and are understood.

rumors Unofficial pieces of information of interest to organizational members but with no identifiable source.

PROVIDE ACCURATE INFORMATION   **Rumors** are unofficial pieces of information of interest to organizational members but with no identifiable source. Rumors spread quickly once they are started, and usually they concern topics that organizational members think are important, interesting, or amusing. Rumors, however, can be misleading and can harm individual employees and their organizations when they are false, malicious, or unfounded. Managers can halt the spread of misleading rumors by giving organizational members accurate information about matters that concern them.

Providing accurate information is especially important in tough economic times like the recession in the late 2000s. During a recession, employees are sometimes laid off or find their working hours or pay levels cut back and often experience high levels of stress. When managers give employees accurate information, this can help reduce their stress levels as well as motivate them to find ways to help their companies weather the tough times.[59] Moreover, when the economy does turn around, employees who received accurate information from their bosses may be more likely to remain with their organizations rather than pursue other opportunities.

Communication Skills for Managers as Receivers

Managers receive as many messages as they send. Thus, managers must possess or develop communication skills that allow them to be effective receivers. Table 16.3 summarizes three of these important skills, which we examine here in greater detail.

PAY ATTENTION   Because of their multiple roles and tasks, managers often are overloaded and forced to think about several things at once. Pulled in many different directions, they sometimes do not pay sufficient attention to the messages they receive. To be effective, however, managers should always pay attention to messages they receive, no matter how busy they are. When discussing a project with a subordinate, for example, an effective manager focuses on the project, not on an upcoming meeting with his or her own boss. Similarly, when managers are reading written communication, they should focus on understanding what they are reading; they should not be sidetracked into thinking about other issues.

BE A GOOD LISTENER   Managers (and all other members of an organization) can do several things to be good listeners. First, managers should refrain from interrupting senders in the middle of a message so that senders do not lose their train of thought and managers do not jump to erroneous conclusions based on incomplete information. Second, managers should maintain eye contact with senders so that senders feel their listeners are paying attention; doing this also helps managers focus on what they are hearing. Third, after receiving a message, managers should ask questions to clarify points of ambiguity or confusion. Fourth, managers should paraphrase, or restate in their own words, points senders make that are important, complex, or open to alternative interpretations; this is the feedback component so critical to successful communication.

Table 16.3

Three Communication Skills for Managers as Receivers of Messages

- Pay attention.
- Be a good listener.
- Be empathetic.

Managers, like most people, often like to hear themselves talk rather than listen to others. Part of being a good communicator, however, is being a good listener—an essential communication skill for managers as receivers of messages transmitted face-to-face and over the telephone.

BE EMPATHETIC   Receivers are empathetic when they try to understand how the sender feels and try to interpret a message from the sender's perspective, rather than viewing the message from only their own point of view. Marcia Mazulo, the chief psychologist in a public school system in the Northwest, recently learned this lesson after interacting with Karen Sanchez, a new psychologist on her staff. Sanchez was distraught after meeting with the parent of a child she had been working with extensively. The parent was difficult to talk to and argumentative and was not supportive of her own child. Sanchez told Mazulo how upset she was, and Mazulo responded by reminding Sanchez that she was a professional and that dealing with such a situation was part of her job. This feedback upset Sanchez further and caused her to storm out of the room.

In hindsight, Mazulo realized that her response had been inappropriate. She had failed to empathize with Sanchez, who had spent so much time with the child and was deeply concerned about the child's well-being. Rather than dismissing Sanchez's concerns, Mazulo realized, she should have tried to understand how Sanchez felt and given her some support and advice for dealing positively with the situation.

Understanding Linguistic Styles

Consider the following scenarios:

- A manager from New York is having a conversation with a manager from Iowa City. The Iowa City manager never seems to get a chance to talk. He keeps waiting for a pause to signal his turn to talk, but the New York manager never pauses long enough. The New York manager wonders why the Iowa City manager does not say much. He feels uncomfortable when he pauses and the Iowa City manager says nothing, so he starts talking again.

- Elizabeth compliments Bob on his presentation to upper management and asks Bob what he thought of her presentation. Bob launches into a lengthy critique of Elizabeth's presentation and describes how he would have handled it differently. This is hardly the response Elizabeth expected.

- Catherine shares with co-members of a self-managed work team a new way to cut costs. Michael, another team member, thinks her idea is a good one and encourages the rest of the team to support it. Catherine is quietly pleased by Michael's support. The group implements "Michael's" suggestion, and it is written up as such in the company newsletter.

- Robert was recently promoted and transferred from his company's Oklahoma office to its headquarters in New Jersey. Robert is perplexed because he never seems to get a chance to talk in management meetings; someone else always seems to get the floor. Robert's new boss wonders whether Robert's new responsibilities are too much for him, although Robert's supervisor in Oklahoma rated him highly and said he is a real "go-getter." Robert is timid in management meetings and rarely says a word.

What do these scenarios have in common? Essentially, they all describe situations in which a misunderstanding of linguistic styles leads to a breakdown in communication. The scenarios are based on the research of linguist Deborah Tannen, who describes linguistic style as a person's characteristic way of speaking. Elements of linguistic style include tone of voice, speed, volume, use of pauses, directness or indirectness, choice of words, credit taking, and use of questions, jokes, and other manners of speech.[60] When people's linguistic styles differ and these differences are not understood, ineffective communication is likely.

The first and last scenarios illustrate regional differences in linguistic style.[61] The Iowa City manager and Robert from Oklahoma expect the pauses that signal turn taking in conversations to be longer than the pauses made by their colleagues in New York and New Jersey. This difference causes communication problems. The Iowan and transplanted Oklahoman think their Eastern colleagues never let them get a word in edgewise, and the Easterners cannot figure out why their colleagues from the Midwest and South do not get more actively involved in conversations.

Differences in linguistic style can be a particularly insidious source of communication problems because linguistic style is often taken for granted. People rarely think about their own

linguistic style A person's characteristic way of speaking.

Cross-cultural differences in linguistic style can lead to misunderstandings.
©LWA/Getty Images

linguistic styles and often are unaware of how linguistic styles can differ. In the example here, Robert did not realize that when dealing with his New Jersey colleagues, he could and should jump into conversations more quickly than he used to do in Oklahoma, and his boss never realized that Robert felt he was not being given a chance to speak in meetings.

The aspect of linguistic style just described, length of pauses, differs by region in the United States. Much more dramatic differences in linguistic style occur cross-culturally.

CROSS-CULTURAL DIFFERENCES Cultural differences play an important role in both verbal and nonverbal communication. Some cultures prefer an indirect method of communication while others prefer a direct style. For example, high-context cultures—typically those found in Asia, South America, and Arab countries—tend to communicate indirectly, talking around the point they're trying to make. Low-context cultures—those found in the United States, German, Scandinavia, and Australia—tend to communicate directly, valuing the content of the message and getting to the point quickly.[62] In addition, a nonverbal gesture such as eye contact is very important to individuals from low-context cultures when communicating with others, while those from high-context cultures tend to avoid eye contact because it is viewed as aggressive and impolite.[63]

Managers from Japan tend to be more formal in their conversations and more deferential toward upper-level managers and people with high status than are managers from the United States. Japanese managers do not mind extensive pauses in conversations when they are thinking things through or when they think further conversation might be detrimental. In contrast, U.S. managers (even managers from regions of the United States where pauses tend to be long) find lengthy pauses disconcerting and feel obligated to talk to fill the silence.[64]

Another cross-cultural difference in linguistic style concerns the appropriate physical distance separating speakers and listeners in business-oriented conversations.[65] The distance between speakers and listeners is greater in the United States, for example, than it is in Brazil or Saudi Arabia. Citizens of different countries also vary in how direct or indirect they are in conversations and the extent to which they take individual credit for accomplishments. Japanese culture, with its collectivist, or group, orientation, tends to encourage linguistic styles in which group rather than individual accomplishments are emphasized. The opposite tends to be true in the United States.

These and other cross-cultural differences in linguistic style can and often do lead to misunderstandings. For example, when a team of American managers presented a proposal for a joint venture to Japanese managers, the Japanese managers were silent as they thought about the implications of what they had just heard. The American managers took this silence as a sign that the Japanese managers wanted more information, so they went into more detail about the proposal. When they finished, the Japanese were silent again, not only frustrating the Americans, but also making them wonder whether the Japanese were interested in the project. The American managers suggested that if the Japanese already had decided they did not want to pursue the project, there was no reason for the meeting to continue. The Japanese were bewildered. They were trying to carefully think out the proposal, yet the Americans thought they were not interested!

Communication misunderstandings and problems like this can be overcome if managers learn about cross-cultural differences in linguistic styles. If the American managers and the Japanese managers had realized that periods of silence are viewed differently in Japan and in the United States, their different linguistic styles might have been less troublesome barriers to communication. Before managers communicate with people from abroad, they should try to find out as much as they can about the aspects of linguistic style that are specific to the country or culture in question. Expatriate managers who have lived in the country in question for an extended time can be good sources of information about linguistic styles because they are likely to have experienced firsthand some of the differences that citizens of a country are not aware of. Finding out as much as possible about cultural differences also can help managers learn about differences in linguistic styles because the two are often closely linked.

GENDER DIFFERENCES   In the four scenarios that open this section, you may be wondering why Bob launched into a lengthy critique of Elizabeth's presentation after she paid him a routine compliment on his presentation, or you may be wondering why Michael got the credit for Catherine's idea in the self-managed work team. Research conducted by Tannen and other linguists has found that the linguistic styles of men and women differ in practically every culture or language.[66] Men and women take their own linguistic styles for granted and, thus, do not realize when they are talking with someone of a different gender that differences in their styles may lead to ineffective communication.

In the United States, women tend to downplay differences between people, are not overly concerned about receiving credit for their own accomplishments, and want to make everyone feel more or less on an equal footing so that even poor performers or low-status individuals feel valued. Men, in contrast, tend to emphasize their own superiority and are not reluctant to acknowledge differences in status. These differences in linguistic style led Elizabeth to routinely compliment Bob on his presentation even though she thought he had not done a particularly good job. She asked him how her presentation was so he could reciprocate and give her a routine compliment, putting them on an equal footing. Bob took Elizabeth's compliment and question about her own presentation as an opportunity to confirm his superiority, never realizing that all she was expecting was a routine compliment. Similarly, Michael's enthusiastic support for Catherine's cost-cutting idea and her apparent surrender of ownership of the idea after she described it led team members to assume incorrectly that the idea was Michael's.[67]

Do some women try to prove they are better than everyone else, and are some men unconcerned about taking credit for ideas and accomplishments? Of course. The gender differences in linguistic style that Tannen and other linguists have uncovered are general tendencies evident in *many* women and men, not in *all* women and men.

Where do gender differences in linguistic style come from? Tannen suggests they begin developing in early childhood. Girls and boys tend to play with children of their own gender, and the ways in which girls and boys play are quite different. Girls play in small groups, engage in a lot of close conversation, emphasize how similar they are to one another, and view boastfulness negatively. Boys play in large groups, emphasize status differences, expect leaders to emerge who boss others around, and give one another challenges to try to meet. These differences in styles of play and interaction result in different linguistic styles when boys and girls grow up and communicate as adults. The ways in which men communicate emphasize status differences and play up relative strengths; the ways in which women communicate emphasize similarities and downplay individual strengths.[68]

Interestingly, gender differences are also turning up in how women and men use email and electronic forms of communication. For example, Susan Herring, a researcher at Indiana University, has found that in public electronic forums such as message boards and chat rooms, men tend to make stronger assertions, be more sarcastic, and be more likely to use insults and profanity than women, whereas women are more likely to be supportive, agreeable, and polite.[69] David Silver, a researcher at the University of Washington, has found that women are more expressive electronic communicators and encourage others to express their thoughts and feelings, while men are briefer and more to the point.[70] Interestingly enough, some men find email to be a welcome way to express their feelings to people they care about. For example, real estate broker Mike Murname finds it easier to communicate with, and express his love for, his grown children via email.[71]

MANAGING DIFFERENCES IN LINGUISTIC STYLES   Managers should not expect to change people's linguistic styles and should not try to. To be effective, managers need to understand differences in linguistic styles. Knowing, for example, that some women are reluctant to speak up in meetings, not because they have nothing to contribute but because of their linguistic style, should lead managers to ensure that these women have a chance to talk. And a manager who knows certain people are reluctant to take credit for ideas can be careful to give credit where it is deserved. As Tannen points out, "Talk is the lifeblood of managerial work, and understanding that different people have different ways of saying what they mean will make it possible to take advantage of the talents of people with a broad range of linguistic styles."[72]

Summary and Review

LO16-1, 16-2

COMMUNICATION AND MANAGEMENT   Communication is the sharing of information between two or more individuals or groups to reach a common understanding. Good communication is necessary for an organization to gain a competitive advantage. Communication occurs in a cyclical process that entails two phases: transmission and feedback.

LO16-3   **INFORMATION RICHNESS AND COMMUNICATION MEDIA**   Information richness is the amount of information a communication medium can carry and the extent to which the medium enables the sender and receiver to reach a common understanding. Four categories of communication media, in descending order of information richness, are face-to-face communication (includes videoconferences), electronically transmitted spoken communication (includes voice mail), personally addressed written communication (includes email), and impersonal written communication (includes corporate newsletters and blogs).

LO16-4   **COMMUNICATION NETWORKS**   Communication networks are the pathways along which information flows in an organization. Four communication networks found in groups and teams are the wheel, the chain, the circle, and the all-channel network. An organization chart summarizes formal pathways of communication, but communication in organizations is often informal, as is true of communication through the grapevine.

LO16-5   **INFORMATION TECHNOLOGY AND COMMUNICATION**   The Internet is a global system of computer networks that managers around the world use to communicate within and outside their companies. The World Wide Web is the multimedia business district on the Internet. Intranets are internal communication networks that managers can create to improve communication, performance, and customer service. Intranets use the same technology that the Internet and World Wide Web are based on. Groupware is computer software that enables members of groups and teams to share information with one another to improve their communication and performance.

LO16-6   **COMMUNICATION SKILLS FOR MANAGERS**   There are various barriers to effective communication in organizations. To overcome these barriers and effectively communicate with others, managers must possess or develop certain communication skills. As senders of messages, managers should send messages that are clear and complete, encode messages in symbols the receiver understands, choose a medium that is appropriate for the message and is monitored by the receiver, avoid filtering and information distortion, include a feedback mechanism in the message, and provide accurate information to ensure that misleading rumors are not spread. Communication skills for managers as receivers of messages include paying attention, being a good listener, and being empathetic. Understanding linguistic styles is also an essential communication skill for managers. Linguistic styles can vary by geographic region, gender, and country or culture. When these differences are not understood, ineffective communication can occur.

Management in Action

Topics for Discussion and Action

Discussion

1. Which medium (or media) do you think would be appropriate for each of the following kinds of messages that a subordinate could receive from his or her boss: (a) a raise, (b) not receiving a promotion, (c) an error in a report prepared by the subordinate, (d) additional job responsibilities, and (e) the schedule for company holidays for the upcoming year? Explain your choices. **[LO16-3]**

2. Discuss the pros and cons of using the Internet and World Wide Web for communication within and between organizations. **[LO16-1, 16-2, 16-3, 16-5]**

3. Why do some organizational members resist using groupware? **[LO16-5]**

4. Why do some managers find it difficult to be good listeners? **[LO16-6]**

5. Explain why subordinates might filter and distort information about problems and performance shortfalls when communicating with their bosses. What steps can managers take to eliminate filtering and information distortion? **[LO16-6]**

6. Explain why differences in linguistic style, when not understood by message senders and receivers, can lead to ineffective communication. **[LO16-6]**

Action

7. Interview a manager in an organization in your community to determine with whom he or she communicates on a typical day, what communication media he or she uses, and which typical communication problems the manager experiences. **[LO16-1, 16-2, 16-3, 16-4, 16-5, 16-6]**

Building Management Skills

Diagnosing Ineffective Communication [LO16-1, 16-2, 16-3, 16-4, 16-5, 16-6]

Think about the last time you experienced very ineffective communication with another person—someone you work with, a classmate, a friend, or a member of your family. Describe the incident. Then answer the following questions:

1. Why was your communication ineffective in this incident?

2. What stages of the communication process were particularly problematic, and why?

3. Describe any filtering or information distortion that occurred.

4. Do you think differences in linguistic styles adversely affected the communication that took place? Why or why not?

5. How could you have handled this situation differently so communication would have been effective?

Managing Ethically [LO16-3, 16-5]

Many employees use their company's Internet connections and email systems to visit websites and send personal email and instant messages.

Questions

1. Either individually or in a group, explore the ethics of using an organization's Internet connection and email system for personal purposes at work and while away from the office. Should employees have some rights to use this resource? When does their behavior become unethical?

2. Some companies track how their employees use the company's Internet connection and email system. Is it ethical for managers to read employees' personal email or to record websites that employees visit? Why or why not?

Small Group Breakout Exercise

Reducing Resistance to Advances in Information Technology [LO16-5]

Form groups of three or four people, and appoint one member as the spokesperson who will communicate your findings to the class when called on by the instructor. Then discuss the following scenario:

You are a team of managers in charge of information and communication in a large consumer products corporation. Your company has already implemented many advances in information technology. Managers and workers have access to email, the Internet, your company's own intranet, groupware, and collaboration software.

Many employees use the technology, but the resistance of some is causing communication problems. A case in point is the use of groupware and collaboration software. Many teams in your organization have access to groupware and are encouraged to use it. While some teams welcome this communication tool and actually have made suggestions for improvements, others are highly resistant to sharing documents in their teams' online workspaces.

Although you do not want to force people to use the technology, you want them to at least try it and give it a chance. You are meeting today to develop strategies for reducing resistance to the new technologies.

1. One resistant group of employees is made up of top managers. Some of them seem computer-phobic and are highly resistant to sharing information online, even with sophisticated security precautions in place. What steps will you take to get these managers to have more confidence in electronic communication?

2. A second group of resistant employees consists of middle managers. Some middle managers resist using your company's intranet. Although these managers do not resist the technology per se and do use electronic communication for multiple purposes, they seem to distrust the intranet as a viable way to communicate and get things done. What steps will you take to get these managers to take advantage of the intranet?

3. A third group of resistant employees is made up of members of groups and teams who do not want to use the groupware that has been provided to them. You think the groupware could improve their communication and performance, but they seem to think otherwise. What steps will you take to get these members of groups and teams to start using groupware?

Be the Manager [LO16-1, 16-2, 16-3, 16-6]

You supervise support staff for an Internet merchandising organization that sells furniture over the Internet. You always thought that you needed to expand your staff, and just when you were about to approach your boss with such a request, business slowed. Thus, your plan to try to add new employees to your staff is on hold.

However, you have noticed a troubling pattern of communication with your staff. Ordinarily, when you want a staff member to work on a task, you email that subordinate the pertinent information. For the last few months, your email requests have gone unheeded, and your subordinates seem to respond to your requests only after you visit them in person and give them a specific deadline. Each time they apologize for not getting to the task sooner but say they are so overloaded with requests that they sometimes even stop answering their phones. Unless someone asks for something more than once, your staff seems to feel the request is not that urgent and can be put on hold. You think this state of affairs is dysfunctional and could lead to serious problems down the road. Also, you are starting to realize that your subordinates seem to have no way of prioritizing tasks—hence, some very important projects you asked them to complete were put on hold until you followed up with them about the tasks. Knowing you cannot add employees to your staff in the short term, what are you going to do to improve communication with your overloaded staff?

Bloomberg Case in the News [LO16-1, 16-2, 16-3]

Don't Skype Me: How Microsoft Turned Consumers Against a Beloved Brand

It's relatively easy these days to find critics of Skype, the popular online calling service that Microsoft acquired in 2011 for $8.5 billion. Former devotees routinely gripe on social media that the software has become too difficult to use. On the Apple App store and Google Play store, negative reviews of the smartphone app are piling up, citing everything from poor call quality to gluttonous battery demand.

In March tech investor and commentator Om Malik summarized the negativity by tweeting that Skype was "a turd of the highest quality" and directing his ire at its owner. "Way to ruin Skype and its experience. I was forced to use it today, but never again."

Microsoft Corp. says the criticism is overblown and reflects, in part, people's grumpiness with software updates. There are also other factors undermining users' affection for an internet tool that 15 years ago introduced the idea of making calls online, radically resetting the telecommunications landscape in the process.

Since acquiring Skype from private equity investors, Microsoft has refocused the online calling service on the corporate market, a change that has made Skype less intuitive and harder to use, prompting many Skypers to defect to similar services operated by Apple, Google, Facebook and Snap.

The company hasn't updated the number of Skype users since 2016, when it put the total at 300 million. Some analysts suspect the numbers are flat at best, and two former employees describe a general sense of panic that they're actually falling. The ex-Microsofters, who requested anonymity to discuss confidential statistics, say that as late as 2017 they never heard a figure higher than 300 million discussed internally.

Chief Executive Officer Satya Nadella has repeatedly said he wants the company's products to be widely used and loved. By turning Skype into a key part of its lucrative Office suite for corporate customers, Microsoft is threatening what made it appealing to regular folks in the first place. "It is like Tim Tebow trying to be a baseball player," Malik says. "The product is so confusing, kludgey and unusable."

Founded in 2003 by a pair of Nordic entrepreneurs, Skype freed tens of millions of people from the tyranny of the phone companies by offering cheap overseas calls. Most chatted free, and Skype made money charging for prepaid calls to regular phones. The company has cycled through various owners, including eBay. By 2011, the company was controlled by a Silver Lake-led consortium of investors and shopping itself to potential acquirers including Google and Microsoft even as it prepared for an initial public offering.

Keen to reduce Microsoft's reliance on the personal computer, former CEO Steve Ballmer saw in Skype an internet brand that was so popular it had become a verb. Having erred previously by acquiring No. 2 players to save money, Ballmer decided to buy the leading incumbent and pay a 40% premium over what Skype valued itself at the time.

"It was the biggest asset in the space at the time with the most recognized brand," says Lori Wright, who joined the Skype team as general manager last year from video-conference rival BlueJeans. "It was an opportunistic way for Microsoft to enter into something that was going to be significant."

After the acquisition, Microsoft executive and former Skype CFO Bill Koefoed was routinely reminded of Skype's popularity as a way to make cheap, or free, international calls. He recalls identifying himself to immigration officers on business trips overseas and constantly hearing variations of: I use Skype to call my grandmother! "Skype was such an iconic brand," he says.

Focusing on corporations was a reasonable strategy and one shared by Skype's prior management. Originally Ballmer and company pledged to let Skype operate independently from Lync, Microsoft's nascent internet phone service for corporations. But two years later the company began merging the two into Skype for Business and folded that into Office.

Today, Microsoft is using Skype for Business to help sell subscriptions to its cloud-based Office 365 and steal customers from Cisco. Microsoft has essentially turned Skype into a replacement for a corporate telephone system—with a few modern features borrowed from instant messaging, artificial intelligence and social networking. Teams, the company's year-old version of Slack, is being merged with Skype for Business. LinkedIn, another acquisition, will provide work bios of the people Skypers are about to call. Drawing on Microsoft's pioneering work in AI, Skype can now translate calls into 12 languages.

As proof that the strategy is working, Microsoft points to a roster of blue-chip customers. Among them is General Electric, which says it rolled out Skype for Business to 220,000 employees late last year and is logging 5.5 million meeting minutes a day. Accenture and some of the largest banks are also big users, according to Office 365 marketing vice president Ron Markezich. In a Forrester survey of 6,259 information workers, 28% said they used Skype for Business for conferencing, compared with 21% for Cisco's products.

Atkins, a U.K. engineering-design company that's part of SNC Lavalin Group, says its 18,500 workers use Skype for telephone service, conferences and sharing projects—to the tune of 10 million minutes a month. "We did a full competitor analysis but we trusted Microsoft's vision," says Atkins collaboration manager Nick Ledger, who says he likes how Skype is integrated with Office. "Very rarely do we have any problems."

But Microsoft has paid a price for prioritizing corporations over consumers. The former seek robust security, search and the ability to host town halls; the latter ease-of-use and decent call quality. Inevitably, the complexity of the corporate software crowds out the simplicity consumers prefer. While the company maintains two separate apps, the underlying technology is the same and it's built with workers in mind.

Skype has tried to be all things to all people, "and almost all those things are executed better elsewhere," says Matthew Culnane, a user experience and content strategist at the U.K.'s Open University.

It doesn't help that Microsoft keeps overhauling the app. A redesign last summer sent ratings plunging. In a scorching Twitter commentary, security journalist Brian Krebs said finding basic buttons was a PITA (pain in the ass) and that the recent update was "probably the worst so far." The tweet—and retweets—got the attention of Skype's social network team. "Brian, we're sorry to hear this," a representative replied. "Would love to hear more feedback and see if there's anything we can help with."

"There was a demographic that loved Skype for what it was; it was clean and simple," says Carolina Milanesi, an analyst at Creative Strategies. "That's no longer the case." Milanesi once paid for a Skype subscription for her mother in Italy. Then her mom got an iPad and now they talk on Apple Facetime. Millions do the same, despite the fact that Skype apps are a download away on iPhone and Android smart phones and tablets.

Microsoft's focus on the corporate market may also have blinded it to the rise of WhatsApp, Facebook Messenger and Tencent's WeChat. Microsoft killed off Windows Live Messenger five years ago, right when WhatsApp was amassing hundreds of millions of users around the globe. The instant messaging service now has 1.5 billion users and has started adding key Skype features. Meanwhile, upstarts like Discord, a free voice and text chat app for gamers, are gaining users.

People who have remained loyal to Skype despite all the alternatives complain most about service quality—calls that don't connect, connections that drop every other word, address books that disappear after software updates. Business customers have similar issues too, according to Forrester analyst Nick Barber. "It's not uncommon for me to talk to companies that have Skype for Business, yet they are still looking at other options because it's not working for them," he said. "It's usually around the call quality and consistency both with audio and video."

Microsoft says it takes quality seriously and tracks dropped calls to ascertain what went wrong. Wright says sometimes the customer's network is at fault, not Skype. She argues that most companies are struggling to perfect the technology. "People get frustrated that it doesn't work like dial-tone and say 'I am just going to switch to the next app or service,' only to find out that the next service has the same issue," she says. "We are making rapid progress."

Downloads of Skype's Android app reached 1 billion in October, although Microsoft doesn't say how often people log on. Ratings are starting to recover from the initial nosedive as customers become accustomed to the changes. "It's a really radical redesign, so we thought there was going to be a pretty negative reaction; we were braced for that," Wright says. "What we are seeing now is they don't hate it anymore."

Questions for Discussion

1. Will Microsoft's decision to refocus Skype to largely a form of business communication help or hurt the app's overall success? Explain your reasoning.

2. How does Skype for Business provide Microsoft with a competitive advance over Cisco and other telecommunication companies?

3. According to the communications process, where does Skype fall short when it comes to individual users?

Source: Dina Bass and Nate Lanxon, "Don't Skype Me: How Microsoft Turned Consumers Against a Beloved Brand," *Bloomberg,* May 10, 2018, https://www.bloomberg.com/news/articles/2018-05-10/don-t-skype-me-how-microsoft-turned-consumers-against-a-beloved-brand. Used with permission of Bloomberg L.P. Copyright © 2017. All rights reserved.

Notes

1. S. Apgar, "Designing for Collaboration: BCG's 'Collision Coefficient,'" *Urban Land,* https://urbanland.uli.org, December 4, 2017.

2. K. Gee, "The Not-So-Creepy Reason More Bosses Are Tracking Employees," *The Wall Street Journal,* www.wsj.com, March 21, 2017; R. Greenfield, "New Office Sensors Know When You Leave Your Desk," *Bloomberg Businessweek,* www.bloomberg.com, February 14, 2017.

3. Gee, "The Not-So-Creepy Reason"; Apgar, "Designing for Collaboration."

4. M. Stohlmeyer Russell and L. Moskowitz Lepler, "How We Closed the Gap between Men's and Women's Retention Rates," *Harvard Business Review,* https://hbr.org, March 19, 2017; A. Elejalde-Ruiz, "To Retain Women, Consulting Firm Targets Gender Communication Differences," *Chicago Tribune,* www.chicagotribune.com, September 9, 2016.

5. Elejalde-Ruiz, "To Retain Women, Consulting Firm Targets Gender Communication Differences"; Russell and Lepler, "How We Closed the Gap."

6. C.A. O'Reilly and L.R. Pondy, "Organizational Communication," in S. Kerr, ed., *Organizational Behavior* (Columbus, OH: Grid, 1979).

7. "About Hyphen," https://gethyphen.com, accessed April 24, 2018; S. Modgil, "How Engagement Startup Hyphen Enables Employees to Be Heard at Work," *People Matters,* https://www.peoplematters.in, April 6, 2018; S. Kashyap, "Hyphen Aims to Answer the Eternal Question: What Do Employees Want?" *YourStory,* https://yourstory.com, June 19, 2017.

8. Ibid.

9. Ibid.

10. Hyphen, "About Hyphen."

11. E.M. Rogers and R. Agarwala-Rogers, *Communication in Organizations* (New York: Free Press, 1976).

12. "Listening to Nonverbal Cues," https://listenlikealawyer.com, accessed April 20, 2018; S.M. Heathfield, "Tips for Understanding Nonverbal Communication," www.thebalancecareers.com, February 17, 2017.

13. N. Zandan, "How Much of Our Workdays Do We Spend Communicating?" *Quantified Communications,* www.quantifiedcommunications.com, accessed April 20, 2018.

14. S. Reinberg, "A Key Thing Doctors Can Do to Reduce Hospital Errors," *CBS News,* www.cbsnews.com, accessed April 20, 2018.

15. B. Newman, "Global Chatter," *The Wall Street Journal,* March 22, 1995, A1, A15.

16. M.L. Wald, "Details Are Added on Pilots in Overflight," *The New York Times,* December 17, 2009, A34; "Pilots Who Missed Airport OK Deal," *Houston Chronicle,* March 16, 2010, A6.

17. "Miscommunications Plague Pilots and Air Traffic Controllers," *The Wall Street Journal,* August 22, 1995, A1.

18. P. Reinert, "Miscommunication Seen as Threat to Space Station," *Houston Chronicle,* September 24, 2003, 6A.

19. W.E. Leary, "NASA Report Says Problems Plague Space Station Program," *The New York Times,* February 28, 2004, A12.

20. R.L. Daft, R.H. Lengel, and L.K. Trevino, "Message Equivocality, Media Selection, and Manager Performance: Implications for Information Systems," *MIS Quarterly* 11 (1987), 355–66; R.L. Daft and R.H. Lengel, "Information Richness: A New Approach to Managerial Behavior and Organization Design," in B.M. Staw and L.L. Cummings, eds., *Research in Organizational Behavior* (Greenwich, CT: JAI Press, 1984).

21. R.L. Daft, *Organization Theory and Design* (St. Paul, MN: West, 1992).

22. "Global Financial Services Firm Cuts Costs, Carbon Emissions (case study)," www.cisco.com, accessed April 28, 2015.

23. Daft, *Organization Theory and Design.*

24. A.S. Wellner, "Lost in Translation," *Inc.,* September 2005, 37–38.

25. Ibid.

26. N. Dixon, "Combining Virtual and Face-to-Face Work," *Harvard Business Review,* https://hbr.org, accessed April 20, 2018.

27. D. Hassell, "Management by Weekly Check-In Is the New 'Wandering Around,'" *Entrepreneur,* www.entrepreneur.com, June 9, 2016.

28. "Cisco Conferencing Products," www.cisco.com, accessed April 20, 2018.

29. D. Rodgers, "How You Can Crush the Video Interview," www.monster.com, accessed April 20, 2018.

30. The Radicati Group, "Email Statistics Report, 2018–2022," www.radicati.com, accessed April 20, 2018.

31. A. Hicks, "Top 10 Ways to Improve Employee Efficiency," *Zenefits Blog,* www.zenefits.com, accessed April 20, 2018.

32. B. W. Reynolds, "4 Remote Work Trends Professionals Should Know for 2018," *Flex Jobs,* www.flexjobs.com, accessed April 20, 2018.

33. M. Bose, "How to Communicate Effectively over Emails at Workplace," *Entrepreneur,* www.entrepreneur.com, accessed April 20, 2018.

34. S. M. Heathfield, "Internet and Email Policy Sample," www.thebalancecareers.com, January 15, 2018.

35. S.M. Heathfield, "Surfing the Web at Work," www.thebalancecareers.com, January 11, 2018; A. Adamczyk, "Yes, Your Employer Knows Exactly What You're Doing Online," *Money,* http://time.com, August 9, 2017.

36. M. Gogan, "How Do Companies Monitor Employee Internet Usage," *TG Daily,* www.tgdaily.com, November 24, 2016.

37. B.R. Sharton and K. L. Neuman, "The Legal Risks of Monitoring Employees Online," *Harvard Business Review,* https://hbr.org, December 14, 2017.

38. M. Anteby and C.K. Chan, "Why Monitoring Your Employees' Behavior Can Backfire," *Harvard Business Review,* https://hbr.org, April 25, 2018.

39. "National Workrights Institute—About NWI," http://workrights.us, April 5, 2016; S.E. Ante, "With Little on Law Books, Employers Have Latitude in Monitoring Workers," *The Wall Street Journal,* October 23, 2013, B6.

40. A. Tugend, "What to Think About Before You Hit Send," *The New York Times,* April 21, 2012, B5.

41. "Three Major Internal Communication Trends for 2016 According to IBM," https://www.orteccommunications.com, January 12, 2016; S. Rodenbaum, "IBM: Communication and Curation Go Hand in Hand," *Forbes,* www.forbes.com, April 30, 2015.

42. "3 of the Best Company Blogs of 2017," www.brafton.com, accessed April 20, 2018.

43. C. J. Benitez, "The Curious Case of Blogging Policy for Employees," www.bloggingtips.com, December 6, 2017.

44. S. Gausepohl, "Don't Let These Social Media Mistakes Ruin Your Career," *Business News Daily,* www.businessnewsdaily.com, December 2, 2016; Pew Research Center, "Social Media and the Workplace," www.pewinternet.org, June 22, 2016.

45. O.W. Baskin and C.E. Aronoff, *Interpersonal Communication in Organizations* (Santa Monica, CA: Goodyear, 1989).

46. T. Gutner, "Move Over, Bohemian Grove," *BusinessWeek,* February 19, 2001, 102.

47. Internet World Stats, "Top 20 Countries in Internet Users vs. Rest of the World—December 31, 2017," www.internetworldstats.com, accessed on April 23, 2018.

48. B. Chakravorti, A. Bhalla, and R. S. Chaturvedi, "60 Countries' Digital Competitiveness, Indexed," *Harvard Business Review,* https://hbr.org, July 12, 2017.

49. G. Rifkin, "A Skeptic's Guide to Groupware," *Forbes ASAP,* 1995, 76–91.

50. Ibid.

51. "Groupware Requires a Group Effort," *BusinessWeek,* June 26, 1995, 154.

52. C. Sun, "The Science of the First Impression: Five Elements of a Great First Impression," *Entrepreneur,* www.entrepreneur.com, March 13, 2018; S. Shellenbarger, "The Mistakes You Make in a Meeting's First Milliseconds," *The Wall Street Journal,* www.wsj.com, January 30, 2018; Vanessa Van Edwards, "How to Hack a First Impression," *Entrepreneur,* May 2017, 46–48.

53. Shellenbarger, "The Mistakes You Make."

54. Shellenbarger, "The Mistakes You Make"; Van Edwards, "How to Hack a First Impression"; Sun, "The Science of the First Impression."

55. Shellenbarger, "The Mistakes You Make"; Van Edwards, "How to Hack a First Impression"; Sun, "The Science of the First Impression."

56. Sun, "The Science of the First Impression."

57. Van Edwards, "How to Hack a First Impression"; Sun, "The Science of the First Impression."

58. K. Shih, "5 Easy Ways to Make Your Workplace Inclusive for Someone Who's Deafblind," www.perkins.org, accessed April 20, 2018.

59. S.E. Needleman, "Business Owners Try to Motivate Employees," *The Wall Street Journal,* January 14, 2010, B5.

60. D. Tannen, "The Power of Talk," *Harvard Business Review,* September–October 1995, 138–48; D. Tannen, *Talking from 9 to 5* (New York: Avon Books, 1995).

61. Tannen, "The Power of Talk."

62. E.T. Hall, *Beyond Culture* (New York: Anchor Books, 1989).

63. M. de Mooji, *Human and Mediated Communication Around the World* (New York: Springer, 2014).

64. R. Bernstein, "7 Cultural Differences in Nonverbal Communication," https://point-park.edu, November 28, 2017.

65. Ibid.

66. Tannen, "The Power of Talk."

67. Ibid.; Tannen, *Talking from 9 to 5.*

68. Tannen, *Talking from 9 to 5.*

69. J. Cohen, "He Writes, She Writes," *Houston Chronicle,* July 7, 2001, C1–C2.

70. Ibid.

71. Ibid.

72. Tannen, "The Power of Talk," 148.

CHAPTER 17

Managing Conflict, Politics, and Negotiation

©Chris Ryan/age fotostock

Learning Objectives

After studying this chapter, you should be able to:

LO17-1 Explain why conflict arises, and identify the types and sources of conflict in organizations.

LO17-2 Describe conflict management strategies that managers can use to resolve conflict effectively.

LO17-3 Understand the nature of negotiation and why integrative bargaining is more effective than distributive negotiation.

LO17-4 Describe ways in which managers can promote integrative bargaining in organizations.

LO17-5 Explain why managers need to be attuned to organizational politics, and describe the political strategies that managers can use to become politically skilled.

How Anjali Sud Became Influential at Vimeo

How do managers influence others in the organization? Successful managers get things done through others. Besides using the authority of their position, successful managers use their understanding of people and organizations to direct conflict in positive directions, negotiate agreements, and gain and use power appropriately. One manager who does this well is Anjali Sud, who at age 34 took the position of CEO at video-editing and sharing platform Vimeo after just three years with the company.[1]

Sud's career has demonstrated her intelligence and interest in business from the start. After graduating from Wharton, the University of Pennsylvania's business school, she worked for Amazon and Time Warner and earned a master's in business administration from Harvard before moving to Vimeo as its vice president of global marketing.[2]

At Vimeo, applying her marketing expertise, Sud determined that what sets Vimeo apart from its competitors is its ad-free context and advanced video-editing tools, which attract submissions from filmmakers who pursue high quality, want to showcase their work, and are willing to pay for a monthly subscription. Sud contributed this view from a marketing standpoint, but as she continually and confidently reinforced it, it gained the power of a corporate strategy. As she expressed her vision, Vimeo should be "a creator's first home," where "every story can be beautifully told"—and, thus, a technology company focused especially on business and professional clients more than an entertainment provider serving consumers.[3]

Sud acknowledges that she was stepping beyond the thinking of a marketing executive. But, she explains, "you just have to give yourself permission and not wait for formal permission"

when you see a void that needs to be filled. Speaking up was a way to build the company's strength as well as foster her own career. When the sitting CEO, Kerry Trainor, left Vimeo, control shifted to the CEO of IAC, the media conglomerate that owns Vimeo. However, IAC did not have a strategic direction in mind for the company. In that risky situation, Sud's strategic thinking made her an attractive candidate for Vimeo's CEO position.[4]

Upon taking over as CEO, Sud immediately began to implement her strategy. The previous leader had planned to make Vimeo an entertainment destination, which would have forced it to compete with the already-popular Netflix, but Sud was determined to carry out her more-focused vision. This required ending some activities and reassigning employees to different projects, a process that inevitably stirs up resistance and conflict. However, Sud ensured that management kept the focus on the vision, not the inconveniences of change.[5]

Sud's ideas for career success are based on contributing to the company's success. She

Vimeo's 30-something CEO Anjali Sud uses her influence to keep the video editing and sharing platform on track and carry out her focused vision.
©Monica Schipper/WireImages/Getty Images

emphasizes that efforts to achieve personal goals must be coupled with "substance"—that is, knowledge and ability to add ideas of value. Thus, the manager is contributing day by day, not bragging but making an impact that he or she can point to when the occasion arises to make a request. This approach makes the manager valuable and credible, which gives him or her an edge in negotiations as well as greater influence on problem solving.[6]

Overview

Successful leaders such as Vimeo's Anjali Sud, in "A Manager's Challenge," can effectively use their power to influence others and to manage conflict to achieve win–win solutions. In Chapter 14 we described how managers, as leaders, influence other people to achieve group and organizational goals and how managers' sources of power enable them to exert such influence. In this chapter we describe why managers need to develop the skills necessary to manage organizational conflict, politics, and negotiation if they are going to be effective and achieve their goals.

LO17-1 Explain why conflict arises, and identify the types and sources of conflict in organizations.

We describe conflict and the strategies managers can use to resolve it effectively. We discuss one major conflict resolution technique, negotiation, in detail, outlining the steps managers can take to be good negotiators. Then we discuss the nature of organizational politics and the political strategies managers can use to maintain and expand their power and use it effectively. By the end of this chapter you will appreciate why managers must develop the skills necessary to manage these important organizational processes if they are to be effective and achieve organizational goals.

Organizational Conflict

Organizational conflict is the discord that arises when the goals, interests, or values of different individuals or groups are incompatible and those individuals or groups block or thwart one another's attempts to achieve their objectives.[7] Conflict is an inevitable part of organizational life because the goals of different stakeholders such as managers and workers are often incompatible. Organizational conflict also can exist between departments and divisions that compete for resources or even between managers who may be competing for promotion to the next level in the organizational hierarchy.

organizational conflict The discord that arises when the goals, interests, or values of different individuals or groups are incompatible and those individuals or groups block or thwart one another's attempts to achieve their objectives.

Not surprisingly, the current business environment continues to evolve at a rapid pace, which intensifies the existence of conflict throughout various parts of any organization. Factors often cited for why finely tuned conflict resolution skills are essential for today's managers include (1) increased pressure on organizations to change and adapt quickly to maintain competitive advantage; (2) increased diversity due to global business expansion, which may cause more conflict; (3) intense use of technology and flexible working arrangements that have reduced face-to-face communications among supervisors, employees, senior management, and business colleagues, which may increase the opportunity for misunderstanding and communication gaps; and (4) increased conflict among members of self-managed teams, who are now making decisions previously the responsibility of other managers in the organization. All of these factors, among others, require greater conflict resolution and negotiation skills at all levels of the organization.[8]

It is important for managers to develop the skills necessary to manage conflict effectively. In addition, the level of conflict present in an organization has important implications for organizational performance. Figure 17.1 illustrates the relationship between organizational conflict and performance. At point A, there is little or no conflict, and organizational performance suffers. Lack of conflict in an organization often signals that managers emphasize conformity at the expense of new ideas, resist change, and strive for agreement rather than effective decision making. As the level of conflict increases from point A to point B, organizational effectiveness is likely to increase. When an organization has an optimum level of conflict, managers are

Figure 17.1

The Effect of Conflict on Organizational Performance

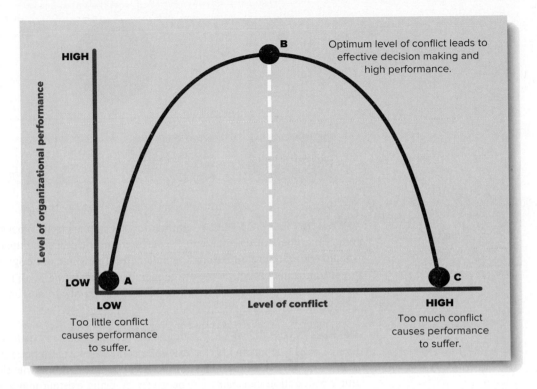

likely to be open to, and encourage, a variety of perspectives; look for ways to improve organizational functioning and effectiveness; and view debates and disagreements as a necessary ingredient of effective decision making and innovation. As the level of conflict increases from point B to point C, conflict escalates to the point where organizational performance suffers. When an organization has a dysfunctionally high level of conflict, managers are likely to waste organizational resources to achieve their own ends, to be more concerned about winning political battles than about doing what will lead to a competitive advantage for their organizations, and to try to get even with their opponents rather than make good decisions.

Conflict is a force that needs to be managed rather than eliminated.[9] Managers should never try to eliminate all conflict but, rather, should try to keep conflict at a moderate and functional level to promote change efforts that benefit the organization. Additionally, managers should strive to keep conflict focused on substantive, task-based issues and minimize conflict based on personal disagreements and animosities. To manage conflict,[10] managers must understand the types and sources of conflict and be familiar with strategies that can be effective in dealing with it.

Types of Conflict

There are several types of conflict in organizations: interpersonal, intragroup, intergroup, and interorganizational (see Figure 17.2).[11] Understanding how these types differ can help managers deal with conflict.

INTERPERSONAL CONFLICT Interpersonal conflict is conflict between individual members of an organization, occurring because of differences in their goals or values. Two managers may experience interpersonal conflict when their values concerning protection of the environment differ. One manager may argue that the organization should do only what is required by law. The other manager may counter that the organization should invest in equipment to reduce emissions, even though the organization's current level of emissions is below the legal limit.

Figure 17.2

Types of Conflict in Organizations

INTRAGROUP CONFLICT   Intragroup conflict arises within a group, team, or department. When members of the marketing department in a clothing company disagree about how they should spend budgeted advertising dollars for a new line of designer jeans, they are experiencing intragroup conflict. Some of the members want to spend all the money on advertisements in magazines; others want to devote half of the money to ads on social media platforms like Facebook and Twitter.

INTERGROUP CONFLICT   Intergroup conflict occurs between groups, teams, or departments. R&D departments, for example, sometimes experience intergroup conflict with production departments. Members of the R&D department may develop a new product that they think production can make inexpensively by using existing manufacturing capabilities. Members of the production department, however, may disagree and believe that the costs of making the product will be much higher. Managers of departments usually play a key role in managing intergroup conflicts such as this.

Sometimes intergroup conflict occurs between founders of companies and their families and supporters on the one hand, and the top managers who run them on the other, as profiled in the following "Management Insight" feature.

MANAGEMENT INSIGHT

Intergroup Conflict at PulteGroup

William ("Bill") Pulte learned about the construction industry from a job he had as a teenager working for a contractor; he turned down a college scholarship to construct and sell his first house in Detroit in 1950. At the end of the 1960s, he had expanded his home construction business to Washington, Atlanta, and Chicago. His company grew and had operations in 25 states in the 1990s. Before the U.S. housing crisis in the late 2000s, PulteGroup had the highest revenues and most houses sold of U.S. homebuilders (after the crisis, it was the third largest homebuilder in the United States).[12] Pulte always concentrated on homebuilding, left administrative matters such as management and finance to executives he had confidence in, and wanted everyone to call him "Bill." He often traveled to homebuilding locations, pointing out problems, and could be seen climbing ladders in his seventies. Pulte was the chairman of the company for many years, until he retired in 2010, and was the company's biggest shareholder until his death in March 2018.[13]

In 2016 Pulte, his grandson, and a director who has since resigned became embroiled in a public intergroup conflict with PulteGroup's chairman and CEO Richard Dugas and the board of directors. Prior to joining PulteGroup in 1994, Dugas had worked at Exxon and PepsiCo in marketing and operations positions and had no

Intergroup conflict at PulteGroup pitted the company's founder against the CEO he hired and the company's board of directors. Eventually the ongoing turmoil caused the embattled CEO to retire early from the homebuilding company.

©Hugh Sitton/Getty Images

experience in the homebuilding industry. Dugas made a good name for himself at PulteGroup as someone who wanted to learn about the company and the housing industry, had a great deal of curiosity, and was a disciplined, hard worker. He relocated to Atlanta to study the business from bottom to top and was named a regional president. In 2002, Pulte promoted Dugas to chief operating officer and then to chief executive in 2003.[14]

Pulte and Dugas's former good working relationship took a turn for the worse in 2016.[15] Pulte (with the support of his grandson, who has the same name, and a director who later resigned) blamed Dugas for the company's lackluster stock performance in comparison with its competitors in the three years leading up to 2016 and called for him to step down. Dugas and the board of directors responded by indicating that Dugas would retire in one year's time. Pulte again called for Dugas to step down immediately. In a letter to the board of directors of the company he had founded, Pulte indicated that it had been a mistake to appoint Dugas to the top position, that he was hurting the company, and that he was an ineffective CEO. He also indicated that Dugas was responsible for the loss of key homebuilding talent to competitors, which resulted in a lack of creativity, innovation, and sales. Initially, the board responded with support for Dugas and his accomplishments. This intergroup conflict between founder Pulte, his grandson, and one director on one side and Dugas and the company board on the other arose from differing views of Dugas's performance as CEO and the company's success under his leadership. In 2017, Dugas retired as a result of Pulte's push to force changes within the company and was replaced by the company's president, Ryan Marshall. In addition, the founder's grandson Bill Pulte was appointed to the company's board of directors.[16]

INTERORGANIZATIONAL CONFLICT   Interorganizational conflict arises across organizations. Sometimes interorganizational conflict occurs when managers in one organization feel that another organization is not behaving ethically and is threatening the well-being of certain stakeholder groups. Interorganizational conflict also can occur between government agencies and corporations.

Sources of Conflict

Conflict in organizations springs from a variety of sources. The ones we examine here are different goals and time horizons, overlapping authority, task interdependencies, different evaluation or reward systems, scarce resources, and status inconsistencies (see Figure 17.3).[17]

DIFFERENT GOALS AND TIME HORIZONS   Recall from Chapter 10 that an important managerial activity is organizing people and tasks into departments and divisions to accomplish an organization's goals. Almost inevitably this grouping creates departments and divisions that have different goals and time horizons, and the result can be conflict. Production managers, for example, usually concentrate on efficiency and cost cutting; they have a relatively short time horizon and focus on producing quality goods or services in a timely and efficient manner. In contrast, marketing managers focus on sales and responsiveness to customers. Their time horizon is longer than that of production because they are trying to be responsive not only to customers' needs today, but also to their changing needs in the future to build long-term customer loyalty. These fundamental differences between marketing and production often breed conflict.

Figure 17.3
Sources of Conflict in Organizations

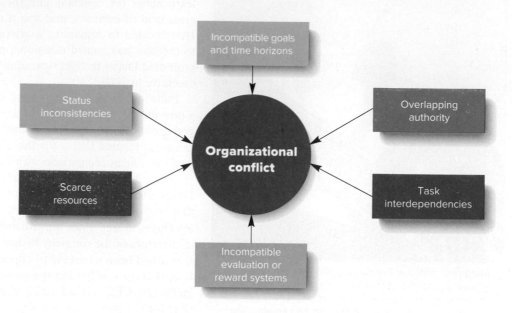

Suppose production is behind schedule in its plan to produce a specialized product for a key customer. The marketing manager believes the delay will reduce sales of the product and therefore insists that the product be delivered on time even if saving the production schedule means increasing costs by paying production workers overtime. The production manager says that she will happily schedule overtime if marketing will pay for it. Both managers' positions are reasonable from the perspective of their own departments, and conflict is likely.

OVERLAPPING AUTHORITY   When two or more managers, departments, or functions claim authority for the same activities or tasks, conflict is likely.[18] This is precisely what happened when heirs of the Forman liquor distribution company, based in Washington, DC, inherited the company from their parents. One of the heirs, Barry Forman, wanted to control the company and was reluctant to share power with the other heirs. Several of the heirs felt they had authority over certain tasks crucial to Forman's success (such as maintaining good relationships with the top managers of liquor companies). What emerged was a battle of wills and considerable conflict, which escalated to the point of being dysfunctional, requiring that the family hire a consulting firm to help resolve it.[19]

TASK INTERDEPENDENCIES   Have you ever been assigned a group project for one of your classes and had one group member who consistently failed to get things done on time? This probably created some conflict in your group because other group members were dependent on the late member's contributions to complete the project. Whenever individuals, groups, teams, or departments are interdependent, the potential for conflict exists.[20] With differing goals and time horizons, the managers of marketing and production come into conflict precisely because the departments are interdependent. Marketing is dependent on production for the goods it markets and sells, and production is dependent on marketing to create demand for the things it makes.

DIFFERENT EVALUATION OR REWARD SYSTEMS   How interdependent groups, teams, or departments are evaluated and rewarded can be another source of conflict.[21] Production managers, for example, are evaluated and rewarded for their success in staying within budget or lowering costs while maintaining quality. So they are reluctant to take any steps that will increase costs, such as paying workers high overtime rates to finish a late order for an important customer. Marketing managers, in contrast, are evaluated and rewarded for their success in generating sales and satisfying customers. So they often think overtime pay is a small price to pay for responsiveness to customers. Thus, conflict between production and marketing is rarely unexpected.

SCARCE RESOURCES   Management is the process of acquiring, developing, protecting, and using the resources that allow an organization to be efficient and effective (see Chapter 1). When resources are scarce, management is more difficult and conflict is likely.[22] For example, divisional managers may be in conflict over who has access to financial capital, and organizational members at all levels may be in conflict over who gets raises and promotions.

STATUS INCONSISTENCIES   The fact that some individuals, groups, teams, or departments within an organization are more highly regarded than others in the organization can also create conflict. In some restaurants, for example, the chefs have relatively higher status than the people who wait on tables. Nevertheless, the chefs receive customers' orders from the waitstaff, and the waitstaff can return to the chefs food that their customers or they think is not acceptable. This status inconsistency—high-status chefs taking orders from low-status waitstaff—can be the source of considerable conflict between chefs and the waitstaff. For this reason, many restaurants require the waitstaff to input food orders directly into an electronic system via iPad or another type of mobile tablet, thereby reducing the amount of direct ordering from the waitstaff to the chefs.[23]

LO17-2 Describe conflict management strategies that managers can use to resolve conflict effectively.

Conflict Management Strategies

If an organization is to achieve its goals, managers must be able to resolve conflicts in a functional manner. *Functional conflict resolution* means the conflict is settled by compromise or by collaboration between the parties in conflict (later in the chapter we discuss other typically less functional ways in which conflicts are sometimes resolved).[24] **Compromise** is possible when each party is concerned about not only its own goal accomplishment, but also the goal accomplishment of the other party and is willing to engage in a give-and-take exchange and to make concessions until a reasonable resolution of the conflict is reached. **Collaboration** is a way of handling conflict in which the parties try to satisfy their goals without making any concessions but, instead, come up with a way to resolve their differences that leaves them both better off.[25]

In addition to compromise and collaboration, there are three other ways in which conflicts are sometimes handled: accommodation, avoidance, and competition.[26] When **accommodation** takes place, one party to the conflict simply gives in to the demands of the other party. Accommodation typically takes place when one party has more power than the other and can pursue its goal attainment at the expense of the weaker party. From an organizational perspective, accommodation is often ineffective: The two parties are not cooperating with each other, they are unlikely to want to cooperate in the future, and the weaker party who gives in or accommodates the more powerful party might look for ways to get back at the stronger party in the future.

When conflicts are handled by **avoidance**, the parties to a conflict try to ignore the problem and do nothing to resolve the disagreement. Avoidance is often ineffective because the real source of the disagreement has not been addressed, conflict is likely to continue, and communication and cooperation are hindered.

Competition occurs when each party to a conflict tries to maximize its own gain and has little interest in understanding the other party's position and arriving at a solution that will allow both parties to achieve their goals. Competition can actually escalate levels of conflict as each party tries to outmaneuver the other. As a way of handling conflict, competition is ineffective for the organization because the two sides to a conflict are more concerned about winning the battle than cooperating to arrive at a solution that is best for the organization and acceptable to both sides. Handling conflicts through accommodation, avoidance, or competition is ineffective from an organizational point of view because the parties do not cooperate with each other and work toward a mutually acceptable solution to their differences.

Another strategy that has been successful in resolving conflict is the problem-solving approach because it focuses on objective outcomes—not individual opinions or views—thus respecting and preserving social relationships within a group. This approach also helps reduce the stress of interpersonal conflict among employees.[27]

compromise A way of managing conflict in which each party is concerned about not only its own goal accomplishment, but also the goal accomplishment of the other party and is willing to engage in a give-and-take exchange and make concessions.

collaboration A way of managing conflict in which both parties try to satisfy their goals by coming up with an approach that leaves them better off and does not require concessions on issues that are important to either party.

accommodation A conflict-handling approach in which one party, typically with weaker power, gives in to the demands of the other, typically more powerful party.

avoidance A conflict-handling approach in which the parties try to ignore the problem and do nothing to resolve their differences.

competition A conflict-handling approach in which each party tries to maximize its own gain and has little interest in understanding the other party's position and arriving at a solution that will allow both parties to achieve their goals.

When the parties to a conflict are willing to cooperate with each other and devise a solution that each finds acceptable, an organization is more likely to achieve its goals.[28] Conflict management strategies managers can use to ensure that conflicts are resolved in a functional manner focus on individuals and on the organization as a whole. Next we describe four strategies that focus on individuals: increasing awareness of the sources of conflict, increasing diversity awareness and skills, practicing job rotation or temporary assignments, and using permanent transfers or dismissals when necessary. We also describe two strategies that focus on the organization as a whole: changing an organization's structure or culture and directly altering the source of conflict.

STRATEGIES FOCUSED ON INDIVIDUALS

INCREASING AWARENESS OF THE SOURCES OF CONFLICT Sometimes conflict arises because of communication problems and interpersonal misunderstandings. For example, different linguistic styles (see Chapter 16) may lead some men in work teams to talk more and take more credit for ideas than women in those teams. These communication differences can cause conflict when the men incorrectly assume that the women are uninterested or less capable because they participate less, and the women incorrectly assume that the men are bossy and are not interested in their ideas because they seem to do all the talking. By increasing people's awareness of this source of conflict, managers can help resolve conflict functionally. Once men and women realize that the source of their conflict is different linguistic styles, they can take steps to interact with each other more effectively. The men can give the women more chances to provide input, and the women can be more proactive in providing this input.

Sometimes personalities clash in an organization. In these situations, too, managers can help resolve conflicts functionally by increasing organizational members' awareness of the source of their difficulties. For example, some people who are not inclined to take risks may come into conflict with those who are prone to taking risks. The non–risk takers might complain that those who welcome risk propose outlandish ideas without justification, whereas the risk takers might complain that their innovative ideas are always getting shot down. When both types of people are made aware that their conflicts are due to fundamental differences in their ways of approaching problems, they will likely be better able to cooperate in coming up with innovative ideas that entail only moderate levels of risk.

In addition, work teams can get sidetracked when trying to resolve conflict within the group and between individual members. Recent research suggests that one possible approach to dealing with conflict within a work group includes assigning work tasks based on skill and relevance, not necessarily on who volunteers to do the task; acknowledging that team members' ability to compromise is an important, positive step toward reaching the team's overall goal; anticipating possible conflicts and working proactively to resolve them rather than reacting to them; and focusing on evidence-based decisions through analysis rather than getting distracted by conflicting views of individual team members.[29] For examples of how team leaders are applying these conflict management principles, read the "Management Insight" feature.

MANAGEMENT INSIGHT

Making Conflict Work for Top-Level Teams

Because team members must work together closely, many people assume that conflict in a team is a problem. But effective team leaders understand that conflict also signals a diversity of perspectives, which is a potential advantage of teamwork. In particular, Orla Leonard of the RHR International consulting group and colleagues who study senior management and coach senior managers have found that effective conflict management is an especially strong predictor of top-team performance. Therefore, executive teams benefit from harnessing conflict and using it as a source of strength.[30]

Executive-level decisions are particularly complex. These decisions cross functional and divisional boundaries, affect every level of the organization, and involve the uncertainty of looking several years into the future. Thus, conflicting views are not just inevitable, but also necessary for interpreting the situation and identifying possible alternatives.[31]

Teams that can meet the challenge combine recognition that conflict is inevitable with a sense of mutual trust and a skill set for navigating conflict. This combination enables team members to recognize conflict when it occurs and feel comfortable in talking about it. To find a way forward, team leaders and members keep in mind the bigger picture: what is best for the organization as a whole and, in particular, what is best for customers. If some participants begin to focus on their own function or division, others reassert the shared vision for the team.[32]

An essential role for the team leader, then, is to ensure that there is a clear and compelling vision for the senior-management team. Rather than focusing on functional activities, the top leader, the CEO, must be able to articulate this vision and make sure that every meeting agenda explicitly addresses it. For example, a CEO of a multinational company started meetings by asking participants to take off their "business-unit hat" and take on the role of a leader focused on the whole enterprise. The CEO would also state that this would inevitably lead to some conflict, but that the team would work toward solutions and then adjourn for some friendly socializing before returning to the groups they lead.[33]

INCREASING DIVERSITY AWARENESS AND SKILLS Interpersonal conflicts also can arise because of diversity. Older workers may feel uncomfortable or resentful about reporting to a younger supervisor, a Hispanic may feel singled out in a group of non-Hispanic workers, or a female top manager may feel that members of her predominantly male top management team band together whenever one of them disagrees with one of her proposals. Whether or not these feelings are justified, they are likely to cause recurring conflicts. Many of the techniques described in Chapter 5 for increasing diversity awareness and skills can help managers effectively manage diversity and resolve conflicts that originate in differences among organizational members.

PRACTICING JOB ROTATION OR TEMPORARY ASSIGNMENTS Sometimes conflicts arise because individual organizational members simply do not understand the work activities and demands that others in an organization face. A financial analyst, for example, may be required to submit monthly reports to a member of the accounting department. These reports have a low priority for the analyst, who typically turns them in a couple of days late. On each due date the accountant calls the financial analyst, and conflict ensues as the accountant describes in detail why she must have the reports on time and the financial analyst describes everything else he needs to do. In situations such as this, job rotation or temporary assignments, which expand organizational members' knowledge base and appreciation of other departments, can be a useful way of resolving the conflict. If the financial analyst spends some time working in the accounting department, he may appreciate better the need for timely reports. Similarly, a temporary assignment in the finance department may help the accountant realize the demands a financial analyst faces and the need to streamline unnecessary aspects of reporting.

Travis Kalanick, Uber's founder, was forced to resign as CEO from the ride-hailing company amid allegations of unethical conduct.
©dpa picture alliance/Alamy Stock Photo

USING PERMANENT TRANSFERS OR DISMISSALS WHEN NECESSARY Sometimes when other conflict resolution strategies do not work, managers need to take more drastic steps, including permanent transfers or dismissals.

Suppose two first-line managers who work in the same department are always at each other's throat; frequent, bitter conflicts arise between them even though they both seem to get along well with other employees. No matter what their supervisor does to increase their understanding of each other, the conflicts keep occurring. In this case the supervisor may want to transfer one or both managers so they do not have to interact as frequently.

When dysfunctionally high levels of conflict occur among top managers who cannot resolve their differences and understand each other, it may be necessary for one of them to leave the company. This is what happened recently when Uber founder, Travis Kalanick, was forced to resign from the ride-hailing company.[34] Amid allegations of sexual harassment made by a female engineer, misuse of technology used to avoid giving rides to officials in cities where Uber's services were illegal, and accusations of stealing trade secrets from Google's self-driving car company, several of Uber's major investors demanded Kalanick resign immediately.[35] Many other senior executives left or were ousted during this same chaotic time period. Uber's board of directors tapped Dara Khosrowshahi, former CEO of Expedia, to transform the company's toxic culture.[36]

STRATEGIES FOCUSED ON THE WHOLE ORGANIZATION

CHANGING AN ORGANIZATION'S STRUCTURE OR CULTURE   Conflict can signal the need for changes in an organization's structure or culture. Sometimes managers can effectively resolve conflict by changing the organizational structure they use to group people and tasks.[37] As an organization grows, for example, the *functional structure* (composed of departments such as marketing, finance, and production) that was effective when the organization was small may cease to be effective, and a shift to a *product structure* might effectively resolve conflicts (see Chapter 10).

Managers also can effectively resolve conflicts by increasing levels of integration in an organization. Recall from Chapter 15 that Hallmark Cards increased integration by using cross-functional teams to produce new cards. The use of cross-functional teams sped new card development and helped resolve conflicts between departments. Now when a writer and an artist have a conflict over the appropriateness of the artist's illustrations, they do not pass criticisms back and forth from one department to another because they are on the same team and can directly resolve the issue on the spot.

Sometimes managers need to take steps to change an organization's culture to resolve conflict (see Chapter 3). Norms and values in an organizational culture might inadvertently promote dysfunctionally high levels of conflict that are difficult to resolve. For instance, norms that stress respect for formal authority may create conflict that is difficult to resolve when an organization creates self-managed work teams and managers' roles and the structure of authority in the organization change. Values stressing individual competition may make it difficult to resolve conflicts when organizational members need to put others' interests ahead of their own. In circumstances such as these, taking steps to change norms and values can be an effective conflict resolution strategy.

ALTERING THE SOURCE OF CONFLICT   When the source of conflict is overlapping authority, different evaluation or reward systems, or status inconsistencies, managers can sometimes effectively resolve the conflict by directly altering its source. For example, managers can clarify the chain of command and reassign tasks and responsibilities to resolve conflicts due to overlapping authority.

LO17-3 Understand the nature of negotiation and why integrative bargaining is more effective than distributive negotiation.

negotiation A method of conflict resolution in which the parties consider various alternative ways to allocate resources to come up with a solution acceptable to all of them.

third-party negotiator An impartial individual with expertise in handling conflicts and negotiations who helps parties in conflict reach an acceptable solution.

mediator A third-party negotiator who facilitates negotiations but has no authority to impose a solution.

arbitrator A third-party negotiator who can impose what he or she thinks is a fair solution to a conflict, which both parties are obligated to abide by.

distributive negotiation Adversarial negotiation in which the parties in conflict compete to win the most resources while conceding as little as possible.

Negotiation

Negotiation is a particularly important conflict resolution technique for managers and other organizational members in situations where the parties to a conflict have approximately equal levels of power. During **negotiation** the parties to a conflict try to come up with a solution acceptable to themselves by considering various alternative ways to allocate resources to each other.[38] Sometimes the sides involved in a conflict negotiate directly with each other. Other times a **third-party negotiator** is relied on. Third-party negotiators are impartial individuals who are not directly involved in the conflict and have special expertise in handling conflicts and negotiations; they are relied on to help the two negotiating parties reach an acceptable resolution of their conflict.[39] When a third-party negotiator acts as a **mediator**, his or her role in the negotiation process is to facilitate an effective negotiation between the two parties; mediators do not force either party to make concessions, nor can they force an agreement to resolve a conflict. **Arbitrators**, on the other hand, are third-party negotiators who can impose what they believe is a fair solution to a dispute, which both parties are obligated to abide by.[40]

Distributive Negotiation and Integrative Bargaining

There are two major types of negotiation—distributive negotiation and integrative bargaining. In **distributive negotiation**, the two parties perceive that they have a "fixed pie" of resources they need to divide. They take a competitive, adversarial stance. Each party realizes that he

In integrative bargaining, conflicts are handled by avoiding a win–lose competitive mindset, and creating a win–win situation for both parties.

©moodboard/SuperStock

integrative bargaining Cooperative negotiation in which the parties in conflict work together to achieve a resolution that is good for them both.

LO17-4 Describe ways in which managers can promote integrative bargaining in organizations.

or she must concede something but is out to get the lion's share of the resources.[41] The parties see no need to interact with each other in the future and do not care if their interpersonal relationship is damaged or destroyed by their competitive negotiation.[42] In distributive negotiations, conflicts are handled by competition.

In integrative bargaining, the parties perceive that they might be able to increase the resource pie by trying to come up with a creative solution to the conflict. They do not view the conflict competitively as a win-or-lose situation; instead, they view it cooperatively, as a win–win situation in which both parties can gain. Trust, information sharing, and the desire of both parties to achieve a good resolution of the conflict characterize integrative bargaining.[43] In integrative bargaining, conflicts are handled through collaboration and/or compromise.

Consider how Adrian Hofbeck and Joseph Steinberg, partners in a successful German restaurant in the Midwest, resolved their recent conflict. Hofbeck and Steinberg founded the restaurant 15 years ago, share management responsibilities, and share equally in the restaurant's profits. Hofbeck recently decided that he wanted to retire and sell the restaurant, but retirement was the last thing Steinberg had in mind; he wanted to continue to own and manage the restaurant. Distributive negotiation was out of the question because Hofbeck and Steinberg were close friends and valued their friendship; neither wanted to do something that would hurt the other or their continuing relationship. So they opted for integrative bargaining, which they thought would help them resolve their conflict so both could achieve their goals and maintain their friendship.

Strategies to Encourage Integrative Bargaining

Managers in all kinds of organizations can rely on five strategies to facilitate integrative bargaining and avoid distributive negotiation: emphasizing superordinate goals; focusing on the problem, not the people; focusing on interests, not demands; creating new options for joint gain; and focusing on what is fair (see Table 17.1).[44] Hofbeck and Steinberg used each of these strategies to resolve their conflict.

EMPHASIZING SUPERORDINATE GOALS *Superordinate goals* are goals that both parties agree to, regardless of the source of their conflict. Increasing organizational effectiveness, increasing responsiveness to customers, and gaining a competitive advantage are just a few of the many superordinate goals that members of an organization can emphasize during integrative bargaining. Superordinate goals help parties in conflict to keep in mind the big picture and the fact that they are working together for a larger purpose or goal despite their disagreements. Hofbeck and Steinberg emphasized three superordinate goals during their bargaining: ensuring that the restaurant continued to survive and prosper, allowing Hofbeck to retire, and allowing Steinberg to remain an owner and manager as long as he wished.

FOCUSING ON THE PROBLEM, NOT THE PEOPLE People who are in conflict may not be able to resist the temptation to focus on the other party's shortcomings and weaknesses, thereby personalizing the conflict. Instead of attacking the problem, the parties to the conflict attack each other. This approach is inconsistent with integrative bargaining and can easily lead both parties into a distributive negotiation mode. All parties to a conflict need to keep

Table 17.1

Negotiation Strategies for Integrative Bargaining

- Emphasize superordinate goals.
- Focus on the problem, not the people.
- Focus on interests, not demands.
- Create new options for joint gain.
- Focus on what is fair.

focused on the problem or on the source of the conflict and avoid the temptation to discredit one another.

Given their strong friendship, this was not much of an issue for Hofbeck and Steinberg, but they still had to be on their guard to avoid personalizing the conflict. Steinberg recalls that when they were having a hard time coming up with a solution, he started thinking that Hofbeck, a healthy 57-year-old, was lazy to want to retire so young: "If only he wasn't so lazy, we would never be in the mess we're in right now." Steinberg never mentioned these thoughts to Hofbeck (who later admitted that sometimes he was annoyed with Steinberg for being such a workaholic) because he realized that doing so would hurt their chances for reaching an integrative solution.

FOCUSING ON INTERESTS, NOT DEMANDS   Demands are *what* a person wants; interests are *why* the person wants them. When two people are in conflict, it is unlikely that the demands of both can be met. Their underlying interests, however, can be met, and meeting them is what integrative bargaining is all about.

Hofbeck's demand was that they sell the restaurant and split the proceeds. Steinberg's demand was that they keep the restaurant and maintain the status quo. Obviously, both demands could not be met, but perhaps their interests could be. Hofbeck wanted to be able to retire, invest his share of the money from the restaurant, and live off the returns on the investment. Steinberg wanted to continue managing, owning, and deriving income from the restaurant.

CREATING NEW OPTIONS FOR JOINT GAIN   Once two parties to a conflict focus on their interests, they are on the road to achieving creative solutions to the conflict that will benefit them both. This win–win scenario means that rather than having a fixed set of alternatives from which to choose, the two parties can come up with new alternatives that might even expand the resource pie.

Hofbeck and Steinberg came up with three such alternatives. First, even though Steinberg did not have the capital, he could buy out Hofbeck's share of the restaurant. Hofbeck would provide the financing for the purchase, and in return Steinberg would pay him a reasonable return on his investment (the same kind of return he could have obtained, had he taken his money out of the restaurant and invested it). Second, the partners could seek to sell Hofbeck's share in the restaurant to a third party under the stipulation that Steinberg would continue to manage the restaurant and receive income for his services. Third, the partners could continue to jointly own the restaurant. Steinberg would manage it and receive a proportionally greater share of its profits than Hofbeck, who would be an absentee owner not involved in day-to-day operations but would still receive a return on his investment in the restaurant.

FOCUSING ON WHAT IS FAIR   Focusing on what is fair is consistent with the principle of distributive justice, which emphasizes the fair distribution of outcomes based on the meaningful contributions that people make to organizations (see Chapter 5). It is likely that two parties in conflict will disagree on certain points and prefer different alternatives that each party believes may better serve his or her own interests or maximize his or her own outcomes. Emphasizing fairness and distributive justice will help the two parties come to a mutual agreement about what the best solution is to the problem.

Steinberg and Hofbeck agreed that Hofbeck should be able to cut his ties with the restaurant if he chose to do so. They decided to pursue the second alternative described and seek a suitable buyer for Hofbeck's share. They were successful in finding an investor who was willing to buy out Hofbeck's share and let Steinberg continue managing the restaurant. And they remained good friends.

When managers pursue these five strategies and encourage other organizational members to do so, they are more likely to be able to effectively resolve their conflicts through integrative bargaining. These skills result in outcomes that benefit the individual participants and the organization as a whole. Furthermore, managers who learn these skills are well prepared for many practical career challenges, including the negotiation of job offers, as described in the "Manager as a Person" feature. In addition, throughout the negotiation process, managers and other organizational members need to be aware of, and on their guard against, the biases that can lead to faulty decision making (see Chapter 7).[45]

Negotiating a Job Offer

Negotiating a job offer can be nerve-racking—for both experienced workers and recent grads. Learning how to negotiate is a legitimate skill that comes in handy during both professional and personal situations.
©fizkes/Shutterstock

A manager's role involves advancing the organization's well being and its overall business success. But like any other person looking for work, managers also find themselves in the labor market, negotiating for a new position. The negotiation skills they apply at work can help them reach employment agreements that benefit both parties. The company acquires talent, and the manager finds an attractive position in exchange for compensation that both parties consider fair.

Especially when currently unemployed, a job seeker might feel safest accepting all the terms in a job offer, thinking the risk of an employer losing interest in him or her might seem too great. But successful managers understand that negotiation is part of decision making. Furthermore, the fact that the company made an offer signals they see the candidate as someone who will add value to the organization. Negotiation is a legitimate skill that can make a major difference in a manager's lifetime earnings.[46]

Negotiation requires information about the situation and the other party, including the going rate of pay for the position. The effective negotiator has in mind a desired salary that is realistic, given the job market and his or her qualifications. If the initial offer is below that amount, the negotiator should respond as objectively as possible, indicating the desired amount and giving reasons why it is reasonable. Reasons should emphasize how the person will contribute to the company's success, including specific examples if possible. If the company representative says the amount of pay is firm, it might help to ask whether demonstrating success on certain measures could be tied to a raise in six months or a year.[47]

Job seekers should look at the complete offer, not just salary. Employee benefits, such as insurance, student-loan repayment, retirement accounts, training or tuition reimbursement, and time off, also have value. People in high-demand jobs might get a signing bonus. If a job requires moving to a new location, then a generous relocation package also can make the offer appealing. Negotiators should consider whether trade-offs on some of these could result in an acceptable offer. If so, the key to a resolution might be a statement such as "If you can get me tuition reimbursement along with that salary, I'll accept your offer today." Human resource professionals advise that candidates using this approach focus on one or two changes that matter most. Picking apart every detail will not win over a team that spent hours putting together what they thought was a fair offer.[48]

Organizational Politics

LO17-5 Explain why managers need to be attuned to organizational politics, and describe the political strategies that managers can use to become politically skilled.

Managers must develop the skills necessary to manage organizational conflict for an organization to be effective. Suppose, however, that top managers are in conflict over the best strategy for an organization to pursue or the best structure to adopt to use organizational resources efficiently. In such situations, resolving conflict is often difficult, and the parties to the conflict resort to organizational politics and political strategies to try to resolve the conflict in their favor.

Organizational politics are the activities that managers (and other members of an organization) engage in to increase their power and to use power effectively to achieve their goals and overcome resistance or opposition.[49] Managers often engage in organizational politics to resolve conflicts in their favor.

Political strategies are the specific tactics that managers (and other members of an organization) use to increase their power and to use power effectively to influence and gain the

organizational politics Activities that managers engage in to increase their power and to use power effectively to achieve their goals and overcome resistance or opposition.

political strategies Tactics that managers use to increase their power and to use power effectively to influence and gain the support of other people while overcoming resistance or opposition.

support of other people while overcoming resistance or opposition. Political strategies are especially important when managers are planning and implementing major changes in an organization: Managers not only need to gain support for their change initiatives and influence organizational members to behave in new ways, but also need to overcome often strong opposition from people who feel threatened by the change and prefer the status quo. By increasing their power, managers are better able to make needed changes. In addition to increasing their power, managers also must make sure they use their power in a way that actually enables them to influence others.

The Importance of Organizational Politics

The term *politics* has a negative connotation for many people. Some think that managers who are political have risen to the top not because of their own merit and capabilities but because of whom they know. Or people may think that political managers are self-interested and wield power to benefit themselves, not their organizations. There is a grain of truth to this negative connotation. Some managers do appear to misuse their power for personal benefit at the expense of their organizations' effectiveness.

Nevertheless, organizational politics are often a positive force. Managers striving to make needed changes often encounter resistance from individuals and groups who feel threatened and wish to preserve the status quo. Effective managers engage in politics to gain support for and implement needed changes. Similarly, managers often face resistance from other managers who disagree with their goals for a group or for the organization and with what they are trying to accomplish. Engaging in organizational politics can help managers overcome this resistance and achieve their goals.

Indeed, managers cannot afford to ignore organizational politics. Everyone engages in politics to a degree—other managers, coworkers, and subordinates, as well as people outside an organization, such as suppliers. Those who try to ignore politics might as well bury their heads in the sand because in all likelihood they will be unable to gain support for their initiatives and goals.

Political Strategies for Gaining and Maintaining Power

Managers who use political strategies to increase and maintain their power are better able to influence others to work toward the achievement of group and organizational goals. (Recall from Chapter 14 that legitimate, reward, coercive, expert, and referent power help managers influence others as leaders.) By controlling uncertainty, making themselves irreplaceable, being in a central position, generating resources, and building alliances, managers can increase their power (see Figure 17.4).[50] We next look at each of these strategies.

CONTROLLING UNCERTAINTY   Uncertainty is a threat for individuals, groups, and whole organizations and can interfere with effective performance and goal attainment. For example, uncertainty about job security is threatening for many workers and may cause top performers (who have the best chance of finding another job) to quit and take a more secure position with another organization. When an R&D department faces uncertainty about customer preferences, its members may waste valuable resources to develop a product that customers do not want. When top managers face uncertainty about global demand, they may fail to export products to countries that want them and, thus, may lose a source of competitive advantage.

Managers who can control and reduce uncertainty for other managers, teams, and departments as well as the organization as a whole are likely to see their power increase.[51] Managers of labor unions gain power when they can eliminate uncertainty over job security for workers. Marketing and sales managers gain power when they can eliminate uncertainty for other departments, such as R&D, by accurately forecasting customers' changing preferences. Top managers gain power when they are knowledgeable about global demand for an organization's products. Managers who can control uncertainty are likely to be in demand and sought after by other organizations.

MAKING ONESELF IRREPLACEABLE   Managers gain power when they have valuable knowledge and expertise that allow them to perform activities no one else can handle. This

Figure 17.4
Political Strategies for Increasing Power

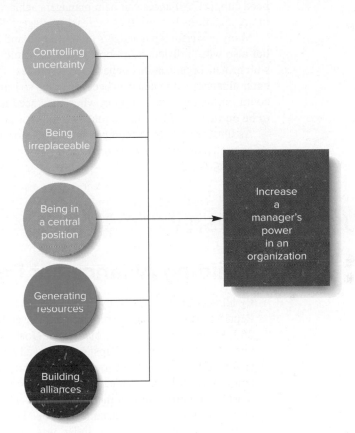

is the essence of being irreplaceable.[52] The more central these activities are to organizational effectiveness, the more power managers gain from being irreplaceable.

BEING IN A CENTRAL POSITION   Managers in central positions are responsible for activities that are directly connected to an organization's goals and sources of competitive advantage and often are located in central positions in important communication networks in an organization.[53] Managers in key positions have control over crucial organizational activities and initiatives and have access to important information. Other organizational members depend on them for their knowledge, expertise, advice, and support, and the success of the organization as a whole is seen as riding on these managers. These consequences of being in a central position are likely to increase managers' power.

Managers who are outstanding performers, have a wide knowledge base, and have made important and visible contributions to their organizations are likely to be offered central positions that will increase their power.

GENERATING RESOURCES   Organizations need three kinds of resources to be effective: (1) input resources such as raw materials, skilled workers, and financial capital; (2) technical resources such as machinery and computers; and (3) knowledge resources such as marketing, information technology, or engineering expertise. To the extent that a manager can generate one or more of these kinds of resources for an organization, that manager's power is likely to increase.[54] In universities, for example, professors who win large grants to fund their research, from associations such as the National Science Foundation and the Army Research Institute, gain power because of the financial resources they generate for their departments and the university as a whole.

BUILDING ALLIANCES   When managers build alliances, they develop mutually beneficial relationships with people both inside and outside the organization, as does Vimeo's Anjali Sud, profiled in "A Manager's Challenge." The parties to an alliance support one another because doing so is in their best interests, and all parties benefit from the alliance. Alliances give managers power because they provide the managers with support for their initiatives. Partners to alliances provide support because they know the managers will reciprocate when their partners need support. Alliances can help managers achieve their goals and implement needed changes in organizations because they increase managers' levels of power.

Many powerful top managers focus on building alliances not only inside their organizations, but also with individuals, groups, and organizations in the task and general environments on which their organizations depend for resources. These individuals, groups, and organizations enter alliances with managers because doing so is in their best interests and they know they can count on the managers' support when they need it. When managers build alliances, they need to be on their guard to ensure that everything is aboveboard, ethical, and legal.

As illustrated in the accompanying "Focus on Diversity" feature, many powerful top managers such as Indra Nooyi, former CEO of PepsiCo, are particularly skilled when it comes to building alliances.

FOCUS ON DIVERSITY

Building Alliances at PepsiCo and Beyond

By all accounts, Indra Nooyi is a powerful business leader. As CEO and chairman of PepsiCo, she oversees a company with over $63 billion in net revenues and around 263,000 employees; Pepsi-Cola, Lay's, Doritos, Tropicana, Mountain Dew, Gatorade, and Quaker are among Pepsi's many well-known brands.[55] She effectively uses her vision for PepsiCo, "Performance with Purpose," to both motivate and guide Pepsi employees and communicate PepsiCo's stance on important issues such as health, obesity, and protection of the natural environment around the world.[56] In 2017 she was ranked 11th on *Forbes* magazine's list of "The World's 100 Most Powerful Women."[57]

Nooyi, born and raised in India, was senior vice president of strategic planning at PepsiCo before assuming the top post in 2006. When the PepsiCo board of directors was deciding who would be the next CEO of the company, two senior executives at PepsiCo were under consideration, Nooyi and Michael White, vice chairman. When Nooyi found out that the board had chosen her, one of her top priorities was to ensure that White would stay at PepsiCo; the two would maintain the great relationship they had with each other, which had evolved from years of working together; and she would have his support and advice. At the time, White was on vacation at his beach house in Cape Cod, Massachusetts. Nooyi flew to Cape Cod and the two walked on the beach, had ice cream together, and even played a duet (Nooyi and White both are fond of music and in this case, he played the piano and she sang). Prior to leaving Cape Cod, she told White, "Tell me whatever I need to do to keep you, and I will."[58] Ultimately, White decided to remain at PepsiCo as CEO of PepsiCo International as well as vice chairman of PepsiCo. At a meeting announcing Nooyi's appointment, Nooyi told employees, "I treat Mike as my partner. He could easily have been CEO." White said, "I play the piano and Indra sings." Nooyi was named chairman of PepsiCo in 2007. In 2009 White retired from the company.[59]

Nooyi excels at building alliances both inside and outside PepsiCo. Given the breadth of her responsibilities, she decided to increase the team of top managers she works closely with. She has good relations with key decision makers around the world in both government and business.[60] Her philosophy is that leaders of top global companies, like PepsiCo, need to work hard to build and maintain collaborative relationships with the countries they operate in and their governments and other organizations and people that have a stake in their operations, such as customers, communities, suppliers, nongovernmental organizations, and

PepsiCo CEO Indra Nooyi is a strong business leader who knows the importance of forging alliances with both internal and external stakeholders. She recently announced she was stepping down from the top job after more than 12 years.
©PepsiCo Inc./AP Images

shareholders. She adopts a long-term approach to do what it takes to build alliances that will enable PepsiCo to achieve its goals and effectively meet the needs of its stakeholders.[61]

Nooyi also excels at gaining the support of PepsiCo's employees (a very important group of stakeholders at PepsiCo). She is down-to-earth, sincere, and genuine in her interactions with employees and comfortable just being herself; she has been known to walk barefoot in the halls of PepsiCo on occasion and sometimes sings at gatherings. Celebrations for employees' birthdays include a cake. As a mother of two daughters, Nooyi also recognizes how employees' families are affected by their work and what a great source of support families can be.[62]

Nooyi has also built alliances to help protect the natural environment and contribute to sustainability in the communities and countries in which PepsiCo operates. Initiatives to reduce PepsiCo's water consumption, reduce waste, and lower the use of plastic help communities and local governments. Her exceptional skills at building alliances and gaining support helped her lead PepsiCo forward on these and other initiatives.[63] After more than 12 years as company CEO, Nooyi recently stepped down. "Growing up in India, I never imagined I'd have the opportunity to lead such an extraordinary company," she said.[64]

Political Strategies for Exercising Power

Politically skilled managers not only understand, and can use, the five strategies to increase their power; they also appreciate strategies for exercising their power. These strategies generally focus on how managers can use their power *unobtrusively*.[65] When managers exercise power unobtrusively, other members of an organization may not be aware that the managers are using their power to influence them. They may think they support these managers for a variety of reasons: because they believe it is the rational or logical thing to do, because they believe doing so is in their own best interests, or because they believe the position or decision the managers are advocating is legitimate or appropriate.

The unobtrusive use of power may sound devious, but managers typically use this strategy to bring about change and achieve organizational goals. Political strategies for exercising power to gain the support and concurrence of others include relying on objective information, bringing in an outside expert, controlling the agenda, and making everyone a winner (see Figure 17.5).[66]

RELYING ON OBJECTIVE INFORMATION   Managers require the support of others to achieve their goals, implement changes, and overcome opposition. One way for a manager to gain this support and overcome opposition is to rely on objective information that supports the manager's initiatives. Reliance on objective information leads others to support the manager because of the facts; objective information causes others to believe that what the manager is proposing is the proper course of action. By relying on objective information, politically skilled managers unobtrusively exercise their power to influence others.

Take the case of Mary Callahan, vice president of Better Built Cabinets, a small cabinet company in the Southeast. Callahan is extremely influential in the company; practically every new initiative that she proposes to the president and owner of the company is implemented. Why is Callahan able to use her power in the company so effectively? Whenever she has an idea for a new initiative that she thinks the company might pursue, she and her subordinates begin by collecting objective information supporting the initiative. Recently, Callahan decided that Better Built should develop a line of high-priced, European-style kitchen cabinets. Before presenting her proposal to Better Built's president, she compiled objective information showing that (1) there was a strong, unmet demand for these kinds of cabinets, (2) Better Built could manufacture them in its existing production facilities, and (3) the new line had the potential to increase Better Built's sales by 20% while not detracting from sales of the company's other cabinets. Presented with this information, the president agreed to Callahan's proposal. Moreover, the president and other members of Better Built whose cooperation was needed to implement the proposal supported it because they thought it would help Better Built gain a competitive advantage. Using objective information to support her position enabled Callahan to unobtrusively exercise her power and influence others to support her proposal.

Figure 17.5

Political Strategies for Exercising Power

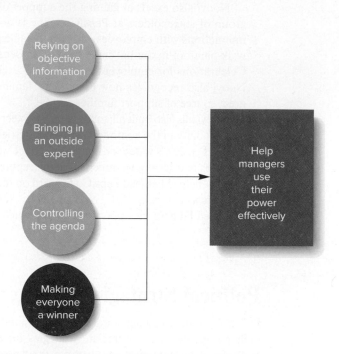

BRINGING IN AN OUTSIDE EXPERT   Bringing in an outside expert to support a proposal or decision can, at times, provide managers with some of the same benefits that the use of objective information does. It lends credibility to a manager's initiatives and causes others to believe that what the manager is proposing is the appropriate or rational thing to do. Suppose Callahan had hired a consultant to evaluate whether her idea was a good one. The consultant reports back to the president that the new European-style cabinets are likely to fulfill Callahan's promises and increase Better Built's sales and profits. As with objective information, this information provided by an objective expert can lend a sense of legitimacy to Callahan's proposal and allow her to unobtrusively exercise power to influence others.

Although you might think consultants and other outside experts are neutral or objective, they sometimes are hired by managers who want them to support a certain position or decision in an organization. For instance, when managers face strong opposition from others who fear that a decision will harm their interests, the managers may bring in an outside expert. They hope this expert will be perceived as a neutral observer to lend credibility and "objectivity" to their point of view. The support of an outside expert may cause others to believe that a decision is indeed the right one. Of course, sometimes consultants and other outside experts actually are brought into organizations to be objective and guide managers on the appropriate course of action.

CONTROLLING THE AGENDA   Managers also can exercise power unobtrusively by controlling the agenda—influencing which alternatives are considered or even whether a decision is made.[67] When managers influence the alternatives that are considered, they can make sure that each considered alternative is acceptable to them and that undesirable alternatives are not in the feasible set. In a hiring context, for example, managers can exert their power unobtrusively by ensuring that job candidates whom they do not find acceptable do not make their way onto the list of finalists for an open position. They do this by making sure that these candidates' drawbacks or deficiencies are communicated to everyone involved in making the hiring decision. When three finalists for an open position are discussed and evaluated in a hiring meeting, a manager may seem to exert little power or influence and just go along with what the rest of the group wants. However, the manager may have exerted power in the hiring process unobtrusively by controlling which candidates have made it to the final stage.

Sometimes managers can prevent a decision from being made. A manager in charge of a community relations committee, for example, may not favor a proposal for the organization to become more involved in local youth groups such as the Boy Scouts and the Girl Scouts. The manager can exert influence in this situation by not including the proposal on the agenda for the committee's next meeting. Alternatively, the manager could place the proposal at the end of the agenda for the meeting and feel confident that the committee will run out of time and not get to the last items on the agenda because that is what always happens. Either approach enables the manager to unobtrusively exercise power. Committee members do not perceive this manager as trying to influence them to turn down the proposal. Rather, the manager has made the proposal into a nonissue that is not even considered.

MAKING EVERYONE A WINNER   Often, politically skilled managers can exercise their power unobtrusively because they make sure that everyone whose support they need benefits personally from providing that support. By making everyone a winner, a manager can influence other organizational members because these members see supporting the manager as being in their best interest.

When top managers turn around troubled companies, some organizational members and parts of the organization are bound to suffer due to restructurings that often entail painful lay-offs. However, the power of the turnaround CEO often accelerates as it becomes clear that the future of the company is on surer footing and the organization and its stakeholders are winners as a result of the change effort.

Making everyone a winner not only is an effective way of exercising power but, when used consistently and forthrightly, also can increase managers' power and influence over time. That is, when a manager actually does make everyone a winner, all stakeholders will see it as in their best interests to support the manager and his or her initiatives.

Summary and Review

LO17-1, 17-2

ORGANIZATIONAL CONFLICT   Organizational conflict is the discord that arises when the goals, interests, or values of different individuals or groups are incompatible and those individuals or groups block or thwart each other's attempts to achieve their objectives. Four types of conflict arising in organizations are interpersonal conflict, intragroup conflict, intergroup conflict, and interorganizational conflict. Sources of conflict in organizations include different goals and time horizons, overlapping authority, task interdependencies, different evaluation or reward systems, scarce resources, and status inconsistencies. Conflict management strategies focused on individuals include increasing awareness of the sources of conflict, increasing diversity awareness and skills, practicing job rotation or temporary assignments, and using permanent transfers or dismissals when necessary. Strategies focused on the whole organization include changing an organization's structure or culture and altering the source of conflict.

LO17-3, 17-4   **NEGOTIATION**   Negotiation is a conflict resolution technique used when parties to a conflict have approximately equal levels of power and try to come up with an acceptable way to allocate resources to each other. In distributive negotiation, the parties perceive that there is a fixed level of resources for them to allocate, and they compete to receive as much as possible at the expense of the other party, not caring about their relationship in the future. In integrative bargaining, both parties perceive that they may be able to increase the resource pie by coming up with a creative solution to the conflict, trusting each other, and cooperating with each other to achieve a win–win resolution. Five strategies that managers can use to facilitate integrative bargaining are to emphasize superordinate goals; focus on the problem, not the people; focus on interests, not demands; create new options for joint gain; and focus on what is fair.

LO17-5   **ORGANIZATIONAL POLITICS**   Organizational politics are the activities that managers (and other members of an organization) engage in to increase their power and to use power effectively to achieve their goals and overcome resistance or opposition. Effective managers realize that politics can be a positive force that enables them to make needed changes in an organization. Five important political strategies for gaining and maintaining power are controlling uncertainty, making oneself irreplaceable, being in a central position, generating resources, and building alliances. Political strategies for effectively exercising power focus on how to use power unobtrusively and include relying on objective information, bringing in an outside expert, controlling the agenda, and making everyone a winner.

Management in Action

Topics for Discussion and Action

Discussion

1. Discuss why too little conflict in an organization can be just as detrimental as too much conflict. [**LO17-1**]

2. Why are compromise and collaboration more effective ways of handling conflict than accommodation, avoidance, and competition? [**LO17-2**]

3. Why should managers promote integrative bargaining rather than distributive negotiation? [**LO17-3**]

4. How can managers promote integrative bargaining? [**LO17-4**]

5. Why do organizational politics affect practically every organization? [**LO17-5**]

6. Why do effective managers need good political skills? [**LO17-5**]

7. What steps can managers take to ensure that organizational politics are a positive force leading to a competitive advantage, not a negative force leading to personal advantage at the expense of organizational goal attainment? [**LO17-5**]

8. Think of a member of an organization whom you know and who is particularly powerful. What political strategies does this person use to increase his or her power? [**LO17-5**]

9. Why is it best to use power unobtrusively? How are people likely to react to power that is exercised obtrusively? [**LO17-5**]

Action

10. Interview a manager in a local organization to determine the kinds of conflicts that occur in his or her organization and the strategies that are used to manage them. [**LO17-1, 17-2**]

Building Management Skills

Effective and Ineffective Conflict Resolution [**LO17-1, 17-2**]

Think about two recent conflicts that you had with other people—one conflict that you felt was effectively resolved (C1) and one that you felt was ineffectively resolved (C2). The other people involved could be coworkers, students, family members, friends, or members of an organization that you are a member of. Answer the following questions:

1. Briefly describe C1 and C2. What type of conflict was involved in each of these incidents?

2. What was the source of the conflict in C1 and in C2?

3. What conflict management strategies were used in C1 and in C2?

4. What could you have done differently to more effectively manage conflict in C2?

5. How was the conflict resolved in C1 and in C2?

Managing Ethically [**LO17-5**]

One political strategy managers can engage in is controlling the agenda by subtly influencing which alternatives are considered or even whether a decision is up for discussion. Some employees believe this can be unethical and can prevent important issues from being raised and points of view from being expressed.

Questions

1. Either individually or in a group, think about the ethical implications of controlling the agenda as a political strategy.

2. What steps can managers and organizations take to ensure that this strategy does not result in important issues and differing points of view being suppressed in an organization?

Small Group Breakout Exercise

Negotiating a Solution [LO17-3, 17-4]

Form groups of three or four people. One member of your group will play the role of Jane Rister, one member will play the role of Michael Schwartz, and one or two members will be observer(s) and spokesperson(s) for your group.

Jane Rister and Michael Schwartz are assistant managers in a large department store. They report directly to the store manager. Today they are meeting to discuss some important problems they need to solve but about which they disagree.

The first problem hinges on the fact that either Rister or Schwartz needs to be on duty whenever the store is open. For the last six months, Rister has taken most of the least desirable hours (nights and weekends). They are planning their schedules for the next six months. Rister thought Schwartz would take more of the undesirable times, but Schwartz has informed Rister that his wife has just gotten a nursing job that requires her to work weekends, so he needs to stay home weekends to take care of their infant daughter.

The second problem concerns a department manager who has had a hard time retaining salespeople in his department. The turnover rate in his department is twice that in the other store departments. Rister thinks the manager is ineffective and wants to fire him. Schwartz thinks the high turnover is just a fluke and the manager is effective.

The last problem concerns Rister's and Schwartz's vacation schedules. Both managers want to take off the week of July 4, but one of them needs to be in the store whenever it is open.

1. The group members playing Rister and Schwartz assume their roles and negotiate a solution to these three problems.

2. Observers take notes on how Rister and Schwartz negotiate solutions to their problems.

3. Observers determine the extent to which Rister and Schwartz use distributive negotiation or integrative bargaining to resolve their conflicts.

4. When called on by the instructor, observers communicate to the rest of the class how Rister and Schwartz resolved their conflicts, whether they used distributive negotiation or integrative bargaining, and their actual solutions.

Be the Manager [LO17-1, 17-2, 17-3, 17-4, 17-5]

You are a middle manager in a large corporation, and lately you have felt that you are caught between a rock and a hard place. Times are tough; your unit has experienced layoffs; your surviving subordinates are overworked and demoralized; and you feel that you have no meaningful rewards, such as the chance for a pay raise, bonus, or promotion, to motivate them with. Your boss keeps increasing the demands on your unit as well as the unit's responsibilities.

Moreover, you believe that you and your subordinates are being unfairly blamed for certain problems beyond your control. You believe that you have the expertise and skills to perform your job effectively and that your subordinates are capable and effective in their jobs. Yet you feel that you are on shaky ground and powerless, given the current state of affairs. What are you going to do?

Bloomberg Case in the News [LO 17-1, 17-2, 17-3]

Buy Now, Pay Later Helps JAB Billionaires Build Beverage Empire

JAB Holding Co., the closely held investment firm that's building a coffee and soft drinks empire, has tapped a simple formula to help it grow: buy now and pay later. Much later.

With Monday's purchase of Dr. Pepper Snapple Group, the investment firm behind the world's No. 2 coffee company has made some

$58 billion of acquisitions in the past six years. One secret to its success concerns its coffee suppliers, who agree to be paid as many as 300 days after selling the beans.

The lengthening payment terms are unprecedented in the commodities industry, where money in many cases still changes hands shortly

after the goods are received. The strategy is squeezing trade houses, from No. 1 Neumann Kaffee Gruppe to Ecom Agroindustrial Corp. and Volcafe Ltd., turning them into bankers supplying credit while leaving JAB cash rich.

"The main purpose of the long payment terms is cash flow," said Jim

Watson, a senior beverages analyst at Rabobank International, a leading financier of the coffee trade. "It just opens up a lot of cash that would be otherwise tied up with suppliers," helping with acquisitions, he said.

JAB has been striking deal after deal since 2012, buying controlling stakes in companies such as Peet's Coffee & Tea, Caribou Coffee, and D.E. Master Blenders 1753, now known as Jacobs Douwe Egberts after a merger with Mondelez International's coffee unit. In 2015, the group acquired Keurig Green Mountain Inc. for almost $14 billion in the coffee industry's biggest-ever deal. Last year, it snapped up U.S. cafe chain Panera for $7.2 billion.

On Monday, Keurig expanded beyond coffee and breakfast foods to pay Dr. Pepper Snapple shareholders $18.7 billion in cash to add some of the biggest soft drink brands.

"Combined, our nationwide distribution system will be unrivaled," Keurig Chief Executive Officer Bob Gamgort said on a call with analysts.

Jacobs Douwe Egberts, or JDE, last year pulled even with Nestle SA in terms of retail coffee volumes, though its sales still lag by value, according to data from London-based consumer research company Euromonitor International Ltd. Some traders estimate all companies acquired by JAB may already be buying more green coffee than the maker of Nespresso.

Alongside its coffee holdings, JAB—run by senior partners Peter Harf, Bart Becht and Olivier Goudet—has invested the fortune of Austria's Reimann family and other investors' funds in a range of consumer-goods companies, including fragrance maker Coty Inc. and Reckitt Benckiser Group Plc.

Four Reimann siblings—Renate Reimann-Haas, Matthias Reimann-Andersen, Stefan Reimann-Andersen and Wolfgang Reimann—each have a net worth of about $4.3 billion, according to the Bloomberg Billionaires Index.

The rapid expansion into coffee has given JAB growing market influence.

Some traders have been asked for up to 300 days of financing, while others provide 260 days, or about three times as long as Nestle typically demands, according to people familiar with the arrangements who asked not to be identified because they fear losing supply contracts. Buyers pay interest on their financed purchases, though rates in Europe remain near historic lows.

Bean Counters

The company doesn't disclose how much coffee it buys, but traders estimate that JDE alone purchases some 720,000 tons annually. While the cost of coffee varies widely with quality and the country of origin, that would amount to about $1.3 billion a year based on the current price of robusta futures. For milder arabica beans, it would total about $2 billion.

JAB had 4.46 billion euros ($5.52 billion) of borrowings and 15.72 billion euros of equity at the end of June, along with 798 million euros of cash, its financial statements show. Moody's Investors Service affirmed JAB's long-term issuer rating of Baa1 after the Dr. Pepper deal, "citing both the sound strategic rationale of the proposed merger and the improvement that this transaction will bring to JAB's portfolio of investments."

As the coffee industry consolidates, following the path of the beer industry, traders are getting squeezed. Only the bigger houses are able to provide such extensive financing and tougher competition will end up leading to a concentration of traders as well, said Michael von Luehrte, secretary general of the Swiss Coffee Trade Association, whose members represent more than half of the bean exports from producing countries.

Brewing Consolidation

"What we have seen on the industry side will replicate itself on the trade side," von Luehrte said. "A lot of companies will have to look at their business models and find out what's the ideal mix between traditional physical

trading, speculative trading and the financing part. But it's clear that the end users, the roasters, they are demanding today many more services that are more banking-related, trade financing-related."

"Our extended payment terms have been in place for many years," said Becht, JDE's chairman. "JDE as buyers have paid for the extra costs that go along with the extended pay periods, so this cannot be used as an argument for the alleged extra pressure some trading houses might now be experiencing."

The longer payment terms do carry risks. Sharply higher interest rates or a sudden spike in futures prices could leave traders with losses or stretch their financing needs as hedging costs go up. While JAB has deep pockets, should its financial standing deteriorate banks could pull or tighten traders' credit lines. And industry consolidation means traders are more exposed to fewer companies.

"The counterpart risk is widely underestimated," von Luehrte said. "We always think one dimensionally. For instance the market is running up and suppliers at origin are defaulting on us. But it can also be the other way around, that suddenly a roaster is having financial problems."

Questions for Discussion

1. Which type(s) of conflict management strategy is/are described in this case?

2. Is JAB's approach to negotiations distributive or integrative? Explain your reasoning.

3. Do you think JAB's approach to negotiating extended payment terms with suppliers will catch on in other industries? Why or why not?

Source: Isis Almeida and Marvin G. Perez, "Buy Now, Pay Later Helps JAB Billionaires Build Beverage Empire," *Bloomberg,* January 30, 2018, https://www.bloomberg.com/news/articles/2018-01-30/buy-now-pay-later-helps-jab-billionaires-build-beverage-empire. Used with permission of Bloomberg L.P. Copyright © 2017. All rights reserved.

Notes

1. A. Cohen, "Anjali Sud: The Vimeo CEO Knows the Customer, Not Content, Is King," *Bloomberg Businessweek,* August 6, 2018, p. 68; R. Feloni and A. Mazarakis, "Vimeo's 34-Year-Old CEO on Why She's Not Worried about YouTube or Netflix, and How She Plans to Bring in $100 Million This Year," *Business Insider,* www.businessinsider.com, April 2, 2018; L. Rose and R. Ford, "Next Gen 2017: Hollywood's Up-and-Coming Execs 35 and Under," *Hollywood Reporter,* www.hollywoodreporter.com, November 8, 2017.

2. Feloni and Mazarakis, "Vimeo's 34-Year-Old CEO"; Rose and Ford, "Next Gen 2017"; L. Gandhi, "How Vimeo CEO Anjali Sud's Star Is Rising High in the Tech World," *Teal Mango,* www.thetealmango.com, April 16, 2018; M. Hahm, "How Anjali Sud Became Vimeo's CEO at 34 Years Old," *Yahoo Finance,* https://finance.yahoo.com, November 9, 2017.

3. Gandhi, "How Vimeo CEO Anjali Sud's Star Is Rising"; Feloni and Anna Mazarakis, "Vimeo's 34-Year-Old CEO."

4. Feloni and Mazarakis, "Vimeo's 34-Year-Old CEO"; Hahm, "How Anjali Sud Became Vimeo's CEO"; T. Spangler, "IAC's Vimeo Appoints Anjali Sud CEO after Yearlong Search," *Variety,* http://variety.com, July 20, 2017.

5. M. Michaels and R. Feloni, "The CEO of Vimeo Landed the Job at 34—and She Learned a Huge Leadership Lesson in Her First 12 Months at the Top," *Business Insider,* www.businessinsider.com, April 26, 2018.

6. Hahm, "How Anjali Sud Became Vimeo's CEO"; C. Wasserman, "Advocate for Yourself at Work with This 3-Step Strategy," *Well and Good,* www.wellandgood.com, January 1, 2018.

7. J.A. Litterer, "Conflict in Organizations: A Reexamination," *Academy of Management Journal* 9 (1966), 178–86; S.M. Schmidt and T.A. Kochan, "Conflict: Towards Conceptual Clarity," *Administrative Science Quarterly* 13 (1972), 359–70; R.H. Miles, *Macro Organizational Behavior* (Santa Monica, CA: Goodyear, 1980).

8. C.K. W. De Dreu and M.J. Gelfand (eds.), *The Psychology of Conflict and Conflict Management in Organizations* (New York: Lawrence Erlbaum Associates, 2008).

9. P. Haapaniemi, "Senior Teams: The Positive Power of Conflict," *Chief Executive,* https://chiefexecutive.net, December 1, 2017; S.P. Robbins, *Managing Organizational Conflict: A Nontraditional Approach* (Englewood Cliffs, NJ: Prentice-Hall, 1974).

10. K.A. Jehn, "A Qualitative Analysis of Conflict Types and Dimensions in Organizational Groups," Cornell University, 1997; K.A. Jehn, "A Multimethod Examination of the Benefits and Detriments of Intragroup Conflict," Cornell University, 1995.

11. L.L. Putnam and M.S. Poole, "Conflict and Negotiation," in F.M. Jablin, L.L. Putnam, K.H. Roberts, and L.W. Porter, eds., *Handbook of Organizational Communication: An Interdisciplinary Perspective* (Newbury Park, CA: Sage, 1987), 549–99.

12. C. Kirkham and J. Jamerson, "A Founder and CEO Spar for Control," *The Wall Street Journal,* April 5, 2016, B1; C. Kirkham, "Pulte at Center of Culture Clash," *The Wall Street Journal,* April 11, 2016, B1; C. Kirkham, "War of Words Heats Up at Pulte," *The Wall Street Journal,* April 12, 2016, B1.

13. C. Dougherty, "William Pulte, Pathbreaking Home Builder, Is Dead at 85," *The New York Times,* www.nytimes.com, March 9, 2018.

14. D. Allison, "Embattled Director James Grosfeld Resigns from PulteGroup," www.bizjournals.com, April 15, 2016.

15. Kirkham and Jamerson, "A Founder and CEO Spar for Control"; Kirkham, "Pulte at Center of Culture Clash"; Kirkham, "War of Words Heats Up at Pulte."

16. P. Gopal, "PulteGroup Names New CEO, Adds Founder's Grandson to Board," *Crain's Detroit Business,* www.crainsdetroit.com, September 9, 2016.

17. L.R. Pondy, "Organizational Conflict: Concepts and Models," *Administrative Science Quarterly* 2 (1967), 296–320; R.E. Walton and J.M. Dutton, "The Management of Interdepartmental Conflict: A Model and Review," *Administrative Science Quarterly* 14 (1969), 62–73.

18. G.R. Jones and J.E. Butler, "Managing Internal Corporate Entrepreneurship: An Agency Theory Perspective," *Journal of Management* 18 (1992), 733–49.

19. T. Petzinger, Jr., "All Happy Businesses Are Alike, but Heirs Bring Unique Conflicts," *The Wall Street Journal,* November 17, 1995, B1.

20. J.A. Wall, Jr., "Conflict and Its Management," *Journal of Management* 21 (1995), 515–58.

21. Walton and Dutton, "The Management of Interdepartmental Conflict."

22. Pondy, "Organizational Conflict."

23. "Restaurant Management Software with Mobile Ordering System," https://possector.com, accessed April 28, 2018.

24. L. Berger, "Five Conflict Management Strategies," *Forbes,* www.forbes.com, June 7, 2017; R.L. Pinkley and G.B. Northcraft, "Conflict Frames of Reference: Implications for Dispute Processes and Outcomes," *Academy of Management Journal* 37(February 1994), 193–206.

25. K.W. Thomas, "Conflict and Negotiation Processes in Organizations," in M.D. Dunnette and L.M. Hough, eds., *Handbook of Industrial and Organizational Psychology,* 2nd ed., vol. 3 (Palo Alto, CA: Consulting Psychologists Press, 1992), 651–717.

26. Thomas, "Conflict and Negotiation Processes in Organizations."

27. M.T.M. Dijkstra, B. Beersma, and A. Evers, "Reducing Conflict-Related Employee Strain: The Benefits of an Internal Locus of Control and a Problem-Solving Conflict Management Strategy," *Work & Stress* 25, no. 2 (2011), 167–84.

28. Pinkley and Northcraft, "Conflict Frames of Reference."

29. K. J. Behfar, "Clash of the Teammates: How the Ideal Team Works Through Conflict," *Darden Ideas to Action,* https://ideas.darden.virginia.edu, accessed May 2, 2018.

30. RHR International, "Our Team: Orla Leonard," https://www.rhrinternational.com, accessed April 30, 2018; O. Leonard, N. Wiita, and C. Milane, "The Best Senior Teams Thrive on Disagreement," *Harvard Business Review,* https://hbr.org, September 18, 2017; https://hbr.org; Haapaniemi, "Senior Teams: The Positive Power of Conflict."

31. Leonard et al., "The Best Senior Teams"; Haapaniemi, "Senior Teams."

32. Leonard et al., "The Best Senior Teams"; RHR International, "Our Team."

33. Haapaniemi, "Senior Teams."

34. M. Isaac, "Uber Founder Travis Kalanick Resigns as C.E.O.," *The New York Times,* www.nytimes.com, June 21, 2017.

35. J. Blackstone, "Uber Accused of Stealing Trade Secrets from Waymo in Groundbreaking Trial," *CBS News,* www.cbsnews.com, February 7, 2018; M. Isaac, "How Uber Deceives the Authorities Worldwide," *The New York Times,* www.nytimes.com, March 3, 2017.

36. S. Kolhatkar, "At Uber, a New C.E.O. Shifts Gears," *The New Yorker,* www.newyorker.com, April 9, 2018; M. Isaac, "Uber Sees

an Executive Exodus as It Faces Questions of Workplace Culture," *The New York Times,* www.nytimes.com, April 12, 2017.

37. P.R. Lawrence, L.B. Barnes, and J.W. Lorsch, *Organizational Behavior and Administration* (Homewood, IL: Irwin,1976).

38. L.K. Stroh, G.B. Northcraft, and M.A. Neale, *Organizational Behavior,* 3rd ed. (Mahwah, NJ: Lawrence Erlbaum Associates, 2002).

39. C. Bendersky, "Organizational Dispute Resolution Systems: A Complementarities Model," *Academy of Management Review* 28 (October 2003), 643–57.

40. "Using Arbitration to Resolve Legal Disputes," https://adr.findlaw.com, accessed May 1, 2018.

41. R.J. Lewicki, S.E. Weiss, and D. Lewin, "Models of Conflict, Negotiation, and Third Party Intervention: A Review and Synthesis," *Journal of Organizational Behavior* 13 (1992), 209–52.

42. Stroh et al., *Organizational Behavior.*

43. Ibid.; Lewicki et al., "Models of Conflict, Negotiation, and Third Party Intervention."

44. "Expanding the Pie—Integrative versus Distributive Bargaining Negotiation Strategies," *Harvard Law School Daily Blog,* www.pon.harvard.edu, accessed May 1, 2018.

45. P.J. Carnevale and D.G. Pruitt, "Negotiation and Mediation," *Annual Review of Psychology* 43 (1992), 531–82.

46. S. Olson, "How to Negotiate a Job Offer," Prudential Financial, www.prudential.com, January 31, 2018; Don Jacobson, "How to Negotiate Once You've Been Offered the Job," *Minneapolis Star Tribune,* www.startribune.com, January 2, 2018; S. Snider, "How to Negotiate Your Salary—and Succeed," *U.S. News and World Report,* https://money.usnews.com, October 4, 2017; R. Apple, "How to Evaluate and Negotiate a Job Offer," APICS, white paper, 2014, www.apics.org.

47. Olson, "How to Negotiate a Job Offer"; Snider, "How to Negotiate Your Salary"; Apple, "How to Evaluate and Negotiate."

48. Olson, "How to Negotiate a Job Offer"; Jacobson, "How to Negotiate"; Apple, "How to Evaluate and Negotiate."

49. M. Jarrett, "The 4 Types of Organizational Politics," *Harvard Business Review,* https://hbr.org, April 24, 2017.

50. D.J. Hickson, C.R. Hinings, C.A. Lee, R.E. Schneck, and D.J. Pennings, "A Strategic Contingencies Theory of Intraorganizational Power," *Administrative Science Quarterly* 16 (1971), 216–27; C.R. Hinings, D.J. Hickson, J.M. Pennings, and R.E. Schneck, "Structural Conditions of Interorganizational Power," *Administrative Science Quarterly* 19 (1974), 22–44; J. Pfeffer, *Power in Organizations* (Boston: Pitman, 1981).

51. Pfeffer, *Power in Organizations.*

52. J. Richman, "How to Make Yourself Irreplaceable," *Fast Company,* www.fastcompany.com, accessed May 1, 2018.

53. M. Crozier, "Sources of Power of Lower Level Participants in Complex Organizations," *Administrative Science Quarterly* 7 (1962), 349–64; A.M. Pettigrew, "Information Control as a Power Resource," *Sociology* 6 (1972), 187–204.

54. Pfeffer, *Power in Organizations;* G.R. Salancik and J. Pfeffer, "The Bases and Uses of Power in Organizational Decision Making," *Administrative Science Quarterly* 19 (1974), 453–73; J. Pfeffer and G.R. Salancik, *The External Control of Organizations: A Resource Dependence View* (New York: Harper & Row, 1978).

55. "PepsiCo Reports Fourth Quarter and Full-Year 2017 Results," www.pepsico.com, accessed May 2, 2018; "PepsiCo 2017 Annual Report," www.pepsico.com, accessed May 2, 2018.

56. "Performance with Purpose," www.pepsico.com, accessed May 2, 2018.

57. "The World's 100 Most Powerful Women: #11 Indra Nooyi," www.forbes.com, accessed May 2, 2018.

58. B. Morris, "The Pepsi Challenge," *Fortune,* http://archive.fortune.com, accessed May 2, 2018.

59. "PepsiCo Announces Upcoming Retirement of Michael White, Vice Chairman and PepsiCo International CEO," www.pepsico.com, September 19, 2009.

60. R. Safian, "How PepsiCo CEO Indra Nooyi Is Steering the Company Toward a Purpose-Driven Future," *Fast Company,* www.fastcompany.com, accessed May 2, 2018.

61. Ibid.

62. M. Ward, "Why Pepsico CEO Indra Nooyi Writes Letters to Her Employees' Parents," *CNBC,* www.cnbc.com, February 1, 2017; Morris, "The Pepsi Challenge."

63. Safian, "How PepsiCo CEO Indra Nooyi Is Steering the Company Toward a Purpose-Driven Future."

64. C. Isidore, "PepsiCo CEO Indra Nooyi Is Stepping Down," *CNN Money,* https://money.cnn.com, August 6, 2018.

65. Pfeffer, *Power in Organizations.*

66. Ibid.

67. Ibid.

CHAPTER 18

Using Advanced Information Technology to Increase Performance

©Sam Edwards/age fotostock

Learning Objectives

After studying this chapter, you should be able to:

LO18-1 Differentiate between data and information, and explain how the attributes of useful information allow managers to make better decisions.

LO18-2 Describe three reasons managers must have access to information to perform their tasks and roles effectively.

LO18-3 Describe the hardware and software innovations that created the IT revolution and changed the way managers behave.

LO18-4 Compare six performance-enhancing kinds of management information systems.

LO18-5 Explain how IT is helping managers build strategic alliances and network structures to increase efficiency and effectiveness.

With Butterfly, Software Becomes an Ever-Present Coach

How can information technology enable managers to get better results? Imagine, for example, the challenges a fast-growing company faces in managing employees. When the company is small, a few people handle their areas of expertise independently. As it grows, those people need help, individual projects become group projects, and someone familiar with the work becomes the manager. The demand for operating on a larger scale often outstrips the new manager's ability to pick up the people skills necessary for leadership, motivation, and control. The organization then wants to develop its managers, but doing so takes time, and training efforts can be difficult to target to the specific needs of a leader at a particular time.[1]

Information technology offers solutions, including software that applies *artificial intelligence*—typically software that has "learned," through massive amounts of trial and error, to analyze situations and propose responses that are associated with good outcomes. The more data the software processes, the better its recommendations become. An example is Butterfly, software that gathers anonymous data from an organization's instant-messaging system and analyzes the data to identify situations calling for more active leadership. The three partners who founded Butterfly were inspired with their own difficulties in learning to lead their teams in prior jobs.[2]

Butterfly's creators describe their product as a management coaching system; the feedback from employees becomes the basis for defining the areas in which a manager needs to improve his or her leadership.[3] This analysis, in turn, becomes the basis of recommendations for improvement. The system also can be set up to deliver alerts when managers need additional support. Because the software uses artificial intelligence to improve its results based on experience, it is designed to increase in value as the company signs on more clients. In its early years, Butterfly has signed up notable clients including Citibank, Coca-Cola, and Ticketmaster. And the frequency of feedback—daily or weekly one-question surveys—also contributes to the pool of data. Cofounder Simon Rakosi says companies using Butterfly have measured increased productivity, decreased absenteeism, and higher levels of employee engagement.[4]

Managers are using Butterfly at Social.Lab, a social-media marketing agency that is part of the advertising giant Ogilvy, where the software is part of the company's instant messaging system. The agency had been growing fast, and management was concerned about keeping

Technology continues to change the way managers do their jobs. Using artificial intelligence, Butterfly software gathers feedback for managers to utilize to bring about positive changes in productivity and employee engagement.
©jirsak/Shutterstock

employees engaged. Butterfly provided a way for managers to gather feedback easily without days of leadership training. Butterfly recommends a question to ask each time—say, asking employees to rate their level of stress. It analyzes the responses and then sends a report to managers, including customized tips and recommendations of articles to read about how to improve.

Benjamin Snyers, who leads the North American operations of Social.Lab, says Butterfly has helped him identify problems and forced him to be "honest about the mood of the company." For example, at one point, he learned that his team was feeling particularly stressed. Snyers learned to express his appreciation and motivate them by reinforcing the importance of their contributions.[5]

Overview

In a world in which business activities of all kinds are increasingly conducted through the Internet, the challenge facing managers is to continually update and improve their use of advancing IT to increase organizational performance. Managers must utilize the most effective IT solutions such as cloud computing and artificial intelligence (AI) to assist their employees and customers, or risk being surpassed by more effective rivals who have developed superior IT competencies. Google and Apple are two of the most valuable companies in the world because they provide advanced IT solutions that increase people's ability to access, search, and use the potential of the web and communicate with others. The most successful brick-and-mortar and online companies, such as Walmart, Best Buy, and Amazon, excel in developing improved company-specific IT solutions. The implication is clear: There are enormous opportunities for managers of all kinds of organizations to find new ways to employ IT to use organizational resources more efficiently and effectively.

In this chapter we begin by looking at the relationship between information and the manager's job and then examine the ongoing IT revolution. Next we examine the impact of rapidly evolving IT on managers' jobs and on an organization's competitive advantage. Then we discuss six types of management information systems, each of which is based on a different sort of IT, which can help managers perform their jobs more efficiently and effectively. By the end of this chapter, you will understand how new developments in IT are profoundly shaping managers' tasks and roles and the way organizations operate.

Information and the Manager's Job

Managers cannot plan, organize, lead, and control effectively unless they have access to information. Information is the source of the knowledge and intelligence they need to make the right decisions. Information, however, is not the same as data.[6] **Data** are raw, unsummarized, and unanalyzed facts such as volume of sales, level of costs, or number of customers. **Information** is data that are organized in a meaningful fashion, such as in a graph showing the changes in sales volume or costs over time. Data alone do not tell managers anything; information, in contrast, can communicate a great deal of useful knowledge to the person who receives it—such as a manager who sees sales falling or costs rising. The distinction between data and information is important because one purpose of IT is to help managers transform data into information to make better managerial decisions.

To further clarify the difference between data and information, consider a supermarket manager who must decide how much shelf space to allocate to two breakfast cereal brands: Dentist's Delight and Sugar Supreme. Most supermarkets use checkout scanners to record individual sales and store the data in an online program. Accessing this program, the manager might find that Dentist's Delight sells 50 boxes per day and Sugar Supreme sells 25 boxes per day. These raw data, however, are of little value in helping the manager decide how to allocate shelf space. The manager also needs to know how much shelf space each cereal currently occupies and how much profit each cereal generates for the supermarket.

data Raw, unsummarized, and unanalyzed facts.

information Data that are organized in a meaningful fashion.

LO18-1 Differentiate between data and information, and explain how the attributes of useful information allow managers to make better decisions.

Suppose the manager discovers that Dentist's Delight occupies 10 feet of shelf space and Sugar Supreme occupies 4 feet and that Dentist's Delight generates 20 cents of profit a box, while Sugar Supreme generates 40 cents of profit a box. By putting these three bits of data together (number of boxes sold, amount of shelf space, and profit per box), the manager gets some useful information on which to base a decision: Dentist's Delight generates $1 of profit per foot of shelf space per day [(50 boxes × $.20)/10 feet], and Sugar Supreme generates $2.50 of profit per foot of shelf space per day [(25 boxes × $.40)/4 feet]. Armed with this information, the manager might decide to allocate less shelf space to Dentist's Delight and more to Sugar Supreme.

Attributes of Useful Information

Four factors determine the usefulness of information to a manager: quality, timeliness, completeness, and relevance (see Figure 18.1).

QUALITY Accuracy and reliability determine the quality of information.[7] The greater its accuracy and reliability, the higher is the quality of information. Technology gives managers access to high-quality, real-time information that they can use to improve long-term decision making and alter short-term operating decisions, such as how much of a particular product to make daily or monthly. Supermarket managers, for example, use handheld bar code readers that are wireless (using Bluetooth technology) or are linked to a server to monitor and record how demand for particular products such as milk, chicken, or bread changes daily so they know how to restock their shelves to ensure the products are always available.

TIMELINESS Information that is timely is available when it is required to allow managers to make the optimal decision—not after the decision has been made. In today's rapidly changing world, the need for timely information often means information must be available on a real-time basis—hence the enormous growth in the demand for mobile devices.[8] **Real-time information** is information that reflects current changes in business conditions. In an industry that experiences rapid changes, real-time information may need to be updated frequently.

real-time information
Frequently updated information that reflects current conditions.

Local transportation systems (buses, subway trains, commuter rail) use real-time information to help commuters track when they can expect their next transit ride. For example, the Transit app (available for Android and iOS devices) helps simplify daily commutes for people in 164 cities in over 12 countries around the world, including the United States, Australia, Iceland, Canada, France, Germany, and the UK. The app updates arrival times of public transportation in your area (thanks to the locations setting/geo-tracking feature of your mobile device), monitors your walking speed, and tells you whether you're going to get to

Figure 18.1
Factors Affecting the Usefulness of Information

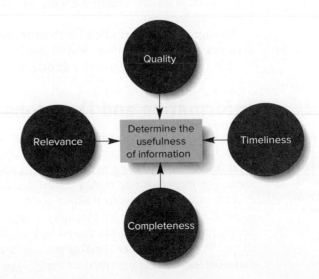

your ride on time. In addition, the app will suggest changing your transit connections based on detours or transportation delays to help you get to your destination on time. And it can even wake you up on your ride before you get to where you're going if you take a quick nap on your journey.[9]

COMPLETENESS   Information that is complete gives managers all the information they need to exercise control, achieve coordination, or make an effective decision. Recall from Chapter 7, however, that managers rarely have access to complete information. Instead, because of uncertainty, ambiguity, and bounded rationality, they have to make do with incomplete information.[10] One function of IT is to increase the completeness of managers' information.

RELEVANCE   Information that is relevant is useful and suits a manager's particular needs and circumstances. Irrelevant information is useless and may actually hurt the performance of a busy manager who has to spend valuable time determining whether information is relevant. Given the massive amounts of information that managers are now exposed to and their limited information-processing capabilities, a company's information systems designers need to ensure that managers receive only relevant information.

What Is Information Technology?

information technology (IT) The set of methods or techniques for acquiring, organizing, storing, manipulating, and transmitting information.

management information system (MIS) A specific form of IT that managers utilize to generate the specific, detailed information they need to perform their roles effectively.

Information technology (IT) is the set of methods or techniques for acquiring, organizing, storing, manipulating, and transmitting information.[11] A **management information system (MIS)** is a specific form of IT that managers select and use to generate the specific, detailed information they need to perform their roles effectively. Management information systems have existed for as long as there have been organizations, which is a long time indeed—merchants in ancient Egypt used clay tablets to record their transactions. Before the computing age, most systems were paper-based: Clerks recorded important information on paper documents (often in duplicate or triplicate) in words and numbers; sent copies of the documents to superiors, customers, or suppliers; and stored other copies in filing cabinets for future reference.

Rapid advances in the power of IT—specifically, the development of ever more powerful and sophisticated hardware and software—have had a fundamental impact on organizations and managers, as suggested by the discussion of artificial intelligence in "A Manager's Challenge." Some IT developments, such as inventory management and customer relationship management (CRM) systems, contribute so much to performance that organizations that do *not* adopt them, or that adopt them ineffectively, become less competitive compared with organizations that do adopt them.[12] IT predictions for the near future include increased use of blockchain technology, advances in AI and machine learning (including the use of chatbots), and more emphasis on data governance, including ongoing privacy challenges.[13] See the "Management Insight" feature for more on blockchain technology and its potential impact on business operations.

Managers need information for three reasons: to make effective decisions, to control the activities of the organization, and to coordinate the activities of the organization. Next we examine these uses of information in detail.

Information and Decisions

LO18-2 Describe three reasons managers must have access to information to perform their tasks and roles effectively.

Much of management (planning, organizing, leading, and controlling) is about making decisions. For example, the marketing manager must decide what price to charge for a product, what distribution channels to use, and what promotional messages to emphasize to maximize sales. The manufacturing manager must decide how much of a product to make and how to make it so that the company makes a profit. The purchasing manager must decide from whom to purchase inputs and what inventory of inputs to hold. The human relations manager must decide how much employees should be paid, how they should be trained, what benefits they should be given, and when it makes sense to hire more workers. The engineering manager must make decisions about new product design. Top managers must decide how to allocate scarce

Blockchain: More than Bitcoin Transactions

You've probably heard the term *Bitcoin,* the digital currency developed over the last decade as a "peer-to-peer electronic cash system," which can be used to buy a variety of goods and services. Bitcoin differs from U.S. currency because this peer-to-peer technology has no central authority (namely, the U.S. Treasury) to issue new money or track transactions. Blockchain is the technology that runs this payment system and records important information in an electronic "public ledger," or database, spread across multiple computers around the world.[14]

Bitcoins are created by the network as a reward for the "mining" process, a mathematic computation in which transactions are verified within the public ledger. Although this process is complicated, the goal is to discover these mathematical solutions so that a new "block" on the chain can be created. Once these blocks are verified, they cannot be removed or altered in the public ledger.[15] In addition, these transactions between two parties do not need third-party authentication and are transparent and time stamped, which enables everyone who accesses the chain to have the same information.[16]

Several years after Bitcoin and blockchain began generating buzz, people started to understand how this technology could be more than just a ledger for virtual currency. Blockchain provides an efficient way to record and track transactions, which could dramatically reduce business costs. In addition, some business professionals believe this technology could potentially have a positive impact on various business sectors, including supply chains, insurance, transportation, and contract management, for starters. Recent estimates suggest, for example, that close to 15% of financial institutions already use the technology as a replacement for paper-based and manual transaction processing.[17]

Blockchain technology could also improve business operations in several ways. Using blockchain could drastically reduce a company's environmental footprint because the electronic ledger would eliminate the need for a paper trail—contracts could be digitized and tracked electronically. In addition, the digitized documents would take less time to manage, freeing up managers and employees to focus their efforts on other tasks. Second, as we discuss in the next section of the chapter, devices controlled by the Internet of Things (IoT) are vulnerable to data leaks, which could be avoided by integrating the security of blockchain in these devices. Not only would this strategy provide additional levels of security, it would also provide a permanent record of the data generated by these devices. It is also likely this increased defense against data leaks could accelerate the adoption of more smart home technology and spur growth in the IoT industry. In addition, blockchain could allow for real-time payments, which would speed up and streamline overall operations including financial management.[18]

The future of digital currency may still be uncertain; however, the blockchain technology that forms the foundation of the digital payment system continues to evolve into an effective and efficient process that may give companies a competitive advantage in this electronic world.

---

financial resources among competing projects, how best to structure and control the organization, and what business-level strategy the organization should be pursuing. And regardless of their functional orientation, all managers have to make decisions about matters such as what performance evaluation to give to a subordinate.

To make effective decisions, managers need information both from inside the organization and from external stakeholders. When deciding how to price a product, for example, marketing

Although technology has changed the way key data are shared with managers, the information is still critical to making informed decisions.
©Image Source Trading Ltd/Shutterstock

managers need information about how consumers will react to different prices. They need information about unit costs because they do not want to set the price below the cost of production. And they need information about competitive strategy because pricing strategy should be consistent with an organization's competitive strategy. Some of this information will come from outside the organization (for example, from gathering consumer data) and some from inside the organization (information about production costs comes from manufacturing). As this example suggests, managers' ability to make effective decisions rests on their ability to acquire and process information.

BIG DATA   The collection and analysis of large sets of data from consumers, competitors, employees, suppliers, and others has become a global industry, with the big data sector expected to top the $40 billion mark in the coming year.[19] *Analytics* is the process of examining all these data to uncover hidden patterns, unknown correlations, market trends, customer preferences, and the like which can help managers make decisions that will advance the organization's business.[20] Analyzing data is no longer done by reviewing a spreadsheet and manually highlighting key bits of information. Instead, powerful software can provide real-time information that assists managers at all levels of an organization in making faster, more effective decisions to help develop new products and services, while reducing costs.[21]

Information and Control

As discussed in Chapter 11, controlling is the process through which managers regulate how efficiently and effectively an organization and its members perform the activities necessary to achieve its stated goals.[22] Managers achieve control over organizational activities by taking four steps (see Figure 11.2): (1) They establish measurable standards of performance or goals, (2) they measure actual performance, (3) they compare actual performance against established goals, and (4) they evaluate the results and take corrective action if necessary.[23] The package delivery company UPS, for example, has a delivery goal: to deliver 99% of the overnight packages it picks up by noon the next day.[24] UPS has thousands of U.S. ground stations (branch offices that coordinate the pickup and delivery of packages in a particular area) that are responsible for the physical pickup and delivery of packages. UPS managers monitor the delivery performance of these stations regularly; if they find that the 99% goal is not being attained, they determine why and take corrective action if necessary.

To achieve control over any organizational activity, managers must have information. To control ground station activities, a UPS manager might need to know what percentage of packages each station delivers by noon. To obtain this information, the manager uses UPS's own information systems; UPS is also a leader in developing proprietary in-house IT. All packages to be shipped to the stations have been scanned with wireless scanners by the UPS drivers who pick them up; then all this information is sent through UPS servers to its headquarters' mainframe computer. When the packages are scanned again at delivery, this information is also transmitted through its computer network. Managers can access this information to quickly discover what percentage of packages were delivered by noon of the day after they were picked up, as well as how this information breaks down station by station so they can take corrective action if necessary.

Management information systems are used to control all divisional and functional operations. In accounting, for example, information systems are used to monitor expenditures and compare them against budgets. To track expenditures against budgets, managers need information about current expenditures, broken down by relevant organizational units; accounting IT is designed to give managers this information. A twist on using IT to improve customer service is being used by several companies, including Disney World and Carnival cruise lines. Disney issues wristbands (called MagicBands) to visitors that work as hotel room keys, parking passes, and charge cards. The data collected when visitors tap the MagicBands throughout the theme park and resorts will help Disney zero in on guest preferences and provide better customer service.[25] Taking the wristband one step further, Carnival Corp. recently introduced Ocean Medallions, quarter-size, waterproof medallions that are encrypted and communicate with thousands of sensors on board and in port to enhance guests' travel experiences. Crew members on Carnival's Princess cruise line are able to access information about guests, family members can use the medallions to track each other, and touch screens throughout the ship will display recommended entertainment or dining options based on guests' information and their interests and activities.[26]

CYBERSECURITY   Technology continues to evolve at a rapid pace. Although the results of such innovations have changed both business and daily life, these changes are not without challenges, particularly when it comes to controlling the information. With advanced IT comes the need for *cybersecurity* to keep all of this information safe and protected against unauthorized use.[27]

In a recent survey conducted by *Security* magazine, 50% of the companies reported their information systems were attacked by hackers using malware to encrypt data, systems, and networks, essentially holding the information hostage until a ransom was paid. In the same survey, more than one-quarter of the companies see cyberattacks and ransom as their biggest threat in the near future.[28]

Another form of cybercrime has become commonplace as businesses collect large amounts of data from individuals. Over the past few years, data breaches have occurred in which information about millions of consumers has been stolen by cyber thieves who figured out how to infiltrate companies, so-called secure information systems. For example, in 2017 Equifax, one of three national credit-reporting companies' suffered one of the biggest data breaches in history: Information for more than 147 million U.S. consumers (nearly half the country's population) was stolen.[29] Findings from a Senate investigation into the data breach revealed (1) Equifax's cybersecurity measures were weak; (2) the company ignored numerous warnings of risk to sensitive data, including a specific warning from the Department of Homeland Security about vulnerability in its systems; (3) the company failed to notify consumers, investors, and regulators in a timely manner about the massive breach; and (4) company assistance and information to affected consumers was inadequate. Recommendations from a Senate investigation include giving the Federal Trade Commission (FTC) supervisory authority to monitor credit-reporting agencies going forward.[30]

Small businesses, in particular, are vulnerable to cyberattacks because they typically do not employ a cybersecurity staff to monitor and protect company data and other vital information. According to the Information Security Forum, as real-time data collection via devices controlled by the Internet of Things (IoT) continues to play an important role in business operations, data leaks from industrial equipment and other digital products such as web cameras, alarm systems, and HVAC systems are easy targets for hackers.[31] The IoT is a network of devices, vehicles, home appliances, and other products embedded with electronics, sensors, and connectivity, which allow these "things" to collect and share data via the Internet.[32]

DATA PRIVACY   Another aspect of controlling information within an organization concerns keeping data private and secure. While many companies are taking steps to make sure security measures outside the company's internal systems are solid, some firms do not use the same aggressive approach to keep their internal networks safe. Once a hacker infiltrates a company's internal networks, it may be difficult for the cyber thief to be detected.[33] In addition, some well-known tech companies seem to be in the news lately for security lapses when it comes to protecting consumers' private data. The "Ethics in Action" feature discusses how Facebook allowed personal data to be mishandled by outside consultants, which caused a serious backlash from users.

Cybersecurity has become a top priority for companies and managers trying to keep business and personal information safe. Credit-reporting firm Equifax found this out the hard way when its information system was breached by cyber thieves who stole the personal data of more than 147 million U.S. consumers.
©Piotr Swat/Shutterstock

Users "Unlike" Facebook over Privacy Issues

Facebook CEO Mark Zuckerberg faced tough questioning when he testified before Congress about how personal data from more than 87 million Facebook users was accessed improperly by Cambridge Analytica.

©Anadolu Agency/Getty Images

More than 200 million people in the United States are regular users of Facebook, the social networking platform created by Mark Zuckerberg and his Harvard classmates back in 2004. Today Facebook has more than 1.8 billion monthly users around the globe who connect with friends and family, share personal stories and photographs, and follow selected national and international news feeds. Being active on Facebook has become a daily if not hourly routine for many people, most of whom assumed that their personal information was secure on the popular social platform.[34]

As a result of ongoing investigations into whether Russia interfered in the 2016 U.S. presidential campaign, Facebook became more than just a connection point for millions of users recently. News reports by *The New York Times, The Intercept,* and *The London Observer,* among others, revealed that over the last several years Facebook allowed a political data and voter-profiling firm, Cambridge Analytica, which was associated with the Trump presidential campaign, to harvest data from nearly 87 million users—without their knowledge.[35] According to reports, more than 300,000 Facebook users downloaded an app that allowed Cambridge Analytica to use their personal information (as well as data from their Facebook friends) to create personality profiles for each user and then embed targeted ads and fake news stories based on personality types within their individual Facebook newsfeeds.[36] Some political observers suggest these ads and fake news influenced voters' decisions in the 2016 election.

After the news broke, Facebook stock price dropped nearly 20%, and CEO Zuckerberg was summoned to testify before Congress to explain the situation and resulting privacy issues. Zuckerberg apologized for the disinformation that appeared on Facebook, at one point saying that the company didn't do enough to keep users' data safe.[37] As a result of the data breach, many Facebook users quit the social media platform.[38] In response to the scandal, Facebook issued a link that appeared at the top of some users' newsfeeds to let them know they were among the members whose data was improperly harvested by Cambridge Analytica. But what about other Facebook users? Experts say all Facebook users should regularly check the social network's privacy settings to see which apps and websites have permission to access their Facebook data. In the meantime, Cambridge Analytica announced it was shutting down its business and filing for bankruptcy.[39]

Information and Coordination

Coordinating department and divisional activities to achieve organizational goals is another basic task of management. As an example of the size of the coordination task that managers face, consider the coordination effort necessary to prepare between 500,000 and 1 million meals for the people who visit Disney parks and resorts every day. Combine that type of volume with Disney's efforts to get food locally, and logistics get complicated fast. According to Lenny DeGeorge, executive chef for culinary development at Walt Disney Parks & Resorts, the supply chain at the Disney parks and resorts worldwide—all 1,040 of them—depends on the location of the resort and what local growers and producers can provide. In Florida, for example, the company works with "Fresh from Florida" to find out what fruits and vegetables are in season and available. In Southern California, Disney works with local growers who provide organic produce for food operations at Disneyland. DeGeorge and his Disney culinary colleagues create their magic in the Flavor Lab, a top secret Orlando facility where they devise, create, and execute every new food and beverage concept for Disney properties around the world.[40]

Starbucks has a program called "Origin Experience" that allows its employees to get involved in the logistics of the supply chain. This experience allows associates to travel overseas and meet Starbucks partners where the coffee beans are grown. The trips provide associates with a new perspective on the supply chain and the coffee that ends up in their stores.

The supply chain at Starbucks runs from the field where the coffee beans are grown to the cup of coffee poured by a friendly barista at a local shop. The supply chain spans 19 countries. From the field, the beans travel to one of six roasting centers, where they are prepared and then shipped to one of 48 regional distribution centers and then on to their final destination. The distribution centers make roughly 70,000 deliveries each week.[41]

For their recent Origin Experience, 35 Starbucks partners from Europe, Africa, and the Middle East flew to Rwanda to become immersed in the coffee industry in this Eastern African nation. The partners visited farms, toured support centers where farmers learn about sustainability, helped plant coffee trees, experienced how the beans are processed, and met the people who work in the fields—picking and drying the beans by hand.[42]

These visits help Starbucks employees learn about the supply chain and how to make it run more smoothly. The visits provide employees at the end of the supply chain with information about how things work at the beginning. The coffee giant recently announced a pilot program with select coffee growers in Costa Rica, Colombia, and Rwanda to develop advanced data technology to share real-time information about the status of coffee bean shipments from the field to Starbucks distribution centers around the world. According to the company, digital communications seem to be everywhere, even within small family farms in faraway places due to the availability of mobile phones.[43]

The IT Revolution

Advances in IT have enabled managers to make gigantic leaps in the way they can collect more timely, complete, relevant, and high-quality information and use it in more effective ways. To better understand the ongoing revolution in IT that has transformed companies, allowing them to improve their responsiveness to customers, minimize costs, and improve their competitive position, we need to examine several key aspects of advanced IT.

LO18-3 Describe the hardware and software innovations that created the IT revolution and changed the way managers behave.

The Effects of Advancing IT

The IT revolution began with the development of the first computers—the hardware of IT—in the 1950s. The language of computers is a digital language of zeros and ones. Words, numbers, images, and sound can all be expressed in zeros and ones. Each letter in the alphabet has its own unique code of zeros and ones, as does each number, each color, and each sound. For example, the digital code for the number 20 is 10100. In the language of computers, it takes a lot of zeros and ones to express even a simple sentence, to say nothing of complex color graphics or moving video images. Nevertheless, modern computers can read, process, and store trillions of instructions per second (an *instruction* is a line of software code) and, thus, vast amounts of zeros and ones. This awesome number-crunching power forms the foundation of the ongoing IT revolution.

The products and services that result from advancing IT are all around us—ever more powerful microprocessors and PCs, high-bandwidth smartphones, sophisticated word-processing software, ever-expanding computer networks, and more and more useful online information and retailing services that did not exist a generation ago. These products are commonplace and are being continuously improved. Many managers and companies that helped develop the new IT have reaped enormous gains.

However, while many companies have benefited from advancing IT, others have been threatened. Traditional landline telephone companies have seen their market dominance threatened by new companies offering Internet, broadband, and wireless technology. They have been forced to respond by buying wireless cell phone companies, building their own high-powered broadband networks, and forming alliances with companies such as Apple and Samsung to make smartphones that will work on their networks. So advancing IT is both an opportunity and a threat, and managers have to move quickly to protect their companies and maintain their competitive advantage.

On one hand, IT helps create new product opportunities that managers and their organizations can take advantage of—such as online travel and vacation booking. On the other hand, IT creates new and improved products that reduce or destroy demand for older, established products—such as the services provided by brick-and-mortar travel agents. Walmart, by developing its own sophisticated proprietary IT, has been able to reduce retailing costs so much that it has put hundreds of thousands of small and medium-size stores out of business. Similarly, thousands of small, specialized U.S. bookstores have closed in the past decade as a result of advances in IT that made online bookselling possible.

IT and the Product Life Cycle

product life cycle The way demand for a product changes in a predictable pattern over time.

When IT is advancing, organizational survival requires that managers quickly adopt and apply it. One reason for this is how IT affects the length of the **product life cycle**, which is the way demand for a product changes in a predictable pattern over time.[44] In general, the product life cycle consists of four stages: the introduction, growth, maturity, and decline stages (see Figure 18.2). In the introduction stage, a product has yet to gain widespread acceptance; customers are unsure what a product, such as a new smartphone, has to offer, and demand for it is minimal.

As a product, like Apple's iPad, becomes accepted by customers (although many products do not, like BlackBerry's tablet), demand takes off and the product enters its growth stage. In the growth stage many consumers are entering the market and buying the product for the first time, and demand increases rapidly. This is the stage iPhones and iPads passed through with great success. Of course, the future success of these products will depend on the

Figure 18.2
A Product Life Cycle

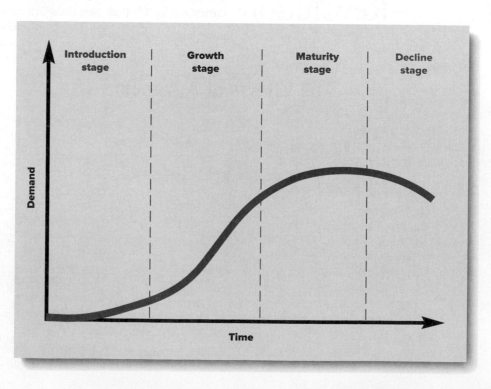

value customers see in the array of apps the products offer—and how quickly competitors such as Samsung and Google move to offer similar and less expensive tablets and smartphones.

The growth stage ends and the maturity stage begins when market demand peaks because most customers have already bought the product (there are relatively few first-time buyers left). At this stage, demand is typically replacement demand. Once demand for a product starts to fall, the decline stage begins. This typically occurs when advancing technology leads to the development of a more advanced product, making the old one obsolete. For example, Apple's iPod music player went into decline when the company developed the iPhone, which could also play music. In 2015 the company introduced the Apple Watch, and its fourth version was released in late 2018. The watch seems to be solidly in the growth stage with a 50% market share for digital watches. Recent sales data indicate Apple shipped more watches in the last quarter of 2017 than the entire Swiss watch industry.[45]

In general, demand for every generation of a digital device such as a smartphone or tablet falls off when the current leaders' technology is superseded by new products that incorporate the most recent IT advances. One reason the IT revolution has been so important for managers is that advances in IT are one of the most significant determinants of the length of a product's life cycle and, therefore, of competition in an industry.[46] One new product still in the introduction phase that has created intense competition among several tech leaders is the digital personal assistant, as described in the following "Management Insight" feature.

MANAGEMENT INSIGHT

Amazon's Alexa Goes to Work

The technology revolution continues to change the way we live and do business—and innovation never seems to end. More than 25 years ago, then CEO of Apple, John Sculley, coined the term *personal digital assistant* (PDA) at the Consumer Electronic Show, which he used to describe the Newton—an Apple device that was the precursor to a combination tablet and smartphone without voice capabilities. Apple's Siri, considered the first modern PDA with voice recognition, was introduced as a feature of the iPhone 4S back in 2011.[47]

Despite these advancing technologies, the PDA that seems to get the most coverage and interest is Alexa, the voice-activated PDA that is part of the Amazon Echo line of home speakers. Introduced in 2014, first to Amazon Prime members, Amazon Echo and Alexa have sparked fierce competition among tech companies. It is estimated that Amazon's Echo currently has 70% of the market for AI-assisted devices, although the competition continues to heat up with Google, Apple, Samsung, and Microsoft all improving their PDA offerings.[48]

PDA technology continues to change our daily lives in so many ways. For example, Alexa can monitor your daily calendar and remind you about important appointments; prepare your shopping list and actually order food items (via Amazon, of course); answer your burning questions about the weather, the time, and even football stats from your fantasy league; and control lighting and temperature in your home. Amazon has set up a rewards program to pay developers around the world to come up with "skills" for Alexa in seven key categories, such as education and reference or trivia and accessories. Already the company has paid out millions to developers for these time-saving apps.[49]

And Alexa's talents are no longer limited to personal activities; the voice-activated device is now taking over

Amazon's voice-activated personal assistant, Alexa, continues to help change people's personal and professional lives. Developers and companies are creating individualized skills that Alexa can take on in the workplace.
©Charles Brutlag/Shutterstock

duties in the office. Recently Amazon rolled out its "Alexa for Business" program, encouraging use of the AI device in the workplace for tasks such as setting up meetings (including reserving the conference room and managing videoconferencing equipment), automatically dialing into conference calls, sending messages and managing calendars, helping people track billable hours, reordering supplies, streaming music, and even reminding people to take a break.[50]

Business applications for Alexa will continue to expand as more and more companies create individualized "skills" for Alexa within their own work environment. Companies already putting Alexa to work include Capital One, WeWork, Vonage, and Brooks Brothers.[51]

The message for managers is clear: The shorter a product's life cycle because of advancing IT, the more important it is to innovate products quickly and continuously. A company that cannot develop a new and improved product line every three to six months will soon find itself in trouble. Increasingly, managers are trying to outdo their rivals by being the first to market with a product that incorporates some advance in IT, such as advanced stability or steering control that prevents vehicle wrecks.[52] In sum, the tumbling price of information brought about by advances in IT is at the heart of the IT revolution. So how can managers use all this computing power to their advantage?

The Network of Computing Power

The tumbling price of computing power and applications has allowed all kinds of organizations, large and small, to invest more to develop networks of servers that are customized with the mix of hardware and software applications that best meets the needs of their current value chain management.

network Interlinked computers that exchange information.

The typical organizationwide computing network that has emerged over time is a four-tier network solution that consists of "external" mobile computing devices such as netbooks, smartphones, and tablet computers, connected to desktops and laptops, and then through rack servers to a company's mainframe or to remote access on the cloud (see Figure 18.3). Through wireless and wired communication, an employee with the necessary permissions can access a company's IT system from any location—in the office, at home, on a boat, on the beach, in the air—anywhere a wireless or wired link can be established.

The internal network is composed of "client" desktop and laptop PCs connected by ethernet or wirelessly to the company's system of servers. The client computers that are linked directly to a server constitute a *local area network* (LAN), and most companies have many LANs—for example, one in every division and function. Large companies that need immense processing power have a mainframe computer at the center or hub of the network that can quickly process vast amounts of information, issue commands, and coordinate computing devices at the other levels. The mainframe can also handle electronic communications between servers and PCs situated in different LANs, and the mainframe can connect to the mainframes of other companies. The mainframe is the master computer that controls the operations of all the other types of computers and digital devices as needed and can link them into one integrated system. It also provides the connection to the *external* IT networks outside the organization; for example, it gives a user access to an organization's cloud computing services—but with high security and reliability and only from recognized and protected computing devices. For instance, a manager with a mobile device or laptop can connect to a four-tier system, accessing data and software stored in the local server, in the mainframe, or through the Internet to a cloud-based computing solution hosted by a third party whose database might be located anywhere in the world.

Just as computer hardware has been advancing rapidly, so has computer software. *Operating system software* tells the computer hardware how to run. *Applications software,* such as programs for word processing, spreadsheets, graphics, and database management, is developed for a specific task or use. The increase in the power of computer hardware has allowed software

Figure 18.3

A Four-Tier Information System with Cloud Computing

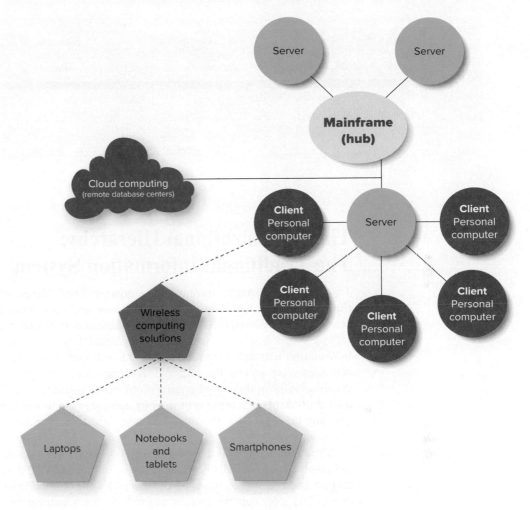

developers to write increasingly powerful programs that are also increasingly user-friendly. By harnessing the rapidly growing power of microprocessors, applications software has vastly increased the ability of managers to acquire, organize, and transmit information. In doing so, it also has improved the ability of managers to coordinate and control the activities of their organization and to make better decisions.

Types of Management Information Systems

LO18-4 Compare six performance-enhancing kinds of management information systems.

Advances in IT have continuously increased managers' ability to obtain the information they need to make better decisions and coordinate and control organizational resources. Next we discuss six types of management information systems (MIS) that have been particularly helpful to managers as they perform their management tasks: transaction-processing systems, operations information systems, decision support systems, expert systems, enterprise resource planning systems, and e-commerce systems (see Figure 18.4). These MIS systems are arranged along a continuum according to the sophistication of the IT they are based on—IT that determines their ability to give managers the information they need to make nonprogrammed decisions. (Recall from Chapter 7 that nonprogrammed decision making occurs in response to unusual, unpredictable opportunities and threats.) We examine each of these systems after focusing on the management information system that preceded them all: the organizational hierarchy.

Figure 18.4

Six Management Information Systems

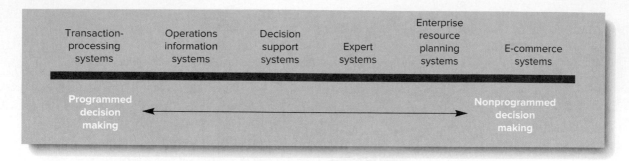

The Organizational Hierarchy: The Traditional Information System

Traditionally, managers have used the organizational hierarchy as the main way to gather the information necessary to make decisions and coordinate and control organizational activities (see Chapter 10 for a detailed discussion of organizational structure and hierarchy). According to business historian Alfred Chandler, the use of the hierarchy as an information network was perfected by U.S. railroad companies in the 1850s.[53] At that time railroads were among the largest U.S. companies, and because of the size of their geographic footprint they faced unique problems of coordination and control. Railroad companies started to solve these problems by designing hierarchical management structures that gave top managers the information they needed to coordinate and control their nationwide operations.

Although hierarchy is a useful information system, it has several drawbacks, as we noted in Chapter 10. First, when too many layers of managers exist, it takes a long time for information and requests to travel up the hierarchy and for decisions and answers to travel back down. The slow communication can reduce the timeliness and usefulness of the information and prevent a quick response to changing market conditions.[54] Second, information can be distorted as it moves from one layer of management to another, and information distortion reduces the quality of information.[55] Third, managers have only a limited span of control, so as an organization grows larger and its hierarchy lengthens, more managers must be hired, and this makes the hierarchy an expensive information system. The popular idea that companies with tall management hierarchies are bureaucratic and unresponsive to the needs of their customers arises from the inability of tall hierarchies to effectively process data and give managers timely, complete, relevant, and high-quality information. The management hierarchy is still the best information system available today—the one that results in the best decisions—*if* managers have access to the other kinds of MIS systems discussed next.

Transaction-Processing Systems

transaction-processing system A management information system designed to handle large volumes of routine, recurring transactions.

A **transaction-processing system** is an MIS designed to handle large volumes of routine, recurring transactions (see Figure 18.4). Transaction-processing systems began to appear in the early 1960s with the advent of commercially available mainframe computers. They were the first type of computer-based IT adopted by many organizations, and today they are commonplace. Bank managers use a transaction-processing system to record deposits into, and payments out of, bank accounts. Supermarket managers use a transaction-processing system to record the sale of items and to track inventory levels. More generally, most managers in large organizations use a transaction-processing system to handle tasks such as payroll preparation and payment, customer billing, and payment of suppliers.

Operations Information Systems

operations information system A management information system that gathers, organizes, and summarizes comprehensive data in a form that managers can use in their nonroutine coordinating, controlling, and decision-making tasks.

Many types of MIS followed hard on the heels of transaction-processing systems in the 1960s as companies like IBM advanced IT. An **operations information system** is an MIS that gathers comprehensive data, organizes them, and summarizes them in a form that is of value to managers. Whereas a transaction-processing system processes routine transactions, an operations information system gives managers information they can use in their nonroutine coordinating, controlling, and decision-making tasks. Most operations information systems are coupled with a transaction-processing system. An operations information system typically accesses data gathered by a transaction-processing system, processes those data into useful information, and organizes that information into a form accessible to managers.

UPS uses an operations information system to track the performance of its thousands of ground stations. Each ground station is evaluated according to four criteria: delivery (to deliver 99% of all packages within the agreed-upon time period), productivity (measured by the number of packages shipped per employee-hour), cost control and efficiency, and station profitability. Each ground station also has specific delivery, efficiency, cost, and profitability targets that it must attain. Every month UPS's operations information system gathers information about these four criteria and summarizes it for top managers, who can then compare the performance of each station against its previously established targets. The system quickly alerts senior managers to underperforming ground stations so they can intervene selectively to help solve any problems that may have given rise to the poor performance.

Decision Support Systems

decision support system An interactive, computer-based management information system that managers can use to make nonroutine decisions.

A **decision support system** provides computer-built models that help managers make better nonprogrammed decisions.[56] Recall from Chapter 7 that nonprogrammed decisions are those that are relatively unusual or novel, such as decisions to invest in new productive capacity, develop a new product, launch a new promotional campaign, enter a new market, or expand internationally. Whereas an operations information system organizes important information for managers, a decision support system gives managers model-building capability and the chance to manipulate information in a variety of ways. Managers might use a decision support system to help them decide whether to cut prices for a product. The decision support system might contain models of how customers and competitors would respond to a price cut. Managers could run these models and use the results as an *aid* to decision making.

The stress on the word *aid* is important—in the final analysis a decision support system is not meant to make decisions for managers. Rather, its function is to give managers valuable information they can use to improve the quality of their decisions.

A good example of a sophisticated decision support system is one developed by Iteris, a software company that specializes in traffic management. Iteris develops technologies and information systems to manage aspects of the transportation industry, such as weather analytics, congestion, and safety. Its decision support system, ClearPath Weather, helps government agencies, local municipalities, and facility managers develop road maintenance strategies that optimize the use of personnel, equipment, and chemicals to keep roadways clear in snowy conditions. The system uses proprietary algorithms and several prediction systems to give managers the information needed to make good decisions about when to plow, the quantity of chemicals to buy, and other key decisions.[57]

Most decision support systems are geared toward aiding middle managers in the decision-making process. For example, a loan manager at a bank might use a decision support system to evaluate the credit risk involved in lending money to a particular client. Rarely does a top manager use a decision support system. One reason for this is that most electronic management information systems have not yet become sophisticated enough to handle effectively the ambiguous types of problems facing top managers. To improve this situation, IT experts have been developing a variant of the decision support system: an executive support system.

executive support system A sophisticated version of a decision support system that is designed to meet the needs of top managers.

An **executive support system** is a sophisticated version of a decision support system that is designed to meet the needs of top managers. One defining characteristic of executive support systems is user-friendliness. Many of them include simple pull-down menus to take a manager through a decision analysis problem. Moreover, they may contain stunning graphics and other visual and interactive features to encourage top managers to use them.[58] Increasingly, executive support systems are used to link top managers virtually so they can function as a team; this type of executive support system is called a **group decision support system**.

Ultimately top managers' intuition, judgment, and integrity will always be needed to decide whether to pursue the course of action suggested by an MIS. There are always many different issues to be factored into a decision, not least of which are its ethical implications.

group decision support system
An executive support system that links top managers so they can function as a team.

Artificial Intelligence and Expert Systems

artificial intelligence Capability of a machine to imitate intelligent human behavior.

As described in "A Manager's Challenge," **artificial intelligence (AI)** can be defined as the capability of a machine to imitate intelligent human behavior.[59] AI has already made it possible to write programs that can solve problems and perform tasks. For example, Google Maps uses artificial intelligence (via location data from smartphones) to analyze the speed of traffic and suggest the fastest routes to and from a destination to reduce driving time behind the wheel.[60] Software programs can be used to perform simple managerial tasks such as sorting through reams of data or incoming email messages to look for important ones. The interesting feature of such technology is that from "watching" a manager sort through data, it can "learn" what the manager's preferences are. Having done this, the software program can take over some of this work from the manager, freeing time for him or her to work on other tasks. Although AI is an ever-evolving technology, many applications have become commonplace in everyday life.[61]

expert system A management information system that employs human knowledge, embedded in a computer, to solve problems that ordinarily require human expertise.

Expert systems, the most advanced management information systems available, incorporate artificial intelligence in their design.[62] An **expert system** is a system that employs human knowledge, embedded in computer software, to solve problems that ordinarily require human expertise.[63] Mimicking human expertise (and intelligence) requires IT that can at a minimum (1) recognize, formulate, and solve a problem; (2) explain the solution; and (3) learn from experience. Although artificial intelligence is still developing, an increasing number of business applications are beginning to emerge in the form of expert systems.

Enterprise Resource Planning Systems

To achieve high performance, it is not sufficient just to develop an MIS inside each of a company's functions or divisions to provide better information and knowledge. It is also vital that managers in the different functions and divisions have access to information about the activities of managers in other functions and divisions. The greater the flow of information and knowledge among functions and divisions, the more learning can take place, and this builds a company's stock of knowledge and expertise. This knowledge and expertise are the source of its competitive advantage and profitability.

enterprise resource planning (ERP) systems Multimodule application software packages that coordinate the functional activities necessary to move products from the design stage to the final customer stage.

Over the past 25 years, another revolution has taken place in IT as software companies have worked to develop enterprise resource planning systems, which essentially incorporate most MIS aspects just discussed, as well as much more. **Enterprise resource planning (ERP) systems** are multimodule application software packages that allow a company to link and coordinate the entire set of functional activities and operations necessary to move products from the initial design stage to the final customer stage. Essentially, ERP systems (1) help each individual function improve its functional-level skills and (2) improve integration among all functions so they work together to build a competitive advantage for the company. Today choosing and designing an ERP system to improve how a company operates is the biggest challenge facing the IT function inside a company. To understand why almost every large global company has installed an ERP system in the last few decades, it is necessary to return to the concept of the value chain, introduced in Chapter 8.

Recall that a company's value chain is composed of the sequence of functional activities that are necessary to make and sell a product. The value chain idea focuses attention on the fact that each function, in sequence, performs its activities to add or contribute value to a product. After one function has made its contribution, it hands the product over to the next function, which makes its own contribution, and so on down the line.

The primary activity of marketing, for example, is to uncover new or changing customer needs or new groups of customers and then decide what kinds of products should be developed to appeal to those customers. It shares, or "hands off," its information to product development, where engineers and scientists work to develop and design the new products. In turn, manufacturing and materials management work to find ways to make the new products as efficiently as possible. Then sales is responsible for finding the best way to convince customers to buy these products.

The value chain is useful in demonstrating the sequence of activities necessary to bring products to the market successfully. In an IT context, however, it suggests the enormous amount of information and communication that needs to link and coordinate the activities of all the various functions. Installing an ERP system for a large company can cost tens of millions of dollars.

As an example of how an ERP system works, let's examine how SAP, one of the world's leading suppliers of ERP software, helps management coordinate activities to speed product development. Suppose marketing has discovered some new unmet customer need, has suggested what kind of product needs to be developed, and forecasts that the demand for the product will be 40,000 units a year. With SAP's IT, engineers in product development use their expert system to work out how to design the new product in a way that builds in quality at the lowest possible cost. Manufacturing managers, watching product development's progress, work simultaneously to find the best way to make the product and thus use their expert system to find out how to keep operating costs at a minimum.

SAP's IT gives all the other functions access to this information; they can tap into what is going on between marketing and manufacturing in real time. So materials management managers, watching manufacturing make its plans, can simultaneously plan how to order supplies of inputs or components from global suppliers or how and when to ship the final product to customers to keep costs at a minimum. At the same time, HRM is tied into the ERP system and uses its expert system to forecast the type and cost of the labor that will be required to carry out the activities in the other functions—for example, the number of manufacturing employees who will be required to make the product or the number of salespeople who will be needed to sell the product to achieve the 40,000 sales forecast.

How does this build competitive advantage and profitability? First, it speeds up product development; companies can bring products to market much more quickly, thereby generating higher sales revenues. Second, SAP's IT focuses on how to drive down operating costs while keeping quality high. Third, SAP's IT is oriented toward the final customer; its customer relationship management (CRM) module watches how customers respond to the new product and then feeds back this information quickly to the other functions.

To see what this means in practice, let's jump ahead three months and suppose that the CRM component of SAP's ERP software reports that actual sales are 20% below target. Further, the software has reasoned that the problem is occurring because the product lacks a crucial feature that customers want. The product is a smartphone, for example, and customers demand a built-in digital camera. The sales group decides this issue deserves major priority and alerts managers in all the other functions about the problem. Now managers can begin to decide how to manage this unexpected situation.

Engineers in product development, for example, use their expert system to work out how much it would cost, and how long it would take, to modify the product so that it includes the missing feature, the digital camera, that customers require. Managers in other functions watch the engineers' progress through the ERP system and can make suggestions for improvement. In the meantime, manufacturing managers know about the slow sales and have already cut back on production to avoid a buildup of the unsold product in the company's warehouse. They are also planning how to phase out this product and introduce the next version, with the digital camera, to keep costs as low as possible. Similarly, materials

A leading supplier of ERP software, SAP provides businesses with application software to link and coordinate cross-functional activities.
©Casimiro PT/Shutterstock

management managers are contacting digital camera makers to find out how much such a camera will cost and when it can be supplied. Meanwhile marketing managers are researching how they missed this crucial product feature and are developing new sales forecasts to estimate demand for the modified product. They announce a revised sales forecast of 75,000 units of the modified product.

It takes the engineers one month to modify the product; but because SAP's IT has been providing information about the modified product to managers in manufacturing and materials management, the product reaches the market only two months later. Within weeks, the sales function reports that early sales figures for the product have greatly exceeded even marketing's revised forecast. The company knows it has a winning product, and top managers give the go-ahead for manufacturing to build a second production line to double production of the product. All the other functions are expecting this decision; in fact, they have already been experimenting with their SAP modules to find out how long it will take them to respond to such a move. Each function gives the others its latest information so they can all adjust their functional activities accordingly.

This quick and responsive action is possible because of the ERP system that gives a company better control of its manufacturing and materials management activities. Quality is increased because a greater flow of information between functions allows a better-designed product. Innovation is accelerated because a company can rapidly change its products to suit the needs of customers. Finally, responsiveness to customers improves because, using its CRM software module, sales can better manage and react to customers' changing needs and provide better service and support to back up the sales of the product. ERP's ability to promote competitive advantage is the reason managers in so many companies, large and small, are moving to find the best ERP solution for their particular companies.

E-Commerce Systems

e-commerce Trade that takes place between companies, and between companies and individual customers, using IT and the Internet.

business-to-business (B2B) commerce Trade that takes place between companies using IT and the Internet to link and coordinate the value chains of different companies.

E-commerce is trade that takes place between companies, and between companies and individual customers, using IT and the Internet. **Business-to-business (B2B) commerce** is trade that takes place between companies using IT and the Internet to link and coordinate the value chains of different companies. (See Figure 18.5.) The goal of B2B commerce is to increase the profitability of making and selling goods and services. B2B commerce increases profitability because it lets companies reduce operating costs and may improve product quality. Recent

Figure 18.5
Types of E-Commerce

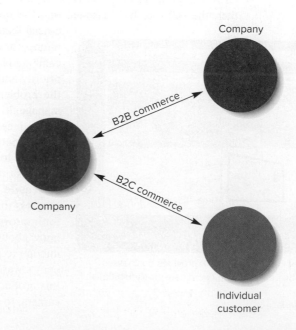

B2B marketplace An Internet-based trading platform set up to connect buyers and sellers in an industry.

estimates suggest that B2B e-commerce sales could top $1.2 trillion by 2021. In addition, according to a recent Google report, 42% of B2B customers use mobile devices for their purchases.[64] A principal B2B software application is **B2B marketplaces**, which are Internet-based trading platforms that have been set up in many industries to connect buyers and sellers. To participate in a B2B marketplace, companies adopt a common software standard that allows them to search for and share information with one another. Then companies can work together over time to find ways to reduce costs or improve quality.

business-to-customer (B2C) commerce Trade that takes place between a company and individual customers using IT and the Internet.

Business-to-customer (B2C) commerce is trade that takes place between a company and individual customers using IT and the Internet. Using IT to connect directly to the customer means companies can avoid having to use intermediaries, such as wholesalers and retailers, who capture a significant part of the profit in the value chain. The use of websites and online stores also lets companies give their customers much more information about the value of their products. This often allows them to attract more customers and thus generate higher sales revenues. Recent estimates suggest that B2C e-commerce sales globally will exceed $2.3 trillion in the coming year.[65]

Software makers, including Microsoft, Oracle, SAP, and IBM, have rushed to use cloud computing to make their products work seamlessly with the Internet and thus respond to global companies' growing demand for e-commerce software. Previously, their software was configured to work only on a particular company's intranet; today their software must be able to network a company's IT systems to other companies, such as their suppliers and distributors. At the same time, as we discussed earlier, companies also need to use software to establish a secure platform their employees can use to share information inside their organizations.

The challenge facing managers now is to select e-commerce software that allows seamless exchange of information between companies anywhere in the world. The stakes are high because global competitive advantage goes to the company first with a major new technological advance. For example, SAP rushed to update its ERP modules to allow transactions over the Internet, and today all its modules have full cloud computing capability. However, Oracle, IBM, and many small specialist companies have also developed ways to provide advanced cloud computing and Internet applications at a lower price, so SAP faces increased global competition.

In summary, by using advanced types of MIS, managers have more control over a company's activities and operations and can work to improve its competitive advantage and profitability. Today the IT function is becoming increasingly important because IT managers select which kind of hardware and software a company will use and then train other functional managers and employees how to use it effectively as part of daily business operations.

The Impact and Limitations of Information Technology

Advances in IT and management information systems are having important effects on managers and organizations. By improving the ability of managers to coordinate and control the activities of the organization and by helping managers make more effective decisions, modern IT has become a central component of any organization's structure. And evidence that IT can be a source of competitive advantage is growing; organizations that do not adopt leading-edge IT are likely to be at a competitive disadvantage. In this section we examine how the rapid advances in IT are affecting organizational structure and competitive advantage. We also examine problems associated with implementing management information systems effectively, as well as the limitations of MIS.

LO18-5 Explain how IT is helping managers build strategic alliances and network structures to increase efficiency and effectiveness.

Strategic Alliances, B2B Network Structures, and IT

Increasing globalization and the use of new IT have brought about two innovations that are sweeping through global companies: electronically managed strategic alliances and B2B network structures. A **strategic alliance** is a formal agreement that commits two or more companies to exchange or share their resources in order to produce and market a product.[66] Most commonly, strategic alliances are formed because the companies share similar interests and believe they can benefit from cooperating. For example, in 2018, Disney entered into a

strategic alliance An agreement in which managers pool or share their organization's resources and know-how with a foreign company, and the two organizations share the rewards and risks of starting a new venture.

strategic alliance with McDonald's that will bring Disney movie toys back to Happy Meals for the first time in more than a decade. This strategic move will give both global brands new ways to market their products to families over the next several years. In 2006 Disney ended an agreement with the fast-food giant because the children's meals didn't meet Disney's nutritional guidelines.[67]

Throughout the 2000s, the growing sophistication of IT using global intranets, cloud computing, and teleconferencing made it much easier to manage strategic alliances and allow managers to share information and cooperate. One outcome of this has been the growth of strategic alliances into an IT-based network structure. A **B2B network structure** is a formal series of global strategic alliances that one or several organizations create with suppliers, manufacturers, and distributors to produce and market a product. Network structures allow an organization to manage its global value chain in order to find new ways to reduce costs and increase the quality of products—without incurring the high costs of operating a complex organizational structure (such as the costs of employing many managers). More and more companies are relying on global network structures to gain access to low-cost foreign sources of inputs, as discussed in Chapter 6.

B2B network structure A series of global strategic alliances that an organization creates with suppliers, manufacturers, and distributors to produce and market a product.

Nike is the largest and most profitable sports shoe manufacturer in the world. The key to Nike's success is the network structure that Nike founder Philip Knight created to allow his company to produce and market shoes. As noted in Chapter 8, the most successful companies today are trying to pursue simultaneously a low-cost and a differentiation strategy. Knight decided early that to do this at Nike he needed to focus his company's efforts on the most important functional activities, such as product design and engineering, and leave the others, such as manufacturing, to other organizations.

By far the largest function at Nike's Oregon headquarters is the design and engineering function, whose members pioneered innovations in sports shoe design such as the air pump and Air Jordans that Nike introduced so successfully. Designers use computer-aided design (CAD) to design Nike shoes, and they electronically store all new product information, including manufacturing instructions. When the designers have finished their work, they electronically transmit the blueprints for the new products to a network of Southeast Asian suppliers and manufacturers with which Nike has formed strategic alliances.[68] Instructions for the design of a new sole may be sent to a supplier in Taiwan; instructions for the leather uppers to a supplier in Malaysia. The suppliers produce the shoe parts and send them for final assembly to a manufacturer in China with which Nike has established another strategic alliance. From China the shoes are shipped to distributors throughout the world. Ninety-nine percent of the over 120 million pairs of shoes that Nike makes each year are made in Southeast Asia.

This network structure gives Nike two important advantages. First, Nike can quickly respond to changes in sports shoe fashion. Using its global IT system, Nike literally can change the instructions it gives each of its suppliers overnight, so that within a few weeks its foreign manufacturers are producing new kinds of shoes.[69] Any alliance partners that fail to perform up to Nike's standards are replaced with new partners through the regular B2B marketplace.

Second, Nike's costs are low because wages in Southeast Asia are a fraction of what they are in the United States, and this difference gives Nike a low-cost advantage. Also, Nike's ability to outsource and use foreign manufacturers to produce all its shoes abroad allows the company to keep the organization's U.S. structure flat and flexible. Nike can use a relatively inexpensive functional structure to organize its activities.

The use of network structures is increasing rapidly as organizations recognize the many opportunities they offer to reduce costs and increase organizational flexibility. Supply chain spending by U.S. firms is expected to exceed $19 billion by 2021.[70] The push to lower costs has led to the development of B2B marketplaces in which most or all of the companies in an industry (for example, carmakers) use the same software platform to link to each other and establish industry specifications and standards. Then these companies jointly list the quantity and specifications of the inputs they require and invite bids from the thousands of potential suppliers around the world. Suppliers also use the same software platform, so electronic bidding, auctions, and transactions are possible between buyers and sellers around the world. The idea is that high-volume standardized transactions can help drive down costs at the industry level. Also, quality will increase as these relationships become more stable as a B2B network structure develops.

Flatter Structures and Horizontal Information Flows

Rapid advances in IT have been associated with a "delayering," or flattening, of the organizational hierarchy, a move toward greater decentralization and horizontal information flows within organizations, and the concept of the boundaryless organization.[71] By electronically giving managers high-quality, timely, relevant, and relatively complete information, modern management information systems have reduced the need for tall management hierarchies. Modern IT has reduced the need for a hierarchy to function as a means of coordinating and controlling organizational activities. Also, by reducing the need for hierarchy, modern IT can directly increase an organization's efficiency because fewer employees are required to perform organizational activities.

The ability of IT to flatten structure and facilitate the flow of horizontal information between employees has led many researchers and consultants to popularize the idea of a **boundaryless organization**. Such an organization is composed of people linked by IT—computers, mobile technology, and videoconferencing—who may rarely, if ever, see one another face-to-face. People are utilized when their services are needed, but they are not formal members of an organization; they are functional experts who form an alliance with an organization, fulfill their contractual obligations, and then move on to the next project.

Large consulting companies, such as Accenture, IBM, and McKinsey & Co., use their global consultants in this way. Consultants are connected to an organization's **knowledge management system**—its company-specific virtual information system that systematizes the knowledge of its employees and facilitates the sharing and integration of expertise within and between functions and divisions through real-time interconnected IT. Knowledge management systems let employees share their knowledge and expertise and give them virtual access to other employees who have the expertise to solve the problems they encounter as they perform their jobs.

Some organizations, especially those that provide complex services and employ highly trained workers, have gone one step further and created what has been called a virtual organization. A *virtual organization* is one in which employees are linked to an organization's centralized information system and rarely see one another face-to-face, if ever.[72] These employees might only infrequently visit the physical premises of their companies; they receive their assignments electronically, report back to their superiors electronically, and operate autonomously.[73] Almost all their employees are out in the field, working anywhere around the globe with clients to solve their problems. The number of teleworkers in the United States increased in the early 2010s, despite the recession.

Despite their usefulness, IT, in general, and management information systems, in particular, have some limitations. A serious potential problem is that in all the enthusiasm for MIS, communication via computer networks might lose the vital human element of communication. There is a strong argument that electronic communication should support face-to-face communication rather than replacing it. For example, it would be wrong to make a judgment about an individual's performance merely by "reading the numbers" provided by an MIS. Instead, the numbers should be used to alert managers to individuals who may have a performance problem. The nature of this problem should then be explored in a face-to-face meeting, during which more detailed information can be gathered. One drawback of using IT, such as email and teleconferencing, is that employees may spend too much time watching their computer screens and communicating electronically—and little time interacting directly with other employees.[74] If this occurs, important and relevant information may not be obtained because of the lack of face-to-face contact, and the quality of decision making may suffer.

boundaryless organization An organization linked by computers, mobile technology, and video teleconferencing and whose employees and associates rarely, if ever, see one another face-to-face.

knowledge management system A company-specific virtual information system that systematizes the knowledge of its employees and facilitates the sharing and integration of their expertise.

Summary and Review

LO18-1, 18-2

INFORMATION AND THE MANAGER'S JOB Computer-based IT is central to the operation of most organizations. By giving managers high-quality, timely, relevant, and relatively complete information, properly implemented IT can improve managers' ability to coordinate and control the operations of an organization and to make effective decisions. Moreover, IT can help the organization attain a competitive advantage through its beneficial impact on productivity, quality, innovation, and responsiveness to customers. Modern IT is an indispensable management tool; however, it comes with several consequences that require managers to control these technological advances. The increase in cybercrimes—events in which data hackers leverage weak security measures and steal company and customer data—have become common in this digital age. In addition, consumers and organizations alike must be vigilant when it comes to ensuring the privacy of key data and information.

LO18-3   THE IT REVOLUTION   Over the last 30 years there have been rapid advances in the power and rapid declines in the cost of IT. Falling prices, wireless communication, computer networks, and software developments have all radically improved the power and efficacy of computer-based IT.

LO18-4   TYPES OF MANAGEMENT INFORMATION SYSTEMS   Traditionally, managers used the organizational hierarchy as the main system for gathering the information they needed to coordinate and control the organization and to make effective decisions. Today managers use six main types of computer-based information systems. Listed in ascending order of sophistication, they are transaction-processing systems, operations information systems, decision support systems, expert systems, enterprise resource planning systems, and e-commerce systems.

LO18-5   THE IMPACT AND LIMITATIONS OF INFORMATION TECHNOLOGY   Modern IT has changed organizational structure in many ways. Using IT, managers can create electronic strategic alliances and form a B2B network structure. A network structure, based on some shared form of IT, can be formed around one company, or a number of companies can join together to create an industry B2B network. Modern IT also makes organizations flatter and encourages more horizontal cross-functional communication. As this increasingly happens across the organizational boundary, the term *boundaryless organizations* has been coined to refer to virtual organizations whose members are linked electronically.

Management in Action

Topics for Discussion and Action

Discussion

1. To be useful, information must be of high quality, be timely, be relevant, and be as complete as possible. Why does a tall management hierarchy, when used as a management information system, have negative effects on these desirable attributes? **[LO18-1]**

2. What is the relationship between IT and competitive advantage? **[LO18-2]**

3. Because of the growth of high-powered, low-cost wireless communications and IT such as videoconferencing, many managers may not need to go into the office to do their jobs. They will be able to work at home. What are the pros and cons of such an arrangement? **[LO18-3, 18-4, 18-5]**

4. Many companies have reported that it is difficult to implement advanced management information systems such as ERP systems. Why do you think this is so? How might the roadblocks to implementation be removed? **[LO18-4]**

5. How can IT help in the new product development process? **[LO18-4]**

6. Why is face-to-face communication between managers still important in an organization? **[LO18-4, 18-5]**

Action

7. Ask a manager to describe the main kinds of IT that he or she uses on a routine basis at work. **[LO18-1, 18-4]**

8. Compare the pros and cons of using a network structure to perform organizational activities versus performing all activities in-house or within one organizational hierarchy. **[LO18-3, 18-4, 18-5]**

9. What are the advantages and disadvantages of business-to-business networks? **[LO18-5]**

Building Management Skills

Analyzing Management Information Systems [LO18-3, 18-4]

Pick an organization about which you have some direct knowledge. It may be an organization you worked for in the past or are in contact with now (such as the college or school you attend). For this organization, answer the following questions:

1. Describe the management information systems that are used to coordinate and control organizational activities and to help make decisions.

2. Do you think that the organization's existing MIS gives managers high-quality, timely, relevant, and relatively complete information? Why or why not?

3. How might advanced IT improve the competitive position of this organization? In particular, try to identify the impact that a new MIS might have on the organization's efficiency, quality, innovation, and responsiveness to customers.

Managing Ethically [LO18-1, 18-2]

The use of management information systems, such as ERPs, often gives employees access to confidential information from all functions and levels of an organization. Employees can see important information about the company's products that is of great value to competitors. As a result, many companies monitor employees' use of the intranet and Internet to prevent an employee from acting unethically, such as by selling this information to competitors. On the other hand, with access to this information employees might discover that their company has been engaging in unethical or even illegal practices.

Questions

1. Ethically speaking, how far should a company go to protect its proprietary information, given that it also needs to protect the privacy of its employees? What steps can it take?

2. When is it ethical for employees to give information about a company's unethical or illegal practices to a third party, such as a newspaper or government agency?

Small Group Breakout Exercise

Using New Management Information Systems [LO18-2, 18-4]

Form groups of three or four people, and appoint one member as the spokesperson who will communicate your findings to the class when called on by the instructor. Then discuss the following scenario:

You are a team of managing partners of a large management consulting company. You are responsible for auditing your firm's MIS to determine whether it is appropriate and up to date. To your surprise, you find that although your organization has a wireless email system in place and consultants are connected into a powerful local area network (LAN) at all times, most of the consultants (including partners) are not using this technology. It seems that most important decision making still takes place through the organizational hierarchy.

Given this situation, you are concerned that your organization is not exploiting the opportunities offered by new

IT to obtain a competitive advantage. You have discussed this issue and are meeting to develop an action plan to get consultants to appreciate the need to learn about and use the new IT.

1. What advantages can you tell consultants they will obtain when they use the new IT?

2. What problems do you think you may encounter in convincing consultants to use the new IT?

3. What steps might you take to motivate consultants to learn to use the new technology?

Be the Manager [LO18-4]

You are one of the managers of a small specialty maker of custom tables, chairs, and cabinets. You have been charged with finding ways to use IT and the Internet to identify new business opportunities that can improve your company's competitive advantage, such as ways to reduce costs or attract customers.

Questions

1. What are the various forces in a specialty furniture maker's task environment that have the most effect on its performance?

2. What kinds of IT or MIS can help the company better manage these forces?

3. In what ways can the Internet help this organization improve its competitive position?

Bloomberg Businessweek Case in the News

Goggles with a Work Crew Inside [LO18-1, 18-2, 18-3]

Replacing parts of an outdated Baker Hughes turbine at a petrochemical plant in Johor Bahru, Malaysia, is about as fun as it sounds. The chore was supposed to halt operations at the facility for at least 10 days and cost $50,000 to fly a specialized U.S. work crew about 9,000 miles. Instead, once the equipment upgrade began last year, it took only five days and zero air travel—just an on-site technician wearing a dorky helmet camera and a few American engineers supervising remotely. They watched

and coached the local crew through the helmet from a Baker Hughes site in Pomona, Calif.

Augmented-reality headsets, which overlay digital images on a real-world field of vision, are driving advances in industrial technology a few steps beyond FaceTime. While the likes of Apple, Amazon.com, Google, and Microsoft race to develop mainstream AR consumer gadgets in the next couple of years, they've been outpaced by oil companies looking for ways to cut costs. Some are simply

buying the goggles and building custom software; others are investing directly in AR startups; still others are making the hardware as well. Baker Hughes, a General Electric Co. subsidiary, calls its rig a Smart Helmet. "Traditionally I would have to pay for two people's travel, two people's accommodations, and so forth to visit the customer's site to do the mentoring," says John McMillan, a regional repairs chief at the company whose team uses the helmet regularly. "It's saved me a lot."

Baker Hughes co-created its AR headset with Italian developer VRMedia S.r.l. and wrote its own software. BP Plc says it's using AR glasses to bring remote expertise to sites across the U.S. Startup RealWear Inc. says it's signed two dozen other energy companies, including Royal Dutch Shell Plc and Exxon Mobil Corp., to test its $2,000 headset. On March 6, AR software maker Upskill announced a fresh $17 million in venture funding from Boeing Co., Cisco Systems Inc., and other investors.

Remote gear can help experienced workers stay on the job even if they can no longer handle the travel or other physical demands of rig maintenance. "With these technologies, it's more about the people than the hardware," says Shell Executive Vice President Alisa Choong. Janette Marx, chief operating officer for industry recruiter Airswift, says remote work is also a good sales pitch to skilled technicians who might be lured by cushier gigs in Silicon Valley.

The bigger prize for oil companies is reduced downtime for equipment. Each day offline for a typical 200,000-barrel-a-day refinery can mean almost $12 million in lost revenue. Offshore oil and gas facilities often halt operations while waiting to fly specialists in by helicopter and, according to industry analyst Kimberlite International Oilfield Research, shut down 27 days a year on average. Little wonder, then, that analyst ABI Research estimates energy and utility companies' annual spending on AR glasses and related technology will reach $18 billion in 2022, among the most of any industry.

Remote AR work doesn't always go smoothly. Oil rigs often lack reliable wireless networks, and many headsets don't yet meet the strict standards for areas near hazardous materials or high-risk jobs. Under certain conditions, for example, the headsets might emit dangerous sparks. That's one reason many of the oil companies' pilot programs remain just that for now.

Baker Hughes hasn't had to worry about those issues yet, says John Westerheide, director of emerging technologies. In Malaysia, engineers were able to view equipment, send images to the headset screen, and talk directly to the on-site workers with few hiccups. "The way that we currently go to work," Westerheide says, "that's going to become much more virtual, interactive, and collaborative."

Questions for Discussion

1. How will advanced technology such as augmented reality transform managerial tasks and decision making?

2. What impact will these AR helmets have on the product life cycle of other tools used in the oil industry?

3. What are possible disadvantages of using this advanced type of technology?

Notes

1. K. Ang, "Companies Use AI to Help Managers Become More Human," *The Wall Street Journal,* www.wsj.com, April 29, 2018; S.F. Gale, "Robot Coaches: New Model for Leadership Training?" *Chief Learning Officer,* www.clomedia.com, August 25, 2017; J. Mannes, "Butterfly Nabs $2.4M Seed Round to Improve Managers with Targeted Tips," *TechCrunch,* https://techcrunch.com, October 6, 2017; H.R. Huhman, "Five Things the Best Leaders Do Every Day," *Entrepreneur,* www.entrepreneur.com, January 30, 2017.

2. T. Greenwald, "What Exactly Is Artificial Intelligence, Anyway?" *The Wall Street Journal,* www.wsj.com, April 30, 2018; Ang, "Companies Use AI to Help Managers"; C. Dessi, "This Startup Will Make You Unbelievably Happy at Work," *Inc.,* www.inc.com, April 25, 2016; Gale, "Robot Coaches."

3. "Work of the Future: Butterfly a.i.," MIT-Solve, https://solve.mit.edu, accessed May 1, 2018.

4. Mannes, "Butterfly Nabs $2.4M Seed Round"; Dessi, "This Startup Will Make You Unbelievably Happy"; Gale, "Robot Coaches."

5. Ang, "Companies Use AI to Help Managers"; Dessi, "This Startup Will Make You Unbelievably Happy"; Gale, "Robot Coaches"; Huhman, "Five Things the Best Leaders Do."

6. "What Is the Difference between Data and Information?" www.computerhope.com, January 24, 2018.

7. J. Cotton, "Data: The Importance of Accuracy, Integrity and Real-Time Integration," http://ww2.informationbuilders.com, accessed May 5, 2018.

8. T. Chen, L. Ravindranath, S. Deng, P. Bahl, and H. Balakrishnan, "Glimpse: Continuous, Real-Time Object Recognition on Mobile Devices," www.microsoft.com, accessed May 5, 2018.

9. "About Transit" and "Regions," https://transit.com, accessed May 3, 2018; M. Lynley, "Transit's Public Transportation Tracking App Gets a Big Overhaul and $2.4M in Funding," *Tech Crunch,* https://techcrunch.com, September 20, 2016.

10. A. Ranadive, "Making Decisions under Uncertainty," https://medium.com, accessed May 5, 2018.

11. E. Turban, *Decision Support and Expert Systems* (New York: Macmillan, 1988).

12. W.H. Davidow and M.S. Malone, *The Virtual Corporation* (New York: Harper Business, 1992); M. E. Porter, *Competitive Advantage* (New York: Free Press, 1984).

13. "8 Tech Predictions for 2018," www.bdo.com, accessed May 3, 2018.

14. B. Marr, "A Very Brief History of Blockchain Technology Everyone Should Read," *Forbes,* www.forbes.com, February 16, 2018.

15. K. Korosec, "This Is Your Guide to Buying Bitcoin," *Fortune,* http://fortune.com, January 3, 2018.

16. Marr, "A Very Brief History of Blockchain Technology."

17. C. Mims, "Why Blockchain Will Survive, Even If Bitcoin Doesn't," *The Wall Street Journal,* www.wsj.com, March 11, 2018.

18. Forbes Finance Council, "Seven Unexpected Blockchain Uses That Will Improve Business," *Forbes,* www.forbes.com, January 31, 2018.

19. D. Parmar, "4 Critical Big Data Developments to Prepare For in 2018," http://

bigdata-madesimple.com, accessed May 3, 2018.

20. "What Is Big Data Analytics?" https://searchbusinessanalytics.techtarget.com, accessed May 3, 2018.

21. "Big Data Analytics: What It Is and Why It Matters," https://www.sas.com, accessed May 3, 2018.

22. S.M. Dornbusch and W.R. Scott, *Evaluation and the Exercise of Authority* (San Francisco: Jossey-Bass, 1975).

23. J. Child, *Organization: A Guide to Problems and Practice* (London: Harper & Row, 1984).

24. Contract Logistics—Retail," http://ups-scs.com, accessed May 5, 2018.

25. "Big Data Meets Walt Disney's Magical Approach," https://datafloq.com, accessed May 3, 2018; A. C. Estes, "How I Let Disney Track My Every Move," *Gizmodo,* https://gizmodo.com, March 28, 2017.

26. "OCEAN FAQs," https://www.princess.com, accessed May 3, 2018; S. Pedicini, "Companies Taking Disney's Tech Concepts a Step Further," *Orlando Sentinel,* www.orlandosentinel.com, January 20, 2017.

27. "What Is Cybersecurity?" *Palo Alto Networks,* www.paloaltonetworks.com, accessed May 3, 2018.

28. "50% of Companies Face Cyber-Attacks Motivated by Ransom," *Security* magazine, www.securitymagazine.com, January 16, 2018.

29. B. Fung, "Equifax's Massive 2017 Data Breach Keeps Getting Worse," *The Washington Post,* www.washingtonpost.com, March 1, 2018.

30. "Bad Credit: Uncovering Equifax's Failure to Protect Americans' Personal Information," https://www.warren.senate.com, February 2018.

31. B.M. Egan, "3 Biggest Cybersecurity Threats Facing Small Businesses Right Now," *Entrepreneur,* www.entrepreneur.com, January 31, 2018.

32. S. Ranger, "What Is the IoT? Everything You Need to Know about the Internet of Things Right Now," *ZDNet,* www.zdnet.com, January 19, 2018.

33. KPMG Voice, "Perspectives: The Next Big Cybersecurity Threats Facing Businesses," *Forbes,* www.forbes.com, April 3, 2018.

34. "Our History," https://newsroom.fb.com, accessed May 5, 2018; "Number of Facebook Users by Age in the U.S. as of January 2018 (in millions)," *Statista,* www.statista.com, accessed May 5, 2018.

35. M. Rosenberg, N. Confessore, and C. Cadwalladr, "How Trump Consultants Exploited the Facebook Data of Millions," *The New York Times,* www.nytimes.com,

March 17, 2018; M. Schwartz, "Facebook Failed to Protect 30 Million Users from Having Their Data Harvested by Trump Campaign Affiliate," https://theintercept.com, March 30, 2017.

36. D. Kurtzleben, "Did Fake News on Facebook Help Elect Trump? What We Know," *NPR,* www.npr.org, April 11, 2018; C. Press, "Facebook Data: How It was Used by Cambridge Analytica (video)," *BBC,* www.bbc.com, April 9, 2018.

37. Bloomberg, "Facebook Cambridge Analytica Scandal: 10 Questions Answered," *Fortune,* http://fortune.com, April 10, 2018; Kurtzleben, "Did Fake News on Facebook Help Elect Trump?"

38. T. Hsu, "For Many Facebook Users, a 'Last Straw' That Led Them to Quit," *The New York Times,* www.nytimes.com, March 21, 2018.

39. L. Bruggeman, "Cambridge Analytica Shutting Down, Files for Bankruptcy," *ABC News,* https://abcnews.go.com, May 2, 2018; J. Temperton, "Check If Your Facebook Data Was Shared with Cambridge Analytica," *Wired,* www.wired.co.uk, April 10, 2018.

40. D. Landsel, "The Most Fascinating Attraction at Disney World You Aren't Allowed to Visit," *Food&Wine,* www.foodandwine.com, January 23, 2018; J. Clampet, "Skift Q&A: The Man Who Feeds More Than 300,000 Disney Guests a Day," *Skift,* http://skift.com, accessed April 27, 2015.

41. J. Trujillo, "Starbucks Origin Trip Builds a Bridge Between Partners and Rwandan Farmers," https://news.starbucks.com, May 1, 2017.

42. "Behind the Scenes at Starbucks Supply Chain Operations: It's Plan, Source, Make & Deliver," *Supply Chain 247,* www.supplychain247.com, accessed May 4, 2018; M. Sargent, "Starbucks' Closely Managed Supply Chain May Be the Key to the Premium Coffee Giant's Success," www.fronetics.com, accessed May 4, 2018.

43. J. Henderson, "Starbucks Adds New Ingredient to 'Bean to Cup' Transparency," *Supply Chain Digital,* www.supplychaindigital.com, March 23, 2018.

44. V.P. Buell, *Marketing Management* (New York: McGraw-Hill, 1985).

45. G. Donnelly, "Apple Is Officially Taking Over the Watch Business," *Fortune,* http://fortune.com, February 20, 2018.

46. See M.M.J. Berry and J.H. Taggart, "Managing Technology and Innovation: A Review," *R & D Management* 24 (1994), 341–53; K.B. Clark and S.C. Wheelwright, *Managing New Product and Process Development* (New York: Free Press, 1993).

47. "A Short History of the Voice Revolution," https://www.voicebot.ai, accessed May 5, 2018.

48. G. Anders, "'Alexa, Understand Me,'" *MIT Technology Review,* www.technologyreview.com, August 9, 2017.

49. A. Montag, "This 22-Year-Old College Student Makes $10,000 a Month Off Amazon's Alexa," *CNBC,* www.cnbc.com, April 12, 2018.

50. T. Martin, "7 Ways to Use Alexa around the Office," *CNET,* www.cnet.com, February 18, 2018; N. Zipkin, "Here's How You Can Use Alexa at Work," *Entrepreneur,* www.entrepreneur.com, December 19, 2017.

51. "Alexa for Business: Overview," https://aws.amazon.com, accessed May 7, 2018.

52. See Berry and Taggart, "Managing Technology and Innovation"; M. Gort and J. Klepper, "Time Paths in the Diffusion of Product Innovations," *Economic Journal* (September 1982), 630–53. Looking at the history of 46 products, Gort and Klepper found that the length of time before other companies entered the markets created by a few inventive companies declined from an average of 14.4 years for products introduced before 1930 to 4.9 years for those introduced after 1949—implying that product life cycles were being compressed. Also see A. Griffin, "Metrics for Measuring Product Development Cycle Time," *Journal of Production and Innovation Management* 10 (1993), 112–25.

53. A.D. Chandler, *The Visible Hand* (Cambridge, MA: Harvard University Press, 1977).

54. C.W.L. Hill and J.F. Pickering, "Divisionalization, Decentralization, and Performance of Large United Kingdom Companies," *Journal of Management Studies* 23 (1986), 26–50.

55. O.E. Williamson, *Markets and Hierarchies: Analysis and Antitrust Implications* (New York: Free Press, 1975).

56. Turban, *Decision Support and Expert Systems.*

57. "ClearPath Weather," www.iteris.com, accessed May 5, 2018.

58. Turban, *Decision Support and Expert Systems.*

59. B. Marr, "The Key Definitions of Artificial Intelligence (AI) That Explain Its Importance," *Forbes,* www.forbes.com, February 14, 2018.

60. G. Narula, "Everyday Examples of Artificial Intelligence and Machine Learning," www.techemergence.com, March 29, 2018.

61. J. Long, "10 Artificial Intelligence Trends to Watch in 2018," *Entrepreneur,* www.entrepreneur.com, January 18, 2018.

62. Narula, "Everyday Examples of Artificial Intelligence and Machine Learning."

63. Turban, *Decision Support and Expert Systems.*

64. J. Carter, "B2B E-Commerce Trends to Take Notice of in 2018," *Forbes,* www.forbes.com, February 15, 2018.

65. "B2C E-Commerce Sales Worldwide from 2012 to 2018 (in Billions U.S. Dollars)," *Statista,* www.statista.com, accessed May 4, 2018.

66. B. Kogut, "Joint Ventures: Theoretical and Empirical Perspectives," *Strategic Management Journal* 9 (1988), 319–32.

67. J. Wohl, "Disney, Now Happy with Happy Meals, Reunites with McDonald's," *Advertising Age,* http://adage.com, February 27, 2018.

68. G. S. Capowski, "Designing a Corporate Identity," *Management Review,* June 1993, 37–38.

69. J. Marcia, "Just Doing It," *Distribution,* January 1995, 36–40.

70. "Gartner Says Supply Chain Management Will Exceed $13 Billion in 2017, Up 11 Percent from 2016," www.gartner.com, June 22, 2017.

71. T. Kastelle, "Hierarchy Is Overrated," *Harvard Business Review,* https://hbr.org, accessed May 4, 2018.

72. J. Fulk and G. Desanctis, "Electronic Communication and Changing Organizational Forms," *Organizational Science,* 6 (1995), 337–49.

73. Y.P. Shao, S.Y. Liao, and H.Q. Wang, "A Model of Virtual Organizations," *Academy of Management Executive,* 12 (1998), 120–28.

74. Forbes Technology Council, "13 Pros and Cons of Having a Distributed Workforce," *Forbes,* www.forbes.com, August 3, 2017.

NAMES INDEX

ORGANIZATION INDEX

SUBJECT GLINDEX

Supply forecasts, 344
Supportive behaviors, 415, 419
SWOT analysis, 222–224
SWOT analysis A planning exercise in which managers identify organizational strengths (S) and weaknesses (W) and environmental opportunities (O) and threats (T), 222–224
Synergy Performance gains that result when individuals and departments coordinate their actions, 47–48
diversification and, 231
from groups, 438
Systematic errors Errors that people make over and over and that result in poor decision making, 193
Systems thinking, 199

T

Tall organizations, 289–291
Tariffs Taxes that a government imposes on imported or, occasionally, exported goods, 167–177
Task analyzability, 276
Task environment The set of forces and conditions that originates with suppliers, distributors, customers, and competitors and affects an organization's ability to obtain inputs and dispose of its outputs. These forces and conditions influence managers daily, 155–162
competitors, 159–160
customers, 159
distributors, 158–159
suppliers, 156–158
Task forces Committees of managers or nonmanagerial employees from various departments or divisions who meet to solve a specific, mutual problem; also called *ad hoc committees*, 293, 441
Task identity, 279
Task interdependence The degree to which the work performed by one member of a group influences the work performed by other members, 446, 502
Task-oriented behaviors, 415
Task-oriented leaders Leaders whose primary concern is to ensure that subordinates perform at a high level, 416
Task significance, 279–280
Task variety, 276
Team A group whose members work intensely with one another to achieve a specific common goal or objective, 436. *See also* Groups and teams; Self-managed work teams
need for soft skills, 437

Team learning, 199
Technical skills The job-specific knowledge and techniques required to perform an organizational role, 13
Technological forces Outcomes of changes in the technology managers use to design, produce, or distribute goods and services, 163–164
Technology The combination of skills and equipment that managers use in designing, producing, and distributing goods and services, 163
influence on organizational structures, 276
management of, and empathy, 3–4
Temporary assignments, 505
Tenure, 41
Terminal values Lifelong goals or objectives that individuals seek to achieve, 64, 74
Theory X A set of negative assumptions about workers that leads to the conclusion that a manager's task is to supervise workers closely and control their behavior, 44–45
Theory Y A set of positive assumptions about workers that leads to the conclusion that a manager's task is to create a work setting that encourages commitment to organizational goals and provides opportunities for workers to be imaginative and to exercise initiative and self-direction, 45
Third-party negotiator An impartial individual with expertise in handling conflicts and negotiations who helps parties in conflict reach an acceptable solution, 506
360-degree appraisal Performance appraisal by peers, subordinates, superiors, and sometimes clients who are in a position to evaluate a manager's performance, 358
Time-and-motion studies, 34
Time horizon The intended duration of a plan, 218–219
conflict over, 501–502
Timeliness of information, 525–526
Times-covered ratio, 317–318
Title VII of the Civil Rights Act (1964), 122, 124–125, 343
Top-down change A fast, revolutionary approach to change in which top managers identify what needs to be changed and then move quickly to implement the changes throughout the organization, 331
Top management team A group composed of the CEO, the COO,

the president, and the heads of the most important departments, 12, 440
Top managers Managers who establish organizational goals, decide how departments should interact, and monitor the performance of middle managers, 12
diversity and securing commitment from, 137–138
Total quality management (TQM) A management technique that focuses on improving the quality of an organization's products and services for competitive advantage, 19
elements of, 47
steps in, 255–256
Trade barriers, 167–177
Training Teaching organizational members how to perform their current jobs and helping them acquire the knowledge and skills they need to be effective performers
as part of human resource management, 341–342, 351–352
types of, 352–353
Trait appraisals, 355
Trait model of leadership, 412–413
Transactional leadership Leadership that motivates subordinates by rewarding them for high performance and reprimanding them for low performance, 423
Transaction-processing system Management information system designed to handle large volumes of routine recurring transactions, 536
Transfers, 505–506
Transformational leadership Leadership that makes subordinates aware of the importance of their jobs and performance to the organization and aware of their own needs for personal growth and that motivates subordinates to work for the good of the organization, 421–423
Transforming, 50
Trans-Pacific Partnership (TPP), 166
Trust The willingness of one person or group to have faith or confidence in the goodwill of another person, even though this puts them at risk, 99–100
Turnaround management The creation of a new vision for a struggling company based on a new approach to planning and organizing to make better use of a company's resources and allow it to survive and prosper, 20